American Casebook Series
Hornbook Series and Basic Legal Texts
Nutshell Series

of

WEST PUBLISHING COMPANY
P.O. Box 64526
St. Paul, Minnesota 55164–0526

ACCOUNTING

Faris' Accounting and Law in a Nutshell, 377 pages, 1984 (Text)

Fiflis, Kripke and Foster's Teaching Materials on Accounting for Business Lawyers, 3rd Ed., 838 pages, 1984 (Casebook)

Siegel and Siegel's Accounting and Financial Disclosure: A Guide to Basic Concepts, 259 pages, 1983 (Text)

ADMINISTRATIVE LAW

Davis' Cases, Text and Problems on Administrative Law, 6th Ed., 683 pages, 1977 (Casebook)

Gellhorn and Boyer's Administrative Law and Process in a Nutshell, 2nd Ed., 445 pages, 1981 (Text)

Mashaw and Merrill's Cases and Materials on Administrative Law–The American Public Law System, 2nd Ed., 976 pages, 1985 (Casebook)

Robinson, Gellhorn and Bruff's The Administrative Process, 3rd Ed., 978 pages, 1986 (Casebook)

ADMIRALTY

Healy and Sharpe's Cases and Materials on Admiralty, 2nd Ed., 876 pages, 1986 (Casebook)

Maraist's Admiralty in a Nutshell, 390 pages, 1983 (Text)

Schoenbaum's Hornbook on Admiralty and Maritime Law, Student Ed., about 675 pages, 1987 (Text)

Sohn and Gustafson's Law of the Sea in a Nutshell, 264 pages, 1984 (Text)

AGENCY—PARTNERSHIP

Fessler's Alternatives to Incorporation for Persons in Quest of Profit, 2nd Ed., 326 pages, 1986 (Casebook)

AGENCY—PARTNERSHIP—Cont'd

Henn's Cases and Materials on Agency, Partnership and Other Unincorporated Business Enterprises, 2nd Ed., 733 pages, 1985 (Casebook)

Reuschlein and Gregory's Hornbook on the Law of Agency and Partnership, 625 pages, 1979, with 1981 pocket part (Text)

Selected Corporation and Partnership Statutes and Forms, about 550 pages, 1987

Steffen and Kerr's Cases and Materials on Agency-Partnership, 4th Ed., 859 pages, 1980 (Casebook)

Steffen's Agency-Partnership in a Nutshell, 364 pages, 1977 (Text)

AGRICULTURAL LAW

Meyer, Pedersen, Thorson and Davidson's Agricultural Law: Cases and Materials, 931 pages, 1985 (Casebook)

ALTERNATIVE DISPUTE RESOLUTION

Kanowitz' Cases and Materials on Alternative Dispute Resolution, 1024 pages, 1986 (Casebook)

Riskin and Westbrook's Dispute Resolution and Lawyers, about 525 pages, 1987 (Coursebook)

Teple and Moberly's Arbitration and Conflict Resolution, (The Labor Law Group), 614 pages, 1979 (Casebook)

AMERICAN INDIAN LAW

Canby's American Indian Law in a Nutshell, 288 pages, 1981 (Text)

Getches and Wilkinson's Cases on Federal Indian Law, 2nd Ed., 880 pages, 1986 (Casebook)

ANTITRUST LAW

Gellhorn's Antitrust Law and Economics in a Nutshell, 3rd Ed., 472 pages, 1986 (Text)

List current as of June, 1987

I

ANTITRUST LAW—Cont'd

Gifford and Raskind's Cases and Materials on Antitrust, 694 pages, 1983 with 1985 Supplement (Casebook)

Hovenkamp's Hornbook on Economics and Federal Antitrust Law, Student Ed., 414 pages, 1985 (Text)

Oppenheim, Weston and McCarthy's Cases and Comments on Federal Antitrust Laws, 4th Ed., 1168 pages, 1981 with 1985 Supplement (Casebook)

Posner and Easterbrook's Cases and Economic Notes on Antitrust, 2nd Ed., 1077 pages, 1981, with 1984–85 Supplement (Casebook)

Sullivan's Hornbook of the Law of Antitrust, 886 pages, 1977 (Text)

See also Regulated Industries, Trade Regulation

ART LAW

DuBoff's Art Law in a Nutshell, 335 pages, 1984 (Text)

BANKING LAW

Lovett's Banking and Financial Institutions in a Nutshell, 409 pages, 1984 (Text)

Symons and White's Teaching Materials on Banking Law, 2nd Ed., 993 pages, 1984, with 1987 Supplement (Casebook)

BUSINESS PLANNING

Painter's Problems and Materials in Business Planning, 2nd Ed., 1008 pages, 1984 with 1987 Supplement (Casebook)

Selected Securities and Business Planning Statutes, Rules and Forms, about 475 pages, 1987

CIVIL PROCEDURE

Casad's Res Judicata in a Nutshell, 310 pages, 1976 (text)

Cound, Friedenthal, Miller and Sexton's Cases and Materials on Civil Procedure, 4th Ed., 1202 pages, 1985 with 1987 Supplement (Casebook)

Ehrenzweig, Louisell and Hazard's Jurisdiction in a Nutshell, 4th Ed., 232 pages, 1980 (Text)

Federal Rules of Civil-Appellate Procedure—West Law School Edition, about 600 pages, 1987

Friedenthal, Kane and Miller's Hornbook on Civil Procedure, 876 pages, 1985 (Text)

Kane's Civil Procedure in a Nutshell, 2nd Ed., 306 pages, 1986 (Text)

Koffler and Reppy's Hornbook on Common Law Pleading, 663 pages, 1969 (Text)

Marcus and Sherman's Complex Litigation—Cases and Materials on Advanced Civil Procedure, 846 pages, 1985 (Casebook)

Park's Computer-Aided Exercises on Civil Procedure, 2nd Ed., 167 pages, 1983 (Coursebook)

CIVIL PROCEDURE—Cont'd

Siegel's Hornbook on New York Practice, 1011 pages, 1978 with 1987 Pocket Part (Text)

See also Federal Jurisdiction and Procedure

CIVIL RIGHTS

Abernathy's Cases and Materials on Civil Rights, 660 pages, 1980 (Casebook)

Cohen's Cases on the Law of Deprivation of Liberty: A Study in Social Control, 755 pages, 1980 (Casebook)

Lockhart, Kamisar, Choper and Shiffrin's Cases on Constitutional Rights and Liberties, 6th Ed., 1266 pages, 1986 with 1987 Supplement (Casebook)—reprint from Lockhart, et al. Cases on Constitutional Law, 6th Ed., 1986

Vieira's Civil Rights in a Nutshell, 279 pages, 1978 (Text)

COMMERCIAL LAW

Bailey's Secured Transactions in a Nutshell, 2nd Ed., 391 pages, 1981 (Text)

Epstein and Martin's Basic Uniform Commercial Code Teaching Materials, 2nd Ed., 667 pages, 1983 (Casebook)

Henson's Hornbook on Secured Transactions Under the U.C.C., 2nd Ed., 504 pages, 1979 with 1979 P.P. (Text)

Murray's Commercial Law, Problems and Materials, 366 pages, 1975 (Coursebook)

Nickles, Matheson and Dolan's Materials for Understanding Credit and Payment Systems, 923 pages, 1987 (Casebook)

Nordstrom and Clovis' Problems and Materials on Commercial Paper, 458 pages, 1972 (Casebook)

Nordstrom, Murray and Clovis' Problems and Materials on Sales, 515 pages, 1982 (Casebook)

Nordstrom, Murray and Clovis' Problems and Materials on Secured Transactions, 594 pages, 1987 (Casebook)

Selected Commercial Statutes, about 1500 pages, 1987

Speidel, Summers and White's Teaching Materials on Commercial Law, 4th Ed., about 1400 pages, 1987 (Casebook)

Speidel, Summers and White's Commercial Paper: Teaching Materials, 4th Ed., about 565 pages, 1987 (Casebook)—reprint from Speidel, et al. Commercial Law, 4th Ed.

Speidel, Summers and White's Sales: Teaching Materials, 4th Ed., about 756 pages, 1987 (Casebook)—reprint from Speidel, et al. Commercial Law, 4th Ed.

Speidel, Summers and White's Secured Transactions—Teaching Materials, 4th Ed., about 463 pages, 1987 (Casebook)—reprint from Speidel, et al. Commercial Law, 4th Ed.

COMMERCIAL LAW—Cont'd

Stockton's Sales in a Nutshell, 2nd Ed., 370 pages, 1981 (Text)

Stone's Uniform Commercial Code in a Nutshell, 2nd Ed., 516 pages, 1984 (Text)

Uniform Commercial Code, Official Text with Comments, 994 pages, 1978

UCC Article 9, Reprint from 1962 Code, 128 pages, 1976

UCC Article 9, 1972 Amendments, 304 pages, 1978

Weber and Speidel's Commercial Paper in a Nutshell, 3rd Ed., 404 pages, 1982 (Text)

White and Summers' Hornbook on the Uniform Commercial Code, 2nd Ed., 1250 pages, 1980 (Text)

COMMUNITY PROPERTY

Mennell's Community Property in a Nutshell, 447 pages, 1982 (Text)

Verrall and Bird's Cases and Materials on California Community Property, 4th Ed., 549 pages, 1983 (Casebook)

COMPARATIVE LAW

Barton, Gibbs, Li and Merryman's Law in Radically Different Cultures, 960 pages, 1983 (Casebook)

Glendon, Gordon and Osakive's Comparative Legal Traditions: Text, Materials and Cases on the Civil Law, Common Law, and Socialist Law Traditions, 1091 pages, 1985 (Casebook)

Glendon, Gordon, and Osakwe's Comparative Legal Traditions in a Nutshell, 402 pages, 1982 (Text)

Langbein's Comparative Criminal Procedure: Germany, 172 pages, 1977 (Casebook)

COMPUTERS AND LAW

Maggs and Sprowl's Computer Applications in the Law, 316 pages, 1987 (Coursebook)

Mason's An Introduction to the Use of Computers in Law, 223 pages, 1984 (Text)

CONFLICT OF LAWS

Cramton, Currie and Kay's Cases-Comments-Questions on Conflict of Laws, 4th Ed., about 925 pages, 1987 (Casebook)

Scoles and Hay's Hornbook on Conflict of Laws, Student Ed., 1085 pages, 1982 with 1986 P.P. (Text)

Scoles and Weintraub's Cases and Materials on Conflict of Laws, 2nd Ed., 966 pages, 1972, with 1978 Supplement (Casebook)

Siegel's Conflicts in a Nutshell, 469 pages, 1982 (Text)

CONSTITUTIONAL LAW

Barron and Dienes' Constitutional Law in a Nutshell, 389 pages, 1986 (Text)

CONSTITUTIONAL LAW—Cont'd

Engdahl's Constitutional Federalism in a Nutshell, 2nd Ed., 411 pages, 1987 (Text)

Lockhart, Kamisar, Choper and Shiffrin's Cases-Comments-Questions on Constitutional Law, 6th Ed., 1601 pages, 1986 with 1987 Supplement (Casebook)

Lockhart, Kamisar, Choper and Shiffrin's Cases-Comments-Questions on the American Constitution, 6th Ed., 1260 pages, 1986 with 1987 Supplement (Casebook)—abridgment of Lockhart, et al. Cases on Constitutional Law, 6th Ed., 1986

Manning's The Law of Church-State Relations in a Nutshell, 305 pages, 1981 (Text)

Miller's Presidential Power in a Nutshell, 328 pages, 1977 (Text)

Nowak, Rotunda and Young's Hornbook on Constitutional Law, 3rd Ed., Student Ed., 1191 pages, 1986 (Text)

Rotunda's Modern Constitutional Law: Cases and Notes, 2nd Ed., 1004 pages, 1985, with 1987 Supplement (Casebook)

Williams' Constitutional Analysis in a Nutshell, 388 pages, 1979 (Text)

See also Civil Rights

CONSUMER LAW

Epstein and Nickles' Consumer Law in a Nutshell, 2nd Ed., 418 pages, 1981 (Text)

Selected Commercial Statutes, about 1500 pages, 1987

Spanogle and Rohner's Cases and Materials on Consumer Law, 693 pages, 1979, with 1982 Supplement (Casebook)

See also Commercial Law

CONTRACTS

Calamari & Perillo's Cases and Problems on Contracts, 1061 pages, 1978 (Casebook)

Calamari and Perillo's Hornbook on Contracts, 3rd Ed., 904 pages, 1987 (Text)

Corbin's Text on Contracts, One Volume Student Edition, 1224 pages, 1952 (Text)

Fessler and Loiseaux's Cases and Materials on Contracts, 837 pages, 1982 (Casebook)

Friedman's Contract Remedies in a Nutshell, 323 pages, 1981 (Text)

Fuller and Eisenberg's Cases on Basic Contract Law, 4th Ed., 1203 pages, 1981 (Casebook)

Hamilton, Rau and Weintraub's Cases and Materials on Contracts, 830 pages, 1984 (Casebook)

Jackson and Bollinger's Cases on Contract Law in Modern Society, 2nd Ed., 1329 pages, 1980 (Casebook)

Keyes' Government Contracts in a Nutshell, 423 pages, 1979 (Text)

Schaber and Rohwer's Contracts in a Nutshell, 2nd Ed., 425 pages, 1984 (Text)

LAW SCHOOL PUBLICATIONS—Continued

CONTRACTS—Cont'd

Summers and Hillman's Contract and Related Obligation: Theory, Doctrine and Practice, 1074 pages, 1987 (Casebook)

COPYRIGHT

See Patent and Copyright Law

CORPORATIONS

Hamilton's Cases on Corporations—Including Partnerships and Limited Partnerships, 3rd Ed., 1213 pages, 1986 with 1986 Statutory Supplement (Casebook)

Hamilton's Law of Corporations in a Nutshell, 2nd Ed., 515 pages, 1987 (Text)

Henn's Teaching Materials on Corporations, 2nd Ed., 1204 pages, 1986 (Casebook)

Henn and Alexander's Hornbook on Corporations, 3rd Ed., Student Ed., 1371 pages, 1983 with 1986 P.P. (Text)

Jennings and Buxbaum's Cases and Materials on Corporations, 5th Ed., 1180 pages, 1979 (Casebook)

Selected Corporation and Partnership Statutes, Regulations and Forms, about 550 pages, 1987

Solomon, Stevenson and Schwartz' Materials and Problems on Corporations: Law and Policy, 1172 pages, 1982 with 1986 Supplement (Casebook)

CORPORATE FINANCE

Hamilton's Cases and Materials on Corporate Finance, 895 pages, 1984 with 1986 Supplement (Casebook)

CORRECTIONS

Krantz's Cases and Materials on the Law of Corrections and Prisoners' Rights, 3rd Ed., 855 pages, 1986 (Casebook)

Krantz's Law of Corrections and Prisoners' Rights in a Nutshell, 2nd Ed., 386 pages, 1983 (Text)

Popper's Post-Conviction Remedies in a Nutshell, 360 pages, 1978 (Text)

Robbins' Cases and Materials on Post Conviction Remedies, 506 pages, 1982 (Casebook)

CREDITOR'S RIGHTS

Bankruptcy Code, Rules and Forms, Law School Ed., about 835 pages, 1988

Epstein's Debtor-Creditor Law in a Nutshell, 3rd Ed., 383 pages, 1986 (Text)

Epstein, Landers and Nickles' Debtors and Creditors: Cases and Materials, 3rd Ed., about 1175 pages, 1987 (Casebook)

LoPucki's Player's Manual for the Debtor-Creditor Game, 123 pages, 1985 (Coursebook)

Riesenfeld's Cases and Materials on Creditors' Remedies and Debtors' Protection, 4th Ed., 914 pages, 1987 (Casebook)

CREDITOR'S RIGHTS—Cont'd

White's Bankruptcy and Creditor's Rights: Cases and Materials, 812 pages, 1985, with 1987 Supplement (Casebook)

CRIMINAL LAW AND CRIMINAL PROCEDURE

Abrams', Federal Criminal Law and its Enforcement, 882 pages, 1986 (Casebook)

Carlson's Adjudication of Criminal Justice, Problems and References, 130 pages, 1986 (Casebook)

Dix and Sharlot's Cases and Materials on Criminal Law, 3rd Ed., 846 pages, 1987 (Casebook)

Federal Rules of Criminal Procedure—West Law School Edition, about 475 pages, 1987

Grano's Problems in Criminal Procedure, 2nd Ed., 176 pages, 1981 (Problem book)

Israel and LaFave's Criminal Procedure in a Nutshell, 3rd Ed., 438 pages, 1980 (Text)

Johnson's Cases, Materials and Text on Criminal Law, 3rd Ed., 783 pages, 1985 (Casebook)

Johnson's Cases on Criminal Procedure, about 790 pages, 1987 (Casebook)

Kamisar, LaFave and Israel's Cases, Comments and Questions on Modern Criminal Procedure, 6th Ed., 1558 pages, 1986 with 1987 Supplement (Casebook)

Kamisar, LaFave and Israel's Cases, Comments and Questions on Basic Criminal Procedure, 6th Ed., 860 pages, 1986 with 1987 Supplement (Casebook)—reprint from Kamisar, et al. Modern Criminal Procedure, 6th ed., 1986

LaFave's Modern Criminal Law: Cases, Comments and Questions, 789 pages, 1978 (Casebook)

LaFave and Israel's Hornbook on Criminal Procedure, Student Ed., 1142 pages, 1985 with 1986 P.P. (Text)

LaFave and Scott's Hornbook on Criminal Law, 2nd Ed., Student Ed., 918 pages, 1986 (Text)

Langbein's Comparative Criminal Procedure: Germany, 172 pages, 1977 (Casebook)

Loewy's Criminal Law in a Nutshell, 2nd Ed., about 350 pages, 1987 (Text)

Saltzburg's American Criminal Procedure, Cases and Commentary, 2nd Ed., 1193 pages, 1985 with 1987 Supplement (Casebook)

Uviller's The Processes of Criminal Justice: Investigation and Adjudication, 2nd Ed., 1384 pages, 1979 with 1979 Statutory Supplement and 1986 Update (Casebook)

LAW SCHOOL PUBLICATIONS—Continued

CRIMINAL LAW AND CRIMINAL PROCEDURE—Cont'd

Uviller's The Processes of Criminal Justice: Adjudication, 2nd Ed., 730 pages, 1979. Soft-cover reprint from Uviller's The Processes of Criminal Justice: Investigation and Adjudication, 2nd Ed. (Casebook)

Uviller's The Processes of Criminal Justice: Investigation, 2nd Ed., 655 pages, 1979. Soft-cover reprint from Uviller's The Processes of Criminal Justice: Investigation and Adjudication, 2nd Ed. (Casebook)

Vorenberg's Cases on Criminal Law and Procedure, 2nd Ed., 1088 pages, 1981 with 1985 Supplement (Casebook)

See also Corrections, Juvenile Justice

DECEDENTS ESTATES

See Trusts and Estates

DOMESTIC RELATIONS

Clark's Cases and Problems on Domestic Relations, 3rd Ed., 1153 pages, 1980 (Casebook)

Clark's Hornbook on Domestic Relations, 754 pages, 1968 (Text)

Krause's Cases and Materials on Family Law, 2nd Ed., 1221 pages, 1983 with 1986 Supplement (Casebook)

Krause's Family Law in a Nutshell, 2nd Ed., 444 pages, 1986 (Text)

Krauskopf's Cases on Property Division at Marriage Dissolution, 250 pages, 1984 (Casebook)

ECONOMICS, LAW AND

Goetz' Cases and Materials on Law and Economics, 547 pages, 1984 (Casebook)

See also Antitrust, Regulated Industries

EDUCATION LAW

Alexander and Alexander's The Law of Schools, Students and Teachers in a Nutshell, 409 pages, 1984 (Text)

Morris' The Constitution and American Education, 2nd Ed., 992 pages, 1980 (Casebook)

EMPLOYMENT DISCRIMINATION

Jones, Murphy and Belton's Cases on Discrimination in Employment, 1116 pages, 1987 (Casebook)

Player's Cases and Materials on Employment Discrimination Law, 2nd Ed., 782 pages, 1984 (Casebook)

Player's Federal Law of Employment Discrimination in a Nutshell, 2nd Ed., 402 pages, 1981 (Text)

Player's Hornbook on the Law of Employment Discrimination, about 575 pages, 1987 (Text)

See also Women and the Law

ENERGY AND NATURAL RESOURCES LAW

Laitos' Cases and Materials on Natural Resources Law, 938 pages, 1985 (Casebook)

Rodgers' Cases and Materials on Energy and Natural Resources Law, 2nd Ed., 877 pages, 1983 (Casebook)

Selected Environmental Law Statutes, about 800 pages, 1987

Tomain's Energy Law in a Nutshell, 338 pages, 1981 (Text)

See also Environmental Law, Oil and Gas, Water Law

ENVIRONMENTAL LAW

Bonine and McGarity's Cases and Materials on the Law of Environment and Pollution, 1076 pages, 1984 (Casebook)

Findley and Farber's Cases and Materials on Environmental Law, 2nd Ed., 813 pages, 1985 (Casebook)

Findley and Farber's Environmental Law in a Nutshell, 343 pages, 1983 (Text)

Rodgers' Hornbook on Environmental Law, 956 pages, 1977 with 1984 pocket part (Text)

Selected Environmental Law Statutes, about 800 pages, 1987

See also Energy Law, Natural Resources Law, Water Law

EQUITY

See Remedies

ESTATES

See Trusts and Estates

ESTATE PLANNING

Kurtz' Cases, Materials and Problems on Family Estate Planning, 853 pages, 1983 (Casebook)

Lynn's Introduction to Estate Planning, in a Nutshell, 3rd Ed., 370 pages, 1983 (Text)

See also Taxation

EVIDENCE

Broun and Meisenholder's Problems in Evidence, 2nd Ed., 304 pages, 1981 (Problem book)

Cleary and Strong's Cases, Materials and Problems on Evidence, 3rd Ed., 1143 pages, 1981 (Casebook)

Federal Rules of Evidence for United States Courts and Magistrates, about 330 pages, 1987

Graham's Federal Rules of Evidence in a Nutshell, 2nd Ed., 473 pages, 1987 (Text)

Kimball's Programmed Materials on Problems in Evidence, 380 pages, 1978 (Problem book)

LAW SCHOOL PUBLICATIONS—Continued

EVIDENCE—Cont'd

Lempert and Saltzburg's A Modern Approach to Evidence: Text, Problems, Transcripts and Cases, 2nd Ed., 1232 pages, 1983 (Casebook)

Lilly's Introduction to the Law of Evidence, 2nd Ed., about 600 pages, 1987 (Text)

McCormick, Sutton and Wellborn's Cases and Materials on Evidence, 6th Ed., 1067 pages, 1987 (Casebook)

McCormick's Hornbook on Evidence, 3rd Ed., Student Ed., 1156 pages, 1984 with 1987 P.P. (Text)

Rothstein's Evidence, State and Federal Rules in a Nutshell, 2nd Ed., 514 pages, 1981 (Text)

Saltzburg's Evidence Supplement: Rules, Statutes, Commentary, 245 pages, 1980 (Casebook Supplement)

FEDERAL JURISDICTION AND PROCEDURE

Currie's Cases and Materials on Federal Courts, 3rd Ed., 1042 pages, 1982 with 1985 Supplement (Casebook)

Currie's Federal Jurisdiction in a Nutshell, 2nd Ed., 258 pages, 1981 (Text)

Federal Rules of Civil-Appellate Procedure—West Law School Edition, about 600 pages, 1987

Forrester and Moye's Cases and Materials on Federal Jurisdiction and Procedure, 3rd Ed., 917 pages, 1977 with 1985 Supplement (Casebook)

Redish's Cases, Comments and Questions on Federal Courts, 878 pages, 1983 with 1986 Supplement (Casebook)

Vetri and Merrill's Federal Courts, Problems and Materials, 2nd Ed., 232 pages, 1984 (Problem Book)

Wright's Hornbook on Federal Courts, 4th Ed., Student Ed., 870 pages, 1983 (Text)

FUTURE INTERESTS

See Trusts and Estates

HEALTH LAW

See Medicine, Law and

IMMIGRATION LAW

Aleinikoff and Martin's Immigration Process and Policy, 1042 pages, 1985, with 1987 Supplement (Casebook)

Weissbrodt's Immigration Law and Procedure in a Nutshell, 345 pages, 1984 (Text)

INDIAN LAW

See American Indian Law

INSURANCE

Dobbyn's Insurance Law in a Nutshell, 281 pages, 1981 (Text)

INSURANCE—Cont'd

Keeton's Cases on Basic Insurance Law, 2nd Ed., 1086 pages, 1977

Keeton's Basic Text on Insurance Law, 712 pages, 1971 (Text)

Keeton's Case Supplement to Keeton's Basic Text on Insurance Law, 334 pages, 1978 (Casebook)

York and Whelan's Cases, Materials and Problems on Insurance Law, 715 pages, 1982, with 1985 Supplement (Casebook)

INTERNATIONAL LAW

Buergenthal and Maier's Public International Law in a Nutshell, 262 pages, 1985 (Text)

Folsom, Gordon and Spanogle's International Business Transactions – a Problem-Oriented Coursebook, 1160 pages, 1986, with Documents Supplement (Casebook)

Frank and Glennon's United States Foreign Relations Law: Cases, Materials and Simulations, about 875 pages, 1987 (Casebook)

Henkin, Pugh, Schachter and Smit's Cases and Materials on International Law, 2nd Ed., 1517 pages, 1987 with Documents Supplement (Casebook)

Jackson and Davey's Legal Problems of International Economic Relations, 2nd Ed., 1269 pages, 1986, with Documents Supplement (Casebook)

Kirgis' International Organizations in Their Legal Setting, 1016 pages, 1977, with 1981 Supplement (Casebook)

Weston, Falk and D'Amato's International Law and World Order—A Problem Oriented Coursebook, 1195 pages, 1980, with Documents Supplement (Casebook)

Wilson's International Business Transactions in a Nutshell, 2nd Ed., 476 pages, 1984 (Text)

INTERVIEWING AND COUNSELING

Binder and Price's Interviewing and Counseling, 232 pages, 1977 (Text)

Shaffer and Elkins' Interviewing and Counseling in a Nutshell, 2nd Ed., 487 pages, 1987 (Text)

INTRODUCTION TO LAW STUDY

Dobbyn's So You Want to go to Law School, Revised First Edition, 206 pages, 1976 (Text)

Hegland's Introduction to the Study and Practice of Law in a Nutshell, 418 pages, 1983 (Text)

Kinyon's Introduction to Law Study and Law Examinations in a Nutshell, 389 pages, 1971 (Text)

See also Legal Method and Legal System

LAW SCHOOL PUBLICATIONS—Continued

JUDICIAL ADMINISTRATION

Nelson's Cases and Materials on Judicial Administration and the Administration of Justice, 1032 pages, 1974 (Casebook)

JURISPRUDENCE

Christie's Text and Readings on Jurisprudence—The Philosophy of Law, 1056 pages, 1973 (Casebook)

JUVENILE JUSTICE

Fox's Cases and Materials on Modern Juvenile Justice, 2nd Ed., 960 pages, 1981 (Casebook)

Fox's Juvenile Courts in a Nutshell, 3rd Ed., 291 pages, 1984 (Text)

LABOR LAW

Atleson, Rabin, Schatzki, Sherman and Silverstein's Collective Bargaining in Private Employment, 2nd Ed., (The Labor Law Group), 856 pages, 1984 (Casebook)

Gorman's Basic Text on Labor Law—Unionization and Collective Bargaining, 914 pages, 1976 (Text)

Grodin, Wollett and Alleyne's Collective Bargaining in Public Employment, 3rd Ed., (the Labor Law Group), 430 pages, 1979 (Casebook)

Leslie's Labor Law in a Nutshell, 2nd Ed., 397 pages, 1986 (Text)

Nolan's Labor Arbitration Law and Practice in a Nutshell, 358 pages, 1979 (Text)

Oberer, Hanslowe, Andersen and Heinsz' Cases and Materials on Labor Law—Collective Bargaining in a Free Society, 3rd Ed., 1163 pages, 1986 with Statutory Supplement (Casebook)

See also Employment Discrimination, Social Legislation

LAND FINANCE

See Real Estate Transactions

LAND USE

Callies and Freilich's Cases and Materials on Land Use, 1233 pages, 1986 (Casebook)

Hagman's Cases on Public Planning and Control of Urban and Land Development, 2nd Ed., 1301 pages, 1980 (Casebook)

Hagman and Juergensmeyer's Hornbook on Urban Planning and Land Development Control Law, 2nd Ed., Student Edition, 680 pages, 1986 (Text)

Wright and Gitelman's Cases and Materials on Land Use, 3rd Ed., 1300 pages, 1982, with 1987 Supplement (Casebook)

Wright and Wright's Land Use in a Nutshell, 2nd Ed., 356 pages, 1985 (Text)

LEGAL HISTORY

Presser and Zainaldin's Cases on Law and American History, 855 pages, 1980 (Casebook)

See also Legal Method and Legal System

LEGAL METHOD AND LEGAL SYSTEM

Aldisert's Readings, Materials and Cases in the Judicial Process, 948 pages, 1976 (Casebook)

Berch and Berch's Introduction to Legal Method and Process, 550 pages, 1985 (Casebook)

Bodenheimer, Oakley and Love's Readings and Cases on an Introduction to the Anglo-American Legal System, 161 pages, 1980 (Casebook)

Davies and Lawry's Institutions and Methods of the Law—Introductory Teaching Materials, 547 pages, 1982 (Casebook)

Dvorkin, Himmelstein and Lesnick's Becoming a Lawyer: A Humanistic Perspective on Legal Education and Professionalism, 211 pages, 1981 (Text)

Greenberg's Judicial Process and Social Change, 666 pages, 1977 (Casebook)

Kelso and Kelso's Studying Law: An Introduction, 587 pages, 1984 (Coursebook)

Kempin's Historical Introduction to Anglo-American Law in a Nutshell, 2nd Ed., 280 pages, 1973 (Text)

Kimball's Historical Introduction to the Legal System, 610 pages, 1966 (Casebook)

Murphy's Cases and Materials on Introduction to Law—Legal Process and Procedure, 772 pages, 1977 (Casebook)

Reynolds' Judicial Process in a Nutshell, 292 pages, 1980 (Text)

See also Legal Research and Writing

LEGAL PROFESSION

Aronson, Devine and Fisch's Problems, Cases and Materials on Professional Responsibility, 745 pages, 1985 (Casebook)

Aronson and Weckstein's Professional Responsibility in a Nutshell, 399 pages, 1980 (Text)

Mellinkoff's The Conscience of a Lawyer, 304 pages, 1973 (Text)

Mellinkoff's Lawyers and the System of Justice, 983 pages, 1976 (Casebook)

Pirsig and Kirwin's Cases and Materials on Professional Responsibility, 4th Ed., 603 pages, 1984 (Casebook)

Schwartz and Wydick's Problems in Legal Ethics, 285 pages, 1983 (Casebook)

Selected Statutes, Rules and Standards on the Legal Profession, about 300 pages, 1987

Smith's Preventing Legal Malpractice, 142 pages, 1981 (Text)

Wolfram's Hornbook on Modern Legal Ethics, Student Edition, 1120 pages, 1986 (Text)

LAW SCHOOL PUBLICATIONS—Continued

LEGAL RESEARCH AND WRITING

Cohen's Legal Research in a Nutshell, 4th Ed., 450 pages, 1985 (Text)

Cohen and Berring's How to Find the Law, 8th Ed., 790 pages, 1983. Problem book by Foster, Johnson and Kelly available (Casebook)

Cohen and Berring's Finding the Law, 8th Ed., Abridged Ed., 556 pages, 1984 (Casebook)

Dickerson's Materials on Legal Drafting, 425 pages, 1981 (Casebook)

Felsenfeld and Siegel's Writing Contracts in Plain English, 290 pages, 1981 (Text)

Gopen's Writing From a Legal Perspective, 225 pages, 1981 (Text)

Mellinkoff's Legal Writing—Sense and Nonsense, 242 pages, 1982 (Text)

Ray and Ramsfield's Legal Writing: Getting It Right and Getting It Written, 250 pages, 1987 (Text)

Rombauer's Legal Problem Solving—Analysis, Research and Writing, 4th Ed., 424 pages, 1983 (Coursebook)

Squires and Rombauer's Legal Writing in a Nutshell, 294 pages, 1982 (Text)

Statsky's Legal Research and Writing, 3rd Ed., 257 pages, 1986 (Coursebook)

Statsky and Wernet's Case Analysis and Fundamentals of Legal Writing, 2nd Ed., 441 pages, 1984 (Text)

Teply's Programmed Materials on Legal Research and Citation, 2nd Ed., 358 pages, 1986. Student Library Exercises available (Coursebook)

Weihofen's Legal Writing Style, 2nd Ed., 332 pages, 1980 (Text)

LEGISLATION

Davies' Legislative Law and Process in a Nutshell, 2nd Ed., 346 pages, 1986 (Text)

Eskridge and Frickey's Cases on Legislation, about 930 pages, 1987 (Casebook)

Nutting and Dickerson's Cases and Materials on Legislation, 5th Ed., 744 pages, 1978 (Casebook)

Statsky's Legislative Analysis and Drafting, 2nd Ed., 217 pages, 1984 (Text)

LOCAL GOVERNMENT

McCarthy's Local Government Law in a Nutshell, 2nd Ed., 404 pages, 1983 (Text)

Reynolds' Hornbook on Local Government Law, 860 pages, 1982, with 1987 pocket part (Text)

Valente's Cases and Materials on Local Government Law, 3rd Ed., 1010 pages, 1987 (Casebook)

MASS COMMUNICATION LAW

Gillmor and Barron's Cases and Comment on Mass Communication Law, 4th Ed., 1076 pages, 1984 (Casebook)

MASS COMMUNICATION LAW—Cont'd

Ginsburg's Regulation of Broadcasting: Law and Policy Towards Radio, Television and Cable Communications, 741 pages, 1979, with 1983 Supplement (Casebook)

Zuckman and Gayne's Mass Communications Law in a Nutshell, 2nd Ed., 473 pages, 1983 (Text)

MEDICINE, LAW AND

Furrow, Johnson, Jost and Schwartz' Health Law: Cases, Materials and Problems, 1005 pages, 1987 (Casebook)

King's The Law of Medical Malpractice in a Nutshell, 2nd Ed., 342 pages, 1986 (Text)

Shapiro and Spece's Problems, Cases and Materials on Bioethics and Law, 892 pages, 1981 (Casebook)

Sharpe, Fiscina and Head's Cases on Law and Medicine, 882 pages, 1978 (Casebook)

MILITARY LAW

Shanor and Terrell's Military Law in a Nutshell, 378 pages, 1980 (Text)

MORTGAGES

See Real Estate Transactions

NATURAL RESOURCES LAW

See Energy and Natural Resources Law

NEGOTIATION

Edwards and White's Problems, Readings and Materials on the Lawyer as a Negotiator, 484 pages, 1977 (Casebook)

Peck's Cases and Materials on Negotiation, 2nd Ed., (The Labor Law Group), 280 pages, 1980 (Casebook)

Williams' Legal Negotiation and Settlement, 207 pages, 1983 (Coursebook)

OFFICE PRACTICE

Hegland's Trial and Practice Skills in a Nutshell, 346 pages, 1978 (Text)

Strong and Clark's Law Office Management, 424 pages, 1974 (Casebook)

See also Computers and Law, Interviewing and Counseling, Negotiation

OIL AND GAS

Hemingway's Hornbook on Oil and Gas, 2nd Ed., Student Ed., 543 pages, 1983 with 1986 P.P. (Text)

Kuntz, Lowe, Anderson and Smith's Cases and Materials on Oil and Gas Law, 857 pages, 1986, with Forms Manual (Casebook)

Lowe's Oil and Gas Law in a Nutshell, 443 pages, 1983 (Text)

See also Energy and Natural Resources Law

PARTNERSHIP

See Agency—Partnership

LAW SCHOOL PUBLICATIONS—Continued

PATENT AND COPYRIGHT LAW

Choate, Francis and Collins' Cases and Materials on Patent Law, 3rd Ed., about 1050 pages, 1987 (Casebook)

Miller and Davis' Intellectual Property—Patents, Trademarks and Copyright in a Nutshell, 428 pages, 1983 (Text)

Nimmer's Cases on Copyright and Other Aspects of Entertainment Litigation, 3rd Ed., 1025 pages, 1985 (Casebook)

PRODUCTS LIABILITY

Noel and Phillips' Cases on Products Liability, 2nd Ed., 821 pages, 1982 (Casebook)

Noel and Phillips' Products Liability in a Nutshell, 2nd Ed., 341 pages, 1981 (Text)

PROPERTY

Bernhardt's Real Property in a Nutshell, 2nd Ed., 448 pages, 1981 (Text)

Boyer's Survey of the Law of Property, 766 pages, 1981 (Text)

Browder, Cunningham and Smith's Cases on Basic Property Law, 4th Ed., 1431 pages, 1984 (Casebook)

Bruce, Ely and Bostick's Cases and Materials on Modern Property Law, 1004 pages, 1984 (Casebook)

Burke's Personal Property in a Nutshell, 322 pages, 1983 (Text)

Cunningham, Stoebuck and Whitman's Hornbook on the Law of Property, Student Ed., 916 pages, 1984, with 1987 P.P. (Text)

Donahue, Kauper and Martin's Cases on Property, 2nd Ed., 1362 pages, 1983 (Casebook)

Hill's Landlord and Tenant Law in a Nutshell, 2nd Ed., 311 pages, 1986 (Text)

Kurtz and Hovenkamp's Cases and Materials on American Property Law, 1296 pages, 1987 (Casebook)

Moynihan's Introduction to Real Property, 2n Ed., about 250 pages, 1987 (Text)

Uniform Land Transactions Act, Uniform Simplification of Land Transfers Act, Uniform Condominium Act, 1977 Official Text with Comments, 462 pages, 1978

See also Real Estate Transactions, Land Use

PSYCHIATRY, LAW AND

Reisner's Law and the Mental Health System, Civil and Criminal Aspects, 696 pages, 1985, with 1987 Supplement (Casebooks)

REAL ESTATE TRANSACTIONS

Bruce's Real Estate Finance in a Nutshell, 2nd Ed., 262 pages, 1985 (Text)

Maxwell, Riesenfeld, Hetland and Warren's Cases on California Security Transactions in Land, 3rd Ed., 728 pages, 1984 (Casebook)

REAL ESTATE TRANSACTIONS—Cont'd

Nelson and Whitman's Cases on Real Estate Transfer, Finance and Development, 3rd Ed., about 1184 pages, 1987 (Casebook)

Nelson and Whitman's Hornbook on Real Estate Finance Law, 2nd Ed., Student Ed., 941 pages, 1985 (Text)

Osborne's Cases and Materials on Secured Transactions, 559 pages, 1967 (Casebook)

REGULATED INDUSTRIES

Gellhorn and Pierce's Regulated Industries in a Nutshell, 2nd Ed., 389 pages, 1987 (Text)

Morgan, Harrison and Verkuil's Cases and Materials on Economic Regulation of Business, 2nd Ed., 666 pages, 1985 (Casebook)

See also Mass Communication Law, Banking Law

REMEDIES

Dobbs' Hornbook on Remedies, 1067 pages, 1973 (Text)

Dobbs' Problems in Remedies, 137 pages, 1974 (Problem book)

Dobbyn's Injunctions in a Nutshell, 264 pages, 1974 (Text)

Friedman's Contract Remedies in a Nutshell, 323 pages, 1981 (Text)

Leavell, Love and Nelson's Cases and Materials on Equitable Remedies and Restitution, 4th Ed., 1111 pages, 1986 (Casebook)

McCormick's Hornbook on Damages, 811 pages, 1935 (Text)

O'Connell's Remedies in a Nutshell, 2nd Ed., 320 pages, 1985 (Text)

York, Bauman and Rendleman's Cases and Materials on Remedies, 4th Ed., 1029 pages, 1985 (Casebook)

REVIEW MATERIALS

Ballantine's Problems

Black Letter Series

Smith's Review Series

West's Review Covering Multistate Subjects

SECURITIES REGULATION

Hazen's Hornbook on The Law of Securities Regulation, Student Ed., 739 pages, 1985, with 1987 P.P. (Text)

Ratner's Securities Regulation: Materials for a Basic Course, 3rd Ed., 1000 pages, 1986 (Casebook)

Ratner's Securities Regulation in a Nutshell, 2nd Ed., 322 pages, 1982 (Text)

Selected Securities and Business Planning Statutes, Rules and Forms, about 470 pages, 1987

LAW SCHOOL PUBLICATIONS—Continued

SOCIAL LEGISLATION

Hood and Hardy's Workers' Compensation and Employee Protection Laws in a Nutshell, 274 pages, 1984 (Text)

LaFrance's Welfare Law: Structure and Entitlement in a Nutshell, 455 pages, 1979 (Text)

Malone, Plant and Little's Cases on Workers' Compensation and Employment Rights, 2nd Ed., 951 pages, 1980 (Casebook)

SPORTS LAW

Schubert, Smith and Trentadue's Sports Law, 395 pages, 1986 (Text)

TAXATION

Dodge's Cases and Materials on Federal Income Taxation, 820 pages, 1985 (Casebook)

Dodge's Federal Taxation of Estates, Trusts and Gifts: Principles and Planning, 771 pages, 1981 with 1982 Supplement (Casebook)

Garbis, Struntz and Rubin's Cases and Materials on Tax Procedure and Tax Fraud, 2nd Ed., 687 pages, 1987 (Casebook)

Gelfand and Salsich's State and Local Taxation and Finance in a Nutshell, 309 pages, 1986 (Text)

Gunn's Cases and Materials on Federal Income Taxation of Individuals, 785 pages, 1981 with 1985 Supplement (Casebook)

Hellerstein and Hellerstein's Cases on State and Local Taxation, 4th Ed., 1041 pages, 1978 with 1982 Supplement (Casebook)

Kahn and Gann's Corporate Taxation and Taxation of Partnerships and Partners, 2nd Ed., 1204 pages, 1985 (Casebook)

Kragen and McNulty's Cases and Materials on Federal Income Taxation: Individuals, Corporations, Partnerships, 4th Ed., 1287 pages, 1985 (Casebook)

McNulty's Federal Estate and Gift Taxation in a Nutshell, 3rd Ed., 509 pages, 1983 (Text)

McNulty's Federal Income Taxation of Individuals in a Nutshell, 3rd Ed., 487 pages, 1983 (Text)

Pennell's Cases and Materials on Income Taxation of Trusts, Estates, Grantors and Beneficiaries, about 400 pages, 1987 (Casebook)

Posin's Hornbook on Federal Income Taxation of Individuals, Student Ed., 491 pages, 1983 with 1987 pocket part (Text)

Selected Federal Taxation Statutes and Regulations, 1576 pages, 1987

Solomon and Hesch's Cases on Federal Income Taxation of Individuals, 1068 pages, 1987 (Casebook)

TAXATION—Cont'd

Sobeloff and Weidenbruch's Federal Income Taxation of Corporations and Stockholders in a Nutshell, 362 pages, 1981 (Text)

TORTS

Christie's Cases and Materials on the Law of Torts, 1264 pages, 1983 (Casebook)

Dobbs' Torts and Compensation—Personal Accountability and Social Responsibility for Injury, 955 pages, 1985 (Casebook)

Green, Pedrick, Rahl, Thode, Hawkins, Smith, and Treece's Advanced Torts: Injuries to Business, Political and Family Interests, 2nd Ed., 544 pages, 1977 (Casebook)

Keeton, Keeton, Sargentich and Steiner's Cases and Materials on Torts, and Accident Law, 1360 pages, 1983 (Casebook)

Kionka's Torts in a Nutshell: Injuries to Persons and Property, 434 pages, 1977 (Text)

Malone's Torts in a Nutshell: Injuries to Family, Social and Trade Relations, 358 pages, 1979 (Text)

Prosser and Keeton's Hornbook on Torts, 5th Ed., Student Ed., 1286 pages, 1984, with 1987 pocket part (Text)

See also Products Liability

TRADE REGULATION

McManis' Unfair Trade Practices in a Nutshell, 444 pages, 1982 (Text)

Oppenheim, Weston, Maggs and Schechter's Cases and Materials on Unfair Trade Practices and Consumer Protection, 4th Ed., 1038 pages, 1983 with 1986 Supplement (Casebook)

See also Antitrust, Regulated Industries

TRIAL AND APPELLATE ADVOCACY

Appellate Advocacy, Handbook of, 2nd Ed., 182 pages, 1986 (Text)

Bergman's Trial Advocacy in a Nutshell, 402 pages, 1979 (Text)

Binder and Bergman's Fact Investigation: From Hypothesis to Proof, 354 pages, 1984 (Coursebook)

Goldberg's The First Trial (Where Do I Sit?, What Do I Say?) in a Nutshell, 396 pages, 1982 (Text)

Haydock, Herr and Stempel's, Fundamentals of Pre-Trial Litigation, 768 pages, 1985 (Casebook)

Hegland's Trial and Practice Skills in a Nutshell, 346 pages, 1978 (Text)

Hornstein's Appellate Advocacy in a Nutshell, 325 pages, 1984 (Text)

Jeans' Handbook on Trial Advocacy, Student Ed., 473 pages, 1975 (Text)

Martineau's Cases and Materials on Appellate Practice and Procedure, about 550 pages, 1987 (Casebook)

LAW SCHOOL PUBLICATIONS—Continued

TRIAL AND APPELLATE ADVOCACY—Cont'd

McElhaney's Effective Litigation, 457 pages, 1974 (Casebook)

Nolan's Cases and Materials on Trial Practice, 518 pages, 1981 (Casebook)

Parnell and Shellhaas' Cases, Exercises and Problems for Trial Advocacy, 171 pages, 1982 (Coursebook)

Sonsteng, Haydock and Boyd's The Trialbook: A Total System for Preparation and Presentation of a Case, Student Ed., 404 pages, 1984 (Coursebook)

TRUSTS AND ESTATES

Atkinson's Hornbook on Wills, 2nd Ed., 975 pages, 1953 (Text)

Averill's Uniform Probate Code in a Nutshell, 2nd Ed., 454 pages, 1987 (Text)

Bogert's Hornbook on Trusts, 6th Ed., Student Ed., about 800 pages, 1987 (Text)

Clark, Lusky and Murphy's Cases and Materials on Gratuitous Transfers, 3rd Ed., 970 pages, 1985 (Casebook)

Gulliver's Cases and Materials on Future Interests, 624 pages, 1959 (Casebook)

Gulliver's Introduction to the Law of Future Interests, 87 pages, 1959 (Casebook)—reprint from Gulliver's Cases and Materials on Future Interests, 1959

McGovern's Cases and Materials on Wills, Trusts and Future Interests: An Introduction to Estate Planning, 750 pages, 1983 (Casebook)

Mennell's Wills and Trusts in a Nutshell, 392 pages, 1979 (Text)

Simes' Hornbook on Future Interests, 2nd Ed., 355 pages, 1966 (Text)

TRUSTS AND ESTATES—Cont'd

Turano and Radigan's Hornbook on New York Estate Administration, 676 pages, 1986 (Text)

Uniform Probate Code, 5th Ed., Official Text With Comments, 384 pages, 1977

Waggoner's Future Interests in a Nutshell, 361 pages, 1981 (Text)

Waterbury's Materials on Trusts and Estates, 1039 pages, 1986 (Casebook)

WATER LAW

Getches' Water Law in a Nutshell, 439 pages, 1984 (Text)

Sax and Abram's Cases and Materials on Legal Control of Water Resources in the United States, 941 pages, 1986 (Casebook)

Trelease and Gould's Cases and Materials on Water Law, 4th Ed., 816 pages, 1986 (Casebook)

See also Energy and Natural Resources Law, Environmental Law

WILLS

See Trusts and Estates

WOMEN AND THE LAW

Kay's Text, Cases and Materials on Sex-Based Discrimination, 2nd Ed., 1045 pages, 1981, with 1986 Supplement (Casebook)

Thomas' Sex Discrimination in a Nutshell, 399 pages, 1982 (Text)

See also Employment Discrimination

WORKERS' COMPENSATION

See Social Legislation

CASES AND MATERIALS ON
PATENT LAW

Including

TRADE SECRETS—COPYRIGHTS—TRADEMARKS

Third Edition

By

Robert A. Choate
Lecturer Emeritus of Patent Law, University of Michigan

William H. Francis
Adjunct Professor of Law, University of Detroit

Robert C. Collins
Member of the Michigan Bar

AMERICAN CASEBOOK SERIES

WEST PUBLISHING CO.
ST. PAUL, MINN., 1987

COPYRIGHT © 1972 ROBERT A. CHOATE
COPYRIGHT © 1973, 1981 WEST PUBLISHING CO.
COPYRIGHT © 1987 By WEST PUBLISHING CO.
                        50 West Kellogg Boulevard
                        P.O. Box 64526
                        St. Paul, Minnesota 55164–0526

Library of Congress Cataloging-in-Publication Data

Choate, Robert A., 1912–
    Cases and materials on patent law.

    (American casebook series)
    Includes index.
        1. Patent laws and legislation—United States—Cases.
2. Copyright—United States—Cases. 3. Trademarks—
United States—Cases. I. Francis, William H.
II. Collins, Robert C., 1946–   . III. Title.
IV. Series.
KF3113.C47   1987   346.7304'8   87–21700
                           347.30648

ISBN 0–314–59993–2

Dedication

To promote the progress of science and useful arts by securing for unlimited times to students and practitioners unexclusive knowledge of the law for protecting writings and discoveries.

*

Preface to the Third Edition

Decisions of the Court of Appeals for the Federal Circuit in pursuit of its goal of patent law uniformity, and changes in the 1952 Patent Act, have prompted revision of the second edition of this casebook. Revision was also prompted by continuing case law development under the 1976 Copyright Act, and a new Act for protection of Semiconductor Chips. Acceptance of prior editions has been most gratifying. It is hoped that this third edition will provide a well-rounded introduction to intellectual property law with particular emphasis on patent law.

We appreciate and gratefully acknowledge the input and suggestions of our partners, students and other teachers. Messrs. Choate and Francis are particularly appreciative of the insightful analysis and effort of their co-author Robert Collins. We acknowledge also the help of Shirley Wisniewski Langley, Marian Brolus and Grace Maceri in preparing drafts of the manuscript and the invaluable effort of Shirley Wisniewski Langley in formulating the manuscript for submission to the publisher.

We gratefully appreciate the encouragement, support and patience of our wives Eileen, Susan, Patricia and our children Anna, Peggy, Kimberly, Robert and David, without which this casebook and many other things would be impossible. "They also serve . . ."

ROBERT A. CHOATE
WILLIAM H. FRANCIS
ROBERT C. COLLINS

Detroit, Michigan
September, 1987

*

Preface to the Second Edition

Supreme Court decisions since 1973, as well as an entirely new Copyright statute, effective Jan. 1, 1978, have dictated a revision of the 1973 edition of this Casebook. The acceptance of the first edition by teachers, lawyers and judges, has been gratifying and it is hoped this second edition will be a helpful introduction to the law of the related fields of patents, trade secrets, copyrights and trademarks.

Because of the extensive new Copyright statute, and its radical changes of prior copyright law, Part III of the Casebook dealing with this subject is focussed mainly on the new statute. This section is still intended, not as an exhaustive treatment, but simply to provide the student with a basic understanding of copyrights in relation to the law of patents and trademarks.

We gratefully acknowledge the assistance of our associates and the suggestions of students, teachers and others relative to a revised edition. We acknowledge also the invaluable help received with respect to the mechanics of preparing a manuscript. Specifically, we mention the assistance of Shirley Wisniewski Langley, Sharon Botzen and Alison Choate Benjamin who have carried the burden relative to the typing, paging, and mounting of the various components to complete the submission to the publisher.

Those who have engaged in the preparing of a Casebook will appreciate that wives and families also contribute, not only with encouragement in times of stress, but with patient indulgence of the necessary shift of the time allotments from home to office. "They also serve . . ."

ROBERT A. CHOATE
WILLIAM H. FRANCIS

Detroit, Michigan
December, 1980

*

Preface to the First Edition

This book has its foundations in Smith's Casebook on Patent Law (1964). Indeed, the exacting and laborious task would not have been undertaken except for the inspiration, leadership, and dedication of the late Judge Arthur M. Smith to his chosen profession. Prior to his appointment to the Court of Customs and Patent Appeals in 1959, Judge Smith was active in the practice of Patent Law as well as Lecturer in Patent Law at the University of Michigan. The written memorials found in volume 422 of the Federal Reporter, Second Series, appropriately reflect his wide influence and pre-eminence.

The purpose of this book is to prepare students for the practice of law with what is intended to be a judicious mixture of historical precedent and its practical application. This is believed to be consistent with the growing emphasis of present day educators not only for the teaching of basic jurisprudence but for a clinical approach which prepares students for the immediate assumption of responsibility after graduation.

For the student who plans a general practice, it is the hope that he will find here enough of the historical background, the policy considerations, and the judicial treatment to enable him to distinguish the various areas of intellectual property and appreciate the need for protection. He should also acquire sufficient confidence that he will embark upon his own analysis of any particular problem. For the student who contemplates specialization, it is the hope that he will find, not only material to give him an overview of the field in general, but also, enough of the theoretical and the practical that he will be able to contribute readily in his chosen specialty as he enters the practice of Patent Law.

For, indeed, this book is directed to the practice of Patent Law. Copyrights and Trademarks are treated only as they affect the every day practice of a patent attorney and also to give some of the flavor of these fascinating branches of the law which can become specialties in themselves. The conviction that creative persons need encouragement and protection has been a motivating force since the author has had a close association over the years with inventors who have created products resulting in growing business organizations and numerous employees. The Patent System, despite its many difficulties, still offers incentive to many whose sole asset is an idea. If some students of law can find in these pages such materials as will lead them to an interest in the practice of patent law and a desire to contribute to the improvement and success of the Patent System, then the effort has not been in vain.

This book is designed for courses having twenty-four to forty-five hours including class time. The division of the parts will allow flexibility in the selection of the assigned material and some teachers may prefer a two semester approach with initial emphasis on patent procurement and final emphasis on patent enforcement. The difficulties of selection of material have been made easier by the observation of Winston Churchill that the maxim, "Nothing avails but perfection," leads to paralysis. There is no claim here to perfection but the resulting product is submitted with the hope that it will prove a helpful tool to teachers and students alike. Miguel de Cervantes has said that "modesty is a virtue not often found among poets" but anyone who has attempted the discipline of selecting appropriate materials for a legal casebook cannot but be humbled as he works with the vast number of well-written and pertinent decisions available.

I owe much to my former students whose interest and questions have made teaching a learning process for me and have suggested new approaches to the presentation of materials. I am especially indebted to my former student and present associate, William H. Francis, who has provided much encouragement and assistance with his incisive analysis and hours of labor in the development of some sections and improvements of others. This I have also acknowledged on the title page. I mention also with gratitude the help of Paul Fisher, student research assistant, whose creative capacities and attention to detail have contributed much to the casebook material and the index. I gratefully acknowledge the painstaking care, and service above and beyond the call of duty, of my secretary, Shirely A. Langley, in the preparation of the manuscript, and the labors of my daughter, Alison M. Choate, who has assisted in the checking of citations and the great task of transforming the manuscript into printable material. The helpful suggestions and unlimited forbearance of my partners and associates should not go unmentioned.

Lastly, I acknowledge the unfailing patience of my wife who encouraged me to initiate this work and who has fearlessly criticized the manuscript while completing three needlework projects during the hours of my absence.

ROBERT A. CHOATE

January, 1973

Format and Acknowledgments

Part II of this book directed to PATENTS is by far the most extensive of the six parts and for this reason has been divided into chapters while the other relatively short parts are simply divided into sections. Footnotes of the inserted cases are marked with the original numbers while footnotes added by the authors are marked with letters. Numerous references are made to the J.P.O.S., The Journal of the Patent Office Society, and to IDEA, The Patent, Trademark and Copyright Journal of Research and Education of The PTC Research Institute of George Washington University.

Acknowledgments of permission to use copyrighted material are gratefully made to the following:

1. The American Law Institute for *Restatement of the Law, Torts;*

2. The Bureau of National Affairs, 1231 25th Street, NW, Wash, DC 20037 for *The United States Patent Quarterly* and a report from *The Southwestern Legal Foundation;*

3. Clarendon Press for Collingwood's *Principles of Art;*

4. Columbia University Press for Kaplan's *An Unhurried View of Copyright;*

5. Doubleday & Co. Inc. for Moore's *Invention, Discovery and Creativity;*

6. The Journal of the Patent Office Society;

7. The Lawyer's Cooperative Publishing Co. for the *Lawyer's Edition of the U.S. Supreme Court Reports; and*

8. INC. Magazine—for use of article entitled *Warning—America Can't Turn Back the Technology Clock* by Jerome B. Weisner (May 1979)—Reprinted with permission—Copyright (©) United Marine Publishing, Inc. 1979.

*

PART III. COPYRIGHTS

PART IV. TRADEMARKS

*

Table of Cases

The principal cases are in bold type. Cases cited or discussed in the text are roman type. References are to pages. Cases cited in principal cases and within other quoted materials are not included.

Summary of Contents

*

Table of Contents

*

CASES AND MATERIALS ON
PATENT LAW
Including
TRADE SECRETS—COPYRIGHTS— TRADEMARKS
Third Edition

*

INTRODUCTION

A. NATURAL RIGHTS TO IDEAS

A legal dictionary defines "natural" as something attributable to the nature of man as distinguished from positive enactments of law.[a] Natural law is defined by Black as a system of rules and principles for the guidance of human conduct which might be discovered by the rational intelligence of man and would be found to grow out of and conform to his nature, i.e., his whole mental, moral and physical constitution.

We are frequently reminded that human nature has not changed much in thousands of years. With reference to natural rights in creations of the mind, to wit, ideas, we can perhaps use our own natures as a test of natural rights. Assume a reasonable, normal person who has shared one of his own ideas, which he thought to be original, with a friend or acquaintance, only to find that person at a later time passing on the idea as his own. What would be his reaction? An altruistic glow that he had been able to contribute to his friend's prestige and reputation, or a slight feeling of inner resentment that credit has not been given where credit was due? The natural reaction untempered by Judeo-Christian charity would probably be the latter one, a feeling of loss and resentment to some degree.

To take the study one step further, assume for the moment that the idea was not just a fleeting thought shared in a mutual exchange but one that had been worked on for quite some time, including many hours of research and background study. Under these conditions, would not the natural reaction to the unauthorized appropriation be a little deeper and more heartfelt even to the point that the originator might be aroused to proclaim the source?

However, the first prehistoric bi-ped who picked up a fallen branch to use as a weapon was probably not greatly surprised when his fellow beings imitated him, particularly if they were in combat at the time. From the beginning of history, ideas have been shared, particularly in the realm of common defense, gathering food, building shelters, and clothing man.

Thus, it is "natural" both that persons with ideas and skills use them to their own advantage, and that other persons copy what they observe. As Thomas Jefferson, one of the writers of the Declaration of Independence of the United States, and a prolific inventor in his own right, stated:

a. Black's Law Dictionary, Revised 5th Edition (1979), West Publishing Co.

If nature has made any one thing less susceptible than all others of exclusive property, it is the action of the thinking power called an idea, which an individual may exclusively possess as long as he keeps it to himself; but the moment it is divulged, it forces itself into the possession of every one, and the receiver cannot dispossess himself of it. Its peculiar character, too, is that no one possesses the less, because every other possesses the whole of it. He who receives an idea from me, receives instructions himself without lessening mine; as he who lights his taper at mine, receives light without darkening me. That ideas should freely spread from one to another over the globe, for the moral and mutual instruction of man, and improvement of his condition, seems to have been peculiarly and benevolently designed by nature * * * [b]

Robinson on Patents [c] (1890) in Sections 24 and 25 elaborates on the natural rights of inventors to use their own inventions and of other persons to copy inventions which they have observed saying:

Section 24.   RIGHTS OF INVENTOR UNDER NATURAL LAW

"In pursuing this investigation the relations of an inventor and the public to an unpatented invention first demand attention. In its earliest stage this invention is a mere addition to the stock of ideas possessed by the inventor. He has imagined or discovered something which to himself, and presumably to all the world, is new, and has conceived a method by which his idea may be so applied as to produce a tangible and valuable result. In this stage he has a natural exclusive right to his invention. No one can compel him to disclose his secret. He may reduce it to actual practice, or preserve it as a matter of subjective contemplation. The law can take no other notice of it than it does of his moral sentiments or his personal recollections. If, however, he endeavors to avail himself of this idea in his exterior life, his position in regard to it is somewhat changed. The material forms in which he then embodies it are his, but the idea itself is not to be imprisoned within their narrow bounds. * * * [W]ith his submission of the tangible result of his idea to the inspection of others, in such a manner that the idea itself becomes apparent, his control over it is gone. An idea once communicated can no longer be exclusively appropriated and enjoyed. Every one who receives it processes it in the same degree as if he alone had apprehended it, and its inventor has no power to restrain him from its practical and useful application. Under the laws of nature the exclusive public use of an invention is thus impossible, and hence there is no natural right to such a use. The inventor, who voluntarily discloses his invention to the public, necessarily and freely dedicates it to the public; and that which formerly

b. 6 Writings of Thomas Jefferson 180–181, H.A. Washington Ed. (1854).

c. Robinson's three volume work on Patents probably contains more original thinking on the law of patents than any other book written before or since on the subject. William C. Robinson was a Professor of Law at Yale University when he published his treatise in 1890. His treatise is still referenced frequently in briefs and decisions of cases currently before the courts.

was his alone by virtue of his sole possession becomes by universal possession the common property of all mankind."

Section 25. RIGHTS OF PUBLIC UNDER NATURAL LAW

"The natural right of the public to appropriate all new ideas that may be voluntarily disclosed is no less evident than that of the inventor to conceal them. It is a law of nature that men should profit by the discoveries and inventions of each other. This is the law which binds society together, and in obedience to which lies all the possibility of moral, intellectual, and material advancement. No man lives, or can live, for himself alone. Every improvement he can make in his appearance, habits, manners, or affairs becomes a guide and stimulus to others, by following which they also can improve themselves in person or estate. * * * This natural right and duty of the public come into existence where the natural right of the inventor ends, the same act which determines his exclusive possession and control delivering the invention to the universal knowledge and service of mankind."

B. PROTECTION OF INTELLECTUAL PROPERTY

As civilization developed from hunting, to agriculture, to specialization and trade, there also developed the artisan or tradesman whose skill in toolmaking or weaving, for example, caused him to devote more time to his trade than to the hunting or growing of food. He would obtain food in barter but at the same time he did not find it advantageous to teach his trade to all comers. He would perhaps pass it on to his son or other members of his family.

Regardless of any "natural" rights that artisans or tradesmen had in their own ideas, skills and inventions, these rights could not be profitably utilized without some means of protection and enforcement due to the "natural" right of others to copy what they observed. Thus, a little later in history, we find these artisans grouped together and organized in guilds for mutual aid and protection. Protecting their skills by secrecy and improving and maintaining the quality of workmanship were the chief functions of the guilds which also regulated hours of labor and terms of admission to the guild, including apprenticeships.

Prager [d], who has studied the history of intellectual property law, indicates that from about the 11th through the 16th centuries:

In Venice as throughout medieval Europe, most of commerce and the arts was dominated by guilds. A guild was a group of masters maintaining a monopoly over their trade. They effected this by fixing prices and standards; trading collectively with other groups, including the taxing powers; defending their trade against masters elsewhere,

d. Prager, A History of Intellectual Property From 1545 to 1787, 26 J.P.O.S., 711 (1944).

and against laborers and journeymen everywhere; and providing some security for aged and disabled members of the guild. In early times, the social security function had been well in the foreground. Later on, the regulation of prices, standards and wages became the main function of the guilds. This line of development was approximately the same in Venice as in all other countries, but reached a mature stage at an early time. Furthermore, in Venice like most other states, other than England, the guilds were gradually degraded to state-supervised, administrative agencies. Complete state control was established in Alexandria about 100 B.C.; in Constantinople about 800 A.D.; in Venice about 1300; and in France about 1650.

This organized effort of the guilds to protect and promote the skills and knowledge of master artisans is the first known attempt to provide trade secret protection.

The guilds also developed and enforced rules for the fair conduct of commerce and trade which were the genesis of the law of unfair competition. Prager [e] indicates:

> Most of the gilds controlling the more refined arts restrained the mutual enticing away of helpers, and theft of tools or goods. As these gilds became more experienced, their articles became more specific. They developed the minimum standards of fair competition, which later on were slowly understood by state courts and legislators and which are now in legal force everywhere.

The guilds used pictures or symbols on the goods produced by their members to identify the goods and their producer, provide a check on quality, identify imitations, and discourage competition by non-members. Incidentally, the guilds virtually never used words on goods because most consumers were illiterate. Thus, trademarks were a part of the organized efforts of the artisans and guilds on the Continent and in Great Britain. Prager [e] states:

> The gild rules sanctioning industrial property can be viewed as an outgrowth of a basic gild principle which required "unity of work." Each product was supposed to come from one producer. Originally and recurrently this principle served to insure the producer's undivided responsibility for so-called true and legal work. However, gradually the notion was developed in the minds of the producers that value as well as responsibility lies in individual craftsmanship. *It is known that this development gave rise to the modern trade mark right.*

The restrictive power of the organized guilds of artisans was felt to be inimical to the state and, hence, some means was sought to encourage the disclosure of the skills of the artisans, as well as to foster the creation and importation of new ideas and devices for the benefit of the general economy. According to Prager [f]:

e. Prager, The Early Growth and Influence of Intellectual Property. 34 J.P.O.S. 106, 111 (1952).

f. Footnote d, supra.

The State attempted to promote the arts in a number of ways, in addition to encouraging the entry of foreigners, and regardless of the general policy which allowed and even forced the guilds to remain stationary. As early as 1332, Venice maintained a special privilege fund, as shown by a document of that year, reciting a payment from that fund to one Bartolomeo Verde, who had promised to erect a windmill. Verde had six months to complete his installation and to make it work. On failure to do so, he had to refund the privilege money at once; otherwise, within 12 years. He had to furnish security. Verde was not necessarily the first inventor of this kind of mills. He was probably the only one who knew how to build them, and the government hoped to spread and promote this knowledge. Payments of the same kind were repeatedly made in the fifteenth century, to persons claiming knowledge of either established or new systems of millwork; the same as to designers of new or improved types of ships, and probably to many others.

Thus, kings, emperors and organized states began to encourage the creation and disclosure of new ideas and devices by providing rewards and the right to exclude others from using the new ideas and devices for a limited time. Prager reports [g] that by about 1432 and perhaps earlier, a statute of Venice provided:

"If somebody invents any machine or process to speed up silkmaking or to improve it, and if the idea is actually useful, the inventor can obtain an exclusive privilege for ten years from the General Welfare Board of the Republic."

*   *   *

The text quoted was a statute of the state, not an internal gild regulation. In Venice the gilds were powerless to grant or allow monopolies by action of their own. *This, accordingly, was the first modern patent statute. It was apparently enacted in response to ideas prevailing in gild circles, which were influenced by the ideas of industrial and intellectual property.*

These early efforts of kings, emperors and states to reward and encourage the disclosure of the intellectual and artistic creations and discoveries of authors and inventors are the beginnings of copyrights and patents. From these early efforts of encouraging and protecting intellectual property have evolved the distinct areas of legal protection of trade secrets, unfair competition, trademarks, patents and copyrights.

While this text is primarily devoted to the law of patents, a brief treatment of these other areas of legal protection of intellectual property is provided to acquaint the student therewith. Such acquaintance will provide the necessary background for the selection of the proper means of legal protection for each particular intellectual creation or discovery and a better understanding of the scope, limitations and terminology of each of the areas of legal protection of intellectual property.

g. Footnote e, supra.

A creator of intellectual property needs to protect his creation or discovery prior to seeking any available patent protection. Accordingly, this text presents the law of trade secrets before the law of patents and copyrights even though chronologically the modern law of trade secrets developed after enactment of the early United States patent and copyright statutes.

Part I

SECRECY AS A PROTECTIVE MEANS

A. IN GENERAL

As noted innumerable times, a secret is information which the possessor has entrusted to nobody. While trust of fellow human beings has not completely deteriorated, nevertheless, the statement illustrates that as the number of persons taken into confidence increases, and as the value of the information increases, the difficulty of maintaining secrecy increases. Without casting aspersions on the general level of morality, it may be observed that in an increasingly mobile society, certain kinds of loyalty often do not have a chance to develop.

In contrast, the patent system encourages disclosure to achieve its primary purpose of advancing the practical arts by increasing public knowledge. It allows free use by the public of a new invention or idea after the inventor has enjoyed exclusive protection for a limited time.[a]

Why then would an inventor or creator of a new idea ever rely on secrecy for protection? There may be several reasons. First, the invention or new idea may be unpatentable because it does not meet the legal requirements for patentability. Second, before a patent is obtained on the new idea, the inventor may want to disclose it to a prospective user, purchaser or financial backer. Third, a belief in what some observers consider to be an anti-patent bias or trend of courts. Fourth, he may prefer secrecy over the great expense of protracted patent litigation, particularly if any patent he might obtain is of doubtful validity.

a. "The outstanding difference is that a patentee has a monopoly as against all the world, while the owner of a secret process has no right, except against those who have contracted, expressly or by implication, not to disclose the secret, or who have obtained it by unfair means." Tower Mfg. Co., Inc. v. Monsanto Chemical Works, 20 F.2d 386, 387 (D.C.N.Y.1927).

"In the area of confidential relationships between partners, employers and employees, licensors and licensees, and the like, the injured party is not required to rely upon an express agreement to hold the trade secret in confidence." Hyde Corp. v. Huffines, 158 Tex. 566, 314 S.W.2d 763, 770, 117 USPQ 44, 49 (Sup.Ct.1958).

The law of trade secrets is too extensive to be fully covered in a patent law course. However, a patent lawyer must understand its basics in order to counsel and advise a client on the type or types of legal protection to pursue for a particular new idea or invention.

The law of trade secrets has been developed largely from the basic legal concepts of the law of torts, restitution, agency, trusts, quasi-contract, property and contracts. Regardless of the particular label or pigeon hole used by a court, the fundamental obligation of secrecy is imposed on another party either involuntarily by operation of law, i.e., tortuous, or voluntarily assumed, i.e., contractual. Sometimes, whether this obligation is tortuous or contractual makes a difference in the remedies afforded, statute of limitation applied, and jurisdiction of the court over the cause of action.

The original Restatement of Torts (1939) of the American Law Institute is the most comprehensive statement of the law of trade secrets and is frequently cited by the courts. Trade secret law was omitted from the second Restatement of Torts (1979) because the Institute believes it has developed into an independent body of law in the specialized field of unfair competition and trade regulation with less reliance on traditional tort principles. Nevertheless, the original Restatement continues to be frequently cited and relied on by courts.

The Commissioners on Uniform State Laws in 1979 approved a Uniform Trade Secrets Act which by 1986 has been enacted by fifteen States.[b] By and large, this Act is in accord with the original Restatement of trade secret law and has been so interpreted by the relatively few courts which have construed this Act.

FOREST LABORATORIES, INC. v. PILLSBURY CO.

United States Court of Appeals, Seventh Circuit, 1971.
452 F.2d 621, 171 USPQ 731.

CUMMINGS, CIRCUIT JUDGE.

Plaintiff, a corporation engaged in producing and packaging effervescent sweetener tablets, sued defendant Pillsbury Company, the well-known manufacturer of food products, alleging that Pillsbury had purloined certain Forest trade secrets.

* * *

After hearing the testimony of various witnesses and considering the exhibits, the district court agreed with plaintiff that it had successfully developed a process for packing effervescent sweetener tablets so as to lengthen their shelf life, Forest Laboratories, Inc. v. Formulations, Inc., 299 F.Supp. 202 (E.D.W.1969). One step of this packaging procedure was adjudged to be plaintiff's confidential trade secret. That step was described as follows: "Before packaging, the tablets are to be

b. As of 1986, the Uniform Trade Secret Act has been adopted, in some instances with minor modifications, by the States of Arkansas, California, Connecti- cut, Delaware, Idaho, Indiana, Kansas, Louisiana, Minnesota, Montana, North Dakota, Oklahoma, Virginia, Washington and Wisconsin.

tempered in a room having 40% or less relative humidity for a period of between 24 to 48 hours."

In determining what is a trade secret, Wisconsin applies the rule of the Restatement of Torts. Abbott Laboratories v. Norse Chemical Corporation, 33 Wis.2d 445, 456, 147 N.W.2d 529 (1967). A trade secret is defined in Section 757, comment (b), of the Restatement as follows:

"A trade secret may consist of any formula, pattern, device, or compilation of information which is used in one's business, and which gives him an opportunity to obtain an advantage over competitors who do not know or use it. It may be a * * * process of * * * treating or preserving materials * * *."

This definition is clearly broad enough to cover the above-described tempering step employed by Forest. The standards for determining trade secrets are well set forth in Cataphote Corporation v. Hudson, 422 F.2d 1290, 1293–1294 (5th Cir.1870). It was there noted that uniqueness in the patent law sense is not an essential element of a trade secret, for the patent laws are designed to encourage invention, whereas trade secret law is designed to protect against a breach of faith. However, the trade secret must "possess at least that modicum of originality which will separate it from everyday knowledge." Cataphote Corporation v. Hudson, 444 F.2d 1313, 1315 (5th Cir.1971). As stated in an authoritative treatise on this subject:

"As distinguished from a patent, a trade secret need not be essentially new, novel or unique; therefore, prior art is a less effective defense in a trade secret case than it is in a patent infringement case. The idea need not be complicated; it may be intrinsically simple and nevertheless qualify as a secret, unless it is in common knowledge and, therefore, within the public domain." 2 Callman, Unfair Competition, Trademarks and Monopolies § 52.1 (3d ed., 1968).

Before finally determining that this tablet-tempering step was a trade secret, the district court weighed the six factors prescribed by *Abbott Laboratories*, supra, and the Restatement. They are:

1. The extent to which the information is known outside of the claimant's business.

2. The extent to which it is known by employees and others involved in his business.

3. The extent of measures taken by him to guard the secrecy of the information.

4. The value of the information to him and his competitors.

5. The amount of effort or money expended by him in developing the information.

6. The ease or difficulty with which the information could be properly acquired or duplicated by others.

The evidence which was discussed in the district court's opinion (299 F.Supp. at 206–207) and will not be reiterated here satisfied the district court and satisfies us that these criteria were met by plaintiff until it had obtained a patent on March 16, 1965, disclosing the tablet-tempering step. Since the element of secrecy evaporated with the issuance of the patent, the district court properly held that Pillsbury should not be held liable after the issuance of the patent.[c]

Even though it allegedly started using Forest's trade secret in Omaha, Nebraska, commencing in January 1964, Pillsbury advances several contentions against liability. First, Pillsbury relies on the fact that its tempering was done in closed containers, whereas Forest's method utilized open containers. However, there was testimony that the tablets would still equilibrate in closed containers, and might do so in a day or two if the container were only in a dry environment. In any event, the user of another's trade secret is liable even "if he uses it with modifications or improvements upon it effected by his own efforts," as long as the substance of the process used by the actor is derived from the other's secret. The purpose of Forest's and Pillsbury's tablet tempering was to place the tablets in an ambient condition. In our opinion, there was insufficient difference in the two methods to absolve Pillsbury from liability.

Pillsbury purchased the assets of Tidy House Corporation on June 1, 1960. The district court found that the trade secret had been divulged by Forest to Tidy House on a confidential basis and that as Tidy House's successor, Pillsbury was bound by the confidential disclosure to Tidy House. On the state of this record we cannot sustain the district court's conclusion. The well settled rule of American jurisdictions, including Wisconsin, is that a corporation which purchases the assets of another corporation does not, by reason of succeeding to the ownership of property, assume the obligations of the transferor corporation. 15 Fletcher, Cyclopedia of the Law of Private Corporations, § 7122 (1961 Rev. Vol.); Pennison v. Chicago, Milwaukee & St. Paul Ry. Co., 93 Wis. 344, 67 N.W. 702 (1896); Kloberdanz v. Joy Mfg. Co., 288 F.Supp. 817, 820 (D.Colo.1968); International Ass'n of Machinists and Local Lodge No. 954 v. Shawnee Indus., Inc., 224 F.Supp. 347, 352 (W.D. Okl.1963). Exceptions to this rule exist where (a) the purchasing corporation expressly or impliedly agrees to assume the liabilities of the seller, (b) the transaction amounts to a consolidation or merger of the two companies, (c) the purchasing corporation is merely a continuation of the selling corporation, or (d) the transaction is entered into fraudu-

---

c. "An application to patent a discovery is not of itself a general disclosure of the discoverer's secret, and hence is not a release of the obligation of a confidential disclosee. A.O. Smith Corp. v. Petroleum Iron Works Co., 6 Cir., 73 F.2d 531, 537. Rule 15 of the Rules of Practice of the United States Patent Office, 35 U.S.C.A. Appendix, provides that 'Pending applications are preserved in secrecy', and that 'No information will be given, without authority, respecting the filing by any particular person of an application for a patent * * * or the subject matter of any particular application, unless it shall be necessary to the proper conduct of business before the office * * *.' If a discovery is one which constitutes invention and for which a patent is issued, the right of further secrecy is, of course, lost, for a legal disclosure and public dedication have then been made, with a right of limited and temporary monopoly granted as the reward." Sandlin v. Johnson, 141 F.2d 660, 61 USPQ 71 (8th Cir.1944).

lently to escape liability. Fletcher, supra, at 191–195; Kloberdanz v. Joy Mfg. Co., supra; International Ass'n of Machinists and Local Lodge No. 954 v. Shawnee Indus., Inc., supra.

* * *

There is no evidence that Pillsbury expressly agreed to assume all the liabilities and obligations of Tidy House, * * *

Since no new corporation emerged from the transaction, a consolidation did not occur. * * *

Apparently Tidy House, Inc. continued its corporate existence after the sale and leased to Pillsbury the buildings housing the facilities it had sold. * * *

Consequently, again on the strength of this record, we cannot conclude that the sale of assets amounted to a merger. * * *

Pillsbury can hardly be said to be a mere continuation of Tidy House since the transfer of assets was not a part of a reorganization. * * *

And finally there is no suggestion whatever that Pillsbury was acting in bad faith when it purchased the Tidy House business. In sum, we are not convinced that Pillsbury subjected itself to the obligation of secrecy as Tidy House's "successor." Moreover, the knowledge of Tidy House's employees cannot properly be imputed to Pillsbury just because they went to work for Pillsbury. Conmar Products Corp. v. Universal Slide Fastener Co., Inc., 172 F.2d 150, 156–157 (2d Cir.1949). See Ferroline Corp. v. General Aniline & Film Corp., 207 F.2d 912, 923 (7th Cir.1953).

Section 757(b) of the Restatement of Torts provides:

"One who discloses or uses another's trade secret, without a privilege to do so, is liable to the other if

* * * * * * * * * *

"(b) his disclosure or use constitutes a breach of confidence reposed in him by the other in disclosing the secret to him * * *."

Since Pillsbury does not stand in the shoes of Tidy House, plaintiff's confidant, Pillsbury's use of the secret does not come within the confines of § 757(b).

* * *

Nevertheless, even though Pillsbury is not liable under § 757(b) of the Restatement of Torts for using Forest's trade secret as Tidy House's successor, the evidence shows that Pillsbury acquired actual knowledge of the confidentiality of the disclosure made by Forest to Tidy House. Thus Mr. Richard Egan, a former employee of Tidy House and of Pillsbury, and considered by the trial judge to be a credible witness, testified that he communicated the trade secret to Dr. Julian Stein, Fred McCarne, and possibly others employed by Pillsbury at a meeting in the middle of 1962. He also told them that the Forest process had been received in confidence by Tidy House.

Section 758(b) of the Restatement states:

"One who learns another's trade secret from a third person without notice that it is secret and that the third person's disclosure is a breach of his duty to the other, or who learns the secret through a mistake without notice of the secrecy and the mistake,

*   *   *

"(b) is liable to the other for a disclosure or use of the secret after the receipt of such notice unless prior thereto he has in good faith paid value for the secret or has so changed his position that to subject him to liability would be inequitable."

Thus under § 758(b) of the Restatement of Torts, Pillsbury would be liable for its use of the secret after receipt of the notice unless prior thereto it had in good faith paid value for the secret. To satisfy this exception, Pillsbury argues that it purchased the trade secret when it acquired Tidy House's assets, and that Mr. Egan's communications did not occur until well after the acquisition. However, the record does not show that Pillsbury paid anything specifically for the trade secret. For all that appears on the record, Pillsbury's purchase of Tidy House assets at most involved only the purchase of its packaging facilities as part of the existing marketing structure, which included plaintiff as supplier. Nothing has been brought to our attention which would show that Pillsbury actually gave value for Tidy House's tempering expertise with a view toward independently exploiting that know-how for its intrinsic value. Comment (e) to § 758(b) of the Restatement states that "not every change of position prevents the recipient of a trade secret from being subjected to the duty not to disclose or use the secret after notice. The issue is whether the imposition of the duty would be inequitable under the circumstances." The mere possibility that some arbitrary portion of the purchase price could *ex post facto* be ascribed to the potential of the trade secret for Pillsbury's later independent use does not demonstrate a change of position which it would be inequitable not to protect under the circumstances. The purpose of Restatement § 758(b) is to protect bona fide purchasers and reasonable reliance, but it may operate harshly on those who have expended substantial sums in development of their trade secrets. See Developments in the Law— Competitive Torts, 77 Harv.L.Rev. 888, 950 (1964). For this reason, we require a specific showing that Pillsbury in good faith paid value for Forest's trade secret at that time, and since there is a dearth of such proof, under § 758(b) of the Restatement, it remained liable to Forest for using the trade secret after the receipt of notice.

Pillsbury next asserts that the special master's assessment of damages in the amount of $75,000 as approved by the district court was erroneous. Both parties agree that the "reasonable royalty" method of computing damages was properly invoked. According to that method, the primary inquiry in fixing a reasonable royalty is "what the parties would have agreed upon, if both were reasonably trying to reach an agreement." Egry Register Co. v. Standard Register Co., 23 F.2d 438, 443 (6th Cir.1928); *   *   * Because of the type of factors considered and the necessarily judgmental process involved in constructing a hypothetical business agreement, we cannot fault any lack of specificity in arriving at what must necessarily be a reasonable approximation.

*   *   *

*   *   * We conclude that the district court's factual determinations were not clearly erroneous and that apart from the award of attorneys' fees, its judgment was correct. Five-sixths of the costs shall be taxed against Pillsbury and one sixth against Forest.

Affirmed in part; reversed in part.

E.I. DU PONT DE NEMOURS & CO., INC. v. CHRISTOPHER

United States Court of Appeals, Fifth Circuit, 1970.
431 F.2d 1012, 166 USPQ 421, cert. denied 400 U.S. 1024, 91 S.Ct. 581, 27
L.Ed.2d 637 (1971).

GOLDBERG, CIRCUIT JUDGE. This is a case of industrial espionage in which an airplane is the cloak and a camera the dagger. The defendants-appellants, Rolfe and Gary Christopher, are photographers in Beaumont, Texas. The Christophers were hired by an unknown third party to take aerial photographs of new construction at the Beaumont plant of E.I. duPont deNemours & Company, Inc. Sixteen photographs of the DuPont facility were taken from the air on March 19, 1969, and these photographs were later developed and delivered to the third party.

DuPont employees apparently noticed the airplane on March 19 and immediately began an investigation to determine why the craft was circling over the plant. By that afternoon the investigation had disclosed that the craft was involved in a photographic expedition and that the Christophers were the photographers. DuPont contacted the Christophers that same afternoon and asked them to reveal the name of the person or corporation requesting the photographs. The Christophers refused to disclose this information, giving as their reason the client's desire to remain anonymous.

Having reached a dead end in the investigation, DuPont subsequently filed suit against the Christophers, alleging that the Christophers had wrongfully obtained photographs revealing DuPont's trade secrets which they then sold to the undisclosed third party. DuPont contended that it had developed a highly secret but unpatented process for producing methanol, a process which gave DuPont a competitive advantage over other producers. This process, DuPont alleged, was a trade secret developed after much expensive and time-consuming research, and a secret which the company had taken special precautions to safeguard. The area photographed by the Christophers was the plant designed to produce methanol by this secret process, and because the plant was still under construction parts of the process were exposed to view from directly above the construction area. Photographs of that area, DuPont alleged, would enable a skilled person to deduce the secret process for making methanol. DuPont thus contended that the Christophers had wrongfully appropriated DuPont trade secrets by taking the photographs and delivering them to the undisclosed third party. In its suit DuPont asked for damages to cover the loss it had already sustained as a result of the wrongful disclosure of the trade secret and sought temporary and permanent injunctions prohibiting any further circulation of the photographs already taken and prohibiting any additional photographing of the methanol plant.

* * *

This is a case of first impression, for the Texas courts have not faced this precise factual issue, and sitting as a diversity court we must sensitize our *Erie* antennae to divine what the Texas courts would do if such a situation were presented to them. The only question involved in this interlocutory appeal is whether DuPont has asserted a claim upon which relief can be granted. The Christophers argued both at trial and before this court that they committed no "actionable wrong" in photographing the DuPont facility and passing these photographs on to their client because they conducted all of their activities in public airspace, violated no government aviation standard, did not breach any confidential relation, and did not engage in any fraudulent or illegal conduct. In short, the Christophers argue that for an appropriation of trade secrets to be wrongful there must be a trespass, other illegal conduct, or breach of a confidential relationship. We disagree.

It is true, as the Christophers assert, that the previous trade secret cases have contained one or more of these elements. However, we do not think that the Texas courts would limit the trade secret protection exclusively to these elements. On the contrary, in Hyde Corporation v. Huffines, 1958, 158 Tex. 566, 314 S.W.2d 763, the Texas Supreme Court specifically adopted the rule found in the Restatement of Torts which provides:

> "One who discloses or uses another's trade secret, without a privilege to do so, is liable to the other if
>
> > (a) he discovered the secret by improper means, or
> >
> > (b) his disclosure or use constitutes a breach of confidence reposed in him by the other in disclosing the secret to him * * *."

Restatement of Torts § 757 (1939).

Thus, although the previous cases have dealt with a breach of a confidential relationship, a trespass, or other illegal conduct, the rule is much broader than the cases heretofore encountered. Not limiting itself to specific wrongs, Texas adopted subsection (a) of the Restatement which recognizes a cause of action for the discovery of a trade secret by any "improper" means.

The defendants, however, read Furr's Inc. v. United Specialty Advertising Co., Tex.Civ.App.1960, 338 S.W.2d 762, writ ref'd n.r.e., as limiting the Texas rule to breach of a confidential relationship. The court in *Furr's* did make the statement that

"The use of someone else's idea is not automatically a violation of the law. It must be something that meets the requirements of a 'trade secret' *and has been obtained through a breach of confidence* in order to entitle the injured party to damages and/or injunction." 338 S.W.2d at 766 (emphasis added).

We think, however, that the exclusive rule which defendants have extracted from this statement is unwarranted. In the first place, in *Furr's* the court specifically found that there was no trade secret involved because the entire advertising scheme claimed to be the trade secret had been completely divulged to the public. Secondly, the court found that the plaintiff in the course of selling the scheme to the defendant had voluntarily divulged the entire scheme. Thus the court was dealing only with a possible breach of confidence concerning a properly discovered secret; there was never a question of any impropriety in the discovery or any other improper conduct on the part of the defendant. The court merely held that under those circumstances the defendant had not acted improperly if no breach of confidence occurred. We do not read *Furr's* as limiting the trade secret protection to a breach of confidential relationship when the facts of the case do raise the issue of some other wrongful conduct on the part of one discovering the trade secrets of another. If breach of confidence were meant to encompass the entire panoply of commercial improprieties, subsection (a) of the Restatement would be either surplusage or persiflage, an interpretation abhorrent to the traditional precision of the Restatement. We therefore find meaning in subsection (a) and think that the Texas Supreme Court clearly indicated by its adoption that there is a cause of action for the discovery of a trade secret by any "improper means." Hyde Corporation v. Huffines, supra.

The question remaining, therefore, is whether aerial photography of plant construction is an improper means of obtaining another's trade secret. We conclude that it is and that the Texas courts would so hold. The Supreme Court of that state has declared that "the undoubted tendency of the law has been to recognize and enforce higher standards of commercial morality in the business world." Hyde Corporation v. Huffines, supra 314 S.W.2d at 773. That court has quoted with approval articles indicating that the *proper* means of gaining possession of a competitor's secret process is "through inspection and analysis" of the product in order to create a duplicate. K & G Tool & Service Co. v. G & G Fishing Tool Service, 1958, 158 Tex. 594, 314 S.W.2d 782, 783, 788. Later another Texas court explained:

"The means by which the discovery is made may be obvious, and the experimentation leading from known factors to presently unknown results may be simple and lying in the public domain. But these facts do not destroy the value of the discovery and will not advantage a competitor who by unfair means obtains the knowledge *without paying the price expended by the discoverer.*" Brown v. Fowler, Tex.Civ.App. 1958, 316 S.W.2d 111, 114, writ ref'd n.r.e. (emphasis added).

We think, therefore, that the Texas rule is clear. One may use his competitor's secret process if he discovers the process by reverse engineering applied to the finished product; one may use a competitor's process if he discovers it by his own independent research; but one may not avoid these labors by taking the process from the discoverer without his permission at a time when he is taking reasonable precautions to maintain its secrecy. To obtain knowledge of a process without spending the time and money to discover it independently is *improper* unless the holder voluntarily discloses it or fails to take reasonable precautions to ensure its secrecy.

In the instant case the Christophers deliberately flew over the DuPont plant to get pictures of a process which DuPont had attempted to keep secret. The Christophers delivered their pictures to a third party who was certainly aware of the means by which they had been acquired and who may be planning to use the information contained therein to manufacture methanol by the DuPont process. The third party has a right to use this process only if he obtains this knowledge through his own research efforts, but thus far all information indicates that the third party has gained this knowledge solely by taking it from DuPont at a time when DuPont was making reasonable efforts to preserve its secrecy. In such a situation DuPont has a valid cause of action to prohibit the Christophers from improperly discovering its trade secret and to prohibit the undisclosed third party from using the improperly obtained information.

We note that this view is in perfect accord with the position taken by the authors of the Restatement. In commenting on improper means of discovery the savants of the Restatement said:

> "f. *Improper means of discovery.* The discovery of another's trade secret by improper means subjects the actor to liability independently of the harm to the interest in the secret. Thus, if one uses physical force to take a secret formula from another's pocket or breaks into another's office to steal the formula, his conduct is wrongful and subjects him to liability apart from the rule stated in this Section. Such conduct is also an improper means of procuring the secret under this rule. But means may be improper under this rule even though they do not cause any other harm than that to the interest in the trade secret. Examples of such means are fraudulent misrepresentations to induce disclosure, tapping of telephone wires, eavesdropping or other espionage. A complete catalogue of improper means is not possible. In general they are means which fall below the generally accepted standards of commercial morality and reasonable conduct." Restatement of Torts § 757, comment f at 10 (1939).

In taking this position we realize that industrial espionage of the sort here perpetrated has become a popular sport in some segments of our industrial community. However, our devotion to free wheeling industrial competition must not force us into accepting the law of the jungle as the standard of morality expected in our commercial relations. Our tolerance of the espionage game must cease when the protections required to prevent another's spying cost so much that the spirit of inventiveness is dampened. Commercial privacy must be protected from espionage which could not have been reasonably anticipated or prevented. We do not mean to imply, however, that everything not in plain view is within the protected vale, nor that all information obtained through every extra optical extension is forbidden. Indeed, for our industrial competition to remain healthy there must be breathing room for observing a competing industrialist. A competitor can and must shop his competition for pricing and examine his products for quality, components, and methods of manufacture. Perhaps ordinary fences and roofs must be built to shut out incursive eyes, but we need not require the discoverer of a trade secret to guard against the unanticipated, the undetectable, or the unpreventable methods of espionage now available.

In the instant case DuPont was in the midst of constructing a plant. Although after construction the finished plant would have protected much of the process from view, during the period of construction the trade secret was exposed to view from the air. To require DuPont to put a roof over the unfinished plant to guard its secret would impose an enormous expense to prevent nothing more than a school boy's trick. We introduce here no new or radical ethic since our ethos has never given moral sanction to piracy. The market place must not deviate far from our mores. We should not require a person or corporation to take unreasonable precautions to prevent another from doing that which he ought not do in the first place. Reasonable precautions against predatory eyes we may require, but an impenetrable fortress is an unreasonable requirement, and we are not disposed to burden industrial inventors with such a duty in order to protect the fruits of their efforts. "Improper" will always be a word of many nuances, determined by time, place, and circumstances. We therefore need not proclaim a catalogue of commercial improprieties. Clearly, however, one of its commandments does say "thou shall not appropriate a trade secret through deviousness under circumstances in which countervailing defenses are not reasonably available."

Having concluded that aerial photography, from whatever altitude, is an improper method of discovering the trade secrets exposed during construction of the DuPont plant, we need not worry about whether the flight pattern chosen by the Christophers violated any federal aviation regulations. Regardless of whether the flight was legal or illegal in that sense, the espionage was an improper means of discovering DuPont's trade secret.

The decision of the trial court is affirmed and the case remanded to that court for proceedings on the merits.

* * *

It has often been said that the courts, in protecting trade secrets, enforce an ever increasing standard of commercial morality.[d] Acquiring secret information by methods which courts find particularly distasteful will be enjoined where no contract or relationship of trust has been created. As the means of obtaining secret information become more sophisticated, which appears inevitable in a society where electronic and scientific information and equipment advance constantly, the judicial task will get increasingly difficult.

E.I. DU PONT de NEMOURS POWDER CO. v. MASLAND

Supreme Court of the United States, 1917.
244 U.S. 100, 37 S.Ct. 575, 61 L.Ed. 1016.

MR. JUSTICE HOLMES delivered the opinion of the court:

This is a bill to prevent the defendant Walter E. Masland from using or disclosing secret processes the knowledge of which was acquired by the defendant while in the plaintiffs' employ. The defendant admits that he intends to manufacture artificial leather, to which some of the plaintiffs' alleged secret processes relate, but denies that he intends to use any inventions, trade secrets, or secret processes of the plaintiffs that he may have learned in any confidential relation, prefacing his denial, however, with the averment that many of the things claimed by the plaintiffs are well known to the trade. A preliminary injunction was refused at first. 216 F. 271. But before the final hearing the defendant proposed to employ one or more experts and to make such disclosures to them as the preparation of the defense might require. Thereupon the district court issued a preliminary injunction against disclosing any of the plaintiffs' alleged processes to experts or witnesses during the taking of proofs, but excepting counsel, with leave to move to dissolve the injunction if occasion to consult experts arose. Later a motion to dissolve was denied and the hearing was continued for a decision by the appellate court. 222 F. 340. The circuit court of appeals reversed the decree. 140 C.C.A. 229, 224 F. 689. Before any further order was entered the writ of certiorari was granted by this court.

d. "Our conclusion that plaintiff may not recover is reached with some reluctance, particularly in view of defendant's reiterated 'moral bond' to secrecy. We have recently expressed the view that cases involving the confidential disclosure of trade secrets must be governed by 'increasingly higher standards of fairness, or commercial morality * * *'." Protexol Corp. v. Koppers Co., Inc., 229 F.2d 635, 637, 108 USPQ 238, 239 (2d Cir.1956).

"The policy reasons for affording protection to these commercial intangibles are to prevent exploitation by reprehensible business methods and to encourage innovation. See Developments in the Law—Competitive Torts, 77 Harv.L.Rev. 888, 947–48 (1964). If a trade secret is protected, the competitive advantage realized by the owner of the secret will enable him to recoup his development costs, hopefully before his competitors can 'reverse-engineer' the product and duplicate it." Water Services, Inc. v. Tesco Chemicals, Inc., 410 F.2d 163, 171, 162 USPQ 321, 327 (5th Cir.1969).

The case has been considered as presenting a conflict between a right of property and a right to make a full defense; and it is said that if the disclosure is forbidden to one who denies that there is a trade secret, the merits of his defense are adjudged against him before he has a chance to be heard or to prove his case. We approach the question somewhat differently. The word "property" as applied to trademarks and trade secrets is an unanalyzed expression of certain secondary consequences of the primary fact that the law makes some rudimentary requirements of good faith. Whether the plaintiffs have any valuable secret or not the defendant knows the facts, whatever they are, through a special confidence that he accepted. The property may be denied, but the confidence cannot be. Therefore the starting point for the present matter is not property or due process of law, but that the defendant stood in confidential relations with the plaintiffs, or one of them. These have given place to hostility, and the first thing to be made sure of is that the defendant shall not fraudulently abuse the trust reposed in him. It is the usual incident of confidential relations. If there is any disadvantage in the fact that he knew the plaintiffs' secrets, he must take the burden with the good.

The injunction asked by the plaintiffs forbade only the disclosure of processes claimed by them, including the disclosure to experts or witnesses produced during the taking of proofs, but excepting the defendant's counsel. Some broader and ambiguous words that crept into the decree, seemingly by mistake, may be taken as stricken out and left on one side. This injunction would not prevent the defendant from directing questions that should bring out whatever public facts were nearest to the alleged secrets. Indeed, it is hard to see why it does not leave the plaintiffs' rights somewhat illusory. No very clear ground as yet has been shown for going further. But the judge who tries the case will know the secrets, and if, in his opinion and discretion, it should be advisable and necessary to take in others, nothing will prevent his doing so. It will be understood that if, in the opinion of the trial judge, it is or should become necessary to reveal the secrets to others, it will rest in the judge's discretion to determine whether, to whom, and under what precautions, the revelation should be made.

Decree reversed and case remanded for further proceedings in conformity with this opinion.[e]

e. "The courts have generally recognized that there is no definite privilege against disclosure of trade secrets but that a disclosure of trade secrets will be required only where such disclosure is relevant and necessary to the prosecution or defense of a particular case. * * *

"If duPont can establish that all or some part of the information sought is relevant and necessary to its proper defense of the action, then in our view it is entitled to an appropriate order incorporating such protective provisions, if any,

as the district court in the exercise of sound discretion may deem proper in light of the showing before it." Hartley Pen Co. v. United States District Court, 287 F.2d 324, 330, 129 USPQ 152, 157 (9th Cir.1961).

"We are of the opinion, however, that it would be appropriate for the defendant to apply to the district judge for such protective orders as may be needed and are permissible under Rule 30(b), (d) and Rule 31(d). If disclosures by it, now required by the broad order of the dis-

B. APPROPRIATION OF TRADE SECRETS

Because of the need to commercialize secret ideas, there is a constant problem of communicating them to others such as prospective purchasers and employees without destroying their value to their owner. There is also a problem surrounding the receiving of such ideas in a way which will not subject the recipient to unjust accusations of improper appropriation. A frank acceptance of a confidential disclosure without advance notice as to the nature of the idea may place the recipient in a difficult legal position. On the other hand, an inventor who must sign away all his rights to a confidential relationship before he makes a disclosure is left with a naked feeling, which tends to be aggravated by his helplessness as to any other avenue for successful commercialization. The following cases are representative of some of the problems in this area of the law.

SMITH v. DRAVO CORP.

United States Court of Appeals, Seventh Circuit, 1953.
203 F.2d 369, 97 USPQ 98.

LINDLEY, CIRCUIT JUDGE. * * *

In the early 1940s Leathem D. Smith, now deceased, began toying with an idea which, he believed, would greatly facilitate the ship and shore handling and transportation of cargoes. As he was primarily engaged in the shipbuilding business, it was quite natural that his thinking was chiefly concerned with water transportation and dock handling. Nevertheless his overall plan encompassed rail shipping as well. He envisioned construction of ships especially designed to carry their cargo in uniformly sized steel freight containers. These devices (which, it appears, were the crux of his idea) were: equipped with high doors at one end; large enough for a man to enter easily; weather and pilfer proof; and bore collapsible legs, which (1) served to lock them (a) to the deck of the ship by fitting into recesses in the deck, or (b) to each other, when stacked, by reason of receiving sockets located in the upper four corners of each container, and (2) allowed sufficient clearance between deck and container or container and container for the facile insertion of a fork of a lift tractor, and (3) were equipped with lifting eyelets, which, together with a specially designed hoist, made possible placement of the containers upon or removal from a ship, railroad car

---

trict court, are made, any secret formulae or processes now actually owned by the defendant will become public property. It may thereby become irreparably damaged. If at the end of this litigation defendant prevails, but in the meantime has made public property of valuable secret formulae, the victory will have been a costly one.

"The district court, likewise, may enter any appropriate order preventing public disclosure of information obtained from defendant through the discovery order here involved, and preventing plaintiff's use of such information, should its asserted cause of action against defendant fail."

The Chemical & Industrial Corp. v. Druffel, 301 F.2d 126, 133 USPQ 133 (6th Cir. 1962).

or truck, while filled with cargo. The outer dimensions of the devices were such that they would fit compactly in standard gauge North American railroad cars, or narrow gauge South American trains, and in the holds of most water vessels.

World War II effectually prevented Smith from developing his conception much beyond the idea stage. Nevertheless blue prints were drawn in 1943, and in 1944, as a result of considerable publicity in trade journals and addresses delivered by Smith before trade associations, Agwilines, one of the principal New York ship operators, displayed great interest in the proposals. Certain refined features, particularly in dimensions and folding legs, were the result of discussions between Smith and Agwilines' officials.

In 1945 production started, and in the fall of that year twelve containers were used by Agwilines in an experimental run. Relative success was experienced, with the result that, by the spring of 1946, Brodin Lines, Grace Lines, Delta Lines and Stockard, in addition to Agwilines, were leasing Safeway containers. (Leathem D. Smith Shipbuilding Company was the owner of the design and manufactured the containers. Safeway Container Corporation purchased the finished containers from the shipbuilding company and leased them to shippers.)

During this period the containers were occasionally seen on the docks. However, in view of their limited number (100) this was far from an every day occurrence. Furthermore, the details of their construction could not be ascertained by casual, distant appraisal. But, in the quest for acceptance, some minor construction details were revealed in the publicity material distributed throughout the shipping trade, including: the outer dimensions, cubic and weight capacities, placement of the lifting lugs, stacking sockets, double doors and the fact that the legs were folding. Three dimensional perspective illustrations demonstrated the use of the containers.

* * *

Defendant was interested in the Safeway container, primarily, it appears, for use by its subsidiary, the Union Barge Lines. In October 1946 it contacted Agwilines seeking information. It watched a loading operation in which Agwilines used the box. At approximately the same time, defendant approached the shipbuilding company and inquired as to the possibility of purchase of a number of the containers. It was told to communicate with Cowan, plaintiffs' eastern representative. This it did, and, on October 29, 1946, in Pittsburgh, Cowan met with defendant's officials to discuss the proposed sale of Safeways. But, as negotiations progressed, defendant demonstrated an interest in the entire container development. Thus, what started as a meeting to discuss the purchase of individual containers ended in the possible foundation for a sale of the entire business.

Based upon this display of interest, Cowan sent detailed information to defendant concerning the business. This included: (1) patent applications for both the "knockdown" and "rigid" crates; (2) blue prints of both designs; (3) a miniature Safeway container; (4) letters of inquiry from possible users; (5) further correspondence with prospective users. In addition, defendant's representatives journeyed to Sturgeon Bay, Wisconsin, the home of the shipbuilding company, and viewed the physical plant, inventory and manufacturing operation.

Plaintiffs quoted a price of $150,000 plus a royalty of $10 per unit. This was rejected. Subsequent offers of $100,000 and $75,000 with royalties of $10 per container were also rejected. Negotiations continued until January 30, 1947, at which time defendant finally rejected plaintiffs' offer.

On January 31, 1947 defendant announced to Agwilines that it "intended to design and produce a shipping container of the widest possible utility" for "coastal steamship application * * * [and] use * * * on the inland rivers and * * * connecting highway and rail carriers." Development of the project moved rapidly, so that by February 5, 1947 defendant had set up a stock order for a freight container which was designed, by use of plaintiffs' patent applications, so as to avoid any claim of infringement. One differing feature was the use of skids and recesses running the length of the container, rather than legs and sockets as employed in plaintiffs' design. However, Agwilines rejected this design, insisting on an adaptation of plaintiffs' idea. In short defendant's final product incorporated many, if not all, of the features of plaintiffs' design. So conceived, it was accepted by the trade to the extent that, by March 1948, defendant had sold some 500 containers. Many of these sales were made to firms who had shown considerable prior interest in plaintiffs' design and had been included in the prospective users disclosed to defendant.

One particular feature of defendant's container differed from plaintiffs: its width was four inches less. As a result plaintiffs' product became obsolete. Their container could not be used interchangeably with defendant's; they ceased production. Consequently the prospects of disposing of the entire operation vanished.

The foregoing is the essence of plaintiffs' cause of action. Stripped of surplusage, the averment is that defendant obtained, through a confidential relationship, knowledge of plaintiffs' secret designs, plans and prospective customers, and then wrongfully breached that confidence by using the information to its own advantage and plaintiffs' detriment.

* * *

In Macbeth-Evans Glass Co. v. Schnelbach, 239 Pa. 76, 86 A. 688, the Supreme Court of Pennsylvania painted, in broad strokes, the general picture of a claim of this nature, holding the essential elements to be: (1) existence of a trade secret, (2) communicated to the defendant (3) while he is in a position of trust and confidence and (4) use by the defendant to the injury of the plaintiff. This, then, is our broad basis for decision.

(1) THE EXISTENCE OF A TRADE SECRET

This is the very basis of plaintiffs' claim. They begin their search for relief with the assertion: "We possessed a trade secret." In order to ascertain whether they are correct, we must first determine just what a trade secret is and the precedent question as to what may be the subject matter of a trade secret.

We assume that almost any knowledge or information used in the conduct of one's business may be held by its possessor in secret. International Industries v. Warren Petroleum Corp., D.C.Del., 99 F.Supp. 907; Restatement, Torts, Sec. 757(b) (1939). Of course, as the term demands, the knowledge cannot be placed in the public domain and still be retained as a "secret". Thus, plaintiffs would not be permitted to copy the design of a known device and claim that the copies are their secret. That which has become public property cannot be recalled to privacy. However, this does not mean that the product must reach the stature of invention. Shellmar Products Co. v. Allen-Qualley Co., 7 Cir., 36 F.2d 623; Booth v. Stutz Motor Car Co., 7 Cir., 56 F.2d 962; A.O. Smith Corp. v. Petroleum Iron Works Co., 6 Cir., 73 F.2d 531. All that is required is that the information or knowledge represent in some considerable degree the independent efforts of its claimant. Clearly plaintiffs' plans and customer lists fall within this broad field of knowledge and may properly be the subject matter of a trade secret. Pressed Steel Car Co. v. Standard Steel Car Co., 210 Pa. 464, 60 A. 4; Chas. H. Elliott Co. v. Skillkrafters, Inc., 271 Pa. 185, 114 A. 488.

We do not understand that defendant seriously contends otherwise. Rather its position is that the structural designs of plaintiffs' containers were disclosed by (1) public use of the containers and (2) publicity material freely circulated. Thus, defendant says, at the crucial time of communication, plaintiffs' knowledge was no longer secret, it had been publicly disclosed. As to the customer lists, defendant denies their very existence.

The second of these assertions can be disposed of readily. The evidence is undisputed that plaintiffs had in their possession, at the time of their negotiations with defendant, original letters of inquiry from numerous shipping companies and a consequential number of files of further correspondence between plaintiffs and the inquirers. Together these comprised a valuable prospective customer list, the existence of which can in no way be challenged.

The continued secrecy of the construction plans presents a different question. The District Court entered the following finding of fact: "* * * the record shows that Plaintiffs had published to the world, through public uses of the containers and unrestricted publications by circulars and in trade magazines, complete information concerning the subject-matter with which the material [the patent applications and plans] * * * was concerned." From this the court concluded that no secrets were confidentially disclosed to defendant.

The publicity material did not, in any way, disclose plaintiffs' design. The outward dimensions were revealed, and the fact that the container employed large double doors, lifting eyelets, stacking sockets and folding legs was publicized. But this was not equivalent to a disclosure of the structural design, the engineering details, of either the container as a whole or its various working parts. These could be obtained only by careful inspection of the article and the drawings. Therefore, in this respect the finding of fact that plaintiffs had, through unrestricted publications in trade magazines and circulars, "Published * * * complete information concerning the subject", was clearly erroneous and must be set aside.

There is no dispute that 100 of plaintiffs' products had been in public use at the time of the communication. There is, however, serious debate over the legal consequences of this fact. The lower court, in refusing plaintiffs' recovery, applied the following conclusion of law: "There can be no confidential disclosure where, as here, the alleged novel container was being manufactured and sold. * * * and all information concerning its construction was available from an inspection of the container." Certain cases appear to give support to this broad statement. See, e.g., Sandlin v. Johnson, 8 Cir., 141 F.2d 660; Northup v. Reish, 7 Cir., 200 F.2d 924; Carver v. Harr, 132 N.J.Eq. 207, 27 A.2d 895. But, close examination reveals that the inquiry is much deeper than whether "all information * * * was *available* from an inspection of the containers."

As a starting point we must look again to Pennsylvania for our guide. In Pressed Steel Car Co. v. Standard Steel Car Co., 210 Pa. 464, 60 A. 4, 7, plaintiff sought to protect its secret construction design for railroad cars. These plans had been obtained by defendant through a known breach of confidence. It was urged by defendant that because it *could have* obtained the design from an inspection of the car (which was in public use) its use of knowledge gained through improper means would be condoned. In short, defendant suggested, as does defendant here, that the existence of a lawful means of acquiring the information precluded recovery for the employment of unlawful means. The court said:

> " * * * these engineers and draftsmen * * * should have been able to measure the cars made by the company, and to produce in a short time detailed and practical drawings from which the cars could be constructed. They did not do this, for the very obvious reason that blue prints of drawings were available and were accurate. * * * "

The court then affirmed recovery for the plaintiff.

Thus, Pennsylvania will not deny recovery merely because the design *could have* been obtained through inspection. Rather, the inquiry in that jurisdiction appears to be: How *did* defendant learn of plaintiffs' design? And this, we regard as the proper test. It recognizes the very nature of the type of wrong with which we are here concerned. Confidential business information is not given protection merely as a reward to its accumulator. If the creator is entitled to reward it is available to him in the patent and copyright statutes.

HISEL v. CHRYSLER CORP.

United States District Court of Missouri, 1951.
94 F.Supp. 996, 88 USPQ 281.

RIDGE, DISTRICT JUDGE. * * *

December 20, 1939, plaintiff sent to defendant Chrysler Corporation a letter, inviting attention to an idea he had concerning the appearance of new cars which he claimed would improve the charm and beauty thereof. The idea was not disclosed in that letter. Under date of January 9, 1940, Chrysler Corporation sent to plaintiff a letter, acknowledging receipt of his letter and calling attention to the "policy of Chrysler Corporation in regard to new ideas" and enclosed therewith a document so entitled, outlining such policy. Said document is as follows:

"It has always been the policy of the Chrysler Corporation to encourage and develop all such improvements for its products as will tend to produce better vehicles at the lowest possible price. During the years of its existence, the Chrysler Corporation has made use of and paid royalties for a large number of inventions which have been submitted to it by persons outside the Corporation. We like to feel that we give equally as much, if not more, consideration to the idea which is submitted to us from outside our Corporation as we do to the idea which is submitted to us by our own engineers.

"As a result of this policy, thousands of ideas are submitted to us each year. They come from people in all walks of life and of every temperament and disposition. To each of them we attempt to give courteous and considerate attention so that those ideas which have merit in our business may be brought to the attention of the proper persons in our organization.

"Because of the number of suggestions which come to us, containing both old and new ideas, and the different types of people with whom we have to deal, it is necessary, before we receive and consider any suggestion, that we prescribe certain conditions upon which we will receive and consider the suggestion. Briefly, these are:

"1. Chrysler Corporation is willing to consider any suggestion which may be made but does so only at the request of the person who has the suggestion.

"2. No obligation of any kind is assumed by, nor may be implied against, the Chrysler Corporation unless or until a formal written contract has been entered into and then the obligation shall be only such as is expressed in the formal written contract.

"3. You do not give Chrysler Corporation any rights under any patents you now have or may later obtain covering your suggestion but do, in consideration of its examining your suggestion, release it from any liability in connection with your suggestion or liability because of use of any portion thereof, except such liability as may accrue under valid patents now or hereafter issued."

Also enclosed with said letter was a form prepared by Chrysler Corporation, addressed to its Engineering Improvements Committee, for execution by plaintiff, providing for the identification of the idea he wished to submit for consideration by Chrysler Corporation, and setting forth the conditions under which the Corporation was to consider it.

About a year later, on December 31, 1940, without intervening events occurring, plaintiff sent a letter to Chrysler Corporation, explaining an idea, which he claimed to be original with him, relative to the placing of a license plate for an automobile in a 1-inch-deep waterproof metal box, covered with a glass, inserted into the right or left front fender thereof; and, the insertion of a rear license plate in a similar metal box inserted in the center of the trunk compartment or turtleback of an automobile, just above the handle. Plaintiff enclosed therein a sketch illustrating his idea and the location on an automobile of such a device. January 3, 1941, Chrysler Corporation sent to plaintiff a letter acknowledging receipt of plaintiff's letter of December 31, 1940, and stated that Chrysler Corporation had not received an executed copy of the agreement under which it would be willing to consider his idea; and called plaintiff's attention to the fact that a form of such an agreement had been forwarded to plaintiff with its letter of January 9, 1940. On January 27, 1941, plaintiff executed and mailed the form agreement last above referred to, which was received by Chrysler Corporation on January 30, 1941. In that agreement, plaintiff identified his idea as "Inserted license-plate holder. The front plate is inserted in front fender in glass-covered, insulated, metal box; the rear plate in trunk compartment in a like box." After so identifying his idea, the following is contained in said agreement over plaintiff's signature:

"I have been informed by your representatives that you are willing to consider all suggestions which may be made to you by persons outside of your Corporation, but that because of the large number of such suggestions, containing both old and new ideas, which are submitted from people in all walks of life and of every temperament and disposition, you require the acceptance by me of certain conditions before considering my suggestion. These conditions are:

"1. Chrysler Corporation is willing to consider any suggestion which may be made but does so only at the request of the person who has the suggestion.

"2. No obligation of any kind is assumed by, nor may be implied against, the Chrysler Corporation, unless or until a formal written contract has been entered into, and then the obligation shall be only such as is expressed in the formal written contract.

"3. I do not hereby give Chrysler Corporation any rights under any patents I now have or may later obtain covering my suggestion but I do hereby, in consideration of its examining my suggestion, release it from any liability in connection with my suggestion or liability because of use of any portion thereof, except such liability as may accrue under valid patents now or hereafter issued.

"I am agreeable to these conditions and ask you to consider my suggestion under them."

February 13, 1941, Chrysler Corporation sent a letter to plaintiff, acknowledging receipt of said agreement and advising plaintiff that his idea for a license-plate holder had been discussed with its engineers, and stated "that the idea is not new to them since others have submitted similar plans in the past." Six years thereafter, on April 14, 1947, plaintiff sent another letter to Chrysler Corporation, again explaining and calling to its attention his idea for mounting license-plates, and stating that the explanation therein contained "has been copywrighted." The "explanation of device" contained in that letter is identical with that contained in plaintiff's previous letter of December 31, 1940, and makes reference thereto. April 18, 1947, Chrysler Corporation acknowledged receipt of said letter from plaintiff, and stated that it was not at present in a position to give consideration to the type of license-plate holder which plaintiff suggested, and expressed the thought to plaintiff as to "whether the idea you suggest is patentable in view of the many similar suggestions which have been made by others." It is admitted that the foregoing correspondence is all the communication that ever passed between plaintiff and defendant relating to the disclosure by plaintiff, to Chrysler Corporation, of plaintiff's idea for mounting license-plates on automobiles.

The answers of defendants in the above actions specifically aver that the alleged idea claimed by plaintiff with respect to the mounting of license-plates was commonly known in the automobile trade and was in the public domain and available for free use by the public long prior to any alleged origination thereof by plaintiff, and prior to any disclosure made by plaintiff to defendants. In the answers, specific reference is made to certain expired United States Letters Patent and to pictures, drawings and articles appearing in various trade journals, published and circulated among members of the automobile industry in the United States and foreign countries as far back as the year 1926.

* * *

Examination of the specifications and drawings of the above letters patent, considered in relation to the idea and claim to invention expressed and described in the letters and documents forwarded to Chrysler Corporation by plaintiff, reveals without question, that plaintiff's idea was anticipated by the grant of the claims allowed in the above-referred-to letters patent. * * *

An examination of the sixteen publications so cited reveals that every feature of the idea and invention here claimed by plaintiff as being original with him was anticipated long prior to the time of any alleged disclosure by plaintiff of his idea to defendants. * * *

The issue raised and presented by the pleadings herein presents the proposition whether, under the foregoing state of facts, plaintiff "in faith and in confidence" disclosed to Chrysler Corporation "the secret nature" of an idea and invention claimed by him, under such circumstances that the Corporation should, in good conscience and fair dealing, be prohibited from making further disclosure thereof, or making use of any novelty contained in plaintiff's claimed idea or invention without additional consent and approval of the plaintiff. * * *

When plaintiff divulged his idea and suggestion to Chrysler Corporation, for the mounting of license-plates on automobiles, it is apparent that plaintiff was fully informed of the "policy of the Chrysler Corporation in regard to new ideas" and the conditions under which that corporation would receive and consider the same.[f] Being so informed, plaintiff disclosed his idea to Chrysler Corporation and executed an agreement compatible with that policy by which he agreed that if Chrysler Corporation would examine his suggestion he would "release it from any liability in connection with (the) suggestion, or liability because of use of any portion thereof, except such liability as may accrue under valid patents now or hereafter issued." Therefore, the relationship existing between plaintiff and defendant Chrysler Corporation, as at issue in this action, is to be determined from the legal effect to be given to the provisions of such agreement. Said agreement is unambiguous in its terms. Consequently, the construction and legal effect to be given thereto is a question of law to be decided by the Court. National Surety Corp. of New York v. Ellison, 8 Cir., 88 F.2d 399.

The clear intent, manifest in the above agreement, is repugnant to any implication of confidential relationship existing between plaintiff and Chrysler Corporation as here contended. By said agreement Chrysler Corporation cannot be held to have established a relationship of "trust and confidence." Before it acceded to plaintiff's request to consider the idea or suggestion plaintiff says he divulged to them, that Corporation made known to plaintiff its policy relative thereto and requested plaintiff to execute an agreement setting forth the conditions under which it would do so. Therefore, rather than establishing a relationship of "trust and confidence," such matters reveal that Chrysler Corporation was dealing with plaintiff at arm's length and was not negotiating with him in such a manner as to bind it in respect to any information disclosed to it by plaintiff, even though it made use thereof, unless a valid patent was issued thereon. Under the facts shown in evidence, the law will not imply a promise on the part of Chrysler Corporation not to make use of said idea, or cast a liability on it by implication of a confidential relationship such as we would be compelled to do to sustain a right of action existing in favor of plaintiff.

f. Hawkins and Udell, Corporation Caution and Unsolicited New Product Ideas: A Survey of Corporate Waiver Requirements, 58 J.P.O.S. 379 (1976).

Even though defendants may be shown to be making use of plaintiff's claimed idea, "they are not indebted to plaintiff, because they did not offer (or) make any agreement to pay for such (idea)" if they used it, unless it was patentable. Lueddecke v. Chevrolet Motor Co., 8 Cir., 70 F.2d 345, 348; Moore v. Ford Motor Co., D.C., 28 F.2d 529.

* * *

C. EMPLOYER–EMPLOYEE RELATIONSHIP

Some of the most difficult problems in the law of trade secrets are involved in the employer-employee relationship. It is an age old problem for an employer to deal with disloyal, untrustworthy and occasionally even dishonest employees. But in a free and democratic society which fosters an open market, how much loyalty can an employer rightfully expect of his employees? Can he rightfully expect them to limit their mobility, employment by others and later use of acquired skills and knowledge to compete with him? The courts must strike a balance between the employer's interest in protecting his trade secrets and the employee's interest in earning a livelihood by the fullest possible utilization of his talents, skills and knowledge. Is the problem any different when the secret information was created by the employee for the employer's benefit rather than imparted to him by the employer?

AMERICAN CHAIN & CABLE CO., INC. v. AVERY
Supreme Court of Connecticut, 1964.
143 USPQ 126.

BARBER, JUDGE. I. The plaintiff, through its Allison-Campbell Division of Bridgeport, is engaged in the manufacture and sale of abrasive cutting wheels. The defendants, Avery, LeBlanc and Pane, are all former employees of the plaintiff. The corporate defendant, Avery Abrasives, Inc., is a new company, formed to manufacture and sell abrasive cutting wheels.

The plaintiff claims that the defendants have misappropriated plaintiff's trade secrets, consisting of the exact nature of supplies purchased from various companies, its formulas, processes and techniques for manufacturing, and information relating to the identity and needs of its customers. This, it claims, has resulted in an unfair competitive advantage to the defendant, Avery Abrasives, Inc., in the sale of abrasive cutting wheels. The defendants claim that they have not used any information which qualifies as a trade secret; and that they did use only such general information as was and is common knowledge in the industry and such technical information as constituted a part of their technical knowledge and skill.

The prayer for relief in this action claims a temporary and permanent injunction restraining the defendants from (a) using or revealing to others any of the formulas, processes and techniques utilized by the plaintiff in the manufacture of cutting wheels, and (b) selling, soliciting orders for, offering for sale or in any manner assisting in the sale of abrasive cutting wheels, utilizing the formulas, processes and techniques of the plaintiff. It also claims an accounting of all profits realized from defendants' sale of abrasive cutting wheels, an order imposing a trust for the benefit of the plaintiff on all contracts for the sale of abrasive cutting wheels which, at the date of judgment are executory, and money damages.

* * *

III. The law is well settled that, in the absence of a restrictive agreement, a former employee can properly compete with his former employer. Town and Country House & Homes Service, Inc. v. Evans, 150 Conn. 314, 317. Even before the termination of his employment, an employee is entitled to make arrangements to compete, except he cannot use confidential information peculiar to his employer's business and acquired therein. Restatement, Agency 2d § 393, comment e. An employee has a right to grow with his experience, and he can carry away for general use his skill and everything that he has learned at his place of employment, except trade secrets. Restatement, Agency 2d § 396, comment b & h. * * *

Not only does the plaintiff claim a misappropriation of certain alleged trade secrets, but it seems to rely upon a misappropriation of all these trade secrets in the sense that they constitute a compilation of information. The burden is upon the plaintiff to prove that it possessed such trade secrets and that they were misappropriated by the defendants in violation of a confidence. Wexler v. Greenberg, 399 Pa. 569, 160 A.2d 430, 125 USPQ 471. There is no doubt but that the individual defendants brought with them to the new company a wealth of skill and a broad background of experience in the specialized field of manufacturing and the selling of abrasive cutting wheels. The sole question for this court to determine is whether they brought with them any trade secrets, as distinguished from just information generally known in the industry. To prevail, the plaintiff must also furnish a basis for appropriate relief.

IV. One of the claims of the plaintiff is that although the existence of the companies which supply the plaintiff with various ingredients are generally known, the exact nature of the supplies purchased from such companies was a trade secret. The complaint refers only to plaintiff's sources of supply. The evidence does show that the Avery Company did order similar specific supplies from the same specific companies as did the plaintiff. However, there is nothing secret or unique about the ingredients used in making abrasive cutting wheels that is unusual or not known generally by the industry and by salesmen doing business with the manufacturers.

V. Another claim of the plaintiff is that the defendants misappropriated its formulas, processes and techniques for manufacturing abrasive cutting wheels. A cutting wheel is produced in accordance with a definite formula. At the plaintiff's plant the formulas for these wheels are coded on small cards or sheets of paper. To a person familiar with the code, these cards or sheets of paper show the prescribed size and type of abrasive grain to be used, the amount and type of bond and the density of the wheel. Plaintiff's cutting wheels are identified by numbers and letters, based primarily upon the "Standard Marking System Chart," used generally in the industry (Exhibit 1, pp. 10 & 11). The grain type, the abrasive type, the grain size, the grain combination, the hardness of the wheel, its density and the bond type are all classified by numbers and letters from the standard chart. The specific manufacturer may also have a special marking pertaining to the manufacturing procedure.

The ingredients used in abrasive cutting wheels manufactured by the plaintiff are commonly known in the industry and there is no secrecy attached to them or to their use in cutting wheels. The abrasives, the bonds and the liquids used as fillers, are all commonly known and used throughout the industry. The plaintiff does not seek to suppress any certain unique mixture or recipe, but the making of any wheels similar to its product. * * * The plaintiff has proved no superior advances or differences in formulas which are protectable as trade secrets. Boost Co. v. Faunce, 17 N.J.Super. 458, 86 A.2d 283, 285; 43 C.J.S. 750, § 148a. It does not seem proper that the jurisdiction of a court should be invoked to prevent competition and employees from utilizing their skills, aptitudes and subjective general knowledge after they have terminated their employment, unless their former employer has made known to them while in employment that the things, subsequently claimed to be a trade secret, should in fact be regarded as trade secrets. Developments in the Law— Competitive Torts, 77 H.L.R. 888, 950 (March 1964); Chaffee & Pound, Cases on Equitable Relief against Torts, 86, note 1. Of course, the court should be permitted to infer such knowledge from circumstantial evidence in the proper case, but in this case the court does not find that such a conclusion by inference is warranted.

Both Avery and LeBlanc were skilled technicians in a specialized industry. They were not under a contract. The totality of the relief demanded by the plaintiff would prevent them from pursuing their occupations and would entirely stifle competition with the plaintiff. Competition must not be stifled unless unfair. In our industrial and economic system allegiance to an employer is not forever. In the absence of a binding agreement, either the employer or the employee can terminate the status at any time. Of course, the longer the employee has served his principal and the more intense the loyalty has been, the greater the irritation to the principal against whom the former employee must compete. This irritation or any resulting harm therefrom, in the absence of an appropriation of property based upon breach of confidence, does not, however, establish a cause of action. Wexler v. Greenberg, supra; Springs Steels, Inc. v. Malloy, 400 Pa. 354, 162 A.2d 370, 373, 126 USPQ 214.

* * *

VI. The plaintiff also claimed that the defendants have misappropriated information relating to the identity and needs of its customers. There is no evidence that any defendant carried away with him a specific list of customers and their needs. The corporate defendant has no salesmen, but does business through manufacturer's agents. After commencing business the defendant concern was voluntarily approached by several customers of the plaintiff with regard to purchasing Avery cut-off wheels. When acquiring agents, Avery made a list of potential customers, noting the type of wheels they would probably be interested in and the quantity. (Exhibit 11). This list contained several of plaintiff's customers. It was given to a manufacturer's agent in the Philadelphia area, and specifically to a Mr. Ahlstrom who was acting for the firm. Mr. Ahlstrom had previous experience with Bay State Abrasive Company and Norton Abrasive Company, competitors of the plaintiff. Mr. Ahlstrom was aware of the existence of every company on the list and had actually done business with forty-two of the hundred companies listed and had solicited business from more than half. Actually the plaintiff has lost only three accounts on this list in their entirety, and in January of 1964, had eighty more accounts in the Philadelphia area than it had in 1960. Such information as Avery had pertaining to plaintiff's customers was only general information which he was able to recall from memory. Nor did the defendant Pane, a salesman for the plaintiff before the termination of his employment, carry away with him a specific list of customers and their needs. In fact, he turned in all his written records and information upon terminating his employment and took a receipt therefor. At the time he terminated with the plaintiff, it had approximately eight hundred accounts in the Metropolitan New York Area. Out of this substantial total, Pane only solicited between fifty and seventy-five of these accounts since he became a manufacturer's representative handling, among other products, the Avery wheel. Only about 20% of the accounts Mr. Pane has solicited have in fact purchased Avery wheels.

Town & Country House & Homes Service, Inc. v. Evans, supra, is the most recent case in this jurisdiction dealing with trade secrets. In this case the court expounds the law on "lists of customers" but was not compelled to clarify to what extent names of customers retained in memory as a result of employment are protectable. In most jurisdictions it has been held that, "(W)here there is no express contract prohibiting the solicitation of such customers by the employee after termination of his employment he cannot be injoined from such solicitation as long as he proceeds from memory rather than by unauthorized use of a list of customers." 43 C.J.S. 755, § 148b; Restatement of Agency 2d § 396, comment b: Customers cannot be owned by a manufacturer. Ellis, Trade Secrets § 67. The plaintiff has not sustained its burden of proof that the competition from the defendant manufacturer was unfair. Ibid. § 76.

* * * It does not appear from the evidence that the plaintiff has been unlawfully harmed or that the defendants have been unlawfully benefited. Judgment may enter for the defendants.

STRUCTURAL DYNAMICS RESEARCH CORP. v. ENGINEERING MECHANICS RESEARCH CORP.

United States District Court of Michigan, 1975.
401 F.Supp. 1102.

FEIKENS, DISTRICT JUDGE.

I.

Structural Dynamics Research Corporation (SDRC) brought this action against three former employees, Kant Kothawala, Karan Surana and Robert Hildebrand, for unfair competition, misappropriation and misuse of confidential and trade secret material, breach of confidential disclosure agreements and interference with SDRC's customer relations, and against Engineering Mechanics Research Corporation (EMRC) for conspiring with the individual defendants to accomplish the above purposes. It seeks both damages and a permanent injunction.

SDRC is an Ohio corporation with its principal place of business at Cincinnati, Ohio. EMRC is a Michigan corporation with its principal place of business at Southfield, Michigan. Kothawala, Surana and Hildebrand are all residents of Michigan.

[All of the individual defendants are now employed by EMRC. Kothawala is the President and sole shareholder. Surana is Vice President of Engineering. Hildebrand is Manager of Applications.]

* * *

Both SDRC and EMRC are engaged in the business of structural analysis and testing. They are also engaged in the development of computer programs for such purposes for use in their business and for lease to other users.

* * *

Structural analysis involves, generally speaking, the prediction of how a physical structure will react when forces are applied to it. One of the methods used to solve structural analysis problems is a finite element computer program. The technical part of this dispute concerns two such programs. These computer programs are used to obtain an approximation of the reaction of a physical structure when forces are applied to it. This approximation is termed a mathematical model. It simulates actual conditions.

* * *

The finite element computer programs generally in use prior to 1971 employed primarily straight sided elements such as triangles and rectangles. When the structure involved curved surfaces, straight sided elements had cost and accuracy limitations as a large number of elements were required to approximate the structure's configuration.

Thus, the concept of employing curved and irregular shaped elements and "higher order" elements with different nodal structures termed "isoparametric elements" was under investigation. Isoparametric elements, in a properly designed program, offer substantial advantages over conventional finite element programs since the use of curved and irregular shaped elements permits the user to achieve at least as accurate results at a lower cost due to the reduction of the number of elements necessary to prepare models of a structure to be tested.

SDRC first became interested in isoparametric elements when, in the fall of 1971, Surana and Russell Henke, vice-president of SDRC attended a conference at Urbana, Illinois, where a number of technical papers were delivered. References to isoparametric elements appeared in some papers. Kothawala, then an employee of General Motors, also attended the conference.

Following the Urbana conference Surana began to investigate isoparametric technology thoroughly, primarily from the literature. Prior to this time Surana did not have a substantial background or knowledge in the field of isoparametric finite element technology. He concluded that an isoparametric program would be useful and advantageous to SDRC and so informed SDRC's management. SDRC encouraged Surana to continue his efforts but also required him to devote time to revenue producing projects. In April, 1972 SDRC gave formal recognition to Surana's isoparametric research by the establishment of a time charge account. By that time Surana had reduced to writing certain preliminary equations, computations and sketches necessary to the development of a program. He continued preliminary development work as time permitted until August.

In August of 1972 Kothawala joined SDRC as a member of the Technical Staff. Beginning a year or more prior to his employment, Kothawala and SDRC had discussed this possibility. SDRC wished to open a Detroit office and Kothawala desired a managerial position in a Detroit-based company which he would wholly or partially own. When Kothawala was hired, both parties anticipated that he would assume management responsibility for an SDRC office in Detroit but the details were left for future resolution. It was agreed that Kothawala would spend six to twelve months in Cincinnati to familiarize himself with SDRC's business and procedures.

Hildebrand was also hired in August of 1972 on Kothawala's recommendation. It was anticipated that he would also be involved in the Detroit office.

In August of 1972, shortly after Kothawala started working at SDRC, Surana showed him the results of his investigation concerning an isoparametric element computer program. Kothawala arranged to have Surana's conclusions reviewed by the Technical Staff.

A meeting of the Technical Staff was held on August 14, 1972. Surana explained to them what he had been doing with respect to isoparametric elements and the advantages he believed a program containing such elements would have over one containing conventional elements. At the conclusion of the meeting, this group gave Surana authority to devote all of his time to develop such a program and assigned to Kothawala and Surana responsibility for drafting a formal written proposal. Kothawala was eventually assigned supervisory responsibility for the project.

* * *

In this case Surana and Kothawala did not obtain the claimed trade secrets through improper means. In substantial measure they were the developers and innovators of a general purpose isoparametric computer program. They were hired by SDRC for research and development activity in this very field, and the manner of their acquisition of knowledge of this technology can in no sense be said to have been obtained improperly.

Does their subsequent use or disclosure of this technology, assuming it to be a trade secret, breach a duty of trust owed by these individual defendants to plaintiff? The Restatement, supra, at 4, suggests this question by its comment: "apart from breach of contract, abuse of confidence or impropriety in the means of procurement, trade secrets may be copied as freely as devices which are not secret".

The relationship giving rise to a duty is not necessarily dependent upon contract; it may be based on agency principles or on specific dealings between parties in which a situation of trust arises and out of which sought-to-be-protected knowledge is acquired. Vital to a consideration of the creation of duty in such situations is the key question as to how the person acquiring such trade secret knowledge obtained it. If the subject matter of the trade secret is in being and an employee learns about it in the course of his employment in a relationship of confidence, the duty not to use or disclose trade secret knowledge adversely to his employer arises. On the other hand, if the subject matter of the trade secret is brought into being because of the initiative of the employee in its creation, innovation or development even though the relationship is one of confidence, no duty arises since the employee may then have an interest in the subject matter at least equal to that of his employer or in any event, such knowledge is a part of the employee's skill and experience. In such a case, absent an express contractual obligation by the employee not to use or disclose such confidential information acquired during his employment adverse to his employer's interest, he is free to use or disclose it in subsequent employment activity.

In Wexler v. Greenberg, 399 Pa. 569, 160 A.2d 430 (1960), the Pennsylvania Supreme Court held that in the absence of a contractual obligation not to use or disclose, no duty arose from the employment relationship itself that would prevent a chemist from using and disclosing secret chemical formulae developed by him in the course of his former employment. The court distinguished the cases in which an employer discloses to his employee a preexisting trade secret from those in which the employee himself develops the trade secret sought to be protected. A further distinction was then drawn within the category of employee-developed secrets. Where the employer assigns the employee to a specific development task and commits considerable resources and supervision to the project, a confidential relationship arises that prevents the employee from using or disclosing the fruits of his research. When, on the other hand, the developments are the product of the application of the employee's own skill, "without any appreciable assistance by way of information or great expense or supervision by [the employer], outside of the normal expenses of his job", 160 A.2d at 436, he has "an unqualified privilege" to use and disclose the trade secrets so developed. 160 A.2d at 437. Accord, New Method Die & Cut-Out Co. v. Milton Bradley Co., 289 Mass. 277, 194 N.E. 80, 82 (1935) (defendant employee not required to maintain secrecy where he "took part to a substantial extent in developing the process", but "was not employed specifically for this purpose".)

While the question is concededly a close one, the court holds that the isoparametric program developed on the initial encouragement—and under the supervision—of Surana and Kothawala falls within the latter category.

Surana and Kothawala do not owe SDRC a duty not to use or disclose its trade secrets by reason of a relationship of confidence in employment. As the substantial developers and innovators of this technology they have an interest in it and unless they expressly contracted with SDRC not to use or disclose such knowledge or information in future employment activity, there is no duty imposed upon them by reason of their employment relationship with SDRC. Nor is such a duty created by any equitable doctrine of quasi-contract; i.e., a contract implied in law.

Accordingly, the court turns to the remaining question. Are there obligations imposed on the individual defendants not to use or disclose confidential information acquired in and during the course of their employment at SDRC because of express contractual agreements into which they entered?

III.

Here, all three individual defendants entered into an Employee Patent and Confidential Information Agreement.

* * *

The agreements not to disclose confidential information impose obligations by their clear terms since these undertakings do not exclude information, technology or knowledge which the employee himself discovers, develops or contributes. See Winston Research Corp. v. Minnesota Mining and Manufacturing Co., 350 F.2d 134, 140 (9th Cir.

1965). Thus, if the contracts are valid and enforceable, defendants are under obligations not to use or disclose confidential information gained while employed at SDRC.

* * *

The contracts in issue are valid *in toto* if governed by Ohio law and valid in part if severable under Michigan law. Ohio permits its courts to enforce covenants not to use or disclose confidential information as well as reasonable covenants not to compete. Raimonde v. Van Vlerah, 42 Ohio St.2d 21, 325 N.E.2d 544 (1975). In Michigan a statute, M.C. L.A. 445.761 [g] declares that covenants not to compete, whether reasonable or unreasonable, are against public policy and are illegal and void.[h] Michigan, however, does recognize and enforce covenants not to use or disclose confidential information. Glucol Manufacturing Co. v. Schulist, 239 Mich. 70, 214 N.W. 152 (1927).

Whether Michigan or Ohio law applies is a question of conflict of laws. A United States District Court in exercising diversity jurisdiction must follow the forum state's rules. Klaxon Co. v. Stentor Electric Manufacturing Co., 313 U.S. 487, 61 S.Ct. 1020, 85 L.Ed. 1477 (1941). Michigan follows the general rule expressed in the Restatement of Conflict of Laws § 332 that the nature, validity, effect and obligation of a contract are governed by the law of the place where the contract was made. Keehn v. Charles J. Rogers, Inc., 311 Mich. 416, 18 N.W.2d 877 (1945); Waldorf v. KMS Industries, Inc., 25 Mich.App. 20, 181 N.W.2d 85 (1970).

There does not seem to be any dispute as to the place of the making of the contracts and in any event the court finds that they were entered into in Ohio.

* * *

This being so, the law of Ohio would govern questions of validity. A number of factors indicate this to be the correct result: (a) It is in accord with principles stated in the Restatement of Conflict of Laws which were recently so forcefully upheld in Michigan in the area of torts. Abendschein v. Farrell, 382 Mich. 510, 170 N.W.2d 137 (1969). (b) The contracts in issue were made, executed and delivered in Ohio. (c) It would further the presumed intent of the parties, in accordance with traditional contract doctrine, to enter into a valid contract. (d) The employment relationship arose and centered in Ohio. (e) The

g. As of 1986, this statute had counterparts in the state codes of Alabama, California, Florida, Louisiana, North Dakota, Oklahoma, South Dakota and Montana.

h. In pertinent part, this statute provided "All agreements and contracts by which any person, co-partnership or corporation promises or agrees not to engage in any avocation, employment, pursuit, trade, profession or business, whether reasonable or unreasonable, partial or general, limited or unlimited, are hereby declared to be against public policy and illegal and void."

(M.C.L.A. '48 § 445.761.) This statute was repealed by the Michigan legislature effective March 19, 1985 when revising the Michigan anti-trust law so it now provides in part "A contract, combination or conspiracy between 2 or more persons in restraint of, or to monopolize, trade or commerce in a relevant market is unlawful." (M.C.L.A. § 445.772.) As of 1986 no Michigan appellate court has considered what effect, if any, these statutory changes have on the enforceability of a covenant by a former employee not to compete.

defendants acquired the confidential information while employed at SDRC's principal place of business in Ohio.

The extent to which an Ohio contract will be enforced in Michigan depends upon the doctrine of judicial comity. McColl v. Wardowski, 280 Mich. 374, 273 N.W. 736 (1937). Defendants argue that even though the contracts are valid where made, the inclusion of a non-competition clause in each, void under M.C.L.A. 445.761, invalidates the contracts and precludes their enforcement.

This court is unable to perceive any reason why contracts, valid *in toto* where made, should not be enforced as a matter of comity to the extent their provisions do not contravene the public policy of the forum. In Glucol Manufacturing Company v. Schulist, 239 Mich. 70, 214 N.W. 152 (1927) the Michigan Supreme Court, in discussing the enforceability of non-disclosure provisions, stated:

> "But we agree with the trial court that this statute [M.C.L.A. 445.761] has no application in the instant case. The reason is obvious. Defendant did not agree not to engage in a similar business, but only that he would not use the formulae of his employer, which, he was given to understand, were the property of plaintiff." 239 Mich. at 74, 214 N.W. at 153.

See O. & W. Thum Co. v. Tloczynski, 114 Mich. 149, 72 N.W. 140 (1897).

The public policy of Michigan does not preclude enforcement of use or non-disclosure provisions. The presence of the non-competition provision, while itself unenforceable, does not make the other logically distinct and separate provisions of these contracts unenforceable when these provisions, standing alone, are valid in both states.

* * *

Tom Arnold, a practicing patent attorney and author of numerous articles on patent law, comments on employer-employee relations in "Rights in Trade Secrets That Are Not Secret", presented at the Institute of Patent Law in 1963 at the Southwestern Legal Foundation [i]:

> So here we find an area where the common law has fumbled the ball as badly as a hippopotamus playing tiddly winks. Even with declaratory judgment procedures, our judicial system does not now afford a clear answer to the right of the former employee in the many in-between areas of know-how necessarily used in new competitive businesses, until *after* the new business has committed its capital to some selected design. And even then the answer obtained is not across the full scope of the employee's knowledge but is specific to only the tools litigated—leaving the former employee still in a quandary as to every new tool he designs thereafter.

* * *

i. Reprinted by permission from "Patent Procurement and Exploitation," Copyright 1963 by The Bureau of National Affairs, Inc., Washington, D.C. 20037.

[On the employer's problem]:

Here I think it significant to note that it is not the laborer who is critical, and often it is not even the typical research engineer who is most critical. The man in the young management group with no special technical trade secret as such, is often the man who can hurt you most by going to a competitor—and this man's know-how is most often totally unprotectable by the law of confidential information, as such.

It does not follow, however, that the employer is helpless to afford itself substantial protection. It can do this by appropriate employment contracts with its critical personnel, including no-competition clauses in appropriate areas for six months, a year or two years, as may be appropriate.

*   *   *

D. LIMITATIONS AND REMEDIES

THE ANACONDA COMPANY v. METRIC TOOL & DIE COMPANY

United States District Court of Pennsylvania, 1980.
485 F.Supp. 410.

BECKER, DISTRICT JUDGE.

I. PRELIMINARY STATEMENT

This is a trade secret case. Plaintiff, The Anaconda Company ("Anaconda"), a Montana corporation, is best known for its mining operations. However, Anaconda is a diversified company also engaged in the fabrication of a varied line of products made from copper, aluminum, steel, and other materials, including a product known as flexible metal hose. One application of flexible metal hose is an item known as telephone cord armor ("TCA"), a strip-wound metal hose familiar to all users of coin telephones. TCA is what protects the telephone cord from wear and tear, abuse, and vandalism. Anaconda fabricates TCA on a sophisticated profile and winding ("P & W") machine which it engineered and built for this purpose, after a considerable and expensive development period.

Anaconda claims that the design of its P & W machine used to make TCA is a trade secret which was misappropriated by the defendant Metric Tool & Die Company ("Metric"). Metric is a Morrisville, Pennsylvania concern which was originally engaged in small scale manufacturing operations, including stamping and drilling and the design and manufacture of sundry machine tools and dies. Metric began to manufacture TCA after it was invited to bid on TCA by Western Electric Company, Inc., ("Western Electric" or "Western"). Western is the principal buyer of TCA in the nation, and Metric has now succeeded Anaconda as Western Electric's principal supplier of TCA. Anaconda claims that the misappropriation was achieved by industrial piracy: the hiring of Anaconda employees from its Mattoon,

Illinois, plant and the unauthorized removal from that plant of certain tooling and drawings which served as a material aid to Metric in the construction of its own P & W machine for the manufacture of TCA.

Metric's principal defense is that it designed, engineered, and built its P & W machine on its own, admittedly with some help from some former Anaconda employees, but essentially on the basis of the expertise of Metric's president and sole stockholder, Edward Hussian ("Hussian"), an experienced tool and die maker. * * *

C. Is Anaconda's Suit Barred by the Statute of Limitations?

The parties agree, and we concur, that the applicable statute of limitations in this diversity action is the Pennsylvania six-year statute, 12 P.S. § 31. Metric argues that the action is barred by the statute of limitations since the acts of misappropriation occurred more than six years before the complaint was filed on August 3, 1976. Anaconda replies that the unauthorized use of a misappropriated trade secret is a continuing tort. In Anaconda's view, each unauthorized use of the trade secret by the misappropriator is a separate tort giving rise to a new cause of action as to which the statute of limitations commences to run anew, and the effect of the statute of limitations is not to bar the action but only to limit plaintiff's recovery to damages sustained during the statutory period preceding the filing of the suit. There are no reported decisions on this issue in the Pennsylvania state courts or in federal courts following Pennsylvania law. Our task, therefore, is to predict how the Pennsylvania courts would decide the issue if it were presented to them. *Becker v. Interstate Properties*, 569 F.2d 1203 (3d Cir.1977), *cert. denied*, 436 U.S. 906, 98 S.Ct. 2237, 56 L.Ed.2d 404 (1978).

Among decisions in other jurisdictions, there is a split in authority on the question whether or not adverse use of a misappropriated trade secret is a continuing tort. *See M & T Chemicals, Inc. v. International Business Machines Corp.*, 403 F.Supp. 1145 (S.D.N.Y.1975), *aff'd mem.*, 542 F.2d 1165 (2d Cir.), *cert. denied*, 429 U.S. 1030, 97 S.Ct. 656, 50 L.Ed. 2d 637 (1976) (collecting cases). *See also Kistler Instruments A.G. v. PCB Piezotronics, Inc.*, 419 F.Supp. 120 (W.D.N.Y.1976). Our examination of the reported decisions reveals that the split in authority on this issue reflects a more fundamental split on the basis for legal protection of trade secrets.

There are two competing views on the theoretical basis for legal protection of trade secrets: the "property" view and the "confidential relationship" view. In *E.I. DuPont de Nemours Powder Co. v. Masland*, 244 U.S. 100, 102, 37 S.Ct. 575, 61 L.Ed. 1016 (1917), Justice Holmes stated that the basis of trade secret protection is the "confidential relations" between the parties, and not the status of the trade secret as intellectual property. The Holmes view has been rejected by the Pennsylvania Supreme Court. *Van Products Co. v. General Welding & Fabricating Co.*, 419 Pa. 248, 268, 213 A.2d 769, 780 (1965). Thus Pennsylvania adheres to the "property" view of trade secret law. *See*

Sims v. Mack Truck Corp., 488 F.Supp. 592 (E.D.Pa.1980) (Lord, C.J.), On that view, the theoretical basis for recovery on a trade secret claim is not merely the breach of a confidential relationship, but also the adverse use of the plaintiff's intellectual property.

As we have previously stated, Pennsylvania trade secret law follows Section 757 of the Restatement of Torts. That section creates a cause of action against a person "who discloses *or uses* another's trade secret." (emphasis added). The American Law Institute's comments explicitly state that "The rule stated in this Section protects the interest in a trade secret against both disclosure *and adverse use.*" Restatement of Torts § 757, Comment c at 8 (1939) (emphasis added). Thus the protection of trade secrets under section 757 and Pennsylvania law is not limited to protection against the initial disclosure, but embraces protection against subsequent unauthorized use as well.

These basic principles of Pennsylvania trade secret law—the treatment of trade secrets as intellectual property and the recognition of a separate cause of action for wrongful use of a misappropriated trade secret—control our decision on the statute of limitations issue. Since recovery may be premised not merely on the breach of the confidential relationship when the secret was disclosed, but also on subsequent wrongful use of the secret, the statute of limitations for the tort of wrongful use begins to run at the time of the wrongful use, and not at the time of the initial misappropriation. In other words, under Pennsylvania law, wrongful use of a misappropriated trade secret is a continuing tort.

* * *

Since Anaconda complains not merely of the misappropriation of its trade secret, but also of its wrongful use, we believe that Pennsylvania would hold that the statute of limitations commences to run anew with each wrongful use. Thus the effect of the statute of limitations is not to bar this action completely because the alleged misappropriation occurred more than six years before this lawsuit was initiated. Instead, its effect is to limit plaintiff's recovery to damages sustained by reason of the defendant's unauthorized use of the trade secret during the statutory six-year period preceding the filing of the suit.

D. IS ANACONDA'S SUIT BARRED BY LACHES?

Metric argues that Anaconda is not entitled to relief because of laches. The essential elements of laches are inexcusable delay in instituting suit and prejudice resulting to the defendant from such delay. *Gruca v. United States Steel Corp.*, 495 F.2d 1252, 1258 (3d Cir. 1974). Laches is an equitable defense; its existence depends on the particular equitable circumstances of each case, and is a question primarily addressed to the discretion of the trial court. *Burke v. Gateway Clipper, Inc.*, 441 F.2d 946, 949 (3d Cir.1971). In recognition of the equitable nature of the defense of laches, courts have also considered whether the party asserting the defense is a conscious wrongdoer.

E.g., TWM Manufacturing Co. v. Dura Corp., 592 F.2d 346 (6th Cir. 1979); *Tisch Hotels, Inc. v. Americana Inn, Inc.,* 350 F.2d 609 (7th Cir. 1965); *John Wright, Inc. v. Casper Corp.,* 419 F.Supp. 292, 323 (E.D.Pa. 1976) (Fullam, J.), *aff'd in part and rev'd in part on other grounds,* 587 F.2d 602 (3d Cir.1978); *Alfred Dunhill of London, Inc. v. Kasser Distillers Products Corp.,* 350 F.Supp. 1341, 1368 (E.D.Pa.1972) (Becker, J.), *aff'd mem.,* 480 F.2d 917 (3d Cir.1973). If laches is invoked by a defendant who is a conscious wrongdoer, he can prevail only if the plaintiff's delay "is so prolonged and inexcusable that it amounts to a virtual abandonment of the right by the plaintiff for a long period of time." *John Wright, supra, quoting Tisch Hotels, supra.*

1. BURDEN OF PROOF OF LACHES

The allocation of the burden of proof of laches depends on the length of the plaintiff's delay. If the delay is shorter than the applicable statute of limitations, then the defendant has the burden of proving laches. If, on the other hand, the delay is longer than the applicable statute of limitations, then the defendant is entitled to a rebuttable presumption of both elements of laches. In that case, the plaintiff has the burden of disproving laches. *Gruca, supra; Miller v. United States,* 438 F.Supp. 514, 524 (E.D.Pa.1977) (Luongo, J.). * * * In fact, by April 15, 1969, more than seven years before it initiated legal action, Anaconda had actual knowledge of all the essential elements of Metric's misappropriation. Since its delay exceeded six years, Anaconda must rebut the presumption of laches by negating one or both of the essential elements of laches. In addition, plaintiff may avoid or diminish the effect of laches by showing that defendant was a conscious wrongdoer.

2. INEXCUSABILITY OF ANACONDA'S DELAY IN INSTITUTING SUIT

Anaconda argues that its delay in bringing suit was reasonable or excusable because it did not know of the misappropriation until 1976, when Sauers provided it with photographs showing that Metric's machine was nearly identical to Anaconda's. It contends that while Anaconda executives may have had some relevant information in 1968 and 1969, they had no "hard evidence" of misappropriation. Although Hogan, the Mattoon plant manager, testified that he suspected at the time that Metric was receiving technical information from former employees of Anaconda, the plaintiff argues that "suspicion is not knowledge," quoting *Kraft v. Cohen,* 32 F.Supp. 821, 825 (E.D.Pa.1940), *rev'd on other grounds,* 117 F.2d 579 (3d Cir.1941).

* * *

We conclude that Anaconda has failed to rebut the presumption that its delay in instituting suit was unreasonable and inexcusable. We add only that the result on this point would be the same even if there were no presumption.

3. Prejudice to the Defendant

Anaconda contends that Metric has not been prejudiced by the delay in bringing suit. It notes that no prejudice has resulted to defendant's ability to defend this action, as might have occurred if, for instance, a witness had died or records had been destroyed. While the defendant claims that he was prejudiced in that he built five P & W machines and invested much of his capital in TCA manufacture, Anaconda points out that Metric received considerable profits on this investment, and argues that Metric cannot have been prejudiced by carrying on a lucrative activity.

The prejudice which is an essential element of laches must be more than the mere continued use of a misappropriated trade secret. *Alfred Dunhill, supra,* 350 F.Supp. at 1368. However, the expansion of one's business and the expenditure of capital to undertake an activity which is later subjected to legal challenge is the kind of change of position which will support the defense of laches. *Continental Coatings Corp. v. Metco, Inc.,* 464 F.2d 1375, 1378 (7th Cir.1972) (Stevens, J.); *Westco-Chippewa Pump Co. v. Delaware Electric & Supply Co.,* 64 F.2d 185 (3d Cir.1933); *Siemens Aktiengesellschaft v. Beltone Electronics Corp.,* 381 F.Supp. 57 (N.D.Ill.1974). By investing more and more of its resources in TCA manufacture, Metric exposed itself to greater damage liability and increased the cost to its business which is likely to result from injunctive relief. Anaconda's prompt action would have made it possible for Metric to devote its resources to other equally profitable business operations, instead of increasing its exposure to liability. Thus the mere fact that Metric's TCA operation was profitable does not preclude a finding of prejudice sufficient to support the defense of laches. While Metric has produced no evidence to show that it ever contemplated expanding its business in other areas, it is entitled to a rebuttable presumption of prejudice because Anaconda's delay exceeded the six-year period of the statute of limitations. Anaconda has failed to rebut that presumption.

4. Conscious Wrongdoing

In balancing the equities to determine whether plaintiff's suit is barred by laches, a court may consider whether the defendant "has engaged in particularly egregious conduct which would change the equities significantly in plaintiff's favor." *TWM Manufacturing, supra,* 592 F.2d at 349. Such egregious conduct may be shown by demonstrating, for example, that the defendant to a claim of patent infringement participated in "deliberate, calculated plagiarism," *id.,* or that the defendant to a claim of trademark infringement "was fully aware of the plaintiff's mark and reputation," *Alfred Dunhill, supra,* 350 F.Supp. at 1368.

We have no difficulty in concluding that Metric was a conscious wrongdoer. The only inference that can be drawn from Hussian's conduct is that after his initial attempts to buy or build a P & W machine failed, he deliberately set out to construct a duplicate of Anaconda's machine. He knew that Anaconda had the only machine in the United States then capable of manufacturing TCA, and he knew or should have known that the machine, and the manufacturing process, were confidential. As we have noted, Hussian treated Metric's P & W machine as confidential, thereby evincing his awareness that the machine was not a matter of public knowledge, and also perhaps demonstrating some fear of apprehension.

5. ANACONDA'S APPARENT ACQUIESCENCE IN METRIC'S MISCONDUCT; THE EFFECT OF ANACONDA'S CONDUCT ON RELIEF

Although we have labeled Metric a "conscious wrongdoer," we view the effect of this categorization as mitigated somewhat by Anaconda's apparent acquiescence in its misconduct. * * *

While Anaconda has failed to rebut the presumption of laches by disproving the existence of inexcusable delay or of prejudice, it has, as we have seen, succeeded in demonstrating that Metric was a conscious wrongdoer. There is some authority to the effect that laches will bar the award of damages against even a conscious wrongdoer, but will not bar injunctive relief. *E.g., Hanover Star Milling Co. v. Metcalf,* 240 U.S. 403, 419, 36 S.Ct. 357, 362, 60 L.Ed. 713 (1916); *Philadelphia Extracting Co. v. Keystone Extracting Co.,* 176 F. 830 (E.D.Pa.1910). On the other hand, most recent decisions discussing the conscious wrongdoer doctrine as a bar to laches assume that conscious wrongdoing, if proved, would totally negate the defense of laches permitting both damages and injunctive relief. *E.g., TWM Manufacturing, supra.*

We do not find it necessary to subscribe to one rule or the other. The essential nature of laches lies in the balancing of equities in light of the particular circumstances of each case. *E.g., Burke v. Gateway Clipper, supra.* Because the egregiousness of Metric's conduct is offset by the unreasonableness of Anaconda's inaction, particularly its inaction after Hussian was aware that Anaconda was aware of his activities, we do not believe that it would be fair either to permit laches to bar the action totally, or to permit the conscious wrongdoer doctrine completely to counteract the laches defense. Given the rather unique facts of this case, the result which we deem appropriate is to bar the plaintiff's damage claim because of laches, but to permit its claim for injunctive relief. * * *

EMERY INDUS., INC. v. COTTIER

United States District Court of Ohio, 1978.
202 USPQ 829.

HOGAN, DISTRICT JUDGE.

The plaintiff Emery Industries, Inc. (hereinafter "Emery") is an Ohio corporation with its principal place of business in Cincinnati, Ohio. It is engaged primarily in the fatty acids and derivative field.[1]

The defendant Dwight A. Cottier is presently a resident and citizen of Philadelphia, Pennsylvania, and the Court's jurisdiction is based on diversity and the necessary diversity and amount in controversy requirements are present.

This action was filed in the State Court and removed to this Court quite recently. It seeks a temporary restraining order, preliminary injunction and permanent injunction enjoining the defendant from working for his present employer Welsbach Ozone Corporation in any area dealing with the product or system hereinafter described for a period of two (2) years, a mandatory injunction compelling specific performance of a confidentiality agreement and damages. The alleged property right or rights which the plaintiff asserts as being violated or threatened with violation is/are trade secrets in the ozone field.

A restraining order, restraining the defendant from engaging in employment with Welsbach in the pertinent field, was granted after notice and informal hearing on July 27, 1978, and plaintiff's motion for a temporary injunction was the subject of an evidentiary hearing which commenced on Monday, August 7, 1978.

* * *

FINDINGS

* * *

Ozone is a gas which is a highly reactive form of oxygen. Its chemical formula is O_3, as contrasted with the usual form of oxygen, O_2. It has a pungent odor, is a toxic, invisible, highly active, unstable gas used in chemical processing. It is widely recognized as a germicide and oxidant for use in water purification, chemical preparation and treatment of wastewater and industrial wastes.

Emery has used ozone in its own chemical processing for at least 25 years. It has been used by Emery mainly for converting high molecular weight unsaturated fatty acids into lower molecular weight acids. Emery is one of the largest industrial users of ozone and has been for a good many years.

* * *

The defendant began working for Emery as a co-op student in 1964. He was graduated from the University of Cincinnati as a chemical engineer in 1967. He worked at Emery and attended that University

---

1. Acid and chemical productions and sales.

for the following year, receiving a master's degree in marketing and, from that time until June 30, 1978, was a full-time employee of Emery.

* * *

Through the first four or five years of his employment the defendant was not particularly connected with the ozone field. His work did include some marketing in the plastics additive field. There is nothing in the record to indicate that the defendant, as a practical matter, is employable in any particular marketing field, other than ozone.

* * *

In 1972, as indicated, Emery's management decided to market ozone systems, i.e., apparatus and related engineering and technical services for using ozone as a reactant material. The defendant was given the initial responsibility more or less as an entrepeneur in this effort. One always judges the extent of the responsibility by the ultimate, i.e., compensation. From that viewpoint, while the defendant, six years ago, was given the responsibility for the entrepreneuring, at least then it did not represent a major effort for Emery. In 1974 came a formal title—"Manager of the Ozone Group." The group started out with one other full-time employee in 1974 and by 1978 consisted of approximately six, with several part time. The ozone technology group since 1974 has been responsible in Emery for the research, development, manufacture and sale of ozone generation equipment and technology used in connection therewith. Defendant devoted full time to supervising the development and marketing of ozone systems for sale to others and was involved with virtually every aspect of the design, manufacture, marketing and selling, as well as the use, of Emery's ozone systems.

* * *

Ozone systems offered by manufacturers are somewhat complex. Typical Emery systems are indicated in Plaintiff's Exhibit 44. For practical purposes, any system would include an ozone generator, a contractor (where the ozone is brought in contact with the material to be treated), an ozone destruct system (to return the O_3 to O_2 to the extent that O_3 is not used—this because of the toxic quality of O_3). The cost of systems is substantial, running from \$100,000 to in excess of \$1,000,000. The systems are practically all custom made.

In developing and marketing its ozone systems, Emery has invested considerable effort and considerable funds in developing processes, designing equipment and systems. In so doing, it has developed a substantial amount of information which it asserts to be trade secrets.

* * *

In all of the instances in the record in which the defendant has had occasion either to be a party to or to know of disclosures of the type of information asserted by the plaintiff as proprietary, the defendant himself has been the asserter, i.e., he signed the agreement and consistently asserted the proprietary feature. In other words, the defendant historically has been thoroughly aware of the assertion of a proprietary interest and has concurred in it consistently until his departure.

In May of 1978, the defendant was approached by an executive employment independent agency. The President of Welsbach expects to retire this fall and the agency sought a replacement for employment with the company some months in advance of that retirement. The defendant was then making $29,000 a year with the plaintiff. He explored the possibility and by the middle of June, 1978, was seriously considering it. At least by June 23rd, he tentatively decided to take the position with Welsbach and so informed the plaintiff. Welsbach is a competitor with Emery in the ozone field in every respect and has been for some years. Welsbach actually was in the field before Emery, and the head-to-head competition has been going on for at least the past five or six years. Welsbach is a subsidiary of a French corporation called Trailigaz Corporation. Welsbach employs about twenty persons.

The defendant's duties with Welsbach as the executive head of the company will include the same general type of work as he performed as manager of the group at Emery. His authority will, of course, be broader. His salary has been fixed at $45,000 a year, plus a $5,000 guaranteed bonus. The defendant is married. The last day he worked at Emery was June 28, 1978. He started work with Welsbach at least by July 12, 1978. He moved to Philadelphia in that interim.

* * *

It could not be claimed that the detail of the proprietary material could be or is carried around by the defendant in his head. It is not. The generality of it is, and the generality is usable for conclusory purposes.

The plaintiff does own proprietary trade secrets in the ozone and ozone systems field. The generality of them is known to the defendant.

The disclosure by the defendant to Welsbach of such secrets and/or generality will cause the plaintiff irreparable damage in that it will cause the plaintiff damage which will not be ascertainable in terms of money.

From the point of view of balance of interest, an injunction simply enjoining disclosure would not cause any presently determinable hardship to the defendant. An injunction prohibiting the defendant from working for Welsbach for any appreciable length of time would obviously cause the defendant irreparable injury. At least on this present record, the defendant's employability, as a practical matter, is limited to the ozone field.

CONCLUSIONS

This is a diversity case removed to this Court and is governed by Ohio law.

* * *

In Ohio—again referring to the Goodrich case [B.F. Goodrich Co. v. Wohlgemuth, 117 Ohio App. 493, 192 N.E.2d 99 (1963)]—the right to an injunction does not depend on the presence or absence of a confidentiality agreement signed by the employee or, for that matter, a non-competent agreement. In that case, too, the defendant had been employed a substantial period of time for a company, working in a specialized and new area. * * *

Under the Ohio law, as established in the same case, 117 Ohio App. at 500, 137 USPQ at 807:

> Equitable intervention is sanctioned when it appears that there exists a present real threat of disclosure, even without actual disclosure.

There can be no doubt of the present threat of disclosure in any case in which the transfer of employment is to a head-to-head competitor and the responsibilities in the employments are comparable.

The similarity between the facts in this case and the facts in the Ohio case lead this Court to the conclusion that the plaintiff in this case has demonstrated sufficient likelihood of success on the merits to warrant a temporary injunction.

* * *

Conclusorily and accepting the Goodrich case as the law of Ohio, which we must, and with or without the express written confidentiality agreement signed by the defendant, the plaintiff would fairly clearly be entitled to an injunction requiring the defendant "to keep secret and confidential any and all proprietary information of the plaintiff received by him during the time of his employment with the plaintiff, including trade secrets pertaining to the ozone systems of the plaintiff and its research development in that field."

The plaintiff, however, contends that, under the facts of this case, such an injunction will not effectively carry out the agreement of the parties and asserts that the only way the specific agreement can be enforced is to bar the defendant from working for Welsbach for a limited period of time because, in the proposed position as president of Welsbach, it would be inevitable that he would use the very trade secret information which he has agreed not to use.

There is considerable support for that position in the books. A case considerably comparable on its facts is Allis-Chalmers v. Continental, 255 F.Supp. 645, 151 USPQ 25 (E.D.Mich.1966). In that case the employee involved was an engineer who had worked for the plaintiff for a considerable length of time in the development of a fuel injection pump. He had had access to and had become familiar with the plaintiff's research, design development and refinements and know-how relating to fuel injection systems in general and its distributor type fuel injection pump in particular. The plaintiff and the defendant Continental were in head-to-head competition in attempting to develop a particular fuel injection system for the armed services. In October of 1965 the engineer accepted a position with the defendant, terminated his employment with the plaintiff on December 15th and was to begin work at Continental in January of the following year. The injunction case was filed during the interim. The Court, without specifying the precise trade secrets involved, pointed out: (255 F.Supp. at 652, 151 USPQ at 31)

> There also exists a body of information concerning these pumps and their design which is not the subject of patent applications, has not been disclosed to the public, has been reduced to concrete form and documents, and would be useful in designing a distributor type fuel injection pump of the performance capabilities * * *. This is detailed and technical information relating, for example, to optimum finishes on surfaces of parts, certain heat treatments, certain configurations * * *. The employee learned about such areas of information while employed by plaintiff. All of this information would be of value to the competitors in the saving of time and money and material.

This case involves certainly the same situation. In the Allis-Chalmers case, the Court pointed out that the basic facts—(255 F.Supp. at 654, 151 USPQ at 32–33)

> all lead to an inference that there is an inevitable and imminent danger of disclosure of Allis-Chalmers trade secrets to Continental and use of the trade secrets by Continental.

> The virtual impossibility of the employee performing all of his prospective duties for Continental to the best of his ability, without in effect giving it the benefit of Allis-Chalmers' confidential information, makes a simple injunction against disclosure and use of this information inadequate.

And so in this case, it is a necessary conclusion based on the facts that there is an inevitable and imminent danger of disclosure of plaintiff's trade secrets. It will be virtually impossible for the defendant to perform his prospective duties for Welsbach without in effect giving Welsbach the benefit of plaintiff's confidential information.

* * *

While it may well be and we think it is true that the only effective protection to the plaintiff involves granting an injunction against the defendant working for Welsbach for a reasonable period of time, that is not, in this Court's view, the end of the matter. The parties to this controversy, some eleven years ago, gave consideration to what sort of agreement should govern their relationship after it terminated. It was their joint decision at that time that their relationship after termination could be covered by a nondisclosure agreement. Both the plaintiff and the defendant have stood on that ever since and only after their relationship was terminated has the plaintiff asserted the necessity of a noncompete agreement. Concededly, a noncompete agreement is more stringent than a nondisclosure agreement. If the circumstances change in such a way as to require noncompetition, it would seem only fair that it be on some basis which would compensate the defendant. It is clear in this case that taking the defendant out of the ozone field practically amounts to removing him from employment. That circumstance has not been present in the Allis-Chalmers and other cases to which we have been referred. (See Appendix I.)

Furthermore, it is axiomatic in the injunction field that the issue of any injunction is subject to a certain amount of discretion and that that discretion may involve the imposition of conditions dictated by requirements of fairness. Finally, those principles are particularly applicable in Ohio. (See Appendix II.) In Ohio a covenant not to compete, such as this Court is in effect asked to write, is enforceable only to the extent necessary to protect an employer's legitimate interest and only to the extent that unreasonable restrictions are not placed upon the employee. In a nutshell in Ohio in the noncompete field, the question is "on the basis of all available evidence what restrictions would be reasonable between the parties." The Ohio Supreme Court has said:

> Among the factors properly to be considered are: the absence or presence of limitations as to time and space, * * * whether the employee is possessed with confidential information or trade secrets; whether the benefit to the employer is disproportional to the detriment to the employee; whether the covenant seeks to eliminate competition which would be unfair to the employer or merely seeks to eliminate ordinary competition; whether the covenant seeks to stifle the inherent skill and experience of the employee; whether the covenant operates as a bar to the employee's sole means of support; whether the employee's talent which the employer seeks to suppress was actually developed during the period of employment; whether the forbidden employment is merely incidental to the main employment. See Raimonde v. Van Vlerah, 42 Ohio St.2d 21 (1975).

It would be useless to attempt to draft an injunction which would permit any employment by Welsbach, since Welsbach is engaged solely in the ozone field. The interest of the public in the mobility of employment and in the freedom of an employee to seek other employment requires that such a nonemployment injunction be limited to the time absolutely essential to the protection of the employer's legitimate interest.

Balancing the breadth of the territorial involvement, the specialization of the occupation involved, the fact that due to the defendant's continuous occupation the field involved offers the sole means of practical support, and bearing in mind that the field involved is only one of a number occupying the efforts of the plaintiff, and a relatively small one at that, a period of, at the most, a year from July 1, 1978 is reasonable.

In the Raimonde case, the Supreme Court of Ohio, 42 Ohio St.2d at 28, said:

> Because this court holds, for the first time, that a trial court may enforce a covenant "to the extent necessary to protect an employer's legitimate interests," we direct that this cause be remanded to the Court of Common Pleas, so that court may ascertain if its initial finding conforms with the test established today. That court is now specifically empowered to construct a reasonable covenant between the parties, and to grant injunctive relief, if appropriate, for the period of time to which appellant may be entitled.

If it is the duty of a trial court in narrowing a noncompete agreement to the boundary of reasonableness in a situation involving an originally unreasonable covenant, it must also be the duty of a trial court in, in effect, writing a noncompete, to construct it in a reasonable fashion.

Under all of the circumstances of this case, it seems to this Court that a reasonable fashion includes the payment by the plaintiff to the defendant of consideration. The plaintiff will therefore be required to pay to the defendant as consideration for the noncompetition and as a condition for the continuance of the injunction the sum of Three Thousand Three Hundred Dollars ($3,300.00) per month, for each month during which the temporary injunction remains in effect (beginning August 1, 1978). The temporary injunction will also be conditioned upon the giving of a bond and the bond is fixed at Twenty-five Thousand Dollars ($25,000.00).

A temporary injunction consistent with the foregoing is being entered this date.

APPENDIX I

In Allis-Chalmers, the employee whose migration from one job to another led to the litigation was able to continue to work for his new employer in other aspects of the new employer's business besides that involving the trade secret. Thus, his right to pursue his chosen vocation was not unduly restrained by the injunction obtained.

In B.F. Goodrich, the space-suit manufacturing division was but one of the competing employer's divisions.

In the case at bar, Welsbach is a small concern involved only in the ozone industry. Welsbach could not employ Cottier in any field but ozone marketing.

* * *

CONMAR PRODUCTS CORP. v. UNIVERSAL SLIDE FASTENER CO.

United States Court of Appeals, Second Circuit, 1949.
172 F.2d 150, 80 USPQ 108.

L. HAND, CHIEF JUDGE. The plaintiff appeals from a judgment so far as it dismissed its complaint for the infringement of Claims 43, 44, 45, 47, 48, 49 and 52 of Patent No. 2,201,068, issued to George Wintritz on May 14, 1940, for the infringement of Claims 1, 2, 4, 9, 10, 11, 17, 21, 22 and 23 of Patent No. 2,221,740, issued to Frederick Ulrich on November 12, 1940; and upon a third cause of action for inducing the plaintiff's employees to divulge its trade secrets. The art to which both the patents and the trade secrets belong was that of "slide fasteners," or "zippers."

* * *

THE TRADE SECRETS

As its third cause of action the plaintiff alleged that the defendants enticed away several of its employees and made use of information which they had acquired while working for it. The plaintiff recognized that this alone would not be enough, and therefore it asserted, as was the fact, that these employees, and particularly the most important among them, Voity, had executed a contract in which they promised not to divulge anything which they might learn of the plaintiff's methods; and that the defendants, knowing of this contract, or at least having notice of its existence, induced the men to divulge the secrets they had learned. It was Voity who devised the offending machine, which the plaintiff says embodied some seven of its secrets, of which six and a part of the seventh were to be found in the disclosures of the two patents in suit. The other part of the seventh was disclosed in two later patents issued to the plaintiff.

* * *

Courts have been accustomed to speak of trade secrets as "property," and at times to deal with them as if they were. That may be permissible and to some extent desirable, when the question is whether the wrongdoer has got access to them by some wrongful means, like breaking into a factory, or copying formulae or blue prints. When, however, the dispute turns, as it does here, upon whether the wrongdoer has acquired a secret from the employee who has himself acquired it lawfully, the wrong consists in inducing him to break his contract, or to be disloyal to a confidence reposed in him; and in either case it is a species of the tort—recognized now for over a century—of inducing an obligor to default upon an obligation. Since the specifications of the patents in suit disclosed the first six secrets and part of the seventh, that much of the secrets upon issue of the patents fell into the public demesne; and, prima facie, the defendants were free to use them. The Seventh Circuit,[3] and apparently the Sixth as well,[4] have, however, held that if before issue one has unlawfully obtained and used information which the specifications later disclose, he will not be free to continue to do so after issue;[j] his wrong deprives him of the right which he would otherwise have had as a member of the public. We have twice refused to follow this doctrine;[5] and we adhere to our decisions. Conceivably an employer might exact from his employees a contract not to disclose the information even after the patent issued. Of what possible value such a contract could be, we find it hard to conceive; but, if an employer did exact it, others would perhaps be obliged to turn to the specifications, if they would use the information. Be that as it may, we should not so construe any secrecy contract unless the intent were put

---

3. Shellmar Products Co. v. Allen-Qualley Co., 87 F.2d 104.

4. A.O. Smith Corp. v. Petroleum Iron Works Co., 74 F.2d 934.

j. Whether this Shellmar rule is still viable in view of the supremacy of federal patent law and policy is considered in the subsequent Federal Pre-emption section.

5. Picard v. United Aircraft Corp., 2 Cir., 128 F.2d 632; Pennington Engineering Co. v. Houde Engineering Corp., 2 Cir., 136 F.2d 210.

in the most inescapable terms; and the plaintiff's contract had none such. In their absence we do not see why a wrongful inducement to divulge the disclosure before issue should deprive the wrongdoer of his right to avail himself of the patentee's dedication; for, as we have just said, the contract is to be construed as imposing secrecy only until issue. The doctrine must rest upon the theory that it is a proper penalty for the original wrong to deny the wrongdoer resort to the patent; and for that we can find no support in principle. Thus, any possible liability for exploiting whatever the patents in suit disclosed, ended with their issue. Since the earliest notice was on November 16, 1940, it is not necessary to resort to this reasoning as to the first six secrets and as to part of the seventh, because the two patents in suit issued before November 16, 1940; but the doctrine does become important as to the remaining part of the seventh secret.

It is almost, if not quite, impossible to learn what was that part of the seventh secret which did remain undisclosed after the issue of the Ulrich patent in suit; but for argument we will assume that the plaintiff proved that some parts did so remain. Whatever these were, they were all disclosed in two later patents to Ulrich: No. 2,338,884, issued January 11, 1944, and No. 2,370,380, issued February 27, 1945; and in any event the right to an injunction against exploiting any secrets whatever had therefore expired before the judgment was entered in November, 1947. All that could remain was the right to an accounting for profits or to a claim for damages between November 16, 1940, and the date of issue of these patents. We think, however, that the defendants had an excuse for exploiting that secret over that period, if they did so. As we have said, by November 16, 1940, they had invested $40,000 in the offending machine; that is, they had either paid or committed themselves to pay that much. The Restatement of Torts [6] makes it an excuse for continued exploitation of a secret that at the time when one, who has theretofore been innocently exploiting it, first learns that he has induced the breach of an obligation, he has substantially changed his position. The opinions which support this are not very satisfactory; so far as we have found, in all but one or two it is doubtful whether what the judges say is more than dictum.[7] However, they do all point the same way, for they assume that the situation is proper for the application of the doctrine that a bona fide purchaser takes free from a trust. The act of inducing the breach is the wrong, and the inducer's ignorance is an excuse only because one is not ordinarily held liable for consequences which one could not have anticipated. Although it is proper to prevent any continued use of the secret after the inducer has learned of the breach, the remedies must

6. § 758(b) Comment (e).

7. Morison v. Moat, 9 Hare 241; Edelsten v. Edelsten, 1 DeG. J. & S. 185; Stewart v. Hook, 118 Ga. 445, 45 S.E. 369, 63 L.R.A. 255; Homer v. Crown Cork & Seal Co., 155 Md. 66, 141 A. 425; Chadwick v. Covell, 151 Mass. 190, 23 N.E. 1068, 6 L.R.A. 839, 21 Am.St.Rep. 442; Vulcan Detinning Co. v. American Can Co., 72 N.J. Eq. 387, 67 A. 339, 12 L.R.A.,N.S., 102, Id., 75 N.J.Eq. 542, 73 A. 603; Lamont, Corliss & Co. v. Bonnie Blend Chocolate Corp., 135 Misc. 537, 238 N.Y.S. 78.

not invade the inducer's immunity over the period while he was ignorant. They may invade it, if the inducer has changed his position on the faith of his ignorance. We agree with the Comment of the Restatement that each case must stand on its facts; the answer depends upon weighing the loss to the inducer against the benefit to the obligee. In the case at bar we have no hesitation in deciding that issue in favor of the defendants. On November 16, 1940, when the defendants were first charged with any duty to desist, they had become free to exploit the major part of the secrets—the first six and an undetermined part of the seventh. Their duty at most extended no further than to change their machines and their methods, so as not to continue to exploit the still protected vestiges of the seventh; and even these would become free when the two other patents issued. Certainly, to compel them to make that change was seriously to invade the immunity they had enjoyed to that time; it would have compelled a disruption of their business and a redesigning of their machines. Opposed to this was a benefit to the plaintiff, the importance of which no one could even guess; for it must be measured by the advantage of suppressing only the use of the yet undisclosed part of the seventh secret, while the defendants remained free to use all the rest. The plaintiff had the burden of showing that the balance was in its favor, and we should be wholly unwarranted in deducing that conclusion from the maze of verbiage which wraps the issue.

* * *

Having acquired the secrets innocently, they were entitled to exploit them till they learned that they had induced the breach of the contract.

Judgment affirmed.

WINSTON RESEARCH CORP. v. MINNESOTA MINING & MFG. CO.

United States Court of Appeals, Ninth Circuit, 1965.
350 F.2d 134, 146 USPQ 422.

BROWNING, CIRCUIT JUDGE:

The Mincom Division of the Minnesota Mining and Manufacturing Company developed an improved precision tape recorder and reproducer. Somewhat later, Winston Research Corporation developed a similar machine. Mincom alleged that the Winston machine was developed by former employees of Mincom, including Johnson and Tobias, by using confidential information which they had acquired while working on the Mincom machine, and sued for damages and an injunction. The district court granted Mincom an injunction, but denied damages. Both sides appealed.

I

Some background is required for an understanding of the issues.

For some uses of precision tape recorder/reproducers, the time interval between coded signals must be recorded and reproduced with great accuracy. To accomplish this, the tape must move at as constant a speed as possible during both recording and reproduction, and any changes in tape speed during recording must be duplicated as nearly as possible during reproduction. The degree to which a particular tape recorder/reproducer accomplishes this result is measured by its "time-displacement error."

* * *

In May 1962, when Mincom had substantially completed the research phase of its program and was beginning the development of a production prototype, Johnson, who was in charge of Mincom's program, left Mincom's employment. He joined Tobias, who had previously been discharged as Mincom's sales manager, in forming Winston Research Corporation. In late 1962, Winston contracted with the government to develop a precision tape reproducer. Winston hired many of the technicians who had participated in the development of the Mincom machine to work on the design and development of the Winston machine.

In approximately fourteen months, Winston completed a machine having the same low time-displacement error as the Mincom machine.

* * *

The district court enjoined Winston Research Corporation, Johnson, and Tobias from disclosing or using Mincom's trade secrets in any manner for a period of two years from the date of judgment—March 1, 1964. The court also required the assignment of certain patent applications to Mincom. No damages were awarded.

* * *

* * * Mincom argues that the injunction should have been permanent, or at least for a substantially longer period. Winston contends that no injunctive relief was appropriate.

Mincom was, of course, entitled to protection of its trade secrets for as long as they remained secret. The district court's decision to limit the duration of injunctive relief was necessarily premised upon a determination that Mincom's trade secrets would shortly be fully disclosed, through no fault of Winston, as a result of public announcements, demonstrations, and sales and deliveries of Mincom machines. Mincom has not seriously challenged this implicit finding, and we think the record fully supports it.

Mincom argues that notwithstanding public disclosure subsequent to its former employees' breach of faith, Mincom was entitled to a permanent injunction under the Shellmar rule. Winston responds that under the competing Conmar rule public disclosure of Mincom's trade secrets would end the obligation of Mincom's former employees to maintain the information in confidence, and that neither the employees nor their privies may be enjoined beyond the date of disclosure.

Thus, Winston's argument would bar any injunction at all once there was public disclosure, and Mincom's argument would require an injunction in perpetuity without regard to public disclosure. The district court rejected both extremes and granted an injunction for the period which it concluded would be sufficient both to deny Winston unjust enrichment and to protect Mincom from injury from the wrongful disclosure and use of Mincom's trade secrets by its former employees prior to public disclosure.

We think the district court's approach was sound. A permanent injunction would subvert the public's interest in allowing technical employees to make full use of their knowledge and skill and in fostering research and development. On the other hand, denial of any injunction at all would leave the faithless employee unpunished where, as here, no damages were awarded; and he and his new employer would retain the benefit of a headstart over legitimate competitors who did not have access to the trade secrets until they were publicly disclosed. By enjoining use of the trade secrets for the approximate period it would require a legitimate Mincom competitor to develop a successful machine after public disclosure of the secret information, the district court denied the employees any advantage from their faithlessness, placed Mincom in the position it would have occupied if the breach of confidence had not occurred prior to the public disclosure, and imposed the minimum restraint consistent with the realization of these objectives upon the utilization of the employees' skills.

* * *

Mincom argues that in any event a two-year injunction from March 1, 1964, was not sufficient to overcome the wrongful advantage obtained by Winston. Mincom points out that four years were required to develop its machine, whereas Winston developed its machine in fourteen months. For this reason, and because the injunction was stayed for some time, Mincom argues that injunctive relief should be granted for at least three years from the completion of appellate review.

As we have noted, the appropriate injunctive period is that which competitors would require after public disclosure to develop a competitive machine. The time (fourteen months) which Winston in fact took with the aid of the very disclosure and use complained of by Mincom would seem to be a fair measure of the proper period. The district court granted an injunction for a somewhat longer period, presumably because the Mincom machine was built in such a way as to require some time for persons unfamiliar with it to determine the details of its construction, and to compensate for delay which Mincom encountered in the final stages of its development program because Winston had hired away Mincom's key personnel. Whether extension of the injunctive period for the latter reason was proper we need not decide, for Winston has not raised that question.

We think it was proper to make the injunctive period run from the date of judgment since public disclosure occurred at about that time. The stays subsequently granted by the district court and this court were limited in scope and do not justify an extension of the injunctive period.

* * *

Mincom argues that the district court should have awarded money damages as well as injunctive relief. We think the district court acted well within its discretion in declining to do so. Since Winston sold none of its machines, it had no past profits to disgorge. The evidence as to possible future profits was at best highly speculative. To enjoin future sales and at the same time make an award based on future profits from the prohibited sales would result in duplicating and inconsistent relief, and the choice which the district court made between these mutually exclusive alternatives was not an unreasonable one. There was evidence that Winston would probably sell its machine and realize profits after the injunction expired, but these sales and profits, as we have seen, would not be tainted by breach of confidence, since Winston could by that time have developed its machine from publicly disclosed information.

* * *

SPERRY RAND CORP. v. A–T–O, INC.

United States Court of Appeals, Fourth Circuit, 1971.
447 F.2d 1387, 171 USPQ 775.

WINTER, CIRCUIT JUDGE:

Sperry Rand Corporation ("Sperry Rand"), invoking the diversity jurisdiction of the district court, sought damages and injunctive relief against Electronic Concepts, Inc. ("ECI"), John E. Zentmeyer, Jr. ("Zentmeyer"), a former employee of Sperry Rand and later president of ECI, and Gus K. Tebell ("Tebell"), also a former employee of Sperry Rand and later an employee of ECI. As a first cause of action, Sperry Rand alleged a misappropriation by defendants of Sperry Rand's confidential manufacturing data, designs and drawings for a slotted array antenna and their use to compete with Sperry Rand; and as a second cause of action, it alleged a misappropriation by defendants of Sperry Rand's confidential bid pricing information in connection with a United States Coast Guard radar contract and the use of this information and other data wrongfully obtained from Sperry Rand to underbid Sperry Rand on the contract. The district judge found liability on the part of defendants under both of Sperry Rand's causes of action, and he awarded compensatory damages, punitive damages and injunctive relief. We agree with his conclusions as to liability and injunctive relief, but we find error in the calculation of the money damages. We will, therefore, vacate the judgment as to the damages awarded and remand the case for reassessment of damages in accordance with our views.

* * *

The district judge awarded the following substantial damages:

$631,012.00—compensatory damages, including attorneys' fees—awarded against all defendants.

$175,000.00—punitive damages—awarded against Zentmeyer and ECI.

$ 10,000.00—punitive damages—awarded against Tebell.

$816,012.00—total damages awarded to Sperry Rand.

The opinion of the district court discloses that the $631,012.00 item of compensatory damages was arrived at as follows:

$175,000.00—value to ECI of misappropriated documents materials and data, excluding bidding data and the manual used in preparing ECI's bid.

$231,012.00—loss of profit to Sperry Rand as a result of being underbid on the Coast Guard contract.

$225,000.00—attorneys' fees.

$631,012.00—total compensatory damages, including attorneys' fees.

We find error in the assessment of damages.

We consider, first, the allowance of $175,000.00 as the value to ECI of the misappropriated items. There are two basic methods for assessing damages for misappropriation of trade secrets: one, the damages sustained by the victim (the traditional common law remedy), and the other, the profits earned by the wrongdoer by the use of the misappropriated material (an equitable remedy which treats the wrongdoer as trustee *ex maleficio* for the victim of the wrongdoer's gains from his wrongdoing). R. Ellis, Trade Secrets § 286 (1953); Restatement of the Law of Torts §§ 746 and 747 (1938); R. Callman, The Law of Unfair Competition, Trademarks and Monopolies § 59.3 (1965). Ordinarily a plaintiff may recover either, but not both, because to allow both would permit double recovery. Ellis, supra, § 287; Restatement, supra, § 747(c); Harley & Lund Corp. v. Murray Rubber Co., 31 F.2d 932 (2 Cir.1929), cert. den., 279 U.S. 872, 49 S.Ct. 513, 73 L.Ed. 1007 (1929); Consolidated Boiler Corp. v. Bogue Elec. Co., 141 N.J.Eq. 550, 58 A.2d 759 (1949). Since the objective in allowing damages is to compensate the plaintiff for the difference in his position before and after the misappropriation of his secret, his probable loss may be the more significant measuring rod than the misappropriator's actual gain. Callman, supra, § 59.3 at 497.

Plaintiff argues that the $175,000.00 was properly allowed under the "comparison of cost method" of assessing damages employed in International Industries, Inc. v. Warren Petroleum Corp., 248 F.2d 696 (3 Cir.1957), appeal dismissed, 355 U.S. 943, 78 S.Ct. 529, 2 L.Ed.2d 523 (1958). In that case defendant was a manufacturer and shipper of liquefied petroleum gas who misappropriated a plan for shipment by waterways which enabled it to cut shipment costs. The court allowed plaintiff to recover the savings defendant obtained in shipping over the method it had previously used, but a close reading of the opinion discloses that the "comparison of cost method" was used to determine the wrongdoer's profits. Indeed, the court remarked at one point that "the *profits* are simply measured by the *savings*." (emphasis supplied.) 248 F.2d at 702. Gordon Form Lathe Co. v. Ford Motor Co., 133 F.2d 487 (6 Cir.1943), aff'd. memo by an equally divided court, 320 U.S. 714, 64 S.Ct. 257, 88 L.Ed. 419 (1943), not cited by the parties but relied on in *International Industries* was a patent infringement case where the "comparison of cost method" of assessing damages was also employed but the opinion makes even clearer than *International Industries* the fact that this method was employed to ascertain the infringer's *profits*. 133 F.2d 492, 494 and 497.

Even if we assume that ECI saved $175,000.00 in research and development costs by using the misappropriated materials and thereby increased its profits by a like amount, it follows that Sperry Rand may not, under the authorities cited, recover both its damages from loss of the Coast Guard contract and ECI's profits derived therefrom because to allow both would be to allow double recovery. And we think that damages to Sperry Rand is the more appropriate measure of recovery than ECI's profits. ECI successfully used the misappropriated data in a single transaction, and it is being required to return the misappropriated material and is being enjoined from unfair competition with Sperry Rand for two years. There is thus no need for further equitable relief when Sperry Rand can prove legal damages in a greater amount.

Double recovery for Sperry Rand cannot be justified on the theory that defendants committed two separate acts giving rise to liability on their part, i.e., misappropriation of general proprietary secrets and misappropriation of bidding data and bidding price. Under the facts of this case, both of these objects of misappropriation were used in combination to inflict a single specific wrong, i.e., underbidding Sperry Rand and depriving it of the Coast Guard contract which it would otherwise have been awarded. Thus, the item of $175,000.00 must be disallowed.

In regard to $231,012.00 awarded for loss of profit to Sperry Rand as a result of losing the Coast Guard contract, we think the amount awarded was proper. Sperry Rand offered evidence that its profit alone (in the strict economic sense) on the contract, had it received the award, would have been $95,955.00, and that if it had gained the contract it would have also recovered fixed overhead costs of $78,592.00, and material overhead costs of $10,264.00. Additionally, there was evidence that Sperry Rand could reasonably have expected a 25% follow-on spares order to supplement the basic contract and, after computing the expected revenues and estimated costs derived from the follow-on spares order that it would have realized, additional profit of $23,989.00, recovery of additional general and administrative expenses of $19,648.00 and material overhead of $2,564.00. These six items total $231,012.00. Thus, we find support for allowance of this total item.

We conclude that the allowance of $225,000.00 for attorneys' fees was error. "[I]n an ordinary diversity case where the state law does not run counter to a valid federal statute or rule of court, and usually it will not, state law denying the right to attorney's fees or giving a right thereto, which reflects a substantial policy of the state, should be followed." (footnotes eliminated.) 6 Moore's Federal Practice ¶ 54.77[2] at 1354 (1965). As we view Virginia law, it would not support the allowance of counsel fees here. The Virginia rule is that "[e]xcept in rare instances, the power of a court to require one party to contribute to the fees of the counsel of another party must be confined to cases where the plaintiff, suing in behalf of himself and others of the same class, discovers or creates a fund which inures to the common benefit of all * * *." McCormick v. Elsea, 107 Va. 472, 475, 59 S.E. 411 (1907), quoted with approval in Norris v. Barbour, 188 Va. 723, 51 S.E.2d 334, 342 (1949).

* * * We think that Virginia would treat this case within the general rule denying counsel fees and not within one of the exceptions.[k]

The award of punitive damages and the amounts of the award seem proper. The district judge found that the acts of Zentmeyer and Tebell, which inured to the benefit of ECI, and were imputed to it, were "calculated," "deliberate," and "reprehensible," that Zentmeyer and Tebell were both guilty of serious breaches of loyalty, fidelity and responsibility to Sperry Rand and that "[t]he acts of the defendants were wilful and deliberate and were committed with the knowledge that they were unlawful and were calculated to result in substantial harm to the plaintiff." On this record we cannot say that these findings are clearly erroneous. There was also evidence that Zentmeyer's net worth was in excess of $750,000.00 and that ECI was a company of undisclosed worth but of "much substance." There was no finding as to Tebell's net worth, but the award of punitive damages against him was relatively nominal. It, therefore, appears that while the total punitive damages assessed were substantial they were not excessive under all of the circumstances. We do not, therefore, find any abuse of the discretion lodged in the district judge to make the award. Day v. Woodworth, 13 How. 363, 371, 14 L.Ed. 181 (1851); Kaufman v. Abramson, 363 F.2d 865 (4 Cir.1966) (applying the law of Virginia.) Cf. American Safety Table Co. v. Schreiber, 415 F.2d 373 (2 Cir.1969).

* * *

k. "Except when overriding considerations of justice compel them, it is the policy of federal and state courts to deny attorneys' fees in the absence of statutory authorization or agreement. Thus in an analogous situation involving unfair competition of the trademark variety, the Supreme Court approved the denial of attorneys' fees to the prevailing party. Fleischmann Distilling Corp. v. Maier Brewing Corp., 386 U.S. 714, 87 S.Ct. 1404, 18 L.Ed.2d 475." Forest Laboratories, Inc. v. Pillsbury Co., 452 F.2d 621, 171 USPQ 731 (7th Cir.1971).

To summarize with respect to damages, we conclude that $400,000.00 of the award against all defendants should not have been granted. On remand, we will direct that compensatory damages against all defendants be reduced to $231,012.00, with punitive damages of $175,000.00 against Zentmeyer and ECI, and $10,000.00 against Tebell.

Part II

PATENTS

Chapter One

HISTORICAL BACKGROUND

A. EARLY GOVERNMENTAL REGULATION AND ENCOURAGEMENT OF INVENTIONS

We have seen that the "natural" right of a person to his own ideas and inventions was strengthened by certain early governmental proclamations and regulations and that the "natural" right to copy was commensurately restrained. Persons who contributed something to a culture rather than being "passive culture carriers" were encouraged in their efforts. For the most part, this protection was limited in time. James Willard Hurst, in one of his Cooley Lectures at the University of Michigan in 1959, comments: [a]

> In largest part * * * culture was an unearned common inheritance of each generation * * * Law recognized the common right of free access to the cultural inheritance when it limited the years of a patent or a copyright * * * However ingenious an inventor, author, or advertiser, he built on too great an inherited stock of accumulated ideas and symbols to claim other than a marginal increment by his own creativity.

In many cases, however, the early forms of government were of an authoritarian nature ruled by monarchs, sovereigns, kings, and emperors with various degrees of power. In keeping with Lord Acton's comment, "Power tends to corrupt; absolute power corrupts absolutely," it was the practice, more prevalent than not, in the early monarchies, that royal favors were granted to certain individuals giving exclusive rights to sell certain commodities, which had previously been available to all. Needless to say, this type of monopoly [monos (alone) + polein (to sell)] did not find favor with the general public. This

a. Law and Social Process in United States History, page 237.

62

practice was the beginning of what is sometimes referred to as an "odious" monopoly. Aristotle reported that the creation of monopolies is "an art often practiced by cities when they are in want of money."

The state or city monopolies, which met with disfavor among all but the privileged few, were outlawed in the Roman Empire in a proclamation by Emperor Zeno in 480 A.D. It read:

> We order that no one will dare exercise a monopoly upon any garment or fish or * * * any kind of thing in that respect, or any material, whether it is already ascertained in a sacred way, or by a later rescript which ascertains it, or by Imperial Decree, or by a sacred notation of our kindness * * * etc.

Similar state or royal monopolies were outlawed in medieval Europe and Great Britain at a much later date.

Nevertheless, despite the prohibitions on state monopolies, which were rather general through the Middle Ages, various practices developed to reward certain individuals for unique ideas. In connection with the right of the state to control mining, forests, rivers, etc., in short, natural resources, there were certain secondary exclusive grants made to individuals. Prager refers to them as building permits but suggests they were the forerunner of modern patents. The archives of Venice indicate protection was granted from about 1200 to dredges, wells, flour mills and other water controlling or water utilizing plants.[b]

For several centuries of the Middle Ages, Venice was an aggressive power by land and sea and a thriving center of commerce. The guilds of Venice, unlike those of most of medieval Europe, encouraged the granting of protection to new devices and arts. Thus, by 1432, and probably about 1400, the Senate of Venice enacted a statute providing:

> If somebody invents any machine or process to speed up silk-making or to improve it, and if the idea is actually useful, the inventor can obtain an exclusive privilege for ten years from the Guild Welfare Board of the Republic.

By general usage, this protection was soon extended to other devices and arts. For example, Venetian patents were granted for flour mills (1443), cookstoves for dye shops (1460), which stoves used only half the fuel previously required, a device for raising water (1460), the art of printing (1469), and mills for grinding corn (1472).[c]

These grants were made not only to encourage citizens of Venice, but to attract ingenious persons from abroad. For example, in 1443, a citizen of France was granted an exclusive right for a period of twenty years to build a number of flour mills, without water, in Venice and surrounding villages. The Senate of Venice ordered that experimental mills be made in one borough, and, if successful, then the grant would extend to other areas.

b. Prager, supra 34 J.P.O.S. 106, 125.

c. Mandich, Venetian Patents (1450–1550), 30 J.P.O.S. 166, 172–174 (1948).

Before granting a patent, the General Welfare Board usually examined the invention to some extent, principally to be certain it was new and indeed useful. Disclosure was made by public use, not filing a written document, and examination proceeded by interview, observation, and the explanations of experts. Guilds that might be affected by the grant had an opportunity to be heard. Often, the grant of a patent was conditioned on the invention proving in practice to be truly useful and to achieve the advantages asserted by the inventor.[d]

These grants and practices form the background for what is believed to be the first general patent statute. In 1474, the Senate of the Republic of Venice reorganized the patent system by enacting a statute with the clear intent of encouraging both native ingenuity and the importation of ideas. This statute is set forth in its entirety since it provides a rather astounding forerunner of modern patent statutes.

March 19, 1474

WE HAVE among us men of great genius, apt to invent and discover ingenious devices; and in view of the grandeur and virtue of our City, more such men come to us every day from divers parts. Now, if provision were made for the works and devices discovered by such persons, so that others who may see them could not build them and take the inventor's honor away, more men would then apply their genius, would discover, and would build devices of great utility and benefit to our commonwealth. Therefore:

BE IT ENACTED that, by the authority of this Council, every person who shall build any new and ingenious device in this City, not previously made in our Commonwealth, shall give notice of it to the office of our General Welfare Board when it has been reduced to perfection so that it can be used and operated. It being forbidden to every other person in any of our territories and towns to make any further device conforming with and similar to said one, without the consent and license of the author, for the term of 10 years. And if anybody builds it in violation hereof, the aforesaid author and inventor shall be entitled to have him summoned before any magistrate of this City, by which magistrate the said infringer shall be constrained to pay him hundred ducats; and the device shall be destroyed at once. It being, however, within the power and discretion of the Government, in its activities, to take and use any such device and instrument, with this condition however that no one but the author shall operate it.

It will be noted this statute requires that the devices be actually constructed and useful, introduces the test of novelty in calling for "new" devices and, perhaps, a further test of innovation when it refers to "ingenious" devices. Remedies are provided for infringement and a definite term for the grant is stipulated. It will be of interest later to compare this statute with statutes of the United States and other countries which are currently in force.

d. Prager, supra 26 J.P.O.S. 711, 714–716.

B. EARLY BRITISH PATENT STATUTES

The English word "patent" is based on the Latin *patens,* the present participle of patere, to be open. The term "Letters Patent" comes from the practice in Great Britain of royal grants being sealed in closed condition (Litterae Clausae) or in open condition (Litterae Patentis). A royal grant sealed in open condition was referred to as "litterae patentis"—open letters—which could be read without breaking the royal seal. Such "litterae patentis" were used for pardons, titles of honor, official appointments and grants to inventors. Thus, patents granted to inventors today in the United States and Great Britain are called Letters Patent.

In Great Britain, as in Venice, there was a history of royal grants prior to the first formal statute establishing patents. Even as the great adventure of Columbus in sailing for America was subsidized by Queen Isabella of Spain, so England sponsored and encouraged commercial ventures at sea and other hazardous undertakings of commerce. Thus, in England, as in other countries, there were special grants and monopolies by the Crown to promote the public interest. Importing of skills from abroad was encouraged in an effort to compete with the progress in other European countries. In the 14th Century, the arts of weaving, shipmaking, glassmaking, and iron working, were stimulated in England by special grants to foreign artisans. In the reign of Queen Elizabeth, which began in 1558, the first elements of a modern patent system appeared. Patents for a dredging machine, the making of soap, alum, and saltpeter were granted.

Of particular interest is a petition in 1559 of Giacopo Acontio, an Italian, to Queen Elizabeth. The petition states that he had an invention in a furnace and a wheel machine "which would be copied in the absence of protection." He stated further:

> [N]othing is more honest than that those who by searching have found out things useful to the public should have some of the fruits of their rights and labors, as meanwhile they abandon all other modes of gain, are at much expense in experiments and often sustain much loss.

Acontio was allowed a pension in 1560 and his patent was granted in 1565.[e]

In England, however, as in other countries, where royal prerogative was the source of the grants, abuses arose and public opinion was reflected in complaints to the House of Commons and in the submission of bills to curb the practice.[f] Despite royal promises to reform abuses,

e. Federico, Origin and Early History of Patents, 11 J.P.O.S. 292 (1929); 18 J.P.O.S. 19 (Centennial Number insert).

f. Robinson, Vol. 1, Sections 4 to 9 (1890).

During the reign of Elizabeth it was the policy of the Crown to raise as little revenue as possible by direct taxation and as much as possible by the sale of monopolies. In the forty-fourth year of her reign the burdens borne by the nation through this method of indirect taxation had become so intolerable that they produced an outbreak in Parliament; and the extraordinary ex-the matter came to the courts in a case involving a monopoly on playing cards referred to as the Case on Monopolies set forth below.

DARCY v. ALLIN (The Case of Monopolies)

11 Coke 84b, 77 Eng.Rep. 1260 (1602).
King's Bench.

This was an action on the case brought by Edward Darcy against Thomas Allin for the infringement of a patent granted in the 30 Eliz., to one Ralph Bowes and his assigns, for the exclusive making and importing and sale of playing-cards during twelve years, and renewed for an additional twelve years to the plaintiff, evidently an assignee of Bowes.

The defendant pleaded that, as a citizen of London, he had a free right to trade in all merchantable things; and to this plea the plaintiff demurred. The argument against the validity of the patent, given at length in the report, is interesting and very forcible. It insists that the crown has no power to grant such a patent, and refers to cases in which monopolies of office, toll, etc., had been held void by the courts. It also denounces the patent as contrary to common right, destroying trade and labor, raising prices, and filling the market with inferior goods. It then states the distinction between lawful and unlawful monopolies, and gives instances thereof as follows: (182) "Now, therefore, I will show you how the judges have heretofore allowed of monopoly patents; which is, that where any man by his own charge and industry, or by his own wit or invention, doth bring any new trade into the realm, or any engine tending to the furtherance of a trade, that never was used before,—and that for the good of the realm,—that in such cases the king may grant to him a monopoly patent for some reasonable time, until the subjects may learn the same, in consideration of the good that he doth bring by his invention to the Commonwealth; otherwise not.

* * *

The same case, but without the argument of counsel, is reported in 11 Coke, R 84b., Trinity Term, 44 Eliz., where it appears that the cause itself was decided in favor of the defendant. 1 Abb.P.C. 1.

Another case, a few years later (1614), involved the weaving art:

tent to which the system had been carried is nowhere so well stated as in the report of the debate on the bill entitled "An act for the explanation of the common law in certain cases of letters patents," moved by Mr. Lawrence Hyde on the 20th November, 1601, a debate in which both Sir Walter Raleigh and "Mr. Francis Bacon" participated.

Sir Robert Wroth said: "There have been divers patents granted since the last Parliament; these are now in being, viz, the patents for currants, iron, powder, cards, ox shin-bones, train oyl, transportation of leather, lists of cloth, ashes, anise-seed, vinegar, seacoals, steel, aqua vitae, brushes, pots, saltpeter, lead, accidences, oyl calumet stone, oyl of blubber, fumathos or dried piltchers in the smoak, and divers others."

* * * "Upon the reading of the patents aforesaid, Mr. Hackwell, of Lincoln's Inn, stood up and asked thus: 'Is not bread there?' 'Bread,' quoth one. 'Bread,' quoth another. 'This voice seems strange,' quoth another. 'This voice seems strange,' quoth a third. 'No,' quoth Mr. Hackwell, 'if order be not taken for these, bread will be there before the next Parliament.'"

THE CLOTHWORKERS OF IPSWICH

Godbolt, 252.
(Decided at Easter Term, 12 James I).
English Reports Full Reprint, Vol. 78, p. 147.

"It was agreed by the court that the king might make corporations, and grant to them that they may make ordinances for the ordering and government of any trade; but thereby they cannot make a monopoly, for that is to take away free trade which is the birthright of every subject. * * * (254) But if a man hath brought in a new invention and a new trade within the kingdom, in peril of his life and consumption of his estate or stock, etc., or if a man hath made a new discovery of anything; in such cases the king, of his grace and favor, in recompense of his costs and travail, may grant by charter unto him, that he only shall use such a trade or traffic for a certain time, because at first the people of the kingdom are ignorant and have not the knowledge or skill to use it. But when that patent is expired, the king cannot make a new grant thereof; for when the trade is become common, and others have been bound apprentices to the same trade, there is no reason that such should be forbidden to use it." 1 Abb.P.C. 6.

In another decade (in 1623) a Statute of Monopolies was passed by Parliament (some authorities report 1624):

STATUTE 21, JAMES I. CHAPTER 3

This statute was in substance, as follows, the passages in quotation marks being in the language of the act itself:

"An Act concerning monopolies and dispensations of penal laws and the forfeiture thereof.

"I. Whereas your majesty, in the year 1610, published a book declaring that all grants of monopolies, and of the benefit of penal laws, and of the power of dispensing with law, and of compounding penalties, are contrary to law; and whereas your majesty then expressly commanded that no suitor should ever apply for such grants; and whereas, nevertheless, such grants have been applied for and allowed: Therefore to make void all these, and to prevent the like in time to come, may it please your majesty that it be declared and enacted by authority of this present parliament 'that all monopolies, charters, and letters-patent, heretofore made or granted, or hereafter to be made or granted, to any person or persons, bodies politic or corporate whatsoever, of or for the sole buying, selling, making, working, or using of anything, within this realm or the dominion of Wales, or of any other monopolies,' and all licenses to do anything contrary to law, or to confer authority on others so to do, and all grants of the power to compound or receive the benefit of any penalty before judgment thereon had, and all warrants or other process for the erection or promotion of the same are altogether contrary to the laws of this realm, and so are and shall be utterly void; and of none effect, and in no wise to be put in use or execution.

* * *

"IV. That at the end of forty days after this present session of parliament, any person who may be aggrieved 'by occasion or pretext of any monopoly,' or other matter or thing tending as aforesaid, may recover in the king's courts, in an action on this statute, treble damages; and such suits shall not be hindered or delayed by any order or injunction issuing out of any other court than that before which such suit is pending, except a writ of error, under penalty of a *premunire*.

* * *

"VI. Provided also, and be it declared and enacted: That any declaration before mentioned shall not extend to any letters-patent and grants of privilege, for the term of fourteen years or under, hereafter to be made, of the sole working or making of any manner of new manufactures, within this realm, to the true and first inventor and inventors of such manufactures, which others, at the time of making such letters-patent and grant, shall not use, so as also they be not contrary to the law, nor mischievous to the state, by raising prices of commodities at home, or hurt of trade, or generally inconvenient: The said fourteen years to be accounted from the date of the first letters-patent or grant of such privilege, hereafter to be made; but that the same shall be of such force as they should be, if this act had never been made and of none other."

* * *

———————◆———————

Blackstone's Commentaries on English law, written after 1750, refers to this statute in the section on personal property which also mentions rights in literary property. Under a section on Title to Things Personal, he lists Copyrights and Patents as having Title by Occupancy such as goods captured from alien enemies, things found, animals wild by nature, literary property, invention, etc.

It is to be noted that Section VI of the Statute James I makes reference, as did the early Venetian statute, to "new manufacturers within the realm" again setting up the requirement of novelty as a prerequisite to protection.

C. THE PATENT CLAUSE OF THE UNITED STATES CONSTITUTION

The colonization of North America resulted in the immigration of many British subjects to the colonies of New England, and, again, the desire to stimulate manufacture led to the adoption of laws to encourage inventions. The experience in England was reflected in the laws of the Colony of Massachusetts, for example, where in 1641 the General Court of Massachusetts adopted the following:

> There shall be no monopolies granted or allowed among us, but of such new inventions as are profitable to the country, and that for a short time.

In Connecticut, a similar provision was adopted in 1672, followed in 1715 by a provision to stimulate importation of commodities.

The first patent in America was granted in 1641 to Samuel Winslow by the General Court of Massachusetts for his invention of a method of manufacturing salt. In 1646 one Joseph Jenks was granted the first machinery patent in Massachusetts for "erecting of engines of mills to go by water."[g]

The Declaration of Independence in 1776 and the successful conclusion of the Revolutionary War brought statehood to the various colonies. The several states granted some patents, for the most part by special acts of their legislatures.[h] South Carolina in 1784 passed an act for the copyright of books which also contained the following:

> And be it further enacted by the authority aforesaid, that the inventors of useful machines shall have a like exclusive privilege of making or vending their machines for the like term of fourteen years, under the same privileges and restrictions hereby granted to and imposed on the authors of books.

While the granting of patents by individual states[i] continued to some degree after the adoption of the Federal Constitution in 1789 and the first Patent Act of 1790, this activity soon ceased.

The framers of the Constitution, as leaders of the various states, were aware of the activities of inventors and authors and the efforts to aid them in the individual state legislatures and the Continental Congress. James Madison, one of the authors of *The Federalist*, and Charles Pinckney of South Carolina, which state had a copyright and patent statute, each submitted proposals to the Constitutional Convention in August of 1787. The resulting provision adopted in September of 1787 became Clause 8 of Section 8, Article I, of the Constitution of the United States:

> The Congress shall have power * * * To promote the progress of science and useful arts, by securing for limited times to authors and inventors the exclusive right to their respective writings and discoveries.

Evidently, this provision was uncontroversial as there is no record of any debate of this matter.

James Madison, writing in *The Federalist*, No. 43, stated with respect to this provision:

> The utility of this clause will scarcely be questioned. The copyright of authors has been solemnly adjudged in Great Britain to be a

---

g. Federico, Colonial Monopolies and Patents, 11 J.P.O.S. 358; See also Deller's Walker on Patents, Early American Patents, Second Edition (1964), Vol. 1, p. 51.

h. Federico, State Patents, 13 J.P.O.S. 166, 176 (1931). In commenting on a decision of the United States Supreme Court in 1825 striking down a New York State law granting an exclusive privilege of navigating steam ferry boats, the author comments: "Thus passed the last of the state patents. States probably have the power to grant patents but they do not exercise it. Such patents would now be of very little value due to their limited jurisdiction and to the possibility of interfering with federal laws and patents." The question of federal preemption of patent protection will be treated, infra, Part V.

i. See Walker on Patents, Deller Ed., Vol. 1, p. 28; Second Edition, Vol. 1, p. 51.

right at Common Law. The right to useful inventions seems with equal reason to belong to the inventors. The public good fully coincides in both cases with the claims of individuals. The States cannot separately make effectual provision for either of the cases, and most of them have anticipated the decision of this point by laws passed at the instance of Congress.

Does an inventor have a right to his invention at common law? Madison, in the language previously quoted, and perhaps the Federal Constitution itself, imply that this right exists. In Part I, dealing with confidential disclosures and trade secrets, we have considered some of the "natural" rights of an inventor which may be protected at common law prior to the issuance of a patent.

Chief Justice Taney observed, in the case of Gayler et al. v. Wilder, 51 U.S. (10 How.) 477, 13 L.Ed. 504 (1850):

> The inventor of a new and useful improvement certainly has no exclusive right to it, until he obtains a patent. This right is created by the patent, and no suit can be maintained by the inventor against anyone for using it before the patent is issued. * * *
>
> Now, the monopoly granted to the patentee is for one entire thing; it is the exclusive right of making, using and vending to others to be used, the improvement he has invented, and for which the patent is granted. The monopoly did not exist at common law, and the rights, therefore, which may be exercised under it cannot be regulated by the rules of the common law. It is created by the act of Congress; and no rights can be acquired in it unless authorized by statute, and in the manner the statute prescribes.

And in 1913, we find the United States Supreme Court saying: [j]

> The right to make, use, and sell an invented article is not derived from the patent law. This right existed before and without the passage of the law, and was always the right of an inventor. The act secured to the inventor the *exclusive* right to make, use, and vend the thing patented, and consequently to prevent others from exercising like privileges without the consent of the patentee. Bloomer v. McQuewan, 14 How. 539, 549, 14 L.Ed. 532, 537; Continental Paper Bag Co. v. Eastern Paper Bag Co., 210 U.S. 405, 425, 28 S.Ct. 748, 52 L.Ed. 1122, 1130. It was passed for the purpose of encouraging useful invention and promoting new and useful improvements by the protection and stimulation thereby given to inventive genius, and was intended to secure to the public, after the lapse of the exclusive privileges granted, the benefit of such inventions and improvements.

D. PATENTS AND PUBLIC POLICY

Prior to perusal of this text, the reader's acquaintance with patents may have been limited to seeing "Patent Applied For" or "Patent Pending" on certain articles of manufacture, or "Patent Medicines" in

j. Bauer & Cie. v. O'Donnell, 229 U.S. 1, 10, 33 S.Ct. 616, 57 L.Ed. 1041, 1043 (1913).

stores which merchandise proprietary or trademarked products most of which are not patented. Some students may have had closer contact with patents through family relationships with inventors, by having been applicants for patents themselves, or, at least, employees who have signed patent agreements with corporate employers.

Accordingly, it is appropriate to examine some of the opinions and writings which have formed the backdrop for the various patent law decisions of the courts and the legislative enactments. The judicial decisions will reflect many of these policies but the comments of others are pertinent.

Robinson on Patents (1890) points out that the patent privilege restricts the natural right of the public to use a disclosed invention (Sec. 26), to independently discover and employ the same invention (Sec. 28), and to improve on the same invention (Sec. 30). Nevertheless, Robinson suggests that the patent privilege differs from an "odious monopoly" in that it does not deprive the public of an existing right but rather prevents only the exercise for a limited time of a new direction marked out by the inventor (Sec. 32). Indeed, Robinson concluded that on balance, the patent privilege is fully justified saying:

> The creation of a monopoly embracing these extraordinary privileges, with their corresponding limitations of the common right, could not be justified unless the ultimate results of its bestowed were, upon the whole, highly advantageous to the public. That this is true, experience has fully demonstrated. The granting of a patent privilege at once accomplishes three important objects; it rewards the inventor for his skill and labor in conceiving and perfecting his invention; it stimulates him, as well as others, to still further efforts in the same or different fields; it secures to the public an immediate knowledge of the character and scope of the invention, and an unrestricted right to use it after the patent has expired. Each of these objects, with its consequences, is a public good, and tends directly to the advancement of the industrial arts. Any system of law which attains these results, without the undue restriction of natural rights, is evidently consonant with reason, justice, and sound public policy. (Sec. 33)

The following excerpts are also of interest.

OPPENHEIM,[k] A NEW APPROACH TO EVALUATION OF THE AMERICAN PATENT SYSTEM

33 Journal of the Patent Office Society 555 (1951).

"The United States has staked its national destiny and welfare upon the basic principle that private initiative, creative talents and venture capital shall be the primary means of determining the recipients of rewards for competitive enterprise. The American Patent System is deeply imbedded in that tradition. The Constitutional provision and the laws relating to

k. S. Chesterfield Oppenheim, Professor Emeritus of Law, University of Michigan.

patent rights give the patentee a limited-time exclusiveness. This temporary protection against free competition is awarded in the faith that it will serve the public interest. The stated objective is to promote progress of science and the industrial arts. The exclusiveness of patent rights is regarded as a short-term public welfare monopoly which promotes the competitive economy of which the Patent System is itself a vital part.

* * *

"My concluding comments go to the heart of the atmosphere which should pervade an evaluation of the Patent System based upon facts and a 'rule of reason' analysis of the facts. Here I express an inner conviction of faith in the traditions by which America has lived under our Constitution. I believe in holding fast to the traditions of private competitive enterprise as the main sparkplug of incentive to seek rewards through risk-taking in expenditure of labor, capital and other resources of the entrepreneur. The Patent System has existed for 160 years along with the competitive economy under which it functions. In that period the citizens of America have enjoyed a progressive elevation of the standards of living.

"I do not argue that because of the interdependence of the free enterprise and the patent systems, this historical development *ipso facto* supports the latter as a matter of cause and effect. But I do say that before challenging the historical premises of the Patent System, it must be factually demonstrated that, first, it has basic deficiencies and second, that suggested alternatives give real promise of eliminating them, without unacceptable sacrifices to a workable competitive system and to American technological supremacy."

NATIONAL PATENT PLANNING COMMISSION FIRST REPORT (1943)

"The American patent system established by the Constitution giving Congress the 'power to promote the progress of science and useful arts,' is over 150 years old. The system has accomplished all that the framers of the Constitution intended. It is the only provision of the government for the promotion of invention and discovery and is the basis upon which our entire industrial civilization rests.

"The American people and their government should recognize the fundamental rightness and fairness of protecting the creations of its inventors by the patent grant. The basic principles of the present system should be preserved. The system has contributed to the growth and greatness of our nation; it has:

(1) encouraged and rewarded inventiveness and creativeness, producing new products and processes which have placed the United States far ahead of other countries in the field of scientific and technological endeavor;

(2) stimulated American inventors to originate a major portion of the important industrial and basic inventions of the past 150 years;

(3) facilitated the rapid development and general application of new discoveries in the United States to an extent exceeding that of any other country;

(4) contributed to the achievement of the highest standard of living that any nation has ever enjoyed;

(5) stimulated creation and development of products and processes necessary to arm the nation and to wage successful war;

(6) contributed to the improvement of the public health and the public safety; and

(7) operated to protect the individual and small business concerns during the formative period of a new enterprise." (pp. 783–84)

REPORT OF PRESIDENT'S COMMISSION [1]
(Nov. 17, 1966)

* * *

"Agreeing that the patent system has in the past performed well its Constitutional mandate 'to promote the progress of * * * useful arts,' the Commission asked itself: What is the basic worth of a patent system in the context of present day conditions? The members of the Commission unanimously agreed that a patent system today is capable of continuing to provide an incentive to research, development, and innovation. They have discovered no practical substitute for the unique service it renders.

"First, a patent system provides an incentive to invent by offering the possibility of reward to the inventor and to those who support him. This prospect encourages the expenditure of time and private risk capital in research and development efforts.

"Second, and complementary to the first, a patent system stimulates the investment of additional capital needed for the further development and marketing of the invention. In return, the patent owner is given the right, for a limited period, to exclude others from making, using, or selling the invented product or process.

"Third, by affording protection, a patent system encourages early public disclosure of technological information, some of which might otherwise be kept secret. Early disclosure reduces the likelihood of duplication of effort by others and provides a basis for further advances in the technology involved.

"Fourth, a patent system promotes the beneficial exchange of products, services, and technological information across national boundaries by providing protection for industrial property of foreign nationals.

THE ROLE OF PATENTS IN THE GROWTH OF NEW COMPANIES [m]
By Dr. Edwin H. Land [†]

"The almost automatic operation of the patent system in a good corporation enables the scientist to discover, to invent, to publish, to participate in the scientific activity of the academic world unselfconsciously

---

l. The President's Commission on the Patent System was established in April of 1965 by President Lyndon B. Johnson.

m. Presented at the Annual Dinner of the Boston Patent Law Association on April 2, 1959.

† President of Polaroid Corporation.

and naturally, knowing that the corporation which is supporting him will be protected, and that the scientific world in which his mind is rooted will be continuously repaid by the prompt publication, both in patents and in scientific journals, of all that he has learned. The horrible, unthinkable alternative to all this is the cesspool of secrecy; and industrial environment filled with spies, and an industrial environment in which a true scientist would be embarrassed to participate because he could not talk freely of what he knew, and he could not use freely what he had learned. Our industrial scientific community has in America proceeded to take its place proudly and properly as a great contributor to pure science by not having to discriminate between the pure and the applied, by having the Patent Department within the company take care of the concern of the stockholders. There is encouraged a continuous interplay between the pure and the applied, an interplay so continuous that there is no boundary between them and no definition to separate them.

* * *

"A retention in secrecy, even for years, of wonderful discoveries by great individuals in industry could lead to disastrous retardation of the general progress of science, and if my thesis is correct that individual greatness is necessary for general progress, then it simply is not true that the same discoveries are likely to be made anyhow, somewhere, at some time. By every definition the things we care about most do not occur spontaneously in multiple because they are the result of a very special way of seeing, by a very special mind.

"It should be the role of our patent system to bring encouragement, a sense of reward, and a stimulus to prompt publication to this potential army of great men in applied science. There are a thousand new fields ready to be opened. Only a handful of these will be explored by large corporations, and without the protection of the patent system these new fields cannot be developed by young scientific entrepreneurs."

WARNING: AMERICA CAN'T TURN BACK THE TECHNOLOGY CLOCK *

By Jerome B. Wiesner [n]
May 19, 1979, P. 10.

I believe that the United States has entered a critical quarter century for human social evolution, in which we face two almost antagonistic needs. The first is the deep human need for genuinely felt purpose that emerges when mere survival no longer dominates our daily lives. The second is the necessity of finding ways to make sure that an industrial society, and the technology needed to support it, evolves to an ever more satisfactory level.

My concern is for the role of technology in an industrial society that we neither fully understand nor know how to manage. Until recently the economic and social climate of the United States encouraged the innovation

* Reprinted with the permission of *INC. Magazine,* May 1979. Copyright © United Marine Publishing, Inc. 1979.

n. The author is president of the Massachusetts Institute of Technology. He served as science adviser to Presidents Kennedy and Johnson and has been involved in a number of the nation's major scientific developments.

that created our spectacular scientific and industrial capabilities. But today we see ever-increasing deterrents to such creative change, and technical development has been much slowed as a result.

* * *

The deterrents to technological progress, as I see it, consist of both conceptual and pragmatic considerations. On the conceptual side, there are fundamental contradictions between the basic conditions of a healthy industrial society and the public understanding and expectations. In my view, this accounts for much of the misunderstanding, the malfunctioning of the system, and the high level of alienation and unhappiness that exists in our industrial societies.

A technological society must be in a continuous state of change. Yet what people want most from their society is stability. We must accept the fact that there is not likely to be a stable state—in the sense that new problems, demanding in turn new technologies for their solutions, will cease to arise. We are participants in an ongoing social process and we cannot turn off the man-made world and its demands for change. Nor can we run the technological clock backward to a simpler time as the small-is-beautiful people would have us do.

On the pragmatic side, the need for more sophisticated technology in a highly industrialized nation requires more complete understanding and a much more effective management of our man-made world than in the past—particularly of that part of the world which is the responsibility of the government.

There is a Catch-22 situation here. We obviously need predicting and planning mechanisms adequate to cope with the size, time scale, and complexity of the technological needs of a modern, interconnected society such as ours. This implies governmental planning and management. Yet extensive governmental planning, control, and regulations do not appear to provide an adequate solution in the nations that depend on them.

* * *

These conceptual and pragmatic difficulties may seem disparate, but they all contribute to deterring innovation. I am troubled because I don't have any answers to these problems, but I do believe that the first step toward reversing the trend and encouraging innovation is to understand the relationship between innovation, productivity, industry, economic welfare, and social well-being.

One thing is clear: we haven't run out of important problems. There is an urgent need for continued innovation to improve the quality of life and to continue economic development. But even more important, innovation is needed just to keep the system we now have working properly, to retain what has been achieved, and to insure that the quality of life doesn't deteriorate drastically because technical and industrial capabilities haven't kept up with our society's changing needs and problems.

E. UNITED STATES PATENT STATUTES

A patent statute was proposed in the very first session of the First Congress and in the second session the first Patent Act was enacted on

April 10, 1790.[o] This first Patent Act of 1790 authorized the issuance of a patent to the "first and true inventor or discoverer" if the invention was "not before known or used" and was deemed by the Attorney General and the Secretaries of War and State to be "sufficiently useful and important" to warrant patent protection. Thus, the first patent statute required an examination as to the newness or novelty and the level of innovation of the invention for which patent protection was sought. Thomas Jefferson, as the first Secretary of the Department of State, had the primary responsibility for administering this patent statute including examination procedures.[p]

The examination required by the Patent Act of 1790 and the deliberations in determining whether to grant a patent were burdensome on the Cabinet officer administrators and resulted in slowness in issuing patents and dissatisfaction of patent applicants with the high standards applied by the administrators of the Act.[q] Thus, the Patent Act of 1793 eliminated the examination to determine if the applicant's invention was "sufficiently useful and important" and substituted a ministerial registration system.[r] The validity of such patents was to be determined by the Federal Courts.

By 1836 this registration system had resulted in many worthless patents, much burdensome litigation, and many frauds involving patent rights. These evils were outlined in an 1836 Senate Committee Report[s] as:

1. A considerable portion of all the patents granted are worthless and void, as conflicting with, and infringing upon one another, or upon, public rights not subject to patent privileges; arising either from a want of due attention to the specifications of claim, or from the ignorance of the patentees of the state of the arts and manufacturers, and of the inventions made in other countries, and even in our own.

2. The country becomes flooded with patent monopolies, embarrassing to bona fide patentees, whose rights are thus invaded on all sides; and not less embarrassing to the community generally, in the use of even the most common machinery and long-known improvements in the arts and common manufactures of the country.

3. Out of this interference and collision of patents and privileges, a great number of lawsuits arise, which are daily increasing in an alarming degree, onerous to the courts, ruinous to the parties, and injurious to society.

4. It opens the door to frauds, which have already become extensive and serious. It is represented to the committee that it is not uncommon for persons to copy patented machines in the model-room; and, having made some slight immaterial alterations, they apply in the

o. Outline of the History of the United States Patent Office, 18 J.P.O.S. (No. 7, Chap. 6) 59–60 (1936) [Hereinafter cited as Outline]

p. Id. at p. 64.

q. Id. at p. 77.

r. Id. at 81.

s. S.Doc. No. 338, 24 Cong., 1st Sess. (Ap. 28, 1836), reprinted in 18 J.P.O.S. 854–63 (1936).

next room for patents. There being no power given to refuse them, patents are issued of course. Thus prepared, they go forth on a retailing expedition, selling out their patent rights for States, counties, and townships, to those who have no means at hand of detecting the imposition, and who find, when it is too late, that they have purchased what the vendors had no right to sell, and which they obtain thereby no right to use. This speculation in patent rights has become a regular business, and several hundred thousand dollars, it is estimated, are paid annually for void patents, many of which are thus fraudulently obtained.

The patent statute accompanying this report was unanimously adopted by the Senate, as amended, and became the Patent Act of 1836 [t] which provided the general outline of the present patent system. This Act established the Patent Office as a Bureau of the Department of State under a Commissioner of Patents and required a novelty examination and a determination of whether the invention was "sufficiently useful and important" to warrant patent protection.

The Patent Act of 1836 was amended to provide for design patents in 1842 and was subsequently revised and consolidated by the Patent Act of 1870 to incorporate some 25 amendments thereto.[u] The Patent Act of 1870 was quite complete, containing some 111 sections, and without any important changes became the Patent Act of 1874 as part of a revision and consolidation of all Federal statutes.[v]

Patent provisions for asexually reproduced plants were added in 1930 and the Patent Act of 1874 was subsequently revised and consolidated as the Patent Act of 1952 (35 U.S.C.A.). Although the 1952 Patent Act is largely a codification of its predecessor, it also contains several important revisions and additions including an express statutory test for innovation of "non-obvious" subject matter which will be studied in a later chapter.[w]

In the last three decades, numerous amendments have been made to the 1952 Patent Act some of which, such as re-examination of the validity of issued patents and a single National Court of Appeals for most patent matters, will be discussed in subsequent chapters.

t. 1836 Senate Committee Report, 18 J.P.O.S. 853 (1936).

u. Outline, supra note 1, at 110.

v. Outline, supra note r. at 110 and 115.

w. From 1861 to 1865 the Confederate Constitution and supporting statutes were the basis for a Confederate Patent Office located at Richmond, Virginia and directed by Rufus R. Rhodes. A total of 266 patents was issued by the Confederacy during the Civil War. Newton, A Forgotten Chapter of Confederate History, 12 J.P.O.S. 248 (1930).

Chapter Two

CONDITIONS FOR A VALID PATENT

A. INTRODUCTION

Some readers may wonder why all patents are not valid. If the Patent Office has an examination procedure, cannot this administrative branch of the Government be relied upon to issue patents which meet the statutory requirements and are therefore valid and enforceable?

There are a number of reasons why this is not true. Perhaps the first reason is occasional deceitfulness. The first U.S. Patent Statute of 1790 recognized that some patents might be "obtained surreptiously by or upon false suggestion", and provided a remedy. This same statute recognized that in litigation a defendant might "prove that the specification filed by plaintiff does not contain the whole of the truth concerning his invention or discovery; * * *". Similarly, today, a defense to a patent may be inequitable conduct in the Patent Office examination which undermines validity or enforcement.

Another reason is the inability of the Patent Office to be completely omniscient in its search for prior patents and printed publications which bear upon the patentability of a particular invention. Moreover, the Patent Office may have no knowledge of a prior sale or public use which would defeat patentability despite lack of any pertinent prior patents or printed publications. While the Patent Office has one of the world's outstanding collections of patents and publications, the proliferation of documents is such that an Examiner cannot always be infallible in his searching efforts and may have insufficient time to make a comprehensive search.

The word "invention" is used in texts and cases with several different meanings. Prior to the 1952 Patent Act, it usually meant the standard of innovation required for patentability or a patentable invention. Currently, it usually designates the particular idea, discovery or subject matter being considered without regard to whether it meets the requirements for patentability.

Section 100 of the 1952 Patent Act defines the word rather ineptly as "The term 'invention' means invention or discovery." The revisors' note indicates this definition was presented simply to avoid repetition in the ensuing statutory provisions. Undoubtedly, this definition was influenced by the constitutional power of Congress "to grant to *inventors* the exclusive right to their *discoveries.*" [a] In any event, under the

---

a. "Discovery" is synonomous with "invention". In re Kemper (C.C.D.C.1841) Fed. Cases No. 7,687. California Research Corp. v. Ladd (D.C.D.C.1966) 260 F.Supp. 752; 151 USPQ 563.

1952 Patent Act, the word "invention" means the idea or subject matter of a patent application or patent. The requirements for patentability of the idea or invention are set forth in other sections of the 1952 Patent Act.

As further background, one should have a general understanding of the terms "written description", "claims", and "specification."

Every utility patent application and every patent issued by the United States Patent Office has, as a first part, a written description which may consist of a brief discussion of the field of the invention including the problem confronted by the inventor, the prior art, i.e., a brief summary of the efforts of others to solve the problem, a summary of the invention including a brief recitation of the objects or advantages of the invention, and a detailed technical description of the invention, accompanied by drawings if the invention may be illustrated by them.

A second part of each patent application and patent is a claim or set of claims which consists of statements at the end of the written description particularly pointing out and defining the subject matter which the inventor considers to be his patentable invention for which he desires a patent grant. The claims define the scope of patent protection. The drafting of claims has an interesting evolution through the years; a kind of common law of claim drafting has developed within the framework of the evolving statutes, resulting in certain established practices, undefined by any rules or statutes, which provide the basis for the form of the claims.

Most patent attorneys and patent agents practicing today have technical training, based on formal education, practical experience, or both, which enables them to work with inventors to compose a specification for presentation to the Patent Office as a part of the patent application.

The specification and claims of a patent, particularly if the invention be at all complicated, constitute one of the most difficult legal instruments to draw with accuracy, and in view of the fact that valuable inventions are often placed in the hands of inexperienced

"We can go a step further on the question of obviousness of the invention. It must be borne in mind that the Patent Law covers two types of results, discoveries and inventions. They are often very similar, but they are two distinct concepts. The Constitution, in Article I, Section 8, authorizes the Congress to grant to inventors the exclusive right to their discoveries. It does not use the word 'inventions'. The pertinent statute uses two terms, both inventions and discoveries, 35 U.S.C.A. § 101.

"A discovery is an unintended or unexpected result found by the discoveror.

An invention, on the other hand, is a product of the intellectual efforts of the inventor, a result that he develops by the use of his mind and possibly with a series of experimentations. If the alleged invention involves the use of the inventive faculty, it is patentable. If it involves merely the use of routine mechanical skill, it does not rise to the dignity of patentability. These remarks have been made in view of the fact that in this case we are dealing with what is claimed to be a discovery rather than an invention, and discoveries are much less common than inventions."

persons to prepare such specifications and claims, it is no matter of surprise that the latter frequently fail to describe with requisite certainty the exact invention of the patentee, and err either in claiming that which the patentee had not in fact invented, or in omitting some element which was a valuable or essential part of his actual invention.[b]

A precise use of language and considerable skill is required to draft claims which define a patentable invention over the "prior art" (prior patents, publications or uses) while still embodying the spirit of the particular invention and embracing all possible variations of the invention within the prescience of the draftsman. When drafting claims, one needs to use imagination and creative ability to envision all possible ways of utilizing the basic concept of the invention so claims can be prepared to provide the full measure of protection to which the inventor is entitled.

It may be unfortunate that an element discarded by the patentee because it "would not work" and from a viewpoint of practical utility probably unimportant in any event affords an automatic insulation to one accused of infringement. But this consequence follows naturally and logically from the nature of a combination patent and the principle that it is the patentee who determines how much he is claiming to be within his monopoly and, on the other hand, how much he is releasing for unrestricted public appropriation. Mahn v. Harwood, 1884, 112 U.S. 354, 361, 5 S.Ct. 174, 6 S.Ct. 451, 28 L.Ed. 665, 668; 2 Walker, Patents, § 256 at 1231 et seq.; § 165 at 769–770. It is the hard lesson so much a part of every breathing moment of a patent solicitor's life— calling for a precision and a prescient forecast encountered in few other facets of the law—of claiming enough but not too much. Reed v. Parrack, 276 F.2d 784, 788, 125 USPQ 256 (5th Cir.1960).

In the Patent Office, an application is examined for compliance with the requirements of the 1952 Patent Act by a person called an Examiner. This examination usually includes a search of the pertinent prior art patents and publications in the Patent Office and an application of the requirements for patentability. If the Examiner concludes the application, either as originally filed or subsequently amended, meets the requirements of the Patent Act, the patent will be granted on payment of an issue fee.

Any final rejection of an application by the Examiner may be appealed to a Board of Patent Appeals and Interferences, which is usually composed of three Chief Examiners of the Patent Office. An adverse decision by this Board may be appealed to either the Circuit Court of Appeals for the Federal Circuit, based on the record made in the Patent Office, or to the District Court for the District of Columbia, where the record made in the Patent Office may be supplemented by additional evidence. The judgments of this District Court are appealed to the Circuit Court of Appeals for the District of Columbia. The Court

b. Topliff v. Topliff, 145 U.S. 156, 12 S.Ct. 825, 36 L.Ed. 658 (1892); Hart, The Art of Communicating Complex Patent Matters, 37 J.P.O.S. 843 (1955).

of Appeals for the Federal Circuit was created November 1, 1982 and, prior thereto, an adverse decision of the Board could be appealed to the Court of Customs and Patent Appeals. The judgments of all these Courts of Appeal may be reviewed by the United States Supreme Court on a Petition for Certiorari.

The Federal Court system has exclusive jurisdiction over patent infringement cases and most cases appearing in this casebook will be decisions of the Federal District Courts, the Circuit Courts of Appeal, including the Federal Circuit, and the Supreme Court of the United States. An occasional case decided by the Court of Claims may also be used. On some issues, and particularly issues relating to title of patents or contracts involving patents, the courts of the respective States may have proper jurisdiction. Nevertheless, the conditions for patentability are governed by the same federal law in connection with both patent applications and issued patents whether they are determined by the Patent Office, Federal Courts, or State Courts.

One other aspect of patent cases deserves comment before the presentation of numerous decisions for reading and study. In every case before the courts, the inventor, or his assignee, as well as the attorneys, are vitally interested and very frequently emotionally involved in the outcome. It might be thought that reading and searching large numbers of patents is dull work indeed; yet, if it is remembered that in most cases, if not all, there are dreams, hopes, aspirations, investments, competition, excitement, possibilities of large rewards, and also large losses, then there is drama enough behind the printed word.

"I think you will agree that patent suits are not instituted to establish validity and infringement. Nor are they resisted in order to establish the converse. Patent suits are fought for money and for the power to make money. When the prize is large there is added zest to the conflict. But always it is a conflict for a prize, and the prize is sometimes very large indeed; frequently, as I believe you who have tried patent cases know, much larger than in the run of the mill civil litigation.

"In this conflict for a prize, the contestants are no longer faceless plaintiffs and defendants, nor, as some of the opinions would make it appear, are they simply claims and anticipations. They are human beings possessed of distinctive virtues and deficiencies. They are emotion-laden individuals. They are frequently picturesque characters with dramatic tales to tell. * * * If only he [the judge] would put upon the printed page the story of the tedious search, the trial and the error, the intuition, the 'A-Ha' phenomenon, the nerve-wracking, patient wait as the confirming experiment is sweated out, the cry of 'Eureka'. Indeed, we would then become aware of the ever-present romance of patent litigation.

"Moreover, patent litigation is invested not only with the story teller's romance, not only with the romance of ever-startling human ingenuity, but also with the peculiar romance which only a judge or lawyer can savor. Sometimes we forget that a patent is a monopoly, that patent rights are property rights, that infringements are but trespasses, and that licenses are but contracts. Each of these fields has its frontier of the law; and there is great excitement in being at the frontier of any body of law; to stand at the place where the pavement ends, and the highway turns into a foot path and dribbles off into the trackless unknown. What sport can match the excitement of stepping out into this unmarked terrain, exploring it for a while, then choosing the new direction and planting the marker which will beckon the next frontiersman on to a selected route." [c]

To assist a student at this stage of study, a United States patent is reproduced as an illustration. The validity of this patent was considered in the following United States Supreme Court decision which provides an overview of the principal conditions for patentability which are dealt with in detail in subsequent chapters. Hopefully, this overview will provide a framework for consideration, organization and synthesis of the policies and rules of patent law.

[c.] The Romance Discoverable in Patent Cases—Hon. Simon H. Rifkind, Federal Rules Decisions, Dec. 1954, West Publishing Co.—Reprinted in Journal of the Patent Office Society, Vol. 37, page 319.

Jan. 27, 1959   B. I. Scoggin, Jr.   2,870,943

PUMP-TYPE LIQUID SPRAYER HAVING HOLD-DOWN CAP

Filed March 4, 1957

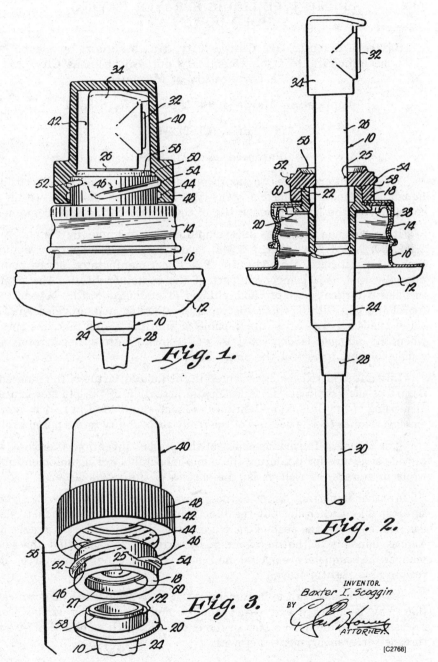

Fig. 1.

Fig. 2.

Fig. 3.

INVENTOR.
Baxter I. Scoggin

BY

ATTORNEY.

[C2768]

UNITED STATES PATENT OFFICE
2,870,943

PUMP–TYPE LIQUID SPRAYER HAVING HOLD–DOWN CAP

Baxter I. Scoggin, Jr., Kansas City, Mo., assignor, by mesne assignments, to Cook Chemical Company, Kansas City, Mo., a corporation of Missouri

Application March 4, 1957, Serial No. 643,711

4 Claims. (Cl. 222–182)

Patented Jan. 27, 1959.

This invention relates to improvements in structures for dispensing liquids wherein is provided a spray-type hand pump mounted within a container for the liquid through use of the closure cap of such container.

It is common practice, as exemplified for example by Patent No. 2,362,080, issued November 7, 1944, to dispense various types of liquids such as insecticides, through use of a finger-manipulated spray pump normally sold as a component part of the container itself. The pump includes a vertically reciprocable plunger extending upwardly beyond the top of the cap within which the pump is mounted and provided with a spray head or nozzle structure capable of emitting a fine mist-like spray when the plunger is depressed by engagement with a finger-receiving saddle forming a part of the spray head.

Difficulties have been experienced in the field by virtue of the inherent nature of such structure since accidental actuation of the plunger causes dispensing of the fluid and oftentimes the material is used in part by store employees prior to sale because of the ready accessibility to the pump itself.

It is the most important object of the present invention, therefore, to provide structure for rendering the pump inoperable during shipment and while in storage, as well as on the shelves of the retail dealer.

Another important object of the present invention is to provide structure capable of carrying out the functions above set forth which is also adapted to enclose the head of the plunger and thereby protect the same, as well as handlers of the merchandise by virtue of the fact that the said plunger is completely enclosed and held at the innermost end of its reciprocable path of travel.

A further object of the instant invention is to provide a hold-down cap that may be quickly and easily applied and removed by virtue of a releasable attachment to a part of the entire unit such as by use of screw-threaded interengagement therewith.

A further object of this invention is to provide improvements of the aforementioned character that advantageously employs a part of the unit which has a secondary function of attaching the barrel of the spray pump to the closure cap of the container.

Other objects include important details of construction to be made clear or become apparent as the following specification progresses, reference being had to the accompanying drawing, wherein:

Figure 1 is a fragmentary, elevational view of a liquid container showing a pump-type sprayer as a part thereof and including the novel hold-down cap of the instant invention, parts being in section for clearness.

Fig. 2 is a fragmentary, vertical, cross-sectional view through the container and its cap showing the pump assembly in its operable position with the hold-down cap removed; and

Fig. 3 is an exploded perspective view showing the hold-down cap and certain parts of the sprayer with which the same is operably associated.

Pump-type sprayer 10 for liquid container 12 is attached to cap 14 for retention thereby when cap 14 is removed from threaded neck 16 of container 12, and if desired, there may be provided sufficient clearance between cup-shaped retainer 18 and annular outturned flange 20 to permit rotation of cap 14 relative to sprayer 10.

Both cap or closure 14 and retainer 18 are received by a cylindrical extension 22 of frusto-conical barrel 24, forming a part of the sprayer 10, extension 22 being integral with flange 20 at the innermost edge of the latter. Flange 20 is integral with barrel 24 near the larger, uppermost edge of the latter and is held against the under side of gasket 38 in the cap 14 when the sprayer 10 is operably associated with container 12.

Retainer 18 is provided with a central opening 25 which receives tubular plunger 26 and has a cavity 27 that accommodates the enlarged extension 22 as is clear in Fig. 2. Retainer 18 is fitted tightly over the extension 22 and maintains the retainer in place with flange 20 against gasket 38 as above set forth.

Reduced end 28 of barrel 24 receives a tube 30 that extends to the bottom of container 12, it being understood that the sprayer 10 is internally constructed in a suitable manner as, for example, in accordance with teachings of the aforementioned patent to pump liquid from the container 12 into the tube 30 and thence through nozzle 32 forming a part of a spray head 34 secured to the uppermost end of plunger 26. The enlarged head 34 is normally depressed by one finger as the operator grasps the container 12 as is well understood in this art.

Cap 14 has a clearance opening therein, as best shown in Fig. 2, for the extension 22 of barrel 24 and when the cap 14 is in screw-threaded engagement with neck 16, the gasket 38 which surrounds barrel 24, is clamped tightly between flange 20 and the under side of the top of cap 14.

A hold-down member broadly designated by the numeral 40, is provided to hold the plunger 26 at the lowermost end of its path of travel within the barrel 24 in the manner illustrated by Fig. 1, it being understood as by reference to said patent, that a spring (not shown) within the barrel 24, yieldably biases the plunger 26 upwardly to the position shown in Fig. 2. The hold-down member 40 is preferably in the nature of a hollow cap so that the same not only encloses or houses the upper end of plunger 26, i.e. spray head 34, but releasably attaches to the retainer 18 and also houses the latter.

A cylindrical bore 42 within the hold-down cap 40 receives the head 34 as seen in Fig. 1, and enlargement of the bore 42 adjacent the lowermost open end of the cap 40 is provided with internal screw threads 44 that mesh with external screw threads 46 on the retainer 18, thereby releasably attaching the cap 40 to the retainer 18.

An enlarged, annular boss 48 on the cap 40 is provided with a ribbed, outermost surface to facilitate mounting and removal of the cap 40 relative to retainer 18. A downwardly-facing shoulder 50 within the cap 40 engages the upper surface of retainer 18, thereby preventing engagement between cap 40 and closure 14 to prevent forcing of the retainer 18 from its tight press-fit engagement with extension 22. As illustrated, the screw threads 46 on the retainer 18 are in the nature of a pair of substantially semi-circular, spirally arranged sections 52 and 54, permitting molding of the retainer 18 with its screw threads 46 as a single unitary part.

In addition to the seal provided between shoulder 50 and the top surface of retainer 18, there is established an additional annular seal between annular rib 56 and the annular surface of cap 40 immediately adjacent to shoulder 50. This seal is clearly illustrated in Figure 1. The cross-sectional contour of rib 56 is as shown in Fig. 2 to present an upwardly and inwardly inclined annular face which snugly fits against the "corner" or line of juncture between shoulder 50 and the adjacent annular inner face of cap 40.

The interfitting surfaces between extension 22 and retainer 18 are as illustrated in Fig. 2. There is an annular notch formed in extension 22 at the outer extremity thereof and this notch 58 receives a similarly formed, continuous annular projection 60 formed integrally with retainer 18 and at a point where elements 58 and 60 will interlock when the parts are in assembled condition.

Thus, any accidental leakage or seepage from container 12 through the parts after they are assembled is obviated.

The material from which retainer 18 is produced is soft enough to be slightly compressed when shoulder 50 and the corner adjacent thereto, rides along the upwardly and inwardly inclined outer face of rib 56 when cap 40 is moved to position.

Having thus described the invention what is claimed as new and desired to be secured by Letters Patent is:

1. In a closure assembly for an open-top container having a perforated cap over said open top thereof mounting a spray unit including a barrel provided with a tubular extension passing coaxially upwardly through the perforation in said cap, a plunger reciprocably carried by the barrel and normally extending therebeyond and a spray head on the upper end of the plunger above said extension, the combination with said spray unit of an annular retainer telescoped over and secured to the extension above said cap and provided with external, circumferentially disposed screw threads and an annular, continuous segment at the upper part of the retainer above said screw threads, and a cup-shaped hold-down member housing the head and holding the plunger depressed at substantially the innermost path of travel thereof within the barrel, said member being provided with

internal screw threads complementally engaging said screw threads on the retainer and having an internal, circumferentially extending, continuous shoulder disposed to engage said segment around the entire periphery thereof and thereby present a liquid-tight seal located between the spray head and said threads on the retainer and said member respectively, said shoulder being spaced from the lower annular peripheral edge of the member a distance at least slightly less than the distance from that portion of said segment normally engaged by said shoulder, to the proximal upper surface of the cap whereby said lower edge of the member is maintained out of contacting relationship with the cap when the member is on the retainer in a position with said shoulder in tight sealing engagement with the segment.

2. A closure assembly as set forth in claim 1 wherein one of the normally interengaged surfaces of the shoulder and segment respectively is substantially conical to present an inclined annular face coaxial with the member and said retainer and of sufficient diameter at the largest end thereof to cause the seal effected between the shoulder and said segment to become tighter as the shoulder slides on said segment during shifting of the member toward the cap.

3. A closure assembly as set forth in claim 2 wherein said retainer is provided with a continuous, annular rib integral with the normally upper edge thereof and defining said segment, said rib having an outwardly facing, inclined surface presenting said conical face and of greatest external diameter at the zone of juncture of the rib with the retainer, said member having a pair of inner, coaxial, longitudinally spaced, cylindrical surfaces, the innermost cylindrical surface having a smaller diameter than the outermost cylindrical surface and presenting said shoulder therebetween lying in a plane perpendicular to the axes of said cylindrical surfaces, the diameter of said innermost cylindrical surface of the member being intermediate the diameters of opposed external end margins of said rib.

4. A closure assembly as set forth in claim 3 wherein the member and retainer are constructed of materials having different coefficients of hardness whereby one of the interengaged faces of the rib and said shoulder respectively is deformed as the member is shifted toward the cap to thereby produce a more effective seal therebetween.

References Cited in the file of this patent
UNITED STATES PATENTS

1,447,712	Cohen	Mar. 6, 1923
2,118,222	Nilson	May 24, 1938
2,119,884	Lohse	June 7, 1938
2,586,687	Mellon	Feb. 19, 1952
2,844,290	Slade	July 22, 1958

GRAHAM v. JOHN DEERE CO.

Supreme Court of the United States, 1966.
383 U.S. 1, 86 S.Ct. 684, 15 L.Ed.2d 545.

MR. JUSTICE CLARK delivered the opinion of the Court.

After a lapse of 15 years, the Court again focuses its attention on the patentability of inventions under the standard of Art. I, § 8, cl. 8, of the Constitution and under the conditions prescribed by the laws of the United States. Since our last expression on patent validity, Great A. & P. Tea Co. v. Supermarket Equipment Corp., 340 U.S. 147, 71 S.Ct. 127, 95 L.Ed. 162 (1950), the Congress has for the first time expressly added a third statutory dimension to the two requirements of novelty and utility that had been the sole statutory test since the Patent Act of 1793. This is the test of obviousness, i.e., whether "the subject matter sought to be patented and the prior art are such that the subject matter as a whole would have been obvious at the time the invention was made to a person having ordinary skill in the art to which said subject matter pertains. Patentability shall not be negatived by the manner in which the invention was made." § 103 of the Patent Act of 1952, 35 U.S.C.A. § 103.

The questions, involved in each of the companion cases before us, are what effect the 1952 Act had upon traditional statutory and judicial tests of patentability and what definitive tests are now required. We have concluded that the 1952 Act was intended to codify judicial precedents embracing the principle long ago announced by this Court in Hotchkiss v. Greenwood, 11 How. 248, 13 L.Ed. 683 (1851), and that, while the clear language of § 103 places emphasis on an inquiry into obviousness, the general level of innovation necessary to sustain patentability remains the same.

I.

THE CASES.

(a). No. 11, Graham v. John Deere Co., an infringement suit by petitioners, presents a conflict between two Circuits over the validity of a single patent on a "Clamp for vibrating Shank Plows." * * *

(b). No. 37, Calmar, Inc. v. Cook Chemical Co., and No. 43, Colgate-Palmolive Co. v. Cook Chemical Co., both from the Eighth Circuit, were separate declaratory judgment actions, but were filed contemporaneously. Petitioner in *Calmar* is the manufacturer of a finger-operated sprayer with a "hold-down" cap of the type commonly seen on grocers' shelves inserted in bottles of insecticides and other liquids prior to shipment. Petitioner in *Colgate-Palmolive* is a purchaser of the sprayers and uses them in the distribution of its products. Each action sought a declaration of invalidity and noninfringement of a patent on similar sprayers issued to Cook Chemical as assignee of Baxter I. Scoggin, Jr., the inventor. By cross-action, Cook Chemical claimed infringement. The actions were consolidated for trial and the patent was sustained by the District Court. 220 F.Supp. 414. The Court of Appeals affirmed, 8 Cir., 336 F.2d 110, and we granted certiorari, 380 U.S. 949, 85 S.Ct. 1082, 13 L.Ed.2d 967. We reverse.

Manifestly, the validity of each of these patents turns on the facts. The basic problems, however, are the same in each case and require initially a discussion of the constitutional and statutory provisions covering the patentability of the inventions.

II.

At the outset it must be remembered that the federal patent power stems from a specific constitutional provision which authorizes the Congress "To promote the Progress of * * * useful Arts, by securing for limited Times to * * * Inventors the exclusive Right to their * * * Discoveries." Art. I, § 8, cl. 8. The clause is both a grant of power and a limitation. This qualified authority, unlike the power often exercised in the sixteenth and seventeenth centuries by the English Crown, is limited to the promotion of advances in the "useful arts." It was written against the backdrop of the practices—eventually curtailed by the Statute of Monopolies—of the Crown in granting monopolies to court favorites in goods or businesses which had long before been enjoyed by the public. See Meinhardt, Inventions, Patents and Monopoly, pp. 30–35 (London, 1946). The Congress in the exercise of the patent power may not overreach the restraints imposed by the stated constitutional purpose. Nor may it enlarge the patent monopoly without regard to the innovation, advancement or social benefit gained thereby. Moreover, Congress may not authorize the issuance of patents whose effects are to remove existent knowledge from the public domain, or to restrict free access to materials already available. Innovation, advancement, and things which add to the sum of useful knowledge are inherent requisites in a patent system which by constitutional command must "promote the Progress of * * * useful Arts." This is the *standard* expressed in the Constitution and it may not be ignored. And it is in this light that patent validity "requires reference to a standard written into the Constitution." Great A. & P. Tea Co. v. Supermarket Equipment Corp., supra, 340 U.S. at 154, 71 S.Ct. at 131, 95 L.Ed., at 168 (concurring opinion).

Within the limits of the constitutional grant, the Congress may, of course, implement the stated purpose of the Framers by selecting the policy which in its judgment best effectuates the constitutional aim. This is but a corollary to the grant to Congress of any Article I power. Gibbons v. Ogden, 9 Wheat. 1, 6 L.Ed. 23. Within the scope established by the Constitution, Congress may set out conditions and tests for patentability. McClurg v. Kingsland, 1 How. 202, 206, 11 L.Ed. 102, 103. It is the duty of the Commissioner of Patents and of the courts in the administration of the patent system to give effect to the constitutional standard by appropriate application, in each case, of the statutory scheme of the Congress.

Congress quickly responded to the bidding of the Constitution by enacting the Patent Act of 1790 during the second session of the First Congress. It created an agency in the Department of State headed by the Secretary of State, the Secretary of the Department of War and the Attorney General, any two of whom could issue a patent for a period not exceeding 14 years to any petitioner that "hath * * * invented or discovered any useful art, manufacture, * * * or device, or any improvement therein not before known or used" if the board found that "the invention or discovery [was] sufficiently useful and important * * *." 1 Stat. 110. This group, whose members administered the patent system along with their other public duties, was known by its own designation as "Commissioners for the Promotion of Useful Arts."

Thomas Jefferson, who as Secretary of State was a member of the group, was its moving spirit and might well be called the "first administrator of our patent system." See Federico, Operation of the Patent Act of 1790, 18 J.Pat.Off.Soc. 237, 238 (1936). He was not only an administrator of the patent system under the 1790 Act, but was also the author of the 1793 Patent Act. In addition, Jefferson was himself an inventor of great note. His unpatented improvements on plows, to mention but one line of his inventions, won acclaim and recognition on both sides of the Atlantic. Because of his active interest and influence in the early development of the patent system, Jefferson's views on the general nature of the limited patent monopoly under the Constitution, as well as his conclusions as to conditions for patentability under the statutory scheme, are worthy of note.

He rejected a natural-rights theory in intellectual property rights and clearly recognized the social and economic rationale of the patent system. The patent monopoly was not designed to secure to the inventor his natural right in his discoveries. Rather, it was a reward, an inducement, to bring forth new knowledge. The grant of an exclusive right to an invention was the creation of society—at odds with the inherent free nature of disclosed ideas—and was not to be freely given. Only inventions and discoveries which furthered human knowledge, and were new and useful, justified the special inducement of a limited private monopoly. Jefferson did not believe in granting patents for small details, obvious improvements, or frivolous devices. His writings evidence his insistence upon a high level of patentability.

As a member of the patent board for several years, Jefferson saw clearly the difficulty in "drawing a line between the things which are worth to the public the embarrassment of an exclusive patent and those which are not." The board on which he served sought to draw such a line and formulated several rules which are preserved in Jefferson's correspondence. Despite the board's efforts, Jefferson saw "with what slow progress a system of general rules could be matured." Because of the "abundance" of cases and the fact that the investigations occupied "more time of the members of the board than they could spare from higher duties, the whole was turned over to the judiciary, to be matured into a system, under which every one might know when his actions were safe and lawful." Letter to McPherson, supra, at 181, 182. Apparently Congress agreed with Jefferson and the board that the courts should develop additional conditions for patentability. Although the Patent Act was amended, revised or codified some 50 times between 1790 and 1950, Congress steered clear of a statutory set of requirements other than the bare novelty and utility tests reformulated in Jefferson's draft of the 1793 Patent Act.

III.

The difficulty of formulating conditions for patentability was heightened by the generality of the constitutional grant and the statutes implementing it, together with the underlying policy of the patent system that "the things which are worth to the public the embarrassment of an exclusive patent," as Jefferson put it, must outweigh the restrictive effect of the limited patent monopoly. The inherent problem was to develop some means of weeding out those inventions which would not be disclosed or devised but for the inducement of a patent.

This Court formulated a general condition of patentability in 1851 in Hotchkiss v. Greenwood, 11 How. 248, 13 L.Ed. 683. The patent involved a mere substitution of materials—porcelain or clay for wood or metal in doorknobs—and the Court condemned it, holding:

> "[U]nless more ingenuity and skill * * * were required * * * than were possessed by an ordinary mechanic acquainted with the business, there was an absence of that degree of skill and ingenuity which constitute essential elements of every invention. In other words, the improvement is the work of the skilful mechanic, not that of the inventor." At p. 267, 13 L.Ed. at p. 691.

Hotchkiss, by positing the condition that a patentable invention evidence more ingenuity and skill than that possessed by an ordinary mechanic acquainted with the business, merely distinguished between new and useful innovations that were capable of sustaining a patent and those that were not. The Hotchkiss test laid the cornerstone of the judicial evolution suggested by Jefferson and left to the courts by Congress. The language in the case, and in those which followed, gave birth to "invention" as a word of legal art signifying patentable inventions. Yet, as this Court has observed, "[t]he truth is the word ['invention'] cannot be defined in such manner as to afford any substantial aid in determining whether a particular device involves an exercise of the inventive faculty or not." McClain v. Ortmayer, 141 U.S. 419, 427, 12 S.Ct. 76, 78, 35 L.Ed. 800, 803 (1891); Great A. & P. Tea Co. v. Supermarket Equipment Corp., supra, 340 U.S. at 151, 71 S.Ct., at 129, 95 L.Ed. at 166. Its use as a label brought about a large variety of opinions as to its meaning both in the Patent Office, in the courts, and at the bar. The Hotchkiss formulation, however lies not in any label, but in its functional approach to questions of patentability. In practice, Hotchkiss has required a comparison between the subject matter of the patent, or patent application, and the background skill of the calling.

It has been from this comparison that patentability was in each case determined.

IV.

THE 1952 PATENT ACT.

The Act sets out the conditions of patentability in three sections. An analysis of the structure of these three sections indicates that patentability is dependent upon three explicit conditions: novelty and utility as articulated and defined in § 101 and § 102, and nonobviousness, the new statutory formulation, as set out in § 103. The first two sections, which trace closely the 1874 codification, express the "new and useful" tests which have always existed in the statutory scheme and, for our purposes here, need no clarification. The pivotal section around which the present controversy centers is § 103. It provides:

"§ 103. *Conditions for patentability; non-obvious subject matter.*

"A patent may not be obtained though the invention is not identically disclosed or described as set forth in section 102 of this title, if the differences between the subject matter sought to be patented and the prior art are such that the subject matter as a whole would have been obvious at the time the invention was made to a person having ordinary skill in the art to which said subject matter pertains. Patentability shall not be negatived by the manner in which the invention was made."

The section is cast in relatively unambiguous terms. Patentability is to depend, in addition to novelty and utility, upon the "non-obvious" nature of the "subject matter sought to be patented" to a person having ordinary skill in the pertinent art.

The first sentence of this section is strongly reminiscent of the language in Hotchkiss. Both formulations place emphasis on the pertinent art existing at the time the invention was made and both are implicitly tied to advances in that art. The major distinction is that Congress has emphasized "nonobviousness" as the operative test of the section, rather than the less definite "invention" language of Hotchkiss that Congress thought had led to "a large variety" of expressions in decisions and writings. In the title itself the Congress used the phrase "Conditions for patentability; *nonobvious subject matter*" (italics added), thus focusing upon "nonobviousness" rather than "invention."
* * *

It is undisputed that this section was, for the first time, a statutory expression of an additional requirement for patentability, originally expressed in *Hotchkiss*. It also seems apparent that Congress intended by the last sentence of § 103 to abolish the test it believed this Court announced in the controversial phrase "flash of creative genius," used in Cuno Engineering Corp. v. Automatic Devices Corp., 314 U.S. 84, 62 S.Ct. 37, 86 L.Ed. 58 (1941).

It is contended, however, by some of the parties and by several of the amici that the first sentence of § 103 was intended to sweep away judicial precedents and to lower the level of patentability. Others contend that the Congress intended to codify the essential purpose reflected in existing judicial precedents—the rejection of insignificant variations and innovations of a commonplace sort—and also to focus inquiries under § 103 upon nonobviousness, rather than upon "invention," as a means of achieving more stability and predictability in determining patentability and validity.

The Reviser's Note to this section, with apparent reference to *Hotchkiss*, recognizes that judicial requirements as to "lack of patentable novelty [have] been followed since at least as early as 1850." The note indicates that the section was inserted because it "may have some stabilizing effect, and also to serve as a basis for the addition at a later time of some criteria which may be worked out." To this same effect are the reports of both Houses, supra, which state that the first sentence of the section "paraphrases language which has often been used in decisions of the courts, and the section is added to the statute for uniformity and definiteness."

We believe that this legislative history, as well as other sources, shows that the revision was not intended by Congress to change the general level of patentable invention. We conclude that the section was intended merely as a codification of judicial precedents embracing the *Hotchkiss* condition, with congressional directions that inquiries into the obviousness of the subject matter sought to be patented are a prerequisite to patentability.

V.

Approached in this light, the § 103 additional condition, when followed realistically, will permit a more practical test of patentability. The emphasis on nonobviousness is one of inquiry, not quality, and, as such, comports with the constitutional strictures.

While the ultimate question of patent validity is one of law, Great A. & P. Tea Co. v. Supermarket Equipment Corp., supra, 340 U.S. at 155, 71 S.Ct. at 131, 95 L.Ed. at 168, the § 103 condition, which is but one of three conditions, each of which must be satisfied, lends itself to several basic factual inquiries. Under § 103, the scope and content of the prior art are to be determined; differences between the prior art and the claims at issue are to be ascertained; and the level of ordinary skill in the pertinent art resolved. Against this background, the obviousness or nonobviousness of the subject matter is determined. Such secondary considerations as commercial success, long felt but unsolved needs, failure of others, etc., might be utilized to give light to the circumstances surrounding the origin of the subject matter sought to be patented. As indicia of obviousness or nonobviousness, these inquiries may have relevancy. See Note, Subtests of "Nonobviousness": A Nontechnical Approach to Patent Validity, 112 U.Pa.L.Rev. 1169 (1964).

This is not to say, however, that there will not be difficulties in applying the nonobviousness test. What is obvious is not a question upon which there is likely to be uniformity of thought in every given factual context. The difficulties, however, are comparable to those encountered daily by the courts in such frames of reference as negligence and scienter, and should be amenable to a case-by-case development. We believe that strict observance of the requirements laid down here will result in that uniformity and definiteness which Congress called for in the 1952 Act.

* * *

VI.

We now turn to the application of the conditions found necessary for patentability to the cases involved here:

A. *The Patent in Issue No. 11.* Graham v. John Deere Co.

* * *

B. THE PATENT IN ISSUE IN NO. 37, CALMAR, INC. V. COOK CHEMICAL CO. AND IN NO. 43, COLGATE-PALMOLIVE CO. v. COOK CHEMICAL CO.

The single patent involved in these cases relates to a plastic finger sprayer with a "hold-down" lid used as a built-in dispenser for containers or bottles packaging liquid products, principally household insecticides. Only the first two of the four claims in the patent are involved here and we, therefore, limit our discussion to them. We do not set out those claims here since they are printed in 220 F.Supp., at 417–418.

In essence the device here combines a finger-operated pump sprayer, mounted in a container or bottle by means of a container cap, with a plastic overcap which screws over the top of and depresses the sprayer (see Appendix, Fig. 3). The pump sprayer passes through the container cap and extends down into the liquid in the container; the overcap fits over the pump sprayer and screws down on the outside of a collar mounting or retainer which is molded around the body of the sprayer. When the overcap is screwed down on this collar mounting a seal is formed by the engagement of a circular ridge or rib located above the threads on the collar mounting with a mating shoulder located inside the overcap above its threads. The overcap, as it is screwed down, depresses the pump plunger rendering the pump inoperable and when the seal is effected, any liquid which might seep into the overcap through or around the pump is prevented from leaking out of the overcap. The overcap serves also to protect the sprayer head and prevent damage to it during shipment or merchandising. When the overcap is in place it does not reach the cap of the container or bottle and in no way engages it since a slight space is left between those two pieces.

The device, called a shipper-sprayer in the industry, is sold as an integrated unit with the overcap in place enabling the insecticide manufacturer to install it on the container or bottle of liquid in a single operation in an automated bottling process. The ultimate consumer simply unscrews and discards the overcap, the pump plunger springs up and the sprayer is ready for use.

The Background of the Patent.

For many years manufacturers engaged in the insecticide business had faced a serious problem in developing sprayers that could be integrated with the containers or bottles in which the insecticides were marketed. Originally, insecticides were applied through the use of tin sprayers, not supplied by the manufacturer. In 1947, Cook Chemical, an insecticide manufacturer, began to furnish its customers with plastic pump dispensers purchased from Calmar. The dispenser was an unpatented finger-operated device mounted in a perforated cardboard holder and hung over the neck of the bottle or container. It was necessary for the ultimate consumer to remove the cap of the container and insert and attach the sprayer to the latter for use.

Hanging the sprayer on the side of the container or bottle was both expensive and troublesome. Packaging for shipment had to be a hand operation, and breakage and pilferage as well as the loss of the sprayer during shipment and retail display often occurred. Cook Chemical urged Calmar to develop an integrated sprayer that could be mounted directly in a container or bottle during the automated filling process and that would not leak during shipment or retail handling. Calmar did develop some such devices but for various reasons they were not completely successful. The situation was aggravated in 1954 by the entry of Colgate-Palmolive into the insecticide trade with its product marketed in aerosol spray cans. These containers, which used compressed gas as a propellent to dispense the liquid, did not require pump sprayers.

During the same year Calmar was acquired by the Drackett Company. Cook Chemical became apprehensive of its source of supply for pump sprayers and decided to manufacture its own through a subsidiary, Bakan Plastics, Inc. Initially, it copied its design from the unpatented Calmar sprayer, but an officer of Cook Chemical, Scoggin, was assigned to develop a more efficient device. By 1956 Scoggin had perfected the shipper-sprayer in suit and a patent was granted in 1959 to Cook Chemical as his assignee. In the interim Cook Chemical began to use Scoggin's device and also marketed it to the trade. The device was well received and soon became widely used.

In the meanwhile, Calmar employed two engineers, Corsette and Cooprider, to perfect a shipper-sprayer and by 1958 it began to market its SS–40, a device very much similar to Scoggin's. When the Scoggin patent issued, Cook Chemical charged Calmar's SS–40 with infringement and this suit followed.

* * *

THE PRIOR ART.

Only two of the five prior art patents cited by the Patent Office Examiner in the prosecution of Scoggin's application are necessary to our discussion, i.e., Lohse U.S. Patent No. 2,119,884 (1938) and Mellon U.S. Patent No. 2,586,687 (1952). Others are cited by Calmar that were not before the Examiner, but of these our purposes require discussion of only the Livingstone U.S. Patent No. 2,715,480 (1953). Simplified drawings of each of these patents are reproduced in the Appendix, Figs. 4–6, for comparison and description.

The Lohse patent (Fig. 4) is a shipper-sprayer designed to perform the same function as Scoggin's device. The differences, recognized by the District Court, are found in the overcap seal which in Lohse is formed by the skirt of the overcap engaging a washer or gasket which rests upon the upper surface of the container cap. The court emphasized that in Lohse "[t]here are no seals above the threads and below the sprayer head." 220 F.Supp., at 419.

The Mellon patent (Fig. 5), however, discloses the idea of effecting a seal above the threads of the overcap. Mellon's device, likewise a shipper-sprayer, differs from Scoggin's in that its overcap screws directly on the container, and a gasket, rather than a rib, is used to effect the seal.

Finally, Livingstone (Fig. 6) shows a seal above the threads accomplished without the use of a gasket or washer. Although Livingstone's arrangement was designed to cover and protect pouring spouts, his sealing feature is strikingly similar to Scoggin's. Livingston uses a tongue and groove technique in which the tongue, located on the upper surface of the collar, fits into a groove on the inside of the overcap. Scoggin employed the rib and shoulder seal in the identical position and with less efficiency because the Livingstone technique is inherently a more stable structure, forming an interlock that withstands distortion of the overcap when subjected to rough handling. Indeed, Cook Chemical has now incorporated the Livingstone closure into its own shipper-sprayers as had Calmar in its SS–40.

THE INVALIDITY OF THE PATENT.

Let us first return to the fundamental disagreement between the parties. Cook Chemical, as we noted at the outset, urges that the invention must be viewed as the overall combination, or—putting it in the language of the statute—that we must consider the subject matter sought to be patented taken as a whole. With this position, taken in the abstract, there is, of course, no quibble. But the history of the prosecution of the Scoggin application in the Patent Office reveals a substantial divergence in respondent's present position.

As originally submitted, the Scoggin application contained 15 claims which in very broad terms claimed the entire combination of spray pump and overcap. No mention of, or claim for, the sealing features was made. All 15 claims were rejected by the Examiner because (1) the applicant was vague and indefinite as to what the invention was, and (2) the claims were met by Lohse. Scoggin canceled these claims and submitted new ones. Upon a further series of rejections and new submissions, the Patent Office Examiner, after an office interview, at least relented. It is crystal clear that after the first rejection, Scoggin relied entirely upon the sealing arrangement as the exclusive patentable difference in his combination. It is likewise clear that it was on that feature that the Examiner allowed the claims. In fact, in a letter accompanying the final submission of claims, Scoggin, through his attorney, stated that "agreement was reached between the Honorable Examiner and applicant's attorney relative to *limitations* which must be in the claims in order to define novelty over the previously applied disclosure of Lohse when considered in view of the newly cited patents of Mellon and Darley, Jr." (Italics added.)

Moreover, those limitations were specifically spelled out as (1) the use of a rib seal and (2) an overcap whose lower edge did not contact the container cap. Mellon was distinguished, as was the Darley patent, infra, n. 18, on the basis that although it disclosed a hold-down cap with a seal located above the threads, it did not disclose a rib seal disposed in such position as to cause the lower peripheral edge of the overcap "to be maintained out of contacting relationship with [the container] cap * * * when * * * [the overcap] was screwed [on] tightly * * *." Scoggin maintained that the "obvious modification" of Lohse in view of Mellon would be merely to place the Lohse gasket above the threads with the lower edge of the overcap remaining in tight contact with the container cap or neck of the container itself. In other words, the Scoggin invention was limited to the use of a rib—rather than a washer or gasket—and the existence of a slight space between the overcap and the container cap.

It is, of course, well settled that an invention is construed not only in the light of the claims, but also with reference to the file wrapper or prosecution history in the Patent Office. Hogg v. Emerson, 11 How. 587, 13 L.Ed. 824 (1850); Crawford v. Heysinger, 123 U.S. 589, 8 S.Ct. 399, 31 L.Ed. 269 (1887). Claims as allowed must be read and interpreted with reference to rejected ones and to the state of the prior art; and claims that have been narrowed in order to obtain the issuance of a patent by distinguishing the prior art cannot be sustained to cover that which was previously by limitation eliminated from the patent. Powers-Kennedy Contracting Corp. v. Concrete Mixing & Conveying Co., 282 U.S. 175, 185–186, 51 S.Ct. 95, 99, 75 L.Ed. 278, 285, 286, (1930); Schriber Co. v. Cleveland Trust Co., 311 U.S. 211, 220–221, 61 S.Ct. 235, 239–240, 85 L.Ed. 132, 137 (1940).

Here, the patentee obtained his patent only by accepting the limitations imposed by the Examiner. The claims were carefully drafted to reflect these limitations and Cook Chemical is not now free to assert a broader view of Scoggin's invention. The subject matter as a whole reduces, then, to the distinguishing features clearly incorporated into the claims. We now turn to those features.

As to the space between the skirt of the overcap and the container cap, the District Court found:

> "Certainly without a space so described there could be no inner seal within the cap, but such a space is not new or novel, but it is necessary to the formation of the seal within the hold-down cap.

> "*To me this language is descriptive of an element of the patent but not a part of the invention.* It is too simple, really, to require much discussion. In this device the hold-down cap was intended to perform two functions—to hold down the sprayer head and to form a solid tight seal between the shoulder and the collar below. In assembling the element it is necessary to provide this space in order to form the seal." 220 F.Supp., at 420. (Italics added.)

The court correctly viewed the significance of that feature. We are at a loss to explain the Examiner's allowance on the basis of such a distinction. Scoggin was able to convince the Examiner that Mellon's cap contacted the bottle neck while his did not. Although the drawings included in the Mellon application show that the cap might touch the neck of the bottle when fully screwed down, there is nothing—absolutely nothing—which indicates that the cap was designed at any time to *engage* the bottle neck. It is palpably evident that Mellon embodies a seal formed by a gasket compressed between the cap and the bottle neck. It follows that the cap in Mellon will not seal if it does not bear down on the gasket and this would be impractical, if not impossible, under the construction urged by Scoggin before the Examiner. Moreover, the space so strongly asserted by Cook Chemical appears quite plainly on the Livingstone device, a reference not cited by the Examiner.

The substitution of a rib built into a collar likewise presents no patentable difference above the prior art. It was fully disclosed and dedicated to the public in the Livingstone patent. Cook Chemical argues, however, that Livingstone is not in the *pertinent* prior art because it relates to liquid containers having pouring spouts rather than pump sprayers. Apart from the fact that respondent made no such objection to similar references cited by the Examiner, so restricted a view of the applicable prior art is not justified. The problems confronting Scoggin and the insecticide industry were not insecticide problems; they were mechanical closure problems. Closure devices in such a closely related art as pouring spouts for liquid containers are at the very least pertinent references. See, II Walker on Patents § 260 (Deller ed. 1937).

Cook Chemical insists, however, that the development of a workable shipper-sprayer eluded Calmar, who had long and unsuccessfully sought to solve the problem. And, further, that the long-felt need in the industry for a device such as Scoggin's together with its wide commercial success supports its patentability. These legal inferences or subtests do focus attention on economic and motivational rather than technical issues and are, therefore, more susceptible of judicial treatment than are the highly technical facts often present in patent litigation. See Judge Learned Hand in Reiner v. I. Leon Co., 285 F.2d 501, 504 (2 Cir.1960). See also Note, Subtests of "Nonobviousness": A Nontechnical Approach to Patent Validity, 112 U.Pa.L.Rev. 1169 (1964). Such inquiries may lend a helping hand to the judiciary which, as Mr. Justice Frankfurter observed, is most ill-fitted to discharge the technological duties cast upon it by patent legislation. Marconi Wireless Co. v. United States, 320 U.S. 1, 60, 63 S.Ct. 1393, 87 L.Ed. 1731, 1763 (1943). They may also serve to "guard against slipping into use of hindsight," Monroe Auto Equipment Co. v. Heckethorn Mfg. & Supply Co., 332 F.2d 406, 412 (1964), and to resist the temptation to read into the prior art the teachings of the invention in issue.

However, these factors do not, in the circumstances of this case, tip the scales of patentability. The Scoggin invention, as limited by the Patent Office and accepted by Scoggin, rests upon exceedingly small and quite nontechnical mechanical differences in a device which was old in the art. At the latest, those differences were rendered apparent in 1953 by the appearance of the Livingstone patent, and unsuccessful attempts to reach a solution to the problems confronting Scoggin made before that time became wholly irrelevant. It is also irrelevant that no one apparently chose to avail himself of knowledge stored in the Patent Office and readily available by the simple expedient of conducting a patent search—a prudent and nowadays common preliminary to well organized research. Mast, Foos & Co. v. Stover Mfg. Co., 177 U.S. 485, 20 S.Ct. 708, 44 L.Ed. 856 (1900). To us, the limited claims of the Scoggin patent are clearly evident from the prior art as it stood at the time of the invention.

We conclude that the claims in issue in the Scoggin patent must fall as not meeting the test of § 103, since the differences between them and the pertinent prior art would have been obvious to a person reasonably skilled in that art.

The judgment of the Court of Appeals in No. 11 is affirmed. The judgment of the Court of Appeals in Nos. 37 and 43 is reversed and the cases remanded to the District Court for disposition not inconsistent with this opinion.

It is so ordered.

MR. JUSTICE STEWART took no part in the consideration or decision of Nos. 37 and 43.

MR. JUSTICE FORTAS took no part in the consideration or decision of these cases.

FIG. 3. SCOGGIN PATENT 2,870,943
(The Patent in Issue)

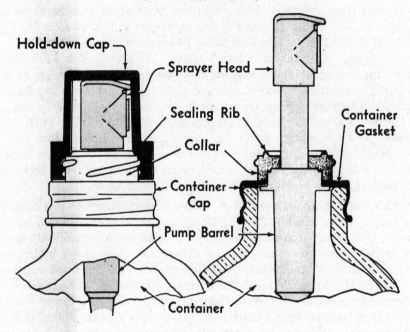

FIG. 4. LOHSE PATENT 2,119,884
(Prior art 1938)

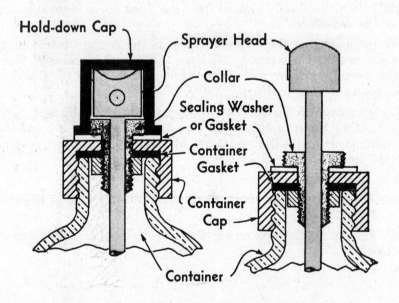

FIG. 5. MELLON PATENT 2,586,687
(Prior art 1952)

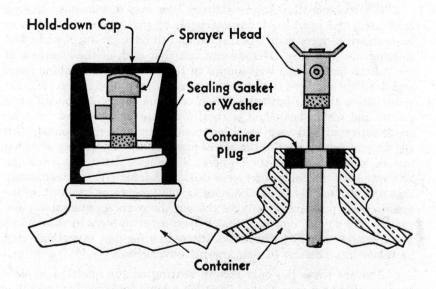

Hold-down Cap

Sprayer Head

Sealing Gasket
or Washer

Container
Plug

Container

FIG. 6. LIVINGSTONE PATENT 2,715,480
(Prior art 1953)

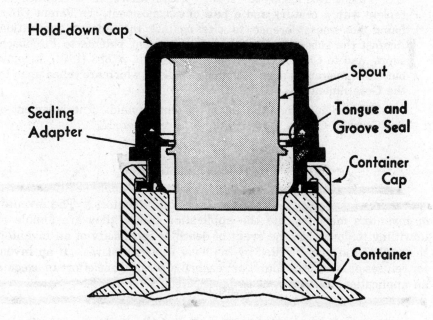

Hold-down Cap

Spout

Tongue and
Groove Seal

Sealing
Adapter

Container
Cap

Container

In the same term of the Supreme Court in which the preceding decision was handed down, the Supreme Court also decided a case, United States v. Adams, 383 U.S. 39, 86 S.Ct. 708, 15 L.Ed.2d 572 (1966), holding a battery patent valid, commenting in part as follows:

"We conclude the Adams battery was also nonobvious. As we have seen, the operating characteristics of the Adams battery have been shown to have been unexpected and to have far surpassed then-existing wet batteries. Despite the fact that each of the elements of the Adams battery was well known in the prior art, to combine them as did Adams required that a person reasonably skilled in the prior art must ignore that (1) batteries which continue to operate on an open circuit and which heated in normal use were not practical; and (2) water-activated batteries were successful only when combined with electrolytes detrimental to the use of magnesium. These long-accepted factors, when taken together, would, we believe, deter any investigation into such a combination as is used by Adams. This is not to say that one who merely finds new uses for old inventions by shutting his eyes to their prior disadvantages thereby discovers a patentable innovation. We do say, however, that known disadvantages in old devices which would naturally discourage the search for new inventions may be taken into account in determining obviousness.

"Nor are these the only factors bearing on the question of obviousness. We have seen that at the time Adams perfected his invention noted experts expressed disbelief in it. Several of the same experts subsequently recognized the significance of the Adams invention, some even patenting improvements on the same system. Fischbach et al., U.S. Patent No. 2,636,060 (1953). Furthermore, in a crowded art replete with a century and a half of advancement, the Patent Office found not one reference to cite against the Adams application. Against the subsequently issued improvement patents to Fischbach, supra, and to Chubb, U.S. Reissue Patent No. 23,883 (1954), it found but three references prior to Adams—none of which are relied upon by the Government.

"We conclude that the Adams patent is valid. The judgment of the Court of Claims is affirmed. It is so ordered."

B. INVENTORSHIP

In the United States, a patent application must be filed in the name of the inventor or, if a joint invention, inventors.[a] The inventor or inventors must execute the application unless they are unable or unwilling to do so. In the event of death or incapacity of an inventor, the application may be filed by his legal representatives. If an inventor refuses or cannot be found or reached after diligent effort to execute an application, it may be filed by a person who has an ownership or proprietary interest in the invention, on behalf of and as an agent for

a. Kennedy v. Hazelton, 128 U.S. 667, 672, 9 S.Ct. 202, 32 L.Ed. 576 (1888); City of Milwaukee v. Activated Sludge, 69 F.2d 577, 21 USPQ 69 (7th Cir.1934); Agawam Woolen Co. v. Jordan, 74 U.S. (7 Wall.) 583, 19 L.Ed. 177 (1869).

the inventor. The United States Patent Office will accept applications from citizens and aliens, and a person need not be of legal age to be a proper applicant.

This is in contrast to the practice in most foreign countries where an application for patent can be filed either by the inventor or by those who are importing an invention into the country. Since in these countries, the first person to file an application will obtain the patent, the development of inventions is usually shrouded by stringent secrecy measures and frequently applications are filed prematurely before the invention is fully developed.

Prior to the 1952 Patent Act, a patent was invalid for failure to name the correct inventor or inventors.[b] Even under this Act, an uncorrectable error in naming the inventor or inventors, invalidates a patent. Thus, an attorney filing a patent application has a responsibility to analyze the invention carefully and investigate the facts surrounding the making of the invention in order to determine proper inventorship.

In general, inventors are the persons who created the patentable (useful, new and non-obvious) subject matter defined by the claims. Of course, it is easy to determine inventorship when only one person created the invention. However, it is frequently difficult to determine inventorship when more than one person participated in creating an invention.

In recognition of these difficulties and the reality that modern team research projects may include many inventors, Congress, in 1984 amended Sec. 116 of the 1952 Patent Act by adding what is now the first paragraph.[c] The first two subparts of this amendment appear to select and codify prior somewhat conflicting case law concepts of joint inventorship and the third subpart adopts a recent case law concept which somewhat expands the traditional scope of joint inventorship.

1. STATUTORY PROVISIONS

35 U.S.C.A. § 102. Conditions for Patentability; Novelty and Loss of Right to Patent

A person shall be entitled to a patent unless—

(f) he did not himself invent the subject matter sought to be patented,

35 U.S.C.A. § 111. Application for Patent

Application for patent shall be made, or authorized to be made, by the inventor, except as otherwise provided in this title, in writing to the Commissioner. Such application shall include (1) a specification as prescribed by section 112 of this title; (2) a drawing as prescribed by section 113 of this title; and (3) an oath by the applicant as prescribed by section

---

b. Kennedy v. Hazelton, 128 U.S. 667, 672, 9 S.Ct. 202, 203, 32 L.Ed. 576 (1888).

c. Section-By-Section Analysis of H.R. 6286, Patent Law Amendments Act of 1984. Congressional Record, 1984, H 10525, H 10527.

115 of this title. The application must be accompanied by the fee required by law. The fee and oath may be submitted after the specification and any required drawing are submitted, within such period and under such conditions, including the payment of a surcharge, as may be prescribed by the Commissioner. Upon failure to submit the fee and oath within such prescribed period, the application shall be regarded as abandoned, unless it is shown to the satisfaction of the Commissioner that the delay in submitting the fee and oath was unavoidable. The filing date of an application shall be the date on which the specification and any required drawing are received in the Patent and Trademark Office.

35 U.S.C.A. § 115. Oath of Applicant

The applicant shall make oath that he believes himself to be the original and first inventor of the process, machine, manufacture, or composition of matter, or improvement thereof, for which he solicits a patent; and shall state of what country he is a citizen. Such oath may be made before any person within the United States authorized by law to administer oaths, or, when made in a foreign country, before any diplomatic or consular officer of the United States authorized to administer oaths, or before any officer having an official seal and authorized to administer oaths in the foreign country in which the applicant may be, whose authority is proved by certificate of a diplomatic or consular officer of the United States, or apostille of an official designated by a foreign country which, by treaty or convention, accords like effect to apostilles of designated officials in the United States. Such oath is valid if it complies with the laws of the state or country where made. When the application is made as provided in this title by a person other than the inventor, the oath may be so varied in form that it can be made by him.

35 U.S.C.A. § 25. Declaration in Lieu of Oath

(a) The Commissioner may by rule prescribe that any document to be filed in the Patent and Trademark Office and which is required by any law, rule, or other regulation to be under oath may be subscribed to by a written declaration in such form as the Commissioner may prescribe, such declaration to be in lieu of the oath otherwise required.

(b) Whenever such written declaration is used, the document must warn the declarant that willful false statements and the like are punishable by fine or imprisonment, or both (18 U.S.C.A. 1001).

35 U.S.C.A. § 116. Inventors

When an invention is made by two or more persons jointly, they shall apply for patent jointly and each make the required oath, except as otherwise provided in this title. Inventors may apply for a patent jointly even though (1) they did not physically work together or at the same time, (2) each did not make the same type or amount of contribution, or (3) each did not make a contribution to the subject matter of every claim of the patent.

If a joint inventor refuses to join in an application for patent or cannot be found or reached after diligent effort, the application may be made by the other inventor on behalf of himself and the omitted inventor. The Commissioner, on proof of the pertinent facts and after such notice to the omitted inventor as he prescribes, may grant a patent to the inventor making the application, subject to the same rights which the omitted inventor would have had if he had been joined. The omitted inventor may subsequently join in the application.

Whenever through error a person is named in an application for patent as the inventor, or through an error an inventor is not named in an application and such error arose without any deceptive intention on his part, the Commissioner may permit the application to be amended accordingly, under such terms as he prescribes.

35 U.S.C.A. § 117.　Death or Incapacity of Inventor

Legal representatives of deceased inventors and of those under legal incapacity may make application for patent upon compliance with the requirements and on the same terms and conditions applicable to the inventor.

35 U.S.C.A. § 118.　Filing by Other Than Inventor[b]

Whenever an inventor refuses to execute an application for patent, or cannot be found or reached after diligent effort, a person to whom the inventor has assigned or agreed in writing to assign the invention or who otherwise shows sufficient proprietary interest in the matter justifying such action, may make application for patent on behalf of and as agent for the inventor on proof of the pertinent facts and a showing that such action is necessary to preserve the rights of the parties or to prevent irreparable damage; and the Commissioner may grant a patent to such inventor upon such notice to him as the Commissioner deems sufficient, and on compliance with such regulations as he prescribes.

35 U.S.C.A. § 256.　Correction of Named Inventor

Whenever through error a person is named in an issued patent as the inventor, or through error an inventor is not named in an issued patent and such error arose without any deceptive intention on his part, the Commissioner may, on application of all the parties and assignees, with proof of the facts and such other requirements as may be imposed, issue a certificate correcting such error.

b. This section of the statute recognizes the situation where the right to a patent might be forfeited under the one-year statutory bar by publication or prior use while the parties entitled to the patent may be litigating their rights to the invention. Under this section, while the application may be filed by someone other than the inventor, the power of the Commissioner is limited to granting the patent to the "inventor." In considering this provision of the statute, it is well to bear in mind that the expense and responsibility of filing and prosecuting the application will be on someone other than the inventor. A court might later decide that the party filing (other than the inventor) is not entitled to legal title to the patent and, hence, title remains in the inventor. The situation also may be complicated further if the court should hold that the applicant's right was that of a shop right or non-exclusive licensee. For a discussion of the proofs required, see In re Gray, 115 USPQ 80 (Comm'r Patents 1956).

The error of omitting inventors or naming persons who are not inventors shall not invalidate the patent in which such error occurred if it can be corrected as provided in this section. The court before which such matter is called in question may order correction of the patent on notice and hearing of all parties concerned and the Commissioner shall issue a certificate accordingly.

2. DETERMINING INVENTORSHIP

MONSANTO COMPANY v. ERNST KAMP

United States District Court, District of Columbia, 1967.
269 F.Supp. 818, 154 USPQ 259.

HOLTZOFF, DISTRICT JUDGE.

This is an action under 35 U.S.C. § 146, to set aside a determination by the Patent Office, in an interference proceeding, awarding to the defendants Kamp and Jahn, rights of priority to a patent. At this time the case was before this Court on a separate trial as to one of the issues.

The invention involved in this controversy relates to plastic bottles, such as are used for pharmaceutical products. Specifically it consists of coating or lining bottles of this type with a resin compound to prevent the loss of liquid contents by permeation or evaporation. The kind of plastic used is known as polyethylene. The resin employed is known as an epoxy resin. There are two counts in the interference. Each of them covers a coated container as an article of manufacture, one of the counts being somewhat broader than the other.

The plaintiffs, Pinsky, Adakonis, and Nielsen, filed an application for a patent on March 28, 1956. Patent No. 2,830,721 was granted to them on April 15, 1958, and was eventually assigned to the plaintiff Monsanto Company.

The defendants, Kamp and Jahn, filed an application for a patent on April 17, 1956, No. 578,846. They had filed a parent application in Germany on April 22, 1955 and were accorded in the United States the benefit of that earlier date. The application submitted in the United States was claimed to be for the same invention and made in behalf of the same inventors as that previously filed in Germany.

An interference was declared between the plaintiffs' patent and the defendants' application, on March 27, 1961. That proceeding terminated on June 29, 1964 by an award of priority to the defendants, on the basis of their earlier German filing date. The plaintiffs then brought this action to set aside that decision. They contend that they are entitled to priority and, therefore, should be permitted to retain their patent and that none should issue to the defendants.

A motion was made by the plaintiffs in this Court for a preliminary injunction to restrain the Commissioner of Patents from issuing a patent to the defendants during the pendency of this action. Another Judge of this Court denied the application. The Court of Appeals reversed his order and held that the Commissioner of Patents was without authority to issue a patent to the defendants until the final outcome of this suit, in effect, staying the issuance of a patent in the meantime, Monsanto Co. v. Kamp, 123 U.S.App.D.C. 365, 360 F.2d 499.

* * *

The next contention of the plaintiffs is that the defendants Kamp and Jahn were not joint inventors in fact. This brings us to a consideration of the pertinent principles. A joint invention is the product of collaboration of the inventive endeavors of two or more persons working toward the same end and producing an invention by their aggregate efforts. To constitute a joint invention, it is necessary that each of the inventors work on the same subject matter and make some contribution to the inventive thought and to the final result. Each needs to perform but a part of the task if an invention emerges from all of the steps taken together. It is not necessary that the entire inventive concept should occur to each of the joint inventors, or that the two should physically work on the project together. One may take a step at one time, the other an approach at different times. One may do more of the experimental work while the other makes suggestions from time to time. The fact that each of the inventors plays a different role and that the contribution of one may not be as great as that of another, does not detract from the fact that the invention is joint, if each makes some original contribution, though partial, to the final solution of the problem.

A pertinent discussion of this subject is found in De Laski & Thropp C. W. T. Co. v. Wm. R. Thropp & Sons Co., D.C., 218 F. 458, 464, and reads as follows:

> "In order to constitute two persons joint inventors, it is not necessary that exactly the same idea should have occurred to each at the same time, and that they should work out together the embodiment of that idea in a perfected machine. The conception of the entire device may be due to one, but if the other makes suggestions of practical value, which assisted in working out the main idea and making it operative, or contributes an independent part of the entire invention, which is united with the parts produced by the other and creates the whole, he is a joint inventor, even though his contribution be of comparatively minor importance and merely the application of an old idea."

The decision of the District Court in that case was affirmed by the Court of Appeals for the Third Circuit, in an opinion by Judge Woolley, who was a leading authority in this field. He stated in Wm. R. Thropp & Sons Co. v. De Laski & Thropp C. W. T. Co., 226 F. 941, 949:

"In a machine containing as many elements as this one, it is not to be thought nor by the law required, that the inventive conceptions of two inventors shall develop simultaneously. One may conceive a general or imperfect outline of an entirely novel thing, which, without the conception of another developing it and giving it body, might never amount to invention; but if the conceptions of one supplement and complement the conceptions of the other, the result might be invention and therefore joint invention."

* * *

With a view to establishing affirmatively that Kamp and Jahn were not in fact joint inventors, counsel for the plaintiffs took their depositions in Germany. The depositions are lengthy. The two defendants were subjected to a thorough and searching interrogation. They had retired from active business and apparently their recollection as to some details was somewhat faded and dim. It was brought out that Alex Kamp and Company was a German manufacturer of various types of chemicals and similar products. The defendant Kamp was the principal proprietor of the business and actively managed it. The defendant Jahn was a chemist in the employ of the concern. Each of the two defendants had his own laboratory. Apparently most of the detailed experimental work was done by Jahn. Some of it, however, was conducted by Kamp. The two co-workers were in frequent consultation with each other concerning various aspects of the project. Jahn reported to Kamp from time to time concerning his laboratory operations and Kamp made suggestions to him. There was an interchange of ideas between the two, until finally a consummation was reached. Each of the two gave credit to the participation of his colleague in the development of the invention. Obviously this evidence not only fails to disprove the position of the defendants Kamp and Jahn that they were joint inventors, but on the contrary it supports their contention.

Finally the plaintiffs claim that Kamp and Jahn were not in fact inventors at all, but merely borrowed and utilized the ideas of other persons. To be sure, the evidence does show that they investigated and studied the literature bearing on the subject in which they were working. This was an intelligent approach. They also visited several manufacturers of similar products, and in conferences and conversations with them, derived some useful ideas that they pursued. This evidence does not disprove the fact that the final concept and its reduction to practice, were their own invention. Intelligent and successful inventors do not ordinarily work in a vacuum. It is natural for them to commence their endeavors by studying and analyzing what had been done by their predecessors and to begin their own operations at that point.

The objections to the award of priority to the defendants Kamp and Jahn are overruled. The Court finds and concludes that the defendants Kamp and Jahn were joint inventors of the invention in suit; * * *

and that the American application was properly filed by them as joint inventors.

* * *

GENERAL MOTORS CORPORATION v. TOYOTA MOTOR COMPANY, LTD.

United States Court of Appeals, Sixth Circuit, 1981.
667 F.2d 504, 212 USPQ 659.

PECK, SENIOR CIRCUIT JUDGE.

* * *

The patented converter was developed at GM by at least three stages:

STAGE	"INVENTORS" AS FOUND BY TRIAL COURT
CM–474 sketch	Moore
CM–714	Banyas, Jabling, [Moore] [1]
014 patent	Moore, Foster, Haggart (pantees)

On appeal, GM argues, in essence, that there was only one invention, the patented converter, and that the two earlier steps in its development should be seen as merging into the final product. Put another way, GM contends that the patented converter is a "joint invention" of most or all of the above GM employees, and that an intermediate step by a subset of this inventive group should not be considered disabling prior art. Toyota argues that the three steps are discrete inventions because the first two steps did not result from the collaboration of the patentees.

GM's argument has the virtue of realism—it provides an accurate description of the manner of the patented converter's invention. The '041 converter's creation was not at the hands of lone-eagle inventors who occasionally flocked together to exchange ideas, but was the product of a concerted effort underwritten and directed by GM.

Toyota's argument that the prior inhouse development must be considered disabling prior art is based largely on Application of Land, 368 F.2d 866, 881, 151 USPQ 621, 634–635 (C.C.P.A.1966), and Application of Bass, 474 F.2d 1276, 1288, 177 USPQ 178, 187–188 (C.C.P.A. 1973), where prior sole inventions of one joint inventor were held to be prior art to the later joint inventions. Neither Land nor Bass indicates that the prior inventions were in any way the product of concerted effort within a business entity. Under the facts of this case, where numerous "inventors" all worked under the aegis of one employer toward a common goal, it is appropriate to define the concept of joint invention broadly. It is not realistic to require in such circumstances that joint inventors work side-by-side, and that each step in the inventive process be taken by all the firm's collaborators. * * * For the

1. The district court found that the CM–714 was conceived solely by Banyas and Jalbing, two GM employees, but that Moore, another GM employee, "also should be given some credit for the CM–714 converter since it was derived from the CM–474 sketch." Thus, Moore participated at least indirectly in all three steps.

reasons outlined above, the CM–714 should not be seen as a "complete invention" sufficient to deprive the named inventors (or GM as their assignee) of the "exclusive property in the perfected improvement."

Toyota's response to GM's joint invention arguments amounts to no more than raising as a defense to GM's infringement allegation the non-joinder of Banyas and Jalbing as coinventors in the patent application. Such defenses are highly technical; courts disfavor these defenses on the strength of the legal presumption that the inventors named in a patent are the true ones. See Jamesbury Corp. v. United States, 518 F.2d 1384, 1395, 187 USPQ 720 (Ct.Cl. 1975); Garrett Corp. v. United States, 422 F.2d 874, 880–81, 164 USPQ 521, 526–527 (Ct.Cl.), cert. denied, 400 U.S. 951, 167 USPQ 705 (1970); Shields v. Halliburton Co., 493 F.Supp. 1376, 1385, 207 USPQ 304, 312–313 (W.D.La.1980). This presumption is only overcome by clear and convincing evidence. Garrett, supra, 422 F.2d at 880–81, 164 USPQ at 526–527; Shields, supra, 493 F.Supp. at 1385, 207 USPQ at 312–313. Toyota has not produced clear and convincing evidence that the contributions of the unnamed "inventors" were any more than improvements on Moore's concept.

Toyota has argued against an expansive definition of "joint invention" in the context of corporate in-house developments, stating that such a reading would bring an "elasticity" to statutory patent law that Congress did not put there. There are two answers to this argument: first, 35 U.S.C. § 103, the statutory ground for invalidating the patent in suit, is but a codification of prior judicial practice. Graham, supra, 383 U.S. at 3–4, 148 USPQ at 461–462. In such circumstances, it would be mindless to reach irrational or inequitable results out of supposed fidelity to statutory language. Second, § 103 ends with the sentence "[p]atentability shall not be negatived by the manner in which the invention was made." Toyota would have us create extra barriers to the patenting of "in-house" developments.

* * *

P & D SALES & MFG. CO. v. WINTER

United States Court of Appeals, Seventh Circuit, 1964.
334 F.2d 830, 142 USPQ 187.

KNOCH, CIRCUIT JUDGE. * * * We feel similarly that the Trial Court erred in holding that Mr. Winter was not the sole inventor and that the patent was invalid for that reason. The findings do not indicate the basis for this conclusion, but perhaps the District Judge considered Mr. Salzman, the engineer employed by Mr. Winter, to be a joint inventor. Mr. Winter is not himself an engineer familiar with specific electrical details, but close scrutiny of his testimony shows that when he retained Mr. Salzman to build a model for exhibition, he did set out exactly what he wanted done. He does not claim invention of specific switches, motors or timers. The patent states that the mechanism is controlled and actuated by conventional electrical components.

Even if Mr. Salzman did make discoveries ancillary to the plan of his employer, Mr. Winter is still the inventor of the original improved principle and the ancillary discoveries may be embodied in his patent. Agawam Woolen Co. v. Jordan, 74 U.S. 583, 603, 19 L.Ed. 177, 182 (1868).

Mr. Salzman's interests are in no way adverse to those of defendants. In return for his efforts in building the exhibition model, he is receiving a portion of the royalties. If Mr. Salzman were a joint inventor here, a conclusion which we do not find supported by this record, then the patent would not necessarily be rendered invalid. A patent may be corrected pursuant to Title 35 U.S.C.A. § 256 which provides for addition of a joint inventor omitted by error.

* * *

C. ESTABLISHING DATE AND PRIORITY OF INVENTION

1. INTRODUCTION

Perhaps under the first Patent Act of 1790, as between two inventors who independently made the same patentable invention, a patent was granted to the first inventor to file an application. However, the Patent Act of 1793 provided for the selection of three arbitrators to determine on which of two or more interfering applications for the same invention, a patent would be granted. The Patent Act of 1836 authorized the Commissioner of Patents to determine priority of invention between interfering applications and unexpired patents. This Act also provided that an issued patent was invalid if obtained for an invention previously "invented or discovered by another, who was using reasonable diligence in adapting and perfecting the same."

All subsequent patent acts have provided for Patent Office interference proceedings and also for invalidation by the Federal Courts of issued patents by the prior invention of another under some circumstances. Section 102(g) of the 1952 Patent Act contains the basic provisions for both interferences and invalidation by the prior invention of another.

In determining when an invention is made and also priority of invention, the Patent Office and Federal Courts have evolved the concepts of conception, reduction to practice, and diligence. In general, conception is the mental activity of inventing or the creation or discovery of the new idea and a specific tangible means or way of carrying out the new idea.

Reduction to practice may be either actual or constructive. Generally, actual reduction is the first construction of the tangible means or way of carrying out the new idea and any testing or operation needed to demonstrate that such means or way is effective. Constructive reduction is the filing of a patent application disclosing the new idea and the means or way of carrying it out. Diligence is reasonable effort of an inventor in trying to reduce the conception of an invention to practice.

The first inventor can lose his right to a patent to a second inventor who makes the same invention at a time when the first inventor is not taking reasonable steps to confer the benefit of the invention on the public such as by filing a patent application or publicly disclosing the invention. Thus, the Patent Office and Courts developed and the Patent Act of 1836 adopted the equitable rule that the second inventor will be granted the patent where the first inventor has abandoned, suppressed, or concealed the invention.

If there are not independent inventors, the person who created or originated the invention can establish his right to a patent by proving that the other person did not independently conceive the same invention as required by § 102(f), but rather derived or obtained his knowledge of the invention from its creator or originator. This question of derivation can also be determined in both a Patent Office interference proceeding or in the federal courts.

An interference proceeding to determine priority of invention between independent inventors is peculiar to the patent systems of the United States and Canada. For many years, in the patent systems of other countries of the world, the first applicant is granted the patent. Of course, this avoids the delay, expense, and uncertainty of an interference proceeding. However, this may also result in more secrecy during development of the invention, failure to actually reduce to practice the conception to make sure it works, and many hastily prepared and inadequate patent applications which are prematurely filed simply to establish priority. While legislation has been proposed in both the United States and Canada to eliminate interference proceedings and adopt a first-to-file patent system, to-date, it has not been enacted.

2. STATUTORY PROVISIONS

§ 102. Conditions for patentability; novelty and loss of right to patent

(g) before the applicant's invention thereof the invention was made in this country by another who had not abandoned, suppressed, or concealed it. In determining priority of invention there shall be considered not only the respective dates of conception and reduction to practice of the invention, but also the reasonable diligence of one who was first to conceive and last to reduce to practice, from a time prior to conception by the other.

§ 104. Invention Made Abroad

In proceedings in the Patent and Trademark Office and in the courts, an applicant for a patent, or a patentee, may not establish a date of invention by reference to knowledge or use thereof, or other activity with respect thereto, in a foreign country, except as provided in sections 119 and 365 of this title. Where an invention was made by a person, civil or military, while domiciled in the United States and serving in a foreign country in connection with operations by or on behalf of the United States, he shall be entitled to the same rights of priority with respect to such inventions as if the same had been made in the United States.

§ 119. Benefit of Earlier Filing Date in Foreign Country; Right of Priority

An application for patent for an invention filed in this country by any person who has, or whose legal representatives or assigns have, previously regularly filed an application for a patent for the same invention in a foreign country which affords similar privileges in the case of applications filed in the United States or to citizens of the United States, shall have the same effect as the same application would have if filed in this country on the date on which the application for patent for the same invention was first filed in such foreign country, if the application in this country is filed within twelve months from the earliest date on which such foreign application was filed; but no patent shall be granted on any application for patent for an invention which had been patented or described in a printed publication in any country more than one year before the date of the actual filing of the application in this country, or which had been in public use or on sale in this country more than one year prior to such filing.

No application for patent shall be entitled to this right of priority unless a claim therefor and a certified copy of the original foreign application, specification and drawings upon which it is based are filed in the Patent and Trademark Office before the patent is granted, or at such time during the pendency of the application as required by the Commissioner not earlier than six months after the filing of the application in this country. Such certification shall be made by the patent office of the foreign country in which filed and show the date of the application and of the filing of the specification and other papers. The Commissioner may require a translation of the papers filed if not in the English language and such other information as he deems necessary.

In like manner and subject to the same conditions and requirements, the right provided in this section may be based upon a subsequent regularly filed application in the same foreign country instead of the first filed foreign application, provided that any foreign application filed prior to such subsequent application has been withdrawn, abandoned, or otherwise disposed of, without having been laid open to public inspection and without leaving any rights outstanding, and has not served, nor thereafter shall serve, as a basis for claiming a right of priority.

Applications for inventors' certificates filed in a foreign country in which applicants have a right to apply, at their discretion, either for a patent or for an inventor's certificate shall be treated in this country in the same manner and have the same effect for purpose of the right of priority under this section as applications for patents, subject to the same conditions and requirements of this section as apply to applications for patents, provided such applicants are entitled to the benefits of the Stockholm Revision of the Paris Convention at the time of such filing.

§ 120. Benefit of Earlier Filing Date in the United States

An application for patent for an invention disclosed in the manner provided by the first paragraph of section 112 of this title in an application previously filed in the United States, or as provided by section 363 of this title, which is filed by an inventor or inventors named in the previously filed application shall have the same effect, as to such invention, as though filed on the date of the prior application, if filed before the patenting or abandonment of or termination of proceedings on the first application or on an application similarly entitled to the benefit of the filing date of the first application and if it contains or is amended to contain a specific reference to the earlier filed application.

§ 135. Interferences

(a) Whenever an application is made for a patent which, in the opinion of the Commissioner, would interfere with any pending application, or with any unexpired patent, an interference may be declared and the Commissioner shall give notice of such declaration to the applicants, or applicant and patentee, as the case may be. The Board of Patent Appeals and Interferences shall determine questions of priority of the inventions and may determine questions of patentability. Any final decision, if adverse to the claim of an applicant, shall constitute the final refusal by the Patent and Trademark Office of the claims involved, and the Commissioner may issue a patent to the applicant who is adjudged the prior inventor. A final judgment adverse to a patentee from which no appeal or other review has been or can be taken or had shall constitute cancellation of the claims involved in the patent, and notice of such cancellation shall be endorsed on copies of the patent distributed after such cancellation by the Patent and Trademark Office.

(b) A claim which is the same as, or for the same or substantially the same subject matter as, a claim of an issued patent may not be made in any application unless such a claim is made prior to one year from the date on which the patent was granted.

(c) Any agreement or understanding between parties to an interference, including any collateral agreements referred to therein, made in connection with or in contemplation of the termination of the interference, shall be in writing and a true copy thereof filed in the Patent and Trademark Office before the termination of the interference as between the said parties to the agreement or understanding. If any party filing the same so requests, the copy shall be kept separate from the file of the interference, and made available only to Government agencies on written request, or to any person on a showing of good cause. Failure to file the copy of such agreement or understanding shall render permanently unenforceable such agreement or understanding and any patent of such parties involved in the interference or any patent subsequently issued on any application of such parties so involved. The Commissioner may, however, on a showing of good cause for failure to file within the time prescribed, permit the filing of the agreement or understanding during the six-month period subsequent to the termination of the interference as between the parties to the agreement or understanding.

The Commissioner shall give notice to the parties or their attorneys of record, a reasonable time prior to said termination, of the filing requirement of this section. If the Commissioner gives such notice at a later time, irrespective of the right to file such agreement or understanding within the six-month period on a showing of good cause, the parties may file such agreement or understanding within sixty days of the receipt of such notice.

Any discretionary action of the Commissioner under this subsection shall be reviewable under section 10 of the Administrative Procedure Act.

(d) Parties to a patent interference, within such time as may be specified by the Commissioner by regulation, may determine such contest or any aspect thereof by arbitration. Such arbitration shall be governed by the provisions of title 9 to the extent such title is not inconsistent with this section. The parties shall give notice of any arbitration award to the Commissioner, and such award shall, as between the parties to the arbitration, be dispositive of the issues to which it relates. The arbitration award shall be unenforceable until such notice is given. Nothing in this subsection shall preclude the Commissioner from determining patentability of the invention involved in the interference.

§ 291. Interfering Patents

The owner of an interfering patent may have relief against the owner of another by civil action, and the court may adjudge the question of the validity of any of the interfering patents, in whole or in part. The provisions of the second paragraph of section 146 of this title shall apply to actions brought under this section.

3. BASIC RULE OF PRIORITY

CHRISTIE v. SEYBOLD

United States Court of Appeals, Sixth Circuit, 1893.
55 Fed. 69.

Statement by TAFT, CIRCUIT JUDGE.

This was an appeal from a decree of the circuit court of the United States for the district of Kentucky, directing the commissioner of patents to issue a patent to Charles Seybold, the appellee and complainant below, for a device in a power press used in bookbinding, * * *

The appellant, Christie, who was respondent below, secured a patent, one claim of which covered the device which Seybold averred that he first invented. Seybold filed his application June 6, 1889, and Christie, his, June 7, 1889. An interference was declared between them in the patent office, * * *

Seybold conceived of his invention in October, 1885, and made a rough sketch of it, which he showed to several persons in January, 1886. He was a machinist and inventor, and engaged in manufacturing numbering machines, perforators, cutting machines, index cutters, pasting machines, glueing machines, wood-staining machines, graining machines, polishing machines, sandpaper machines, and general repair work. At the time of his conception he says that he did not have the proper tools in his shop to make the machine. It would have required a planer, a long lathe, and a boring mill. He did not have the requisite tools until he moved into his new shop, on Webster Street, in the month of March, 1889. From October, 1885, until October, 1888, he did nothing towards reducing his machine to practice. At the latter date he had full-sized drawings made, and his first machine was made in April, 1889. He applied for a patent June 6, 1889.

* * *

Christie claimed to have conceived of his invention in the summer of 1886. He had working drawings made and patterns ordered for the production of his press in the spring and early summer of 1888, and his press was completed about July 12th of that year. The machine was set up and put in operation in the Methodist Book Concern of Cincinnati about that date, and continued in operation until the bill herein was filed. A second machine was built in October, and put in operation in that building. He filed an application for a patent June 7, 1889.

* * *

TAFT, CIRCUIT JUDGE, (after stating the facts.) The questions arising in this case, covered by the assignments in error, are two: First, * * * and, second, * * * which one of the two, Seybold or Christie, was the first or true inventor, within the meaning of the patent laws?

The patent statutes have always required such particularity of description in the applications for a patent as to leave no doubt that in the eye of the law he is the first and true inventor who first reduces the conception of a new invention or discovery to practical and operative form. In Bedford v. Hunt, 1 Mason, 302–304, Mr. Justice Story said:

"The first inventor who has put the invention into practice, and he only, is entitled to a patent."

And again, on page 305, he says:

"The intent of the statute was to guard against defeating patents by the setting up of a prior invention which had never been reduced to practice. If it were the mere speculation of a philosopher or a mechanician, which had never been tried by the test of experience, and never put into actual operation by him, the law would not deprive a subsequent inventor, who had employed his labors and his talents in putting it into practice, of the reward due to his ingenuity and enterprise."

So in Agawam Co. v. Jordan, 7 Wall. 583, Mr. Justice Clifford states the rule as follows:

"The settled rule of law is that whoever first perfects a machine is entitled to a patent, and is the real inventor, although others may have previously had the idea, and made some experiments towards putting it in practice. He is the inventor, and is entitled to the patent, who first brought the machine to perfection, and made it capable of useful operation."

So in Whitely v. Swayne, 7 Wall. 685, 687, Mr. Justice Nelson said:

"He is the first inventor and entitled to the patent who, being an original discoverer, has first perfected and adapted the invention to actual use."

This is the general rule, and had no exception under the statutes in force down to the act of July 4, 1836, (5 St. p. 117.) The fifteenth section of that act, in specifying the defenses which a defendant might set up in an action for infringement, permitted him to plead that the patentee "had surreptitiously and unjustly obtained the patent for that which was in fact invented or discovered by another who was using reasonable diligence in adapting and perfecting the same." The effect of the change made by the act of 1836 was considered by Mr. Justice Story in the case of Reed v. Cutter, 1 Story, 590, where, referring to the words "was using reasonable diligence in adapting and perfecting his invention," he said:

"These latter words were copied from the fifteenth section of the act of 1836, c. 357, and constitute a qualification of the preceding language of that section; so that an inventor who has first actually perfected his invention will not be deemed to have surreptitiously or unjustly obtained a patent for that which was in fact first invented by another, unless the latter was at that time using reasonable diligence in adapting and perfecting the same. And this I take to be clearly the law; for he is the first inventor in the sense of the act, and entitled to a patent for his invention, who has first adapted and perfected the same to use; and until the invention is so perfected and adapted for use it is not patentable. An imperfect and incomplete invention, existing in mere theory or in intellectual notion, or in uncertain experiments, and not actually reduced to practice, and embodied in some distinct machinery, apparatus, manufacture, or composition of matter, is not, and indeed cannot be, patentable under our patent acts, since it is utterly impossible, under such circumstances, to comply with the fundamental requisites of those acts. In a race of diligence between two independent inventors, he who first reduces his invention to a fixed, positive, and practical form would seem to be entitled to a priority of right to a patent therefor. Woodcock v. Parker, 1 Gall. 438. The clause now under consideration seems to qualify that right by providing that in such case he who invents first shall have the prior right, if he is using reasonable diligence in adapting and perfecting the same, although the second inventor, has in fact, first perfected the same, and reduced the same to practice in a positive form. It thus gives full effect to the well-known maxim that he has the better right who is prior in point of time, namely, in making the discovery or invention."

Reed v. Cutter is a leading case, and has been followed by Mr. Justice Clifford in White v. Allen, 2 Cliff. 224, 2 Fish. Pat. Cas. 440, and in later cases.

It is obvious from the foregoing that the man who first reduces an invention to practice is prima facie the first and true inventor, but that the man who first conceives, and, in a mental sense, first invents, a machine, art, or composition of matter, may date his patentable invention back to the time of its conception, if he connects the conception with its reduction to practice by reasonable diligence on his part, so that they are substantially one continuous act. The burden is on the second reducer to practice to show the prior conception, and to establish the connection between that conception and his reduction to practice by proof of due diligence. It has sometimes been held, in the decisions in the patent office, that the necessity for diligence on the part of the first conceiver does not arise until the date of the second conception; but this, we think, cannot be supported on principle. The diligence of the first reducer to practice is necessarily immaterial. It is not a race of diligence between the two inventors in the sense that the right to the patent is to be determined by comparing the diligence of the two, because the first reducer to practice, no matter what his diligence or want of it, is prior in right unless the first conceiver was using reasonable diligence at the time of the second conception and the first reduction to practice. The language of the statute, (section 4920,) in the use of the imperfect tense, "was using reasonable diligence," shows the legislative intent to confer a prior right on a first conceiver in a case where, after his mental act of invention, and pending his diligent reduction to practice, another inventor enters the field and perfects the invention before his rival. The reasonable diligence of the first conceiver must be pending at the time of the second conception, and must therefore be prior to it. Reasonable diligence by the first conceiver, beginning when his rival enters the field, could only carry his invention back to the date of the second conception, and in the race from that time the second conceiver must win because of his first reduction to practice. See Rob. Pat. §§ 384–386; Millward v. Barnes, 11 O.G. 1060. The elaborate opinion of the commissioner of patents, Mr. Mitchell, in the interference proceeding between Christie and Seybold, reported in 54 O.G. 957, cites all the authorities, and is quite convincing on this point. We fully concur therein. As Christie reduced the invention to practice nearly a year before Seybold's press was made, the burden is on Seybold to show that from the time of his original conception, which antedated that of Christie, he was using reasonable diligence in adapting and perfecting his idea to practical use. Has he sustained that burden? It is quite clear to us that he has not. The question of reasonable diligence in any case depends, of course, upon all the circumstances. A complicated invention, requiring many experiments and much study to give it practical form, would reasonably delay a reduction to practice after the first conception for a greater length of time than where the idea and the machine embodying it were of a simple character. Bradford v. Corbin, 6 O.G. 223. Then, too, the sickness of the inventor, his poverty, and his engagement in other inventions of a similar kind are all circumstances which may affect the question of reasonable diligence. See Webster v. Carpet Co., 5 O.G. 522; Cox v. Griggs, 1 Biss. 362, 2 Fish. Pat. Cas. 174; Munger v. Connell, 1 O.G. 491; Proctor v. Ackroyd, 6 O.G. 603; Cushman v. Parham, 9 O.G. 1108.

In this case, Seybold's first conception was in October, 1885, and he did not reduce his machine to practical form until April, 1889, three years and a half later. He made a rough sketch in January, 1886, which he subsequently lost. In October, 1888, three years after his first conception, he had working drawings made, and six months later a press was manufactured. His excuse for his delay is that until the spring of 1889 he could not afford to buy the necessary tools for the manufacture of the press, and, if he had been able to do so, his shop was not large enough to permit the use of them. He does not say, however, that he had not the means to have the press made at some other shop, where the proper tools were to be had, but, on the contrary, intimates that he might have done so, but for the fact that there would have been no profit for him to sell machines made by others according to his invention. Now, we do not think this is a good excuse for failing to make at least one machine, in accordance with his conception. It is as much as to say that in his view his new conception, when reduced to practice, would not have sufficient value and utility to bring him any return commensurate with the outlay required to reduce it to practice, and in consequence he indefinitely postponed putting it into practical form until circumstances should change. This is a temporary abandonment of the idea, (White v. Allen, 2 Cliff. 224,) and is not the due diligence which entitles him to the favor of the public, for whose benefit, primarily, the patent laws were enacted, (Wright v. Postel, 44 Fed.Rep. 352.)

* * *

On the whole case we find, therefore, that Seybold is not the true and first inventor. The decree of the court below is reversed, with instructions to dismiss the bill at the costs of the complainant.

HULL v. DAVENPORT

United States Court of Customs and Patent Appeals, 1937.
24 CCPA 1194, 90 F.2d 103, 33 USPQ 506.

BLAND, ASSOCIATE JUDGE.

This is an appeal by the party Hull from a decision of the Board of Appeals of the United States Patent Office, in which priority of invention relating to refrigerating apparatus was awarded to the party Davenport. The Board reversed the decision of the Examiner of Interferences which had awarded priority in the invention of the count to the junior party Hull.

Hull was the first to conceive and the last to reduce to practice. He was awarded a date of conception of June 3, 1930, and he filed his application January 31, 1931. The party Davenport filed his application December 30, 1930, and this date is his only date for conception and reduction to practice. Neither party actually reduced the invention to practice, and both rely upon a constructive reduction to practice which consists of the filing of their respective applications.

The question of diligence of the party Hull was the only question considered by the Board and is the only question presented here.

* * *

In Patent Office practice the rule with respect to diligence is an old one and one which we think is well settled and generally understood by those familiar with patent law. In the Patent Act of 1836, 5 Stat. 117, provision was made for certain defenses to be set up in actions for patent infringement. Among the defenses which might be pleaded was "that he [the patentee] had surreptitiously or unjustly obtained the patent for that which was in fact invented or discovered by another, who *was using reasonable diligence* in adapting and perfecting the same. [Italics ours]" Section 15. This was, in substantially the same language, re-enacted into the Patent Act of 1870, 16 Stat. 198, § 61, which became section 4920 of the Revised Statutes (35 U.S.C.A. § 69). Soon after the passage of the act of 1836, the courts were called upon in infringement suits to determine who were the first inventors of the inventions there involved. We find in the decisions from that time to this day much discussion of the question, and, while courts have used different language in stating the rule, there has been but little change in the rule as originally announced.

Clearly it was the intent of Congress to assure the first inventor who had completed the mental act of invention that he should not be deprived of his reward by reason of delays which he could not reasonably avoid in giving his invention to the public. But we must bear in mind that it was not alone to reward the inventor that the patent monopoly was granted. The public was to get its reward and have the advantage of the inventor's discovery as early as was reasonably possible. See Robinson on Patents, § 385. It will be noticed that the act of 1836, which is the genesis of the rule of diligence as applied in Patent Office practice, said: "who was using reasonable diligence in adapting and perfecting the same." As applied by the Patent Office and the courts in most instances, the rule has finally crystallized to be that the first conceiver who is last to reduce to practice must couple his conception to his reduction to practice with reasonable diligence. In some cases it is stated that he must so act as to make his conception of the invention and the perfecting it a single inventive act. The weight of authority, however, regards his diligence sufficiently shown if it be found that he was diligent from a time just prior to the second conceiver's entrance into the field to the first conceiver's reduction to practice either actually or constructively. Christie v. Seybold (C.C.A.) 55 F. 69; Woods v. Poor, 29 App.D.C. 397; Grundy v. Van Leir, 75 F.(2d) 503, 22 C.C.P.A. (Patents) 1034; Wilson et al. v. Shorts et al., 81 F.(2d) 755, 23 C.C.P.A. (Patents) 914.

His lack of diligence from the time of conception to the time immediately preceding the conception date of the second conceiver is not regarded as of importance except as it may have a bearing upon his subsequent acts, for the reason that he has not forfeited his right to a patent by his delay when no adverse interests are involved, and it follows that his adversary should only be concerned with what happened immediately prior to and after his entry into the field. Evidence of diligence during the critical period may be shown either by affirmative acts or acceptable excuses or reasons for failure of action. See Christensen v. Ellis, 17 App.D.C. 498.

* * *

Now, measuring the facts at hand by the principles above announced, we, after most careful consideration, have arrived at the conclusion that the appellant here has not shown such reasonable diligence as the law requires and that the decision of the Board in denying the appellant priority of invention in the count at issue on account of his lack of diligence was not erroneous.

LAAS v. SCOTT

United States Circuit Court of Wisconsin, 1908.
161 Fed. 122.

QUARLES, DISTRICT JUDGE.

[Excerpt Only]

* * *

The present controversy involves the question, which of two rival inventors was the first and true inventor of the device embodied in letters patent 757,754?

* * * From all the cases I deduce the following principles applicable to this controversy: Under our patent system, he who first arrives at a complete conception of the inventive thought is entitled to recognition and reward, unless and until the interest of the public is compromised by his lack of diligence in demonstrating that his invention is capable of useful operation. The public may justly demand of the inventor who seeks a legal monopoly that within a reasonable time the invention be brought to such a state of perfection as to be adapted to actual use. To that extent the public interest is paramount. Actual reduction to practice is preferable to that which is constructive merely, as more to the interest of the public and reasonable indulgence ought to be extended to one pursuing that course in good faith. Therefore the inventor who first reduces the discovery to practical operation is held to be prima facie the true inventor, without regard to the date of his conception. But the earlier inventor may overcome this presumption and prevail, if he can show by satisfactory evidence continuous diligence to perfect and utilize the invention. Thus with nicety and fairness has the law adjusted the respective rights of rival inventors consistently with the general welfare. When the inventor who is first to conceive is also the first to reduce to practice within the statutory period, he is clearly entitled to priority, although a junior inventor may anticipate him by earlier application at the Patent Office, and may have secured letters patent. Agawam Woolen Co. v. Jordan, 7 Wall. 583, 19 L.Ed. 177; Christie v. Seybold, 55 Fed. 69, 5 C.C.A. 33; Coffin v.

Ogden, 18 Wall. 120, 21 L.Ed. 821; National Cash Register v. Lamson Co. (C.C.) 60 Fed. 603.

4. CONCEPTION AND DILIGENCE

TOWNSEND v. SMITH

United States Court of Customs and Patent Appeals, 1929.
17 CCPA 647, 36 F.2d 292, 4 USPQ 269.

GRAHAM, PRESIDING JUDGE. Harry P. Townsend, the appellant, presented his application to the Patent Office on January 13, 1922, praying that a patent might be issued to him on improvements in machines for cutting multiple threads on wood screws. On December 8, 1924, an interference proceeding was instituted and declared between his application and a patent issued to one Henry L. Smith, the appellee, No. 1,452,986, granted April 24, 1923, for a similar invention.

The Examiner of Interferences rendered a decision awarding priority of invention to said Townsend on July 10, 1926. On appeal, the Board of Examiners in Chief rendered a decision on April 15, 1927, reversing the said decision of the Examiner of Interferences, and which decision of said board was afterward, on December 7, 1927, affirmed by the Commissioner of Patents. From the decision of said Commissioner this appeal was perfected.

The sole question at issue in this case is the question of priority as between the appellant and appellee. Townsend claims to have conceived the idea of his invention on or about June 1, 1921. The Examiner of Interferences found that he had done so, while the Board of Examiners in Chief and the Commissioner of Patents, respectively, held that he had not proved such conception by such clear and convincing evidence as is required in such cases.

As both applications were co-pending at the time of the inadvertent issuance of the patent to appellee, and as but a short time intervened between the respective dates of application, the burden upon the appellant to prove prior conception is slight, and it is sufficient if he establish his case by a mere preponderance of the evidence. Having this rule, which we consider to be a reasonable one, in mind, we have examined the record carefully to ascertain what the facts are in this regard. The three tribunals in the Patent Office differing in their views as to what this evidence shows, the rule does not obtain here that obtains where all the tribunals agree, namely, that it must clearly and affirmatively appear that there has been some oversight, or mistake, or wrong construction of material facts, or some mistake or misapplication of some controlling principle of law, to justify this court in reversing the decision appealed from. Hien v. Buhoup, 11 App.D.C. 293; Kennicott v. Caps, 49 App.D.C. 187, 262 F. 641; Greenawalt v. Dwight (App. D.C.) 258 F. 982.

Townsend testifies that, while building wood screw threaders for the Ewing Bolt & Screw Company, on or about June 1, 1921, there was trouble with one of his screw threading machines. Townsend was an experienced builder of such machines, and understood them thoroughly at that time. He states that one of the gears had been cut with the wrong number of teeth, with the result that the threading tool, on the moment of initiating each cut on the screw blank, did not start in the same spot that it formerly did, and made a new mark each time the tool passed over the screw. He conceived the idea at the time, and mentioned it to the workmen around him, that this was the way to make a double threaded screw. At that time he was well acquainted with the Caldwell invention of double threaded wood screws. He says he explained it to two workmen, Pond and Clark, but that these men did not recollect it, except Clark recollected that some of the gears were cut wrong. He changed the machine at that time, putting on another gear, after which it cut single threaded screws, as it should have. He states that he thought nothing more about it until October 21, 1921, when he visited Smith and Caldwell at Providence, in answer to a letter informing him that they were interested in a machine for cutting a double threaded screw. He then promised them he would change one of his single threaded wood screw machines, which he was building for a Japanese order, and make it into a double threaded screw machine; that he did this on or about the 10th or 11th of November 1921, and wrote to Swift November 14th to come and see the machine. On the same day he wrote out the details of his invention for his attorney, for the purpose of making application for a patent. On November 21st the machine was demonstrated, and was afterwards changed back to a single thread machine and shipped to Japan on November 30, 1921.

It is said by the Board of Examiners in Chief and the Commissioner that this testimony lacks corroboration of any kind. Townsend testifies that he did not know that a man by the name of Oscar J. Reeves had witnessed his occurrence of June 1st until about six weeks before the time of the hearing in May, 1925, but that Reeves, at that time, told him he had been present. The Board of Examiners in Chief and the Commissioner both reject the testimony of Reeves on the ground that it is not in harmony with Townsend's testimony, and is not to be relied upon as corroborative. Reeves is not related to either of the parties, and has no interest in the result of the proceeding. He testifies he was not well, and, in order to put in the time on frequent occasions visited Townsend's shop where he was much interested in the operation of automatic machinery; that some time before June 17, 1921, which date he fixes by the fact that a short time thereafter he purchased a car and went to the country for his health, staying all summer, he was in Townsend's shop, and Townsend and his helpers were having trouble with a screw threading machine; that they had a wrong set of gearing in the machine which caused it to cut a double thread screw instead of a single thread; that Townsend made adjustments on the machine, and explained each adjustment to those about the machine; that he said at that time the trouble was caused by a wrong set of gears in the machine; that he explained to the men the changes he would have to make on the machine before it was ready for shipment, and so adjusted it that it worked before the witness left, making a single threaded screw after adjustment. Reeves testified, on being shown the drawings, that the adjustments were made on gears No. 42 and No. 43, which are the gears involved in the issue before us. On cross-examination he stated that double threaded screws were made with the machine, at that time, before the gears were changed, and that some of these were distributed among the bystanders.

It is said that, because Reeves goes further in this matter than Townsend, and states that double threaded screws were actually made and distributed at that time, that he must be in error; that his testimony is in conflict with that of Townsend in this respect; and that therefore it should be rejected as corroboration.

The rule is well settled in this jurisdiction as to what is required to constitute a conception and disclosure of an invention. It is well stated in Mergenthaler v. Scudder, 11 App.D.C. 264. A complete conception as defined in an issue of priority of invention is a matter of fact, and must be clearly established by proof. The conception of the invention consists in the complete performance of the mental part of the inventive act. All that remains to be accomplished in order to perfect the act or instrument belongs to the department of construction, not invention. It is therefore the formation in the mind of the inventor of a definite and permanent idea of the complete and operative invention as it is thereafter to be applied in practice that constitutes an available conception within the meaning of the patent law. A priority of conception is established when the invention is made sufficiently plain to enable those skilled in the art to understand it.

Does the alleged conception and disclosure of Townsend, in June, meet these requirements? We are inclined to the belief that it does. It will be remembered that Townsend, accidentally, it is true, had before him, at the time he claims to have conceived the invention, a machine which was actually cutting the threads upon the screw blank in the same manner as the final invention. The only thing required to change the single thread screw machine to a double thread screw machine was the change in gears, which was already an accomplished fact by the error that had occurred. There can be no doubt that Townsend, and those about him, understood perfectly, at that time, just how such a machine could be constructed. This is not such a case as arises when an alleged inventor mentally conceives of some invention and makes an oral disclosure to another, which disclosure may or may not be complete. Here the parties had a complete working model, and there was nothing left to the imagination. The demonstration and disclosure were complete. We can see no reason for discarding the testimony of Reeves on the theory that he testifies screws were made and distributed, while Townsend does not. Townsend did not deny that this happened, nor did any one else. The fact that Reeves went further than Townsend in this regard is not a sufficient fact upon which we should conclude that he committed perjury or was totally mistaken in all that he said.

Another circumstance which leads us to believe Townsend's story has foundation is the fact that, when he was finally called upon to construct a machine on the Swift and Caldwell order, Townsend disclosed fully to these men just how he proposed to make the machine. He went to his shop, according to the testimony of Clark, and informed him that he wanted to set up one of the machines in the shop to cut a double thread; that thereupon the witness Clark said Townsend, "simply took the machine we had, cut a new cam, changed the gears, and cut a double thread on our regular machine." This was but a few days after his interview with Swift and Caldwell, and at this time the idea was so well developed in Townsend's mind that there were no preliminary difficulties in the preparation of the double threaded screw machine. In Townsend's explanation to Swift, according to the testimony of the witness, John W. Caldwell, Townsend was definite and clear as to the method of converting one of his own machines for this purpose.

For these reasons we conclude that the Examiner of Interferences correctly held that Townsend had established conception of this invention in June, 1921. It is agreed that Townsend reduced to practice on November 14, 1921, when he prepared and operated his machine. It is held by all the tribunals in the Patent Office that appellee, Smith, conceived the invention on the 19th or 20th of October, 1921. Appellee does not insist upon any earlier date. Whether this was the exact date of conception we are not now called upon to say, in view of our conclusion in the matter generally. After Smith's conception, no question is raised as to his diligence. He made the necessary drawings and started construction of his machine. According to the preliminary statement in this interference, the appellee, Smith, completed a fully operative machine and operated the same on or about December 12, 1921. This, appellee concedes in his argument, he must rely upon as his date for formal reduction to practice. His preliminary statement is his pleading and he is bound by it. Lindmark v. De Ferranti, 34 App. D.C. 445; Browne v. Dyson, 39 App.D.C. 415. Appellant, Townsend, filed his application for a patent in the Patent Office on January 13, 1922. The Smith application was made on January 3, 1922. No question arises in the case as to the diligence of either Townsend or Smith after October, 1921, when they were each requested to prepare plans for double threaded screw machines by the Commercial Service Company. From that time forward each party moved with all the diligence required by the law.

* * * This being so, and there being no abandonment or negligence since reduction to practice, Townsend is entitled to priority.

* * *

We are of the opinion that the Examiner of Interferences arrived at the correct conclusion in the matter, and the decision of the Commissioner of Patents is therefore reversed and priority is awarded to Townsend, the appellant.

Reversed.

AUTOMATIC WEIGHING MACHINE CO. v. PNEUMATIC SCALE CORP.

United States Court of Appeals, First Circuit, 1909.
166 Fed. 288.

COLT, CIRCUIT JUDGE. This is a bill in equity brought under section 4920 of the Revised Statutes (U.S.Comp.St.1901, p. 3394) for infringement of the first seven claims of the Thomas patent, No. 766,004, for improvements in automatic weighing machines. The invention consists, broadly speaking, in the addition of a second hopper with a time valve to the previous single-hopper weighing machine of the Doble and Watson patent, No. 556,258.

The only defense is priority of invention by Thomas W. Watson, to whom a patent was issued for the same invention. It is admitted that both Thomas and Watson were independent inventors of this improvement.

* * *

Thomas filed his application December 17, 1896, and his patent issued July 26, 1904.

Watson conceived his invention, illustrated it by a drawing, and disclosed it to others, as early as January 10, 1896. He reduced his invention to practice by the building of a machine in April, 1897. He filed his application March 11, 1898, and his patent issued September 26, 1899.

* * *

On April 24, 1901, the Patent Office declared an interference between the Thomas application and the Watson patent, under section 4904 of the Revised Statutes (U.S.Comp.St.1901, p. 3389).

* * *

Under a rule of the Patent Office, the filing of an allowable application is a constructive reduction to practice. In accordance with this rule, the date of the Thomas invention was fixed as of December 17, 1896, the date of his application; and the burden of proof was thrown upon Watson to establish the fact of reasonable diligence from the date of his prior conception, January 10, 1896, to the time Thomas filed his application. Upon this issue of diligence on the part of Watson, the Examiner of Interferences and the Commissioner of Patents, two of the three Patent Office tribunals which passed upon the question, and the Court of Appeals of the District of Columbia, found against Watson, and adjudged Thomas to be the prior inventor; and accordingly a patent was issued to Thomas under section 4904. As a result of the interference proceedings, there are two outstanding patents for the same invention issued to independent inventors.

The decision in interference proceedings is not conclusive on the question of priority of invention. The same question may arise in subsequent suits instituted under sections 4915, 4918, and 4920 ° of the Revised Statutes (U.S.Comp.St.1901, pp. 3392, 3394).

* * *

Section 4920 provides that the defendant in a suit for infringement may prove any of the special matters of defense therein enumerated.

Second. We have now to consider the question whether Watson can carry the date of his invention back to the time of his conception, January 10, 1896. This question must be viewed from two standpoints: First, can it be said that Watson's conception, drawing, and disclosure to others, of themselves, or without regard to his subsequent acts, constitute a complete invention within the meaning of the patent laws? Second, can Watson as a patentee carry back the date of his invention to the time of his conception?

(1) The law appears to be well established that a conception evidenced by disclosure, drawings, and even a model, confers no rights upon an inventor unless followed by some other act, such as actual reduction to practice, or filing an application for a patent. A conception of this character is not a complete invention under the patent laws. It may constitute an invention in a popular sense, but it does not make the inventor the "original and first inventor" under the statutes. If it did constitute an invention under the statutes, then an inventor might stop with his drawings and disclosure, and hold the field for all time against a subsequent inventor who has reduced his invention to practice, or who has obtained a patent. The law will not permit this. An inventor must not stop with this stage of his invention, but he must proceed with reasonable diligence to perfect his invention, either by actual reduction to practice, or by filing his application for a patent.

This rule of the patent law is both reasonable and just. It secures to the first conceiver the right to his invention. It is not uncommon for two persons to conceive an improvement in an existing device about the same time, and all the law exacts of the first conceiver in order to protect him in his right to the invention is that he shall proceed with reasonable diligence to reduce the invention to practice, or to file an application for a patent in conformity with the statutes.

The authorities seem to be conclusive upon the point that a conception evidenced by disclosure and drawings does not constitute an invention under the patent laws. * * *

We come now to the remaining question, whether Watson was reasonably diligent in adapting and perfecting his invention.

Upon this question of fact the decision of the Patent Office tribunals and the Court of Appeals of the District of Columbia is entitled to great weight, if it is not absolutely controlling.

c. Now 35 U.S.C.A. 146, 291, 282.

In Morgan v. Daniels, 153 U.S. 120, 125, 14 Sup.Ct. 772, 773, 38 L.Ed. 657, a suit was brought under section 4915 of the Revised Statutes by the party who was refused a patent in interference proceedings, to determine the question whether he should not be adjudged entitled to a patent. In that case the court used the following language:

"Upon principle and authority, therefore, it must be laid down as a rule that, where the question decided in the Patent Office is one between contesting parties as to priority of invention, the decision there made must be accepted as controlling upon that question of fact in any subsequent suit between the same parties, unless the contrary is established by testimony which in character and amount carries thorough conviction."

There are four admitted facts with respect to Watson's diligence; (1) Watson conceived the invention, illustrated it by a drawing, and disclosed it to Doble as early as January 10, 1896; (2) he made working drawings some time between January 10, 1896, and the early part of January, 1897, when the exhibit blue print which was taken from the working drawings was handed to the pattern maker, Frazer; (3) he completed the building of a machine in April, 1897; (4) the main reason for the delay was business considerations arising from the fact that John F. Cushing had made a contract with the Electric Scale Company to build 10 single-hopper machines under the Doble and Watson patent.

Watson assigned his application to the Electric Scale Company, and the patent issued to that company as assignee. W. H. Doble was the manager of the Electric Scale Company. The Cushing contract with the Electric Scale Company was made January 28, 1896. The additional evidence taken in this case relates to the time during 1896 when these working drawings were made. In our opinion this is immaterial; and it may be assumed, as stated by Watson, and now testified to by Doble, that these drawings were made in the fall of 1896.

The main point against Watson on the question of diligence is that for business reasons nothing was done with respect to his invention between January, 1896, and January, 1897, except to make working drawings, or, upon the evidence as it now stands, nothing was done until September, 1896, when Watson began on the working drawings. As to the reason for this delay, Mr. Doble testified in the interference proceedings as follows:

"As he [Cushing] guaranteed the speed and accuracy, and was the responsible party, I did not care whether he accomplished this with one hopper or a dozen."

"Before January, 1897, they had done nothing except complete the drawings. This contract with John P. Cushing which practically gave, if carried out, all the results that could be accomplished under the double hopper, kept them from acting during the early part of the year, and the fact that they were held to Cushing by this contract kept them from acting later. I would say that I was practically the only one in the company who knew just what was going on and took an active part in the affairs of the company. In January we had the patterns made for the double hopper and the casting made from same on 1st of February."

"After receiving the drawings from Mr. Watson, in 1896, nothing was done in an active way, as I was trying to induce Mr. Cushing to put the double hopper onto the machines he had constructed, and which failed to do the work for which they were designed. Individually, I had no money to manufacture with myself, and the company had but a limited amount, and were practically bound to Mr. Cushing by his contract until such time as he threw up the same."

Mr. Watson also testified as follows:

"In the late summer of 1896, Mr. Cushing had proceeded with his contract until a part of the machines had been finished, and he was experimenting at that time with devices which he was called upon to furnish under his contract for the remaining machines. At the same time he had told me that it was his intention to discontinue his business at the close of the year 1896, and had so told me that I might be on the lookout for other employment. At that time I mentioned to Mr. Cushing the idea of the double hopper, and suggested to him that such an arrangement would assist him in fulfilling his contract in the completion of the remaining machines. As the result of my interview with Mr. Cushing, I thought that he was favorably impressed with the idea that the double hopper would be of use to him in completing the remaining machines; and with the idea that he thought such an arrangement would be useful to him I went to work making drawings of the additional hopper and its mechanism, so that it might be applied to the machines that he was building. A portion of this time so spent was while actively employed on Mr. Cushing's work, and a portion of it on outside time. I consulted with Mr. Cushing and showed him some of these drawings, but he finally concluded that it would not be necessary for him to use the idea in the completion of his contract."

Upon the state of facts presented in the interference proceedings and in this record, we agree with the conclusion of the Patent Office tribunals and the Court of Appeals of the District of Columbia that Watson failed to use such diligence as the law requires.

In its decision the Court of Appeals said:

"The determination of the question depends upon the action or inaction of Watson during the period intermediate between the date of his conception of the invention, January 10, 1896, and the filing date of Thomas' application. December 17, 1896. But during all this period we find no evidence whatever of action on the part of Watson to reduce his conception to practice, beyond the making of some working drawings and a blue print taken from them, if indeed these were made during that interval; for their date is left in extreme doubt by the testimony, and it is not at all certain that they were made before January of 1897. Even if they had been made before the filing of Thomas' application, they could scarcely be held to have been a manifestation of due diligence on the part of Watson. During the whole of the year 1896 he was busy with the single-hopper machine; and during the year he took out a patent for that machine. If he had the device of the double hopper perfected in his own mind, no reason is shown why it could not have been reduced to practice; nor is there any reason shown why he could not have applied for a patent." Watson v. Thomas, 23 App.D.C. 65, 68.

Since infringement is not denied as to the defendant's machine complained of, it follows that a decree should be entered for the complainant for an injunction and an account, as prayed for in its bill.

The decree of the Circuit Court is reversed, and the case is remanded to that court for proceedings in accordance with this opinion, and the appellant recovers its cost of appeal.

5. ACTUAL REDUCTION TO PRACTICE

"In science the credit goes to the man who convinces the world, not to the man to whom the idea first occurs."

—Sir William Osler

BENNETT v. FITZGERALD

United States Court of Customs and Patent Appeals, 1931.
18 CCPA 1201, 48 F.2d 917, 9 USPQ 211.

LENROOT, ASSOCIATE JUDGE. * * *

The testimony concerning the result of the tests of said containers amounted to conclusions of the witnesses, except as to the witness Wilson, who testified that some of the sample cans were filled with water and some were filled with paint; that some of them were dropped two feet and others were dropped three feet; that the result of the tests was that "some of them had a slight leak and some were tight"; that "about six" were closed by the No. 7 closing tool and "about four" were closed by hand; that pails closed by the No. 7 closing machine would be more likely to leak than pails closed by the new No. 8 closing machine; that he would not care to furnish to the trade pails embodying this invention with closing machines such as were used in December, 1923.

It also appears from testimony offered on behalf of appellant that tests were made in 1927 of pails purchased in the open market, embodying appellee's device, and that the same kind of tests were applied to them as had been applied to appellant's sample containers in December, 1923; that the result of the tests was that they broke open and their contents were largely lost.

The first question for consideration is whether appellant reduced the invention to practice in December, 1923, as claimed.

Appellant contends that the making of a dozen containers, exactly as specified in the counts in issue, in itself constitutes a reduction to practice, and that no tests of the containers were necessary, but that, if it should be held that tests were necessary to constitute a reduction to practice, then the evidence establishes that such tests were made and that they were successful.

We think the requirements of tests in reduction to practice were correctly stated by the Court of Appeals of the District of Columbia in the case of Sydeman v. Thoma, 32 App.D.C. 362, wherein the court said:

> "Decisions involving this often-litigated question of actual reduction to practice may be divided into three general classes. The first class includes devices so simple and of such obvious efficacy that the complete construction of one of a size and form intended for and capable of practical use is held sufficient without test in actual use. [Citing cases]. The second class consists of those where a machine embodying every essential element of the invention, having been tested and its practical utility for the intended purpose demonstrated to reasonable satisfaction, has been held to have been reduced to practice notwithstanding it may not be a mechanically perfect machine. In other words, it is sufficient reduction to practice, although a more desirable commercial result may be obtained by some simple and obvious mechanical improvement, or by substituting another well-known material for the one used in the original construction, as, for example, metal for wood, cast metal for sheet metal, and the like. [Citing cases]. The third class includes those where the machine is of such a character that the particular use for which it is intended must be given special consideration, and requires satisfactory operation in the actual execution of the object."

We are of the opinion that the invention here in issue belongs to the second class of devices above referred to. It was, we think, essential to determine by actual tests if the cover of the container embodying the invention here involved would resist severe shocks, as when dropped, with minimum danger of leakage because of loosening of the top. Both of the parties hereto seem to have recognized this, because appellant did subject the 1923 container to tests and also the same type of container brought out by him in 1926, and appellee also tested his container embodying the invention in issue.

The next question is, Did the tests, in December, 1923, of appellant's device, demonstrate its practicability sufficiently to constitute a reduction to practice of the invention?

As heretofore noted, the testimony of most of appellant's witnesses upon this point consists of conclusions, rather than statements of fact from which we might draw our own conclusion. The witness Wilson, however did testify that the results of the tests were such that he would not care to offer to the trade containers embodying this invention, with closing machines such as the company then had, and also that the tests revealed that some of the containers had a slight leak. Also, appellant testified that the closing machine used upon the sample containers was very weak and ineffective. This testimony, standing alone, would not be sufficient to negative a successful reduction to practice. A device need not be mechanically perfect, or in its exact form a commercial success. We think it proper, however, to consider said testimony in connection with other circumstances revealed by the record bearing upon the question of reduction to practice.

Of course, if reduction to practice is established, other circumstances or conduct of a party would not warrant us in making a contrary finding; but, if reduction to practice is not clearly established, the facts and circumstances shown by the record may be resorted to for the purpose of determining whether there was in fact a reduction to practice, or whether the alleged reduction to practice was only an abandoned experiment.

The circumstances shown by the record, which we deem material on this point, are:

(1) In December, 1923, appellant's company was manufacturing a container, No. 7, which was not patented, and which it preferred to appellant's 1923 device.

(2) Appellant's device was, after the tests in December, 1923, referred to, turned over to the development department of the Wilson Company "for further development."

(3) In 1925 appellant's 1923 device was discussed by the officers of the Wilson Company, and it was again determined not to manufacture the same.

(4) In 1925 appellant invented another container for which he made application for patent in December, 1925, and the Wilson Company then entered upon the manufacture of said type of container.

(5) In 1925 appellant invented a closing device and applied for a patent thereon, which closing device was the type used in closing appellant's device here in issue when the Wilson Company began its manufacture. The testimony on behalf of appellant is to the effect that this closing device made appellant's container here involved commercially practicable.

(6) In the fall of 1926 appellant was aware that appellee's device was upon the market, as was also a ring seal device of the American Can Company, but said last-named device was of a different character than the device here in question.

(7) Appellant did not place his device upon the market until 1927, and did not file his application for a patent upon the device here involved until April 30, 1927.

Considering the foregoing facts in connection with the lack of positive evidence of the success of the tests in 1923, we are compelled to agree with the tribunals of the Patent Office that the claimed reduction to practice in December, 1923, constituted only an abandoned experiment.

* * *

It is a significant circumstance that, if the tests of 1923 by appellant were successful, and the only bar to commercial success of the device was the type of closing machine used in 1923, appellant waited for more than a year after perfecting a closing machine which would successfully operate upon the device here in issue before bringing out as a commercial proposition the device here involved. It is also a significant fact that, although in 1925 appellant applied for a patent for another container, and also for a patent for a closing device, he did not apply for a patent on the device here in issue until long after appellee's device was upon the market.

In the case of Paul v. Hess, 24 App.D.C. 462, the court said:

"Long delay in making use of an invention claimed to have been reduced to practice, or in applying for a patent, have always been regarded as potent circumstances tending to show that the alleged reduction to practice was nothing more than an unsatisfactory or abandoned experiment. Traver v. Brown, 14 App.D.C. 34, 41; Reichenbach v. Kelley, 17 App.D.C. 333, 344; Latham v. Armat, 17 App.D.C. 345. And this is specially the case where, in the meantime, the inventor has been engaged in the prosecution of similar inventions (Fefel v. Stocker, 17 App.D.C. 317, 321), or others, without reasonable explanation, have been adopted for manufacture and commercial use."

*   *   *

FARRAND OPTICAL CO. v. UNITED STATES

United States Court of Appeals, Second Circuit, 1963.
325 F.2d 328, 139 USPQ 249.

LEONARD P. MOORE, CIRCUIT JUDGE.

Plaintiff seeks compensation under the Invention Secrecy Act of 1951, 35 U.S.C.A. § 183, for the disclosure and use of its invention by the Government. *   *   *

The basis of the relief sought is claim 32 of the Tripp patent application, now claim 4 of patent No. 2,719,457, which describes a device used by airplane gunners and bombers for scanning the horizon and sighting their targets. *   *   *

THE BROWN BOX MOCK-UP

Farrand's claim to reduction to practice rests upon the construction prior to March 10, 1945, of a device which embodied the optical principles set forth in claim 4. It was housed in a brown box. By placing the box on a window sill with one end protruding beyond the building line, the observer was able to view an entire hemisphere from his position within the building. To this extent this mock-up, referred to by Ferrand as "crude," demonstrated the optical principles of the Tripp invention. If anything were reduced to practice at this stage, it could only have been the basic prismatic device because obviously the Air Force did not desire to order the manufacture of a series of brown boxes so that his (sic) its fighter pilots could sit at window sills and scan hemispheres.

*   *   *

The device had never been incorporated into a gunsight or a bombsight, had never been tested in such a sight and had never been subjected to any of the actual conditions in or out of an airplane which it would have to meet in use. The trial court, however, held that the brown box mock-up constituted "reduction to practice" under the law. The court's theory was expressed as follows: "After it was inspected, examined and operated, the invention was found by these men skilled in the art to be a satisfactory answer and a solution to the problem the Air Force could not resolve. Nothing more is required to constitute reduction to practice, and more could not be asked for or expected of an inventor. There was nothing conjectural about being able to look through plaintiff's device and being able to scan a 180° hemisphere. What the Air Force was searching for had reached its point of consummation in plaintiff's device." 175 F.Supp. at 243. The court concluded that the mock-up performed "the functions claimed for it and in the manner claimed." 175 F.Supp. at 244. And so it did. In its brown box the optical arrangement invented by Tripp illustrated the optical principles covered by claim 4. But is this "reduction to practice"?

What constitutes "reduction to practice" has been the subject matter of many decisions. "The general rule is well established that tests under actual working conditions are necessary to establish reduction to practice." Kruger v. Resnick, 197 F.2d 348, 39 CCPA Patents, 994, and cases there cited. Gaiser v. Linder, 253 F.2d 433, 436 (CCPA 1958).

A review of the relevant cases decided over the last fifteen years by appellate courts indicates the importance of the "reduction to practice" element. Gaiser v. Linder, supra, involved an airplane windshield provided with a transparent electroconductive film through which electric current would be passed to heat the windshield and prevent icing. The court rejected the contention that since the only tests necessary were those showing that the film would produce uniform temperatures, laboratory tests were sufficient, saying:

> "[T]he purpose for which the articles tested were designed was not to give uniform temperatures in a laboratory, but under service conditions in an airplane. It is entirely possible that a coating which would operate satisfactorily under laboratory conditions might fail to do so under the varying conditions of sun, wind, precipitation, vibration, and pressure encountered in actual use." At 435 of 253 F.2d.

Radio Corp. of America v. International Stand. Elec. Corp., 232 F.2d 726 (3d Cir.1956) involved a radar system. The court found that there had been no reduction to practice, saying:

> "The claimed invention was talked about as something to use on ships and large airplanes. Despite the obvious differences in the conditions on top of an office building and that on a moving ship at sea or in an airplane there was no experimentation done in either place." At 731 of 232 F.2d.

Chandler v. Mock, 202 F.2d 755 (CCPA 1953) involved an aircraft carburetor embodying a new automatic unit for the control of air and fuel mixtures. In holding the device not reduced to practice, the court said:

> "The board in reaching its conclusion properly proceeded in accordance with an established principle of patent law that tests of a complex mechanical device consisting of an aircraft carburetor must establish that the carburetor would satisfactorily operate under conditions of use, real or simulated, for which it was intended to function; namely, flight conditions * * *". At 757 of 202 F.2d.

> "The practicability of the invention should have been established by timely tests which adequately embraced the essential conditions which the carburetor would be required to meet in actual service on an airplane." [c] At 758 of 202 F.2d.

> * * * Judge Learned Hand in Sinko [Sinko Tool & Mfg. Co. v. Automatic Devices Corp., 157 F.2d 974, 977 (2d Cir.1946)] stated the doctrine succinctly:

> "[A] test under service conditions is necessary in those cases, and in those only, in which persons qualified in the art would require such a test before they were willing to manufacture and sell the invention, as it stands."

* * *

In the reduction to practice cases, particularly where the device was intended for airplane installation, the courts quite obviously were influenced by the lack of demonstration that the devices in question could perform their intended function when subjected to the peculiarities of actual flight conditions, such as vibration, temperature, pressure, moisture and air flow. But it does not follow that any invention which is to become a part of a device to be used in an airplane cannot be reduced to practice by means other than actual flight testing. The essential inquiry here is whether the advance in the art represented by the invention, the so-called "flash of genius," was imbodied in a workable device that demonstrated that it could do what it was claimed to be capable of doing. The "tests under actual conditions" rule cannot be an absolute requirement. Its applicability must depend on the nature of the device, the circumstances of its intended use, and the state of the art. Resolution of the question must depend on the particular facts of each case.

c. Thus, Elmore v. Schmitt, 278 F.2d 510, 47 CCPA 958, relied on by both the board and appellee, is not controlling. In that case, which involved subject matter very similar to that here in issue, we held that the tests there relied upon to show reduction to practice were insufficient because it was not shown that the test arrangement was designed to simulate any practical application of the invention. In other words, we did not hold that laboratory testing is unacceptable as a means of proving a reduction to practice, but rather that, for such tests to be acceptable proof of such reduction to practice, a relationship must be established which relates the test conditions to the intended functional setting of the invention. In the present case, as distinguished from the situation in Elmore v. Schmitt, we think such a relationship has been clearly established.

Paivinen v. Sands, 52 CCPA 906, 1030, 339 F.2d 217, 144 USPQ 1 (1964).

In the present case, what represented an advance in the art was a device that would solve the optical problems of a broad vision gun and bomb sight. Tripp's invention, the use of a cylindrical lens in the telescope that permitted the use of small prisms without requiring a reduction in the size of the entrance pupil and a consequent reduction in angle of view, did this and his mock-up demonstrated that his concept provided the answer. This was the essence of the invention and, as the trial court said, it was "probable" that the problems remaining could be resolved by application of the existing art. Further, those eminent in the art considered the mock-up a significant advance and a satisfactory answer to the problem presented.

In the "airplane" cases, the inventions in question were designed primarily for use in airplanes and the advances in the art that they represented were their ability to overcome the peculiarities and rigors of flight. Here, problems of application to flight conditions remained, but the advance lay not in overcoming peculiar optical problems encountered in flight; rather it was construction of a device that would, in effect, put the viewer's eye immediately outside the structure that he occupied.

This court has no desire to disregard or weaken the uniform body of law that has developed for generations in reduction to practice cases, particularly in the "airplane" cases (see the forceful criticism of Judge Ryan's decision by Nemerovski, in Reduction to Practice: The Farrand Optical Illusion, 43 J.Pat.Off.Soc'y 99 (1961)). However, Tripp's invention can be considered to have been sufficiently reduced to practice if the scope of that invention is limited to the components embodied in the mock-up, namely, to claim 4.[d]

6. CORROBORATION

Deuteronomy, Chapter 17, Verse 6, King James Version

At the mouth of two witnesses, or three witnesses, shall he that is worthy of death be put to death; but at the mouth of one witness he shall not be put to death.

Shakespeare's MacBeth, Act V, Scene 1

Doctor: * * * What at any time have you heard her say?

Gentlewoman: That, Sir, which I will not repeat after her.

Doctor: You may, to me; and 'tis most meet you should.

Gentlewoman: Neither to you or anyone; having no witness to confirm my speech.

d. See Editorial Note, Grauer, The Legally Complete Invention: A Study of the Requirement of Testing to Establish an Actual Reduction to Practice, George Washington Law Review, Vol. 33, No. 3, p. 740 (Mar. 1965).

WEBER v. GOOD AND PUTZRATH

Patent Office Board of Patent Interferences, 1960.
129 USPQ 32, 42.

* * *

We have been concerned here with corroboration.

The doctrine of corroboration of the testimony of an inventor began with Commissioner Fisher's holding in Doughty v. Clark, 1869 C.D. 14, that definite and corroborated testimony must prevail over indefinite and uncorroborated testimony, and became a positive rule of law (Akers v. Pabst, 27 CCPA 1400, 1940, C.D. 738, 46 USPQ 211) based upon public policy. Stevens v. Putnam, 1880 C.D. 164. But corroboration is not a fixed quantity (Mathieson Alkali Works, Inc. v. Crowley, Alien Property Custodian, 59 USPQ 177) and there is no positive requirement that the corroborating testimony must be in any particular form. It may at least in part be supplied by "independent circumstances." Podlesak et al. v. McInnerney, 1906 C.D. 558, 26 App.D.C. 399. It must be such as to carry conviction and serve to remove the determination of dates of inventive acts from the exclusive control of the inventor and from dependence upon statements emanating from him. Otherwise, as the early cases on corroboration point out, each inventor could set the dates to suit himself and there would be no check upon them. We are of the opinion that as to the dates we have accorded Weber, conception and reduction to practice are sufficiently corroborated.

PATTERSON v. HAUCK

United States Court of Customs and Patent Appeals, 1965.
341 F.2d 131, 133, 144 USPQ 481, 484.

Drawing what we deem to be unduly rigid principles of law primarily from the case of Thurston v. Wulff, 164 F.2d 612, 35 CCPA 794, and applying then to the facts, the board concluded that no actual reduction to practice had been proved. On a review of *all* the evidence, and considering it as a whole, we do not have the slightest doubt that the invention was reduced to practice several times before December 23, 1954 or that the proof thereof is legally sufficient.

Thurston v. Wulff was a case in which the appellant argued that the rule of independent corroboration of inventors' testimony or notebook evidence was a harsh one and "should not be applied with its usual strictness in chemical cases where new compounds emanate from large and well-conducted laboratories in the ordinary course of business * * *." This court flatly rejected that proposition but said, in doing so:

> "An inventor's testimony, however, might be corroborated *by facts and circumstances other than by an independent witness.* Such proof or evidence should be independent of the testimony of the inventor and should not consist of self-serving documents prepared by him or under his direction, nor should it be based upon facts the truth of which

depends upon information received from the inventor." [Emphasis added.]

On other occasions we have been faced with similar applications of Thurston v. Wulff, as we were recently in Hasselstrom v. McKusick, 324 F.2d 1013, 51 CCPA 1008, wherein we reversed a finding of no corroboration and said:

"＊ ＊ ＊ we are in complete agreement with the necessity for corroboration of an inventor's testimony. However, the purpose of corroborative evidence is to confirm and to strengthen the testimony of the inventor. [Quoting in a footnote Revise and Caesar, Interference Law and Practice, Vol. 3, p. 2127.] Obviously the amount and quality of corroborative evidence that is necessary in any given case will vary with the facts of that case. As we observed in Phillips and Paul S. Starcher v. Arthur W. Carlson, 278 F.2d 732, 47 CCPA 1007 there can be no fixed single formula in determining the sufficiency of corroborative evidence."

MINNESOTA MINING & MFG. CO. v. GENERAL ELEC. CO.

United States District Court, District of Columbia, 1958.
167 F.Supp. 37, 40, 119 USPQ 65, 67.

The plaintiff is required to establish corroboration of all essential points by independent witnesses or other positive evidence. As stated by the Court of Appeals in Goolman v. Hobart, 31 App.D.C. 286, 292:

"Appellant is the junior applicant. The burden rests upon him to remove the presumption of prior invention that always attaches to the senior applicant. This presumption cannot be overcome by the uncorroborated evidence of the junior applicant alone. *He must be corroborated directly on all points necessary to establish priority.* ＊ ＊ ＊" (Italics supplied.)

This rule also applies to joint inventors. In Sundberg v. Schmitt, 58 App.D.C. 292, 29 F.2d 880, the Court said: ＊ ＊ ＊

COLEMAN v. DINES

United States Court of Appeals, Federal Circuit, 1985.
754 F.2d 353, 224 USPQ 857.

DAVIS, CIRCUIT JUDGE.

＊ ＊ ＊

The subject matter of the interference is directed to a method of separating isotopes of an element. Prior to the current applications, those skilled in the art had tried to take advantage of the fact that the absorption spectra of atoms of an element exhibit an isotopic shift, and that it should be possible to excite isotopes of those elements with light of a selected wavelength. However, production of these light sources was not economically feasible, the atoms were not attainable in the vapor phase, and the shift exhibited overlapping bands. In addition, excitation was difficult, if not impossible, without the required volatility and vibrational characteristics existing in a compound. The current applications relate to a volatile uranyl compound which is useful in such a separation process, seemingly overcomes these obstacles, and meets the desired parameters.

* * * It is settled that in establishing conception a party must show possession of every feature recited in the count, and that every limitation of the count must have been known to the inventor at the time of the alleged conception. *Davis v. Reddy,* 620 F.2d 885, 889, 205 USPQ 1065, 1069 (CCPA 1980). Conception must be proved by corroborating evidence which shows that the inventor disclosed to others his "completed thought expressed in such clear terms as to enable those skilled in the art" to make the invention. *Field v. Knowles,* 183 F.2d 593, 601, 37 CCPA 1211, 1222, 86 USPQ 373, 379 (1950).

Coleman asserts that the 1973 letters corroborate his claim to a conception date of late 1973. He argues that in his letter to Kovac on December 18, 1973, he proposed the use of laser energy for uranium isotope separation. In addition, it is claimed that in the December 11, 1973 letter, Coleman's proposed use of a high power CO_2 laser is confirmed. Finally, Coleman contends that, under the "rule of reason" used to corroborate conception, uranyls were a well-known major class of uranium compounds in 1973, and that fact (by itself) should be considered adequate corroboration. The Board noted that "[i]n Coleman's view it is inconceivable that Coleman, a scientific man well versed in the art, was not aware of and did not contemplate uranyls as candidates for the process which he had in mind. * * *"

This "rule of reason," which was developed over the years in order to ease the requirement of corroboration, usually is applied when establishing actual reduction to practice. *See Mikus v. Wachtel,* 542 F.2d 1157, 191 USPQ 571 (CCPA 1976). Even so, Coleman's attempt to apply the rule to establish conception fails in this present case. The rule suggests a reasoned examination, analysis and evaluation of all pertinent evidence so that a sound determination of the credibility of the inventor's story may be reached. *See Mann v. Werner,* 347 F.2d 636, 52 CCPA 1578, 146 USPQ 199 (CCPA 1965). The rule of reason, however, does not dispense with the requirement for some evidence of independent corroboration. Coleman has not presented any evidence of an independent nature to support his testimony that one of ordinary skill in the art, at the time of his purported conception, would contemplate the use of volatile uranyl compounds. Thus, the Board did not err in ruling that Coleman failed to establish conception in late 1973.

Coleman also attacks the Board's finding that Marks' testimony does not indicate that the use of volatile uranyl compounds set forth in the 1975 ERDA proposal was the invention of Coleman alone. He argues that, in light of the Board's finding that the ERDA proposal discloses the invention and also of the asserted fact that he was one of the authors of that proposal, it is undeniable that he is entitled to a date of conception no later than 1975 (when the ERDA proposal was made).

The fact is that Marks' testimony does not establish that any of the uranyl compounds were suggested by Coleman. Marks testified, rather, that the ideas between the authors were "intermingled." The parties even stipulated that Weitz collaborated in and participated in the preparation of the ERDA proposal. Further, as noted above (note 2, *supra*), Coleman's name or signature is absent from the list of principal investigators on the title page of the proposal.

Appellant has pointed us toward no authority standing for the proposition that one who *may* be a *co*-author of a document can be considered the *sole* inventor of any invention disclosed in that document, without some further proof. As was set forth in *Gunter, supra*, it is the formation "in the mind of the inventor," not in the mind of another, that establishes conception. It is insufficient to argue, without offering independent corroboration of the particular source of the invention, that one who attains a definite and permanent idea of the complete and operative invention—after the document is completed—is necessarily the inventor. By just *reading* the ERDA proposal, anyone, including Coleman, could have a "definite and permanent idea." Coleman cites *Van Otteren v. Hafner and Cork*, 278 F.2d 738, 742, 47 CCPA 993, 126 USPQ 151, 154 (Bd.Pt.Int.1950), as support for the proposition that one who was "the spark which lead to the final satisfactory result" is the inventor. The difficulty here is that initial formation in Coleman's mind must be, but was not, firmly established. The evidence did not show that Coleman's "completed thought" was disclosed to others. *See Field v. Knowles, supra*. What was shown here, at best, was that the ideas were "intermingled," and not that Coleman was the "spark." For that reason we cannot say the Board erred in finding that the ERDA proposal did not establish Coleman's own conception.

Thus, on the basis of Dines' June 17, 1976 constructive reduction to practice and Coleman's failure to establish conception prior to that date, the Board properly concluded that Dines is entitled to priority.

* * *

7. ABANDONED, SUPPRESSED, OR CONCEALED

✓ MASON v. HEPBURN

United States Court of Appeals, District of Columbia, 1834.
13 App.D.C. 86, 1834 C.D. 510.

SHEPARD, J.:

First. This is an appeal from the decision of the Commissioner of Patents in the interference proceeding with the following issue:

"In a magazine-firearm, the detachable end piece closing the outer end of the magazine provided with upwardly-projecting curved arms to clasp the sides of the barrel, sustantially as described."

The device is a clip made in one piece instead of two, as formerly, one end of which is made to fit closely in the upper end of the magazine. The other is split or divided into two curved arms, which are elastic and clasp each side of the gun-barrel far enough around to hold securely without meeting each other. A side screw at the junction of magazine and barrel holds tight the clasp or releases it, as desired.

Hepburn received a patent for this invention September 11, 1894. Having taken no testimony, his date of invention must be confined to that of his application, filed April 3, 1894.

Mason's application was filed December 31, 1894. Mason offered testimony tending to show that he conceived the invention about June 28, 1887, on which date he made a complete drawing showing the device; that a working drawing was traced from that in July, 1887, and the clip made in the shops of the Winchester Repeating Arms Company; that during the same month a new "take-down" shotgun was made with this clip attached, which was tested, probably, in the shooting-gallery. This gun was stored in the model-room of the same company until produced in the course of the trial of this controversy. No clips of the kind were manufactured for any other purpose and no similar gun was made. No exhibition of the gun and clip was made to the public, and no one saw it besides the inventor and one or two other employees of the Winchester Company.

It appears that Mason filed an application for a detachable or "take-down" gun April 4, 1892, and the same was issued to him December 6, 1892. In this no mention is made of the device for clipping the upper end of the magazine to the barrel. On the same day, however, he received a patent for a clip, for which he applied August 1, 1892. This is made with projecting curved arms, as in the device of the controversy, to clasp the gun-barrel; but at the other end it has a hole made to receive the end of a pin on a separate piece that closes the end of the magazine.

Second. The testimony is sufficient to warrant the conclusion, in which all of the tribunals of the Patent Office have concurred, that Mason conceived the idea of this invention at the time claimed and that the gun, with the device attached, was actually completed and ready for use in July, 1887. They have not agreed, however, in respect of the sufficiency of the evidence to show with the required certainty that the gun, when constructed, was actually tested by firing in a manner that demonstrated the completeness and practical utility of the device of the controversy.

*   *   *

In reaching our own conclusion we regard the examination of the evidence in respect of the actual firing test of the gun as immaterial, because, in our opinion, the reduction to practice of the clip was accomplished by its perfect construction and attachment to a gun apparently completely finished and ready for sale and use. It was demonstrably capable of producing the result sought to be accomplished—namely, that of closing the magazine and clipping it to the barrel. As admitted by the Examiners—

"the clip evidently performs its expected office."

Actual test of the restraining power under the strain of repeated firing of the gun might be of importance in demonstrating the value of the clip, but was not necessary to the completion of the inventive act. (Hall v. MacNeale, C.D., 1883, 191; 23 O.G., 937; 107 U.S., 90, 97.)

* * *

The remaining question is, can the decision be upheld upon the ground that Mason's right to claim of priority has become barred by his designed or negligent concealment of his invention from the public and the subsequent entry of his rival in the apparently unoccupied field?

We concur with the Commissioner in the answer to this question, that under the circumstances Hepburn must be held to be the first inventor in the sense of the law regulating the grant of patents. (Rev. Stat., sec. 4886.)

A liberal interpretation of the words of the statute is demanded in the interest of the public, for the advancement of which the patent laws were enacted. (Kendall v. Winsor, 21 How., 322, 327, 328.) In the opinion in that case it was said:

"The true policy and ends of the patent laws enacted under this Government are disclosed in that article of the Constitution, the source of all these laws, viz., 'to promote the progress of science and the useful arts,' contemplating and necessarily implying their extension and increasing adaptation to the uses of society. (*Vide* Constitution of the United States, Art. 1, sec. 8, clause 8.) By correct induction from these truths it follows that the inventor who, designedly, and with a view of applying it indefinitely and exclusively for his own profit, withholds his invention from the public, comes not within the policy or objects of the Constitution or acts of Congress. He does not promote and, if aided in his design, would impede the progress of science and the useful arts; and with a very bad grace could he apply for favor or protection to that society which, if he had not injured, he certainly had neither benefited nor intended to benefit. Hence, if during such a concealment an invention similar to or identical with his own should be made and patented or brought into use without a patent, the latter could not be inhibited nor restricted upon proof of its identity with a machine previously invented and withheld and concealed by the inventor from the public. The rights and interests, whether of the public or individuals, can never be made to yield to schemes of selfishness or cupidity; moreover, that which is once given to or is invested in the public cannot be recalled nor taken from them."

That case was, it is true, an action for infringement by a patentee against one who before the application for the patent had made use of his invention without claim, himself, of discovery. The right was claimed in the patentee, on the one hand, as against the right of the public on the other. Nevertheless we think that our conclusion is in strict conformity with the principles which it enounces, and there is nothing in it inconsistent with the spirit of indulgence that has always been manifested toward those who in good faith delay application for patent while engaged in a diligent effort to perfect their inventions. (Idem, p. 329; Agawam Co. v. Jordan, 7 Wall., 583, 607; Yates v. Huson, C.D., 1896, 278; 74 O.G., 1732; 8 App.D.C., 93, 98.)

Considering, then, this paramount interest of the public in its bearing upon the question as presented here, we think it imperatively demands that a subsequent inventor of a new and useful manufacture or improvement who had diligently pursued his labors to the procurement of a patent in good faith and without any knowledge of the preceding discoveries of another shall, as against that other, who has deliberately concealed the knowledge of his invention from the public, be regarded as the real inventor and as such entitled to his reward.

This right of second discoverer has been recognized with considerable uniformity for a number of years in the administration of the Patent Office. (Duncan, Acting Commissioner, in Monce v. Adams, 1 O.G., 1; Paine, Commissioner, in Mallett v. Cogger, C.D., 1879, 100; 16 O.G., 45, and Farmer v. Brush, C.D., 1880, 5; 17 O.G., 150; Marble, Commissioner, in Sheridan v. Latus, C.D., 1883, 76; 25 O.G., 501.) And again recently by Commissioner Duell, in whose decision the authorities are extensively reviewed. (Mower v. Crisp & Copeland, ante, 41; 83 O.G., 155.)

It has the sanction also of the following judicial decisions: Rowley v. Mason, (2 Am.Law Times Rep., 106;) Consolidated Fruit Jar Co. v. Wright, (6 O.G., 327; 12 Blatch., 149;) U.S. Rifle and Cartridge Co. v. Whitney Arms Co., (C.D., 1877, 197; 11 O.G., 373; 14 Blatch., 94, 101;) Boyd v. Cherry, (4 McCreery, 70, 77;) Cahoon v. Ring, (1 Cliff., 610;) White v. Allen, (2 Fish., 440, 454).

In Bates v. Coe (C.D., 1879, 365; 15 O.G., 337; 98 U.S., 31, 46) the point was not directly involved; but Mr. Justice Clifford in affirming the right of the inventor to keep his invention secret for any length of time without modifying his right to a patent coupled it with the following exception, as if one of unquestioned application, namely:

> "Unless another in the meantime has made the same invention, and secured by patent the exclusive right to make, use and vend the patented improvement. Within that rule and subject to that exception, inventors may delay to apply for a patent."

See also 1 Robinson on Patents, section 390.

In some of the decisions the first inventor is regarded as having abandoned the field to other inventors, while in others he is held to have lost his right by sleeping too long upon it.

Strictly speaking, abandonment after the completion of an inventive act applies in a case where the right of the public to the use is involved and not in one where the contention is between rival claimants merely of the monopoly.

The true ground of the doctrine, we apprehend, lies in the spirit and policy of the patent laws and in the nature of the equity that arises in favor of him who gives the public the benefit of the knowledge of his invention, who expends his time, labor, and money in discovering, perfecting, and patenting in perfect good faith that which he and all others have been led to believe has never been discovered by reason of the indifference, supineness, or willful act of one who may, in fact, have discovered it long before.

It follows that the decision of the Commissioner must be affirmed. It is so ordered, and this decision will be certified to the Commissioner of Patents, in accordance with the law.

✓ YOUNG v. DWORKIN

United States Court of Customs and Patent Appeals, 1974.
489 F.2d 1277, 180 USPQ 388.

MILLER, JUDGE.

This is an appeal from the Board of Patent Interferences which awarded priority to the senior party-appellee on the grounds that the junior party-appellant had suppressed or concealed the invention. 35 U.S.C.A. § 102(g). We affirm.

FACTS

The invention is an expansible envelope formed from single blanks of foldable material. The envelope is open at the top and has a gusset (an inward bellow-type fold forming a triangular insert) on each of the two sides plus one at the bottom, thereby permitting expansion into a box-like configuration.

It appears that sometime prior to November 4, 1965, appellant conceived the invention which, according to his testimony, would be adaptable to machine folding and gluing of the bottom gusset. Existing three-gusseted envelopes, which were of a different construction from the invention, were only partially manufactured, by machine, the bottom gusset requiring a hand folding and gluing operation. Thus, appellant's objective was to design a three-gusseted envelope which could be entirely machine-manufactured. Upon receipt by his company of an order for 15,000 three-gusseted filing envelopes from the School District of Philadelphia on November 4, 1965, appellant constructed a model of the envelope. This was introduced into evidence and found by the board to be a completed article, capable of actual use, and further found to have constituted a reduction to practice.

In November, 1965, appellant showed the model to the company vice-president for production and to the plant superintendent, who made a drawing and had a die prepared for the new design. Using the die, paper blanks for the entire order were prepared, and about the last week of November, 1965, were run through one of the company machines. However, the glue did not register in the right positions, the paper blanks were scrapped, new blanks were re-die-cut for hand-fold manufacture, and the order was completed by hand. Nothing further was done with the invention until after August 26, 1966, when an order for 6,000 envelopes was received from the School District of Philadelphia. Appellant decided to make this run with the new design on another company machine, with new gears and new belts designed to overcome the glue problem encountered in the first run nine months earlier. However, the glue problem was not overcome, and this run (made in September, 1966) was unsuccessful. The paper blanks were thrown away, and again the order was completed by hand, using new blanks for hand-fold manufacture.

No further attempt was made by appellant to produce the invention on the company's existing machines. However, some eight months later appellant attended an international paper-converting machinery show in Dusseldorf, Germany, for the purpose, as he testified, of looking for a standard folding and gluing machine which would answer the glue problem. Appellant testified that he felt all of the machines that he saw there would handle the problem, but, upon his return, he directed his vice-president for production to get in touch with the International Paper Box Machine Company in New Hampshire, because it was the only company from the United States at the show and would probably provide better service. In the first week of August, 1967, the vice-president visited the International plant in New Hampshire. He made subsequent trips to the plant and ordered a machine on September 13, 1967. The machine was delivered late in December, 1967, assembled, and put into operation in January, 1968. Appellant testified that approximately 25,000 envelopes of the invention design were successfully run off during January.

Meanwhile, on October 31, 1967, some five months after attending the show in Dusseldorf, appellant wrote to his patent lawyer, enclosing samples "to show the style and construction of the expanding envelopes which can be manufactured on the new machine" and saying, "I think we should apply for a patent very soon." However, no showing was made of when the lawyer was directed to proceed in drawing up the application. It was not until February 7, 1968, following the successful runs on the new machine the month before, that appellant filed his application for a patent.

Under cross-examination appellant testified that he had been in touch with his patent lawyer prior to writing the letter of October 31, 1967, and that "I told him I had invented a new design and that we had experimented with it; *we knew that it was a practical design* but we were unable to manufacture it with our present equipment." (Emphasis supplied.)

When asked on cross-examination whether it was his usual practice to delay a period of two years after conception before taking up an invention with his patent solicitor, appellant responded: "I do not apply for a patent until I am positive that we can manufacture the item."

When asked on cross-examination whether it was correct that his reason for not seeking out the services of his patent solicitor in 1965 was his "doubts" that the envelope could be manufactured at that time, appellant testified: "I had no doubts that it could be manufactured. My doubts were that we could not manufacture it with our present equipment, and the patent itself would be of no value to us unless we could manufacture it."

Under cross-examination appellant testified, "Oh, yes," in response to the question: "During the time from November, 1965, to May, 1967, was there a continuous demand for gusseted envelopes?" He also said, "That is correct," in response to the question: " * * * I understand that it is much cheaper to make these envelopes by machine than it is by hand; is that correct?"

OPINION

The record before us supports the board's finding that appellant's invention was reduced to practice and, further, that this occurred in November, 1965.

The sole remaining question is whether the board correctly held that junior party-appellant suppressed or concealed his invention within the meaning of 35 U.S.C.A. § 102(g). Here, senior party-appellee bears the burden of proof by a preponderance of the evidence, notwithstanding junior party-appellant's burden on the issue of priority of invention which he has sustained. Gallagher v. Smith, 206 F.2d 939, 41 CCPA 734 (1953).

In considering the question, we point out that section 102(g) is concerned with the subject of priority of invention and, for interference purposes, provides that a person shall be entitled to a patent unless "before the applicant's invention thereof the invention was made in this country by another who had not abandoned, suppressed, or concealed it." By its enactment as part of the Patent Act of 1952, Congress codified the body of law which had accumulated on the subject of priority of invention, including the legal concept of "suppression or concealment."

We note that commencing with the first edition of Webster's dictionary in 1828 and continuing to the present the definition of "suppress" has included the idea of keeping from public knowledge. It is to be expected, of course, that the courts would be aware of the definition, which fits very well with their statements on the clear policy against suppression underlying our interference laws, both prior to and including 35 U.S.C.A. § 102(g). Long ago this policy was explained by the U.S. Supreme Court in Kendall v. Winsor, 62 U.S. (21 How.) 322, 328, 16 L.Ed. 165 (1858) as follows:

The true policy and ends of the patent laws enacted under this Government are disclosed in that article of the Constitution, the source of all these laws, viz: "to promote the progress of science and the useful arts," contemplating and necessarily implying their extension, and increasing adaptation to the uses of society. * * * By correct induction from these truths, it follows, that the inventor who designedly, and with the view of applying it indefinitely and exclusively for his own profit, withholds his invention from the public, comes not within the policy or objects of the Constitution or acts of Congress. He does not promote, and, if aided in his design, would impede, the progress of science and the useful arts.

Mason v. Hepburn, 13 App.D.C. 86, 1898 C.D. 510 (1898) has generally been regarded as the origin of the suppression and concealment doctrine. There the court (13 App.D.C. at 96), after quoting from Kendall v. Winsor, emphasized the "policy and spirit of the patent laws" underlying the doctrine as follows:

> The true ground of the doctrine, we apprehend, lies in the policy and spirit of the patent laws and in the nature of the equity that arises in favor of him who gives the public the benefit of the knowledge of his invention, who expends his time, labor, and money in discovering, perfecting, and patenting, in perfect good faith, that which he and all others have been led to believe has never been discovered, by reason of the indifference, supineness, or wilful act of one who may, in fact, have discovered it long before.

In Thomson v. Weston, 19 App.D.C. 373, 1902 C.D. 521 (1902), the court reaffirmed its Mason v. Hepburn doctrine—again in reference to "the true policy and ends of the patent laws":

> [B]y deliberate concealment or suppression of the knowledge of his [the inventor's] invention he subordinates his claim, in accordance with the general policy of the law in the promotion of the public interest, to that of another and *bona fide* inventor who during the period of inaction and concealment shall have given the benefit of the discovery to the public. Viewed in the light of "the true policy and ends of the patent laws," the latter is the first to invent, and therefore entitled to the reward.

This court has clearly followed the Mason v. Hepburn doctrine. Brokaw v. Vogel, 429 F.2d 476, 57 CCPA 1296 (1970); Woofter v. Carlson, 367 F.2d 436, 54 CCPA 917 (1966). It has, to be sure, cautioned that the doctrine is to be applied only where the record sustains the burden of proving suppression or concealment. Frey v. Wagner, 87 F.2d 212, 24 CCPA 823 (1937); Woofter v. Carlson, supra. At the same time, the court has declared that application of the Mason v. Hepburn doctrine is not to be confined to "extreme cases" and that it—

> * * * is a very healthy rule to be invoked in the public interest whenever the fact situation warrants it. While the law may abhor a forfeiture, the Mason v. Hepburn principle is not a forfeiture in the true sense; rather, it is a rule according to which the patent right goes to the most deserving.

Brokaw v. Vogel, supra. Needless to say, evidence of one party's being "first to file" would hardly satisfy his burden of proving suppression by the other party.

As we have done before, we emphasize here that each case involving the issue of suppression or concealment must be considered on its own particular set of facts. Myers v. Feigelman, 455 F.2d 596, 59 CCPA 834 (1972); Engelhardt v. Judd, 369 F.2d 408, 54 CCPA 865 (1966). In such consideration, two guideposts have been firmly established:

First, the length of time from reduction to practice to filing of an application for a patent is not determinative. Woofter v. Carlson, supra; Schnick v. Fenn, 277 F.2d 935, 47 CCPA 1174 (1960). Mere delay, without more, is not sufficient to establish suppression or concealment. Gallagher v. Smith, supra. However, the warning has been sounded that one who delays filing his application does so at the peril of a finding of suppression or concealment due to the circumstances surrounding the delay. Woofter v. Carlson, supra. See also Watson, Commissioner of Patents v. Allen, 103 U.S.App.D.C. 5, 254 F.2d 342 (1958); International Glass Co., Inc. v. United States, 408 F.2d 395, 187 Ct.Cl. 376 (1968).[3]

Second, spurring into filing an application for a patent by knowledge of another's entry into the field (e.g. by issuance of a patent) is not essential to a finding of suppression or concealment. Dewey v. Lawton, 347 F.2d 629, 52 CCPA 1573 (1965); Brokaw v. Vogel, supra; Gallagher v. Smith, supra.

Bearing these points in mind, we now turn to the question of appellant's intent to suppress. This, if established by the evidence of record, coupled with the delay in filing his application for patent, would support the board's finding of "suppression" for purposes of 35 U.S.C.A. § 102(g). The facts show a delay from reduction to practice in November of 1965 until February 7, 1968, when appellant's application for a patent was filed. During this period there was a "continuous demand" for gusseted envelopes which, if machine-produced, would cost less.

The delay was *not* for the purpose of perfecting appellant's invention—a critical point of distinction from other cases holding that delay was justifiable and, therefore, suppression or concealment had not been proved. Frey v. Wagner, supra ("The law does not punish an inventor for attempting to perfect his process before he gives it to the public. * * * reasonable experimentation is frequently encouraged."); Altorfer v. Haag, 74 F.2d 129, 22 CCPA 806 (1934) (following reduction to practice, frequent and comparative tests of machines equipped with the invention with a view to determining best materials for manufacture of invention and refinements that should be made); Dewey v. Lawton,

---

3. Thus, when the delay period is determined to be "unreasonable," there is a basis for inferring an intent to suppress. Brokaw v. Vogel, supra. The activities of an inventor during the delay period (e.g. steps to improve or perfect the invention after it has been reduced to practice) may well *excuse* the delay and, thereby, support a finding that it was "reasonable." Frey v. Wagner, supra.

supra (testing and refinement of invention for more than a year after reduction to practice); Schnick v. Fenn, supra ("mitigating circumstances" included continuing development, after reduction to practice, of best design and tests in further perfecting the invention); Watson, Commissioner of Patents v. Allen, supra.

Instead, the evidence discloses that the delay here resulted from appellant's intent to wait, without disclosing his invention—not to perfect the invention, but: first, to determine whether the invention could be produced with his company's own equipment; then, when that could not be done (after two attempts nine months apart), some eight months later to locate a machine which would enable his company to manufacture it; and, finally, some eight months after that, to have a successful run on the new machine. Appellant argues that a "generalized search" went on for a machine to produce his envelope.

Aside from appellant's trip to the Dusseldorf show over a year and a half after reduction to practice and the follow-on visits to the International plant in New Hampshire by the company's vice-president, the record is devoid of any meaningful evidence to support appellant's "generalized search" argument. Rather, it supports a finding of total inactivity. For example, appellant has made no showing that an equipment catalog was consulted or that even one telephone call or letter of inquiry was made to a machine manufacturer prior to his trip to Dusseldorf where, interestingly, he located a machine produced by a U.S. manufacturer. Considering the two unsuccessful runs on the machines of appellant's company, we believe some such evidence should have been forthcoming to establish ordinary business prudence on the part of appellant in locating a suitable machine during the over a year and a half period following reduction to practice.

In his own words, appellant's excuse for the delay in filing his application was simply: "I do not apply for a patent until I am positive we can manufacture it." And, indeed, appellant delayed filing his application until after the successful run, when he was positive that the invention could be produced on his company's new machine. Unlike Schnick v. Fenn, supra, where early in the delay period the inventor had his patent attorney make a preliminary search for which his company was billed, appellant delayed some twenty months after reduction to practice before furnishing his patent lawyer samples of his invention. This was five months after the Dusseldorf show where, appellant testified, he thought all the machines he saw would satisfy his problem. Even then, appellant merely told his patent lawyer that he thought "we should apply for a patent very soon." And it was not until over three months later, after the successful runs on the new machine, that appellant filed his application.

Meanwhile, as found by the board, appellee, without knowledge of appellant's activities, conceived and reduced his invention to practice between January 31, 1967, and October 6, 1967, at which time he delivered and explained to his patent lawyer an envelope constructed according to the count. Less than three months later, he filed his patent application. Also, the record shows that in early March, 1967, appellee sent samples of blanks for envelopes to the International plant in New Hampshire to be run on an experimental machine (which was built for exhibition at the Dusseldorf show later in the year). Appellee made a downpayment for one of the machines by check dated May 1, 1967, and the machine was delivered in late July or early August, 1967. We believe the nature and tempo of appellee's activities were in accord with ordinary business prudence.

In view of the foregoing and considering the record as a whole, we hold that junior party-appellant suppressed his invention within the meaning of 35 U.S.C.A. § 102(g).

The decision of the board is affirmed.

Affirmed.

[Concurring opinion of Judge Rich is omitted.]

PAULIK v. RIZKALLA

United States Court of Appeals, Federal Circuit, 1985.
760 F.2d 1270, 226 USPQ 224.

NEWMAN, CIRCUIT JUDGE.

This appeal is from the decision of the United States Patent and Trademark Office Board of Patent Interferences (Board), awarding priority of invention to the senior party Nabil Rizkalla and Charles N. Winnick (Rizkalla), on the ground that the junior party and de facto first inventors Frank E. Paulik and Robert G. Schultz (Paulik) had suppressed or concealed the invention within the meaning of 35 U.S.C. § 102(g). We vacate this decision and remand to the Board.

I.

Rizkalla's patent application has the effective filing date of March 10, 1975, its parent application. Paulik's patent application was filed on June 30, 1975. The interference count is for a catalytic process for producing alkylidene diesters such as ethylidene diacetate, which is useful to prepare vinyl acetate and acetic acid. Paulik presented deposition testimony and exhibits in support of his claim to priority; Rizkalla chose to rely solely on his filing date.

The Board held and Rizkalla does not dispute that Paulik reduced the invention of the count to practice in November 1970 and again in April 1971. On about November 20, 1970 Paulik submitted a "Preliminary Disclosure of Invention" to the Patent Department of his assignee, the Monsanto Company. The disclosure was assigned a priority designation of "B", which Paulik states meant that the case would "be taken up in the ordinary course for review and filing."

Despite occasional prodding from the inventors, and periodic review by the patent staff and by company management, this disclosure had a lower priority than other patent work. Evidence of the demands of other projects on related technology was offered to justify the patent staff's delay in acting on this invention, along with evidence that the inventors and assignee continued to be interested in the technology and that the invention disclosure was retained in active status.

In January or February of 1975 the assignee's patent solicitor started to work toward the filing of the patent application; drafts of the application were prepared, and additional laboratory experiments were requested by the patent solicitor and were duly carried out by an inventor. The evidentiary sufficiency of these activities was challenged by Rizkalla, but the Board made no findings thereon, on the basis that these activities were not pertinent to the determination of priority. The Board held that "even if Paulik demonstrated continuous activity from prior to the Rizkalla effective filing date to his filing date * * * such would have no bearing on the question of priority in this case", and cited 35 U.S.C. § 102(g) as authority for the statement that "[w]hile diligence during the above noted period may be relied upon by one alleging prior conception and subsequent reduction to practice, it is of no significance in the case of the party who is not the last to reduce to practice." * * *

The Board then held that Paulik's four-year delay from reduction to practice to his filing date was prima facie suppression or conceal-ment under the first clause of section 102(g), that since Paulik had reduced the invention to practice in 1971 and 1972 he was barred by the second clause of section 102(g) from proving reasonable diligence leading to his 1975 filing, and that in any event the intervening activities were insufficient to excuse the delay. The Board refused to consider Paulik's evidence of renewed patent-related activity.

II.

The Board's decision converted the case law's estoppel against reliance on Paulik's early work for priority purposes, into a forfeiture encompassing Paulik's later work, even if the later work commenced before the earliest activity of Rizkalla. According to this decision, once the inference of suppression or concealment is established, this infer-ence cannot be overcome by the junior party to an interference. There is no statutory or judicial precedent that requires this result, and there is sound reason to reject it.

United States patent law embraces the principle that the patent right is granted to the first inventor rather than the first to file a patent application. The law does not inquire as to the fits and starts by which an invention is made. The historic jurisprudence from which 35 U.S.C. § 102(g) flowed reminds us that "the mere lapse of time" will not prevent the inventor from receiving a patent. *Mason v. Hepburn*, 13 App.D.C. 86, 91, 1898 C.D. 510, 513 (1898). The sole exception to this principle resides in section 102(g) and the exigencies of the priority contest.

There is no impediment in the law to holding that a long period of inactivity need not be a fatal forfeiture, if the first inventor resumes work on the invention before the second inventor enters the field. We deem this result to be a fairer implementation of national patent policy, while in full accord with the letter and spirit of section 102(g).

The Board misapplied the rule that the first inventor does not have to show activity following reduction to practice to mean that the first inventor will not be allowed to show such activity. Such a showing may serve either of two purposes: to rebut an inference of abandonment, suppression, or concealment; or as evidence of renewed activity with respect to the invention. Otherwise, if an inventor were to set an invention aside for "too long" and later resume work and diligently develop and seek to patent it, according to the Board he would always be worse off than if he never did the early work, even as against a much later entrant.

Such a restrictive rule would merely add to the burden of those charged with the nation's technological growth. Invention is not a neat process. The value of early work may not be recognized or, for many reasons, it may not become practically useful, until months or years later. Following the Board's decision, any "too long" delay would constitute a forfeiture fatal in a priority contest, even if terminated by extensive and productive work done long before the newcomer entered the field.

We do not suggest that the first inventor should be entitled to rely for priority purposes on his early reduction to practice if the intervening inactivity lasts "too long," as that principle has evolved in a century of judicial analysis. Precedent did not deal with the facts at bar. There is no authority that would estop Paulik from relying on his resumed activities in order to pre-date Rizkalla's earliest date. We hold that such resumed activity must be considered as evidence of priority of invention. Should Paulik demonstrate that he had renewed activity on the invention and that he proceeded diligently to filing his patent application, starting before the earliest date to which Rizkalla is entitled—all in accordance with established principles of interference practice—we hold that Paulik is not prejudiced by the fact that he had reduced the invention to practice some years earlier.

III.

This appeal presents a question not previously treated by this court or, indeed, in the historical jurisprudence on suppression or concealment. We take this opportunity to clarify an apparent misperception of certain opinions of our predecessor court which the Board has cited in support of its holding.

There is over a hundred years of judicial precedent on the issue of suppression or concealment due to prolonged delay in filing. From the earliest decisions, a distinction has been drawn between deliberate suppression or concealment of an invention, and the legal inference of suppression or concealment based on "too long" a delay in filing the patent application. Both types of situations were considered by the courts before the 1952 Patent Act, and both are encompassed in 35 U.S.C. § 102(g). The result is consistent over this entire period—loss of the first inventor's priority as against an intervening second inventor— and has consistently been based on equitable principles and public policy as applied to the facts of each case.

The earliest decisions dealt primarily with deliberate concealment. In 1858, the Supreme Court in *Kendall v. Winsor*, 62 U.S. (21 How.) 322, 328, 16 L.Ed. 165 (1858) held that an inventor who "designedly, and with the view of applying it indefinitely and exclusively for his own profit, withholds his invention from the public" impedes "the progress of science and the useful arts".

In *Mason v. Hepburn*, supra, the classical case on inferred as contrasted with deliberate suppression or concealment, Hepburn was granted a patent in September 1894. Spurred by this news Mason filed his patent application in December 1894. In an interference, Mason demonstrated that he had built a working model in 1887 but showed no activity during the seven years thereafter. The court held that although Mason may have negligently rather than willfully concealed his invention, the "indifference, supineness, or wilful act" of a first inventor is the basis for "the equity" that favors the second inventor when that person made and disclosed the invention during the prolonged inactivity of the first inventor. 13 App.D.C. at 96, 1898 C.D. at 517.

Other early cases affirmed these principles. *Thomson v. Weston*, 19 App.D.C. 373, 381, 1902 C.D. 521, 527, (1902) discussed the situation where a second inventor appeared "during the period of inactivity and concealment". The decisions are consistent, and were codified in section 102(g) of the 1952 Patent Act.

The legislative history of section 102(g) makes clear that its purpose was not to change the law. As described in H.R.Rep. No. 1923, 82d Cong., 2d Sess. 17–18 (1951), section 102(g) "retains the present rules of [the case] law governing the determination of priority of invention". The pre-1952 cases all dealt with situations whereby a later inventor made the same invention during a period of either prolonged inactivity or deliberate concealment by the first inventor, after knowledge of which (usually, but not always, by the issuance of a patent to the second inventor) the first inventor was "spurred" into asserting patent rights, unsuccessfully.

The decisions after the 1952 Act followed a similar pattern, as the courts considered whether to extinguish a first inventor's priority under section 102(g). The cases show either intentional concealment or an unduly long delay after the first inventor's reduction to practice. Some cases excused the delay, and some did not. A few examples will illustrate the application of the statute:

* * *

IV.

The decisions applying section 102(g) balanced the law and policy favoring the first person to make an invention, against equitable considerations when more than one person had made the same invention: in each case where the court deprived the de facto first inventor of the right to the patent, the second inventor had entered the field during a period of either inactivity or deliberate concealment by the first inventor. * * *

In no case where the first inventor had waited "too long" did he end his period of inactivity before the second inventor appeared. We affirm the long-standing rule that too long a delay may bar the first inventor from reliance on an early reduction to practice in a priority contest. But we hold that the first inventor will not be barred from relying on later, resumed activity antedating an opponent's entry into the field, merely because the work done before the delay occurred was sufficient to amount to a reduction to practice.

This result furthers the basic purpose of the patent system. The exclusive right, constitutionally derived, was for the national purpose of advancing the useful arts—the process today called technological innovation. As implemented by the patent statute, the grant of the right to exclude carries the obligation to disclose the workings of the invention, thereby adding to the store of knowledge without diminishing the patent-supported incentive to innovate.

But the obligation to disclose is not the principal reason for a patent system; indeed, it is a rare invention that cannot be deciphered more readily from its commercial embodiment than from the printed patent. The reason for the patent system is to encourage innovation and its fruits: new jobs and new industries, new consumer goods and trade benefits. We must keep this purpose in plain view as we consider the consequences of interpretations of the patent law such as in the Board's decision.

A foreseeable consequence of the Board's ruling is to discourage inventors and their supporters from working on projects that had been "too long" set aside, because of the impossibility of relying, in a priority contest, on either their original work or their renewed work. This curious result is neither fair nor in the public interest. We do not see that the public interest is served by placing so severe a sanction on failure to file premature patent applications on immature inventions of unknown value. In reversing the Board's decision we do not hold that such inventions are necessarily entitled to the benefits of their earliest dates in a priority contest; we hold only that they are not barred from entitlement to their dates of renewed activity.

* * *

VI.

Having established the principle that Paulik, although not entitled to rely on his early work, is entitled to rely on his renewed activity, we vacate the decision of the Board and, in the interest of justice, remand to the PTO for new interference proceedings in accordance with this principle.

Vacated and Remanded.

8. INVENTIONS MADE ABROAD AND DERIVATION

JAMES B. CLOW & SONS, INC. v. UNITED STATES PIPE AND FOUNDRY CO.

United States Court of Appeals, Fifth Circuit, 1963.
313 F.2d 46, 136 USPQ 397.

BELL, CIRCUIT JUDGE. Appellant, defendant below, and appellee, plaintiff below, are large manufacturers of cast iron pressure pipe. Appellee sells a push-on joint under the trademark "Tyton-Joint" for use in joining pipe, while appellant sells a similar joint under the trademark "Bell-Tite" for the same use. This is an appeal from a judgment on a suit for patent infringement brought by appellee and entered in favor of appellee, owner of United States Letters Patent No. 2,953,398, holding claims 1, 2, 4, 5, 7, and 8 of that patent valid and infringed by the "Bell-Tite" joint of appellant.

The patent in suit relates to joints of the type used to connect sections of pipe made of metal, ceramic material, concrete, cement-asbestos, plastic and other compositions. The invention of the patent is a joint embodying a gasket holding means in the bell of a pipe, enabling the insertion of a spigot to effect a seal under radial compression. The seal is effected in spite of tolerances between the bell and spigot, and with the result that the pipe may be deflected or curved as it is being laid. The patent was issued to Haugen and Henrikson, employees of appellee, and assigned upon issuance to appellee.

* * *

Appellant contends that the patent in suit is invalid as not having been issued to the first inventor, and that it is also invalid as lacking invention over the prior art.

* * *

The question of whether the patent was issued to the first inventor depends in its entirety on circumstances having to do with the application of Yves Mathieu for a patent filed on May 25, 1956, three days ahead of the application for the patent in suit, with appellant relying— not on the three day priority—but on a Brazilian application filed there on July 25, 1955. Appellant claims priority under 35 U.S.C.A. § 119, based on the filing date in Brazil. The application for the patent in suit was filed on May 28, 1956 and the earliest date of the invention established for it on the trial was December 23, 1955. It is not disputed that Haugen and Henrikson were original inventors as distinguished from first inventors.

The position of appellant is that Mathieu was entitled to constructive reduction to practice under the statute as of the date on which he filed his application in Brazil, and resulting priority. An interference was set up in the Patent Office, 35 U.S.C.A. § 135, between the two applications regarding what is now Claim 5 of the patent in suit.

* * *

The interference was settled by appellee with Mathieu and his assignee under a lump sum arrangement which included the grant of licenses to appellee under other patents of the assignee. Mathieu and his assignee then filed a disclaimer of the subject matter in interference under Rule 262(a) of the Patent Office. Judgment of priority was thereafter awarded to Haugen and Henrikson, assignors of appellee, and the patent in suit, including Claim 5, issued to appellee. The application of Mathieu was later abandoned. * * *

There was evidence that the invention of the Brazilian application differed from what was embraced in Claim 5 of the patent in suit in that the gasket, differing in form, did not seal as a result of radial compression, and thus that application, so the argument went, could not have served as a basis for an earlier filing date under Sec. 119, supra, assuming that the American application made the same disclosure. That the American application read on Claim 5 would be the first step, but only the first step to set up the Brazilian filing date. The next and necessary step was to show that the Brazilian application was for the same invention. This was all in issue under the defense of the assignors of appellee not having been the first inventors, and there are no findings relative to this defense regarding the role of the Brazilian application or otherwise.

* * *

It is the position of appellee that this issue has been precluded by the disclaimer as well as by the abandonment of the Mathieu American application. But the question of who is a first inventor may not be conclusively settled between private parties. No third party is bound by such a settlement, and the patent that issues may be subjected to the question of priority by others. Congress made the public interest dominant in requiring that a patent issue only to the first inventor in fact—not the first inventor by arrangement or agreement. We are unfamiliar with any doctrine that would permit the vesting of the monopoly of a patent in such a manner. The philosophy of the patent law is to reward only the first and original inventor, and for a limited period only, as an incentive for the resulting public good obtained. Nor is it any answer to say that the application of Mathieu was abandoned. The question of who, in fact, was the first inventor remained to be raised on another day, as it was, notwithstanding the disclaimer or abandonment.

Appellant was entitled to prove, if it could, that the assignors of appellee were not the first inventors. This it sought to do by a defense in terms thusly couched, and by showing fraud. It failed to show fraud, but the other defense was not resolved and the case must be remanded for that limited purpose.

CTS CORPORATION v. PIHER INTERNATIONAL CORPORATION

United States Court of Appeals, Federal Circuit, 1984.
727 F.2d 1550, 221 USPQ 11.

KASHIWA, CIRCUIT JUDGE.

* * *

The district court, in its oral findings of fact and conclusions of law, held that Piher failed to meet its burden of proving by the greater weight of the evidence that the parties had entered into an understanding or agreement which was required to be filed and was not filed with the PTO prior to the termination of the interference. * * *

In determining the facts of this case, the district court, after hearing conflicting testimony, found that the evidence did not demonstrate a causal relationship between the settlement and the termination of the interference. * * *

35 U.S.C. § 135(c) was enacted to promote competition in the patent law area. As a means to prevent anti-competitive settlements between parties involved in patent interferences, any settlement agreements between parties must be filed with the PTO. Such agreements can therefore be reviewed by the Department of Justice's Antitrust Division by means of a "Civil Investigative Demand." *See generally United States v. FMC Corp.*, 717 F.2d 775, 777–78, 219 USPQ 761, 763–64 (3rd Cir.1983). The underlying motivation for the statute was clearly stated in the House Report. It stated:

> Recent experience has indicated that parties have sometimes used these interference proceedings in derogation of the public interest, in that interference settlement agreements have been entered into for the purpose of restricting competition. By requiring the filing of settlement agreements, the bill would make it more difficult for patent applicants and owners to use an interference settlement agreement as a means of secretly violating the antitrust law.

H.R.Rep. No. 1983, 87th Cong., 2d Sess. 1 (1962), U.S.Code Cong. & Admin.News 1962, 3286.

Section 135(c) requires that any agreement or understanding made in connection with or in contemplation of the termination of an interference must be filed with the PTO. *See Moog, Inc. v. Pegasus Laboratories, Inc.*, 376 F.Supp. 439, 444, 180 USPQ 4, 8 (E.D.Mich.1973), *aff'd*, 521 F.2d 501, 187 USPQ 279 (6th Cir.1975), *cert. denied*, 424 U.S. 968, 96 S.Ct. 1464, 47 L.Ed.2d 735 (1976) ("[A]ll agreements, whether initial or supplemental, with actual or potential anti-trust implications, must be filed in accordance with Section 135(c) or suffer the penalty of unenforceability."). Failure to file with the PTO renders such agreement or understanding and any patent involved in, or subsequently issued on an application involved in, the interference unenforceable.

The appellants argue that the district court misinterpreted section 135(c) and that the settlement agreements are clearly within the scope of the statute. Piher contends that the agreements were made in connection with or in contemplation of the termination and, as such, were the direct cause of the termination. Whereas the district court found there was no causal relationship between the agreements and the termination, the appellants contend otherwise. We disagree with the appellants.

We agree with the district court that, pursuant to section 135(c), there must be a causal relationship between the agreements and the termination of the interference. *See United States v. FMC Corp.,* 215 USPQ 43, 51–53 (E.D.Pa.1982), *rev'd on other grounds,* 717 F.2d 775, 219 USPQ 761 (3rd Cir.1983); *cf. Moog,* 521 F.2d at 506 ("The District Court was right in finding a causal relationship between the withholding [of an agreement] and the termination of the interference.").

* * *

Since the district court's findings of fact are not clearly erroneous and it did not abuse its discretion in denying the various motions, we affirm the district court's decision.

Affirmed.

HEDGEWICK v. AKERS

United States Court of Customs and Patent Appeals, 1974.
497 F.2d 905, 182 USPQ 167.

MILLER, JUDGE.

This appeal is from the decision of the Board of Patent Interferences awarding priority to appellee (Akers), the senior party, who is involved through application serial No. 710,032, filed March 4, 1968. Appellant (Hedgewick), the junior party, is involved through application serial No. 715,391, filed March 22, 1968. We affirm.

The interference concerns a safety package comprising a container and a cap which is disengageable therefrom by combined axial and rotative motion. Inasmuch as derivation is the only dispositive issue raised on appeal, further discussion of the invention is unnecessary except to note that it involves a relatively narrow difference from appellant's prior art Palm-N-Turn cap, the subject of his patent No. 3,344,942, issued October 3, 1967.

Hedgewick was president of International Tools Ltd. (ITL) of Windsor, Ontario, Canada, which is a subsidiary of ITL Industries. Reflex Corporation of Canada Ltd. (Reflex) is another subsidiary which was established for the production of the Palm-N-Turn cap. Reflex is assignee of the Palm-N-Turn patent and also of Hedgewick's present application.

Alternative constructions to the Palm-N-Turn cap were discussed and sketched among Hedgewick, McBride (an engineer for Reflex), and Morillo (manager of Reflex). The sketches, some of which satisfy the limitations of the two counts in interference, were kept in McBride's personal files in a cabinet in the engineering area at Reflex. Although employees of the engineering area had access to them, the files were dormant after January 1, 1967.

Because of Akers' experience with plastic closures and safety caps, he was hired by Hedgewick as a consultant for Reflex to design tooling for the Palm-N-Turn cap and to review production procedures, quality control, and other problems encountered in the Palm-N-Turn cap program. Akers was present on the premises of ITL and Reflex at various times from January to August, 1967, and had access to McBride's "dormant" files. McBride, Morillo, and another employee were instructed not to withhold any information from Akers, but, on the other hand, no instruction was given to directly reveal anything to him. Morillo testified that he showed sketches to Akers of alternative cap constructions to the Palm-N-Turn cap, some of which satisfy the limitations of count 1. However, he could not produce any of the sketches and could not recall anyone else who saw them.

Akers testified that he did not recall seeing or discussing the contents of any of the documents introduced by Hedgewick prior to the interference; that he paid no attention to sketches, such as those allegedly shown him by Morillo, because they were not drawn to scale and did not show the locking action of the container and cap; and that he did not recall seeing any of the sketches allegedly shown him by Morillo, although he conceded that anything was possible.

Akers testified that subsequent to his employment at Reflex he conceived his invention, as evidenced by various corroborated engineering drawings. Akers' cap, as conceived and constructively reduced to practice, differs in form and design from the cap covered by Hedgewick's application, although the functioning of the essential elements is the same.

OPINION

As noted above, the only dispositive issue is derivation. In considering this issue, we point out that evidence of activity, knowledge or use concerning an invention in a foreign country is not precluded by 35 U.S.C.A. § 104 in establishing derivation. That section merely provides:

> In proceedings in the Patent Office and in the courts, an applicant for a patent, or a patentee, may not establish a *date of invention* by reference to knowledge or use thereof, or other activity with respect thereto, in a foreign country, except as provided in section 119 of this title. [Emphasis supplied.]

Evidence of derivation has to do with origin of the invention—not date of invention. See In re Krank, 438 F.2d 609, 58 CCPA 976 (1971). As stated in Federico, Commentary on the New Patent Act, 35 U.S.C.A., page 24:

It should be noted that proof of acts abroad is not barred when the object is not to establish a date of invention, that is when the object is not to antedate a printed publication or public use or the date of invention of another; in a case where an applicant for patent, in an interference, is trying to show that the adverse party was not an inventor at all but derived the invention from him, the fact that the events took place in a foreign country would be immaterial.

The legislative history of 35 U.S.C.A. § 104 confirms this analysis. The predecessor statute (35 U.S.C.A. § 109, § 9 of the Boykin Act, P.L. 690, 60 Stat. 940 (1946)) was enacted to eliminate the anomalous situation resulting from Electric Storage Battery Co. v. Shimadzu, 307 U.S. 5, 59 S.Ct. 675, 83 L.Ed. 1071 (1939). As a result of the decision in that case, evidence of activity abroad was admissible for the purpose of proving a patentee's date of invention in a patent infringement case in which the alleged infringer sought to defend on the ground of public knowledge or use prior to the patentee's date of invention; whereas as the Supreme Court pointed out, in an interference proceeding, such evidence was not admissible.

Thus, the testimony presented on behalf of Hedgewick relating to acts, knowledge, or use of the invention in Canada was admissible for the purpose of the derivation issue. Although Hedgewick himself did not testify, his testimony would have been relevant and admissible for this purpose.

The issue of derivation is one of fact, and the party asserting derivation has the burden of proof. Beall v. Ormsby, 154 F.2d 663, 33 CCPA 959 (1946). That burden is independent of the senior or junior party status of the parties. Fritz v. Hawn, 37 F.2d 430, 17 CCPA 796 (1930). Derivation is shown by a prior, complete conception of the claimed subject matter and communication of the complete conception to the party charged with derivation. Egnot v. Looker, 387 F.2d 680, 55 CCPA 782 (1967); MacMillan v. Moffett, 432 F.2d 1237, 58 CCPA 792 (1970). Communication of a complete conception must be sufficient to enable one of ordinary skill in the art to construct and successfully operate the invention. Agawam Co. v. Jordan, 74 U.S. (7 Wall.) 583, 19 L.Ed. 177 (1869); DeGroff v. Roth, supra. All the circumstances in the record must be considered in evaluating the sufficiency of the communication. Bartsch v. Baker, 134 F.2d 487, 30 CCPA 919 (1942).

It should be emphasized that mere proof of motive and opportunity (e.g. access) is not sufficient to carry the burden of proving derivation. Rider v. Griffith, 154 F.2d 193, 33 CCPA 884 (1946). Under the proper circumstances, differences between the embodiments of the parties may demonstrate that their inventions were independently made. St. Pierre v. Harvey, 233 F.2d 337, 43 CCPA 918 (1956).

The board held that Hedgewick failed to satisfy his burden of proving that sufficient information was communicated to Akers to constitute a complete conception, bearing in mind the narrow difference between the invention and the prior art Palm-N-Turn cap. For this purpose, it assumed, without deciding, that Hedgewick possessed the necessary complete conception prior to the alleged disclosure to Akers.

That Akers had access to the files in the engineering area is, without more, insufficient to establish derivation. Any inference of derivation that could possibly arise from such access is dispelled by the differences in form and design between the embodiments of the parties. Morillo's alleged communication of sketches of the invention to Akers is uncorroborated and was, for all practical purposes, denied by Akers.

In view of the foregoing, we conclude that the board correctly held that Hedgewick failed to meet his burden of proof on the derivation issue.

D. NOVELTY AND PRIOR ART

1. INTRODUCTION

As previously noted, the earliest known patent statutes limited patent protection to those inventions which were "new" or "novel". The English Statute of James I limited patent protection to the "sole working or making of any manner of *new* manufacture within this realm." The first United States Patent Act of 1790 limited patent protection to inventions which were "not before known or used" anywhere. The Patent Act of 1793 limited patent protection to any "*new* and useful art, machine, manufacture, or composition of matter, or any *new* and useful improvement" thereof "not known or used before the application" for patent, and provided that the courts of the United States could declare any issued patent void if the invention "had been in use, or had been described in some public work anterior to the supposed discovery of the patentee."

The basic requirement that a patentable invention be "new" or novel is now set forth in 35 U.S.C.A. § 101 and qualified and limited in § 102.

The Patent Act of 1836 limited patent protection to inventions "not know or used by others" before the applicant's discovery or invention thereof, not "described in some public work anterior to the supposed discovery thereof by the patentee", and not "in public use or on sale with the consent and allowance of the patentee before his application for a patent." The Patent Act of 1836 also provided that a patent shall not be void on account of the invention "having been before known or used in any foreign country, it not appearing that the same or any substantial part thereof had before been patented or described in any printed publication." Thus, the Patent Act of 1836 limited invalidating prior knowledge or use to that within the geographical boundaries of the United States. The substance of the provisions of the Patent Act of 1836 relating to the requirement that a patentable invention be new or "novel" at the time the invention is made, was embodied in subsequent patent acts and is now contained in 35 U.S.C.A. § 102(a).

The Patent Acts of 1790 and 1793 were interpreted as precluding patent protection if an invention was not new or novel (a) when the invention was made and (b) when an application for patent was filed. The requirement of novelty when the application was filed is often referred to as a statutory bar. The Patent Act of 1839 changed the time of the statutory bar to more than two years before filing an application, and, in 1939, the time was changed to more than one year before filing. The present statutory bar is embodied in 35 U.S.C.A. § 102(b) which is discussed in the next section of this textbook.

In none of the United States Patent Acts has Congress ever formulated a definition of novelty, and hence, there has developed a common law or judicial definition of the novelty requirement of the patent statutes. As is to be expected, there is a lack of uniformity in the judicial interpretations of the novelty requirement. Some courts define novelty as requiring that the invention be new in the sense that the same thing has not been previously known, while other courts use the term in referring to the quality of the difference between the new invention and what was previously known or used before, i.e., as a reference to what is now the non-obvious subject matter requirement of 35 U.S.C.A. § 103. Some courts have used the terms "patentable novelty" and "invention" to refer to the nonobviousness requirement. Likewise, some courts have used the term "anticipation" to refer to the nonobviousness requirement while other courts have used the terms "anticipation" and "complete anticipation" to refer to novelty in the first sense of being simply new or different from prior inventions. For example, the Court in Westinghouse Electric Corp. v. Bulldog Electric Products Co., 106 F.Supp. 819, 876 (N.D.W.Va.1952) observed: "In order to anticipate and find invalid a patent for want of invention, it is not necessary that a complete anticipation be found in a single prior patent." Thus, it is usually necessary to consider the precise context in which these terms are used by a particular court in order to determine their meaning. This is particularly true of cases which were decided under the predecessors to the 1952 Patent Act because prior to 1952 there was no express statutory requirement of nonobvious subject matter as one of the conditions for patentability.

There is an apparent split of case authority as to whether prior references and devices can be combined to negate the novelty of an invention or whether all of the elements of the invention must be disclosed within the four corners of a single reference or by a single device. Most of the cases cited as support for combining references and devices to negate novelty actually refer to combining references and devices for "anticipation". When read in context, it is evident that "anticipation" is used in these cases in the sense of the nonobviousness requirement of what is now 35 U.S.C.A. § 103. It has always been permissible to combine prior references and devices to demonstrate nonobviousness. Therefore, this split or contradiction in case authority is more apparent than real.

The definite trend of the cases decided under the 1952 Patent Act is that to negate novelty, the invention must be disclosed within the four corners of a single reference or by a single device. Under this Patent Act, prior references and devices are usually combined only under 35 U.S.C.A. § 103 in applying the nonobvious subject matter test.

Section 102 defines both a variety of acts resulting in loss of the right to a patent and what is prior art for applying the novelty and non-obviousness tests in determining the patentability of an invention.

As in earlier statutes, 35 U.S.C.A. § 102(a) generally prescribes the place of origination, types and forms of documents and things which can be relied on as evidence tending to negate novelty and nonobviousness and requires that such documents and things be in existence before the creation of the invention under consideration. Judicial interpretations as to which documents and things are within the scope of this section of the statute have varied to fit the exigencies of the particular case according to the conviction of the court as to what will best "promote the progress of * * * useful arts" and thus the public interest.

---

§ 102. Conditions for Patentability; Novelty and Loss of Right to Patent

A person shall be entitled to a patent unless—

(a) the invention was known or used by others in this country, or patented or described in a printed publication in this or a foreign country, before the invention thereof by the applicant for patent, or

(b) the invention was patented or described in a printed publication in this or a foreign country or in public use or on sale in this country, more than one year prior to the date of the application for patent in the United States, or

applied against inventor — S/L

(c) he has abandoned the invention, or

(d) the invention was first patented or caused to be patented, or was the subject of an inventor's certificate, by the applicant or his legal representatives or assigns in a foreign country prior to the date of the application for patent in this country on an application for patent or inventor's certificate filed more than twelve months before the filing of the application in the United States, or

(e) the invention was described in a patent granted on an application for patent by another filed in the United States before the invention thereof by the applicant for patent, or on an international application by another who has fulfilled the requirements of paragraphs (1), (2), and (4) of section 371(c) of this title before the invention thereof by the applicant for patent, or

(f) he did not himself invent the subject matter sought to be patented, or

(g) before the applicant's invention thereof the invention was made in this country by another who had not abandoned, suppressed, or concealed it. In determining priority of invention there shall be considered not only the respective dates of conception and reduction to practice of the invention, but also the reasonable diligence of one who was first to conceive and last to reduce to practice, from a time prior to conception by the other.

KALMAN v. KIMBERLY–CLARK CORPORATION

United States Court of Appeals, Federal Circuit, 1983.
713 F.2d 760, 218 USPQ 781.

RICH, CIRCUIT JUDGE.

This appeal is from the September 17, 1982, judgment of the District Court for the Eastern District of Wisconsin, sitting without a jury, holding claims 1, 3, 15, 18, 20, 23, and 25 of appellee Kalman's U.S. Patent No. 3,471,017, issued October 7, 1969, entitled "Filtering Process and Apparatus," valid and infringed by appellant Kimberly-Clark Corp. ("KC"). 561 F.Supp. 628. We affirm.

The Kalman patent describes and claims a process and apparatus for filtering a heat-softened substance, for example, a thermoplastic, by introducing a filter ribbon across a passage through which the substance flows. * * *

The principal prior art reference relied upon, which is not listed in the Kalman patent, is U.S. Patent No. 3,112,525, issued December 3, 1963, to Moziek for an "Apparatus for Extruding Thermoplastic Material." The patent describes an extrusion device that utilizes single slidable cartridge filter assemblies each of which consists of a perforated screen holder, a screen, and a ribbed screen retainer. The filter is said to be changed without interrupting extrusion, but changing is done by opening valve means located on either side of the filter receiving passage and inserting a fresh filter cartridge, which pushes the clogged filter cartridge out through the opposite valve means. * * *

KC's principal argument is that the Kalman invention, as defined in the claims in suit, is anticipated by Moziek * * *

A party asserting that a patent claim is anticipated under 35 U.S.C. § 102 must demonstrate, among other things, identity of invention. In cases like this, identity of invention is a question of fact, *e.g.,* *Coupe v. Royer,* supra, 155 U.S. at 578–79, 15 S.Ct. at 204–05, and one who seeks such a finding must show that each element of the claim in issue is found, either expressly described or under principles of inherency, in a single prior art reference, or that the claimed invention was previously known or embodied in a single prior art device or practice. Preliminary to this determination, of course, is construction of the claims to determine their meaning in light of the specification and prosecution history, which construction is a matter of law for the court.

Although the claims make no mention of continuous movement of the filter, the district court distinguished the claimed invention from Moziek on the basis that that reference

* * * discloses a variation on the screen changer method of filtering plastic. It does not call for continuous movement of the filter; rather, as in screen changers, the change is done all at once—that is, an entire new filter is placed across the flow.

The court continued:

Although Moziek teaches that the valves can be cooled to prevent leakage, the theory of the cooling is different from that in the Kalman patent. In Moziek, leakage is primarily prevented by using closely fitting metal parts. The cooling helps prevent leakage past the valves. This is vastly different from relying on the plastic itself, as in Kalman, to form plugs.

Accordingly, after consideration of the Kalman and Moziek *inventions,* the district court concluded that "The Moziek patent falls far short of anticipating the Kalman *patent,*" for the reason that "Moziek, as written, does not *teach* what Kalman does." (Emphasis ours.) Citing *Illinois Tool Works, Inc. v. Sweetheart Plastics, Inc.,* 436 F.2d 1180, 1182–83 (7th Cir.1971), the district court had previously emphasized that "To be an anticipation a prior patent must include all the teachings necessary to accomplish what the allegedly invalid *patent* succeeds in doing." (Emphasis ours.)

This was a somewhat incorrect analysis of the law of anticipation, which requires that a distinction be made between the invention described or taught and the invention claimed. The law of anticipation does not require that the reference "teach" what the subject patent teaches. Assuming that a reference is properly "prior art," it is only necessary that the claims under attack, as construed by the court, "read on" something disclosed in the reference, i.e., all limitations of the claim are found in the reference, or "fully met" by it.

While the court erred in stating that Moziek must, to anticipate, disclose the same invention as that *described* by Kalman, it still found that one element of the *claimed* invention was not disclosed in Moziek, which is enough. The court concluded that "Moziek makes no provision for a band or ribbon or any length of filter." KC has not persuaded us that this finding was erroneous. Our study of the Moziek patent confirms it.

* * * Given the district court's summary judgment conclusion on the interpretation of "band or ribbon," we are unable to find clear error in the court's decision that KC did not sustain its burden of demonstrating anticipation.

* * *

TITANIUM METALS CORPORATION OF AMERICA v. BANNER

United States Court of Appeals, Federal Circuit, 1985.
778 F.2d 775, 227 USPQ 773.

RICH, CIRCUIT JUDGE.

* * *

We are left in no doubt that the court was impressed by the totality of the evidence that the applicants for patent had discovered or invented and disclosed knowledge which is not to be found in the reference, nor do we have any doubt about that ourselves. But those facts are beside the point. The patent law imposes certain fundamental conditions for patentability, paramount among them being the condition that what is sought to be patented, as determined by the claims, be new. The basic provision of Title 35 applicable here is § 101, providing in relevant part: "Whoever invents or discovers any *new* * * * composition of matter, or any *new* * * * improvement thereof, may obtain a patent therefor, subject to the conditions and requirements of this title." (Emphasis ours.) The title of the application here involved is "Titanium Alloy," a composition of matter. Surprisingly, in all of the evidence, nobody discussed the key issue of whether the alloy was new, which is the essence of the anticipation issue, including the expert Dr. Williams. * * *

Section 102, the usual basis for rejection for lack of novelty or anticipation, lays down certain principles for determining the novelty required by § 101, among which are the provisions in § 102(a) and (b) that the claimed invention has *not* been "described in a printed publication in this or a foreign country," either (a) before the invention by the applicant or (b) more than one year before the application date to which he is entitled (strictly a "loss of right" provision similar to novelty). Either provision applies in this case, the Russian article having a date some 5 years prior to the filing date and its status as "prior art" not being questioned. The PTO was never specific as to what part of § 102 applies, merely rejecting on § 102. The question, therefore, is whether claims 1 and 2 encompass and, if allowed, would enable plaintiff-appellee to exclude others from making, using, or selling an alloy *described* in the Russian article. *See* 35 U.S.C. § 154. *Kalman v. Kimberly-Clark Corp.,* 713 F.2d 760, 218 USPQ 781 (Fed.Cir.1983).

To answer the question we need only turn to the affidavit of James A. Hall, a metallurgist employed by appellee's TIMET Division, who undertook to analyze the Russian article disclosure by calculating the ingredient percentages shown in the graph data points, which he presented in tabular form. There are 15 items in his table. The second item shows a titanium base alloy containing 0.25% by weight Mo and 0.75% Ni and this is squarely within the ranges of 0.2–0.4% Mo and 0.6–0.9% Ni of claims 1 and 2. As to that disclosed alloy of the prior art, there can be no question that claims 1 and 2 read on it and would be infringed by anyone making, using, or selling it. Therefore, *the statute prohibits* a patent containing them. This seems to be a case either of not adequately considering the novelty requirement of the statute, the true meaning of the correlative term "anticipation," or the meaning of the claims.

*   *   *

As we read the situation, the court was misled by the arguments and evidence to the effect that the inventors here found out and disclosed in their application many things that one cannot learn from reading the Russian article and that this was sufficient in law to justify granting them a patent for their contributions—such things as what good corrosion resistance the claimed alloys have against hot brine, which possibly was not known, and the range limits of the Ni and Mo content, outside of which that resistance diminishes, which are teachings of very useful information. These things the applicants teach the art and the Russian article does not. Indeed, appellee's counsel argued in his opening statement to the trial court that the PTO's refusal of a patent was "directly contrary to the requirement of Article I, Section 8, of the Constitution," which authorizes Congress to create a patent law. But throughout the trial counsel never came to grips with the real issues: (1) what do the claims cover and (2) is what they cover new? Under the laws Congress wrote, they must be considered. Congress has not seen fit to permit the patenting of an old alloy, known to others through a printed publication, by one who has discovered its corrosion resistance or other useful properties, or has found out to what extent one can modify the composition of the alloy without losing such properties.

*   *   *

The trial court and appellee have relied on *In re Wilder,* supra, but they have both failed to note those portions of that opinion most relevant to the present case. The issue there, as here, was anticipation of certain claims. Wilder argued "that even though there may be a technical anticipation, the discovery of the new property and the recitation of this property in the claims 'lends patentable novelty' to the claims." The court answered:

> However, recitation, in a claim to a composition, of a particular property said to be possessed by the recited composition, be that property newly-discovered or not, does not necessarily change the scope of the subject matter otherwise defined by that claim. [429 F.2d at 450, 57 C.C.P.A. 1314, 166 UPSQ at 548.]

The court in that case also said:

> [W]e start with the proposition that claims cannot be obtained to that which is not new. This was the basis of the holding in *In re Thuau* [135 F.2d 344, 30 C.C.P.A. 979, 57 USPQ 324 (CCPA 1943)]. It was the law then, is now and will be until Congress decrees otherwise. [Id.]

It is also an elementary principle of patent law that when, as by a recitation of ranges or otherwise, a claim covers several compositions, the claim is "anticipated" if *one* of them is in the prior art. *In re Petering,* 301 F.2d 676, 682, 49 C.C.P.A. 993, 1001, 133 USPQ 275, 280 (1962).

For all of the foregoing reasons, the court below committed clear error and legal error in authorizing the issuance of a patent on claims 1 and 2 since, properly construed, they are anticipated under § 102 by the Russian article which admittedly discloses an alloy on which these claims read.

* * *

2. KNOWN OR USED BY OTHERS IN THIS COUNTRY

GAYLER v. WILDER

Supreme Court of the United States, 1850.
51 U.S. (10 How.) 477, 491, 495, 13 L.Ed. 504, 512.

[The patent in suit was issued to Fitzgerald in 1843 for fireproof chests or safes in which plaster of paris was used in the construction of the walls thereof. The Circuit Court held the patent valid and a majority of the Supreme Court affirmed in an opinion by Chief Justice Taney.]

* * *

The remaining question is upon the validity of the patent on which the suit was brought.

It appears that James Conner, who carried on the business of a stereotype founder in the City of New York, made a safe for his own use between the years 1829 and 1832, for the protection of his papers against fire; and continued to use it until 1838, when it passed into other hands. It was kept in his counting-room and known to the persons engaged in the foundry; and after it passed out of his hands, he used others of a different construction.

It does not appear what became of this safe afterwards. And there is nothing in the testimony from which it can be inferred that its mode of construction was known to the person into whose possession it fell, or that any value was attached to it as a place of security for papers against fire; or that it was ever used for that purpose.

Upon these facts the court instructed the jury, "that if Conner had not made his discovery public, but had used it simply for his own private purpose, and it had been finally forgotten or abandoned, such a discovery and use would be no obstacle to the taking out of a patent by Fitzgerald or those claiming under him, if he be an original, though not the first, inventor or discoverer.

The instruction assumes that the jury might find from the evidence that Conner's safe was substantially the same with that of Fitzgerald, and also prior in time. And if the fact was so, the question then was whether the patentee was "the original or first inventor or discoverer," within the meaning of the act of Congress.

The Act of 1836, ch. 357, sec. 6, authorizes a patent where the party has discovered or invented a new and useful improvement, "not known or used by others before his discovery or invention." And the 15th section provides that, if it appears on the trial of an action brought for the infringement of a patent that the patentee "was not the original and first inventor or discoverer of the thing patented," the verdict shall be for the defendant.

Upon a literal construction of these particular words, the patentee in this case certainly was not the original and first inventor or discoverer, if the Conner safe was the same with his, and preceded his discovery.

But we do not think that this construction would carry into effect the intention of the Legislature. It is not by detached words and phrases that a statute ought to be expounded. The whole act must be taken together, and a fair interpretation given to it, neither extending nor restricting it beyond the legitimate import of its language, and its obvious policy and object. And in the 15th section, after making the provision above mentioned, there is a further provision, that, if it shall appear that the patentee at the time of his application for the patent believed himself to be the first inventor, the patent shall not be void on account of the invention or discovery having been known or used in any foreign country, it not appearing that it had been before patented or described in any printed publication.

In the case thus provided for, the party who invents is not, strictly speaking, the first and original inventor. The law assumes that the improvement may have been known and used before his discovery. Yet his patent is valid if he discovered it by the efforts of his own genius, and believed himself to be the original inventor. The clause in question qualifies the words before used, and shows that by knowledge and use the Legislature meant knowledge and use existing in a manner accessible to the public. If the foreign invention had been printed or patented, it was already given to the world and open to the people of this country, as well as of others, upon reasonable inquiry. They would therefore derive no advantage from the invention here. It would confer no benefit upon the community, and the inventor therefore is not considered to be entitled to the reward. But if the foreign discovery is not patented, nor described in any printed publication it might be known and used in remote places for ages, and the people of this country be unable to profit by it. The means of obtaining knowledge would not be within their reach; and, as far as their interest is concerned, it would be the same thing as if the improvement had never been discovered. It is the inventor here that brings it to them, and places it in their possession. And as he does this by the effort of his own genius, the law regards him as the first and original inventor, and protects his patent, although the improvement had in fact been invented before, and used by others.

So, too as to the lost arts. It is well known that centuries ago discoveries were made in certain arts the fruits of which have come down to us, but the means by which the work was accomplished are at this day unknown. The knowledge has been lost for ages. Yet it would hardly be doubted, if anyone now discovered an art thus lost, and it was a useful improvement, that, upon a fair construction of the act of Congress, he would be entitled to a patent. Yet he would not literally be the first and original inventor. But he would be the first to confer on the public the benefit of the invention. He would discover what is unknown, and communicate knowledge which the public had not the means of obtaining without his invention.

Upon the same principle and upon the same rule of construction, we think that Fitzgerald must be regarded as the first and original inventor of the safe in question. * * *

COFFIN v. OGDEN

Supreme Court of the United States, 1873.
85 U.S. (18 Wall.) 120, 21 L.Ed. 821.

Mr. Justice Swayne stated the case, recited the evidence, and delivered the opinion of the court.

The appellant was the complainant in the court below, and filed this bill to enjoin the defendants from infringing the patent upon which the bill is founded. The patent is for a door lock with a latch reversible, so that the lock can be applied to doors opening either to the right or the left hand. It was granted originally on the 11th of June, 1861, to Charles R. Miller, assignee of William S. Kirkham, and reissued to Miller on the 27th of January, 1863.

* * * The answer alleges that the thing patented, or a material and substantial part thereof, had been, prior to the supposed invention thereof by Kirkham, known and used by divers persons in the United States, and that among them were Barthol Erbe, residing at Birmingham, near Pittsburg, and Andrew Patterson, Henry Masta, and Bernard Brossi, residing at Pittsburg, and that all these persons had such knowledge at Pittsburg. The appellees insist that Erbe was the prior inventor, and that this priority is fatal to the patent. This proposition, in its aspects of fact and of law, is the only one which we have found it necessary to consider.

Kirkham made his invention in March, 1861. This is clearly shown by the testimony, and there is no controversy between the parties on the subject.

It is equally clear that Erbe made his invention not later than January 1st, 1861. This was not controverted by the counsel for the appellant; but it was insisted that the facts touching that invention were not such as to make it available to the appellees, as against the later invention of Kirkham and the patent founded upon it. This renders it necessary to examine carefully the testimony upon the subject.

Erbe's deposition was taken at Pittsburg upon interrogatories agreed upon by the parties and sent out from New York. He made the lock marked H.E. (It is the exhibit of the appellees, so marked.) He made the first lock like it in the latter part of the year 1860. He made three such before he made the exhibit lock. The first he gave to Jones, Wallingford & Co. The second he sent to Washington, when he applied for a patent. The third he made for a friend of Jones. He thinks the lock he gave to Jones, Wallingford & Co. was applied to a door, but is not certain.

Brossi [another witness.] In 1860, he was engaged in lockmaking for the Jones & Nimmick Manufacturing Company. He had known Erbe about seventeen years. In 1860 Erbe was foreman in the lockshop of Jones, Wallingford & Co. at Pittsburg. In that year, and before the 1st of January, 1861, he went to Erbe's house. Erbe there showed him a lock, and how it worked so that it could be used right or left. * * * He had then been a lockmaker eight years. He examined the lock carefully. He had never seen a reversible lock before. He has examined the exhibit lock. It is the same in construction. The only difference is, that the original lock was made of rough wrought iron. It was a complete lock, and capable of working. Erbe thought it a great thing. Erbe showed him the lock twice afterwards at Jones, Wallingford & Co. He saw such a lock attached to the office door there and working, but didn't know whether it was the first lock made or one made afterwards.

* * *

There is no proof that Erbe made any locks according to his invention here in question but those mentioned in his testimony. He applied for a patent in 1864, and failed to get it. Why, is not disclosed in the record.

The appellants called no witnesses at Pittsburg or elsewhere to contradict or impeach those for the appellees. * * *

We entertain no doubt that the testimony of all these witnesses is true in every particular, including the statement of Brossi as to putting the lock on the door. * * *

The case arose while the Patent Act of 1836 was in force, and must be decided under its provisions. The sixth section of that act requires that to entitle the applicant to a patent, his invention or discovery must be one "not known or used by others before his invention or discovery thereof." The fifteenth section allowed a party sued for infringement to prove, among other defences, that the patentee "was not the original and first inventor of the thing patented, or of a substantial and material part thereof claimed to be new."

The whole act is to be taken together and construed in the light of the context. The meaning of these sections must be sought in the import of their language, and in the object and policy of the legislature in enacting them. The invention or discovery relied upon as a defence, must have been complete, and capable of producing the result sought to be accomplished; and this must be shown by the defendant. The burden of proof rests upon him, and every reasonable doubt should be resolved against him. If the thing were embryotic or inchoate; if it rested in speculation or experiment; if the process pursued for its development had failed to reach the point of consummation, it cannot avail to defeat a patent founded upon a discovery or invention which was completed, while in the other case there was only progress, however near that progress may have approximated to the end in view. The law requires not conjecture, but certainty. If the question relate to a machine, the conception must have been clothed in substantial forms which demonstrate at once its practical efficacy and utility. The prior knowledge and use by a single person is sufficient. The number is immaterial. Until his work *is done,* the inventor has given nothing to the public.

* * *

Here it is abundantly proved that the lock originally made by Erbe "was complete and capable of working." The priority of Erbe's invention is clearly shown. It was known at the time to at least five persons, including Jones, and probably to many others in the shop where Erbe worked; and the lock was put in use, being applied to a door, as proved by Brossi. It was thus tested and shown to be successful. These facts bring the case made by the appellees within the severest legal tests which can be applied to them. The defence relied upon is fully made out.

Decree affirmed.

WESTINGHOUSE MACHINE CO. ET AL. v. GENERAL ELEC. CO. ET AL.

United States Court of Appeals, Second Circuit, 1913.
207 Fed. 75.

LACOMBE, CIRCUIT JUDGE. This case grows out of an interference in the Patent Office entitled De Kando v. Armstrong, which was decided adversely to De Kando, and his assignee, the Westinghouse Machine Company. The interference was between an application of De Kando filed July 3, 1906, and a patent to defendant Armstrong No. 811,758, dated February 6, 1906, on an application filed June 28, 1905.

Quoting from the opinion below the facts there found are:

"(1) That De Kando actually made his invention in a foreign country and reduced it to actual practice and put it in actual use, prior to the spring of 1904 on the Valtellina Railway in Italy.

"(2) It was therefore an invention which could be and was seen, understood, and known to be practical. There was not only the patentable conception but the idea of means and means.

"(3) That on March, 1904, Waterman went from the United States to Europe and met De Kando at Budapest, where the details of the invention were explained to him, and then, proceeding to Italy, Waterman saw the invention in actual use. In addition De Kando then furnished Waterman with an elaborate written description of the invention.

"(4) It appears from the evidence that Waterman was learned and skilled and fully capable of fully understanding and that he did understand the invention.

"(5) Waterman therefore 'knew' that the invention had been conceived and actually made and reduced to actual and successful practice.

"(6) That Waterman not only brought the information he had gained in Europe with him to the United States, when he arrived May 5, 1904, but also the said written description of such invention and notes which he had made relating to such invention while in Europe.

"(7) That Waterman made a written report as to this invention to Stillwell June 7, 1904, and during the year following he described same in the United States to a number of electrical engineers of standing, all capable of understanding same, and June 19, 1905, Waterman explained the invention to the American Institute of Electrical Engineers in the United States.

"(8) Prior to 1901 or 1902 Armstrong had conceived the same invention and in * * * June, 1905, he filed his application for a patent. There is no claim or pretense that Armstrong exercised reasonable diligence, or any diligence, or that he made any effort whatever to reduce his invention to practice prior to filing his application for a patent."

Defendants, it may be noted, especially controvert the findings 3, as to what Waterman saw in Italy, and 8, as to the date of Armstrong's conception and the measure of his diligence. Waterman was an eminent electrician who went abroad to inform himself as to De Kando's invention on behalf of parties here who contemplated buying it. The testimony warrants a further finding of fact which complainant suggests, viz., that:

"(9) The knowledge of De Kando's invention and its use abroad was communicated by De Kando to Waterman for the specific purpose of introducing such knowledge into the United States and of having the invention put into use in the United States."

Whatever other questions there are in the case, and many have been argued, it is manifest that the fundamental and crucial one is whether upon the facts shown Armstrong was entitled to the grant of his patent; it not being disputed that his invention and De Kando's are substantially the same, nor that the invention of each was made independently of any knowledge of the other's. If Armstrong's patent was properly issued, that ends the cause. The question thus presented involves the construction of two sections of the United States Revised Statutes, which have been frequently before the courts:

"Sec. 4886. Any person who has invented or discovered any new and useful art, machine, manufacture, or composition of matter, or any new and useful improvements thereof, not known or used by others in this country, before his invention or discovery thereof, and not patented or described in any printed publication in this or any foreign country, before his invention or discovery thereof, or more than two years prior to his application, and not in public use or on sale in this country for more than two years prior to his application, unless the same is proved to have been abandoned, may, upon payment of the fees required by law, and other due proceedings had, obtain a patent therefor."

"Sec. 4923. Whenever it appears that a patentee, at the time of making his application for the patent, believed himself to be the original and first inventor or discoverer of the thing patented, the same shall not be held to be void on account of the invention or discovery, or any part thereof, having been known or used in a foreign country, before his invention or discovery thereof, if it had not been patented or described in a printed publication." U.S.Comp.St.1901, pp. 3382, 3396.

The proposition of law for which complainants contend is that De Kando's date of invention in this country is May, 1904, when Waterman, arriving here with knowledge of the completed invention, disclosed that knowledge to others here skilled in the art capable of understanding the same. That by reason of his knowledge and disclosures to others in this country prior to June 28, 1905, the invention was "known" in the legal sense in this country before Armstrong's application was filed. This proposition has been discussed at great length in the opinions of the two judicial tribunals which have had to do with this case; we are inclined to affirm on the opinion of the Court of Appeals of the District of Columbia, which, in substance, holds that, for the purpose of defeating a patent application, reduction to practice in a foreign country is a nullity unless the invention is patented or described in a printed publication.

If section 4886 stood alone, we might be inclined to the conclusion that upon this record Armstrong was not entitled to a patent because although, prior to his date, his art or machine had not been used here, it was known by others in this country. A machine is certainly knowable when its various component parts are brought together and, cooperating with each other, function successfully. De Kando's device was knowable in this sense when it was installed in Italy. It would become known to any competent person who examined it, saw what its component parts were and what function it performed. Waterman, upon the facts as found above, acquired that knowledge and he carried his knowledge with him wherever he went. When he was here he was a person in this country by whom the De Kando device was known. And when he imparted his knowledge to others here they also became persons in this country by whom the De Kando device was known. Considering this section only, it might seem to make little difference where the knowable machine be located, provided the persons who know it are themselves in this country.

But the Patent Law is contained in many sections, and they must be construed together to get at the precise code which they set forth. Section 4886 states generally the conditions which must exist in order to entitle an inventor to the grant of a patent. Section 4923 deals specifically with the effect of knowledge and use in a foreign country, and it makes no distinction whether such use is made or such knowledge is acquired by persons who, after using the thing or acquiring the knowledge, remain abroad or come here. This section (4923) provides that the patent taken out by an applicant for the same thing here shall not be void on account of such knowledge or use unless the invention had been patented or described in a printed publication. As we construe this section, reduction to practice in a foreign country can never operate to destroy a patent applied for here, however widely known such reduction to practice may be, either among foreigners or among persons living here, unless the invention be patented or described in a printed publication. To that extent section 4923 qualifies the language of section 4886, which without such qualification might well lead to a different result.

The decree is affirmed, with costs.

JOSEPH BANCROFT & SONS CO. v. BREWSTER FINISHING CO.

United States District Court of New Jersey, 1953.
113 F.Supp. 714, 98 USPQ 187, aff'd 210 F.2d 677 (1954).

[Excerpt Only]

According to this section, an application in a foreign country does not suffice to establish priority of invention over a United States application. The foreign patent must have issued or a description published. The wording is clear. There is nothing in the legislative history of the Act that indicates any intention other than the plain meaning of that section. In fact, Mr. Lanham's Report on the Bill for the Committee on Patents recorded in U.S. Code Congressional Service, 79th Congress, Second Session 1946, page 1498, states:

> "* * * It is deemed preferable to refuse evidence of foreign activities; *not published or patented,* in all cases, as this is the greater convenience in trials and other proceedings held in this country. It is pointed out in the hearings that this change is more in line with foreign laws, since foreign countries pay no attention to acts done outside of their own borders." (Emphasis Supplied.)

APPLICATION OF BORST

United States Court of Customs and Patent Appeals, 1965.
52 CCPA 1398, 345 F.2d 851, 145 USPQ 554.

SMITH, JUDGE. The invention for which appellant seeks a patent comprises means for safely and effectively controlling a relatively large neutron output by varying a small and easily controlled neutron input source. The application, serial No. 654,837, filed April 24, 1957, is aptly titled "Neutron Amplifier."

* * *

Appellant asserts that the claimed invention affords a revolutionary approach to the safety problem in the nuclear reactor art. As the amplifier is said to be inherently safe from divergent nuclear chain reaction, the intricate systems needed to monitor and control the operation of conventional neutron amplifiers to prevent an explosion are unnecessary.

The single reference relied upon by the Patent Office in rejecting the appealed claims is an Atomic Energy Commission document entitled "KAPL–M–RWS–1, A Stable Fission Pile with High Speed Control." The document is in the form of an unpublished memorandum authored by one Samsel, and will hereinafter be referred to as "Samsel." Samsel is dated February 14, 1947 and was classified as a secret document by the Commission until March 9, 1957, when it was declassified.

* * *

Samsel is prefaced by a statement that it was made to record an idea, and it nowhere indicates that the idea had been tested in an operating reactor.

The Patent Office does not invoke Samsel as a publication (which it apparently was not, at any pertinent date). Rather, the contention is that Samsel constitutes evidence of prior knowledge within the meaning of 35 U.S.C.A. § 102(a).

While there seems to be some disagreement on the part of the solicitor, we think the most reasonable interpretation of the examiner's rejection, and one which is concurred in by the board and by appellant, is that claims 27, 30, 31 and 32 are fully met by Samsel and thus the subject matter defined therein is unpatentable because it was known by another in this country prior to appellant's invention thereof.

* * *

Our own independent consideration of Samsel has convinced us that it contains adequate enabling disclosure of the invention of claims 27 and 30–32, see In re Sheppard, 339 F.2d 238, 52 CCPA 859, and In re LeGrice, 301 F.2d 929, 49 CCPA 1124, and appellant does not appear to contend otherwise. Rather, appellant contends that Samsel is not available as evidence of prior knowledge under sections 102(a) and 103.

* * *

In the case of In re Schlittler, 234 F.2d 882, 43 CCPA 986, this court was presented with the following situation: A manuscript containing an anticipatory disclosure of the appellants' claimed invention had been submitted to The Journal of the American Chemical Society and was later published. The date to which the appellants' application was entitled for purposes of constructive reduction to practice was earlier than the publication date of the Journal article, and therefore the Patent Office did not contend that the "printed publication" portion of section 102(a) was applicable. However, the manuscript bore a notation that it had been received by the publisher on a date prior to the effective filing date of the appellants' application. On the basis of this notation the Patent Office argued that the article constituted sufficient evidence of prior knowledge under section 102(a).

After an exhaustive review of the authorities, and of the legislative history of the Patent Act of 1952, this court rejected the contention of the Patent Office, and concluded that such a document was not proper evidence of prior knowledge. In reversing, the court stated (234 F.2d at 886, 433 CCPA at 992):

> "In our opinion, one of the essential elements of the word 'known' as used in 35 U.S.C. § 102(a) is knowledge of an invention which has been completed by reduction to practice, actual or constructive, and is not satisfied by disclosure of a conception only."

And therefore, since the Journal article, "at best, could be evidence of nothing more than conception and disclosure of the invention," the

> "* * * placing of the Nystrom article in the hands of the publishers did not constitute either prima facie or conclusive evidence of knowledge or use by others in this country of the invention disclosed by the article, within the meaning of Title 35, § 102(a) of the United States Code, since the knowledge was of a conception only and not of a reduction to practice."

Another aspect of the court's discussion in Schlittler involved the well-established principle that "prior knowledge of a patented invention would not invalidate a claim of the patent unless such knowledge was available to the public." After reaffirming that principle, the court went on to state:

> "Obviously, in view of the above authorities, the mere placing of a manuscript in the hands of a publisher does not necessarily make it available to the public within the meaning of said authorities."

However, the court did not go on to determine whether the Journal article was in fact available to the public, since such determination was deemed unnecessary for disposition of the case, under the court's theory.

We shall consider first the public availability aspect of the Schlittler case. Although that portion of the Schlittler opinion is clearly dictum, we think it just as clearly represents the settled law. The knowledge contemplated by section 102(a) must be accessible to the public. In addition to Schlittler and cases cited therein, see, e.g., Minneapolis-Honeywell Regulator Co. v. Midwestern Instruments, Inc., 7 Cir., 298 F.2d 36 (7th Cir.1961); Rem-Cru Titanium, Inc. v. Watson, 152 F.Supp. 282 (D.D.C.1957).

In the instant case, Samsel was clearly not publicly available during the period it was under secrecy classification by the Atomic Energy Commission. We note that the date of declassification, however, was prior to appellant's filing date, and it is perhaps arguable that

Samsel became accessible to the public upon declassification. But we do not find it necessary to decide that difficult question, for there is a statutory provision which is, we think, dispositive of the question of publicity. Section 155 of the Atomic Energy Act of 1954 (42 U.S.C.A. § 2185) provides:

> "In connection with applications for patents covered by this subchapter, the fact that the invention or discovery was known or used before shall be a bar to the patenting of such invention or discovery even though such prior knowledge or use was under secrecy within the atomic energy program of the United States."

We think the meaning and intent of this provision is so clear as to admit of no dispute: With respect to subject matter covered by the patent provisions of the Atomic Energy Act, prior knowledge or use under section 102(a) *need not* be accessible to the public. Therefore, Samsel is available as evidence of prior knowledge insofar as the requirement for publicity is concerned.

The remaining consideration regarding the status of Samsel as evidence of prior knowledge directly calls into question the correctness of the unequivocal holding in Schlittler that the knowledge must be of a reduction to practice, either actual or constructive. After much deliberation, we have concluded that such a requirement is illogical and anomalous, and to the extent Schlittler is inconsistent with the decision in this case, it is hereby expressly overruled.

The mere fact that a disclosure is contained in a patent or application and thus "constructively" reduced to practice, or that it is found in a printed publication, does not make the disclosure itself any more meaningful to those skilled in the art (and thus, ultimately, to the public). Rather, the criterion should be whether the disclosure is *sufficient to enable one skilled in the art to reduce the disclosed invention to practice.* In other words, the disclosure must be such as will give possession of the invention to the person of ordinary skill. Even the act of publication or the fiction of constructive reduction to practice will not suffice if the disclosure does not meet this standard. See In re Sheppard and In re LeGrice, supra.

Where, as is true of Samsel, the disclosure constituting evidence of prior knowledge contains, in the words of the Board of Appeals, "a description of the invention fully commensurate with the present patent application," we hold that the disclosure need not be of an invention reduced to practice, either actually or constructively. We therefore affirm the rejection of claims 27, 30, 31 and 32.

* * *

Notes

1. "Subsection (a) [of section 102] is the language of the existing law, recognizing that the interpretation by the courts excludes various kinds of private knowledge not known to the public." H.R.Rep. No. 1923, 82d Cong, 2d Sess. 6 (1952).

2. The Reviser's Note for 35 U.S.C.A. § 102 provides in part that "the interpretation by the courts of paragraph (a) as being more restricted than the actual language would suggest (for example 'known' has been held to mean 'publicly known') is recognized but no change in the language is made at this time."

3. "Under this statute [a predecessor of § 102(a)] the testimony as to the practice in foreign countries, none of which practice was shown to be known to Pauling [the Patentee] was incompetent to invalidate his patent." Southern Electro-Chem. Co. v. E.I. Du Pont De Nemours & Co., 20 F.2d 97, 99 (3d Cir.1927). "Reduction to practice in a foreign country of a previous foreign invention cannot operate to invalidate a patent granted in the United States unless the foreign invention has either been patented or described in a printed publication, neither of which conditions existed here." City of Milwaukee v. Activated Sludge, 69 F.2d 577, 589, 21 USPQ 69 (7th Cir.1934).

4. In Gillman v. Stern, 114 F.2d 28, 46 USPQ 430 (2d Cir.1940), Judge Learned Hand in holding that a commercial use in secret of a prior invention by another does not invalidate a patent said at page 31:

"We are to distinguish between a public user which does not inform the art (Hall v. Macneale, 107 U.S. 90, 97, 2 S.Ct. 73, 27 L.Ed. 367) and a secret user; some confusion has resulted from the failure to do so. It is true that in each case the fund of common knowledge is not enriched, and that might indeed have been good reason originally for throwing out each as anticipations. But when the statute made any 'public use' fatal to a patent, and when thereafter the court held that it was equally fatal, whether or not the patentee had consented to it, there was no escape from holding—contrary to the underlying theory of the law—that it was irrelevant whether the use informed the public so that they could profit by it. Nevertheless, it was still true that secret uses were not public uses, whether or not public uses might on occasion have no public value. Perhaps it was originally open to argument that the statute merely meant to confine prior 'public uses' to the prospective patentee and to be evidence of abandonment, and that 'first inventor' meant to include anyone who first conceived the thing in tangible enough form to be persuasive. But, rightly or wrongly, the law did not develop so, and it is now too late to change. Hence the anomaly that, by secreting a machine one may keep it from becoming an anticipation, even though its public use would really have told nobody anything about it."

5. "Defendant selected certain work on a 'magnetograph,' carried on in 1943 for the United States Government by the Department of Terrestrial Magnetism (DTM) of the Carnegie Institute of Washington, as its best non-patented reference against the Heiland patent [in suit]. This work is relied on by defendant solely as a statutory bar (35 U.S.C.A. § 102(a)) on the ground the invention of the Heiland patent ' * * * was known or used by others in this country * * * before the invention thereof * * *'. The trial court held the DTM work was not proof of prior knowledge or use by others on two grounds, 1) the DTM work was classified as 'restricted' and was not publicly available, and 2) * * *. We approve the trial court's findings and conclusions on both grounds." Minneapolis-Honeywell Reg.

Co. v. Midwestern Instruments, Inc., 298 F.2d 36, 38, 131 USPQ 402, 403 (7th Cir.1961).

6. "Mere belief, or even confidence, that a device will work if it is constructed and tried is not enough to bring into operation the statute which renders unpatentable an invention 'known * * * by others in this country' before the invention thereof by the applicant for a patent. An invention is 'known' as that word is used in the statute, when it is 'reduced to practice.' It follows here, on the same principle, that Mudd and his associates and his employer cannot be found to have 'known' the practical advantages of a rolling spring as an electrode before they ever rolled a spring for that purpose." Stearns v. Tinker & Rasor, 220 F.2d 49, 56, 104 USPQ 234, 239 (9th Cir.1955).

7. "When [the statutory predecessor of 102(a)], prescribes that a patentable invention must not be 'known or used' by others, it means something quite different from the prior public use by which it may be abandoned. In the case at bar Nathan clearly did not use the pads before January 16, 1919; indeed none were made. Were they 'known' in the sense which the statutes used the term? The word has acquired a somewhat esoteric meaning, imputed by the courts to accomplish the purpose of the statute. Mere acquaintance with the invention, even if disclosed, is not enough; nothing short of 'reduction to practice' will do, whatever that may mean. [Citations omitted.] All this is very old law, though it is by no means always easy to ascertain just when 'reduction' has taken place, for the books, perhaps wisely, are reticent of positive definition." Judge Learned Hand speaking for the Court in Block v. Nathan Anklet Support Co., 9 F.2d 311, 312–13 (2d Cir.1925).

8. "The mere fact that the earlier invention was not the subject of patent is not material, nor is it material that the inventor may have been ignorant of the anticipatory invention. The invention, however, must have been known to the public, or there must have been an opportunity to acquire such knowledge as would enable one skilled in the art to reproduce it without exercising further invention of his own. While actual construction or use of the prior method of apparatus is the best evidence of its prior discovery, yet this is not essential if the discovery has been so manifested publicly that one skilled in the particular art would be able to reproduce it. Generally, the invention must be tested and found satisfactory." Simmons v. Hansen, 117 F.2d 49, 51, 48 USPQ 345, 348 (8th Cir.1941).

3. PATENTED OR DESCRIBED IN A PRINTED PUBLICATION

a. Introduction

Patents and printed publications are considered under both 35 U.S. C.A. §§ 102(a) and 102(b). While Sections 102(a) and (b) focus on different points of time, they both seek to "promote the progress of * * * useful arts" by requiring that patent protection be limited to inventions which were novel and nonobvious at both the date of invention and more than one year prior to filing a patent application thereon. The phrase "patented or described in a printed publication" is considered to have generally the same meaning and scope in both

Sections 102(a) and (b) and thus, the following cases interpreting this phrase may arise under either of these sections or their statutory predecessors.

To negate novelty or establish obviousness, the prior art patents and publications must give possession of the invention to the public. As the Supreme Court observed in Seymour v. Osborne, 78 U.S. (11 Wall.) 516, 555, 20 L.Ed. 33, 42 (1871):

> Patented inventions cannot be superseded by the mere introduction of a foreign publication of the kind, though of prior date, unless the description and drawings contain and exhibit a substantial representation of the patented improvement, in such full, clear, and exact terms as to enable any person skilled in the art or science to which it appertains, to make, construct, and practice the invention to the same practical extent as they would be enabled to do if the information was derived from a prior patent. Mere vague and general representations will not support such a defence, as the knowledge supposed to be derived from the publication must be sufficient to enable those skilled in the art or science to understand the nature and operation of the invention, and to carry it into practical use. Whatever may be the particular circumstances under which the publication takes place, the account published, to be of any effect to support such a defence, must be an account of a complete and operative invention capable of being put into practical operation.

and in Cohn v. United States Corset Co., 93 U.S. 366, 370, 23 L.Ed. 907, 908 (1876):

> * * * [U]nless the earlier printed and published description does exhibit the later patented invention in such a full and intelligible manner as to enable persons skilled in the art to which the invention is related to comprehend it without assistance from the patent, or to make it, or repeat the process claimed, it is insufficient to invalidate the patent.

Whether a particular prior art patent or publication contains an "enabling" disclosure or description of an invention and thus negates novelty or demonstrates obviousness must be determined in the particular factual context of each case.

b. *Patented*

REEVES BROS., INC. v. UNITED STATES LAMINATING CORP. ET AL.

United States District Court of New York, 1968.
282 F.Supp. 118, 157 USPQ 235, aff'd 417 F.2d 869 (2d Cir.1969).

[Excerpts Only]

BARTELS, DISTRICT JUDGE. * * *

THE GEBRAUCHSMUSTER AS ANTICIPATION

Before analyzing all the prior art references it is proper to adjudicate the effect of the Gebrauchsmuster 1,691,026 (hereinafter referred

to as "GM") issued by Germany in January, 1955, which defendants
claim falls within the purview of Section 102(a) and (b) and also Section
103 as anticipation and prior art patents.

* * *

The questions which arise are whether (1) the GM is a patent
within the purview of Section 102(a) and (b); (2) the GM as a patent
constitutes anticipation only for what is claimed or also for what is
disclosed; and (3) the GM actually anticipates the Dickey invention and
to what extent it can be used as prior art under Section 103.

THE GM IS A PATENT

A patent has been repeatedly defined as a franchise granting the
right to exclude everyone from making, using or selling the patented
invention without the permission of the patentee. Bloomer v. McQue-
wan, et al., 1852, 55 U.S. 539, 549, 14 How. 539, 14 L.Ed. 532; 1 Walker
on Patents (Deller's Ed.1937) § 6 at 22. According to the testimony of
the experts, a Gebrauchsmuster is registered under the German law
after an application filed in the German Patent Office. If the application meets the requirements of form and content, the GM is issued
without any novelty search and is accompanied by the publication of an
official notice in the German Official Gazette that it has been so issued.
There is no requirement of nonobviousness in order to obtain a GM,
and its purpose is to enable the applicant to obtain a speedy protection
for a new article and if desirable, to concurrently seek a regular patent,
a procedure which would consume much more time. After registration
the specifications and claims become available to the public and anyone
has free and open access to the same. The GM was not a printed
publication at any time and is referred to as a utility model. It is
limited to a maximum of six years instead of eighteen years, covers
only articles and never can cover processes as such, and grants to the
inventor the exclusive right to prevent others from making, using or
selling his article and also to recover damages for any infringement.

* * *

By a directive issued to its examiners in 1965, the United States
Patent Office resolved certain prior inconsistent practices as to the
treatment of GMs and stated that GMs may be considered as patents
for anticipation purposes within the purview of Section 102. Official
Gazette of the United States Patent Office, No. 2, 1965, Vol. 820, No. 1.
In American Infra-Red Radiant Co. v. Lambert Industries, Inc., 8 Cir.
1966, 360 F.2d 977, cert. denied, 385 U.S. 920, 87 S.Ct. 233, 17 L.Ed.2d
144, the court held that a GM was a patent under Section 102(d), citing
also Permutit Co. v. Graver Corp., N.D.Ill.1930, 37 F.2d 385, affirmed on
other grounds, 43 F.2d 898, affirmed, 1931, 284 U.S. 52, 52 S.Ct. 53, 76
L.Ed. 163, and Safety Gas Lighter Co. v. Fischer Bros. & Corwin, D.N.J.
1916, 236 F. 955, affirmed, 1918, 247 F. 1005. Plaintiff, however,
contends that the words "patented * * * in a foreign country" (as
used in Section 102(a) and (b) of Article 35 of the Patent Act of 1952)
have been taken without change from several of the prior enactments

from as early as the Act of 1836, and that the legislative history of the
various patent acts shows that Congress accorded no consideration to
the enactment in various foreign countries of Utility Model Laws that
came into existence in the latter part of the Nineteenth Century (see
Sec. 7, Patent Act of 1836; R.S. 4886 of 1874; R.S. 4886 of 1897; R.S.
4929 of 1902). To support this argument plaintiff cites Permutit v.
Wadham, 6 Cir.1926, 13 F.2d 454; rearg. 15 F.2d 20 (covering the same
patent as Permutit Co. v. Graver Corp., supra), which suggested that
Congress did not intend to include GMs as foreign patents.

No place in the Patent Act or elsewhere did Congress indicate that
only certain types or classes of patents may be considered under Section
102(a) and (b), and it did not distinguish between one particular type of
foreign patent and another. If in effect the foreign document grants a
patent right to exclude others from producing, using, or selling the
invention, process, or article for a specified period of time, it clearly
falls within the accepted definition of a patent which may be considered
under Section 102(a) and (b). Accordingly, a GM must be deemed an
effective patent under the above section as of its registration date.
American Infra-Red Radiant Co., supra, pp. 993–994, supports this
postulate.

THE EFFECT OF A GM

Another problem results from the necessity of determining to what
extent a GM may be used as an anticipatory reference under Section
102(a) and (b). There is respectable authority to the effect that under
this section an American patent is a reference not only for its claims
but also for its disclosures as revealed in its specifications. Lanyon v.
M.H. Detrick Co., 9 Cir.1936, 85 F.2d 875, 877; Mershon v. Sprague
Specialties Co., 1 Cir.1937, 92 F.2d 313, cert. denied, 1938, 304 U.S. 561,
58 S.Ct. 943, 82 L.Ed. 1528; 1 Walker on Patents (Deller's Ed.1937) § 51
at 272. But this principle is apparently not applicable to foreign
patents which, for anticipation purposes, are limited to their claims and
cannot be used as references for the disclosures in their specifications.
American Tri-Ergon Corp. v. Paramount Publix Corp., 2 Cir.1934, 71
F.2d 153, reversed on other grounds, 1935, 294 U.S. 464, 55 S.Ct. 449, 79
L.Ed. 997; General Electric Co. v. Alexander, 2 Cir.1922, 280 F. 852,
cert. denied, 260 U.S. 727, 43 S.Ct. 89, 67 L.Ed. 484; Carter Products v.
Colgate-Palmolive Company, D.Md.1955, 130 F.Supp. 557, affirmed, 230
F.2d 855, cert. denied, 1956, 352 U.S. 843, 77 S.Ct. 43, 1 L.Ed.2d 59;
Permutit Co. v. Wadham, supra; Leeds & Catlin Co. v. Victor Talking
Mach. Co., 1909, 213 U.S. 301, 29 S.Ct. 495, 53 L.Ed. 805. So that what
is publicly known or used but not printed in a foreign country is not a
bar to an American patent. Defendants rely upon Application of Fuge,
47 CCPA 735, 1959, 272 F.2d 954, and Ex Parte Ovist, P.O.Bd.App.1963,
152 USPQ 709, as authorities to the contrary. Application of Fuge does
not reach that far but only holds that a "patent even though it is not a
printed publication is a reference to the extent that it protects the

rejected invention". 272 F.2d 956. Ex Parte Ovist rests its authority upon Application of Fuge without further reasons.

The Court concludes that for anticipation purposes under Section 102 a GM, which is a foreign patent but not a printed publication, is a reference only for what is patented, i.e., for what it claims and not, for what is disclosed in its specifications. This is consistent with the language of Section 102(a) and (b) which juxtaposes "patented * * * in a foreign country" with the phrase "described in a printed publication in * * * a foreign country". To permit the effect of such a foreign patent to extend beyond what is actually patented, would appear to indirectly effectuate a form of use and knowledge in a foreign country which is not statutorily allowable as an anticipatory reference to an American patent.

* * *

To treat the GM as a prior art reference under Section 103 for all it discloses would render the claims restriction of Section 102 meaningless because such treatment would accomplish indirectly what is proscribed directly. The legislative history of Section 103 makes clear that the term "prior art" as used in that section refers only to "what was known before as described in section 102". S.Rep. No. 1979, 82 Cong., 2d Sess. (1952) at 6; H.R.Rep. No. 1923, 82d Cong., 2 Sess. (1952) at 7, U.S. Congressional and Administrative Code, p. 2399. Therefore, the GM can be treated as a prior art reference under Section 103 only for what is claimed therein.

BENDIX CORP. v. BALAX, INC.

United States Court of Appeals, Seventh Circuit, 1970.
421 F.2d 809, 164 USPQ 485.

HASTINGS, SENIOR CIRCUIT JUDGE. * * *

Defendants urge several reasons for the invalidity of the reissue patent. Their first contention is that it is anticipated by the 1939 German Gebrauchsmuster Patent 1,455,626 (GM). Section 102(b) of Title 35, U.S.C.A. provides: * * *

A GM is clearly a patent within the meaning of this section, but it is not a printed publication. American Infra-Red Radiant Co. v. Lambert Industries, Inc., 8 Cir., 360 F.2d 977, 991–994, cert. denied, 385 U.S. 920, 87 S.Ct. 233, 17 L.Ed.2d 144 (1966); Permutit Co. v. Wadham, 6 Cir., 13 F.2d 454, 458 (1926); Reeves Bros., Inc. v. United States Laminating Corp., 282 F.Supp. 118, 134–136 (E.D.N.Y.1968); Permutit Co. v. Graver Corp., 37 F.2d 385, 390 (N.D.Ill.1930), aff'd on other grounds, 7 Cir., 43 F.2d 898, 902 (1930), aff'd 284 U.S. 52, 52 S.Ct. 53, 76 L.Ed. 163 (1931); and Safety Gas Lighter Co. v. Fischer Bros. & Corwin, 236 F. 955, 962 (D.N.J.1916), aff'd 3 Cir., 247 F. 1005, 159 C.C.A. 652 (1918).

On this basis, all parties agree that only that which is "patented" by a GM may be considered as prior art under Section 102(b), supra. Subject matter which is ancillary to, but not a part of, the patented subject matter may not be considered. The district court so held. The disagreement between the parties concerns the method of determining what is "patented" by the Gebrauchsmuster in question.

issue

The trial court held that a GM "patents" only that which is disclosed by the bare words of its claims. It relied on language in *Reeves,* supra, in holding that it is never permissible to look to the specifications of a GM in construing its claims. The *Reeves* court had said: " * * * for anticipation purposes under Section 102 a GM * * * is a reference only for what is patented, i.e., for what it claims and not, for what is disclosed in its specifications." 282 F.Supp. at 136.

Defendants maintain that the claims of a GM are to be construed in light of its specifications and seek to distinguish *Reeves.* They note that in *Reeves* a GM was cited as a reference against a process patent and that a GM is by definition a patent only on an article and never on a process. From this they conclude the *Reeves* court ignored the specifications only because they referred to a process.

However, the *Reeves* court clearly recognized that an article patent may in some cases anticipate a process. Such would be the case where "a process in one patent can produce only one article and that article is definitely covered by what is claimed in another patent [e.g., in an earlier GM] * * *. [B]ut this alone may not be sufficient to treat the article patent as an anticipation of the process patent, if many processes are described in the article patent while only one specific process is described in the process patent." 282 F.Supp. at 136–137.

The patent in suit in *Reeves* claimed a method of laminating a sheet of plastic foam to a sheet of fabric by the application of heat from a gas flame. The GM cited against it claimed a fabric lined foam material with the fabric bonded directly to the foam. The specifications of the GM described the process by which the article could be made indicating the application of heat from heated rollers, hot gas, infrared light, or high frequency current.

When the language of *Reeves* is read in light of these facts, it is clear to us that it calls for neither an absolute rule that GM specifications may never be resorted to, nor an absolute rule that they may always be resorted to in interpreting the claims. Rather, it is consistent with our own judgment as to the correct rule. We conclude that the specifications of a GM may be resorted to for the purpose of clarifying the meaning of the language used in the claims, but may not be resorted to for the purpose of adding completely new material to that which is disclosed by the claims.

For example, in *Reeves* the GM claims disclosed an article which could have been produced by several processes. The court had held that in such a case the article patent could not anticipate any one of those processes when cited against a patent specifically claiming one of them. Therefore, resort to the specifications there to learn in what manner the claimed article was actually produced would have added wholly new matter to the claims. Without the specifications, the

Reeves claims could anticipate no process, but with them, the claims would anticipate a process as well as an article. *Reeves* was thus a particularly clear case of specifications adding new matter to what was "patented" by the claims, rather than simply giving meaning to the words of the claims for the purpose of determining what was "patented" by them.

Each case will, of course, turn on its own facts. In each case the question will be "What is 'patented'?" The specifications of the GM may be resorted to if necessary to clarify the meaning of the words of the claim—*to determine what* it is that the claims "patent" *but not to add to* what they patent.

Thus, the double question here is whether resort to the specifications is necessary to determine what is patented and whether such resort may be taken without increasing the scope of what is patented.

The claims of the GM cited against the reissue patent in suit are:

"1. Thread pressing tap for the chipless production of inner threads, characterized in that the thread tap (a) provided with a continuous, *i.e.,* uninterrupted thread along the circumference of its thread cross section (b, c, d) is undulatingly formed over its entire length or partly, and, consequently, has continuous or interrupted depressions (f, f ', f ") extending longitudinally axially, as well as spirally axially or otherwise, which though they recede with respect to the outer circumference (g, g ', g "), nevertheless have the thread extend over their circumferential surface in the profiling of the thread to be cut and otherwise along the circumference of the tap.

"2. Thread pressing tap for the chipless production of inner threads in accordance with claim 1, characterized by the shape, disposition and arrangement reflected by the drawing and the specification."

These claims make clear that what is patented is a swaging tap, i.e., a "tap for the chipless production of inner threads." They also make clear that the patented tap is of a particular form and shape— one "characterized by the shape, disposition and arrangement reflected by the drawing and the specification." However, by this cross reference, the words of the claims leave unclear exactly what the "shape, disposition and arrangement" of the patented article is meant to be. Thus, it is plainly necessary in this case to resort to the specifications to determine what is "patented" by the claims.

It is just as plainly possible to take such resort without increasing the scope of what is patented by the claims. The claims clearly profess to patent a particular article of a particular shape, disposition and arrangement. They also clearly indicate how such particular shape, disposition and arrangement is to be determined. Claim 2 is an obvious incorporation by reference and makes the specifications and drawings as much a part of the claim as if they were reproduced verbatim in the claim. Without such an incorporation, Claim 2 would be meaningless.

The trial court completely disregarded Claim 2. It reasoned that to give it any effect would undermine its conclusion as to the proper construction of a Gebrauchsmuster: "Claim 1 is the only real claim of the GM. Claim 2 incorporates by cross reference 'the shape, disposition and arrangement reflected by the drawing and the specification.' However, to allow such a cross reference would defeat the limited use which this court has concluded must be made of the GM."

We do not agree that allowing the obviously intended cross reference to the specifications here defeats the limitations to which Gebrauchsmusters are admittedly subject. We allow such cross reference not to increase the scope of what is patented by the Gebrauchsmuster claims but only to accomplish the task at hand of determining what it is that those claims patent.

The use of GM specifications which we here find proper is fully supported by the German practice. Under that practice, while claims are frequently used, they are not required, and the entire specification will be construed in determining what is patented. The advisory explanations accompanying the German Regulations regarding "the application for Gebrauchsmuster" provide:

> "Indication of Novelty.
>
> According to sec. 2 paragraph 2 of the statute, the application must specify 'what purpose of work, or utility, the new form or device is intended to serve.' Since this indication is of importance for the range of the legal protection corresponding with the recording, applicant will do well in many cases, even tho the law does not prescribe the setting of a protection claim, to summarize separately from the description, in the type of construction of a patent claim, the legally protectable characteristics of the model." Patents and Gebrauchsmuster in International Law, Emerson Stringham, Pacot Publications, Madison, Wisconsin, 1935, p. 248.

Stringham comments:

> "Scope of protection involves much the same problems which arise everywhere in patent law. The German statute requires no claim for Gebrauchsmuster. The tendency, during a decade or so, of the Reichsgericht to hold itself not bound by the statutory claim of the long-term patent, finds freer play with Gebrauchsmuster; * * *." Id. at 255.

Having concluded that what is patented by Gebrauchsmuster Patent 1,455,626 should have been determined by construing its claims in the light of its specifications rather than on the bare words of the claims, it becomes necessary to determine whether that patent, properly construed, does anticipate, and thus invalidate, plaintiff's Patent Re. 24,572 in suit.

* * *

Thus we conclude that all claims of the plaintiff's reissue patent can be found in the Gebrauchsmuster Patent 1,455,626 which was issued more than one year prior to plaintiff's application for its patent. We hold that the claims of plaintiff's Patent Re. 24,572 are invalid because of anticipation by the 1939 GM.

* * *

Notes

1. All of the cases cited as authority for limiting the effect of foreign patents to what is claimed therein in negating novelty appear to rely ultimately on decisions of the Supreme Court of the United States in Guar. Ins. Trust and Safe Deposit Co. v. Sellers, 123 U.S. 276, 8 S.Ct. 117, 31 L.Ed. 153 (1887); Bate Refrigerating Co. v. Sulzberger, 157 U.S. 1, 15 S.Ct. 508, 39 L.Ed. 601 (1894); and Leeds & Catlin Co. v. Victor Talking Machine Co., 213 U.S. 301, 29 S.Ct. 495, 53 L.Ed. 805 (1909). These three Supreme Court cases interpreted and applied Sections 6 and 25 of the Patent Acts of 1839 and 1870 respectively which limited the term of a U.S. patent on an invention which had been previously patented in a foreign country before filing the application for the U.S. patent. Under the Patent Act of 1839, the term of the U.S. patent was limited in such a situation to 14 years from the date of publication of the foreign patent. Under the Patent Act of 1870, the term of the U.S. patent expired at the same time as the first to expire foreign patent, but in no event was the term longer than 17 years.

In *Leeds* the Supreme Court observed at 213 U.S. 319 that the policy of Section 25 of the Patent Act of 1870 was "that an American patent is not precluded by a foreign patent for the same invention, but, if a foreign patent be granted, an American patent is granted upon the condition that the 'invention shall be free to the American people whenever, by reason of the expiration of the foreign patent, it becomes free to the people abroad.' Bate Refrigerating Co. v. Sulzberger, [citation omitted]." Thus, the Patent Acts of 1839 and 1870 did not preclude an application for a U.S. patent on an invention which was patented in a foreign country, and, hence, disclosed to the public and no longer novel when the U.S. application was filed. Rather, the Patent Acts of 1839 and 1870 simply provided a more limited term for the U.S. patent in this situation.

In view of the different purpose and policy of Sections 6 and 25 of the Patent Acts of 1839 and 1870, should these cases be considered as precedent for limiting the disclosure of a foreign patent to what is claimed therein for negating novelty under 35 U.S.C.A. § 102(a) and (b)? Does the limitation of the disclosure of a foreign patent to what is actually claimed therein for negating novelty "promote the progress of * * * useful arts"?

2. "Foreign patents are to be construed more strictly than domestic patents." National Latex Products Co. v. Sun Rubber Co., 274 F.2d 224, 236, 123 USPQ 279, 287 (6th Cir.1959). "The disclosures in foreign patents when asserted against a [United States] patent are strictly construed and are restricted in their teaching to exactly what they clearly and fully disclose, without alterations." Eversharp Inc. v. Fisher Pen Co., Inc., 204 F.Supp. 649, 659, 132 USPQ 423, 431 (N.D.Ill.1961).

3. "Appellant further attempts to disparage the value of the French patent as a reference on the ground that it is a 'foreign patent,' and is good 'for only what it clearly and definitely discloses.' That statement is true with respect to any reference, patent or others, foreign or domestic. There is no basis in the statute (35 USC § 102 or § 103) for discriminating either in favor of or against prior art references on the basis of nationality. We do know that some opinions have looked askance at foreign patents but

that is for the reason that the patents of some countries have been notorious for containing inadequate and incomplete disclosures. A consideration of cases will show that this type of argument has not borne fruit in this court for the past 30 years." Application of Moreton, 288 F.2d 708, 711, 129 USPQ 227, 230 (CCPA 1961).

4. Although a prior art patent may be utilized to negate novelty and unobviousness even if its invention was not reduced to practice, its use for such purpose is greatly impaired where its invention was not reduced to commercial practice in spite of a long felt want for a solution to the problem. See, e.g., University of Illinois Foundation v. Block Drug Co., 241 F.2d 6, 112 USPQ 204 (7th Cir.1957); Young v. Watson, 168 F.Supp. 856, 119 USPQ 312 (D.D.C.1958).

5. "Neither the age of the prior patent, its commercial success, nor its utility will destroy its anticipatory effect." Wittlin v. Remco Inc., 132 F.Supp. 57, 59, 105 USPQ 323, 325 (E.D.Ill.1955). "It is not material whether a prior patent ever went into actual use, or is more than a paper patent." Kester Solder Co. v. Berry Solder Co., 14 F.Supp. 863, 867, 29 USPQ 565, 569 (S.D.N.Y.1936).

c. *Printed Publication*

PHILLIPS ELECTRONIC & PHARMACEUTICAL INDUS. CORP. v. THERMAL & ELECTRONICS INDUS., INC.

United States District Court of New Jersey, 1970.
311 F.Supp. 17, 165 USPQ 185.

SHAW, DISTRICT JUDGE.

[Excerpts Only]

* * * The initial issue raised by the Lorenz application is the status of the application as a printed publication under the statute. It was filed in the German patent office on November 3, 1941 and its availability for public inspection appeared in a German document entitled "Patentblat" on July 30, 1942 (D–20b(1)). The application was microfilmed by the U.S. Office of Military Government for Germany and identified by reel Number 831, Class 32b, on page 13 in Fiat Technical Bulletin T–50, dated May 29, 1947 (D–20B–4). The microfilm was accessible in the Library of Congress in Washington, D.C. on reel No. 831, identified by frames 8374, 8375, 8376, 8377 and available to the general public June 4, 1948. A document entitled "Bibliography of Scientific and Industrial Reports," Vol. 9, No. 10, dated June 4, 1948 which was received in the Library of Congress on June 21, 1948 lists the Lorenz microfilm under the heading "Patents" and subheading "Minerals and Mineral Products" on pages 906–911. The title of the Lorenz Application is on page 907, No. 8374, 8377: "*Vacuum fusions of metal and glass, not affected by temperature,* German patent application L99347VI32b, dated November 3, 1941. In German." (D–20B–3). A printed abstract of the Lorenz application was also lodged in the British Patent Office and available to the public on November 1, 1948 (D–20B–

5) and the bibliography indexing the microfilm was also available in a library in Stockholm, Sweden (D–20B–7).

[handwritten margin note: Patent App. not a printed publication]

A patent application, foreign or domestic, that is merely open for inspection in a patent office (and not ultimately resulting in a patent) should not be regarded as a printed publication under the statute. Ex parte Haller, 103 USPQ 332 (Pat.Off.Bd. of App.1953); Celanese Corporation of America v. Ribbon Narrow Fabrics Co., Inc., 117 F.2d 481 (2nd Cir.1941). See White Cap Co. v. Owens-Illinois Glass Co., 203 F.2d 694, 696 (6th Cir.1953); Package Devices, Inc. v. Sun Ray Drug Co., 301 F.Supp. 768, 779 (E.D.Pa.1969). Cf. Ellis-Foster Co. v. Reichhold Chemicals, 198 F.2d 42 (3rd Cir.1952). A patent application, however, could be a printed publication if it was "printed" and "published" outside of patent office files in a manner complying with the statute. In Application of Tenney, 254 F.2d 619, 622, 45 CCPA 894 (1958) it was held that a German patent application reproduced on microfilm and filed in the Library of Congress could not be considered "printed" because "there is no probability, from a mere showing that a microfilm copy of a disclosure has been produced, that the disclosure has achieved wide circulation and that, therefore, the public has knowledge of it." Id. at 627. The concurring opinion in *Tenney* agreed with the result but stressed that a literal interpretation of "printed publication" should not be the only factor considered, but that availability, accessibility, and dissemination are also relevant. It should be noted that the microfilm was misclassified in *Tenney* under a misleading label. This same issue was again raised in I.C.E. Corporation v. Armco Steel Corporation, 250 F.Supp. 738 (S.D.N.Y.1966). That case also involved a German patent application reproduced upon microfilm and stored in the Library of Congress. The Court stated:

> * * * it is no longer reasonable to assume as the majority of the Court in *Tenney* apparently did, that the traditional methods of 'printing' are the only acceptable methods, for the purposes of Section 102. In the light of modern developments, a preferable rationale for the result in *Tenney* would have been that the microfilmed material, whether 'printed' or not, was not shown to be sufficiently accessible to the public so as to constitute a 'publication' within the meaning of the statute.

* * *

[handwritten margin note: printed publication, defined]

> * * * the term "printed publication" * * * can include a document printed, reproduced or duplicated by modern day methods, including microfilming, upon a satisfactory showing that such document has been *disseminated or otherwise made available to the extent that persons interested and ordinarily skilled in the subject matter or art, exercising reasonable diligence, can locate it* and recognize and comprehend therefrom the essentials of the claimed invention without the need of further research or experimentation. Id. at 742–743. (Emphasis supplied.)

The reasoning in *I.C.E. Corp.*, supra, appears sound. There is no persuasive testimony to establish that a person interested and ordinarily skilled in the art could locate this microfilm by the exercise of reasonable diligence or whether the filing index was erroneous or misleading. The evidence supplied by exhibits will be reviewed in an effort to decide this question. The Library of Congress certified that the microfilm was available to the general public as indexed by the bibliography discussed previously (D–20B–2). The Bibliography of Scientific Reports lists the microfilm under the general heading "patents". This does not appear to be misleading or a misfiling. The subheading listed is "minerals and mineral products." Such a classification might seem inappropriate and misleading as a reference to glass-to-metal seals, but a review of the other patent applications located on the same index page as the Lorenz microfilm index indicates that they all involve devices or processes involving glass or glass-metal combinations. One citation mentions annealing, and another mentions fusion of glass and metal. It should not be concluded that all of these references were misfiled. It appears that it was proper to file this application under the above mentioned subheading and that this was neither a misfiling nor misleading. The final title of the microfilm was "vacuum fusions of metal and glass, not affected by temperature" (D–20B–3). The basic field of art involved in this case concerns the fusing of glass and metal through a controlled heating and cooling procedure. The seals involved are used to insure vacuum tight electrical products. It is concluded that this microfilm, as indexed, was available to persons interested and could be located by persons ordinarily skilled in the subject matter with the exercise of reasonable diligence. Accordingly, the microfilm is a printed publication under the statute. * * *

⊢ IN RE WYER

United States Court of Customs and Patent Appeals, 1981.
655 F.2d 221, 210 USPQ 790.

RICH, JUDGE.

This appeal is from the decision of the United States Patent and Trademark Office (PTO) Board of Appeals (board) sustaining the examiner's rejection of all claims under 35 U.S.C. § 102(b), on the ground that applicant's invention was described in a printed publication in a foreign country more than one year prior to the U.S. filing date of his application serial No. 740,343, filed November 9, 1976, for a patent on a "Cable Junction Box." We affirm.

This appeal was heard on an agreed statement of the case, pursuant to CCPA Rule 5.5, which presents the following facts. On March 13, 1972, appellant filed Australian Patent Application No. PA 8273 accompanied by a provisional specification, that is, one without claims. On February 28, 1973, appellant filed a specification with claims and on August 29, 1974, more than two years before filing of the application at bar, the entire application, renumbered as patent application 52,691/ 73, was laid open to public inspection by the Australian Patent Office and a printed abstract thereof was published. The disclosure of the instant U.S. application corresponds to that of the Australian application.

Involved here are: (1) a microfilm copy of the Australian application preserved in the Australian Patent Office as a security reel, (2) a microfilm copy of the application that is cut up and used to make diazo copies, and (3) the diazo copies. * * *

ISSUE

The sole issue is whether what occurred in the Australian Patent Office resulted in the production of a "printed publication" within the meaning of 35 U.S.C. § 102(b).

* * *

It has been stated by this and other courts that to constitute a "printed publication," as that term is used in § 102, a reference must be both "printed" and "published." *In re Bayer,* 568 F.2d 1357, 1359, 196 USPQ 670, 673 (CCPA 1978); *In re Tenney,* 45 CCPA 894, 898, 254 F.2d 619, 622, 117 USPQ 348, 351 (1958); *General Tire & Rubber Co. v. Firestone Tire Co.,* 349 F.Supp. 345, 355, 174 USPQ 427, 442 (N.D.Ohio 1972), *modified,* 489 F.2d 1105, 180 USPQ 98 (6th Cir.1973). *See generally* 1 Chisum, *Patents* § 3.04 (1978); Rose, *Do You Have A "Printed Publication?" If Not, Do You Have Evidence Of Prior "Knowledge Or Use?",* 61 JPOS 643 (1979); Herbster, *It's Time To Take The "Printing" Out Of "Printed Publications",* 49 JPOS 38 (1967).

With regard to the "printing" requirement, it has been stated that the "only realistic distinction that we can see as between 'handwritten' and 'printed' publications relates to the *method* of producing them." *Tenney,* supra at 901, 254 F.2d at 625, 117 USPQ at 353 (emphasis in original). In other words, the requirement of printing increases the probability that a reference will be available to the public, for "Congress no doubt reasoned that one would not go to the trouble of printing a given description of a thing unless it was desired to print a number of copies of it." *Id.* at 902, 254 F.2d at 626, 117 USPQ at 354.

The "publication requirement," said to be "so connected with [the "printing" requirement] that treatment of the one cannot be satisfactorily done without overstepping into the bounds of the other," *Id.* 45 CCPA at 898 n. 4, 254 F.2d at 622 n. 4, 117 USPQ 351 n. 4, has been equated with public accessibility to the "printed document." *In re Bayer,* supra 568 F.2d at 1359, 196 USPQ at 673.

On the other hand, there are a number of cases which eschew this two-tiered approach and view the unitary concept of "printed publication" in the context of dissemination or accessibility alone. *Philips Electronics & Pharmaceutical Industries Corp. v. Thermal & Electronic Industries, Inc.,* 450 F.2d 1164, 1170, 171 USPQ 641, 645 (3d Cir.1971); *I.C.E. Corp. v. Armco Steel Corp.,* 250 F.Supp. 738, 742, 743, 148 USPQ 537, 540 (S.D.N.Y.1966). It was reasoned in *Philips* that:

The traditional process of "printing" is no longer the only process synonymous with "publication." The emphasis, therefore, should be

> *public dissemination* of the document, *and its availability and accessibility* to persons skilled in the subject matter or art. [Emphasis ours.]

We agree that "printed publication" should be approached as a unitary concept. The traditional dichotomy between "printing" and "publication" is no longer valid. Given the state of technology in document duplication, data storage, and data-retrieval systems, the "probability of dissemination" of an item very often has little to do with whether or not it is "printed" in the sense of that word when it was introduced into the patent statutes in 1836. In any event, interpretation of the words "printed" and "publication" to mean "probability of dissemination" and "public accessibility," respectively, now seems to render their use in the phrase "printed publication" somewhat redundant. This becomes clear upon examination of the purpose of the § 102 printed publication bar.

As this court pointed out in *In re Bayer,* supra 568 F.2d at 1359, 196 USPQ at 675, the printed publication provision was designed to prevent withdrawal by an inventor, as the subject matter of a patent, of that which was already in the possession of the public. Thus, the question to be examined under § 102(b) is the accessibility to at least the pertinent part of the public, of a perceptible description of the invention, in whatever form it may have been recorded. Access involves such factual inquiries as classification and indexing. In other words, such a reference is a "printed publication" and a bar to patentability

> * * * upon a satisfactory showing that such document has been disseminated or otherwise made available to the extent that persons interested and ordinarily skilled in the subject matter or art, exercising reasonable diligence, can locate it and recognize and comprehend therefrom the essentials of the claimed invention without need of further research or experimentation. [*I.C.E. Corp.,* supra [250 F.Supp.] at 743, 148 USPQ at 540.]

Appellant filed an application for an Australian patent which resulted in copies of that application being classified and laid open to public inspection at the Australian Patent Office and each of its five "sub-offices" over one year before he filed his application in the United States. Appellant himself informs us that:

> Equipment was available to the public in the Patent Office and in the sub-offices for providing an enlarged reproduction of the diazo copies on a display screen. Equipment was also available for producing enlarged paper copies for purchase by the public. Moreover, diazo copies were also available for sale to the public upon application to the Australian Patent Office, these latter diazo copies being produced to order from the second microfilm copy * * *.

Even though no fact appears in the agreed statement respecting actual viewing or dissemination of any copy of the application, there is no dispute that the records were maintained for this purpose. Given that there is also no genuine issue as to whether the application was properly classified, indexed, or abstracted, we are convinced that the contents of the application were sufficiently accessible to the public and to persons skilled in the pertinent art to qualify as a "printed publication," notwithstanding those cases holding that a foreign patent application laid open for public inspection is not a printed publication.

While intent to make public, activity in disseminating information, production of a certain number of copies, and production by a method allowing production of a large number of copies may aid in determining whether an item may be termed a "printed publication," they are neither always conclusive nor requisite. Each case must be decided on the basis of its own facts. Accordingly, whether information is printed, handwritten, or on microfilm or a magnetic disc or tape, etc., the one who wishes to characterize the information, in whatever form it may be, as a "printed publication"

> * * * should produce sufficient proof of its dissemination or that it has otherwise been available and accessible to persons concerned with the art to which the document relates and thus most likely to avail themselves of its contents. [*Philips Electronic Corp.*, supra 450 F.2d at 1171, 171 USPQ at 646.]

Through demonstration of the accessibility of reproductions of appellant's application in the Australian Patent Office and in each of its sub-offices, the PTO has met this burden.

* * *

The decision of the board affirming the rejection of claims 1–5 and 7–13 is *affirmed.*

IN RE HALL

United States Court of Appeals, Federal Circuit, 1986.
781 F.2d 897, 228 USPQ 453.

BALDWIN, CIRCUIT JUDGE.

This is an appeal from the decision of the U.S. Patent and Trademark Office's (PTO) former Board of Appeals, adhered to on reconsideration by the Board of Patent Appeals and Interferences (board), sustaining the final rejection of claims 1–25 of reissue Application No. 343,922, filed January 29, 1982, based principally on a "printed publication" bar under 35 U.S.C. § 102(b). The reference is a doctoral thesis. Because appellant concedes that his claims are unpatentable if the thesis is available as a "printed publication" more than one year prior to the application's effective filing date of February 27, 1979, the only issue is whether the thesis is available as such a printed publication.

* * *

The statutory phrase "printed publication" has been interpreted to give effect to ongoing advances in the technologies of data storage, retrieval, and dissemination. *In re Wyer*, 655 F.2d 221, 226, 210 USPQ 790, 794 (CCPA 1981). Because there are many ways in which a reference may be disseminated to the interested public, "public accessibility" has been called the touchstone in determining whether a reference constitutes a "printed publication" bar under 35 U.S.C. § 102(b). *See, e.g., In re Bayer,* 568 F.2d at 1359, 196 USPQ at 673; *In re Wyer,* 655 F.2d at 224, 210 USPQ at 792. The § 102 publication bar is a legal determination based on underlying fact issues, and therefore must be approached on a case-by-case basis. *See id.* at 227, 210 USPQ at 795. The proponent of the publication bar must show that prior to the critical date the reference was sufficiently accessible, at least to the public interested in the art, so that such a one by examining the reference could make the claimed invention without further research or experimentation. *See In re Donohue,* 766 F.2d 531, 533, 226 USPQ 619, 621 (Fed.Cir.1985); *In re Bayer,* 568 F.2d at 1361, 196 USPQ at 674; *In re Wyer,* 655 F.2d at 226–27, 210 USPQ at 794–95.

Relying on *In re Bayer,* appellant argues that the Foldi thesis was not shown to be accessible because Dr. Will's affidavits do not say when the thesis was indexed in the library catalog and do not chronicle the procedures for receiving and processing a thesis in the library.

* * *

In the present case, Dr. Will's affidavits give a rather general library procedure as to indexing, cataloging, and shelving of theses. Although no specific dates are cited (except that the thesis was received on November 4, 1977), Dr. Will's affidavits consistently maintain that inasmuch as the Foldi dissertation was received by the library in early November 1977, the dissertation "most probably was available for general use toward the beginning of the month of December, 1977." The only reasonable interpretation of the affidavits is that Dr. Will was relying on his library's general practice for indexing, cataloging, and shelving theses in estimating the time it would have taken to make the dissertation available to the interested public. Dr. Will's affidavits are competent evidence, and in these circumstances, persuasive evidence that the Foldi dissertation was accessible prior to the critical date. Reliance on an approximation found in the affidavits such as "toward the beginning of the month of December, 1977" works no injustice here because the critical date, February 27, 1978, is some two and one half months later. Moreover, it is undisputed that appellant proffered no rebuttal evidence.

Based on what we have already said concerning "public accessibility," and noting that the determination rests on the facts of each case, we reject appellant's legal argument that a single cataloged thesis in one university library does not constitute sufficient accessibility to those interested in the art exercising reasonable diligence.

We agree with the board that the evidence of record consisting of Dr. Will's affidavits establishes a prima facie case for unpatentability of the claims under the § 102(b) publication bar. It is a case which stands unrebutted.

Accordingly, the board's decision sustaining the rejection of appellant's claims is *affirmed.*

Notes

1. "It will be observed that the same statute uses different phraseology in describing the kind of publication which is to have this effect. In the body of the fifteenth section of the act of 1836 it is declared to be a description in 'some public work'; and in the proviso of the same section it is declared to be 'any printed publication.' This renders it somewhat doubtful, as to what kind of publication is intended. The phrase 'some public work' would seem to point to a class of regular, established publications, or to some book, publicly printed and circulated, so as to be open to the public; while the phrase 'any printed publication,' is broad enough to include any description printed in any form and published or circulated to any extent and in any manner. Taking the whole section together, however, and looking to the apparent policy of the statute, it is probable that the intention of Congress was to make it a conclusive presumption that the patentee had seen any printed description of the thing, which had been so printed and published as to be accessible to the public; but not to adopt that presumption in cases of printed descriptions published and circulated in such a manner as not to be accessible either to the public or to him." Curtis, Law of Patents § 376 (3rd ed., 1867).

2. In Hamilton Laboratories Inc. v. Massengill, 111 F.2d 584, 585, 45 USPQ 594, 595 (6th Cir.1940), the court held that a patentee's typewritten thesis submitted for his Master's Degree and put on file in the Library of Iowa State College and available to students there and through other libraries having exchange arrangements therewith was part of the prior art because "intent that the fruits of research be available to the public is determinative of publication under the statute whether the paper be printed or typewritten, although the court below decided otherwise." Accord, Ex parte Hershberger, 96 USPQ 54 (Pat.Office Bd.Appeals, 1952) and Gulliksen v. Halberg v. Edgerton v. Scott, 75 USPQ 252 (POBA 1937).

3. A document allegedly published by the Government of the Union of Soviet Socialist Republics, a copy of which was obtained only after months of diplomatic endeavor by the United States was not a printed publication in the absence of proof that the document was accessible to the public. Badowski v. United States, 143 Ct.Cl. 23, 164 F.Supp. 252, 118 USPQ 358 (1958).

d. *Effective Dates of Patents and Printed Publications*

APPLICATION OF EKENSTAM

United States Court of Customs and Patent Appeals, 1958.
45 CCPA 1022, 256 F.2d 321, 118 USPQ 349.

WORLEY, JUDGE. This is an appeal from the decision of the Board of Appeals of the United States Patent Office, one member dissenting, affirming the rejection by the Primary Examiner of claims 1 to 4, inclusive, and 6 to 9, inclusive, of appellant's application for a patent on a method of oxidizing cyclic compounds. The rejection is based on a single reference, namely the patent to Du Pont (Belgium) 494,439, having a "brevet octroyé" date of March 31, 1950, and a "brevet publié" date of July 1, 1950.

Since it is not disputed that the reference discloses the invention defined by the appealed claims, it is unnecessary to consider such disclosure or the claims. The sole issue is whether the effective date of the reference is March 31, 1950, or July 1, 1950. If it is the former then the reference is a statutory bar under 35 U.S.C.A. § 102(b) to the allowance of the claims in appellant's application, which was not filed until June 2, 1951. If it is the latter, then there is no statutory bar, and the reference is overcome by appellant's Swedish application filed June 12, 1950, a certified copy of which has been made of record in the Patent Office, and which has been held to disclose the rejected invention. It follows that if the board correctly held March 31, 1950, to be the effective date of the reference the decision appealed from should be affirmed, but if, as contended by appellant, the effective date is July 1, 1950, it should be reversed.

The majority of the Board of Appeals, relying on the board's prior decision in Ex parte Scalera et al., 104 USPQ 75, was of the opinion that availability to the public was not an essential feature of patenting. Neither in the Scalera et al. decision nor in the majority opinion of the board in the instant case was the matter extensively discussed. In each case it was recognized that the authorities were in conflict, but the decision of the United States District Court for the Southern District of New York in General Electric Company v. Hygrade Sylvania Corporation, 61 F.Supp. 476, was adopted as setting forth the proper conclusion. Accordingly, the "brevet octroyé" date of March 31, 1950, was held to be the effective date of the Du Pont Belgian patent here involved.

The significance of the "brevet octroyé" and "brevet publié" dates of a Belgian patent is fully pointed out in the carefully documented and well-reasoned opinion of the dissenting member of the board, which has been of great help in our review of this appeal. His statements of fact with respect to the significance of those dates appear to have been accepted without controversy by both parties. From those statements it appears that on the "brevet octroyé" date (March 31, 1950, in the instant case), which is normally less than a month after the application is filed, there is issued a decree which does not expressly grant specific rights but merely certifies that the application complies with the formal requirements. Nothing is sent to the applicant at that time, but he may ask for and receive as many official copies of the decree as he desires at any time after the "brevet octroyé" date. If he does not ask for such copies, a copy is mailed to him about six months after the date of the decree. The term of the patent begins on the day the application is filed but, as a practical matter, no court would grant relief unless it were presented with a copy of the decree, thus no suit could be effectively brought prior to the "brevet octroyé" date.

The application is deliberately kept secret from the public until the "brevet publié" date (July 1, 1950, in the instant case), which is approximately three months after the "brevet octroyé" date. During that period the applicant may, if he desires, withdraw his application, in which case the decree is cancelled and the application is not made public. In the absence of such a request, the application papers are made available to the public on the "brevet publié" date. It is agreed here that at least as early as that date the application becomes a patent.

The applicable Belgian law provides that the decree above referred to "shall constitute the patent" and the expression "brevet octroyé," which appears on the printed copies of the specification, may properly be translated "patent granted." In our opinion, however, the Belgian interpretation as to the "patent granted" is not in any wise binding on us as to whether the invention is patented there within the meaning of 35 U.S.C.A. § 102. It seems to us that section relates to the substance of what is actually done in a foreign country, rather than to the form or the literal meaning of language used in connection therewith. It is extremely difficult for us to believe that Congress intended anything which might happen to be called a "patent" in foreign countries should *ipso facto* be a bar to applicants in this country regardless of how remote it might be from what is generally understood here as being a patent. * * *

It is also noted that in each instance in which prior patenting is made a statutory bar by Title 35 U.S.C.A., it is coupled with publication, by the use of the expression "patented or described in a printed publication" (35 U.S.C.A. §§ 102(a) and (b) and 119), which would seem to indicate a connection between patenting and availability to the public. In the recent case of In re Tenney, 45 CCPA, Patents, —, 254 F.2d 619, it was pointed out that the apparent reason for making a prior description of an invention in a printed publication a bar to the granting of a patent on an invention was that if knowledge of the invention was already available to the public there was no consideration for the patent grant. We think it reasonable to assume that prior patenting was made a bar for the same reason and on the assumption that a patented invention would be available to the public.

There seems to be no logical reason why the granting of a secret patent abroad should be a bar to patenting in this country. Such a foreign patent is of no value to persons in this country unless and until it is made available to the public. It is to be noted that even a widespread prior knowledge of an invention abroad does not alone bar the grant of a patent in this country, and it is not reasonable to suppose that Congress intended to give greater effect to secret patenting abroad than to public knowledge there.

While the decisions as to whether availability to the public is essential to constitute patenting are somewhat conflicting, most of them appear to hold that a secret foreign patent is not a proper reference against an application for a patent in this country.

* * *

It is also argued on behalf of the Commissioner that if patenting within the meaning of the statute is limited to patents which are open to the public, then a patent is merely a special form of printed publication, and the expression "patented or described in a printed publication" is redundant. That argument, however, overlooks the fact that there is nothing in the nature of a patent which requires it to be printed. In fact it agreed by appellant and the Patent Office that the Du Pont patent here was a patent on its "brevet publié" date of July 1, 1950, even though it was not printed at that time and was only open to inspection in typewritten form, a form which has been held not to be a printed publication. It is thus quite possible for a document to be a patent without also being a printed publication.

For the reasons given, we are of the opinion, both on principle and authority, that the word "patented" as used in 35 U.S.C.A. § 102(a) and (b) is limited to patents which are available to the public. Since the Belgian patent relied on was not so available prior to July 1, 1950, it did not become a patent until that date, within the meaning of those paragraphs, and hence is not properly available as a reference against appellant's application.

The decision of the Board of Appeals is accordingly reversed.

Reversed.

✓ MILBURN CO. v. DAVIS-BOURNONVILLE CO.

Supreme Court of the United States, 1926.
270 U.S. 390, 70 L.Ed. 651, 46 S.Ct. 324.

MR. JUSTICE HOLMES delivered the opinion of the court:

This is a suit for the infringement of the plaintiff's patent for an improvement in welding and cutting apparatus alleged to have been the invention of one Whitford. The suit embraced other matters but this is the only one material here. The defense is that Whitford was not the first inventor of the thing patented, and the answer gives notice that to prove the invalidity of the patent evidence will be offered that one Clifford invented the thing, his patent being referred to and identified. The application for the plaintiff's patent was filed on March 4, 1911, and the patent was issued on June 4, 1912. There was no evidence carrying Whitford's invention further back. Clifford's application was filed on January 31, 1911, before Whitford's, and his patent was issued on February 6, 1912. It is not disputed that this application gave a complete and adequate description of the thing patented to Whitford, but it did not claim it. The district court gave the plaintiff a decree, holding that while Clifford might have added this claim to his application, yet as he did not, he was not a prior inventor. 297 F. 846. The decree was affirmed by the circuit court of appeals. 1 F.2d 227. There is a conflict between this decision and those of the other circuit courts of appeal, especially the sixth. Lemley v. Dobson-Evans Co., 156 C.C.A. 171, 243 F. 391; Naceskid Service Chain Co. v. Perdue (C.C.A.6th) 1

F.2d 924. Therefore, a writ of certiorari was granted by this court. 266 U.S. 596, 45 S.Ct. 93, 69 L.Ed. 459.

The patent law authorizes a person who has invented an improvement like the present, "not known or used by others in this country, before his invention," etc., to obtain a patent for it. Rev.Stat. § 4886, amended March 3, 1897, chap. 391, § 1, 29 Stat. at L. 692, Comp.Stat. § 9430, 7 Fed.Stat.Anno.2d ed. p. 23. Among the defenses to a suit for infringement the fourth specified by the statute is that the patentee "was not the original and first inventor or discoverer of any material and substantial part of the thing patented." Rev.Stat. § 4920, amended March 3, 1897, chap. 391, § 2, 29 Stat. at L. 692, Comp.Stat. § 9466, 7 Fed.Stat.Anno.2d ed. p. 309. Taking these words in their natural sense as they would be read by the common man, obviously one is not the first inventor if, as was the case here, somebody else had made a complete and adequate description of the thing claimed before the earliest moment to which the alleged inventor can carry his invention back. But the words cannot be taken quite so simply. In view of the gain to the public that the patent laws mean to secure we assume for purposes of decision that it would have been no bar to Whitford's patent if Clifford had written out his prior description and kept it in his portfolio uncommunicated to anyone. More than that, since the decision in the case of The Corn-Planter Patent (Brown v. Guild) 23 Wall. 181, 23 L.Ed. 161, it is said, at all events for many years, the Patent Office has made no search among abandoned patent applications, and by the words of the statute a previous foreign invention does not invalidate a patent granted here if it has not been patented or described in a printed publication. Rev.Stat. § 4923. See Westinghouse Mach. Co. v. General Electric Co., 126 C.C.A. 575, 207 F. 75. These analogies prevailed in the minds of the courts below.

On the other hand publication in a periodical is a bar. This as it seems to us is more than an arbitrary enactment, and illustrates, as does the rule concerning previous public use, the principle that, subject to the exceptions mentioned, one really must be the first inventor in order to be entitled to a patent. Coffin v. Ogden, 18 Wall. 120, 21 L.Ed. 821. We understand the circuit court of appeals to admit that if Whitford had not applied for his patent until after the issue to Clifford, the disclosure by the latter would have had the same effect as the publication of the same words in a periodical, although not made the basis of a claim. 1 F.2d 233. The invention is made public property as much in the one case as in the other. But if this be true, as we think that it is, it seems to us that a sound distinction cannot be taken between that case and a patent applied for before but not granted until after a second patent is sought. The delays of the Patent Office ought not to cut down the effect of what has been done. The description shows that Whitford was not the first inventor. Clifford had done all that he could do to make his description public. He had taken steps that would make it public as soon as the Patent Office did its work, although, of course, amendments might be required of him before the end could be reached. We see no reason in the words or policy of the law for allowing Whitford to profit by the delay and make himself out to be the first inventor when he was not so in fact, when Clifford had shown knowledge inconsistent with the allowance of Whitford's claim (Webster Loom Co. v. Higgins, 105 U.S. 580, 26 L.Ed. 1177), and when otherwise the publication of his patent would abandon the thing described to the public unless it already was old (McClain v. Ortmayer, 141 U.S. 419, 424, 12 S.Ct. 76, 35 L.Ed. 800, 802; Underwood v. Gerber, 149 U.S. 224, 230, 13 S.Ct. 854, 37 L.Ed. 710, 713).

The question is not whether Clifford showed himself by the description to be the first inventor. By putting it in that form it is comparatively easy to take the next step and say that he is not an inventor in the sense of the statute unless he makes a claim. The question is whether Clifford's disclosure made it impossible for Whitford to claim the invention at a later date. The disclosure would have had the same effect as at present if Clifford had added to his description a statement that he did not claim the thing described because he abandoned it or because he believed it to be old. It is not necessary to show who did invent the thing in order to show that Whitford did not.

* * *

As to the analogies relied upon below, the disregard of abandoned patent applications however explained cannot be taken to establish a principle beyond the rule as actually applied. As an empirical rule it no doubt is convenient if not necessary to the Patent Office, and we are not disposed to disturb it, although we infer that originally the practice of the Office was different. The policy of the statute as to foreign inventions obviously stands on its own footing and cannot be applied to domestic affairs. The fundamental rule we repeat is that the patentee must be the first inventor. The qualifications in aid of a wish to encourage improvements or to avoid laborious investigations do not prevent the rule from applying here.

Decree reversed.[d]

IN RE WERTHEIM

United States Court of Customs and Patent Appeals, 1981.
646 F.2d 527, 209 USPQ 554.

RICH, JUDGE.

This appeal is from the decision of the Patent and Trademark Office (PTO) Board of Appeals (board) affirming the final rejection under 35 U.S.C. § 103 of claims 37, 38, and 44 in application serial No. 96,285, filed by Wertheim and Mishkin (Wertheim) December 8, 1970, entitled "Drying Method." We reverse.

* * *

d. The Reviser's Note on Section 102 of the 1952 Patent Act states in part that "Paragraph (e) is new and enacts the rule of Milburn v. Davis-Bournonville, 270 U.S. 390, 46 S.Ct. 324, 70 L.Ed. 651, by reason of which a United States patent disclosing an invention dates from the date of filing the application for the purpose of anticipating a subsequent inventor." Is 102(e) a codification of the Milburn case?

The primary reference, cited by the examiner under 35 U.S.C. § 102(e), is the Pfluger patent which issued on the last of a series of four applications, as shown above. The patent discloses a foam/freeze-dried coffee process for retaining volatile aromatics during the foaming and freezing steps.

* * *

The Pfluger application chain developed as follows: Pfluger IV was designated a continuation of Pfluger III, which was designated a continuation-in-part (CIP) of Pfluger II, which was designated a CIP of Pfluger I.

Pfluger I did not support all of the limitations of the claims copied from the Pfluger patent. Specifically, it did not disclose concentrating the extract to a solids content of between 35% and 60% prior to foaming. Express disclosure of this limitation did not occur until Pfluger III. It also did not expressly disclose always creating the foamed extract at at least atmospheric pressure, a limitation first found in Pfluger II.

* * *

A different situation arises where, unlike *Milburn* or *Hazeltine,* the reference patent issues not after only one application, but after a series of applications. In other words, after permitting the use of a patent reference in both § 102(e) and §§ 102(e)/103 rejections as of the reference filing date, the next question confronting the courts was what filing date was to be accorded a reference patent which issues after a series of applications. How far back can one extend the effective date of a reference patent as "prior art" in such a case?

II. 102(e) AND CONTINUATION APPLICATIONS

In *In re Lund,* 54 CCPA 1361, 376 F.2d 982, 153 USPQ 625 (1967), this court was called upon to decide whether a certain compound disclosed in Example 2 of an application filed by Margerison on September 29, 1958, was available as prior art as of that filing date to reject Lund's claims, which were presented in an application filed almost a year later. Although Margerison abandoned the application, he had filed a continuation-in-part application, without Example 2, which resulted in issuance of the reference patent. The court stated it to be

> * * * well settled that where a patent purports on its face to be a "continuation-in-part" of a prior application, the continuation-in-part application is entitled to the filing date of the parent application as to all subject matter *carried over* into it from the parent application, whether for purposes of obtaining a patent or subsequently utilizing the *patent* disclosure as evidence to defeat another's right to a patent. [Emphasis in original.]

In deciding what had been "carried over," the court held that merely designating an application as a continuation-in-part was not sufficient to incorporate by reference the disclosure of the abandoned application into the patent disclosure, "as if fully set out therein." The court concluded that:

It seems to us that the sine qua non of § 102(e) and the *Milburn* case is that, consistent with the gain to the public which the patent laws mean to secure, a *patent must issue* which contains, explicitly or implicitly, the description of an invention which is to be relied on to defeat a later inventor's patent rights. It does not appear that the patentee here has done "all that he could do to make his description public," *Milburn,* supra, for the language Margerison employs is not sufficient to incorporate the description of his earlier application into the patent and the description which the Patent Office relies upon appears only in the earlier application. [Emphasis in original.]

* * *

We now come to the situation in the instant case, one which we believe has not heretofore been before us. What patent disclosure, or portion thereof, which has been "carried over" through a chain of applications, may be traced back to an earlier application and given its effective date, and then combined with a secondary reference to reject later filed claims under §§ 102(e)/103?

issue

* * *

We are asked by the PTO to apply the "carried over" principle set forth in *Klesper* to the present §§ 102(e)/103 rejection. Specifically, the solicitor argues that since this court said in *Wertheim I* that Pfluger II was "carried forward" into the Pfluger patent, and Pfluger I discloses essentially the same invention as Pfluger II, the Pfluger reference patent must be awarded the benefit of the Pfluger I filing date.

* * *

Although this court apparently embraced this procedure in *Wertheim I,* such an approach in a situation where there are continuation-in-part applications ignores the rationale behind the Supreme Court decisions in *Milburn* and *Hazeltine* that "but for" the delays in the Patent Office, the patent would have earlier issued and would have been prior art known to the public. The patent disclosure in *Milburn* was treated as prior art as of its filing date because at the time the application was filed in the Patent Office the inventor was presumed to have disclosed an invention which, but for the delays inherent in prosecution, would have been disclosed to the public on the filing date. A continuation-in-part application, by definition, adds new matter to the parent application previously filed. Thus, the type of new matter added must be inquired into, for if it is critical to the patentability of the claimed invention, a patent could not have issued on the earlier filed application and the theory of Patent Office delay has no application.

Additionally, it is at this point in the analysis that § 120 enters the picture, for the phrase in § 102(e), "on an *application* for patent," necessarily invokes § 120 rights of priority for prior co-pending applications. If, for example, the PTO wishes to utilize against an applicant a part of that patent disclosure found in an application filed earlier than the date of the application which became the patent, it must demonstrate that the earlier-filed application contains §§ 120/112 support for the invention claimed in the reference patent. For if a patent *could not* theoretically have issued the day the application was filed, it is not entitled to be used against another as "secret prior art," the rationale of *Milburn* being inapplicable, as noted above. In other words, we will extend the "secret prior art" doctrine of *Milburn* and *Hazeltine* only as far as we are required to do so by the logic of those cases.

* * *

Thus, the determinative question here is whether the invention claimed in the Pfluger patent finds a *supporting disclosure in compliance with § 112*, as required by § 120, in the 1961 Pfluger I application so as to entitle that invention in the Pfluger patent, as "prior art," to the filing date of Pfluger I. Without such support, the invention, and its accompanying disclosure, cannot be regarded as prior art as of that filing date. * * * The only date the Pfluger patent has *under § 102(e)* is February 10, 1969, the filing date of Pfluger IV, the application on which the patent issued. Any earlier U.S. filing date for the patent necessarily depends on further compliance with §§ 120 and 112. The board appears to have assumed the existence of the very point at issue here—whether the patent reference *is* entitled to a March 24, 1961, filing date.

We take note of two claim limitations missing from Pfluger I but present in the Pfluger patent which answer the question of whether to award the 1961 filing date to the § 102(e) reference patent disclosure. Pfluger I did not expressly disclose either concentrating the coffee extract to a 35% to 60% solids content, or avoiding evaporative cooling during the foaming and freezing steps. If either limitation, later added as new matter, resulted in the disclosure of a patentable invention for the first time, it is relevant to our determination of whether the Pfluger patent receives the benefit of the Pfluger I filing date.

* * *

A closer examination of the Pfluger file history reveals that the above limitations were relevant, indeed, critical new matter. From Pfluger II on, the patentee argued with the examiner over that feature of his process which he believed made the invention patentable—the avoidance of evaporative cooling. However, it was not until after the filing of Pfluger III that the first allowance of claims occurred. There the patentee successfully distinguished the prior art by expressly stating the conditions under which such cooling is avoided. Both at least a 35% solids content and foaming under "conditions which avoid the evaporation of water" were allegedly necessary for allowance. It was the combination of these steps, and others, which was held to be a patentable invention and deemed allowable by the examiner in Pfluger III. In fact, during the prosecution of Pfluger IV, the examiner required that Pfluger specify the minimum level of concentration for the coffee extract—at least 35%.

The board erred in ruling that since "the substance of the relevant disclosure in Pfluger I was carried forward into the patent," that same disclosure in the reference patent was entitled to the Pfluger I filing date, *even though the entire patent was not.* While some of the reference patent disclosure can be traced to Pfluger I, such portions of the original disclosure cannot be found "carried over" for the purpose of awarding filing dates, unless that disclosure constituted a full, clear, concise and exact description in accordance with § 112, first paragraph, of the invention claimed in the reference patent, else the application could not have matured into a patent, within the *Milburn* § 102(e) rationale, to be "prior art" under § 103.

The two claim limitations of the reference patent missing from Pfluger I were a necessary part of the only patentable invention ever set forth in the Pfluger file history. These limitations, however, were neither expressly nor inherently part of the original Pfluger disclosure. Absent these steps, the Pfluger I filing date cannot be accorded to the Pfluger patent reference. Without that date, the reference does not antedate Wertheim's alleged actual reduction to practice and cannot be combined with another reference to support a § 103 rejection.

To look at it another way, without the benefit of the Pfluger I filing date, that part of the reference patent disclosure relied upon cannot be said to have been incipient public knowledge as of that date "but for" the delays of the Patent and Trademark Office, under the *Milburn* rationale. Here, it cannot be said to have been "carried over" into the reference patent for purposes of defeating another's application for patent under §§ 102(e)/103.

The dictum in *Lund,* supra, that

> * * * the continuation-in-part application is entitled to the filing date of the parent application as to all subject matter *carried over* into it from the parent application * * * for purposes of * * * utilizing the *patent* disclosure as evidence to defeat another's right to a patent * * * [emphasis in original]

is hereby modified to further include the requirement that the application, the filing date of which is needed to make a rejection, must disclose, pursuant to §§ 120/112, the invention claimed in the reference patent. Where continuation-in-part applications are involved, the logic of the *Milburn* holding as to secret prior art would otherwise be inapplicable. Without the presence of a patentable invention, no patent could issue "but for the delays of" the PTO.

CONCLUSION

Since the patent disclosure used in the present rejection is not effective as a reference as of the Pfluger I filing date, the decision of the board affirming the §§ 102(e)/103 rejection of claims 37, 38, and 44 is *reversed.*

APPLICATION OF BAYER

United States Court of Customs and Patent Appeals, 1978.
568 F.2d 1357, 196 USPQ 670.

BALDWIN, JUDGE.

* * *

Appellant does not dispute that his thesis is printed. Accordingly, the dispositive issue is whether appellant's uncatalogued, unshelved thesis, by virtue of its accessibility to the graduate committee, is a "publication" within the meaning of 35 U.S.C.A. § 102(b).

OPINION

It is well settled that in determining whether a printed document constitutes a publication bar under 35 U.S.C.A. § 102(b) the touchstone is public accessibility. This follows logically from the theory that the patent grant is in the nature of a contract between the inventor and the public. Hence, if knowledge of the invention is already accessible to the public there is a failure of consideration and no patent may be granted. In re Tenney, 254 F.2d 619, 45 CCPA 894, 117 USPQ 348 (1958).

We are here concerned with a question of degree, namely, what degree of public accessibility is required for a printed document to qualify as a publication under the statute. Appellant maintains that accessibility to the general public is required, whereas the board expressed the view that accessibility to any part of the public will suffice. Authority can be mustered to support either position.

The essential requisites for publication set forth in 1 W. Robinson, The Law of Patents § 325 at 446 (1890), insofar as are here pertinent, are that the publication be: "(1) A work of public character intended for general use; (2) within reach of the public * * *." With respect to the first of these requisites, it is stated:

A work of public character is such a book or other printed document as is intended and employed for the communication of ideas to persons in general, as distinguished from particular individuals. Private communications, although printed, do not come under this description, whether designed for the use of single persons or of a few restricted groups of persons.

Id. § 326 at 447.

That the publication be within the reach of the public is amplified as follows:

[I]t must have been actually published in such a manner that any one who chooses may avail himself of the information it contains.

Id. § 327 at 448.

Of similar import is the following excerpt from Popeil Brothers, Inc. v. Schick Electric, Inc., 494 F.2d 162, 166, 181 USPQ 482, 485 (C.A.7 1974):

To constitute a printed publication for purposes of the publication bar all that is required is that the document in question be printed and so disseminated as to provide wide public access to it.

Needless to say, appellant relies on the foregoing authorities to support his position.

The board's holding, in essence, is founded on the proposition enunciated in Pickering v. Holman, 459 F.2d 403, 407, 173 USPQ 583, 585 (C.A.9 1972) (citing 1 A. Deller, Deller's Walker on Patents § 60 at 272 (2d ed. 1964)) that "[a]nything that is printed and made accessible to any part of the public is a printed publication." However, a review of the cases cited in Deller's as standing for that proposition reveals that the board's reliance thereon is misplaced.

The printed documents relied upon to show patent invalidity in Imperial Glass Co. v. A. H. Heisey & Co., supra note 10, were glass manufacturers' catalogues. The trial court refused to consider the catalogues, thinking that they were not publications within the meaning of the statute because they were not found in a library. The appellate court held that to be error, reasoning that "manufacturer's catalogues so circulated are more effective in spreading information among persons skilled in that art than if the same catalogues were only on file in some public library." Id. at 269. This rationale was followed in Jockmus v. Leviton, 28 F.2d 812, 813–14 (C.A.2 1928), wherein it was stated:

> On principle we are entirely in accord, for the purpose of the statute is apparent, and we ought to effect it so far as its language will allow. While it is true that the phrase, "printed publication," presupposes enough currency to make the work part of the possessions of the art, it demands no more. A single copy in a library, though more permanent, is far less fitted to inform the craft than a catalogue freely circulated, however ephemeral its existence; for the catalogue goes direct to those whose interests make them likely to observe and remember whatever it may contain that is new and useful.

From the foregoing authorities, we think it apparent that a printed document may qualify as a "publication" under 35 U.S.C.A. § 102(b), notwithstanding that accessibility thereto is restricted to a "part of the public," so long as accessibility is sufficient "to raise a presumption that the public concerned with the art would know of [the invention]." Camp Bros. & Co. v. Portable Wagon Dump & Elevator Co., supra note 10, at 607. Cf. Garrett Corp. v. United States, 422 F.2d 874, 190 Ct.Cl. 858, cert. denied, 400 U.S. 951, 91 S.Ct. 242, 27 L.Ed.2d 257 (1970). Accessibility to appellant's thesis by the three members of the graduate committee under the circumstances of the present case does not raise such a presumption.[11]

---

11. Although the board stated that members of the graduate committee could have transmitted the information necessary for obtaining the thesis to others, the record is devoid of any enlightenment concerning that possibility.

Moreover, since appellant's thesis could have been located in the university library only by one having been informed of its existence by the faculty committee, and not by means of the customary research aids available in the library, the "probability of public knowledge of the contents of the [thesis]," In re Tenney, supra, 254 F.2d at 626, 45 CCPA at 902, 117 USPQ at 354, was virtually nil.

The board's opinion does not specifically address the examiner's argument that the library's inefficiency should not redound to appellant's benefit, and the solicitor has reasserted it in his brief, paraphrasing Alexander Milburn Co. v. Davis Bournonville Co., 270 U.S. 390, 46 S.Ct. 324, 70 L.Ed. 651 (1926), thus, "the delays of the university library ought not to cut down the effect of what has been done[;] and appellant had taken steps that would make his thesis public as soon as the university library did its work." However, this argument overlooks conceptual differences between 35 U.S.C.A. § 102(b) and 35 U.S.C.A. § 102(e), the latter providing that: * * *

The concept underlying 35 U.S.C.A. § 102(e) is that a complete description of an applicant's invention in an earlier filed application of another, which subsequently matures into a patent, constitutes prima facie evidence that the applicant is *not the first inventor* of the invention in controversy. The Supreme Court in *Milburn* was of the opinion that administrative delays in the Patent Office should not detract from the anticipatory effect of such evidence.[13]

The publication bar of 35 U.S.C.A. § 102(b), as mentioned previously, operates upon the theory that the *invention in controversy is in the public domain*, and once there, is no longer patentable by anyone. The date on which the public actually gained access to the invention by means of the publication is the focus of inquiry. As stated in In re Tenney, supra, 254 F.2d at 626, 45 CCPA at 902, 117 USPQ at 354, "the public is not to be charged with knowledge of a subject until such time as it is available to it." Accordingly, under 35 U.S.C.A. § 102(b), delays within a university library, or within any other organization responsible for the publication of printed documents, are of utmost significance because public access to the document is thereby deferred, thus postponing the commencement of the one year time bar.

* * *

We have carefully reviewed the board's decision and the solicitor's arguments in support thereof, however, we are unconvinced that appellant's thesis defense before the graduate committee in its official capacity as arbiter of appellant's entitlement to a master's degree was somehow transmuted into a patent-defeating publication merely by depositing the thesis in the university library where it remained uncatalogued and unshelved as of the critical date in question. We believe that the board has attempted to draw too fine a line of

13. The rationale of *Milburn* is manifestly inapplicable to the case at bar because the thesis, being appellant's own work product, cannot provide any evidence whatever that appellant was not the first inventor of the subject matter of the appealed claims.

distinction here, and in so doing, has unjustifiably denied appellant's claims.

In view of the foregoing, we conclude that the board erred in holding that appellant's thesis constituted a "publication" within the meaning of 35 U.S.C.A. § 102(b).

Reversed.

JOSEPH BANCROFT & SONS CO. v. BREWSTER FINISHING CO.

United States District Court of New Jersey, 1953.
113 F.Supp. 714, 98 USPQ 187, affirmed 210 F.2d 677 (1954).

MODARELLI, DISTRICT JUDGE.

This is an action arising under the Patent Laws. The plaintiff, a Delaware corporation, charges that defendant, a New Jersey corporation, has infringed Claims 2 and 3 of United States Letters Patent No. 2,121,005, issued June 21, 1939, to Christian Bener, assignor to Raduner & Co. A.–G., Horn, Switzerland.

* * *

The Bener Patent in suit teaches a process of imparting a durable mechanical finish to goods, durable in that it is relatively fast to repeated dry cleanings or washings.

* * *

Before examining the prior art, the court must dispose of three questions of law.

* * *

II. THE ABANDONED LANTZ AND MORRISON UNITED STATES APPLICATION IS NOT TO BE CONSIDERED.

Messrs. Lantz and Morrison filed a United States application for a patent on a process for "Glazing, Embossing and Finishing of Textile Fabrics." The Lantz and Morrison United States application was filed two days before the United States Bener application. Lantz and Morrison United States was filed on October 2, 1934; Bener United States was filed on October 4, 1934. The Lantz and Morrison application was later abandoned; a United States patent never issued. Our intention is focused then on the question: Is an abandoned application a part of the body of prior art?

This is not a question of novel impression. In Monarch Marking System Co. v. Dennison Mfg. Co., 6 Cir., 1937, 92 F.2d 90, it was held that an abandoned application is not proof of prior invention: * * *

The rule is somewhat mollified by the fact that if the subject of an abandoned application was *reduced to practice* in this country, then the abandoned application itself is admissible as evidence of prior knowledge of the technique. U.S. Blind Stitch Mach. Corp. v. Reliable Mach. Works, Inc., 2 Cir., 1933, 67 F.2d 327. See particularly pp. 328–329. See also Journal of the Patent Office Society, Vol. 28, No. 3, Page 160. Defendant states in his brief that the Lantz and Morrison British

Patent No. 425,032, filed June 6, 1933, and covering the same process, indicates an intention of making the invention available to the public. Defendant states further that they would, in fact, make the invention available to the public. But it does not follow, therefore, that the subject of the abandoned United States application *was* made available to the public. We note also Interurban Ry. & Terminal Co. v. Westinghouse Electric & Mfg. Co., 6 Cir., 1911, 186 F. 166. That court quotes from Walker on Patents, 4th Edition, c. 3, Section 58:

"Novelty is not negatived by any prior abandoned application for a patent. Abandoned applications for patents are not, by the statutes, made bars to patents to later applicants. They furnish no evidence that the processes or things they describe were ever made or used anywhere. Being only pen and ink representations of what may have existed only as mental conceptions of the men who put them upon paper, they do not prove that the processes or things which they depict were ever known in any country. Nor can they be classed among printed publications, for they are usually in writing, and are not published by the Patent Office." 186 F. at page 168.

The court holds that the abandoned United States application by Lantz and Morrison is not to be considered in a study of the prior art to determine the validity of the Bener Patent in suit.

III. LANTZ AND MORRISON BRITISH APPLICATION NO. 425,032 CANNOT BE CONSIDERED AS PRIOR ART.

Bener United States was filed October 4, 1934. Prior to that date, Lantz and Morrison filed their provisional specifications in Britain, to wit, on June 6, 1933. The complete specifications were filed on June 20, 1934, and the British Patent accepted on March 6, 1935. The important sequence to note is that the Bener United States application was filed before the Lantz and Morrison British Patent was accepted, or issued, as we term it.

R.S. § 4923, 35 U.S.C.A. § 72, read:

"Whenever it appears that a [United States] patentee, at the time of making his application for the patent, believed himself to be the original and first inventor or discoverer of the thing patented, the same shall not be held to be void on account of the invention or discovery, or any part thereof, having been known or used in a foreign country, before his invention or discovery thereof, if it had not been *patented or described in a printed publication.*" (Emphasis Supplied.)

According to this section, an application in a foreign country does not suffice to establish priority of invention over a United States application. The foreign patent must have issued or a description published. The wording is clear. There is nothing in the legislative history of the Act that indicates any intention other than the plain meaning of that section. In fact, Mr. Lanham's Report on the Bill for the Committee on Patents recorded in U.S. Code Congressional Service, 79th Congress, Second Session 1946, page 1498, states:

"* * * It is deemed preferable to refuse evidence of foreign activities; *not published or patented,* in all cases, as this is the greater convenience in trials and other proceedings held in this country. It is pointed out in the hearings that this change is more in line with foreign laws, since foreign countries pay no attention to acts done outside of their own borders." (Emphasis Supplied.)

The Patent Code Act of July 19, 1952, c. 950, 66 Stat. 792, became effective January 1, 1953. The Patent Code, 35 U.S.C.A. § 102 reads:

"A person shall be entitled to a patent unless—

"(a) the invention was known or used by others in this country, or *patented or described in a printed publication in this or a foreign country,* before the invention thereof by the applicant for patent". (Emphasis Supplied.)

The crucial words are the same under the code as under its earlier counterpart, 35 U.S.C.A. Section 31.

In Westinghouse Mach. Co. v. General Electric Co., 2 Cir., 1913, 207 F. 75, the court following 35 U.S.C.A. Sections 31 and 72 held that "for the purpose of defeating a patent application, reduction to practice in a foreign country is a nullity unless the invention is patented or described in a printed publication." 207 F. at page 77. The court stated further 207 F. at page 78:

"* * * As we construe this section, reduction to practice in a foreign country can never operate to destroy a patent applied for here, however widely known such reduction to practice may be, either among foreigners or among persons living here, unless the invention be patented or described in a printed publication. To that extent section 4923 [35 U.S.C.A. § 72] qualifies the language of section 4886 [35 U.S. C.A. § 31], which without such qualification might well lead to a different result." To like effect: Vacuum Engineering Co. v. Dunn, 2 Cir., 1913, 209 F. 219.

The court holds that the Lantz and Morrison British application does not establish prior invention with respect to the Bener application later filed in the United States Patent Office.

APPLICATION OF HILMER [e]

United States Court of Customs and Patent Appeals, 1966.
359 F.2d 859, 149 USPQ 480, appeal after remand 424 F.2d 1108 (CCPA 1970).

RICH, JUDGE. The sole issue is whether a majority of the Patent Office Board of Appeals erred in overturning a consistent administrative practice and interpretation of the law of nearly forty years standing by giving a United States patent effect as prior art as of a foreign filing date to which the *patentee* of the reference was entitled under 35 U.S.C.A. § 119.

e. This case has been greatly reduced from the original 15–page decision. A student interested in scholarly legislative interpretation will profit by a reading of the full decision.

Because it held that a U.S. patent, cited as a prior art reference under 35 U.S.C.A. § 102(e) and § 103, is effective as of its foreign "convention" filing date, relying on 35 U.S.C.A. § 119, the board affirmed the rejection of claims 10, 16, and 17 of application serial No. 750,887, filed July 25, 1958, for certain sulfonyl ureas.

This opinion develops the issue, considers the precedents, and explains why, on the basis of legislative history, we hold that section 119 does not modify the express provision of section 102(e) that a reference patent is effective as of the date the application for it was "filed in the United States."

* * *

* * * We find it indeed strange that it has suddenly become imperative to reinterpret a statute which was enacted in 1903, later construed in the light of a Supreme Court decision of 1926, and to invert a practice under which a generation of lawyers since the latter date has obtained for clients close to two million United States patents, counting for their validity on a construction of the statutory law not only followed but promulgated by the Patent Office. Furthermore, in 1952 this law, already a quarter of a century old in toto, was carried forward by Congressional action without change, insofar as it was already statutory, and insofar as it was case law it was codified without change, the particulars of which will be dealt with later. This change in long and continuous administrative practice has also been made without any advance notice, hearing, or stated basis in policy, economics, or international relations. While it may be that the world is shrinking and the very concept of "foreign" should be abolished for the good of mankind, this is not a constitution we are expounding but specific statutes enacted to accomplish specific purposes, the meaning of which should stay put, absent intervening Congressional modifications, for well-understood reasons.

* * *

Section 102(e) was a codification of the *Milburn* doctrine. The *Milburn* case accorded a U.S. patent effect as a reference as of its U.S. filing date and stated that the policy of the statute on domestic inventions "cannot be applied to foreign affairs." No foreign date was involved in the case. The codifying statute specifies that the date as of which the patent has effect is the date of filing *"in the United States."*

R.S. 4887, predecessor of section 119, was in effect from 1903 to 1952 when it was incorporated unchanged in the present statutes. An examination of the legislative history of that statute fails to reveal a scintilla of evidence that it was ever intended to give "status" to an application or to serve as a patent-defeating provision except insofar as the application, or patent issuing thereon, becomes involved in a priority contest. The *Milburn* rule, under which U.S. patents are used as prior art references for all matter disclosed in them as of their U.S. filing dates has been consistently and continuously applied since its inception in 1926, if not earlier under lower court decisions, by the

United States Patent Office, the agency charged with the administration of the patent system, in accordance with the view expressed by the Commissioner of Patents in 1935 in the *Viviani* case. That view was that R.S. 4887, and later section 119, does not make a U.S. patent effective as a reference as of a foreign priority date to which it may be entitled. This view was further actively promulgated by the Patent Office in the *first edition* of its Manual of Patent Examining Procedure, Section 715.01, November, 1949, and so continued until May 27, 1964, after the expression by the board of its new view as exemplified in this case.

There is no case "law" on the issue here worth considering. Some seven cases have been cited pro and con, the most that can be found in a period of thirty-four years from 1926 to 1960. We believe they can be accurately summarized as follows: * * *

If any "weight of authority" is to be found in this we would say the scales tip more than perceptibly in favor of the restriction of U.S. patents *as references* to their filing dates *in the United States,* as stated in section 102(e) and in accordance with "in this country" limitations of 102(a), (g), and the prohibitions of section 104.

But over and above this as a basis of decision we feel there is a paramount principle which controls. The administrative agency known as the Patent Office pursued a uniform policy and interpretation contrary to the new view of the board for the 26 years from 1926 to 1952, at least. That interpretation was well publicized and well known and must be assumed to have been known to Congress in 1952 when it revised and codified the patent statutes into present Title 35, United States Code. In that codification section 119 reenacted R.S. 4887 with no change in substance, as above shown.

This legislative ratification of the interpretation of the statutes by the Patent Office determines the meaning and effect of section 119 for the future. Helvering v. Winmill, 305 U.S. 79, 59 S.Ct. 45, 83 L.Ed. 52 (1938), United States v. Dakota-Montana Oil Co., 288 U.S. 459, 53 S.Ct. 435, 77 L.Ed. 893 (1933). Under that interpretation, section 119 does not affect the express provision of 102(e) as to filing "*in the United States*" and the decision of the board that the Swiss filing date of Habicht is the effective date of his U.S. patent as a reference must be reversed.

* * *

APPLICATION OF SCHLITTLER

United States Court of Customs and Patent Appeals, 1956.
234 F.2d 882, 110 USPQ 304.

Before JOHNSON, ACTING CHIEF JUDGE, and WORLEY, COLE, and JACKSON, retired, ASSOCIATE JUDGES.

WORLEY, JUDGE. This is an appeal from the decision of the Board of Appeals of the United States Patent Office, affirming the rejection by the Primary Examiner of claims 11 to 15, inclusive, of appellants' application for a patent on "Amines and Process for the Preparation of Amines."

* * *

Since issues of law only are involved in this appeal, it is unnecessary to discuss the disclosure of appellants' application or to reproduce any of the claims on appeal.

* * *

The single reference relied on by the Patent Office in rejecting appellants' application is an article by Nystrom et al. which appeared in the November 1948 issue of the publication "The Journal of the American Chemical Society." Since appellants' application is admittedly entitled to the benefit of its filing date in Switzerland as of May 21, 1948, it is conceded the Nystrom et al. article cannot be used as a proper reference on the basis of its publication date alone. However, at the end of the published article is the notation "Received April 30, 1948."

The rejection is based on Section 102(a) of the Patent Act of 1952, 35 U.S.C.A. § 102(a), which provides that a patent shall not be granted if "the invention was known or used by others in this country * * * before the invention thereof by the applicant for patent." While no one contends the Nystrom article is a "publication" within the meaning of 35 U.S.C.A. § 102(a), as of April 30, 1948, it was the position of the Patent Office, notation of that date constitutes prima facie evidence that the invention claimed by appellants was "known" by others in this country prior to May 21, 1948. It is not disputed that the invention recited in appealed claims 11 and 13 is disclosed in the Nystrom et al. publication.

Although appellants, as well as amicus curiae, stress the alleged criticality of the notation purportedly reflecting the date of receipt of the article, it seems to us, in view of the decisions hereinafter cited, the basic question here is whether the Nystrom article, regardless of the date received, constitutes sufficient evidence of prior knowledge or use of the claimed invention by others in this country within the meaning of 35 U.S.C.A. § 102(a).

The Nystrom article contains descriptions of various experiments. It has been held by this court, however, that even a printed publication does not constitute a reduction to practice, but is evidence of conception only, Kear v. Roder, 115 F.2d 810, 28 CCPA, Patents, 774. Obviously the same would certainly be true of the manuscript on which a publication is based. Moreover, it was not held below, nor is it contended in the brief for the Commissioner of Patents, that the Nystrom et al. article per se is evidence of reduction to practice of the invention claimed. Accordingly, that article, at best, could be evidence of nothing more than conception and disclosure of the invention.

Before enactment of the Patent Act of 1952, it was repeatedly held that prior knowledge, in order to defeat a claim for a patent, must be knowledge of a complete and operative device, as distinguished from knowledge of a conception only.

* * *

[Citation and discussion of numerous cases and commentary of learned authors omitted.]

The reviser's note on Section 102 of the Patent Act of 1952, 35 U.S. C.A. § 102, contains the following statement:

> "No change is made in these paragraphs [102(a), (b), and (c)] other than that due to division into lettered paragraphs. The interpretation by the courts of paragraph (a) as being more restricted than the actual language would suggest (for example, "known" has been held to mean "publicly known") is recognized but no change in the language is made at this time."

Apparently, therefore, the 1952 act contemplated no change in the meaning of "known," as fixed by former judicial interpretation, and also recognized it as being even more limited than the ordinary meaning of the word.

* * *

The foregoing authorities are clearly to the effect that reduction to practice is an essential part of the prior knowledge or use by others which is necessary to anticipate a claim of a patent application within the meaning of the involved statute.

* * *

In our opinion, one of the essential elements of the word "known" as used in 35 U.S.C.A. § 102(a) is knowledge of an invention which has been completed by reduction to practice, actual or constructive, and is not satisfied by disclosure of a conception only.

It was also held in numerous decisions prior to the Patent Act of 1952 that prior knowledge of a patented invention would not invalidate a claim of the patent unless such knowledge was available to the public. Gayler v. Wilder, 10 How. 477, 13 L.Ed. 504; Pennock and Sellers v. Dialogue, 2 Pet. 1, 27 U.S. 1, 7 L.Ed. 327; Simmons v. Hansen, 8 Cir., 117 F.2d 49. That principle is stated by Robinson, Law of Patents, in Section 227:

> "It is to be remembered, however, that 'knowledge' in this sense means such an acquaintance with the invention on the part of the public as renders it available to them as a practically operative means."

and in Walker on Patents, Deller's Edition, page 281, it is said:

> "Novelty of a machine or manufacture is not negatived by any prior unpublished drawings, no matter how completely they may exhibit the patented invention—nor by any model no matter how fully it may coincide with the thing covered by the patent."

Obviously, in view of the above authorities, the mere placing of a manuscript in the hands of a publisher does not necessarily make it available to the public within the meaning of said authorities.

In view of the extensive discussion by all parties of the Milburn case, supra, it is desirable to consider that decision in some detail. Involved there was the validity of a patent to Whitford granted June 4, 1912, on an application filed March 4, 1911, in view of a patent to Clifford, disclosing but not claiming the invention claimed by Whitford, and granted February 6, 1912, on an application filed January 31, 1911. Thus, Clifford's patent was granted after Whitford's application was filed, but his application was filed prior to that of Whitford. The court held that the prior disclosure of the invention in the Clifford application rendered the Whitford patent invalid, saying [270 U.S. 390, 46 S.Ct. 325]:

> " * * * We understand the Circuit Court of Appeals to admit that if Whitford had not applied for his patent until after the issue to Clifford, the disclosure by the latter would have had the same effect as the publication of the same words in a periodical, although not made the basis of a claim. [Davis-Bournonville Co. v. Alexander Milburn Co., 2 Cir.,] 1 F.2d [227] 233. The invention is made public property as much in the one case as in the other. But if this be true, as we think that it is, it seems to us that a sound distinction cannot be taken between that case and a patent applied for before but not granted until after a second patent is sought. The delays of the patent office ought not to cut down the effect of what has been done. * * * "

It seems to us from the quoted language that the court did not hold that prior knowledge, to be anticipatory, need not be public, but did hold that the filing of a patent application on which a patent is later granted makes the invention disclosed public property as much as an actual publication in a periodical. The situation is different with respect to the submission of a manuscript to a private publisher who may make it public or not as he sees fit.

* * *

It is to be noted that in addition to Section 102(a), previously considered, the Patent Act of 1952 contains a further Section 102(e) which precludes the granting of a patent if "the invention was described in a patent granted on an application for patent by another filed in the United States before the invention thereof by the applicant for patent." The reviser's note with respect to the latter section reads:

> "Paragraph (e) is new and enacts the rule of Milburn Co. v. Davis-Bournonville, 270 U.S. 390 [46 S.Ct. 324, 70 L.Ed. 651], by reason of which a United States patent disclosing an invention dates from the date of filing the application for the purpose of anticipating a subsequent inventor."

This court has previously considered the Milburn decision. In Conover v. Downs, 35 F.2d 59, 61, 17 CCPA Patents, 587, it was pointed out that the Milburn decision "should be construed and applied in accordance with the precise issue before the court." We think that admonition is clearly appropriate here. Since the issues in the Milburn case are completely distinct from those here, we do not think the dicta there contemplated the precise issues here, nor that the conclusion there is properly applicable here.

*   *   *

Accordingly it becomes necessary to *reverse* the decision of the Board of Appeals.

Reversed.

Notes

1. "Appellants urge that the Swiss patent is not a proper reference because Switzerland was 'surrounded by the enemy' from the time the patent was granted until within one year of the filing of appellants' application. As to that matter, however, we are in agreement with the Board that the patent statutes make no distinction as to the availability to residents of the United States of a regularly issued and published foreign patent, and that the Swiss patent is therefore a proper reference." Application of Ward & Switzer, 43 CCPA 1007, 236 F.2d 428, 430–431, 111 USPQ 101, 103 (1956).

2. In Ex parte Harris, Hoffman and Folkers, 79 USPQ 439 (Bd.App. 1948), the Board of Appeals held that printed reports prepared in connection with research subsidized by the United States Government and classified as secret and confidential did not become a "printed publication" until the date on which they were released to the general public rather than the earlier date on which the reports were declassified since the group of persons who had received confidential copies of the reports were requested to refrain from disclosing the reports until an orderly procedure for publication could be developed.

3. In Ex parte Carnahan, 76 USPQ 335 (Bd.App.1948), the Board of Appeals held that a printed magazine was published on the date it was received by the addressee rather than when mailed by the publisher since "as a rule, the contents of the mails are preserved in secrecy until delivered to the addressee."

4. PRIOR INVENTION UNDER § 102(g) AS PRIOR ART

Controversy has raged among commentators as to whether a prior invention of another can be prior art under § 102(g) for negating novelty and nonobviousness of a patented invention. Unlike § 102(a), under § 102(g), the prior invention of another need not be publicly known or used by others before the patented invention was made.

The difference in the two sections can be dramatized by a situation in which a first inventor has a conception of an invention which is well documented in a written disclosure accompanied by drawings fully witnessed and corroborated. In addition, he has completely, successfully, and diligently reduced his invention to practice in a working device and has documented and corroborated complete test data and pictures of successful operation of the device. None of the work has been publicized and, in fact, care has been taken to keep it confidential. Due to the annual model change of his company's product line, the time required to design and test a commercial version of his invention, and the time required to construct a mass production facility, it is first introduced to the public and offered for sale about a year after it was reduced to practice. No patent application is contemplated by the first inventor. A second inventor conceives and reduces to practice the same invention within the aforesaid year period and is granted a patent on an application filed prior to any production or sale of the first inventor's invention.

Is the work of the first inventor available as prior art against the patent of the second inventor? Recently, several courts have concluded that it is, without expressly considering whether this "promotes the progress of * * * useful arts." Frequently, the following case is cited in support of this conclusion.

CORONA CORD TIRE CO. v. DOVAN CHEM. CORP.

Supreme Court of the United States, 1928.
276 U.S. 358, 48 S.Ct. 380, 72 L.Ed. 610.

The patent in suit relates to accelerators used in the vulcanization of rubber. A defense to this action was set up alleging prior knowledge by Dr. Kratz of the invention claimed. In 1916, Kratz prepared an accelerator referred to as D.P.G. and demonstrated its utility as a rubber accelerator by using it in making test slabs of vulcanized or cured rubber. Every time that he produced such a slab, he recorded his tests in cards which he left with the Norwalk Company. By these tests, he determined the superiority of D.P.G. over other known accelerators.

This work was known to his associate in the Norwalk Company who confirmed Kratz' records and statements. In 1918, Kratz conducted at another plant further tests which served as the basis for a paper which he read in 1919 before a meeting of the American Chemical Society. There also was evidence of sales of 300 inner tubes in 1917 which Kratz testified were made with D.P.G., although he did not tell anyone of this fact.

Weiss, the patentee, recorded data for tests which he conducted on February 10, 1919. This date in the record books had been tampered with, and there was some question of its accuracy. Weiss filed his application for patent in November, 1921.

Chief Justice TAFT, speaking for the U.S. Supreme Court, held that the Kratz paper, while read in 1919, was not published until April, 1920, and therefore, was not a bar since it was not published more than two years prior to the application. He then went on to say at a later portion of the opinion:

"But even if we ignore this evidence of Kratz' actual use of D.P.G. in these rubber inner tubes which were sold, what he did at Norfolk, supported by the evidence of Dr. Russell, his chief, and by the indubitable records that are not challenged, leave no doubt in our minds that he did discover in 1916 the strength of D.P.G. as an accelerator as compared with the then known accelerators, and that he then demonstrated it by a reduction of it to practice in production of curved or vulcanized rubber.

"This constitutes priority in this case."

Still later in the decision he stated:

"It is a mistake to assume that reduction to use must necessarily be a commercial use. If Kratz discovered, and completed as we are convinced that he did, the first use of D.P.G. as an accelerator in making vulcanized rubber, he does not lose his right to use this discovery when he chooses to do so for scientific purposes or purposes of publication or because he does not subsequently sell the rubber thus vulcanized or use his discovery in trade or does not apply for a patent for it. It is not an abandoned experiment because he confines his use of the rubber thus produced to his laboratory or to his lecture room. It is doubtless true that Kratz by his course in respect to his discovery as to the use of D.P.G. has abandoned any claim as against the public for a patent, but that is a very different thing from saying that it was abandoned as against a subsequent discoverer or patentee.

"The conclusion we reach then is that, so far as this record shows, the first discovery that D.P.G. was a useful accelerator of the vulcanization of rubber was made by George Kratz, and not by Weiss. * * *"

DUNLOP HOLDINGS LTD. v. RAM GOLF CORP.

United States Court of Appeals, Seventh Circuit, 1975.
524 F.2d 33, 188 USPQ 481.

STEVENS, CIRCUIT JUDGE.

Plaintiff sued Ram for infringement of its patent covering an unusually durable golf ball.[1] Ram convinced the district court that the patent was invalid because the invention had been made by a third party named "Butch" Wagner.

* * *

As noted, the date of invention claimed by plaintiff is February 10, 1965. In April of 1964, duPont was trying to find a commercial use for its Surlyn, a recently developed product. Shortly thereafter, Butch Wagner, who was in the business of selling re-covered golf balls, began to experiment with Surlyn as a golf ball cover. He first made some sample balls by hand and then, using a one-iron, determined that the material was almost impossible to cut. He obtained more Surlyn and made several dozen experimental balls, trying different combinations of additives to achieve the proper weight, color, and a texture that could easily be released from an injection molding machine. By November 5, 1964, he had developed a formula which he considered suitable for commercial production and had decided to sell Surlyn covered balls in

1. U.S. Patent No. 3,454,280 covering "Golf Balls Having Covers of Ethylene— Unsaturated Monocarboxylic Acid Copolymer Compositions," issued to Dunlop Rubber Company Limited, a British company, as the assignee of the two individual inventors, pursuant to a U.S. Patent Application filed February 2, 1966, and a British application filed on February 10, 1965.

large quantities. The date is established by a memorandum recording his formula, which Wagner wrote in his own hand and gave to his daughter for safekeeping on the occasion of her son's birthday.

During the fall of 1964, Wagner provided friends and potential customers with Surlyn covered golf balls. By the end of the year he had purchased enough Surlyn to produce more than 20,000 balls, and by February of 1965 he had received orders for over 1,000 dozen Surlyn covered balls. By the end of 1965, he had ordered enough Surlyn to produce more than 900,000 such balls. Without commenting further on the evidence, we note our conclusion that there is ample support in the record for the district court's findings that Wagner had discovered the use of Surlyn as a golf ball cover before November 5, 1964, had reduced the discovery to practice before February of 1965, and did not abandon the invention before his death in October of 1965.

We recognize that Wagner continued to experiment with different formulae after his decision to go into commercial production and that he encountered some problems with cracked covers. These facts do not undermine any of the district court's findings on the prior invention issue. The patent claims are broad enough to encompass any golf ball cover made principally of Surlyn, and there is no doubt that Wagner had made a large number of such golf balls and successfully placed them in public use.[2] The only novel feature of this case arises from the fact that Wagner was careful not to disclose to the public the ingredient that made his golf ball so tough. For that reason plaintiff argues that he "suppressed or concealed" the invention within the meaning of § 102(g).

Since 1850 it has been settled that a patentee may be entitled to credit for making a new discovery or invention even though someone else actually made the discovery before he did. Gayler v. Wilder, 10 How. 509, 51 U.S. 477, 13 L.Ed. 504. That case established the proposition that an abandoned invention will not defeat the patentability of the rediscovery of "lost art." The case has also been cited for the proposition that an inventor who had merely made a secret use of his discovery should not be regarded as the first inventor. Gillman v. Stern, 114 F.2d 28, 31 (2d Cir.1940).

Gillman involved a patent on a machine which had previously been developed by a man named Haas; Haas had used the machine in his own factory under tight security. The output from the machine had been sold, but the public had not been given access to the machine itself. In holding that Haas was not the first inventor, Judge Hand

2. The evidence identifies at least three golfers who used Surlyn covered balls during the fall of 1964 for rounds of golf played at Riveria Country Club in Los Angeles. (Tr. 366–377; Fredericks Deposition, pp. 4–9; Keller Deposition, pp. 5–11) By February, 1965, two of these golfers, both of whom were favorably impressed with the play of the new ball, had placed orders with Wagner for more than 1000 dozen Surlyn covered balls; they began to distribute them commercially although they both lacked knowledge of the Surlyn content in the cover construction. (Tr. 365–377; Keller Deposition, pp. 5–11; DX 7, 8, 13, and 24–27.)

drew a distinction between a secret use and a noninforming public use. There had been only a secret use of the Haas machine and therefore he was not regarded as the first inventor.

This case certainly involves neither abandonment nor a mere secret use. For the evidence clearly demonstrates that Wagner endeavored to market his golf balls as promptly and effectively as possible. The balls themselves were in wide public use. Therefore, at best, the evidence establishes a noninforming public use of the subject matter of the invention.

If Wagner had applied for a patent more than a year after commencing the public distribution of Surlyn covered golf balls, his application would have been barred notwithstanding the noninforming character of the public use or sale. Egbert v. Lippmann, 104 U.S. 333, 336, 26 L.Ed. 755; Magnetics, Inc. v. Arnold Engineering Co., 438 F.2d 72, 74 (7th Cir.1971). For an inventor must exercise reasonable diligence if he is to be rewarded with patent protection.

The question of diligence is especially significant in cases arising out of a dispute between two applicants for a patent on the same discovery. For in such a case, when the issue is which of the two applicants is entitled to the monopoly reward, it is often appropriate to weigh the later inventor's diligence in enabling the public to obtain the benefit of the concept more heavily than the earlier date of unexploited conception. Cf. Mason v. Hepburn, 13 App.D.C. 86, 91 (1898). But in this case, although Wagner may have failed to act diligently to establish his own right to a patent, there was no lack of diligence in his attempt to make the benefits of his discovery available to the public. In view of his public use of the invention, albeit noninforming, we do not believe he concealed or suppressed the discovery within the meaning of § 102(g).

We recognize, as appellant argues, that portions of Judge Rich's opinion in Palmer v. Dudzik, 481 F.2d 1377 (C.C.P.A.1973), suggest that a public use which does not disclose the inventive concept may amount to concealment within § 102(g). But that case, like *Gillman,* involved a patent on a machine; the benefits of using the machine were not made available to anyone except the inventor. Moreover, the case arose out of an interference proceeding in which the dispute was between two applicants for a patent, the earlier of the two having been less diligent than the later. In this case, Wagner was not only the first inventor, but also "the first to confer on the public the benefit of the invention," Gayler v. Wilder, 51 U.S. at 497.

There are three reasons why it is appropriate to conclude that a public use of an invention forecloses a finding of suppression or concealment even though the use does not disclose the discovery. First, even such a use gives the public the benefit of the invention. If the new idea is permitted to have its impact in the marketplace, and thus to "promote the Progress of Science and useful Arts," it surely has not been suppressed in an economic sense. Second, even though there may be no explicit disclosure of the inventive concept, when the article itself is freely accessible to the public at large, it is fair to presume that its secret will be uncovered by potential competitors long before the time when a patent would have expired if the inventor had made a timely application and disclosure to the Patent Office.[3] Third, the inventor is under no duty to apply for a patent; he is free to contribute his idea to the public, either voluntarily by an express disclosure, or involuntarily by a noninforming public use. In either case, although he may forfeit his entitlement to monopoly protection, it would be unjust to hold that such an election should impair his right to continue diligent efforts to market the product of his own invention.

We hold that the public use of Wagner's golf balls forecloses a finding of suppression or concealment; that holding is consistent with both the decided cases and the underlying purposes of the statute.

Affirmed.

KIMBERLY–CLARK CORPORATION v. JOHNSON & JOHNSON

United States Court of Appeals, Federal Circuit, 1984.
745 F.2d 1437, 223 USPQ 603.

RICH, CIRCUIT JUDGE.

This appeal is from the February 4, 1983, March 15, 1983 (219 USPQ 214), and April 5, 1983, 573 F.Supp. 1179 (219 USPQ 217), judgments of the United States District Court for the Northern District of Illinois, Eastern Division, sitting without a jury, holding that Kimberly-Clark Corporation's Roeder patent No. 3,672,371 ('371) issued June 27, 1972, for "Sanitary Napkin with Improved Adhesive Fastening Means" was not infringed, "unenforceable" because of "fraud on the PTO," and invalid under 35 U.S.C. § 103. We affirm the holding of non-infringement, reverse the holdings of obviousness and fraud, and remand.

Kimberly-Clark Corporation (K–C), which manufactures and sells MAXI–PADS under its KOTEX and NEW FREEDOM marks, sued Johnson & Johnson (J & J) and its wholly owned subsidiary, Personal Products Company (PPC), which manufactures and sells similar products under its STAYFREE and SURE & NATURAL marks. The patent in suit discloses a sanitary napkin having pressure-sensitive adhesive strips to secure it temporarily to a supporting undergarment, e.g., panties * * *

K–C contends that the district court incorrectly included as prior art the in-house work at K–C by Champaigne and Mobley and incor-

---

3. In this case, for example, it is not unreasonable to assume that competing manufacturers of golf balls in search of a tough new material to be used as a cover, might make inquiries of Wagner's Surlyn supplier that would soon reveal his secret ingredient. After all, duPont certainly had a motive to expand the market for Surlyn.

rectly determined the scope of the remaining prior art. We address these contentions separately.

The work of Champaigne found by the district court to be prior art related to a pad with a single wide line of attachment adhesive. To qualify as prior art, this work must meet the requirements of § 102(g) which, in relevant part, reads:

* * * Section 102(g) "relates to prior inventorship by another in this country as preventing the grant of a patent * * *. It * * * retains the rules of law governing the determination of priority of invention. * * *" P.J. Federico, *Commentary on the New Patent Act,* 35 U.S.C.A. page 1, at 19 (1954).

Thus, under § 102(g), one of the issues now before us is the question of priority as between Champaigne and Roeder. K–C argues that the district court incorrectly determined Champaigne's work to be prior art on the ground that "Roeder's work preceded * * * Champaigne's filing date," citing *In re Clemens,* 622 F.2d 1029, 206 USPQ 289 (CCPA 1980). *Clemens* was an appeal from the PTO Board of Appeals (board) of a §§ 102(g)/103 rejection on an invention shown in a Barrett patent, issued to a common assignee, having an earlier filing date. The dispositive issue in *Clemens,* as here, was whether there had been a prior reduction to practice of Barrett's invention relied on as invalidating art. Our predecessor court reversed the board, saying:

> Because the record does not support a finding that Barrett made his invention before appellants [Clemens et al.] made the invention * * *, the present 35 USC 102(g)/103 rejection * * * must fall. [622 F.2d 1029, 206 USPQ at 299.]

Here, K–C relies on Roeder's experimental conclusions on the location of the adhesive strips as proof of Roeder's prior reduction to practice. Those Roeder conclusions, however, make no reference to the adhesive's multiple functions which the examiner, the board and the trial court correctly determined to be critical limitations of the '371 patent claims. We are therefore not persuaded that the record supports a reduction to practice of Roeder's *claimed* invention prior to Champaigne's filing date. Accordingly, the district court's finding that Champaigne's invention was a prior reduction to practice was not legally wrong. Since Champaigne's invention meets the other requirements of § 102(g)[1] his work can be considered as prior art to Roeder under § 103.

The second item of K–C in-house work, that of Carolyn Mobley, consisted of laboratory experiments, documented in lab notebooks, designed to test various adhesive mixtures to find an adhesive composition that would alleviate the prior art problems ranging from insufficient tack to the undergarment to transfer of the adhesive to the

---

1. As discussed infra, the timely filing of a patent application, and subsequent issuance of a patent thereon, covering the Champaigne pad, constitutes sufficient proof that his invention was not abandoned, suppressed, or concealed.

undergarment. To qualify as prior art, this work also has to fit within the requirements of § 102(g).

* * *

K–C argues Mobley's experiments were not reduced to practice. J & J counters that such a suggestion is "absurd" stating:

> The actual making of these napkins is recorded in numerous lab notebooks * * *. In fact, hundreds of the napkins were actually *worn* by women participating in tests conducted by Champaigne, Mobley and outside consultants * * *.

While evidence of in-house testing may be prima facie evidence of conception, reduction to practice requires that an invention be sufficiently tested to demonstrate that it will work for its intended purpose. *Barmag Barmer Maschinenfabrik v. Murata Machinery, Ltd.,* 731 F.2d 831, 838, 221 USPQ 561, 567 (Fed.Cir.1984); *Shurie v. Richmond,* 699 F.2d 1156, 1159, 216 USPQ 1042, 1045 (Fed.Cir.1983). The record shows that the usefulness of the adhesive mixtures for their intended purpose was not inherently apparent, so that utility must have been demonstrated by actual testing of various adhesive mixtures. Mobley's experiments failed to set forth a single adhesive mixture that performed with sufficient success. As is the case here, "When the invention has not quite passed beyond experiment and has not quite attained certainty and has fallen short of demonstrating the capacity of the invention to produce the desired result, the invention itself is still inchoate." 1 *Deller's Walker on Patents,* § 46 at 202 (2d ed. 1964). We hold the Mobley experiments were not prima facie evidence of a reduction to practice. Under § 102(g), proof of a conception alone does not suffice to establish Mobley's work as prior to Roeder's invention. We therefore agree with K–C that Mobley's work was unavailable as § 103 "prior art" under § 102(g).

In addition, both parties have responded to the district court's finding that Roeder was *aware* of the foregoing in-house research. We need consider this point only with respect to Mobley's work since we have already decided, above, that Champaigne's work is § 103 prior art under § 102(g). K–C argues that "there is no evidence that Roeder was aware of any specific Champaigne or Mobley work on which the court could have relied. *In re Clemens,* 622 F.2d 1029, 1039–40 (C.C.P.A. 1980)." J & J counters, stating there is "substantial evidence to support the Court's finding that the Mobley and Champaigne work was known to Roeder. * * * Accordingly, this work by Champaigne and Mobley clearly qualifies as prior art. *In re Clemens* * * *; *In re Bass,* 474 F.2d 1276 [177 USPQ 178] (CCPA 1973)."

Both parties are citing *Clemens* for the legal proposition that personal knowledge of non-public work is sufficient to qualify that work as § 103 "prior art." *Clemens,* as previously discussed, involved a §§ 102(g)/103 rejection in which the reference, Barrett, was determined not to be *prior* under § 102(g) and therefore was not available as § 103 prior art. As § 102(g) contains no personal knowledge requirement, the court's sole discussion of personal knowledge was dictum in the course of a discussion which distinguished the facts before it from those in a previous opinion of the court also dealing with §§ 102(g)/103, namely, *In re Bass*. In that § 103 discussion, the court said:

> [W]here this other invention is unknown to both the applicant and the art at the time the applicant makes his invention, treating it as 35 USC 103 prior art would establish a standard for patentability in which an applicant's contribution would be measured against secret prior art. [622 F.2d at 1040, 206 USPQ at 299.]

The key factor in the above statement is the reference to "secret prior art." As *Clemens* points out, the use of such secret art—as § 103 "prior art"—except as required by § 102(e), is not favored for reasons of public policy.

In conclusion, the district court's finding that Roeder was aware of Mobley's work is irrelevant to a §§ 102(g)/103 analysis. It is still not prior art.

The in-house "work" which we find to be prior art is therefore that of Champaigne alone, whose patent is before us, the work thus having become public.   * * *

AKTIEBOLAGET KARLSTADS MEKANISKA WERKSTAD v. UNITED STATES INTERNATIONAL TRADE COMMISSION

United States Court of Appeals, Federal Circuit, 1983.
705 F.2d 1565, 217 USPQ 865.

RICH, CIRCUIT JUDGE.

This appeal is from the final determination of the United States International Trade Commission (ITC) of November 18, 1981, in Investigation No. 337–TA–82A, USITC Publication No. 1197 (November 1981), entitled "In the Matter of Certain Headboxes and Papermaking Machine Forming Sections for the Continuous Production of Paper, and Components Thereof." We affirm in part, reverse in part, vacate in part, and remand.

The underlying basis of the ITC's investigation resides in two patents owned by appellee Beloit Corporation (Beloit), a leading domestic manufacturer of papermaking machinery. They are Reissue patent No. 28,269 (the '269 patent) granted December 10, 1974, a reissue of original patent No. 3,607,625 to Hill, Parker, and Hergert (the '625 patent), issued September 21, 1971, on application serial No. 698,633 filed January 17, 1968; and Verseput patent No. 3,923,593 (the '593 patent), issued December 2, 1975, on application serial No. 434,048 filed January 17, 1974, as a continuation-in-part of an earlier application filed December 3, 1971. Both of these patents in suit issued to Beloit as assignee.   * * *

A third patent asserted by KMW to be prior art is U.S. patent No. 3,939,037 (the '037 patent) issued in 1976 to Hill, a named coinventor in the '269 patent, as a sole inventor on application serial No. 451,225, which was a continuation of a continuation-in-part of a division of the application which matured into the patent reissued as the '269 patent. As might be expected, the specifications of the '037 and '269 patents strongly resemble one another. Specifically, the '037 patent teaches a headbox with self-positionable trailing elements, and mentions that

> * * * it may be more convenient to have the flexible members
> * * * extend transversely of the slice chamber in the form of a full
> width sheet * * * where the transverse dimension of the preslice
> flow chamber is relatively narrow.

As developed later in this opinion, it is necessary to make a distinction between Hill's sole invention (later explained) as "prior art" under 35 U.S.C. §§ 102(g)/103 and the *disclosure* of the Hill '037 patent, as such, which is not § 103 "prior art."

* * *

KMW contends that the subject matter of claims 1 and 12 of the '269 patent is anticipated by the '037 patent's disclosure of the use of full width trailing elements in a narrow headbox. It also contends that the invention claimed in the '269 patent would have been obvious from the German patent. * * *

Underlying KMW's argument of anticipation is the premise that the '037 *patent* is prior art with respect to the '269 patent. KMW cites no statutory basis for this premise nor is one presented by the facts of record. The '037 and '269 patents, being derived from the same parent application, have the *same* effective filing date. It apparently is based instead on Beloit's statement that "the ['037] patent is unquestionably the most pertinent prior art with respect to the headbox claimed in the '269 patent." Appellants present this statement as an admission that the '037 *patent,* as such, is prior art.

Beloit admits making the quoted statement but disagrees with KMW's interpretation. When asked at oral argument whether Beloit admitted the '037 *patent* was technical prior art, its counsel responded:

> Only as far as the dangling or trailing element concept [is concerned]. It is not technical prior art for the entire wording of the specification because the two cases were copending. They go back to exactly the same filing date. They derive from the same basic application. You cannot take the words, all the words of the specification, and say they are prior art because you cannot use the words and go to a date earlier than the Hill et al. ['269] patent. And we say they are prior art, that Hill alone ['037] is prior art, because it taught the dangling element, but that was the generic concept of an unsupported self-positionable element.

Thus, the parties agree that there has been an admission, but disagree over what has been admitted. In resolving this disagreement, we cannot take an arguably ambiguous statement and construe it in the manner most detrimental to Beloit, regardless of its explanations and attempted clarifications. Rather, it is necessary to consider everything that has been said about what is prior art. *In re Nomiya,* 509 F.2d 566, 571, 184 USPQ 607, 612 (Cust. & Pat.App.1975). Beloit's statements of record in this case include those already quoted, as well as a longer discussion of what part of the '037 patent is prior art, similar to its remarks at oral argument, in its post-hearing brief to the Commission, as well as remarks in its brief and additional remarks at oral argument. These statements taken together demonstrate that Beloit has consistently insisted that Hill alone did not invent a headbox having full width trailing elements, despite the fact that Beloit has used some language which might suggest otherwise. They lead us to conclude that Beloit has admitted only that Hill's work was prior to that of the joint inventors, and that he invented a headbox having self-positionable trailing elements, but not full width trailing elements. The record, taken as a whole, supports only this view.

Having determined the extent of Beloit's admission of Hill's prior invention, it must now be resolved whether, as KMW alleges, Hill alone invented *more* than Beloit has admitted. Specifically, KMW argues that the description of full width trailing members in the '037 patent, in which Hill is named as the sole inventor, demonstrates that Hill by himself invented a headbox incorporating such full width trailing members. The short answer to this argument is that there is no presumption, or any reason to assume, that everything disclosed in a patent specification has been invented by the patentee. *In re Clemens,* 622 F.2d 1029, 1036, 206 USPQ 289, 297 (Cust. & Pat.App.1980). *See In re DeBaun,* 687 F.2d 459, 214 USPQ 933 (Cust. & Pat.App.1982). This is especially significant in this case. The embodiment comprising full width trailing members is an improvement on, and thus the best mode of practicing, what has been conceded by Beloit to be Hill's prior invention. This improvement was unquestionably known to Hill, who participated in its development. Thus, 35 U.S.C. § 112, which requires an inventor to set forth the best mode contemplated by him of carrying out his invention, required Hill in this instance to retain the description of full width trailing sheets in his application when it was divided out of the joint application, regardless of whether it was his invention. Under these circumstances, there is no reason to believe that Hill's invention is anything more than Beloit has conceded.

The above analysis leads us to conclude that Beloit has admitted, and admitted accurately, that Hill by himself invented a headbox having self-positionable trailing elements before the invention of other embodiments of that concept by Hill, Parker, and Hergert; but that his headbox did *not* have full width trailing elements. This is an admission of prior invention by another in this country, and so Hill's headbox becomes prior art by virtue of this admission and 35 U.S.C. § 102(g). Hill's headbox is therefore prior art for the purpose of determining obviousness under 35 U.S.C. § 103, especially here where the joint inventors Hill et al. were undeniably aware of Hill's prior work, and the evidence of priority, an admission, is conclusive. *In re Clemens*, 622 F.2d 1029, 206 USPQ 289 (Cust. & Pat.App.1980).

* * *

With regard to the specific issue now under consideration, whether the invention claimed in the '269 patent would have been obvious to one of ordinary skill in the art when made, our conclusion, the same as that of the ITC, is that it would not have been. Knowledge of Hill's sole invention would not have suggested a headbox having the pond-side-to-pondside elements recited in the '269 patent claims in suit.

* * *

In 1984 the Patent Act of 1952 was amended to preclude use as prior art under 102(f) and (g) of an earlier invention not publicly known in applying the non-obvious subject matter test of Section 103 to a later invention of another if both inventions were owned by the same entity. The amendment added to Section 103 the provision that:

> Subject matter developed by another person, which qualifies as prior art only under subsection (f) or (g) of section 102 of this title, shall not preclude patentability under this section where the subject matter and the claimed invention were, at the time the invention was made, owned by the same person or subject to an obligation of assignment to the same person.

This provision was added by Section 104 of the bill which became the Patent Law Amendments Act of 1984. With respect to Section 104, House Report 6286 [g] states in part:

> Section 104 of the bill changes a complex body of case law which discourages communication among members of research teams working in corporations, universities or other organizations. * * *

> "Prior art" is the existing technical information against which the patentability of an invention is judged. Publicly known information is always considered in determining whether an invention is obvious. However, under *In re Bass*, 474 F.2d 1276, 177 USPQ 178, (C.C.P.A. 1973), and *In re Clemens*, 622 F.2d 1029, 206 USPQ 289 (C.C.P.A.1980), an earlier invention which is not public may be treated under section 102(g), and possibly under 102(f), as prior art with respect to a later invention made by another employee of the same organization.

> New technology often is developed by using background scientific or technical information known within an organization but unknown to the public. The bill by disqualifying such background information from prior art, will encourage communication among members of research teams, and patenting, and consequently public dissemination, of the results of "team research."

> The subject matter which is disqualified as prior art under section 103 is strictly limited to subject matter which qualifies as prior art only under sections 102(f) or (g). If the subject matter qualifies as prior art under any other subsection—e.g., subsection 102(a), (b) or (e)—it

g. Cong.Rec., H 10525–H 10529 (Oct. 1, 1984).

would not be disqualified as prior art under the amendment to section 103.

The amendment applies only to consideration of prior art for purposes of section 103. It does not apply to or affect subject matter which qualifies as prior art under section 102. A patent applicant urging that subject matter was disqualified has the burden of establishing that it was commonly owned at the time the claimed invention was made.

Section 104 is not intended to permit anyone other than the inventor to be named in a patent application or patent. Also, the amendment is not intended to enable appropriation of the invention of another.

* * *

The language in section 104 is parallel to but also is more precise than the language of H.R. 4525. For example, section 104 makes clearer that information learned from or transmitted to persons outside the inventor's immediate organization is not disqualified as prior art.

The term "subject matter" as used in section 104 is intended to be construed broadly in the same manner as the term is construed in the remainder of section 103. The term "another" as used in this amendment means any inventive entity other than the inventor. The term "developed" is to be read broadly and is not limited by the manner in which the development occurred.

E. LOSS OF THE RIGHT TO PATENT AN INVENTION

1. DELAY IN FILING A U.S. PATENT APPLICATION

a. Introduction

The first Patent Act of 1790 and the Patent Act of 1793 limited patent protection to inventions which were "not before known or used" anywhere and "not known or used before the application" anywhere, respectively. The United States Supreme Court, in Pennock & Sellers v. Dialogue, 27 U.S. (2 Pet.) 1, 7 L.Ed. 327 (1829), interpreted both of these Patent Acts as meaning that patent protection was limited to inventions not "publicly" known or used anywhere before the date of application for a patent. Thus, the very first Patent Act was interpreted as barring patent protection for an invention which was not novel and nonobvious when the application for a patent was filed. This preclusion of patent protection, even if the invention was novel and nonobvious when made, is commonly called a statutory bar.

The Patent Act of 1836 barred patent protection if the invention "had been in public use or on sale with the applicant's consent or allowance prior to the application". Thus, this act explicitly limited the statutory bar to public use and on sale occurring with the "applicant's consent or allowance" and may have eliminated all other "public knowledge or use" prior to the application as a statutory bar.

In 1839, the Patent Act was amended by adding a provision that no patent shall be invalid by reason of the purchase, sale, or use by any corporation or person of an invention prior to an application for a patent therefor, unless "such purchase, sale or prior use has been for more than two years prior to such application for a patent." This provision appears to have introduced considerable uncertainty as to the applicable period of time for the bars to patent protection and as to whether the applicant's consent or allowance was necessary for public use or on sale to be a statutory bar.

The Patent Act of 1870 barred patent protection if the invention was "in public use or on sale in this country for more than two years before the application for a patent." Hence, this Act eliminated the requirement of "the applicant's consent or allowance", clearly specified the period of time as two years, and limited the public use or on sale to that occurring "in this country."

In 1897, the Patent Act was amended to limit patent protection to a patentee's invention "not patented or described in any printed publication in this or any foreign country * * * more than two years prior to his application and not in public use or on sale in this country for more than two years prior to his application." The two-year period was decreased to one year in 1939 and the substance of this provision was retained in subsequent patent acts and is presently found in 35 U.S.C.A. § 102(b) which provides that:

A person shall be entitled to a patent unless—

(b) the invention was patented or described in a printed publication in this or a foreign country or in public use or on sale in this country, more than one year prior to the date of the application for patent in the United States.

Due to the substantial statutory changes and modifications of these provisions prior to 1897, the cases decided under these prior statutory provisions must be carefully scrutinized in determining their value as controlling precedents.

As previously noted, a valid patent cannot be obtained on an invention unless it is novel and nonobvious, both when made, and just prior to one year before the effective date of the application for patent. Hence, even though an invention is novel and nonobvious when made, patent protection may be barred by Section 102(b).

The meaning and scope of the expression "patented or described in a printed publication" of Section 102(b) is generally considered to be the same as that of Section 102(a), which was explored in the preceding Section D of Chapter Two, and thus will not be repeated here. The following cases present some of the judicial interpretations of the policy and the scope of "in public use or on sale in this country" of Section 102(b) and its statutory predecessors. This terminology merely identifies a general category of acts which can bar the granting of valid patent protection. The judicial interpretations of this language are not uniform, and they vary with the particular factual context of the case at hand and the court's determination of what result will best "promote the progress of * * * useful arts."

b. In Public Use or on Sale

SHAW v. COOPER

Supreme Court of the United States, 1833.
32 U.S. (7 Pet.) 292, 8 L.Ed. 689.

MR. JUSTICE MCLEAN delivered the opinion of the court:

* * *

From the facts in the case, it appears that the plaintiff, while residing in England, in 1813 or 1814, invented the instrument secured by his patent. That before he came to the United States, he made known his invention to his brother, to Mr. Manton, a gun-maker in London, and to others. That shortly after he came to the United States, in 1817, he disclosed his invention to a gun-maker in Philadelphia, and that in 1817 or 1818, the plaintiff's brother sold the invention to a gun-maker in London. That in 1819 the invention was sold and used in England; and that in the two following years it was in public use there, and in the latter year also in France. That on the 19th of June, 1822, his first patent was obtained.

It also appears that in April, 1807, a patent was granted in England to one Forsyth for fourteen years, for an invention on the same subject. This fact was shown by the plaintiff, it is presumed, as a reason why he did not take out a patent in England.

The question arises from these facts, and others which belong to the case, whether there was such a use in the public of this invention at the date of the plaintiff's first patent as to render it void.

* * *

The question what use in the public before the application is made for a patent shall make void the right of the patentee, was brought before this court by the case of Pennock and Sellers v. Dialogue, reported in 2 Peters, 1. In this case the court say (sic) says that "it has not been, and indeed cannot be denied, that an inventor may abandon his invention and surrender or dedicate it to the public. This inchoate right, thus gone, cannot afterwards be resumed at his pleasure; for when gifts are once made to the public in this way, they become absolute." And again, "if an invention is used by the public with the consent of the inventor at the time of his application for a patent, how can the court say that his case is nevertheless such as the act was intended to protect? If such a public use is not a use within the meaning of the statute, how can the court extract the case from its operation and support a patent when the suggestions of the patentee were not true, and the conditions on which alone the grant was authorized do not exist?"

rule

"The true construction of the patent law is," the court say (sic) says "that the first inventor cannot acquire a good title to a patent if he suffers the thing invented to go into public use, or to be publicly sold for use before he makes application for a patent."

x application

In this case it appeared that the thing invented had been in use by the public, with the consent of the inventors, and through which they derived a profit, for seven years before the emanation of a patent. And this use was held by the court to be an abandonment of the right by the patentees.

The policy of granting exclusive privileges in certain cases was deemed of so much importance in a national point of view, that power was given to Congress in the federal Constitution, "to promote the progress of science and useful arts, by securing for limited times to authors and inventors the exclusive right to their respective writings and discoveries."

This power was exercised by Congress in the passage of the acts which have been referred to.

* * *

The patent law was designed for the public benefit as well as for the benefit of inventors. For a valuable invention, the public, on the inventor's complying with certain conditions, give him for a limited period the profits arising from the sale of the thing invented. This holds out an inducement for the exercise of genius and skill in making discoveries which may be useful to society, and profitable to the discoverer. But it was not the intention of this law to take from the public that of which they were fairly in possession.

In the progress of society, the range of discoveries in the mechanic arts, in science, and in all things which promote the public convenience, as a matter of course, will be enlarged. This results from the aggregation of mind, and the diversity of talents and pursuits, which exist in every intelligent community. And it would be extremely impolitic to retard or embarrass this advance, by withdrawing from the public any useful invention or art, and making it a subject of private monopoly. Against this consequence, the Legislature have carefully guarded in the laws they have passed on the subject.

* * *

A strict construction of the act, as it regards the public use of an invention before it is patented, is not only required by its letter and spirit, but also by sound policy. A term of fourteen years was deemed sufficient for the enjoyment of an exclusive right of an invention by the inventor; but if he may delay an application for his patent at pleasure, although his invention be carried into public use, he may extend the period beyond what the law intended to give him.

* * *

conclusion

Whatever may be the intention of the inventor, if he suffers his invention to go into public use, through any means whatsoever, without an immediate assertion of his right, he is not entitled to a patent: nor will a patent, obtained under such circumstances, protect his right.

The judgment of the Circuit Court must be affirmed with costs.

CITY OF ELIZABETH v. AMERICAN NICHOLSON PAVEMENT CO.

Supreme Court of the United States, 1878.
97 U.S. (7 Otto) 126, 24 L.Ed. 1000.

MR. JUSTICE BRADLEY delivered the opinion of the court.

* * *

The next question to be considered is, whether Nicholson's invention was in public use or on sale, with his consent and allowance, for more than two years prior to his application for a patent, within the meaning of the 6th, 7th and 15th sections of the Act of 1836, as qualified by the 7th section of the Act of 1839, which were the Acts in force in 1854, when he obtained his patent. It is contended by the appellants that the pavement which Nicholson put down by way of experiment, on Mill-dam Avenue in Boston, in 1848, was publicly used for the space of six years before his application for a patent, and that this was a public use within the meaning of the law.

To determine this question, it is necessary to examine the circumstances under which this pavement was put down, and the object and purpose that Nicholson had in view. It is perfectly clear from the evidence that he did not intend to abandon his right to a patent. He had filed a caveat in August, 1847, and he constructed the pavement in question by way of experiment, for the purpose of testing its qualities. The road in which it was put down, though a public road, belonged to the Boston and Roxbury Mill Corporation, which received toll for its use; and Nicholson was a stockholder and treasurer of the corporation. The pavement in question was about seventy-five feet in length, and was laid adjoining to the toll-gate and in front of the toll-house. It was constructed by Nicholson at his own expense, and was placed by him where it was, in order to see the effect upon it of heavily loaded wagons, and of varied and constant use; and also to ascertain its durability, and liability to decay. Joseph L. Lang, who was toll-collector for many years, commencing in 1849, familiar with the road before that time, and with this pavement from the time of its origin, testified as follows: "Mr. Nicholson was there almost daily, and when he came he would examine the pavement, would often walk over it, cane in hand, striking it with his cane, and making particular examination of its condition. He asked me very often how people liked it, and asked me a great many questions about it. I have heard him say a number of times that this was his first experiment with this pavement, and he thought that it was wearing very well. The circumstances that made this locality desirable for the purpose of obtaining a satisfactory test of the durability and value of the pavement were: that there would be a better chance to lay it there; he would have more room and a better chance than in the city; and, besides, it was a place where most everybody went over it, rich and poor. It was a great thoroughfare out of Boston. It was frequently traveled by teams having a load of five or six tons, and some larger. As these teams usually stopped at the toll-house, and started again, the stopping and starting would make as severe a trial to the pavement as it could be put to."

* * *

But, in this case, it becomes important to inquire what is such a public use as will have the effect referred to. That the use of the pavement in question was public in one sense cannot be disputed. But can it be said that the invention was in public use? The use of an invention by the inventor himself, or of any other person under his direction, by way of experiment, and in order to bring the invention to perfection, has never been regarded as such a use. Curt.Pat., sec. 381; Shaw v. Cooper, 7 Pet., 292.

Now, the nature of a street pavement is such that it cannot be experimented upon satisfactorily except on a highway, which is always public.

When the subject of invention is a machine, it may be tested and tried in a building, either with or without closed doors. In either case, such use is not a public use, within the meaning of the statute, so long as the inventor is engaged, in good faith, in testing its operation. He may see cause to alter it and improve it or not. His experiments will reveal the fact whether any and what alterations may be necessary. If durability is one of the qualities to be attained, a long period, perhaps years, may be necessary to enable the inventor to discover whether his purpose is accomplished. And though, during all that period, he may not find that any changes are necessary, yet he may be justly said to be using his machine only by way of experiment; and no one would say that such a use, pursued with a bona fide intent of testing the qualities of the machine, would be a public use, within the meaning of the statute. So long as he does not voluntarily allow others to make it and use it, and so long as it is not on sale for general use, he keeps the invention under his own control, and does not lose his title to a patent.

It would not be necessary, in such a case, that the machine should be put up and used, only in the inventor's own shop or premises. He may have it put up and used in the premises of another, and the use may inure to the benefit of the owner of the establishment. Still, if used under the surveillance of the inventor, and for the purpose of enabling him to test the machine and ascertain whether it will answer the purpose intended, and make such alterations and improvements as experience demonstrates to be necessary, it will still be a mere experimental use and not a public use, within the meaning of the statute.

Whilst the supposed machine is in such experimental use, the public may be incidentally deriving a benefit from it. If it be a grist-mill, or a carding-machine, customers from the surrounding country may enjoy the use of it by having their grain made into flour, or their wool into rolls, and still it will not be in public use, within the meaning of the law.

But if the inventor allows his machine to be used by other persons generally, either with or without compensation, or if it is, with his consent, put on sale for such use, then it will be in public use and on public sale, within the meaning of the law.

If, now, we apply the same principles to this case, the analogy will be seen at once. Nicholson wished to experiment on his pavement. He believed it to be a good thing, but he was not sure; and the only mode in which he could test it was to place a specimen of it in a public roadway. He did this at his own expense, and with the consent of the owners of the road. Durability was one of the qualities to be attained. He wanted to know whether his pavement would stand, and whether it would resist decay. Its character for durability could not be ascertained without its being subjected to use for a considerable time. He subjected it to such use, in good faith, for the simple purpose of ascertaining whether it was what he claimed it to be. Did he do anything more than the inventor of the supposed machine might do, in testing his invention? The public had the incidental use of the pavement, it is true; but was the invention in public use, within the meaning of the statute? We think not. The proprietors of the road alone used the invention, and used it at Nicholson's request, by way of experiment. The only way in which they could use it was by allowing the public to pass over the pavement.

Had the city of Boston, or other parties, used the invention, by laying down the pavement in other streets and places, with Nicholson's consent and allowance, then, indeed, the invention itself would have been in public use, within the meaning of the law; but this was not the case. Nicholson did not sell it, nor allow others to use it or sell it. He did not let it go beyond his control. He did nothing that indicated any intent to do so. He kept it under his own eyes, and never for a moment abandoned the intent to obtain a patent for it.

* * *

It is sometimes said that an inventor acquires an undue advantage over the public by delaying to take out a patent, inasmuch as he thereby preserves the monopoly to himself for a longer period than is allowed by the policy of the law; but this cannot be said with justice when the delay is occasioned by a bona fide effort to bring his invention to perfection, or to ascertain whether it will answer the purpose intended. His monopoly only continues for the allotted period, in any event; and it is the interest of the public, as well as himself, that the invention should be perfect and properly tested, before a patent is granted for it. Any attempt to use it for a profit, and not by way of experiment, for a longer period than two years before the application, would deprive the inventor of his right to a patent.

EGBERT v. LIPPMANN

Supreme Court of the United States, 1881.
104 U.S. (14 Otto) 333, 26 L.Ed. 755.

MR. JUSTICE WOODS, delivered the opinion of the court:

* * *

The evidence on which the defendants rely to establish a prior public use of the invention, consists mainly of the testimony of the complainant herself, who is the executrix of the original patentee.

She testifies that Barnes invented the improvement covered by his patent between January and May, 1855; that between the dates named the witness and her friend, Miss Cugier, were complaining of the breaking of their corset steels. Barnes, who was present, and was an intimate friend of the witness, said he thought he could make her a pair that would not break. At their next interview he presented her with a pair of corset steels which he himself had made. The witness wore these steels a long time. In 1858 Barnes made and presented to her another pair, which she also wore a long time. When the corsets in which these steels were used wore out, the witness ripped them open and took out the steels and put them in new corsets. This was done several times.

It is admitted and, in fact, is asserted, by complainant that these steels embodied the invention afterward patented by Barnes and covered by the re-issued patent on which this suit is brought.

Joseph H. Sturgis, another witness for complainant, testifies that in 1863 Barnes spoke to him about two inventions made by himself, one of which was a corset steel, and that he went to the house of Barnes to see them. Before this time, and after the transactions testified to by the complainant, Barnes and she had intermarried. Barnes said his wife had a pair of steels made according to his invention in the corsets which she was then wearing, and if she would take them off he would show them to witness. Mrs. Barnes went out and returned with a pair of corsets and a pair of scissors and ripped the corsets open and took out the steels. Barnes then explained to witness how they were made and used.

This is the evidence presented by the record, on which defendants rely to establish the public use of the invention by the patentee's consent and allowance.

The question for our decision is, whether this testimony shows a public use within the meaning of the statute.

We observe in the first place that to constitute the public use of a patent it is not necessary that more than one of the patented articles should be publicly used. The use of a great number may tend to strengthen the proof of public use, but one well defined case of public use is just as effectual to annul the patent as many.

For instance, if the inventor of a mower, a printing press or a railway car, makes and sells only one of the articles invented by him, and allows the vendee to use it for two years, without restriction or limitation, the use is just as public as if he had sold and allowed the use of a great number.

We remark, secondly, that, whether the use of an invention is public or private, does not necessarily depend upon the number of persons to whom its use is known. If an inventor, having made his device, gives or sells it to another, to be used by the donee or vendee, without limitation or restriction, or injunction of secrecy, and it is so used, such use is public, within the meaning of the statute, even though the use and knowledge of the use may be confined to one person.

We say thirdly, that some inventions are by their very character only capable of being used where they cannot be seen or observed by the public eye. An invention may consist of a lever or spring, hidden in the running gear of a watch, or of a ratchet, shaft or cog-wheel covered from view in the recesses of a machine for spinning or weaving. Nevertheless, if its inventor sells a machine of which his invention forms a part, and allows it to be used without restriction of any kind, the use is a public one, within the meaning of the law. So, on the other hand, a use necessarily open to public view, if made in good faith solely to test the qualities of the invention, and for the purpose of experiment, is not a public use within the meaning of the patent law. Elizabeth v. Pavement Co., 97 U.S., 126 [XXIV., 1000]; Shaw v. Cooper, 7 Pet., 292.

Tested by these principles, we think the evidence of the complainant herself shows that there was a public use of the invention, covered by the original patent to Barnes, for more than two years before the application for the patent, and by his consent and allowance. He made and gave the complainant two pairs of corset steels, constructed according to his device one in 1855 and one in 1858. They were presented to her for use. He imposed no obligation of secrecy, or any condition or restriction whatever. They were not presented for the purpose of experiment or to test their qualities. No such claim is set up in the testimony of complainant. The invention was at the time complete, and there is no evidence that it was afterwards changed or improved. The donee of the steels used them for years for the purpose and in the manner designed by the inventor. They were not capable of any other use. She might have exhibited them to any person she pleased, or might have made other steels of the same kind, and used or sold them without violation of any condition or restriction imposed on her by the inventor.

According to the testimony of complainant, the invention was completed and put in use in 1855. The inventor slept on his rights for eleven years. The patent was not applied for till March, 1866. In the meantime, the invention had found its way into general, and almost universal use. A great part of the record is taken up with the testimony of the manufacturers and venders of corset steels, showing that before Barnes applied for his patent the principle of his device was almost universally used in the manufacture of corset steels. It is fair to presume that having learned from this general use that there was some value in his invention, Barnes attempted to resume, by an application for a patent, what by his acts he had clearly dedicated to the public.

* * *

We are of opinion that the defense of two years' public use, by the consent and allowance of the inventor, before he made application for his patent, is satisfactorily established by the evidence. The decree of the Circuit Court is, therefore, affirmed.

HALL v. MACNEALE

Supreme Court of the United States, 1883.
107 U.S. 90, 2 S.Ct. 73, 27 L.Ed. 367.

MR. JUSTICE BLATCHFORD delivered the opinion of the court:

This suit is brought on letters patent No. 67046, granted to Joseph L. Hall, the appellant, July 23, 1867, for an improvement in connecting doors and casings of safes. The only claim alleged to have been infringed is claim 3, which is in these words: "3. The conical or tapering arbors 1, in combination with two or more plates of metal, in the doors and casings of safes and other secure receptacles, the arbors being secured in place in the plates by keys, 2, or in other substantial manner." In regard to what is embraced in this claim the specification says: "The nature of this invention consists in * * * securing a series of plates forming a casing or door of the safe by means of conical or tapering arbors, which, being tapped in from the outside of the door or casing and keyed upon the inside, present serious obstacles to the removal of successive plates forming the body of the safe.

* * *

The introduction of arbors for the purpose of more effectually binding in one compact mass the series of alternate iron and steel plates in the doors or bodies of safes will very much protract the labors of the burglar; indeed, it will be necessary, in order to remove one sheet in succession, to cut out the arbors, which are made of the hardest steel.

* * *

In his testimony in the present suit, the appellant states that he made three safes between 1859 and 1864 which were burglar proof, and had conical bolts for fastening together the different plates of metal. One of them had the double conical bolt and no single bolt, and was sold to a firm in Dayton, Ohio. One was made in 1858 or 1859, to be exhibited at a fair in Ohio, and was sold to a banker in Lafayette, Indiana. It had the single, drill proof conical arbors in the doors. The third one was made to be exhibited at a fair held in 1860, and was sold to the treasurer of Loraine County, Ohio. It had a few of the single conical arbors.

* * *

The application for that patent was made in March 1867, and the patent was granted under the provisions of the Act of July 4, 1836, 5 Stat. at L., 117, and of the Act of March 3, 1839, 5 Stat. at L., 353. Within the meaning of sections 7 and 15 of the Act of 1836, as modified by section 7 of the Act of 1839, the invention covered by claim 3 of the patent in suit was in use and on sale more than two years before the appellant applied for that patent, and such use and sale were, also, with the consent and allowance of the appellant, and the use was a public use. It is contended that the safes were experimental and that the use was a use for experiment. But we are of opinion that this was not so and that the case falls within the principle laid down by this court in Coffin v. Ogden, 18 Wall, 120 [85 U.S., XXI., 821]. The invention was complete in those safes. It was capable of producing the results sought to be accomplished, though not as thoroughly as with the use of welded steel and iron plates. The construction and arrangement and purpose and mode of operation and use of the bolts in the safes were necessarily known to the workmen who put them in. They were, it is true, hidden from view, after the safes were completed, and it required a destruction of the safe to bring them into view. But this was no concealment of them or use of them in secret. They had no more concealment than was inseparable from any legitimate use of them. As to the use being experimental, it is not shown that any attempt was made to see if the plates of the safes could be stripped off, and thus to prove whether or not the conical bolts were efficient. The safes were sold and, apparently, no experiment and no experimental use were thought to be necessary. The idea of a use for experiment was an afterthought. An invention of the kind might be in use and no burglarious attempt be ever made to enter the safe, and it might be said that the use of the invention was always experimental until the burglarious attempt should be made, and so the use would never be other than experimental. But it is apparent that there was no experimental use in this case, either intended or actual. The foregoing views, which are controlling to show that claim 3 of the patent in suit cannot be sustained, are in accordance with those announced by this court in Egbert v. Lippmann, 104 U.S. 333 [XXVI., 735].

The decree of the Circuit Court dismissing the bill is affirmed, and the same decision is made in No. 165.

TP LABORATORIES, INC. v. PROFESSIONAL POSITIONERS, INC.

United States Court of Appeals, Federal Circuit, 1984.
724 F.2d 965, 220 USPQ 577.

NIES, CIRCUIT JUDGE.

These appeals are from the October 27, 1982 judgment of the United States District Court for the Eastern District of Wisconsin (Warren, J.) dismissing a charge of infringement of a patent for an orthodontic appliance. Sitting without a jury, the court held U.S.

Theory of the [handwritten margin note]

Patent No. 3,178,820 ('820), owned by TP Laboratories, Inc. (TP), invalid under 35 U.S.C. § 102(b), on the ground that a public use occurred more than one year prior to the filing date of the application for the subject patent.

TP appeals the holding of invalidity. TP admits that the inventor used the dental appliance on three orthodontal patients during the critical period but asserts that such use was non-barring experimental use. On this issue we agree with appellant and reverse. * * *

issue: Experimental? [handwritten margin note]

I

Appellant-plaintiff, TP Laboratories, Inc., makes and sells orthodontic supplies and appliances to the dental profession. TP Laboratories is a separate business from the professional practice of the Kesling and Rocke Orthodontic Group (K & R), a group of four orthodontists, Doctors Harold D. Kesling, Robert A. Rocke, Peter C. Kesling and David L. Kesling, but the firms are closely connected. The record before us shows that Dr. Harold Kesling, now deceased, (Kesling), who is the inventor named in the patent in suit, was an officer and one of the owners of TP Laboratories. Dr. Peter Kesling is president. The two businesses share a small building and employ the same office manager.

* * *

The use of tooth positioners with C's in the treatment of three K & R patients during the period 1958–61 led to the issues under 35 U.S.C. § 102(b). It is undisputed that these three devices fell within the language of the '820 claims and no modification of design was made as a consequence of these uses. * * *

The initial use in each of the above cases occurred prior to the critical date of February 19, 1961. During the years 1958–60, K & R placed 606 tooth positioners, of which only the three described above were within the claims of '820. In 1961, after the critical date, 28 tooth positioners with C's were prescribed by K & R out of a total of 151.

The above devices were made for the K & R patients by TP, including C's handmade by Kesling. There is no evidence that K & R charged patients specifically for any positioner. With two of the three patients, K & R followed its regular practice of setting a fixed total fee for professional services, which included necessary appliances. One patient (Furst), whose father was a dentist, received free treatment as a professional courtesy.

Sales of the patented device to other orthodontists began in 1966, that is, only after TP's acquisition of the patent. Appellees, Huge and Allessee, had no knowledge of the invention even though employed at TP prior to 1961.

* * *

II

A

The patent statute provides in pertinent part in 35 U.S.C. § 102:
* * * Decisions under this provision and comparable provisions in earlier statutes are marked by confusion and inconsistency.

"The general purpose behind all the [§ 102(b)] bars is to require inventors to assert with due diligence their right to a patent through the prompt filing * * * of a patent application." 2 D. Chisum, *Patents* § 601 (1981 & Supp.1983).

More specifically, courts have discerned a number of factors which must be weighed in applying the statutory bar of § 102(b). Operating against the inventor are the policies of 1) protecting the public in its use of the invention where such use began prior to the filing of the application, 2) encouraging prompt disclosure of new and useful information, 3) discouraging attempts to extend the length of the period of protection by not allowing the inventor to reap the benefits for more than one year prior to the filing of the application. In contrast to these considerations, the public interest is also deemed to be served by allowing an inventor time to perfect his invention, by public testing, if desired, and prepare a patent application.

The district court's consideration of the issue of public use proceeded according to the following two-step analysis:

Consequently, the first step in analyzing PRO's 35 U.S.C. § 102(b) assertion is to determine whether a public use occurred. If a public use is found, then the Court must ascertain whether the use was not a public use under the statute because it was experimental.

As to the first step, the district court reasoned: * * *

On the second issue as perceived by the district court, the court placed a heavy burden of proof on the patent owner to prove that the inventor's use had been experimental and expressly found that TP did not carry that "burden." In the words of the court:

The inventor bears a heavy burden of showing that the public use was bona fide experimentation.

*   *   *   *   *   *   *   *   *

The experimental exception is unavailable to plaintiff TP for two reasons. First, the evidence presented does not establish that the patentee was conducting a bona fide experiment. On the contrary, the record shows that the uses were random and poorly monitored.
* * *

Assuming, however, that the use was experimental, the delay in filing the patent application was unreasonable. The first use of the invention was in August of 1958. By April of 1959, Dr. H. Kesling knew that the precision seating springs operated as designated * * *. Nevertheless, Dr. H. Kesling waited until February 19, 1962 to file his patent application. * * *

We disagree with this analysis and the shift in the burden of proof which led the district court to an erroneous result.

B

It is not public knowledge of his invention that precludes the inventor from obtaining a patent for it, but a public use or sale of it.

The above quotation is from *City of Elizabeth v. American Nicholson Pavement Co.,* 97 U.S. 126, 136, 24 L.Ed. 1000 (1877), which is the starting place for analysis of any case involving experimental use. There, a toll road, built according to the invention of the patent in suit, was in daily use for a period of 6 years before the inventor filed for a patent. In upholding the validity of the patent, the Supreme Court spoke with clarity but through the years the guidelines set forth therein have been obfuscated. Returning to the original, we quote the following passages which are particularly pertinent to our analysis here:

That the use of the pavement in question was public in one sense cannot be disputed. But can it be said that the invention was in public use? The use of an invention by the inventor himself, or of any other person under his direction, by way of experiment, and in order to bring the invention to perfection, has never been regarded as such a use. Curtis, Patents, sect. 381; *Shaw v. Cooper,* 7 Pet. 292 [8 L.Ed. 689].

Now, the nature of a street pavement is such that it cannot be experimented upon satisfactorily except on a highway, which is always public.

When the subject of invention is a machine, it may be tested and tried in a building, either with or without closed doors. In either case, such use is not a public use, within the meaning of the statute, so long as the inventor is engaged, in good faith, in testing its operation.

* * *

Whilst the supposed machine is in such experimental use, the public may be incidentally deriving a benefit from it. If it be a gristmill, or a carding-machine, customers from the surrounding country may enjoy the use of it by having their grain made into flour, or their wool into rolls, and still it will not be in public use, within the meaning of the law.

But if the inventor allows his machine to be used by other persons generally, either with or without compensation, or if it is, with his consent, put on sale for such use, then it will be in public use and on public sale, within the meaning of the law.

97 U.S. at 134–35.

In the decision on appeal, the trial court looked for proof of an exception to the public use bar. However, in *Elizabeth,* the Supreme Court did not refer to "experimental use" as an "exception" to the bar otherwise created by a public use. More precisely, the Court reasoned that, if a use is experimental, even though not secret, "public use" is negated. This difference between "exception" and "negation" is not

merely semantic.   Under the precedent of this court, the statutory
presumption of validity provided in 35 U.S.C. § 282 places the burden
of proof upon the party attacking the validity of the patent, and that
burden of persuasion does not shift at any time to the patent owner.   It
is constant and remains throughout the suit on the challenger.   As
stated in *Richdel, Inc. v. Sunspool Corp.,* 714 F.2d 1573, 1579, 219 USPQ
8, 11–12 (Fed.Cir.1983):

> 35 USC 282 *permanently* places the burden of proving facts necessary
> to a conclusion of invalidity on the party asserting such invalidity.
> *Stratoflex, Inc. v. Aeroquip Corp.,* 713 F.2d 1530, 218 USPQ 871 (Fed.
> Cir.1983); *Solder Removal,* supra, 582 F.2d [628] at 633, 199 USPQ at
> 133.

Under this analysis, it is incorrect to impose on the patent owner,
as the trial court in this case did, the burden of proving that a "public
use" was "experimental."   These are not two separable issues.   It is
incorrect to ask: "Was it public use?" and then, "Was it experimental?"
Rather, the court is faced with a single issue: Was it public use under
§ 102(b)?

Thus, the court should have looked at all of the evidence put forth
by both parties and should have decided whether the entirety of the
evidence led to the conclusion that there had been "public use."   This
does not mean, of course, that the challenger has the burden of proving
that the use is not experimental.   Nor does it mean that the patent
owner is relieved of explanation.   It means that if a *prima facie* case is
made of public use, the patent owner must be able to point to or must
come forward with convincing evidence to counter that showing.   *See
Strong v. General Electric Co.,* 434 F.2d 1042, 1044, 168 USPQ 8, 9 (5th
Cir.1970).   The length of the test period is merely a piece of evidence to
add to the evidentiary scale.   The same is true with respect to whether
payment is made for the device, whether a user agreed to use secretly,
whether records were kept of progress, whether persons other than the
inventor conducted the asserted experiments, how many tests were
conducted, how long the testing period was in relationship to tests of
other similar devices.   In other words, a decision on whether there has
been a "public use" can only be made upon consideration of the entire
surrounding circumstances.

While various objective indicia may be considered in determining
whether the use is experimental, the expression by an inventor of his
subjective intent to experiment, particularly after institution of litigation, is generally of minimal value.   *In re Smith,* 714 F.2d at 1127, 218
USPQ at 976.

C

Applying the principles set forth above to this case, that non-secret
uses of the device were made prior to the critical date is not in itself
dispositive of the issue of whether activity barring a patent under 35
U.S.C. § 102(b) occurred.   *Minnesota Mining & Manufacturing Co. v.*

Johnson & Johnson, 179 USPQ 216, 220 (N.D.Ill.1973). The fact that the device was not hidden from view may make the use not secret but non-secret use is not *ipso facto* "public use" activity. *City of Elizabeth v. American Nicholson Pavement Co.,* 97 U.S. at 136. Nor, it must be added, is all secret use *ipso facto* not "public use" within the meaning of the statute, if the inventor is making commercial use of the invention under circumstances which preserve its secrecy.

Turning to the instant case, we note first that disclosure of the seating device to patients could not be avoided in any testing. In some circumstances, no doubt it would be significant that no pledge of confidentiality was obtained from the user. In the circumstances of use by orthodontal patients, we attach no importance to the fact that the doctor did not ask a patient to swear to secrecy. As in *City of Elizabeth,* testing of the device had to be public to some extent and it is beyond reasonable probability that a patient would show the device to others who would understand the function of the C's or would want to duplicate the device. One is all that is needed and, if lost or broken, the patient would expect it to be replaced by the treating dentist.

In any event, a pledge of confidentiality is indicative of the inventor's continued control which here is established inherently by the dentist-patient relationship of the parties. Nothing in the inventor's use of the device on his patients (or the transfer to them) is inconsistent with experimentation. Similarly, the routine checking of patients by one of the other K & R orthodontists does not indicate the inventor's lack of control or abandonment to the public.

Secondly, the finding is clearly erroneous that the invention "proved satisfactory immediately," or "by April of 1959." In this connection, it is noted that the '820 patent itself describes a utility of the patented device for correcting orthodontal irregularities as "urging teeth into preselected positions." The patent records discussed above indicate that treatment to correct such orthodontal irregularities can range from two to six years. Moreover, while results appeared to be good within six months use by one patient, the variable of patient cooperation cannot be checked by one patient alone. Use on three patients is not an obviously excessive number. In other words, the test for success of the improvement was not whether it could be used at all, but whether it could be said to work better on patients than a positioner without C's. Again, as in *City of Elizabeth,* the test of necessity had to run for a considerable time and on several patients before the inventor could know whether "it was what he claimed it to be" and would "answer the purpose intended."

A factor in favor of the patentee is that during this critical time the inventor had readily available all of the facilities of TP to commercially exploit the device. Yet, no positioners with C's were offered competing orthodontists despite the fact this was one facet of the inventor's total business activity. Further, the inventor made no extra charge for fitting the three patients with the improved positioners although that in itself is not critical. The facts here indicate the inventor was testing the device, not the market. No commercial exploitation having been made to even a small degree prior to filing the patent application, the underlying policy of prohibiting an extension of the term is clearly not offended in this respect.

Indeed, none of the policies which underlie the public use bar and which, in effect, define it have been shown to be violated. At most, the record shows that the uses were not secret, but when the evidence as to the facts of use by the inventor is considered as a whole, we conclude that appellees failed to prove that the inventor made a public use of the subject invention within the meaning of 35 U.S.C. § 102(b). The patent may not be held invalid on this ground.

* * *

WATSON v. ALLEN

United States Court of Appeals, District of Columbia Circuit, 1958.
103 U.S.App.D.C. 5, 254 F.2d 342, 117 USPQ 68.

BURGER, CIRCUIT JUDGE. From an adverse decision in the Patent Office, appellee invoked the jurisdiction of the District Court under 35 U.S.C.A. § 145, where the issue of patentability of his invention was tried de novo. The District Court rejected Patent Office claims that the invention had been in non-experimental public use, and authorized the Patent Office to issue a patent.

A person is not entitled to a patent where "the invention was * * * in public use * * * more than one year prior to the date of the application for patent. * * *" An exception to this is recognized and "public use" is no bar to patentability where that use was incidental to experiment. The issue on this appeal is whether the District Court erred in finding that the prior use of the invention was incidental to experiment, contrary to the findings of the Patent Office.

The invention is a shim, which is a thin metal plate designed to be inserted between an engine bearing and bearing holder so as to compensate for wear in the bearing, thus reducing oil consumption in worn automobile engines. In 1939, appellee installed a set of his shims in his 1934 Oldsmobile, for the purpose of experiment. After investigating their performance, he stopped using the car. With minor exceptions, the car lay idle for a year, finally being sold for $75 in 1942, still containing the shims. Appellee did not tell the buyer of their presence, and made no effort to follow up performance of the shims in the hands of the purchaser. The car passed to several other owners, none being aware of the shims. Appellee continued to improve the design of the shims, working on other models, and in April 1946 applied for a patent. After extended proceedings his application was denied because the Patent Office found (1) his shims had been in public use, in that members of the public (the car buyers) had used the shims without any restrictions, even though unwittingly; and (2) such public use was not incidental to experiment, because after the sale, appellee did not actually experiment with those shims. The Patent Office apparently would have required appellee either to remove the shims when he was finished experimenting with them, or else apply for a patent within one year after he sold the car containing them.

The trial court found that the use of appellee's invention "was experimental and did not constitute public use regardless of whether he removed them or not. Further, his continued efforts to make shims which would be an improvement over those he had installed likewise was experimental and this experimental period extended to a date less than one year prior to the filing of his application." The trial court relied on Goodwin v. Borg-Warner Corp., also known as the Daukus case, wherein the inventor installed an improved clutch in a friend's car without profit. The use was held experimental, and the fact that the car was later sold to a stranger, apparently without restriction, did not constitute a non-experimental public use. The Patent Office relies on a case precisely contra, which was handed down by the Court of Customs and Patent Appeals a few days after the decision of the court below. [Application of Blaisdell, 44 CCPA 846, 242 F.2d 779, 113 USPQ 289 (CCPA 1957)].

* * *

rule

In order to understand the reason for the extremely broad construction of "public use," and the judicial exception read into seemingly absolute statutory words, it is necessary to examine the policy involved. The cases seem to be hospitable to the inventor *during the experimental stage* of his invention, but become disposed to construe the law against him thereafter. The judicial policy underlying this rule has been said to be that an inventor acquires an undue advantage over the public by delaying to take out a patent, inasmuch as he thereby preserves the monopoly to himself for a longer period than the law allows. * * *

On the other hand, the law also recognizes that the inventor may wish to perfect his idea before applying for patent, and indeed, it is in the public interest that he do so. Hence, facts which may well be fatal to patentability *after* experimentation are frequently excused if they occurred *during* experimentation. A sale which is primarily for the purpose of experiment will not bar patentability. During experiment, use by assistants under no obligation of secrecy will probably not bar a patent, although after the experiments are ended, use or knowledge by assistants or workmen under no obligation of secrecy may well bar patentability. Our conclusion is that the courts accord considerable hospitality to the inventor during the experimental stage. However, as a limitation, we note that his hospitality disappears even during the experimental stage when the "experimental motive" wanes, or is superseded by a profit motive, or is tainted by careless acts of the inventor.

* * *

The Patent Office claims that the public use was not incidental to experiment because the inventor did not actually experiment with those very shims after the sale. There is force to this argument, but we believe that reasonable disposal of discarded prototypes of a still-experimental invention must, viewed favorably, be considered as incidental to experiment. What amounts to a reasonable disposal depends upon the facts of each case, keeping in mind the physical nature of the device, and the likelihood that the method of disposal chosen will lead to discovery of the secret by the public in general.

Here the shims were minute, inexpensive, fragile (so that removal might have damaged them beyond further use), and had no salvage value. They were located deep in the heart of an old automobile engine, a place difficult of access and seldom opened to examination. The transferees of the automobile were not told of the presence of the shims, and they did not discover them in fact. There was little likelihood that they ever would be discovered except by one who dismantled the engine, and perhaps not even then. Even if discovered, it is not certain that the discoverer would have understood or recognized the purpose of the shims. Taken together, these circumstances made it reasonable that the shims be left in the car; this was a reasonable method of disposal in this case just as discarding might be in other cases, and falls short of being such carelessness as would taint the experimental motive which continued unabated throughout. We believe the protective umbrella of the experimental use doctrine should include reasonable disposal of models and prototypes of the invention once their usefulness to the inventor has ended—reasonable in view of the nature of the device and the probability of discovery and appropriation of the invention by strangers.

reasonable disposal

This conclusion, however, does not resolve the issues as to claimed public use of the same idea by a third person unknown to Allen. It is claimed by the Patent Office that one Blaisdell had also put into public use shims similar to appellee's device. If this use was public use, and was not incident to experiment, then the use of Blaisdell's shims "more than one year prior to the date of" appellee's application would bar appellee from securing a patent, at least as to the elements common to both inventions. Blaisdell performed work for used car dealers and in 1934 he installed his shims in three cars sent to him for repairs. He told the dealers what he had done, and kept in touch with the cars for several months, and in 1936, he applied for a patent. He prosecuted the application to allowance of a patent but forfeited for failure to pay the final fee. He resumed work on the shims, made improvements and in March 1945 again applied for patent. In September 1945 he placed his shims on the market. The trial court found that "Blaisdell's activities prior to one year before the filing of Allen's application were * * * experimental and not public use." For the reasons outlined in the discussion dealing with the appellee's use, i.e., that there is substantial evidence which supports the trial court findings, we affirm the finding of experimental use.

Our holding with respect to public use cannot be reconciled with that of the Court of Customs and Patent Appeals. We recognize the special competence of that court to deal with matters relating to patents and as to technical or highly specialized patent matters, we would accord substantial weight to its views. However, the issues presently involved are not technical or in any sense within the areas of special expertise; hence, the views of the Court of Customs and Patent Appeals are those of a coordinate appellate court having perhaps, approximately the standing of another circuit court of appeals; they are persuasive and entitled to deference, but are not authoritatively binding. On the other hand we are bound to treat the District Court's findings and conclusion in this matter as we would on any appeal, that is, as presumptively correct. While the result is by no means free from doubt, we think the fact findings of the trial court are not clearly erroneous, and that the District Court correctly applied the law of public use.

Affirmed.

BAZELON, CIRCUIT JUDGE (dissenting).

I would follow Application of Blaisdell, Cust. & Pat.App.1957, 242 F.2d 779, where, upon precisely the same facts presented here, the United States Court of Customs and Patent Appeals upheld a determination of public use by the Board of Appeals of the United States Patent Office.

CONNECTICUT PAPER PRODUCTS v. NEW YORK PAPER CO.

United States District Court of Maryland, 1941.
39 F.Supp. 127, 50 USPQ 180, modified 127 F.2d 423 (4th Cir.1942).

WILLIAM C. COLEMAN, DISTRICT JUDGE.

This is a patent suit involving three patents having related subject matter; that is to say, one patent is for a paper drinking cup (Ericson patent No. 1940406, issued December 19, 1933, upon application of June 30, 1932); one is for a metal device for dispensing such cups one at a time as required, from a nested stack of them (Emerson patent No. 2206838, issued July 2, 1940, upon application of April 15, 1940); and the third patent is for a design for a paper cup dispenser (design patent to the same W.J. Emerson No. 118578, issued January 16, 1940, upon application of November 4, 1939).

The plaintiff is a corporation of Connecticut owned and controlled largely by W.J. Emerson, the patentee of the dispenser and design patents in suit, and manufactures and sells paper cups at wholesale. The defendant, the New York Paper Company, is a Maryland corporation and is not a manufacturer of cups or dispensers, but is a small jobber obtaining its products from the Boston Drinking Cup Company, an affiliate of the Boston Envelope Company, of Dedham, Massachusetts.

* * *

In addition to the claim of invalidity on the ground of anticipation by the prior art, defendant maintains that the Emerson dispenser patent is nevertheless invalid by virtue of the provisions of the patent law, 35 U.S.C.A. § 31, because, as is claimed, it was on sale more than two years before the filing date of the application.

* * *

In 1939, the two year limitation in the statute just quoted was reduced to one year, Act of August 5, 1939, c. 450, sec. 1, 53 Stat. 1212, but the amendment is not retroactive.

Public use or sale within the meaning of the statute must be conclusively shown to have occurred. Maibohm v. RCA Victor Co., 4 Cir., 89 F.2d 317. We are not satisfied that such is true in the present case, because the weight of the credible evidence indicates that whereas there were negotiations looking towards a sale of the Emerson dispenser to the Boston Drinking Cup Company as early as the latter part of February or the first part of March, 1938, that is, more than two years prior to the patent application, we do not believe that these negotiations are sufficient to establish that the dispenser was actually in public use or on sale at such time. It is true that an imperfect model of the Emerson dispenser was prepared by Mr. Emerson and shown to the sales manager of the Boston Drinking Cup Company prior to March 3, 1938, as a result of which, on that date, if not somewhat earlier, an agreement was reached whereby, after thirty days, the Emerson dispenser would be supplied to the Boston Drinking Cup Company in conformity with the demonstrated model, that company having, on March 3rd, ordered 15,000,000 Ericson cups from Mr. Emerson and it being understood that, according to common practice, these new dispensers were to be furnished with every order obtained by the Boston Drinking Cup Company for 5,000 of such cups. However, there is no evidence that any of these Emerson dispensers were actually delivered to the Boston Drinking Cup Company or to any of its customers, or that there were any sales orders taken for them, prior to July or August, 1938, or that any of them had, in fact, been fabricated prior to August, 1938. Mr. Emerson, who gave the impression of being a truthful witness, stated that none of the dispensers, completely finished and ready for delivery to customers, were received by him from his manufacturer until August 28th, 1938; and that all sales of these dispensers occurred between August 29, 1938, and a date about a year later, when he severed business relations with the Boston Drinking Cup Company. The sales manager of that Company, who was called to testify by the defendant, likewise, was not able to fix by documentary evidence or otherwise, any earlier date of actual sale.

An article for which a patent is sought and which is on hand, ready for delivery under contract of purchase, at a date prior to the two (now one) year period named in the statute, may be said to have then been "on sale", within the meaning of the statute. So it has been held. See Covert v. Covert, C.C., 106 F. 183; National Cash Register Co. v.

American Cash-Register Co., 2 Cir., 178 F. 79; Wende v. Horine, 7 Cir., 225 F. 501. However, if the article is not on hand, ready for delivery, it cannot be said to be "on sale." Such was the situation in the present case. An agreement to sell, made prior to the statutory period, is not in itself sufficient to invoke the bar of the statute, if the goods were not in fact on hand prior to that period, and therefore could not have been delivered prior to that period. So it was held, and we think correctly, in Burke Electric Co. v. Independent Pneumatic Tool Co., 234 F. 93 (certiorari denied, 241 U.S. 682, 36 S.Ct. 728, 60 L.Ed. 1234), by the Circuit Court of Appeals for the Second Circuit, and the First Circuit Court of Appeals in McCreery Engineering Co. v. Massachusetts Fan Co., 195 F. 498. The precise point appears never to have been passed upon in this Circuit, although, inferentially, we interpret the decision in Maibohm v. RCA Victor Co., supra, to support the conclusion here reached.

We quote the following from the Burke Electric Co. case, supra, 234 F. 93: "The proofs in this case show that the patented motors were ordered two years and a few days before the application for the patent was filed, but were not delivered and could not have been delivered until a time within the two-year period. The question is as to the proper construction of the words 'not in public use or on sale' in Rev.St. § 4886 (Comp.St.1913, § 9430 [35 U.S.C.A. § 31]). The combination of the words indicates that the sale contemplated is such as creates an opportunity for present public use. It is a situation quite different from the reduction to practice necessary to sustain anticipation. * * * The provision ought to be construed favorably to patentees. If patented articles are on hand ready to be delivered to any purchaser, they are on sale, whether any of them has been sold or not. But, if they are not, they cannot be said to be on sale within the meaning of the act, though the invention itself has ceased to be experimental and is complete. This certainly should be true of articles which can be carried in stock, like the motors in question."

* * *

KING INSTRUMENT CORPORATION v. OTARI CORPORATION

United States Court of Appeals, Federal Circuit, 1985.
767 F.2d 853, 266 USPQ 402.

DAVIS, CIRCUIT JUDGE.

King Instrument Corporation (King), the plaintiff below, charged Otari Corporation (Otari) with infringement of its U.S. Patent Nos. 3,637,153 ('153) issued January 25, 1972, and 3,737,358 ('358) issued June 5, 1973. King now appeals from final judgment by the United States District Court for the Northern District of California, following a bench trial, that held the '358 patent invalid because the invention claimed was found to be "on sale" under 35 U.S.C. § 102(b). We affirm.

* * *

The patents at issue relate to an automated apparatus for loading magnetic (blank or pre-recorded audio or video) tape into closed cassettes. Before loading, a closed cassette consists of an outer plastic case containing two winding hubs (spools) and a short length of leader tape wound around each hub. After loading, the finished product has a much longer length of magnetic supply ("use") tape which has been spliced to the leader tape. The patents claim an apparatus for automatically cutting, splicing, and winding magnetic use tape into closed cassettes.

The tape loading machine embodying the invention of the earlier '153 patent came to be known as the "swing arm" machine. * * *

The device disclosed in the '358 patent has been called a "shift block" machine. * * * *

The '358 patent application was filed on May 27, 1971. A tape loading device was offered for sale in a written price quotation on May 22, 1970 to Morningstar. The offer for two "King Turbo-matic 300–EC" cassette loaders contained a description of the specifications for the leader tape, the required power supply, a discount for two of Morningstar's old tape loaders, and a price quotation for a spare automatic splicer. This offer resulted in an acceptance confirmed by a purchase order dated June 8, 1970. The two loaders arrived at Morningstar on June 17, 1970. The district court found that, since the offer embodied the '358 claimed invention which had been reduced to practice by April 27, 1970, the '358 patent was invalid under 35 U.S.C. § 102(b).

King argues that the district court failed to apply the three-part test enunciated in *Timely Products Corp. v. Arron,* 523 F.2d 288, 187 USPQ 257 (2d Cir.1975), which it says this court adopted as the standard for determining "on sale" under § 102(b) in *Barmag Barmer Maschinenfabrik v. Murata Machinery, Ltd.,* 731 F.2d 831, 221 USPQ 561 (Fed.Cir.1984). This three-part test requires that: (1) the complete invention claimed must have been embodied in or obvious in view of the thing offered for sale; (2) the invention must have been tested sufficiently to verify that it is operable and commercially marketable; and (3) the sale must be primarily for profit rather than for experimental purposes. 523 F.2d at 302, 187 USPQ at 267–268. However, this court expressly held in *Barmag* that *Timely Products* is not adopted for all cases, and a less stringent standard might be appropriate in some circumstances where the underlying statutory policies might otherwise be frustrated. *Accord Western Marine Electronics v. Furano Electric Co.,* 764 F.2d 840 (Fed.Cir.1985).

These underlying policies include: (1) discouraging removal of inventions from the public domain which the public justifiably comes to believe are freely available; (2) favoring prompt and widespread disclosure of inventions; (3) giving the inventor a reasonable amount of time following the sales activity to determine the value of a patent, *see In re Caveney,* 761 F.2d 671, 676 (Fed.Cir.1985), and (4) prohibiting an extension of the period for exploiting the invention. Consistent with these policies, the district court properly relied on two factors as evidence of "on sale": (1) a sale or offer of sale of the invention, and (2) an existing reduction to practice of the invention by the time of the offer. *See generally Barmag, supra.* An offer to sell is sufficient under the policies animating the statute, which proscribes not a sale, but a placing "on sale." *D.L. Auld Co. v. Chroma Graphics Corp.,* 714 F.2d 1144, 1147, 219 USPQ 13, 18 (Fed.Cir.1984). Although it argues in the context of *Timely Products,* King's position is essentially that there was never an offer of sale before the critical date, nor was the '358 invention reduced to practice before that date.

To support its position that there was no such offer to sell the '358 invention, King asserts that the alleged offer for sale was phrased in language consistent with that used in concurrent quotations made to other companies for the '153 swing arm machines, not the '358 shift block machines. Moreover, there was no reference in the offer as to how the machine worked. Other purchasers who received quotations containing the same general performance language could not say specifically which type of machine was being offered for sale. Robert Hunt of Morningstar, who allegedly received the '358 shift block machines in June, 1970, admitted he was "surprised" to receive the new device. The alleged offer becomes even more ambiguous, argues King, when one considers that the earlier swing arm and later shift block machines were both referred to as a "King Turbo-matic Cassette Loader 300–EC". It is said, therefore, that no intent existed to make such an offer, nothing in the offer identified the subject matter of the invention, and no notice was given to the purchaser that a new or different machine existed.

While a bare, unexplained offer, not explicitly shown to be of the new invention, may be insufficient, the totality of the circumstances must always be considered in order to ascertain whether an offer of the new invention was in fact made. *Accord Barmag, supra.* When an executory sales contract is entered into (or offered) before the critical date, the purchaser must know how the invention embodied in the offer will perform. *See In re Dybel,* 524 F.2d 1393, 1400, 187 USPQ 593, 598 (CCPA 1975). The policies underlying the on sale bar, however, concentrate on the attempt by the inventor to exploit his invention, not whether the potential purchaser was cognizant of the invention. Accordingly, the purchaser need not have actual knowledge of the invention for it to be on sale. *In re Blaisdell,* 242 F.2d 779, 783, 44 CCPA 846, 850, 113 USPQ 289, 292 (1957). In this case, from the descriptions contained in the quotation (*e.g.,* "The loader measures tape in one foot increments from 2 feet to 999 feet"), the purchaser generally knew how the machine would perform. King's argument that nothing in the quotation distinguishes the offer from any other offer for a swing arm machine is inaccurate. Comparison of the Morningstar quotation to those made to other companies reveals that only the offer to Morningstar included a 40% allowance for old machines. Although this distinction does not establish the existence of an offer to replace old swing arm machines with a "new" type of machine, such a possibility is another factor for the trier to consider.

As evidence that no offer was made before the critical date, King also argues that Morningstar did not receive two shift block machines in June 1970, but in fact received two swing arm machines embodying the invention claimed in the '153 patent. However, Hunt of Morningstar was convinced that the two machines received on June 17, 1970 were horizontal shift block machines. Review of Hunt's testimony shows that he was continuously connected with the cassette winding operation during this period of time. His unbiased live testimony is a sufficient basis for the district court to have concluded that the machines received embodied the '358 shift block invention. The fact that Morningstar received two shift block machines is further support that the earlier ambiguous offer made on May 22, 1970 was in fact for shift block machines.

Even if there was an offer, King argues that the '358 invention was not reduced to practice before the critical date. The district court's conclusion that the invention was reduced to practice was based on the following findings of fact: (1) James King, Sr. testified that he had horizontal shift blocks on April 27, 1970; (2) it was the custom at King to make sales of machines prior to the completion of drawings; (3) the assembly drawing of the '358 horizontal shift block device was prepared on May 16, 1970; and (4) it was the custom and practice of King to have assembly drawings prepared from an existing assembled machine.

* * *

Our predecessor court has recognized that the invention must have been "sufficiently tested to demonstrate that it will work for its intended purpose." *General Electric Co. v. United States,* 654 F.2d 55, 60, n. 8, 228 Ct.Cl. 192, 201, n. 8, 211 USPQ 867, 872, n. 8 (1981). But, in order for there to be a reduction to practice, there is no requirement that the invention when tested be in a commercially satisfactory stage of development. *Barmag, supra,* 731 F.2d at 838, 221 USPQ at 567. Moreover, the district court might have considered that "[s]ome devices are so simple and their purpose and efficacy so obvious that their complete construction is sufficient to demonstrate workability." *Eastern Rotorcraft Corp. v. United States,* 384 F.2d 429, 431, 181 Ct.Cl. 299, 305, 155 USPQ 729, 730 (1967). Here, testimony and other evidence supports the district court's finding that King prepared assembly drawings from a completed and workable device. Accordingly, the district court did not err in inferring that the '358 invention embodied in an existing machine was sufficiently tested to constitute a reduction to practice. Rather, we are persuaded that the district court's conclusion that the '358 patent is invalid as being "on sale" under § 102(b) is supported by clear and convincing evidence.

* * * *

UMC ELECTRONICS COMPANY v. UNITED STATES

United States Court of Appeals, Federal Circuit, 1987.
816 F.2d 647.

NIES, CIRCUIT JUDGE.

UMC Electronics Company brought this action, pursuant to 28 U.S.C. § 1498(a), to recover compensation for use of its patented invention by the United States. UMC is the owner of Patent No. 3,643,513, issued February 22, 1972, by assignment from the inventor Preston Weaver. The United States Claims Court, 8 Cl.Ct. 604, 228 USPQ 396 (1985), upheld the validity of all claims (1–4) but dismissed the complaint on the ground of no infringement or, more accurately, no use of the patented invention by the United States. Both parties appeal. We reverse the Claims Court's holding that the patented invention was not on sale within the meaning of 35 U.S.C. § 102(b). Accordingly, we affirm the judgment in favor of the government, but on different grounds.

I

BACKGROUND

The claimed invention is an aviation counting accelerometer (ACA), a device for sensing and for recording the number of times an aircraft has been subjected to predetermined levels of acceleration. The sensor component is mounted on the aircraft in a direction to measure acceleration loading and is connected electrically to the recorder component. Records produced by an ACA can indicate an aircraft's remaining useful life and show the need for structural inspection, overhaul, or rotation to less demanding service.

The patent application which became the patent in this suit ('513) was filed on August 1, 1968. Under 35 U.S.C. § 102(b) the commercial exploitation and the state of development of the invention one year before the filing of the application for the subject invention are critical to resolution of the on-sale issue.

Prior to the late 1960's when UMC first entered this field, the U.S. Navy had procured ACA's from Maxson Electronics Company and from Giannini Controls Corporation. The Navy was dissatisfied with these ACA's because they sometimes recorded data that defied common sense, failed to count accelerations, or counted accelerations that never occurred. In 1966 the Navy contacted Preston Weaver, an employee of UMC, told him of the problems with existing ACA's and informed him of the Navy's interest in buying improved devices. Weaver designed an accelerometer, model UMC–A, and in late 1966, UMC was awarded a contract to supply the Navy with approximately 1600 units.

In early 1967, UMC concluded that its model UMC–A would not meet the Navy's performance specification required by its contract. Like the Maxson and Giannini ACA's, the UMC–A accelerometer utilized, as part of its sensor, an electromechanical transducer to mechanically generate signals to indicate levels of acceleration. Like the Maxson and Giannini devices, the UMC–A device sometimes counted and sometimes did not count the same acceleration load. The problem lay in the inherent frequency of the mass-spring system in the transducer. The devices could not distinguish between acceleration due to inflight maneuvers, which determines actual stress, and acceleration from other sources, e.g., windgusts or weapons release.

To prevent UMC from losing the ACA contract, Weaver began work to improve the sensor portion of an ACA and conceived his invention which uses an analog transducer in the sensor. An analog transducer electrically generates a varying signal (in contrast to the mechanically produced signal of prior devices) which can be filtered electronically to selectively remove the effects of superimposed vibrations. The Claims Court found that in April-May of 1967 Weaver built and tested an engineering prototype of his ACA containing a commercial analog transducer, a filter, a timing circuit and a voltage sensor that measured one load level. UMC sought to modify the existing contract for ACA's to substitute an analog transducer for the electromechanical transducer specified in the contract, but was unsuccessful in negotiating a modification.

In late May, 1967, the Navy issued new specifications and in July, 1967, requested proposals from contractors to deliver ACA's built to the new specification (Mil–A–22145B). Technically, the request for proposals called separately for a certain number of sensor components of an ACA system and a certain number of recorders, the two units being compatible in combination. UMC responded to the request on July 27, 1967, the final date for making a proposal, with an offer to supply $1,668,743 worth of its improved ACA (hereinafter model UMC–B). UMC represented as part of its proposal that the sensor portion "has been constructed and tested in conjunction with voltage sensing and time controlled circuitry." In response to a Navy inquiry, on August 2, 1967, after the critical date, UMC submitted a technical proposal which described the model UMC–B in detail and included test results and schematic drawings. On August 9, 1967, UMC gave a demonstration of its device to the Navy at the UMC facility.

In early 1968 the Navy canceled the request to which the above submission of UMC was directed, and in July 1968, it issued another. The latter request eventually led to a contract with Systron-Donner Corporation, which company has been providing the Navy with ACA's utilizing analog transducers since 1970.

* * *

As an initial matter, UMC is correct in pointing out the inconsistency between the Claims Court's conclusion that the claimed invention was "reduced to practice" before the critical date and its separate finding that no physical embodiment of the invention existed at that time. It is not sufficient for a reduction to practice that Weaver built and tested only a part of the later-claimed model UMC–B accelerometer. Under our precedent there cannot be a reduction to practice of the invention here without a physical embodiment which includes all limitations of the claim. *See, e.g., Correge v. Murphy*, 705 F.2d 1326, 1329, 217 USPQ 753, 755 (Fed.Cir.1983); 1 C. Rivise & A. Caesar, *Interference Law and Practice* § 137 (1940) and cases cited therein. Because the court found and the parties do not dispute that there was no physical embodiment containing all limitations of the claimed invention before the critical date, we conclude that the Claims Court erred in holding that there had been a reduction to practice.

The clarification of that issue, however, does not resolve the precise dispute here. Per the government, UMC's substantial attempted commercial exploitation of the claimed invention contravenes the policies of the on-sale bar despite the absence of a complete embodiment and, thus, raises an on-sale bar under section 102(b). For this proposition the government relies on the decision of this court in *Barmag*. On the other hand, UMC maintains that, as a matter of law, there is no on-sale bar unless the claimed invention had been reduced to practice before the critical date, and urges that we here reject the contrary suggestion in *Barmag*. Thus, we address first the issue whether reduction to practice of the claimed invention before the critical date is required to invoke the on-sale bar, and conclude, for reasons that follow, that reduction to practice is not always a requirement of the on-sale bar.[6] This leads to the issue whether there is an on-sale bar in this case. On the undisputed facts, we hold that the invention of the '513 patent was on sale within the meaning of section 102(b).

IV

Whether a reduction to practice is a requirement of the on-sale bar of 35 U.S.C. § 102(b) requires a review of our precedent. However, the issue has been directly addressed by this court or its predecessors in only two cases, *Barmag* and *General Electric Co. v. United States*, 654 F.2d 55, 60–61, 211 USPQ 867, 872–73 (Ct.Cl.1981) (en banc), although the issue has surfaced in others. In *General Electric Co. v. United States*, 654 F.2d at 61–64, 211 USPQ at 873–75, the Court of Claims, one of this court's predecessors, analyzed an on-sale bar issue by focusing on the policies underlying the bar to determine whether application of the bar would further those policies. Those policies were stated to be: * * * On the facts of that case, the court held that the policies were violated and that there was a reduction to practice before the critical date. 654 F.2d at 62, 211 USPQ at 874. The latter holding obviated the need to agree or disagree with a detailed analysis of the trial judge, who had concluded that reduction to practice was not "indispensable in every case."

In *Barmag*, the court went out of its way to reserve the question whether a physical embodiment should be a requirement of the on-sale

---

6. The public use bar of section 102(b) implicates different considerations and nothing said here should be construed to encompass that part of the statute.

bar in all cases. 731 F.2d at 836–37, 221 USPQ at 565. Without a physical embodiment, as stated above, there can be no reduction to practice. * * *

In *Western Marine Elecs., Inc. v. Furuno Elec. Co.,* 764 F.2d 840, 844, 226 USPQ 334, 337 (Fed.Cir.1985), the argument was made that the patented invention, a gravity stabilized sonar device used on fishing boats, had not been reduced to practice and, thus, had not been on sale before the critical date. Because the device had not been mounted on a boat, it was argued, the device had not been sufficiently tested and, thus, had not been reduced to practice. In holding the invention to be on sale, the court did not directly answer that issue, stating that the "totality of the circumstances" determined whether the device was on sale. It reiterated:

> Rigid standards are especially unsuited to the on sale provision where the policies underlying the bar, in effect, define it. *See TP Laboratories, Inc. v. Professional Positioners, Inc.,* 724 F.2d 965, 973, 220 USPQ 577, 583 (Fed.Cir.1984) [*cert. denied,* 469 U.S. 826 (1985)] (public use).

> As a result, this court has been careful to avoid erecting rigid standards for section 102(b). . . . While approving of the *Timely Products* criticism of the "on hand" doctrine because the doctrine often produces results contrary to the basic policies underlying the on sale bar, this court [in *Barmag*] nevertheless declined to adopt the *Timely Products* test for all cases.

Accord J.A. LaPorte Inc. v. Norfolk Dredging Co., 787 F.2d 1577, 1580 n.4, 229 USPQ 435, 437 (Fed.Cir.1986), *cert denied,* 107 S.Ct. 274 (1986); *King Instrument,* 767 F.2d 853, 226 USPQ 402; *In re Caveney,* 761 F.2d 671, 226 USPQ 1.

* * * In *General Electric* and *Barmag,* consideration of the issue was dicta, however well considered. In *Western Marine,* the court did not explicitly hold that there was or was not a reduction to practice of the claimed invention. It, therefore, cannot be said that this court has taken a definitive position either way on the issue we address here. *Cf. NLRB v. Boeing Co.,* 412 U.S. 67, 72 (1973) (premise assumed in earlier cases is rejected when court was, at last, "squarely presented with the issue"); *Lear, Inc. v. Adkins,* 395 U.S. 653, 663, 162 USPQ 1, 5 (1969) (Court receded from earlier endorsements of "licensee estoppel" as not "considered").

* * *

Finally, a major flaw in reduction to practice as a *per se* requirement of the on-sale bar in all cases is disclosed by a close analysis of *Timely Products,* the leading case which purports to adopt that requirement. A significant development with respect to the scope of section 102(b) occurred in a series of decisions beginning with those of another of our predecessors, the Court of Customs and Patent Appeals, when it recognized the operation of the bar in conjunction with the obviousness determination under section 103. In *In re Foster,* 343 F.2d at 988, 145 USPQ at 173, that court held:

[S]ince the purpose of the statute has always been to require filing of the application within the prescribed period after the time the public came into possession of the invention, we cannot see that it makes any difference *how* it came into such possession, whether by a public use, a sale, a single patent or publication, or by combinations of one or more of the foregoing. In considering this principle, *we assume*, of course, that by these means *the invention has become obvious* to that segment of the "public" having ordinary skill in the art. Once this has happened, the purpose of the law is to give the inventor only a year within which to file and this would seem to be liberal treatment.

Accord Argus Chem. v. *Fibre Glass-Evercoat*, 759 F.2d 10, 14, 225 USPQ 1100, 1103 (Fed.Cir.1985); *In re Kaslow*, 707 F.2d 1366, 1374, 217 USPQ 1089, 1095 (Fed.Cir.1983); *In re Corcoran*, 640 F.2d at 133, 208 USPQ at 869.

Implicit in the operation of a sections 102(b)/103 bar is the *absence* of reduction to practice of the *claimed invention* as a requirement for the bar to operate. The invention, i.e., as claimed with all elements, is not the subject of the sale. If it were, section 103 would not be involved. With respect to non-claimed subject matter of the sale in a sections 102(b)/103 situation, it is meaningless to speak of "reduction to practice" of what was sold. "Reduction to practice" relates only to the precise invention expressed *in a claim*. Thus, the second requirement of *Timely Products*, reduction to practice of the *claimed invention*, is inherently inconsistent with the first requirement under which the bar is applicable if the claimed invention is merely "obvious in view of the thing offered for sale."

In view of all of the above considerations, we conclude that reduction to practice of the claimed invention has not been and should not be made an absolute requirement of the on-sale bar.

We hasten to add, however, that we do not intend to sanction attacks on patents on the ground that the inventor or another offered for sale, before the critical date, the mere concept of the invention. Nor should inventors be forced to rush into the Patent and Trademark Office prematurely. On the other hand, we reject UMC's position that as a matter of law no on-sale bar is possible unless the claimed invention has been reduced to practice in the interference sense.

We do not reject "reduction to practice" as an important analytical tool in an on-sale analysis. A holding that there has or has not been a reduction to practice of the claimed invention before the critical date may well determine whether the claimed invention was in fact the subject of the sale or offer to sell or whether a sale was primarily for an experimental purpose. A holding that there is a reduction to practice of the claimed invention "may, of course, lighten the burden of the party asserting the bar." *General Electric*, 206 USPQ at 271. Thus, we simply say here that the on-sale bar does not necessarily turn on whether there was or was not a reduction to practice of the claimed invention. All of the circumstances surrounding the sale or offer to sell, including the stage of development of the invention and the nature of the invention, must be considered and weighed against the policies underlying section 102(b). *See In re Brigance*, 792 F.2d 1103, 1107–08, 229 USPQ 988, 991 (Fed.Cir.1986); *Western Marine*, 764 F.2d at 845, 226 USPQ at 337.

* * *

We do not attempt here to formulate a standard for determining when something less than a complete embodiment of the invention will suffice under the on-sale bar. However, the development of the subject invention was far beyond a mere conception. Much of the invention was embodied in tangible form. The prior art devices embodied each element of the claimed invention, save one, and that portion was available and had been sufficiently tested to demonstrate to the satisfaction of the inventor that the invention as ultimately claimed would work for its intended purpose. Thus, we conclude from the unchallenged facts with respect to the commercial activities of UMC, coupled with the extent to which the invention was developed, the substantial embodiment of the invention, the testing which was sufficient to satisfy the inventor that his later claimed invention would work, and the nature of the inventor's contribution to the art, that the claimed invention was on sale within the meaning of section 102(b).

Accordingly, we hold all claims of the '513 patent invalid. That issue being determinative of the case, we vacate the remainder of the Claims Court opinion.

Affirmed on different grounds, vacated-in-part.

ROBBINS CO. v. LAWRENCE MFG. CO.

United States Court of Appeals, Ninth Circuit, 1973.
482 F.2d 426, 178 USPQ 577.

JAMES M. CARTER, CIRCUIT JUDGE:

[Excerpt only].

After Lawrence filed its motion for summary judgment, Robbins for the first time contended that its offers for sale and sales were solely for experimental use. Robbins submitted three affidavits, * * *.

Even if we were inclined to credit these conclusory and subjective statements, they do not establish that the transactions were *substantially* for purposes of experimentation. *Smith & Griggs Mfg. Co.,* supra; *FMC Corp.,* supra.

At best, the import of the affidavits is that fully developed prototypes of the new cutters were sold for commercial exploitation; but because the particular configuration of bearings and seals (the innovations covered in the patent) had not been placed into such use before, Robbins and Sugden, as prudent engineers, considered the new cutters to be experimental. However, similar cutters had previously been successfully used to cut rock, and the innovations in seals and bearings, both obtained from suppliers' stock, were apparently not anticipated to have a fatal effect upon that ultimate function. Indeed, they did not, as seen from the Tasmania experience prior to the critical date herein.

* * *

There are certain categories in which it is clear that the fact of a sale, or an offering for sale, does not eliminate the experimental exception.

(A) CONDITIONAL SALES

"A sale which reserves to the inventor a right of experimentation and substitution does not place the invention on sale * * *." 2 Deller's Walker on Patents § 147, at 711 (2d ed. 1964). Austin Machinery Co. v. Buckeye Traction Ditcher Co., supra, 13 F.2d at 699–700, is such a case. There was a sale and use, supervised by the inventor as a joint vendee, which was held to be a conditional sale. The lower court's judgment, holding the patent invalid because of sale or use, was reversed. In Ushakoff v. United States (1964), 164 Ct.Cl. 455, 327 F.2d 669, a purchase by the Air Force prior to the critical date, stated the purchase was to be an "experimental procurement" for comparative or service tests, id. at 677, and the defense of invalidity of the patent was rejected.

(B) SALES WITH NO REQUIREMENTS OF SECRECY OR REPORTING

Wilkie v. Manhattan Rubber Mfg. Co. (3 Cir.1926) 14 F.2d 811, 812, held a patent invalid under both the "public use" and "on sale" defenses to an infringement action. The court said:

> "[T]he inference of the inventor's intention, before the grant of the patent, to abandon his invention to the public is established (and the patent subsequently granted is invalid) unless successfully controverted by full, unequivocal and convincing proof that such use and sale were not of the completed and commercially operative device subsequently patented, or that such use and *sale were not absolute and unconditional* but were principally and primarily for the purpose of perfecting the uncompleted invention by tests and experiments." 14 F.2d at 812. [Emphasis added]

The court noted that although both the inventor and the buyer may have hopefully awaited reports on the success of the invention, there was no showing of actual follow-up by the inventor, nor of conditions on the sale. The court said "there is no indication that the rolls were sold * * * for durability tests or experiments of any kind." The rolls were sold "absolutely and unconditionally * * *." There was no follow-up by the inventor. Id. at 812. "To that extent the use was problematical rather than experimental." Id. at 813.

* * *

(C) SALES WHERE DEVICE NOT COMPLETE

In Amerio Contact Plate Freezers, Inc. v. Belt-Ice Corp. (9 Cir.1963) 316 F.2d 459, the Ninth Circuit recognized that where no fully operative device is in existence prior to the critical date, a contract to sell the device, prior to that date, is not a placing of the invention on sale under the statute. Id. at 464. The court held no contract existed, and there were no special circumstances requiring the court, absent a prototype, to hold that the invention was "on sale." In *B.F. Sturtevant Co.,* supra, 124 F.2d at 97, a contract to construct from plans and deliver in the future, a machine not proven to have been previously completed, did not constitute putting the invention "on sale."

* * *

Accordingly, we adopt the following rule to determine whether a sale or offering for sale precludes patentability.

rule

A sale or an offering for sale

precludes any inquiry into the experimental nature of the sale *unless* the contract of sale or the offering for sale contains an express or clearly implied condition that the sale or offering is made primarily for experimental use.

Thus the sale or offering would not ipso facto invalidate the patent nor preclude further inquiry into the experimental nature of the use where the contract or the offer stated that the sale was for experimental purposes (*Austin* and *Ushakoff,* supra); or showed that the device was still experimental and that no workable prototype had been made (*Americo Contact Plate Freezers,* supra); or required that the invention should be kept confidential or from public view, or that reports on the use of the invention should be supplied to the inventor (*Ajem Laboratories, Cataphote,* and *Piet,* supra); or other similar statements appeared from which it could clearly be implied that the sale or the offering was made for an experimental purpose.

In cases where the exceptions did *not* appear in the sale or offering for sale, summary judgment would be permissible and proper. If the exceptions did appear, then a trial on the merits could dispose of exceptions made falsely or collusively and, generally, the merits of the claimed exceptions.

Where there has been commercial exploitation, the courts have generally found there was "public use" and not experimental use. Smith & Griggs Mfg. Co. and FMC Corp., supra. But even in case of a sale where the real purpose was experimentation, the patent is still valid. Watson v. Nelson, supra. Thus obtaining some monetary return from a sale made primarily for experimental purposes may not constitute in every case a "commercial exploitation" which invalidates the patent.

Under this rule, where there was some commercial exploitation, a showing that a sale or offering for sale was conditioned upon experimentation would preclude summary judgment against patentability. The court could then hear proof on the merits and determine whether the case came within the experimental exception.

The rule we rely on clarifies the problem for inventors. The sale or offering for sale of a later-patented item places it "on sale," within the statute, *unless* there is the express or clearly implied condition of experimentation.

Applying this rule to the facts of this case, it is clear that in both the Hydro-Electric and the Bles transactions there were sales and offerings for sale, with no express or clearly implied condition that they were for an experimental purpose. The device had been completed and was in existence. No requirements of secrecy were imposed on Hydro-Electric or Bles, nor were they required to report on the results of the supposed experimentation. Summary judgment was therefore proper.

Notes

1. The installation and use of patentee Cloud's vacuum food packaging machine in a food packaging plant producing more than 50,000 packages sold to retail food stores without the patentee receiving any rental or profits was an experimental use since " * * * it was necessary to send out thousands of vacuum packaged products to the stores marketing such products so as to obtain results, over a period of time, on so-called 'shelf life' of the products. Many were returned as 'leakers' and as being unsatisfactory. The results of the tests proved so unsatisfactory that Ostrow eventually stopped using the machine and Cloud asked him to return the machine." Cloud v. Standard Packaging Corp., 236 F.Supp. 981, 985, 144 USPQ 172, 174 (N.D.Ill.1965), reversed on other grounds 376 F.2d 384 (7th Cir.1967).

2. "While usable samples of a product or device disclosing the invention later patented may be sufficient to place the invention 'on sale' even though the samples are not production models, and even though the display of a mockup may be sufficient to place the invention on a design patent 'on sale,' Philco Corp. v. Admiral Corp., 199 F.Supp. 797 (D.C.Del.1961), a model of a scrap metal baling press built to a reduced scale rendering it commercially unusable is not available for present public use and accordingly is not sufficient to render the invention disclosed therein 'on sale.' The additional factor of a sales contract having been made in September of 1955, more than one year prior to the patent application, does not alter the situation, since no usable baling press was ever on hand and ready for delivery more than one year prior to the patent application date." Galland-Henning Mfg. Co. v. Dempster Bros., Inc., 315 F.Supp. 68, 81, 165 USPQ 688, 696 (E.D. Tenn.1970).

3. "Sales in the automobile clock market are initiated by presentation of samples to potential customers. Preparation for production does not begin until the customer approves the samples, agrees on a price, and gives a firm order. The procedure followed by Borg in the instant case is consistent with this sale-by-sample trade custom.

"Given the sale-by-sample method employed by the industry, the supplier-customer relationship between Borg and Cadillac, and a transfer of the resilient escapement device to Cadillac in a manner identical to the industry's method of sale, we find that the defendant established a prima facie defense that the Borg resilient escapement was 'on sale' to Cadillac in 1960. Once such a prima facie defense is established, the burden of coming forward with evidence falls on the plaintiff to show that the submission of samples was not an 'on sale' event." Amphenol Corp. v. General Time Corp., 275 F.Supp. 903, 905, 155 USPQ 246, 247 (N.D.Ill.1967).

4. "[T]here is convincing testimony that Bros did not intend to offer the roller for sale until it had been thoroughly tested. The testimony of defendant's witnesses regarding the testing as a prerequisite for sale and the fact that such tests did take place later is persuasive on this issue. It is true that an actual sale is not required under the statute, in that the law provides that if the device was placed on sale more than one year prior to the date of the application for the patent, the patentee would not be entitled to a patent. The Court concludes, however, that the plaintiffs have not sustained the burden of proof in establishing that the machine was 'on sale'. Granted that the exhibition of the machine at the Road Show, with distribution of the pamphlet which states that the price of the roller was $12,500, tends to lend credence to plaintiffs' contentions in this regard. A sound analysis of the entire testimony, however, would indicate that Bros' activities upon which the plaintiffs rely were directed at sounding out the industry's reaction to the machine and indicated the price at which it would be sold after the company had fully tested the machine, and if the tests proved satisfactory then the company would be ready thereafter to place the machine on the market for sale at the proposed price." Browning Mfg. Co. v. Bros, Inc., 134 USPQ 231, 235 (C.D.Minn.1962), affirmed 317 F.2d 413 (8th Cir.1963).

5. "The facts as fully set forth in the district court's findings, reveal that appellant had instituted a period of market testing, well beyond the product experimental stage, substantially in advance of the critical date. * * * in the spring and summer of 1956 Cataphote began negotiations with public agencies in many parts of the country for sales of the newly-developed thermoplastic process. The sales that eventually evolved from these negotiations, in August and September 1956, were concededly of a limited volume and at a reduced price. But these factors are not conclusive evidence that the product was still being treated experimentally as that term is used in patent law. Rather these factors are consistent with a program of market testing, product introduction, and sales promotion that is consistent with a stage of product development well beyond the experimental. The principal purpose of these sales to public agencies was commercialization of the product, not further experimentation and testing of the ultimately patented product. At this stage of commencement of negotiations, the product was sufficiently developed that its commercial promotion could have been the primary motivation behind appellant's course of conduct." Cataphote Corp. v. DeSoto Chem. Coatings, Inc., 356 F.2d 24, 26–27, 148 USPQ 527, 529 (9th Cir.1966).

6. Defendant also contends that the method claims covered in the Marshall method patent were "on sale" or in "public use" more than one year prior to the filing of the application on February 11, 1963. 35 U.S. C.A. § 102(b). * * * Marshall was essentially submitting his *apparatus* to various companies for testing and evaluation with the purpose of developing the device for manufacture and production. It was not "on sale" in the traditional sense. See, e.g., Amphenol Corp. v. General Time Corp., 397 F.2d 431 (7th Cir.1968); Chemithon Corp. v. Procter & Gamble Co., 287 F.Supp. 291 (D.Md.1968), affirmed per curiam 427 F.2d 893 (4th Cir.1970), cert. denied 400 U.S. 925, 91 S.Ct. 186, 27 L.Ed.2d 185 (1970). Rather, Marshall had but one model of his apparatus invention, which he

was in the process of developing over the period. This was not a submission by sample to a prospective purchaser; instead, Marshall was looking for a company to acquire the rights *under his patent application,* to produce and distribute his apparatus which could practice his methods. Aside from the difficulty with the concept of these particular methods ever being "on sale" in such a situation, I find that Marshall's disclosure of the methods in his pursuit of a manufacturer for his *apparatus* did not constitute public use or sale such as to invalidate his patent.

7. Choate, "On Sale"—Review and Circumspection, 47 J.P.O.S. 906 (1965).

c. Effective Date of Application for a Patent

Under certain conditions, an application for a U.S. patent is entitled to the benefit of the date of a previously filed U.S. application disclosing the same invention. Most of these conditions were developed by Patent Office practice and court decisions presumably beginning with Godfrey v. Eames, 68 U.S. (1 Wall.) 317, 17 L.Ed. 684 (1864) and were first embodied in statutory form in Section 120 of the 1952 Patent Act.

When applicable, this section determines the effective "date of the application for patent" under the statutory provisions of 35 U.S.C.A. § 102(b) and (d), and constructive reduction to practice under § 102(a), (e) and (g).

In considering Section 120, an understanding of certain terminology is helpful. If a subsequent patent application is filed before the patenting, abandonment, or termination of proceedings on an earlier filed application by at least one of the same inventors, it is commonly referred to as a "copending" application. If a copending application discloses and claims only the invention disclosed and claimed in the earlier application, it is referred to as a "continuation" application. If a copending application includes at least a portion of the disclosure of the earlier application and also subject matter not disclosed therein, it is referred to as a "continuation-in-part" application. If a copending application claims only a portion of the subject matter disclosed in the earlier application, it is referred to as a "divisional" application.

35 U.S.C.A. § 120. Benefit of earlier filing date in the United States

An application for patent for an invention disclosed in the manner provided by the first paragraph of section 112 of this title in an application previously filed in the United States, or as provided by section 363 of this title, which is filed by an inventor or inventors named in the previously filed application shall have the same effect, as to such invention, as though filed on the date of the prior application, if filed before the patenting or abandonment of or termination of proceedings on the first application or on an application similarly entitled to the benefit of the filing date of the first application and if it contains or is amended to contain a specific reference to the earlier filed application.

GODFREY v. EAMES

Supreme Court of the United States, 1864.
68 U.S. (1 Wall.) 317, 17 L.Ed. 684.

IN ERROR to the Circuit Court of the United States for the District of Massachusetts.

This action was originally brought by the plaintiff in error, to recover damages for the alleged infringement of certain letters patent issued upon the application of one Lewis, consisting of his petition, specification, oath, model, & c. These papers and model were filed with the Commissioner of Patents, on the 24th of April, 1857.

Prior to that time the said Lewis had made an application to the Commissioner of Patents, consisting of another petition, specification, oath, and model; which said application, having been refused, was, at the election of the applicant, withdrawn, and the fee returned, pursuant to section 7 of the Act of 1836, before the making of the new application, which was successful.

This prior application was filed in the Patent Office, Jan. 30, 1855. It was refused by the commissioner or, in technical language, "rejected" by him, May 17th, 1855, and no further proceedings thereon having been had, was finally withdrawn as above, April 24, 1857, pursuant to statute, by election of the applicant.

These applications thus made at different times by the said Lewis, were made through different agents or attorneys, and the papers used, description of the invention, claims of novelty, and models, were different.

The patentee, in 1854, and more than two years before the filing of the application, filed April 24, 1857, had put his alleged invention in public use and on sale, and thus had lost all right to obtain a patent therefor, under the saving clause of Act of 1839, section 7, unless it shall appear that "the application" referred to in that section is not necessarily the application in pursuance of which the patent was granted, but might as well mean any preceding application by the same person, for a like purpose, which had come to nought.

* * *

MR. JUSTICE SWAYNE delivered the opinion of the court:

* * *

In this case the patentee filed his application in the Patent Office on the 31st of January, 1855, and from that time it was constantly before the office, until the patent was issued on the 2d of March, 1858, except that on the 24th of April, 1857, it was withdrawn and refiled on the same day with an amended specification. It was admitted and proved "that the patentee, in the summer and fall of 1854, and since, publicly manufactured and sold, boot-trees containing his alleged invention." The sales and use, as thus shown, were less than two years before the first application was filed, and hence, according to the letter of the Act of March 3, 1839, cannot effect the validity of the patent.

In answer to this, two propositions are relied upon by the plaintiff in error:

1. It is said the original and the renewed application are for patents for different things.

Both specifications are before us, and it is our duty to construe them.

The act of July 4, 1836, gives the applicant a right to change his specification after receiving the suggestions of the commissioner. Doubtless, this right exists and may be exercised independently of such suggestions, at any time before the commissioner has given his formal judgment upon the application; and the inventor may "persist in his application for a patent, with or without any alteration of his specification." A change in the specification as filed in the first instance, or the subsequent filing of a new one, whereby a patent is still sought for the substance of the invention as originally claimed, or a part of it, cannot in any wise affect the sufficiency of the original application or the legal consequence, flowing from it. To produce that result the new or amended specification must be intended to serve as the basis of a patent for a distinct and different invention, and one not contemplated by the specification, as submitted at the outset.

We are satisfied that there was here such substantial identity in the two specifications as brings the case within the rule thus laid down. This objection cannot be sustained.

2. It is said that the withdrawal of the first application broke the continuity of the claim, and that the case stands as if the only application were the one of the 24th of April, 1857.

* * *

In our judgment, if a party choose to withdraw his application for a patent, and pay the forfeit, intending at the time of such withdrawal to file a new petition, and he accordingly do so, the two petitions are to be considered as parts of the same transaction, and both as constituting one continuous application, within the meaning of the law.

The question of the continuity of the application should have been submitted to the jury. In directing them to return a verdict for the defendant, we think the learned judge, who tried the cause in the court below, committed an error.

The judgment is, therefore, reversed, and a venire de novo awarded.

GENERAL TALKING PICTURES CORP. v. WESTERN ELEC. CO.

Supreme Court of the United States, 1938.
304 U.S. 175, 58 S.Ct. 849, 82 L.Ed. 1273, reh. granted 304 U.S. 587, 58 S.Ct. 1051, 82 L.Ed. 1548 (1938).

MR. JUSTICE BUTLER delivered the opinion of the Court.

Three suits were brought by respondents against petitioner in the district court for the southern district of New York to restrain infringements, based on different patents for inventions in vacuum tube amplifiers which have been used in wire and radio telephony, talking motion pictures, and other fields. In all there were in suit seven patents. The cases were tried together and are treated as one. The lower courts held one of the patents invalid, and that ruling is not challenged here. They concurred in holding six of the patents valid and infringed by petitioner. 16 F.Supp. 293; 91 F.2d 922. This Court granted a writ of certiorari 302 U.S. 674, ante, 520, 58 S.Ct. 49.

* * *

3. Petitioner's affirmative statement of its third question is: "An inventor who has filed an application for patent showing and describing, but not claiming, certain inventions cannot obtain a valid patent for said inventions by voluntarily filing a 'divisional' or 'continuation' application for said unclaimed inventions more than two years subsequent to public use of the said unclaimed inventions by him or his assignee or licensee." It makes that contention as to four patents: Arnold Patent No. 1,403,475, dated January 17, 1922; Arnold Patent No. 1,465,332, dated April 21, 1923; Arnold Patent No. 1,329,283, dated January 27, 1920; and Arnold Patent No. 1,448,550, dated March 13, 1923.

The district court and circuit court of appeals found that there was no public use of either of the inventions of the first two patents prior to the filing dates of the divisional applications upon which they issued. These findings were made upon adequate evidence and petitioner's contentions as to them will not be considered here.

The subject matter of the claims of the other two patents were disclosed in the original applications and were claimed in the continuation applications upon which they issued. The patentee's use was the only "public use" of the inventions covered by them. And that did not precede by as much as two years the filing of the original applications. The effective dates of the claims of the continuation applications are those of the original applications. In the absence of intervening adverse rights for more than two years prior to the continuation applications, they were in time. Rev.Stat. § 4886 (35 U.S.C.A. § 31); Crown Cork & Seal Co. v. Ferdinand Gutmann Co. decided this day [304 U.S. 159, ante, 1265, 58 S.Ct. 842].

Held [handwritten marginal note]

Affirmed.

* * *

MUNCIE GEAR WORKS v. OUTBOARD, MARINE & MFG. CO.

Supreme Court of the United States, 1942.
315 U.S. 759, 62 S.Ct. 865, 86 L.Ed. 1171.

MR. JUSTICE JACKSON delivered the opinion of the Court:

We are required in this case to determine the validity of claims numbered 11, 12, 13 and 14 of letters patent No. 1,716,962, granted on June 11, 1929, to Harry L. Johnson for invention in a "water propulsion device." Respondent Johnson Brothers Engineering Corporation is the owner of the patent, and respondent Outboard, Marine Manufacturing Company, is the exclusive licensee thereunder. Petitioner Muncie Gear Works, Inc., manufactured outboard motors which are claimed to infringe, and petitioner Bruns & Collins, Inc., sold them.

Respondents contend that this is a validly issued patent covering an invention which solved the problems of "cavitation" by relatively large and fast outboard motors. "Cavitation" is the drawing of air by the propeller from above the surface of the water to the propeller itself. Air so drawn reduces the propulsive effect of the propeller and causes "racing" of the motor with consequent risk of its disintegration and danger to the user. Increased speed or power entails a greater tendency to cavitate. Cavitation may be diminished by setting the propeller deeper in the water, but this increased projection increases resistance and retards speed.

Long before the patent in question, it was known that cavitation could be controlled, and in practice it was controlled, in at least all but relatively large and fast outboard motors, by setting a flat plate horizontally above the propeller and beneath the surface of the water, to act as a baffle and prevent the propeller from drawing air. Respondents presented expert testimony to the effect that relatively large and fast water-cooled outboard motors cannot be successful unless they embody the asserted invention which respondents say is the subject matter of the claims in question. In general, this may be said to consist in the use of an anti-cavitation plate on a housing for the engine and propeller shafts enclosing the water passages for the cooling system, shaped both above and below the plate so as to reduce water displacement and resistance and thus to reduce or eliminate eddy currents forming vortexes through which air can be sucked into the propeller. This permits adequate control of cavitation by means of a not unduly large anti-cavitation plate.

Harry L. Johnson, an experienced engineer and manufacturer of outboard motors, filed his application for the patent on August 25, 1926, but in no way suggested the combination now asserted as his invention. The single sheet of drawing accompanying the application was not changed during the prosecution of the application, and is the same as the drawing of the issued patent. This drawing showed an outboard motor assembly comprising, among other things, an engine at the top connected with a propeller at the bottom, with an anti-cavitation plate located horizontally above the propeller approximately midway between top and bottom of the housing for the engine and propeller shafts. All water passages for the cooling system beneath the normal water level were shown to be enclosed in the housing. No cross section of this housing was drawn or indicated, and for all that appears from the drawing it might have been circular, triangular or rectangular. The drawing showed an arched member extending from the housing and anti-cavitation plate over the top and to the rear of the propeller, containing openings and passages for the intake and discharge of water, and ending in a curved "deflection plate" extending rearwardly like a fixed rudder. From the specifications and claims it appeared that the purpose of the deflection plate was to compensate for the side and pivotal force of the moving propeller, which tended to draw the boat off its course unless the operator made constant adjustment to offset the "side throw." The specifications and drawings both indicated an anti-cavitation plate which the specification said "prevents cavitation," but it was in no way asserted that the cavitation plate was new, or that it was being employed in any novel cooperative relation to the other elements.

All of the claims of the application as originally made were rejected on December 15, 1926. On December 13, 1927, Johnson offered amendments which retained and amended the prior claims and added others directed to the feature of the deflection plate. In urging allowance, he said, among other things: "It is conceded that cavitation plates are old in the art as shown in the patent to Johnson cited," and he proceeded to urge as an invention the combination of the cavitation plate and the arching member or deflection plate. A similar supplemental amendment was filed on January 19, 1928. Several of the original claims as amended were allowed, and the rest of the claims rejected, on June 7, 1928.

On December 8, 1928, Johnson came forward with new claims. Claims 20 to 25 offered by this amendment made no mention of the deflection plate or of the arching members, but did not even suggest the presently asserted invention. On March 30, 1929, Johnson cancelled these claims and offered further amendments to his original application, together with a supplemental oath that he had invented the subject matter of the application as so amended, prior to the filing of the original amendment. The effect of those changes was aptly described by the patent examiner: "The amendments have been such that the claims now emphasize the anti-cavitation plate rather than the anti-torque plate." With changes which are immaterial here, the new claims so offered became the claims in issue. In them Johnson for the first time made claims relating to the exterior surface of the housing. Claim 12 described the housing as having "unbroken outer wall surfaces at each side," and claim 14 as having "smooth and unbroken walls." Claims 11 and 13 were silent on the subject. The amendment also set forth an addition to the description which was incorporated in the description of the patent as issued. Here we find the expression "relatively smooth and substantially stream-line surfaces." Other than these, no indication of the nature of the surface or cross section of the housing was given at any time during the prosecution of the application.

The petitioners interposed defenses to all of the eight patents upon which respondents sued them in the District Court for the Northern District of Illinois, Eastern Division which we take to have put in issue the question whether the claims were void because made more than two years after the first public use of the device. At the trial two of the officers of respondent Outboard, Marine & Manufacturing Company testified on direct examination as respondents' witnesses to the effect that in January or February of 1926 one of this respondent's predecessors put on the market licensed outboard motors equipped with smooth-walled housings, anti-cavitation plates, and internal water passages as described in the claims in suit; and that at least one competitor (which was also a predecessor) had brought out a substantially similar, but unlicensed, motor about a year later.

* * *

Section 4886 of the Revised Statutes, as amended and applicable to the present case, provided for the issuance of a patent to an inventor upon certain conditions, one of which was that his invention was "not in public use or on sale in this country for more than two years prior to his application."

In an effort to avoid the effect of this provision, respondents contend that the question of its applicability was not raised either in the District Court or in the Circuit Court of Appeals; that there was no opportunity to meet the issue; and that the invention as finally claimed was disclosed by the application as originally made or in any event as amended on December 8, 1928.

However, the evidence of public use and sale, given, as we have pointed out, by respondents' own officers and witnesses, has not been questioned or contradicted, and is interpreted by respondents' counsel in accordance with our view of it.

* * *

It is clear to us, however, that the amendments of December 8, 1928, like the original application, wholly failed to disclose the invention now asserted.

The claims in question are invalid if there was public use, or sale, of the device which they are claimed to cover, more than two years before the first disclosure thereof to the Patent Office. Cf. Chicago & N.W.R. Co. v. Sayles, 97 U.S. 554, 557, 559, 563, 564, 24 L.Ed. 1053–1057; Schriber-Schroth Co. v. Cleveland Trust Co., supra (305 U.S. 57, 59 S.Ct. 8, 83 L.Ed. 39). Section 4886 of the Revised Statutes would in terms provide for their invalidity had they been offered by application rather than by amendment; and whatever may be the efficacy of an amendment as a substitute for an application, it surely can effect no more than the application itself.

We think the conclusion is inescapable that there was public use, or sale, of devices embodying the asserted invention, more than two years before it was first presented to the Patent Office. We are not foreclosed from a decision under § 4886 on the point by the obscurity of its presentation in the courts below. This issue has been fully presented to this Court by the petition for a writ of certiorari, and in subsequent briefs and argument; and there is not the slightest indication that respondents have been prejudiced by such obscurity. To sustain the claims in question upon the established and admitted facts would require a plain disregard of the public interest sought to be safeguarded by the patent statutes, and so frequently present but so seldom adequately represented in patent litigation.

We therefore hold that the claims in question are invalid under *Held* § 4886 of the Revised Statutes, and accordingly have no occasion to decide any other question in the case.

Reversed.

June 11, 1929. H. L. JOHNSON 1,716,962
WATER PROPULSION DEVICE
Filed Aug. 25, 1926

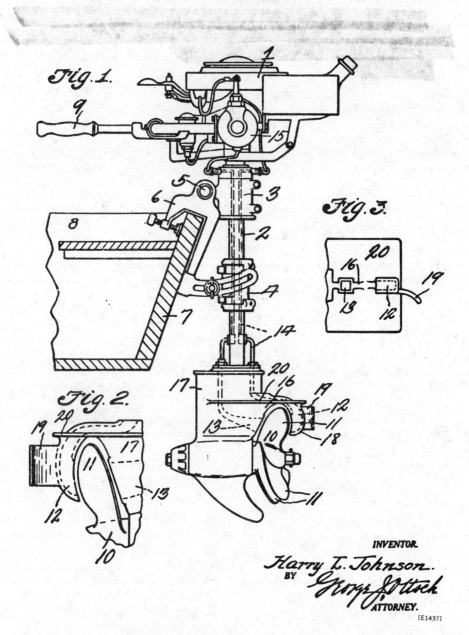

Fig. 1.

Fig. 3.

Fig. 2.

INVENTOR.
Harry L. Johnson.
BY
George J. Fitch
ATTORNEY.
[E1437]

§ 132. Notice of rejection; reexamination

Whenever, on examination, any claim for a patent is rejected, or any objection or requirement made, the Commissioner shall notify the applicant thereof, stating the reasons for such rejection, or objection or requirement, together with such information and references as may be useful in judging of the propriety of continuing the prosecution of his application; and if after receiving such notice, the applicant persists in his claim for a patent, with or without amendment, the application shall be reexamined. No amendment shall introduce new matter into the disclosure of the invention.

Notes

1. "Assuming the common inventorship, copendency, and cross-reference required by section 120, that section further requires only that the invention be disclosed in the parent application in such manner as to comply with the first paragraph of section 112 and *be* the same invention as that disclosed in the later application. It does not require that the invention be described in the same way, or comply with section 112 in the same way, in both applications. And to determine what is the invention under consideration, one must be governed by the claims of the later application, because it is there one must look to determine what invention the 'application for patent' referred to in the opening words of section 120 is for." In re Kirchner, 49 CCPA 1234, 305 F.2d 897, 904, 134 USPQ 324, 330 (1962).

2. "If any claim covers subject matter disclosed in both the parent application and the continuation-in-part application (hereinafter referred to as the CIP) the priority date of the claim is the filing date of the parent application, January 30, 1956. 35 U.S.C.A. § 120. As for a claim containing subject matter disclosed for the first time in the CIP application, that claim has a priority date corresponding to the filing of that application, June 11, 1957. In other words, the priority date is determined not by the date the invention was claimed, but rather when it was first disclosed in an application." Chemithon Corp. v. Procter & Gamble Co., 287 F.Supp. 291, 299, 159 USPQ 139, 145 (D.C.D.Md.1968), affirmed per curiam 427 F.2d 893, 165 USPQ 678 (4th Cir.1970).

3. "A continuation in part application is entitled to the filing date of the parent application to the extent of subject matter common to both." Indiana Gen. Corp. v. Lockheed Aircraft Corp., 408 F.2d 294, 297, 160 USPQ 6, 8 (9th Cir.1968).

4. "The question for our consideration, therefore, is whether, in a case like the present, where it appears that a joint application has been filed through mistake or inadvertence and without fraudulent intent, the sole inventor, one of the joint applicants, is estopped from taking any advantage of that application.

* * *

"The joint application of Roberts and Roberts answered every requirement of this section, except that one of the applicants, as it subsequently developed, did not contribute anything to the subject-matter here involved. All that was sought in the new application was the elimination of one of the joint applicants, to whom credit mistakenly had been given for the particular invention involved. There was identity of subject-matter, and it is difficult to perceive any reason for not permitting the rectification of such a mistake by an amendment eliminating the superfluous applicant. Surely, if such an amendment would have been proper, then the filing of what in substance and effect was a duplicate application by the sole inventor should have been regarded as a continuation of the former application. When one joint applicant admitted that this particular subject-matter was the sole invention of the other applicant, to all intents and purposes the application as to this subject-matter was the application of the sole inventor, who still was a party to the proceeding. The Patent Office, in our view, has failed to give proper weight to the fact that there is identity of subject-matter here, that there is no conflict of interest, and that the second application is filed merely to correct a formal error.

*   *   *

"To prevent a possible failure of justice, the present application should have been considered as a continuation of the abortive application. As already suggested, we perceive no reason why the mistake could not have been rectified by a simple amendment, but in any event the sole inventor should not be deprived of his day in court by the raising of artificial barriers against him. He claimed his invention, and, through mistake, gave his son credit where no credit was due. The elimination of the son ought not to deprive the father, the sole inventor, of the benefit of his original application; and we so rule." In re Roberts, 263 Fed. 646, 49 App. D.C. 250 (1920). To the same effect under 35 U.S.C.A. § 120 see Johnson & Johnson v. C.B. Stenvall, Inc., 193 F.Supp. 128, 129 USPQ 120 (S.D.N.Y. 1961).

5. The claims of a patent issued on an application of a sole inventor as a continuation-in-part of an earlier filed and subsequently abandoned application of the sole and another inventor as joint inventors, disclosing but not claiming the subject matter of the patent claims, are not entitled, under 35 U.S.C.A. § 120, to the filing date of the joint application and hence are invalid in view of an intervening public use and sale under § 102(b) and failure to name the other inventor, where the other inventor fails to acknowledge that he is not and in fact may be asserting his rights as a joint inventor of the subject matter of the patent claims. Merry Manufacturing Co. v. Burns Tool Co., 335 F.2d 239, 142 USPQ 342 (5th Cir. 1964).

6. "Defendants concede that if the patent in suit is not entitled to the benefit of a 1953 filing date [of an abandoned first application to which it does not specifically refer], it is invalid on the ground of public use during the latter part of the summer of 1953. To avoid the statutory bar of 35 U.S.C.A. § 102(b), they argue that the patent is not only entitled to the [February 25, 1957] filing date of the second application [to which it specifically referred] but also to the 1953 filing date of the abandoned [first] application. * * * We hold that under this statute [35 U.S.C.A. § 120] the patent in suit is limited to an effective filing date of February 25, 1957, because neither the application nor patent contains 'a specific reference' to the 1953 application. This holding is consistent with the 9th Circuit's ruling in Hovlid v. Asari, 305 F.2d 747 (9th Cir.1962), which was recently approved in Application of Henriksen, 399 F.2d 253, 256 (CCPA 1968). Section 201.11 of the Manual of Patent Examining Procedure (3d ed. rev. 1968) has adopted the same construction." Sticker Industrial Supply Corp. v. Blaw-Knox Co., 405 F.2d 90, 160 USPQ 177 (7th Cir.1968).

7. "The sole issue presented by this appeal is the interpretation of 35 U.S.C.A. § 120. Simply stated, the question is whether the language of section 120 *limits* an applicant to the benefit of the filing date of the second preceding application in a chain of copending applications. We reverse the decision of the Patent Office Board of Appeals, 154 USPQ 53 (Pat.Off.Bd. App.1966). We hold here that under that section of the statute, in view of its long-standing interpretation by the Patent Office and the patent bar, there is no statutory basis for fixing an arbitrary limit to the *number* of prior applications through which a chain of copendency may be traced to obtain the benefit of the filing date of the earliest of a chain of copending applications, provided applicant meets all the other conditions of the statute." In re Henriksen, 399 F.2d 253, 158 USPQ 224 (CCPA 1968).

d. Antedating Prima Facie Prior Art

Something which qualifies under Section 102(b) as prior art, namely, patented, printed publication, in public use, or on sale, having an effective date *more than one year prior to the date of an application for patent,* must be considered in determining the novelty and nonobviousness of the invention of an application or a patent issued thereon. Such art is considered under the statutory bar of § 102(b) regardless of the date of the invention of the application or patent issued thereon.

However, something which does not qualify under § 102(b) is prior art only if it has an effective date prior to the date the invention was made of the particular application or patent under consideration. Thus, even though this type of art has an effective date prior to the date of the application in question, it is only prima facie prior art, since it does not qualify under § 102(b), and if an earlier date for the invention of the application or patent is established, such art will not be considered in determining novelty and nonobviousness. Examples of prima facie prior art are patents, printed publications, and knowledge or use by others referenced in § 102(a), a subsequently granted U.S. patent issuing on a prior application, § 102(e), and a prior invention of another which was not abandoned, § 102(g).

Establishing the date of invention involves consideration of the factors of conception, reduction to practice, and diligence presented in Section C of Chapter Two. As previously noted, activities in a foreign country cannot be relied on in establishing the date of an invention except to the extent permitted by Sections 104 and 119.

The need to establish a date of invention prior to the date of prima facie art can occur in both a suit on an issued patent and in connection with a pending application. Prima facie art can be antedated in the Patent Office by an affidavit pursuant to Rule 131 of the Patent Office Rules of Practice which provides:

§ 1.131 Affidavit or Declaration of Prior Invention to Overcome Cited Patent or Publication

(a) When any claim of an application or a patent under reexamination is rejected on reference to a domestic patent which substantially shows or describes but does not claim the rejected invention, or on reference to a foreign patent or to a printed publication, and the inventor of the subject matter of the rejected claim, the owner of the patent under reexamination, or the person qualified under §§ 1.42, 1.43 or 1.47, shall make oath or declaration as to facts showing a completion of the invention in this country before the filing date of the application on which the domestic patent issued, or before the date of the foreign patent, or before the date of the printed publication, then the patent or publication cited shall not bar the grant of a patent to the inventor or the confirmation of the patentability of the claims of the patent, unless the date of such patent or printed publication is more than one year prior to the date on which the inventor's or patent owner's application was filed in this country.

(b) The showing of facts shall be such, in character and weight, as to establish reduction to practice prior to the effective date of the reference, or conception of the invention prior to the effective date of the reference coupled with due diligence from said date to a subsequent reduction to practice or to the filing of the application. Original exhibits of drawings or records, or photocopies thereof, must accompany and form part of the affidavit or declaration or their absence satisfactorily explained.

If the prima facie art cited by the Patent Office is a United States patent which *claims* the rejected invention, it can only be overcome by a priority contest (an interference proceeding) and not by a Rule 131 affidavit.

The following cases are intended to provide an acquaintance with antedating prima facie prior art.

BULLOCK ELEC. MFG. CO. v. CROCKER–WHEELER CO.

United States Circuit Court of New Jersey, 1905.
141 Fed. 101.

[A suit for infringement of a patent to Leonard filed November 27, 1891 and issued July 5, 1892. One of the defenses was lack of novelty in view of a patent to Smith filed November 11, 1891 and issued March 15, 1892. Most of the opinion by Judge Lanning has been omitted.]

* * *

The question on this branch of the case therefore is: Was Leonard or Smith, in contemplation of the law, the original or first inventor?

* * *

* * * The earliest date that Mr. Smith satisfactorily fixes for the disclosure of his invention to any one is November 5, 1891. Leonard, on the other hand, has introduced in evidence a description of his invention written out by him and containing also illustrative drawings. The written matter and the drawings are on pages 199 to 212 of a record book kept by him. At the end of the description, on page 212, are the following entries:

"Matters on pp. 199 to 212 explained to me by Mr. Leonard Oct. 3, 1891.

"[Signed]   H. W. Seeley."

"Matters on pp. 199–212, inclusive, explained to me by Mr. Leonard prior to this date, viz., Oct. 5, 1891.

"[Signed]   A.D. Vance.
                                                   "H.J. Westover.
                                                   "C.H. Bloomer.

"Oct. 5, 1891."

Mr. Seeley was Leonard's patent solicitor and is now dead, but his signature was duly proven. Mr. Vance and Mr. Westover have been sworn and testify to the genuineness of their signatures and the appended dates. Vance also testifies to the genuineness of Bloomer's signature. The first part of the written description is dated September 15, 1891. On September 16th Leonard wrote to William Sellers & Co. of Philadelphia, concerning his invention, and on October 30th, pursuant to arrangements with them, he went to Philadelphia to have his invention tested at their works. On November 2d Leonard wrote them requesting an early report on the test. On November 24th Leonard's application for a patent was sworn to by him. On November 27th the application was filed. And on November 28th Sellers & Co. sent to Leonard a report of the test made October 30th. I am satisfied that the test there made was the multiple-voltage system of the Leonard patent. Nor do I think the objection that the description of the invention in Leonard's record book, connected as it was with his explanation of it to four different persons, is incompetent evidence to carry the date of the invention back of the time when he filed his application in the patent office.

* * *

Leonard also was diligent in adapting and perfecting his invention. Whatever delay there was in the filing of his application, which was less than two months after he had disclosed it to other persons, seems to have been due to the illness of his patent solicitor. Disregarding the proofs on the question as to whether Smith did not "surreptitiously and unjustly" obtain a patent for what Leonard had invented, and assuming the utmost good faith on the part of Smith, it appears that Leonard was the first inventor of the system described in his patent, for, as already observed, there is nothing in the case to show that Smith ever disclosed his invention to any person whomsoever before November 5, 1891.

* * *

IN RE MULDER

United States Court of Appeals, Federal Circuit, 1983.
716 F.2d 1542, 219 USPQ 189.

RICH, CIRCUIT JUDGE.

* * *

This ex parte appeal from the PTO involves appellants' patent application on an integrated circuit, the appealed claims of which stand rejected for obviousness under § 103 in view of prior art disclosed in an article by Rodgers et al., published in the IEEE Journal of Solid State

Circuits, Vol. SC–9, No. 5, pages 247 and 248 (Rodgers), combined with one or more of the following: * * *

The real party in interest here is the assignee of appellants, U.S. Philips Corporation, which is affiliated with N.V. Philips Gloei-lampenfabrieken of the Netherlands, where the applicants are located. The U.S. patent application was prepared in the Netherlands and sent to the patent department of U.S. Philips Corporation in Briarcliff Manor, N.Y., where it was received on July 15, 1974. A corresponding Netherlands patent application was filed on October 9, 1974. The U.S. application was filed within a year under the International Convention on August 6, 1975, claiming the benefit of the Netherlands filing date under 35 U.S.C. § 119. The PTO has accorded applicants that date. There is no question that applicants complied with all of the formalities required by § 119 and related PTO rules.

Confronted with rejections of claims based in part, if not primarily, on Rodgers, appellants attempted to antedate, and thus remove, that reference as prior art, by filing declarations under 37 CFR 1.131 (Rule 131). * * *

Applicants proved to the satisfaction of the PTO the receipt in this country of the draft patent application which was accepted as a fact showing conception of the invention prior to Rodgers' publication date, which date is taken by the PTO to be the receipt of the IEEE Journal containing the Rodgers article by the PTO on October 7, 1974. * * *

The foregoing facts can be better visualized from the following chart, adapted from one in appellants' brief:

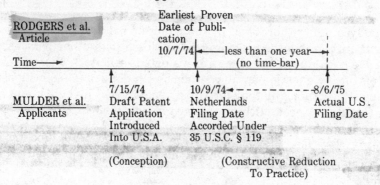

ISSUES

The primary issue is the obviousness of the invention as defined in the appealed claims in view of the references relied on. Preliminary thereto is the question whether the Rodgers article has been overcome as a reference, and involved in that issue is the question whether appellants are entitled to their Netherlands filing date as a constructive reduction to practice. These questions will be considered in the reverse order of their statement.

OPINION

Adverting to Rule 131, supra, as appellants have shown no actual reduction to practice of the invention in this country and no constructive reduction prior to the date of Rodgers, what Rule 131(b) says they have to show is conception in this country prior to Rodgers' date coupled with "due diligence from said date to ＊ ＊ ＊ the filing of the application." The first question, therefore, is the date of conception in this country. The PTO (both the examiner and the board) have accepted July 15, 1974, the date of receipt in the U.S. of the draft application, as a conception date.

The next question is whether appellants are entitled, as a date of constructive reduction to practice, to the Netherlands or only to the actual U.S. filing date. The examiner said it was the former, the board the latter. We agree with the examiner.

The board cited no authority for depriving appellants of the benefit of their convention filing date; it only remarked that "the events of concern under 37 CFR 1.131 are events that occur in this country." It made no reference to § 119 of the statute. We note that Rule 131 refers to "facts showing a completion of the invention in this country" but we also note that in (b) it makes a distinction between an *actual* reduction to practice (which has to be "in this country") and the "filing of the application." We are also aware of the statute which prohibits reliance on "activity ＊ ＊ ＊ in a foreign country" in establishing "a date of invention," 35 U.S.C. § 104. But that same statute has an express exception—"except as provided in sections 119 and 365 of this title." It is § 119 with which we are concerned. It provides that when a U.S. application has been filed, as was the application in this case, within a year from an application in a convention country such as the Netherlands, the formalities all being complied with, the U.S. application

> ＊ ＊ ＊ shall have the same effect as the same application would have if filed in this country on the date on which the application for patent for the same invention was first filed in such foreign country ＊ ＊ ＊.

§119

We hold that this provision entitles appellants to rely on their Netherlands filing date for a constructive reduction to practice. Section 119 is a "patent-saving" provision for the benefit of applicants, and an applicant is entitled to rely on it as a constructive reduction to practice to overcome the date of a reference under Rule 131. *In re Ziegler*, 347 F.2d 642, 52 CCPA 1473, 146 USPQ 76 (1965) (convention German filing dates available to overcome references under § 119). If entitlement to a foreign filing date can completely overcome a reference we see no reason why it cannot partially overcome a reference by providing the constructive reduction to practice element of proof required by Rule 131. It is a *statutory* priority right which cannot be interfered with by a construction placed on a PTO rule. *Cf. In re Hilmer*, 359 F.2d 859, 878, 53 CCPA 1288, 1312, 149 USPQ 480, 496 (1966).

This brings us to the next question under Rule 131. Referring to the time chart, supra, appellants have their conception date of July 15,

1974, and their constructive reduction to practice date of October 9, 1974, and Rule 131 requires that these dates must be "coupled with due diligence." Appellants would have us treat this case as though it were an interference between them and Rodgers, treating Rodgers as an applicant for a patent. But Rodgers is not an applicant and this is not an interference. Rodgers is a printed publication which is prior art under 35 U.S.C. § 102(a), unless shown not to be prior, and thus also "prior art" under § 103. Interference rules do not necessarily apply; nothing is to be gained by treating the situation as though it were something it is not. Interferences involve policy questions not present when antedating a reference. The argument is that *if* this were an interference, and *if* Rodgers were an applicant who has not reduced to practice at all, appellants were first to conceive and first to reduce to practice and would not have to prove diligence. This argument "won't fly." This is not an interference. Rule 131 requires proof of diligence coupling conception to the filing of the application.

The next argument is that there is only a two-day period between the Rodgers' effective date and the filing date, that diligence need be shown only from *just prior* to Rodgers' date, that the gap is very short, and that Rule 131 should be "liberally construed." A liberal construction of the rule, which is clearly intended to benefit applicants, will permit applicants to show diligence from just prior to the date of the reference to their convention filing date, rather than all the way from their proven conception date, but liberality cannot be extended to the point of eliminating all proof of diligence, no matter how short the period to be covered. Appellants' difficulty, as they have had to admit, is that there is no evidence whatever of record showing diligence, and therefore they cannot comply with the rule. Focussing on the shortness of the gap is misleading. During the period between the time the draft application was received in this country and the time the application was filed in the U.S. PTO, the record shows no activity of any kind in this country. The only intervening event of record respecting this invention is the filing of the patent application in the Netherlands. Even that was not done until nearly 3 months after the draft U.S. application was dispatched. Under the circumstances, the PTO's refusal to accept the declarations as meeting the requirements of Rule 131 must be affirmed because of a total lack of evidence of diligence to *couple* conception to the filing date—leaving a hiatus—and Rodgers must be treated as prior art.

* * *

IN RE COSTELLO

United States Court of Appeals, Federal Circuit, 1983.
717 F.2d 1346, 219 USPQ 389.

EDWARD S. SMITH, CIRCUIT JUDGE.

This is an appeal from the December 5, 1979, decision of the U.S. Patent and Trademark Office (PTO) Board of Appeals (board) sustaining two rejections under section 103 of claims 1, 4–10, 12, 13, and

17–20 of application serial No. 488,900, filed July 22, 1974. The invention relates to "foamskin" communication cable insulation. The principal reference relied on is Cereijo, U.S. patent No. 3,914,357, filed January 4, 1973. We affirm the rejections.

I.

On April 12, 1971, appellants filed application serial No. 132,968 for "Communication Cable Having Dual Insulated Conductors" (the original application). Appellants failed to respond to an office action and the original application was abandoned on October 19, 1972. No attempt has been made to revive the original application.

Shortly thereafter, during the period December 5–7, 1972, three of appellants' coworkers at Northern Telecom Ltd. (Northern) presented a paper [Gouldson] on foam-skin telephone cable insulation at the 21st International Wire and Cable Symposium in Atlantic City, New Jersey. The authors of that paper filed with the PTO a declaration under 37 C.F.R. § 1.132 [2] on June 20, 1978, stating that the subject matter of that publication is believed to be the invention of appellants and was disclosed to the authors by appellants while all were employed at Northern.

On January 4, 1973, Cereijo, *et al.*, filed application serial No. 321,082 for "Method of Monitoring the Application of Cellular Plastic Insulation to Elongated Conductive Material." That application issued October 21, 1975, as Cereijo, U.S. patent No. 3,914,357, the principal reference. Appellants filed application serial No. 488,900 (the second application), which was accorded an effective filing date of March 9, 1973, pursuant to section 120.[3] The second application is substantially similar to the original application. The second application, however, was not co-pending with the original application nor does it reference the original application.

Cereijo discloses but does not claim the invention that is the subject matter of the second application. Claims 1, 4–10, 12, 13, and 17–20 of

2. 37 C.F.R. § 1.132 (1982) provides in pertinent part:

"§ 1.132 Affidavits or declarations traversing grounds of rejection.

"When any claim of an application is rejected on reference to a domestic patent which substantially shows or describes but does not claim the invention, * * * affidavits or declarations traversing these references or objections may be received."

3. 35 U.S.C. § 120 (1976) provides in pertinent part:

"§ 120. Benefit of earlier filing date in the United States

"An application for patent for an invention disclosed in the manner provided by the first paragraph of section 112 of this title in an application previously filed in the United States, * * * by the same inventor shall have the same effect, as to such invention, as though filed on the date of the prior application, *if filed before* the patenting or *abandonment of* or termination of proceedings on *the first application* * * * *and if it contains* or is amended to contain *a specific reference to the earlier filed application.*" (Emphasis supplied.)

Application serial No. 339,631 was filed March 9, 1973. The second application, serial No. 488,900, filed July 22, 1974, was a continuation of that application.

the second application were rejected under 35 U.S.C. § 103 in view of Cereijo, or Cereijo taken with Moody.

Because the requirements of section 120 had not been satisfied, the board refused to recognize the filing of the original application as a constructive reduction to practice of the invention. The remainder of the evidence was found insufficient to establish invention by appellants prior to the effective date of Cereijo. The board noted that, even if the original application was considered to establish conception of the invention, appellants failed to prove diligence.

II.

This appeal presents the question whether appellants are entitled to rely on an application, abandoned prior to the effective date of a reference, as a constructive reduction to practice to overcome that reference, where appellants later filed a substantially identical application which is not entitled under section 120 to the date of the abandoned application.

* * *

III.

In section 120, Congress set forth two requirements that an applicant must satisfy in order for a later filed application to be accorded the same effect as if it were filed on the same date as an earlier application by the same inventor disclosing the same invention. Those conditions are (1) copendency of the applications, and (2) reference in the later filed to the earlier filed application.

Even if an applicant is unable to secure an effective filing date previous to the effective date of a prior art reference under section 120, the applicant may overcome a reference by evidence of prior invention. A prior art reference that is not a statutory bar may be overcome by two generally recognized methods. "The most common way to 'antedate' a reference is to submit an affidavit satisfying the requirements of Rule 131." (Footnotes omitted.) Rule 131, however, is only one way of overcoming a reference that is not a statutory bar. An applicant may also overcome a reference by showing that the relevant disclosure is a description of the applicant's own work. The pertinent inquiry is under 35 U.S.C. § 102(e). Appellants can overcome a reference by showing that they were in possession of their invention prior to the effective date of the reference. "The real issue is whether *all* the evidence, including the references, truly shows knowledge by another *prior to the time appellants made their invention* or whether it shows the contrary." (Emphasis in original.)

Rule 131 governs whether an applicant has proved a date of invention "before" the effective date of the reference. Appellants urge this court to find prior invention on the basis of evidence that does not satisfy either the substantive requirements of Rule 131 or the standard of proof required to eliminate the reference. We decline to do so for the reasons set forth below.

The effective date of Cereijo is January 4, 1973, prior to the effective filing date of the second application (March 9, 1973). Therefore, Cereijo is properly cited as prior art under section 102(e). In order to overcome Cereijo appellants must either (1) comply with the substantive requirements of Rule 131, or (2) establish that the relevant disclosure is of their own work.

A.

Rule 131 requires proof of either "reduction to practice prior to the effective date of the reference, or conception of the invention prior to the effective date of the reference coupled with due diligence from said date to a subsequent reduction to practice or to the filing of the application."

Appellants actually reduced the invention to practice in Canada. The invention has never been actually reduced to practice in the United States.

Appellants' principal contention is that the filing of the later abandoned original application constitutes a constructive reduction to practice of the invention. Appellants cite no authority, nor can they, to support their argument. It has long been settled, and we continue to approve the rule, that an abandoned application, with which no subsequent application was copending, cannot be considered a constructive reduction to practice. It is inoperative for any purpose, save as evidence of conception.

While the filing of the original application theoretically constituted a constructive reduction to practice at the time, the subsequent abandonment of that application also resulted in an abandonment of the benefit of that filing as a constructive reduction to practice. The filing of the original application is, however, evidence of conception of the invention. Appellants were able to reduce the invention to writing. That writing therefore constitutes documentary evidence that appellants had conceived of the invention as of the filing date. As the board found, however, appellants did not establish diligence in reducing the invention to practice. Appellants do not contest that finding. Thus, the evidence is not sufficient to antedate Cereijo under Rule 131.

B.

Appellants submitted an affidavit under Rule 132 to establish that Gouldson discloses appellants' own invention. Appellants argue that, having "antedated" Gouldson which has an effective date prior to that of Cereijo, appellants have *ipso facto* antedated Cereijo. Appellants' proof that Gouldson discloses appellants' own work does not enable appellants to step into Gouldson's shoes with respect to the date of publication of the Gouldson article as the date of invention. Only Gouldson is eliminated as a reference by the showing that Gouldson describes appellants' invention. Appellants did not antedate Gouldson. Appellants' evidence, at best, establishes conception and communication of the invention to Gouldson, *et al.*, prior to the date of publication.

This has no relation at all to appellants' attempt to antedate the principal reference, Cereijo.

C.

Finally, appellants argue that two Bell Laboratories articles that reference Gouldson, and the fact that Cereijo discloses the invention as prior art rather than as part of his invention, establish prior invention by appellants. Appellants have submitted no affidavit or declaration to establish that the relevant disclosure of Cereijo is of appellants' invention.

It is not sufficient that the relevant disclosure is recognized as prior art. In order to sustain their claim, appellants must adduce evidence that *appellants* invented the relevant items in the disclosure. Appellants have not done so.

IV.

In summary, in order to overcome a prior art reference under section 102(e) appellants must either satisfy the substantive requirements of Rule 131 or establish that the relevant disclosure describes their own invention. In establishing prior invention to overcome the Cereijo reference, appellants cannot rely on their earlier filed abandoned application as a constructive reduction to practice of the invention. The evidence presented by appellants is not sufficient to establish invention prior to the effective date of the reference under Rule 131. Similarly unavailing is appellants' attempt to establish that the relevant disclosure of Cereijo describes appellants' own work. Thus, appellants have not established on this record that they invented the subject matter of the invention prior to the effective date of the reference. The rejections under 35 U.S.C. § 103 in view of Cereijo are, therefore, proper.

Affirmed.

APPLICATION OF FOSTER

United States Court of Customs and Patent Appeals, 1965.
52 CCPA 1808, 343 F.2d 980, 145 USPQ 166.

ALMOND, JUDGE. This is an appeal from the decision of the Board of Appeals affirming the rejection of the claims in appellant's patent application.

The invention relates to elastomeric synthetic polymers said to combine the desirable properties of natural Hevea rubber and the presently employed synthetic rubbers.

* * *

The examiner and the Board of Appeals rejected all of the claims on the basis of the Binder reference. The record indicates that Binder, an employee of appellant's assignee, wrote an article in the magazine "Industrial and Engineering Chemistry."

* * *

It is assumed by both parties—and it is unquestionably true—that when a reference fully discloses in every detail the subject matter of a claim, the statutory basis of a rejection on that reference is 35 U.S.C.A. § 102(a) if the reference date is before the applicant's *date of invention,* thereby establishing want of novelty, and section 102(b) if the reference date is more than one year prior to the actual United States *filing date,* thereby establishing a so-called "statutory bar," more accurately, a one-year time-bar which results in loss of right to a patent, regardless of when the invention was made. In either of these situations, it is often said that the invention is "anticipated" by the reference and the reference is termed an "anticipation."

Proofs submitted in this case under Patent Office Rule 131 with respect to a reference not before us (because it was overcome thereby) have established that the applicant's invention date was prior to December 26, 1952. The Binder reference is the August 1954 issue of a periodical. It is seen, therefore, that it is subsequent to the date of invention but more than one year prior to the filing date, which was August 21, 1956.

* * *

Since the date of invention is earlier than the reference date, section 102(a) is necessarily inapplicable because the printed publication was not "before the invention thereof by the applicant" and there is statutory novelty. This leaves paragraph (b) of section 102 as the only paragraph of that section having possible relevancy.

* * *

Sections 101, 102 and 103, generally speaking, deal with two different matters: (1) the factors to be considered in determining whether a patentable invention has been *made,* i.e., novelty, utility, unobviousness, and the categories of patentable subject matter; and (2) "loss of right to patent" as stated in the heading of section 102, even though an otherwise patentable invention has been made. On the subject of loss of right, appellant's brief contains a helpful review of the development of the statutory law since 1793. It says:

> "In 1897 the patent laws were amended to make the * * * two-year bar period apply to all public uses, publications and patents *regardless of the source* from which they emanated. The change was a consequence, primarily, of greatly improved communications within the country which had rendered inventors easily able to acquire knowledge of the public acts of others within their own fields. It was reasoned that any inventor who *delayed in filing* a patent application for more than two years after a public disclosure of the invention would obtain *an undeserved reward in derogation of the rights of the public* if he were granted a patent.

> "In 1939, in recognition of further improvements in communications, Congress reduced the two-year bar period to one year. * * *

> "That 1939 Act was carried over unchanged in the 1952 recodification of the patent laws as 35 U.S.C. § 102(b). * * *

"Manifestly, Section 102(b) from its earliest beginnings has been and was intended to be directed toward the encouragement of *diligence* in the filing of patent applications and the protection of the public from monopolies on subject matter which had already been fully disclosed to it."

These statements are in accord with our understanding of the history and purposes of section 102(b). It presents a sort of statute of limitations, which an inventor, even though he has made a patentable invention, must act on penalty of loss of his right to patent. What starts the period running is clearly the availability of the invention *to the public* through the categories of disclosure enumerated in 102(b), which include "a printed publication" anywhere describing the invention. There appears to be no dispute about the operation of this statute in "complete anticipation" situations but *the contention seems to be that 102(b) has no applicability where the invention is not completely disclosed in a single patent or publication,* that is to say where the rejection involves the addition to the disclosure of the reference of the ordinary skill of the art or the disclosure of another reference which indicates what those of ordinary skill in the art are presumed to know, *and to have known for more than a year before the application was filed.* Upon a complete reexamination of this matter, we are convinced that the contention is contrary to the policy consideration which motivated the enactment by Congress of a statutory bar. On logic and principle we think this contention is unsound, and we also believe it is contrary to the patent law as it has actually existed since at least 1898.

First, as to principle, since the purpose of the statute has always been to require filing of the application within the prescribed period after the time the public came into possession of the invention, we cannot see that it makes any difference *how* it came into such possession, whether by a public use, a sale, a single patent or publication, or by combinations of one or more of the foregoing. In considering this principle *we assume*, of course, that by these means *the invention has become obvious* to that segment of the "public" having ordinary skill in the art. Once this has happened, the purpose of the law is to give the inventor only a year within which to file and this would seem to be liberal treatment. Whenever an applicant undertakes, under Rule 131, to swear back of a reference having an effective date more than a year before his filing date, he is automatically conceding that he made his invention more than a year before he filed. If the reference contains enough disclosure to make his invention obvious, the principle of the statute would seem to require denial of a patent to him. The same is true where a combination of two publications or patents makes the invention obvious and they both have dates more than a year before the filing date.

* * *

Notes

1. When a domestic patent, without claiming, discloses only a single species of an invention and the applicant for patent submits an affidavit

under Rule 131 showing completion of the invention of that species prior to the effective date of the domestic patent, it cannot be used for rejecting generic claims of the patent application. Application of Stempel, 44 CCPA 820, 241 F.2d 755, 113 USPQ 77 (1957).

2. "Appellants indulge in some ingenious but specious reasoning based on the Stempel case. They point out that there the reference *sworn back of* disclosed only a single species and that we held that when that species was antedated by a Rule 131 affidavit, the reference was disposed of. They then say that here the British specification [filed by appellants and published on May 13, 1953 in Great Britain] discloses but one species, that their United States parent application antedates it as to all it discloses and therefore it is disposed of as a reference. The two situations, however, are not thus comparable.

"There is one fundamental which appellants consistently overlook, namely that what they are here claiming was first disclosed and claimed by them in their third application and that they are entitled to no date, *as to this subject matter,* earlier than May 9, 1955 when that application was filed. Copendency with earlier filed applications disclosing different subject matter, viz. the tantalum species of the invention only, avails them nothing on the appealed claims. It is of significance only as to the tantalum species. Antedating the reference as to this species does not remove it from the category of a printed publication, published in 1953. As such it is quite unlike the reference in the Stempel case.

"There, if the Amos patent had been issued more than a year before Stempel's filing date, he could not have sworn back of it. Rule 131 in terms would have prohibited it and, even though he could have established *priority,* the Amos patent would have stood as a statutory bar to his claim. It is precisely in this way that the British specification stands as a bar to the claims of the appellants.

* * *

"The principle applicable in this case * * * was applied by the Supreme Court under slightly different circumstances in Muncie Gear Works, Inc. v. Outboard Marine & Mfg. Co., 315 U.S. 759, 53 USPQ 1. There a certain device had been put on sale and had gone into public use after the filing of the patent application but the claims to that device were not made in the application, until they were inserted by amendment two years after such public use, by reason of which they were held invalid. The pendency of the application prior to the commencement of the statutory bar was of no avail.

"In the Muncie Gear Works case the court predicated its decision on that part of R.S. 4886 which is now codified in section 102(b) dealing with events which constitute bars to a patent if they occur more than a year before the applicant's effective filing date in the United States. A filing date, to be effective, must be that of an application which *supports the claims.* Appellants' earlier applications fail them in this respect.

"Of course, it is of no moment whether the bar of a patent, printed publication, public use or sale results from the acts of the applicant or of others, so the circumstance that the British specification was applicants' own cannot be taken into account." Application Ruscetta and Jenny, 45 CCPA 968, 255 F.2d 687, 118 USPQ 101 (1958).

3. "The contention that the self-serving declarations of the [now Rule 131] affidavit filed in the Patent Office five years after Cort's application should be given weight as evidence or should shift the burden of proof to the defendant [alleged infringer] is to say the least surprising. Under the rule of the Patent Office it served the purpose of securing an issue of the patent in suit in spite of the earlier disclosure by Cort. But the issue under such circumstances in no sense was the equivalent of an adjudication of priority, nor did it involve any exercise of discretion by the Patent Office, for the mere filing of the affidavit required the issue under the rule irrespective of any merits." Messler v. United States Rubber Co., 148 F.2d 734, 65 USPQ 145 (2d Cir.1945).

2. ABANDONMENT

The early United States Supreme Court cases of Pennock & Sellers v. Dialogue, 27 U.S. (2 Peters) 1, 7 L.Ed. 327 (1829) and Shaw v. Cooper, 32 U.S. (7 Peters) 292 (1833), in holding patents invalid for public use and sale of the inventions before filing the applications for patent, also indicate that such acts abandoned or dedicated the inventions and the inchoate right to a patent to the public. This abandonment terminology was first embodied in express statutory form in the Patent Act of 1839 which invalidated a patented invention "on proof of abandonment of such invention to the public." Subsequent patent acts provided for obtaining a patent on an invention "unless the same is proved to have been abandoned" and that an issued patent was invalid if the invention "had been abandoned to the public". Apparently, no distinction was made between applications and issued patents based on this difference in terminology. The "to the public" phrase is omitted from Section 102(c) of the 1952 Patent Act which provides:

A person shall be entitled to a patent unless—

(c) he has abandoned the invention.

Over the years, the concept of abandonment has been evolved by judicial precedent to encompass a variety of acts by the inventor which are so repugnant to the basic purpose of the patent statutes of "promoting the progress of * * * useful arts" that the inventor is denied patent protection. Thus, abandonment as a common law development was molded to cover a variety of acts by inventors which conflict with the basic purpose of the patent statutes and undoubtedly can be applied to new types of acts by inventors which to date have not been considered by the courts. In Electric Storage Battery Co. v. Shimadzu, 307 U.S. 5, 59 S.Ct. 675, 83 L.Ed. 1071 (1939), the Supreme Court categorized these various acts saying that "abandonment may be evidenced by the express and voluntary declaration of the inventor; it may be inferred from negligence or unexplained delay in making application for patent; it may be declared as a consequence of the inventor's concealing his invention and delaying application for patent in an endeavor to extend the term of the patent protection beyond the period fixed by the statute. In any case, the question whether the invention has been abandoned is one of fact."

MACBETH–EVANS GLASS CO. v. GENERAL ELEC. CO.

United States Court of Appeals, Sixth Circuit, 1917.
246 Fed. 695.

WARRINGTON, CIRCUIT JUDGE. This was a suit for infringement of letters patent reissue 13,766, bearing date July 7, 1914, to George A. Macbeth, assignor to Macbeth-Evans Glass Company, a corporation of Pennsylvania. The invention relates to a "method and batch or mixture for making glass for illuminating purposes such as in electric and other shades and globes." The pleadings present the usual issues of a patent suit, except that a distinct defense was introduced and made the basis of the decision. This was brought about in pursuance of Equity Rule 29 (198 Fed. xxvi, 115 C.C.A. xxvi), and on motion of defendant below, the General Electric Company, separately to hear and dispose of the defense set up in paragraph 14 of its answer; the facts, for purposes of the motion and hearing, being stated in a written admission of plaintiff below, Macbeth-Evans Glass Company, which was filed with the motion. According to the facts so shown, George A. Macbeth discovered and perfected the formula and process in issue prior to the fall of 1903. About the fall of that year, the appellant company (with which Macbeth was connected as president and stockholder) commenced to use the formula and process "as secret inventions for making illuminating glass," and thereafter continued such use until the application of Macbeth for the original letters patent (No. 1,097,600) was filed, May 9, 1913. Throughout this period the products of the formula and process were "put upon the market and sold in this country in large quantities as regular articles of trade and commerce."

In May, 1910, one of the plaintiff company's employés, who had been intrusted with the secrets of the invention set out in the reissued letters patent, left the company's employ and without its knowledge and in fraud of its rights disclosed these secrets to officials of the Jefferson Glass Company; and prior to the 17th of the following December that company began a secret use of the invention and continued such use until after application was made for the patent as stated, May 9, 1913, and placed the products upon the market and sold them in this country as "regular articles of trade and commerce continuously from and after a date prior to December 17, 1910."

* * *

The question is whether one who has discovered and perfected an invention can employ it secretly more than nine years for purposes only of profit, and then, upon encountering difficulty in preserving his secret, rightfully secure a patent, and thus in effect extend his previous monopoly for the further period fixed by the patent laws. Are both of these courses consistent with a reasonable interpretation of the constitutional provision and the statutes of the United States in relation to patents?

It is earnestly contended for appellant that its rights under the patent in issue are to be tested (1) by the use that was made of the invention, rather than of the product of the invention, prior to the application for a patent, and (2) by the acts if any of appellant and its assignor Macbeth, which would evince an intent to abandon the invention as distinguished from the right to patent the invention. The argument is that, when the acts of Macbeth and appellant are tested by the language of the patent laws, the secret use made of the invention could not have been a public use, and the constant effort made to preserve the secret was inconsistent with intent to abandon the invention; and consequently that the public use and the abandonment contemplated by the patent laws are inapplicable to the present case.

* * *

No decision has come to our attention upon facts precisely like those here involved; in a word, the case is sui generis. It is not necessary, we may observe, to consider the portion of the decision below which deals with the question of public use. Our consideration will be limited to questions pertinent to abandonment.

* * *

It is in substance urged for appellee that there is distinct inconsistency between the right to a trade secret and the right to a patent; and that Macbeth, having elected to use his invention as a trade secret for some ten years instead of applying for a patent, could not under settled principles of the doctrine of election turn around and assert the inconsistent right to a patent.

* * * When a patent expires, the right to practice the invention thus becomes available to everybody. The object of such a limitation and disclosure was to secure to the public the full benefits of patented objects as speedily as was consistent with reasonable stimulation of invention. If then we assume that the course adopted by the present inventor and his assignee did not contemplate an intent to abandon the right to secure a patent, it certainly did contemplate an indefinite delay in disclosure of the invention and a practical and substantial enlargement of any period of monopoly recognized by statute. Can it be doubted that this was opposed to a declared and subsisting public policy?

Enough, however, has been shown of the practical construction and effect of the right to practice an invention in secret and for profit and the right to obtain a patent on the invention fairly to test the soundness of the claim that the rights are not inconsistent. They of course are now to be considered with reference to a scheme which includes an effort to secure a patent. And so regarded we may safely add to what we have already said of these rights that the first is in its nature and essence susceptible of exercise only in a way to evade, or at least unduly to delay, a disclosure of the invention in the interest of science and the useful arts, and with an intent to expand the statutory period of monopoly and thereby reap additional profits. The second is a means simply to acquire a monopoly subject to all the conditions and limitations of the patent laws. Such rights in our opinion are inconsistent in themselves—notably in the matter of profits available through use as distinguished from sale of the invention—and in their respective relations to the patent laws. It is not conceivable that an inventor can consistently hold both rights throughout the same period of time, where the design is to use them for purposes and with results like or similar to those here shown.

* * * Here the choice made was deliberate and is unmistakable; it was the secret use for profit and was persisted in for years. If the right to secure protection of the patent laws can be effectively repudiated, it certainly has been here.

This conclusion is reinforced by other considerations of a kindred character which lead to a like result. When the application for a patent was made we think the invention had in legal effect been abandoned. This is plainly related to the question whether there was an election, equivalent to an abandonment, and is of course a question individual to each case. True, as we have seen, it is contended that the efforts made here to preserve the secret were not reconcilable with an intent to abandon the invention. This is based on the theory that in the absence of intervening rights of other inventors a perfected invention may in point of time be indefinitely used in secret and for profit and also in entire consistency with the right to secure a patent on the invention; in a word, that persistence in such secret use, no matter for what length of time, will not justify an inference of abandonment of the invention. The abandonment contemplated by the patent laws naturally has reference to the advantages and protection alike which are obtainable under those laws. Abandonment in this sense must have been intended to signify a relinquishment of patent privileges. Kendall v. Winsor, 62 U.S. (21 How.) 322, 329, 16 L.Ed. 165. As Macomber says:

> "Abandonment must reside in the acts of the inventor by which he has deprived himself of the right to establish or enjoy the monopoly which he might have secured." Macomber, Fixed Law of Pat. (2d Ed.) 2; Walker on Patents (5th Ed.) § 91, at page 110.

Otherwise stated, abandonment of patent privileges is in every sense material to the patent laws tantamount to abandonment of the invention itself; and, of course, proof of such relinquishment or abandonment may be shown by conduct inconsistent with any other purpose. Rifle & Cartridge Co. v. Whitney Arms Co., 118 U.S. 22, 24, 25, 6 S.Ct. 950, 30 L.Ed. 53; Planing Machine Co. v. Keith, 101 U.S. 479, 484, 25 L.Ed. 939.

What has already been shown in respect of appellant's and its assignor's conduct in connection with the question of election is clearly pertinent to the question of abandonment and so need not be repeated.

* * *

There is still another view to be taken of the course pursued by the present inventor and his assignee. Their conduct was inconsistent with the duty of diligence resting upon an inventor desiring to patent his invention. This duty was in effect defined by the Supreme Court as early as 1829, when, speaking through Mr. Justice Story, it was in substance declared that withholding disclosure of an invention for a long period of time and for purposes only of profit was opposed to the intent and policy of the constitutional provision and the statutes in relation to patents. At that time the patent laws contained no provision respecting abandonment of an invention; this, however cannot be important since an abandoned invention could never have been intended to be made the subject of a patent. Moreover, this rule of diligence was also declared by Mr. Justice Daniel, speaking for the Supreme Court, in 1858 in respect of a patent which had been issued after the introduction into the patent statutes of a provision in effect the same as the present one concerning abandonment. In Pennock v. Dialogue, 2 Pet. 1, 7 L.Ed. 327, an infringement suit, the invention involved was perfected in 1811 and the patent obtained in 1818; the patent was for an improvement in the art of making water hose. In this interval the inventors had permitted one Jenkins, under an agreement as to price, to use the invention and to sell the product so derived. During much of the time Jenkins was in the service of the inventors and had been instructed by them in the art of making the hose. Verdict and judgment were recovered by defendant in the court below. The statute then applicable authorized a patent to be granted upon application of any citizen who should allege that he had invented a new and useful art, machine, etc., "not known or used before the application." The true meaning of these words was the ultimate question for decision. It was held that, since it would have defeated the object of the law to apply to the inventor the words "known or used," the clause meant that the thing invented was "not known or used by the public, before the application." After determining the question of use as stated, and presumably in view of the lapse of some seven years between the time the invention was perfected and the patent issued, Mr. Justice Story, in announcing the opinion of the court affirming the judgment of the court below, said:

> "And thus construed, there is much reason for the limitation thus imposed by the act. While one great object was, by holding out a reasonable reward to inventors, and giving them an exclusive right to their inventions for a limited period, to stimulate the efforts of genius; the main object was 'to promote the progress of science and useful arts'; and this could be done best, by giving the public at large a right to make, construct, use and vend the thing invented, at as early a period as possible, having a due regard to the rights of the inventor. If an inventor should be permitted to hold back from the knowledge of the public the secrets of his invention; if he should, for a long period of years, retain the monopoly, and make and sell his invention publicly, and thus gather the whole profits of it, relying upon his superior skill

and knowledge of the structure; and then, and then only, when the danger of competition should force him to secure the exclusive right, he should be allowed to take out a patent, and thus exclude the public from any further use than what should be derived under it, during his fourteen years; it would materially retard the progress of science and the useful arts, and give a premium to those who should be least prompt to communicate their discoveries."

The rule of diligence thus declared in respect of an inventor who has perfected his invention was affirmed in Kendall v. Winsor, 62 U.S. (21 How.) 322, 328, 16 L.Ed. 165; Mr. Justice Daniel saying:

"＊ ＊ ＊ The inventor who designedly, and with the view of applying it indefinitely and exclusively for his own profit, withholds his invention from the public, comes not within the policy or objects of the Constitution or acts of Congress. He does not promote, and, if aided in his design, would impede, the progress of science and the useful arts. And with a very bad grace could he appeal for favor or protection to that society which, if he had not injured, he certainly had neither benefited nor intended to benefit."

And again (329):

"＊ ＊ ＊ He may forfeit his rights as an inventor by a willful or negligent postponement of his claims. ＊ ＊ ＊"

＊ ＊ ＊

We are thus led to conclude that whatever view may be taken of the conditions existing at the time the patent in suit was applied for, the invention had been abandoned.

Accordingly, upon this ground the decree will be affirmed.

W. L. GORE & ASSOCIATES, INC. v. GARLOCK, INC.

United States Court of Appeals, Federal Circuit, 1983.
721 F.2d 1540, 220 USPQ 303.

MARKEY, CHIEF JUDGE.

Appeal from a judgment of the District Court for the Northern District of Ohio holding U.S. Patents 3,953,566 ('566) and 4,187,390 ('390) invalid. ＊ ＊ ＊

Tape of unsintered polytetrafluorethylene (PTFE) (known by the trademark TEFLON of E.I. du Pont de Nemours, Inc.) had been stretched in small increments. W.L. Gore & Associates, Inc. (Gore), assignee of the patents in suit, experienced a tape breakage problem in the operation of its "401" tape stretching machine. Dr. Robert Gore, Vice President of Gore, developed the invention disclosed and claimed in the '566 and '390 patents in the course of his effort to solve that problem. The 401 machine was disclosed and claimed in Gore's U.S. Patent 3,664,915 ('915) and was the invention of Wilbert L. Gore, Dr. Gore's father. PTFE tape had been sold as thread seal tape, i.e., tape used to keep pipe joints from leaking. ＊ ＊ ＊

(ii) § 102(b) AND THE CROPPER MACHINE

In 1966 John W. Cropper (Cropper) of New Zealand developed and constructed a machine for producing stretched and unstretched PTFE thread seal tape. In 1967, Cropper sent a letter to a company in Massachusetts, offering to sell his machine, describing its operation, and enclosing a photo. Nothing came of that letter. There is no evidence and no finding that the present inventions thereby became known or used in this country.

In 1968, Cropper sold his machine to Budd, which at some point thereafter used it to produce and sell PTFE threat seal tape. The sales agreement between Cropper and Budd provided:

ARTICLE "E"—PROTECTION OF TRADE SECRETS ETC.

1. BUDD agrees that while this agreement is in force it will not reproduce any copies of the said apparatus without the express written permission of Cropper nor will it divulge to any person or persons other than its own employees or employees of its affiliated corporations any of the said known-how or any details whatsoever relating to the apparatus.

2. BUDD agrees to take all proper steps to ensure that its employees observe the terms of Article "E" 1 and further agrees that whenever it is proper to do so it will take legal action in a Court of competent jurisdiction to enforce any one or more of the legal or equitable remedies available to a trade secret plaintiff.

Budd told its employees the Cropper machine was confidential and required them to sign confidentiality agreements. Budd otherwise treated the Cropper machine like its other manufacturing equipment.

A former Budd employee said Budd made no effort to keep the secret. That Budd did not keep the machine hidden from employees legally bound to keep their knowledge confidential does not evidence a failure to maintain the secret. Similarly, that du Pont employees were shown the machine to see if they could help increase its speed does not itself establish a breach of the secrecy agreement. There is no evidence of when that viewing occurred. There is no evidence that a viewer of the machine could thereby learn anything of which process, among all possible processes, the machine is being used to practice. As Cropper testified, looking at the machine in operation does not reveal whether it is stretching, and if so, at what speed. Nor does looking disclose whether the crystallinity and temperature elements of the invention set forth in the claims are involved. There is no evidence that Budd's secret use of the Cropper machine made knowledge of the claimed process accessible to the public.

The district court held all claims of the '566 patent invalid under 102(b), *supra*, note 3, because "the invention" was "in public use [and] on sale" by Budd more than one year before Gore's application for patent. Beyond a failure to consider each of the claims independently, 35 U.S.C. § 282; *Altoona Publix Theatres, Inc. v. American Tri-Ergon*

Corp., 294 U.S. 477, 487, 55 S.Ct. 455, 459, 79 L.Ed. 1005 (1935), and a failure of proof that the claimed inventions as a whole were practiced by Budd before the critical May 21, 1969 date, it was error to hold that Budd's activity with the Cropper machine, as above indicated, was a "public" use of the processes claimed in the '566 patent, that activity having been secret, not public.

Assuming, arguendo, that Budd sold tape produced on the Cropper machine before October 1969, and that that tape was made by a process set forth in a claim of the '566 patent, the issue under § 102(b) is whether that sale would defeat Dr. Gore's right to a patent on the process inventions set forth in the claims.

If Budd offered and sold anything, it was only tape, not whatever process was used in producing it. Neither party contends, and there was no evidence, that the public could learn the claimed process by examining the tape. If Budd and Cropper commercialized the tape, that could result in a forfeiture of a patent granted them for their process on an application filed by them more than a year later. *D.L. Auld Co. v. Chroma Graphics Corp.*, 714 F.2d 1144, at 1147–48 (Fed.Cir. 1983); *See Metallizing Engineering Co. v. Kenyon Bearing & Auto Parts Co.*, 153 F.2d 516, 68 USPQ 54 (2d Cir.1946). There is no reason or statutory basis, however, on which Budd's and Cropper's secret commercialization of a process, if established, could be held a bar to the grant of a patent to Gore on that process.

Early public disclosure is a linchpin of the patent system. As between a prior inventor who benefits from a process by selling its product but suppresses, conceals, or otherwise keeps the process from the public, and a later inventor who promptly files a patent application from which the public will gain a disclosure of the process, the law favors the latter. *See Horwath v. Lee*, 564 F.2d 948, 195 USPQ 701 (CCPA 1977). The district court therefore erred as a matter of law in applying the statute and in its determination that Budd's secret use of the Cropper machine and sale of tape rendered all process claims of the '566 patent invalid under § 102(b).

* * *

CROWN CORK & SEAL CO. v. FERDINAND GUTMANN CO.

Supreme Court of the United States, 1938.
304 U.S. 159, 58 S.Ct. 842, 82 L.Ed. 1265.

MR. JUSTICE BUTLER delivered the opinion of the Court.

Petitioner sued respondent in the district court for eastern New York to enjoin infringements of patents, two of which are here involved. One is Warth Reissue Patent, No. 19,117, dated March 20, 1934. The other is Warth Patent, No. 1,967,195, dated July 17, 1934, a divisional patent. Both relate to methods for applying small disks of paper or foil, known as center spots, to cork cushions of crown caps. These caps are used to seal bottles containing pressure beverages. The center spot prevents contact of the liquid with the cork. The district court adjudged both patents valid and infringed. 14 F.Supp. 255. The circuit court of appeals reversed, holding the reissue patent not infringed and the divisional one invalid because of laches in filing the application on which it was granted. 86 F.2d 698.

The questions presented by the petition for the writ, granted 302 U.S. 664, ante, 513, 58 S.Ct. 12, are these:

1. "Does this Court's decision in Webster Electric Co. v. Splitdorf Electrical Co. [264 U.S. 463, 44 S.Ct. 342, 68 L.Ed. 792] mean that, even in the absence of intervening adverse rights, an excuse must be shown for a lapse of more than two years in presenting claims in a divisional application regularly filed and prosecuted in accordance with patent office rules?"

* * *

The first [question] calls for decision upon a single point. It specifically assumes the absence of intervening rights and that the application was appropriately made. There is no question as to the validity of either the original or reissue patents.

* * *

The important feature is simultaneous application of pressure and heat to the center spot to make it stick to the cork cushion in the cap. Neither these nor any other claims of the patent specify means to be employed to furnish the heat. The claims in suit of the divisional patent cover means to supply heat to be applied to the center spots when subjected to pressure. The important feature is "heating the pads [cork cushions] in the caps" before placing the spots upon them.

* * *

The district court found no adverse use of the preheating method prior to the filing date of the application for the reissue patent. The circuit court of appeals did not disturb that finding. It found that Warth's disclosure of the preheating method was continuously before the patent office from the date of his first application, but that there was no claim for the preheating method on file from December 3, 1930, until April 4, 1933, when he filed application for the divisional patent. It held, citing Webster Electric Co. v. Splitdorf Electrical Co., 264 U.S. 463, 44 S.Ct. 342, 68 L.Ed. 792, supra, that prima facie the two year limit applies to divisional applications, and that an applicant who waits longer before claiming an invention disclosed in his patent must justify his delay by proof of some excuse. It said (86 F.2d 702), "No such excuse appears here. Had Warth chosen to retain in his parent application broad generic claims which might cover the preheating method, then indeed the Splitdorf rule might not be applicable. * * * But * * * for a period of more than two years Warth apparently did not wish to claim the preheating method, having deliberately canceled the preheating specification from his original application and shaped his claims so as to exclude it and his patent having been granted January 6, 1931. He made no claim for preheating until more than two years thereafter, namely, April 4, 1933. In the meantime a patent containing claims for the preheating method had been granted to Johnson on April 5, 1932, and it was Warth's discovery of this fact which stirred him to action. As in the Splitdorf Electrical Co. Case, had it not been for this competitor, Warth might never have considered the subject worth claiming as an invention." The court meant that Warth had really abandoned his invention. See Western Electric Co. v. General Talking Pictures Corp. (C.C.C.A.2d) 91 F.2d 922, 927.

But, as abandonment was not pleaded as a defense, Rev.Stat. § 4920, 35 U.S.C.A. § 69, and as Warth's disclosure was continuously before the patent office, clearly without any significance adverse to the petitioner is the fact that Warth formally canceled one disclosure from his first application and with it claims thought by the circuit court of appeals broad enough to cover the disclosure. The continuity so maintained shows that Warth intended to retain, not to abandon, the disclosed invention. See Godfrey v. Eames, 1 Wall. 317, 325, 326, 17 L.Ed. 684, 686; Clark Blade & Razor Co. v. Gillette Safety Razor Co. (C.C.A.3d) 194 F. 421, 422.

This case is not like Webster Electric Co. v. Splitdorf Electrical Co., 264 U.S. 463, 44 S.Ct. 342, 68 L.Ed. 792, supra. In that case, there came here the question of the validity of claims of a patent issued to Kane in 1918. * * *

This Court pointed out (p. 465) that the claims in question "were for the first time presented to the Patent Office, by an amendment to a divisional application eight years and four months after the filing of the original application, five years after the date of the original Podlesak patent, disclosing the subject-matter, and three years after the commencement of the present suit." We suggested that it was doubtful whether the claims were not so enlarged as to preclude allowance under the original application; we found that Kane, deeming their subject-matter not invention, did not intend to assert them, and, prior to 1918, did not entertain an intention to have them covered by patent. During all of this time their subject matter was disclosed and in general use; Kane and his assignee simply stood by and awaited developments. It was upon the reasons so stated that this Court declared (p. 466) "We have no hesitation in saying that the delay was unreasonable, and, under the circumstances shown by the record, constitutes laches, by which the petitioner lost whatever rights it might otherwise have been entitled to."

* * * It is clear that, in the absence of intervening adverse rights, the decision in Webster Electric Co. v. Splitdorf Electrical Co., does not mean that an excuse must be shown for a lapse of more than two years in presenting the divisional application. Where there is no abandonment, mere delay in filing a divisional application for not more than two years after an intervening patent or publication, does not operate to enlarge the patent monopoly beyond that contemplated by

the statute. By Rev.Stat. § 4886, 35 U.S.C.A. § 31, delay in filing an application for not more than two years after an intervening patent or publication does not bar a patent unless the invention "is proved to have been abandoned." See Wirebounds Patents Co. v. Saranac Automatic Mach. Corp. (C.C.A.6th) 37 F.2d 830, 840, 841, 65 F.2d 904–906.

* * *

Notes

1. In Metallizing Engineering Co. v. Kenyon Bearing & Auto Parts Co., 153 F.2d 516, 68 USPQ 54 (2d Cir.1946) the court in an opinion by Judge Learned Hand held that a use in secret for profit by an inventor for more than one year before filing a patent application forfeited his right to a patent. Judge Hand distinguished the effect of such a secret prior use for profit of an invention on its inventor's right to a patent from its effect on another subsequent inventor's right to a patent saying:

Both do indeed come within the phrase, "prior use"; but the first is a defence for quite different reasons from the second. It had its origin—at least in this country—in the passage we have quoted from Pennock v. Dialogue, supra, 2 Pet. 1, 7 L.Ed. 327; i.e., that it is a condition upon an inventor's right to a patent that he shall not exploit his discovery competitively after it is ready for patenting; he must content himself with either secrecy, or legal monopoly. It is true that for the limited period of two years he was allowed to do so, possibly in order to give him time to prepare an application; and even that has been recently cut down by half. But if he goes beyond that period of probation, he forfeits his right regardless of how little the public may have learned about the invention; just as he can forfeit it by too long concealment, even without exploiting the invention at all.

2. "Undoubtedly, an inventor may abandon his invention, and surrender or dedicate it to the public; but mere forbearance to apply for a patent during the progress of experiments, and until the party has perfected his invention and tested its value by actual practice affords no just grounds for any such presumption. [Citations omitted]

"Application for a patent in this case was probably filed in the Patent Office before the middle of November, 1826, and the proofs are full and satisfactory to the court that the inventor, up to that time, was constantly engaged in perfecting his improvements, and in making the necessary preparations to apply for a patent." Agawam Woolen Co. v. Jordan, 74 U.S. (7 Wall.) 583, 607–608, 19 L.Ed. 177, 183 (1869).

3. In Celluloid Mfg. Co. v. Crofut, 24 Fed. 796, 799 (C.C.D.N.J.1885), the court held that a delay of eight years in filing a patent application after the invention was first reduced to practice was not an abandonment because "continued poverty, sickness and mental alienation are always regarded as sufficient excuses for delay and not a fact or circumstance has been brought into the case showing any intention of abandonment."

4. In Foster v. Magnetic Heating Corp., 297 F.Supp. 512, 160 USPQ 246 (D.C.S.D.N.Y.1968) affirmed per curiam on other grounds 410 F.2d 12, 161 USPQ 133 (2d Cir.1969), the court held in a patent infringement suit

that there was no abandonment of the invention and right to a patent by allowing a first application to be abandoned for failure to pay the final issue fee where the inventor was concerned with the adequacy of his technical knowledge and understanding of the invention and thus attended college to acquire such knowledge and 11 years later filed a second patent application which matured into the patent in suit. The court noted that there was no evidence of either any intervening invention by another or that the alleged infringers had relied on or been lulled into any prejudicial position due to the delay in filing the second patent application.

5. A claim of an issued patent was held void on the ground of abandonment where it was unexplained why the original claim to the same subject matter was cancelled by amendment and, after a delay of four years, reinserted only at the suggestion of the Patent Office for the purpose of an interference with a patent which had issued fifteen months before the original claim was cancelled. Victor Talking Machine Co. v. Brunswick-Balke-Collender Co., 290 F. 565 (D.C.D.Del.1923), affirmed per curiam 8 F.2d 41 (3d Cir.1925) and 273 U.S. 671, 47 S.Ct. 474, 71 L.Ed. 832 (1927).

6. "There is a wide difference between the abandonment of an invention and the abandonment of an application for it. An abandonment of an application is not necessarily an abandonment of the invention, and, after the application has been abandoned, a valid patent for the invention may nevertheless be secured upon a new application, provided the invention has not gone into public use or been upon sale for more than two years prior to the filing of the latter. In cases in which the first application has not been abandoned, subsequent applications and amendments constitute a continuance of the original proceeding, and the two years' public use or sale which may avoid the patent must be reckoned from the presentation of the first application, and not from the filing of subsequent applications or amendments.

"But the abandonment of an application destroys the continuity of the solicitation of the patent. After abandonment a subsequent application institutes a new and independent proceeding, and the two years' public use or sale which may invalidate the patent issued upon it must be counted from the filing of the later application". Hayes-Young Tie Plate Co. v. St. Louis Transit Co., 137 Fed. 80 (8th Cir.1905).

7. "Appellant's brief asserts that each of the publications relied on 'furnishes nothing more than a starting point for further experiments and research', and in another sub-paragraph alleges that "The record is devoid of any showing that the Hrynakowski and Wood-LaWall publications amount to anything more than accounts of abandoned experiments.'

"This indicates that appellant regards a publication as being somewhat akin to a patent application. The researchers in the references did not seek patents. They gave the public what they discovered as a result of experiments. The results they obtained meet appellant's claims. To the extent that they donated their discoveries to the public and sought no patents on them, they may be said to have abandoned them, but that is not a kind of abandonment which inures to appellant's benefit. It was an abandonment to the public. The public became the possessor of the discoveries with freedom to use or not use such discoveries as it (the public) elected." Application of Shackell, 194 F.2d 720, 93 USPQ 34 (CCPA 1952).

3. FILING A FOREIGN APPLICATION ON A DOMESTIC INVENTION WITHOUT GOVERNMENT AUTHORIZATION

In 1917, Congress provided that whenever the United States was at war and the disclosure of an invention by patenting would be "detrimental to the public safety or defense, or might assist the enemy, or endanger the successful prosecution of the war", the Commissioner of Patents could "order that the invention be kept secret and withhold the grant of a patent until termination of the war." If the invention was published or an application for a foreign patent therefor was filed without a license or approval of the Commissioner or Secretary of Commerce, the United States application was abandoned. The Invention Security Act of 1951 which is now 35 U.S.C.A. §§ 181–188 is based on the provisions of the Act of 1917. A fundamental purpose of the Invention Security Act was to continue in peacetime the authority to prevent disclosure of information in applications which would jeopardize national security.

Section 181 of Title 35 provides in part that:

35 U.S.C.A. § 181. Secrecy of Certain Inventions and Withholding of Patent

Whenever publication or disclosure by the grant of a patent on an invention in which the Government has a property interest might, in the opinion of the head of the interested Government agency, be detrimental to the national security, the Commissioner upon being so notified shall order that the invention be kept secret and shall withhold the grant of a patent therefor under the conditions set forth hereinafter.

Whenever the publication or disclosure of an invention by the granting of a patent, in which the Government does not have a property interest, might, in the opinion of the Commissioner, be detrimental to the national security, he shall make the application for patent in which such invention is disclosed available for inspection to the Atomic Energy Commission, the Secretary of Defense, and the chief officer of any other department or agency of the Government designated by the President as a defense agency of the United States.

The Atomic Energy Commission has been abolished and its functions are now transferred to the Secretary of Energy. For purposes of enforcement, the Department of Justice is designated a defense agency by Executive Order.

Section 182 provides that if a secrecy order issued pursuant to Section 181 is violated by the inventor filing a foreign patent application for the invention, or by publication or disclosure thereof, the United States patent application may be held to be abandoned.

Section 183 provides a right to compensation for damage caused by the order of secrecy and/or use of the invention by the United States after the domestic application for patent is in a condition for allowance. However, under Section 182, this right to compensation is forfeited by violation of a secrecy order. Sections 186 and 187 provide for criminal penalties for willful violation of a secrecy order.

Section 184 prohibits filing of a patent application in a foreign country on *any* invention made in this country except when authorized by a license from the Commissioner or more than six months after filing a United States patent application on the invention. The purpose of this section is to afford the U.S. Government an opportunity to determine if the invention relates to national security and should be made the subject of a secrecy order. Under Section 184 a license can be retroactively granted where "an application has been inadvertently filed abroad" and "does not disclose an invention within the scope of Section 181." If Section 184 is violated and a retroactive license is not subsequently obtained, Section 185 bars United States patent protection.

Notes

1. "The second paragraph of Sec. 184 provides: 'The term "application" when used in this chapter includes applications and any modifications, amendments, or supplements thereto, or divisions thereof.' By this paragraph the term 'application' as employed in the statute includes 'any modifications, amendments, or supplements thereto, or divisions thereof.' Even under plaintiffs' theory, it is not open to doubt that the subject matter of the second application was a modification, amendment or supplement to the first. It follows that the foreign applications filed within six months after the filing of the second application, without obtaining a license, invalidated the patent." Beckman Instruments, Inc. v. Coleman Instruments, Inc., 338 F.2d 573, 143 USPQ 278 (7th Cir.1964).[a]

2. "The plaintiff is incorrect (and I think plaintiff's counsel so conceded now) in its contention of yesterday that Sections 184 and 185 apply only to cases of inventions involving the national security. The statutory language is clear. Sections 184 and 185 apply to all cases where foreign patent applications are filed within six months after an application is filed in the United States. Those sections are not limited to inventions involving the national security. On the contrary, the very purpose of the six-month period established by those sections is to provide the Commissioner with an opportunity to screen out patents involving national security. See Minnesota Mining and Mfg. Co. v. Norton Co., 366 F.2d 238, 240 (6th Cir. 1966).

"For that reason, Section 184 gives the Commissioner less discretion to grant retroactive licenses in national security cases than otherwise. Consequently, I hold that this case is governed by Sections 184 and 185 of Title

---

a. In a subsequent petition for a retroactive license for the patent involved in the Beckman case, the Commissioner of Patents denied the petition [In re Application filed November 22, 1952, 153 USPQ 410 (1967)].

35 U.S.C.A., regardless of whether the invention in issue might involve national security." Thermovac Indus. Corp. v. Virtis Co., 285 F.Supp. 113, 158 USPQ 558 (S.D.N.Y.1968).

3. "[T]he question for decision on Microtron's motion for summary judgment is whether the retroactive license procured on February 28, 1966, by Maisel (some nine years after the issuance of the patent) cured the invalidity imposed for foreign filing without a license prior to the end of six months after the United States application was filed.

* * *

"The purpose of Sections 184 and 185, as clearly pointed out by their legislative history, was to prevent inadvertent disclosure of information which might prove detrimental to the safety and welfare of this country. That a retroactive license was granted in this case clearly indicates that the prohibited foreign filing was inadvertent and not detrimental to the national interest of the United States. Certainly the safety of the country has not been placed in jeopardy. To hold the patent invalid on the technicality urged would be unduly harsh and contrary to the better reasoned cases.

"It is adjudged that the granting of the retroactive license was effective to cure the patent's invalidity caused by foreign filing within the six months period." Union Carbide Corp. v. Microtron Corp., 254 F.Supp. 299, 149 USPQ 827 (D.C.W.D.N.Carolina 1966), affirmed per curiam 375 F.2d 438, 153 USPQ 152 (4th Cir.1967).

4. FIRST PATENTED IN A FOREIGN COUNTRY

The Patent Act of 1836 limited domestic patent protection to inventors who had not been granted a foreign patent on their invention more than six months before filing a domestic application for their invention. The Patent Act of 1839 further provided that where the domestic application was filed more than six months after a foreign patent was granted, the domestic patent would not be barred but its term would be limited to fourteen years from the date of granting or publication of the foreign patent.

The Patent Act of 1870 provided that domestic patent protection was not barred where the inventor first patented his invention in a foreign country but that the term of the domestic patent expired with the first to expire foreign patent and in no event was longer than seventeen years.

Under the Patent Act of 1897, an inventor was barred from domestic patent protection where his invention was first patented in a foreign country on an application filed more than seven months before he filed a domestic patent application for the invention. The Patent Act of 1903 extended this period to twelve months. This provision of the Patent Act of 1897 as modified by the Act of 1903 barred domestic patent protection even though the domestic patent application was filed before the foreign patent issued. This was the law until enactment of Section 102(d) of the 1952 Patent Act which provides that:

A person shall be entitled to a patent unless—

(d) the invention was first patented or caused to be patented, or was the subject of an inventor's certificate, by the applicant or his legal representatives or assigns in a foreign country prior to the date of the application for patent in this country on an application for patent or inventor's certificate filed more than twelve months before the filing of the application in the United States, or

GENERAL ELEC. CO. v. ALEXANDER

United States Court of Appeals, Second Circuit, 1922.
280 Fed. 852.

Before HOUGH and MANTON, CIRCUIT JUDGES, and GARVIN, DISTRICT JUDGE.

HOUGH, CIRCUIT JUDGE. The subject-matter of this litigation is the commercial article known as the tungsten-nitrogen lamp, in making which both the patents in suit are used, as is also the Coolidge Patent 1,082,933, lately considered at length and broadly upheld in General Electric Co. v. Independent, etc., Co. (D.C.) 267 F. 824. * * *

The defenses urged against the Just and Hanaman patent are:

(1) That the same patentees obtained German patent, 154,262, valid from April 15, 1903, for substantially the same invention as is revealed by their patent in suit applied for July 6, 1905; wherefore the patent at bar is invalidated under Rev.Stat. § 4887 (Comp.St. § 9431).

* * *

1. The defense of invalidity under section 4887 puts a heavy burden on a defendant. The various amendments to that section have not changed the truth of Judge Putnam's statement in Westinghouse, etc., Co. v. Stanley, 138 F. 823, 71 C.C.A. 189, that the act applies only to cases where the inventions actually claimed in the foreign and domestic patents are identical. It is not sufficient that the foreign patent may disclose the invention of the later United States patent where it is not therein claimed. We agree also with the somewhat similar language of Judge Coxe on this subject in Brush, etc., Co. v. Accumulator Co. (C.C.) 47 F. 48.

The claim of the German patent is for a process, and we agree with the court below (vide 277 F. 295–299) that the German process is wholly inoperative, in that it cannot produce the product covered by the patent in suit. The essential reason for this conclusion is that doing what the German patent calls upon one to do will never replace carbon by tungsten. The process rests upon the theory of replacement, and that theory has no substratum of fact.

The German patent being for a process, and the one at bar for a product, it is true that, if the only use of the process is to make the product, such foreign process patent would and should affect an attempt to get American protection for the product. But that is not here true; this German process patent will not make, and never has made, anybody's incandescent lamp filament, and especially will it not make the product of the patent in suit. Therefore in no sense are the two patents for the same invention (Holmes, etc., Co. v. Metropolitan, etc., Co. [C.C.] 22 F. 341) whether one regards the proven facts, or the language of disclosures and claims.

* * *

F. NON–OBVIOUS SUBJECT MATTER

1. INTRODUCTION

In addition to utility and novelty, the third principal condition for patentability is non-obvious subject matter. This condition deals with the level of innovation required for patentability. Granted an invention is novel, does it represent sufficient innovation over the prior art to warrant patent protection?

After the adoption of the United States Constitution, the first patent act in the United States, passed in 1790, provided for the issuance of Letters Patent if the Secretaries of State or the Department of War, or the Attorney General, or any two of them, "shall deem the invention or discovery sufficiently useful or important, * * *." This language was omitted from the Act of 1793, which eliminated examination of an application to determine if a patent should be granted, and reappeared in the Statute of 1836, which reinstituted such examination. The language also was included in subsequent Acts preceding the 1952 Patent Act.

Apparently, this was a statutory basis for evaluating innovation. However, this provision was universally ignored by the courts. Nevertheless, the courts, in dealing with patents, instituted some criteria for innovation above and beyond the test of novelty.

Accordingly, a body of case law began to develop around the test for "invention" over and above the requirement for novelty. The decided cases contain a great variety of definitions relating to the requirement for innovation. They also have produced a variety of holdings as to validity or invalidity depending on the conviction of a particular court as to what will best "promote the progress * * * of useful arts." The essential problem has always been to determine whether a novel invention is a sufficient advance in the art that its disclosure to the public warrants granting the right to exclude others from its use for a limited period of time.

The test of non-obvious subject matter was first embodied in statutory form in the 1952 Patent Act in Section 103 which provides:

Conditions for Patentability; Non-obvious Subject Matter

A patent may not be obtained though the invention is not identically disclosed or described as set forth in section 102 of this title, if the differences between the subject matter sought to be patented and the prior art are such that the subject matter as a whole would have been obvious at the time the invention was made to a person having ordinary skill in the art to which said subject matter pertains.

Patentability shall not be negatived by the manner in which the invention was made. Subject matter developed by another person, which qualifies as prior art only under subsection (f) or (g) of section 102 of this title, shall not preclude patentability under this section where the subject matter and the claimed invention were, at the time the invention was made, owned by the same person or subject to an obligation of assignment to the same person.

The Reviser's Note to the first two sentences of this section states:

There is no provision corresponding to the first sentence explicitly stated in the present statutes, but the refusal of patents by the Patent Office, and the holding of patents invalid by the courts, on the ground of lack of invention or lack of patentable novelty has been followed since at least as early as 1850. This paragraph is added with the view that an explicit statement in the statute may have some stabilizing effect, and also to serve as a basis for the addition at a later time of some criteria which may be worked out.

The second sentence states that patentability as to this requirement is not to be negatived by the manner in which the invention was made, that is, it is immaterial whether it resulted from long toil and experimentation or from a flash of genius.

Professor A.D. Moore, Emeritus, University of Michigan Engineering School, has written a book on Invention, Discovery, and Creativity [a] containing a wealth of personal experience with inventing as well as a bountiful bibliography. With respect to the creative process, this excerpt is of interest:

In 1939 at a banquet in Ann Arbor, I had the good fortune to be seated next to a very personable young chap of twenty-nine who was already on his way to fame and fortune. I had a good long talk with this college dropout. After a freshman year at Harvard, he quit, to perfect his first invention; and he never finished college. He now holds over two hundred patents. Discoveries, he says, are made "by some individual who has freed himself from a way of thinking that is held by friends and associates who may be more intelligent, better educated, better disciplined, but who have not mastered the art of the fresh, clean look at the old, old knowledge." He himself often spends prolonged periods working on projects in his plant's laboratory. *Fortune* magazine says that he and his wife are worth over half a billion dollars. This is Edwin H. Land, inventor of Polaroid, and maker of Polaroid cameras.

2. BACKDROP FOR SECTION 103

HOTCHKISS v. GREENWOOD

Supreme Court of the United States, 1850.
52 U.S. (11 How.) 248, 13 L.Ed. 683.

NELSON, JUSTICE. On the trial, evidence was given on the part of the plaintiffs tending to prove the originality and usefulness of the invention, and also the infringement by the defendants; and on the part of the defendants, tending to show the want of originality; and that the mode of fastening the shank to the knob, as claimed by the

a. From Invention, Discovery & Creativity, by A.D. Moore, p. 36, Copyright 1969 by Doubleday and Company, Inc. Reprinted by permission of the publisher.

plaintiffs, had been known and used before, and had been used and
applied to the fastening of the shanks to metallic knobs.

And upon the evidence being closed, the counsel for the plaintiffs
prayed the court to instruct the jury that, although the clay knob, in
the form in which it was patented, may have been before known and
used, and also the shank and spindle by which it is attached may have
been before known and used, yet if such shank and spindle have never
before been attached in this mode to a knob of potter's clay, and it
required skill and invention to attach the same to a knob of this
description, so that they would be firmly united, and make a strong and
substantial article, and which, when thus made, would become an
article much better and cheaper than the knobs made of metal or other
materials, the patent was valid, and the plaintiffs would be entitled to
recover.

The court refused to give the instruction, and charged the jury
that, if knobs of the same form and for the same purposes as that
claimed by the patentees, made of metal or other material, had been
before known and used; and if the spindle and shank, in the form used
by them, had been before known and used, and had been attached to
the metallic knob by means of a cavity in the form of dovetail and
infusion of melted metal, the same as the mode claimed by the patentees, in the attachment of the shank and spindle to their knob; and the
knob of clay was simply the substitution of one material for another,
the spindle and shank being the same as before in common use, and
also the mode of connecting them by dovetail to the knob the same as
before in common use, and no more ingenuity or skill was required to
construct the knob in this way than that possessed by an ordinary
mechanic acquainted with the business, the patent was invalid, and the
plaintiffs were not entitled to a verdict.

This instruction, it is claimed, is erroneous, and one for which a
new trial should be granted.

* * *

Now, it may very well be, that, by connecting the clay or porcelain
knob with the metallic shank in this well-known mode, an article is
produced better and cheaper than in the case of the metallic or wood
knob; but this does not result from any new mechanical device or
contrivance, but from the fact that the material of which the knob is
composed happens to be better adapted to the purpose for which it is
made. The improvement consists in the superiority of the material,
and which is not new, over that previously employed in making the
knob.

But this, of itself, can never be the subject of a patent. No one will
pretend that a machine, made, in whole or in part, of materials better
adapted to the purpose for which it is used than the materials of which
the old one is constructed, and for that reason better and cheaper, can
be distinguished from the old one; or, in the sense of the patent law,
can entitle the manufacturer to a patent.

The difference is formal, and destitute of ingenuity or invention. It may afford evidence of judgment and skill in the selection and adaptation of the materials in the manufacture of the instrument for the purposes intended, but nothing more.

* * *

Now, if the foregoing view of the improvement claimed in this patent be correct, it is quite apparent that there was no error in the submission of the question presented at the trial to the jury; for unless more ingenuity and skill in applying the old method of fastening the shank and the knob were required in the application of it to the clay or porcelain knob than were possessed by an ordinary mechanic acquainted with the business, there was an absence of that degree of skill and ingenuity which constitute essential elements of every invention. In other words, the improvement is the work of the skillful mechanic, not that of the inventor.

We think, therefore, that the judgment is, and must be, affirmed.

ATLANTIC WORKS v. BRADY

Supreme Court of the United States, 1882.
107 U.S. 192, 2 S.Ct. 225, 27 L.Ed. 438.

MR. JUSTICE BRADLEY delivered the opinion of the court.

This case arises upon a bill in equity filed by Edwin L. Brady against The Atlantic Works, a corporation of Massachusetts, having workshops and a place of business in Boston, praying for an account of profits for building a dredge-boat in violation of certain letters-patent granted to the complainant bearing date Dec. 17, 1867, and for an injunction to restrain the defendants from making, using, or selling any dredge-boat in violation of said letters-patent. * * *

The most important question, and first to be considered, is the validity of the patent.

It is obvious from reading the specification that the alleged invention consists mainly in attaching a screw (which the patentee calls a mud-fan) to the forward end of a propeller dredge-boat, provided with tanks for setting her in the water. It is operated by sinking the boat until the screw comes in contact with the mud or sand, which, by the revolution of the screw, is thrown up and mingled with the current. The use of a series of tanks for the purpose of keeping the vessel level whilst she settles is an old contrivance long used in dry docks, and is shown, by the evidence, to have been used in many light-draft monitors during the late war. * * *

The process of development in manufactures creates a constant demand for new appliances, which the skill of ordinary head-workmen and engineers is generally adequate to devise, and which, indeed, are the natural and proper outgrowth of such development. Each step forward prepares the way for the next, and each is usually taken by spontaneous trials and attempts in a hundred places. To grant to a

no patent for slight advances

single party a monopoly of every slight advance made, except where the exercise of invention, somewhat above ordinary mechanical or engineering skill, is distinctly shown, is unjust in principle and injurious in its consequences.

The design of the patent laws is to reward those who make some substantial discovery or invention, which adds to our knowledge and makes a step in advance in the useful arts. Such inventors are worthy of all favor. It was never the object of those laws to grant a monopoly for every trifling device, every shadow of a shade of an idea, which would naturally and spontaneously occur to any skilled mechanic or operator in the ordinary progress of manufactures. Such an indiscriminate creation of exclusive privileges tends rather to obstruct than to stimulate invention. It creates a class of speculative schemers who make it their business to watch the advancing wave of improvement, and gather its foam in the form of patented monopolies, which enable them to lay a heavy tax upon the industry of the country, without contributing anything to the real advancement of the arts. It embarrasses the honest pursuit of business with fears and apprehensions of concealed liens and unknown liabilities to lawsuits and vexatious accountings for profits made in good faith. * * *

GOODYEAR TIRE & RUBBER CO.
v. RAY–O–VAC CO.

Supreme Court of the United States, 1944.
321 U.S. 275, 64 S.Ct. 593, 88 L.Ed. 721.

MR. JUSTICE ROBERTS delivered the opinion of the Court:

This case involves the validity and alleged infringement of the Anthony Patent No. 2,198,423, issued April 23, 1940. The District Court held the patent valid and infringed and its judgment was affirmed by the Circuit Court of Appeals.

The patent, a very narrow one in a crowded art, is for a leakproof dry cell for a flash light battery.

* * *

No patent in the prior art addressed itself to the problem of preventing both leakage and swelling in a dry cell. At the time of the Anthony application flash light cells were commonly encased in a paper coating which might, or might not be waterproofed, or in some other similar casing for purposes of insulation from the case.

* * * To accomplish his objects Anthony used the ordinary type of dry cell having circuit terminals at opposite ends, one electrode being a cylindrical zinc cup, the other a centrally placed carbon electrode, in electrolyte and depolarizing mix, the bottom closure affording a terminal for one electrode and the top for the other. Around this conventional combination he placed an insulating material and an outside protecting metal sheath which would enclose the insulated side walls of the zinc cup and tightly embrace both upper and lower closures to prevent leakage.

* * *

Viewed after the event, the means Anthony adopted seem simple and such as should have been obvious to those who worked in the field, but this is not enough to negative invention. During a period of half a century, in which the use of flash light batteries increased enormously, and the manufacturers of flash light cells were conscious of the defects in them, no one devised a method of curing such defects. Once the method was discovered it commended itself to the public as evidenced by marked commercial success. These factors were entitled to weight in determining whether the improvement amounted to invention and should, in a close case, tip the scales in favor of patentability. Accepting, as we do, the findings below, we hold the patent valid and infringed.

Decree affirmed.

CUNO ENGINEERING CORPORATION v. AUTOMATIC DEVICES CORPORATION

United States Supreme Court, 1941.
314 U.S. 84, 62 S.Ct. 37, 86 L.Ed. 58.

MR. JUSTICE DOUGLAS delivered the opinion of the Court:

This is an action in equity brought by respondent for infringement, inter alia, upon claims 2, 3, and 11 of patent No. 1,736,544, granted November 19, 1929, on the application of H.E. Mead, filed August 24, 1927, for a cigar lighter. * * *

The claims in question are for improvements in lighters, commonly found in automobiles, for cigars, cigarettes and pipes. There were earlier lighters of the "reel type." The igniter unit was connected with a source of current by a cable which was wound on a spring drum so that the igniter unit and cable could be withdrawn from the socket and be used for lighting a cigar or cigarette. As the removable plug was returned to the socket the wires were reeled back into it. The circuit was closed either by manual operation of a button or by withdrawal of the igniter from its socket. In 1921 the Morris patent (No. 1,376,154) was issued for a so-called "wireless" or "cordless" lighter. This lighter eliminated the cables and the mechanism for winding and unwinding them, it provided for heating the ignited unit without removing it from its socket, and it eliminated all electrical and mechanical connection of the igniter unit with the socket once it was removed therefrom for use. * * * Mead added to the so-called "wireless" or "cordless" lighter a thermostatic control responsive to the temperature of the heating coil. In operation it automatically returned the plug to its "off" position after the heating coil had reached the proper temperature. * * * The plug might then be manually removed for use in the manner of a match, torch, or ember. When replaced in the socket after use, it was held in open-circuit position until next needed.

* * * *

Thermostatic controls of a heating unit, operating to cut off an electric current energizing the unit when its temperature had reached the desired point, were well known to the art when Mead made his device.

* * * Copeland (No. 1,844,206), filed April 18, 1927, before Mead, showed an electric lighter for cigars and cigarettes with thermostatic control. * * * The advance of Mead over Copeland was the use of the removable plug bearing the heating unit, as in Morris, to establish the automatically controlled circuit of Copeland.

And so the question is whether it was invention for one skilled in the art and familiar with Morris and Copeland, and with the extensive use of the automatic thermostatic control of an electric heating circuit, to apply the Copeland automatic circuit to the Morris removable heating unit in substitution for a circuit manually controlled. * * *

We may concede that the functions performed by Mead's combination were new and useful. But that does not necessarily make the device patentable. Under the statute (35 U.S.C.A. § 31, R.S. § 4886) the device must not only be "new and useful," it must also be an "invention" or "discovery." Thompson v. Boisselier, 114 U.S. 1, 11, 5 S.Ct. 1042, 29 L.Ed. 76, 79. Since Hotchkiss v. Greenwood, 52 U.S. (11 How.) 248, 267, 13 L.Ed. 683, 691, decided in 1851, it has been recognized that if an improvement is to obtain the privileged position of a patent more ingenuity must be involved than the work of a mechanic skilled in the art. * * * The principle of the Hotchkiss case applies to the adaptation or combination of old or well known devices for new uses. * * * That is to say the new device, however useful it may be, must reveal the flash of creative genius not merely the skill of the calling. If it fails, it has not established its right to a private grant on the public domain.

Tested by that principle Mead's device was not patentable. We cannot conclude that his skill in making this contribution reached the level of inventive genius which the Constitution (Art. 1, § 8) authorizes Congress to reward. He merely incorporated the well-known thermostat into the old "wireless" lighter to produce a more efficient, useful, and convenient article. Cf. Electric Cable Joint Co. v. Brooklyn Edison Co., 292 U.S. 69, 54 S.Ct. 586, 78 L.Ed. 1131, supra. A new application of an old device may not be patented if the "result claimed as new is the same in character as the original result" (Blake v. San Francisco, 113 U.S. 679, 683, 5 S.Ct. 692, 28 L.Ed. 1070, 1072) even though the new result had not before been contemplated. Pennsylvania R. Co. v. Locomotive Engine Safety Truck Co., 110 U.S. 490, 494, 4 S.Ct. 220, 28 L.Ed. 222, 223, and cases cited. Certainly the use of a thermostat to break a circuit in a "wireless" cigar lighter is analogous to or the same in character as the use of such a device in electric heaters, toasters, or irons, whatever may be the difference in detail of design. Ingenuity was required to effect the adaptation, but no more than that to be expected of a mechanic skilled in the art.

Strict application of that test is necessary lest in the constant demand for new appliances the heavy hand of tribute be laid on each slight technological advance in an art. The consequences of the alternative course were forcefully pointed out by Mr. Justice Bradley in Atlantic Works v. Brady, 107 U.S. 192, 200, 2 S.Ct. 225, 27 L.Ed. 438, 441: "Such an indiscriminate creation of exclusive privileges tends rather to obstruct than to stimulate invention. It creates a class of speculative schemers who make it their business to watch the advancing wave of improvement, and gather its foam in the form of patented monopolies, which enable them to lay a heavy tax upon the industry of the country, without contributing anything to the real advancement of the arts. It embarrasses the honest pursuit of business with fears and apprehensions of concealed liens and unknown liabilities to lawsuits and vexatious accountings for profits made in good faith." Cf. Mr. Justice Campbell dissenting in Winans v. Denmead, 56 U.S. (15 How.) 330, 344, 345, 347, 14 L.Ed. 717, 722–724; Hamilton, Patents and Free Enterprise, Mon. No. 31, Investigation of Concentration of Economic Power, Temporary National Economic Committee, 76th Cong. 3d Sess. chap. VIII (1941).

Such considerations prevent any relaxation of the rule of the Hotchkiss Case as respondent would seem to desire.

Reversed.

GREAT ATLANTIC & PAC. TEA CO. v. SUPERMARKET EQUIPMENT CORP.

Supreme Court of the United States, 1950.
340 U.S. 147, 71 S.Ct. 127, 95 L.Ed. 162.

MR. JUSTICE JACKSON delivered the opinion of the Court.

Two courts below have concurred in holding three patent claims to be valid, and it is stipulated that, if valid, they have been infringed. The issue, for the resolution of which we granted certiorari, is whether they applied correct criteria of invention. We hold that they have not, and that by standards appropriate for a combination patent these claims are invalid.

Stated without artifice, the claims assert invention of a cashier's counter equipped with a three-sided frame, or rack, with no top or bottom, which, when pushed or pulled, will move groceries deposited within it by a customer to the checking clerk and leave them there when it is pushed back to repeat the operation. It is kept on the counter by guides. That the resultant device works as claimed, speeds the customer on his way, reduces checking costs for the merchant, has been widely adopted and successfully used, appear beyond dispute. * * * What indicia of invention should the court seek in a case where nothing tangible is new, and invention, if it exists at all, is only in bringing old elements together?

* * *

The negative rule accrued from many litigations was condensed about as precisely as the subject permits in Lincoln Engineering Co. v. Stewart-Warner Corp., 303 U.S. 545, 549, 58 S.Ct. 662, 82 L.Ed. 1008,

⅄ 1010: "The mere aggregation of a number of old parts or elements which, in the aggregation, perform or produce no new or different function or operation than that theretofore performed or produced by them, is not patentable invention." To the same end is Toledo Pressed Steel Co. v. Standard Parts, Inc., 307 U.S. 350, 59 S.Ct. 897, 83 L.Ed. 1334, and Cuno Engineering Corp. v. Automatic Devices Corp., 314 U.S. 84, 62 S.Ct. 37, 86 L.Ed. 58.

* * *

Neither court below has made any finding that old elements which made up this device perform any additional or different function in the combination that they perform out of it. This counter does what a store counter always has done—it supports merchandise at a convenient height while the customer makes his purchases and the merchant his sales. The three-sided rack will draw or push goods put within it from one place to another—just what any such a rack would do on any smooth surface—and the guide rails keep it from falling or sliding off from the counter, as guide rails have ever done. Two and two have been added together, and still they make only four.

Courts should scrutinize combination patent claims with a care proportioned to the difficulty and improbability of finding invention in an assembly of old elements. The function of a patent is to add to the sum of useful knowledge. Patents cannot be sustained, when on the contrary, their effect is to subtract from former resources freely available to skilled artisans. A patent for a combination which only unites old elements with no change in their respective functions, such as is presented here, obviously withdraws what already is known into the field of its monopoly and diminishes the resources available to skillful men. This patentee has added nothing to the total stock of knowledge, but has merely brought together segments of prior art and claims them in congregation as a monopoly.

* * * The defect that we find in this judgment is that a standard of invention appears to have been used that is less exacting than that required where a combination is made up entirely of old components. It is on this ground that the judgment below is reversed.

MR. JUSTICE DOUGLAS, with whom MR. JUSTICE BLACK agrees, concurring.

It is worth emphasis that every patent case involving validity presents a question which requires reference to a standard written into the Constitution. Article 1, § 8 contains a grant to the Congress of the power to permit patents to be issued. But unlike most of the specific powers which Congress is given that grant is qualified. The Congress does not have free reign, for example, to decide that patents should be easily or freely given. The Congress acts under the restraint imposed by the statement of purpose in Art. 1, § 8. The purpose is "To promote the Progress of Science and useful Arts." The means for achievement of that end is the grant for a limited time to inventors of the exclusive right to their inventions.

Every patent is the grant of a privilege of exacting tolls from the public. The Framers plainly did not want those monopolies freely granted. The invention to justify a patent had to serve the ends of science—to push back the frontiers of chemistry, physics, and the like; to make a distinctive contribution to scientific knowledge. That is why through the years the opinions of the Court commonly have taken "inventive genius" as the test. It is not enough that an article is new and useful. The Constitution never sanctioned the patenting of gadgets. Patents serve a higher end—the advancement of science. An invention need not be as startling as an atomic bomb to be patentable. But it has to be of such quality and distinction that masters of the scientific field in which it falls will recognize it as an advance.

* * *

The question of invention goes back to the constitutional standard in every case. We speak with final authority on that constitutional issue as we do on many others.

The attempts through the years to get a broader, looser conception of patents than the Constitution contemplates have been persistent. The Patent Office, like most administrative agencies, has looked with favor on the opportunity which the exercise of discretion affords to expand its own jurisdiction. And so it has placed a host of gadgets under the armour of patents—gadgets that obviously have had no place in the constitutional scheme of advancing scientific knowledge.

* * *

3. SECTION 103 IN GENERAL

LYON v. BAUSCH & LOMB OPTICAL CO.[b]

United States Court of Appeals, Second Circuit, 1955.
224 F.2d 530, 106 USPQ 1.

HAND, CIRCUIT JUDGE. This is an appeal from a judgment of the District Court for the Western District of New York (Burke, J., presiding), sustaining the validity of Patent No. 2,398,382, granted to the plaintiff, Lyon, on April 16, 1946, upon an application filed November 17, 1942. Of the nine claims all but 6 and 7 are in suit; the judgment held all seven valid, and the defendant concedes infringement. Judge Burke, in a long and careful opinion, 119 F.Supp. 42, has stated the evidence in such detail that we may, as we shall, assume familiarity with it in our discussion of the issues involved.

* * *

Therefore we at length come to the question whether Lyon's contribution, his added step, was enough to support a patent. It certainly would have done so twenty or thirty years ago; indeed it conforms to the accepted standards of that time. The most competent workers in the field had for at least ten years been seeking a hardy,

b. See also: Gentzel v. Manning, Maxwell & Moore, 230 F.2d 341, 108 USPQ 353 (2d Cir.1956); Welsh Mfg. Co. v. Sunware Products Co., 236 F.2d 225, 110 USPQ 161 (2d Cir.1956); Brown v. Brock, 240 F.2d 723, 112 USPQ 199 (4th Cir.1956).

tenacious coating to prevent reflection; there had been a number of attempts, none satisfactory; meanwhile nothing in the implementary arts had been lacking to put the advance into operation; when it appeared, it supplanted the existing practice and occupied substantially the whole field. We do not see how any combination of evidence could more completely demonstrate that, simple as it was, the change had not been "obvious * * * to a person having ordinary skill in the art"— § 103. On the other hand it must be owned that, had the case come up for decision within twenty, or perhaps, twenty-five, years before the Act of 1952 went into effect on January 1, 1953, it is almost certain that the claims would have been held invalid. The Courts of Appeal have very generally found in the recent opinions of the Supreme Court a disposition to insist upon a stricter test of invention than it used to apply— indefinite it is true, but indubitably stricter than that defined in § 103. Indeed, some of the justices themselves have taken the same view. The Act describes itself as a codification of existing law, as it certainly is in the sense that the structure of the system remains unchanged. Moreover those decisions that have passed upon it have uniformly referred to it as a codification, although so far as we have found none of them has held that § 103 did not change the standard of invention. And so the question arises whether we should construe § 103 as restoring the law to what it was when the Court announced the definition of invention, now expressly embodied in § 103, or whether we should assume that no change whatever was intended.

* * *

In the first place § 103 only restores the original gloss, substantially in ipsissimis verbis; which has never been overruled; but on the contrary for seventy or eighty years had continued to be regarded as authoritative. Moreover—and this is the important consideration— although it may have ceased in practice to be followed, and had come to enjoy no more than lip service, there never has been the slightest intimation of any definite substitute; nothing more than an unexpressed and unacknowledged misgiving about the increased facility with which patents were being granted. Such judicial attitudes are indeed the stuff of which much of the law is made; but we cannot agree that, however controlling upon the lower courts, they are a warrant for that solid assurance, the disappointment of which will make a statute invalid. Courts again and again shift their position; and, although they are apt to do so under cover of nice distinctions, they impose the risk of anticipating the changes upon those who may have acted upon the faith of the original. Certainly a legislature, whose will the courts have undertaken to proliferate, must be free to reinstate the courts' initial interpretation, even though it may have been obscured by a series of later comments whose upshot is at best hazy.

* * *

We agree with Judge Burke's searching and comprehensive analysis, and the judgment will be affirmed.

Judgment affirmed.[c]

c. See also: Palmer Co. v. Luden, 236 F.2d 496, 111 USPQ 1 (3rd Cir.1956); Was- serman v. Burgess & Blacher Co., 217 F.2d 402, 103 USPQ 368 (1st Cir.1954); Cold

GRAHAM v. JOHN DEERE CO.

Supreme Court of the United States, 1966.
383 U.S. 1, 86 S.Ct. 684, 15 L.Ed.2d 545.

MR. JUSTICE CLARK delivered the opinion of the Court.

After a lapse of 15 years, the Court again focuses its attention on the patentability of inventions under the standard of Art. I, § 8, cl. 8, of the Constitution and under the conditions prescribed by the laws of the United States. Since our last expression on patent validity, Great A. & P. Tea Co. v. Supermarket Equipment Corp., 340 U.S. 147, 71 S.Ct. 127, 95 L.Ed. 162 (1950), the Congress has for the first time expressly added a third statutory dimension to the two requirements of novelty and utility that had been the sole statutory test since the Patent Act of 1793. This is the test of obviousness, i.e., * * *.

The questions, involved in each of the companion cases before us, are what effect the 1952 Act had upon traditional statutory and judicial tests of patentability and what definitive tests are now required. We have concluded that the 1952 Act was intended to codify judicial precedents embracing the principle long ago announced by this Court in Hotchkiss v. Greenwood, 11 How. 248, 13 L.Ed. 683 (1851), and that, while the clear language of § 103 places emphasis on an inquiry into obviousness, the general level of innovation necessary to sustain patentability remains the same.

Graham v. John Deere Co., an infringement suit by petitioners, presents a conflict between two Circuits over the validity of a single patent on a "Clamp for vibrating Shank Plows." The invention, a combination of old mechanical elements, involves a device designed to absorb shock from plow shanks as they plow through rocky soil and thus to prevent damage to the plow. In 1955, the Fifth Circuit had held the patent valid under its rule that when a combination produces an "old result in a cheaper and otherwise more advantageous way," it is patentable. Jeoffroy Mfg., Inc. v. Graham, 219 F.2d 511, cert. denied 350 U.S. 826, 76 S.Ct. 55, 100 L.Ed. 738. In 1964, the Eighth Circuit held, in the case at bar, that there was no new result in the patented combination and that the patent was, therefore, not valid. 333 F.2d 529, reversing D.C., 216 F.Supp. 272. We granted certiorari, 379 U.S. 956, 85 S.Ct. 652, 13 L.Ed.2d 553. Although we have determined that neither Circuit applied the correct test, we conclude that the patent is invalid under § 103 and, therefore, we affirm the judgment of the Eighth Circuit.

* * *

[The court here sets forth the historical background of the patent clause of the Constitution, prior Patent Acts, and the judicial test of Hotchkiss v. Greenwood, 52 U.S. (11 How.) 248, 13 L.Ed. 683.]

* * *

Metal Products Co. v. Newport Steel Corp., 226 F.2d 19, 107 USPQ 59 (6th Cir.1955).

THE 1952 PATENT ACT.

The Act sets out the conditions of patentability in three sections. An analysis of the structure of these three sections indicates that patentability is dependent upon three explicit conditions: novelty and utility as articulated and defined in § 101 and § 102, and nonobviousness, the new statutory formulation, as set out in § 103. The first two sections, which trace closely the 1874 codification, express the "new and useful" tests which have always existed in the statutory scheme and, for our purposes here, need no clarification. The pivotal section around which the present controversy centers is § 103. It provides:

"§ 103. *Conditions for patentability; non-obvious subject matter*

"A patent may not be obtained though the invention is not identically disclosed or described as set forth in section 102 of this title, if the differences between the subject matter sought to be patented and the prior art are such that the subject matter as a whole would have been obvious at the time the invention was made to a person having ordinary skill in the art to which said subject matter pertains. Patentability shall not be negatived by the manner in which the invention was made."

The section is cast in relatively unambiguous terms. Patentability is to depend, in addition to novelty and utility, upon the "non-obvious" nature of the "subject matter sought to be patented" to a person having ordinary skill in the pertinent art.

The first sentence of this section is strongly reminiscent of the language in *Hotchkiss*. Both formulations place emphasis on the pertinent art existing at the time the invention was made and both are implicitly tied to advances in that art. The major distinction is that Congress has emphasized "nonobviousness" as the operative test of the section, rather than the less definite "invention" language of *Hotchkiss* that Congress thought had led to "a large variety" of expressions in decisions and writings. In the title itself the Congress used the phrase "Conditions for patentability; *non-obvious subject matter*" (italics added), thus focusing upon "nonobviousness" rather than "invention."

The Senate and House Reports, S.Rep. No. 1979, 82d Cong., 2d Sess. (1952); H.Rep. No. 1923, 82d Cong., 2d Sess. (1952), reflect this emphasis in these terms:

"Section 103, for the first time in our statute, provides a condition which exists in the law and has existed for more than 100 years, but only by reason of decisions of the courts. An invention which has been made, and which is new in the sense that the same thing has not been made before, may still not be patentable if the difference between the new thing and what was known before is not considered sufficiently great to warrant a patent. That has been expressed in a large variety of ways in decisions of the courts and in writings. Section 103 states this requirement in the title. It refers to the difference between the subject matter sought to be patented and the prior art, meaning what was known before as described in section 102. If this difference is such that the subject matter as a whole would have been obvious at the time to a person skilled in the art, then the subject matter cannot be patented.

"That provision paraphrases language which has often been used in decisions of the courts, and the section is added to the statute for uniformity and definiteness. This section should have a stabilizing effect and minimize great departures which have appeared in some cases." H.R.Rep., supra, at 7; S.Rep., supra, at 6.

It is undisputed that this section was, for the first time, a statutory expression of an additional requirement for patentability, originally expressed in *Hotchkiss*. It also seems apparent that Congress intended by the last sentence of § 103 to abolish the test it believed this Court announced in the controversial phrase "flash of creative genius," used in Cuno Engineering Corp. v. Automatic Devices Corp., 314 U.S. 84, 62 S.Ct. 37, 86 L.Ed. 58 (1941).

It is contended, however, by some of the parties and by several of the *amici* that the first sentence of § 103 was intended to sweep away judicial precedents and to lower the level of patentability. Others contend that the Congress intended to codify the essential purpose reflected in existing judicial precedents—the rejection of insignificant variations and innovations of a commonplace sort—and also to focus inquiries under § 103 upon nonobviousness, rather than upon "invention," as a means of achieving more stability and predictability in determining patentability and validity.

The Reviser's Note to this section, with apparent reference to *Hotchkiss*, recognizes that judicial requirements as to "lack of patentable novelty [have] been followed since at least as early as 1850." The note indicates that the section was inserted because it "may have some stabilizing effect, and also to serve as a basis for the addition at a later time of some criteria which may be worked out." To this same effect are the reports of both Houses, supra, which state that the first sentence of the section "paraphrases language which has often been used in decisions of the courts, and the section is added to the statute for uniformity and definiteness."

We believe that this legislative history, as well as other sources,[9] shows that the revision was not intended by Congress to change the general level of patentable invention. We conclude that the section was intended merely as a codification of judicial precedents embracing the *Hotchkiss* condition, with congressional directions that inquiries into the obviousness of the subject matter sought to be patented are a prerequisite to patentability.

9. See Efforts to Establish a Statutory Standard of Invention, Study No. 7, Senate Subcommittee on Patents, Trademarks, and Copyrights, 85th Cong., 1st Sess. (Committee Print, 1958); Hearings, Subcommittee No. 3, House Committee on the Judiciary, on H.R. 3760, 82d Cong., 1st Sess. (1951).

Approached in this light, the § 103 additional condition, when followed realistically, will permit a more practical test of patentability. The emphasis on nonobviousness is one of inquiry, not quality, and, as such, comports with the constitutional strictures.

While the ultimate question of patent validity is one of law, Great A. & P. Tea Co. v. Supermarket Equipment Corp., supra, 340 U.S. at 155, 71 S.Ct. at 131, the § 103 condition, which is but one of three conditions, each of which must be satisfied, lends itself to several basic factual inquiries. Under § 103, the scope and content of the prior art are to be determined; differences between the prior art and the claims at issue are to be ascertained; and the level of ordinary skill in the pertinent art resolved. Against this background, the obviousness or nonobviousness of the subject matter is determined. Such secondary considerations as commercial success, long felt but unsolved needs, failure of others, etc., might be utilized to give light to the circumstances surrounding the origin of the subject matter sought to be patented. As indicia of obviousness or nonobviousness, these inquiries may have relevancy. See Note, Subtests of "Nonobviousness": A Nontechnical Approach to Patent Validity, 112 U.Pa.L.Rev. 1169 (1964).

This is not to say, however, that there will not be difficulties in applying the nonobviousness test. What is obvious is not a question upon which there is likely to be uniformity of thought in every given factual context. The difficulties, however, are comparable to those encountered daily by the courts in such frames of reference as negligence and scienter, and should be amenable to a case-by-case development. We believe that strict observance of the requirements laid down here will result in that uniformity and definiteness which Congress called for in the 1952 Act.

* * *

We now turn to the application of the conditions found necessary for patentability to the cases involved here:

A. THE PATENT IN ISSUE IN NO. 11, GRAHAM V. JOHN DEERE CO.

This patent, No. 2,627,798 (hereinafter called the '798 patent) relates to a spring clamp which permits plow shanks to be pushed upward when they hit obstructions in the soil, and then springs the shanks back into normal position when the obstruction is passed over. The device, which we show diagrammatically in the accompanying sketches (Appendix, Fig. 1), is fixed to the plow frame as a unit. The mechanism around which the controversy center is basically a hinge. The top half of it, known as the upper plate (marked 1 in the sketches), is a heavy metal piece clamped to the plow frame (2) and is stationary relative to the plow frame. The lower half of the hinge, known as the hinge plate (3), is connected to the rear of the upper plate by a hinge pin (4) and rotates downward with respect to it. The shank (5), which is bolted to the forward end of the hinge plate (at 6), runs beneath the plate and parallel to it for about nine inches, passes through a stirrup (7), and then continues backward for several feet curving down toward

the ground. The chisel (8), which does the actual plowing, is attached
to the rear end of the shank. As the plow frame is pulled forward, the
chisel rips through the soil, thereby plowing it. In the normal position,
the hinge plate and the shank are kept tight against the upper plate by
a spring (9), which is atop the upper plate. A rod (10) runs through the
center of the spring, extending down through holes in both plates and
the shank. Its upper end is bolted to the top of the spring while its
lower end is hooked against the underside of the shank.

When the chisel hits a rock or other obstruction in the soil, the
obstruction forces the chisel and the rear portion of the shank to move
upward. The shank is pivoted (at 11) against the rear of the hinge
plate and pries open the hinge against the closing tendency of the
spring. (See sketch labeled "Open Position," Appendix, Fig. 1) This
closing tendency is caused by the fact that, as the hinge is opened, the
connecting rod is pulled downward and the spring is compressed.
When the obstruction is passed over, the upward force on the chisel
disappears and the spring pulls the shank and hinge plate back into
their original position. The lower, rear portion of the hinge plate is
constructed in the form of a stirrup (7) which brackets the shank,
passing around and beneath it. The shank fits loosely into the stirrup
(permitting a slight up and down play). The stirrup is designed to
prevent the shank from recoiling away from the hinge plate, and thus
prevents excessive strain on the shank near its bolted connection. The
stirrup also girds the shank, preventing it from fishtailing from side to
side.

In practical use, a number of spring-hinge-shank combinations are
clamped to a plow frame, forming a set of ground-working chisels
capable of withstanding the shock of rocks and other obstructions in the
soil without breaking the shanks.

BACKGROUND OF THE PATENT.

Chisel plows, as they are called, were developed for plowing in
areas where the ground is relatively free from rocks or stones. Originally, the shanks were rigidly attached to the plow frames. When such
plows were used in the rocky, glacial soils of some of the Northern
States, they were found to have serious defects. As the chisels hit
buried rocks, a vibratory motion was set up and tremendous forces were
transmitted to the shank near its connection to the frame. The shanks
would break. Graham, one of the petitioners, sought to meet that
problem, and in 1950 obtained a patent, U.S. No. 2,493,811 (hereinafter
'811), on a spring clamp which solved some of the difficulties. Graham
and his companies manufactured and sold the '811 clamps. In 1950,
Graham modified the '811 structure and filed for a patent. That
patent, the one in issue, was granted in 1953. This suit against
competing plow manufacturers resulted from charges by petitioners
that several of respondents' devices infringed the '798 patent.

THE PRIOR ART.

Five prior patents indicating the state of the art were cited by the Patent Office in the prosecution of the '798 application. Four of these patents, 10 other United States patents and two prior-use spring-clamp arrangements not of record in the '798 file wrapper were relied upon by respondents as revealing the prior art. The District Court and the Court of Appeals found that the prior art "as a whole in one form or another contains all of the mechanical elements of the '798 Patent." One of the prior-use clamp devices not before the Patent Examiner—Glencoe—was found to have "all of the elements."

We confine our discussion to the prior patent of Graham, '811, and to the Glencoe clamp device, both among the references asserted by respondents. The Graham '811 and '798 patent devices are similar in all elements, save two: (1) the stirrup and the bolted connection of the shank to the hinge plate do not appear in '811; and (2) the position of the shank is reversed, being placed in patent '811 above the hinge plate, sandwiched between it and the upper plate. The shank is held in place by the spring rod which is hooked against the bottom of the hinge plate passing through a slot in the shank. Other differences are of no consequence to our examination. In practice the '811 patent arrangement permitted the shank to wobble or fishtail because it was not rigidly fixed to the hinge plate; moreover, as the hinge plate was below the shank, the latter caused wear on the upper plate, a member difficult to repair or replace.

Graham's '798 patent application contained 12 claims. All were rejected as not distinguished from the Graham '811 patent. The inverted position of the shank was specifically rejected as was the bolting of the shank to the hinge plate. The Patent Office examiner found these to be "matters of design well within the expected skill of the art and devoid of invention." Graham withdrew the original claims and substituted the two new ones which are substantially those in issue here. His contention was that wear was reduced in patent '798 between the shank and the heel or rear of the upper plate.[11] He also emphasized several new features, the relevant one here being that the bolt used to connect the hinge plate and shank maintained the upper face of the shank in continuing and constant contact with the under-face of the hinge plate.

Graham did not urge before the Patent Office the greater "flexing" qualities of the '798 patent arrangement which he so heavily relied on in the courts. The sole element in patent '798 which petitioners argue

11. In '811, where the shank was above the hinge plate, an upward movement of the chisel forced the shank up against the underside of the rear of the upper plate. The upper plate thus provided the fulcrum about which the hinge was pried open. Because of this, as well as the location of the hinge pin, the shank rubbed against the heel of the upper plate causing wear both to the plate and to the shank. By relocating the hinge pin and by placing the hinge plate between the shank and the upper plate, as in '798, the rubbing was eliminated and the wear point was changed to the hinge plate, a member more easily removed or replaced for repair.

before us is the interchanging of the shank and hinge plate and the consequences flowing from this arrangement. The contention is that this arrangement—which petitioners claim is not disclosed in the prior art—permits the shank to flex under stress for its *entire* length. As we have sketched (see sketch, "Graham '798 Patent" in Appendix, Fig. 2), when the chisel hits an obstruction the resultant force (A) pushes the rear of the shank upward and the shank pivots against the rear of the hinge plate at (C). The natural tendency is for that portion of the shank between the pivot point and the bolted connection (i.e., between C and D) to bow downward and away from the hinge plate. The maximum distance (B) that the shank moves away from the plate is slight—for emphasis, greatly exaggerated in the sketches. This is so because of the strength of the shank and the short—nine inches or so—length of that portion of the shank between (C) and (D). On the contrary, in patent '811 (see sketch, "Graham '811 Patent" in Appendix, Fig. 2), the pivot point is the upper plate at point (c); and while the tendency for the shank to bow between points (c) and (d) is the same as in '798, the shank is restricted because of the underlying hinge plate and cannot flex as freely. In practical effect, the shank flexes only between points (a) and (c), and not along the entire length of the shank, as in '798. Petitioners say that this difference in flex, though small, effectively absorbs the tremendous forces of the shock of obstructions whereas prior art arrangements failed.

The Obviousness of the Differences.

We cannot agree with petitioners. We assume that the prior art does not disclose such an arrangement as petitioners claim in patent '798. Still we do not believe that the argument on which petitioners' contention is bottomed supports the validity of the patent. The tendency of the shank to flex is the same in all cases. If free-flexing, as petitioners now argue, is the crucial difference above the prior art, then it appears evident that the desired result would be obtainable by not boxing the shank within the confines of the hinge.[12] The only other effective place available in the arrangement was to attach it below the hinge plate and run it through a stirrup or bracket that would not disturb its flexing qualities. Certainly a person having ordinary skill in the prior art, given the fact that the flex in the shank could be utilized more effectively if allowed to run the entire length of the shank, would immediately see that the thing to do was what Graham did, i.e., invert the shank and the hinge plate.

Petitioners' argument basing validity on the free-flex theory raised for the first time on appeal is reminiscent of Lincoln Engineering Co. of Illinois v. Stewart-Warner Corp., 303 U.S. 545, 58 S.Ct. 662, 82 L.Ed.

12. Even petitioners' expert testified to that effect:

"Q. Given the same length of the forward portion of the clamp * * * you would anticipate that the magnitude of flex [in '798] would be precisely the same or substantially the same as in 811, wouldn't you?

"A. I would think so."

1008 (1938), where the Court called such an effort "an afterthought. No such function ＊ ＊ ＊ is hinted at in the specifications of the patent. If this were so vital an element in the functioning of the apparatus, it is strange that all mention of it was omitted." At p. 550, 58 S.Ct. at p. 665. No "flexing" argument was raised in the Patent Office. Indeed, the trial judge specifically found that "flexing is not a claim of the patent in suit ＊ ＊ ＊" [d] and would not permit interrogation as to flexing in the accused devices. Moreover, the clear testimony of petitioners' experts shows that the flexing advantages flowing from the '798 arrangement are not, in fact, a significant feature in the patent.[13]

We find no nonobvious facets in the '798 arrangement. The wear and repair claims were sufficient to overcome the patent examiner's original conclusions as to the validity of the patent. However, some of the prior art, notably Glencoe, was not before him. There the hinge plate is below the shank but, as the courts below found, all of the elements in the '798 patent are present in the Glencoe structure. Furthermore, even though the position of the shank and hinge plate appears reversed in Glencoe, the mechanical operation is identical. The shank there pivots about the underside of the stirrup, which in Glencoe is *above* the shank. In other words, the stirrup in Glencoe serves exactly the same function as the heel of the hinge plate in '798. The mere shifting of the wear point to the heel of the '798 hinge plate from the stirrup of Glencoe—itself a part of the hinge plate—presents no operative mechanical distinctions, much less nonobvious differences.

＊ ＊ ＊

Judgment of Court of Appeals in No. 11 affirmed.

MR. JUSTICE FORTAS took no part in the consideration or decision of these cases.

---

d. Claim 1 provided in part "means connecting the elongated plate portion with the shank for maintaining the upper face of the shank in constant continuous contact with the underface of said plate portion of the shank attaching member."

13. "Q. ＊ ＊ ＊ Do you regard the small degree of flex in the forward end of the shank that lies between the pivot point and the point of spring attachment to be of any significance or any importance to the functioning of a device such as 798? A. Unless you are approaching the elastic limit, I think this flexing will reduce the maximum stress at the point of pivot there, where the maximum stress does occur. I think it will reduce that. I don't know how much.

"Q. Do you think it is a substantial factor, a factor of importance in the functioning of the structure? A. Not a great factor, no."

Figure 1.—GRAHAM '798 PATENT

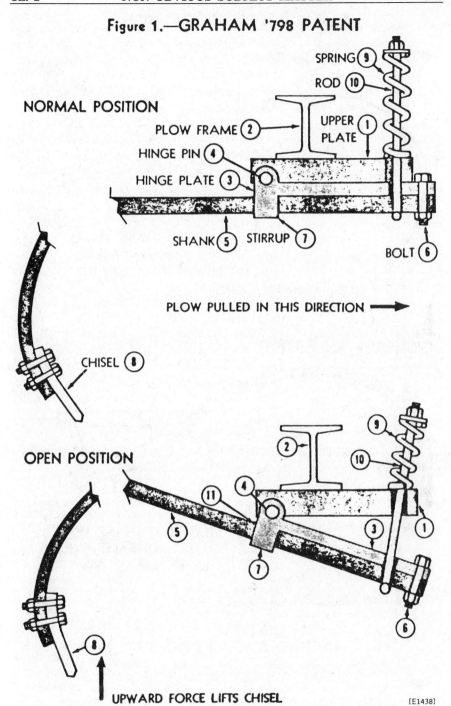

NORMAL POSITION

SPRING ⑨
ROD ⑩
PLOW FRAME ②
UPPER PLATE ①
HINGE PIN ④
HINGE PLATE ③
SHANK ⑤   STIRRUP ⑦
BOLT ⑥

PLOW PULLED IN THIS DIRECTION ➡

CHISEL ⑧

OPEN POSITION

UPWARD FORCE LIFTS CHISEL

[E1438]

Figure 2.—FLEX COMPARISON

GRAHAM '798 PATENT

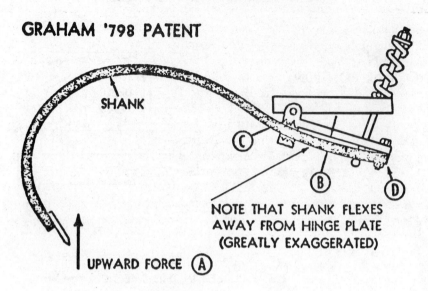

SHANK

C

B

D

NOTE THAT SHANK FLEXES
AWAY FROM HINGE PLATE
(GREATLY EXAGGERATED)

UPWARD FORCE Ⓐ

GRAHAM '811 PATENT

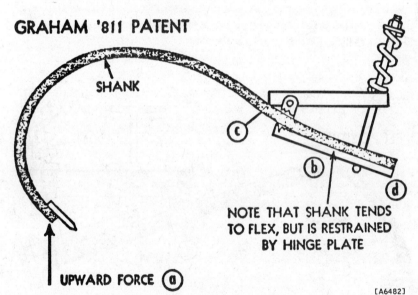

SHANK

c

b

d

NOTE THAT SHANK TENDS
TO FLEX, BUT IS RESTRAINED
BY HINGE PLATE

UPWARD FORCE ⓐ

[A6482]

SAKRAIDA v. AG PRO, INC.

Supreme Court of the United States, 1976.
425 U.S. 273, 96 S.Ct. 1532, 47 L.Ed.2d 734.

Mr. Justice Brennan delivered the opinion of the Court.

[Excerpt Only].

The Court of Appeals concluded that "the facts presented at trial clearly do not support [the District Court's] finding of obviousness under the three-pronged *Graham* test * * *." 474 F.2d, at 172. We disagree and hold that the Court of Appeals erroneously set aside the District Court's findings.   *   *   *

We cannot agree that the combination of these old elements to produce an abrupt release of water directly on the barn floor from storage tanks or pools can properly be characterized as synergistic, that is, "result[ing] in an effect greater than the sum of the several effects taken separately." Anderson's-Black Rock v. Pavement Co., 396 U.S. 57, 61, 90 S.Ct. 305, 308, 24 L.Ed.2d 258, 261 (1969). Rather, this patent simply arranges old elements with each performing the same function it had been known to perform, although perhaps producing a more striking result than in previous combinations. Such combinations are not patentable under standards appropriate for a combination patent. Great A. & P. Tea Co. v. Supermarket Corp., supra; Anderson's-Black Rock v. Pavement Co., supra. Under those authorities this assembly of old elements that delivers water directly rather than through pipes or hoses to the barn floor falls under the head of "the work of the skillful mechanic, not that of the inventor." Hotchkiss v. Greenwood, 11 How., at 267, 13 L.Ed., at 691. Exploitation of the principle of gravity adds nothing to the sum of useful knowledge where there is no change in the respective functions of the elements of the combination; this particular use of the assembly of old elements would be obvious to any person skilled in the art of mechanical application. See Dann v. Johnston, 425 U.S., at 229, 96 S.Ct., at 1399, 47 L.Ed.2d, at 699.

Though doubtless a matter of great convenience, producing a desired result in a cheaper and faster way, and enjoying commercial success, Dairy Establishment "did not produce a 'new or different function' *   *   * within the test of validity of combination patents." Anderson's-Black Rock v. Pavement Co., supra, 396 U.S., at 60, 90 S.Ct., at 308, 24 L.Ed.2d, at 261. These desirable benefits "without invention will not make patentability." Great A. & P. Tea Co. v. Supermarket Corp., 340 U.S., at 153, 71 S.Ct., at 130, 95 L.Ed., at 167. See Dann v. Johnston, 425 U.S., at 229, 96 S.Ct., at 1399, 47 L.Ed.2d, at 699 n. 4.

Reversed.

REPUBLIC INDUS., INC. v. SCHLAGE LOCK CO.

United States Court of Appeals, Seventh Circuit, 1979.
592 F.2d 963, 200 USPQ 769.

SWYGERT, CIRCUIT JUDGE.

*   *   *

This appeal presents a recurrent problem: the proper criteria by which a combination patent is measured for nonobviousness. Increasingly, the district courts in this circuit, not without some confusion emanating from this court, have taken the view that synergism and not the criteria articulated in Graham v. John Deere Co., 383 U.S. 1, 86 S.Ct. 684, 15 L.Ed.2d 545 (1966), is the controlling test in combination patent claims.

*   *   *

The Patent Act of 1793 required that a device had to be both new and useful to be patentable. Act of February 21, 1793, ch. XI, § 1, 1 Stat. 318. Thereafter a third criterion was judicially created: a device had to be an "invention" as well. Defining "invention" proved to be elusive. Nearly a century ago, the Supreme Court said as much about the term:

> The truth is the word cannot be defined in such manner as to afford any substantial aid in determining whether a particular device involves an exercise of the inventive faculty or not. In a given case we may be able to say that there is present invention of a very high order. In another we see that there is lacking that impalpable something which distinguishes invention from simple mechanical skill. Courts, adopting fixed principles as a guide, have by a process of exclusion determined that certain variations in old devices do or do not involve invention; but whether the variation relied upon in a particular case is anything more than ordinary mechanical skill is a question which cannot be answered by applying the test of any general definition.

McClain v. Ortmayer, 141 U.S. 419, 427, 12 S.Ct. 76, 78, 35 L.Ed. 800 (1891). The imprecision of the "invention" standard resulted in an inconsistent and unpredictable body of law because it required that the decision of patentability be based ultimately upon the subjective whims of the reviewing court.

Congress revised the patent laws in 1952. The novelty and utility requirements were maintained and recodified. 35 U.S.C.A. §§ 101, 102. The retention of these requirements did not, however, completely define the concept of patentability; missing was that essential quality which goes beyond mere newness or usefulness—the "something" that the courts had unsuccessfully strived for by the use of the term "invention." In order to start afresh in a semantic sense and to promote uniformity in the application of the patent laws, Congress added section 103. That provision replaced the judicially imposed requirement of "invention" with that of "nonobviousness": * * *

Section 103 received its definitive interpretation in Graham v. John Deere Co., 383 U.S. 1, 86 S.Ct. 684, 15 L.Ed.2d 545 (1966). There, the Court, in calling for "strict observance" of its requirements, laid out the analysis to be followed in cases involving the obviousness standard: * * *

It is against this backdrop that *Black Rock* and *Sakraida* must be read.

Black Rock involved a combination patent in which each of the elements were known in the prior art.[14] In that case the Court recited that it would adhere to the guidelines it had developed in *Graham*. 396 U.S. at 61–63, 90 S.Ct. 305. Using such analysis, the Court held the

14. The claimed invention in *Black Rock* was the placement of a radiant-heat burner, a bituminous paving machine, and an asphalt shaper apparatus on one chassis. All three elements were old in the paving art. The alleged contribution was the combining of these three elements into a single paving machine.

patent at issue invalid because "the combination was reasonably obvious to one with ordinary skill in the art." Id. at 60, 90 S.Ct. at 307. Although during the course of its discussion the Court noted that a combination "may result" in a synergistic effect, the Court went on to hold that the device in question "was not an invention by the obvious-nonobvious standard," id. at 63, 90 S.Ct. at 309; this phrase could only refer to *Graham* and section 103.

Similarly in *Sakraida,* the Court scrutinized the combination patent in issue by considering the scope and content of the prior art together with the differences between that art and the claimed invention. In holding the patent invalid, the Court held: "[T]his particular use of the assembly of old elements would be obvious to any person skilled in the art of mechanical application." 425 U.S. at 282, 96 S.Ct. at 1537. Although the Court again discussed synergism, it is apparent from the context of the opinion that the Supreme Court raised the topic only in response to the court of appeals' assertion that synergism was present; the Court simply did not agree that the effect produced by the claimed invention in that case was synergistic.

* * *

The district court, while agreeing that *Black Rock* and *Sakraida* did not establish synergism as a requisite for patentability, nonetheless interpreted cases from this court as requiring that every combination invention must have a synergistic effect to be patentable.

The synergism test necessarily involves a two-pronged hypothesis: (1) the subject matter of the patent claim comprises a combination of several elements, each of which was known in the prior pertinent art, and (2) the combination is synergistic or at least produces a synergistic "effect." One premise of this hypothesis, at least as applied to mechanical or hydraulic devices, is that all such inventions are merely new applications of known elements and materials in different combinations. As Judge Learned Hand observed:

It is idle to say that combinations of old elements cannot be inventions; substantially every invention is for such a "combination": that is to say, it consists of former elements in a new assemblage.

Reiner v. I. Leon Co., 285 F.2d 501, 503 (2d Cir.1960), cert. denied, 366 U.S. 929, 81 S.Ct. 1649, 6 L.Ed.2d 388 (1961). If this be true (and if new nonobvious combinations are not patentable), then almost nothing would be patentable. See Reeves Instrument Corp. v. Beckman Instruments, Inc., 444 F.2d 263, 270 (9th Cir.), cert. denied, 404 U.S. 951, 92 S.Ct. 283, 30 L.Ed.2d 268 (1971).

Once it has been determined that all of the elements in the combination are known, the next inquiry under the synergism approach is whether the claimed patent is synergistic or produces a synergistic effect. This has been no easy task. Courts have long wrestled with the meaning of synergism and have formulated a number of definitions. The two most common have been that one of the elements functions differently in combination than it did previously, e.g., Burland v. Trippe Manufacturing Co., 543 F.2d 588, 592 (7th Cir. 1976), and that the combination results in an effect greater than the sum of the several parts taken separately. E.g., St. Regis Paper Co. v. Bemis Co., 549 F.2d 833, 838 (7th Cir.), cert. denied, 434 U.S. 833, 98 S.Ct. 119, 54 L.Ed.2d 94 (1977). A realistic appraisal of these formulations, however, reveals that synergism is only a figure of speech, for in its literal sense synergism never has existed and never can exist in mechanical or hydraulic inventions when the term is defined as a whole result greater than the sum of its constituent parts.

There is, in fact, no such thing as a mechanical or hydraulic element functioning differently in combination than it did outside the combination. A spring or valve will always function as a spring or valve, alone or in concert with other components. Moreover, mechanical elements can do no more than contribute to the combination the mechanical functions of which they are inherently capable. See Application of Menough, 323 F.2d 1011, 1015, 51 C.C.P.A. 741 (1963). Thus, the overall performance of the combination is always equal to the sum of the functions of its individual components. As Judge William Conner of the Southern District of New York observed: "In the real world, two plus two never equals five." Some Highly Personal Reflections on Section 103, 5 Am.Pat.L.Q. 77, 85 (1977). Compare Great A & P Tea Co. v. Supermarket Equipment Co., 340 U.S. 147, 152, 71 S.Ct. 127, 130, 95 L.Ed. 162 (1950) ("Two and two have been added together and they still make only four.").

* * *

Putting the definitional aspects aside, there are more fundamental flaws in the use of synergism as a standard for patentability. In enacting section 103, Congress expressly mandated nonobviousness, not synergism, as the sole test for the patentability of novel and useful inventions: indeed, synergism is not even mentioned in the Patent Act of 1952. Moreover, as section 103 applies to all patent claims, there is no justification why patentability of a combination patent should be measured by a different standard than any other type of invention.

More importantly, when using the synergism approach to determine whether one element functions differently or whether the whole somehow exceeds the parts, one is required to look solely to the operation of the elements *after* they are combined. This analysis suffers from two defects. First, a test which looks exclusively to the functioning of the individual components after they are combined must necessarily be premised on the assumption that it is always obvious to take known elements and combine them. We find this assumption unsound and not based in fact. It may be that in certain circumstances the very choice of the elements to be selected is not obvious. Again, as Judge Hand noted:

> All machines are made up of the same elements; rods, pawls, pitmans, journals, toggles, gears, cams, and the like, all acting their parts as they always do and always must. All compositions are made of the

same substances, retaining their fixed chemical properties. But the elements are capable of an infinity of permutations and the selection of that group which proves serviceable to a given need may require a high degree of originality. *It is that act of selection which is the invention* * * *.

B:G. Corp. v. Walter Kidde & Co., 79 F.2d 20, 22 (2d Cir.1935) (emphasis added). See also Application of Menough, 323 F.2d 1011, 1015, 51 C.C. P.A. 741 (1963).

The second and more basic defect with synergism is that section 103 sets as the standard of patentability the nonobviousness of the invention "at the time the invention was made to a person having ordinary skill in the art * * *." This provision therefore compels the courts to view the invention from the vantage point of the field of art at a specific point in time, i.e., the time the invention was made. See Rich, Principles of Patentability, 28 Geo.Wash.L.Rev. 393, 405–06 (1960). From this vantage point the critical question becomes whether the level of skill in the art was such that the combining of the elements in the manner claimed would have been obvious, not in retrospect, but at the time it was done by the inventor. As the Supreme Court stated in United States v. Adams, 383 U.S. 39, 50, 86 S.Ct. 708, 713, 15 L.Ed.2d 572 (1966), a companion case to *Graham:*

> It begs the question * * * to state merely that magnesium and cuprous chloride were individually known battery components. If such a combination is novel, the issue is whether bringing them together as taught by [the inventor] was obvious in the light of the prior art.

Synergism, however, precludes this analysis. Because synergism centers exclusively on the performance of the elements *after* combination and without regard to the obviousness or nonobviousness of *making the combination,* synergism does not comport with the *Graham* mandate to apply section 103.

Regrettably, we have heretofore failed to provide clear and consistent guidance regarding the standards appropriate for combination patents. Although we have in fact continued, either explicitly or implicitly, to judge patent validity according to the *Graham* analysis, we have also from time to time commented on the presence or absence of a requirement akin to synergism in the claimed invention under review. * * * However, because synergism has prevented the development of a consistent, predictable body of law under section 103, and because the concept does not bear any logical *ipso facto* relationship to obviousness, the term has little, if any, utility. Therefore until Congress shall otherwise legislate or the Supreme Court shall otherwise specifically hold, this court will continue to apply the *Graham* analysis as the exclusive means by which to measure nonobviousness under section 103.

STRATOFLEX, INC. v. AEROQUIP CORPORATION

United States Court of Appeals, Federal Circuit, 1983.
713 F.2d 1530, 218 USPQ 871.

MARKEY, CHIEF JUDGE.

[Excerpt Only].

Appeal from a judgment of the District Court for the Eastern District of Michigan, 561 F.Supp. 618, declaring Claims 1, 3, 4, 6, and 7 of U.S. Patent No. 3,473,087 to Winton Slade ('087 patent) invalid and not infringed. We affirm.

* * *

"SYNERGISM" AND "COMBINATION PATENTS"

Judge Boyle said "synergism" is "a symbolic reminder of what constitutes nonobviousness when a combination patent is at issue," and that under "either standard (*Graham* analysis or synergism) the combination * * * simply lacks the unique essence of authentic contribution to the Teflon art which is the heart of invention."

A requirement for "synergism" or a "synergistic effect" is nowhere found in the statute, 35 U.S.C. When present, for example in a chemical case, synergism may point toward nonobviousness, but its absence has no place in evaluating the evidence on obviousness. The more objective findings suggested in *Graham,* supra, are drawn from the language of the statute and are fully adequate guides for evaluating the evidence relating to compliance with 35 U.S.C. § 103. *Bowser Inc. v. United States,* 388 F.2d 346, 181 Ct.Cl. 834, 156 USPQ 406 (Ct.Cl. 1967). Judge Boyle treated synergism as an alternative consideration. Hence the error of its analytical inclusion is harmless in view of Judge Boyle's employment of the *Graham* aids.

The reference to a "combination patent" is equally without support in the statute. There is no warrant for judicial classification of patents, whether into "combination" patents and some other unnamed and undefined class or otherwise. Nor is there warrant for differing treatment or consideration of patents based on a judicially devised label. Reference to "combination" patents is, moreover, meaningless. Virtually *all* patents are "combination patents," if by that label one intends to describe patents having claims to inventions formed of a combination of elements. It is difficult to visualize, at least in the mechanical-structural arts, a "non-combination" invention, i.e., an invention consisting of a *single* element. Such inventions, if they exist, are rare indeed. Again, however, Judge Boyle's inclusion in her analysis of a reference to the '087 patent as a "combination" patent was harmless in view of her application of *Graham* guidelines.

Similarly, Judge Boyle's reference to "the heart of invention" was here a harmless fall-back to the fruitless search for an inherently amorphous concept that was rendered unnecessary by the statute, 35

U.S.C. The *Graham* analysis here applied properly looked to *patentability*, not to "invention."

We sit to review judgments, not opinions. The analysis reflected in an opinion filed with the judgment appealed from may on occasion be so flawed, however, as to obfuscate the true basis for the judgment or to establish that the judgment was erroneously based. Such might have here been the case if the judgment had not been accompanied by the alternative and proper analysis under *Graham* described above. In light of that alternative analysis, in which we see no error, we affirm the judgment declaring claims 1, 3, 4, 6, and 7 invalid for obviousness.

AMERICAN HOIST & DERRICK COMPANY v. SOWA & SONS, INC.

United States Court of Appeals, Federal Circuit, 1984.
725 F.2d 1350, 220 USPQ 771.

RICH, CIRCUIT JUDGE.

[Excerpt Only].

In ending its jury charge on the § 103 nonobviousness requirement, the court said:

> You must next determine whether the differences between plaintiff's claimed invention and the prior art, if any, and as you have found them to be, produce a new and unexpected result. That is, you must determine whether the elements making up plaintiff's claimed invention combine so as to perform in some way or manner, a new and unexpected function in combination than they perform separately. The reason for this is that a patented invention which unites only old elements without producing either a new and unexpected result merely withdraws from the public's use that which was known before.

Instructing a jury that the presence of such a "new and unexpected function in combination" is a requirement of patentability—and reasoning that were the law otherwise a claimed combination of old elements would "merely [withdraw] from the public's use that which was known before"—is wholly erroneous.

While the *existence* of a new and unexpected result or function or a so-called "synergistic" effect may *support* a holding of nonobviousness, *e.g.*, *Clark Equipment Co. v. Keller*, 570 F.2d 778, 789, 197 USPQ 209, 217 (8th Cir.1978) ("in the patent law context, 'synergism' has no talismanic power; 'synergism' is merely one indication of nonobviousness"), our predecessor courts have considered and rejected the notion that a new result or function or synergism is a requirement of patentability. It was emphasized that "under this standard * * * one would focus solely on the product created rather than on the obviousness or nonobviousness of its creation, as required under § 103." *General Motors Corp. v. U.S. International Trade Commission*, 687 F.2d 476, 482–83, 215 USPQ 484, 489 (CCPA 1982). *See In re Sponnoble*, 405 F.2d 578, 585, 56 CCPA 823, 160 USPQ 237, 243 (1969) ("A patentable invention * * * *may* result even if the inventor *has,* in effect, merely combined features, old in the art, for their known purpose, without producing anything beyond the results inherent in their use."); *Bowser, Inc. v. United States,* 388 F.2d 346, 349–350, 181 Ct.Cl. 834, 56 USPQ 406, 409 (1967). We agree with the Seventh Circuit's analysis of the "fundamental flaws" in the theory that synergism is essential to patentability. *Republic Industries, Inc. v. Schlage Lock Co.,* 592 F.2d 963, 967–72, 200 USPQ 769, 774–79 (7th Cir.1979). *See Stratoflex, Inc. v. Aeroquip Corp.,* 713 F.2d 1530, 218 USPQ 871 (Fed.Cir.1983).

KIMBERLY–CLARK CORPORATION v. JOHNSON & JOHNSON

United States Court of Appeals, Federal Circuit, 1984.
745 F.2d 1437, 223 USPQ 603.

RICH, CIRCUIT JUDGE.

[Excerpt Only].

WHO IS PRESUMED TO KNOW THE PRIOR ART

* * *

It would suffice, perhaps, to say that the presumption of the inventor's knowledge of the prior art, long treated as axiomatic in patent law, is not to be applied in connection with the duty of candor and the obligation to disclose material prior art to the PTO—limiting the obligation to disclose material prior art actually known to the inventor or his assigns, agents, and attorneys. *See* 37 CFR 1.56. However, since it has actually happened that the axiom has been combined with the obligation to disclose—a tactic likely to be repealed—we are moved to analyze this old axiom (as we have analyzed equally venerable dogmas from the past for the purpose of burying them) to see what, if any, validity or vitality it possesses today.

The germ of the idea is very old, going back at least to *Eaton v. Evans,* 16 U.S. (3 Wheat.) 210, 4 L.Ed. 454 (1818). * * * In *Duer v. Corbin Cabinet Lock Co.,* 149 U.S. 216, 223, 13 S.Ct. 850, 853, 37 L.Ed. 707 (1893), which involved a lock for a cabinet drawer or the like patented by Mr. Orum, Justice Brown said:

> In view of the fact that Mr. Orum had no actual knowledge of the Gory patent, he may rightfully claim *the quality of invention* in the conception of his own device, *but as he is deemed in a legal point of view to have had this and all other prior patents before him,* his *title to invention* rests upon modifications of these, too trivial to be the subject of serious consideration. [Our emphasis.]

In these opinions, we witness the age-old struggle of the courts with the philosophical problem of reconciling the *fact* of patentees having truly made "inventions," when seen from the standpoint of what their personal efforts were, while having at the same time to hold that they were not "inventors" in the eyes of the law and their production not "inventions," because, under the law, they were not entitled to patents.

In those days, the invention could not be regarded as having involved "invention," the sine qua non of patentability.

* * *

It is therefore not surprising that our predecessor Court of Customs and Patent Appeals would say, even after the effective date of the 1952 Patent Act, in discussing its new § 103:

> We think the proper way to apply the 103 obviousness test to a case like this is to first picture the inventor as working in his shop with the prior art references *which he is presumed to know*—hanging on the walls around him. *In re Winslow,* 365 F.2d 1017, 1020, 151 USPQ 48, 51 (CCPA 1966). [Our emphasis.]

[margin handwritten:] objective std.

The court later found it necessary to qualify that overly picturesque statement, which has met with unfortunate popularity, in *In re Antle,* 444 F.2d 1168, 1171–72, 170 USPQ 285, 287–88 (CCPA 1971), and even then reiterated the statement about the presumption, saying, "As we also said in *Winslow,* 'Section 103 requires us to presume full knowledge by the inventor of the *prior* art *in the field of his endeavor*'," adding, however, that "it only requires us to presume that the inventor would have that ability to select and utilize knowledge * * * pertinent to his particular problem which would be expected of *a man of ordinary skill in the art* to which the subject matter pertains." That man, of course, is the *hypothetical* person postulated by § 103.

* * *

Before 1952, the statutes contained no such provision as § 103. Its requirement of nonobviousness as a prerequisite to patentability existed in the form of the case law requirement for "invention." To be entitled to a patent, the inventor was required to have made an "invention"—inversely, he had to be "an inventor." This requirement was in addition to the requirements of novelty and utility, which were always statutory. This was law made by the courts. In essence, it required that an applicant for patent, when presented with the problem, must have done more than would have been done by "an ordinary mechanic acquainted with the business." *Hotchkiss v. Greenwood,* supra 52 U.S. at 265.

As the above collection of quotations makes clear, the courts were constantly faced with situations where the applicant or patentee had actually made a new and useful invention, and therefore was an inventor, in every sense of the word but one—he had invented something which the courts, viewing prior art, felt did not involve the quality of "invention" and a reason for denying a patent had to be rationalized. There seems to have been a felt need to find a reason for saying the applicant or patentee either had not made an "invention" or should not be called "an inventor." In the lack of novelty cases it was easy enough to say the "statute is inexorable," because it required novelty; but in a "lack of invention" case there was no statute and to show that "an invention" had not been made, or that the requirement for "invention" had not been met, the applicant or patentee was, in effect, viewed from on high and treated as though *he* knew things he really did not know in order to determine his rights from a social point of view. There was no one other than the inventor to pin it on. By *presuming* he knew all the prior art, *he* could be said not to have made "an invention" and, not being "an inventor," he could be denied a patent or, if he had one, it could be invalidated, as well-developed law required. This line of reasoning having been once established, the courts, including our predecessor court as in *Winslow,* mentioned above, decided cases on the basis of the axiom—the applicant (or patentee) is presumed to have knowledge of all material prior art—without giving the situation further thought. But a bad axiom is like a noxious weed, a thriving plant in the wrong place interfering with the growth of more desirable plants.

Basing the rationalization of decisions on a fiction—which the presumption of knowledge is—it has been unusual that opinions have explained the real reason for the denial of patent rights, which is the basic principle (to which there are minor exceptions) that no patent should be granted which withdraws from the public domain technology already available to the public. *Graham v. John Deere Co.,* 383 U.S. 1, 6, 86 S.Ct. 684, 688, 15 L.Ed.2d 545, 148 USPQ 459, 462 (1966). It is available, in legal theory at least, when it is described in the world's accessible literature, including patents, or has been publicly known or in the public use or on sale "in this country." 35 U.S.C. § 102(a) and (b). That is the real meaning of "prior art" in legal theory—it is knowledge that is available, including what would be obvious from it, at a given time, to a person of ordinary skill in an art. Society, speaking through Congress and the courts, has said "thou shalt not take it away."

Since January 1, 1953, the effective date of the 1952 Patent Act, the implementation of that social policy has not required courts to use the legal fiction that *an inventor* must be presumed to know the "prior art." The inventor, for the purposes of legal reasoning, has been replaced, as some courts have discovered, by the statutory hypothetical "person having ordinary skill in the art" who has been provided by 35 U.S.C. § 103. Since that date, *there has been no need to presume that the inventor knows anything* about the prior art.

Since we believe that progress in legal thinking is not only possible but highly desirable when it simplifies such thinking, we believe the time has come to discontinue this particular fiction of the patent law. Congress has given us in § 103 a substitute for the former "requirement for invention," which gave rise to the presumption, and that substitute, being statutory, should be used exclusively. We hereby declare the presumption that the inventor has knowledge of all material prior art to be dead.

What controls the patentability of the fruits of the inventor's labors are the statutory conditions of novelty, utility, and unobviousness "to a person having ordinary skill in the art to which said subject matter pertains" as stated in § 103. It should be clear that that hypothetical person is not the inventor, but an imaginary being possessing "ordinary skill in the art" created by Congress to provide a *standard of patentability,* a descendant of the "ordinary mechanic acquainted with the business" of *Hotchkiss v. Greenwood.* Realistically, courts never have judged patentability by what the real inventor/applicant/patentee could or would do. Real inventors, as a class, vary in their capacities from ignorant geniuses to Nobel laureates; the courts have always applied a standard based on an imaginary worker of their own devising whom they have equated with the inventor.

* * *

4. SCOPE OF PRIOR ART

UNION CARBIDE CORPORATION v. AMERICAN CAN COMPANY

United States Court of Appeals, Federal Circuit, 1984.
724 F.2d 1567, 220 USPQ 584.

NIES, CIRCUIT JUDGE.

This case is an appeal from the grant of summary judgment by the United States District Court for the Northern District of Illinois, Eastern Division (Marshall, J.), entered March 4, 1983, holding United States Patent Nos. 4,262,803 ('803) and 4,277,930 ('930) invalid for obviousness under 35 U.S.C. § 103. Union Carbide appeals from that judgment, contesting the ruling of invalidity and asserting that material issues of fact remain to be tried in this case.

* * *

The subject patents are concerned with the packaging of plastic bags customarily used in the meat packing industry. In the packaging of primal cuts of beef, individual bags must be available to workers to place around each meat cut. The inventions of the patents in suit involve holding a stack of bags held together by an elongate flexible binding, such as a plastic tube, which passes through holes in the bags to form a loop. By being secured to the bottom of the stack of bags, the loop serves as a handle for carrying the bags and, upon being severed, continues to hold the stack of bags together while allowing the bags to be easily removed, one at a time. The record indicates that in other dispensing arrangements actually used in the industry, bags were supplied either in a loose stack, or in a continuous roll with perforations between them, or taped together in shingle fashion, or in dispenser boxes.

Appellant asserts that its invention solved the various problems of carrying the stack of bags, keeping the bags neatly together at the work station, separating the bags easily one at a time, and allowing the bags to be dispensed without tearing, disadvantages associated with other dispensing systems.

* * *

The patented apparatus and method are illustrated by the drawings shown below:

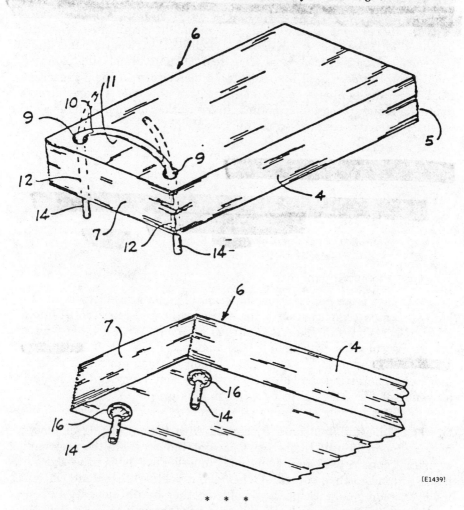

[E1439]

* * *

With respect to the *Graham v. John Deere* inquiries, the principal attack by Union Carbide is that an issue of fact was raised by the Fischer affidavit concerning the scope and content of the prior art. If this position were correct, the trial court's determination of obviousness under § 103, which is dependent on the teaching of certain patent references said by Fischer to come from non-analogous arts, would fail.

In particular, the trial court relied upon Million, Roberts and Hunt, admittedly prior art, and Chamberlin '950, Sutcliffe, Aikin and Stebbins, each of the latter being asserted in the Fischer affidavit to be improper references had the trial court properly defined the scope of the art. In Fischer's opinion, Chamberlin is non-analogous, being directed to retaining paper sheets, not dispensing them. * * *

The district court considered the Million patent (shown below) to be the most pertinent prior art reference cited by the examiner and, accordingly, used Million as its primary reference. The district court noted that Million "used a wicket type fastener to hold the bags together" and that "with the exception of the lack of a hand-grippable loop, the diagram of this part of Million appears identical to the '803 patent." The fasteners and general shape of the wicket in Million supports the court's view.

MILLION U.S. PATENT No. 3,311,399
FLEXIBLE BAGS AND BAGGING MEANS

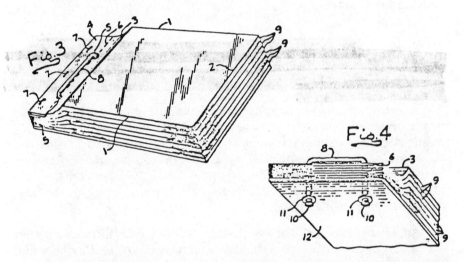

The court further noted that Million did not disclose severability of the binding member, requiring instead that the bags be torn for removal. Focusing on that feature, the district court found that the Chamberlin '950, Sutcliffe, Aikin, and Stebbings patents each employed a "binding member that may be separated in the middle to allow for removal of the items bound."

* * * [T]he Chamberlin reference (shown below) teaches that which Million lacks.

CHAMBERLIN U.S. PATENT No. 3,822,950
FILE FOLDER PAPER FASTENER

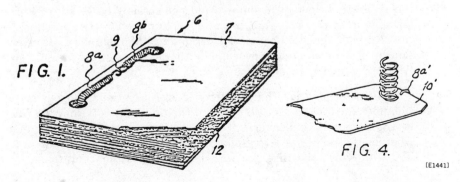

[E1441]

Chamberlin discloses a holder with two coil springs anchored to a back leaf and joined on top to hold a stack of "regular paper, *plastic* sheets, cardboard or the like." (Emphasis added.)

The coil springs of Chamberlin satisfy appellant's demand for a teaching of an "elongate flexible binding member" which, when severed, forms "upwardly extending free-ended wickets," as shown by the drawings above. Moreover, contrary to appellant's argument that Chamberlin's only function is to "retain * * * paper sheets together," Chamberlin specifically sets forth that its fastener is designed to "facilitat[e] the removal and/or addition of sheets from the bound stack."

* * * [T]he court rejected the substance of Union Carbide's position that only art relating to "dispensing of flexible bags and bagging means" was analogous as an "amazingly restrictive characterization" of the prior art. The court looked to the problem addressed by the inventor, as stated by him in his patent application and as indicated by the prosecution history, to establish the scope and content of the art, noting that the examiner (and it must be noted by us, also the applicant) cited Chamberlin '066 for a flexible loop paper fastener, and Tarnoff for a display rack, as pertinent art. The problems of the inventor here, the court noted, included binding and carrying the bags as well as dispensing them.

Appellant does not dispute that a basis for determining whether art is analogous under the standards of the Court of Customs and Patent Appeals is to look at whether it deals with a problem similar to that being addressed by the inventor. Indeed, the trial court relied on the following analysis from *In re Wood*, 599 F.2d 1032, 1036, 202 USPQ 171, 174 (CCPA 1979), *quoted in In re Pagliaro*, 657 F.2d 1219, 1224, 210 USPQ 888, 892 (CCPA 1981):

> In resolving the question of obviousness under 35 U.S.C. § 103, we presume full knowledge by the inventor of all the prior art in the field of his endeavor. However, with regard to prior art outside the field of his endeavor, we only presume knowledge from those arts reasonably pertinent to the particular problem with which the inventor was involved. The rationale behind this rule precluding rejections based on combination of teachings from references from non-analogous arts is the realization that an inventor could not possibly be aware of every teaching in every art. Thus, we attempt to more closely approximate the reality of the circumstances surrounding the making of an invention by only presuming knowledge by the inventor of prior art in the field of his endeavor and in analogous arts.
>
> The determination that a reference is from a nonanalogous art is therefore two-fold. First, we decide if the reference is within the field of the inventor's endeavor. If it is not, we proceed to determine whether the reference is reasonably pertinent to the particular problem with which the inventor was involved. [Citation omitted.]

To the same effect are *Stratoflex, Inc. v. Aeroquip Corp.*, 713 F.2d 1530, 1535, 218 USPQ 871, 876 (Fed.Cir.1983), *In re Mlot-Fijalkowski*, 676 F.2d 666, 670, 213 USPQ 713, 716 (CCPA 1982), and *Republic Industries v. Schlage Lock Co.*, 592 F.2d 963, 975, 200 USPQ 769, 781 (7th Cir.1979).

With the problems clearly defined by the inventor, we see no basis to hold that the district court erred in determining the scope and content of the prior art. Contrary to Union Carbide's view, the Fischer affidavit expressed no more than an unsupported conclusory opinion which ignored, rather than conflicted with, the evidence of record. Thus, no genuine issue of material fact was raised by appellant on the scope and content of the prior art and the district court correctly considered the art submitted by American Can in resolving the issue of obviousness.

BOTT v. FOUR STAR CORPORATION

United States District Court, E.D. Michigan, 1983.
218 USPQ 358.

COHN, DISTRICT JUDGE.

* * *

Plaintiff John A. Bott (Bott) is a Michigan resident and the owner of U.S. Patent No. 4,099,658 (the '658 patent) and U.S. Patent No. 4,182,471 (the '471 patent). The patents-in-suit disclose an article carrier for an automotive vehicle. (Article carriers are also known as carriers, luggage racks or simply racks; the terms are interchangeable).

* * *

Except for the apparent sincerity which Four Star has pursued Kalajian's '097 patent (the easel) I would reject it out of hand since it is clearly not analogous prior art and therefore not relevant to the issues in this case. The test for relevant or analogous prior art is "similarity of element, problems and purposes". *Universal Electric Co. v. A.O. Smith Corp.*, 643 F.2d 1240, 1246, 209 USPQ 1077, 1081 (6th Cir.1981). "Analogous art is that field of art which a person of ordinary skill in the art would have been apt to refer in attempting to solve the problem solved by a proposed invention", *The Black & Decker Co. v. Sears, Roebuck & Co.*, 679 F.2d 1101 (4th Cir.1982).

Four Star's position that the artist's easel disclosed in the '097 patent is relevant prior art against a luggage rack for an automobile is based on no more than a lawyer's imaginative use of a schematic drawing, clever cross-examination and a naive witness. The cross-examination of Bott in a discovery deposition in which he said that the basic structure of the easel taught the essence of his invention is quoted in Dx12D. Important to consideration of this testimony is (a) the lack of the reference to time, (b) the clear implication that the device Bott was shown was mounted on the roof of a car, and (c) the use of the phrase "article holding system". The article, of course, is the "rectangular stretcher frame for canvas" used by the artist.

not same b prior art

A stationary artist's easel does not have the same problems and purposes as a luggage rack for an automobile even if it can be said that it contains the same elements. The easel is not mounted on an automobile. It does not have slats, but rather two channel shaped rails capable of standing vertically on their own but also substantial enough to support additional loading when in an upright position. There is nothing low profile about it.

Lastly, there was no evidence at all that a person of ordinary skill in the field of article carriers or luggage racks would say the artist's easel has such similarity of elements, problems, and purposes as would make it relevant art. To be relevant the area or art should be "where one of ordinary skill in the art would be aware that similar problems exist", Stevenson v. ITC, 612 F.2d 546, 550, 204 USPQ 276, 280 (C.C.P.A. 1979).

However the term "art" is expanded, Geo. J. Meyer Manufacturing Co. v. San Marino Electronic Corp., 422 F.2d 1285, 1288, 155 USPQ 231, 236 (9th Cir.1970), the field of "artist easel adapted for adjustably supporting a framed canvas and a pallette" simply has no relevance to the field of "an article carrier for an automobile" or "an article carrier system" for an automobile, and Four Star has not shown by a preponderance of the evidence anything to the contrary.

* * *

5. THE SUBJECT MATTER AS A WHOLE

a. *Claimed Invention*

JONES v. HARDY

United States Court of Appeals, Federal Circuit, 1984.
727 F.2d 1524, 220 USPQ 1021.

MARKEY, CHIEF JUDGE.

Appeal from a judgment of the United States District Court for the Central District of California holding the patents in suit invalid and dismissing pendent unfair competition claims. We *reverse* and *remand.*

BACKGROUND

In construction, some concrete walls have been cast in a horizontal containing form. A polystyrene plastic sheet with a design carved or cut into it, was laid in the form with the design uppermost. Concrete was poured into the form, and after it hardened, the wall was tilted upright and the sheet was removed, leaving a decorated concrete wall surface. The sheet tended to adhere to the wall. Its removal was done in pieces and presented methodology and time-consumption problems.

Robert L. Jones (Jones), in 1963 molded a design in a polystyrene sheet. After concrete poured on the molded sheet had cured, the sheet could be air blown off in one piece. He applied for and obtained U.S. Patents 3,515,779 ('779 patent) entitled "Mold and Method for Casting

Concrete Panels", and 3,702,180 ('180 patent) entitled "Mold for Casting Concrete Panels".

* * *

Independent product claim 1 of the '779 patent recites the combination of an outer frame structure of the containing form and a molded plastic sheet (a "mold") having a "molded intaglio pattern" of artistic relief, and a very limited but flex resistant thickness (from 0.005 to 0.2 times its length, i.e., a "thin face" mold). Claims 2–6 are dependent on claim 1 and add various details of the mold.

Independent method claim 7 recites the steps of forming a thin-face mold by molding a plastic foam against an artistic pattern, positioning the mold in a form, pouring concrete into the form, permitting the concrete to cure, and separating the form and mold from the concrete wall. Dependent claim 8 requires that the plastic be of cellular, expandable polystyrene beads of limited sizes. Dependent claim 9 adds the step of selecting the bead size of the polystyrene beads to control the texture of artistic relief in the concrete wall. Dependent claim 10 recites the added step of vibrating the concrete.

Independent product claim 1 of the '180 patent recites a thin-face plastic foam mold with an intaglio pattern of relief "molded therein". Dependent claims 2–6 add details of the mold.

On August 23, 1974, Jones and Labrado sued Alexander Hardy and Vefo, Inc. (Hardy) for infringement and unfair trade practices. Hardy admitted infringement and defended on the ground that the patents were invalid.

* * *

CLAIMED INVENTION

The invention cannot be tested on the basis of whether the "idea" of using molded polystrene foam is patentable. Under the patent statute, Title 35 U.S.C., "ideas" are not patentable; claimed structures and methods are. Reducing a claimed invention to an "idea", and then determining patentability of that "idea" is error. *W.L. Gore & Associates, Inc. v. Garlock, Inc.,* 721 F.2d 1540, 220 USPQ 303, 308–09 (Fed. Cir.1983). Analysis properly begins with the claims, for they measure and define the invention. *Aro Manufacturing Co. v. Convertible Top Replacement Co.,* 365 U.S. 336, 339, 81 S.Ct. 599, 600–601, 5 L.Ed.2d 592 (1961). Further, each claim must be considered as defining a separate invention. 35 U.S.C. § 282, *supra,* note 1; *Altoona Publix Theaters, Inc. v. American Tri-Ergon Corp.,* 294 U.S. 477, 487, 55 S.Ct. 455, 459, 79 L.Ed. 1005 (1935).

Both patents were characterized as relating to "a method" of constructing a concrete wall. The record contains no discussion of the individual product and method claims of the '779 and '180 patents. There is present an indication that the present invention is the use of a pattern formed by molding polystyrene foam against a positive design because all other aspects of the claim are well known in the art.

Though it is proper to note the difference in a claimed invention from the prior art, because that difference may serve as one element in determining the obvious/nonobviousness issue, it is improper (even if erroneously suggested by a party) to consider the *difference* as the *invention*. The "difference" may have seemed slight (as has often been the case with some of history's great inventions, e.g., the telephone), but it may also have been the key to success and advancement in the art resulting from the invention. Further, it is irrelevant in determining obviousness that all or all other aspects of the claim may have been well known in the art. *Medtronic, Inc. v. Cardiac Pacemakers, Inc.,* 721 F.2d 1563, 220 USPQ 97, 99–100 (Fed.Cir.1983). Hence the statute, the law established not by judges but by Congress, requires that the invention as claimed be considered "as a whole" when considering whether that invention would have been obvious when it was made. 35 U.S.C. § 103.

* * *

The test under § 103 is not whether an improvement or a use set forth in a patent would have been obvious or nonobvious. The test is whether the claimed invention, considered as a whole, would have been obvious or nonobvious. 35 U.S.C. § 103; *Carl Schenck, A.G. v. Nortron Corp.,* 713 F.2d 782, 785, 218 USPQ 698, 700 (Fed.Cir.1983). Failure to consider the claimed invention as a whole is an error of law. *W.L. Gore, supra,* 721 F.2d 1540, 220 USPQ at 309 (error in considering claims in less than their entireties).

* * *

That Jones had not invented a molding process, and that molded plastic has a smooth outer skin, are insufficient bases for the view that "what plaintiffs are actually claiming is the discovery of a new use for an inherent quality of a product long in use in the trade". The difficulty is that that is not what the claims say. Further, the uncontradicted evidence establishes that the claimed product was never used in the trade before Jones invented it.

The "actually claiming" statement appears to have been occasioned by Jones' emphasis at trial on one of the *advantages* of the claimed invention, i.e., releasability or "strippability". But Jones is not "actually claiming" (in the patent sense) releasability. That the claimed invention has the asserted advantage in some installations is not actually contested. That the same advantage went unrecognized for years by users of cut foam and other means of forming relief designs in concrete walls argues for, not against, nonobviousness.

Further, as above indicated, treating the advantage as the invention disregards the statutory requirement that the invention be viewed "as a whole", ignores the problem-recognition element, and injects an improper "obvious to try" consideration. *In re Antonie,* 559 F.2d 618, 195 USPQ 6 (Cust. & Pat.App.1977). * * *

Judges are not constitutionally empowered to legislate their individual subjective views respecting degrees of inventiveness, a distinct approach from that of determining validity on the basis of the evidence and procedural rules. What is required to uphold validity of a patent challenged under § 103 is what Congress in §§ 103 and 282 has said is required, namely, that the patent challenger shall have failed to show that the claimed subject matter as a whole would have been obvious at the time the invention was made to a person having ordinary skill in the art. 35 U.S.C. § 103.

*   *   *

b. Discovery of Problem

EIBEL PROCESS CO. v. MINNESOTA & ONTARIO PAPER CO.

Supreme Court of the United States, 1923.
261 U.S. 45, 43 S.Ct. 322, 67 L.Ed. 523.

This was a bill in equity charging the infringement of a patent and seeking an injunction, an accounting and damages. The patent No. 845,224 issued to William Eibel, February 26, 1907. The application was filed August 22, 1906. The specifications described the patent as for an improvement for Fourdrinier machines for paper making and say that it "has for its object to construct and arrange the machine whereby it may be run at a very much higher speed than heretofore and produce a more uniform sheet of paper which is strong, even, and well formed." The contention of the plaintiff, the petitioner here, is that the improvement was an important step in the art of paper making, and increased the daily product from twenty to thirty per cent.

*   *   *

The Fourdrinier machine has for many years been well known and most widely used for making newsprint paper. Its main feature is an endless wire cloth sieve known as the "wire" is woven with 60 or 70 meshes to the inch. It may be 70 feet or more in length and is often more than 100 inches in width. Its working surface with the total length of 70 feet is about 30 feet, the rest being taken up in the return of the wire underneath. At what is called the breast roll, at one end of the machine, there is discharged upon the wire from a flow box or pond, a constant stream of paper making stock of fibres of wood pulp mixed with from 135 to 200 times their weight of water of the consistency and fluidity of diluted milk. As this stream moves along the wire, the water drains through its meshes and fibres are deposited thereon. The process is stimulated by a device to shake the wire with constant and rapid sidewise thrusts, forward and back, which insures the proper interlocking and felting of the stock as it progresses, the water continuing to drain from it. At the end of the surface length of the wire, the stock reaches what are called the couch rolls between which it is pressed and then in the form of a sheet of uniformly distributed pulp, felted sufficiently to hold together, it leaves the wire and is carried through a series of rolls or calendars by which the sheet is pressed and

dried and from which it emerges to be rolled up as a finished paper.
* * *

Between the breast roll where the stream of liquid stock strikes the wire, and the couch rolls at the end of the surface length of the wire, there is a series of parallel horizontal rolls supporting the wire, called table rolls, and, twenty feet from the breast roll, there are placed under the wire and in contact with it, three suction boxes in succession, in which a partial vacuum is maintained, and through them is sucked out the greater part of the water remaining in the wet sheet of the pulp.
* * *

These machines are very large, some of them weighing more than a million pounds, and their cost will range as high as one hundred twenty-five thousand dollars. They are run night and day in order that the capital invested in them may yield a proper return. Speed which increases production is therefore of the highest importance. Eibel's patent had for its avowed purpose the increase of this speed. * * *

MR. CHIEF JUSTICE TAFT, after stating the case as above, delivered the opinion of the Court.

The evidence in the case establishes that before Eibel entered that field, continued high speeds in the wire of the Fourdrinier machine much beyond five hundred feet a minute resulted in defective paper. Eibel concluded that this was due to the disturbance and ripples in the stock as it was forming at a point between the breast roll and the first suction box, caused by the fact that at that point the wire was traveling much faster than the stock, and that if at that point the speed of the flowing stock could be increased approximately to the speed of the wire, the disturbance and rippling in the stock would cease and the defects would disappear from the paper product. Accordingly he proposed to add to the former speed of the stock by substantially tilting up the wire and giving the stock the added force of the downhill flow. He thought that as long as he could thus maintain equality of speed between stock and wire at the crucial point, and prevent the disturbance and rippling there, a further increase in the speed of the wire would not result in a defective product. He confirmed this by actual trial.

The first and most important question is whether this was a real discovery of merit. The Circuit Court of Appeals thought not. The prior art and the obvious application of the principle that water will run downhill in their opinion robbed it of novelty or discovery. The issue is one largely of evidence. * * *

What Eibel tried to do was to enable the paper maker to go to six or seven hundred feet and above in speed and retain a good product. Did he do it? Eibel was the superintendent of a paper mill at Rhinelander, Wisconsin. Before August, 1906, he raised the pitch of the wire from two or three inches to twelve inches and greatly increased the speed with a satisfactory product, and in that month he applied for a patent. The defendant's witnesses without exception refer to that disclosure as something that surprised and startled the paper-making trade. It spread, to use the expression of one witness, like wildfire. There were those who hesitated to take the venturesome step to give such an unheard-of pitch to the wire and waited until others assumed the risk, but the evidence is overwhelming that within a short interval of a year or two all of the fast machines were run with wires at a pitch of twelve inches and that this pitch has been increased to fifteen and eighteen and even twenty-four inches, that the speed of the machines with satisfactory product has increased to six hundred, six hundred and fifty, and even seven hundred feet, with plans now even for a thousand feet and that the makers of two-thirds of the print paper of the country are licensees of Eibel.

* * *

The Circuit Court of Appeals questions the assumption that gravity was a new factor with Eibel, because the head of the flow box is only another application of the force of gravity. This is a mere criticism of a term which whether accurate or not is not misleading. What Eibel was dealing with in his patent as a new factor was the additional force acquired by the pitch of the wire and that he called gravity, and Judge Hale in the passage quoted uses the word with the same meaning and without any confusion to the reader.

We think, then, that the Eibel patent is to be construed to cover a Fourdrinier machine in which the pitch of the wire is used as an appreciable factor, in addition to the factors of speed theretofore known in the machine, in bringing about an approximation to the equal velocity of the stock and wire at the point where but for such approximation, the injurious disturbance and ripples of the stock would be produced. * * *

The invention was not the mere use of a high or substantial pitch to remedy a known source of trouble. It was the discovery of the source not before known and the application of the remedy for which Eibel was entitled to be rewarded in his patent. Had the trouble which Eibel sought to remedy been the well-known difficulty of too great wetness or dryness of the web at the Dandy roll and had he found that a higher rather than a low pitch would do that work better, a patent for this improvement might well have been attacked on the ground that he was seeking monopoly for a mere matter of degree. But that is not this case. On the other hand, if all knew that the source of the trouble Eibel was seeking to remedy was where he found it to be and also knew that increased speed of the stock would remedy it, doubtless it would not have been invention on his part to use the pitch of the wire to increase the speed of the stock when such pitch had been used before to do the same thing although for a different purpose and in a less degree. We cannot agree with the Circuit Court of Appeals that the causal connection between the unequal speeds of the stock and the wire, and the disturbance and rippling of the stock and between the latter and the defective quality of the paper in high speeds of the machine was so obvious that perception of it did not involve discovery which will support a patent. The fact that in a decade of an eager quest for higher speeds this important chain of circumstances had escaped observation, the fact that no one had applied a remedy for the consequent trouble until Eibel, and the final fact that when he made known his discovery, all adopted his remedy, leave no doubt in our minds that what he saw and did was not obvious and did involve discovery and invention.

* * *

IN RE KASLOW

United States Court of Appeals, Federal Circuit, 1983.
707 F.2d 1366, 217 USPQ 1089.

KASHIWA, CIRCUIT JUDGE.

[Excerpt Only].

In reviewing decisions of the Board which are based on section 103 obviousness grounds, our focus must be whether "the differences between the subject matter sought to be patented and the prior art are such that the *subject matter as a whole* would have been obvious at the time the invention was made." [Emphasis added]. 35 U.S.C. § 103. *See Graham v. John Deere Co.,* 383 U.S. 1, 13, 86 S.Ct. 684, 691, 15 L.Ed. 2d 545 (1966); *Lockheed Aircraft Corp. v. United States,* 553 F.2d 69, 77, 213 Ct.Cl. 395, 193 USPQ 449, 454 (Ct.Cl.1977); *In re Buehler,* 515 F.2d 1134, 1140, 185 USPQ 781, 786 (Cust. & Pat.App.1975). Moreover, the discovery of the source of a problem is a part of the "subject matter as a whole" inquiry. In *In re Sponnoble,* 405 F.2d 578, 585, 56 CCPA 823, 160 USPQ 237, 243 (1969), the Court of Customs and Patent Appeals stated:

> It should not be necessary for this court to point out that a patentable invention may lie in the discovery of the source of a problem even though the remedy may be obvious once the source of the problem is identified. This is *part* of the "subject matter as a whole" which should always be considered in determining the obviousness of an invention under 35 U.S.C. § 103. [Emphasis in original].

See also In Re Peehs, 612 F.2d 1287, 1290, 204 USPQ 835, 837 (Cust. & Pat.App.1980).

c. Simplicity

In considering the expression "the subject matter as a whole" found in Section 103 of the Patent Act of 1952, it is appropriate to examine some of the cases relative to "simple" inventions.

In 1908, the United States Supreme Court observed, in Expanded Metal Co. v. Bradford, 214 U.S. 366, 381, 29 S.Ct. 652, 53 L.Ed. 1034, 1039:

> It is suggested that Golding's improvement, while a step forward, is nevertheless only such as a mechanic skilled in the art, with the previous inventions before him, would readily take; and that the invention is devoid of patentable novelty. It is often difficult to

determine whether a given improvement is a mere mechanical advance, or the result of the exercise of the creative faculty amounting to a meritorious invention. The fact that the invention seems simple after it is made does not determine the question; if this were the rule, many of the most beneficial patents would be stricken down.

In 1959, Circuit Judge Medina, in a case in the Second Circuit Court of Appeals (American Safety Table Co. v. Schreiber, 269 F.2d 255, 263, 122 USPQ 29, 36), made this statement:

> In the last analysis the burden of Schreiber & Goldberg's attack on the first patent for lack of invention comes down to its simplicity. But experience in practically every field of human endeavor has demonstrated that the very simplicity of a new idea is the truest and most reliable indication of novelty and invention, when others have devoted extensive effort and exhausted their resourcefulness in a futile search for the solution of the same vexing problem. Potts v. Creager, 1895, 155 U.S. 597, 608, 15 S.Ct. 194, 39 L.Ed. 275; Lyon v. Bausch & Lomb Optical Co., 2 Cir., 1955, 224 F.2d 530, 534, certiorari denied 350 U.S. 911, 76 S.Ct. 193; H.C. White Co. v. Morton E. Converse & Son Co., 2 Cir., 1927, 20 F.2d 311, 313, certiorari denied, 275 U.S. 547, 48 S.Ct. 85, 72 L.Ed. 419.

CHESAPEAKE & OHIO RY. CO. v. KALTENBACH

United States Court of Appeals, Fourth Circuit, 1938.
95 F.2d 801, 804, 37 USPQ 288, 291.

It is apparent to us that the Kaltenbach patent was a distinct advance in the art that possessed many advantages and arose to the dignity of an invention. Because an idea, once demonstrated, seems simple, it does not follow that it only involves mechanical skill and is not an invention. As was said by Mr. Justice Story in Ryan v. Goodwin, 3 Sumn. 514, Fed.Cas. No. 12,186: "The combination is apparently very simple; but the simplicity of an invention, so far from being an objection to it, may constitute its great excellence and value."

d. Slight Physical Changes

Another aspect of the phrase "the subject matter as a whole," in Section 103, is found in cases which have indicated that a slight physical change can sometimes result in a patentable invention.

TOPLIFF v. TOPLIFF

Supreme Court of the United States, 1892.
145 U.S. 156, 12 S.Ct. 825, 36 L.Ed. 658.

But there is a further distinction between the two devices which ought not to be overlooked. Under the Augur patent, the front ends of the springs are supported upon standards rising from the bolster, and the rear ends upon the links of the connecting-rod, rising perpendicularly above the rear axle. In other words, the links are turned upward, instead of down. This arrangement would evidently be inoperative if the springs were hung at both ends upon links, so placed, since the body of the vehicle would fall down at once upon the axles. In the Topliff and Ely patent, to obviate this, and to enable the device to be applied at both ends of the springs, the links are turned horizontally, or somewhat dependent, so that the springs can rest upon them at both ends, and thus secure a more perfect equalization. Trifling as this deviation seems to be, it renders it possible to adapt the Augur device to any side spring wagon of ordinary construction.

While the question of patentable novelty in this device is by no means free from doubt, we are inclined, in view of the extensive use to which these springs have been put by manufacturers of wagons, to resolve that doubt in favor of the patentees, and sustain the patent.

SCHENCK v. NORTRON CORPORATION

United States Court of Appeals, Federal Circuit, 1983.
713 F.2d 782, 218 USPQ 698.

MARKEY, CHIEF JUDGE.

Appeal from a judgment of the District Court for the Middle District of Tennessee holding U.S. Patent No. 3,182,511 ('511 patent) valid and finding claims 1, 2, and 5 of that patent infringed by Nortron Corporation (Nortron). We *affirm*.

* * *

Nortron points to recognition in the '511 patent of a prior support structure in which legs and cross-pieces are bolted together with notch-and-tooth engaging faces. From that it argues that the present invention was merely the forming of that structure in one piece, a step, Nortron says, that would have been obvious to those skilled in the art at the time the invention was made.

The unchallenged testimony of record establishes that the legs of the notch-and-tooth design are broad leaf springs. Thus, far from eliminating damping (as Nortron asserts) the notch-and-tooth design *introduces* damping, as was pointed out to and accepted by the examiner during prosecution of the application that resulted in the '511 patent.

The uncontested testimony of record further establishes that those skilled in the art believed that damping was required in hard-bearing balancers. Judge Nixon's finding that "many practitioners introduced damping into their measuring devices in order to suppress resonance" is amply supported in the record. * * *

Nortron has pointed to nothing of record that would suggest the replacement of a structure formed of bolted leaf springs and cross bars with a single, unitary, gapless (and thus rigid) structure. On the contrary, the record reflects that that step would remove the flexibility present and thought to be necessary in the former.

In its argument that the invention here is but making integral what had earlier been made in four bolted pieces, Nortron seeks to limit the focus of inquiry to a structural difference from the prior art and then to show that that difference *alone* would have been obvious. That effort is not proper under the statute, which requires that an invention be considered "as a whole," 35 U.S.C. § 103. As Judge Nixon recognized, "the emphasis on nonobviousness is one of inquiry, not quality". *Graham v. John Deere Co.,* 383 U.S. 1, 86 S.Ct. 684, 15 L.Ed. 2d 545 (1966). The inquiry here establishes that the present invention includes the inventor's elimination of the need for damping. Because that insight was contrary to the understanding and expectations of the art, the structure effectuating it would not have been obvious to those skilled in the art. *United States v. Adams,* 383 U.S. 39, 86 S.Ct. 708, 15 L.Ed.2d 572 (1966).

Indeed, hard-bearing balancers had been known since the early 1920's, but had not been successful because of the art-perceived need for mechanisms to dampen resonance. That the *means* of eliminating the need for damping was the one-piece gapless support structure described in the claims detracts in no manner from the contribution to the art made by the inventor. The present invention was a key to the unlocking of a pre-accepted barrier and to the resurrection of hard-bearing balancers, which then replaced widely-used soft-bearing balancers. Nortron was and is at liberty to employ, as it once did, a support formed of separate elements bolted together. That it felt impelled to abandon earlier devices and to employ the unitary structure of the invention is evidence of the latter's value.

*   *   *

While the preceding cases in this section have dealt with physical changes, the next case is directed to chemical compounds wherein the prior art is a homologue of the claimed subject matter.

A homologous series defines a family of chemical compounds whose structure is related and differs regularly by some radical such as ethylene (CH_2). Usually, but not invariably, adjacent homologues have similar properties.

APPLICATION OF PAPESCH

United States Court of Customs and Patent Appeals, 1963.
315 F.2d 381, 137 USPQ 43.

RICH, JUDGE. This appeal is from the decision of the Patent Office Board of Appeals affirming the rejection of claims 1–3, the only claims presented in appellant's application Ser. No. 836,870, filed August 31, 1959, for "2,4,6–TRIALKYLPYRAZOLO [4,3–d]–4,5,6,7–TE-TRAHYDROPYRIMIDINE–5,7–DIONES."

The specification, which is brief and occupies less than three pages of the printed record, states:

"The trialkyl compounds of this invention have been found to possess unexpectedly potent anti-inflammatory activity in contrast to the related trimethyl compound. The instant compounds are also diuretic agents."

Claim 1 reads:

"A compound of the structural formula

[A6655]

wherein R is a lower alkyl radical containing more than one and less than five carbon atoms."

Claim 2 is specific to a compound within claim 1 wherein each R is an ethyl radical (which has, inter alia, 2 carbon atoms) and claim 3 is specific to the n-butyl compound wherein the alkyl radicals each contain 4 carbon atoms. There are no other claims and the legal issue is such that it is unnecessary to distinguish between the claims.

* * *

We have before us, therefore, a single clean-cut issue of law. The claims are rejected only on the ground that they are unpatentable over a single reference which discloses what is conceded to be a lower homologue of the claimed compounds (whether or not all chemists would so consider it) and proof has been given showing that the compound of claim 2, "a representative member of" the group of compounds claimed, possesses an advantageous pharmacological property shown not to be possessed by the prior art compound. In filing the affidavit, appellant stated in his response to the office action that the compounds of his claims 1 and 3 included more distantly related compounds than the triethyl compound tested and submitted that the showing of unpredictable and "completely dissimilar biological properties" established the patentability of the compounds he claimed.

* * *

OPINION

The problem of "obviousness" under section 103 in determining the patentability of new and useful chemical compounds, or, as it is sometimes called, the problem of "chemical obviousness," is not really a problem in chemistry or pharmacology or in any other related field of science such as biology, biochemistry, pharmacodynamics, ecology, or others yet to be conceived. It is a problem of *patent law.*

As everyone knows, section 103 is the statutory version of what was, prior to January 1, 1953, the effective date of the latest revision of the patent statutes, the judge-made requirement of "invention." We are not unaware that we are, in this case, in the field of what has come to be called the "Hass-Henze Doctrine," though the briefs do not mention it by name.[3] The Hass and Henze cases, which *are* mentioned, antedate section 103 and suggest, by way of dicta, that proof of the existence of unobvious or unexpected beneficial properties in a new compound, which would otherwise appear to be obvious (along with its properties), is indicative of the presence of "invention" and hence of patentability. What this comes down to, in final analysis, is a rather simple proposition: If that which appears, at first blush, to be obvious though new is shown by evidence *not* to be obvious, then the evidence prevails over surmise or unsupported contention and a rejection based on obviousness must fall. Many cases, both before and after the enactment of section 103, have been decided according to such reasoning and we shall now discuss a few of them.

Schering Corp. v. Gilbert, 153 F.2d 428 (C.C.A.2d) was decided in 1946. The claim sustained was to a specific chemical compound. It was proved to possess unobvious and highly useful properties as an X-ray contrast agent in cholecystography. The court characterized the claimed invention, "a short claim for one definite chemical compound not found in nature and never previously synthesized," as a "seemingly slight departure from the old." Its approach to the question of patentability was stated thus:

> " * * * it is necessary to understand what the inventors did as well as what they sought to accomplish and *give recognition to their end result* as a novel and useful improvement, *not in the art of organic chemistry but in that of cholecystography.*" [Emphasis added.]

[Discussion of specific case omitted.]

In re Petering and Fall, 301 F.2d 676, 49 CCPA 993, also dealt with compounds stated to have antimetabolite activity as riboflavin antagonists. The rejection of claims 5, 11, and 12 on art was reversed. Judge Martin, again speaking for a unanimous court, said:

> "Although it is also true that some of the specific compounds of Karrer [the reference] * * * are *structurally rather similar* to the compounds defined in claims 5, 11 and 12, * * * there is a *significant difference in properties* between appellants' compounds and Karrer's compounds. [Emphasis added.]

> * * *

> "We do not agree with the board that the unexpected properties of the compounds defined in claims 5, 11 and 12 should not be considered in determining the patentability of these claims. The compounds are

---

3. This "doctrine" was evolved by the bar from this court's opinions in the three cases called In re Hass et al., 141 F.2d 122, 127, 130, 31 CCPA 895, 903, 908, and in In re Henze, 181 F.2d 196, 37 CCPA 1009. See "The Hass-Henze Doctrine," by Alvin Guttag, Dec. 1961 JPOS, Vol. XLIII, No. 12, p. 808. This article commences with a discussion of what is meant by "homolog" and sets forth a definition which would exclude the compounds involved in the present case. In spite of all the talking and writing on the subject, we are not quite sure what the doctrine is but, whatever, it is, insofar as the Hass and Henze cases are concerned, it appears to be based on dicta, since all of those cases affirmed the Patent Office rejections. For some observations on the limitations of the Henze case and the significance of homology, see In re Mills, 281 F.2d 218, 47 CCPA 1185.

not *described* in Karrer within the meaning of 35 U.S.C. § 102(b). In determining whether the claimed compounds are *obvious* within the meaning of 35 U.S.C. § 103, we think their properties may and should be considered, and having considered the properties, we are convinced the compounds * * * are patentable over Karrer."

In that case, the board had taken essentially the same position it took in the present case, saying, "we are not convinced that the ascertainment of the property referred to could make such obvious compounds unobvious as compounds."

From the foregoing cases it will be seen that this and other courts, both before and after the enactment of section 103, have determined the unobviousness and patentability of new chemical compounds by taking into consideration their biological or pharmacological properties. Nine of the ten cases above considered, directly and indirectly, involved such properties. Patentability has not been determined on the basis of the obviousness of structure alone. In fact, where patentability was found in the above cases it was found in spite of close similarity of chemical structure, often much closer similarity than we have here.

Returning now to the decision of the board in this case, we think that it rests on one fundamental error of law, namely, the failure to take into consideration the biological or pharmaceutical property of the compounds as anti-inflammatory agents on the ground that to chemists the structure of the compounds would be *so* obvious as to be beyond doubt, and that a showing of such properties is to be used only to resolve doubt.

From the standpoint of patent law, a compound and all of its properties are inseparable; they are one and the same thing. The graphic formulae, the chemical nomenclature, the systems of classification and study such as the concepts of homology, isomerism, etc., are mere symbols by which compounds can be identified, classified, and compared. But a formula is not a compound and while it may serve in a claim to *identify* what is being patented, as the metes and bounds of a deed identify a plot of land, the *thing* that is patented is not the formula but the compound identified by it. And the patentability of the thing does not depend on the similarity of its formula to that of another compound but of the similarity of the former compound to the latter. There is no basis in law for ignoring any property in making such a comparison. An assumed similarity based on a comparison of formulae must give way to evidence that the assumption is erroneous.

The argument has been made that patentability is here being asserted only on the basis of *one* property, the anti-inflammatory activity, and that the compounds claimed and the compound of the prior art presumably have many properties in common. *Presumably* they do, but presumption is all we have here. The same is true of all of the compounds of the above cases which were held patentable over compounds of the prior art, many of which must have had more in common by way of properties than the compounds here because the relationships, structurally, were even closer than here.

As to the examiner's view that in a case such as this the applicant should claim his invention as a process utilizing the newly discovered property, the board appears to have ignored it, properly we think. It is contrary to practically all of the above decisions wherein no fault was found with granting product claims. Such claims have well-recognized advantages to those in the business of making and selling compounds, in contrast to process-of-use claims, because competitors in the sale of compounds are not generally users.

The solicitor relies heavily on In re Finley and similar cases which we will now consider, arguing that there may be other factors to consider than a difference of a single advantageous property, which is true.

* * * The passage in the Finley opinion relied on by the Patent Office is:

"Obviously appellant construes our holding in those [Hass et al.] cases to mean that if a new and useful product does show unobvious or unexpected beneficial properties it follows that such a product is patentable. We did not affirmatively, or even by implication, so state in our decisions there. Our statement meant merely that unless a product does show the defined characteristics it is not patentable. Even if they be shown, the consideration of other factors may be required. As we said in our decision in the second Hass et al. case, supra, 'Whether novel chemical compounds are patentable over prior art isomers and homologues, is a question to be determined in each case.' "

The principle of the above passage was also reiterated the next year in In re Henze, 181 F.2d 196, 37 CCPA 1009, in the following words:

"Patentability is not resolved conclusively even where unexpected or unobvious beneficial properties are established to exist in novel members of a homologous series over prior art members, as the circumstances of the case *may* require a consideration of other factors. [citing Finley] *A mere difference in degree* is not the marked superiority which ordinarily will remove the unpatentability of adjacent homologues of old substances. In re Loring Coes, Jr., supra [36 CCPA 1067, 173 F.2d 1012, 81 USPQ 369]." [Emphasis added.]

* * *

The other factor of importance which was present in the Finley, Henze, and Coes cases and others of their type is that the prior art disclosure was not merely of a structurally similar compound but also, at least to a degree, of *the same desired property* relied on for patentability in the new compound. Such an "other factor" must of course be considered because it bears on the obviousness of the compound, which is, realistically and legally, a composite of both structure and properties.

As should be apparent from the foregoing, we regard the board's opinion and decision as contrary to well established law. We see no reason to change that law. The decision is therefore reversed.

Reversed.[d]

6. ORDINARY SKILL IN THE ART

The landmark case of Hotchkiss v. Greenwood, 52 U.S. (11 How.) 248, 13 L.Ed. 683 (1850) spoke of "ingenuity or skill * * * possessed by an ordinary mechanic acquainted with the business." This expression or others similar to it have been used by the courts for over a century and finally were incorporated in Section 103 of the Patent Act of 1952.

Clearly, one cannot evaluate the skill of an ordinary mechanic without becoming familiar with the particular art and invention in question. And once this has been accomplished, the particular judge or jury must attempt to determine the level of ordinary skill in solving problems in the art. Until recently, few courts focused on this issue.

ENVIRONMENTAL DESIGNS, LTD. v. UNION OIL COMPANY OF CALIFORNIA

United States Court of Appeals, Federal Circuit, 1983.
713 F.2d 693, 218 USPQ 865.

MARKEY, CHIEF JUDGE.

[Excerpt Only].

LEVEL OF ORDINARY SKILL

Factors that may be considered in determining level of ordinary skill in the art include: (1) the educational level of the inventor; (2) type of problems encountered in the art; (3) prior art solutions to those problems; (4) rapidity with which innovations are made; (5) sophistication of the technology; and (6) educational level of active workers in the field. *Orthopedic Equipment Co., Inc. v. All Orthopedic Appliances, Inc.,* 707 F.2d 1376 at 1381–1382 (Fed.Cir.1983). Not all such factors may be present in every case, and one or more of these or other factors may predominate in a particular case. The important consideration lies in the need to adhere to the statute, *i.e.,* to hold that an invention would or would not have been obvious, as a whole, when it was made, to a person of "ordinary skill in the art"—not to the judge, or to a layman, or to those skilled in remote arts, or to geniuses in the art at hand.

Judge Pfaelzer discussed various factors involved in determining ordinary skill in the art, but did not specify a particular level applicable here. Nor need she have done so, for the parties are in agreement that their respective chemical expert witnesses with extensive backgrounds in sulfur chemistry are persons of ordinary skill in the art.

---

d. See Monsanto Co. v. Rohm and Haas Co., 312 F.Supp. 778, 164 USPQ 556 (D.C. Pa.1970).

7. COMBINING PRIOR ART REFERENCES AND ELEMENTS

ACS HOSPITAL SYSTEMS, INC. v. MONTEFIORE HOSPITAL

United States Court of Appeals, Federal Circuit, 1984.
732 F.2d 1572, 221 USPQ 929.

EDWARD S. SMITH, CIRCUIT JUDGE.

[Excerpt Only].

Turning now to the determination of obviousness under section 103, we conclude that none of the references, either alone or in combination, would have disclosed or suggested to one of ordinary skill in the art the use of override switching means in a television rental system [The claimed invention of the Sonnenberg patent in suit]. The trial court's heavy reliance on the widespread use of override switches appears to be no more than hindsight reconstruction of the claimed invention. The court below identified no source, other than the Sonnenberg patent itself, for the suggestion to use override switching means in a television rental system.

Obviousness cannot be established by combining the teachings of the prior art to produce the claimed invention, absent some teaching or suggestion supporting the combination. Under section 103, teachings of references can be combined *only* if there is some suggestion or incentive to do so. The prior art of record fails to provide any such suggestion or incentive. Accordingly, we hold that the court below erred as a matter of law in concluding that the claimed invention would have been obvious to one of ordinary skill in the art under section 103.

FROMSON v. ADVANCE OFFSET PLATE, INC.

United States Court of Appeals, Federal Circuit, 1985.
755 F.2d 1549, 225 USPQ 26.

MARKEY, CHIEF JUDGE.

Consolidated appeal and cross appeal from a judgment of the United States District Court for the District of Massachusetts, declaring claims 1, 4, 6, 7, 12, and 16 of [Fromson] United States Patent No. 3,181,461 (the '461 patent) invalid and infringed. The judgment of invalidity is reversed; the judgment of infringement is affirmed.

* * *

In modern photo-lithographic printing, a substrate is prepared, light-sensitized, exposed, and then developed. A post-development treatment may be applied to highlight the image so that the printer may see the prepared printing surface. The plate is then mounted on a roller to receive successive water and ink treatments. The prepared and treated surface is then used to print, directly or with an offset mechanism.

* * *

In deciding the question of "whether a patent is invalid for obviousness," the [District] court said it must consider the differences inquiry mandated by the Supreme Court in *Graham v. John Deere Co.,* 383 U.S. 1, 17, 86 S.Ct. 684, 693, 15 L.Ed.2d 545 (1966):

> The Fromson Patent is a combination patent comprised of old elements. The use of aluminum as a substrate in printing is old art. The forming of oxide coatings on aluminum, whether by anodization or other means, was old art. The use of alkali metal silicates, especially sodium silicate, in conjunction with an aluminum base sheet and the subsequent coating with diazo resins was old art with the Jewett patent. The use of light-sensitive coatings generally in lithography was old art. The only difference between the Fromson Patent and the prior art * * * is that the Fromson Patent combines anodization, silication, and application of a sight-sensitive substance into one process. The advantage of the Fromson process is that the oxide layer protects the aluminum base from corrosion, giving it much longer press life, while the silicate layer provides an insoluble, hydrophilic surface that acts as a good anchor for the light-sensitive compound.

* * *

The basic error of law extant here lies in the district court's evaluation of the claimed invention. That evaluation is reflected in the court's statement that the difference between the Fromson invention and the prior art "is that the Fromson patent combines anodization, silication, and application of a light-sensitive substance into one process." At no point did the court indicate, nor does the record indicate, a basis on which it can be said that the making of that combination would have been obvious when it was made.

In a statement conceded by Advance to have been "perhaps unfortunate," the district court characterized the '461 patent as "a combination patent comprised exclusively of old elements." That each "element" was old at the time the invention was made was undisputed in the PTO, at trial, and before this court. There is no basis in the law, however, for treating combinations of old elements differently in determining patentability. *See Stratoflex, Inc. v. Aeroquip Corp.,* 713 F.2d at 1540, 218 USPQ at 880.

The critical inquiry is whether "there is something in the prior art as a whole *to suggest* the desirability, and thus the obviousness, of making the combination." *Lindeman Maschinenfabrik GMBH v. American Hoist & Derrick Co.,* 730 F.2d at 1462, 221 USPQ at 488 (emphasis added).

Where, as here, nothing of record plainly indicates that it would have been obvious to combine previously separate process steps into one process, it is legal error to conclude that a claim to that process is invalid under § 103.

IN RE SERNAKER

United States Court of Appeals, Federal Circuit, 1983.
702 F.2d 989, 217 USPQ 1.

NICHOLS, CIRCUIT JUDGE.

This case is before us on appeal from the decision of the Patent and Trademark Office Board of Appeals (board). In a 2–1 decision, the board affirmed the examiner's rejection, under 35 U.S.C. § 103, of claims 1–6 and 8–11 in appellant's application serial No. 916,018, filed June 15, 1978, entitled "Embroidered Transfer and Method of Making." These claims comprise all the claims in the case. We *reverse.*

I

BACKGROUND

A. The Invention

Appellant has invented a type of embroidered emblem and a method of making the same. * * *

The emblem produced by appellant's method resembles an emblem initially embroidered with different colored threads. Appellant's method, however, circumvents the need to embroider the desired pattern with these different colored threads. Rather, a manufacturer following appellant's method first embroiders the pattern with thread of one color on a substrate, separates the embroidery and its associated substrate from the rest of the substrate, and then essentially dyes the threads different colors by use of a transfer print. Such a transfer print consists of two or more dyestuffs on a piece of paper arranged in a pattern mirroring in shape or "mating" the pattern of the embroidery. By placing the transfer print over the embroidery so that the dyestuffs face the embroidery and match its pattern, and then by applying heat and pressure or vacuum conditions, the dyestuffs on the paper will sublime and then adhere to the matching portion of the embroidery.

Before appellant's invention, a manufacturer would use the Schiffli embroidery machine alone to mass produce embroidery. This large machine, however, cannot stitch thread of more than one color at a time. Thus, to create multicolored patterns, the machine would be shut down after each separate color had been embroidered so its 684 needles could be rethreaded with the next color thread. Since each rethreading procedure takes about 45 minutes, the number of different colors that were commercially feasible to use in a single emblem was limited. With appellant's invented method, on the other hand, a manufacturer can produce an emblem of many colors because he need not rethread the machine anew for each desired color. Instead, only one color (usually white) is used for the entire embroidered pattern, and then the pattern is dyed different colors with one multicolored transfer print.

B. The References

The references relied upon by the board are: * * * The British patent discloses a process of transfer printing on all types of textile articles regardless of their fibers, and a like process of printing on a variety of non-textile articles. * * * The British patent does not specifically mention embroidery as an article susceptible to transfer printing. This patent does, however, teach that a multicolored design may be transferred to textile articles, generally, from a transfer print:

> * * * [S]everal dyes of different colours can be applied on the same support [of the transfer print], these dyes being either intimately mixed *or distributed in order to form the designs* which are to be transferred to the textile articles.

[British, page 2, lines 44–48, emphasis supplied.]

The Miles reference teaches that transfer printing can be done on a variety of substrates, such as substrates of polyester and of carpet tile. Miles specifically states that when transferring designs from a paper transfer print to fiber, perfect contact is not necessary because of the vapor state of the dye when it transfers. * * *

The remainder of the references concern various embroidery techniques and methods of producing embroidered emblems, rather than teachings about transfer printing.

* * *

II

OPINION

A. Whether the board correctly deduced obviousness from the prior art.

We may assume, for purposes of this decision, that all the prior art references in this case are sufficiently related to one another and to a related and common art, that the hypothetical person skilled in the art must be presumed to be familiar with all of them. That being so, the next questions are (a) whether a combination of the teachings of all or any of the references would have suggested (expressly or by implication) the possibility of achieving further improvement by combining such teachings along the line of the invention in suit, and (b) whether the claimed invention achieved more than a combination which any or all of the prior art references suggested, expressly or by reasonable implication. These manifestly related tests are indicated as appropriate by the following decisions of the former Court of Customs and Patent Appeals reviewing, as we do here, decisions of the board denying patentability under § 103 on obviousness grounds.

Cases reversing the board and holding the invention patentable—
* * *

Cases affirming the board and holding the invention unpatentable for obviousness—* * * And there are many others. All these cases are binding precedents in this tribunal, as much as our own will be.

South Corp. v. United States, 690 F.2d 1368 (Fed.Cir.1982). None can be treated as discredited merely because expressions in them can be taken out of their context and construed as in conflict with expressions in other cases. Some minds will prefer the results of the first trio, others of the second. The tests stated above, (a) and (b), were the tests applied in all six cases.

The board majority misdescribed the invention by confusing the embroidery with the substrate and in supposing the inventor just applied a print to a rough substrate instead of a smooth one. It compared the invention with the prior art on the basis of the elements employed being print and substrate. Actually, by both claim 1 and claim 10, there are three component elements. The embroidery is introduced between the print and the substrate. No print is applied to the substrate. It is all applied to the embroidery. The pattern, being "sculptured," intercepts the colors in the print according to the designer's intentions. The print and the pattern (embroidery) are made to "register" (claims 1 and 10 both use this word), *i.e.,* conform. They "mate."

Certainly the board pointed to no prior art that separately suggested expressly or by implication a three-element combination made up in this way. British in general teaches transfer prints on the substrate, as do Miles and Vellins. The remainder do not teach at all about transfer printing. When one skilled in the art at the time of the invention is considering all the prior art in combination, we wholly fail to perceive what more he would have found. The most that would have appeared to have been suggested was the use of transfer prints on rough substrates by which, no doubt, a variety of designs might have been achieved. Mating or registering are suggested nowhere in the prior art. Therefore, it does not show how to approach the results this inventor achieved. No prior art suggests expressly or by implication keeping the print off the substrate and providing a "sculptured" embroidery in a pattern to mate and register with the print.

Although British teaches transfer printing on lace, this patent does not envision the use of a pattern inserted between the transfer print and the lace substrate that would "mate" with the transfer print. Of course the lace substrate itself has an inherent pattern, but British makes no mention of it and does not even hint at mating the transfer print with this pattern. Without some express or implied suggestion, we cannot assume that one of ordinary skill in the art would have found it obvious to mate the transfer print with this pattern. * * *

The conclusion is the same under test (b) as it is under test (a). Under test (b), the person who considered merely combining the teachings of prior art references would not expect from the references or any implication to be drawn therefrom that the great advance made by appellant's invention could be attained. The board never showed how the teachings of the prior art could be combined to make the invention.

* * *

In re Imperato, supra, may be taken as an example of a case when combination of the teachings of prior art references did not suggest the inventor's result. The court therefore reversed the board's holding of obviousness. The invention related to an improvement in the process of "beneficiating" low grade ore to prepare it for the blast furnace. Beneficiation requires grinding the ore to a finely divided state in order to facilitate the removal of impurities. Then, however, it must be recombined into lumps for the furnace. The prior art used various carbonates for bonding to which the inventor added free sulphur. Other prior art taught use of free sulphur only for bonding. The board thought it obvious to combine the two. The court, however, noted that combining both carbonates and sulphur achieved an unexpected result. Both prior processes resulted in lump ore having high strength at low temperatures, but not at high temperatures, whereas the combination obtained a lump ore having high strength in both situations, an unexpected and unobvious result. The lesson of this case appears to be that prior art references in combination do not make an invention obvious unless something in the prior art references would suggest the advantage to be derived from combining their teachings. It does not appear from the opinion that the inventor actually did anything not disclosed somewhere in the prior art references, and in that regard the case was less favorable for unobviousness than the case at bar, where none of the prior art references disclosed an embroidery inserted between the print and the substrate, "registered" or mated the print with the embroidery, not the substrate, and transferred the print to the insert, not to the substrate.

For the foregoing reasons, it is clear that the principal rejection of claims 1, 4–6, and 9–11 cannot be sustained. The four references relied upon by the board for this rejection (British, Miles, Vellins, and Butterick), either separately or in combination, do not suggest that transfer printing techniques should be combined with embroidery techniques in the specific manner claimed in appellant's application.

* * *

8. SECONDARY CONSIDERATIONS

STRATOFLEX, INC. v. AEROQUIP CORPORATION

United States Court of Appeals, Federal Circuit, 1983.
713 F.2d 1530, 218 USPQ 871.

MARKEY, CHIEF JUDGE.

Appeal from a judgment of the District Court for the Eastern District of Michigan, 561 F.Supp. 618, declaring Claims 1, 3, 4, 6, and 7 of U.S. Patent No. 3,473,087 to Winton Slade ('087 patent) invalid and not infringed. We affirm.

When Stratoflex filed suit seeking a declaration of invalidity and non-infringement of the '087 patent, Aeroquip, as assignee, counterclaimed for infringement of claims 1, 3, 4, 6, and 7. After a non-jury trial, Judge Boyle declared those claims invalid and found them not infringed.

* * *

SECONDARY CONSIDERATIONS

It is jurisprudentially inappropriate to disregard any relevant evidence on any issue in any case, patent cases included. Thus evidence rising out of the so-called "secondary considerations" must always when present be considered en route to a determination of obviousness. *In re Sernaker,* 702 F.2d 989, 217 USPQ 1 (Fed.Cir.1983) citing *In re Fielder and Underwood,* 471 F.2d 640, 176 USPQ 300 (Cust. & Pat.App.1973), *see In re Mageli et al.,* 470 F.2d 1380, 1384, 176 USPQ 305, 307 (Cust. & Pat.App.1973) (evidence bearing on issue of nonobviousness "is never of 'no moment', is always to be considered and accorded whatever weight it may have.") Indeed, evidence of secondary considerations may often be the most probative and cogent evidence in the record. It may often establish that an invention appearing to have been obvious in light of the prior art was not. It is to be considered as part of all the evidence, not just when the decisionmaker remains in doubt after reviewing the art.

Judge Boyle made findings on secondary considerations, but said she did not include them in her analysis because she believed the claimed inventions were plainly obvious and "those matters without invention will not make patentability" and should be considered only in a close case. That was error.

Enroute to a conclusion on obviousness, a court must not stop until *all* pieces of evidence on that issue have been fully considered and each has been given its appropriate weight. Along the way, some pieces will weigh more heavily than others, but decision should be held in abeyance, and doubt maintained, until all the evidence has had its say. The relevant evidence on the obviousness-nonobviousness issue, as the Court said in *Graham,* supra, and as other courts had earlier emphasized, includes evidence on what has now been called "secondary considerations." It is error to exclude that evidence from consideration.

* * *

The evidence and findings on secondary considerations being present in the record, the interests of judicial economy dictate its consideration and evaluation on this appeal. The result being unchanged, a remand for reconsideration of the evidence would in this case constitute a waste of resources for the courts and the parties.

A nexus is required between the merits of the claimed invention and the evidence offered, if that evidence is to be given substantial weight enroute to conclusion on the obviousness issue. *Solder Removal Co. v. USITC,* 582 F.2d 628, 637, 65 CCPA 120, 199 USPQ 129, 137 (CCPA 1978) and cases cited therein.

Aeroquip says commercial success is shown because: the "entire industry" makes the tubing claimed in the '087 patent; only Stratoflex is not licensed under the '087 patent; Curtiss-Wright retrofitted 10,000 engines with conductive tubing; and military specifications for conductive tubing are met only by tubing claimed in the '087 patent. We are not persuaded.

Recognition and acceptance of the patent by competitors who take licenses under it to avail themselves of the merits of the invention is evidence of nonobviousness. Here, however, Aeroquip does not delineate the make-up of the "entire industry." The record reflects only two manufacturers, Titeflex and Resistoflex, in addition to the parties. Titeflex has a royalty-free license, resulting from the interference settling agreement described above. Resistoflex has a license that includes several other patents and the right to use the trademark "HI-PAC" for complete hose assemblies. Aeroquip has shown neither a nexus between the merits of the invention and the licenses of record, nor that those licenses arose out of recognition and acceptance of the patent.

No evidence of record establishes that tubing covered by the claims of the '087 patent was used in the Curtiss-Wright retrofit. It cannot therefore be given weight in respect of commercial success.

The military specifications were promulgated after the claimed invention was known. Thus the invention did not meet a longfelt but unfilled need expressed in the specifications. Moreover, the record does not support Aeroquip's assertion that the specifications can be met only by tubing covered by the claims of the '087 patent. The nexus required to establish commercial success is therefore not present with respect to the military specifications.

Nor is there evidence that others skilled in the art tried and failed to find a solution for the problem. Aeroquip cites Abbey and Upham, but their effort was limited to investigation of the problem and its cause, and was not directed to its solution.

Upon full consideration of the evidence respecting the secondary considerations in this case, and of Aeroquip's arguments, we are persuaded that nonobviousness is not established by that evidence. Judge Boyle's error in refusing to include that evidence in her analysis was therefore in this case harmless.

* * *

ROSEMOUNT, INC. v. BECKMAN INSTRUMENTS, INC.

United States Court of Appeals, Federal Circuit, 1984.
727 F.2d 1540, 221 USPQ 1.

MARKEY, CHIEF JUDGE.

Appeals from a judgment of the District Court, Central District of California, that Rosemount's patent No. 3,440,525 ('525 patent) is valid and infringed by Beckman (No. 83–947), and from a judgment of that court that Beckman's post-trial infringement violated its injunction, but denying damages to Rosemount for that infringement (Nos. 83–1238, 83–1251). We *affirm.*

BACKGROUND

In 1965, when Charles Cardeiro made the inventions claimed in the '525 patent, Beckman was the leading manufacturer of pH meters, with 40% of the process pH market. Beckman had a continuous development program designed to maintain and preferably increase its market share. Universal Interlock, Inc. (Uniloc), Rosemount's predecessor in interest, began marketing the pH meter of the '525 patent shortly after Cardeiro invented it. By 1975, Uniloc's annual sales of the patented inventions had grown from zero to many millions of dollars, and Uniloc employees had increased from its 5 founders to 170. Uniloc sold $25,000,000 worth of the patented inventions.

Beginning in 1966, within a year of Uniloc's first sales, Beckman's engineers and salesmen were sending a stream of reports to Beckman about the superiority of Uniloc's pH meters over Beckman's and those of other manufacturers, about customer preference for the patented pH meters, and about sales lost to Uniloc. The reports and Beckman's internal memos praised the patented pH meters as offering "unique and advantageous features", as preferred by users because of no "downtime" and "complete lack of maintenance", and as "low in price".

Having lost sales of the Model "J" it was selling when Cardeiro made his invention, Beckman unsuccessfully attempted to design and market improved pH meters. After studying designs it found in the prior art, Beckman developed a pH meter embodying Cardeiro's concept in 1968. It modified that design upon issuance of the '525 patent in 1969. By 1973, Beckman found its market share had dropped to 27%, due principally to the advent of the patented pH meter, which had captured 25% of the market and was selling at 10% less than Beckman's pH meter. At that point, after evaluating the pH meters of six manufacturers, including its own and Uniloc's, Beckman elected to make and sell the pH meters found to have infringed claims of the '525 patent.

*   *   *

§ 103

As above indicated, Beckman's defense under § 103 consists of an effort to establish that each element of the inventions claimed in the '525 patent can be found in one of four places: Cameron patent disclosing a laboratory pH meter; two Zimmerli articles; literature of a parts manufacturer; and the Fein article. The district court found, and we agree, that this prior art array was not more pertinent than that considered by the PTO and was merely cumulative with the considered art.

Beckman's effort to establish that each element may be found somewhere in the prior art is unavailing. As this court has held, a combination may be patentable whether it be composed of elements all new, partly new, or all old. *Connell v. Sears, Roebuck & Co.,* 722 F.2d 1542, 220 USPQ 193, 199 (Fed.Cir.1983); *Environmental Designs, Ltd. v. Union Oil Co.,* 713 F.2d 693, 218 USPQ 865 (Fed.Cir.1983).

Fatal to Beckman's cause is its inability at trial and here to cite anything in the prior art items, individually or together, that can be seen as suggesting Cardeiro's solution to the drifting problem. Indeed, the facts of real world experience establish the contrary. The art now extolled by Beckman was available to all skilled in the art, including Beckman's own development staff, yet the solution to the drifting problem found by Cardeiro was not obvious to any of them. The same facts refute Beckman's assertion that the advent of field effect transistors rendered the inventions claimed in the '525 patent obvious.

The objective evidence, again composed of real world facts, is worthy of great weight in this case. As found by the district court, that evidence included tremendous commercial success, the filling of a long felt need, failure of others, including Beckman, to solve the problem, copying by Beckman, Beckman's praise of the invention, Cardeiro's departure from expert-accepted principles, and widespread recognition of the invention's significance in the industry. Beckman's argument that a nexus between commercial success and Cardeiro's invention is lacking and its conjecture that some of the commercial success here proven may have been due to elements in non-asserted claims are inadequate to overcome the objective evidence of record.

In sum, Beckman's attack on the validity of the patent under § 103 wholly failed to meet the burden imposed on Beckman under 35 U.S.C. § 282.

9. AT THE TIME THE INVENTION WAS MADE

For many years, the courts have been aware of the dangers of hindsight,—wisdom after the fact,—in the evaluation of an invention. Mr. Justice Frankfurter registered some rather deep feelings on the subject in his now famous and oft quoted dissent in Marconi Wireless Telegraph Co. v. United States, 320 U.S. 1, 60, 63 S.Ct. 1393, 1421, 87 L.Ed. 1731, 1763 (1943):

* * *

It is an old observation that the training of Anglo-American judges ill fits them to discharge the duties cast upon them by patent legislation. The scientific attainments of a Lord Moulton are perhaps unique in the annals of the English-speaking judiciary. However, so long as the Congress, for the purposes of patentability, makes the determination of originality a judicial function, judges must overcome their scientific incompetence as best they can. But consciousness of their limitations should make them vigilant against importing their own notions of the nature of the creative process into congressional legislation, whereby Congress "to promote the Progress of Science and useful Arts" has secured "for limited Times to * * * Inventors the exclusive Right to their * * * Discoveries." Above all, judges must avoid the subtle temptation of taking scientific phenomena out of their contemporaneous setting and reading them with a retrospective eye.

The discoveries of science are the discoveries of the laws of nature, and like nature do not go by leaps. Even Newton and Einstein, Harvey and Darwin, built on the past and on their predecessors. Seldom indeed has a great discoverer or inventor wandered lonely as a cloud. Great inventions have always been parts of an evolution, the culmination at a particular moment of an antecedent process. So true is this that the history of thought records striking coincidental discoveries—showing that the new insight first declared to the world by a particular individual was "in the air" and ripe for discovery and disclosure.

The real question is how significant a jump is the new disclosure from the old knowledge. Reconstruction by hindsight, making obvious something that was not at all obvious to superior minds until someone pointed it out,—this is too often a tempting exercise for astute minds. The result is to remove the opportunity of obtaining what Congress has seen fit to make available.

The inescapable fact is that Marconi in his basic patent hit upon something that had eluded the best brains of the time working on the problem of wireless communication—Clerk Maxwell and Sir Oliver Lodge and Nikola Tesla. * * * But it is now held that in the important advance upon his basic patent Marconi did nothing that had not already been seen and disclosed.

To find in 1943 that what Marconi did really did not promote the progress of science because it had been anticipated is more than a mirage of hindsight. Wireless is so unconscious a part of us, like the automobile to the modern child, that it is almost impossible to imagine ourselves back into the time when Marconi gave to the world what for us is part of the order of our universe. And yet, because a judge of unusual capacity for understanding scientific matters is able to demonstrate by a process of intricate ratiocination that anyone could have drawn precisely the inferences that Marconi drew and that Stone hinted at on paper, the Court finds that Marconi's patent was invalid although nobody except Marconi did in fact draw the right inferences that were embodied into a workable boon for mankind. For me it speaks volumes that it should have taken forty years to reveal the fatal bearing of Stone's relation to Marconi's achievement by a retrospective reading of his application to mean this rather than that. This is for me, and I say it with much diffidence, too easy a transition from what was not to what became.

PANDUIT CORPORATION v. DENNISON MANUFACTURING CO.

United States Court of Appeals, Federal Circuit, 1985.
774 F.2d 1082, 227 USPQ 337.
Vacated and Remanded Per Curiam on Other Grounds, 475 U.S. ___, 106 S.Ct.
1578, 89 L.Ed.2d 817 (1986), and Decision Adhered to on Remand, 810
F.2d 1561, 1 USPQ 2d 1593 (Fed.Cir.1987).

MARKEY, CHIEF JUDGE.

Appeal from a judgment of the United States District Court for the Northern District of Illinois, Eastern Division, holding * * * United States Patent No. 3,537,146 ('146 patent), * * * United States Patent No. 3,660,869 ('869 patent), and * * * United States Patent No. 3,965,538 ('538 patent) invalid on the ground of obviousness, * * *. We reverse.

BACKGROUND

(1) The Art

One-piece cable ties are used to bind a bundle of cables or insulated wires. Looped around the bundle, a strap has one end passed through an opening in a frame at the other end. Teeth on the strap engage with a locking device at the frame. The strap and device operate to permit tensioning of the strap end to prevent its loosening or withdrawal.

Prior art cable ties with rigid locking devices had a desired high strap withdrawal force, but an undesired high strap insertion force. Conversely, those with flexible locking devices had an undesired low withdrawal force and a desired low insertion force.

(2) The Real World Story

As stated in *Rosemount, Inc. v. Beckman Instruments, Inc.*, 727 F.2d 1540, 1544, 221 USPQ 1, 5 (Fed.Cir.1984), many patent suits "arise out of the affairs of people, real people facing real problems." That is true of the present suit.

Jack E. Caveney founded Panduit in the basement of his home in 1955, making first a plastic wiring duct. In 1958, he developed and began selling a two-piece plastic cable tie. In 1961, he began a research program to develop a one-piece plastic cable tie. That program lasted nine years and cost several million dollars. The end result of that program is the tie of the '538 patent, which includes the features of all three patents in suit. Primary among its advantages are the minimal force required to deflect the locking member when the strap is inserted through the frame and the high force required to withdraw the strap from the frame. Jack Caveney was the first to envision and achieve a cable tie having a higher ratio of low strap insertion force and high strap withdrawal force than anyone else had ever achieved or thought possible. Panduit's commercial embodiment of the patents in suit achieves an insertion force of one-half pound and a withdrawal force of 80 pounds.

First sold in 1970, the tie of the '538 patent had by 1984 achieved annual sales of $50 million, and was accounting for half of Panduit's total profits and 80 percent of its cable tie sales.

Beginning in 1968, Dennison Manufacturing Corporation (Dennison) put its staff of engineers and designers to work on a one-piece cable tie development program. It carried that program on at considerable expense for ten years, developing many ties and patenting some. None was successful. With the '869 patent before it, Dennison copied the tie claimed in that patent in 1976. When the '538 patent issued in 1976, Dennison thereupon copied the tie claimed in that patent. Having failed to succeed for over ten years with ties of its own design, Dennison achieved such success with its copy of the '538 tie as to make Dennison the second or third largest supplier of one-piece cable ties.

(3) The Patents in Suit

* * *

The '538 patent issued June 29, 1976 on an application filed May 5, 1969. Figure 9 is representative:

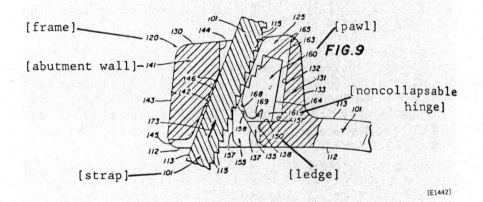

[E1442]

* * *

(1) Hindsight

The record compels the conclusion that the district court, having heard many days of testimony from the inventor Caveney, was unable to cast the mind back to the "time the invention was made." 35 U.S.C. § 103. The court did not, as the statute requires, view the prior art from the perspective of one skilled in the art and uninformed by that testimony. Caveney described in detail the shortcomings of prior art cable ties and the superiority of cable ties constructed in accord with the claims in suit. In deciding the obviousness question, the district court looked to knowledge taught by the inventor Caveney, in his patents and in his testimony, and then used that knowledge against its teacher.

The test is whether the subject matter of the claimed inventions would have been obvious to one skilled in the art at the time the inventions were made, *not* what would be obvious to a judge after reading the patents in suit and hearing the testimony. In the present case, for example, there is no way that one skilled in the art in 1961 and 1968 (necessarily unaided by knowledge of the patents in suit and Caveney's testimony) would find in the prior art either a teaching or a suggestion of the claimed inventions.

Though hindsight was applied to all of the claims and references, a few examples are illustrative. There is no way one skilled in the art would have focused on an incomprehensible phrase in Fein, and ignored his disclosure of a rigid pawl; or would have focused on multiple teeth in Fein and Litwin, while ignoring how those reference structures function and the total absence of an abutment wall; or would have known that the teeth must be "in a straight line and equidistant from the surface of the abutment wall"; or would have learned from the Japanese and Litwin patents, which disclose manually releasable pawls, how to design the non-releasable pawls of the claimed inventions. *W.L. Gore & Assocs., Inc. v. Garlock, Inc.,* 721 F.2d 1540, 1550, 220 USPQ 303, 311 (Fed.Cir.1983). Most importantly, nothing whatever in the prior art would have suggested to one skilled in the art how to produce a cable tie with a one-half pound insertion force and an 80 pound withdrawal force.

The use of hindsight was the more egregious here, where, as discussed below, the court applied a subjective view based on "engineering principles and general principles of physics" and "the common experience of mankind" in the face of a record establishing that those "principles" and that "experience" did not for years suggest the claimed inventions to numerous earlier workers skilled in the art, including Dennison's engineers.

This court and one of its predecessors have cautioned against the use of hindsight:

> It is difficult but necessary that the decisionmaker forget what he or she has been taught at trial about the claimed invention and cast the mind back to the time the invention was made (often as here many years), to occupy the mind of one skilled in the art who is presented only with the references, and who is normally guided by the then-accepted wisdom in the art.

W.L. Gore & Assocs., Inc. v. Garlock, Inc., 721 F.2d at 1553, 220 USPQ at 313.

> It is impermissible to first ascertain factually what appellants *did* and then view the prior art in such a manner as to select from the random facts of that art only those which may be modified and then utilized to reconstruct appellants' invention from such prior art.

In re Shuman, 361 F.2d 1008, 1012, 150 USPQ 54, 57 (CCPA 1966).

In *Stratoflex, Inc. v. Aeroquip Corp.*, 713 F.2d 1530, 1538, 218 USPQ 871, 879 (Fed.Cir.1983), this court noted the conflict with the statute, 35 U.S.C. § 103, when the test applied is whether the claimed invention would have been obvious, not to one skilled in the art when the invention was made, but "to a judge or other layman after learning all about the invention."

10. MANNER IN WHICH THE INVENTION WAS MADE

A man is searching for a way to treat latex, the sap of a rubber tree, in such a way that it will be useful to mankind beyond simply serving as an eraser (rubber). His mental efforts have not produced the answer. He accidentally drops some natural rubber mixed with sulphur on a hot stove and discovers the vulcanization process. Was Charles Goodyear in 1839 using his mind or his imagination? Was he an ordinary mechanic skilled in the art? Was he momentarily using skill beyond that of the ordinary mechanic? Did he have a "flash of genius"? Probably we can answer "no" to all these questions. He was just lucky. Or in finer terms, he experienced "serendipity," defined in the Oxford Universal Dictionary (1964) as the faculty of making happy and unexpected discoveries by accident. Goodyear, of course, knew what he was looking for, and, in this respect, he was able to recognize the vulcanized rubber when he found it.

Thus, ideas, inventions, discoveries, can come as a result of laborious experiments and trial and error efforts, from "happy thoughts" or lucky accidents, from the imagination bridging the gaps of logical deduction as distinguished from a reasoned answer. A person with ordinary skill in the art accomplishes something requiring extraordinary skill on that particular day when the answer he has been seeking finally appears.

The Supreme Court in Cuno Engineering Corp. v. Automatic Devices Corporation, supra in determining patentability indicated that a new device "must reveal the flash of creative genius, not merely the skill of the calling." Similarly, Justice Douglas made reference to "creative genius" in his concurring opinion in *The Great Atlantic & Pacific Tea Co.* case, supra.

In the 1952 Patent Act, the "flash of genius", as a test of level of innovation, was explicitly rejected in the second sentence of Section 103 which in part states:

Patentability shall not be negatived by the manner in which the invention was made.

In Graham v. John Deere Co., 383 U.S. 1, 15, 86 S.Ct. 684, 692, 15 L.Ed. 2d 545 (1966), the Supreme Court indicated that no connotation of the frame of mind of an inventor was intended by this controversial phrase, rather, it was a rhetorical embellishment of the "skill of the calling" test, and had been abolished by Congress.

11. A QUESTION OF LAW OR FACT

In perusing the last section, the reader would clearly recognize that a judge or jury, in determining the state of a particular art and the skill of an ordinary mechanic in that art, would be examining facts. Likewise, consideration of what prior art references disclose, and such testimony as experts might give, involves the evaluation of facts. Is there then any need for review of the question of nonobviousness? Should the ultimate decision as to this question by the trier of fact, who has observed the demeanor of the witnesses and heard the evidence, be sustained in the absence of a determination that such decision is totally unsupported by the evidence?

MOORE v. WESBAR CORPORATION

United States Court of Appeals, Seventh Circuit, 1983.
701 F.2d 1247, 217 USPQ 684.

CUDAHY, CIRCUIT JUDGE.

[Excerpt Only].

An initial question confronting us in this case is that of the scope of our review of the district court's findings on obviousness. The defendants here assert that our task is limited to assessing whether Judge Reynolds followed the legal standard prescribed in *Graham v. John Deere*, 383 U.S. 1, 86 S.Ct. 684, 15 L.Ed.2d 545 (1966), and maintain that findings based on that standard may not be overturned unless they are clearly erroneous. Plaintiffs, on the other hand, insist that validity of a patent, including the question of obviousness, is a question of law, which this court may decide *de novo*. A clarification of this issue is clearly a prerequisite to our addressing the issue of obviousness. The ultimate legal question which this court must answer, of course, is that posed by the statute: "[whether] the differences between the subject matter sought to be patented and the prior art are such that the subject matter as a whole would have been obvious at the time the invention was made to a person having ordinary skill in the art to which said subject matter pertains." 35 U.S.C. § 103 (1976). On this question—nonobviousness as a condition for the validity of a patent—this court is entitled—in fact, obliged—to make an independent judgment. *E-T Industries v. Whittaker Corp.*, 523 F.2d 636 (7th Cir.1975), *cert. denied*, 429 U.S. 870, 97 S.Ct. 182, 50 L.Ed.2d 150 (1976); *see also Dual Manufacturing & Engineering, Inc. v. Burris Industries*, 619 F.2d 660, 663 (7th Cir.) (en banc), *cert. denied*, 449 U.S. 870, 101 S.Ct. 208, 66 L.Ed.2d 90 (1980).

Nonetheless, in the *Graham* case, the Supreme Court has directed that a district court considering the *legal* question of obviousness must undertake a preliminary, three-part *factual* inquiry into the scope and content of the prior art, the differences between the prior art and the claim at issue and the level of ordinary skill in the pertinent art. 383 U.S. at 17, 86 S.Ct. at 693. This tripartite inquiry is intended to establish a background of fact against which the ultimate statutory question may be answered; and the findings made by the district court pursuant to this inquiry are findings of fact, which may not be set aside unless clearly erroneous. Fed.R.Civ.P. 52(a). An exception is sometimes made in cases where the evidence on these findings is wholly documentary or involves the actual examination of a product or device in operation, *Deep Welding, Inc. v. Sciaky Bros.,* 417 F.2d 1227, 1229 (7th Cir.1969), *cert. denied,* 397 U.S. 1037, 90 S.Ct. 1354, 25 L.Ed.2d 648 (1970). But, where the district court's findings instead rest, as here, upon a combination of documentary and testimonial evidence, we must accept those findings, unless they are clearly erroneous. *LaSalle Street Press v. McCormick & Henderson, Inc.,* 445 F.2d 84, 87 (7th Cir.1971). In this case, Judge Reynolds listened to five days of testimony before making the findings of fact required by the *Graham* case; and we would not presume to overturn those findings unless it were clear to us that they were in error. Instead, we think the judge's findings were well-supported. Accepting those findings, however, we must nonetheless independently review his conclusion that the Bloodgood patent was obvious and thus invalid.

12. PRESUMPTION AND BURDEN

AMERICAN HOIST & DERRICK COMPANY v. SOWA & SONS, INC.

United States Court of Appeals, Federal Circuit, 1984.
725 F.2d 1350, 220 USPQ 763.

RICH, CIRCUIT JUDGE.

[Excerpt Only].

American Hoist and Derrick Co. (AmHoist) appeals from the unpublished decision of the United States District Court for the District of Oregon holding for Sowa & Sons, Inc. (Sowa) on AmHoist's suit for infringement of claims 3, 5, and 7 of its Shahan U.S. Patent No. 4,079,584, issued March 21, 1978, for a "Heavy Duty Shackle." * * *

1. 35 U.S.C. § 282

With respect to the burden of proof, the court instructed the jury as follows:

> If you find the prior art references which defendant has cited are no more pertinent than the art utilized by the examiner when examining the Shahan patent[,] then defendant has the burden of establishing obviousness by "clear and convincing evidence." If, on the other hand, you find any of the prior art references which defendant has cited are more pertinent than the art utilized by the examiner when examining the Shahan patent, then that presumption of validity *disappears* as to that issue of obviousness and the *plaintiff has the burden of proof* by a preponderance of the evidence. [Emphasis ours.]

That instruction was erroneous in two respects. First, it misassigned the burden of proof. The final sentence of 35 U.S.C. § 282 mandates that "The burden of establishing invalidity of a patent or any claim thereof shall rest on the party asserting such invalidity." Precedent adopted by this court pursuant to *South Corp. v. United States,* 690 F.2d 1368, 1369, 215 USPQ 657, 658 (Fed.Cir.1982), declares that burden to be permanent, emphasizing that § 282

> * * * mandates not only a presumption shifting the burden of going forward in a purely procedural sense, but also *places the burden of persuasion on the party who asserts that the patent is invalid.* To speak of the presumption as "no longer attaching" is to risk a concomitant, and unspoken, assumption that the burden of persuasion is thereafter no longer upon him who asserts invalidity. That view is contrary to the meaning of § 282, for *the burden of persuasion is and remains always upon the party asserting invalidity,* whether the most pertinent prior art was or was not considered by the examiner. [Emphasis ours.]

Solder Removal Co. v. U.S. International Trade Commission, 582 F.2d 628, 632–33, 199 USPQ 129, 133 (CCPA 1978) (footnotes omitted). *SSIH Equipment, S.A. v. U.S. International Trade Comm.,* 718 F.2d 365, 375, 218 USPQ 678, 687 (1983). On this point we, like the CCPA, disagree with the Ninth Circuit position stated in *Tveter,* supra note 1, which was that because the examiner did not have certain prior art patents before him when examining the application for the patent in suit, which patents were closer art than he cited, the burden of proving nonobviousness was on the patentee. Our position is that this is never so because it would be contrary to the statute.

The second and more general error in the above jury instruction was that it failed to explain accurately the "presumption of validity," which is not surprising. The prevailing confusion in the cases over its meaning and effect has been engendered by assertions that under some circumstances the presumption is retained and under others it is destroyed, or that the presumption is strengthened or weakened, as a result of which, it has been said, the burden of proof shifts from one party to another or the standard of proof changes.

The presumption was, originally, the creation of the courts and was a part of the judge-made body of patent law when the Patent Act of 1952 was written. That act, for the first time, made it statutory in § 282, first paragraph, which, before the amendments of 1965 and 1975, was of the utmost simplicity. It read:

A patent shall be presumed valid. The burden of establishing invalidity of a patent shall rest on the party asserting it.

* * *

The two sentences of the original § 282, which, though added to, have not been changed, amount in substance to different statements of the same thing: the burden is on the attacker. And, as this court has been saying in other cases, that burden never shifts. The only question to be decided is whether the attacker is successful. When no prior art other than that which was considered by the PTO examiner is relied on by the attacker, he has the added burden of overcoming the deference that is due to a qualified government agency presumed to have properly done its job, which includes one or more examiners who are assumed to have some expertise in interpreting the references and to be familiar from their work with the level of skill in the art and whose duty it is to issue only valid patents. In some cases a PTO board of appeals may have approved the issuance of the patent.

When an attacker, in sustaining the burden imposed by § 282, produces prior art or other evidence *not* considered in the PTO, there is, however, *no reason to defer* to the PTO so far as *its* effect on validity is concerned. Indeed, new prior art not before the PTO may so clearly invalidate a patent that the burden is fully sustained merely by proving its existence and applying the proper law; but that has no effect on the presumption or on who has the burden of proof. They are static and in reality different expressions of the same thing—a single hurdle to be cleared. Neither does the *standard* of proof change; it must be by clear and convincing evidence or its equivalent, by whatever form of words it may be expressed. *See Radio Corp.,* supra. What the production of new prior art or other invalidating evidence not before the PTO does is to eliminate, or at least reduce, the element of deference due the PTO, thereby partially, if not wholly, *discharging* the attacker's burden, but neither shifting nor lightening it or changing the standard of proof. When an attacker simply goes over the same ground travelled by the PTO, part of the *burden* is to show that the PTO was wrong in its decision to grant the patent. When new evidence touching validity of the patent not considered by the PTO is relied on, the tribunal considering it is not faced with having to *disagree* with the PTO or with *deferring* to its judgment or with taking its expertise into account. The evidence may, therefore, carry more weight and go further toward sustaining the attacker's unchanging burden.

To summarize on this point, § 282 creates a presumption that a patent is valid and imposes the burden of proving invalidity on the attacker. That burden is constant and never changes and is to convince the court of invalidity by clear evidence. Deference is due the Patent and Trademark Office decision to issue the patent with respect to evidence bearing on validity which it considered but no such deference is due with respect to evidence it did not consider. All evidence bearing on the validity issue, whether considered by the PTO or not, is to be taken into account by the tribunal in which validity is attacked.

IN RE ETTER

United States Court of Appeals, Federal Circuit, 1985.
756 F.2d 852, 225 USPQ 1.

MARKEY, CHIEF JUDGE.

[Excerpt Only].

Etter's basic contention—that § 282 must be applied in reexamination proceedings—misconstrues the purposes for which that statute and the reexamination statutes were enacted. Review of the statutes, legislative history, regulations, and case law compels the view that § 282 is not applicable to claims about which "a substantial new question of patentability," 35 U.S.C. § 305, is under consideration in a reexamination proceeding. * * *

No statutory language and no legislative history indicates any support for a requirement that the provisions of 35 U.S.C. § 282 must be applied in the consideration of claims involved in reexamination proceedings. Indeed, all available indications are to the contrary. We hold, therefore, that § 282 has no application in reexamination proceedings.

It is at best incongruous to apply a trial court procedural rule to the examination of claims in the PTO. Moreover, because this court and one of its predecessors has consistently held that the PTO examiner has the burden of showing a basis under the statute, 35 U.S.C., for each rejection, injection of the presumption into the examination process could add nothing but legalistic confusion.

* * *

G. UTILITY

The Constitutional provision, Art. 1, Sec. 8, gives Congress the power to "promote the progress of science and the useful arts." United States patent statutes since 1790 have included the word "useful" as a qualification for a patentable invention. The present statute reads (Section 101)

Whoever invents or discovers any new and useful process, machine, manufacture, or composition of matter, or any new and *useful* improvement thereof, may obtain a patent therefor, subject to the conditions and requirements of this title.

As a practical matter, one can conclude that a patent on a useless device would be worthless and, accordingly, present no problems in litigation. In addition, the patent grant itself, which is sometimes said to be a contract between the inventor and government, would fail for lack of consideration if what is disclosed is useless. The Patent Office should not be required to process applications on devices of no utility since this would be a waste of its facilities and manpower. Since applicants for a patent must spend a considerable sum in government fees, drawing expense and attorney's fees to present an application to the Patent Office, one is led to wonder how the question of utility or usefulness could arise. Why would a person or company spend time and money promulgating a patent application unless there was advance evidence that the device was practical?

Despite the logic of the matter, there have been a number of intriguing questions which have arisen in the cases surrounding the meaning of the word "useful" in the statute. Can a person patent an article or composition of matter which has no present utility but may in the future become very useful? Does a patentable device have to be useful to all, or just to a special group, and does the use have to be a generally beneficial one? What tests will be used for utility?

The early statutes required the presentation of a model "if the nature of the invention or discovery will admit of a model" (1790); if the Secretary of State "shall deem such model to be necessary" (1793); "in all cases which admit of a representation of a model, of a convenient size to exhibit advantageously its several parts" (1836). With the presentation of a model, an Examiner could determine to some degree the utility of an invention. However, later statutes have omitted this requirement for a model, and it must be recognized that many patent applications are presented prior to any "reduction to practice," that is, prior to any practical and actual demonstration of the subject invention.[a]

An early treatment of the issue of utility is found in the instructions to the Jury by Circuit Justice Story in Bedford v. Hunt, 1 Mason, 302, 3 Fed.Cas. 37 (No. 1217) (C.C.D.Mass.1817).

> By useful invention, in the statute, is meant such a one as may be applied to some beneficial use in society, in contradistinction to an invention, which is injurious to the morals, the health, or the good order of society. It is not necessary to establish, that the invention is of such general utility, as to supersede all other inventions now in practice to accomplish the same purpose. It is sufficient, that it has no obnoxious or mischievous tendency, that it may be applied to practical uses, and that so far as it is applied, it is salutary. If its practical utility be very limited, it will follow, that it will be of little or no profit to the inventor; and if it be trifling, it will sink into utter neglect. The law, however, does not look to the degree of utility; it simply requires, that it shall be capable of use, and that the use is such as sound morals and policy do not discountenance or prohibit. In the present case there cannot be the slightest doubt, upon the evidence, that the patent is for a useful invention, in a very large sense.

Courts have in some instances talked of "morals, health, and good order of society" in determining utility. Anyone whose life has spanned a decade or two in the 20th Century has witnessed how moral standards can change in a period of a few years. Gambling devices, frowned upon early in the century, are legalized in several states; race

---

a. 35 U.S.C.A. § 114 provides—"The Commissioner may require the applicant to furnish a model of convenient size to exhibit advantageously the several parts of his invention. When the invention relates to a composition of matter, the Commissioner may require the applicant to furnish specimens or ingredients for the purpose of inspection or experiment." Rule 92 of the Rules of Practice in patent cases promulgated by the Commissioner provides: "A model, working model, or other physical exhibit, may be required if deemed necessary for any purpose on examination of the application." The Manual of Patent Examining Procedure, 5th Edition, August 1983, as revised December 1985, in Section 608.03 states with respect to Rule 92 that "With the exception of cases involving perpetual motion, a model is not ordinarily required by the Office to demonstrate the operativeness of a device. If operativeness of a device is questioned, the applicant must establish it to the satisfaction of the Examiner, but he may choose his own way of so doing."

tracks and lotteries are now used to generate substantial amounts of income in many states. Birth control devices, in a period of thirty to forty years, have come from a position of illegality to a position where they are welcomed by some as a means of curbing a population explosion. Thus, in determining "utility" based on public mores, the courts should apply a test which will not penalize an inventor who may be prescient enough to be anticipating basic needs of a society changed by forces yet unrecognized by the general public.

When an application for a patent is directed to a well-known product such as a hammer or pair of pliers, a bicycle or even an airplane, there would probably be no necessity for stating what the device was to be used for. There is, in a sense, an implied statement of utility which would not be challenged by the Patent Office or an infringer. Indeed, one rarely sees a portion of a patent specification entitled "Utility" although the objects of the invention and a description of the operation usually found in a patent specification will generally make clear what is the purpose of the device being described. However, there must be an expression of utility either by implication or directly, In re Christmann et al., 128 F.2d 596, 53 USPQ 634 (CCPA 1942).[b] As pointed out in the decision of the Court of Customs and Patent Appeals, In re Bremmer et al., 182 F.2d 216, 217, 86 USPQ 74, 75 (1950):

> It is our view that no "hard and fast" ruling properly may be made fixing the extent of the disclosure of utility necessary in an application, but we feel certain that *the law requires that there be in the application an assertion of utility and an indication of the use or uses intended.*

> It was never intended that a patent be granted upon a product, or a process producing a product, unless such product be useful. See subsection 8 of section 8 of Article I, United States Constitution;

In some instances, the expressed utility may be based on an intellectual speculation or a theory which cannot be accepted by the Patent Office or a court.[c] Here again, the tests that are used by the

---

b. In re Hitchings et al., 342 F.2d 80, 87, 144 USPQ 637, 643 (CCPA 1965): With regard to the question of the "how to use" requirement of section 112, we note that the parent application contains no information whatever concerning methods or manner of administration, dosages, etc. In short, there is a complete absence of *express* disclosure of how to use the claimed compounds. Such a lack, however, does not per se render the disclosure inadequate under section 112. All the statute requires is that the disclosure be one which will "enable any person skilled in the art to which it pertains, or with which it is most nearly connected," to make and use the invention. Thus, where the manner of using a claimed compound is obvious to one of ordinary skill in the particular art, even though the specification is utterly barren of any express teaching of how to use, this court has found compliance with section 112. In re Johnson, 48 CCPA 733, 282 F.2d 370, 127 USPQ 216.

c. Mahler v. Animarium Co., 111 Fed. 530 (8th Cir.1901) for treatment of human diseases by disturbance of the electrical equilibrium of the body; In re Perrigo, 48 F.2d 965, 9 USPQ 152 (CCPA 1931) relating to an electromotive force, and In re Oberweger, 115 F.2d 826, 47 USPQ 455 (CCPA 1940) relating to a composition for producing hair growth. See also Radoev v. Brenner, Com'r of Patents, 253 F.Supp. 923, 148 USPQ 702 (D.D.C.1966); Ex parte Paschal, 88 USPQ 131 (Pat. Office Bd. Appeals 1950); and Ex Parte Timmis, 123 USPQ 581 (Pat. Office Bd. Appeals 1959).

reviewing body must be examined. Cases which involve therapeutic or pharmaceutical devices or compositions present greater difficulties.

The following cases or brief excerpts illustrate some of the requirements for, and some of the problems which arise in the determination of "utility" of the subject matter of patent applications and patents.

EX PARTE MURPHY ET AL.

United States Patent and Trademark Office Board of Appeals, 1977.
200 USPQ 801.

MESSENHEIMER, EXAMINER-IN-CHIEF.

This is an appeal from the final rejection of claims 1 through 7, which are all of the claims in the application.

The application discloses an amusement device having three symbol-bearing wheels which are activated by the insertion of a coin or token and the pull of a handle. An electrical circuit having feelers which detect the position of the wheels when stopped is employed to determine whether a player has won, and, if so, to what extent that player has won.

We view the disclosed amusement device to be what is commonly referred to as a "slot machine" or "one-armed bandit."   *   *   *

The sole basis of the rejection of all of the claims is under 35 U.S. C.A. § 101 as lacking patentable utility. Reliance was placed on Chicago Patent Corporation v. Genco, Inc., 124 F.2d 725, 52 USPQ 3 (7th Circuit, 1941); Davies, Sheriff v. Mills Novelty Co., 70 F.2d 424 (8th Circuit, 1934); and Ex parte Segers, Appeal No. 906–38, Board of Appeals, 1970, unpublished but available under the provisions of 37 CFR 1.14(d).

In making the rejection the examiner stated that the instant apparatus is, in fact, a gambling device operated by money, dependent upon chance, with a payoff in money. He continued by asserting that all twenty-nine pages of the specification relate solely to a gambling machine. Nowhere is there a disclosure of its being used for amusement only.

Appellants argue that there is no statutory basis for this rejection; it involves the passing of a moral judgment by the Patent and Trademark Office, a judgment which it is in no way qualified to make. Appellants point out that gambling including the use of coin-operated gambling machines is legal in many jurisdictions in the United States, that the manufacture and shipment of coin-operated gambling machines in interstate commerce is perfectly legal in the United States and, to the extent there was a prevailing public or judicial view that coin-operated gambling devices were harmful to public morals or to the public welfare, that view is long gone and that the rejection of the claims on the ground stated is inconsistent with the treatment given by the Patent and Trademark Office to similar devices over a long period of time.

We find ourselves in agreement with appellants and recognize that while some may consider gambling to be injurious to the public morals and the good order of society, we cannot find any basis in 35 U.S.C.A. § 101 or related sections which justify a conclusion that inventions which are useful only for gambling ipso facto are void of patentable utility.

From a historical standpoint, we think the guiding principles were set forth in Fuller v. Berger, 120 F.2d 274 (7th Circuit, 1903), cert. denied 193 U.S. 668 where the court stated:

"* * * With regard to the defense of no utility (available equally at law and in equity), we hold that the true inquiry is, Was the Government improvident in making the grant? Does the opposing evidence, the grant itself being prima facie proof of utility, go to the extent of establishing not merely that the device has been used for pernicious purposes, *but that it is incapable of serving any beneficial end?* As the just criterion, we approve and adopt Mr. Walker's conclusion (section 82 (3d Ed.)), with the additions to his text which we note by parentheses:

"An important question, relevant to utility in this aspect, may hereafter arise and call for judicial decision. It is perhaps true, for example, that the invention of Colt's revolver was injurious to the morals, and injurious to the health, and injurious to the good order of society. That instrument of death may have been injurious to morals, in tending to tempt and to promote the gratification of private revenge. It may have been injurious to health, in that it is very liable to accidental discharge, and thereby to cause wounds, and even homicide. It may also have been injurious to good order, especially in the newer parts of the country, because it facilitates and increases private warfare among frontiersmen. On the other hand, the revolver, by furnishing a ready means of self-defense, may sometimes have promoted morals and health and good order. By what test, therefore, is utility to be determined in such cases? Is it to be done by balancing the good functions with the evil functions? *Or is everything useful within the meaning of the law, if it is used (or is designed and adapted to be used) to accomplish a good result, though in fact it is oftener used (or is as well or even better adapted to be used) to accomplish a bad one?* Or is utility negatived by the mere fact that the thing in question is sometimes injurious to morals, or to health, or to good order? The third hypothesis cannot stand, because if it could, it would be fatal to patents for steam engines, dynamos, electric railroads, and indeed many of the noblest inventions of the nineteenth century. [And what of such things as automobiles, airplanes, tires, power tools, explosives, lawn mowers, and drugs in the twentieth century?] The first hypothesis cannot stand, because if it could, it would make the validity of the patents to depend on a question of fact to which it would often be impossible to give a reliable answer. *The second hypothesis is the only one which is consistent with the*

> *reason of the case, and with the practical construction which the courts have given to the statutory requirement of utility.*

We deem the additions to the second hypothesis necessary to complete statement of the acceptable test, for, to continue with Colt's revolver as an example, if at the time of a suit for infringement the defendant should prove that the only uses to which 'that instrument of death' had been put were vicious, the patent should not be held void for want of utility, if the court for itself should see, or be convinced by experts, that the instrument was susceptible of good uses, though in fact never put to such before the suit was begun. And, if utility is found, the cases seem to be uniform that courts will not set up a measure of utility which must be filled." [Emphasis supplied.]

* * *

For the reasons stated above, the rejection under 35 U.S.C.A. § 101 based on lack of patentable utility will not be sustained.

Reversed.

BRENNER, COMM'R OF PATENTS v. MANSON

Supreme Court of the United States, 1966.
383 U.S. 519, 86 S.Ct. 1033, 16 L.Ed.2d 69.

MR. JUSTICE FORTAS delivered the opinion of the Court.

This case presents two questions of importance to the administration of the patent laws: First, * * * and second, whether the practical utility of the compound produced by a chemical process is an essential element in establishing a prima facie case for the patentability of the process. The facts are as follows: * * *

A Patent Office examiner denied Manson's application, and the denial was affirmed by the Board of Appeals within the Patent Office. The ground for rejection was the failure "to disclose any utility for" the chemical compound produced by the process. Letter of Examiner, dated May 24, 1960. This omission was not cured, in the opinion of the Patent Office, by Manson's reference to an article in the November 1956 issue of the Journal of Organic Chemistry, 21 J.Org.Chem. 1333–1335, which revealed that steroids of a class which included the compound in question were undergoing screening for possible tumor-inhibiting effects in mice, and that a homologue adjacent to Manson's steroid had proven effective in that role. Said the Board of Appeals, "It is our view that the statutory requirement of usefulness of a product cannot be presumed merely because it happens to be closely related to another compound which is known to be useful."

The Court of Customs and Patent Appeals (hereinafter CCPA) reversed, Chief Judge Worley dissenting. 52 CCPA (Pat.) 739, 745, 333 F.2d 234, 237–238. The court held that Manson was entitled to a declaration of interference since "where a claimed process produces a known product it is not necessary to show utility for the product," so long as the product "is not alleged to be detrimental to the public interest." Certiorari was granted, 380 U.S. 971, 85 S.Ct. 1334, 14 L.Ed. 2d 267, to resolve this running dispute over what constitutes "utility" in chemical process claims, * * *

Our starting point is the proposition, neither disputed nor disputable, that one may patent only that which is "useful." In Graham v. John Deere Co., 383 U.S. 1, at 5–10, 86 S.Ct. 684, 15 L.Ed.2d 545, at 549–552, we have reviewed the history of the requisites of patentability, and it need not be repeated here. Suffice it to say that the concept of utility has maintained a central place in all of our patent legislation, beginning with the first patent law in 1790 and culminating in the present law's provision that "Whoever invents or discovers any new and useful process, machine, manufacture, or composition of matter, or any new and useful improvement thereof, may obtain a patent therefor, subject to the conditions and requirements of this title."

As is so often the case, however, a simple, everyday word can be pregnant with ambiguity when applied to the facts of life. That this is so is demonstrated by the present conflict between the Patent Office and the CCPA over how the test is to be applied to a chemical process which yields an already known product whose utility—other than as a possible object of scientific inquiry—has not yet been evidenced. * * *

Respondent does not—at least in the first instance—rest upon the extreme proposition, advanced by the court below, that a novel chemical process is patentable so long as it yields the intended product and so long as the product is not itself "detrimental." Nor does he commit the outcome of his claim to the slightly more conventional proposition that any process is "useful" within the meaning of § 101 if it produces a compound whose potential usefulness is under investigation by serious scientific researches, although he urges this position, too, as an alternative basis for affirming the decision of the CCPA. Rather, he begins with the much more orthodox argument that his process has a specific utility which would entitle him to a declaration of interference even under the Patent Office's reading of § 101. The claim is that the supporting affidavits filed pursuant to Rule 204(b), by reference to Ringold's 1956 article, reveal that an adjacent homologue of the steroid yielded by his process has been demonstrated to have tumor-inhibiting effects in mice, and that this discloses the requisite utility. We do not accept any of these theories as an adequate basis for overriding the determination of the Patent Office that the "utility" requirement has not been met.

Even on the assumption that the process would be patentable were respondent to show that the steroid produced had a tumor-inhibiting effect in mice, we would not overrule the Patent Office finding that respondent has not made such a showing. The Patent Office held that, despite the reference to the adjacent homologue, respondent's papers did not disclose a sufficient likelihood that the steroid yielded by his process would have similar tumor-inhibiting characteristics. Indeed, respondent himself recognized that the presumption that adjacent homologues have the same utility has been challenged in the steroid field because of "a greater known unpredictability of compounds in that field." In these circumstances and in this technical area, we would not overturn the finding of the Primary Examiner, affirmed by the Board of Appeals and not challenged by the CCPA.

* * *

Whatever weight is attached to the value of encouraging disclosure and of inhibiting secrecy, we believe a more compelling consideration is that a process patent in the chemical field, which has not been developed and pointed to the degree of specific utility, creates a monopoly of knowledge which should be granted only if clearly commanded by the statute. Until the process claim has been reduced to production of a product shown to be useful, the metes and bounds of that monopoly are not capable of precise delineation. It may engross a vast, unknown, and perhaps unknowable area. Such a patent may confer power to block off whole areas of scientific development, without compensating benefit to the public. The basic quid pro quo contemplated by the Constitution and Congress for granting a patent monopoly is the benefit derived by the public from an invention with substantial utility. Unless and until a process is refined and developed to this point—where specific benefit exists in currently available form—there is insufficient justification for permitting an applicant to engross what may prove to be a broad field.

These arguments for and against the patentability of a process which either has no known use or is useful only in the sense that it may be an object of scientific research would apply equally to the patenting of the product produced by the process. Respondent appears to concede that with respect to a product, as opposed to a process, Congress has struck the balance on the side of nonpatentability unless "utility" is shown. Indeed, the decisions of the CCPA are in accord with the view that a product may not be patented absent a showing of utility greater than any adduced in the present case. We find absolutely no warrant for the proposition that although Congress intended that no patent be granted on a chemical compound whose sole "utility" consists of its potential role as an object of use-testing, a different set of rules was meant to apply to the process which yielded the unpatentable product. That proposition seems to us little more than an attempt to evade the impact of the rules which concededly govern patentability of the product itself.

This is not to say that we mean to disparage the importance of contributions to the fund of scientific information short of the invention of something "useful," or that we are blind to the prospect that what now seems without "use" may tomorrow command the grateful attention of the public. But a patent is not a hunting license. It is not a reward for the search, but compensation for its successful conclusion.

"[A] patent system must be related to the world of commerce rather than to the realm of philosophy. * * *"

The judgment of the CCPA is

Reversed.

RAYTHEON COMPANY v. ROPER CORPORATION

United States Court of Appeals, Federal Circuit, 1983.
724 F.2d 951, 220 USPQ 592.

MARKEY, CHIEF JUDGE.

Roper Corporation (Roper) appeals from a judgment of the United States District Court for the District of Massachusetts declaring U.S. Patent No. 4,028,520 ('520 patent), issued to Sumner H. Torrey and assigned to Roper, invalid for lack of utility and * * * We reverse in part, affirm in part, and remand.

BACKGROUND

A. Prior Technology

The Roper patent is directed to a "common cavity" oven capable of conventional thermal cooking, microwave cooking, and pyrolytic self-cleaning (*i.e.*, heating the walls to about 900° F. to break down soil baked thereon). Those three "modes" of operation (thermal cooking, microwave cooking, and self-cleaning) are not totally compatible.

At the time of the Torrey invention, cooking in a thermal oven required minimal amounts of air. * * *

Microwave cooking produced more moisture than thermal cooking. To remove moisture vapors from the cavity of a conventional microwave oven, a blower or fan was employed to blow them out a vent at the cavity top. Microwave cooking also required maximum sealing of the cavity to prevent escape of microwave energy. Thus, the opening in the oven door of a thermal oven was not desirable in a microwave oven.

Inclusion of a self-cleaning mode further complicated the ventilation of an oven operable in the thermal and microwave modes. Though a limited air supply was needed to flush smoke and volatile products of self-cleaning, excess air caused combustion of those products. That combustion, known as "autoignition", produced sudden pressure that sought release through any opening, including "backflow" through the waveguide. Although autoignition occurred only occasionally, backflow was thought to contaminate ("foul") the waveguide with burnt food particles cleaned from the cavity walls. Moreover, if autoignition were fueled by even greater amounts of excess air, as when forced air removed moisture produced in the microwave mode, fire or explosion could result.

* * *

B. The Torrey Invention

In 1973, Roper began work on a self-cleaning common cavity oven. Under Torrey's supervision, Roper developed an oven with proper ventilation during the microwave, thermal, and self-cleaning modes, and which, to Torrey's surprise, had no fouling problems.

In the summer of 1976, Roper marketed its oven nationally under its own name and through Sears, Roebuck & Company under the Kenmore label. About 24,000 have been sold, with no complaints respecting contamination of the microwave feed system. The Roper oven was and is a successful product.

* * *

B. Invalidity for Lack of Utility

Utility is a fact question, *see e.g.*, *Wilden Pump v. Pressed & Welded Products Co.*, 655 F.2d 984, 988, 213 USPQ 282, 285 (9th Cir.1981); *Nickola v. Peterson*, 580 F.2d 898, 911, 198 USPQ 385, 399 (6th Cir. 1978), *cert. denied*, 440 U.S. 961, 99 S.Ct. 1504, 59 L.Ed.2d 774 (1979). In determining utility, however, the claims must first be interpreted to define the invention to be tested for utility. Claim interpretation is a legal matter subject to review free of the clearly erroneous standard applicable to fact findings. *Fromson v. Advance Offset Plate, Inc.*, 720 F.2d 1565 at 1569 (Fed.Cir.1983).

In this case, the district court's holding that claim 1 is invalid must be affirmed, but its holding of invalidity for lack of utility in the inventions set forth in claims 2–7 must be reversed because the latter rests on an erroneous interpretation of those claims, as well as on other incorrect legal bases.

1. *The district court correctly interpreted and held invalid claim 1 but erroneously interpreted claims 3 and 4 as requiring prevention of backflow during autoignition.*

In *Linde Air Products Co. v. Graver Tank & Mfg. Co.*, 86 F.Supp. 191, 197, 75 USPQ 231, 235 (N.D.Ind.1947), *rev'd*, 167 F.2d 531, 536–37, 77 USPQ 207, 212 (7th Cir.1948), *aff'd*, *Graver Mfg. Co. v. Linde Co.*, 336 U.S. 271, 277–79, 69 S.Ct. 535, 538–39, 93 L.Ed. 672 (1949), certain process claims were held invalid because they included incorrect ideas and:

> To make a claim for a * * * process in which these erroneous ideas are incorporated is to stake out a process * * * which does not in point of fact exist within the invention. While a patent covering a meritorious invention should not be struck down because the patentee has misconceived the scientific principle of his invention, the error cannot be overlooked when the misconception is embodied in the claim.

Accord, Noma Lites Canada Ltd. v. Westinghouse Electric Corp., 399 F.Supp. 243, 253, 186 USPQ 485, 493 (D.D.C.1975) ("When an incorrect or questionable theory of operation is included in a patent claim, that claim is invalid. 35 U.S.C. § 112."). Because it is for the invention as claimed that enablement must exist, and because the impossible cannot be enabled, a claim containing a limitation impossible to meet may be held invalid under § 112. Moreover, when a claim requires a means for accomplishing an unattainable result, the claimed invention must be considered inoperative as claimed and the claim must be held invalid under either § 101 or § 112 of 35 U.S.C. *See e.g., General Electric Co. v. United States,* 572 F.2d 745, 755, 198 USPQ 65, 93, 215 Ct.Cl. 636 (1978); *In re Harwood,* 390 F.2d 985, 989, 156 USPQ 673, 676, 55 CCPA 922 (1968); *CPC International, Inc. v. Standard Brands, Inc.,* 385 F.Supp. 1057, 1061, 184 USPQ 332, 335 (D.Del.1974); *Novelart Mfg. Co. v. Carlin Container Corp.,* 363 F.Supp. 58, 76, 179 USPQ 17, 29 (D.N.J.1973). Whether the appropriate basis for holding claim 1 invalid be failure of compliance with the utility requirement of § 101 or with the enablement requirement of § 112, therefore, that holding must be affirmed.

In the present case, the district court interpreted claims 1, 3 and 4 as requiring that the inventions set forth in those claims include a means for continuing convection during autoignition. The district court found, however, that convection did not in fact occur during occasional autoignition in the Roper oven, a finding which is not clearly erroneous. Given that claim interpretation and finding, the district court was compelled under the above authorities to hold those claims invalid. However, though the district court was correct in interpreting and holding invalid claim 1, it legally erred in interpreting claims 3 and 4.

Claim 1 specifically provides: "the blower inlet being located at a level below the bottom wall of the cavity so that when the blower and magnetron are turned off and the thermal element is turned on air is thermally convected from the blower inlet through the air passages into the waveguide and *into the cavity for exiting through the cavity air vent notwithstanding the autoignition pressure* which exists in the cavity under high temperature self-cleaning conditions" (emphasis added).

* * *

The district court impermissibly read the above-quoted language from claim 1 into claims 3 and 4. The impropriety of reading limitations into claims is dramatized where, as here, the limitation sought to be added is already present in another claim. *Environmental Designs, Ltd. v. Union Oil Co. of California,* 713 F.2d 693, 699, 218 USPQ 865, 870–71 (Fed.Cir.1983). *Accord, Fromson v. Advance Offset Plate, Inc., supra,* at 1570; *Caterpillar Tractor Co. v. Berco, S.P.A.,* 714 F.2d 1110, 1116, 219 USPQ 185, 188 (Fed.Cir.1983); *Kalman v. Kimberly Clark Corp.,* 713 F.2d 760, 770, 218 USPQ 781, 788 (Fed.Cir.1983). * * *

3. A CLAIMED INVENTION NEED NOT ACCOMPLISH ALL OBJECTIVES STATED IN THE SPECIFICATION.

The district court held the '520 patent invalid in part because Roper's oven, as set forth in claims interpreted by the district court as requiring prevention of backflow and autoignition, failed to accomplish all objectives stated in the patent. Raytheon urged at oral argument that that holding is compelled by *Mitchell v. Tilghman,* 86 U.S. (19

Wall.) 287, 396–97, 22 L.Ed. 125 (1873) (a patent is void "if the described result cannot be obtained by the described means"). In *Mitchell,* the described result was production of fatty acids and glycerin from fatty or oily substances by the action of water at high temperature and pressure. *Id.* at 296, 380, 22 L.Ed. 125. That was the single result stated and was an element of the *claim. Id.* at 296, 22 L.Ed. 125. To interpret *Mitchell* as requiring that all claims must set forth inventions satisfying all objectives would make no sense. When a properly claimed invention meets at least one stated objective, utility under § 101 is clearly shown. *See e.g., Standard Oil Co. (Indiana) v. Montedison, S.P.A.,* 664 F.2d 356, 375, 212 USPQ 327, 344 (3rd Cir. 1981), *cert. denied,* 456 U.S. 915, 102 S.Ct. 1769, 72 L.Ed.2d 174 (1982); *E.I. du Pont de Nemours & Co. v. Berkley & Co.,* 620 F.2d 1247, 1258 n. 10, 1260 n. 17, 205 USPQ 1, 8 n. 10, 10 n. 17 (8th Cir.1980); *Krantz and Croix v. Olin,* 148 USPQ 659, 661–62 (CCPA 1966); Chisum on Patents, ¶ 4.04[4] [1983].

Here, the Torrey invention as set forth in claims 2–7 clearly accomplished at least one, and a major one, of the patent's stated objectives, *i.e.,* a "ventilating system for a common cavity oven usable in all three modes of operation and which is safe in all three modes and which runs no risk of violent explosion of the products of combustion in the self-clean mode". The incorrectness of Torrey's theory explaining the absence of fouling (i.e., that continued convection prevented backflow during autoignition) does not undermine the unchallenged accomplishment of the quoted objective by the ovens set forth in claims 2–7. Torrey was attempting to explain in his specification why his tests showed no fouling, and a patentee is not responsible for the correctness of such theories and explanations when their correctness is not related to validity of the claims under consideration. *See e.g., Fromson v. Advance Plate, Inc., supra,* at 1570. (In *Fromson,* the sole issue was infringement, and validity of non-asserted claims including a limitation based on the patentee's theory that an alumino-silicate layer was produced, was not before the court.)

4. LACK OF UTILITY CANNOT CO-EXIST WITH INFRINGEMENT AND COMMERCIAL SUCCESS.

The wisdom of the trial court in deciding validity and infringement, and the interrelationship of those issues, are manifested in the present case. *See, Medtronic, Inc. v. Cardiac Pacemakers,* 721 F.2d 1563 at 1582 (Fed.Cir.1983); *Gore v. Garlock, supra,* at 1559.

The district court's finding on infringement of claim 1 was clearly erroneous because Raytheon's proof established the impossibility of its oven having a means to continue convection during autoignition. However, the court's finding on infringement of claims 2–7 was not clearly erroneous. *See* section E, *infra.* That finding compels the conclusion that claims 2–7 cannot be held invalid for lack of utility.

A correct finding of infringement of otherwise valid claims mandates as a matter of law a finding of utility under § 101. *See e.g., E.I.*

du Pont de Nemours & Co. v. Berkley & Co., supra, 620 F.2d at 1258–61, 205 USPQ at 8–11; *Tapco Products Co. v. Van Mark Products Corp.,* 446 F.2d 420, 428, 170 USPQ 550, 555–56 (6th Cir.), *cert. denied,* 404 U.S. 986, 92 S.Ct. 2151, 30 L.Ed.2d 370 (1971). The rule is not related, as Raytheon argues, to whether a defendant may simultaneously assert nonutility and non-infringement; a defendant may do so. The rule relates to the time of decision not to the time of trial, and is but a common sense approach to the law. If a party has made, sold, or used a properly claimed device, and has thus infringed, proof of that device's utility is thereby established. People rarely, if ever, appropriate useless inventions.

Proof of such utility is further supported when, as here, the inventions set forth in claims 2–7 have on their merits been met with commercial success. *See e.g., Medtronic, Inc., supra,* at 1582; *Wilden Pump v. Pressed & Welded Products Co., supra,* 655 F.2d at 988, 213 USPQ at 285; *CTS Corp. v. Piher International Corp.,* 527 F.2d 95, 105, 188 USPQ 419, 428 (7th Cir.1975), *cert. denied,* 424 U.S. 978, 96 S.Ct. 1485, 47 L.Ed.2d 748 (1976).

In sum, we hold in this section B that claims 2–7 are not invalid for lack of utility.[d]

E. I. DuPONT de NEMOURS & COMPANY v. BERKLEY AND COMPANY, INC.

United States Court of Appeals, Eighth Circuit, 1980.
620 F.2d 1247, 205 USPQ 1.

MARKEY, CHIEF JUDGE [*]

[Excerpt Only.]

It is axiomatic that "one who appropriates the teachings of a patent may not deny the utility of the invention." *Tapco Products Co. v. Van Mark Products Corp.,* 446 F.2d 420, 428 (6th Cir.), *cert. denied,* 404 U.S. 986, 92 S.Ct. 451, 30 L.Ed.2d 370 (1971); *Monogram Manufacturing Co. v. Glemby,* 136 F.2d 961, 963 (2d Cir.), *cert. denied,* 320 U.S.

---

d. Quite obviously if an alleged infringer is making, using or selling the invention of a patent, it comes with ill grace that he deny the utility. See Deering, Milliken & Co. v. Temp-Resisto Corp., 160 F.Supp. 463, 116 USPQ 386 (S.D.N.Y.1958): "Furthermore, as the Special Master pointed out, the defendants paid to the patented fabric the tribute of imitation, and in their advertising and their sales promotion extolled the novelty and value of the lining and attributed to it the advantage of heat insulation which they now, in the midst of litigation, deny. * * *"

Also in Seymour v. Ford Motor Co., 44 F.2d 306, 7 USPQ 182 (C.C.A.Mich.1931): "Considered apart from the question of the exercise of invention, this is essentially the defense of want of utility—the lack of any useful function—an in this aspect it is correctly claimed by the appellant that an infringer is estopped to assert the defense. The patent is itself evidence of such utility, and the use of the patented device by the defendant has long been recognized as an admission of this fact, and as creating an estoppel upon the defendant to deny such utility."

See also, Enterprise Mfg. Co. v. Shakespeare Co., 141 F.2d 916, 61 USPQ 201 (6th Cir.1944).

[*] The Honorable Howard T. Markey, Chief Judge, United States Court of Customs and Patent Appeals, sitting by designation.

778, 64 S.Ct. 93, 88 L.Ed. 467 (1943); *Kansas City Southern Railway v. Silica Products Co.,* 48 F.2d 503, 505 (8th Cir.), *cert. denied,* 284 U.S. 626, 52 S.Ct. 11, 76 L.Ed. 533 (1931). Hence, the first flaw was the failure to recognize that Berkley's admission, that its fishing line fell within the scope of claims 2, 5 and 6, is an admission of utility in the invention there claimed and that Berkley, as an infringer, was thereby estopped from asserting that those claims are invalid for lack of utility.

The second flaw was the failure to recognize that the presumption of utility created by issuance of the patent, 35 U.S.C. § 282, *Dashiell v. Grosvenor,* 162 U.S. 425, 432, 16 S.Ct. 805, 807, 40 L.Ed. 1025 (1896); *Strong-Scott Manufacturing Co. v. Weller,* 112 F.2d 389, 394 (8th Cir. 1940); *Metropolitan Engineering Co. v. Coe,* 64 App.D.C. 315, 317, 78 F.2d 199, 201 (D.C.Cir.1935); *Superior Hay Stacker Manufacturing Co. v. Dain Manufacturing Co.,* 208 F. 549, 557 (8th Cir.1913), is strengthened when others, as Berkley did here, have copied the invention, *Superior Hay Stacker Manufacturing Co. v. Dain Manufacturing Co., id.* at 557, and when, as it did here in both DuPont's and Berkley's hands, the invention has achieved commercial success, *Western Electric Co. v. LaRue,* 139 U.S. 601, 608, 11 S.Ct. 670, 672, 35 L.Ed. 294 (1891); *Continental Can Co. v. Anchor Hocking Glass Corp.,* 362 F.2d 123, 124 (7th Cir.1966); *Panduit Corp. v. Stahlin Bros. Fibre Works, Inc.,* 298 F.Supp. 435, 442 (W.D.Mich.1969), *aff'd,* 430 F.2d 221 (6th Cir.1970), *cert. denied,* 401 U.S. 939, 91 S.Ct. 932, 28 L.Ed.2d 218 (1971).

Berkley, for the first time on appeal, says its non-utility position relates to the "ceases to glow" language of withdrawn claims 1 and 8. The evidence respecting utility was insufficient, however, for any purpose. * * *

Perfection under all conditions is not required,[17] whether the patent does or does not suggest that the invention is imperfect or inoper-

---

17. A small degree of utility is sufficient. *In re Oberweger,* 115 F.2d 826, 828, 28 CCPA 749, 752 (1940). The claimed invention must only be capable of performing *some* beneficial function. *National Slug Rejectors, Inc. v. A.B.T. Manufacturing Corp.,* 164 F.2d 333, 335 (7th Cir.1947), *cert. denied,* 333 U.S. 832, 68 S.Ct. 459, 92 L.Ed. 1116 (1948); *In re Oberweger, supra* at 828; 28 CCPA at 752; *Panduit Corp. v. Stahlin Bros. Fibre Works, Inc., supra* at 435. An invention does not lack utility merely because the particular embodiment disclosed in the patent lacks perfection or performs crudely. *Hildreth v. Mastoras,* 257 U.S. 27, 34, 42 S.Ct. 20, 23, 66 L.Ed. 112 (1921); *Decca Ltd. v. United States,* 544 F.2d 1070, 1077, 210 Ct.Cl. 546 (1976); *Field v. Knowles,* 183 F.2d 593, 600, 37 CCPA 1211, 1221 (1950); *Plant Products Co. v. Charles Phillips Chemical Co.,* 96 F.2d 585, 586 (2d Cir.1938); *Besser v. Merrilat Culvert Core Co.,* 243 F. 611, 612 (8th Cir.1917). A commercially successful product is not required. *Hildreth v. Mastoras, supra* at 34, 42 S.Ct. at 23; *In re Anthony,* 414 F.2d 1383, 1396, 56 CCPA 1443, 1460 (1969). Nor is it essential that the invention accomplish all its intended functions, *Conner v. Joris,* 241 F.2d 944, 947, 44 CCPA 772, 776 (1957), *Panduit Corp. v. Stahlin Bros. Fibre Works, Inc., supra* at 442, or operate under all conditions, *Decca Ltd. v. United States, supra* at 1077, partial success being sufficient to demonstrate patentable utility, *Freedman v. Overseas Scientific Corp.,* 248 F.2d 274, 276 (2d Cir.1957), *Emery Industries, Inc. v. Schumann,* 111 F.2d 209, 210 (7th Cir.1940), *Cummins Engine Co. v. General Motors Corp.,* 299 F.Supp. 59, 90 (D.Md.1969), *aff'd,* 424 F.2d 1368 (4th Cir.1970). In short, the defense of non-utility cannot be sustained without proof of total incapacity. *Scovill Manufacturing Co. v. Satler,* 21 F.2d 630, 634 (D.Conn.1927). Proof of inoperativeness or non-utility must be strong, *Steinfur Patents Corp. v. William Beyer, Inc.,* 62 F.2d

able under certain conditions. *See Conner v. Joris, supra* note 17, at 946–48; 44 CCPA at 775–76; *Plant Products Co. v. Charles Phillips Chemical Co., supra* note 17, at 586. Dr. Johnson's report showed the DuPont line no more visible than non-fluorescent line under some water conditions. Berkley did not challenge those test results, but relied on *ex parte* tests it conducted exclusively in crystal clear water. Assuming that Berkley's evidence establishes what it claims, *i.e.*, that DuPont's line is more visible than non-fluorescent line in crystal clear water, that evidence is insufficient as a matter of law to establish non-utility. At most, it might demonstrate that DuPont's commercial embodiment of the invention does not work perfectly under a particular condition and is thus not a model of perfection.

It is instructive on the issue of utility that any imperfections respecting some continued glow under visible light in clear water did not deter Berkley from copying the invention and selling it for over 7½ million dollars during 1976–1978.

Thus, the issue of whether the patent was invalid for lack of utility should not have gone to the jury and should have been decided as a matter of law in DuPont's favor. Its submission, for any purpose, constituted prejudicial error.

APPLICATION OF HARTOP

United States Court of Customs and Patent Appeals, 1962.
50 CCPA 780, 311 F.2d 249, 135 USPQ 419.

MARTIN, JUDGE. This is an appeal from a decision of the Patent Office Board of Appeals affirming the examiner's rejection of appealed claims 30–34, 38 and 39 of appellants' application, Serial No. 418,468, for a patent on a "Therapeutic Composition."

* * *

According to appellants' specification, thiobarbituric acid compounds and salts thereof are important as anesthetic and hypnotic agents, especially for inducing surgical anesthesia of relatively short duration. For the latter purpose, dilute aqueous solutions of water-soluble thiobarbiturate salts are injected parenterally. These aqueous solutions are unstable and must be prepared shortly before use by dissolving the dry salts in water. Appellants consider it uneconomical to use small, individual-dose ampoules of the dry salts and inconvenient to weigh and otherwise handle solid materials when preparing these solutions.

Appellants have discovered that certain concentrated, alkaline, non-aqueous solutions of thiobarbiturate salts are relatively stable, have a suitable shelf life, and, just before parenteral administration, can be easily and conveniently diluted with water to produce a clear solution with a therapeutically effective concentration of the thiobar-

238, 240 (2d Cir.1932), every reasonable doubt being resolved in favor of the paten- tee, *Strong-Scott Manufacturing Co. v. Weller, supra* at 394.

biturate but yet with a concentration of organic solvents and alkaline material sufficiently low for safe injection.

* * *

The Patent Office has insisted on *clinical tests,* i.e. tests with human patients, to "prove" that appellants' solutions are "safe" for human therapy. We do not know what sort of clinical tests would have satisfied the Patent Office, i.e. how many subjects of what age, sex, physical conditions, etc. and what degree of vascular damage, if any, would have been permissible in a "proof" of "safety," but it is unnecessary to concern ourselves with that matter because *no* clinical evidence whatever has been submitted. But that fact does not mean that there is no *evidence* of "safety" in the case at bar. On the basis of tests with rabbits, Spruth has stated in his affidavit:

> "* * * there are no significant differences between the safety * * * of regular 'Pentothal' powder, reconstituted, and any of the compositions of the specific examples of [the application at bar] * * *."

There are three important points involved in that statement. The qualifications of Spruth to express such an opinion have not been questioned; the rabbit tests involve a side-by-side comparison of what appellants are claiming with a widely used, commercially and medically acceptable material; in our opinion, rabbits are "standard experimental animals" for testing the safety of thiobarbituric anesthetics.

Bearing in mind that *absolute proof* of such a proposition as "safety" of a drug or medicament is impossible and that "proof" of "safety" is relative with the degree of "proof" dependent on the quantity and quality of the available evidence, bearing in mind what evidence of "safety" has been submitted in the case at bar, and bearing in mind that inherent in the concept of the "standard experimental animal" is the ability of one skilled in the art to make the appropriate correlations between the results actually observed with the animal experiments and the probable results in human therapy, we hold that appellants' claimed solutions have been shown to be useful within the meaning of 35 U.S.C.A. § 101. In holding as we do, we realize that no *clinical* evidence has been submitted as to the "safety" of these solutions. Therefore there is lacking that degree of "proof" which such evidence would provide. However, we do not believe that such a degree of "proof" is necessary in view of the *factual situation* in the case at bar. We think that a sufficient *probability* of safety in human therapy has been demonstrated in the case at bar to satisfy the requirement of 35 U.S.C.A. § 101 that appellants' invention be useful.

* * *

However, regardless of the issuance of the patent under the circumstances of the case at bar, there is no question but that the public must be protected absolutely against the advertising and sale and other distribution of harmful drugs, medicines and the like in all situations, including this one if such be the case. We believe that Congress has recognized this problem and has clearly expressed its intent to give statutory authority and responsibility in this area to Federal agencies different than that given to the Patent Office. This is so because the standards established by statute for the advertisement, use, sale or distribution of drugs are quite different than the requirements under the Patent Act for the issuance of a patent. For example, the Federal Trade Commission has been given the responsibility of enforcing the Wheeler-Lea amendments to the Federal Trade Commission Act. Also, the Food and Drug Administration has been given the responsibility of enforcing the Federal Food, Drug, and Cosmetic Act.

* * * As we said in In re Krimmel, supra:

"* * * It is not for us or the Patent Office to legislate and if the Congress desires to give this responsibility to the Patent Office, it should do so by statute."

Therefore, in our judgment, the board has erred in rejecting the appealed claims. We have held that appellants disclose in their specification that their invention is useful in human therapy. The Patent Office has expressed doubt that the invention will be "safe" for that purpose. Although appellants have not supplied clinical data concerning the actual use of their invention in human therapy, they have supplied evidence and *expert opinion* based on laboratory experiments with rabbits, the "standard experimental animal" for their purpose, that their invention is as safe as a widely used, commercially and medically acceptable material. In our opinion, this evidence indicates a sufficient *probability* that the invention will be as safe as this latter material in human therapy to satisfy the statutory requirement that the invention be useful.

Although it is true that the advertising and sale or other distribution of appellants' invention for human therapy in interstate and much of the intrastate commerce will not be legally permissible until experiments with humans have been carried out, we do not think it is within the authority or responsibility of the Patent Office to demand such tests *in this particular case* in view of the evidence of record. However, no implication is intended here that clinical evidence should not be demanded by the Patent Office under different circumstances. Each case must be decided on its own set of facts.

For the foregoing reasons, we *reverse* the decision of the Board of Appeals.

Reversed.

IN RE JOLLES

United States Court of Customs and Patent Appeals, 1980.
628 F.2d 1322, 206 USPQ 885.

BALDWIN, JUDGE.

This appeal is from the decision of the Patent and Trademark Office Board of Appeals (board) affirming the examiner's rejection of claims 7–14, 16, 27–34 and 36 under 35 U.S.C. § 101 and 35 U.S.C. § 112, first paragraph, for lack of proof of utility. We reverse.

*   *   *

Proof of utility is sufficient if it is convincing to one of ordinary skill in the art. *In re Irons,* 52 CCPA 938, 340 F.2d 974, 144 USPQ 351 (1965). The amount of evidence required depends on the facts of each individual case. *In re Gazave,* 54 CCPA 1524, 379 F.2d 973, 154 USPQ 92 (1967). The character and amount of evidence needed may vary, depending on whether the alleged utility appears to accord with or to contravene established scientific principles and beliefs. *In re Chilowsky,* 43 CCPA 775, 229 F.2d 457, 108 USPQ 321 (1956).

*   *   *

The board avoided the examiner's assertion of incredible utility, but did question the operativeness of the claimed subject matter. When utility as a drug, medicant, and the like in human therapy is alleged, it is proper for the examiner to ask for substantiating evidence unless one with ordinary skill in the art would accept the allegations as obviously correct. *In re Novak,* 49 CCPA 1283, 306 F.2d 924, 134 USPQ 335 (1962).

However, in considering the evidence proffered by appellant, the board dismissed the Maral declarations as not relevant to establish the claimed human utility. The Jacquillat clinical tests were accepted by the board solely for the establishment of utility for the specific composition tested.

We believe the board erred in dismissing the Maral evidence as not relevant to human utility. This court recognizes "that a demonstration that a compound has desirable or beneficial properties in the prevention, alleviation, or cure of some disease or manifestation of a disease in experimental animals does not necessarily mean that the compound will have the same properties when used with humans." *In re Krimmel,* 48 CCPA 1116, 1123, 292 F.2d 948, 953, 130 USPQ 215, 219 (1961). However, this is by no means support for the board's position that such evidence is not relevant to human utility.

To the contrary, this court has accepted tests on experimental animals as sufficient to establish utility in *In re Bergel,* 48 CCPA 1102, 292 F.2d 955, 130 USPQ 206 (1961). Utility was recognized by this court in *Bergel* not because of any concern with the health or existence of the experimental animals, but rather because of the widespread pharmacological work in animals recognized as a screening procedure for testing new drugs. It is clear that such testing is relevant to utility in humans. Evidence showing substantial activity against experimental tumors in mice in tests customarily used for the screening of anticancer agents of potential utility in the treatment of humans is relevant to utility in humans and is not to be disregarded. *In re Buting,* 57 CCPA 777, 418 F.2d 540, 163 USPQ 689 (1969). *   *   * The board erred in this finding by failing to give sufficient weight to the similarity of the remaining claimed derivatives to the derivative in allowed claims 15 and 35 when considered with the Maral animal tests.

The similarities of the claimed derivatives to each other are represented in the tabulation of differences provided supra for the eight compounds tested by Dr. Maral. The Maral declarations establish that the eight compounds have substantial activity against experimental tumors in mice. The board found that the successful clinical tests in humans of the one derivative shown in the Jacquillat declarations sufficiently established utility for claims 15 and 35. The claimed compounds have a close structural relationship to daunorubicin and doxorubicin, both known to be useful in cancer chemotherapy. Considering these facts in the record before us, we conclude that one of ordinary skill in the art would accept appellant's claimed utility in humans as valid and correct. The decision of the board is *reversed*.

REVERSED.

YASUKO KAWAI ET AL. v. METLESICS

United States Court of Customs and Patent Appeals, 1973.
480 F.2d 880, 178 USPQ 158.

ALMOND, SENIOR JUDGE.

In each of these appeals, the board involved concluded that the foreign application must satisfy the requirements of section 112 if it is to be the basis of a claim for priority under section 119. We affirm those decisions. * * *

The examiner refused to accord the United States applications the benefit of the filing dates of the earlier British applications. The basis for this refusal was his determination that the British provisional specifications were not adequate to meet the disclosure requirements found in the first paragraph of section 112. * * *

THE REQUIREMENTS OF SECTION 112 AND FOREIGN APPLICATIONS

This court has extensively discussed the history and purpose of section 119 in In re Hilmer, 359 F.2d 859, 53 CCPA 1288 (1966). * * *

It is well understood that the act of filing a United States patent application can be regarded as being a constructive reduction to practice of an invention described therein as of the filing date. It follows naturally from this that the written specification in the application is the evidence proving the invention of that which is reduced to practice, i.e., the subject matter to which properly supported claims can be drawn.

We think it is now settled that an invention cannot be considered as having been reduced to practice in the sense that a patent can be granted for it unless a practical utility for the invention has been discovered where such utility would not be obvious. See 35 U.S.C.A. § 101; Brenner v. Manson, 383 U.S. 519, 86 S.Ct. 1033, 16 L.Ed.2d 69

(1966); In re Kirk, 376 F.2d 936, 54 CCPA 1119 (1967); In re Joly, 376 F.2d 906, 54 CCPA 1159 (1967). Therefore, a constructive reduction to practice, as opposed to an actual reduction to practice, is not proven unless the specification relied upon discloses a practical utility for the invention where one would not be obvious. We also think that *proof* of a constructive reduction to practice would also require that there be sufficient disclosure in the specification to enable any person skilled in the art to take advantage of that utility where it would not be obvious how this is done. * * *

If these are requirements which a United States specification must meet if it is to be adequate to support a reduction to practice by the act of filing the application, it follows that a foreign application must meet the same requirements if it is to be used to prove a date of invention. * * *

The net effect of not requiring the foreign application to meet the disclosure requirements of United States law would be that an inventor could file a patent application for promising chemical compounds in a foreign country not requiring a disclosure of utility and have up to one year to determine a practical utility before filing in the United States and yet claim an earlier date of invention. We do not think section 119 should be construed as permitting this. * * *

Because we hold that section 119 requires that a foreign application must meet the disclosure requirement of section 112 in the same way that a United States application must before the benefit of its filing date is accorded to a later United States application, the decisions of the Board of Appeals and the Board of Interferences in each appeal before us must be affirmed.

Affirmed.

H. SUFFICIENCY OF SPECIFICATION

1. ENABLING DISCLOSURE

A patent is frequently referred to as a contract [a] or franchise [b] with the consideration to the Government being disclosure of the invention to the public and the right to use it after the grant expires. Accordingly, there is a failure of consideration invalidating the patent if the disclosure is insufficient to enable a skilled person to make and use the invention.

This requirement of an enabling disclosure of the invention was embodied in the first Patent Act of 1790 which provided in part:

> [W]hich specification shall be so particular as * * * to enable a workman or other person skilled in the art of manufacture, whereof it is a branch, or wherewith it may be nearest connected, to make,

a. Century Electric Co. v. Westinghouse, 191 Fed. 350 (8th Cir.1911).

b. Seymour v. Osborne, 78 U.S. 516, 533, 20 L.Ed. 33, 35 (1871).

construct or use the same, to the end that the public may have the full benefit thereof, after the expiration of the patent term;

This requirement is now found in 35 U.S.C. 112 which provides in part:

The specification shall contain a written description of the invention, and of the manner and process of making and using it, in such full, clear, concise, and exact terms as to enable any person skilled in the art to which it pertains, or with which it is most nearly connected, to make and use the same, and shall set forth the best mode contemplated by the inventor of carrying out his invention.

The United States Supreme Court in Grant v. Raymond, 31 U.S. (6 Pet.) 218, 8 L.Ed. 376 (1832) stated:

An enabling disclosure is necessary in order to give the public, after the privilege shall expire, the advantage for which the privilege is allowed, and is the foundation of the power to issue the patent.

Under an earlier Patent Act, the United States Supreme Court held the disclosure was sufficient in a patent specification on a process for making railroad wheels, saying:

Whitney conceived a process and practiced it. That process may have been a highly useful invention and, therefore, patentable, and yet he may have failed so to describe it as to teach the public how to practice it. The law requires every inventor, before he can receive a patent, to furnish a specification or a written description of his invention or discovery, and of the manner and process of making, constructing, using and compounding the same, in such full, clear, and exact terms, avoiding unnecessary prolixity, as to enable any person skilled in the art or science to which it appertains, or with which it is most nearly connected, to make, construct, compound, and use the same. The specification, then, is to be addressed to those skilled in the art, and is to be comprehensible by them. It may be sufficient, though the unskilled may not be able to gather from it how to use the invention. And it is evident that the definiteness of a specification must vary with the nature of its subject. Addressed as it is, to those skilled in the art, it may leave something to their skill in applying the invention, but it should not mislead them. Mowry v. Whitney, 81 U.S. 620, 644, 20 L.Ed. 860, 863 (1872).

The United States Supreme Court also stated with respect to a process for treatment of fats and oils:

If the mode of doing it or the apparatus in or by which it may be done is sufficiently obvious to suggest itself to a person skilled in the particular art, it is enough, in the patent, to point out the process to be performed, without giving supererogatory directions as to the apparatus or method to be employed. If the mode of applying the process is not obvious, then a description of a particular mode by which it may be applied is sufficient. There is, then, a description of the process and of one practical mode in which it may be applied. Perhaps the process is susceptible of being applied in many modes and by the use of many forms of apparatus. The inventor is not bound to describe them all in order to secure to himself the exclusive right to the process, if he is really its inventor or discover[er] [sic]. But he must describe some particular mode, or some apparatus, by which the process can be applied with at least some beneficial result, in order to show that it is capable of being exhibited and performed in actual experience. Tilghman v. Proctor, 102 U.S. 707, 728, 26 L.Ed. 279, 287 (1881).

Determining the sufficiency of a disclosure requires consideration of the particular invention, nature and state of development of the prior art, and knowledge and kinds and degree of skills and experience of one skilled in the art. As the Court said in A.B. Dick Co. v. Barnett, 288 Fed. 799 (2d Cir.1923):

> We further think that, in judging the sufficiency of a patent disclosure, it is necessary to consider, not only the art to which the invention may be assigned, but its relation to other and especially older arts, and the nature of the alleged new thought. It is upon the difficulty, obscurity, or even novelty of the art concerned that depends the kind and degree of skill or knowledge which must be possessed by those who assume to apply it.

> And all these attributes of the art must be ascertained from the evidence in a particular case, plus matters of common knowledge concerning which the court may take judicial notice. * * *

> Judges, as triers of the facts, have said that a disclosure, to be good, must be clear to a manufacturer, or a workman, or a mechanic, or even a journeyman (Leonard v. Maxwell, 252 Fed. 584, 164 C.C.A. 500); but the word used is quite meaningless unless the nature of the patent and the art involved be carefully investigated, when it will be found, e.g., that the journeyman of the Maxwell Case was a person whose accomplishments would be much admired by most men.

> It is not possible to formulate a rule in this matter, though it may be safely said that it is by no means enough to condemn a patent disclosure that even a skilled man might find it necessary to make several tests or trials before arriving at success. Malignani v. Jasper, etc., Co. (C.C.) 180 Fed. 442. The nearest approach to a rule is the summary declaration so characteristic of the rude sense of Jessel, M.R., that "the specification of a patent is not addressed to people who are ignorant about the subject-matter. It is addressed to people who know something about it." Plimpton v. Malcolmson, 3 Ch.Div. 531. But how much said people must know about it is a matter of degree, and always relative.

Any drawings accompanying the written description are to illustrate the principles and construction of the invention. Drawings usually are not to scale and need not be if a person of ordinary skill would know how to proportion the dimensions and component parts to construct a practical operating embodiment of the invention.[c] Some courts have held that drawings alone, unsupported by a written description,

---

    c. Crown Cork & Seal Co. of Baltimore City v. Aluminum Stopper Co., 108 Fed. 845 (4th Cir.1901).

cannot provide a sufficient disclosure to support an element of a claim. However, most courts hold drawings alone can do so if they in fact provide an enabling disclosure or teaching to a person of ordinary skill in the art.[d]

While new matter cannot be added to an original specification as filed of a pending application (35 U.S.C.A. § 132), all new language and changes are not necessarily new matter if they simply render explicit what was implicitly disclosed [e] or add material already known to the public when the application was filed.[f] An original specification can also be amended to conform its written description to the claims and drawings as originally filed and the drawings can be amended or added to conform to the original written description and claims.[g] While original claims may be relied on as part of the disclosure, it is preferable that the written description be amended to set forth properly their subject matter as a basis for the claims.[h]

An original specification can also incorporate by reference subject matter disclosed in another patent application which is pending before the Patent Office and hence unavailable to the public.[i] If the referenced application was abandoned, normally it would never be available to the public. However, if a patent issues which has incorporated an application by reference, the referred application will be made available to the public even if abandoned. Therefore, consent of the applicant or owner of the referenced application should be obtained if not implicitly granted because of the same inventorship or common ownership of the issued patent and referenced abandoned application.[j]

Preferably, a specification is a model of clarity, leaves nothing to doubt or speculation, and does not require any experiments to make

---

d. In re Wolfensperger, 302 F.2d 950, 133 USPQ 537 (CCPA 1962).

e. U.S. Pipe & Foundry Co. v. Woodward Iron Co., 327 F.2d 242, 247, 140 USPQ 208, 212 (4th Cir.1963); In re Wright, 343 F.2d 761, 767, 145 USPQ 182, 188 (CCPA 1965); Brian Jackson Associates v. San Manuel Copper Corp., 259 F.Supp. 793, 817, 151 USPQ 5, 10 (D.C.Ariz. 1966); Canaan Products, Inc. v. Edward Don & Co., 273 F.Supp. 492, 500, 154 USPQ 393, 399 (D.C.Ill.1966).

f. In re Georg Stauber, 45 F.2d 661, 7 USPQ 258 (CCPA 1930); In re Heritage, 182 F.2d 639, 643, 86 USPQ 160, 164 (CCPA 1950), In re Hirsch, 295 F.2d 251, 131 USPQ 198 (CCPA 1961).

g. Patent Office Rules of Practice

118. Amendment of disclosure.

(a) No amendment shall introduce new matter into the disclosure of an application after the filing date of the application (§ 1.53(b)). All amendments to the specification, including the claims, and the drawings filed after the filing date of the application

cation must conform to at least one of them as it was at the time of the filing of the application. Matter not found in either, involving a departure from or an addition to the original disclosure, cannot be added to the application after its filing date even though supported by an oath or declaration in accordance with § 1.63 or § 1.67 filed after the filing date of the application.

h. Application of Gardner, 480 F.2d 879, 178 USPQ 149 (CCPA 1973); Bolyard v. Watson, 181 F.Supp. 882, 886, 124 USPQ 165, 168 (D.C.D.C.1959); In re Frey et al., 166 F.2d 572, 575, 77 USPQ 116, 119 (CCPA 1948); Ex Parte Wilson et al., 116 USPQ 595, 597 (P.O.Bd.App.1957); Ex Parte Fritz Gosslau, 25 USPQ 373, 374 (P.O. Bd.App.1935).

i. Ex Parte Jordan & Shapiro, 90 USPQ 41 (P.O.Bd.App.1950); Ex Parte Teter et al., 105 USPQ 192 (P.O.Bd.App.1948).

j. Orenbuch, The Doctrine of Incorporation by Reference in the Law of Patents, 43 J.P.O.S. 467 (1961).

and use the invention. However, it need not set forth minutiae of details or procedures which are clear to a person skilled in the art even though unfamiliar to laymen.[k] Moreover, a specification will be sufficient even though a skilled person might have to make several trials or experiments before successfully making and using the invention as long as only the exercise of ordinary skill is required to do so.[l] Furthermore, every patentee may be his own lexicographer and utilize terms other than in the strict dictionary sense as long as he defines them and is consistent in their use and interpretation.[m]

It is unnecessary for an inventor to understand or disclose the scientific principles of his invention as long as the specification enables a skilled person to make and use the invention.

> * * * A patentee may be baldly empirical, seeing nothing beyond his experiments and the result; yet if he has added a new and valuable article to the world's utilities, he is entitled to the rank and protection of an inventor. And how can it take from his merit that he may not know all of the forces which he has brought into operation? It is certainly not necessary that he understand or be able to state the scientific principles underlying his invention, and it is immaterial whether he can stand a successful examination as to the speculative ideas involved. * * * He must, indeed, make such disclosure and description of his invention that it may be put into practice. In this he must be clear. He must not put forth a puzzle for invention or experiment to solve, but the description is sufficient if those skilled in the art can understand it. This satisfies the law, which only requires as a condition of its protection that the world be given something new and that the world be taught how to use it. It is no concern of the world whether the principle upon which the new construction acts be obvious or obscure, so that it inheres in the new construction. * * *—Diamond Rubber Co. v. Consolidated Rubber Tire Co., 220 U.S. 428, 435, 31 S.Ct. 444, 55 L.Ed. 527, 532 (1911).

Section 112 U.S.C. says nothing about the disclosure of advantages, features and unexpected results of an invention which frequently come to light when the validity of an issued patent is being contested. Some courts have precluded reliance on undisclosed advantages and results [n], but most courts have permitted the patent holder to do so. The

---

k. In re Folkers et al., 344 F.2d 970, 976, 145 USPQ 390, 394 (CCPA 1965); In re Gay, 309 F.2d 769, 774; 135 USPQ 311, 316 (CCPA 1962).

l. A.B. Dick Co. v. Barnett, 288 Fed. 799 (2d Cir.1923).

It is well settled that the apparatus disclosed in an application need not necessarily be operative in the exact form in which it is shown and described. It is sufficient if it can be rendered operative by adjustments and corrections which would naturally occur to a skilled worker in the art attempting to construct the apparatus on the basis of the application disclosure.

Trumbull et al. v. Kirschbraun, 21 CCPA 758, 67 F.2d 974, 20 USPQ 46; Creed et al. v. Potts, 25 CCPA 1084, 96 F.2d 317, 37 USPQ 512; Bennett v. Halahan, 285 F.2d 807, 811, 128 USPQ 398, 401 (CCPA 1961).

m. Dennis v. Pitner, 106 F.2d 142, 148, 42 USPQ 248, 254 (7th Cir.1939); Turchan v. Bailey Meter Co., 167 F.Supp. 58, 65, 119 USPQ 165, 170 (D.C.Del.1958); Martin v. Ford Alexander Corp., 160 F.Supp. 670, 682, 117 USPQ 378, 387 (D.C.Cal.1958).

n. Tinnerman Products, Inc. v. George K. Garrett, Inc., 292 F.2d 137, 129 USPQ 438 (3d Cir.1961); In re Stewart, 222 F.2d 747, 106 USPQ 115 (CCPA 1955).

rationale for allowing reliance on them was well stated by Judge Buffington in Mead-Morrison Mfg. Co. v. Exeter Machine Works, 225 Fed. 489, 496 (3d Cir.1915).

We have not overlooked the fact that there was no mention in the patent of the lessening of vibration which now appears to be the most striking advantage of the patent. But we do not think the failure to disclose all the merits of a device should now serve to defeat it. Very often subsequent use shows that claimed advantages did not materialize, and in the same way use sometimes brings to light unsuspected merits in a device. In either case the presence or absence of asserted advantages is of evidential weight in securing the patent. The gist of a disclosure is that it be so full as will enable those versed in the art to thereafter use the device, and where such use, practice, mechanism, formula, etc., are fully disclosed, the requirements of the law are satisfied, without claiming every advantage such device may have. If subsequent use discloses unsuspected additional benefits the patentee is the gainer during the life of the patent, and the public when it expires.[o]

Thus, while the exposition of all the advantages and features of an invention, apart from basic utility, is not a statutory requirement, a good draftsman will include as many as possible to avoid the condemnation of "afterthoughts" when the patent is brought to court.[p]

TANNAGE PATENT CO. v. ZAHN

United States Circuit Court of New Jersey, 1895.
66 Fed. 986, 988, reversed 70 Fed. 1003.

DISTRICT JUDGE GREEN. * * *

The purpose of the specification, as contradistinguished from a claim, in letters patent, is to describe clearly the invention sought to be protected by them, and the manner of making, using, and constructing the same. The letters patent constitute a contract between the patentee and the public. On the one hand is granted an exclusive use of the invention for a specified term. On the other, by way of consideration, a full disclosure of the invention, in all its parts, must be made. It is through the instrumentality of the specifications that this disclosure is made, and the invention thereby fully placed within the knowledge of the public. Necessarily, upon their thoroughness in that respect, and upon their accuracy in statement, depends the validity of the contract of the letters patent. If there be material failure in either respect, there necessarily results such failure of consideration as must vitiate the contract. It follows, then, that a specification failing in any material respect to make the invention fully known and accessible to the public must be held fatally defective, and the patent based upon it,

o. Putnam v. Yerrington, 20 Fed.Cas. 92 (No. 11,486) (D.C.N.J.1876); McCormick Harvesting Machine Co. v. Aultman & Co., 69 F. 371, 378 (6th Cir.1895); Westmoreland Specialty Co. v. Hogan, 167 F. 327 (3d Cir.1909); Jackson Fence Co. v. Peerless Wire Fence, 228 F. 691, 696 (6th Cir.1915); Simplex Piston Ring Co. v. Horton Gallo Creamer Co., 61 F.2d 748, 750, 16 USPQ 157, 160 (2d Cir.1932).

p. Choate, Invention and Obviousness— "Afterthoughts"—Reliance on Features and Advantages Undisclosed at Original Filing, 49 J.P.O.S. 619 (1967).

ipso facto, becomes void. Wayne v. Holmes, 2 Fish.Pat.Cas. 20, Fed.Cas. No. 17,303. But it should be borne in mind, in judging of the sufficiency of the specifications of letters patent, that while the language and the methods of statement used by the inventor must be such as will fully place the invention in the intelligible possession of the public generally, it is not necessary that it should be so minutely and exactly described as to be readily understood by every person going to make up the public. The specifications of letters patent are addressed primarily to those skilled in the art to which the invention relates, and not to those who are wholly ignorant of the subject-matter. In Plimpton v. Malcolmson, 3 Ch.Div. 531, Sir. George Jessel, the master of the rolls, thus states the principle:

> "In the first place, it is plain that the specification of a patent is not addressed to people who are ignorant of the subject-matter. It is addressed to people who know something about it. If it is mechanical invention, as this is, you have, first of all, the scientific mechanicians of the first class,—eminent engineers. Then you have scientific mechanicians of the second class, managers of great manufactories; great employers of labor; persons who have studied mechanics, not to the same extent as those of the first class, the scientific engineers, but still to a great extent, for the purpose of conducting manufactories of complicated and unusual machines. * * * And then the third class, consisting of the ordinary workman, using that amount of skill and intelligence which is fairly to be expected from him,—not a careless man, but a careful man, though not possessing that great scientific knowledge or power of invention which would enable him by himself, unaided, to supplement a defective description or correct an erroneous description. Now, as I understand, to be a good specification it must be intelligible to the third class I have mentioned, and that is the result of the law. It will be a bad specification if the first two classes only understand it, and if the third class do not."

And in the case of Morgan v. Seaward, 1 Webst.Pat.Cas. 174, Mr. Baron Aderson used this language:

> "The specification ought to be framed so as not to call on a person to have recourse to more than those ordinary means of knowledge (not invention) which a workman of competent skill in his art may be presumed to have. You may call upon him to exercise all the actual existing knowledge common to the trade, but you cannot call upon him to exercise anything more. You have no right to call upon him to tax his ingenuity or invention."

From which it seems to follow that persons skilled in the art to which the specification is addressed are in fact those of ordinary and fair information, but not to those having very great technical knowledge relating to the subject-matter of the invention. And if, to them, the specification sufficiently and well describes the invention or process, it is quite sufficient.

* * *

[Patent held valid and infringed on appeal]

W.L. GORE & ASSOCIATES, INC. v. GARLOCK, INC.

United States Court of Appeals, Federal Circuit, 1983.
721 F.2d 1540, 220 USPQ 303.

MARKEY, CHIEF JUDGE.

* * *

Tape of unsintered polytetrafluorethylene (PTFE) (known by the trademark TEFLON of E.I. du Pont de Nemours, Inc.) had been stretched in small increments. W.L. Gore & Associates, Inc. (Gore), assignee of the patents in suit, experienced a tape breakage problem in the operation of its "401" tape stretching machine. Dr. Robert Gore, Vice President of Gore, developed the invention disclosed and claimed in the '566 and '390 patents in the course of his effort to solve that problem.

* * *

(C) § 112 AND THE '566 AND '390 PATENTS

The patents in suit resulted from a single application and thus have substantially identical specifications. The holding of invalidity on the basis of § 112 is common to both patents.

The district court found that the patents did not disclose sufficient information to enable a person of ordinary skill in the art to make and use the invention, as required by § 112, first paragraph, and that certain claim language was indefinite, presumably in light of § 112, second paragraph, because: (1) there was no definition in the specification of "stretch rate", different formulae for computing stretch rate having been developed and presented at trial; (2) there was no way taught in the specification to calculate the minimum rate of stretch above 35°C; (3) the phrase "matrix tensile strength" is indefinite; and (4) the phrase "specific gravity of the solid polymer" is indefinite.

The findings rest on a misinterpretation of § 112, its function and purpose. The district court considered whether certain terms would have been enabling to the public and looked to formula developments and publications occurring well after Dr. Gore's filing date in reaching its conclusions under § 112. Patents, however, are written to enable those skilled in the art to practice the invention, not the public, *In re Storrs,* 245 F.2d 474, 478, 114 USPQ 293, 296–97 (CCPA 1957), and § 112 speaks as of the application filing date, not as of the time of trial. *In re Mott,* 539 F.2d 1291, 1296, 190 USPQ 536, 541 (CCPA 1976). There was no evidence and no finding that those skilled in the art would have found the specification non-enabling or the claim language indefinite on May 21, 1970, when the application which resulted in issuance of Dr. Gore's patents was filed. Indeed, the expert quoted by the district court and whose testimony was primarily relied upon respecting formulae, was still in school at that time.

There is uncontradicted evidence in the record that at the time the application was filed "stretch rate" meant to those skilled in the art the percent of stretch divided by the time of stretching, and that the latter was measurable, for example, with a stopwatch. Concern for the absence from the specification of a formula for calculating stretch rate is therefore misplaced, and the post-filing date development of varying formulae, including Dr. Gore's later addition of a formula in his corresponding Japanese patent, is irrelevant.

Section 112 requires that the inventor set forth the best mode of practicing the invention known to him at the time the application was filed. Calculating stretch rate at that time was accomplished by actually measuring the time required to stretch the PTFE material. That was the only mode then used by the inventor, and it worked. The record establishes that calculation by that mode would have been employed by those of ordinary skill in the art at the time the application was filed. As indicated, Dr. Gore's disclosure must be examined for § 112 compliance in light of knowledge extant in the art on his application filing date.

The district court, though discussing enablement, spoke also of indefiniteness of "stretch rate", a matter having to do with § 112, second paragraph, and relevant in assessment of infringement. The use of "stretching * * * at a rate exceeding about 10% per second" in the claims is not indefinite. Infringement is clearly assessable through use of a stopwatch. No witness said that could not be done. As above indicated, subsequently developed and therefore irrelevant formulae cannot be used to render non-enabling or indefinite that which was enabling and definite at the time the application was filed.

Similarly, absence from the specification of a method for calculating the minimum rate of stretch above 35°C does not render the specification non-enabling. The specification discloses that "[t]he lower limit of expansion rates interact with temperature in a roughly logarithmic fashion, being much higher at higher temperatures." Calculation of minimum stretch rate above 35°C is nowhere in the claims, and it is the *claimed* invention for which enablement is required. The claims require stretching at a rate greater than 10% per second at temperatures between 35°C and the crystalline melt point of unsintered PTFE. That the minimum rate of stretch may increase with temperature does not render non-enabling Dr. Gore's specification, particularly in the absence of convincing evidence that those skilled in the art would have found it nonenabling at the time the application was filed.

The district court invalidated both patents for indefiniteness because of its view that some "trial and error" would be needed to determine the "lower limits" of stretch rate above 10% per second at various temperatures above 35°C. That was error. Assuming some experimentation were needed, a patent is not invalid because of a need for experimentation. *Minerals Separation, Ltd. v. Hyde,* 242 U.S. 261, 270–71, 37 S.Ct. 82, 86, 61 L.Ed. 286 (1916). A patent is invalid only when those skilled in the art are required to engage in *undue* experimentation to practice the invention. *In re Angstadt,* 537 F.2d 498, 503–

04, 190 USPQ 214, 218 (CCPA 1976). There was no evidence and the court made no finding that undue experimentation was required.

Moreover, the finding here rested on confusion of the role of the specification with that of the claims. The court found that the specification's failure to state the lower limit of stretch rate (albeit above 10% per second) at each degree of temperature above 35°C (a requirement for at least hundreds of entries in the specification) did not "distinguish processes performed above the 'lower limit' from those performed below the 'lower limit'". The claims of the '390 patent say nothing of processes and lower limits. Distinguishing what infringes from what doesn't is the role of the claims, not of the specification. It is clear that the specification is enabling, *In re Storrs, supra,* and that the claims of both patents are precise within the requirements of the law. *In re Moore,* 439 F.2d 1232, 169 USPQ 236 (CCPA 1971).

The finding that "matrix tensile strength" is indefinite, like the other findings under § 112, appears to rest on a confusion concerning the roles of the claims and the specification. While finding "matrix tensile strength" in the claims indefinite, the district court at the same time recognized that the specification itself disclosed how to compute matrix tensile strength, in stating "to compute matrix tensile strength of a porous specimen, one divides the maximum force required to break the sample by the cross sectional area of the porous sample, and then multiplies this quantity by the ratio of the specific gravity of the solid polymer divided by the specific gravity of the porous specimen." Further, the specification provided the actual matrix tensile strength in several examples. It is well settled that a patent applicant may be his own lexicographer. In light of the disclosure of its calculation in the specification, we cannot agree that "matrix tensile strength" is either indefinite or non-enabling.

Nor does absence from the specification of a definition for "specific gravity of the solid polymer", a part of the computation of matrix tensile strength, render that computation indefinite. It is undisputed that in the many examples in the application the specific gravity values used for unsintered and sintered PTFE were 2.3 and 2.2, respectively. There was no testimony that those values were not known to persons of ordinary skill in the art or could not be calculated or measured. There is simply no support for the conclusion that "specific gravity of the solid polymer" is indefinite or that absence of its definition renders the specification non-enabling. *See In re Wertheim,* 541 F.2d 257, 191 USPQ 90 (CCPA 1976).

We conclude that Garlock has failed to prove that at the time the application was filed, the specification was not enabling or that the claims were indefinite within the meaning of § 112.

*   *   *

WHITE CONSOLIDATED INDUSTRIES, INC. v.
VEGA SERVO–CONTROL, INC.

United States Court of Appeals, Federal Circuit, 1983.
713 F.2d 788, 218 USPQ 961.

MARKEY, CHIEF JUDGE.

White Consolidated Industries, Inc. (White) appeals from a judgment of the United States District Court for the Eastern District of Michigan that U.S. Patent No. 3,668,653 (the '653 patent) issued June 6, 1972 for a "Control System" was invalid and not infringed. * * *

We affirm. * * *

THE '653 PATENT

The '653 patent is directed to a numerical control (NC) system for machine tools. * * *

White markets an NC system under the name "Omnicontrol". That system, the subject of the '653 patent, links the computer and machine tool and provides for two-way communication between the operator and the computer, so that the operator may dynamically (i.e., while the program is running) modify the controlling part program.

The '653 system also includes a universal input feature so that a single part program can be used to control a plurality of machine tools, thus eliminating the need to create a new part program for each tool. This feature is accomplished by writing the part program in a universal NC language (i.e., machine tool independent) and employing a language translator in the control system to translate the program into machine code to control the tool. Describing the language translator, the '653 patent reads:

> The language TRANSLATOR used in the RUN mode may be a known translator capable of converting, in a single pass, a part program in programming language form into a part program in machine language form, as for example SPLIT (Sundstrand Program Language Internally Translated). In the CONVERSATIONAL mode, where each source or language part instruction is individually translated into machine language form, the TRANSLATOR program is modified by the additions shown in FIG. 12.

At the time the application that resulted in the '653 patent was filed, SPLIT was a trade secret of Sundstrand, White's predecessor in interest, and was available only by purchase from Sundstrand.

In holding the '653 patent invalid, Judge Cohn determined that (1) the language translator was an integral part of the '653 system; (2) SPLIT was the only single pass language known to work in the '653 system at the time and was considered by the inventors to be the best mode; and (3) by failing to disclose SPLIT, the '653 patent failed of compliance with the enablement and best mode requirements of 35 U.S.C. § 112.

* * *

(1) ENABLEMENT UNDER 35 U.S.C. § 112

35 U.S.C. § 112 requires that the invention be described "in such full, clear, concise, and exact terms as to enable any person skilled in the art * * * to make and use the same." White does not claim that SPLIT was disclosed, but rather that the specification contains an enabling disclosure notwithstanding its omission. White says the '653 patent calls for a known or standard single pass translator "as for example SPLIT" and specifies the characteristics of such a translator; that SPLIT was only an example; and that there were other known single pass translators interchangeable with SPLIT. White says because those other translators, e.g., ACTION and COMPACT, were known to those skilled in the art and available to them, the enablement requirement is satisfied.

We disagree. Though one may refer to an element of a claimed invention held as a trade secret by name only and yet satisfy 35 U.S.C. § 112 if equivalent elements are known, and known to be equivalents, and available to those skilled in the art, *In re Gebauer-Fuelnegg, et al.,* 50 USPQ 125, 28 Cust. & Pat.App. 1359, 121 F.2d 505 (1941), there is insufficient evidence here from which to conclude that suitable substitutes for SPLIT were known and widely available. Testimony that ACTION and COMPACT were "take-offs" of, i.e., patterned upon, SPLIT, does not, for example, establish that those translators were known to be suitable substitutes for SPLIT. That other translators were available when the application was filed is unavailing where there is no basis in the record for finding that a person skilled in the art on reading the specification would know that another single pass processor would be suitable. Indeed, the record here is to the contrary. The statements of Sundstrand, White's predecessor in interest, suggest that the inventors themselves (then employed by Sundstrand) originally considered SPLIT the *only* language suitable for operation in the "conversational" mode of the invention. * * *

White's assertion that SPLIT was itself widely available, albeit only upon purchase from Sundstrand, misses the mark. The sine qua non of a valid patent is a full, clear, *enabling* description of the invention. *Kewanee Oil Co. v. Bicron Corp.,* 416 U.S. 470, 480, 94 S.Ct. 1879, 1885, 40 L.Ed.2d 315 (1974). Though the "language translator" by itself is not the claimed invention, it is an integral part of the disclosure necessary to enable those skilled in the art to "make and use the same." Were Sundstrand (now White) to maintain SPLIT as a trade secret, it could, as Judge Cohn noted, theoretically extend its exclusionary rights beyond the 17 year life of the patent by controlling access to SPLIT, a result inconsistent with the objectives of the patent system. Sundstrand was therefore obliged to disclose the details of SPLIT or some other language translator, unless suitable substitutes were known and available to those skilled in the art or unless a suitable substitute could be obtained without undue experimentation.

Respecting the latter alternative, White correctly says a disclosure is sufficient even if it would require that one skilled in the art conduct some experimentation. The amount of required experimentation, however, must be reasonable. *In re Brandstadter,* 484 F.2d 1395, 1404, 179 USPQ 286, 294 (CCPA 1973). Richard Stitt, a skilled programmer in the NC field, testified in this case that development of a single pass language translator would require from 1½ to 2 man years of effort, a clearly unreasonable requirement. Though White says that estimate is irrelevant because it concerns development of a commercially profitable single pass translator and suitable commercial translators were readily available, the language of the '653 patent, "a known translator * * * as for example SPLIT", is insufficient to identify which language translators could be satisfactorily used and White presented no evidence that one skilled in the art would be able to select or develop a suitable translator without undue experimentation and delay.

It is immaterial that commercial use made, and publications issued, after the October 1968 filing date of the '653 patent may have established the suitability of other language translators (e.g., ACTION, ADAPT, APT, AUTOSPOT, COMPACT and UNIAPT). A sufficient disclosure must exist as of the application filing date. *In re Glass,* 492 F.2d 1228, 1232, 181 USPQ 31, 34 (CCPA 1974). That the listed language translators were not specifically identified at that time as suitable substitutes for SPLIT renders futile their citation by White in this case.

* * *

White has not demonstrated on this appeal that Judge Cohn erred in concluding that the '653 patent failed to meet the enablement requirement of 35 U.S.C. § 112.

* * *

ATLAS POWDER COMPANY v. E.I. DU PONT DE NEMOURS & COMPANY

United States Court of Appeals, Federal Circuit, 1984.
750 F.2d 1569, 224 USPQ 409.

BALDWIN, CIRCUIT JUDGE.

This is an appeal by E.I. du Pont De Nemours & Co. and its customer Alamo Explosives Co., Inc. (collectively, "Du Pont"). The appeal is from a final judgment of the United States District Court for the Northern District of Texas holding product claims 1–5, 7, 12–14, and 16–17 of U.S. Patent No. 3,447,978 ('978 patent), issued to Harold Bluhm on June 3, 1969 and assigned to the Atlas Powder Co. ("Atlas"), not invalid under 35 U.S.C. §§ 102, 103, and 112, not fraudulently procured, and infringed. We affirm.

* * *

Briefly, the '978 patent relates to blasting agents, *i.e.*, chemical mixtures that are relatively insensitive to normal modes of detonation

but can be made to detonate with a high strength explosive primer.
* * *

In light of the differences between the claimed invention and prior art, the '978 solution to a troublesome problem, and the unexpected result that a water-in-oil emulsion of ammonium nitrate, fuel oil, and a water-in-oil emulsifying agent can serve as a blasting agent in the presence of occluded air, we agree with the district court's conclusion of nonobviousness.

* * *

V. ENABLEMENT

The district court rejected Du Pont's arguments of "overly broad", "overclaiming", and "non-enablement", and its argument that the broad scope of the claims is not supported by the limited disclosure present. In essence, those arguments are one: the '978 disclosure does not enable one of ordinary skill in the art to make and use the claimed invention, and hence, the claimed invention is invalid under 35 U.S.C. § 112, ¶ 1.

To be enabling under § 112, a patent must contain a description that enables one skilled in the art to make and use the claimed invention. *Raytheon Co. v. Roper Corp.,* 724 F.2d at 960, 220 USPQ at 599. That some experimentation is necessary does not preclude enablement; the amount of experimentation, however, must not be unduly extensive. *See, e.g., W.L. Gore & Associates, Inc. v. Garlock, Inc.,* 721 F.2d 1540, 1557, 220 USPQ 303, 316 (Fed.Cir.1983), *cert. denied,* ___ U.S. ___, 105 S.Ct. 172, 83 L.Ed.2d 107 (1984); *In re Angstadt,* 537 F.2d 498, 503, 190 USPQ 214, 218 (CCPA 1976). Determining enablement is a question of law. *Raytheon Co. v. Roper Corp.,* 724 F.2d at 959–60, 220 USPQ at 599.

Du Pont argues that the patent disclosure lists numerous salts, fuels, and emulsifiers that could form thousands of emulsions but there is no commensurate teaching as to which combination would work. The disclosure, according to Du Pont, is nothing more than "a list of candidate ingredients" from which one skilled in the art would have to select and experiment unduly to find an operable emulsion.

The district court held it would have been impossible for Bluhm to list all operable emulsions and exclude the inoperable ones. Further, it found such list unnecessary, because one skilled in the art would know how to select a salt and fuel and then apply "Bancroft's Rule" to determine the proper emulsifier. Bancroft's Rule was found by the district court to be a "basic principle of emulsion chemistry," and Du Pont has not shown that finding to be clearly erroneous.

We agree with the district court's conclusion on enablement. Even if some of the claimed combinations were inoperative, the claims are not necessarily invalid. "It is not a function of the claims to specifically exclude * * * possible inoperative substances * * *." *In re Dinh-Nguyen,* 492 F.2d 856, 858–59, 181 USPQ 46, 48 (CCPA 1974) (emphasis omitted). *Accord, In re Geerdes,* 491 F.2d 1260, 1265, 180 USPQ 789, 793 (CCPA 1974); *In re Anderson,* 471 F.2d 1237, 1242, 176 USPQ 331, 334–35 (CCPA 1973). Of course, if the number of inoperative combinations becomes significant, and in effect forces one of ordinary skill in the art to experiment unduly in order to practice the claimed invention, the claims might indeed be invalid. *See, e.g., In re Cook,* 439 F.2d 730, 735, 58 CCPA 1049, 169 USPQ 298, 302 (1971). That, however, has not been shown to be the case here.

Du Pont contends that, because the '978 examples are "merely prophetic", they do not aid one skilled in the art in making the invention.[1] Because they are prophetic, argues Du Pont, there can be no guarantee that the examples would actually work.

Use of prophetic examples, however, does not automatically make a patent non-enabling. The burden is on one challenging validity to show by clear and convincing evidence that the prophetic examples together with other parts of the specification are not enabling. Du Pont did not meet that burden here. To the contrary, the district court found that the "prophetic" examples of the specification were based on actual experiments that were slightly modified in the patent to reflect what the inventor believed to be optimum, and hence, they would be helpful in enabling someone to make the invention.

Du Pont argues that of some 300 experiments performed by Atlas before the filing of the '978 patent application, Atlas' records indicated that 40 percent failed "for some reason or another". The district court agreed that Atlas' records showed 40 percent "failed", but found that Atlas' listing of an experiment as a "failure" or "unsatisfactory" was misleading. Experiments were designated "failures", the district court found, in essence because they were not optimal under all conditions, but such optimality is not required for a valid patent. *Decca Ltd. v. United States,* 544 F.2d 1070, 1077, 210 Ct.Cl. 546, 191 USPQ 439, 444–45 (1976). *Accord, E.I. du Pont de Nemours & Co. v. Berkley & Co.,* 620 F.2d 1247, 1260, 205 USPQ 5, 10 (8th Cir.1980). *Cf. Raytheon Co. v. Roper Co.,* 724 F.2d at 958, 220 USPQ at 598. The district court also found that one skilled in the art would know how to modify slightly many of those "failures" to form a better emulsion. Du Pont has not persuaded us that the district court was clearly erroneous in those findings.

* * *

1. The PTO Manual of Patent Examining Procedure (MPEP) § 608.01(p)(D) (5th ed. 1983), states:

Simulated or predicted test results and prophetical examples (paper examples) are permitted in patent applications. Working examples correspond to work actually performed and may describe tests which have actually been conducted and results that were achieved. Paper examples describe the manner and process of making an embodiment of the invention which has not actually been conducted. Paper examples should not be represented as work actually done. Paper examples should not be described using the past tense.

In sum, we conclude that Du Pont has failed to show that the district court erred in determining enablement.

* * *

2. BEST MODE

The Patent Act of 1793 required "in the case of a machine" the inventor "shall fully explain the principle and the several modes in which he contemplated the application of that principle". This Act also invalidated a patent if the specification "does not contain the whole truth concerning his invention" or "contains more than is necessary to produce the effect described" and "shall appear to have been intended to mislead, or shall actually mislead the public".

The Patent Act of 1870 changed this provision from "several modes" to the "best mode" with respect to machines. Presumably, this was a statutory basis for invalidating machine patents for failure to disclose the "best mode" contemplated by the inventor. However, several authors report that no Court did so prior to 1965.

The 1952 Patent Act broadened this "best mode" disclosure requirement to all kinds of inventions, not just machines, by providing in part in Section 112:

> The specification * * * shall set forth the best mode contemplated by the inventor of carrying out his invention.

STUDIENGESELLSCHAFT KOHLE mbH v. EASTMAN KODAK CO.

United States Court of Appeals, Fifth Circuit, 1980.
616 F.2d 1315, 206 USPQ 577.

COLEMAN, CHIEF JUDGE.

[Excerpt Only].

Eastman also challenges the validity of the '792 patent on the grounds that it fails to comply with § 112's requirement that the patent "set forth the best mode contemplated by the inventor of carrying out his invention." SGK and Eastman apparently agree that the '792 patent does not teach how to obtain the highly crystalline, isotactic polypropylene. According to Eastman, this process, discovered by Professor Natta, constitutes the best mode of carrying out the invention. Since Ziegler and his co-workers, as a result of their collaboration with Natta, were aware of Natta's use of δ–$TiCl_3$ as a catalyst component, Eastman argues, the trial court was correct in finding that Ziegler failed to set forth the best mode as required by 35 U.S.C. § 112.

In interpreting § 112, the courts have emphasized the obligation of the inventor to disclose the best method contemplated by him to carry out the invention, as of the time he executes his application. *Dale Electronics, Inc. v. R.C.L. Electronics, Inc.,* 488 F.2d 382, 388–89 (1st Cir. 1973); *Application of Glass,* 492 F.2d 1228, 1233–34 (Cust. & Pat.App. 1974); *Application of Gay,* 309 F.2d 769, 50 CCPA 725 (1962); *Benger*

Laboratories, Ltd. v. R.K. Laros Co., 209 F.Supp. 639, 644 (E.D.Pa.1962), *affirmed per curiam,* 317 F.2d 455 (3rd Cir.1963).

On the other hand, the courts have not required the mode disclosed by the inventor be in fact the optimum mode of carrying out the invention. *Application of Gay,* 309 F.2d at 773. Even if there is a better method, the failure to disclose it will not invalidate the patent if the inventor does not know of it or does not appreciate that it is the best method. *See Benger Laboratories, Ltd. v. R.K. Laros Co.,* 209 F.Supp. at 644, *affirmed per curiam,* 317 F.2d at 456. Instead, the thrust of the decisions in this area has been to require that the inventor act in good faith with no attempt to conceal what he feels is the best method of using the invention. *Benger Laboratories, Ltd. v. R.K. Laros Co.,* 317 F.2d at 456; *Application of Gay,* 309 F.2d at 772.

From our examination of the record we are unable to find sufficient evidence to justify the conclusion that Ziegler knew that the method employed by Natta was the best mode of carrying out the invention. Neither are we able to conclude that Ziegler acted without good faith or in an attempt to conceal what he believed to be the best use of his catalytic process. Under the statute, Ziegler was not required to disclose every known modification of his process. This is particularly true when those modifications are developed by other people. The mere fact that Ziegler knew of other uses of his catalysts does not create a presumption that he contemplated or appreciated those uses to be the best mode of carrying out his invention. In the absence of evidence that Ziegler felt the use of δ–$TiCl_3$ was the best mode of using his catalyst process, we cannot conclude that the '792 patent is invalid for failure to state the best mode.

BENGER LABORATORIES, LTD. v. R.K. LAROS CO.

United States District Court of Pennsylvania, 1962.
209 F.Supp. 639, 644, 135 USPQ 11, 15, affirmed 317 F.2d 455 (3d Cir.1963).

KIRKPATRICK, Judge.   *   *   *

The next attack upon the validity of the patent is that the specification does not disclose the best mode contemplated by the inventor of carrying out his invention as required by 35 U.S.C.A. § 112. The defendants' argument depends for most of its force upon the fact that the plaintiff has from the beginning used in its commercial production a method differing in some particulars from any method of manufacture disclosed by the patent and has been conspicuously successful in marketing its product on a world-wide scale. Of course, there may be many reasons why the plaintiff adopted this method in preference to others, and I do not regard the fact that a patent owner adopts a certain method for its commercial production as by any means conclusive or as compelling a finding that it is the best method although it must, of course, be considered. There is also always a question as to what is meant by the "best" method. There could easily be cases where reasons of economy or other considerations would call for the use of a certain method for production on a large commercial scale, although a greatly superior product might be produced if smaller quantities were desired.

A patentee must disclose the best method known to him to carry out the invention. Even if there is a better method, his failure to disclose it will not invalidate his patent if he does not know of it or if he does not appreciate that it is the best method. It is enough that he act in good faith in his patent disclosure. On the other hand, if he knows at the time the application is filed, of a better method to practice the invention and knows it for the best, it would make no difference whether or not he was the discoverer of that method. The answer to the question of sufficiency of disclosure of best method must be determined in the present case as of the time that the American application was filed.

It appears that after the patentees had disclosed their invention to their employer a controversy arose between them and another scientist who was in charge of commercial production. The latter (Fowler) wanted a method of production which would be efficient and give reliable and consistent results. The methods used by the patentees in their laboratory work produced the desired results but not consistently and Mr. Fowler became engaged with the patentees in a dispute as to the best method to achieve *his* objective. The patent applications were filed while this dispute was going on and, though commercial production proceeded in accordance with Fowler's method, London and Twigg remained unconvinced for some time.

* * *

Under these circumstances, I cannot say that either the Fowler method or that of Example 3 was "contemplated by the inventor" as the best method of carrying out the invention.

* * * [T]he only ground upon which it could be held that the insertion of Example 3 in the application for reissue was the introduction of new matter is that Example 3 was the only disclosure of the best method of practicing the invention. It has already been held that the proof falls short of establishing that fact. The fact that the processes of Examples 1 and 2 were demonstrated to have produced a usable product, the fact that the defendant Laros produces an infringing product on a large commercial scale by a different process than Example 3, and the fact that the very successful commercial production of the plaintiff differs in some respects from Example 3 all seem to make it at least a matter of grave doubt whether Example 3 is the best mode. At any rate, the defendants have failed to meet the burden of proving by evidence satisfactory to the Court that the inventors at the time the application was filed thought it was.

I, therefore, conclude that the reissue of the patent was proper and in accordance with the provisions of 35 U.S.C.A. § 251.

INDIANA GEN. CORP. v. KRYSTINEL CORP.[m]

United States District Court of New York, 1969.
297 F.Supp. 427, 161 USPQ 82, affirmed 421 F.2d 1023 (2d Cir.1970).

TENNEY, JUDGE. [Patent infringement action. The District Court, Tenney, J., held, inter alia, that Patent No. 3,036,009 relating to a ferro-magnetic, ceramic body with high quality at high frequency was invalid in that the specification failed to contain language adequately describing best mode contemplated by inventor of carrying out his invention so as to enable persons skilled in the relevant art to make and use the same.]

*   *   *

It has been well established that: " *   *   * the patentee is required to draft his specifications and claims as precisely as the subject matter permits, and his failure to do so may result in judicial invalidation of his patent." Georgia-Pacific Corp. v. United States Plywood Corp., 258 F.2d 124, 136 (2d Cir.1958).

As a corollary to that proposition, it is established as well that "a patentee cannot arbitrarily select a range in a known progressive change and maintain a patent monopoly on the products falling within that range on the ground that the designated range produces optimum results." Georgia-Pacific Corp. v. United States Plywood Corp., supra at 132; Kwik Set v. Welch Grape Juice Co., 86 F.2d 945, 947 (2d Cir. 1936).

It appears from a careful examination of the patent in suit that with regard to its description of the claimed invention it fails to set forth the best mode contemplated by the inventor. Although the *preferred* composition, which itself may have been an advance in the development of ferrite materials, was known prior to the effective filing date of the 1954 parent application, it was effectively obscured in both the parent application and the patent in suit. Rather than disclose its specific recipe, plaintiff merely included the elements of the preferred composition within the series of broad ranges claimed by the patent in suit, which ranges extended beyond the area representing significant technological advancement.

*   *   *

[T]he significant advance could not be determined by a consideration of the patent in suit in spite of the possibility that an inventive combination was lurking somewhere therein. Therefore, this Court is constrained to pronounce the patent in suit invalid for failing to comply with the requirements of 35 U.S.C.A. § 112.

*   *   *

m. Affirmed 421 F.2d 1023, 164 USPQ 321 (2d Cir.1970).

3. CLAIMS PARTICULARLY POINTING OUT AND DISTINCTLY CLAIMING THE SUBJECT MATTER

a. *Introduction*

The first Patent Act of 1790 provided that the specification "distinguish the invention or discovery from other things before known and used". Even more specifically, the Patent Act of 1836 provided that the inventor "shall particularly specify and point out the part, improvement, or combination which he claims as his own invention or discovery."

Despite these provisions, claims defining the invention as they are known today did not immediately appear in the issuing patents. Rather, patent claims have had a gradual evolution influenced and molded more by Court decisions and Patent Office regulations than by statutory requirements.[r] In the early case of Evans v. Eaton, 20 U.S. (7 Wheat.) 356, 434, 5 L.Ed. 472, 491 (1822), the United States Supreme Court invalidated a patent issued in 1804 on flour milling equipment, saying:

> The other object of the specification is, to put the public in possession of what the party claims as his own invention, so as to ascertain if he claimed anything that is in common use, or is already known, and to guard against prejudice or injury from the use of an invention which the party may otherwise innocently suppose not to be patented. It is, therefore, for the purpose of warning an innocent purchaser or other person using a machine, of his infringement of the patent; and at the same time of taking from the inventor the means of practicing upon the credulity or the fears of other persons, by pretending that his invention is more than what it really is, or different from its ostensible objects, that the patentee is required to distinguish his invention in his specification. Nothing can be more direct than the very words of the act. The specification must describe the invention "in such full, clear, and distinct terms, as to distinguish the same from all other things before known." How can that be a sufficient specification of an improvement in a machine, which does not distinguish what the improvement is, nor state in what it consists, nor how far the invention extends? Which describes the machine fully and accurately, as a whole, mixing up the new and old, but does not in the slightest degree explain what is the nature or limit of the improvement which the party claims as his own? It seems to us perfectly clear that such a specification is indispensable.

In 1853, the Supreme Court considered the patent issued to Samuel Morse on his renowned telegraph invention. The Morse patent had been held valid by the Kentucky District Court and on appeal the Supreme Court considered the propriety of the eighth claim which read:

r. Historical background for the United States system of claiming is found in the following articles:

Brumbaugh, History and Purpose of Claims in United States Patent Law, 14 J.P.O.S. 273, 426 (1932); Lutz, Evolution of the Claims of U.S. Patents, 20 J.P.O.S. 134, 377, 457 (1938); Rossman, Patent Claim Practice Needs Overhauling, 45 J.P.O.S. 363 (1963).

Eighth. I do not propose to limit myself to the specific machinery or parts of machinery described in the foregoing specification and claims; the essence of my invention being the use of the motor power of the electric or galvanic current, which I call electro-magnetism, however developed for marking or printing intelligible characters, signs, or letters, at any distances, being a new application of that power of which I claim to be the first inventor or discoverer.

In O'Reilly v. Morse, 56 U.S. (15 How.) 62, 112, 14 L.Ed. 601, 623 (1853), the Supreme Court found valid the first seven claims of the Morse patent and invalidated the eighth claim, saying:

It is impossible to misunderstand the extent of this claim. He claims the exclusive right to every improvement where the motive power is the electric or galvanic current, and the result is the marking or printing intelligible characters, signs, or letters at a distance.

If this claim can be maintained, it matters not by what process or machinery the result is accomplished. For aught that we now know some future inventor, in the onward march of science, may discover a mode of writing or printing at a distance by means of the electric or galvanic current, without using any part of the process or combination set forth in the plaintiff's specification. His invention may be less complicated—less liable to get out of order—less expensive in construction, and in its operation. But yet if it is covered by this patent the inventor could not use it, nor the public have the benefit of it without the permission of this patentee.

Nor is this all, while he shuts the door against inventions of other persons, the patentee would be able to avail himself of new discoveries in the properties and powers of electro-magnetism which scientific men might bring to light. For he says he does not confine his claim to the machinery or parts of machinery, which he specifies; but claims for himself a monopoly in its use, however developed, for the purpose of printing at a distance. New discoveries in physical science may enable him to combine it with new agents and new elements, and by that means attain the object in a manner superior to the present process and altogether different from it. And if he can secure the exclusive use by his present patent he may vary it with every new discovery and development of the science, and need place no description of the new manner, process, or machinery, upon the records of the patent office. And when his patent expires, the public must apply to him to learn what it is. In fine he claims an exclusive right to use a manner and process which he has not described and indeed had not invented, and therefore could not describe when he obtained his patent. The court is of opinion that the claim is too broad, and not warranted by law.

Thus, early in the evolution of patent claims, courts required they both particularly point out and distinctly define an invention and not be broader than the invention actually disclosed by the patent specification. Indeed, by 1891, the Supreme Court in McClain v. Ortmayer, 141 U.S. 419, 424, 12 S.Ct. 76, 77, 35 L.Ed. 800, 802 (1891) stated it was well settled that the claim must point out and distinctly define the invention, saying:

> Nothing is better settled in the law of patents than that the patentee may claim the whole or only a part of his invention, and that if he only describe and claim a part, he is presumed to have abandoned the residue to the public. The object of the patent law in requiring the patentee to "particularly point out and distinctly claim the part, improvement, or combination which he claims as his invention or discovery," is not only to secure to him all to which he is entitled, but to apprise the public of what is still open to them. The claim is the measure of his right to relief, and while the specification may be referred to to limit the claim, it can never be made available to expand it.

Unlike many European countries, in the United States, a modern patent claim is characterized by a so-called peripheral definition, i.e., a delineation of the outer limits or boundaries of the invention defined by the claim. This peripheral definition is often analogized to defining real property by a metes and bounds deed. In some circumstances, courts will provide limited relief from this concept of a peripheral definition under the judicially created doctrine of equivalents which is discussed in Chapter 6.

The relatively meager statutory provisions of the 1952 Patent Act pertaining to claims are set forth in Sec. 112 which provides:

§ 112. Specification

The specification shall contain a written description of the invention, and of the manner and process of making and using it, in such full, clear, concise, and exact terms as to enable any person skilled in the art to which it pertains, or with which it is most nearly connected, to make and use the same, and shall set forth the best mode contemplated by the inventor of carrying out his invention.

The specification shall conclude with one or more claims particularly pointing out and distinctly claiming the subject matter which the applicant regards as his invention.

A claim may be written in independent or, if the nature of the case admits, in dependent or multiple dependent form.

Subject to the following paragraph, a claim in dependent form shall contain a reference to a claim previously set forth and then specify a further limitation of the subject matter claimed. A claim in dependent form shall be construed to incorporate by reference all the limitations of the claim to which it refers.

A claim in multiple dependent form shall contain a reference, in the alternative only, to more than one claim previously set forth and then specify a further limitation of the subject matter claimed. A multiple dependent claim shall not serve as a basis for any other multiple dependent claim. A multiple dependent claim shall be construed to incorporate by reference all the limitations of the particular claim in relation to which it is being considered.

An element in a claim for a combination may be expressed as a means or step for performing a specified function without the recital of structure, material, or acts in support thereof, and such claim shall be construed to cover the corresponding structure, material, or acts described in the specification and equivalents thereof.

APPLICATION OF MOORE

United States Court of Customs and Patent Appeals, 1971.
439 F.2d 1232, 169 USPQ 236.

BALDWIN, JUDGE.

The sole issue in this appeal is whether the Patent Office Board of Appeals was correct in affirming the rejection of claims 1–7 in appellants' application as failing to comply with the requirements of 35 U.S.C. § 112. * * *

For the sake of completeness we will treat the claims on appeal as if they were rejected under both the first and second paragraphs of § 112. Any analysis in this regard should begin with the determination of whether the claims satisfy the requirements of the second paragraph. It may appear awkward at first to consider the two paragraphs in inverse order but it should be realized that when the first paragraph speaks of "the invention", it can only be referring to that invention which the applicant wishes to have protected by the patent grant, *i.e.,* the *claimed* invention. For this reason the claims must be analyzed first in order to determine exactly what subject matter they encompass. The subject matter there set out must be presumed, in the absence of evidence to the contrary, to be that "which the applicant regards as his invention."

This first inquiry therefore is merely to determine whether the claims do, in fact, set out and circumscribe a particular area with a reasonable degree of precision and particularity. It is here where the definiteness of the language employed must be analyzed—not in a vacuum, but always in light of the teachings of the prior art and of the particular application disclosure as it would be interpreted by one possessing the ordinary level of skill in the pertinent art.[2]

Once having determined that the subject matter defined by the claims is particular and definite, the analysis then turns to the first paragraph of section 112 to determine whether the scope of protection sought is supported and justified by the specification disclosure. This first paragraph analysis in itself contains several inquiries. Considering the language of the statute, it should be evident that these inquiries include determining whether the subject matter defined in the claims is described in the specification, whether the specification disclosure as a

---

2. It is important here to understand that under this analysis claims which on first reading—in a vacuum, if you will—appear indefinite may upon a reading of the specification disclosure or prior art teachings become quite definite. It may be less obvious that this rule also applies in the reverse, making an otherwise definite claim take on an unreasonable degree of uncertainty. See In re Cohn, Cust. & Pat. App., 438 F.2d 989 (1971); In re Hammack, 427 F.2d 1378, 57 CCPA 1225 (1970).

whole is such as to enable one skilled in the art to make and use the claimed invention, and whether the best mode contemplated by the inventor of carrying out that invention is set forth.

Two of the first paragraph requirements indicated above, *i.e.*, the "description of the invention" and the "best mode" requirements, are relatively simple to comply with and thus will ordinarily demand minimal concern on the part of the Patent Office. * * *

What is of maximum concern in any analysis of whether a particular claim is supported by the disclosure in an application is whether that disclosure contains sufficient teaching regarding the subject matter of the claims as to enable one skilled in the pertinent art to make *and* to use the claimed invention. These two requirements, "how to make" and "how to use" have sometimes been referred to in combination as the "enablement" requirement, but, in one form or another, have been the subject of extended discussion in this court of recent years. The relevant inquiry may be summed up as being whether the scope of enablement provided to one of ordinary skill in the art by the disclosure is such as to be commensurate with the scope of protection sought by the claims.

Applying now the analysis outlined above to the case before us, the position of the Board of Appeals regarding the definiteness of the claims before us can be justified only if it can be concluded that one of ordinary skill in this art, having appellants' disclosure and claims before him, would not be possessed of a reasonable degree of certainty as to the exact subject matter encompassed within the claims. We must conclude that the board's position cannot stand. * * *

Considering now any assertions that the claims are not supported by an adequate enabling disclosure and thus are unduly broad, we also find these to be not well taken. * * *

The decision of the Board of Appeals is reversed.

Reversed.

IN RE HYATT

United States Court of Appeals, Federal Circuit, 1983.
708 F.2d 712, 218 USPQ 195.

RICH, CIRCUIT JUDGE.

* * *

The proper statutory basis for the rejection of a single means claim is the requirement of the first paragraph of § 112 that the enabling disclosure of the specification be commensurate in scope with the claim under consideration.

The long-recognized problem with a single means claim is that it covers every conceivable means for achieving the stated result, while the specification discloses at most only those means known to the inventor. *See O'Reilly v. Morse,* 56 U.S. (15 How.) 62, 112, 14 L.Ed. 601 (1853). Thus, the claim is properly rejected for what used to be known as "undue breadth," but has since been appreciated as being, more accurately, based on the first paragraph of § 112. As stated in *In re Borkowski*, 422 F.2d 904, 909, 164 USPQ 642, 645–46 (CCPA 1970) (footnotes omitted, emphasis in original):

> The first sentence of the second paragraph of § 112 is essentially a requirement for *precision and definiteness* of claim language. If the scope of subject matter embraced by a claim is clear, and if the applicant has not otherwise indicated that he intends the claim to be of a different scope, then the claim does particularly point out and distinctly claim the subject matter which the applicant regards as his invention. That is to say, if the "enabling" disclosure of a specification is not commensurate in scope with the subject matter encompassed by a claim, that fact does not render the claim imprecise or indefinite or otherwise not in compliance with the *second* paragraph of § 112; rather, the claim is based on an *insufficient disclosure* (§ 112, first paragraph) and should be rejected on that ground. See *In re Fuetterer*, 50 CCPA 1453, 319 F.2d 259, 138 USPQ 217 (1963); *In re Kamal*, 55 CCPA 1409, 398 F.2d 867, 158 USPQ 320 (1968); and *In re Wakefield* (PA 8192), decided concurrently herewith. [422 F.2d 897, 164 USPQ 636 (CCPA 1970).] Thus, just as a claim which is of such breadth that it reads on subject matter disclosed in the prior art is rejected under § 102 rather than under the second paragraph of § 112, a claim which is of such breadth that it reads on subject matter as to which the specification is not "enabling" should be rejected under the first paragraph of § 112 rather than the second. We do not intend hereby to suggest that rejections under § 112 must be labeled "first paragraph" or "second paragraph." What we do suggest is that it should be made clear exactly which of the several requirements to § 112 are thought not to have been met. Is the claim unclear or is the specification's disclosure inadequate to support it?

The final paragraph of § 112 saves *combination* claims drafted using means-plus-function format from this problem by providing a construction of that format narrow enough to avoid the problem of undue breadth as forbidden by the first paragraph. But no provision saves a claim drafted in means-plus-function format which is not drawn to a combination, i.e., a single means claim.

*   *   *

D.M.I., INC. v. DEERE & CO.

United States Court of Appeals, Federal Circuit, 1985.
755 F.2d 1570, 225 USPQ 236.

Markey, Chief Judge.

D.M.I., Inc. (DMI) appeals from a grant of summary judgment of noninfringement by the United States District Court for the Central District of Illinois. We reverse and remand.

*   *   *

The district court said claim 1, "as thus interpreted," was not infringed by the accused Deere structure. As this court stated in

Raytheon Co. v. Roper Corp., 724 F.2d 951, 956, 220 USPQ 592, 596 (Fed. Cir.1983), "Claim interpretation is a legal matter subject to review free of the clearly erroneous standard applicable to fact findings."

The interpretation adopted here by the district court is in law twice flawed. It was adopted in contravention of the statute, 35 U.S.C. § 112, and it involved a reading into independent claim 1 of a limitation appearing in dependent claim 4.

Paragraph 6 of 35 U.S.C. § 112 reads:

> An element in a claim for a combination may be expressed as a means or step for performing a specified function without the recital of structure, material, or acts in support thereof, and such claim *shall be construed* to cover the corresponding structure, material, or acts described in the specification *and equivalents thereof.* [Emphasis added.]

The first flaw occurred here when the district court apparently lost sight of the *function* appearing in the involved claims. That function is clearly expressed in the language "for maintaining said steering wheel * * * lateral settings of said plow units" (claim 1) and "for correcting the disposition * * * for all lateral adjustments of said units" (claim 8). Its attention having been focused on a felt, but non-existent, need to find a "definition" of "compensating means" *per se* in the *claim* and on an unfounded fear that a "result" rather than a function might be covered, the court looked to the specification. No basis was cited by the district court, and none appears in the record, for limiting the means plus function limitation of the independent claims to compensating means formed of a parallelogram. *See Schenck v. Nortron Corp.,* 713 F.2d 782, 787, 218 USPQ 698, 702 (Fed.Cir.1983). To interpret "means plus function" limitations as limited to a particular means set forth in the specification would be to nullify the provision of § 112 requiring that the limitation *shall* be construed to cover the structure described in the specification *and* equivalents thereof. Patentees are required to disclose in the specification some enabling means for accomplishing the function set forth in the "means plus function" limitation. At the same time, there is and can be no requirement that applicants describe or predict every possible means of accomplishing that function. The statute, § 112–6, was written precisely to avoid a holding that a means-plus-function limitation must be read as covering only the means disclosed in the specification.

* * *

GEORGIA–PACIFIC CORPORATION v. UNITED STATES PLYWOOD CORPORATION

United States Court of Appeals, Second Circuit, 1958.
258 F.2d 124, 118 USPQ 122.

LUMBARD, CIRCUIT JUDGE.

* * *

The district judge, however, went further, holding that the description in the specification of the patent is fatally vague and indefinite and that none of the claims, including claim 1, particularly points out and distinctly claims the subject matter which the applicant regards as his invention. These conclusions appear to be predicated upon the lack of objective measurements both in the specification and claims and the inability of expert witnesses precisely to delimit the scope of the Deskey claims.

We think that the district court was too rigorous in applying the requirement of precision. This requirement serves two primary purposes: those skilled in the art must be able to understand and apply the teachings of the invention and enterprise and experimentation must not be discouraged by the creation of an area of uncertainty as to the scope of the invention. On the other hand, the policy of the patent statute contemplates granting protection to valid inventions, and this policy would be defeated if protection were to be accorded only to those patents which were capable of precise definition. The judicial function requires a balancing of these competing considerations in the individual case.

It is true that the Supreme Court has stated that "(a)n invention must be capable of accurate definition, and it must be accurately defined, to be patentable," United Carbon Co. v. Binney & Smith Co., 1942, 317 U.S. 228, 237, 63 S.Ct. 165, 170, 87 L.Ed. 232, * * *

On the other hand, patentable inventions cannot always be described in terms of exact measurements, symbols and formulae, and the applicant necessarily must use the meager tools provided by language, tools which admittedly lack exactitude and precision. If the claims, read in the light of the specifications, reasonably apprise those skilled in the art both of the utilization and scope of the invention, and if the language is as precise as the subject matter permits, the courts can demand no more. See Lever Bros. Co. v. Procter & Gamble Mfg. Co., 4 Cir., 1943, 139 F.2d 633, 639; H.H. Robertson Co. v. Klauer Mfg. Co., 8 Cir., 1938, 98 F.2d 150, 153. That an area of uncertainty necessarily exists in such a situation cannot be denied, but the existence of an inescapable area of uncertainty is not sufficient justification for denying to the patentee the fruits of his invention. * * * The patent covers a striated plywood surface formed by gouging out "a multitude of closely spaced grooves," a varying but considerable number of which must extend to or through the median of the ply. The number of grooves, their size and configuration, the size of the ribs, and the depth of the grooving are all variable within limits, and the infinite permutations of variables preclude a definite statement of these limitations.

This inevitable imprecision, however, is not fatal. Claim 1, read, as it must be, in the light of the specifications and drawings [H.H. Robertson Co. v. Klauer Mfg. Co., supra; Chicago Pneumatic Tool Co. v. Hughes Tool Co., supra; Raytheon Mfg. Co. of Newton, Mass. v. Coe, 1938, 68 App.D.C. 255, 96 F.2d 527] reasonably indicates to the industry the teachings and the scope of the patent. * * * Although the two drawings of the patent are concededly diagrammatic rather than to scale, they convey a visual perspective which aids in the interpretation of the claim.

This case has considerable similarity to Eibel Process Co. v. Minnesota & Ontario Paper Co., 1923, 261 U.S. 45, 43 S.Ct. 322, 67 L.Ed. 523, where the Court upheld an improvement patent in the paper industry. The patentee discovered that by increasing the height or pitch of an element of a machine the speed of the flow of paper could be increased so as to increase production and eliminate or minimize certain problems which had previously plagued the industry. The Court, pointing to the general adoption of the discovery, held the discovery patentable in the face of an attack that it constituted no more than a change in degree over the prior art. Further, the words "substantial" and "high" were held not to be too indefinite inasmuch as they were necessitated by variations in the practice of the patent and because those skilled in the art, in view of the drawing and their knowledge of the prior art, could understand the scope of the patent. See also Lever Bros. Co. v. Procter & Gamble Mfg. Co., supra.

Here both the specification and the claim to some extent interrelate a description of configuration and function, but we think the latter merely aids in understanding the scope of the patent. The patentee is not attempting to claim a function, stress relief, and all the manifold ways of obtaining it, thus claiming more than his invention. See Philip A. Hunt Co. v. Mallinckrodt Chemical Works, supra. Rather, his claim, as amplified by the specification, is restricted to striation, and the functional aspects of the description are a suitable supplementary means of indicating the breadth of the patent grant.

Nor does it seem that the industry has had any difficulty in understanding the meaning of the patent or its general scope. The long continued acquiescence in the defendant's unilateral and highly successful promotion of a striated panel strongly suggests that those skilled in the art considered the Deskey patent not only inventive but also sufficiently definite to withstand judicial scrutiny. We think it may truly be said, "It is impossible to suppose that anyone who really wished to respect the patent would have any difficulty in identifying what the claim covered." Musher Foundation v. Alba Trading Co., 2 Cir., 1945, 150 F.2d 885, 889, certiorari denied 326 U.S. 770, 66 S.Ct. 175, 90 L.Ed. 465.

* * *

RADIO STEEL & MFG. CO. v. MTD PRODUCTS, INC.

United States Court of Appeals, Federal Circuit, 1984.
731 F.2d 840, 221 USPQ 657.

FRIEDMAN, CIRCUIT JUDGE.

[Excerpt Only].

MTD contends that the '600 patent is invalid under *Lincoln Engineering Co. v. Stewart Warner Corp.*, 303 U.S. 545, 58 S.Ct. 662, 82 L.Ed.

1008 (1938). In that case the Supreme Court held that, where the invention was only an improvement in a single element of a combination of old elements, a patent claiming the entire combination was "void as claiming more than the applicant invented." 303 U.S. at 549, 58 S.Ct. at 664. The Court reasoned that "the improvement of one part of an old combination gives no right to claim that improvement in combination with other old parts which perform no new function in the combination." *Id.* at 549–50, 58 S.Ct. at 664–65 (footnote omitted). MTD argues that under *Lincoln Engineering,* the '600 patent is invalid since the only novel element of the invention is the channel-shaped portion at the ends of the cross brace, but the claims cover an entire wheelbarrow, all the other elements of which are old and well-known.

We disagree with MTD that *Lincoln Engineering* requires the invalidation of the claims of the '600 patent.

Contrary to MTD's argument, the channel-shaped portion of the cross brace is not the essence of the invention or its only novel element. To the contrary, as the district court stated in its discussion of obviousness, "[i]t is the totality of all the elements and their interaction with each other which is the inventor's contribution to the art of wheelbarrow making." The "new type of wheelbarrow" that, according to the district court, the '600 patent describes, was the result of a number of novel elements, including (in addition to the channel-ended cross brace) the two-piece handles, their joinder at the middle of the underside of the bowl, the support and the strengthening of that joinder by the cross brace, and attachment to the bowl. In sum, as the district court held, the '600 patent "descri[bed] * * * a new and improved complete wheelbarrow."

Lincoln Engineering does not control this case for another reason. *Lincoln Engineering* was decided more than 20 years before the present patent code was enacted in 1952. The question, therefore, is what significance, if any, that decision has on interpreting and applying the different statutory provisions of the present law.

In *In re Bernhart and Fetter,* 417 F.2d 1395, 163 USPQ 611 (CCPA 1969), the Court of Customs and Patent Appeals, whose decisions bind us, *South Corp. v. United States,* 690 F.2d 1368, 215 USPQ 657 (Fed.Cir. 1982), after discussing *Lincoln Engineering,* held that under the present statute the only proper basis for an old combination rejection is "that portion of section 112 which requires that the claims specifically point out and distinctly claim the invention." 417 F.2d at 1403, 163 USPQ at 618.

In the present case the district court did not discuss the application of that provision of section 112 to the claims at issue. It ruled, however, that each of the claims (other than claim 1 here at issue), "no specific deficiencies in which have been asserted * * * is in compliance with § 112." We conclude that claim 2 meets the statutory requirement that it "particularly point[ ] out and distinctly claim[ ] the subject matter which the applicant regards as his invention."

Claim 2 covers "[a] wheelbarrow comprising" a number of elements, which it discussed in detail and which fully point out and describe the elements of the invention. MTD, which did not even cite *In re Bernhart and Fetter,* despite the obvious significance of that decision on this point, has not rebutted the presumption of validity of the '600 patent, *Stratoflex, Inc. v. Aeroquip Corp.,* 713 F.2d 1530, 218 USPQ 871 (Fed.Cir.1983); *TP Laboratories, Inc. v. Professional Positioners,* 724 F.2d 965, 220 USPQ 577 (Fed.Cir.1984), which covers this requirement of section 112.

b. Claim Drafting

The struggle of inventors and their attorneys to draft proper claims caused the following comment of the Supreme Court in 1892 in Topliff v. Topliff, 145 U.S. 156, 171, 12 S.Ct. 825, 831, 36 L.Ed. 658, 664:

> The specification and claims of a patent, particularly if the invention be at all complicated, constitute one of the most difficult legal instruments to draw with accuracy, and in view of the fact that valuable inventions are often placed in the hands of inexperienced persons to prepare such specifications and claims, it is no matter of surprise that the latter frequently fail to describe with requisite certainty the exact invention of the patentee, and err either in claiming that which the patentee had not in fact invented, or in omitting some element which was a valuable or essential part of his actual invention.

Evidence that this struggle continues is the perceptive comment of Circuit Judge Brown in 1960 in Reed v. Parrack: [v]

> It is the hard lesson so much a part of every breathing moment of a patent solicitor's life—calling for a precision and a prescient forecast encountered in few other facets of the law—of claiming enough but not too much.

The art of drafting patent claims is usually learned by neophyte attorneys working with experienced practicing patent attorneys. There are few books which actually attempt to teach the novice how to write claims. An elementary approach is found in Drafting Patent Claims by Gray, Jackson and Morris (PLI 1966).[w] It is not the province of this text to teach claim drafting. However, some basic rules can be outlined:

1. A claim is a single sentence and usually has a preamble, a transition and a body.

2. Preferably, the language used in claims shall find its counterpart in the written description of the specification.

---

v. 276 F.2d 784, 788, 125 USPQ 256, 259 (5th Cir.1960).

w. Other Treatises on Claims are: Ellis, Patent Claims (1949); Deller, Patent Claims, 2nd Edition (1971); Stringham, Outline of Patent Law (1937).

3. The words "consisting of" are limiting in that they exclude other elements, while the word "comprising" does not exclude other ingredients or elements.

4. Claims should not be multiplied to the point that the differences or variations are so trifling as to be unreasonable.

5. Claims are usually sequenced with broad claims first and progressively narrower claims following.

6. Principal elements of a claim are preferably set out positively, i.e., each element is introduced by itself before reference is made to it. For example, a claim on an ordinary paper stapler might read:

> A device for stapling paper comprising: a base, a forming anvil carried by said base, etc.,—rather than "a base having a forming anvil."

7. Each element of a claim should be related to one or more of the other elements, i.e., the various elements of the combination should not be simply listed with no reference to how they relate to each other. In the above example, the forming anvil is recited as being "carried by said base". The claim might continue:

> a rigid actuator arm pivotally carried by said base and having a portion overlying said forming anvil.

8. Openings, recesses, grooves, slots and holes are usually recited indirectly as "in" or "formed in" a particular part. When the part has been positively recited, it may be described as "provided with" a certain opening, recess, etc. Thus, the stapler claim might read:

> An actuator arm pivotally carried by said base, having a portion overlying said forming anvil and provided with a storage recess extending along said arm for receiving and storing staples and a discharge slot open to said recess and positioned on said arm to register with said forming anvil.

9. Elements in a claim are not to be recited in the alternative.

10. Negative limitations are not generally used. For example, "a rigid actuator arm" as contrasted with "an actuator arm which is not resilient."

11. An element of a combination may be defined as a "means" plus a "functional" statement. (See Section 112) For example:

> means movable on said actuator arm for urging staples in said recess toward said slot, and means carried by said actuator arm to drive a staple from said recess through said slot into contact with said forming anvil.

Thus, a complete claim on a paper stapler might read as follows:

1. A device for stapling paper comprising:

> (a) a base,

> (b) a forming anvil carried by said base and having spaced recesses for shaping the legs of a U-shaped staple moved against said anvil,

> (c) a rigid actuator arm pivotally carried by said base at a point spaced from said anvil, having a portion overlying said anvil and

provided with a storage recess extending along said actuator arm for receiving and storing U-shaped staples and a discharge slot open to said recess and positioned on said actuator arm to register with said forming anvil,

(d) means movable on said actuator arm for urging staples in said recess toward said slot, and

(e) retractable means on said arm to drive a staple from said recess through said slot into contact with said forming anvil.

Dependent claims may also be used. For example—

2. A device for stapling paper as defined in claim 1 in which said retractable means comprises a blade movable in said slot and having a driving end movable from a first position above said recess to a second position through said slot, and resilient means carried by said actuator arm to return said blade to said first position.

The Patent Office permits a so called "Markush" claim (Ex parte Markush, 1925 Commissioner's Decision 126) in which, lacking a subgeneric term for some of a group of related substances, an applicant may use an expression—"a group consisting of" certain specified substances. This is used in chemical cases when all members of a certain group may not perform in the combination. For example, if certain members of the halogen family operate in a particular combination, but iodine does not, the claim could use the phrase "a group consisting of flourine, chlorine, bromine and astatine". This type of claim was discussed in Ex parte Dahlen, 1934 Commissioner's Decisions 9, where the Commissioner said:

The position of the examiner is that, a generic claim being allowed, there is no need of a subgeneric claim of the Markush type to fully cover the invention.

* * *

Even though a generic claim be allowable, by reason of a sufficient showing in the specification to justify the conclusion that there are properties common to all species of the genus which make them useful for applicant's purpose, such emergency may exist where, as here, the genus is of vast extent and comprises substances of rare occurrence or not easily obtainable for experimentation. In such a situation there is always the possibility that there may exist some little-known substance within the genus which is inoperative in the applicant's process (or composition) and which would consequently defeat a generic claim. It seems only fair to permit the use of a claim of the Markush type under such conditions. Such a "Markush" claim must be restricted to the members of the generic class which applicant has shown in his application to be operative for his purpose. Such a claim is analogous to a "preferred form" claim, as for example to a claim specifying a narrow range of temperatures where a broader range is stated in the specification and is included in another claim.

Another form of claim is called the Jepson type (Ex parte Jepson, 1917 Commissioner's Decisions 62) in which a certain addition is being made to a well-known apparatus. The following excerpt from the decision constitutes a succinct explanation:

> The claims in question are drawn to an invention which consists in adding a certain solenoid-coil in certain relation to old and well-known apparatus for operating the lights of a car from a storage battery and charging the battery from a variable-speed generator driven from the axle of the car. They are worded as follows:

> 16. In an electrical system of distribution of the class wherein a variable speed generator charges a storage battery and when the battery becomes sufficiently charged a voltage coil becomes effective to regulate the generator for constant potential, the combination with said voltage coil of a coil traversed by current flowing to the battery which is acted upon by decreasing battery current to reduce the potential maintained constant by the voltage coil.

> * * *

> I agree with the applicant's contention that the old elements should not be catalogued with equal emphasis with the new and that the claim should be so written as to make at once apparent a clear line of demarcation between the old structure and those elements which really constitute the invention. * * * I can see no reason why the preamble of the claim should not perform the double function of completing the setting of the real invention claimed and also disclaiming the old parts of the apparatus, which constitute nothing but setting. This is, in effect, what this applicant attempts to do. I have no doubt it would meet with the approval of the courts, because it seems to me nothing can be so important as to remove all uncertainty as to the exact location of the forbidden field covered by a patent. The Supreme Court very early emphasized this duty in *Evans v. Eaton*, 20 U.S. (7 Wheat.) 356, 5 L.Ed. 472 (1822).

> * * *

> The common German and English practice is to state briefly the old general structure in the claim, followed by such an expression as "characterized by" the certain particular structure which constitutes the patentee's invention. This language is much like that in our own statutes of 1790 and 1836—"that principle or character by which it may be distinguished." In the particular case before me I think this form of claim makes it unnecessary to analyze the claim in order to find out what is the life and essence of the invention. The claim is at once self-analyzing and self-classifying and, above all, it does what to my mind is the primary requirement of the statute and the essential condition of the contract between the inventor and the public—namely, it points out what parts of the described apparatus are and what parts are not the subject-matter of the patent monopoly. * * *

As some courts have indicated, drafting claims is an exacting discipline. It is at the same time fascinating and engrossing work which can be challenging in searching for words which will replace phrases and in attempting to envision and include devices which will fall within the spirit of the invention while still excluding the known prior art. The following cases are illustrative of certain claiming problems.

FROMSON v. ADVANCE OFFSET PLATE, INC.

United States Court of Appeals, Federal Circuit, 1983.
720 F.2d 1565, 219 USPQ 1137.

MARKEY, CHIEF JUDGE.

Appeal from four judgments of the U.S. District Court for the District of Massachusetts holding that claims 1, 4, 6, 7, 12 and 16 of U.S. Patent 3,181,461 issued to Fromson are not infringed or contributorily infringed. We vacate and remand.

* * *

In *Autogiro Co. of America v. United States,* 384 F.2d 391, 397, 155 USPQ 697, 702 (Ct.Cl.1967), our predecessor court recognized that patentees are not confined to normal dictionary meanings:

> The dictionary does not always keep abreast of the inventor. It cannot. Things are not made for the sake of words but words for things. To overcome this lag, patent law allows the inventor to be his own lexicographer. (Citations omitted.)

A patentee's verbal license "augments the difficulty of understanding the claims", and to understand their meaning, they must be construed "in connection with the other parts of the patent instrument and with the circumstances surrounding the inception of the patent application". *Id.* Accord, *General Electric Co. v. United States,* 572 F.2d 745, 751–53, 198 USPQ 65, 70–73 (Ct.Cl.1978).

This appeal hinges on construction of "reaction". The specification discloses a new and improved method of forming plates for use in lithography. Fromson discovered that the treatment of anodized aluminum with an aqueous solution of water soluble alkali metal silicate produces a water insoluble, hydrophilic, organophobic layer on the aluminum, a layer having exceptional lithography-related properties. Fromson's invention included the formation of the layer, not its exact structure. Though Fromson referred to the disclosed treatment as involving a "reaction", he also referred to it in the specification as an "application" and as "adsorption". Not all references to "reaction" were accompanied by a reference to formation of an aluminosilicate.

Fromson did theorize that his new, improved layer was an aluminosilicate believed "to be in the nature of a commercial zeolite", having "properties of a molecular sieve", but expressed that theory as merely a "belief". There is no basis or warrant for incorporating that belief as a limitation in the claims. It is undisputed that inclusion of Fromson's theory and belief was unnecessary to meet the enablement requirement of 35 U.S.C. § 112 (that a patentee describe how to make and use the invention). Moreover, it is axiomatic that an inventor need not comprehend the scientific principles on which the practical effectiveness of his invention rests. *See, e.g., Diamond Rubber Co. v. Consolidated*

Rubber Co., 220 U.S. 428, 435–36, 31 S.Ct. 444, 447–48, 55 L.Ed. 527 (1911).

Significant evidence of the scope of a particular claim can be found on review of other claims. *General Electric v. United States, supra,* 572 F.2d at 752, 198 USPQ at 70. Here, claim 5 (not asserted) limits the layer described in claim 1 to "an aluminosilicate structure in the nature of a zeolite molecular sieve", *i.e.,* to Fromson's theory of what is formed. In *Kalman v. Kimberly-Clark Corp., supra,* 713 F.2d at 770, 218 USPQ at 788, this court said "where some claims are broad and others narrow, the narrow claim limitations cannot be read into the broad whether to avoid invalidity or to escape infringement". *Accord, Environmental Designs, Ltd. v. Union Oil Co. of California,* 713 F.2d 693, 699, 218 USPQ 865, 871 (Fed.Cir.1983); *Caterpillar Tractor Co. v. Berco, S.P.A.,* 714 F.2d 1110, 1115, 219 USPQ 185, 188 (Fed.Cir.1983). The aluminosilicate limitation of narrow claim 5 cannot, therefore, be read into broader claim 1.

* * *

That "reaction" in the claims need not be confined to production of an aluminosilicate is consistent with the dictionary definition. That in Webster's New Collegiate Dictionary (1974) includes both "chemical transformation or change", and "interaction of chemical entities", which are consistent with the definitions appearing in Hackh's Chemical Dictionary (1969) and the American Heritage Dictionary (1970).

When an oxide coated aluminum surface is contacted with an aqueous solution of water soluble alkali metal silicate, chemical change occurs in at least two ways. First, ions or other chemical units in solution have somehow interacted to form a solid structure. Second, the water insoluble solid structure, whatever may be its precise nature (*e.g.,* silica or aluminosilicate), is not identical to the water soluble alkali metal silicate and oxidized aluminum that interacted to produce it. Moreover, there is clearly present an "interaction of chemical entities".

The foregoing is fully consistent with long-standing use of "reaction" in the lithography art. Claims are normally construed as they would be by those of ordinary skill in the art. *See e.g., Schenck v. Nortron Corp.,* 713 F.2d 782, 785, 218 USPQ 698, 701–02 (Fed.Cir.1983). Jewett interchangeably uses terms such as "treating", "treatment", and "react", to describe a lithographic plate producing process. Jewett's claims use "reacting", "treatment", and "reaction product". Jewett makes no attempt to define the structure of the layer there disclosed (as an aluminosilicate compound or otherwise), although it does mention the hydrophilic layer as being chemically bonded to the aluminum surface. Jewett refers to the layer as "silicate treatment", as "silicate or silicon containing" film, or as "an inorganic material such as silicate". It is not unreasonable to conclude that one of ordinary skill in the lithography art would interpret "react" in Fromson to mean the same thing it appears to mean in Jewett, *i.e.,* the treatment of a metal substrate with an aqueous solution to yield a layer, regardless of the chemical structure of the layer or the proper label for the phenomena that produced it.

We hold, therefore, that the district court erred as a matter of law in interpreting the claims as limited to the product of a chemical reaction producing a new chemical compound in the restrictive sense of those terms. * * *

IN RE MAROSI
United States Court of Appeals, Federal Circuit, 1983.
710 F.2d 799, 218 USPQ 289.

JACK R. MILLER, CIRCUIT JUDGE.

* * *

Initially, we note that appellants' invention, simply put, is the discovery that zeolites may be synthesized without the presence in the reaction mixture of alkali metal. The PTO does not appear to dispute appellants' point that the prior art syntheses of zeolitic compounds required, as an essential ingredient, alkali metal compounds. At the same time, the parties agree that there are minute but, nevertheless, measurable quantities of alkali metal (however undesired) in the re-agents utilized in appellants' synthesis. Thus, this appeal raises the practical question of whether and in what manner appellants may, in their claims, particularly point out and distinctly claim *their* invention.

Appellants have chosen to distinguish their invention from the prior art with the limitation "essentially free of alkali metal." It is well established that "claims are not to be read in a vacuum, and limitations therein are to be interpreted in light of the specification in giving them their 'broadest *reasonable* interpretation.'" *In re Okuzawa*, 537 F.2d 545, 548, 190 USPQ 464, 466 (CCPA 1976). The specification sets forth a method for synthesizing zeolites "in the absence of alkali metal." However, it recognizes that "industrial chemicals always contain traces of sodium," and, in recognition thereof, specifically defines the claim terminology in question, thus:

> Free from alkali metal, for the purposes of the invention, means essentially free from sodium ions. The residual alkali metal content of such zeolites is in principle only attributable to impurities of the chemicals used as starting materials. * * * Thus, commercial pyrogenic silica (Aerosil), which is a particularly suitable starting material, contains about 4 ppm of Na_2O.

The difficulty the PTO has with this definition which, appellants say, includes a process using pyrogenic silica having 4 ppm sodium but excludes a process using 3,819 ppm sodium (the lower limit disclosed by Rollmann et al.), is summarized in the Commissioner's brief: "[W]e challenge appellants to show on this record where one skilled in the art would draw the 'essentially free of alkali metal' line between 4 ppm and 3,819 ppm."

Insofar as it requires appellants to specify a particular *number* as the cutoff between their invention and the prior art, the PTO's position is impractical. Appellants' invention does not reside in such a number. The PTO's challenge is reminiscent of the argument advanced by the board in *In re Mattison,* 509 F.2d 563, 184 USPQ 484 (CCPA 1975). * * * The board said: "How much is a substantial increase? Is it 3%, 30%, 300%, or something else?" *Id.* at 564, 184 USPQ at 485. Reading the claims in light of the specification, the Court of Customs and Patent Appeals reversed, saying:

> General guidelines are disclosed [in the specification] for a proper choice of the substituent Ep together with a representative number of examples. If the prior art [compound] is modified by the inclusion of * * * substituent Ep as claimed, resulting in substantially increased efficiency * * *, the compound is within the scope of the claims. Hypothesizing whether an increase in efficiency of 3%, 30%, or 300% is necessary for said increase to be classified as substantial is not determinative of the issue of whether the claims satisfy 35 U.S.C. § 112, second paragraph.

Id. at 565, 184 USPQ at 486. (Footnote omitted.)

As in *Mattison,* appellants have provided a general guideline and examples sufficient to enable a person of ordinary skill in the art to determine whether a process uses a silicon dioxide source "essentially free of alkali metal" to make a reaction mixture "essentially free of alkali metal" to produce a zeolitic compound "essentially free of alkali metal." We are persuaded that such a person would draw the line between unavoidable impurities in starting materials and essential ingredients.

* * *

APPLICATION OF SWINEHART ET AL.

United States Court of Customs and Patent Appeals, 1971.
439 F.2d 210, 169 USPQ 226.

BALDWIN, JUDGE. This appeal is from the decision of the Patent Office Board of Appeals, adhered to on reconsideration, which affirmed the rejection of claim 24 in appellants' application as failing to meet the requirements of 35 U.S.C.A. § 112. The board reversed the rejection of two other claims.

THE INVENTION

The subject matter of the appealed claim is a composition of matter essentially made up of barium fluoride and calcium fluoride in approximately eutectic proportions. The record indicates, and appellants confirm, that "[e]utectic compositions of barium fluoride and calcium fluoride are well known in the prior art." However, appellants are apparently the first to discover that when crystalline forms of these two components are melted together in eutectic proportion and then resolidified by "conventional crystal-growing techniques," there results a multi-phase crystalline body characterized by an intimate matrix of large, visible crystals, which, unlike the prior art materials, does not cleave, is resistant to thermal shock and impact and approaches maximum density for the overall composition. In addition, and allegedly unexpectedly, these crystalline bodies "are capable of transmitting collimated light," especially in the infrared wave range.

The appealed claim recites:

24. A new composition of matter, transparent to infrared rays and resistant to thermal shock, the same being a solidified melt of two components present in proportion approximately eutectic, one of said components being BaF_2 and the other being CaF_2.

According to their brief, "[t]he exact point of novelty between appellants' claimed composition and that of the prior art is transparency."

THE GROUNDS FOR REJECTION

The examiner rejected claim 24 "for failing to particularly point out and distinctly claim the invention as required in 35 U.S.C. 112." His asserted reasons were as follows:

Claim 24 is functional and fails to properly point out the invention. Applicants point out on page 2 of the specification, lines 24–27 that when the components are merely fused and cast as an integral body, said body is opaque. This claim in reciting "transparent to infrared rays" is thus improperly functional. * * * It should also be noted that this claim does not require more than one phase.

The board agreed, adding:

Claim 24 stands rejected as improperly functional in that it distinguishes over the unsatisfactory material of appellants' figure 3 merely in the functional term "transparent to infrared rays."

* * *

We are convinced that there is no support, either in the actual holdings of prior cases or in the statute, for the proposition, put forward here, that "functional" language, in and of itself, renders a claim improper. We have also found no prior decision of this or any other court which may be said to hold that there is some other ground for objecting to a claim on the basis of *any* language, "functional" or otherwise, beyond what is already sanctioned by the provisions of 35 U.S.C.A. § 112.[5]

Assuming that an applicant is claiming what he regards as his invention, there are in reality only two basic grounds for rejecting a

5. Compare the following language quoted from the opinion in Locklin v. Switzer Bros., Inc., 125 USPQ 515, 519 (N.D. Cal., 1959), aff'd 299 F.2d 160 (9th Cir. 1961):

"Plaintiffs cite a multitude of cases in support of the argument that this functional expression invalidates the claims. But, none of these cases holds that claims employing functional expressions to define the claimed invention are per se invalid. In all of the cases relied upon by Plaintiff the claims were disapproved because under the particular circumstances the use of functional expressions either left the description of the invention too vague or made the claim broader than the invention."

claim under § 112. The first is that the language used is not precise and definite enough to provide a clear-cut indication of the scope of subject matter embraced by the claim. This ground finds its basis in the second paragraph of section 112, the rationale for which was discussed by us recently in In re Hammack, 427 F.2d 1378, 57 CCPA 1225 (1970). The second is that the language is so broad that it causes the claim to have a potential scope of protection beyond that which is justified by the specification disclosure. Cf. General Electric Co. v. Wabash Appliance Corp., 304 U.S. 364, 58 S.Ct. 899, 82 L.Ed.2d 1402 (1938). This ground of rejection is now recognized as stemming from the requirements of the first paragraph of 35 U.S.C.A. § 112. See In re Robins, 429 F.2d 452, 57 CCPA 1321 (1970); In re Borkowski, 422 F.2d 904, 57 CCPA 946 (1970). Cf. In re Halleck, supra. The merits of the "functional" language in the claim before us must be tested in the light of these two requirements alone.

"Functional" terminology may render a claim quite broad. By its own literal terms a claim employing such language covers *any and all* embodiments which perform the recited function. Legitimate concern often properly exists, therefore, as to whether the scope of protection defined thereby is warranted by the scope of enablement indicated and provided by the description contained in the specification. This is not to say, however, that every claim containing "functional" terminology is broad. Indeed, in many cases it will be obvious that only a very limited group of objects will fall within the intended category. Such appears to be the case here, since we do not sense any concern by the Patent Office that appellants are claiming more than they are entitled to claim under the first paragraph of section 112. We need not, therefore, consider whether there are any problems with the appealed claim arising under that paragraph.

* * *

It follows that when appellants' claim is read in light of that disclosure the limits it purports to define are made sufficiently clear.

The decision of the board is reversed.

Reversed.

IN RE THORPE

United States Court of Appeals, Federal Circuit, 1985.
777 F.2d 695, 227 USPQ 964.

PAULINE NEWMAN, CIRCUIT JUDGE.

We affirm the judgment of the United States Patent and Trademark Office Board of Appeals (the Board), which upheld the examiner's rejection of product-by-process claims 44, 45, 46, and 47 of U.S. Patent Application Serial No. 132,739 of Donald H. Thorpe *et al.* (Thorpe), filed March 24, 1980 for "Improved Process for Metal-Modified Phenolic Novolac Resin".

* * *

Product-by-process claims are not specifically discussed in the patent statute. The practice and governing law have developed in response to the need to enable an applicant to claim an otherwise patentable product that resists definition by other than the process by which it is made. For this reason, even though product-by-process claims are limited by and defined by the process, determination of patentability is based on the product itself. *In re Brown*, 459 F.2d 531, 535, 173 USPQ 685, 688 (CCPA 1972); *In re Pilkington*, 411 F.2d 1345, 1348, 162 USPQ 145, 147 (CCPA 1969); *Buono v. Yankee Maid Dress Corp.*, 77 F.2d 274, 279, 26 USPQ 57, 61 (2d Cir.1935).

The patentability of a product does not depend on its method of production. *In re Pilkington*, 411 F.2d 1345, 1348, 162 USPQ 145, 147 (CCPA 1969). If the product in a product-by-process claim is the same as or obvious from a product of the prior art, the claim is unpatentable even though the prior product was made by a different process. *In re Marosi*, 710 F.2d 799, 803, 218 USPQ 289, 292–93 (Fed.Cir.1983); *Johnson & Johnson v. W.L. Gore*, 436 F.Supp. 704, 726, 195 USPQ 487, 506 (D.Del.1977); *see also In re Fessman*, 489 F.2d 742, 180 USPQ 324 (CCPA 1974).

* * *

Thorpe acknowledges the controlling precedent of this court and the Court of Customs and Patent Appeals, as discussed *supra,* and invites us to overrule this precedent. Thorpe argues that as a matter of public policy a patent applicant should be entitled to product-by-process claims whether or not the same product was previously produced by some other process. He argues that no harm is done thereby, no patent rights are extended, and that the case law is unduly restrictive.

Thorpe reminds us of the principle that an inventor is entitled to claim an invention in the inventor's choice of terms, and argues that this entitles him to claim the product as produced by his admittedly patentable process. Thorpe states that a product-by-process claim is only infringed when the process of the claim is used, and that the grant of product-by-process claims merely enables a fairer scope of enforcement to an inventor's statutory right to exclude.

Thorpe has directed our attention to pending legislation, which he states would change the law we are here applying. It is the province of Congress to make changes in law based on public policy. We do not agree with Thorpe that we should act in anticipation of possible action by the legislature. To the contrary. It is inappropriate for a court to abandon long-standing precedent, were it in our power and inclination to do so, on the eve of congressional consideration. *Roche Products v. Bolar Pharmaceutical Co.*, 733 F.2d 858, 865, 221 USPQ 937, 942 (Fed. Cir.1984), *cert. denied,* __ U.S. __, 105 S.Ct. 183, 83 L.Ed.2d 117 (1984).

AFFIRMED.

c. Double Patenting

MILLER v. EAGLE MFG. CO.

Supreme Court of the United States, 1894.
151 U.S. 186, 196, 14 S.Ct. 310, 314, 38 L.Ed. 121, 127.

MR. JUSTICE JACKSON. * * *

The novelty of Wright's invention consists, as held by the court below, in the application of a double acting spring to assist the operator in either lifting the plow beams, or the plows attached thereto, or in sinking them deeper in the earth, as occasion might require, while the cultivator is in service. The first patent, issued in 1879, covered both the lifting and depressing actions or operations, while the second patent covered only the lifting effect. The spring device which was designed to accomplish these effects, or operations, is the same in both patents. The drawings in each of the patents are identical, and the specification in each is substantially the same. Under these circumstances can it be held that the second patent has any validity, or must it be treated as having been anticipated by the grant of the 1879 patent? If, upon a proper construction of the two patents—which presents a question of law to be determined by the court (Heald v. Rice, 104 U.S. 749 [26:914]) and which does not seem to have been passed upon and decided by the court below—they should be considered as covering the same invention, then the later must be declared void, under the well settled rule that two valid patents for the same invention cannot be granted either to the same or to a different party.

* * *

The result of the foregoing and other authorities is that no patent can issue for an invention actually covered by a former patent, especially to the same patentee, although the terms of the claims may differ; that the second patent, although containing a broader claim, more generical in its character, than the specific claims contained in the prior patent, is also void; but that where the second patent covers matter described in the prior patent essentially distinct and separable from the invention covered thereby, and claims made thereunder, its validity may be sustained.

In the last class of cases it must distinctly appear that the invention covered by the later patent was a separate invention distinctly different and independent from that covered by the first patent; in other words, it must be something substantially different from that comprehended in the first patent. It must consist in something more than a mere distinction of the breadth or scope of the claims of each patent. If the case comes within the first or second of the above classes, the second patent is absolutely void.

* * *

A single invention may include both the machine and the manufacture it creates, and in such cases, if the inventions are really separable, the inventor may be entitled to a monopoly of each. It is settled also that an inventor may make a new improvement on his own invention of a patentable character, for which he may obtain a separate patent, and the cases cited by the appellee come to this point, and to this point only, that a later patent may be granted where the invention is clearly distinct from, and independent of, one previously patented.

It clearly appears from a comparison of the two patents, and their respective specifications and drawings, that the first function or object of the patent of 1879, relating to the lifting power of the spring, is identical with the sole object or function covered by the patent of 1881, and that the improved device and combination for the accomplishment of the lifting operation are identical in both patents.

The invention covered by the first patent, as stated in the specification, consists in a spring which serves the double purpose of *lifting* or *holding* down the plcws at will; and it is further stated that one spring may be adapted to serve all, or either one, or more, of the offices above enumerated.

The patent of 1879 thus embraces both the lifting and the depressing effects or operations of the spring device, while that of 1881 seeks to cover only the increased lifting effect of the same device. The first patent clearly includes the second. No substantial distinction can be drawn between the two, which have the same element in combination, and the same spring arrangement and adjustment to accomplish precisely the same lifting effect, increasing as the beams are raised from their operative positions. The matter sought to be covered by the second patent is inseparably involved in the matter embraced in the former patent, and this, under the authorities, renders the second patent void.

APPLICATION OF VOGEL

United States Court of Customs and Patent Appeals, 1970.
422 F.2d 438, 164 USPQ 619.

LANE, JUDGE. This appeal is from the decision of the Patent Office Board of Appeals affirming the rejection of all claims (7, 10 and 11) in appellants' patent application serial No. 338,158, filed January 16, 1964, for "Process of Preparing Packaged Meat Products for Prolonged Storage."

The ground of rejection for each claim is double patenting, based upon the claims of appellants' U.S. patent 3,124,462, issued March 10, 1964, in view of a reference patent to Ellies, Re. 24,992, reissued May 30, 1961. No terminal disclaimer has been filed.

THE APPEALED CLAIMS

Claims 7 and 10 are directed to a process of packaging meat generally. Claim 10 is illustrative: * * * The invention is based on appellants' discovery that spoilage and discoloration of meat are markedly accelerated if the meat is allowed to reach ambient temperature before packaging.

Claim 11 is directed to a similar process specifically limited to beef.

* * *

THE PATENT

Appellants' patent, which is not prior art, claims a method of processing pork. Claim 1 of the patent is illustrative.

* * *

OPINION

The proceedings below in this case indicate the advisability of a restatement of the law of double patenting as enunciated by this court.

The first question in the analysis is: Is the same invention being claimed twice? 35 U.S.C.A. § 101 prevents two patents from issuing on the same invention. See, e.g., Application of Boylan, 392 F.2d 1017, 55 CCPA 1041 (1968). As we have said many times, "invention" here means what is defined by the claims, whether new or old, obvious or unobvious; it must *not* be used in the ancient sense of "patentable invention," or hopeless confusion will ensue. By "same invention" we mean identical subject matter. Thus the invention defined by a claim reciting "halogen" is not the *same* as that defined by a claim reciting "Chlorine," because the former is broader than the latter. On the other hand, claims may be differently worded and still define the same invention. Thus a claim reciting a length of "thirty-six inches" defines the same invention as a claim reciting a length of "three feet," if all other limitations are identical. In determining the meaning of a word in a claim, the specification may be examined. It must be borne in mind, however, especially in non-chemical cases, that the words in a claim are generally not limited to their meaning by what is shown in the disclosure. Occasionally the disclosure will serve as a dictionary for terms appearing in the claims, and in such instances the disclosure may be used in interpreting the coverage of the claim. In re Baird, supra. A good test, and probably the only objective test, for "same invention," is whether one of the claims could be literally infringed without literally infringing the other. If it could be, the claims do not define identically the same invention. This is essentially the test applied in In re Eckel, 393 F.2d 848, 55 CCPA 1068 (1968). There the court rejected the idea of "colorable variation" as a comparison category and stated that inventions were either the same, or obvious variations, or unobvious variations. The court's holding in *Eckel* was that same invention means identically same invention.

If it is determined that the same invention is being claimed twice, 35 U.S.C.A. § 101 forbids the grant of the second patent, regardless of the presence or absence of a terminal disclaimer. If the same invention is not being claimed twice, a second question must be asked.

The second analysis question is: Does any claim in the application define merely an obvious variation of an invention disclosed and claimed in the patent? In considering the question, the patent disclosure may not be used as prior art. In re Boylan, supra; In re Aldrich,

398 F.2d 855, 55 CCPA 1431 (1968). This does not mean that the disclosure may not be used at all. As pointed out above, in certain instances it may be used as a dictionary to learn the meaning of terms in a claim. It may also be used as required to answer the second analysis question above. We recognize that it is most difficult, if not meaningless, to try to say what is or is not an obvious variation of a claim. A claim is a group of words defining only the boundary of the patent monopoly. It may not describe any physical thing and indeed may encompass physical things not yet dreamed of. How can it be obvious or not obvious to modify a legal boundary? The disclosure, however, sets forth at least one tangible embodiment within the claim, and it is less difficult and more meaningful to judge whether that thing has been modified in an obvious manner. It must be noted that this use of the disclosure is not in contravention of the cases forbidding its use as prior art, nor is it applying the patent as a reference under 35 U.S.C.A. § 103, since only the disclosure of the invention claimed in the patent may be examined.

If the answer to the second question is no, there is no double patenting involved and no terminal disclaimer need be filed. If the answer is yes, a terminal disclaimer is required to prevent undue timewise extension of monopoly.

We now apply this analysis to the case before us.

The first question is: Is the same invention being claimed twice? The answer is no. The patent claims are limited to pork. Appealed claims 7 and 10 are limited to meat, which is not the same thing. Claims 7 and 10 could be infringed by many processes which would not infringe any of the patent claims. Claim 11 is limited to beef. Beef is not the same thing as pork.

We move to the second question: Does any appealed claim define merely an obvious variation of an invention disclosed and claimed in the patent? We must analyze the claims separately.

As to claim 11 the answer is no. This claim defines a process to be performed with beef. We must now determine how much of the patent disclosure pertains to the invention claimed in the patent, which is a process to be performed with pork, to which all the patent claims are limited. The specification begins with certain broad assertions about meat sausages. These assertions do not support the patent claims. The patent claims recite "pork" and "pork" does not read on "meat." To consider these broad assertions would be using the patent as prior art, which it is not. The specification then states how the process is to be carried out with pork. This portion of the specification supports the patent claims and may be considered. It describes in tabular form the time and temperature limits associated with the pork process. Appealed claim 11, reciting beef, does not read on the pork process disclosed and claimed in the patent. Further, we conclude that claim 11 does not define merely an obvious variation of the pork process. The specific time and temperature considerations with respect to pork might not be applicable to beef. There is nothing in the record to indicate that the spoliation characteristics of the two meats are similar. Accordingly, claim 11 does not present any kind of double patenting situation.

Appealed claim 10, supra, will now be considered. It recites a process to be performed with "meat." "Meat" reads literally on pork. The only limitation appearing in claim 10 which is not disclosed in the available portion of the patent disclosure is the permeability range of the packaging material; but this is merely an obvious variation as shown by Ellies. The answer to the second analysis question, therefore, is yes, and the claim is not allowable in the absence of a terminal disclaimer. The correctness of this conclusion is demonstrated by observing that claim 10, by reciting "meat," includes pork. Its allowance for a full term would therefore extend the time of monopoly as to the pork process. It is further noted that viewing the inventions in reverse order, i.e. as though the broader claims issued first, does not reveal that the narrower (pork) process is in any way unobvious over the broader (meat) invention disclosed and claimed in the instant application. The same considerations and result apply to claim 7.

The decision of the board is *affirmed* as to claims 7 and 10 and *reversed* as to claim 11.

Modified.

IN RE LONGI

United States Court of Appeals, Federal Circuit, 1985.
759 F.2d 887, 225 USPQ 645.

DAVIS, CIRCUIT JUDGE.

* * *

A. DOUBLE PATENTING—IN GENERAL

A double patenting rejection precludes one person from obtaining more than one valid patent for either (a) the "same invention," or (b) an "obvious" modification of the same invention. A rejection based on double patenting of the "same invention" type finds its support in the language of 35 U.S.C. § 101, which states that "Whoever invents or discovers any new and useful process * * * may obtain a patent therefor * * *" (Emphasis added.) Thus, the term "same invention," in this context means an invention drawn to identical subject matter. *In re Vogel*, 422 F.2d 438, 57 C.C.P.A. 920, 164 USPQ 619 (1970).

On the other hand, a rejection based upon double patenting of the *obviousness type* ((b), *supra*) is a judicially created doctrine grounded in public policy (a policy reflected in the patent statute) rather than based purely on the precise terms of the statute. The purpose of this rejection is to prevent the extension of the term of a patent, even where an express statutory basis for the rejection is missing, by prohibiting the issuance of the claims in a second patent not patentably distinct from the claims of the first patent. *Carman Industries Inc. v. Wahl,* 724 F.2d 932, 220 USPQ 481 (Fed.Cir.1983); and *In re Thorington,* 418 F.2d 528, 57 C.C.P.A. 759, 163 USPQ 644 (1969), *cert. denied,* 397 U.S. 1038, 90 S.Ct. 1356, 25 L.Ed.2d 649 (1970). Fundamental to this doctrine is the policy that:

> The public should * * * be able to act on the assumption that upon the *expiration* of the patent it will be free to use not only the invention claimed in the patent but also modifications or variants which would have been *obvious* to those of ordinary skill in the art at the time the invention was made, taking into account the skill of the art and prior art other than the invention claimed in the issued patent. (Emphasis in original.)

In re Zickendraht, 319 F.2d 225, 232, 50 C.C.P.A. 1529, 1536, 138 USPQ 23, 27 (1963) (Rich, *J.,* concurring). Under that facet of the doctrine of double patenting, we must direct our inquiry to whether the claimed invention in the application for the second patent would have been obvious from the subject matter of the claims in the first patent, in light of the prior art. *Carman Industries,* 724 F.2d at 940, 220 USPQ at 487.

Appellants argue that clear lines of division among the respective groups of claims in the several applications have been maintained. They conclude that because there are no "conflicting claims" and the claims in these applications do not "overlap," double patenting does not exist. However, appellants confuse the difference between the two types of double patenting. Overlapping and conflicting claims are considerations more significant in a § 101 "same invention" double patenting analysis. These are not "significant or controlling" factors in an obviousness type double patenting analysis where a rejection may be applied to "clearly distinct inventions." *In re Jentoft,* 392 F.2d 633, 640, 55 C.C.P.A. 1026, 1036, 157 USPQ 363, 369 (1968); *see also In re Siu,* 222 F.2d 267, 42 C.C.P.A. 864, 105 USPQ 428 (1955). This type of double patenting rejection has been applied where there are separate inventions, each of which is considered patentable over the prior art absent the first patent. *In re Bowers,* 359 F.2d 886, 53 C.C.P.A. 1590, 149 USPQ 571 (1966). Thus, appellants' argument that the claimed inventions do not overlap is irrelevant.

Appellants also maintain that the entire doctrine of double patenting of the obviousness type should not apply to commonly-owned applications with different inventive entities. A rejection based upon such a doctrine, appellants say, is unduly restrictive and discourages group research. Moreover, each inventor in a research department should be entitled to separate patents for his or her own independent contribution to the basic objective of the overall research project. Such a broad position has been previously rejected, and it is inconsistent with both our precedents and recent legislation.

Many times our predecessor court, the Court of Customs and Patent Appeals, has treated commonly-owned applications by different inventors as though they were filed by the same inventor, and then relied upon the doctrine of double patenting of the obviousness type to deny a second patent on subject matter not patentably distinct from the claims of the first patent. *See In re Newton,* 414 F.2d 1400, 56 C.C.P.A. 1463, 163 USPQ 35 (1969); *In re Frilette,* 412 F.2d 269, 56 C.C.P.A. 1262, 162 USPQ 163 (1969); *In re Rogers,* 394 F.2d 566, 55 C.C.P.A. 1092, 157 USPQ 569 (1968); *In re Bowers,* 359 F.2d 886, 53 C.C.P.A. 1590, 149 USPQ 570 (1966); *In re Borcherdt,* 197 F.2d 550, 39 C.C.P.A. 1045, 94 USPQ 175 (1952); and *In re Borg,* 392 F.2d 642, 55 C.C.P.A. 1021, 157 USPQ 359 (1968). In fact, the appellant in *In re Rogers* made an argument similar to the one the present appellant makes here. In that case, Rogers asserted that the obviousness type double patenting rejection was "distressing" to corporate practitioners and did not take into account the considerable exchange of information between inventors. The result, as the argument goes, would be that a corporation would find itself in a "box" because patent protection for both inventions would not be possible.

As we declared in that case, appellants, and those in like situations, are not in an inescapable "box." *In re Rogers, supra,* 394 F.2d at 571, 55 C.C.P.A. at 1099, 157 USPQ at 573. A patent may still issue if an applicant faced with such a rejection were to file a terminal disclaimer under 35 U.S.C. § 253, disclaiming "any terminal part of the term * * * of the patent," thereby guaranteeing that the second patent would expire at the same time as the first patent. It is well-established that a common assignee is entitled to proceed with a terminal disclaimer to overcome a rejection based on double patenting of the obviousness type. *In re Bowers, supra,* 359 F.2d 886, 53 C.C.P.A. 1590, 149 USPQ 571. Since the second patent would expire simultaneously with the first, this use of a terminal disclaimer is consistent with the policy that the public should be free to use the invention as well as any obvious modifications at the end of the patent's term. *In re Robeson,* 331 F.2d 610, 614, 51 C.C.P.A. 1271, 1275, 141 USPQ 485, 486 (1964).

* * *

As a last resort, appellants argue that under the recent legislative changes to 35 U.S.C. § 103, the "tenuous and untenable" double patenting rejection is unsupportable in light of the "fierce spotlight of the now-so-clearly revealed Congressional intent." To respond to this contention, we inquire whether the recent legislation changes or in any way affects the doctrine of double patenting of the obviousness type.

Certainly the mere words of the new statute do not compel the elimination of that type of double patenting objection. The objective of this amendment was to deal with citation of a co-worker's research development, *see In re Bass,* 474 F.2d 1276, 59 C.C.P.A. 1342, 177 USPQ 178 (1973) and *In re Clemens,* 622 F.2d 1029, 206 USPQ 289 (CCPA 1980), not with double patenting. *See* 130 CONG.REC. H10925 (October 1, 1984); PATENT LAW AMENDMENTS ACT of 1984, Pub.L. No. 98–622, § 104, 98 Stat. 3385, *reprinted in* 1984 U.S.Code Cong. & Ad.News

5827, 5833. Indeed, the present problem is definitively resolved by important legislative history of that legislation. Of particular interest are Congressman Kastenmaier's remarks, incorporated into the Senate Report, on the effect the legislation would have on the judicially created double patenting doctrine:

> The Committee expects that the Patent and Trademark Office will reinstitute in appropriate circumstances the practice of rejecting claims in commonly owned applications of different inventive entities on the ground of double patenting. This will be necessary in order to prevent an organization from obtaining two or more patents with different expiration dates covering *nearly identical* subject matter. In accordance with established patent law doctrines, double patenting rejections can be overcome in certain circumstances by disclaiming the terminal portion of the term of the later patent, thereby eliminating the problem of extending patent life. (Emphasis added.)

130 CONG.REC. H10525 (daily ed. October 1, 1984); SENATE COMMITTEE ON THE JUDICIARY, PATENT LAW AMENDMENTS ACT OF 1984, S.Rep. 98–663, 98th Cong., 2d Sess. 8 (1984), *reprinted in* 1984 U.S.Code Cong. & Ad.News 5834 (section-by-section analysis of the Patent Law Amendments of 1984). Although it would seem clear from this statement that the recent amendment was not intended to affect the doctrine of double patenting, but seems rather to reaffirm its viability, appellants argue otherwise. They assert that in referring to "nearly identical subject matter," Mr. Kastenmaier was coining a new term of art different from the established test utilized in the obviousness type double patenting doctrine.

There is no substantial support for this argument. As we have previously discussed, double patenting of the same invention type under § 101 questions whether the respective claims cover "identical" subject matter. In referring to "nearly identical subject matter," we believe Congressman Kastenmaier and the Committees were referring to subject matter which "would have been obvious" from the subject matter of the claims of the first patent, in accordance with the established existing doctrine of double patenting of the obviousness type. That the doctrine was left unaffected but reaffirmed is further supported by the "PTO's Initial Guidelines as to Implementation of Patent Law Amendments" which state:

> (14) Double patenting rejections may now be made in applications based on commonly owned patents of different inventive entities and double patenting rejections of the obviousness type can be overcome by terminal disclaimers.

> *   *   *   *   *   *   *   *   *

> (16) The Commissioner's Notice of January 9, 1967, "Double Patenting," 834 O.G. 1615 (Jan. 31, 1967) is withdrawn to the extent that it does not authorize a double patenting rejection where different inventive entities are present.

Reprinted in 29 BNA's *Pat.T.M. & Copy.J.* 214 (December 20, 1984). For these reasons, we hold that double patenting of the obviousness type, as applied to commonly-owned applications made by different inventive entities, is still a viable doctrine.

* * *

CARMAN INDUSTRIES, INC. v. WAHL
United States Court of Appeals, Federal Circuit, 1983.
724 F.2d 932, 220 USPQ 481.

EDWARD S. SMITH, CIRCUIT JUDGE.

* * *

As a matter of legal theory, double patenting between a design and a utility patent presents significant problems. Judicial and scholarly criticism has been leveled at the concept of applying double patenting between a design and a utility patent. Design and utility patents are based on different statutory provisions and involve different subject matter. The scope of protection afforded by each type of patent is different. It has been asserted that these differences entirely obviate double patenting in the design-utility setting. However, there exists CCPA precedent to the effect that a double patenting rejection of a pending design or utility patent application can be sustained on the basis of a previously issued utility or design patent, respectively.

* * *

Double patenting, as applied between a design and a utility patent, is a judicially created doctrine based purely on the public policy of preventing extension of the term of a patent, even where an express statutory basis for the doctrine is lacking. Double patenting may be found in a design/utility setting "irrespective of whether the patent relied on in the rejection and the application [or patent] on appeal involve the same invention, or whether they involve inventions which are obvious variations of one another." In the former situation ("same invention"-type) the test is whether the design and the utility patent claim the same subject matter. In the latter situation ("obviousness"-type), the test is whether the subject matter of the claims of the patent sought to be invalidated would have been obvious from the subject matter of the claims of the other patent, and vice versa. In considering that question, the disclosure of the "reference" patent may not be used as prior art. In certain situations, however, it may be used to define terms in a claim and to determine whether the embodiment claimed has been modified in an obvious manner.

In applying the above tests, there is a heavy burden of proof on one seeking to show double patenting. Double patenting is rare in the context of utility versus design patents.

We now turn to examine the facts relating to double patenting in terms of the above guidelines. The '068 (design) patent claims the visible external surface configuration of a storage bin flow promoter, as shown in the drawing below.

Front view

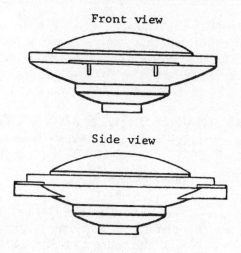

Side view

Wahl '068 design patent

The claims of the '508 (utility) patent, on the other hand, are drawn to the interior construction of a flow promoter. The exterior appearance of the invention claimed in the '068 patent does not dictate the interior structure, nor does the exterior appearance disclose the function, of the invention claimed in the '508 patent. It is possible, and fully in accordance with the construction given the claims by the district court, to practice the invention claimed in the '508 patent without utilizing the claimed design. Moreover, the court found that Vibra had indeed practiced the invention claimed in the '508 patent without utilizing the design claimed in the '068 patent. Thus, the '508 patent does not claim the "same" invention as does the '068 patent.

The question then becomes whether one patent claims an obvious variation of that which the other patent claims, and vice versa. With respect to that question, Carman has failed to sustain the heavy burden referred to above. The record is wholly inadequate to establish that it would have been obvious to a person of ordinary skill in the art to make the interior of the device according to the claims of the '508 (utility) patent simply from knowledge of the exterior configuration of the device claimed in the '068 (design) patent. Thus, even if it would have been obvious to make the invention claimed in the design patent in view of the subject matter claimed in the utility patent by simply designing the exterior and interior walls of the material-receiving member to be parallel, as Carman has attempted to prove, that alone is insufficient to establish double patenting in accordance with the two-way test set forth above.

We hold that, under the above guidelines, the '508 patent does not claim the same invention as, or an obvious variation of, the invention claimed in the '068 patent. Thus, the design patent did not, in effect, extend the beginning of the term of the utility patent. For the above reasons, the '508 patent is not invalid for double patenting.

* * *

Chapter Three

SUBJECT MATTER PATENTABLE
UNDER THE STATUTE

A. INTRODUCTION

The first Patent Act of 1790 was entitled "An Act to Promote the Progress of the Useful Arts" and defined patentable subject matter as "any useful art, manufacture, engine, machine or device or any improvement therein * * *" The language was changed slightly in 1793 to read "any new and useful art, machine, manufacture or composition of matter * * *" Essentially, the same language has been used in various succeeding patent statutes until 1952 when the word "process" was substituted for "art". Relevant Sections of 35 U.S. C.A. read as follows:

35 U.S.C.A. § 100. Definitions

When used in this title unless the context otherwise indicates—

(a) The term "invention" means invention or discovery.

(b) The term "process" means process, art or method, and includes a new use of a known process, machine, manufacture, composition of matter, or material.

35 U.S.C.A. § 101. Inventions Patentable

Whoever invents or discovers any new and useful process, machine, manufacture, or composition of matter, or any new and useful improvement thereof, may obtain a patent therefor, subject to the conditions and requirements of this title.

"The Committee Reports accompanying the 1952 Act inform us that Congress intended statutory subject matter to include anything under the sun made by man." [a] The Court of Customs and Patent Appeals, now the Court of Appeals for the Federal Circuit, indicates that "any process, machine, manufacture or composition of matter constitutes statutory subject matter *unless* it falls within a judicially determined exception to Section 101." [b]

Several writers [c] have dissected the Constitutional provision to conclude that it was the intention to promote "science" (meaning

---

a. Diamond v. Chakrabarty, infra, page 506.

b. In re Pardo, 684 F.2d 912, 916, 214 USPQ 673, 677 (1982).

c. DeWolf, An Outline of Copyright Law (1925); Lutz, Patents and Science, A

Clarification of the Patent Clause of the U.S. Constitution, 18 George Wash.Law Review, p. 50–55 (1949); Crosskey, Politics and the Constitution in the History of the United States, University of Chicago Press,

knowledge) by securing to authors copyright protection for their writings, and to promote progress in the "useful arts" by securing to inventors patent protection for their discoveries. The term "Useful Arts" has been used in the title of all of the patent statutes from 1790 to 1866 after which titles of this nature were discontinued. A subsequent section herein will deal with scientific discoveries but we might at this stage point out that one Supreme Court Justice [d] in 1950 stated that the invention "had to serve the ends of science—to push back the frontiers of chemistry, physics, and the like; to make a distinctive contribution to scientific knowledge." The results reached in determining validity of a patent can well be influenced by the attitude of a court as to the original and present purpose of the Constitution and the enabling statutes.

There seems to be agreement at the present time that the patent laws are not intended to secure protection for principles or abstractions. In Burr v. Duryee [e] the Supreme Court of the United States in a decision by Justice Grier, after quoting the statute relative to patentable subject matter, stated: "We find here no authority to grant a patent for a 'principle' or a 'mode of operation,' or an idea, or any other abstraction."

In Fuller v. Yentzer,[f] the Supreme Court carried this thought further in saying:

Patents for a machine will not be sustained if the claim is for a result, the established rule being that the invention, if any, within the meaning of the Patent Act, consists in the means or apparatus by which the result is obtained, and not merely in the mode of operation, independent of the mechanical devices employed; nor will a patent be held valid for a principle or for an idea, or any other mere abstraction. Burr v. Duryee, 1 Wall., 531, 17 L.Ed. 650.

DETMOLD v. REEVES

United States Circuit Court of Pennsylvania, 1851.
7 Fed.Cases 547 (No. 3,831).

KANE, DISTRICT JUDGE. The complainant, Mr. Detmold, is the assignee, and as such, the patentee in this country, of an invention made by M. Faber Du Faur, and patented by him in 1840 and 1841, in Bavaria and Wurtemburg. The American patent was issued in 1842, but it was amended and reissued in 1845. It was for "a new and useful invention for generating and applying heat," and its immediate subject is a new mode of collecting, conducting and using the combustible gases that ordinarily escape from the tunnel-head of the blast furnace. The defendants are extensively engaged in the manufacture of iron, and, it

1953; See also, Walker, Deller's Second Ed., Vol. 1, Section 10.

d. Justice Douglas in concurring opinion in Great A & P Tea Co. v. Supermarket

Equip. Corp., 340 U.S. 147, 71 S.Ct. 127, 95 L.Ed. 162 (1950).

e. 68 U.S. 531, 17 L.Ed. 650 (1864).

f. 94 U.S. 288, 24 L.Ed. 103 (1877).

is charged, that they are availing themselves of a part of the patented invention.   *   *   *

There is no doubt, that he who has discovered some new element or property of matter, may secure to himself the ownership of his discovery, so soon as he has been able to illustrate it practically, and to demonstrate its value. His patent, in such a case, will be commensurate with the principles, which it announces to the world, and may be as broad as the mental conception itself. But, then, the mental conception must have been susceptible of embodiment, and must have been, in fact, embodied in some mechanical device, or some process of art. The abstract must have been resolved into the concrete. The patent must be for a thing—not for an idea merely.

*   *   *

DOLBEAR v. AMERICAN BELL TEL. CO. (THE TELEPHONE CASES)

Supreme Court of the United States, 1888.
126 U.S. 1, 533, 8 S.Ct. 778, 31 L.Ed. 863, 988.

MR. CHIEF JUSTICE WAITE delivered the opinion of the court:

The important question which meets us at the outset in each of these cases is as to the scope of the fifth claim of the patent of March 7, 1876, which is as follows:

> "The method of, and apparatus for, transmitting vocal or other sounds telegraphically, as herein described, by causing electrical undulations, similar in form to the vibrations of the air accompanying the said vocal or other sounds, substantially as set forth."

It is contended that this embraces the art of transferring to or impressing upon a current of electricity the vibrations of air produced by the human voice in articulate speech, in a way that the speech will be carried to and received by a listener at a distance on the line of the current. Articulate speech is not mentioned by name in the patent. The invention, as described, "consists in the employment of a vibratory or undulatory current of electricity, in contradistinction to a merely intermittent or pulsatory current, and of a method of, and apparatus for, producing electrical undulations upon the line-wire." A "pulsatory current" is described as one "caused by sudden or instantaneous changes of intensity," and an "electrical undulation" as the result of "gradual changes of intensity exactly analogous to the changes in the density of air occasioned by simple pendulous vibrations."

Among the uses to which this art may be put is said to be the "telegraphic transmission of noises or sounds of any kind," and it is also said that the undulatory current, when created in the way pointed out, will produce through the receiver at the receiving end of the line "a similar sound to that uttered into" the transmitter at the transmitting end. One of the means of imparting the necessary vibrations through the transmitter, to produce the undulations, may be the human voice.

Articulate speech is certainly included in this description, for it is an "uttered" "sound" produced by the "human voice."

* * *

In his art—or, what is the same thing under the patent law, this process, this way of transmitting speech—electricity, one of the forces of nature, is employed; but electricity, left to itself, will not do what is wanted. The art consists in so controlling the force as to make it accomplish the purpose. It had long been believed that if the vibrations of air caused by the voice in speaking could be reproduced at a distance by means of electricity, the speech itself would be reproduced and understood. How to do it was the question.

Bell discovered that it could be done by gradually changing the intensity of a continuous electric current, so as to make it correspond exactly to the changes in the density of the air caused by the sound of the voice. This was his art. He then devised a way in which these changes of intensity could be made and speech actually transmitted. Thus his art was put in a condition for practical use.

In doing this, both discovery and invention, in the popular sense of those terms, were involved; discovery in finding the art, and invention in devising the means of making it useful.

* * *

What Bell claims is the art of creating changes of intensity in a continuous current of electricity, exactly corresponding to the changes of density in the air caused by the vibrations which accompany vocal or other sounds, and of using that electrical condition thus created for sending and receiving articulate speech telegraphically. For that, among other things, his patent of 1876 was in our opinion issued; and the point to be decided is, whether as such a patent it can be sustained.

In O'Reilly v. Morse, 56 U.S., 15 How. 62 [14:601], it was decided that a claim in broad terms (p. 86) [611] for the use of the motive power of the electric or galvanic current called "electro-magnetism, however developed, for making or printing intelligible characters, letters, or signs, at any distances," although "a new application of that power" first made by Morse, was void, because (p. 120) [626] it was a claim "for a patent for an effect produced by the use of electro-magnetism, distinct from the process or machinery necessary to produce it;" but a claim (p. 85) for "making use of the motive power of magnetism, when developed by the action of such current or currents, substantially as set forth in the foregoing description, * * * as means of operating or giving motion to machinery, which may be used to imprint signals upon paper or other suitable material, or to produce sounds in any desired manner, for the purpose of telegraphic communication at any distances," was sustained. The effect of that decision was, therefore, that the use of magnetism as a motive power, without regard to the particular process with which it was connected in the patent, could not be claimed, but that its use in that connection could.

In the present case the claim is not for the use of a current of electricity in its natural state as it comes from the battery, but for putting a continuous current in a closed circuit into a certain specified condition suited to the transmission of vocal and other sounds, and using it in that condition for that purpose. So far as at present known, without this peculiar change in its condition it will not serve as a medium for the transmission of speech, but with the change it will. Bell was the first to discover this fact, and how to put such a current in such a condition, and what he claims is its use in that condition for that purpose, just as Morse claimed his current in his condition for his purpose. We see nothing in Morse's case to defeat Bell's claim; on the contrary, it is in all respects sustained by that authority. It may be that electricity cannot be used at all for the transmission of speech except in the way Bell has discovered, and that, therefore, practically, his patent gives him its exclusive use for that purpose, but that does not make his claim one for the use of electricity distinct from the particular process with which it is connected in his patent. It will, if true, show more clearly the great importance of his discovery, but it will not invalidate his patent.[g]

* * *

CINCINNATI TRACTION CO. v. POPE

United States Court of Appeals, Sixth Circuit, 1913.
210 Fed. 443.

KNAPPEN, CIRCUIT JUDGE. This is a suit for the infringement of claims 1, 3, 4, 7, and 8 of United States patent to Pope, No. 805,153, November 21, 1905. The defenses are: (a) Nonpatentable subject-matter; (b) anticipation; (c) lack of invention; and (d) noninfringement. The district court held the patent valid and infringed, and made the usual decree for injunction and accounting, from which this appeal is taken.

1. *Is the subject-matter patentable?* The invention relates particularly to "time limit" transfer tickets for use by street railways, traction companies, etc. The stated objects of the invention are, in substance, to enable the railroad company to make the transfer as quickly as possible, and to keep check on conductors and passengers; and thereby be able to determine whether a given transfer has been correctly issued and whether lawfully presented by the passenger; as well as to provide a transfer ticket which when used can prove with certainty the correctness of the passenger's claim, thereby preventing litigation in case a transfer issued for forenoon use is presented for afternoon fare, and for this reason refused by the conductor.

g. "The use and purpose sought to be accomplished by the Hall patent was the radial expansion of the dress form, but is well settled by the authorities that the end or purpose sought to be accomplished by the device is not the subject of a patent. The invention covered thereby must con-sist of new and useful means of obtaining that end. In other words, the subject of a patent is the device or mechanical means by which the desired result is to be secured." Knapp v. Morss, 150 U.S. 221, 14 S.Ct. 81, 37 L.Ed. 1059.

The specifications disclose a ticket consisting of a strip of suitable material (presumably paper) divided into a body portion and a single afternoon coupon, the latter being separated, on the one side from the body portion and on the other from the stub, by lines or perforations or indentations, enabling the ready separation of the body from the coupon, as well as of the latter from the stub.

* * *

Claim 1 reads:

"1. A transfer ticket comprising a body portion and a coupon, said body portion and coupon bearing conventional indications to constitute an antemeridian transfer ticket when said body portion is used separately and a postmeridian transfer ticket when used together."

Claims 3, 4, and 7 do not differ from claim 1 in respects material here.

Claim 8 reads:

"8. A transfer ticket comprising a body portion and a coupon and further provided with conventional indications to constitute a complete transfer ticket for one part of the day when said body portion is used separately and a complete transfer ticket for another part of the day when said body portion and coupon are used together."

The patent is assailed as relating merely to "a method of transacting business, a form of contract, a mode of procedure, a rule of conduct, a principle or idea, or a permissive function, predicated upon a thing involving no structural law"; and counsel say that the ticket in question "has no physical characteristics which enable it to be distinguished from any other transfer ticket or from any other printed slip of paper." If this criticism is well taken, the subject-matter is not within the patent statute.[1]

But while the case is perhaps near the border line, we think the device should be classed as an article to be used in a method of doing business, and thus a "manufacture" within the statute (Rev.St. § 4886 [U.S.Comp.St.1901, p. 3382]). Broadly stated:

"The term 'manufacture,' as used in the patent law, has a very comprehensive sense, embracing whatever is made by the art or industry of man, not being a machine, a composition of matter, or a design."[2]

The device of the patent clearly involves physical structure. The claims themselves are, in a proper sense, limited to such structure.

The specifications describe a distinctive physical structure, viz., a given combination and general arrangement of body and coupon (with

1. In re Moeser (Ct. of App.D.C.) 123 O.G. 655; Hotel, etc., Co. v. Lorraine (C.C.A. 2) 160 F. 467, 87 C.C.A. 451; United States Credit System Co. v. American Credit Indemnity Co. (D.C.) 53 F. 818; s.c., 59 F. (C.C.A. 2) 139, 8 C.C.A. 49.

2. Language of Judge Acheson in Johnson v. Johnston (C.C.) 60 F. 618, 620. See, also, Riter-Comey Mfg. Co. v. Aiken (C.C.A. 3) 203 F. 699, 703, 121 C.C.A. 655, and cases there cited.

the suggestion that the two parts may be printed in different colors), accompanied by "conventional indications" and instructions for the use and interpretation of the ticket. But the alleged patentable novelty does not reside in the arrangement of the printed text, nor does such text constitute merely a printed agreement. The argument to that effect overlooks the important consideration that the body alone is good at one time, and that the body and coupon are required for the other portion of the day; and that the ticket bears on its face, whether the body is used alone or with the coupon, the distinguishing indications. Nor is there merely an attempt to patent a form of a contract. The specifications do not confine the construction to either the style, or printed arrangement or language of the legends. The essential thing is that the required information be conveyed on the face of the ticket. The authorities cited in the margin sustain, to a greater or less degree, the patentability of this device.[3]

Rand, McNally & Co. v. Exchange Scrip-Book Co. involved the patentability of an exchange scrip-book containing the essential feature that the units are expressed in money instead of miles as in ordinary mileage tickets, and avoided the necessity for calculation "by adopting a standard, expressed on the face of the ticket, that indicates to both carrier and traveller, without calculation, just what each one is entitled to." The language of Judge Grosscup seems peculiarly applicable here:

"Nor do we think that this patented concept is nothing more than a business method. Its use is a part of a business method. The ticket patented is not a method at all, but a physical tangible facility, without which the method would have been impracticable, and with which it is practicable."

The Benjamin Menu Card Case involved a combination of menu card with meal check. To the objection that it was "only for a piece of cardboard paper, with printed matter or composition on both sides thereof, and divided on one side by perforated lines employed in the system of doing business," Judge Seaman said:

"The fact that the structure may be of cardboard with printed matter upon it does not exclude the device from patentability, according to the patent office. * * *"

The presence of conventional indications and legends does not rob the structure of patentability. In more than one of the cases cited, the structures sustained as patentable bore conventional indications and information.

* * *

The decree of the District Court is affirmed, with costs.

---

3. Johnson v. Johnston, supra; Rand, McNally & Co. v. Exchange Scrip-Book Co. (C.C.A. 7) 187 F. 984, 986, 110 C.C.A. 322; Thomson v. Citizens' National Bank (C.C.A. 8) 53 F. 250, 255, 3 C.C.A. 518; Benjamin Menu Card Co. v. Rand, McNally & Co., 210 F. 285 (opinion by Judge Seaman); Ex parte Wm. E. Watkins, decision of Duell, Commissioner of Patents.

GREENEWALT v. STANLEY CO. OF AMERICA

United States Court of Appeals, Third Circuit, 1931.
54 F.2d 195, 12 USPQ 122.

THOMPSON, CIRCUIT JUDGE. This is an appeal by the appellant, the plaintiff below, from a decree dismissing a bill charging infringement of appellant's reissue patent No. 16,825 for a method of and means for associating light and music. The original issue was on January 15, 1924, upon an application filed August 30, 1918. The patent was reissued upon application on December 20, 1927. The issues upon hearing involved infringement of method claims 8 to 17 of the reissued patent. The defenses set up were invalidity and noninfringement.

* * *

It is urged, however, by the appellee that the association of light and color with rhythmic sound or music, sought to be monopolized by the appellant, as set out in her claims in suit, is not a statutory subject-matter for patent. It is conceded that method claim 10 is typical. It is as follows: "The method of combining sound and light for aesthetic expression, consisting in producing audible sounds in timed, rhythmic relationship, flooding with light an area within the area of audibility of the sound and simultaneously producing gradual variations in the color and intensity of the light in timed relationship with the emotional or aesthetic content of a succession of such sounds." * * *

We do not find authority in the law for the issuance of a patent for results dependent upon such intangible, illusory, and nonmaterial things as emotional or aesthetic reactions. An emotional or aesthetic timed relationship between music and light, thus dependent, is not a statutory "art, machine, manufacture, or composition of matter" susceptible of protection under the patent laws. R.S.Sec. 4886 (35 U.S.C.A. Sec. 31).

* * *

We conclude that the method claims are void for want of patentable subject-matter.

B. DISCOVERIES OF SCIENTIFIC PRINCIPLES AND NATURAL PHENOMENA

If we start with the premise that the patent system is to promote the progress of the "useful arts," the conclusion may follow that it does not reward basic scientific discoveries except as incorporated in useful devices. Could a discoverer of a basic principle such as Boyle's theory relative to relationship of gas volume to pressure be rewarded by the patent system? Could Einstein obtain a patent on his theory of relativity? Or Maxwell receive protection for his famous equations which describe the behavior of electric and magnetic fields? Much has been written on this subject [a] and a few decisions will be illustrative of the manner in which the courts have treated the problem.

MORTON v. NEW YORK EYE INFIRMARY

United States Circuit Court of New York, 1862.
5 Blatchford 116, 17 Fed.Cases 879 (No. 9,865).

[This case relates to a patent granted on a new and useful improvement in surgical operations on animals and involved the discovery that sulphuric ether when inhaled would produce an insensibility to pain which made it possible to perform major surgical operations with much greater facility and much less danger of shock to the patient. In rejecting the patentability of the subject matter, the court stated in part:]

SHIPMAN, J. * * * The means, that is, the process of the inhalation of vapors, existed among the animals of the geologic ages preceding the creation of our race. That process, in connection with these vapors, is as old as the vapors themselves. We come, therefore, to the same point, only by a different road. We have, after all, only a new or more perfect effect of a well-known chemical agent, operating through one of the ordinary functions of animal life.

It is curious and instructive to observe the perpetual struggle, in the specification, to draw from the surgical operation some support to the patent, beyond that of its utility. "We are fully aware," says the paragraph immediately preceding the claim, "that narcotics have been administered to patients undergoing surgical operations, and, as we believe, always, by introducing them into the stomach. This we consider in no respect to embody our invention, as we operate through the lungs and air passages." An examination of this single passage in the specification will demonstrate the impossibility of sustaining this patent on any grounds known to the law. Now, suppose these agents had been fluids instead of elastic vapors, and their effect had been known, when taken into the stomach, to be the same as that now long known to have resulted from their inhalation, namely, a state of partial intoxication—would the discovery that an increased quantity of the fluid produced a more perfect effect, by rendering intoxication complete, accompanied by total insensibility to pain, have rendered the discovery patentable? We think clearly not. In this view of the subject, we here lay out of the case the application of the new effect to surgical operations. We will allude to that again, in a moment. Now, a precisely parallel case is presented, by the actual facts before us, to the one just supposed. The inhalation of the ethers had long been known. By increasing their quantity, it was discovered that a new or more complete effect was produced, by which the subject was rendered

a. Charles W. Rivise: What's Patentable in Paper Making? (1929) 11 J.P.O.S. 494, 503; William J. Wyman: Patents for Scientific Discoveries (1929) 11 J.P.O.S. 533; A.S. Greenberg: Quasi-Patent Rights: A Proposal for the Future (1930) 12 J.P. O.S. 13, 65, 115; Arthur M. Smith: Protection of Scientific Property (1932) 14 J.P. O.S. 336; Spencer: Scientific Property (1932) 13 Am.Bar Assn. Jr. 79.

wholly insensible. This can be no more patentable than the discovery that the increased quantity of liquor, taken into the stomach, would produce a like result. In both cases, there is only a naked discovery of a new effect, resulting from a well-known agent, working by a well-known process. This effect is a temporary suspension of sensibility and motion in the animal body. What is new in the alleged invention begins and ends here. The fact that the surgeon can operate upon the body in the condition to which it is thus reduced, forms no part of the invention or discovery. It simply furnishes evidence that it can be applied to at least one useful purpose—a fact quite independent of the other elements necessary to make a discovery patentable.

Before dismissing this case, it may not be amiss to speak of the character of the discovery upon which the patent is founded. Its value in securing insensibility during the surgical operation, and thus saving the patient from sharp anguish while it is proceeding, and mitigating the shock to his system, which would otherwise be much greater, was proved, on the trial, by distinguished surgeons of the city of New York. They agreed in ranking it among the great discoveries of modern times; and one of them remarked that its value was too great to be estimated in dollars and cents. Its universal use, too, concurs to the same point. Its discoverer is entitled to be classed among the greatest benefactors of mankind. But the beneficent and imposing character of the discovery cannot change the legal principles upon which the law of patents is founded nor abrogate the rules by which judicial construction must be governed. These principles and rules are fixed, and uninfluenced by shades and degrees of comparative merit. They secure to the inventor a monopoly in the manufacture, use, and sale of very humble contrivance, of limited usefulness, the fruits of indifferent skill and trifling ingenuity, as well as of those grander products of his genius which confer renown on himself and extensive and lasting benefits on society. But they are inadequate to the protection of every discovery, by securing its exclusive control to the explorer to whose eye it may be first disclosed. A discovery may be brilliant and useful, and not patentable. No matter through what long, solitary vigils, or by what importunate efforts, the secret may have been wrong from the bosom of nature, or to what useful purposes it may be applied. Something more is necessary. The new force or principle brought to light must be embodied and set to work, and can be patented only in connection or combination with the means by which, or the medium through which, it operates. Neither the natural functions of an animal, upon which or through which it may be designed to operate, nor any of the useful purposes to which it may be applied, can form any essential parts of the combination, however they may illustrate and establish its usefulness.[b]

NELSON, J. concurred.

Motion for new trial denied.

---

b. Could this discovery have been protected as a process if discovery had been made after Section 101 of the 1952 Patent Statute had been enacted?

Now, what about those discoveries which are not applied by the discoverer to a useful purpose embodied in an art, machine, manufacture or composition of matter? Even these discoveries must be grouped into two classes before a solution can be proposed. Anticipating what is to be analyzed in detail in the next part of this paper, Professor Wigmore is quoted: "It must be obvious therefore that, even if we are ready to concede to scientists the right to a share of the profits for some of their discoveries, a sure line must be drawn *between those discoveries which lead to novel applications based exclusively on the discoveries,* and those discoveries which *explain practices* already *existing in industry* generally." And cannot this line of distinction be employed in rationalizing a constitutional system of legislative reward for discoverers of the first group, *without necessarily extending to them an exclusive right to their discoveries?* Greenberg, Quasi-Patent Rights, 12 J.P.O.S. 115, 127 (1930).

WISCONSIN ALUMNI RESEARCH FOUNDATION v. VITAMIN TECHNOLOGISTS, INC.

United States District Court of California, 1941.
41 F.Supp. 857, 51 USPQ 345, reversed 146 F.2d 941, 63 USPQ 262 (1944).

CAVANAH, DISTRICT JUDGE. The suit involves the validity and infringement of three patents issued to Dr. Harry Steenbock of the University of Wisconsin, who transferred his interest in them to the plaintiff, Wisconsin Alumni Research Foundation of Madison, Wisconsin, a non-profit affair, which was organized in 1925 for the purpose of promoting scientific research at the University in assisting in the development of inventions and discoveries made by the faculty and students of the University. The defendant Vitamin Technologists is a corporation organized under the laws of the State of California, and the defendant H.F.B. Roessler is a director and officer of the defendant corporation.

* * *

LAW OR PROCESS OF NATURE

The argument is pressed that the inventions of the patents in suit cover only a law or process of nature and the foundation of the argument is that they cover the use of sunlight and nature's practices as sunlight, as "Mother nature forms vitamin D in foods eaten by man and animal and forms vitamin D in man and animal whenever exposed to the sun", and is not patentable, presents the interesting question as to whether or not the process covered by the patents may utilize a law of nature by means of an art and put it in a certain specified condition and then use it in that condition for a practical purpose. The process claims in the patents utilize ultra violet light. It did not discover or invent ultra violet light, but invented processes in which ultra violet light is utilized and invented products derived from the utilization of ultra violet light. The patents are not directed to what nature was doing, as it was not known prior to then that the sunlight, unaided by man, was efficient to treat edible products or inactive substances so as to activate the provitamin in such substances or products and thereby make them a preventative or cure of rickets.

* * *

These terms of the patent and the evidence disclose that Dr. Steenbock whose discoveries concerned with the effects of sunlight followed them up by inventing a new method by which to accomplish through artificial means what sunlight could not do. It appears clear that prior to the Steenbock discoveries and invention it was not known that it was possible to treat edible products with ultra violet rays so as to make such products a preventative or cure of rickets, and such process was practical through the use of sunlight, or that the ultra violet rays of the sun could not antirachitically process medicine or food with any distinction as to selection of substances, or of intensity, or of time, or that ultra violet rays of the sun could not practically impart the antirachitic principle to medicine or foods as the only then recognized edible, antirachitic substance was cod liver oil.

* * *

rule

The principle of law is settled that if one has gone beyond the *domains* of discovery and laid hold of a new force and connected it with some *mechanical contrivance* through which it acts, he is entitled to secure control of it, for the existence in nature of a force that can be and is used by man does not argue against invention unless the invention consists simply in adopting what nature, unaided, gave. It is the use that is patentable, the utilizing of a law of nature by means of a method. The process covered by the patent is patentable if it is one where, as said by Judge Lacombe of the Second Circuit Court of Appeals: "The process is one which puts a force of nature into a certain specified condition and then uses it in that condition for a practical purpose." Cameron Septic Tank Co. v. Village of Saratoga Springs et al., 2 Cir., 159 F. 453, 463; Telephone Cases, 126 U.S. 1, 8 S.Ct. 778, 31 L.Ed. 863; American Chemical Paint Co. v. C.R. Wilson Body Co., D.C., 298 F. 310.

In respect to the yeast and essence patent, nature never provided any unsaponifiable lipoid extract, activated, or prepared a concentrate to be activated to be used as a cure or preventative for rickets, or that yeast was ever antirachitically activated by subjecting it to the action of the ultra violet rays of the sun. It was not known prior to the Steenbock inventions that edible products or inactive substances could be treated with ultra violet rays so as to make them a preventative or cure of rickets. Prior to the plaintiff's patents, rickets were increasing among infants and neither the sun nor man had an antirachitic food or medicine activated by ultra violet light or an essence antirachitically activated for prevention and cure of rickets. The claims of it do not cover sunlight and is limited to the employment of "artificially produced ultra violet rays" and are supported by the specification of the second patent and are not based upon any new matter.

* * *

In view of what has been said as disclosed by the evidence, the patents of the plaintiff are valid, and have been infringed by the defendants, who are each enjoined from further infringement, and for an accounting to be made by the defendant Vitamin Technologists, Inc., for profits and damages, if any, with costs, and findings of fact and conclusions of law to that effect will be made.

VITAMIN TECHNOLOGISTS, INC. v. WISCONSIN ALUMNI RESEARCH FOUNDATION

United States Court of Appeals, Ninth Circuit, 1944.
146 F.2d 941, 63 USPQ 262.

(The majority opinion and parts of the concurring opinion are omitted)

HEALY, CIRCUIT JUDGE (concurring).

I agree with the result of the main opinion and with much that is said in it. I think, though, that we should confine ourselves to the issues actually presented by counsel. Further, it appears to me doubtful that the claims are fairly subject to the criticism that they broadly include a monopoly of the use of sunlight. The patents should be adjudged invalid on the less questionable ground of anticipation.

* * *

I think the Steenbock patents are subject to an infirmity still more fundamental. Ultra violet light is a natural form of energy. Like the sun, which is the source of that energy, and like the air we breathe, ultra violet rays are the property of all mankind. Men may devise or improve machines for their more effective utilization and may obtain patents upon the machine or the improvement. But it would be a monstrous thing if the energy itself could be made the subject of a monopoly. It must be remembered that sunlight by its own inherent process activates the vitamin D principle in both inert and living tissues and substances, albeit, because of unfavorable atmospheric conditions, sunlight is not effective in all cases. Nevertheless it is clear that the artificial process differs in no essential particular from the natural one. The intervention of the mercury vapour lamp—developed long prior to Steenbock—may adapt the natural process to wider fields, but in a patentable sense the process itself is as ancient as the sun.

It seems to me doubtful that the claims should be held invalid because lacking in particularity in respect of the period of time of exposure. It may be that they are sufficiently specific to enable those skilled in the art to understand what is intended. I assume, therefore, that Steenbock discovered and sufficiently disclosed in his claims the most effective time period of exposure. Nevertheless such a discovery would not amount to a patentable invention. It would amount to no more than the ascertainment of a naked fact or principle in nature existing independently of the efforts of the discoverer. Cf. O'Reilly v. Morse, 15 How. 62, 14 L.Ed. 601; Tilghman v. Proctor, 102 U.S. 707, 722–729, 26 L.Ed. 279. If the discovery were patentable, it would be broader than the process itself in that it "would cover all processes which aim at the same result," including even the purposeful exposure of dietary substances to the direct rays of the sun. * * *

✓ C. DISCOVERY OF NEW USE OR ADVANTAGE

The following cases are inserted as illustrative of the doctrine that discovery of a new use for, or advantage of, an old product or composition does not make the old product or composition patentable.

IN RE THUAU

United States Court of Customs and Patent Appeals, 1943.
135 F.2d 344, 57 USPQ 324.

LENROOT, ASSOCIATE JUDGE. This is an appeal from a decision of the Board of Appeals of the United States Patent Office affirming a decision of the Primary Examiner rejecting claim 1 to 4, inclusive, 7 and 25 of appellant's application for a patent.

* * *

As stated in appellant's brief: "The invention of the appeal claims relates to a therapeutic product for the treatment of diseased tissue, which product comprises a water-soluble condensation product of metacresolsulfonic acid and an aldehyde, such as formaldehyde. This therapeutic product is especially useful in the treatment of cervicitis, cervical erosions, and related ailments."

* * *

Claim 1 is illustrative of the claims rejected upon the cited prior art. "1. A new therapeutic product for the treatment of diseased tissue, comprising a condensation product of metacresolsulfonic acid condensed through an aldehyde."

* * *

The composition here claimed is a condensation product of metacresolsulfonic acid condensed through an aldehyde. This product had long been known, but so far as the references disclose, its use had only been for tanning purposes.

Some of the references disclosing the composition are patents which have long since expired, and the other references are publications.

Appellant discovered that this old composition is useful for the treatment of diseased tissue. He has in no way changed the composition for such new use, and as stated the question before us is whether a new and unobvious use for an old composition, without change in or addition to that composition, is patentable.

* * *

The doctrine is so familiar as not to require citation of authority that a patentee is entitled to every use of which his invention is susceptible, whether such use be known or unknown to him. Likewise, with regard to an unpatentable article or substance long in use, any member of the public has the right to every use of which the article or substance is susceptible so long as it is unchanged in any way, regardless of whether or not such uses were known prior to his own use.

To allow a patent for an old composition without change in any way, merely because it may be used for a specified purpose, would result in a situation where two compositions of exactly the same character could be sold by merchants to consumers, but if one of the compositions was not made by the patentee or his assignee or licensee, the merchant might be liable to suit for infringement if the composition was used by the purchaser for therapeutic purposes, and the user would certainly be liable to such a suit.

In our opinion the patent laws do not contemplate that two identical substances or devices may be legally sold side by side, only one of which is the subject of a valid patent, and we are in agreement with the view expressed in the case of H.K. Regar & Sons, Inc., v. Scott & Williams, Inc., supra, that a patent for a new use for an old substance quite unchanged is not authorized by the patent laws because such use is not the invention or discovery of "any *new* and useful art, machine, manufacture, or *composition of matter,* or any new and useful improvements thereof" as required by Section 4886 of the Revised Statutes, U.S.C. Title 35, Sec. 31, 35 U.S.C.A. § 31. (Italics ours.)

That appellant has made a valuable discovery in the new use of the composition here involved we have no doubt, and it is unfortunate for him if he cannot make claims adequate to protect such discovery, but to hold that every new use of an old composition may be the subject of a patent upon the composition would lead to endless confusion and go far to destroy the benefits of our patent laws.

For the reasons stated we find no error in the decision of the board respecting claims 1 to 4, inclusive, 7 and 25.

* * *

For the reasons stated herein the decision appealed from is affirmed.

Affirmed.[a]

APPLICATION OF HACK [b]

United States Court of Customs and Patent Appeals, 1957.
44 CCPA 954, 245 F.2d 246, 114 USPQ 161.

JACKSON, JUDGE. This is an appeal from the decision of the Board of Appeals of the United States Patent Office affirming the final

a. See Ansul Co. v. Uniroyal, 301 F.Supp. 273, 290; 162 USPQ 525, 539 (D.C. N.Y.1969), where the court sustained validity of a patent on a material known since 1894 which was discovered to have plant growth inhibiting properties when used with a wetting agent. "An inventor who discovers a basic new use is not required specifically to disclose, or even be aware of, all the uses of his invention. B.G. Corporation v. Walter Kidde & Co., Inc., 79 F.2d 20, 22, 26 USPQ 288, 289–290 (2d Cir.1935). Despite the discoveries by others of variations on the patentee's invention, the significant invention will receive patent protection to encourage the type of sampling and disclosures which occurred here. Patents are granted to encourage the ready availability of new knowledge to the public."

b. See also: Rohm & Haas Co. v. Roberts Chemicals, Inc., 245 F.2d 693; 113 USPQ 423 (4th Cir.1957); and Elrick Rim Co. v. Reading Tire Machinery Co., Inc., 264 F.2d 481, 120 USPQ 514 (9th Cir.1959).

rejection of claims 3 and 5 of patent application 208,449, filed January 29, 1951, for a brazing alloy.

The rejected claims, the only ones remaining in the case, read as follows:

"3. A brazing alloy composed entirely of approximately 35% by weight of gold, approximately 62% by weight of copper, and approximately 3% by weight of nickel.

"5. A brazing alloy for use under conditions of elevated temperatures and high vacuum which is characterized by low surface tension characteristics, low vapor pressure, flowability and fine crystalline structure composed entirely of gold, copper and nickel, said alloy comprising between 25% to 50% by weight of gold and from 1% to 5% by weight of nickel."

The references relied upon are:

Peterson,	2,164,938,	July 4, 1939,
Nelson,	2,426,467,	Aug. 26, 1947,
German Patent	575,257	Apr. 26, 1933.

The new alloy is characterized by its low surface tension characteristic and flowability which is superior to that of previous alloys consisting only of copper and gold. The addition of nickel also imparts a fine crystalline structure to the composition, thereby minimizing leakage when it is used as a soldering alloy in the production of vacuum tube equipment.

* * *

The prior art cited clearly, in our view, discloses the claimed composition of gold, copper and nickel. Peterson, disclosing an alloy of gold, copper and cobalt, suggests that nickel can be substituted for cobalt if the practitioner is not concerned with the "paling" effect which would be the result of such a substitution. The German patent explicitly discloses and claims an alloy in which the ingredients are gold, copper and nickel. Nowhere in the course of the prosecution of this case has applicant contended that the percentage proportion of each metal used in his alloy is critical. Such selection would seem but a matter of choice. The precise percentages claimed, moreover, fall within the range disclosed by Peterson. These references alone, without reliance on the patent to Nelson, show that the claimed composition of matter is neither new nor unsuggested by the art.

* * *

[Cases cited and discussed.]

These cases are merely expressive of the principle that the grant of a patent on a composition or machine cannot be predicated on a new use of that machine or composition. We did not in those cases deny a patent to applicant because there was necessarily any lack of *inventiveness* in adapting the known composition to a new use. We recognize that it often requires perceptivity and intuitive genius of the highest order to grasp the idea that a device or material in one art may be utilized in another. The inventive faculties may be brought as fully into play in this regard as they would be in the creation of a device *de novo.* But a patent on an old product, based on its new use, has never been authorized by the patent laws which provided for patents only on a new and useful art, machine, manufacture, or *composition of matter,* or any new and useful improvement thereof (R.S. § 4886). As declared in Old Town Ribbon & Carbon Co. v. Columbia Ribbon & Carbon Mfg. Co., Inc., 2 Cir., 159 F.2d 379, 382:

> " * * * it makes not the slightest difference how beneficial to the public the new function may be, how long a search it may end, how many may have shared that search, or how high a reach of imaginative ingenuity the solution may have demanded. All the mental factors which determine invention may have been present to the highest degree, but it will not be patentable because it will not be within the terms of the statute. * * * "

The new patent statute of 1952, 35 U.S.C.A. § 1 et seq., in no way limits or modifies the doctrine of those cases. While it recognizes (Secs. 100(b) and 101) that the discovery or invention of a *new use* of a known process machine, manufacture, composition of matter or material may be patentable, it is obvious that such use can be nothing other than a method or process.[1] As a matter of claim drafting, therefore, the discoverer of a new use must protect his discovery by means of process or method claims and not product claims.

Applicant is here attempting to procure a patent based on his discovery that a known composition of matter can be adapted to use as a brazing alloy. His claims are product claims. To entitle him to a patent the composition claimed must be both new and unobvious to one skilled in the art. In our view it is neither.

For the foregoing reasons, the decision of the board is affirmed.

Affirmed.

D. PROCESS

1. INTRODUCTION

Section 100(b) of 35 U.S.C.A.:

The term "process" means process, art or method, and includes a new use of a known process, machine, manufacture, composition of matter, or material.

---

1. See Revision Notes to Section 101, contained in the appendix to H.R.Rep. No. 1923 and Sen.Rep. No. 1979, 82d Cong., 2d Sess.1952 U.S.Code Cong. & Adm.News 1952, p. 2410: "The remainder of the definition clarifies the status of processes or methods which involve merely the new use of a known process, machine, manufacture, composition of matter, or material; they are processes or methods under the statute * * *."

EX PARTE TURNER

Decisions of the Commissioner of Patents, 1894 C.D. 36.

SEYMOUR, COMMISSIONER. This is an appeal from the decision of the Examiners-in-Chief affirming the rejection by the Primary Examiner of the following claims:

1. The improvement in the art of advertising, which consists in issuing publications or supplements distinguished from each other and publishing a series of advertisements, some or all of which are accompanied by offers for certain publications or supplements, substantially as described.

* * *

The appellant claims to have invented a process to secure the reading of advertisements in newspapers. A numbered picture is issued with each paper and the advertiser prints as a part of his advertisement an offer of some article of his stock in return for some one of the numbered pictures.

* * *

It is assumed that the advertisements will be read by a purchaser of the paper in order to see whether any advertiser makes an offer for the picture bearing the particular number issued to him with his paper.

Is this series of acts an art, such as is intended to be protected and its growth promoted by the patent law?

Again, if this process is practiced by one taking the prescribed steps in the order mentioned, the process will not produce any physical effect. A patentable process must accomplish some change in the character or condition of material objects; hence a plan or theory of action which, if carried into practice, could produce no physical results proceeding direct from the operation of the theory or plan itself is not an art within the meaning of the patent laws. (1 Rob. on Pats., 249.)

Several cases are cited by the appellant in support of his contention that a process producing no physical effect may nevertheless be patentable, among them the Telephone Cases, (C.D., 1888, 321; 43 O.G., 377; 126 U.S.,) where the method of producing a variable current and using it to reproduce sound-waves at a distance was sustained; but the reproduction of sound-waves in air is just as truly a physical effect as the production of pig-iron.

* * *

Since the process if carried out produces no physical effect, but only a state of mind in the purchaser of the newspaper amounting to a predisposition to read the advertisements and there ends, unless the reader wills otherwise, and since the process is not specified to include any fair and legal method of selecting the number of the picture of which the holder is to be rewarded, it is considered that claims 1, 2, and 3 cannot be allowed.

*   *   *

The decision of the Examiners-in-Chief is affirmed.

EXPANDED METAL CO. v. BRADFORD
Supreme Court of the United States, 1909.
214 U.S. 366, 29 S.Ct. 652, 53 L.Ed. 1034.

MR. JUSTICE DAY delivered the opinion of the court:

*   *   *

The patent in controversy relates to what is known as expanded sheet metal. Expanded metal may be generally described as metal openwork, held together by uncut portions of the metal, and constructed by making cuts or slashes in metal and then opening them so as to form a series of meshes or latticework. In its simplest form sheet metal may be expended by making a series of cuts or slits in the metal in such relation to each other as to break joints, so that the metal, when opened or stretched, will present an open mesh appearance. It may be likened to the familiar woven wire openwork construction, except that the metal is held together by uncut portions thereof, uniting the strands, and the whole forms a solid piece.

*   *   *

Golding testifies that he at first executed his process by hand. Other witnesses, skilled in the art, say that they could do likewise from the information found in the patent.

*   *   *

It is lastly contended, and this is perhaps the most important question in the case, that in view of the former declarations and opinions of this court, what is termed a process patent relates only to such as are produced by chemical action, or by the operation or application of some similar elemental action, and that such processes do not include methods or means which are affected by mere mechanical combinations, *   *   *

An examination of the extent of the right to process patents requires consideration of the object and purpose of the Congress in exercising the constitutional power to protect for a limited period meritorious inventions or discoveries. Section 4886 of the Revised Statutes provides:

> "Any person who has invented or discovered any new and useful art, machine, manufacture, or composition of matter, or any new and useful improvement thereof *   *   * may obtain a patent therefor."

This is the statute which secures to inventors the right of protection, and it is not the province of the courts to so limit the statute as to deprive meritorious inventors of its benefits. The word "process" is not used in the statute. The inventor of a new and useful art is distinctly entitled to the benefit of the statute as well as he who invents a machine, manufacture, or composition of matter. The word "process" has been brought into the decisions because it is supposedly an equivalent form of expression or included in the statutory designation of a new and useful art.

When then is the statutory right to a patent for a "process" when the term is properly considered? * * *

It is undoubtedly true, and all the cases agree, that the mere function or effect of the operation of a machine cannot be the subject-matter of a lawful patent. But it does not follow that a method of doing a thing, so clearly indicated that those skilled in the art can avail themselves of mechanism to carry it into operation, is not the subject-matter of a valid patent. The contrary has been declared in decisions of this court. A leading case is Cochrane v. Deener, 94 U.S. 780, in which this court sustained a process patent involving mechanical operations, and in which the subject was discussed by Mr. Justice Bradley, speaking for the court. On page 787 that learned justice said:

> "That a process may be patentable, irrespective of the particular form of the instrumentalities used, cannot be disputed. * * * Either may be pointed out; but if the patent is not confined to that particular tool or machine, the use of the others would be an infringement, the general process being the same. A process is a mode of treatment of certain materials to produce a given result. It is an act, or a series of acts, performed upon the subject matter to be transformed and reduced to a different state or thing. If new and useful, it is just as patentable as a piece of machinery. In the language of the patent law, it is an art. The machinery pointed out as suitable to perform the process may or may not be new or patentable; whilst the process itself may be altogether new, and produce an entirely new result. The process requires that certain things should be done with certain substances, and in a certain order; but the tools to be used in doing this may be of secondary consequence."

This clear and succinct statement of the rule was recognized and applied (Mr. Justice Bradley again speaking for the court) in the case of Tilghman v. Proctor, 102 U.S. 707. In the course of the opinion the learned justice tersely says:

> "A machine is a thing. A process is an act, or a mode of acting. The one is visible to the eye—an object of perpetual observation. The other is a conception of the mind, seen only by its effects when being executed or performed. Either may be the means of producing a useful result."

That this court did not intend to limit process patents to those showing chemical action or similar elemental changes is shown by subsequent cases in this court.

In Westinghouse v. Boyden Company, 170 U.S. 537, the opinion was written by the same eminent justice who wrote the opinion in Risdon Locomotive Works v. Medart, 158 U.S. supra, and delivering the opinion of the court, he said (p. 557):

"These cases (158 U.S. 68, and 103 U.S. 461) assume, although they do not expressly decide, that a process to be patentable must involve a chemical or other similar elemental action, and it may be still regarded as an open question whether the patentability of processes extends beyond this class of inventions."

And added these significant words:

"Where the process is simply the function or operative effect of a machine, the above cases are conclusive against its patentability; but where it is one which, though ordinarily and most successfully performed by machinery, may also be performed by simple manipulation, such, for instance, as the folding of paper in a peculiar way for the manufacture of paper bags, or a new method of weaving a hammock, there are cases to the effect that such a process is patentable, though none of the powers of nature be invoked to aid in producing the result. * * *"

We therefore reach the conclusion that an invention or discovery of a process or method involving mechanical operations, and producing a new and useful result, may be within the protection of the Federal statute, and entitle the inventor to a patent for his discovery.

We are of opinion that Golding's method was a substantial improvement of this character, independently of particular mechanism for performing it, and the patent in suit is valid as exhibiting a process of a new and useful kind.

* * *

Decrees accordingly.

2. FUNCTION OF A MACHINE

APPLICATION OF TARCZY-HORNOCH

United States Court of Customs and Patent Appeals, 1968.
55 CCPA 1441, 397 F.2d 856, 158 USPQ 141.

RICH, JUDGE. This appeal is from a decision of the Patent Office Board of Appeals affirming the examiner's rejection of claims 31–35 and 40 in appellant's application serial No. 23,739, filed April 21, 1960, entitled "Pulse Sorting Apparatus and Method." Claims 16–28, 29, 30, and 36–39 have been allowed.

The invention of the claims on appeal is a method for sorting or counting electrical pulses, effective in counting of such pulses of varying amplitudes even at extremely high repetition rates, i.e., at rates greater than 50,000,000 (50 megacycles) per second. Appellant's method envisions the use of a multi-stage apparatus. The first stage counts every pulse within its capacity. Cancelling orders in the form of "inhibit" pulses are then sent to each of the succeeding stages to prevent another counting of those same pulses. Should the initial stage be unable to handle a pulse, no cancellation order is given the second stage. The pulse, then, is counted by the second stage. Thereupon, cancellation orders are sent to succeeding stages.

Claim 31 is illustrative:

31. In a method for sorting a plurality of imput pulses by utilizing a plurality of serially connected stages adapted to accept pulses, causing each input pulse to be applied to each stage sequentially in time, generating an inhibit pulse in each stage which accepts an input pulse and applying the inhibit pulse to each succeeding stage in substantial coincidence with the input pulse so that the input pulse is canceled to thereby prevent registration of the same input pulse in a succeeding stage.

The examiner allowed appellant's apparatus claims. However, he rejected all the method claims on the ground that they merely defined the function of appellant's apparatus. In appeal to the board, appellant argued mainly against the propriety of the "function of the apparatus" rejection. However, this point, in the board's opinion, was foreclosed: "[T]he previous decisions by the Court of Customs and Patent Appeals are binding on us until overruled." The board did reverse the rejection of two of the method claims on a showing that the defined methods were capable of performance by apparatus other than that disclosed. The rejection of the other claims was affirmed.

The issue, therefore, is whether a process claim, otherwise patentable, should be rejected because the application, of which it is a part, discloses apparatus which will *inherently* carry out the recited steps. There is no contention that the claims on appeal can be saved by the "exceptions" to the doctrine, exempting claims for those processes capable of performance either manually or by another, dissimilar apparatus. See In re Parker, 79 F.2d 908, 23 CCPA 721 (1935).

We have determined that our decisions requiring the rejection of such claims are justified neither by history nor policy. Today we overrule those decisions.

The expression "function of an apparatus" [2] is our legacy of 19th century controversy over the patentability of processes. Early cases proscribed a kind of overweening claim in which the desirable result first effected by an invention was itself appropriated by the inventor. Two notorious examples will suffice.

Wyeth had obtained a patent for a machine for cutting ice into blocks of uniform size. His specification read: "It is claimed as new, to cut ice of a uniform size, by means of an apparatus worked by any other power than human. The invention of this art, as well as the particular method of the application of the principle, are claimed by * * * [Wyeth]." In an infringement suit, in 1840, Justice Story, sitting on circuit, held the claimed matter "unmaintainable" in point of law and a patent, granted for such, void as for an abstract principle and broader than the invention. "A claim broader than the actual invention of the patentee is, for that very reason, upon the principles of the common

2. Alternatively, especially in early cases, "function of a machine."

law, utterly void, and the patent is a nullity." Wyeth v. Stone, Fed.Cas. No. 18,107, 1 Story 273, 285–286 (C.C.Mass.1840).

The first comprehensive review of process patents by the Supreme Court was occasioned some thirteen years later by Morse's attempt to enforce his telegraph patent. Chief Justice Taney wrote the opinion for the Court, which held several apparatus claims valid and infringed. O'Reilly v. Morse, 56 U.S. (15 How.) 62, 14 L.Ed. 601 (1853). The only process claim in the Morse patent was the subject of separate discussion. ＊ ＊ ＊ The Chief Justice commented:

> If this claim can be maintained, it matters not by what process or machinery the result is accomplished. For aught that we now know some future inventor, in the onward march of science, may discover a mode of writing or printing at a distance by means of the electric or galvanic current, without using any part of the process or combination set forth in the plaintiff's specification. His invention may be less complicated—less liable to get out of order—less expensive in construction, and in its operation. But yet if it is covered by this patent the inventor could not use it, nor the public have the benefit of it without the permission of this patentee.
>
> ＊ ＊ ＊
>
> No one we suppose will maintain that Fulton could have taken out a patent for his invention of propelling vessels by steam, describing the process and machinery he used, and claimed under it the exclusive right to use the motive power of steam, however developed, for the purpose of propelling vessels.[3]

The claim was, of course, held invalid because it did not correspond in scope to Morse's invention. "[Professor Morse] ＊ ＊ ＊ has not discovered that the electro-magnetic current, used as motive power, in any other method and with any other combination, will do as well." [4] The Chief Justice also summarized the law in this area:

> Whoever discovers that a certain useful result will be produced, in any art, machine, manufacture, or composition of matter, by the use of certain means, is entitled to a patent for it; provided he specifies the means he uses in a manner so full and exact, that any one skilled in the science to which it appertains, can, by using the means he specifies, without any addition to, or subtraction from them, produce precisely the result he describes. And if this cannot be done by the means he describes, the patent is void. ＊ ＊ ＊

The latter exposition apparently cast some doubt on the validity of claims for processes generally, whether mechanical or not. It shortly became clear, however, that the patentability of chemical processes at least had been unaffected. In Corning v. Burden, 56 U.S. (15 How.) 252, 14 L.Ed. 683 (1853), a case decided after *Morse* but during the same term, the issue was whether Burden's ambiguous claim was properly interpreted as for a process. The patent was ostensibly directed toward a machine for rolling puddle balls in the manufacture of iron. ＊ ＊ ＊

---

3. 56 U.S. (15 How.) at 113.   **4.** 56 U.S. (15 How.) at 117.

In an influential aside on the way to this conclusion, Justice Grier, for a unanimous Court, discussed the patentability of processes:

> A process, *eo nomine,* is not made the subject of a patent in our act of Congress. It is included under the general term "useful art." An art may require one or more processes or machines in order to produce a certain result or manufacture. * * *

> * * * It is for the discovery or invention of some practicable method or means of producing a beneficial result or effect, that a patent is granted, and not for the result or effect itself. It is when the term process is used to represent the means or method of producing a result that it is patentable, and it will include all methods or means which are not effected by mechanism or mechanical combinations.

> But the term process is often used in a more vague sense, in which it cannot be the subject of a patent. Thus we say that a board is undergoing the process of being planed, grain of being ground, iron of being hammered, or rolled. Here the term is used subjectively or passively as applied to the material operated on, and not to the method or mode of producing that operation, which is by mechanical means, or the use of a machine, as distinguished from a process.

> In this use of the term it represents the function of a machine, or the effect produced by it on the material subjected to the action of the machine. But it is well settled that a man cannot have a patent for the function or abstract effect of a machine, but only for the machine which produces it.

* * *

Several subsequent cases upheld process patents. Cochrane v. Deener, 94 U.S. 780, 24 L.Ed. 139 (1876); Tilghman v. Proctor, 102 U.S. 707, 26 L.Ed. 279 (1880). In the first of these a patent for a process for sifting flour was held valid and infringed. Justice Bradley wrote for the Court:

> That a process may be patentable, irrespective of the particular form of the instrumentalities used, cannot be disputed. * * * The machinery pointed out as suitable to perform the process may or may not be new or patentable; whilst the process itself may be altogether new, and produce an entirely new result. The process requires that certain things should be done with certain substances, and in a certain order; but the tools to be used in doing this may be of secondary consequence.[6]

This discussion as well as the validation itself of the flour-sifting process seemed to show that the connotation of the "function of a machine" rejection was not an objection to mechanical processes but rather to mere effects masquerading as processes.

* * *

Only a few years later, however, the Court seemed to turn away from the means-result dichotomy. In Risdon Locomotive Works v.

6. 94 U.S. at 787–788.

Medart, 158 U.S. 68, 15 S.Ct. 745, 39 L.Ed. 899 (1894), the validity of a patent for a process of manufacturing belt pulleys was in issue.

* * *

It was at this unfortunate time that our predecessor in jurisdiction of appeals from the Patent Office, the Court of Appeals of the District of Columbia, attempted a synthesis of the cases on "function of an apparatus." In re Weston, 17 App.D.C. 431 (1901). The Commissioner of Patents had rejected certain claims for a process of manufacturing devices used in electrical measuring instruments. The question before the court on appeal from the Commissioner was "the greatly-vexed one, how far a method or a process is patentable, and when it is a subject of patentability."

The court reviewed the case law, * * * and came to the following conclusion.

> It seems to us from all these authorities the deductions to be drawn are these: First, that processes involving a chemical or other elemental action, if new and useful, are patentable; second, that a process, which amounts to no more than the mere function of a machine, is not patentable; third, that a process or method of a mechanical nature, not absolutely dependent upon a machine, although perhaps best illustrated by mechanism, may, if new and useful, be the proper subject of a patent, even though it involves no chemical or other elemental action.

* * *

In the Court of Customs and Patent Appeals, the *Weston* views have more than survived, they have flourished. In In re Ernst, 71 F.2d 169, 21 CCPA 1235 (1934), the *Weston* doctrine was embraced by this court. Appellant's reliance on *Expanded Metal* was unavailing—the court relied on the possibility of manual operation and distinguished that case. The "mere function of an apparatus" rejection was regularly upheld thereafter. See, e.g., In re McCurdy, 76 F.2d 400, 22 CCPA 1140 (1935); In re Wadman, 94 F.2d 993, 25 CCPA 936 (1938); In re Mead, 127 F.2d 302, 29 CCPA 1001 (1942); In re Solakian, 155 F.2d 404, 33 CCPA 1054 (1946); In re Nichols, 171 F.2d 300, 36 CCPA 759 (1948); In re Ashbaugh, 173 F.2d 273, 36 CCPA 902 (1949); In re Horvath, 211 F.2d 604, 41 CCPA 844 (1954); In re Gartner, 223 F.2d 502, 42 CCPA 1022 (1955).

* * *

The issue in this case, therefore, is whether this court will continue to insist upon the connotation its decisions and those of its predecessor in jurisdiction have breathed into the "function of an apparatus" symbol or will restore to that phrase its former meaning.

Appellant argues that the "function of the apparatus" doctrine as it is presently conceived is historically unsound, devoid of statutory basis, and at variance with the new Congressional policy evidenced by the Patent Act of 1952.

The solicitor, on the other hand, argues that the present doctrine is required by Expanded Metal Co. v. Bradford, supra. He urges, in rebuttal, that no specific prohibition is required to reject a claim as embracing non-statutory subject matter, and that there has been no shift in Congressional policy.

Our present view of the major precedents has persuaded us that the decisions of the Supreme Court have not required the rejection of process claims merely because the process apparently could be carried out only with the disclosed apparatus. These rejections have been the product of decisions in the lower courts and especially in this court. We decide today that we will no longer follow those decisions.

3. MENTAL STEPS AND COMPUTERS

HALLIBURTON OIL WELL CEMENTING CO. v. WALKER

United States Court of Appeals, Ninth Circuit, 1944.
146 F.2d 817, 64 USPQ 278, certiorari granted 326 U.S. 705, 66 S.Ct. 90, 90 L.Ed. 416 (1945).
Affirmed 326 U.S. 696, 66 S.Ct. 482, 90 L.Ed. 410 (1946), modified as to apparatus patent 329 U.S. 1, 67 S.Ct. 6, 91 L.Ed. 3 (1946).

HEALY, CIRCUIT JUDGE. * * * *Patent No. 2,209,944.* The court held this patent invalid for want of invention, finding that its novelty lay only in the performance of certain mental steps.

This is a method patent. The steps involved are described in the claims by the following descriptive words "determining," "registering," "counting," "observing," "measuring," "comparing," "recording," "computing." There are 9 claims, all of which are in suit. Claim 2, copied below, may be taken as typical:

> "2. The method of determining the unknown location of an obstruction in a well having a string of tubing therein, which consists in creating an acoustical impulse in the annular space between the tubing and the well casing to produce echoes from portions of the tubing string distinguishable from each other and from the echo from the unknown obstruction, observing the lapse of time between the arrival at a predetermined point of the echoes from successive portions of the tubing string to thereby determine the velocity of the pressure wave through the particular well under measurement, and measuring the lapse of time between the creation of the pressure impulse and the arrival at said predetermined point of the echo from the unknown obstruction."

In substance, Walker's method here claimed consists in setting down three knowns in a simple equation and from them determining or computing an unknown. The three knowns are: (a) the distance from the well head to the tubing catcher (for example); (b) the length of time it takes an echo to return from that obstruction; and (c) the length of time it takes an echo to return from the fluid surface. From these three knowns can then be determined the distance of the fluid surface from the well head.

We think these mental steps, even if novel, are not patentable. Cf. Don Lee, Inc. v. Walker, 9 Cir., 61 F.2d 58. A patent may be obtained only upon an invention of a "new and useful art, machine, manufacture, or composition of matter" 35 U.S.C.A. § 31. As said in Cochrane v. Deener, 94 U.S. 780, 788, 24 L.Ed. 139: "A process is a mode of treatment of certain materials to produce a given result. It is an act, or a series of acts, performed upon the subject-matter to be transformed and reduced to a different state or thing. If new and useful, it is just as patentable as is a piece of machinery. In the language of the patent law, it is an art." Cf. also Corning v. Burden, 15 How. 252, 267, 14 L.Ed. 683.

It must be remembered that this is purely a method patent. No apparatus is claimed. Given an apparatus for initiating an impulse wave in a well and a means for differentiating between and for recording echoes returned from obstructions in it, anybody with a rudimentary knowledge of arithmetic will be able to do what Walker claims a monopoly of doing. If his method were patentable it seems to us that the patentee would have a monopoly much broader than would the patentee of a particular apparatus. To sum the matter up, we think Walker's apparatus patent No. 2,156,519 gives him all the protection his inventive genius entitles him to.

* * *

[The Supreme Court later held the apparatus claims invalid as not meeting statutory requirements]

APPLICATION OF BERNHART

United States Court of Customs & Patent Appeals, 1969.
57 CCPA 737, 417 F.2d 1395.
163 USPQ 611.

LANE, JUDGE.

This appeal is from the decision of the Patent Office Board of Appeals affirming the examiner's rejection of claims 8, 13 and 18–21 in patent application serial No. 151,909, filed November 13, 1961, entitled "Planar Illustration Method and Apparatus" and disclosing a method of and apparatus for automatically making a two-dimensional portrayal of a three-dimensional object from any desired angle and distance and on any desired plane of projection.

THE DISCLOSURE

The starting point for the method and the input for the apparatus is a set of data defining the three-dimensional positions of various points on or in the object relative to some convenient fixed point, plus information as to which of the various points should be connected by lines. The disclosure provides equations definitive of the geometric relationships between the three-dimensional coordinates of each point of interest and the corresponding two-dimensional coordinates which determine the location of that point on a planar portrayal or drawing to be made. The equations are sufficiently general to allow the resulting drawing to represent a view of the object as projected on any selected plane and as viewed from any point in space. The disclosure then teaches that the original data on point positions and connecting lines can be written in a form acceptable as input to a general purpose digital computer; that the equations disclosed in the application can be used to control the operation of the computer on the input data, i.e. the equations can be programmed into the computer; that an operator can select particular values for certain terms in the programmed equations, thereby determining the kind of portrayal to be produced; that the computer output will be a sequence of signals representative of the locations of points on the desired portrayal; and that those signals can be used to control the operation of a plotting machine which will produce the desired view of the object on paper.

Applicants concede that they did not invent the computer or the plotting machine. Nor do they claim any special method of feeding input data on point positions into the computer. Most importantly, they do not claim as their invention *merely* a set of equations even though, as we shall later see, those equations were not known in the prior art.

In order to know what the invention is we must, of course, look to the claims which point it out. We find that claims 8 and 18–21 define apparatus and claim 13 defines a method.

THE REJECTIONS

* * *

The apparatus claims were further rejected by the examiner as failing to define a machine within the statutory class (35 U.S.C.A. § 101) "since for patentability they were predicated on mental steps," citing a patent to Tripp[2] which, said the examiner, showed that it was old to combine a programmed digital computer with a plotting device. The examiner indicated that the novelty in applicants' claims therefore lay in the equations with which the computer was programmed, and that this is not a *structural* difference over the prior art. The examiner concluded that since the programming was not structural, the claims were "predicated for patentability on mental steps." As to the method claim, the examiner similarly argued that since the novelty of applicants' claimed invention lay in the particular equations to be solved, the invention is non-statutory, citing Ex parte Meinhardt, 1907 C.D. 238; In re Abrams, 188 F.2d 165, 38 CCPA 945 (1951); In re Yuan, 188 F.2d 377, 38 CCPA 967 (1951); and In re Middleton, 167 F.2d 1012, 35 CCPA 1166 (1948). The board affirmed these rejections, but it reasoned with respect to the apparatus claims that the issues were analogous to

2. U.S. Patent 3,066,868, filed Nov. 15, 1956, issued Dec. 4, 1962.

the "printed matter" cases such as Ex parte Gwinn, 112 USPQ 439 (PO Bd.App.1955). Regarding these cases, the board said:

> The rationale of these cases appears to be that the law does not favor the granting of a patent for non-statutory subject matter by indirection, and this should be applicable to a mathematical formula or an algorithm as well as to printed text, when the real substance of the contribution by its originator clearly is unpatentable in its own right.

Looking first at the apparatus claims, we see no recitation therein of mental steps, nor of any element requiring or even permitting the incorporation of human faculties in the apparatus. These claims recite, and can be infringed only by, a digital computer in a certain physical condition, i.e., electro-mechanically set or programmed to carry out the recited routine. The claims also define the invention as having plotting means for drawing lines or for illustrating an object. When such functional language is used in a claim, 35 U.S.C.A. § 112 states that "such claim shall be construed to cover the corresponding structure, material, or acts described in the specification and equivalents thereof." The specification here mentions only mechanical drafting machines. The claims therefore cover, under section 112, only such mechanical drafting machines and their equivalents. We know of no authority for holding that a human being, such as a draftsman, could ever be the equivalent of a machine disclosed in a patent application, and we are not prepared to so hold in this case. Accordingly, we think it clear that applicants have not defined as their invention anything in which the human mind could be used as a component. Nor are the "printed matter" cases, cited by the board, supra, controlling as to these apparatus claims either on the facts or in principle. On their facts, those cases dealt with claims defining as the invention certain novel arrangements of printed lines or characters, useful and intelligible only to the human mind. Here the invention as defined by the claims *requires* that the information be processed not by the mind but by a machine, the computer, and that the drawing be done not by a draftsman but by a plotting machine. Those "printed matter" cases therefore have no factual relevance here.

A much closer question arises, however, when we consider the *principle* extracted by the examiner from the mental step cases and by the board from the printed matter cases. The principle may, we think, be fairly stated as follows: If, in an invention defined by a claim, the novelty is indicated by an expression which does not itself fit in a statutory class (in this case not a machine or a part thereof), then the whole invention is non-statutory since all else in the claim is old. We do not believe this view is correct under the Patent Act and the case law thus far developed.

We think it is clear that in enacting section 101 Congress meant to exclude principles or laws of nature and mathematics, of which equations are an example, from even temporary monopolization by patent. Accordingly, no rule of law should be announced which would impress a monopoly upon all uses of the equations disclosed by appellants here in their patent application. To allow the claims in issue here would not prohibit all uses of those equations. As we have pointed out above, a member of the public would have to do much more than use the equations to infringe any of these claims. He would have to use them in the physical equipment recited in the claim. Moreover, all machines function according to laws of physics which can be mathematically set forth if known. We cannot deny patents on machines merely because their novelty may be explained in terms of such laws if we are to obey the mandate of Congress that a machine is subject matter for a patent. We should not penalize the inventor who makes his invention by discovering new and unobvious mathematical relationships which he then utilizes in a machine, as against the inventor who makes the *same machine* by trial and error and does not disclose the laws by which it operates. The mandate of Congress in 35 U.S.C.A. § 103 is that "patentability shall not be negatived by the manner in which the invention was made." For the foregoing reasons, we conclude that under the statute the apparatus herein claimed constitutes statutory subject matter.

* * *

There is one further rationale used by both the board and the examiner, namely, that the provision of new signals to be stored by the computer does not make it a new machine, i.e. it is *structurally* the same, no matter how new, useful and unobvious the result. This rationale really goes more to novelty than to statutory subject matter but it appears to be at the heart of the present controversy. To this question we say that if a machine is programmed in a certain new and unobvious way, it is physically different from the machine without that program; its memory elements are differently arranged. The fact that these physical changes are invisible to the eye should not tempt us to conclude that the machine has not been changed. If a new machine has not been invented, certainly a "new and useful improvement" of the unprogrammed machine has been, and Congress has said in 35 U.S. C.A. § 101 that such improvements are statutory subject matter for a patent. It may well be that the vast majority of newly programmed machines are obvious to those skilled in the art and hence unpatentable under 35 U.S.C.A. § 103. We are concluding here that such machines are statutory under 35 U.S.C.A. § 101, and that claims defining them must be judged for patentability in light of the prior art.

GOTTSCHALK v. BENSON

Supreme Court of the United States, 1972.
409 U.S. 63, 93 S.Ct. 253, 34 L.Ed.2d 273.
No. 71–485

Robert Gottschalk, Acting Commissioner of Patents, Petitioner,

v.

Gary R. Benson and Arthur C. Tabbot.

On Writ of Certiorari to the United States Court of Customs and Patent Appeals.

[November 20, 1972]

MR. JUSTICE DOUGLAS delivered the opinion of the Court.

Respondents filed in the Patent Office an application for an invention which was described as being related "to the processing of data by program and more particularly to the programmed conversion of numerical information" in general purpose digital computers. They claimed a method for converting binary-coded-decimal (BCD) numerals into pure binary numerals. The claims were not limited to any particular art or technology, to any particular apparatus or machinery, or to any particular end use. They purported to cover any use of the claimed method in a general purpose digital computer of any type. Claims 8 [1] and 13 were rejected by the Patent Office but sustained by the Court of Customs and Patent Appeals, 441 F.2d 682. The case is here on a petition for a writ of certiorari. 405 U.S. 915.

The question is whether the method described and claimed is a "process" within the meaning of the Patent Act.

* * *

The patent sought is on a "method of programming" a general purpose digital computer to convert signals from binary coded decimal form into pure binary form. A procedure for solving a given type of mathematical problem is known as an "algorithm." The procedures set forth in the present claims are of that kind; that is to say, they are a generalized formulation for programs to solve mathematical problems

---

1. Claim 8 reads as follows:

"8. The method of converting signals from binary coded decimal form into binary which comprises the steps of

"(1) storing the binary coded decimal signals in a reentrant shift register,

"(2) shifting the signals to the right by at least three places, until there is a binary '1' in the second position of said register,

"(3) masking out said binary '1' in said second position of said register,

"(4) adding a binary '1' to the first position of said register,

"(5) shifting the signals to the left by two positions,

"(6) adding a '1' to said first position, and

"(7) shifting the signals to the right by at least three positions in preparation for a succeeding binary '1' in the second position of said register."

of converting one form of numerical representation to another. From the generic formulation, programs may be developed as specific applications.

*   *   *

*   *   * The method sought to be patented varies the ordinary arithmetic steps a human would use by changing the order of the steps, changing the symbolism for writing the multiplier used in some steps, and by taking subtotals after each successive operation. The mathematical procedures can be carried out in existing computers long in use, no new machinery being necessary. And, as noted, they can also be performed without a computer.

The Court stated in MacKay Co. v. Radio Corp., 306 U.S. 86, 94, 59 S.Ct. 427, 83 L.Ed. 506, that "While a scientific truth, or the mathematical expression of it, is not a patentable invention, a novel and useful structure created with the aid of knowledge of scientific truth may be." That statement followed the long-standing rule that "An idea of itself is not patentable." Rubber-Tip Pencil Co. v. Howard, 20 Wall. 498, 507, 87 U.S. 498, 22 L.Ed. 410. "A principle, in the abstract, is a fundamental truth; an original cause; a motive; and these cannot be patented, as no one can claim in either of them an exclusive right." LeRoy v. Tatham, 14 How. 156, 175, 55 U.S. 156, 14 L.Ed. 367. Phenomena of nature, though just discovered, mental processes, abstract intellectual concepts are not patentable, as they are the basic tools of scientific and technological work. As we stated in Funk Bros. Seed Co. v. Kalo Co., 333 U.S. 127, 130, 68 S.Ct. 440, 92 L.Ed. 588. "He who discovers a hitherto unknown phenomenon of nature has no claim to a monopoly of it which the law recognizes. If there is to be invention from such a discovery, it must come from the application of the law of nature to a new and useful end." We dealt there with a "product" claim, while the present case deals only with a "process" claim. But we think the same principle applies.

Here the "process" claim is so abstract and sweeping as to cover both known and unknown uses of the BCD to pure-binary conversion. The end use may (1) vary from the operation of a train to verification of drivers' licenses to researching the law books for precedents and (2) be performed through any existing machinery or future-devised machinery or without any apparatus.

It is argued that a process patent must either be tied to a particular machine or apparatus or must operate to change articles or materials to a "different state or thing."

We do not hold that no process patent could ever qualify if it did not meet the requirements of our prior precedents. It is said that the decision precludes a patent for any program servicing a computer. We do not so hold. It is said that we have before us a program for a digital computer but extend our holding to programs for analogue computers. We have, however, made clear from the start that we deal with a program only for digital computers. It is said we freeze process patents to old technologies, leaving no room for the revelations of the new, onrushing technology. Such is not our purpose. What we come down to in a nutshell is the following.

It is conceded that one may not patent an idea. But in practical effect that would be the result if the formula for converting binary code to pure binary were patented in this case. The mathematical formula involved here has no substantial practical application except in connection with a digital computer, which means that if the judgment below is affirmed, the patent would wholly pre-empt the mathematical formula and in practical effect would be a patent on the algorithm itself.

It may be that the patent laws should be extended to cover these programs, a policy matter to which we are not competent to speak. The President's Commission on the Patent System [4] rejected the proposal that these programs be patentable: [5]

"Uncertainty now exists as to whether the statute permits a valid patent to be granted on programs. Direct attempts to patent programs have been rejected on the ground of nonstatutory subject matter. Indirect attempts to obtain patents and avoid the rejection, by drafting claims as a process, or a machine or components thereof programmed in a given manner, rather than as a program itself, have confused the issue further and should not be permitted.

"The Patent Office now cannot examine applications for programs because of a lack of a classification technique and the requisite search files. Even if these were available, reliable searches would not be feasible or economic because of the tremendous volume of prior art being generated. Without this search, the patenting of programs would be tantamount to mere registration and the presumption of validity would be all but nonexistent.

"It is noted that the creation of programs has undergone substantial and satisfactory growth in the absence of patent protection and that copyright protection for programs is presently available."

If these programs are to be patentable,[6] considerable problems are raised which only committees of Congress can manage, for broad powers of investigation are needed, including hearings which canvass the wide variety of views which those operating in this field entertain. The technological problems tendered in the many briefs before us [7] indicate to us that considered action by the Congress is needed.

Reversed.

4. To Promote the Progress of Useful Arts, Report of the President's Commission on the Patent System (1966).

5. Id., at 13.

6. See Wild, Computer Program Protection: The Need to Legislate a Solution, 54 Corn.L.Rev. 586, 604–609 (1969); Bender, Computer Programs: Should They Be Patentable, 68 Col.L.Rev. 241 (1968); Buckman, Protection of Proprietary Interest in Computer Programs, 51 J.Pat.Off.Soc'y 135 (1969).

7. Amicus briefs of 16 interested groups have been filed in this case.

MR. JUSTICE STEWART, MR. JUSTICE BLACKMUN, and MR. JUSTICE POWELL took no part in the consideration or decision of this case.

* * *

APPLICATION OF FREEMAN

United States Court of Customs and Patent Appeals, 1978.
573 F.2d 1237, 197 USPQ 464.

MARKEY, CHIEF JUDGE.

Appeal from the decision of the Patent and Trademark Office (PTO) Board of Appeals (board), affirming the rejection of claims 1–10, all of the claims in application serial No. 32,025, filed May 6, 1970, and entitled "Computer Typesetting." We reverse.

THE INVENTION

The subject matter of Freeman's invention is a system for typesetting alphanumeric information, using a computer-based control system in conjunction with a phototypesetter of conventional design. * * *

Freeman's system is especially useful in printing mathematical formulae. Its particular advantage over prior computer-aided printing systems is its positioning of mathematical symbols in an expression in accordance with their appearance, while maintaining the mathematical integrity of the expression.

* * *

In sum, appellant's invention includes three signal-processing steps. First, the input codes are read, and a tree structure of symbols representing the mathematical expression is built. Second, the signals specifying the relative concatenation point positions of the symbols are composed by application of the local positioning algorithm. Third, an image of the expression, with all symbols in proper position, is generated on the CRT or other output device.

* * *

ISSUE

The sole issue is whether the systems recited in claims 1–7 and the methods recited in claims 8–10 constitute statutory subject matter under 35 U.S.C.A. § 101.

OPINION

The Board's Application of Benson

The board looked to the "nutshell" holding in *Benson*:

It is conceded that one may not patent an idea. But in practical effect that would be the result if the formula for converting BCD numerals to pure binary numerals were patented in this case. The mathematical formula involved here has no substantial practical application except in connection with a digital computer, which means that if the judgment below is affirmed, the patent would wholly pre-empt the mathematical formula and in practical effect would be a patent on the algorithm itself. [409 U.S. at 71–72, 93 S.Ct. at 257, 175 USPQ at 676.]

In applying the "principles set down" in *Benson,* the board decided that "the novelty resides in the program," and concluded, without further analysis of the claims themselves, that the results foreseen in the "nutshell" holding would ensue. We disagree with the approach taken and the conclusion reached by the board.

We have indicated the inappropriateness of the "point of novelty" approach in determining whether a claimed invention is statutory subject matter under 35 U.S.C.A. § 101. See In re de Castelet, 562 F.2d 1236, 1240, 195 USPQ 439, 443 (Cust. & Pat.App.1977); In re Chatfield, 545 F.2d 152, 158, 191 USPQ 730, 736 (Cust. & Pat.App.1976), cert. denied, 434 U.S. 875, 98 S.Ct. 226, 54 L.Ed.2d 155, 195 USPQ 465 (1977). Though the solicitor refers to language appearing in In re Christensen, 478 F.2d 1392, 178 USPQ 35 (Cust. & Pat.App.1973), we clarified that language in In re Chatfield, supra, 545 F.2d at 158, 191 USPQ at 736:

> Our reference in *Christensen* to the mathematical equation as being "at the point of novelty" does not equate to a holding that a claim may be dissected, the claim components searched in the prior art and, if the only component found novel is outside the statutory classes of invention, the claim may be rejected under 35 U.S.C.A. § 101. That procedure is neither correct nor within the intent of Congress, for the reasons we stated in [In re Bernhart, 417 F.2d 1395, 57 CCPA 737, 163 USPQ 611 (1969)].

In reversing the examiner, the board considered In re Christensen, supra, inapposite because the data here operated upon, i.e., symbols and their concatenation points, were not in the prior art. "Thus" said the board, "the instant case involves more than the mere practice of an algorithm or formula on data considered to be old and well known."

The solicitor contends that Graham v. John Deere Co., 383 U.S. 1, 32–33, 86 S.Ct. 684, 15 L.Ed.2d 545, 148 USPQ 459, 472–73 (1966), supports the board's "point of novelty" approach. The issue in *Graham,* however, was obviousness under 35 U.S.C.A. § 103, a statutory provision specifically requiring that the subject matter sought to be patented be considered "as a whole." Nothing in *Graham* can be read as an effort to redraft the statute so as to delete the words "as a whole" from 35 U.S.C.A. § 103,[4] and nothing therein had anything to do with whether particular subject matter constitutes a machine, manufacture, composition of matter or process under 35 U.S.C.A. § 101. Analyses of specific facts in a § 103 case cannot serve as an "example" to be followed in determining whether claimed subject matter is within a statutory class of § 101.

---

4. "The question under § 103 is whether the *subject matter as a whole* would have been obvious, not whether the *differences* [point of novelty] would have been obvious." In re Buehler, 515 F.2d 1134, 1140, 185 USPQ 781, 786 (Cust. & Pat.App. 1975). See In re Van Venrooy, 412 F.2d 250, 253 n. 4, 56 CCPA 1199, 1203 n. 4, 162 USPQ 37, 39 n. 4 (1969).

The board chose to read *Benson* much too broadly. The solicitor states the PTO's view of the *Benson* holding as being "that a patent should not be granted where the only novelty resides in a program for a general purpose digital computer." That overly broad reading, whatever purpose it may be intended to serve in the PTO, is unjustified. That computer programs are not patentable was neither the holding nor the "thrust" of *Benson*. In re de Castelet, supra; In re Chatfield, supra. Neither this court nor the PTO is at liberty to disregard the words of the Court in *Benson:* "It is said that the decision precludes a patent for any program servicing a computer. We do not so hold." 409 U.S. at 71, 93 S.Ct. at 257, 175 USPQ at 676.[5] Nor is this court or the PTO at liberty to ignore the Court's own characterization of its *Benson* holding: "Our limited holding ∗ ∗ ∗ was that respondent's method was not a patentable 'process' as that term is defined in 35 U.S.C.A. § 100(b)." Dann v. Johnston, 425 U.S. 219, 224, 96 S.Ct. 1393, 1396, 47 L.Ed.2d 692, 189 USPQ 257, 259 (1976).

The fundamental flaw in the board's analysis in this case lies in a superficial treatment of the claims. With no reference to the nature of the algorithm involved, the board merely stated that the coverage sought "in practical effect would be a patent on the algorithm itself." Though the board gave no clear reasons for so concluding, its approach would appear to be that every implementation with a programmed computer equals "algorithm" in the *Benson* sense. If that rubric be law, every claimed method that can be so implemented would equal nonstatutory subject matter under 35 U.S.C.A. § 101. That reasoning sweeps too wide and is without basis in law. The absence, or inadequacy, of detailed claim analysis in the present case is further illustrated by the conclusion that "the novelty resides in the program" when, as here, the claims recite no particular computer program. In the present case, it is not the claims but the *specification* that discloses implementation of the claimed invention with computer programs.[6]

As a bare minimum, application of *Benson* in a particular case requires a careful analysis of the claims, to determine whether, as in *Benson,* they recite a "procedure for solving a given type of *mathemati-*

---

5. In In re Chatfield, supra, 545 F.2d at 156, 191 USPQ at 734, and in In re Noll, 545 F.2d 141, 148–49 n. 6, 191 USPQ 721, 726 n. 6 (Cust. & Pat.App.1976), cert. denied, 434 U.S. 875, 98 S.Ct. 226, 54 L.Ed.2d 155, 195 USPQ 465 (1977), this court pointed out that the phrase "these programs" in the *Benson* opinion necessarily referred to the specific type of program there involved, not to computer programs in general. Though the present invention is not merely a "program," the solicitor contends that the responsible course would be to deny patents on "software inventions" until Congress sanctions them. The constitutionally responsible course, however, was

stated in In re de Castelet, supra, 562 F.2d at 1240, 195 USPQ at 443:

"Absent contrary directions, no basis exists for a moratorium on protection of inventions embodying or using computer programs. Such broad prohibition could subject meritorious statutory inventions to unabatable piracy, and could forestall invention disclosure, the hallmark of the patent system, until Congress chooses to act."

6. Appellant characterizes the board's approach as "effectively a rejection of the disclosure and not of the claims."

cal problem."   409 U.S. at 65, 93 S.Ct. at 254, 175 USPQ at 674 (emphasis added).

THE METHOD CLAIMS

Appellant's claims 8–10 define methods of controlling a computer display system. Claim 8 sets forth a process of assigning concatenation points to each character to appear on the display device and specifying which of the concatenation points for adjacent characters will coincide. Claim 9 adds the process limitation of testing and modifying the spatial relationship between adjacent characters to provide minimum clearance therebetween. Claim 10 adds the process limitation of employing a hierachical tree structure to establish the spatial relationships among a group of characters to appear on the display device.

Determination of whether a claim preempts nonstatutory subject matter as a whole, in the light of *Benson,* requires a two-step analysis. First, it must be determined whether the claim directly or indirectly recites an "algorithm" in the *Benson* sense of that term, for a claim which fails even to recite an algorithm clearly cannot wholly preempt an algorithm. Second, the claim must be further analyzed to ascertain whether in its entirety it wholly preempts that algorithm. We do not reach the second step in this case because method claims 8–10 do not recite an algorithm in the *Benson* sense.

We are not unmindful of the need for clear understanding of the term "algorithm." As we stated in In re Chatfield, supra, 545 F.2d at 156 n. 5, 191 USPQ at 734 n. 5:

> Over-concentration on the word "algorithm" alone, for example, may mislead. The Supreme Court carefully supplied a definition of the particular algorithm before it, i.e., "[a] procedure for solving a given type of mathematical problem." The broader definition of algorithm is "a step-by-step procedure for solving a problem or accomplishing some end." *Webster's New Collegiate Dictionary* (1976). It is axiomatic that inventive minds seek and develop solutions to problems and step-by-step solutions often attain the status of patentable invention. It would be unnecessarily detrimental to our patent system to deny inventors patent protection on the *sole* ground that their contribution could be broadly termed an "algorithm."

Because every process may be characterized as "a step-by-step procedure ＊ ＊ ＊ for accomplishing some end," a refusal to recognize that *Benson* was concerned only with *mathematical* algorithms leads to the absurd view that the Court was reading the word "process" out of the statute.

The manner in which a claim recites a mathematical algorithm may vary considerably. In some claims, a formula or equation may be expressed in traditional mathematical symbols so as to be immediately recognizable as a mathematical algorithm. See, e.g., In re Richman, 563 F.2d 1026, 195 USPQ 340 (Cust. & Pat.App.1977); In re Flook, 559 F.2d 21, 195 USPQ 9 (Cust. & Pat.App.1977), cert. granted sub nom, Parker v. Flook, 434 U.S. 1033, 98 S.Ct. 764, 54 L.Ed.2d 780 (1978).

Other claims may use prose to express a mathematical computation or to indirectly recite a mathematical equation or formula by means of a prose equivalent therefor. See, e.g., In re de Castelet, supra (claims 6 and 7); In re Waldbaum, 559 F.2d 611, 194 USPQ 465 (Cust. & Pat.App. 1977). A claim which substitutes, for a mathematical formula in algebraic form, "words which mean the same thing," nonetheless recites an algorithm in the *Benson* sense. In re Richman, supra, 563 F.2d at 1030, 195 USPQ at 344. Indeed, the claims at issue in *Benson* did not contain a formula or equation expressed in mathematical symbols. When considered as a whole, each of the claims in *Benson* did, however, recite in prose a formula for converting binary coded decimal numbers into binary numbers.

* * *

THE APPARATUS CLAIMS

Though a claim expressed in "means for" (functional) terms is said to be an apparatus claim, the subject matter as a whole of that claim may be indistinguishable from that of a method claim drawn to the steps performed by the "means." For example, present claim 8 recites process steps of assigning concatenation points to each symbol and specifying which of the concatenation points for adjacent symbols will coincide and claim 1 merely recites "means for" accomplishing each of these same steps. As another example, claim 3 adds a "means for storing input data in a hierarchical tree structure," paralleling the process step added by claim 10. We agree with the solicitor's contention that if allowance of a method claim is proscribed by *Benson,* it would be anomalous to grant a claim to apparatus encompassing any and every "means for" practicing that very method.

The apparatus claims do not directly or indirectly recite any mathematical equation, formula, or calculation and thus do not preempt the use of any mathematical problem solving algorithm. It is unnecessary, therefore, to consider the effect of specific apparatus limitations in some of the apparatus claims.

Because neither the present apparatus claims nor the present method claims recite or preempt a mathematical algorithm as forbidden by *Benson,* both sets of claims are immune from a rejection based solely on the opinion in that case.

Accordingly, the decision of the board, rejecting claims 1–10 under 35 U.S.C.A. § 101, is *reversed.*

Reversed.

LANE, J., dissents.

DIAMOND v. DIEHR

Supreme Court of the United States, 1981.
450 U.S. 175, 101 S.Ct. 1048, 67 L.Ed.2d 155.
209 USPQ 1.

JUSTICE REHNQUIST delivered the opinion of the Court.

We granted certiorari to determine whether a process for curing synthetic rubber which includes in several of its steps the use of a mathematical formula and a programmed digital computer is patentable subject matter under 35 U.S.C. § 101.

* * *

The patent examiner rejected the respondents' claims on the sole ground that they were drawn to nonstatutory subject matter under 35 U.S.C. § 101.[5] He determined that those steps in respondents' claims that are carried out by a computer under control of a stored program constituted nonstatutory subject matter under this Court's decision in *Gottschalk v. Benson,* 409 U.S. 63, 93 S.Ct. 253, 34 L.Ed.2d 273 (1972). The remaining steps—installing rubber in the press and the subsequent closing of the press—were "conventional and necessary to the process and cannot be the basis of patentability." The examiner concluded that respondents' claims defined and sought protection of a computer program for operating a rubber-molding press.

* * *

II

Last Term in *Diamond v. Chakrabarty,* 447 U.S. 303, 100 S.Ct. 2204, 65 L.Ed.2d 144 (1980), this Court discussed the historical purposes of the patent laws and in particular 35 U.S.C. § 101. As in *Chakrabarty,* we must here construe 35 U.S.C. § 101 * * * Unless otherwise defined, "words will be interpreted as taking their ordinary, contemporary, common meaning," *Perrin v. United States,* 444 U.S. 37, 42, 100 S.Ct. 311, 314, 62 L.Ed.2d 199 (1979), and, in dealing with the patent laws, we have more than once cautioned that "courts 'should not read into the patent laws limitations and conditions which the legislature has not expressed.'" *Diamond v. Chakrabarty, supra,* at 308, 100

---

5. Respondents' application contained 11 different claims. Three examples are claims 1, 2, and 11 which provide:

"1. A method of operating a rubber-molding press for precision molded compounds with the aid of a digital computer, comprising:

"providing said computer with a data base for said press including at least,

"natural logarithm conversion data (ln),

"the activation energy constant (C) unique to each batch of said compound being molded, and

"a constant (x) dependent upon the geometry of the particular mold of the press,

"initiating an interval timer in said computer upon the closure of the press for monitoring the elapsed time of said closure,

"constantly determining the temperature (Z) of the mold at a location closely adjacent to the mold cavity in the press during molding,

"constantly providing the computer with the temperature (Z),

"repetitively calculating in the computer, at frequent intervals during each cure, the Arrhenius equation for reaction time during the cure, which is

"ln $v = CZ + x$

"where v is the total required cure time,

"repetitively comparing in the computer at said frequent intervals during the cure each said calculation of the total required cure time calculated with the Arrhenius equation and said elapsed time, and

"opening the press automatically when a said comparison indicates equivalence.

"2. The method of claim 1 including measuring the activation energy constant for the compound being molded in the press with a rheometer and automatically updating said data base within the computer in the event of changes in the compound being molded in said press as measured by said rheometer.

* * * * *

S.Ct., at 2207 quoting *United States v. Dubilier Condenser Corp.,* 289 U.S. 178, 199, 53 S.Ct. 554, 561, 77 L.Ed. 1114 (1933).

The Patent Act of 1793 defined statutory subject matter as "any new and useful art, machine, manufacture or composition of matter, or any new or useful improvement [thereof]." Act of Feb. 21, 1793, ch. 11, § 1, 1 Stat. 318. Not until the patent laws were recodified in 1952 did Congress replace the word "art" with the word "process." It is that latter word which we confront today, and in order to determine its meaning we may not be unmindful of the Committee Reports accompanying the 1952 Act which inform us that Congress intended statutory subject matter to "include anything under the sun that is made by man." S.Rep. No. 1979, 82d Cong., 2d Sess., 5 (1952).

Although the term "process" was not added to 35 U.S.C. § 101 until 1952 a process has historically enjoyed patent protection because it was considered a form of "art" as that term was used in the 1793 Act. In defining the nature of a patentable process, the Court stated:

> "That a process may be patentable, irrespective of the particular form of the instrumentalities used, cannot be disputed. * * * A process is a mode of treatment of certain materials to produce a given result. It is an act, or a series of acts, performed upon the subject-matter to be transformed and reduced to a different state or thing. If new and useful, it is just as patentable as is a piece of machinery. In the language of the patent law, it is an art. The machinery pointed out as suitable to perform the process may or may not be new or patentable; whilst the process itself may be altogether new, and produce an entirely new result. The process requires that certain things should be done with certain substances, and in a certain order; but the tools to be used in doing this may be of secondary consequence." *Cochrane v. Deener,* 94 U.S. 780, 787–788, 24 L.Ed. 139 (1877).

Analysis of the eligibility of a claim of patent protection for a "process" did not change with the addition of that term to § 101. Recently, in *Gottschalk v. Benson,* 409 U.S. 63, 93 S.Ct. 253, 34 L.Ed.2d 273 (1972), we repeated the above definition recited in *Cochrane v. Deener,* adding: "Transformation and reduction of an article 'to a different state or thing' is the clue to the patentability of a process claim that does not include particular machines." 409 U.S., at 70, 93 S.Ct., at 256.

Analyzing respondents' claims according to the above statements from our cases, we think that a physical and chemical process for molding precision synthetic rubber products falls within the § 101 categories of possibly patentable subject matter. That respondents' claims involve the transformation of an article, in this case raw, uncured synthetic rubber, into a different state or thing cannot be disputed. The respondents' claims describe in detail a step-by-step method for accomplishing such, beginning with the loading of a mold with raw, uncured rubber and ending with the eventual opening of the press at the conclusion of the cure. Industrial processes such as this are the types which have historically been eligible to receive the protection of our patent laws.[8]

III

Our conclusion regarding respondents' claims is not altered by the fact that in several steps of the process a mathematical equation and a programmed digital computer are used. This Court has undoubtedly recognized limits to § 101 and every discovery is not embraced within the statutory terms. Excluded from such patent protection are laws of nature, natural phenomena, and abstract ideas. See *Parker v. Flook,* 437 U.S. 584, 98 S.Ct. 2522, 57 L.Ed.2d 451 (1978); *Gottschalk v. Benson, supra,* at 67, 93 S.Ct., at 255; *Funk Bros. Seed Co. v. Kalo Inoculant Co.,* 333 U.S. 127, 130, 68 S.Ct. 440, 441, 92 L.Ed. 588 (1948). "An idea of itself is not patentable," *Rubber-Tip Pencil Co. v. Howard,* 20 Wall. 498, 507, 22 L.Ed. 410 (1874). "A principle, in the abstract, is a fundamental truth; an original cause; a motive; these cannot be patented, as no one can claim in either of them an exclusive right." *Le Roy v. Tatham,* 14 How. 156, 175, 14 L.Ed. 367 (1853). Only last Term, we explained:

> "[A] new mineral discovered in the earth or a new plant found in the wild is not patentable subject matter. Likewise, Einstein could not patent his celebrated law that $E = mc^2$, nor could Newton have patented the law of gravity. Such discoveries are 'manifestations of * * * nature, free to all men and reserved exclusively to none.'" *Diamond v. Chakrabarty,* 447 U.S., at 309, 100 S.Ct., at 2208, quoting *Funk Bros. Seed Co. v. Kalo Inoculant Co., supra,* at 130, 68 S.Ct., at 441.

Our recent holdings in *Gottschalk v. Benson, supra,* and *Parker v. Flook, supra,* both of which are computer-related, stand for no more than these long-established principles. In *Benson,* we held unpatentable claims for an algorithm used to convert binary code decimal numbers to equivalent pure binary numbers. The sole practical application of the algorithm was in connection with the programming of a general purpose digital computer. We defined "algorithm" as a "procedure for solving a given type of mathematical problem," and we concluded that such an algorithm, or mathematical formula, is like a law of nature, which cannot be the subject of a patent.

Parker v. Flook, supra, presented a similar situation. The claims were drawn to a method for computing an "alarm limit." An "alarm

---

8. We note that as early as 1854 this Court approvingly referred to patent eligibility of processes for curing rubber. See *id.,* at 267; n. 7, *supra.* In *Tilghman v. Proctor,* 102 U.S. 707, 26 L.Ed. 279 (1881) we referred to the original patent Charles Goodyear received on his process for "vulcanizing" or curing rubber. We stated:

"That a patent can be granted for a process, there can be no doubt. The patent law is not confined to new machines and new compositions of matter, but extends to any new and useful art or manufacture. A manufacturing process is clearly an art, within the meaning of the law. Goodyear's patent was for a process, namely, the process of vulcanizing india-rubber by subjecting it to a high degree of heat when mixed with sulphur and a mineral salt. The apparatus for performing the process was not patented, and was not material. The patent pointed out how the process could be effected, and that was deemed sufficient." *Id.,* at 722.

limit" is simply a number and the Court concluded that the application sought to protect a formula for computing this number. Using this formula, the updated alarm limit could be calculated if several other variables were known. The application, however, did not purport to explain how these other variables were to be determined, nor did it purport "to contain any disclosure relating to the chemical processes at work, the monitoring of process variables, or the means of setting off an alarm or adjusting an alarm system. All that it provides is a formula for computing an updated alarm limit." 437 U.S., at 586, 98 S.Ct., at 2523.

In contrast, the respondents here do not seek to patent a mathematical formula. Instead, they seek patent protection for a process of curing synthetic rubber. Their process admittedly employs a well-known mathematical equation, but they do not seek to pre-empt the use of that equation. Rather, they seek only to foreclose from others the use of that equation in conjunction with all of the other steps in their claimed process. These include installing rubber in a press, closing the mold, constantly determining the temperature of the mold, constantly recalculating the appropriate cure time through the use of the formula and a digital computer, and automatically opening the press at the proper time. Obviously, one does not need a "computer" to cure natural or synthetic rubber, but if the computer use incorporated in the process patent significantly lessens the possibility of "overcuring" or "undercuring," the process as a whole does not thereby become unpatentable subject matter.

Our earlier opinions lend support to our present conclusion that a claim drawn to subject matter otherwise statutory does not become nonstatutory simply because it uses a mathematical formula, computer program, or digital computer. In *Gottschalk v. Benson*, we noted: "It is said that the decision precludes a patent for any program servicing a computer. We do not so hold." 409 U.S., at 71, 93 S.Ct., at 257. Similarly, in *Parker v. Flook*, we stated that "a process is not unpatentable simply because it contains a law of nature or a mathematical algorithm." 437 U.S., at 590, 98 S.Ct., at 2526. It is now commonplace that an *application* of a law of nature or mathematical formula to a known structure or process may well be deserving of patent protection. See, *e.g., Funk Bros. Seed Co. v. Kalo Inoculant Co.,* 333 U.S. 127, 68 S.Ct. 440, 92 L.Ed. 588 (1948); *Eibel Process Co. v. Minnesota & Ontario Paper Co.,* 261 U.S. 45, 43 S.Ct. 322, 67 L.Ed. 523 (1923); *Cochrane v. Deener,* 94 U.S. 780, 24 L.Ed. 139 (1877); *O'Reilly v. Morse,* 15 How. 62, 14 L.Ed. 601 (1854); and *Le Roy v. Tatham,* 14 How. 156, 14 L.Ed. 367 (1853). As Justice Stone explained four decades ago:

> "While a scientific truth, or the mathematical expression of it, is not a patentable invention, a novel and useful structure created with the aid of knowledge of scientific truth may be." *Mackay Radio & Telegraph Co. v. Radio of America,* 306 U.S. 86, 94, 59 S.Ct. 427, 431, 83 L.Ed. 506 (1939).

We think this statement in *Mackay* takes us a long way toward the correct answer in this case. Arrhenius' equation is not patentable in isolation, but when a process for curing rubber is devised which incorporates in it a more efficient solution of the equation, that process is at the very least not barred at the threshold by § 101.

In determining the eligibility of respondents' claimed process for patent protection under § 101, their claims must be considered as a whole. It is inappropriate to dissect the claims into old and new elements and then to ignore the presence of the old elements in the analysis. This is particularly true in a process claim because a new combination of steps in a process may be patentable even though all the constituents of the combination were well known and in common use before the combination was made. The "novelty" of any element or steps in a process, or even of the process itself, is of no relevance in determining whether the subject matter of a claim falls within the § 101 categories of possibly patentable subject matter.[12]

It has been urged that novelty is an appropriate consideration under § 101. Presumably, this argument results from the language in § 101 referring to any "new and useful" process, machine, etc. Section 101, however, is a general statement of the type of subject matter that is eligible for patent protection "subject to the conditions and requirements of this title." Specific conditions for patentability follow and § 102 covers in detail the conditions relating to novelty. The question therefore of whether a particular invention is novel is "wholly apart from whether the invention falls into a category of statutory subject matter." *In re Bergy,* 596 F.2d 952, 961 (Cust. & Pat.App., 1979) (emphasis deleted). See also *Nickola v. Peterson,* 580 F.2d 898 (CA6 1978). The legislative history of the 1952 Patent Act is in accord with this reasoning. The Senate Report stated:

> "Section 101 sets forth the subject matter that can be patented, 'subject to the conditions and requirements of this title.' The conditions under which a patent may be obtained follow, and *Section 102 covers the conditions relating to novelty.*" S.Rep. No. 1979, 82d Cong., 2d Sess., 5 (1952), U.S.Code Cong. & Admin.News, 1952, p. 2399 (emphasis supplied).

12. It is argued that the procedure of dissecting a claim into old and new elements is mandated by our decision in *Flook* which noted that a mathematical algorithm must be assumed to be within the "prior art." It is from this language that the petitioner premises his argument that if everything other than the algorithm is determined to be old in the art, then the claim cannot recite statutory subject matter. The fallacy in this argument is that we did not hold in *Flook* that the mathematical algorithm could not be considered at all when making the § 101 determina-tion. To accept the analysis proffered by the petitioner would, if carried to its extreme, make all inventions unpatentable because all inventions can be reduced to underlying principles of nature which, once known, make their implementation obvious. The analysis suggested by the petitioner would also undermine our earlier decisions regarding the criteria to consider in determining the eligibility of a process for patent protection. See, *e.g., Gottschalk v. Benson, supra;* and *Cochrane v. Deener,* 94 U.S. 780, 24 L.Ed. 139 (1877).

It is later stated in the same Report:

> "Section 102, in general, may be said to describe the statutory novelty required for patentability, and includes, in effect, an amplification and definition of 'new' in section 101." *Id.*, at 6, U.S.Code Cong. & Admin.News, 1952, p. 2399.

Finally, it is stated in the "Revision Notes":

> "The corresponding section of [the] existing statute is split into two sections, section 101 relating to the subject matter for which patents may be obtained, and section 102 defining statutory novelty and stating other conditions for patentability." *Id.*, at 17, U.S.Code Cong. & Admin.News, 1952, p. 2409.

See also H.R.Rep. No. 1923, 82d Cong., 2d Sess., at 6, 7, and 17 (1952).

In this case, it may later be determined that the respondents' process is not deserving of patent protection because it fails to satisfy the statutory conditions of novelty under § 102 or nonobviousness under § 103. A rejection on either of these grounds does not affect the determination that respondents' claims recited subject matter which was eligible for patent protection under § 101.

IV

We have before us today only the question of whether respondents' claims fall within the § 101 categories of possibly patentable subject matter. We view respondents' claims as nothing more than a process for molding rubber products and not as an attempt to patent a mathematical formula. We recognize, of course, that when a claim recites a mathematical formula (or scientific principle or phenomenon of nature), an inquiry must be made into whether the claim is seeking patent protection for that formula in the abstract. A mathematical formula as such is not accorded the protection of our patent laws, *Gottschalk v. Benson,* 409 U.S. 63, 93 S.Ct. 253, 34 L.Ed.2d 273 (1972), and this principle cannot be circumvented by attempting to limit the use of the formula to a particular technological environment. *Parker v. Flook,* 437 U.S. 584, 98 S.Ct. 2522, 57 L.Ed.2d 451 (1978). Similarly, insignificant post-solution activity will not transform an unpatentable principle into a patentable process. *Ibid.*[14] To hold otherwise would

---

14. Arguably, the claims in *Flook* did more than present a mathematical formula. The claims also solved the calculation in order to produce a new number or "alarm limit" and then replaced the old number with the number newly produced. The claims covered all uses of the formula in processes "comprising the catalytic chemical conversion of hydrocarbons." There are numerous such processes in the petrochemical and oil refinery industries and the claims therefore covered a broad range of potential uses, 437 U.S., at 586, 98 S.Ct., at 2523. The claims, however, did not cover every conceivable application of the formula. We rejected in *Flook* the argument that because all possible uses of the mathematical formula were not preempted, the claim should be eligible for patent protection. Our reasoning in *Flook* is in no way inconsistent with our reasoning here. A mathematical formula does not suddenly become patentable subject matter simply by having the applicant acquiesce to limiting the reach of the patent for the formula to a particular technological use. A mathematical formula in the abstract is nonstatutory subject matter regardless of whether the patent is intended to cover all uses of the formula or only limited uses. Similarly, a mathematical formula does not become patentable sub-

allow a competent draftsman to evade the recognized limitations on the type of subject matter eligible for patent protection. On the other hand, when a claim containing a mathematical formula implements or applies that formula in a structure or process which, when considered as a whole, is performing a function which the patent laws were designed to protect (*e.g.,* transforming or reducing an article to a different state or thing), then the claim satisfies the requirements of § 101. Because we do not view respondents' claims as an attempt to patent a mathematical formula, but rather to be drawn to an industrial process for the molding of rubber products, we affirm the judgment of the Court of Customs and Patent Appeals.[15]

It is so ordered.

JUSTICE STEVENS, with whom JUSTICE BRENNAN, JUSTICE MARSHALL, and JUSTICE BLACKMUN join, dissenting.

*   *   *

Prior to 1968, well-established principles of patent law probably would have prevented the issuance of a valid patent on almost any conceivable computer program. Under the "mental steps" doctrine, processes involving mental operations were considered unpatentable. See, *e.g., In re Heritage,* 150 F.2d 554, 556–558, 32 CCPA (Pat.) 1170, 1173–1177 (1945); *In re Shao Wen Yuan,* 188 F.2d 377, 380–383, 38 CCPA (Pat.) 967, 972–976

ject matter merely by including in the claim for the formula token postsolution activity such as the type claimed in *Flook.* We were careful to note in *Flook* that the patent application did not purport to explain how the variables used in the formula were to be selected, nor did the application contain any disclosure relating to chemical processes at work or the means of setting off an alarm or adjusting the alarm unit. *Ibid.* All the application provided was a "formula for computing an updated alarm limit." *Ibid.*

15. The dissent's analysis rises and falls on its characterization of respondents' claims as presenting nothing more than "an improved method of calculating the time that the mold should remain closed during the curing process." *Post,* at 1066. The dissent states that respondents claim only to have developed "a new method of programming a digital computer in order to calculate—promptly and repeatedly—the correct curing time in a familiar process." *Post,* at 1069. Respondents' claims, however, are not limited to the isolated step of "programming a digital computer." Rather, respondents' claims describe a process of curing rubber beginning with the loading of the mold and ending with the opening of the press and the production of a synthetic rubber product that has been perfectly cured—a result heretofore unknown in the art. See n. 5, *supra.* The fact that one or more of the steps in re-

spondents' process may not, in isolation, be novel or independently eligible for patent protection is irrelevant to the question of whether the claims as a whole recite subject matter *eligible* for patent protection under § 101. As we explained when discussing machine patents in *Deepsouth Packing Co. v. Laitram Corp.,* 406 U.S. 518, 92 S.Ct. 1700, 32 L.Ed.2d 273 (1972):

"The patents were warranted not by the novelty of their elements but by the novelty of the combination they represented. Invention was recognized because Laitram's assignors combined ordinary elements in an extraordinary way—a novel union of old means was designed to achieve new ends. Thus, for both inventions 'the whole in some way exceed[ed] the sum of its parts.' *Great A. & P. Tea Co. v. Supermarket Equipment Corp.,* 340 U.S. 147, 152 [71 S.Ct. 127, 130, 95 L.Ed. 162] (1950)." *Id.,* at 521–522, 92 S.Ct., at 1703–1704 (footnote omitted).

In order for the dissent to reach its conclusion it is necessary for it to read out of respondents' patent application all the steps in the claimed process which it determined were not novel or "inventive." That is not the purpose of the § 101 inquiry and conflicts with the proposition recited above that a claimed invention may be entitled to patent protection even though some or all of its elements are not "novel."

(1951). The mental-steps doctrine was based upon the familiar principle that a scientific concept or mere idea cannot be the subject of a valid patent. See *In re Bolongaro,* 62 F.2d 1059, 1060, 20 CCPA (Pat.) 845, 846–847 (1933). The doctrine was regularly invoked to deny patents to inventions consisting primarily of mathematical formulae or methods of computation. It was also applied against patent claims in which a mental operation or mathematical computation was the sole novel element or inventive contribution; it was clear that patentability could not be predicated upon a mental step. * * *

Beginning with two decisions in 1968, a dramatic change in the law as understood by the Court of Customs and Patent Appeals took place. By repudiating the well-settled "function of a machine" and "mental steps" doctrines, that court reinterpreted § 101 of the Patent Code to enlarge drastically the categories of patentable subject matter. This reinterpretation would lead to the conclusion that computer programs were within the categories of inventions to which Congress intended to extend patent protection.

In *In re Tarczy-Hornoch,* 397 F.2d 856, 55 CCPA (Pat.) 1441 (1968), a divided Court of Customs and Patent Appeals overruled the line of cases developing and applying the "function of a machine" doctrine. The majority acknowledged that the doctrine had originated with decisions of this Court and that the lower federal courts, including the Court of Customs and Patent Appeals, had consistently adhered to it during the preceding 70 years. Nonetheless, the court concluded that the doctrine rested on a misinterpretation of the precedents and that it was contrary to "the basic purposes of the patent system and productive of a range of undesirable results from the harshly inequitable to the silly." *Id.,* at 867, 55 CCPA (Pat.), at 1454. Shortly thereafter, a similar fate befell the "mental steps" doctrine. In *In re Prater,* 415 F.2d 1378, 56 CCPA (Pat.) 1360 (1968), modified on rehearing, 415 F.2d 1393, 56 CCPA (Pat.) 1381 (1969), the court found that the precedents on which that doctrine was based either were poorly reasoned or had been misinterpreted over the years. 415 F.2d, at 1382–1387, 56 CCPA (Pat.), at 1366–1372. The court concluded that the fact that a process may be performed mentally should not foreclose patentability if the claims reveal that the process also may be performed without mental operations. *Id.,* at 1389, 56 CCPA (Pat.), at 1374–1375. This aspect of the original *Prater* opinion was substantially undisturbed by the opinion issued after rehearing. However, the second *Prater* opinion clearly indicated that patent claims broad enough to encompass the operation of a programmed computer would not be rejected for lack of patentable subject matter. 415 F.2d, at 1403, n. 29, 56 CCPA (Pat.), at 1394, n. 29.[14]

---

14. It is interesting to note that the Court of Customs and Patent Appeals in the second *Prater* opinion expressly rejected the Patent Office's procedure for analyzing the apparatus claim pursuant to which the mathematical principle was treated as though it were within the prior art. 415 F.2d, at 1405–1406, 56 CCPA (Pat.), at 1397. This precise procedure, of course, was later employed by this Court in *Parker v. Flook,* 437 U.S. 584, 98 S.Ct. 2522, 57 L.Ed.2d 451 (1978).

The Court of Customs and Patent Appeals soon replaced the overruled doctrines with more expansive principles formulated with computer technology in mind. In *In re Bernhart,* 417 F.2d 1395, 57 CCPA (Pat.) 737 (1969), the court reaffirmed *Prater,* and indicated that all that remained of the mental-steps doctrine was a prohibition on the granting of a patent that would confer a monopoly on all uses of a scientific principle or mathematical equation. *Id.,* at 1399, 57 CCPA (Pat.), at 743. The court also announced that a computer programmed with a new and unobvious program was physically different from the same computer without that program; the programmed computer was a new machine or at least a new improvement over the unprogrammed computer. *Id.,* at 1400, 57 CCPA (Pat.), at 744. Therefore, patent protection could be obtained for new computer programs if the patent claims were drafted in apparatus form.

The Court of Customs and Patent Appeals turned its attention to process claims encompassing computer programs in *In re Musgrave,* 431 F.2d 882, 57 CCPA (Pat.) 1352 (1970). In that case, the court emphasized the fact that *Prater* had done away with the mental-steps doctrine; in particular, the court rejected the Patent Office's continued reliance upon the "point of novelty" approach to claim analysis. *Id.,* at 889, 57 CCPA (Pat.), at 1362.[15] The court also announced a new standard for evaluating process claims under § 101: any sequence of operational steps was a patentable process under § 101 as long as it was within the "technological arts." *Id.,* at 893, 57 CCPA (Pat.), at 1366–1367. This standard effectively disposed of any vestiges of the mental-steps doctrine remaining after *Prater* and *Bernhart.* The "technological arts" standard was refined in *In re Benson,* 441 F.2d 682, 58 CCPA (Pat.) 1134 (1971), in which the court held that computers, regardless of the uses to which they are put, are within the technological arts for purposes of § 101. *Id.,* at 688, 58 CCPA (Pat.), at 1142.

4. NEW USE

CONTINENTAL CAN CO., INC. v. CROWN CORK AND SEAL, INC.

United States District Court of Pennsylvania, 1967.
281 F.Supp. 474, 156 USPQ 80, vacated 3d Cir., 415 F.2d 601.

KIRKPATRICK, SENIOR DISTRICT JUDGE. This is an action for the infringement of two patents,[1] 2654913 and 2654914, issued to Maier, both applied for July 27, 1950 and issued October 13, 1953, and both

---

15. Under the "point of novelty" approach, if the novelty or advancement in the art claimed by the inventor resided solely in a step of the process embodying a mental operation or other unpatentable element, the claim was rejected under § 101 as being directed to nonstatutory subject matter. See Blumenthal & Riter, Statutory or Non-Statutory?: An Analysis of the Patentability of Computer Related Inventions, 62 J.Pat.Off.Soc. 454, 457, 461, 470 (1980).

1. The rather complicated pleadings by which the issue was finally arrived at need not be recited in detail. The action, as now presented for trial, amounts to a simple infringement suit with counterclaim challenging validity.

being method patents for making sealing members[2] or liners for metal caps of beverage bottles. In both, the liners are molded in the crown or metal shell of the cap, of a synthetic material known as plastisol. The only important difference between them is that the 914 patent calls for a second step, namely "curing" the molded liners in an oven, whereas in the 913 patent the curing is accomplished in a single step by the same means as the molding.

The defenses are invalidity for obviousness, invalidity for indefiniteness, non-infringement and double-patenting. The challenge on the ground of obviousness presents the main issue in the case.

* * *

Both patents disclose and claim a process in which plastisol in a flowable state is deposited in the metal shell or crown cap which is then positioned upon a heated platen where a heated plunger comes down upon it to apply light pressure, producing a wafer-like disc having a thickened circumference which will form a seal between the crown and the lips of the bottle. In patent 913, the plunger remains on the plastisol for approximately six seconds, with the result that a solid liner ready for use is produced. In patent 914, the plunger is removed after two or three seconds, and final curing takes place in an oven further along the line.

* * *

There is no dispute that in the manufacture of liners for bottle caps, a two-step process consisting of first molding and then curing in an oven is old. Production of discs of solid material by this method was well known, and crown liners so produced were in commercial production before the Maier patents issued. It was also admitted that the means disclosed in the patents by which the molding of the liners was accomplished, namely, heated plungers cooperating with heated platens, was not new. The characteristics of plastisol, its suitability for use as crown liners and its performance under heat and pressure, including its ability to solidify quickly after being heated to certain high temperatures, had been studied and the results published.

Thus, it appears that practically every major step of the process is to be found somewhere in the prior art. However, the combination claimed by the patents is nowhere disclosed. Specifically, there is no evidence of any prior art plunger-and-platen process in which plastisol was deposited in the metal cap in a semi-liquid or flowable state and molded in situ.[3]

The defendant's case for invalidity is based largely upon the textbook principle of patent law that the use of a new material whose characteristics are well known in an old process is not a patentable

---

2. Also referred to in the record as "crown liners", "gasket liners", "sealing pads" and "cushion pads".

3. U.S. Patents 2489407 and 2528506 to Foye were issued in 1949 and 1950 for a method of making crown liners from plas-

tisol introduced into the metal cap in a more or less fluid form. However, the method was an entirely different one from that of the patents in suit, the molding being carried out not by plunger and platen but by spinning the cap.

advance even though the new material is superior to the old and a better result is obtained. This principle has met with many exceptions or modifications since Hotchkiss v. Greenwood, 52 U.S. 248 (a decision generally accepted as its origin), with the result, that today there is no such inflexible rule of law if there ever was one. The authorities dealing with substitution of materials are simply a branch of the law relating to obviousness as enacted into Section 103 of the Patent Statute.

Decisions in the Third Circuit, both before and since the Patent Act of 1952, make it clear that patentability of a process may be found although the only new thing about it is the substitution of a new material, if such change is unobvious.

In Yablick v. Protecto, etc. Corp., 21 F.2d 885, 887, the court said—

"It is also the law, as exceptions to this general rule, that, if the substitution involved a new mode of construction, or if it developed new properties and uses of the article made, or where it produces a new mode of operation, or results in a new function, or *when it is the first practical success in the art in which the substitution is made,* or where the practice shows its superiority to consist not only in greater cheapness and greater utility, but also in more efficient action, it may amount to invention." (Emphasis added).

In Ellis-Foster v. Gilbert Spruance Co., 28 F.Supp. 375, 378, 42 USPQ 9, 11–12, a decision affirmed by the Circuit Court of Appeals, 114 F.2d 771, 46 USPQ 535, this court said, "That the substitution of one known material for another in a known combination may amount to invention, depending upon whether the step went beyond what was obvious to persons skilled in the art, is too well settled to require citation of authority."

I doubt that any court today would deny patentability to a process the only novelty of which consisted of the substitution of one material for another in a case where the new material was an unobvious choice.

* * *

[The Court then proceeded to examine the evidence and concluded that both patents were valid. On appeal in the Third Circuit, the patents were held invalid on the ground of obviousness with a vigorous dissent by Judge McLaughlin. See 415 F.2d 601, 163 USPQ 1 (1969).]

APPLICATION OF ZIERDEN

United States Court of Customs and Patent Appeals, 1969.
411 F.2d 1325, 162 USPQ 102.

RICH, ACTING CHIEF JUDGE. This appeal is from the decision of the Patent Office Board of Appeals, adhered to on reconsideration, affirming the rejection of claims 1, 2, and 6 of application serial No. 352,337, filed March 16, 1964, entitled "Methods and Compositions for Removing Alluvium and Other Deposits in Water Systems." Six claims have been allowed.

The appealed claims are for a method (claims 1 and 2) and composition (claim 6) useful for removing and preventing alluvium deposits in water systems where the water employed is derived from "rivers, ponds, lakes or other sources of impure natural waters," as, for example, in industrial cooling systems. The meaning which appellant ascribes to the term "alluvium" appears from the following excerpt from his specification:

> * * * silt, mud, and/or organic wastes and other accumulations [in natural waters] which deposit on heat exchange surfaces and create problems of corrosion, loss of heat transfer efficiency, and the like, as well as reducing the area of the passageways and thus the amount of cooling water which can be circulated.

Locations where such alluvium may present such problems, mentioned in the specification, include cooling systems in blast furnaces, open-hearth furnaces and the like in the steel industry; cooling towers in the oil industry; surface condensers associated with turbine generators; pipes, sewers, and heated water lines; and ship ballast tanks into which river water may be pumped.

Appellant has discovered that deposits of alluvium in such water systems can be removed and prevented by adding to the water in the systems "insoluble potassium metaphosphate and a solubilizing agent therefor."

The appealed claims read:

1. The method of removing and preventing alluvium deposits in water systems which comprises adding to such systems insoluble potassium metaphosphate and a solubilizing agent therefor.

2. The method of removing and preventing alluvium deposits in water systems which comprises adding to such systems insoluble potassium metaphosphate, a solubilizing agent therefor and a compatible dispersing agent.

6. A composition for removing and preventing alluvium deposits in water systems consisting essentially of insoluble potassium metaphosphate, a solubilizing agent therefor and a compatible dispersing agent.

[There follows a discussion of the references including a French Patent.]

Appellant necessarily concedes that his composition, as defined in composition claim 6, is to be patentably distinguished, if at all, from the compositions disclosed in the French patent only by the statement of intended use in the claim: "A composition for removing and preventing alluvium deposits in water systems * * *." A mere statement of a new use for an otherwise old or obvious composition cannot render a claim to the composition patentable. As we said in In re Lemin, 326 F.2d 437, 51 CCPA 942 (1964),

> Appellants are clearly correct in demanding that the subject matter as a whole must be considered under 35 U.S.C.A. § 103. But in applying the statutory test, the differences over the prior art must be

more substantial than a statement of the intended use of an old composition. * * * It seems to us that the composition * * * would be exactly the same whether the user were told to cure pneumonia in animals with it * * * or to promote plant growth with it (as here). The directions on the label will not change the composition * * *.

Since the composition recited in claim 6 is not rendered patentable by the recitation of intended use, the rejection of claim 6 must be *affirmed*.

As to the method claims 1 and 2, the situation is different. First of all, there is express statutory authority for a patent on a process which is a new use of a known process, composition of matter, or material, 35 U.S.C.A. §§ 100(b)[1] and 101,[2] provided, of course, the process predicated on the new use is new and unobvious and not subject to a statutory one-year time bar. 35 U.S.C.A. §§ 102 and 103. We come back, therefore, to the question of whether it would have been obvious to *use* the admittedly old composition, disclosed in the French patent as useful to prevent *scale* formation in water systems, to prevent the settling out of alluvium and to remove previously deposited alluvium in view of the references. If it would not be obvious to use the old composition for this purpose, then we think appellant is entitled to his process or method claims.

* * *

Since we do not find the process, as claimed, obvious or anticipated, the rejection of claims 1 and 2 is *reversed*. The rejection of claim 6 is *affirmed*.

Modified.

* * *

E. MACHINE

There is seldom controversy in the courts at this stage of development of patent law as to whether a subject of a patent is or is not a machine. Webster's New International Dictionary, Second Edition, has the following definition:

a construction or contrivance of a mechanical sort; any device consisting of two or more resistant, relatively constrained parts, which, by a certain predetermined intermotion, may serve to transmit and modify force and motion so as to produce some given effect or to do some desired kind of work; * * *

A sewing machine, a paper-making machine, a printing machine, a hoisting machine, and a flying machine, are examples.

1. 35 U.S.C.A. § 100(b) reads:

(b) The term "process" means process, art or method, and includes a new use of a known process, machine, manufacture, composition of matter, or material.

2. 35 U.S.C.A. § 101 reads (emphasis ours):

Whoever invents or discovers any new and useful *process*, machine, manufacture, or composition of matter, or any new and useful improvement thereof, may obtain a patent therefor, subject to the conditions and requirements of this title.

Walker on Patents (Deller's Second Edition, Section 16), in a discussion on machines, reads in part as follows:

Inventions pertaining to machines may, a court pointed out for purposes of explanation, be divided into four classes. The first class embraces the entire machine, such as a car for a railway or a sewing-machine. The second class of inventions relating to machines is that which embraces one or more of the elements of the machine, but not the entire machine, such as the coulter of the plough or the divider of the reaping-machine. The third class of machines is that which embraces both a new element and a new combination of elements, some of which may have been previously used and well known. The fourth class of machines is that where all the elements of the machine are old and where the invention involves a new combination of those old elements whereby a new and useful result is obtained or an old result is produced in a new and better way.[a]

CANTRELL v. WALLICK

Supreme Court of the United States, 1886.
117 U.S. 689, 6 S.Ct. 970, 29 L.Ed. 1017.

Mr. Justice Woods delivered the opinion of the court:

This was a bill in equity filed by Wallick, the appellee to restrain the infringement by Cantrell and Petty, the appellants, of letters patent granted to Wallick, dated May 25, 1875, for an "improvement in apparatus for enameling moldings," on an application filed October 16, 1874.

* * *

The first defense is based on the theory that a patent cannot be valid unless it is new in all its elements as well as in the combination, if it is for a combination. But this theory cannot be maintained. If it were sound no patent for an improvement on a known contrivance or process could be valid. And yet the great majority of patents are for improvements in old and well known devices, or on patented inventions. Changes in the construction of an old machine which increase its usefulness are patentable. Seymour v. Osborne, 11 Wall. 516 [78 U.S. bk. 20, L.Ed. 33]. So a new combination of known devices, whereby the effectiveness of a machine is increased, may be the subject of a patent. Loom Co. v. Higgins, 105 U.S. 580 [Bk. 26, L.Ed. 1177]; Hailes v. Van Wormer, 20 Wall. 353 [87 U.S. bk. 22, L.Ed. 241]. Two patents may both be valid when the second is an improvement on the first, in which event, if the second includes the first, neither of the two patentees can lawfully use the invention of the other without the other's consent. Star Salt Caster Co. v. Crossman, 4 Cliff. 568.

Therefore, letters patent for an improvement on a patented invention cannot be declared void because they include such patented inven-

a. Union Sugar Refinery v. Matthesson,
(2 Fisher Case 600), 24 F.Case 686 (No.
14,399) (C.C.Mass.1865).

tion. Much less does it lie in the mouth of a party who is infringing both the improvement and the original invention to set up the existence of the first patent as an excuse for infringing the improvement: It is only the patentee of the original invention who has the right to complain of the use made of his invention. We are, therefore, of opinion that the first defense to the suit must fail.

* * *

Decree affirmed.

F. MANUFACTURE

"The species of inventions belonging to this class are very numerous, comprehending every article devised by man except machinery upon the one side, and compositions of matter and designs upon the other. Thus the parts of a machine considered separately from the machine itself, all kinds of tools and fabrics, and every other vendible substance which is neither a complete machine nor produced by the mere union of ingredients, is included under the title 'manufacture.' The mechanical effects which they are intended to produce are of all varieties, from the simple interruption of the action of natural forces to the direction and application of forces artificially developed. In this wide field of inventions many articles must, of course, be found lying so close to the dividing line that doubt may well arise whether they do not more properly belong to the class which follows or precedes it; but even here careful attention to the exact idea of means which the inventor has intended to express will usually remove all ambiguity." Sec. 183. Robinson on Patents (1890).

JOHNSON v. JOHNSTON
United States Circuit Court of Pennsylvania, 1894.
60 Fed. 618.

ACHESON, CIRCUIT JUDGE. The plaintiffs sue for the infringement of letters patent No. 461,787, dated October 20, 1891, granted to Montgomery H. Watson, for an improvement in general indexes. The patented index is designed for use in connection with books in which are recorded the names of individuals, and facts and transactions; for example, entries in the order book or appearance docket of a court, or the record of deeds or mortgages in the books of a recorder.

* * *

No matter at what page of the index volume the searcher may open it, he will there find a ready and accurate reference to the particular page on which will be found the name for which he is searching. Indeed, every page is a complete index. The claims of the patent are:

"(1) As a new article of manufacture, an index book or volume consisting of numbered pages suitably ruled, headed, and numbered, and of a table composed of the letters of the alphabet appearing on said pages, such letters representing the initials of Christian names, and a figure or figures associated with each of said initial letters, and corresponding with a page or pages in said book, the book being designated by a letter of the alphabet. (2) As a new article of manufacture, the herein described index book or volume, the same being designated by a letter of the alphabet, and consisting of a suitable number of pages consecutively numbered, one or more pages of such book being devoted to Christian names commencing with a certain letter of the alphabet, and each page being suitably headed and ruled, and a table on each page, consisting of the letters of the alphabet progressively arranged, and a figure or figures corresponding with a page or pages of said book."

Infringement is clearly shown. In truth, the index books which the defendant made for and sold to the county of Allegheny, Pa., for use in the prothonotary's office (the act of infringement here complained of) are identical with the index of the patent. Two defenses have been urged: First, that the patent in suit is not for a patentable subject-matter; second, that the patent lacks invention, especially in view of the prior state of the art.

1. The term "manufacture," as used in the patent law, has a very comprehensive sense, embracing whatever is made by the art or industry of man, not being a machine, a composition of matter, or a design. Curt.Pat. § 27; 1 Rob.Pat. § 183. In Waring v. Johnson, 6 F. 500, letters patent for an improvement in pocket check books were sustained by Judge Blatchford; and in Norrington v. Bank, 25 F. 199, Judge Colt sustained a patent whose subject-matter was of a like nature. In Dugan v. Gregg, 48 F. 227, a combined book and index, so connected as to facilitate the more ready and convenient handling thereof, was held to be a patentable improvement by Judge Coxe, who, also, in Carter & Co. v. Wollschlaeger, 53 F. 573, upheld a patent for an improvement in duplicate memorandum sales slips, following a decision of Judge Colt in Carter & Co. v. Houghton, 53 F. 577, sustaining the same patent. In Thomson v. Bank, 3 C.C.A. 518, 53 F. 250, the United States circuit court of appeals for the eighth circuit sustained a patent for a bank account book, the improvement consisting in a suitable number of full leaves and alternate series of short leaves, each of the latter being creased or perforated for folding in such a manner as to transfer the column of balances on the right-hand page to the succeeding left-hand page. I have no difficulty in holding that the subject-matter of the patent in suit is patentable.

[The court proceeded to evaluate the invention and concluded with a holding of validity.]

———

We have seen in the decision of Cincinnati Traction Co. v. Pope (210 F. 443, 6th Cir.1913), supra, 447, that the court, in dealing with a transfer ticket, considered the question of patentable subject matter and concluded that "while the case is perhaps near the borderline, we think the device should be classed as an article to be used in a method of doing business, and thus a 'manufacture' within the statute." The question of the combination of "indicia" or "printed matter" with other structure has been frequently treated by the various tribunals having jurisdiction over patents or patent applications. See Jacobs, Patentability of Printed Matter, 18 George Washington Law Review 475 (1950). The following case is illustrative.

FLOOD v. COE

United States District Court, District of Columbia, 1940.
31 F.Supp. 348, 45 USPQ 72.

LUHRING, JUSTICE. This is a suit under Section 4915 of the Revised Statutes, U.S.C. Tit. 35, § 63, 35 U.S.C.A. § 63, to direct the Commissioner of Patents to issue to Dennison Manufacturing Company a patent on the application of Carl A. Flood, Serial No. 43,205, filed October 2, 1935, containing the three claims 11, 16 and 17 set forth in the bill of complaint. These claims were held to be unpatentable over the prior art.

The subject matter of the Flood application is a price ticket particularly intended for tagging garments in retail stores. The ticket is like prior tickets in that it is formed in two parts with a line of perforations between the two parts and in that each part carries a series of identification indicia and also a price mark, the marking on the two parts being the same. When a garment is sold one part of the ticket is torn off and retained by the store while the other part is left attached to the garment taken by the customer.

The applicant's ticket, however, differs from the prior art in that the line of perforations extends lengthwise of the ticket instead of crosswise; in that the series of identification indicia is arranged in a row extending lengthwise of the line of perforation instead of being tabulated in a column extending perpendicularly to the line of perforations; in that the price marks of the two sections are printed in alignment crosswise of the line of perforations at one end of the ticket instead of merely being included in the columns of other indicia; and in that fastening means (such as a pin or an opening for a string loop) is provided in one section of the ticket in a space bordered by the perpendicular rows of indicia.

By virtue of the novel shape of the ticket and the unique relationship between the indicia and the physical characteristics of the ticket, when the ticket is divided along one straight line (the line of perforations) it is separated into two sections carrying duplicate indicia, and when divided along another straight line extending perpendicular to the line of perforations both price marks may be severed and new price marks may be printed in the space left for that purpose, without removing the ticket from the garment and without interfering with the other indicia on the two sections. It is only by the novel shape of the ticket, the disposition of the weakened line lengthwise of the sections, and the unique relationship of the indicia to the structural features that the ticket can be re-marked by severing the ticket along another line transversely of the first.

None of the references cited by the Patent Office contains any suggestion of applicant's unique relationship between the physical structure and the printed matter nor any tags which can be re-marked in the manner above described.

The invention here is more than an arrangement of printed matter on a piece of paper. There is definite and decided relationship between the physical structure and the printed matter. The one depends upon the other. In other words, there is cooperative relationship between the printed indicia and the structural features of the ticket, without which it would be impossible to quickly reprice both sections of each tag without removing it from the merchandise and without leaving the old mark showing on either section of the tag.

By virtue of this unique relationship between the physical structure and the printed matter great savings of time and money are effected by the use of these tags in department stores; and as a consequence the sales of these tags have rapidly mounted during the few years they have been on the market.

This is a new and useful inventive concept and is therefore patentable. Cincinnati Traction Co. v. Pope, 6 Cir., 210 F. 443; Benjamin Menu Card Co. v. Rand, McNally & Co., C.C., 210 F. 285; Rand, McNally & Co. v. Exchange Script-Book Co., 7 Cir., 187 F. 984.

The claims in issue will be allowed, and counsel will prepare and submit formal findings of fact and conclusions of law accordingly.

✓ PARK–IN THEATRES, INC. v. ROGERS ET AL.

United States Court of Appeals, Ninth Circuit, 1942.
130 F.2d 745, 55 USPQ 103.

WILBUR, CIRCUIT JUDGE. Appellant sued appellees for alleged infringement of a patent for a drive-in theater. After answering, appellees moved for summary judgment under rule 56, Rules of Civil Procedure, 28 U.S.C.A. following section 723c, on the grounds that appellant's patent was void on its face for want of patentable subject matter, want of patentable combination, want of invention, and undue multiplicity of claims. The motion was heard on the pleadings and on affidavits filed by appellant. The court made findings of fact and found that the patent, as to claims in suit, was for an architectural design and was not for an art, machine, manufacture or composition of matter, or any new and useful improvement thereof, and dismissed the complaint on the ground that the subject of the patent was not a patentable subject matter and the invention was not a patentable invention or improvement within the meaning of 35 U.S.C.A. § 31, 46 Stat. 376.

* * *

The appellant claims that the drive-in theater conceived by the patentee is a manufacture, a machine and an art, and is patentable as either under the express language of the statute authorizing the issue of patents. 35 U.S.C.A. § 31.

In reaching the contrary conclusion the trial court relied heavily upon the decision by this court in American Disappearing Bed Co. v. Arnaelsteen, 9 Cir., 182 F. 324, 325, as authority for holding that if the subject matter of the patent was in the nature of architecture it did not come within the meaning of the patent law. The court in that case had under consideration a construction of rooms in an apartment house whereby a recess was made under the floor of one room and over the floor of another, wherein a bed could be kept when not in use. The claim thus was confined to a mere arrangement of partitions in a building. In that connection the court said:

> "It would be a gross misuse of the word [manufacture] to say that a house, or a room in a house, is manufactured. While many devices and many novel combinations of materials used in the construction of houses are within the protection of the patent laws, it has never been held, so far as we are advised, that any particular form of construction of a room in a house, or of a recess in a room, is patentable, whether considered by itself or taken in combination with any conceivable use to which it may be put."

*   *   *

It should be noted that the decision in the American Disappearing Bed Co. v. Arnaelsteen, supra, referred to two decisions by the Supreme Court involving the construction of a jail and assumes that the Supreme Court held that such a structure was not patentable. An examination of those cases shows that the court was doubtful whether or not such structure was patentable but held that the patent was invalid for anticipation. Jacobs v. Baker, 7 Wall. 295, 74 U.S. 295, 19 L.Ed. 200; Fond du Lac County v. May, 137 U.S. 395, 11 S.Ct. 98, 34 L.Ed. 714.

We think the rule is correctly stated in the opinion of the Third Circuit Court of Appeals by Judge Buffington in Riter-Conley Mfg. Co. v. Aiken, 3 Cir., 203 F. 699, 702, wherein the court said: "But, considering the question as unaffected by this long course of practice [of the Patent Office], we are clear that the term 'manufacture' in the patent law embraces buildings. To say that a roof falls within the domain of architecture is not to decide the question; for the question is not whether a roof construction is included in architecture, which, of course, it is, but whether the roof section here in question is, in view of its several constituent and cooperating elements, a manufacture. We must not be misled by the factors of size and immobility. The pyramids, by reason of their bulk and solidity, are none the less a manufacture, as distinguished from a natural object."

*   *   *

In the case at bar the patent provides for a system of arranging automobiles facing the stage or screen so that the various automobiles will not enter the line of sight of those in other automobiles and that the automobiles going and coming will also be below the line of sight of those which remain.

The main problem involved is in arranging the position of the automobile so that all the persons therein may be able to look through the windshield and see the entire stage or screen. This is accomplished by tilting the automobile. The patent claims do not specify the means for tilting the automobile but the drawings indicate that one method is by driving the automobile on planes of varying inclination.

The material utilized in constructing the drive-in theater is not important in determining whether or not the finished project is manufactured within the meaning of the patent law.

We conclude that the outdoor theater comes under a patentable classification, as a manufacture or machine.

* * * We return the case to the district court for a trial of the case and a decision not inconsistent with the above determination of this court.[a]

STEPHENS, CIRCUIT JUDGE.

I dissent.

STEINFUR PATENTS CORP. v. WILLIAM BEYER, INC.

United States Court of Appeals, Second Circuit, 1932.
62 F.2d 238, 16 USPQ 219.

SWAN, CIRCUIT JUDGE. The patents in suit relate to the art of bleaching and dyeing furs and the like. One patent is for a process of treating fur skins; the other for the product resulting from the practice of the process. The product patent No. 1,564,378 was issued December 8, 1925, and some two months before the process patent, No. 1,573,200, although both applications were filed in the Patent Office on the same date, May 3, 1924. All the claims of each patent were held valid and infringed by the District Judge, whose careful and thorough discussion of the issues below is reported in 56 F.2d 372.

The patented process discloses a method of bleaching naturally dark-colored fur skins without impairment of the leather or hair. The skins so bleached may then be dyed the same colors as formerly could be successfully applied only to white or naturally light-colored furs. This resulted in a commercial advantage, as the dark-colored skins were cheaper.

There are three stages in the process: The first relating to treatment of the unbleached skins; the second to bleaching them; and the third to dyeing the bleached skins. * * *

The product patent describes the same method of treatment as the process patent, and claims the product of the several steps as "an article of manufacture." There are twenty-four claims; one group

a. In the First Circuit, the patent in suit was held invalid for lack of invention, and, while the court conceded that a drive-in-theater structure may be the subject of a patent, the discussion revolves around the thought that the patent was primarily directed to a system of doing business. Loew's Drive-In-Theatres v. Park-In Theatres, 174 F.2d 547, 81 USPQ 149 (1949).

relating to an unbleached fur skin impregnated with a solution of the protective agent, another group relating to a bleached fur skin which had previously been treated with the protective agent, and a third group relating to a bleached and dyed skin. * * *

[The court considered contentions that the patents were invalid because (1) the specification did not sufficiently describe the process, (2) the process as described was "inoperative," and (3) the product patent did not relate to "any new and useful * * * manufacture, or composition of matter."

In respect of this last contention, the defendant relied upon Am. Fruit Growers v. Brogdex Co., 283 U.S. 1, which had "held that an orange, the rind of which was impregnated with borax by immersion in a solution, and thereby rendered resistant to blue mold decay, was not a 'manufacture' within the meaning of the statute."

not a manufacture

This court held the patent in suit not invalid because of indefiniteness or inoperativeness, and continued:—]

It can hardly be doubted that a naturally dark-colored skin which has been bleached and dyed a light color is an article of manufacture. Certainly it cannot be said of it, as of the orange, that there is no change in its "name, appearance or general character." In none of the three stages sought to be protected by the present patent were the dressed skins in their natural state. While it was true of the orange that impregnation of its rind with borax only protected the natural article against deterioration by mold and gave it no new beneficial uses, the same cannot be said of impregnation of the unbleached skin with ferrous sulphate. By such impregnation the skin attains a new quality which gives it a new beneficial use; it fits it to be used for bleaching by a method which could not without such impregnation be successfully employed. An orange has the same use whether or not impregnated with borax. A fur skin unimpregnated with ferrous sulphate cannot be used in the same way as one which has been so impregnated. The orange case does not, in our opinion, require a decision that the product patent in suit is invalid.[b]

* * *

BINNEY & SMITH CO. v. UNITED CARBON CO. ✓

United States Court of Appeals, Fourth Circuit, 1942.
125 F.2d 255, 52 USPQ 205.
(Reversed 317 U.S. 228, 63 S.Ct. 165, 87 L.Ed. 232.)[c]

PARKER, CIRCUIT JUDGE. This is a suit for infringement of Wiegand and Venuto Patent No. 1,889,429, covering carbon black pellets and a process for making them. * * *

b. For an informative discussion of the patentability of a "product" as such, independent of the process of its production, see Upham, "Does 'Composition of Matter' clause in Patent Statute Include Chemical Compounds Per Se?" 16 Geo.Wash.L.Rev. 351 (1948). The article is a comment on Schering Corp. v. Gilbert, 153 F.2d 428 (1946), so holding.

c. The reversal by the Supreme Court was on the basis that the claims were not sufficiently definite to meet the requirements of the statute.

From an order dismissing the suit, the plaintiff has appealed.
* * *

Claims one and two of the patent, being the product claims here relied on, are as follows:

"1. Substantially pure carbon black in the form of commercially uniform, comparatively small, rounded, smooth aggregates having a spongy porous interior.

"2. As an article of manufacture a pellet of approximately one-sixteenth of an inch in diameter and formed of a porous mass of substantially pure carbon black." * * *

The first question which arises with respect to the product claims in suit is whether such a product was patentable, not being a "combination of matter," but being composed of pure carbon black. We think that it was. It was patentable as a "manufacture." As said by Judge Acheson in Johnson v. Johnson, C.C., 60 F. 618, 620:

"The term 'manufacture,' as used in the patent law, has a very comprehensive sense, embracing whatever is made by the art or industry of man, not being a machine, a composition of matter, or a design. Curt.Pat. Sec. 27; 1 Rob.Pat. Sec. 183." In J.E. Baker Co. v. Kennedy Co. et al., 3 Cir., 253 F. 739, a patent was sustained covering magdolite, a product which was no more than dolomite rock with certain objectionable features removed. And in Union Carbide Co. v. American Carbide Co., 2 Cir., 181 F. 104, it was held that calcium carbide in the form of crystals was patentable as a new product, although the chemical combination in other forms was well known. And there can be no question as to the patentability of the product as distinguished from the process for making it, which was also patentable. Providence Rubber Co. v. Goodyear, 9 Wall. 788, 796, 19 L.Ed. 566; Leeds & Catlin Co. v. Victor Talking Mach. Co., 213 U.S. 301, 319, 29 S.Ct. 495, 53 L.Ed. 805; Hide-Ite Leather Co. v. Fiber Products Co., 1 Cir., 226 F. 34, 36. As said in the case last cited:

"It is a well-recognized rule that a new product, having definite characteristics by which it may be identified, and which distinguish it apart from the process by which it was produced, may be properly described by such characteristics, and when so claimed and described the claims are not limited to the process. Maurer v. Dickerson [3 Cir.], 113 F. 870, 51 C.C.A. 494."

We entertain no doubt as to the patentability of the product here involved. What we have is not an obvious change of form which anyone could make, once the desirability of such change was recognized, as was the breaking up of the flakes of glue in Milligan & Higgins Glue Co. v. Upton, 87 U.S. 3, 24 L.Ed. 985, but the manufacture of an entirely new form of a product, having new characteristics and advantages, and solving problems in connection with the use of the product which had long baffled those most highly skilled in the art. Although a form of carbon black in which the dust nuisance would be eliminated had been sought diligently, it had not been found up to that time. The product of the patent solved not only this problem but also problems connected with handling and transportation. It did this by agglomerating the tiny particles of the powdered product into small granules or pellets which were ductless, which were flowable and which would disintegrate in the process of rubber manufacture so as to preserve the advantages of the dispersability of the tiny particles. Carbon black in such form was a new and highly useful product; and we see no reason why those who first made it should not be protected with respect to the new product which they had brought forth as well as with respect to the process which they had devised for making it.

*   *   *

EX PARTE GRAYSON

United States Patent Office Board of Appeals, 1941.
51 USPQ 413.

Before LANDERS, EDINBURG and CLIFT, EXAMINERS IN CHIEF.

LANDERS, EXAMINER IN CHIEF.

This is an appeal from the action of the Primary Examiner finally rejecting claim 9.

Claim 9 reads as follows:

> 9. A fresh shrimp product comprising a shrimp having the head removed and a narrow channel cut through the shell thereof along the crest or back portion of the shrimp, extending from the cut head portion to a point adjacent the tail and to a depth sufficient to remove the vein and the waste matter contained therein, the remainder of the shell remaining intact and protecting the body of the shrimp from contact with the oxygen of the air.

The claim has been rejected as lacking invention over the ordinary shrimp of commerce. In such shrimp, the head and digestive organs have been removed. The claim requires also that the sand vein be removed. The examiner points out that this vein is in reality a part of the alimentary canal of the shrimp, and holds its omission is insufficient to render the shrimp of the application patentably different from that of commerce. We concur in this view.

The claim has also been rejected as in substance defining a product of nature, under authority of the decision in the case of American Fruit Growers Inc. v. Brogdex Company, 283 U.S. 1 [8 USPQ 131]. Applicant is not claiming the whole shrimp. However, the part he is claiming is still in its natural state which has been changed in no manner. We consider this ground of rejection to be sound.

The decision of the examiner is affirmed.[d]

d. See also, In re McKee, 64 F.2d 379, 17 USPQ 293 (CCPA 1933), and In re McKee, 75 F.2d 991, 25 USPQ 12 (CCPA 1935), where meat products bearing identifying marks did fall into the statutory class of a manufacture.

APPLICATION OF VENEZIA

United States Court of Customs and Patent Appeals, 1976.
530 F.2d 956, 189 USPQ 149.

LANE, JUDGE.

This is an appeal from the decision of the Patent and Trademark Office Board of Appeals (board) affirming the rejections of claims 31 through 36 in application serial No. 31,500 filed April 24, 1970, for "Method of Splicing High Voltage Shielded Cables and Splice Connector Therefor." We reverse.

THE INVENTION

Appellant's invention is a splice connector having interrelated parts adapted to be assembled in the field to provide a splice connection between a pair of high voltage shielded electric cables.

Appellant's application contains claims drawn to the completed connector and to the method of making the splice connection, which have been allowed by the Patent and Trademark Office. On appeal before us are claims drawn to a splice connector "kit" consisting of the parts which are used in making the splice in their unassembled condition.

* * *

THE REJECTIONS

Claims 31–36 were rejected under 35 U.S.C.A. § 112, second paragraph, as indefinite and incomplete in not defining a completed article of manufacture. The examiner particularly relied on In re Collier, 397 F.2d 1003, 55 C.C.P.A. 1280 (1968), as support for this rejection.

Claims 31–36 were additionally rejected under 35 U.S.C.A. § 101 because they were drawn to a plurality of separately and discretely listed and defined manufactures instead of a manufacture.

* * *

OPINION

Section 112 Rejection

We have reviewed the disputed claims and in particular the language criticized by the examiner and the board. We conclude that the claims do define the metes and bounds of the claimed invention with a reasonable degree of precision and particularity, and that they are, therefore, definite as required by the second paragraph of section 112. In re Conley, 490 F.2d 972 (C.C.P.A.1974); In re Miller, 441 F.2d 689, 58 C.C.P.A. 1182 (1971); In re Borkowski, 422 F.2d 904, 57 C.C.P.A. 946 (1970). As we view these claims, they precisely define a group or "kit" of interrelated parts. These interrelated parts may or may not be later assembled to form a completed connector. But what may or may not happen in the future is *not* a part of the claimed invention. The claimed invention does include present structural limitations on each part, which structural limitations are defined by how the parts are to be interconnected in the final assembly, if assembled. However, this is not to say that there is anything futuristic or conditional in the "kit" of parts itself.

* * *

We also fail to see any basis for rejecting appellant's claims for being incomplete in failing to recite a completed assembly. Appellant's invention is a "kit" of parts which may or may not be made into a completed assembly. Since all of the essential parts of the "kit" are recited in the claims, there is no basis for holding the claims incomplete.

We cannot leave our discussion of the section 112 rejection without discussing In re Collier, supra, relied on by both the examiner and the board as support for this rejection. * * *

In *Collier* appellant argued that we were to regard the italicized portions of claim 17 about intended uses, capabilities, and structures which would result upon the performance of future acts, as positive structural limitations. However, we found that the claim did not positively recite any structural relationship between the two elements identified as [1] and [2], in its recitation of what may or may not occur. We concluded that the claim failed to comply with section 112, second paragraph, in "failing distinctly to claim what appellant in his brief insists is his actual invention."

* * *

Section 101 Rejection

35 U.S.C.A. § 101 provides in pertinent part:

> Whoever invents or discovers any new and useful process, machine, manufacture, or composition of matter * * * may obtain a patent therefor * * *.

Both the examiner and the board construed the language "any * * * manufacture" as excluding from its ambit claims drawn to a "kit" of parts, reasoning that a "kit" would be a plurality of separate manufactures, not a single manufacture.

The solicitor in his brief recognizes that the Patent and Trademark Office has in the past issued patents containing similar claims drawn to "kits" of interrelated parts.[1] He argues, however, that double patenting decisions by this court, holding that an inventor may obtain only one patent on a single invention, show that this court has interpreted portions of section 101 in the singular. From this he reasons that the word "manufacture" in section 101 is to be similarly interpreted.

We do not find our decisions on double patenting to be applicable to an interpretation of the words "any manufacture" in section 101. Suffice it to say that the two situations are totally dissimilar. In the

1. There are copies of several patents in the record which contain "kit" claims exemplifying this prior practice, including patent No. 3,108,803, claiming a basketball goal set kit, patent No. 3,041,778, claiming a puppet kit, patent No. 1,974,838, claiming a toy construction set, and patent No. 3,355,837, also claiming a toy construction set.

section 101 "same invention" type double patenting cases, all we were construing was the phrase "a patent therefor."

No other authority has been cited, either by the board or the solicitor, to support the narrow construction which the Patent and Trademark Office now seeks to impose on the words "any manufacture" in section 101.

We do not believe the words in question are to be so narrowly construed. To hold that the words "any manufacture" exclude from their meaning groups or "kits" of interrelated parts would have the practical effect of not only excluding from patent protection those "kit" inventions which are capable of being claimed as a final assembly (e.g., a splice connector), but also many inventions such as building blocks, construction sets, games, etc., which are incapable of being claimed as a final assembly. We do not believe Congress intended to exclude any invention from patent protection merely because it is a group or "kit" *Held* of interrelated parts. We therefore hold that a group or "kit" of interrelated parts is a "manufacture" as that term is used in section 101.

Accordingly, the decision of the board is reversed.

Reversed.

PATENTABILITY OF MICROORGANISMS

By the use of genetic engineering, certain micro-organisms (bacteria) can be modified to meet the practical needs of man. One example is a micro-organism useful in the production of the antibiotic lincomycin. Application of Bergy, Coats, and Malik, 563 F.2d 1031, 195 USPQ 344 (CCPA 1977). Another example is a micro-organism with a capacity for degrading several different components of crude oil. Application of Chakrabarty, 571 F.2d 40, 199 USPQ 72 (CCPA 1978). In the cited cases, the Court of Customs and Patent Appeals held these micro-organisms were industrial products patentable as a manufacture under Section 101 of the Patent Statute.

The Supreme Court granted certiorari in both Bergy and Chakrabarty. Following reconsideration by the CCPA, however, the patent application in Bergy was abandoned.

DIAMOND v. CHAKRABARTY

Supreme Court of the United States, 1980.
447 U.S. 303, 100 S.Ct. 2204,
65 L.Ed.2d 144, 206 USPQ 193.

Mr. Chief Justice Burger delivered the opinion of the Court.

We granted certiorari to determine whether a live, human-made micro-organism is patentable subject matter under 35 U.S.C.A. § 101.

I

In 1972, respondent Chakrabarty, a microbiologist, filed a patent application, assigned to the General Electric Company. The application asserted 36 claims related to Chakrabarty's invention of "a bacterium from the genus *Pseudomonas* containing therein at least two stable energy-generating plasmids, each of said plasmids providing a separate hydrocarbon degradative pathway."[1] This human-made, genetically engineered bacterium is capable of breaking down multiple components of crude oil. Because of this property, which is possessed by no naturally occurring bacteria, Chakrabarty's invention is believed to have significant value for the treatment of oil spills.[2]

Chakrabarty's patent claims were of three types: first, process claims for the method of producing the bacteria; second, claims for an inoculum comprised of a carrier material floating on water, such as straw, and the new bacteria; and third, claims to the bacteria themselves. The patent examiner allowed the claims falling into the first two categories, but rejected claims for the bacteria. His decision rested on two grounds: (1) that micro-organisms are "products of nature," and (2) that as living things they are not patentable subject matter under 35 U.S.C.A. § 101.

Chakrabarty appealed the rejection of these claims to the Patent Office Board of Appeals and the Board affirmed the Examiner on the second ground.[3] Relying on the legislative history of the 1930 Plant Patent Act, in which Congress extended patent protection to certain asexually reproduced plants, the Board concluded that § 101 was not intended to cover living things such as these laboratory created micro-organisms.

The Court of Customs and Patent Appeals, by a divided vote, reversed on the authority of its prior decision in In re Bergy, 563 F.2d 1031 (1978), which held that "the fact that micro-organisms * * * are alive * * * [is] without legal significance" for purposes of the patent law.[4] Subsequently, we granted the Government's petition for certiorari in *Bergy*, vacated the judgment, and remanded the case "for further consideration in light of Parker v. Flook, 437 U.S. 584." 438 U.S. 902 (1978). The Court of Customs and Patent Appeals then vacated its

1. Plasmids are hereditary units physically separate from the chromosomes of the cell. In prior research, Chakrabarty and an associate discovered that plasmids control the oil degradation abilities of certain bacteria. In particular, the two researchers discovered plasmids capable of degrading camphor and octane, two components of crude oil. In the work represented by the patent application at issue here, Chakrabarty discovered a process by which four different plasmids, capable of degrading four different oil components, could be transferred to and maintained stably in a single *Pseudomonas* bacteria, which itself has no capacity for degrading oil.

2. At present, biological control of oil spills requires the use of a mixture of naturally occurring bacteria, each capable of degrading one component of the oil complex. In this way, oil is decomposed into simpler substances which can serve as food for aquatic life. However, for various reasons, only a portion of any such mixed culture survives to attack the oil spill. By breaking down multiple components of oil, Chakrabarty's micro-organism promises more efficient and rapid oil-spill control.

3. The Board concluded that the new bacteria were not "products of nature," because *Pseudomonas* bacteria containing two or more different energy-generating plasmids are not naturally occurring.

4. *Bergy* involved a patent application for a pure culture of the micro-organism *Streptomyces vellosus* found to be useful in the production of lincomycin, an antibiotic.

judgment in *Chakrabarty* and consolidated the case with *Bergy* for reconsideration. After re-examining both cases in the light of our holding in *Flook*, that court, with one dissent, reaffirmed its earlier judgments. 596 F.2d 952 (1979).

The Government again sought certiorari, and we granted the writ as to both *Bergy* and *Chakrabarty*. 494 U.S. 924, 100 S.Ct. 261, 62 L.Ed. 2d 180 (1979). Since then, *Bergy* has been dismissed as moot, 444 U.S. 1028, 100 S.Ct. 696, 62 L.Ed.2d 664 (1980), leaving only *Chakrabarty* for decision.

II

The Constitution grants Congress broad power to legislate to "promote the Progress of Science and the useful Arts, by securing for limited times to authors and inventors the exclusive right to their respective writings and discoveries." Art. I, § 8. The patent laws promote this progress by offering inventors exclusive rights for a limited period as an incentive for their inventiveness and research efforts. Kewanee Oil Co. v. Bicron Corp., 416 U.S. 470, 480–481 (1974); Universal Oil Co. v. Globe Co., 322 U.S. 471, 484 (1944). The authority of Congress is exercised in the hope that "[t]he productive effort thereby fostered will have a positive effect on society through the introduction of new products and processes of manufacture into the economy, and the emanations by way of increased employment and better lives for our citizens." *Kewanee*, supra, at 480.

The question before us in this case is a narrow one of statutory interpretation requiring us to construe 35 U.S.C.A. § 101, which provides:

> "Whoever invents or discovers any new and useful process, machine, manufacture, or composition of matter, or any new and useful improvement thereof, may obtain a patent therefor, subject to the conditions and requirements of this title."

Specifically, we must determine whether respondent's micro-organism constitutes a "manufacture" or "composition of matter" within the meaning of the statute.[5]

III

In cases of statutory construction we begin, of course, with the language of the statute. Southeastern Community College v. Davis, 442 U.S. 397, 405 (1979). And "unless otherwise defined, words will be interpreted as taking their ordinary, contemporary, common meaning." Perrin v. United States, 444 U.S. 37, 42 (1979). We have also cautioned that courts "should not read into the patent laws limitations and conditions which the legislature has not expressed." United States v. Dubilier Condenser Corp., 289 U.S. 178, 199 (1933).

---

5. This case does not involve the other "conditions and requirements" of the patent laws, such as novelty and nonobviousness. 35 U.S.C.A. §§ 102, 103.

Guided by these canons of construction, this Court has read the term "manufacture" in § 101 in accordance with its dictionary definition to mean "the production of articles for use from raw materials prepared by giving to these materials new forms, qualities, properties, or combinations whether by hand labor or by machinery." American Fruit Growers, Inc. v. Brogdex Co., 283 U.S. 1, 11 (1931). Similarly, "composition of matter" has been construed consistent with its common usage to include "all compositions of two or more substances and * * * all composite articles, whether they be the results of chemical union, or of mechanical mixture, or whether they be gases, fluids, powders, or solids." Shell Dev. Co. v. Watson, 149 F.Supp. 279, 280 (DC 1957) (citing 1 A. Deller, Walker on Patents § 14, p. 55 (1st ed. 137)). In choosing such expansive terms as "manufacture" and "composition of matter," modified by the comprehensive "any," Congress plainly contemplated that the patent laws would be given wide scope.

The relevant legislative history also supports a broad construction. The Patent Act of 1793, authored by Thomas Jefferson, defined statutory subject matter as "any new and useful art, machine, manufacture, or composition of matter, or any new or useful improvement [thereof]." Act of Feb. 21, 1793, ch. 11, § 1, 1 Stat. 318. The Act embodied Jefferson's philosophy that "ingenuity should receive a liberal encouragement." V Writings of Thomas Jefferson, at 75–76. See Graham v. John Deere Co., 383 U.S. 1, 7–10 (1966). Subsequent patent statutes in 1836, 1870, and 1874 employed this same broad language. In 1952, when the patent laws were recodified, Congress replaced the word "art" with "process," but otherwise left Jefferson's language intact. The Committee Reports accompanying the 1952 act inform us that Congress intended statutory subject matter to "include anything under the sun that is made by man." S.Rep. No. 1979, 82d Cong., 2d Sess., 5 (1952); H.R.Rep. No. 1923, 82d Cong., 2d Sess., 6 (1952).[6]

This is not to suggest that § 101 has no limits or that it embraces every discovery. The laws of nature, physical phenomena, and abstract ideas have been held not patentable. See Parker v. Flook, 437 U.S. 584 (1978); Gottschalk v. Benson, 409 U.S. 63, 67 (1973); Funk Seed Co. v. Kalo Co., 333 U.S. 127, 130 (1948); O'Reilly v. Morse, 15 How. 61, 112–121 (1853); Le Roy v. Tatham, 14 How. 155, 175 (1852). Thus, a new mineral discovered in the earth or a new plant found in the wild is not patentable subject matter. Likewise, Einstein could not patent his celebrated law that $E = mc^2$; nor could Newton have patented the law of gravity. Such discoveries are "manifestations of * * * nature, free to all men and reserved exclusively to none." *Funk*, supra, at 130.

---

6. This same language was employed by P.J. Federico, a principal draftsman of the 1952 recodification, in his testimony regarding that legislation: "[U]nder section 101 a person may have invented a machine or manufacture, which may include any-thing under the sun that is made by man. * * *" Hearings on H.R. 3760 before Subcommittee No. 3 of the House Committee on the Judiciary, 82d Cong., 1st Sess., 37 (1951).

Judged in this light, respondent's micro-organism plainly qualifies as patentable subject matter. His claim is not to a hitherto unknown natural phenomenon, but to a nonnaturally occurring manufacture or composition of matter—a product of human ingenuity "having a distinctive name, character [and] use." Hartranft v. Wiegmann, 121 U.S. 609, 615 (1887). The point is underscored dramatically by comparison of the invention here with that in *Funk*. There, the patentee had discovered that there existed in nature certain species of root-nodule bacteria which did not exert a mutually inhibitive effect on each other. He used that discovery to produce a mixed culture capable of inoculating the seeds of leguminous plants. Concluding that the patentee had discovered "only some of the handiwork of nature," the Court ruled the product nonpatentable:

> "Each of the species of root-nodule bacteria contained in the package infects the same group of leguminous plants which it always infected. No species acquires a different use. The combination of the six species produces no new bacteria, no change in the six bacteria, and no enlargement of the range of their utility. Each species has the same effect it always had. The bacteria perform in their natural way. Their use in combination does not improve in any way their natural functioning. They serve the same ends nature originally provided and act quite independently of any effort by the patentee." 333 U.S., at 127.

Here, by contrast, the patentee has produced a new bacterium with markedly different characteristics from any found in nature and one having the potential for significant utility. His discovery is not nature's handiwork, but his own; accordingly it is patentable subject matter under § 101.

IV

Two contrary arguments are advanced, neither of which we find persuasive.

(A)

The Government's first argument rests on the enactment of the 1930 Plant Patent Act, which afforded patent protection to certain asexually reproduced plants, and the 1970 Plant Variety Protection Act, which authorized patents for certain sexually reproduced plants but excluded bacteria from its protection.[7] In the Government's view, the passage of these Acts evidences congressional understanding that

7. The Plant Patent Act of 1930, 35 U.S.C.A. § 161, provides in relevant part:

"Whoever invents or discovers and asexually reproduces any distinct and new variety of plant, including cultivated sports, mutants, hybrids, and newly found seedlings, other than a tuber propogated plant or a plant found in an uncultivated state, may obtain a patent therefor. * * * *"

The Plant Variety Protection Act of 1970, provides in relevant part:

"The breeder of any novel variety of sexually reproduced plant (other than fungi, bacteria, or first generation hybrids) who has so reproduced the variety, or his successor in interest, shall be entitled to plant variety protection therefor * * * *" 7 U.S.C.A. § 2402(a).

the terms "manufacture" or "composition of matter" do not include living things; if they did, the Government argues, neither Act would have been necessary.

We reject this argument. Prior to 1930, two factors were thought to remove plants from patent protection. The first was the belief that plants, even those artificially bred, were products of nature for purposes of the patent law. This position appears to have derived from the decision of the Patent Office in Ex parte Latimer, 1889 C.D. 123, in which a patent claim for fiber found in the needle of the *Pinus australis* was rejected. The Commissioner reasoned that a contrary result would permit "patents [to] be obtained upon the trees of the forests and the plants of the earth, which of course would be unreasonable and impossible." Id., at 126. The *Latimer* case, it seems, came to "set[ ] forth the general stand taken in these matters" that plants were natural products not subject to patent protection. H. Thorne, Relation of Patent Law to Natural Products, 6 J.Pat.Off.Soc. 23, 24 (1923).[8] The second obstacle to patent protection for plants was the fact that plants were thought not amendable to the "written description" requirement of the patent law. See 35 U.S.C.A. § 112. Because new plants may differ from old only in color or perfume, differentiation by written description was often impossible. See Hearings on H.R. 11372 before the House Committee on Patents, 71 Cong., 2d Sess., 4 (1930), p. 7 (memorandum of Patent Commissioner Robertson).

In enacting the Plant Patent Act, Congress addressed both of these concerns. It explained at length its belief that the work of the plant breeder "in aid of nature" was patentable invention. S.Rep. No. 315, 71st Cong., 2d Sess., 6–8 (1930); H.R.Rep. No. 1129, 71st Cong., 2d Sess., 7–9 (1930). And it relaxed the written description requirement in favor of "a description * * * as complete as is reasonably possible." 35 U.S.C.A. § 162. No Committee or Member of Congress, however, expressed the broader view, now urged by the Government, that the terms "manufacture" or "composition of matter" exclude living things. The sole support for that position in the legislative history of the 1930 Act is found in the conclusory statement of Secretary of Agriculture Hyde, in a letter to the Chairmen of the House and Senate committees considering the 1930 Act, that "the patent laws * * * at the present time are understood to cover only inventions or discoveries in the field of inanimate nature." See S.Rep. No. 315, supra, at Appendix A; H.R. Rep. No. 1129, supra, at Appendix A. Secretary Hyde's opinion, however, is not entitled to controlling weight. His views were solicited on the administration of the new law and not on the scope of patentable

---

See generally, 3 A. Deller, Walker on Patents, Chapter IX (2d ed. 1964); R. Allyn The First Plant Patents (1934).

8. Writing three years after the passage of the 1930 Act, R. Cook, Editor of the Journal of Heredity, commented: "It is a little hard for plant men to understand why [Article I § 8] of the Constitution should not have been earlier construed to include the promotion of the art of plant breeding. The reason for this is probably to be found in the principle that natural products are not patentable." Florists Exchange and Horticultural Trade World, July 15, 1933, at 9.

subject matter—an area beyond his competence. Moreover, there is language in the House and Senate Committee reports suggesting that to the extent Congress considered the matter it found the Secretary's dichotomy unpersuasive. The reports observe:

> "There is a clear and logical distinction *between the discovery of a new variety of plant and of certain inanimate things,* such, for example, as a new and useful natural mineral. The mineral is created wholly by nature unassisted by man. * * * On the other hand, a plant discovery resulting from cultivation is unique, isolated, and is not repeated by nature, nor can it be reproduced by nature unaided by man. * * *" S.Rep. No. 315, supra, at 6; H.R.Rep. No. 1129, supra, at 7 (emphasis added).

Congress thus recognized that the relevant distinction was not between living and inanimate things, but between products of nature, whether living or not, and human-made inventions. Here, respondent's microorganism is the result of human ingenuity and research. Hence, the passage of the Plant Patent Act affords the Government no support.

Nor does the passage of the 1970 Plant Variety Protection Act support the Government's position. As the Government acknowledges, sexually reproduced plants were not included under the 1930 Act because new varieties could not be reproduced true-to-type through seedlings. Brief for United States 27, n. 31. By 1970, however, it was generally recognized that true-to-type reproduction was possible and that plant patent protection was therefore appropriate. The 1970 Act extended that protection. There is nothing in its language or history to suggest that it was enacted because § 101 did not include living things.

In particular, we find nothing in the exclusion of bacteria from plant variety protection to support the Government's position. See supra, at n. 7. The legislative history gives no reason for this exclusion. As the Court of Customs and Patent Appeals suggested, it may simply reflect congressional agreement with the result reached by that court in deciding In re Arzberger, 112 F.2d 834 (1940), which held that bacteria were not plants for the purposes of the 1930 Act. Or it may reflect the fact that prior to 1970 the Patent Office had issued patents for bacteria under § 101.[9] In any event, absent some clear indication that Congress "focused on [the] issues * * * directly related to the one presently before the Court," SEC v. Sloan, 436 U.S. 103, 120–121 (1978), there is no basis for reading into its actions an intent to modify the plain meaning of the words found in § 101. See TVA v. Hill, 437 U.S. 153, 189–193 (1978); United States v. Price, 361 U.S. 304, 313 (1960).

9. In 1873, the Patent Office granted Louis Pasteur a patent on "yeast, free from organic germs of disease, as an article of manufacture." And in 1967 and 1968, immediately prior to the passage of the Plant Variety Protection Act, that office granted two patents which, as the Government concedes, state claims for living micro-organisms. See Reply Brief of United States, at 3, and n. 2.

(B)

The Government's second argument is that micro-organisms cannot qualify as patentable subject matter until Congress expressly authorizes such protection. Its position rests on the fact that genetic technology was unforeseen when Congress enacted § 101. From this it is argued that resolution of the patentability of inventions such as respondent's should be left to Congress. The legislative process, the Government argues, is best equipped to weigh the competing economic, social, and scientific considerations involved, and to determine whether living organisms produced by genetic engineering should receive patent protection. In support of this position, the Government relies on our recent holding in Parker v. Flook, 437 U.S. 584 (1978), and the statement that the judiciary "must proceed cautiously when * * * asked to extend patent rights into areas wholly unforeseen by Congress." Id., at 596.

It is, of course, correct that Congress, not the courts, must define the limits of patentability; but it is equally true that once Congress has spoken it is "the province and duty of the judicial department to say what the law is." Marbury v. Madison, 1 Cranch 137, 177 (1803). Congress has performed its constitutional role in defining patentable subject matter in § 101; we perform ours in construing the language Congress has employed. In so doing, our obligation is to take statutes as we find them, guided, if ambiguity appears, by the legislative history and statutory purpose. Here, we perceive no ambiguity. The subject matter provisions of the patent law have been cast in broad terms to fulfill the constitutional and statutory goal of promoting "the Progress of Science and the useful Arts" with all that means for the social and economic benefits envisioned by Jefferson. Broad general language is not necessarily ambiguous when congressional objectives require broad terms.

Nothing in *Flook* is to the contrary. That case applied our prior precedents to determine that a "claim for an improved method of calculation, even when tied to a specific end use, is unpatentable subject matter under § 101." 437 U.S., at 595, n. 18. The Court carefully scrutinized the claim at issue to determine whether it was precluded from patent protection under "the principles underlying the prohibition against patents for 'ideas' or phenomena of nature." Id., at 593. We have done that here. *Flook* did not announce a new principle that inventions in areas not contemplated by Congress when the patent laws were enacted are unpatentable *per se*.

To read that concept into Flook would frustrate the purposes of the patent law. This Court frequently has observed that a statute is not to be confined to the "particular application[s] * * * contemplated by the legislators." Barr v. United States, 324 U.S. 83, 90 (1945). Accord, Browder v. United States, 312 U.S. 335, 339 (1941); Puerto Rico v. Shell Co., 302 U.S. 253, 257 (1937). This is especially true in the field of patent law. A rule that unanticipated inventions are without protection would conflict with the core concept of the patent law that anticipation undermines patentability. See Graham v. John Deere Co., 383 U.S., at 12–17. Mr. Justice Douglas reminded that the inventions most benefiting mankind are those that "push back the frontiers of chemistry, physics, and the like." A. & P. Tea Co. v. Supermarket Corp., 340 U.S. 147, 154 (1950) (concurring opinion). Congress employed broad general language in drafting § 101 precisely because such inventions are often unforeseeable.[10]

To buttress its argument, the Government, with the support of *amicus,* points to grave risks that may be generated by research endeavors such as respondent's. The briefs present a gruesome parade of horribles. Scientists, among them Nobel laureates, are quoted suggesting that genetic research may pose a serious threat to the human race, or, at the very least, that the dangers are far too substantial to permit such research to proceed apace at this time. We are told that genetic research and related technological developments may spread pollution and disease, that it may result in a loss of genetic diversity, and that its practice may tend to depreciate the value of human life. These arguments are forcefully, even passionately presented; they remind us that, at times, human ingenuity seems unable to control fully the forces it creates—that with Hamlet, it is sometimes better "to bear those ills we have than fly to others that we know not of."

It is argued that this Court should weigh these potential hazards in considering whether respondent's invention is patentable subject matter under § 101. We disagree. The grant or denial of patents on micro-organisms is not likely to put an end to genetic research or to its attendant risks. The large amount of research that has already occurred when no researcher had sure knowledge that patent protection would be available suggests that legislative or judicial fiat as to patentability will not deter the scientific mind from probing into the unknown any more than Canute could command the tides. Whether respondent's claims are patentable may determine whether research efforts are accelerated by the hope of reward or slowed by want of incentives, but that is all.

What is more important is that we are without competence to entertain these arguments—either to brush them aside as fantasies generated by fear of the unknown, or to act on them. The choice we are urged to make is a matter of high policy for resolution within the legislative process after the kind of investigation, examination, and study that legislative bodies can provide and courts cannot. That process involves the balancing of competing values and interests, which in our democratic system is the business of elected representatives.

---

10. Even an abbreviated list of patented inventions underscores the point: telegraph (Morse, No. 1647); telephone (Bell, No. 174,465); electric lamp (Edison, No. 223,898); airplane (the Wrights, No. 821,393); transistor (Bardeen & Brattain, No. 2,524,035); neutronic reactor (Fermi & Szilard, No. 2,708,656); laser (Schawlow & Townes, No. 2,929,922). See generally Revolutionary Ideas, Patents & Progress in America, Office of Patents (1976).

Whatever their validity, the contentions now pressed on us should be addressed to the political branches of the government, the Congress and the Executive, and not to the courts.[11]

We have emphasized in the recent past that "[o]ur individual appraisal of the wisdom or unwisdom of a particular [legislative] course * * * is to be put aside in the process of interpreting a statute." TVA v. Hill, 437 U.S. 153, 194 (1978). Our task, rather, is the narrow one of determining what Congress meant by the words it used in the statute; once that is done our powers are exhausted. Congress is free to amend § 101 so as to exclude from patent protection organisms produced by genetic engineering. Compare 42 U.S.C.A. § 2181, exempting from patent protection inventions "useful solely in the utilization of special nuclear material or atomic energy in an atomic weapon." Or it may choose to craft a statute specifically designed for such living things. But, until Congress takes such action, this Court must construe the language of § 101 as it is. The language of that section fairly embraces respondent's invention.

Accordingly, the judgment of the Court of Customs and Patent Appeals is affirmed.

Affirmed.

MR. JUSTICE BRENNAN, with whom MR. JUSTICE WHITE, MR. JUSTICE MARSHALL, and MR. JUSTICE POWELL join dissenting.

I agree with the Court that the question before us is a narrow one. Neither the future of scientific research, nor even the ability of respondent Chakrabarty to reap some monopoly profits from his pioneering work, is at stake. Patents on the processes by which he has produced and employed the new living organism are not contested. The only question we need decide is whether Congress, exercising its authority under Art. I, § 8, of the Constitution, intended that he be able to secure a monopoly on the living organism itself, no matter how produced or how used. Because I believe the Court has misread the applicable legislation, I dissent.

The patent laws attempt to reconcile this Nation's deep-seated antipathy to monopolies with the need to encourage progress. Deepsouth Packing Co. v. Laitram Corp., 406 U.S. 518, 530–531 (1972);

---

11. We are not to be understood as suggesting that the political branches have been laggard in the consideration of the problems related to genetic research and technology. They have already taken action. In 1976, for example, the National Institutes of Health released guidelines for NIH-sponsored genetic research which established conditions under which such research could be performed. 41 Fed.Reg. 27902. In 1978 those guidelines were revised and relaxed. 43 Fed.Reg. 60080, 60108, 60134. And committees of the Congress have held extensive hearings on these matters. See, *e.g.,* Hearings on genetic engineering before the Subcommittee on Health of the Senate Committee on Labor and Public Welfare, 94th Cong., 1st Sess. (1975); Hearings before the Subcommittee on Science, Technology, and Space of the Senate Committee on Commerce, Science, and Transportation, 95th Cong., 1st Sess. (1978); Hearings before the Subcommittee on Health and the Environment of the House Committee on Interstate and Foreign Commerce, 95th Cong., 1st Sess. (1977).

Graham v. John Deere Co., 383 U.S. 1, 7–10 (1966). Given the complexity and legislative nature of this delicate task, we must be careful to extend patent protection no further than Congress has provided. In particular, were there an absence of legislative direction, the courts should leave to Congress the decisions whether and how far to extend the patent privilege into areas where the common understanding has been that patents are not available.[1] Cf. Deepsouth Packing Co. v. Laitram Corp., supra.

In this case, however, we do not confront a complete legislative vacuum. The sweeping language of the Patent Act of 1793, as re-enacted in 1952, is not the last pronouncement Congress has made in this area. In 1930 Congress enacted the Plant Patent Act affording patent protection to developers of certain asexually reproduced plants. In 1970 Congress enacted the Plant Variety Protection Act to extend protection to certain new plant varieties capable of sexual reproduction. Thus, we are not dealing—as the Court would have it—with the routine problem of "unanticipated inventions." Ante, at 12. In these two Acts Congress has addressed the general problem of patenting animate inventions and has chosen carefully limited language granting protection to some kinds of discoveries, but specifically excluding others. These Acts strongly evidence a congressional limitation that excludes bacteria from patentability.[2]

First the Acts evidence Congress' understanding, at least since 1930, that § 101 does not include living organisms. If newly developed living organisms not naturally occurring had been patentable under § 101, the plants included in the scope of the 1930 and 1970 Acts could have been patented without new legislation. Those plants, like the bacteria involved in this case, were new varieties not naturally occurring.[3] Although the Court ante, at 7, rejects this line of argument, it does not explain why the Acts were necessary unless to correct a pre-

---

1. I read the Court to admit that the popular conception, even among advocates of agricultural patents, was that living organisms were unpatentable. See ante, at 7–8, and n. 8.

2. But even if I agreed with the Court that the 1930 and 1970 Acts were not dispositive, I would dissent. This case presents even more cogent reasons than *Deepsouth Packing Co.* not to extend the patent monopoly in the face of uncertainty. At the very least, these Acts are signs of legislative attention to the problems of patenting living organisms, but they give no affirmative indication of congressional intent that bacteria be patentable. The caveat of Parker v. Flook, 437 U.S. 584, 596 (1978), an admonition to "proceed cautiously when we are asked to extend patent rights into areas wholly unforeseen by Congress," therefore becomes pertinent. I

should think the necessity for caution is that much greater when we are asked to extend patent rights into areas Congress has foreseen and considered but has not resolved.

3. The Court refers to the logic employed by Congress in choosing not to perpetuate the "dichotomy" suggested by Secretary Hyde. Ante, at 9. But by this logic the bacteria at issue here are distinguishable from a "mineral * * * created wholly by nature" in exactly the same way as were the new varieties of plants. If a new act was needed to provide patent protection for the plants, it was equally necessary for bacteria. Yet Congress provided for patents on plants but not on these bacteria. In short, Congress decided to make only a subset of animate "human-made inventions," ibid. patentable.

existing situation.[4] I cannot share the Court's implicit assumption that Congress was engaged in either idle exercises or mere correction of the public record when it enacted the 1930 and 1970 Acts. And Congress certainly thought it was doing something significant. The committee reports contain expansive prose about the previously unavailable benefits to be derived from extending patent protection to plants.[5] H.R.Rep. No. 91–1605, 91st Cong., 2d Sess., 1–3 (1970); S.Rep. No. 315, 71st Cong., 2d Sess., 1–3 (1930). Because Congress thought it had to legislate in order to make agricultural "human-made inventions" patentable and because the legislation Congress enacted is limited, it follows that Congress never meant to make patentable items outside the scope of the legislation.

Second, the 1970 Act clearly indicates that Congress has included bacteria within the focus of its legislative concern, but not within the scope of patent protection. Congress specifically excluded bacteria from the coverage of the 1970 Act. 7 U.S.C.A. § 2402(a). The Court's attempts to supply explanations for this explicit exclusion ring hollow. It is true that there is no mention in the legislative history of the exclusion, but that does not give us license to invent reasons. The fact is that Congress, assuming that animate objects as to which it had not specifically legislated could not be patented, excluded bacteria from the set of patentable organisms.

The Court protests that its holding today is dictated by the broad language of § 101, which "cannot be confined to the 'particular application[s] * * * contemplated by the legislators.'" Ante, at 12, quoting Barr v. United States, 324 U.S. 83, 90 (1945). But as I have shown, the Court's decision does not follow the unavoidable implications of the statute. Rather, it extends the patent system to cover living material even though Congress plainly has legislated in the belief that § 101 does not encompass living organisms. It is the role of Congress, not this Court, to broaden or narrow the reach of the patent laws. This is especially true where, as here, the composition sought to be patented uniquely implicates matters of public concern.

---

4. If the 1930 Act's only purpose were to solve the technical problem of description referred to by the Court, ante, at 8, most of the Act, and in particular its limitation to asexually reproduced plants, would have been totally unnecessary.

5. Secretary Hyde's letter was not the only explicit indication in the legislative history of these Acts that Congress was acting on the assumption that legislation was necessary to make living organisms patentable. The Senate Judiciary Committee Report on the 1970 Act states the Committee's understanding that patent protection extended no further than the explicit provisions of these Acts.

"Under the patent law, patent protection is limited to those varieties of plants which reproduce asexually, that is, by such methods as grafting or budding. No protection is available to those varieties of plants which reproduce sexually, that is, by seeds." S.Rep. No. 91–1246, 91st Cong., 2d Sess., 3 (1970).

Similarly, Representative Poage, speaking for the 1970 Act, after noting the protection accorded asexually developed plants, stated that "for plants produced from seed, there has been no such protection." 122 Cong.Rec. 40295 (1970).

Notes

1. See also Ex parte Hibberd, infra, page 674.

2. The following notice was published by the Commissioner of Patents and Trademarks in the April 21, 1987 issue of the Official Gazette, 1077 O.G. 24:

A decision by the Board of Patent Appeals and Interferences in *Ex parte Allen*, 2 USPQ 2d 1425 (Bd.App. & Int. April 3, 1987), held that claimed polyploid oysters are nonnaturally occurring manufactures or compositions of matter within the meaning of 35 U.S.C. 101. The Board relied upon the opinion of the Supreme Court in *Diamond v. Chakrabarty*, 447 U.S. 303, 206 USPQ 193 (1980) as it had done in *Ex parte Hibberd*, 227 USPQ 443 (Bd.App. & Int., 1985), as controlling authority that Congress intended statutory subject matter to "include anything under the sun that is made by man." The Patent and Trademark Office now considers nonnaturally occurring non-human multicellular living organisms, including animals, to be patentable subject matter within the scope of 35 U.S.C. 101.

The Board's decision does not affect the principle and practice that products found in nature will not be considered to be patentable subject matter under 35 U.S.C. 101 and/or 102. An article of manufacture or composition of matter occurring in nature will not be considered patentable unless given a new form, quality, properties or combination not present in the original article existing in nature in accordance with existing law. See e.g. *Funk Bros. Seed Co. v. Kalo Inoculant Co.*, 333 U.S. 127, 76 USPQ 280 (1948); *American Fruit Growers v. Brogdex*, 283 U.S. 1, 8 USPQ 131 (1931); *Ex parte Grayson*, 51 USPQ 413 (Bd.App.1941).

A claim directed to or including within its scope a human being will not be considered to be patentable subject matter under 35 U.S.C. 101. The grant of a limited, but exclusive property right in a human being is prohibited by the Constitution. Accordingly, it is suggested that any claim directed to a non-plant muticellular organism which would include a human being within its scope include the limitation "non-human" to avoid this ground of rejection. The use of a negative limitation to define the metes and bounds of the claimed subject matter is a permissible form of expression. *In re Wakefield*, 422 F.2d 897, 164 USPQ 636 (CCPA 1970).

Accordingly, the Patent and Trademark Office is now examining claims directed to multicellular living organisms, including animals. To the extent that the claimed subject matter is directed to a non-human "nonnaturally occurring manufacture or composition of matter—a product of human ingenuity" (*Diamond v. Chakrabarty*), such claims will not be rejected under 35 U.S.C. 101 as being directed to nonstatutory subject matter.

G. COMPOSITION OF MATTER

In Section 101 of Title 35 U.S.C.A. is found the term "composition of matter" among the list of patentable inventions. The word "matter" is defined as "any body, substance or particle which is subject to gravitation; hence any substance, either solid or liquid or gaseous, which occupies space" (Hackh's Chemical Dictionary). This use seems to eliminate any suggestion of a composition of words, numbers, or music. The word "composition" is defined in Webster's International Dictionary, Second Edition, as:

> An aggregate, mixture, mass, or body formed by combining two or more elements or ingredients; as, a *composition* of several acids. A substance so composed; a composite substance; esp. one artificially made.

> The nature of a compound or mixture as regards the kind and amounts of its constituents. It is usually expressed in numbers of atoms of each element in its molecule, or in percentages of each element by weight.

The courts have not had great difficulty with the definition of a composition of matter and most cases dealing with this class of inventions have been directed more to the problems of patentability.

Two early cases dealt with the patentability of a product which was known in nature but ultimately "made artificially." The subject matter of American Wood–Paper Co. v. Fibre Disintegrating Co., 90 U.S. 566, 23 L.Ed. 31 (1874) was a process of producing paper pulp from wood by chemical agencies alone. The same material had been previously obtained from vegetable substances by other processes. A patent on the product was refused. In the second case, Cochrane v. Badische Anilin and Soda Fabrik, 111 U.S. 293, 4 S.Ct. 455, 28 L.Ed. 433 (1884), the Supreme Court referenced the Paper Pulp case in making the following statement:

> There is another view of the case. According to the description in No. 95465, and in No. 4321, and the evidence, the article produced by the process described was the alizarine of madder, having the chemical formula $C_{14}H_8O_4$. It was an old article. While a new process for producing it was patentable, the product itself could not be patented, even though it was a product made artifically for the first time in contradistinction to being eliminated from the madder root. Calling it artificial alizarine did not make it a new composition of matter, and patentable as such, by reason of its having been prepared artificially for the first time from anthracine, if it was set forth as alizarine, a well known substance. The Wood Paper Patent, 23 Wall., 566, 593 [90 U.S., XXIII., 31, 39]. There was, therefore, no foundation for re-issue No. 4321, for the product, because, on the description given, no patent for the product could have been taken out originally.

The problems of patentability relative to purification or synthesization of known products are still relevant today. In some cases, it will be found that the problems of scientific discovery or discovery of a law or product of nature are intertwined in the discussion. Inasmuch as the student has studied cases relating to Section 103 of Title 35 U.S.

C.A., it is not out of place to include cases which deal with these aspects
of the patentability of compositions of matter.

P.E. SHARPLESS CO. v. CRAWFORD FARMS

United States Court of Appeals, Second Circuit, 1923.
287 Fed. 655.

MANTON, CIRCUIT JUDGE. Appellant sues for infringement of patent
No. 1,258,438 granted to Nusbaum, applied for May 22, 1917, and
granted March 5, 1918. It is a grant of a monopoly for a process and a
product. The bill also asks for injunctive relief, claiming unfair competition in trade in the packaging and marketing of the product.

The appellant is a Pennsylvania corporation and makes cheese and
sells the same commercially in packages. The appellee is a New York
corporation and also makes cheese and markets the same commercially
in similar sized packages. The inventor, Nusbaum, says he invented
the new composition of matter and process of producing it in the
autumn of 1916. In the trade, there are two types of cheese, one soft
and uncured, and the other hard and cured. These were not thought to
be capable of blending into a single composition. The desirability of
the invention was, if possible, to retain the physical character of the
soft and uncured element, and impart to it the characteristic taste and
flavor of the cured cheese, without its physical presence in the composition. He says in the specifications of the patent that his invention
relates to the production of a new variety of soft or uncured cheese, and
it results in a new composition of matter having for its principal object
to impart to the composition the characteristic flavor of the well-known
Roquefort cheese, combined with and modified by the commercial soft
or uncured cream cheese, made usually from unskimmed milk, while
retaining the characteristic physical and other inherent qualities which
identify the latter, and to this end the composition of matter consists of
elements stated and combined in the manner and substantially in the
proportions set forth.

* * *

After this the composition is sufficiently hard to be molded into
small cylinders or rectangular cakes. The identifying characteristics of
a homogeneous composition wherein the cured element, the Roquefort
cheese, has not only lost its physical characteristics as such, but has
imparted such part of that quality to the resultant composition, so as to
increase the keeping qualities and obtained the flavor and taste of the
Roquefort cheese, it has the characteristics of the soft cream cheese,
and is capable of being molded into the commercial form required, and
is then wrapped in tinfoil and sold.

* * *

What the inventor has done by his process is not merely admixing two
radically different ingredients normally incapable of admixture and not
known to be miscible, nor is it for a method of effecting a general
combination or composite of them, but is for producing a specific

combination of them wherein one element acts on the other to produce an ultimate product.

* * *

Did the inventor teach the art something new? And did the product become recognized by those familiar with the art as a new and useful thing? If so, then that result should be resolved in favor of patentable novelty. The question is presented of whether or not a food product or a process of producing it may properly be considered as the subject-matter for the grant of a patent, within the meaning of the statute authorizing the grant for a new and useful composition of matter, or "any new and useful improvement thereof" (as to the product), or any new and useful art, being interpreted to mean or include a method or a process within the lay meaning of those terms. It is to be observed Congress provided for invention in respect "of composition of matter" as one of the four classes of invention. There is no restriction as to the nature of the composition which may be patented. The only limitation is they must be new, useful, and the result of invention.

Issue

We think the meritorious result of a method or process has been disclosed by what the inventor here conceived. It is new. It should be given patent protection. A patentable composition of matter may well result or be formed by the intermixture of two or more ingredients, which develop a different or additional property or properties which the several ingredients individually do not possess in common.

Held

* * *

Decree modified accordingly.[a]

SCHERING CORP. v. GILBERT

United States Court of Appeals, Second Circuit, 1946.
153 F.2d 428, 68 USPQ 84.

CHASE, CIRCUIT JUDGE. The appellee is a New Jersey corporation and the owner of U.S. Patent No. 2,345,384 which was granted to it on March 28, 1944 as the assignee of the inventors whose application was filed on April 6, 1940. It sued the appellants, Jules R. Gilbert and William Bell, partners in business under the firm name of National Synthetics, in the District Court for the Southern District of New York for infringement of the patent, relying at the trial only on Claim 2.

* * *

[a] "This court has taken the position that new recipes or formulas for cooking food which involve the addition or elimination of common ingredients, or for treating them in ways which differ from the former practice, do not amount to invention merely because it is not disclosed that, in the constantly developing art of preparing food, no one else ever did the particular thing upon which the applicant asserts his right to a patent. In all such cases, there is nothing patentable unless the applicant by a proper showing further establishes a coaction or cooperative relationship between the selected ingredients which produces a new, unexpected, and useful function. In re White, 39 F.2d 974, 17 CCPA, Patents, 956; In re Mason et al., 156 F.2d 189, 33 CCPA, Patents, 1144." In re Levin, 178 F.2d 945, 84 USPQ 232 (CCPA 1949).

As stated in the specifications, the invention relates to "poly iodized derivatives of the hydroxy diphenyl carboxylic acids and a process for preparing the same," but the patent contains only product claims. Claim 2 is a short claim for one definite chemical compound not found in nature and never previously synthesized. It is for the beta-(4-hydroxy-3, 5-diiodophenyl)-alpha-phenyl propionic acid which melts at 159° C.

* * * *

The inventors were trying to improve the art of cholecystography and were using known principles of organic chemistry as their tools. The problem was not the mere construction of a chemical formula followed by experiments to see if what had been formulated could be synthesized. They had so to contrive that a stable compound would be produced with ingredients which would after oral administration so act upon the gall bladder, without much, if any, distressing effect upon the person whose gall bladder was being so treated, that sufficiently revealing X-ray pictures of it could be taken. * * *

To any suggestion that that was a simple problem whose solution should have been obvious to the skillful the sufficient answer seems to be that it eluded all in that class for many long years while persons with diseased gall bladders waited in vain for relief from the harmful effects of distressing methods of diagnosis.

* * *

Previously the most notable advance in the art of cholecystography had followed the discovery in 1923 or 1924 by Drs. Graham and Cole that good X-ray visualization of the gall bladder could be obtained by the administration of purified tetraiodophenolphthalein or its related compounds.

* * *

Though a contrast agent which was much better physiologically and perhaps somewhat better otherwise was much needed, no one succeeded in producing one until some nineteen years later when these inventors did so. With astonishing rapidity after the product of Claim 2 of the patent in suit became available to the medical profession under the trade-name of Priodax it, according to the uncontradicted testimony in this record, practically supplanted the older preparations. Both of the specialists in radiology who testified, one called by the plaintiff and one by the defendants, used it exclusively. And the defendants, who were in the business of making and purveying such contrast agents, soon copied Priodax and marketed an identical product under the trademark Dikol. The trial judge's finding of utility was overwhelmingly supported by the evidence.

* * *

[Defendants] say that this new and useful composition of matter is not patentable because Claim 2 covers a new molecule and that a molecule is the inevitable result of the action of so-called laws of nature which are immutable by man and remain free for the use of all unrestricted by patent law. If this were wholly true the corollary would be that the process by which a result is reached, involving as it does the application of natural laws, would be likewise unpatentable and that there could be no valid patents for new compositions of matter. Similarly, there could be no valid patents for new machines or for new methods for making them since so-called natural laws of physics, such as those relating to gravity and friction, to mention only two, always play their part. Obviously, such an advanced position cannot be maintained in the face of the patent statute and the multitude of authoritative decisions to the contrary.

MERCK & CO. v. OLIN MATHIESON CHEM. CORP.

United States Court of Appeals, Fourth Circuit, 1958.
253 F.2d 156, 116 USPQ 484.

HAYNSWORTH, CIRCUIT JUDGE. This is a suit upon the product claims of patent No. 2,703,302, entitled "Vitamin B_{12}-Active Composition and Process of Preparing Same," issue to Rickes and Wood, assignors of the plaintiff, Merck, on March 1, 1955, upon an application dated December 8, 1952. The District Court held the product claims invalid, upon the grounds that they covered a "product of nature" and that there was lack of invention. Merck & Company, Inc., v. Olin Mathieson Chemical Corp., D.C.W.D.Va., 152 F.Supp. 690.

* * *

We are concerned with the three product claims, which are identical except that the minimal active strength is specified in the three claims, respectively, as 440, 1500 and 65,000 LLD units per milligram.

Claim 1 is in the following language:

"1. A vitamin B_{12}-active composition comprising recovered elaboration products of the fermentation of a vitamin B_{12}-activity producing strain of Fungi selected from the class consisting of Schizomycetes, Torula, and Eremothecium, the L.L.D. activity of said composition being at least 440 L.L.D. units per milligram and less than 11 million L.L.D. units per milligram."

In 1926 it was found that pernicious anemia patients were benefited by the addition to their diets of substantial amounts of the liver of cattle. In the succeeding twenty years intensive efforts were made to isolate and identify the substance or substances in liver responsible for the anti-pernicious anemia effect.

* * *

The claims of this patent do not reach pure, crystalline vitamin B_{12}, for they are restricted to compositions having a maximum LLD activity which is less than that of the pure substance. The claims do not cover vitamin B_{12} compositions derived from liver or any source other than the specified fermentates.

* * *

It can hardly be doubted that, as was said in "The Wood-Paper Patent case", "* * * if one should discover a mode or contrive a process by which prussic acid could be obtained from a subject in which it is not now known to exist, he might have a patent for his process, but not for prussic acid." The fact that the product, itself, is not a "new and useful * * * machine, manufacture, or composition of matter," within the meaning of § 101, is fatal to the product claims. The facts here, however, are far from the premise of the principle. Until the patentees produced them, there were no such B_{12} active compositions. No one had produced even a comparable product. The active substance was unidentified and unknown. The new product, not just the method, had such advantageous characteristics as to replace the liver products. What was produced was, in no sense, an old product.

The second aspect of the defense is equally inapplicable to the facts. Each slight step in purification does not produce a new product. What is gained may be the old product, but with a greater degree of purity. Alpha alumina purified is still alpha alumina, In re Ridgway, 76 F.2d 602, 22 CCPA, Patents, 1169 and ultramarine from which flotable impurities have been removed is still ultramarine, In re Merz, 97 F.2d 599, 25 CCPA, Patents, 1314. The fact however, that a new and useful product is the result of processes of extraction, concentration and purification of natural materials does not defeat its patentability.

[Cited cases omitted.]

The compositions of the patent here have all of the novelty and utility required by the Act for patentability. They never existed before; there was nothing comparable to them. If we regard them as a purification of the active principle in natural fermentates, the natural fermentates are quite useless, while the patented compositions are of great medicinal and commercial value. The step from complete uselessness to great and perfected utility is a long one. That step is no mere advance in the degree of purity of a known product. From the natural fermentates, which for this purpose, were wholly useless and were not known to contain the desired activity in even the slightest degree, products of great therapeutic and commercial worth have been developed. The new products are not the same as the old, but new and useful compositions entitled to the protection of the patent.

For the reasons stated and without resort to the presumption arising from the action of the Patent Office, which was taken only after full consideration of all the matters here relied on by the appellee, we think the invention is meritorious, the product claims of the patent valid and entitled to a liberal construction. That presumption of validity, however should not be disregarded especially in a case of this sort where the intricate questions of bio-chemistry involved are peculiarly within the particular competence of the experts of the Patent Office. Nor should we overlook the presumptions arising from the fact that the product of the patent filled a long felt want, went into immediate use and promptly displaced the competing liver products. Florence-Mayo Nuway Co. v. Hardy, 4 Cir., 168 F.2d 778, 782. The patentees have given us for the first time a medicine which can be used successfully in the treatment of pernicious anemia, a medicine which avoids the dangers and disadvantages of the liver extracts, the only remedies available prior to this invention, a medicine subject to accurate standardization and which can be produced in large quantities and inexpensively, a medicine which is valuable for other purposes, as well as for the treatment of pernicious anemia. It did not exist in nature in the form in which the patentees produced it and was produced by them only after lengthy experiments. Nothing in the prior art either anticipated or suggested it. The assay of Dr. Shorb, upon which defendant relies, did not anticipate; while it gave the patentees a useful tool for conducting experiments, it did not suggest the product of the patent. As said by the Supreme Court in Diamond Rubber Company v. Consolidated Rubber Tire Company, 220 U.S. 428, 435, 31 S.Ct. 444, 447, 55 L.Ed. 527, 532:

"Knowledge after the event is always easy, and problems once solved present no difficulties, indeed, may be represented as never having had any, and expert witnesses may be brought forward to show that the new thing which seemed to have eluded the search of the world was always ready at hand and easy to be seen by a merely skillful attention. But the law has other tests of the invention than subtle conjectures of what might have been seen and yet was not. It regards a change as evidence of novelty, the acceptance and utility of change as a further evidence, even as demonstration."

As the issue of infringement was not passed upon in the court below, we will not consider it here. The decree of the District Court will be reversed and the case will be remanded for further proceedings not inconsistent herewith.

Reversed and remanded.[b]

H. IMPROVEMENTS

The first patent statute in the United States passed in 1790 defined the subject matter of patents as "any useful art, manufacture, engine, machine, or device, or any *improvement* therein" (Emphasis added). The word "improvement" has remained in the statutes to the present and appears in Section 101 of Title 35 U.S.C.A. There is a qualitative connotation to the use of the word since there is an implication that, in

b. "Merely because there is evidence that a product exists in nature with other substances is not invariably sufficient reason for denying claims to such product. On the other hand, mere purity of an old product normally does not entitle one to a patent on the pure product. Appellants on page 2 of the disclosure state that their novel factor does not exist as such in the source material because 'the testing of those materials does not reveal the presence of pyruvate oxidation factors.' Further, the publications of record indicate that large quantities of liver, as alleged, are needed to obtain the claimed potent factor in effective amounts. The facts herein do not convince us that appellants have merely obtained a pure product of the same utility as the substance from which it was isolated and consequently differs therefrom only in purity but they have recovered a compound having a new utility on which invention may rest." Ex parte Reed and Gunsalus, 135 USPQ 105 (Pat. Office Board of Appeals, 1961).

addition to a basic invention as patentable subject matter, an improvement on a basic invention can be considered.

✓ Robinson [a] provides the following definition:

> An improvement is an addition to or alteration in some existing means, which increases its efficiency without destroying its identity. It includes two necessary ideas: first, the idea of a complete and practically operative art or instrument, either natural or artificial, as the original to be improved; and second, the idea of some change in such art or instrument, not affecting its essential character, but enabling it to produce its appropriate results in a more perfect or a more economical manner. When such a change involves the exercise of the inventive faculties it is a true invention and is known as an improvement.

There is clear indication in the cases that an improvement will be subject to the same requirements for patentability as any other patentable subject matter. Winans v. Denmead, 56 U.S. 330, 14 L.Ed. 717 (1853); Packing Co. Cases, 105 U.S. 566, 26 L.Ed. 1172 (1882); Diamond Rubber Co. v. Consolidated Rubber Tire Co., 220 U.S. 428, 31 S.Ct. 444, 55 L.Ed. 527 (1911). Some later decisions have been construed as suggesting that a more stringent test for innovation should be applied to combinations of old elements and improvements. Great A & P Tea Co. v. Supermarket Equip. Corp., 340 U.S. 147, 71 S.Ct. 127, 95 L.Ed. 162 (1950), ("Courts should construe combination patent claims with a care proportional to the difficulty and improbability of finding invention in an assembly of old elements * * *. A patent for a combination which only unites old elements with no change in their respective functions * * * obviously withdraws what already is known into the field of its monopoly and diminishes the resources available to skillful men."); Anderson's-Black Rock, Inc. v. Pavement Salvage Co., Inc., 396 U.S. 57, 90 S.Ct. 305, 24 L.Ed.2d 258 (1969); Sakraida v. Ag Pro, Inc., 425 U.S. 273, 96 S.Ct. 1532, 47 L.Ed.2d 784 (1976) ("We cannot agree that the combination of these old elements * * * can properly be characterized as synergistic, that is, result[ing] in an effect greater than the sum of the effects taken separately.") However, recent decisions of the Court of Appeals for the Federal Circuit indicate only the same statutory test of nonobviousness is applicable to all inventions including improvements and combinations of old elements.

↳ WILLIAMS MFG. CO. v. UNITED SHOE MACHINERY CORP.

Supreme Court of the United States, 1942.
316 U.S. 364, 62 S.Ct. 1179, 86 L.Ed. 1537.

MR. JUSTICE ROBERTS delivered the opinion of the Court.

The suit was for the infringement of Claims 6, 23, 42, 85, and 91 of the McFeely Patent No. 1,558,737 for improvements in automatic heel

---

a. Robinson on Patents (1890) Sec. 210.

lasting machines. The District Court held the claims valid and infringed. The Circuit Court of Appeals affirmed.

District Ct. rule

The defendant sought certiorari on the ground that the claims were invalid under recent decisions of this court because they constituted attempts to repatent a broad combination of old devices—bed lasters and automatic tackers—and embodied only aggregations of new unpatentable mechanisms with old mechanical combinations. In pressing us to grant the writ, the petitioner insisted that it desired no retrial of the facts but merely a proper application of the law to the facts found by the courts below. We granted the writ.

* * *

We come to the petitioner's contention that the courts below have held the patent valid and infringed on the theory that the improvements and adjustments disclosed in the claims entitle McFeely to repatent the entire combination of the old devices, known as bed lasters and automatic tackers. * * *

The contention is not in accord with the holdings below. It is true that both courts found that manual adjustments are provided which are not found in the earlier McFeely patent or in the prior art as applied to the three combinations embodied in the claims in suit. But the findings do not stop there. In respect of each claimed combination, both courts have found that they embody other improvements, in addition to mere manual preliminary adjustments and that each combination exhibits invention in that its elements cooperate in a new and useful way to accomplish an improved result.

* * *

We think, however, that each of the claims is confined to a combination of specified means applicable only to a restricted portion and function of the whole machine.

* * *

It would be difficult to describe an improvement in a washing machine without naming such a machine as the thing to which the patent is addressed and equally difficult to refrain from referring to various parts of the machine, such as the tub or the motor which actuates the washer. But it has never been thought that a claim limited to an improvement in some element of the machine is, by such reference, rendered bad as claiming a monopoly of tubs or motors used in washing machines.

* * *

The decree is affirmed.

MR. JUSTICE BLACK, dissenting, with whom MR. JUSTICE DOUGLAS and MR. JUSTICE MURPHY concur.

* * *

APPLICATION OF RATTI

United States Court of Customs and Patent Appeals, 1959.
46 CCPA 976, 270 F.2d 810, 123 USPQ 349.

SMITH, JUDGE. This is an appeal from the decision of the Board of Appeals of the United States Patent Office affirming the rejection by the Primary Examiner of claims 1, 4, 7 and 10 of appellant's application serial No. 359,325, filed June 3, 1953, for a patent on an "Oil Seal" for sealing the space between a bore in a housing and a relatively movable shaft centrally located in the bore.

* * *

The Chinnery et al. patent is the reference principally relied upon by the Patent Office.

* * *

The seal construction disclosed in Chinnery et al. is such that the "interference press fit" which that patent calls for is alone relied on to keep the seal tight. There is nothing in the Chinnery et al. patent to show how the resilient sealing element is *maintained* in resilient contact with the bore otherwise than by the resiliency of the rubber. If and when that resiliency is lost, the sealing effect will be impaired.

* * *

We, therefore, find that Chinnery et al. did not teach the shaft sealing art how to solve the problems which existed in that art at the time of appellant's invention. We hold, further, that the combination of Jepson with Chinnery et al. is not a proper ground for rejection of the claims here on appeal. This suggested combination of references would require a substantial reconstruction and redesign of the elements shown in Chinnery et al. as well as a change in the basic principles under which the Chinnery et al. construction was designed to operate.

* * *

* * * We fully agree, of course, with the board's statement that novelty alone is not enough for patentability.

With the next statement of the board, in explanation of its affirmance of the rejection of claim 10, we do not agree. It reads:

In order to *properly* define invention [meaning, of course, *patentable* invention], a claim should clearly define a structure *which possesses some definite advantage over the prior art.* As far as we can determine there is *no better* combination of housing and seal produced by using a series of snap fastener connections to connect the seal to the housing, as in appellant's structure, over using a series of bolts, as in the structure shown by Chinnery et al. Both act to merely detachably connect one element to another element and as far as we can find are merely equivalent connecting means especially in the absence of any unexpected result *or advantage* being obtained, by using one means in preference to the other, on which the record before us is entirely silent." (Emphasis ours.)

If we may extract from the foregoing what we understand to be the essence of the board's position in the matter, it is that claim 10 is not patentable, though it defines a combination which is novel over the disclosures of the references, because the claimed combination has not been shown to be any better than, or to possess any advantage over, what was known to the art.

As was pointed out in In re Stempel, Jr., 241 F.2d 755, 44 CCPA 820, an applicant is entitled to a patent, under the statutes, unless one of the prohibitory provisions of the statutes applies. The statutory requirements for patentability, broadly stated, are novelty, usefulness and unobviousness, as provided in 35 U.S.C.A. sections 101, 102, and 103. While it is true that proof that an invention *is* better or *does* possess advantages may be persuasive of the existence of any one or all of the foregoing three requirements, and hence be indicative of patentability, Congress has not seen fit to make such proof a prerequisite to patentability.[1]

Appellant's invention, as defined in claim 10, has been held by the board to possess novelty over the disclosure of Chinnery et al. Just what the board thought about the pertinency of Norton is obscure but it seems to have regarded this reference as of little moment. Appellant in his brief here said that Norton was held by the board to have no bearing on the invention and the Patent Office brief said that the appellant was correct in so stating and that the court need not consider it. We are, therefore, virtually without any reference against claim 10 except Chinnery et al. and the rejection thereon is predicated solely on a theory of patentability we find to be outside of the patent statutes, namely, that the combination of claim 10 is, by reason of the use of spring retaining hooks instead of a series of bolts, *no better* than the combination of Chinnery et al. However intriguing such a ground of rejection may be, it is the duty of the tribunals of the Patent Office and of this court to apply the law as Congress has written it. While the provisions of the former R.S. 4893 may be said to have given the Commissioner some discretion in refusing to grant a patent on an otherwise patentable invention unless "the same is sufficiently useful and important," when the Patent Codification Act of 1952 was enacted, Congress removed this provision from old section 36 of title 35, now

1. A critical essay on the existing law has recently appeared under the title "A Proposal for: A Standard of Patentability; Consonant Statutory Changes; A Manual on Determination of Patentability," by Malcolm F. Bailey, 41 J.P.O.S. 192–225, 231–257. It advocates, as we understand it, that the present law should be changed to set up as the test for patentability, in place of the requirement of section 103 that an invention be unobvious, a requirement that the invention involve *progress*, which the author finds in the constitutional provisions. Congress has not seen fit to include in the statutes, at any time during the past 169 years so far as we are aware, a requirement that each and every patentable *invention* shall involve "progress" in this sense, i.e., that each new invention must also be shown to possess some definite advantage over the prior art. The author relates the term "progress" to individual inventions and then gives it the connotation that each such invention should be a technical advance, improvement or betterment. The very making of the suggestion to change the law is an indication that the existing law is otherwise.

section 131. We take this as a further indication that it is the intent of Congress that patentability be determined solely by the provisions of sections 101, 102 and 103. We therefore reverse the board on this ground of rejection of claim 10.

* * *

For the foregoing reasons we reverse the rejection of claim 10. The rejections of claims 1, 4, 7 and 10 are reversed.

Reversed.[b]

MARTIN, JUDGE, concurs in result.

KIRKPATRICK, DISTRICT JUDGE, dissenting, in which WORLEY, CHIEF JUDGE, joins.

One of the avowed purposes of the Patent System is promotion of progress of the useful arts. The issuance of one patent stimulates others to develop non-infringing devices or processes and at the same time to improve on that which has gone before. It has been said that "books and movies are seldom equal to those to which they are a sequel." With inventions, sometimes the improvement proves to be far superior to the predecessor concepts. An improvement patent cannot receive strength from the basic or parent idea. It must stand or fall on its own merit. The Supreme Court of the United States expressed this well in Washburn and Moen Mfg. Co. v. The Beat 'Em All Barbed Wire Co., 143 U.S. 275, 282, 12 S.Ct. 443, 36 L.Ed. 154, 158 (1892):

> The vital difference in the two patents is in the shape of the barb itself. In one case a flat bit of metal is used of an elongated diamond shape, through which a hole is pierced, by means of which it is strung upon the wire, requiring something more than the aid of a second wire twisted upon the first to render it immovable. In the other the barb is a piece of wire coiled about one of the fence wires, and held rigidly in place by the twisting of another wire about the first.

> It is true that the affixing of barbs to a fence wire does not apparently give a wide scope to the ingenuity of the inventor; but from the crude device of Hunt to the perfected wire of Glidden, each patent has marked a step in the progress in the art. The difference between the Kelly fence and the Glidden fence is not a radical one, but slight as it may seem to be, it was apparently this which made the barbed-wire fence a practical and commercial success. The inventions of Hunt and Smith appear to be scarcely more than tentative, and never to have gone into general use. The sales of the Kelly patent never seem to have exceeded 3,000 tons per annum, while plaintiff's manufacture and sales of the Glidden device (substituting a sharp barb for a blunt one) rose rapidly from 50 tons in 1874 to 44,000 tons in 1886, while those of its licensees in 1887 reached the enormous amount of 173,000 tons. Indeed, one who has traveled upon the western plains of this continent cannot have failed to notice the very large amount of territory enclosed

b. See also Application of Fay and Fox, 347 F.2d 597, 146 USPQ 47 (CCPA 1965).

by these fences which otherwise, owing to the great scarcity of wood, would have to be left unprotected.

Under such circumstances courts have not been reluctant to sustain a patent to the man who has taken the final step which has turned a failure into a success. In the law of patents it is the last step that wins. It may be strange that, considering the important results obtained by Kelly in his patent, it did not occur to him to substitute a coiled wire in place of the diamond shape prong, but evidently it did not; and to the man to whom it did ought not to be denied the quality of inventor. There are many instances in the reported decisions of this court where a monopoly has been sustained in favor of the last of a series of inventors, all of whom were groping to attain a certain result, which only the last one of the number seemed able to grasp. Conspicuous among these is the case of Webster Loom Co. v. Higgins, 105 U.S. (15 Otto) 580, 591, 26 L.Ed. 1177 (1881) [26:1177, 1181], where an improvement in looms for weaving pile fabrics, consisting of such a new combination of known devices as to give to a loom the capacity of weaving fifty yards of carpet a day, when before it could only weave forty, was held to be patentable. It was said by the court, in answer to the argument that the combination was a mere aggregation of old and well known devices, that " 'this argument would be sound if the combination claimed by Webster was an obvious one for attaining the advantages proposed—one which would occur to any mechanic skilled in the art. But it is plain from the evidence, and from the very fact that it was not sooner adopted and used, that it did not, for years, occur in this light to even the most skillful persons. It may have been under their very eyes, they may almost be said to have stumbled over it; but they certainly failed to see it, to estimate its value, and to bring it into notice. * * * Now that it has succeeded, it may seem very plain to any one that he could have done it as well. This is often the case with inventions of the greatest merit. It may be laid down as a general rule, though perhaps, not an invariable one, that if a new combination and arrangement of known elements produce a new and beneficial result never attained before, it is evidence of invention.' "

I. INVENTIONS RELATING TO ATOMIC WEAPONS AND UTILIZATION OF NUCLEAR MATERIAL

42 U.S.C.A. § 2181. Inventions Relating to Atomic Weapons, and Filing of Reports

(a) *Denial of Patent; Revocation of Prior Patents.* No patent shall hereafter be granted for any invention or discovery which is useful solely in the utilization of special nuclear material or atomic energy in an atomic weapon. Any patent granted for any such invention or discovery is revoked, and just compensation shall be made therefor.

(b) *Denial of Rights; Revocation of Prior Rights.* No patent hereafter granted shall confer any rights with respect to any invention or discovery to the extent that such invention or discovery is used in the utilization of special nuclear material or atomic energy in atomic weapons. Any rights conferred by any patent heretofore granted for any invention or discovery are revoked to the extent that such invention or discovery is so used, and just compensation shall be made therefor.

(c) *Report of Invention to Commissioner of Patents.* Any person who has made or hereafter makes any invention or discovery useful in the production or utilization of special nuclear material or atomic energy, shall file with the Commission a report containing a complete description thereof unless such invention or discovery is described in an application for a patent filed with the Commissioner of Patents by such person within the time required for the filing of such report. The report covering any such invention or discovery shall be filed on or before the one hundred and eightieth day after such person first discovers or first has reason to believe that such invention or discovery is useful in such production or utilization.

(d) *Report to Commission by Commissioner of Patents.* The Commissioner of Patents shall notify the Commission of all applications for patents heretofore or hereafter filed which, in his opinion, disclose inventions or discoveries required to be reported under subsection (c) of this section, and shall provide the Commission access to all such applications.

(e) *Confidential Information; Circumstances Permitting Disclosure.* Reports filed pursuant to subsection (c) of this section, and applications to which access is provided under subsection (d) of this section, shall be kept in confidence by the Commission, and no information concerning the same given without authority of the inventor or owner unless necessary to carry out the provisions of any Act of Congress or in such special circumstances as may be determined by the Commission. (Aug. 1, 1946, ch. 724, sec. 151, as added Aug. 30, 1954, ch. 1073, sec. 1, 68 Stat. 943; as amended Sept. 6, 1961, Pub.L. 87–206, secs. 7, 8, 9, 75 Stat. 477.)

HOBBS v. UNITED STATES, ATOMIC ENERGY COMM'N

United States Court of Appeals, Fifth Circuit, 1967.
376 F.2d 488, 153 USPQ 378.

The Board held that Hobbs' inventions "were developed completely through federally financed work, whether it be called 'research' or some other name." The statute uses the word "research", not the word "work" or any other word. To us, "research" implies more than work. It involves the notion of lengthy, complex technical investigation.[8] We conclude, therefore, that an invention developed in connection with a federal contract is not necessarily the product of "federally financed research" as that term is used in the Act.

In this case, the invention of the two valves was not the product of an intensive investigation. Rather the idea came to Hobbs suddenly one night in a Chicago hotel room, and was reduced to practice quickly, without exhaustive experimentation, and at very little cost to the Government. The Board should take these considerations into account

---

8. Webster's Second New International Dictionary defines "Research" as: "[C]ritical and exhaustive investigation or experimentation * * *".

when on remand it considers the "federally financed research" clause of section 11(a)(3).

PIPER AND JOHNSTON v. ATOMIC ENERGY COMM.

United States Court of Customs and Patent Appeals, 1974.
502 F.2d 1393, 183 USPQ 235.

In our view, the decisive question is whether the language in section 152, "useful in the production or utilization of special nuclear material or atomic energy," reaches appellants' invention, which is described below.

* * *

The board held that appellants' invention is "useful in the production or utilization of special nuclear material or atomic energy," because it is "proximately related" thereto as a protective agent for personnel engaged in such activities. However, we can find no basis in the legislative history or in the statute itself for such interpretation, and no presumption of correctness attaches to such interpretation. See Fitch v. Atomic Energy Commission, 491 F.2d 1392, 181 USPQ 41 (CCPA 1974).

* * * we hold that appellants' invention is not "useful in the production or utilization of special nuclear material or atomic energy," within the meaning of section 152 of the Atomic Energy Act of 1954.

The decision of the board is reversed.

IN RE BRUECKNER

United States Court of Customs and Patent Appeals, 1980.
623 F.2d 184, 206 USPQ 415.

MILLER, JUDGE.

This appeal is from a decision of the Patent and Trademark Office ("PTO") Board of Appeals ("board") affirming the examiner's rejection of appellant's claims under section 151 of the Atomic Energy Act of 1954, as amended (42 U.S.C.A. § 2181), on the ground that the claims are to an invention useful solely in the utilization of atomic energy in an atomic weapon. We reverse.

* * *

The board recognized that the proper test under section 2181(a) is whether the invention is "useful solely in the utilization of * * * atomic energy in an atomic weapon," and then correctly looked to section 2014(d) for the definition of atomic weapon. However, it erred in then ignoring the word "solely" in section 2181(a) and the complementary provisions in section 2181(b). United States v. Blasius, 397 F.2d 203, 207 n. 9, 158 USPQ 371, 373 n. 9 (2d Cir.1968), cert. dismissed 393 U.S. 1008, 89 S.Ct. 615, 21 L.Ed.2d 557, 160 USPQ 832 (1969).

Even assuming that appellant's invention meets the definition of "atomic weapon" in section 2014(d), it is necessary to determine whether the invention is "useful *solely*" in an atomic weapon. The record is clear, and the PTO does not argue to the contrary, that appellant's invention has nonweapon utility. Therefore, we hold that the restrictions of section 2181(a) are not applicable.[5]

The examiner suggested that, if the claims recited a "peaceful purpose" limitation, section 2181(a) would not be applicable. However, this ignores the phrase "to the extent" in section 2181(b) and would require that each atomic energy type claim include a boilerplate phrase, such as "used only for peaceful or nonweapon purposes." Such a limitation is already impliedly incorporated into every such claim by section 2181(b).

The decision of the board is *reversed.*

Reversed.

---

5. Unlike the statutory language involved in Piper v. Atomic Energy Comm'n., 502 F.2d 1393, 183 USPQ 235 (CCPA 1974), the meaning of the language involved in this case is clear on its face. Therefore, we need not resort to legislative history. United States v. Oregon, 366 U.S. 643, 648, 81 S.Ct. 1278, 1281, 6 L.Ed.2d 575 (1961).

Chapter Four

PROCEDURES IN THE PATENT OFFICE

A. APPLICATIONS AND APPEALS

The Patent Office is a division of the Department of Commerce where records are maintained (35 U.S.C.A. § 1). The Commissioner of Patents is appointed by the President, by and with the advice and consent of the Senate (35 U.S.C.A. § 3). The Commissioner establishes regulations for the conduct of proceedings in the Patent Office including the maintenance of a classification system to aid in the determining of novelty and he is authorized to issue patents under the official seal of the Office (35 U.S.C.A. §§ 2, 6, 9). The Commissioner issues a book entitled "Rules of Practice in Patent Cases" which contains about 450 numbered paragraphs establishing procedures to be followed by inventors and attorneys in the presentation of patent applications and in the conduct of business before the patent examiners, and the Board of Patent Appeals and Interferences (35 U.S.C.A. §§ 131, 132, 134, 135).

Correspondence relative to an application is based on Sections 132 and 133 of the statute which read:

35 U.S.C.A. § 132. Notice of Rejection; Reexamination

Whenever, on examination, any claim for a patent is rejected, or any objection or requirement made, the Commissioner shall notify the applicant thereof, stating the reasons for such rejection, or objection or requirement, together with such information and references as may be useful in judging of the propriety of continuing the prosecution of his application; and if after receiving such notice, the applicant persists in his claim for a patent, with or without amendment, the application shall be reexamined. No amendment shall introduce new matter into the disclosure of the invention.

35 U.S.C.A. § 133. Time for Prosecuting Application

Upon failure of the applicant to prosecute the application within six months after any action therein, of which notice has been given or mailed to the applicant, or within such shorter time, not less than thirty days, as fixed by the Commissioner in such action, the application shall be regarded as abandoned by the parties thereto, unless it be shown to the satisfaction of the Commissioner that such delay was unavoidable.

———◆———

Under certain circumstances, a patent application may be divided into two or more applications, each of which will receive the benefit of the first filing date as governed by the following:

35 U.S.C.A. § 121. Divisional Applications

If two or more independent and distinct inventions are claimed in one application, the Commissioner may require the application to be restricted to one of the inventions. If the other invention is made the subject of a divisional application which complies with the requirements of section 120 of this title it shall be entitled to the benefit of the filing date of the original application. A patent issuing on an application with respect to which a requirement for restriction under this section has been made, or on an application filed as a result of such a requirement, shall not be used as a reference either in the Patent Office or in the courts against a divisional application or against the original application or any patent issued on either of them, if the divisional application is filed before the issuance of the patent on the other application. If a divisional application is directed solely to subject matter described and claimed in the original application as filed, the Commissioner may dispense with signing and execution by the inventor. The validity of a patent shall not be questioned for failure of the Commissioner to require the application to be restricted to one invention.

It is not generally appreciated that patent applications are maintained under secrecy by the Patent Office throughout the entire prosecution and until a patent actually issues. The successful applicant may ultimately control whether or not the patent will issue since he must authorize issuance by payment of the final government fee due after a notice of allowance. The allowance generally follows correspondence between the applicant (or his attorney) and the examiner in charge of the application. This correspondence is usually called the "prosecution" of the application. Section 122 of 35 U.S.C.A. reads:

Confidential status of applications

Applications for patents shall be kept in confidence by the Patent Office and no information concerning the same given without authority of the applicant or owner unless necessary to carry out the provisions of any Act of Congress or in such special circumstances as may be determined by the Commissioner.

The Freedom of Information Act (FOIA) does not abrogate this long established policy of secrecy for patent applications in the Patent and Trademark Office. In Iron & Sears v. Dann, the Court of Appeals of the District of Columbia (1979), 202 USPQ 798, 801, dealt with this question:

> "On August 27, 1975 appellant filed suit in the District Court seeking disclosure of all filing date decisions withheld, along with pertinent indices. The District Court granted summary judgment in favor of the PTO on January 23, 1978. The court found that Exemption 3 of the FOIA, 5 U.S.C. § 552(b)(3) (1976), in conjunction with the provision of the patent statute requiring that patent applications be maintained in confidence, 35 U.S.C. § 122 (1976), shields the bulk of

the decisions in suit from disclosure under the FOIA. This appeal followed.

"The FOIA combines a strong disclosure mandate with nine rather specific exemptions. It is commonplace that the former is to be generously construed while the latter are narrowly circumscribed. The key question posed by the instant litigation is whether patent applications and information concerning them qualify by virtue of 35 U.S.C. § 122 as materials 'specifically exempted from disclosure by statute' for purposes of the third exemption to the FOIA, 5 U.S.C. § 552(b)(3), and thus may be kept in confidence by the PTO. The District Court held that they do so qualify, and we concur."

EX PARTE BONNIE–B CO. INC.

313 O.G. 453, 1922.
1923 C.D. 42.

ROBERTSON, COMMISSIONER. A petition has been filed by the Bonnie-B Co., Inc., for access to applications of M. in view of a notice of infringement given to petitioner by the attorney for M. under date of October 23, 1922. A photostat copy of said notice accompanied the petition.

It is of course the practice of this Office to preserve all applications in secrecy to the extent stated in the rules so long as the applications are not used to unjustly interfere with the business affairs of others.

Where a competitor is marketing a device for which an inventor has an application pending, it is not considered improper for the inventor to notify the competitor that he, the inventor, has an application pending for said invention, when such notice is merely intended to put the competitor on notice as to making substantial investments and expenditure in the marketing of the device. The inventor, however, should not in any way interfere with the business of the competitor in this matter. To do so will justify this Office in giving the competitor access to the pending applications upon which the notice is based, or at least in giving him photostat copies of the drawings.

The petition for access is denied without prejudice to its renewal in case the applicant makes further demands that petitioner or his customers stop marketing the device.

IN RE GERARD

Commissioner of Patents, 1960.
127 USPQ 337.

CROCKER, FIRST ASSISTANT COMMISSIONER. This is a petition requesting access to the above-identified abandoned applications on the ground that Serial No. 418,705 was involved in Interference No. 88,524, and Serial No. 436,030 was involved in Interference No. 88,606, with an application of J. Oppenheimer which matured into Patent No. 2,926,559. Petitioner states that a question of infringement has arisen in connection with the patent; that claims of the patent appear to have been based upon the disclosures of the instant applications; and that access to the instant cases is necessary to understand and interpret the patent claims.

Applicant, through counsel, opposes the petition contending that the instant applications contain subject matter not shown and disclosed in the patent; that if it were not possible to understand or interpret claims of the patent from a study thereof the claims should not have been granted to the patentee during the interference proceeding; and that it does not appear that claims in the patent can be legally bound by or interpreted by any statement made by Gerard during the prosecution of the instant applications. A supplemental petition for access to the instant applications states that the terminology of the counts of the interferences, which now constitute claims of the patent, is quite foreign to that employed in the patent. A response to the aforesaid supplemental petition reiterates applicant's position with respect to the granting of access.

Section 122 of Title 35 United States Code provides that applications for patent shall be kept in confidence. Rule 14 based thereon states that both pending and abandoned applications are not open to public inspection, but that under certain circumstances abandoned applications may be inspected and copies obtained. Clearly the instant case is not within the exception of Rule 14(b). While petitioner contends that the terminology of the patent claims is foreign to that employed in the patent, and that access is necessary to understand and interpret the patent claims, it is fundamental that each application must be complete in itself, and the grant of a patent carries with it the presumption that the requirements of the statute with respect to a full and clear description of the manner of making and using the invention has been met. Petitioner has not shown that he is entitled to access; therefore, in view of applicant's opposition, access cannot be granted.

The petition is denied.[a]

After an application is received by the Patent Office and a date stamp applied, it is checked for compliance with the requirements with respect to formal and technical matters, i.e., condition of copy, necessary fee, oath, etc.[b] and then passed to the classification division where

a. See also In re W.D. Allen Mfg. Co., 765 O.G. 939; 1961 C.D. 6 (1960).

b. "Rule 56 [Patent Office Rules of Practice] states that any application altered after being signed or sworn to may be stricken from the files (cf. Ames v. Lindstrom, 1911 C.D. 68, 167 O.G. 241); and Rule 52(c) requires the initialing and dating of any alteration in order to insure that the changes were made by the applicant before the application was signed and sworn to. Alterations are not considered to be minor informalities, since there is some doubt as to whether a valid patent could issue on an application in which the papers were altered after execution—Vandenberg v. Reynolds, 44 CCPA 873, 242 F.2d 761, 113 USPQ 275. For that reason it has been the settled practice of this Office to refuse a filing date to any application which has an unexplained Rule 52(c) alteration therein, and to permit the applicant to file an affidavit later to explain whether the alteration was made by him prior to execution of the papers. Hence there was no error on the part of the

it will be examined for subject matter and dispatched to the proper Examining Group for assignment to an Examiner. Applications are usually taken up in the order received but examination may be advanced upon the filing of a petition to the Commissioner with a verified showing of reasons for special action. Advanced age or illness of an applicant may be one basis for the petition, or, as another basis, the possibility of the raising of capital and establishment of a manufacturing facility which is dependent on a patent issuing. Also, if there is actual or threatened infringement, a petition to make special may be granted. Usually the Commissioner requires that a novelty search be made by or in behalf of the applicant and the presentation of a statement that the claimed invention is believed to be patentable.

A Manual of Patent Examining Procedure, prepared by the Patent Office and issued by the Department of Commerce, is designed especially for the guidance of Patent Office Examiners but is found by patent attorneys to be very helpful in meeting Patent Office requirements. The Commissioner of Patents conducts examinations for persons who seek to qualify to practice before the Office as a registered agent or attorney. This examination, directed both to substantive law and to Patent Office rules and regulations, is given at various geographical locations around the United States on a date set by the Commissioner. Successful applicants are assigned a registration number and allowed to represent applicants in the various matters dealing with the Patent Examiners and Boards. An applicant may always file *pro se* and prosecute his own patent application.

Petitions may be made to the Commissioner on matters relating to procedural regulations including requirements for restriction (e.g., election of one of a plurality of inventions or election of species), and to invoke the supervisory authority of the Commissioner in appropriate circumstances. Decisions of the Examiners relating to substantive rejection of the claims are appealable to the Board of Patent Appeals and Interferences. From the Board of Patent Appeals and Interferences, there are mutually exclusive optional routes of appeal, one, to the Court of Appeals for the Federal Circuit (CAFC) based entirely on the record developed in the Patent Office (35 U.S.C.A. §§ 141–144), two, to the District Court for the District of Columbia on a record which may include the proceedings before the Patent Office supplemented by additional evidence if good reason is shown why it was not earlier presented (35 U.S.C.A. § 145).

With respect to appeals from the Board decisions on interferences under Section 146, jurisdiction may lie in District Courts other than the District of Columbia if proper service can be obtained. Appeal may be taken from the CAFC to the Supreme Court,[c] and, in the usual manner, from the District Courts to the CAFC and the Supreme Court.

Application Branch in denying a filing date to the papers presented on October 13, 1960." In re Swanberg, 129 USPQ 364 (Comr.Pats.).

c. Brenner v. Manson, 383 U.S. 519, 86 S.Ct. 1033, 16 L.Ed.2d 69 (1966).

Patent fees are set by statute (35 U.S.C.A. § 41) and may be adjusted by the Commissioner of Patents and Trademarks at three-year intervals to reflect fluctuations in the Consumer Price Index. An adjustment effective October 1, 1985 set a basic fee of $340.00 for filing an application for utility patent, and a fee of $560.00 to issue the patent after the application is allowed. Additional fees are payable $3\frac{1}{2}$, $7\frac{1}{2}$ and $11\frac{1}{2}$ years after issue to maintain the patent in force. However, Sec. 1 of P.L. 97–247, August 27, 1982, 96 Stat. 317, authorizes appropriations of general government funds to operate the Patent Office, and requires that such funds be used to reduce fees by 50% for independent inventors, non-profit organizations and small businesses as defined under the Small Business Act. Generally, a small business is one having less than 500 employees.

B. RESPONSIBILITY OF APPLICANT AND ATTORNEY TO THE PATENT OFFICE

The practice of patent law is a recognized specialty along with the practice of admiralty law. Attorneys in this specialty are permitted to announce their branch of the law on letterheads, business cards, and the like.

Patent agents, that is, those qualified to represent applicants in the Patent Office, if they are not members of the bar in the state in which they practice, are permitted to render opinions and perform such services are incident to the preparation and prosecution of patent applications, but they are restricted in the matters of drafting contracts and giving opinions as to infringement and other substantive matters relating to patents.[a]

The responsibility of patent attorneys and patent agents to the Patent Office was dramatically presented in a case related to patents on glass making where it was shown that an article published in a trade journal relating to the subject had been presented to the patent examiner in the course of the prosecution of the patent to advance the cause of patentability. The article proved to be spurious and certain of the attorneys for Hartford-Empire Co.[b] were implicated in the preparation and presentation of the article. The Supreme Court[c] set aside a final judgment stating:

> The total effect of all this fraud, practiced both on the Patent Office and the courts, calls for nothing less than a complete denial of relief to Hartford for the claimed infringement of the patent thereby procured and enforced.

a. Sperry v. Florida, 373 U.S. 379, 83 S.Ct. 1322, 10 L.Ed.2d 428 (1963).

b. One of the patent attorneys was subsequently disbarred by the Commissioner of Patents, the action being affirmed by the Supreme Court in Kingsland, Comr.

Pats. v. Dorsey, 338 U.S. 318, 70 S.Ct. 123, 94 L.Ed. 123 (1949).

c. Hazel-Atlas Glass Co. v. Hartford-Empire Co., 322 U.S. 238, 250, 64 S.Ct. 997, 88 L.Ed. 1250, 1258 (1944).

In 1945, the Supreme Court, in Precision Instrument Mfg. Co. v. Automotive Maintenance Machinery Co.,[d] also a patent case wherein it was urged that critical information had been withheld from the Patent Office, said:

> Those who have applications pending with the Patent Office or who are parties to Patent Office Proceedings have an uncompromising duty to report to it all facts concerning possible fraud or inequitableness underlying the application in issue.

Twenty years later the Supreme Court had occasion to deal with a patent case wherein allegations, as yet unproven, were made as to misrepresentations in the Patent Office. There was a suggestion that the urging of a patent which had been fraudulently obtained might be a violation of the antitrust laws. A portion of the decision in Walker Process Equipment, Inc. v. Food Machinery and Chemical Corp.[e] reads:

> Walker's counterclaim alleged that Food Machinery obtained the patent by knowingly and willfully misrepresenting facts to the Patent Office. Proof of this assertion would be sufficient to strip Food Machinery of its exemption from the antitrust laws. By the same token, Food Machinery's good faith would furnish a complete defense. This includes an honest mistake as to the effect of prior installation upon patentability—so-called "technical fraud."

> To establish monopolization or attempt to monopolize a part of trade or commerce under § 2 of the Sherman Act, it would then be necessary to appraise the exclusionary power of the illegal patent claim in terms of the relevant market for the product involved. Without a definition of that market there is no way to measure Food Machinery's ability to lessen or destroy competition. It may be that the device—knee-action swing diffusers—use in sewage treatment systems does not comprise a relevant market. There may be effective substitutes for the device which do not infringe the patent. This is a matter of proof, as is the amount of damages suffered by Walker.

As a result of the above Supreme Court decision, and seemingly precipitated by the sentiments expressed in the *Walker Process* case, there has been a popular trend on the part of defendants in infringement suits to attack patents on the grounds of fraudulent misrepresentation in the Patent Office. The following excerpts from patent cases illustrate the approach which the courts have taken.

37 CFR § 1.56 Duty of Disclosure; Fraud; Striking or Rejection of Applications

(a) A duty of candor and good faith toward the Patent and Trademark Office rests on the inventor, on each attorney or agent who prepares or prosecutes the application and on every other individual who is substantively involved in the preparation or prosecution of the application and who is associated with the inventor, with the assignee or with anyone to whom there is an obligation to assign the application. All such individuals have a

---

d. 324 U.S. 806, 818, 65 S.Ct. 993, 89 L.Ed. 1381, 1388 (1945).

e. 382 U.S. 172, 177, 86 S.Ct. 347, 15 L.Ed.2d 247, 251 (1965).

duty to disclose to the Office information they are aware of which is material to the examination of the application. Such information is material when there is a substantial likelihood that a reasonable examiner would consider it important in deciding whether to allow the application to issue as a patent. The duty is commensurate with the degree of involvement in the preparation or prosecution of the application.

* * *

AMERICAN HOIST & DERRICK COMPANY v. SOWA & SONS, INC.

United States Court of Appeals, Federal Circuit, 1984.
725 F.2d 1350, 220 USPQ 763, Certiorari denied, 469 US 821, 105 S.Ct. 95, 83 L.Ed.2d 41 (1984).

RICH, CIRCUIT JUDGE.

* * *

Defending against AmHoist's suit for infringement of these claims, Sowa denied infringement and counterclaimed for a declaratory judgment of invalidity. Sowa later brought to AmHoist's attention what it deemed new prior art, leading AmHoist to file an application for reissue of its patent. Sowa then amended its answer and counterclaimed for damages for unfair competition and for violation of federal antitrust law, asserting that AmHoist committed fraud in the PTO by not disclosing to the examiner the prior art that Sowa discovered.

* * *

Reverting to the court's recitation of a "duty to disclose all facts pertinent to the prosecution of an application," it is also clear that an applicant for patent is under no obligation to disclose "all pertinent prior art or other pertinent information" of which he is aware. *Digital Equipment Corp. v. Diamond,* 653 F.2d 701, 716, 210 USPQ 521, 538 (1st Cir.1981) ("It is not enough that the information be simply 'relevant' in some general sense to the subject matter of the claimed invention, or even to the invention's patentability."). Nor does an applicant for patent, who has no duty to conduct a prior art search, have an obligation to disclose any art of which, in the court's words, he "reasonably should be aware." The former portion of the court's instruction ignores the requirement of materiality and the latter portion overlooks the intent requirement.

It has been noted that courts have utilized at least three distinct orders of materiality: (1) an objective "but for" standard; (2) a subjective "but for" standard; and, (3) a "but it may have" standard. *E.g., Plastic Container Corp. v. Continental Plastics of Oklahoma, Inc.,* 607 F.2d 885, 899, 203 USPQ 27, 38–39 (10th Cir.1979); *Gemveto Jewelry Co. v. Lambert Bros., Inc.,* 542 F.Supp. 933, 939–40, 216 USPQ 976, 981 (S.D. N.Y.1982). Criterion (3) endorses inquiry into whether the involved facts "might reasonably have affected the examiner's decision as to patentability." *Gemveto Jewelry,* supra.

Although strikingly similar to the "but it may have" guideline, there is yet another and official "standard." PTO Rule 1.56(a), explains materiality. It says that information "is material where there is [1] a *substantial likelihood* that [2] a *reasonable examiner* [3] would consider it *important* [4] in deciding *whether to allow the application to issue* as a patent." (Emphasis ours.) 37 CFR 1.56(a), third sentence (1983).

The PTO "standard" is an appropriate starting point for any discussion of materiality, for it appears to be the broadest, thus encompassing the others, and because that materiality boundary most closely aligns with how one ought to conduct business with the PTO. There is no reason, however, to be bound by any single standard, for the answer to any inquiry into fraud in the PTO does not begin and end with materiality, nor can materiality be said to be unconnected to other considerations:

> Questions of "materiality" and "culpability" are often interrelated and intertwined, so that a lesser showing of the materiality of the withheld information may suffice when an intentional scheme to defraud is established, whereas a greater showing of the materiality of withheld information would necessarily create an inference that its nondisclosure was "wrongful." [*Digital Equipment Corp. v. Diamond,* supra at 716, 210 USPQ at 538.]

Thus, for example, where an objective "but for" inquiry is satisfied under the appropriate standard of proof, and although one is not necessarily grossly negligent in failing to anticipate judicial resolution of validity, a lesser showing of facts from which intent can be inferred may be sufficient to justify holding the patent invalid or unenforceable, in whole or in part. Conversely, where it is demonstrated that a reasonable examiner would merely have considered particular information to be important but not crucial to his decision not to reject, a showing of facts which would indicate something more than gross negligence or recklessness may be required, and good faith judgment or honest mistake might well be a sufficient defense.

* * *

J.P. STEVENS & CO., INC. v. LEX TEX LTD., INC.

United States Court of Appeals, Federal Circuit, 1984.
747 F.2d 1553, 223 USPQ 1089.

MARKEY, CHIEF JUDGE.

* * *

"Common law fraud" requires (1) misrepresentation of a material fact, (2) intent to deceive or a state of mind so reckless respecting consequences as to be the equivalent of intent (scienter), (3) justifiable reliance on the misrepresentation by the party deceived, inducing him to act thereon, and (4) injury to the party deceived, resulting from reliance on the misrepresentation. *Norton v. Curtiss,* 433 F.2d 779, 793, 167 USPQ 532, 543 (CCPA 1970).[5]

---

5. In *American Hoist & Derrick Co. v. Sowa & Sons,* 725 F.2d 1350, 1367, 220 USPQ 763, 776 (Fed.Cir.), *cert. denied,* 469 U.S. 821, 105 S.Ct. 95, 83 L.Ed.2d 41 (1984),

Conduct before the PTO that may render a patent unenforceable is broader than "common law fraud". *Norton v. Curtiss*, 433 F.2d at 793, 167 USPQ at 543–44. It includes failure to disclose material information, or submission of false material information, with an intent to mislead. Because the "fraud" label can be confused with other forms of conduct, this opinion avoids that label and uses "inequitable conduct" as a more accurate description of the proscribed activity, it being understood that the term encompasses affirmative acts of commission, *e.g.*, submission of false information, as well as omission, *e.g.*, failure to disclose material information.

"Inequitable conduct" requires proof by clear and convincing evidence of a threshold degree of materiality of the nondisclosed or false information. It has been indicated that the threshold can be established by any of four tests: (1) objective "but for"; (2) subjective "but for"; (3) "but it may have been"; and (4) PTO Rule 1.56(a), *i.e.*, whether there is a substantial likelihood that a reasonable examiner would have considered the omitted reference or false information important in deciding whether to allow the application to issue as a patent. *American Hoist*, 725 F.2d at 1362, 220 USPQ at 772–73. The PTO standard is the appropriate starting point because it is the broadest and because it most closely aligns with how one ought to conduct business with the PTO. *American Hoist*, 725 F.2d at 1363, 220 USPQ at 773. It served as the focus of inquiry in *Hycor Corp. v. The Schlueter Co.*, 740 F.2d 1529, 1539, 222 USPQ 553, 560 (Fed.Cir.1984), and in *Driscoll v. Cebalo*, 731 F.2d 878, 884, 221 USPQ 745, 750 (Fed.Cir.1984). Under the standard, a reference that would have been merely cumulative is not material. *Kimberly-Clark Corp. v. Johnson & Johnson*, 745 F.2d 1437 at 1455–1456 (Fed.Cir.1984).

"Inequitable conduct" also requires proof of a threshold intent. That intent need not be proven with direct evidence. *Hycor*, 740 F.2d at 1540, 222 USPQ at 561. It may be proven by showing acts the natural consequences of which are presumably intended by the actor. *American Hoist*, 725 F.2d at 1363, 220 USPQ at 773; *Kansas Jack, Inc. v. Kuhn*, 719 F.2d 1144, 1151, 219 USPQ 857, 862 (Fed.Cir.1983). Proof of deliberate scheming is not needed; gross negligence is sufficient. *Hycor*, 740 F.2d at 1540, 222 USPQ at 561. Gross negligence is present when the actor, judged as a reasonable person in his position, should have known of the materiality of a withheld reference. *Driscoll v. Cebalo*, 731 F.2d at 885, 221 USPQ at 751; *Kansas Jack, Inc. v. Kuhn*, 719 F.2d at 1152, 219 USPQ at 862. On the other hand, simple negligence, oversight, or an erroneous judgment made in good faith, is insufficient. *Orthopedic Equip. Co. v. All Orthopedic Appliances*, 707 F.2d 1376, 1383, 217 USPQ 1281, 1286 (Fed.Cir.1983).

Once the thresholds of materiality and intent are established, the court must balance them and determine as a matter of law whether the

this court stated that *Norton* erroneously referred to "technical" instead of common law fraud, and vowed not to use "technical".

scales tilt to a conclusion that inequitable conduct occurred. *American Hoist,* 725 F.2d at 1364, 220 USPQ at 774. If the court reaches that conclusion, it must hold that the patent claims at issue are unenforceable.

Whether the holding should be one of invalidity or unenforceability has had no practical significance in cases thus far presented to this court and has not therefore been addressed. * * *

The Supreme Court has discussed inequitable conduct, as a defense to a claim of patent infringement, in terms of enforceability, *see, e.g., Precision Instrument Manufacturing Co. v. Automotive Maintenance Machinery Co.,* 324 U.S. 806, 814–16, 65 S.Ct. 993, 997–98, 89 L.Ed. 1381 (1945). In *Walker Process Equip., Inc. v. Food Mach. & Chem. Corp.,* 382 U.S. 172, 176, 86 S.Ct. 347, 349, 15 L.Ed.2d 247 (1965), in addressing a claim for damages under § 4 of the Clayton Act based, *inter alia,* on alleged willfully fraudulent procurement of a patent, the Court spoke of "invalidity". Some courts have extrapolated from *Walker Process* two categories of defenses: (1) "fraud", rendering the patent invalid and (2) "other inequitable conduct", rendering the patent unenforceable. *See, e.g., Timely Products Corp. v. Arron,* 523 F.2d 288, 297, 187 USPQ 257, 264 (2d Cir.1975); *In re Multidistrict Litigation Involving Frost Patent,* 398 F.Supp. 1353, 1367–68, 185 USPQ 729, 740 (D.Del.1975), *aff'd in part,* 540 F.2d 601, 191 USPQ 241 (3rd Cir.1976).

Focusing on the effect of inequitable conduct as a defense, we conclude that it results in unenforceability. The Patent Act of 1952 states in 35 U.S.C. § 282 the defenses to a patent infringement suit:

(1) Noninfringement, absence of liability for infringement, or unenforceability.

(2) Invalidity of the patent or any claim in suit "on any ground specified in part II of this title as a condition for patentability" [*i.e.,* "novelty and loss of right" under § 102 and "non-obvious subject matter" under § 103].

(3) Invalidity under sections 112 or 251 of this title.

(4) Any fact or other act made a defense by this title.

Paragraph (1) includes "equitable defenses such as laches, estoppel and unclean hands". P.J. Federico, "Commentary On The New Act", 35 U.S.C.A. at 55. Because at the time the Patent Act was enacted Supreme Court cases had treated inequitable conduct as an "unclean hands" type defense, *see, e.g., Precision Instrument, cf., Driscoll v. Cebalo,* 731 F.2d at 884, 221 USPQ at 750–51, the defense fits best in the "unenforceability" phrase of paragraph (1). That approach accords, also, with the specification of particular bases for invalidity in paragraphs (2) and (3) in § 282.

* * *

Once a court concludes that inequitable conduct occurred, all the claims—not just the particular claims to which the inequitable conduct is directly connected—are unenforceable. *See generally,* cases collected in 4 Chisum, PATENTS, ¶ 19.03[6] at 19–85 n. 10 (1984). Inequitable conduct "goes to the patent right as a whole, independently of particular claims". *In re Clark,* 522 F.2d 623, 626, 187 USPQ 209, 212 (CCPA 1975). As stated in *Gemveto Jewelry Co. v. Lambert Bros., Inc.,* 542 F.Supp. 933, 943, 216 USPQ 976, 984 (S.D.N.Y.1982):

> The gravamen of the fraud defense is that the patentee has failed to discharge his duty of dealing with the examiner in a manner free from the taint of 'fraud or other inequitable conduct'. If such conduct is established in connection with the prosecution of a patent, the fact that the lack of candor did not directly affect *all* the claims in the patent has never been the governing principle. It is the inequitable conduct that generates the unenforceability of the patent and we cannot think of any cases where a patentee partially escaped the consequences of his wrongful acts by arguing that he only committed acts of omission or commission with respect to a limited number of claims. It is an all or nothing proposition. [Emphasis in original.]

* * *

PFIZER, INC. v. INTERNATIONAL RECTIFIER CORP.

United States Court of Appeals, Eighth Circuit, 1976.
538 F.2d 180, 190 USPQ 273, cert. denied 192 USPQ 543 (1977).

GIBSON, CHIEF JUDGE.

This patent infringement case was initially filed by Pfizer, Inc. seeking damages and declaratory and injunctive relief in the Central District of California. The defendants, International Rectifier Corp. (IRC) and USV Pharmaceutical Corp. (USV), answered, pleading that Pfizer's United States Patent No. 3,200,149 is invalid and unenforceable for failure to meet statutory requirements of patentability and for fraud and misconduct before the Patent Office.

* * *

The basic issues in this case are the validity and enforceability of the patent alleged to have been infringed. An infringement defendant in complex litigation should not be permitted to sidestep these main issues by nit-picking the patent file in every minute respect with the effect of trying the patentee personally, rather than the patent. A patentee's oversights are easily magnified out of proportion by one accused of infringement seeking to escape the reach of the patent by hostilely combing the inventor's files in liberal pretrial discovery proceedings. Unjustified damage to professional and social reputations can result, as here, without fostering any corresponding public benefit in the form of inhibiting future improvident grants of patent monopolies.

* * *

The judgment of the District Court is reversed and the case remanded for completion of pretrial proceedings consistent with this opinion, and a plenary trial in a district to be selected by the Judicial Panel on Multidistrict Litigation.

Costs are assessed against defendants.

———

In Eltra Corp. v. Basic, Inc., the District Court in Ohio, 193 USPQ 426 (1977), suggested that an unfounded allegation of fraud "as a smoke screen to divert attention" from basic issues might provide a basis for attorney's fees for the aggrieved party. This case was reversed in the Sixth Circuit, 202 USPQ 630 (1979), the Appeals Court suggesting that "only the most frivolous of allegations should give rise to an award of attorney's fees."

———

TESTIMONY OF THE PATENT EXAMINER:

The testimony of a Patent Examiner has been received in a Federal Trade Commission case with respect to whether misrepresentations were made in the Patent Office proceedings.[f] District Judge Watkins (D.C.Maryland) had this to say when requested to reopen a case to receive testimony of Patent Office Examiners: [g]

> Plaintiff further asks for a reopening of the case to permit the examination of the examiner and assistant examiner who processed both the Bennett and the 2,694,182 and 2,694,183 patents. Affidavits of telephone conversations with these persons are filed. The examiner is reported as saying that if he had not considered 2,694,182 and 2,694,183 patentable over Bennett, he would not have allowed the 2,694,182 and 2,694,183 patents; the assistant examiner is reported as saying that before 2,694,182 and 2,694,183 were issued, he considered that Bennett application. The court sees no reason to reopen the case to receive such evidence, even if it were admissible, which is quite doubtful (despite the court's curiosity as to how examiners, after citing apparently sound bases for objection, finally capitulate without explanation as to how and why their doubts have been overcome). The ex parte affidavits embody nothing more than a claim that the examiners did their duty—which the court assumes—and if the contents were proved, could carry no greater—and dependent upon the experience and ability of the particular examiner, quite possibly less—persuasion than the statutory presumption arising from the mere grant of the patents.

Patent Commissioner Gottschalk, on March 13, 1972, issued an order stating conditions under which a Patent Examiner will be permitted to testify on deposition in patent suits without the need of a subpoena as follows:

> (1) The party proposing to take the testimony will state in writing, that the questions to be asked of the examiner will be phrased to

f. Chas. Pfizer & Co., Inc. v. Federal Trade Commission, 401 F.2d 574, 159 USPQ 193 (6th Cir.1968).

g. Entron of Maryland, Inc. v. Jerrold Electronics Corp., 186 F.Supp. 483, 495, 126 USPQ 328, 337 (D.C.D.Md.1960).

comply with the permissible scope of inquiry as outlined in the protective orders contained in the Court opinions in In re Mayewsky, 162 USPQ 86, 89, and Shaffer Tool Works v. Joy Manufacturing Co., 167 USPQ 170, 171:

> " * * * the scope of the oral depositions of the patent examiners is hereby limited to matters of fact and must not go into hypothetical or speculative areas or the bases, reasons, mental processes, analyses or conclusions of the patent examiners in acting upon the patent applications maturing into the patent [in suit]." 167 USPQ 171.

(2) That in addition to complying with the requirements of Rule 30 of the Federal Rules of Civil Procedure, the party taking the testimony will agree to give notice of the taking of the deposition of the patent examiner to the Solicitor, at least thirty days prior to the date on which the taking of the deposition is desired.

(3) That the party taking the deposition arrange with the Solicitor to notice the deposition at a place convenient to the Patent Office.

Chapter Five

AMENDMENT AND CORRECTION OF PATENTS

A. REISSUE

1. HISTORY AND GENERAL PRINCIPLES

In the early 1800's, the Patent Committee developed the practice of cancelling a surrendered original patent with a defective specification and issuing a new patent with a corrected specification for the remainder of the term of the surrendered patent. This practice which developed without any express statutory authorization was approved by the U.S. Supreme Court in Grant v. Raymond, 31 U.S. (6 Peters) 218, 8 L.Ed. 376 (1832) saying:

> * * * [I]t cannot be doubted that the settled purpose of the United States has ever been, and continues to be, to confer on the authors of useful inventions an exclusive right in their inventions for the time mentioned in their patent. * * * That sense of justice and of right which all feel, pleads strongly against depriving the inventor of the compensation thus solemnly promised, because he has committed an inadvertent or innocent mistake.

> If the mistake should be committed in the Department of State, no one would say that it ought not to be corrected. All would admit that a new patent, correcting the error, and which would secure to the patentee the benefits which the law intended to secure, ought to be issued. And yet the act does not in terms authorize a new patent, even in this case. Its emanation is not founded on the words of the law, but is indispensably necessary to the faithful execution of the solemn promise made by the United States. Why should not the same step be taken for the same purpose, if the mistake has been innocently committed by the inventor himself?

> * * *

In 1832 Congress, presumably in response to Grant v. Raymond, enacted the first reissue statute which embodied the spirit of this decision. The provisions of the reissue statute of 1832 were amplified by the Patent Act of 1836 which was amended in 1837 to allow a patentee to receive several reissue patents for the distinct parts of the subject matter of the surrendered patent and to provide for re-examination of applications for reissue patents. The Patent Act of 1870 added a prohibition on introducing new matter into the specification with further elaboration in the Patent Act of 1874. The reissue provisions of the 1952 Patent Act added an express statutory period of limitation of two years for seeking a reissue patent with broadened claims and changed the effect of a reissue patent as to those who had started to use the invention prior to the reissue.

Sections 251 and 252 of the current Patent Statutes provide for reissue of a patent when the patent is "deemed wholly or partly inoperative or invalid, by reason of a defective specification or drawing, or by reason of the patentee claiming more or less than he had a right to claim" in the patent "through error without any deceptive intention". The patent is reissued "for the invention disclosed in the original patent * * * for the unexpired part of the term of the original patent" upon surrender of the original.

If the reissue application seeks "to enlarge the scope of the claims," it must be filed within two years of grant of the original patent and must be executed by the inventor. Otherwise, the application may be filed by the assignee.

As to any claims or cause of action for infringement of the original patent, "the reissued patent, to the extent that its claims are identical with the original patent, shall constitute a continuation thereof and have effect continuously from the original patent." Section 252 also provides for intervening rights of third parties where "substantial preparation (for manufacture, use or sale) was made before grant of reissue * * * to the extent and under such terms as the court deems equitable for the protection of investments or business commenced before the grant of reissue".

BALL CORPORATION v. THE UNITED STATES

United States Court of Appeals, Federal Circuit, 1984.
729 F.2d 1429, 221 USPQ 289.

SMITH, CIRCUIT JUDGE.

This case presents the question whether a patentee is barred by the recapture rule from securing, through reissue, claims to subject matter previously canceled from the original application. * * *

The invention covered by the Krutsinger patent relates to a dual slot antenna assembly intended for use on missiles. * * *

Following the second office action, Ball added limitations to the claims requiring that a plurality of leads be connected to an edge of the outer conductor. These leads were recited to be spaced-apart at intervals substantially equal to one wavelength at the anticipated operating frequency of the antenna. * * * U.S. patent No. 3,810,183 (the original patent) issued on May 7, 1974, to Ball as assignee, on the basis of the original application, as amended.

Subsequently, Ball decided that it was entitled to claims broad enough to include the single feedline. On July 16, 1975, within the 2-year statutory period for broadened reissue provided in 35 U.S.C. § 251, Ball filed a reissue application. * * *

In support of its reissue application Ball stated that the original patent was partially inoperative because it claimed less than Ball had a right to claim. Ball identified as error the undue limitation of the claims of the original patent to a plurality of feedlines:

> [T]he unwarranted limited scope of our original patent claims were errors [sic] that arose without any deceptive intention as a result of inadequate and/or ineffective communication with our former patent attorney, * * * and/or as a result of an inadequate understanding on our part of the potential effect of recitations in the original patent claim language under United States laws; * * *

U.S. patent No. Re. 29,296 issued on July 5, 1977, on the basis of the reissue application.

* * *

Two issues are raised in this appeal: (1) whether the error alleged by Ball is sufficient as a matter of law under 35 U.S.C. § 251 (1976) to support reissue; and (2) whether Ball is estopped from securing, through reissue, claims covering the single feedline feature.

The Government contends that Ball's deliberate cancelation of the single feedline claims was not error. That act was taken to avoid a prior art rejection and, in the Government's view, the recapture rule bars Ball from securing similar claims through reissue. The Government also contends that the deliberate nature of Ball's acts estops Ball from securing similar claims through reissue. Ball did not appeal the denial of its summary judgment motion but, rather, defends the trial judge's opinion as correct as a matter of law. Resolution of this controversy involves a substantial body of precedent. The parties differ in their interpretation of the law and in their application of it to the facts of this case.

Reissue is not a substitute for Patent Office appeal procedures. Reissue is an extraordinary procedure and must be adequately supported by the circumstances detailed in 35 U.S.C. § 251 (1976) and in the implementing regulations, 37 C.F.R. § 1.175 (1982). The Government asserts that the nature of error that will justify reissue is narrowly circumscribed to ensure that reissue remains the exception and not the rule. Relying on *Edward Miller & Co. v. Bridgeport Brass Co.,* the Government contends that "a mere error of judgment" is not adequate to support reissue; rather the error must be "a real *bona fide* mistake, inadvertently committed."

The 1952 revision of the patent laws made no substantive change in the definition of error under section 251. While deliberate cancellation of a claim cannot ordinarily be considered error, the CCPA has repeatedly held that the deliberate cancellation of claims *may* constitute error, if it occurs without deceptive intent. In *In re Petrow,* the CCPA went so far as to state that error is sufficient where the deliberate cancellation of claims does not amount to an admission that the reissue claims were not patentable at the time the original claims were canceled. Similarly, in *In re Wesseler,* the CCPA stated that error is established where there is no evidence that the appellant intentionally omitted or abandoned the claimed subject matter. Thus, the CCPA has construed the term error under section 251 broadly.

The Ninth Circuit employed a more rigid standard in *Riley v. Broadway-Hale Stores, Inc.* stating: "when the chief element added by reissue has been abandoned while seeking the original patent, the reissue is void." The trial judge sought to determine whether Ball had made a deliberate judgment that claims of substantially the same scope as the new reissue claims would have been unpatentable. The Government, arguing from *Riley*, submits that the trial judge's approach loses sight of the feature given up by a patentee in order to secure the original patent. We decline to adopt the rigid standard applied in *Riley*, in favor of the more liberal approach taken by the CCPA. *Petrow* clearly establishes the vitality of the standard employed by the trial judge under this court's precedent.

Further, the Government argues that we need not reach the issue of claim scope because the sufficiency of error is a threshold issue. While claim scope is no oracle on intent, the Government fails to apprehend its role. Rarely is evidence of the patentee's intent in canceling a claim presented. Thus, the court may draw inferences from changes in claim scope when other reliable evidence of the patentee's intent is not available. Claim scope is not the lodestar of reissue. Rather, the court's reliance on that indicator in the case law appears to be born of practical necessity as the only available reliable evidence.

The Government relies heavily on *Haliczer v. United States,* which also involved a suit under 28 U.S.C. § 1498. The Court of Claims in that case held the reissue claims invalid because the patentee sought to acquire through reissue the *same* claims that had earlier been canceled from the original application. The recapture rule bars the patentee from acquiring, through reissue, claims that are of the *same* or of *broader scope* than those claims that were canceled from the original application. On the other hand, the patentee is free to acquire, through reissue, claims that are *narrower* in scope than the canceled claims. If the reissue claims are narrower than the canceled claims, yet broader than the original patent claims, reissue must be sought within 2 years after grant of the original patent.

Thus, the applicability of the recapture rule and the sufficiency of error under section 251 turn in this case, in the absence of other evidence of the patentee's intent, on the similarity between the reissue and the canceled claims. Narrower reissue claims are allowable; broader reissue claims or reissue claims of the same scope as the canceled claims are not. The subject matter of the claims is not alone controlling. Similarly, the focus is not, as the Government contends, on the specific limitations or on the elements of the claims but, rather, on the *scope* of the claims. * * * He determined that the reissue claims were intermediate in scope—broader than the claims of the original patent yet narrower than the canceled claims.

* * *

The reissue claims are, however, broader in one respect. The canceled claims are limited to an antenna of cylindrical configuration, whereas the reissue claims are not so limited. We are aware of the principle that a claim that is broader in any respect is considered to be broader.

Pursuant to section 251, broadened reissue must be sought within 2 years after issuance of the original patent. The CCPA, in *In re Rogoff*, noted that section 251

> contains no exceptions or qualifications as to time or extent of enlargement. The sole issue, therefore, is whether the claims on appeal enlarge, i.e., broaden, the patent claim.
>
> It is well settled that a claim is broadened, so far as the question of right to reissue is concerned, if it is so changed as to bring within its scope any structure which was not within the scope of the original claim. In other words, a claim is broadened if it is broader in any respect than the original claim, even though it may be narrowed in other respects. * * *

Thus, the principle that a claim is broadened if it is broader in any respect than the original claim serves to effect the bar of section 251 against reissue filed later than 2 years after issuance of the original patent. In this case, Ball filed its application for reissue within the 2-year period for broadened reissue specified in section 251.

We know of no authority applying the above rule to reissue claims relative to the scope of canceled claims within the 2-year period for broadened reissue. Nor do we perceive the wisdom of such extension in this case. The rule is rigid and properly so in that it effects an express statutory limitation on broadened reissue. The recapture rule, however, is based on equitable principles. The rigidity of the broader-in-any-respect rule makes it inappropriate in the estoppel situation presented in this appeal.

Hence, we decline to apply that rule here, where the broader feature relates to an aspect of the invention that is not material to the alleged error supporting reissue. In *Willingham*, the CCPA reversed the rejection of a claim that was narrower than the canceled claim as to one element, although broader as to another element. "The extent to which [deliberate cancellation of a claim from the original application] may also prevent [a patentee] from obtaining other claims differing in form or substance from that cancelled necessarily depends upon the facts in each case and particularly on the reasons for the cancellation." Accordingly, we hold that the reissue claims are not substantially identical in scope to the canceled claims.

As noted *supra*, there is widespread agreement that reissue claims that are narrower than the canceled claims are allowable. In *In re Wadlinger*, the CCPA faced a situation in which the reissue claims were, as the trial judge found here, of "different" scope from the canceled claims. While both the reissue and canceled claims were directed to the same process in *Wadlinger,* the canceled claims were considered broader, resulting in claims of different scope. The reissue claims were held valid. Similarly, we find that the non-material, broader aspects of Ball's reissue claims do not deprive them of their fundamental narrowness of scope relative to the canceled claims. Thus, the reissue claims are sufficiently narrower than the canceled claims to avoid the effect of the recapture rule.

* * *

IN RE WEILER

United States Court of Appeals, Federal Circuit, 1986.
790 F.2d 1576, 229 USPQ 673.

MARKEY, CHIEF JUDGE.

* * * [O]ne of our predecessor courts said "the whole purpose of the [reissue] statute, so far as claims are concerned, is to permit limitations to be added to claims that are too broad or to be taken from claims that are too narrow." *In re Handel,* 312 F.2d 943, 948, 136 USPQ 460, 464 (CCPA 1963).

* * *

Language appearing first in the opinion in *U.S. Industrial Chemicals, Inc. v. Carbide & Carbon Chemicals Corp.,* 315 U.S. 668, 676, 53 USPQ 6, 9–10 (1942), has been picked up and has metamorphosed into a requirement that an applicant show his original "intent to claim" the subject matter of the reissue claim sought. The phrase "intent to claim" does not appear in the statute. It is but judicial shorthand, signifying a means of measuring whether the statutorily required *error* is present. Clearly, a showing that an applicant had an intent to claim matter he did not claim can go a long way to support a finding that error occurred; and, conversely, a showing that an applicant never had any such intent makes a finding of error extremely difficult if not impossible.

* * *

This court has recently moved the "intent to claim" approach toward closer conformity with the statute, describing it as merely one factor "that sheds light upon whether the claims of the reissue application are directed to the same invention as the original patent *and the reissue would correct an inadvertent error in the original patent.*" *In re Hounsfield,* 669 F.2d 1320, 1323, 216 USPQ 1045, 1048 (Fed.Cir.1982) (emphasis added).

* * *

Thus, we arrive at the central question in this appeal, which is not whether there is disclosure, but whether Weiler has established "error" which can be remedied by reissue. The reissue statute was not enacted as a panacea for all patent prosecution problems, nor as a grant to the patentee of a second opportunity to prosecute *de novo* his original application.

The language of *U.S. Industrial Chemicals, Inc. v. Carbide & Carbon Chemicals Corp.*, 315 U.S. at 676, 53 USPQ at 9–10, is relevant here:

> [I]t is not enough that an invention *might have been claimed* in the original patent because it was suggested or indicated in the specification. It must appear from the face of the instrument that what is covered by the reissue was intended to have been *covered* and *secured* by the original. [Emphasis added.]

Weiler and the Solicitor argue as though the "error" to be corrected by reissue were a subjective error. It is not. We do not here deal with "deceptive intention".

Though the term "error" is to be interpreted liberally, *In re Wessler,* 367 F.2d 838, 849, 151 USPQ at 339, 348 (CCPA 1966), Congress did not intend to alter the test of "inadvertence, accident, or mistake" established in relation to the pre-1952 statutes. *In re Wadlinger,* 496 F.2d 1200, 1207, 181 USPQ 826, 831 (CCPA 1974). *See In re Mead,* 581 F.2d 251, 257, 198 USPQ 412, 418 (CCPA 1978) ("conscious choice" not to file continuing application not "error"); *In re Clark,* 522 F.2d 623, 626, 187 USPQ 209, 212 (CCPA 1975) (dereliction in duty of candor not "error"); *In re Byers,* 230 F.2d 451, 454, 109 USPQ 53, 55 (CCPA 1956) (deliberate amendment of claim not "error"). *See also In re Petrow,* 402 F.2d 485, 159 USPQ 449 (CCPA 1968) (cancellation of claim in original application was "error"); *In re Willingham,* 282 F.2d 353, 127 USPQ 211 (CCPA 1960) (cancellation of claim was "error").

* * *

The board's notation that the subject matter of claims 13 and 19 was "not claimed at all" in the original application, and its finding that nothing in the original patent evidences Weiler's "intent to claim" that subject matter, reflect non-statutory language used by courts and others to support and convey the concept that an inventor's failure to claim particular subject matter was not the result of the "error" required by § 251. Having made that notation and finding, the board should have stated the resulting basis (no error) for its decision. That it did not do so does not require reversal in this case, in which the record clearly supports the notation and finding, Weiler has not shown that either was clearly erroneous, and Weiler has shown nothing in the record that would have required the board to determine that his failure to claim the subject matter of claims 13 and 19 was the result of error.

SEATTLE BOX COMPANY, INC. v. INDUSTRIAL CRATING & PACKING, INC.

United States Court of Appeals, Federal Circuit, 1984.
731 F.2d 818, 221 USPQ 568.

NICHOLS, SENIOR CIRCUIT JUDGE.

* * *

I

BACKGROUND

Plaintiff-appellee Seattle Box Company, Inc. ("Seattle Box") and defendant-appellant Industrial Crating and Packing, Inc. ("Industrial") are Washington State corporations which provide oil pipe bundling services to oil companies. * * *

Seattle Box filed this action on July 2, 1980, alleging that Industrial infringed U.S. Patent No. 4,099,617 ("the '617 patent") entitled "Shipping Bundle for Numerous Pipe Lengths." Seattle Box brought the action in its capacity as assignee of the rights in the '617 patent. On August 19, 1980, the United States Patent and Trademark Office ("PTO") reissued the '617 patent, with broadened claims, in U.S. Patent No. Re. 30,373 ("the '373 reissue patent"). Seattle Box also was the assignee of the rights in this patent. On October 10, 1980, Seattle Box amended its complaint to allege infringement of the '373 reissue patent. Industrial answered and counterclaimed, alleging patent invalidity, noninfringement, and patent misuse.

* * *

[Briefly, the patented invention defines a system of stacking ("bundling") tiers of pipes across parallel horizontal beams or sleepers. To ensure that adjacent pipes remain separated, double-concave wooden spacer blocks are used. Stacking these tiers results in a pipe "bundle." The weight of the overhead load is absorbed by the spacer blocks.]

Seattle Box filed an application for a patent on Nist's invention on February 17, 1977. Claim 1 of this application stated that the double-concave spacer block had a "height substantially equal to the thickness of the tier of pipe lengths."

Seattle Box's patent attorney, however, narrowed Claim 1 during the application's prosecution so as to specify that the spacer block had a height only "greater than the diameter of the pipe." Soon after the attorney made this narrowing amendment, although not necessarily because of it, the patent examiner allowed each of the application's claims. The '617 patent issued on July 11, 1978.

On December 1, 1978, Seattle Box filed an application to have the '617 patent reissued with broader claims. Nist averred in support of this application that neither the patent examiner nor the cited prior art required the narrow scope of the issued claims, and that the limitation on the height of the spacer block in his Claim 1 was unnecessary and "arose through inadvertence by counsel." Nist additionally stated that "in reality each overlying or superposed sleeper need only be separated from its underlying companion a distance equal to but not less than the diameter (i.e., the thickness) of the pipes in each tier interposed between the sleepers to avoid forces being applied to squeeze the pipe in bundle stacks or handling operations * * *."

The PTO granted the application for the reissue patent and issued the '373 reissue patent on August 19, 1980. In addition to allowing

Seattle Box to amend Claim 1 to specify a spacer block "of a height *substantially equal to or* greater than the thickness of the tier of pipe length" [emphasis in original], the PTO also allowed five wholly new claims, Claims 8–12.

*   *   *

C. Recapture Rule

Industrial argues that the PTO incorrectly allowed the broadened reissue claims with a scope equivalent to the scope of the preamended claims in the original patent application. The recapture rule does not apply here, however, because there is no evidence that Seattle Box's amendment of its originally filed claims was in any sense an admission that the scope of that claim was not in fact patentable. *See In re Petrow*, 402 F.2d 485, 488, 159 USPQ 449, 451 (CCPA 1968); *see also Ball Corp. v. United States*, 729 F.2d 1429 (Fed.Cir.1984).

IV

LIABILITY

The court must consider Industrial's liability for infringement, if any, during two distinct time frames. The first period extends between the date the original patent issued, July 11, 1978, and the date the reissue patent issued, August 19, 1980. Seattle Box's only enforceable patent rights during this period arise from 35 U.S.C. § 252, which allows claims in a reissue patent to reach back under certain circumstances to the date the original patent issued. The second period begins on the date the reissued patent issued, August 19, 1980. During this period, Seattle Box's broadened patent claims cover a double-concave block with a height "substantially equal to or greater than" the diameter of the separated pipes. We consider the two time periods *seriatim*.

A. Activities Occurring Before the '373 Reissue Patent Issued.

Industrial asserts that the district court erred in finding it liable for infringement done before the '373 reissue patent issued. We agree.

An original patent cannot be infringed once a reissue patent has issued, for the original patent is surrendered. At one point in the history of the American patent law, this surrender precluded any action for infringement for acts done prior to the surrender. Courts would not allow a patentee to *bring* an action in response to acts done before the reissue patent issued since no patent existed upon which one could allege infringement. Courts, moreover, would dismiss for a failure to state a cause of action any action *filed* before the patent was surrendered since the patent sued on no longer existed. Courts acted, in other words, as if the original patent never was. *See* Federico, *Intervening Rights in Patent Reissues*, 30 Geo.Wash.L.Rev. 603, 605 (1962).

To ameliorate the harsh effect of a patent's surrender, Congress has legislated that under certain circumstances claims of the original patent have a form of continuity if carried over to the reissue patent. Congress has incorporated its most recent version of this rule into 35 U.S.C. § 252, the first paragraph of which provides that:

> The surrender of the original patent shall take effect upon the issue of the reissued patent, and every reissued patent shall have the same effect and operation in law, on the trial of actions for causes thereafter arising, as if the same had been originally granted in amended form, but *in so far as the claims of the original and reissued patents are identical,* such surrender shall not affect any action then pending nor abate any cause of action then existing, and the reissued patent, *to the extent that its claims are identical with the original patent,* shall constitute a continuation thereof and have effect continuously from the date of the original patent. [Emphasis supplied.]

Congress, in this statute, has explicitly limited claim continuity to claims in the reissued patent *identical* to claims in the original patent. The statute does not allow the claims of the original patent some other form of survival. The original claims are dead. The statute permits, however, the claims of the reissue patent to reach back to the date the original patent issued, *but only if* those claims are identical with claims in the original patent. With respect to new or amended claims, an infringer's liability commences only from the date the reissue patent is issued.

At issue in this case is Congress' meaning of the word "identical." The district court interpreted "identical" to mean "essentially identical," noting that other courts have interpreted the word "identical" in section 252 in a way which does not limit claim continuity to literally identical claims. It cited *Austin v. Marco Dental Products, Inc.,* 560 F.2d 966, 195 USPQ 529 (9th Cir.1977), *cert. denied,* 435 U.S. 918, 98 S.Ct. 1477, 55 L.Ed.2d 511 (1978) and *Akron Brass Co. v. Elkhart Brass Manufacturing Co.,* 353 F.2d 704, 147 USPQ 301 (7th Cir.1965).

Akron Brass and *Austin* permitted changes in a reissue patent's claims, however, only if *without substance.* In *Akron Brass,* a reissued claim substituted the word "outlet" for the word "inlet" in the original claim. Since it was already clear what was intended, the court there noted, substitution of "outlet" for "inlet" in no way enlarged or modified the substance of the claim. In *Austin,* the court found a claim in the reissued patent "identical" to one in the original patent where a modification was made to "make more precise the language used without substantive changes in the claims." 560 F.2d at 973, 195 USPQ at 534.

Since we are not asked to, we do not have to decide exactly what "identical" does mean. It is clear, though, that "identical" means, *at most,* "without substantive change." Seattle Box, in broadening its claims' scope to cover not only spacer blocks "greater than" but also "substantially equal to" the diameter of the pipes in a bundle, has, in our view, made substantive change to its claims. The original claims cannot reasonably be read as intending, but for some inaccuracy in their expression, the same coverage as the reissue claims. Here, the addition is not a matter of a mere clarification of language to make specific what was always implicit or inherent.

We hold, therefore, that Seattle Box's broadened reissue claims, with the added words "substantially equal to," are not "identical" to its original claims, assuming "identical" means "without substantive change." The district court erred in interpreting "identical" in section 252 to mean "essentially identical." Thus, Seattle Box cannot collect damages for any activities performed before its new and broadened claims issued in the reissue patent. We reverse the trial court's award of damages against Industrial for acts done prior to the date the reissue patent issued.

B. Activities Occurring After the '373 Reissue Patent Issued.

* * * Industrial contends, furthermore, that even if we affirm the district court's finding of infringement under the doctrine of equivalents, the doctrine of intervening rights, 35 U.S.C. § 252, saves Industrial from liability. We consider the infringement argument first.

* * *

2. Section 252—Intervening Rights

When a reissue patent issues, a new patent with presumably valid claims exists. The reissue patent has "the same effect and operation in law, on the trial of actions for causes *thereafter arising,* as if the same had been originally granted in amended form, * * *" 35 U.S.C. § 252 [emphasis supplied].

The language quoted above expressly prevents a court from giving any consideration to the protection of intervening rights. The second paragraph of section 252 modifies the first paragraph, however, so as to protect intervening rights. The second paragraph provides, in pertinent part:

> No reissued patent shall abridge or affect the right of any person * * * who made * * * or used prior to the grant of a reissue anything patented by the reissued patent, to continue the use of * * * the specific thing so made * * * or used, unless the making [or] using * * * of such thing infringes a valid claim of the reissued patent which was in the original patent * * *.

The statute sets forth a single straight-forward test for determining whether the doctrine of intervening rights protects an alleged infringer. The only question to ask under this test is whether claims of the original patent which are repeated in the reissue patent are infringed. Section 252 assumes that a patentee having valid claims in a patent will retain those claims in the reissued patent. If valid claims in the original patent appear unaltered in the reissue patent, the doctrine of intervening rights affords no protection to the alleged infringer.

We have already held, however, that the claims appearing in Seattle Box's reissued patent are substantively different than those in the original patent. That is, Seattle Box repeats *no* claim from its original patent in its reissued patent. Industrial, therefore, may properly raise a defense of intervening rights. *See Cohen v. United States,* 487 F.2d 525, 203 Ct.Cl. 57, 179 USPQ 859 (1973).

When the doctrine of intervening rights is properly raised, the court must consider whether to use its broad equity powers to fashion an appropriate remedy. The second paragraph of section 252 states:

> [The court] may provide for the continued manufacture, use or sale of the thing made * * * or used as specified, or for the manufacture, use or sale of which substantial preparation was made before the grant of the reissue, and it may also provide for the continued practice of any process patented by the reissue, practiced * * * prior to the grant of the reissue, to the extent and under such terms as the court deems equitable for the protection of investments made or business commenced before the grant of the reissue.

The court is given the discretion to fashion a remedy from a wide range of options available to it. The court may, for example, (1) confine Industrial to the use of those double-concave blocks already in existence, (2) permit Industrial to continue in business under conditions which limit the amount, type, or geographical location of its activites, or (3) permit Industrial to continue in business unconditionally.

The trial court, properly to exercise its equity powers, must carefully weigh standard equitable considerations. Since the trial court incorrectly held section 252 inapplicable here, it has yet to make any findings as to the equities of this case. Accordingly, we vacate this portion of the district court's judgment and remand the case for further proceedings consistent with this opinion.

* * *

SEATTLE BOX COMPANY, INC. v. INDUSTRIAL CRATING AND PACKING INC.

United States Court of Appeals, Federal Circuit, 1985.
756 F.2d 1574, 225 USPQ 357.

DAVIS, CIRCUIT JUDGE.

We have before us a sequel to this court's decision in *Seattle Box Co. v. Industrial Crating & Packing, Inc.,* 731 F.2d 818, 221 USPQ 568 (Fed.Cir.1984). * * *

After considering Industrial's argument that intervening rights under 35 U.S.C. § 252 should preclude an award of damages for 224 of the 919 post-reissue bundles, the district court merely stated in its final order on July 19, 1982 that:

> [The 224 bundles] were made after the grant of plaintiff's reissue patent. Defendant has failed to persuade the court that good and valid reasons exist for the court to exercise its discretionary powers in favor of the Defendant as to intervening rights. The Court therefore declines to exercise its discretion in according any intervening rights as to [the 224] bundles.

It is from this order and the ensuing judgment that Industrial appeals.

*   *   *

III.

INTERVENING RIGHTS

The doctrine of intervening rights finds its roots in the second paragraph of 35 U.S.C. § 252: *   *   * This section provides that when certain conditions are present a reissue shall not abridge or affect certain rights of those who acted before the reissue was granted. *See* Federico, *Commentary on the New Patent Act,* 35 U.S.C.A. 1, 46 (1954). Because of such pre-reissue activity, an infringer might enjoy a "personal intervening right" to continue what would otherwise be infringing activity after reissue. *See* 3 Chisum, *Patents,* § 15.02[6] (1984). The underlying rationale for intervening rights is that the public has the right to use what is not specifically claimed in the original patent. *Sontag Chain Stores Co. v. National Nut Co.,* 310 U.S. 281, 290, 60 S.Ct. 961, 965, 84 L.Ed. 1204 (1940). Recapture through a reissue patent of what is dedicated to the public by omission in the original patent is permissible under specific conditions, but not at the expense of innocent parties. *Id.* at 293, 60 S.Ct. at 967 (the defendant, who had built and begun to operate its machines in a form not covered by the original patent, was allowed to continue the post-reissue activity which infringed the reissue patent). Therefore, one may be able to continue to infringe a reissue patent if the court decides that equity dictates such a result.

As we said in our first opinion, once the doctrine of intervening rights is properly raised, the court must consider whether to use its broad equity powers to fashion an appropriate remedy. We also held that the second sentence of the second paragraph in 35 U.S.C. § 252 was to be applied in this case in accordance with equity. Accordingly, the district court should have considered the relevant facts as applied to the portion of the statute which questions whether "substantial preparation was made [by the infringer] before the grant of the reissue." Specifically, the district court's inquiry should have been—and it is now our burden to decide—whether the post-reissue use of the 224 bundles which were made from pre-reissue spacer blocks constituted "substantial preparation" to merit the protection afforded by intervening rights, so as to protect "investments made *   *   * before the grant of reissue." We stress that all those spacer blocks were on hand when the reissue patent issued.

Two sets of the district court's factual findings weigh heavily in the present equitable determination of the application of intervening rights. First, in the district court's initial findings in its first decision, it was established that, prior to the Re '373 patent, Industrial and its patent attorney were fully aware of the '617 patent. Second, the district court found that Industrial continued manufacturing after reissue on the advice of its patent counsel. *Seattle Box Co.,* 217 USPQ at 349–350. This advice-of-counsel was given to Industrial in April 1980, while the '617 patent was still extant, some 3 months before the Re '373 patent issued (August 17, 1980), and over two months before Industrial's patent counsel was even informed by Seattle Box's patent counsel (July 9, 1980) of the reissue patent claims which had been allowed by the examiner. This pre-reissue advice, followed by Industrial, was to hold the concave block height to about 1/16 of an inch shorter than the pipe diameter. *See* 217 USPQ at 349 (W.D.Wash.); and 731 F.2d at 828–29, 221 USPQ at 576 (Fed.Cir.). From these facts, it is apparent that Industrial was attempting to design its spacer blocks (including those it held on the date of the reissue patent) "around" the original '617 patent claims which called for a spacer block with a height "*greater* than the diameter of the pipe" (emphasis added). It turned out that these blocks infringed the reissue patent (Re '373), but they plainly did *not* literally infringe the original '617 patent (and probably did not infringe that patent under the doctrine of equivalents).

To enable Seattle Box now to recapture (in the form of damages for post-reissue use of the 224 bundles made from pre-reissue spacer blocks) matter which Seattle Box had already dedicated to the public in the original patent, at the expense of Industrial which knew of the precise claims of that '617 patent, could open the door to a "gross injustice." *Sontag Stores Co.,* 310 U.S. at 293–94, 60 S.Ct. at 966–67; *see also Gerhardt v. Kinnaird,* 162 F.Supp. 858, 117 USPQ 474 (E.D.Ky.1958) (pre-reissue advice of counsel in building a non-infringing item was one of the equitable factors supporting an application of intervening rights). In these circumstances, the new reissue claims in this case present a compelling case for the application of the doctrine of intervening rights because a person should be able to make business decisions secure in the knowledge that those actions which fall outside the original patent claims are protected. 4 Pat.L.Persp. § 10.8 (2d ed. 1983). Here, the spacer blocks involved were made or acquired, before the reissue, so as not to infringe the then existing '617 patent.

Another fact which weighs heavily is that at the time of reissue Industrial had existing orders for 114 bundles. As we have noted, the remedy of intervening rights is calculated to protect an infringer's preexisting investments and business. Prior business commitments, such as previously placed orders and contracts, are one such example. Silverman, *To Err is Human—Patent Reissues and the Doctrine of Intervening Rights,* 48 J.P.O.S. 696 (1966).

Another important factor courts have considered is whether non-infringing goods can be manufactured from the inventory used to manufacture the infringing product. *Plastic Container Corp. v. Continental Plastics of Oklahoma, Inc.,* 607 F.2d 885, 203 USPQ 27 (10th Cir. 1979) (Miller, J., sitting by designation), *cert. denied,* 444 U.S. 1018, 100 S.Ct. 672, 62 L.Ed.2d 648 (1980). The cost and ease of converting infringing items to non-infringing items is an important equitable consideration because the "infringer" can then avoid a total loss of his good faith investment. * * *

After weighing the facts and factors, we conclude that Industrial should clearly have been allowed to dispose of old inventory remaining on hand at the time of reissue, without liability to Seattle Box. * * *

As Industrial went right on infringing after filling 114 orders and using up the 12,100 blocks, and other items in its inventory on the reissue date, necessarily purchasing more as needed, it is apparent it never intended to exercise equitable intervening rights as such. It does not come into equity with clean hands. Its attitude was one of complete contempt for both the original patent and the reissue. * * * Our suggested possible options in the first opinion respecting application of § 252 were predicated, at least in this author's mind, on Industrial's making a far more impressive show of its equities than it did in fact make. The statute, too, seems to me to visualize equities more impressive than unfilled orders and the mere existence in Industrial's inventory of so many 60 cent blocks, bought in face of the plainest warnings. It seems to contemplate plants built, and matters of that sort.

* * *

Notes

1. There was a suggestion in Ex parte Varga (PTO Bd. of Appeals), 189 USPQ 204 (1973) that the doctrine of Blonder-Tongue Laboratories, Inc. v. University of Illinois Foundation, 402 U.S. 313, 91 S.Ct. 1434, 28 L.Ed.2d 788 (1971), would permit rejection of reissue claims which had been held invalid in a judicial proceedings. This position was modified by the Court of Customs and Patent Appeals, In re Varga, 185 USPQ 47 (1975), which affirmed the rejection of the claims on other grounds. However, the Blonder-Tongue doctrine was held applicable to a reissue application when the patent subject to reissue was held invalid, among other things, for "failure to disclose material facts of which" the inventor was aware. In re Kahn, 202 USPQ 772 (Commr. of Patents and Trademarks, 1979).

2. Reissue applications become subject to public notice in the Official Gazette of the Patent and Trademark Office. The reissue serial number is published together with the filing date, number of the patent being reissued, the name of the applicant and his attorney, and the Examining Group to which the reissue application has been assigned. The reissue applications are subject to inspection by the general public and copies may be made. According to the introduction to the regulations, the public notice "will give interested members of the public an opportunity to submit to the examiner information pertinent to patentability of the reissue application." Vol. 955, page 1054, of Official Gazette, Feb. 22, 1977. Patent Office Rule 11(b).

3. In re Bennett, 766 F.2d 524, 226 USPQ 413 (Fed.Cir.1985): A reissue application which sought to "enlarge the scope" of the original patent claims was filed within two years of the patent date, and executed by the assignee but not the inventor. The Patent Office Board of Patent

Appeals and Interferences refused to permit correction by entry of a declaration by the inventor after the statutory two-year period had elapsed. Relying upon Stoddard v. Dann, infra page 578, the Federal Circuit, sitting en banc, reversed.

4. In re Wilder, 736 F.2d 1516, 222 USPQ 369 (Fed.Cir.1984): In a reissue application, applicant's attorney filed a statement that he "did not fully appreciate" the true nature and scope of the invention * * * and thus did not prepare claims of broad enough scope." The court held:

An attorney's failure to appreciate the full scope of the invention is one of the most common sources of defects in patents. The fact that the error could have been discovered at the time of prosecution with a more thorough patentability search or with improved communication between the inventors and the attorney does not, by itself, preclude a patent owner from correcting defects through reissue. * * * We accordingly reverse the board's rejection for failure to allege error correctable through reissue.

5. In re Anthony, 230 USPQ 467 (PO BA 1986): Deliberate filing of a terminal disclaimer to overcome a double patenting is not "error" that would permit reissue to cancel the disclaimer.

B. REEXAMINATION

Sections 301–307 of the Patent Statutes, enacted in 1980, provide a vehicle through which the patentee or a third party may request the Commissioner to reexamine an issued patent on the basis of prior art patents or printed publications. The request must be in writing, accompanied by the established fee ($1,770.00 in the fee schedule of 1985), and a detailed application of the cited art to each claim to be reexamined. (§§ 301 and 302)

The Commissioner must decide within three months whether "a substantial new question of patentability" is presented (§ 303). If the Commissioner decides against ordering reexamination, a portion ($1,200.00) of the fee is refunded.

If the request is filed by a third party, a copy of the request is served on the patent owner (§ 302), but the patent owner may not respond until (and unless) the Commissioner orders reexamination. The patent owner may then respond, requesting amendment of the patent claims if appropriate, and serving the response on the requester (§ 304). The reexamination process then proceeds ex parte as with a normal application (§§ 304 and 305) except that such prosecution and any appeal must be "conducted with special dispatch within the Office."

Reexamination proceedings are terminated by issuance of a certificate showing any changes of or additions to the patent claims (§ 307). Reexamination requests and certificates are published weekly in the Patent Office Official Gazette, and the files are open to the public (Rule 11(c) and (d)).

"No proposed amendment or new claim enlarging the scope of a claim of the patent will be permitted" in a reexamination proceeding

(§ 305). Furthermore, any amended or new claim is subject to "intervening rights" with the same effect "as that specified in section 252 * * * for reissued patents" (§ 307).

IN RE ETTER

United States Court of Appeals, Federal Circuit, 1985.
756 F.2d 852, 221 USPQ 1.

MARKEY, CHIEF JUDGE.

Appeal from a decision of the Board of Appeals (board) of the United States Patent and Trademark Office (PTO) affirming the examiner's final rejection in a reexamination proceeding of claims 1 through 9, all of the claims of United States Patent No. 4,133,034 (the '034 patent), issued January 2, 1979 to Berwyn E. Etter, as nonpatentable under 35 U.S.C. § 103 in view of prior art. We *affirm.*

* * *

The examiner accepted Etter's contention that the '034 patent enjoyed a statutory presumption of validity, 35 U.S.C. § 282, during reexamination, but viewed the presumption as having been overcome. Further, he said the presumption had been weakened by prior art (Azure and Lowell) not earlier cited to nor considered by the PTO.

* * *

Respecting the presumption of validity, the board noted numerous reasons for holding that it did not attach to claims undergoing reexamination. * * *

Etter's basic contention—that § 282 must be applied in reexamination proceedings—misconstrues the purposes for which that statute and the reexamination statutes were enacted. Review of the statutes, legislative history, regulations, and case law compels the view that § 282 is not applicable to claims about which "a substantial new question of patentability," 35 U.S.C. § 305, is under consideration in a reexamination proceeding. Though the board decision here would be correct in any event, we discuss the issue because of its foundational relationship to Etter's appeal and the need for clarification of guidance offered the board and bar.

* * *

It is true that the question has "tempest in a teapot" overtones, for the PTO will reject or cancel claims it considers unpatentable, as is its duty, whether § 282 is or is not considered applicable. The need for clarity in the law and for avoidance of unnecessary disputes, however, has prompted this court to consider the question *in banc.*

Section 282 provides that "[t]he burden of establishing invalidity of a patent or any claim thereof shall rest on the party *asserting such invalidity.*" (Emphasis added.). As this court noted in *Stratoflex, Inc. v. Aeroquip Corp.,* 713 F.2d 1530, 218 USPQ 718 (Fed.Cir.1983):

    The presumption, like all legal presumptions, is a procedural device, not substantive law. It does require the decisionmaker to employ a decisional approach that starts with the acceptance of the patent claims as valid and that looks to *the challenger* for proof of the contrary. Thus *the party asserting invalidity* not only has the procedural burden of proceeding first and establishing a prima-facie case, but the burden of persuasion on the merits remains with that party until final decision * * * With all evidence in, *the trial court* must determine whether the party on which the statute imposes the burden of persuasion has carried that burden. [Emphasis added.]

713 F.2d at 1534, 218 USPQ at 875.

The foregoing description in *Stratoflex* coincides with the inclusion of § 282 in Chapter 29 of title 35, entitled "Remedies for Infringement of Patent, and Other Actions". Both recognize that the presumption is operative to govern procedure in *litigation* involving validity of an *issued* patent. A statute setting rules of procedure and assigning burdens to litigants in a court trial does not automatically become applicable to proceedings before the PTO. Nor can it acquire an independent evidentiary role in any proceeding.

As said in the legislative history of Chapter 30 of title 35 ("Prior Art Citations to Office and Reexamination of Patents"), reexamination "will permit any party to petition the patent office to review the efficacy of a patent, following its issuance, on the basis of new information about pre-existing technology which may have *escaped review at the time of the initial examination* of the application." House Report No. 66–1307, 96th Cong., 2d Sess. (1980), 3–4, *reprinted in* 1980 U.S.Code Cong. & Ad.News 6460, 6462 (emphasis added). Reexamination is thus neutral, the patentee and the public having an equal interest in the issuance and maintenance of valid patents.

The statute, 35 U.S.C. § 305, provides that "reexamination will be conducted according to the procedures established for initial examination under the provisions of sections 132 and 133 of this title." The actual reexamination is conducted *ex parte*. 37 CFR 1.550(a) (1983). Patent claims are reexamined only in light of patents or printed publications under 35 U.S.C. §§ 102, 103, and only new or amended claims are also examined under 35 U.S.C. §§ 112 and 132. 37 CFR 1.552; MPEP § 2258.[4] The focus of the limited proceedings under Chapter 30 thus returns essentially to that present in an initial examination, i.e., to a time at which no presumption of validity had been created.

The innate function of the reexamination process is to increase the reliability of the PTO's action in issuing a patent by reexamination of patents thought "doubtful." House Report at 3. When the patent is

4. If a patent owner requests reexamination, but desires consideration of wider issues, e.g., prior public use or sale, he must obtain such consideration by filing a reissue application. 37 CFR 1.552; MPEP §§ 2212, 2258. The present case involves a non-patentee requestor; it should be remembered, however, that reexamination may be a boon to patentees whose patents may be thereby strengthened, and that the actual reexamination procedure itself should be the same whoever be the requestor.

concurrently involved in litigation, an auxiliary function is to free the court from any need to consider prior art without the benefit of the PTO's initial consideration. In a very real sense, the intent underlying reexamination is to "start over" in the PTO with respect to the limited examination areas involved, and to *re* examine the claims, and to *examine* new or amended claims, as they would have been considered if they had been originally examined in light of all of the prior art of record in the reexamination proceeding. That intent is reflected in 35 U.S.C. § 303, which requires the Commissioner to determine whether "a substantial new question of patentability" has been raised, and in 35 U.S.C. § 304, which provides for initiation of reexamination by the Commissioner *sua sponte*.

The intent that reexamination proceedings and court actions involving challenges to validity be distinct and independent is reflected in the legislative history of § 303, which notes that denial of a request for reexamination does not deprive the requestor (if not the patent owner) "of any legal right" to contest validity in subsequent court proceedings. House Report at 6466. That "legal right" may be exercised as a matter of right, but determination of whether a "substantial new question of patentability" exists, and therefore whether reexamination may be had, is discretionary with the Commissioner, and, as § 303 provides, that determination is final, i.e., not subject to appeal.[5]

That a patentee may request reexamination, and has the opportunity in the PTO of distinguishing art newly cited by the examiner, 37 CFR 1.530(c), and may amend his claims under reexamination, 35 U.S.C. § 305, further distinguish reexamination from litigation. It is of no moment that the examiner's burden of showing a basis for rejection in the examination and reexamination processes is not described in the "clear and convincing" terms applicable under § 282 to a litigant challenging validity of an issued patent. During the examination processes, allowances of claims raise no presumption and may be withdrawn. That one challenging validity in court bears the burden assigned by § 282, that the same party may request reexamination upon submission of art not previously cited, and that, if that art raises a substantial new question of patentability, the PTO may during reexamination consider the same and new and amended claims in light of that art free of any presumption, are concepts not in conflict. On the contrary, those concepts are but further indication that litigation and reexamination are distinct proceedings, with distinct parties, purposes, procedures, and outcomes. In the former, a litigant who is attacking the validity of a patent bears the burden set forth in § 282.

5. The inquiry occasioned by a request for reexamination is solely whether a reexamination order should issue and is not directed toward resolution of validity. The requestor's burden is simply to show a basis for issuance of the order, a burden unrelated to that assigned in § 282. A refusal of reexamination leaves untouched the § 282 presumption to which the patent is entitled in the courtroom. Similarly, a reexamination may involve only certain claims, e.g., those in litigation, and the newly cited prior art may bear no relation to other claims, to which the presumption of validity would remain attached in future litigation involving those claims.

In the latter, an examiner is not attacking the validity of a patent, but is conducting a subjective examination of claims in the light of prior art.

In *In re Yamamoto*, 740 F.2d 1569, 222 USPQ 934 (Fed.Cir.1984), this court said that claims subject to reexamination will "be given their broadest reasonable interpretation consistent with the specification, and limitations appearing in the specification are not to be read into the claims." 740 F.2d at 1571, 222 USPQ at 936. That standard is applied in considering rejections entered in the course of prosecution of original applications for patent. *See In re Prater*, 415 F.2d 1393, 1404–05, 162 USPQ 541, 550–51 (CCPA 1969). As noted in *Yamamoto*:

> [a]n applicant's ability to amend his claims to avoid cited prior art distinguishes proceedings before the PTO from proceedings in federal district courts on issued patents. When an application is pending in the PTO, the applicant has the ability to correct errors in claim language and adjust the scope of claim protection as needed. This opportunity is not available in an infringement action in district court * * *.
>
> The same policies warranting the PTO's approach to claim interpretation when an original application is involved have been held applicable to reissue proceedings because the reissue provision, 35 U.S.C. § 251, permits amendment of the claims to avoid prior art. [Citation omitted.] The reexamination law * * * gives patent owners the same right * * *

740 F.2d at 1572, 222 USPQ at 936.

Claims in a reissue application enjoy no presumption of validity. *In re Sneed*, 710 F.2d 1544, 1550 n. 4, 218 USPQ 385, 389 n. 4 (Fed.Cir. 1983). Though reissue and reexamination proceedings are distinct, the focus of both is on curing defects which occurred during a proceeding in the PTO, which was responsible for original issuance of the patent.

Etter cites language in *In re Andersen*, 743 F.2d 1578, 223 USPQ 378 (Fed.Cir.1984), as appearing to require application of § 282 in reexamination proceedings. At oral argument, the PTO solicitor indicated that *Andersen* has been understood by and accepted in the PTO as establishing that requirement.

The court in *Andersen* dealt with Andersen's argument that any doubt must be resolved in his favor under (1) a judicially imposed "rule of doubt," or (2) as "part of the presumption of validity." The court rejected (1), citing *In re Naber*, 503 F.2d 1059, 183 USPQ 245 (CCPA 1974), and rejected (2), noting that the presumption does not embrace a rule of doubt. The court agreed with Andersen's statement that reexamination should not circumvent the burden "placed on an infringer during litigation." As above indicated, that is a truism, the litigation and reexamination processes being distinct. The court's discussion of the workings of the presumption in the face of new art, and the cases cited, all related to operation of the presumption in litigation.

Nonetheless, recognizing that *Andersen* may be and has been read as holding that claims must be presumed valid under § 282 in reexamination proceedings, the court has *sua sponte* taken this case *in banc* to clarify the law as set forth in this opinion.

No statutory language and no legislative history indicates any support for a requirement that the provisions of 35 U.S.C. § 282 must be applied in the consideration of claims involved in reexamination proceedings. Indeed, all available indications are to the contrary. We hold, therefore, that § 282 has no application in reexamination proceedings.

It is at best incongruous to apply a trial court procedural rule to the examination of claims in the PTO. Moreover, because this court and one of its predecessors has consistently held that the PTO examiner has the burden of showing a basis under the statute, 35 U.S.C., for each rejection, injection of the presumption into the examination process could add nothing but legalistic confusion.

This court has repeatedly pointed out that the § 282 presumption is a rule of procedure placing the burden of persuasion on him who attacks a patent's validity. There is no such attacker in a reexamination, and hence no one on whom that burden may be placed.[6] In litigation, where a patentee cannot amend his claims, or add new claims, the presumption, and the rule of claim construction (claims shall be construed to save them if possible), have important roles to play. In reexamination, where claims can be amended and new claims added, and where no litigating adversary is present, those roles and their rationale simply vanish.

The patent right is a right to exclude. The statute, 35 U.S.C. § 261, says that "patents shall have the attributes of personal property." The essence of all property is the right to exclude, and the patent property right is certainly not inconsequential. It is, nonetheless, created by a grant from the government. When a "substantial question" exists respecting the correctness of that grant, it does not conflict but coincides with the nature of the grantee's right when the government reexamines the propriety of the grant it has made, and thereafter reaffirms the grant, substitutes a new grant (amended or new claims), or withdraws the grant in whole or in part (the last being subject to review in this court).

*   *   *

6. No third party is involved when reexamination is requested by the patentee or initiated *sua sponte* by the Commissioner. When a third party (whether or not an alleged infringer, and whether or not suit has been filed) is the requestor, that party is heard only on whether "a substantial new question" exists. Absent a "substantial new question", an alleged infringer cannot "force" a patentee back into the PTO. Contrary to indications in the concurrence, the reexamination *per se* of the claims is entirely *ex parte*. Whether a requestor, or other party, is permitted to intervene in an appeal to this court (the intervenor being thereby bound by the decision on appeal) is discretionary with this court. In all events, concentration on those instances when an alleged infringer is present at the requesting stage should not influence a decision on whether § 282 applies in the ex parte reexamination proceeding.

NIES, CIRCUIT JUDGE, with whom SMITH and BISSELL, CIRCUIT JUDGES, join, concurring.

*   *   *

This case illustrates the advantage of the new reexamination procedure. It worked here precisely as proponents of the legislation envisaged. What has resulted, however, in my view, is an easy case making bad law, not unusual with dicta. The majority decision finds a negation of the statutory presumption that is not expressed in the statute. Further, the majority opinion cannot be justified on the grounds that it is necessary to achieve the statutory objectives. Indeed, this decision can only have a chilling effect on voluntary use of the new procedure by patent owners, which was to be one of its prime objectives. H.R.Rep. No. 1307, 96th Cong., 2d Sess. 4, *reprinted in* 1980 U.S.Code Cong. & Ad.News 6460, 6463.

*   *   *

The statutory provision in 35 U.S.C. § 282 is absolute:

A patent shall be presumed valid.

Nothing in the reexamination chapter, 35 U.S.C. §§ 301–307, states otherwise. Nothing in the legislative history indicates that Congress intended a patent owner involved in reexamination to "start over" to resecure his patent. On the contrary, the chapter is directed simply to resolution of a new question of patentability under 35 U.S.C. §§ 102 or 103. *   *   *

The presumption of validity places on the challenger of a patent the burden of coming forward with evidence to establish facts which may lead to the conclusion that the patent is invalid. *SSIH Equipment S.A. v. U.S. Int'l Trade Comm'n,* 718 F.2d 365, 375, 218 USPQ 678, 687 (Fed.Cir.1983). The challenger bears the burden of proof of such facts, as well as the ultimate burden of persuasion on the legal issue of validity. *Stratoflex, Inc. v. Aeroquip Corp.,* 713 F.2d 1530, 1534, 218 USPQ 871, 875 (Fed.Cir.1983). The PTO acknowledges that it bears these burdens in examination of an original application or in reexamination of patent claims. *   *   *

Notes

1. Ex parte Neuwirth, 229 USPQ 71, 72–73 (BPAI 1985):

Having considered the entire record in this matter, we agree with the examiner that the introduction of the term "substantially" as a modifier for "rounded bottom wall" in claim 16 added by way of amendment in this reexamination proceeding constitutes a broadening and hence an enlargement of the scope of claim 1. While the decision of the examiner finally rejecting claim 16 was on the basis of 35 U.S.C. § 112, first paragraph, the proper basis for a rejection based on broadening a claim in a reexamination proceeding is 35 U.S.C. § 305.

35 U.S.C. § 305 states, in part,

No proposed amended or new claim enlarging the scope of a claim of the patent will be permitted in a reexamination proceeding under this chapter.

"Substantially rounded" must mean something different than "rounded" to preclude an identity between claims 1 and 16. The scope of claim 16 with a "substantially rounded" bottom wall would encompass both "rounded" and "less rounded" bottom walls. That is, the expression "substantially rounded bottom wall" would encompass bottom walls not previously encompassed by language specifying a "rounded bottom wall." Accordingly, we hold introduction of the term "substantially" as a modifier for "rounded bottom wall" broadens the scope of the claim contrary to this statutory provision.

We therefore affirm the decision of the examiner finally rejecting claim 16 on the basis that it constitutes a broadened claim in contravention of 35 U.S.C. § 305.

* * *

2. In Kaufman Co., Inc. v. Lantech, 807 F.2d 970, 1 USPQ2d 1202 (Fed.Cir.1986), referring to Seattle Box II, supra, the court concluded that the test for claim "identity" in a reexamination patent, for purposes of pre-reexamination infringement liability, is the same as that applied to a reissued patent under § 252—i.e. "without substantive change."

GOULD v. CONTROL LASER CORPORATION

United States Court of Appeals, Federal Circuit, 1983.
705 F.2d 1340, 217 USPQ 985.

Markey, Chief Judge.

* * *

Appellants appealed from a February 3, 1983 order of the United States District Court for the Middle District of Florida staying proceedings before it until conclusion of a reexamination by the Patent and Trademark Office (PTO) of appellants' U.S. Patent No. 4,053,845. Appellees have moved for dismissal for lack of jurisdiction, asserting that the order for stay is not a "final" decision and is not therefore reviewable by this court.

* * *

The present stay is not for such a protracted or indefinite period as to render its issuance an abuse of discretion. "[R]eexamination proceedings * * * including any appeal to the Board of Appeals, will be conducted with special dispatch. * * *" 35 U.S.C. § 305 (Supp. V 1981). Assuming the PTO decision on reexamination is adverse to the patent holder and may therefore be appealed to this court, the stay would not be for a protracted or indefinite period of sufficient length to render its issuance a "final" decision.

* * *

The present stay has thus not terminated the action but has merely shifted to the PTO an issue (patent claim validity) involved in the dispute before the district court. One purpose of the reexamination procedure is to eliminate trial of that issue (when the claim is canceled) or to facilitate trial of that issue by providing the district court with the expert view of the PTO (when a claim survives the reexamination proceeding). Early versions of what became the reexamination statute, 35 U.S.C. §§ 301–307 (Supp. V 1981), expressly provided for a stay of court proceedings during reexamination. S. 1679, 96th Cong., 1st Sess. § 310 (1979); H.R. 5075, 96th Cong., 1st Sess. § 310 (1979); S. 2446, 96th Cong., 2d Sess. § 310 (1980). An express provision was deemed unnecessary, however, as explained in the House report:

> The bill does not provide for a stay of court proceedings. It is believed by the committee that *stay provisions are unnecessary in that such power already resides with the Court* to prevent costly pretrial maneuvering which attempts to *circumvent* the reexamination procedure. It is anticipated that these measures provide a useful and necessary *alternative* for challengers and for patent owners to test the validity of United States patents in an efficient and relatively inexpensive manner. (emphasis added).

H.R.Rep. No. 1307 Part I, 96th Cong., 2d Sess. 4 (1980), U.S.Code Cong. & Admin.News 1980, pp. 6460, 6463.

When a district court stays patent validity proceedings before it until completion of a reexamination proceeding, that stay must be accepted if the purpose of the reexamination statute is to be preserved.

* * *

NATIONAL TRACTOR PULLERS ASS'N INC. v. WATKINS

United States District Court of Illinois, E.D., 1980.
205 USPQ 892.

[Excerpt Only]

The weight to be given to a finding made by the Patent Office in a contested proceeding was considered by the Supreme Court in Morgan v. Daniels, 152 U.S. 120 (1894). The court adopted a test requiring that the Patent Office decision must be accepted as controlling upon that question of fact in any subsequent suit between the same parties unless the contrary is established by testimony which in character and amount carries thorough conviction.

Consistent with the "thorough conviction" test enunciated in Morgan v. Daniels, the less new evidence there is before the district court in a subsequent proceeding, the more blatant the factual errors of the Patent Office must be before the district court is justified in reversing the Patent Office decision. Rex Chainbelt Inc. v. Borg-Warner Corp., 477 F.2d 481, 177 USPQ 549 (7th Cir., 1973).

This court, therefore, finds that where the validity of a patent has been tested in a protested reissue proceeding in the United States Patent and Trademark Office, and where that Office has determined that the original patent was properly granted, this court will not find contrary to the findings of the Patent Office absent a thorough conviction supported by clear and convincing evidence that the Patent Office's decision was erroneous.[*]

JOHNSON & JOHNSON, INC. v. WALLACE A. ERICKSON & CO.

United States Court of Appeals, Seventh Circuit, 1980.
627 F.2d 57, 206 USPQ 873.

SPRECHER, CIRCUIT JUDGE.

The question in this appeal is whether a patentee can be compelled to initiate reissue proceedings in the Patent Office prior to, or as a condition precedent to, adjudication of the judicial proceedings.

In addition to the court in this case, several district courts have compelled reissue proceedings, usually in company with the granting of a stay of judicial proceedings. See Alpine Engineering Products, Inc. v. Automated Building Components, Inc., No. 77–6291–Civ–JLK (S.D.Fla. February 1, 1978); K–Jack Engineering Co. v. Pete's Newsrack, Inc., No. 77–3184–HP (C.D.Cal. June 6, 1978); Lee-Boy Mfg. Co. v. Puckett, 202 U.S.P.Q. 573 (N.D.Ga. September 15, 1978); Choat v. Rome Industries, Inc., 480 F.Supp. 387 (N.D.Ga.1979); In re Yarn Processing Patent Validity Litigation, 448 P.T.C.J. 7 (S.D.Fla. September 7, 1979); Sheller Globe Corp. v. Mobay Chemical Corp., No. 78–70563 (E.D.Mich. January 24, 1980).

Other district courts have denied motions by alleged infringers to compel patentees to initiate reissue proceedings. See RCA Corp. v. Applied Digital Data Systems, 467 F.Supp. 99 (D.Del.1979); Bielomatik Leuze & Co. v. Southwest Tablet Mfg. Co., 204 U.S.P.Q. 226 (N.D.Tex. August 22, 1979); Antonious v. Kamata-Ri & Co., 204 U.S.P.Q. 294 (D.Md. October 2, 1979).

*   *   *

None of the district court cases cited above, nor Erickson in its briefs, has advised us by what authority a district court, prior to a trial on the merits, can require a patentee to submit and surrender his patent right to the Patent Office as a condition to pursuing his remedies against an alleged infringer. If such power were authorized, it would be a taking of property without due process of law. If such power were authorized to be exerted upon the discretion of the district court, it would raise problems of equal protection.

We do not reach these constitutional questions, however, because neither Congress nor the Commissioner of Patents and Trademarks has authorized reissue proceedings to be initiated by anyone other than the inventor or the assignees of the patent right. Congress has not yet deemed it proper to vest district courts with the power to initiate reissue proceedings, nor do courts possess inherent power which extends to compulsion upon patentees to seek reissue. The Commissioner

[*] But see Mooney v. Brunswick Corp., 489 F.Supp. 544, 206 USPQ 121 (D.C.E.Wis. 1980).

can only proceed as far as Congress has declared, and he consequently has established in his regulations that patentees alone may initiate reissue proceedings.

C. DISCLAIMERS

The first disclaimer statute was enacted in 1837 to ameliorate the previously developed common law rule that if any one claim of a patent was invalid, all of the claims were invalid. The disclaimer statute of 1837 in effect provided that if without unreasonable neglect or delay the invalid claims were cancelled, an action for infringement could be brought on any of the remaining claims which might be valid. Under the first disclaimer statute and its successors in the Patent Acts of 1870 and 1874, patentees filed disclaimers which attempted to broaden the scope of original combination claims by deleting elements thereof or to add elements materially altering and narrowing the claimed combination to include improvements developed by the patentee or even his competitors after the patent issued. These inequitable and sometimes fraudulent uses of disclaimers produced much confusion and uncertainty in the reported decisions and in 1942 probably influenced the United States Supreme Court to declare that:

> * * * [T]he revised claims change the combination set out in the original claims. The disclaimers do more than delete a "distinct and separable matter * * * without mutilating or changing what is left standing"; they change the character of the claimed invention and are therefore unauthorized by the disclaimer statute. Hailes v. Albany Stove Co., 123 U.S. 582, 587.

> If an alteration of one of the essential elements of a claimed combination were permissible at all, it would be under the reissue statute, Rev.Stat. § 4916, 35 U.S.C.A. § 64, which grants rights only from the date of reissue and after consideration by the patent office. Altoona Theatres v. Tri-Ergon Corp., supra, 491. To permit such substantial alterations under the disclaimer statute, which, where applicable, gives effect to the revised claims from the date of the original issue without any consideration by the patent office, would be contrary to the policy of the patent laws. In the words of Mr. Justice Bradley, it would permit "a man * * * by merely filing a paper drawn up by his solicitor, [to] make to himself a new patent." Hailes v. Albany Stove Co., supra, 587. Cf. Brooks v. Fiske, 15 How. 212, 219. It would also retroactively create possibilities of innocent infringement where no one would reasonably have suspected them to exist.

> The courts below properly decided that the attempted disclaimers here invalidated the claims in controversy.

Hence, the Patent Act of 1952 restricted disclaimers to whole or complete claims, eliminated the need to disclaim invalid claims of a patent in order to bring an action to recover on the claims thereof which may be valid, and omitted the provision regarding delay. Thus, under the 1952 Patent Act, revision of the scope of a claim of an issued patent must be accomplished by a reissue patent. The 1952 Patent Act also added an entirely new provision authorizing disclaimer or dedication to the public of the entire or any terminal part of the term of a patent. These terminal disclaimer provisions have been used primarily in situations involving double patenting which are discussed in Chapter Two, Section H, 3, C.

The 1952 Patent Act provides:

35 U.S.C.A. § 253. Disclaimer

Whenever, without any deceptive intention, a claim of a patent is invalid the remaining claims shall not thereby be rendered invalid. A patentee, whether of the whole or any sectional interest therein, may, on payment of the fee required by law, make disclaimer of any complete claim, stating therein the extent of his interest in such patent. Such disclaimer shall be in writing and recorded in the Patent Office; and it shall thereafter be considered as part of the original patent to the extent of the interest possessed by the disclaimant and by those claiming under him.

In like manner any patentee or applicant may disclaim or dedicate to the public the entire term, or any terminal part of the term, of the patent granted or to be granted.

35 U.S.C.A. § 288. Action for Infringement of a Patent Containing an Invalid Claim

Whenever, without deceptive intention, a claim of a patent is invalid, an action may be maintained for the infringement of a claim of the patent which may be valid. The patentee shall recover no costs unless a disclaimer of the invalid claim has been entered at the Patent Office before the commencement of the suit.

Notes

1. The '449 patent in suit issued on June 12, 1956. On June 28, 1956, plaintiff, as assignee of the '449 patent, filed a disclaimer disclaiming claim 10 of the '449 patent. Claim 10 is dependent upon claim 6, one of the '449 claims in suit. Defendant contends that plaintiff is estopped to charge infringement of claim 6 because of the disclaimer of claim 10. Defendant's contention is without merit. The Patent Office allows an invention to be defined through varying the scope of claim coverage. Through this practice, structures defined by a claim which has been disclaimed may be covered by other claims not disclaimed. The construction of a patent, after a disclaimer has been properly entered, must be the same that it would have been if the matter so disclaimed had never been claimed. Dunbar v. Myers, 94 U.S. (4 Otto) 187, 194, 24 L.Ed. 34 (1876). Soundscriber Corp. v. United States, 360 F.2d 954, 148 USPQ 298, 175 Ct.Cl. 644 (1966).

2. Defendant argues that by thus disclaiming plaintiff admitted the invalidity of the patent and its unenforceability against defendant's structure. No case is cited in support of this contention and we do not think it is the law. In fact, plaintiff cites cases which appear to support a contrary rule. Dunbar v. Myers, 94 U.S. (4 Otto) 187, 194, 24 L.Ed. 34; Smith, Kline

& French Laboratories v. Clark & Clark, 62 F.Supp. 971, 986 (D.N.J.1945) (modified by the court of appeals on other grounds, 157 F.2d 725 (3d Cir. 1946)). Neither will we go as far as defendant would have us do and hold that the disclaimer action entirely destroyed the presumption of validity as to the remaining claims. We do think, however, that it materially detracts from the weight to be attached to such presumption and negates plaintiff's argument of an enhanced presumption arising from the careful and meticulous scrutiny exercised by the Patent Office. * * * The most that can be said for the remaining claims is that they carry no more than the ordinary presumption. Hoover Co. v. Mitchell Mfg. Co., 269 F.2d 795, 122 USPQ 314 (7th Cir.1959).

D. MISTAKES

The following provisions for correcting mistakes in issued patents are self-explanatory and hence no cases or materials interpreting these sections are provided.

35 U.S.C.A. § 254. Certificate of Correction of Patent Office Mistake

Whenever a mistake in a patent, incurred through the fault of the Patent Office, is clearly disclosed by the records of the Office, the Commissioner may issue a certificate of correction stating the fact and nature of such mistake, under seal, without charge, to be recorded in the records of patents. A printed copy thereof shall be attached to each printed copy of the patent, and such certificate shall be considered as part of the original patent. Every such patent, together with such certificate, shall have the same effect and operation in law on the trial of actions for causes thereafter arising as if the same had been originally issued in such corrected form. The Commissioner may issue a corrected patent without charge in lieu of and with like effect as a certificate of correction.

35 U.S.C.A. § 255. Certificate of Correction of Applicant's Mistake

Whenever a mistake of a clerical or typographical nature, or of minor character, which was not the fault of the Patent Office, appears in a patent and a showing has been made that such mistake occurred in good faith, the Commissioner may, upon payment of the required fee, issue a certificate of correction, if the correction does not involve such changes in the patent as would constitute new matter or would require re-examination. Such patent, together with the certificate, shall have the same effect and operation in law on the trial of actions for causes thereafter arising as if the same had been originally issued in such corrected form.

Section 255 and the last sentence of Section 254 were new provisions added by the 1952 Patent Act. The first two sentences of Section 254 codify the substance of a practice developed by the Patent Office which was first specifically authorized by statute in 1925 (March 4, 1952, c. 535, § 1, 43 Stat. 1268). In 1975 these statutes were amended to substitute for "Patent Office" the extended title "Patent and Trademark Office."

E. CORRECTING ERRORS IN NAMING INVENTORS

The 1952 Patent Act provided in section 256 (supra, p. 105–6) for the first time for the correction of errors in the naming of inventors in issued patents. Section 256 is a companion to Section 116 which permits the correction of errors in naming inventors in pending patent applications. The requirements of this section that the omission or misjoinder of an inventor occur by "error and without any deceptive intention" is generally considered to have the same meaning as the corresponding requirements of Sections 116 and 251.

Notes

1. Control Data Corp. v. Iowa State Univ. Research Foundation, Inc., 444 F.2d 406, 170 USPQ 374 (4th Cir.1971): The principal issue raised in this interlocutory appeal is whether a district court may correct a patent by adding the name of a joint inventor when the named inventor, or his assignee, does not agree to the correction.   *   *   *

Section 256 is a remedial provision of the Patent Act of 1952. Because Article I, § 8 of the Constitution authorizes an exclusive right in discoveries to inventors and none others, the law has been strictly construed to grant patents only to the true inventors. Thus, a patent issued to but one of joint inventors, upon representation that he is the sole inventor, is void. Similarly, if more persons than the true inventors are named, the patent is void. See Shreckhise v. Ritchie, 160 F.2d 593, 595 (4th Cir.1947); 1 Deller's Walker on Patents 184 (2d ed. 1964). Whether a patent is the work of one or several inventors acting jointly is often a question that is not free from difficulty. See, e.g., Wm. R. Thropp & Sons Co. v. De Laski & Thropp C.W.T. Co., 226 F. 941, 947 (3d Cir.1915); Monsanto Co. v. Kamp, 269 F.Supp. 818 (D.D.C.1967). And it was to mitigate the hardship of mistake that § 256 was enacted.

*   *   *

We conclude, therefore, that a literal reading of the statute is proper to achieve the broad remedial purposes Congress intended. In short, when the Commissioner is asked to correct innocent errors of misjoinder or nonjoinder, all parties must apply for relief to comply with the requirements of the first and second paragraphs of § 256. But when relief is sought in court, as allowed by the third paragraph, notice and an opportunity for all parties to be heard are the only requisites for judicial action that Congress expressly prescribed. We are not pursuaded that we should engraft another.

2. In Dee v. Auckerman, 625 F.Supp. 1427, 228 USPQ 600 (S.D.Ohio 1986), the court held that it possessed subject matter jurisdiction under 35 U.S.C.A. § 256 and 28 U.S.C.A. § 1338(a) in a suit in which plaintiff sought to be named as a joint inventor in an issued patent, even in the absence of an infringement or validity controversy, but that plaintiff must allege omission or error through inadvertence rather than deceptive intent by the defendant joint inventor.

3. A.F. Stoddard & Co., Ltd. v. Dann, 564 F.2d 556, 195 USPQ 97 (D.C.Cir.1977):

In this case of first impression, the sole question of law is: If, *through innocent error,* W was named as the inventor in a patent application and it is later discovered that H was the true inventor, can the error be corrected by diligent action upon its discovery? The District Court answered in the negative. We reverse and remand.

* * *

It must be emphasized that the present case involves an *innocent* error, i.e., an error "without any deceptive intention" as reflected in the language of 35 U.S.C.A. §§ 116, 251, and 256.

* * *

Applying the views of Chief Justice Marshall and Chief Justice Burger, we note first that there has been a full and adequate disclosure of the inventions in the present case. On the record here the inventions are themselves patentable. One patent has issued and its reissue is now sought. A patent based on the continuation application appears warranted. The filing documents show Walser as the inventor. We now know that the inventor was Hospied. To permit the requested substitution of names would on this record harm no one. To deny the requested correction, on the other hand, would serve no useful purpose, would frustrate the constitutional objective, would exalt form over substance, and would punish Stoddard's commendable candor, all to the injury of the patent system and to him to whom it must appeal, i.e., the inventor. The United States has fully received its *quid pro quo,* the disclosures, one of which has been published and the other is to be published upon correction of the inventor's name, and should not now deny the formal step requested. A denial would, in sum, violate that "sense of justice" which Chief Justice Marshall saw as pleading "strongly against depriving the inventor" just "because he has committed an inadvertent or innocent mistake," Grant v. Raymond, supra, and could preclude the "positive effect on society" referred to by Chief Justice Burger in *Kewanee,* supra.

F.   REVOCATION OF PATENTS

UNITED STATES v. AMERICAN BELL TEL. CO.

Supreme Court of the United States, 1897.
167 U.S. 224, 17 S.Ct. 809, 42 L.Ed. 144.

* * *

But, further, Congress has established the Patent Office, and thereby created a tribunal to pass upon all questions of novelty and utility. It has given to that office exclusive jurisdiction in the first instance, and has specifically provided under what circumstances its decisions may be reviewed, either collaterally or by appeal. * * *

[T]he government is as much bound by the laws of Congress as an individual, and when Congress has created a tribunal to which it has given exclusive determination in the first instance of certain questions of fact and has specifically provided under what circumstances that determination may be reviewed by the courts, the argument is a forcible one that such determination should be held conclusive upon the government, subject to the same limitations as apply in suits between individuals.

There is nothing in United States v. American Bell Teleph. Co., 128 U.S. 315 [32:450], and United States v. American Bell Teleph. Co., 159 U.S. 548 [40:255], to conflict with the views above expressed. In the former case * * * it was decided that where a patent for a grant of any kind issued by the United States has been obtained by fraud, by mistake, or by accident, a suit by the United States against the patentee is the proper remedy for relief, and that in this country, where there is no kingly prerogative, but where patents for lands and inventions are issued by the authority of the government, and by officers appointed for that purpose, who may have been imposed upon by fraud or deceit, or may have erred as to their power, or made mistakes in the instrument itself, the appropriate remedy is by proceedings by the United States against the patentee.

But while there was thus rightfully affirmed the power of the government to proceed by suit in equity against one who had wrongfully obtained a patent for land or for an invention there was no attempt to define the character of the fraud, or deceit, or mistake, or the extent of the error as to power which must be established before a decree could be entered canceling the patent. It was not affirmed that proof of any fraud, or deceit, or the existence of any error on the part of the officers as to the extent of their power, or that any mistake in the instrument was sufficient to justify a decree of cancellation. Least of all was it intended to be affirmed that the courts of the United States, sitting as courts of equity, could entertain jurisdiction of a suit by the United States to set aside a patent for an invention on the mere ground of error of judgment on the part of the patent officials. That would be an attempt on the part of the courts in collateral attack to exercise an appellate jurisdiction over the decisions of the Patent Office, although no appellate jurisdiction has been by the statutes conferred. We are of opinion, therefore, that the question, as stated, is not open for consideration in this case.

We see no error in the decision of the Court of Appeals, and its decree dismissing the bill is affirmed.

———

While recognizing that the Government cannot sue for revocation of a patent, two lines of cases have provided the public with protection against patents obtained by fraud, or otherwise not validly granted. The first line of cases deals with an attempt to hold patentees to the limits set by antitrust laws. The following case is illustrative.

UNITED STATES v. UNITED STATES GYPSUM CO.

Supreme Court of the United States, 1948.
333 U.S. 364, 68 S.Ct. 525, 92 L.Ed. 746.

MR. JUSTICE REED delivered the opinion of the court.

[Excerpt Only]

Appellees admit that in the absence of whatever protection is afforded by valid patents the licensing arrangements described would be in violation of the Sherman Act. Accordingly, the government sought to amend its complaint to allege that the "bubble board" patents were not valid. The trial court held that the government was estopped to attack the validity of the patents in the present proceeding, on the ground that such attack would constitute a review of action by the Commissioner of Patents which was not authorized by statute.[4] The trial court thought that the issue was controlled by United States v. Bell Teleph. Co., 167 U.S. 224, 17 S.Ct. 809, 42 L.Ed. 144, in which the United States was held without standing to bring a suit in equity to cancel a patent on the ground of invalidity.

While this issue need not be decided to dispose of this case, it seems inadvisable to leave the decision as a precedent. Hurn v. Oursler, 289 U.S. 238, 240, 53 S.Ct. 586, 77 L.Ed. 1148, 1150. We cannot agree with the conclusion of the trial court. The United States does not claim that the patents are invalid because they have been employed in violation of the Sherman Act and that a decree should issue canceling the patents; rather the government charges that the defendants have violated the Sherman Act because they granted licenses under patents which in fact were invalid. If the government were to succeed in showing that the patents were in fact invalid, such a finding would not in itself result in a judgment for cancellation of the patents.[5]

In an antitrust suit instituted by a licensee against his licensor we have repeatedly held that the licensee may attack the validity of the patent under which he was licensed, because of the public interest in free competition, even though the licensee has agreed in his license not to do so. Sola Electric Co. v. Jefferson Electric Co., 317 U.S. 173, 63 S.Ct. 172, 87 L.Ed. 165; Edward Katzinger Co. v. Chicago Metallic Mfg. Co., 329 U.S. 394, 67 S.Ct. 416, 424, 91 L.Ed. 374; MacGregor v. Westinghouse Electric & Mfg. Co., 329 U.S. 402, 67 S.Ct. 421, 424, 91 L.Ed. 380. In a suit to vindicate the public interest by enjoining violations of the Sherman Act, the United States should have the same opportunity to show that the asserted shield of patentability does not exist. Of course, this appeal must be considered on a record that assumes the validity of all the patents involved.

---

4. 53 F.Supp. 889.

5. Compare Becher v. Contoure Laboratories, 279 U.S. 388, 49 S.Ct. 356, 73 L.Ed. 752.

The second line of cases deals with the denial of patent enforcement when the patent was obtained fraudulently. It is best illustrated by Hazel-Atlas Glass Co. v. Hartford-Empire Co., 322 U.S. 238, 64 S.Ct. 997, 88 L.Ed. 1250 (1944), in which Hartford secured publication of an article prepared by its agents and attorneys to be presented as evidence of the importance of its "gob feeding" machine. They induced the president of the Flint Glass Workers' Union to sign the article. The patent was issued and Hartford pressed an infringement claim, using the fraudulent article as evidence, through the Circuit Court. Mr. Justice Black had this to say:

> The total effect of all this fraud, practiced both on the Patent Office and the courts, calls for nothing less than a complete denial of relief to Hartford for the claimed infringement of the patent thereby procured and enforced.

> Since the judgments of 1932 therefore must be vacated, the case now stands in the same position as though Hartford's corruption had been exposed at the original trial. In this situation the doctrine of the Keystone Driller Co. Case, supra, requires that Hartford be denied relief.

> To grant full protection to the public against a patent obtained by fraud, that patent must be vacated. It has previously been decided that such a remedy is not available in infringement proceedings, but can only be accomplished in a direct proceeding brought by the government. United States v. Bell Teleph. Co., 128 U.S. 315, 9 S.Ct. 90, 32 L.Ed. 459, supra.[a]

G. EXTENSION OF PATENT TERM

Only Congress can extend the term of a patent grant, and the instances in which this has been done are few. Extensions are usually allowed only to aid men and women who served the country in the military services during time of war. No action has yet been taken in behalf of those who served in the United States military service during the Vietnam conflict, although legislation is pending.

Public Law 598 (approved June 30, 1950, 64 Stat. 316; amended July 1, 1952, 66 Stat. 321) in behalf of World War II veterans is an example of such Congressional action. The statute has been construed strictly.

A veteran holding 79% of the stock in a corporation owning a patent issued to him originally was denied an extension of his term. In re Field, 190 F.2d 268, 90 USPQ 233 (CCPA 1951). Similarly, where the veteran's interest was 52%, In re Blood, 197 F.2d 545, 94 USPQ 189 (CCPA 1952).

[a]. See also Part II, Chapter Four, Section B, on the Responsibilities of Attorneys to the Patent Office.

Where the patent was returning a bigger income to a veteran during the war, an extension was denied. In re Walker, 195 F.2d 531, 93 USPQ 225 (CCPA 1952); Also, when the veteran assigned the patent to another, and later took a re-assignment, the veteran was held not entitled to an extension. In re Miller, 193 F.2d 339, 92 USPQ 213 (CCPA 1951).

Service in the Merchant Marines is not service "in the military or naval forces of the United States" within the meaning of Public Law 598. In re Martin, 195 F.2d 303, 93 USPQ 173 (CCPA 1952).

Sections 155 and 155A of the Patent Statutes (35 U.S.C.A.) were enacted in 1983 to extend the terms of patents on the drugs aspertame and Forane as compensation to manufacturers of these specific drugs for administrative delay during review by the Federal Food and Drug Administration.

Section 156, enacted in 1984, applies in general to manufacture of "human drug products" or other products "subject to regulation under the Federal Food, Drug and Cosmetic Act." A patent owner may obtain an extension of the patent term of up to five years when commercialization is delayed by "administrative review". The patent owner must apply for an extension to the Commissioner of Patents, who notifies the Secretary of Health and Human Services. The application is published in the Federal Register, and hearings are held if objections are filed. A major consideration in whether the application will be granted, and the length of the extension, is whether the applicant exercised "due diligence" during the regulatory review period.

The Patent and Trademark Office has published detailed regulations governing conditions, eligibility and applications for patent term extensions. 37 CFR 1.710 through 1.785 (1987).

Chapter Six

INFRINGEMENT

A. INTRODUCTION

With respect to a utility patent, the United States Government grants, for the term of 17 years, the right to exclude others from making, using, or selling the patented invention in the United States.[a] Violation of this right is a tort[b] analogous to trespass[c] for which the patent holder may bring a civil action[d] in a Federal Court. Injunctive relief, damages, and other remedies for violation of this right are discussed in Chapter Nine.

Violation of this right to exclude others by making, using, or selling the patented invention in the United States is direct infringement. In accordance with general tort theory, liability is also imposed for actively inducing infringement and for contributory infringement by aiding, abetting, encouraging, or contributing to direct infringement by another.

In determining the existence of direct infringement, the fundamental question is whether, without authorization by the patent holder, another has made, used, or sold the patented invention. In considering this question, it is necessary to determine the nature and scope of the invention defined by the claims. In determining the scope of the claims, resort is usually made to the written description and any drawings of the patent, the prior art, and the proceedings or prosecution in the Patent Office of the application for patent.

In prosecuting a patent application, the claims may be and usually are altered by amendment, deleting claims, or adding new claims. These alterations may be made for a variety of reasons such as correcting informalities, improving form, clarity or specificity to comply with Section 112, or to define a novel and non-obvious invention over the prior art cited by the Patent Office. A record is maintained by the Patent Office of the correspondence and the substance of any oral communications and personal interviews[e] between the Patent Office Examiner in charge of the application and the applicant or his representative. This record is often called the "file history" or "file wrapper" and is available at the Patent Office for examination and copying by the public after the patent issues. This file wrapper provides a

a. 35 U.S.C.A. § 154.

b. Carbice Corp. v. American Patents Development Corp., 283 U.S. 27, 33, 51 S.Ct. 334, 336, 75 L.Ed. 819, 823 (1930).

c. Thompson-Houston Elec. Co. v. Ohio Brass Co., 80 Fed. 712, 721 (6th Cir.1897).

d. 35 U.S.C.A. § 281.

e. 37 C.F.R. 1.133 (1979).

record of the negotiations or arguments and contentions made with respect to the claims, prior art, written description, etc., in procuring the patent. Hence, a file wrapper is often helpful in interpreting the claims of an issued patent.

Initially, patents did not have any claims, and, historically, most patent cases were tried to a judge sitting in equity without a jury. Even when tried to a jury, the judge usually gave instructions regarding the invention and the scope of the claims. Thus, in determining infringement, courts have considered the essential character of the invention disclosed by the patent and the claims, have not been bound by the literal meaning of the words of the claims, and have sought to make an equitable and just determination of the question of infringement.

In determining whether accused subject matter (process, machine, manufacture, or composition of matter) infringes a claim, it is necessary to consider the meaning of the words of the claim and the nature or essential character of the invention as disclosed by the written description of the patent and defined by the claim. The usual test for determining whether the accused subject matter embodies the essential character of the invention is whether they perform substantially the same function in substantially the same way to obtain the same result. These two factors can result in four different situations, each presenting a question of infringement.

First, if the words of a claim do not literally read on or encompass the accused subject matter, and such subject matter does not embody the essential character of the invention defined by the claim, there is no infringement. Second, if the words of the claim literally read on the accused subject matter, but such subject matter does not embody the essential character of the invention defined by the claim, there is no infringement. This result is reached under the so-called doctrine of equivalents in reverse. This doctrine simply recognizes that regardless of the scope of the words of the claim, the invention of the patent is not embodied in the accused subject matter and, thus, there is no infringement.

Third, if the words of the claim literally read on the accused subject matter and such subject matter embodies the essential character of the invention defined by the claim, there is infringement. Fourth, if the words of the claim do not literally read on the accused subject matter, but such subject matter embodies the essential character of the invention defined by the claim, there is infringement under the doctrine of equivalents unless the patent holder is estopped to enlarge the scope of the claim beyond the literal meaning of its words.

An amendment of a claim made in order to obtain the patent, and statements made in the written description of the patent, may result in an estoppel precluding application of the doctrine of equivalents and, hence, no infringement. The patent holder will not be permitted to repudiate these amendments and statements since they were made to the Patent Office in order to obtain the patent, are available to the public, and may well be relied on by others in interpreting the scope of the claims. An estoppel, based on amendments of the claims made to obtain the patent, is usually referred to as "file wrapper estoppel." An estoppel based on a statement in the written description is usually referred to as the doctrine of D'Arcy Spring Co. v. Marshall Ventilated Mattress Co., 259 F. 236 (6th Cir.1919).

The following cases illustrate the various judicial rules of interpretation of claims of utility patents.

B. INTERPRETATION OF PATENT CLAIMS

McGILL INCORPORATED v. JOHN ZINK COMPANY

United States Court of Appeals, Federal Circuit, 1984.
736 F.2d 666, 221 USPQ 944.

KASHIWA, CIRCUIT JUDGE.

* * *

The patented invention relates to a process for recovering hydrocarbon vapors from an air-hydrocarbon mixture. It is a pollution-prevention process for recovering hydrocarbon vapors that have been vented from a storage tank. * * *

In determining patent infringement, two inquiries are involved—(1) the scope of the claims and (2) whether the claimed invention has been infringed. *SSIH Equipment S.A. v. USITC,* 718 F.2d 365, 376, 218 USPQ 678, 688 (Fed.Cir.1983); *Autogiro Co. of America v. United States,* 384 F.2d 391, 401, 155 USPQ 697, 705 (Ct.Cl.1967). The first inquiry, a determination of the scope of the claims, is a question of law. *SSIH Equipment, supra.* If the language of the claims is undisputed, the district court could interpret or construe the undisputed claims as a matter of law. *Singer Manufacturing Co. v. Cramer,* 192 U.S. 265, 275, 24 S.Ct. 291, 295, 48 L.Ed. 437 (1904); *see Super Products Corp. v. D P Way Corp.,* 546 F.2d 748, 756, 192 USPQ 417, 423 (7th Cir.1976); *cf. Chemical Construction Corp. v. Continental Engineering, Ltd.,* 407 F.2d 989, 991 (5th Cir.1969). If, however, the meaning of a term of art in the claims is disputed and extrinsic evidence is needed to explain the meaning, construction of the claims could be left to a jury. *Envirotech Corp. v. Al George, Inc.,* 730 F.2d 753 (Fed.Cir.1984); *cf. Hong Kong Export Credit Insurance Corp. v. Dun & Bradstreet,* 414 F.Supp. 153, 157 (S.D.N.Y.1975). In the latter instance, the jury cannot be directed to the disputed meaning for the term of art. *Cf. Butler v. Local Union 823, International Brotherhood of Teamsters,* 514 F.2d 442, 452 (8th Cir.), *cert. denied,* 423 U.S. 924, 96 S.Ct. 265, 46 L.Ed.2d 249 (1975).

Where, as here, the overall question of infringement was answered by a jury and the losing party's motion for JNOV was denied, an appellate court's review of the denial is limited. *Connell v. Sears,*

Roebuck & Co., 722 F.2d 1542, 1546, 220 USPQ 193, 197 (Fed.Cir.1983). The appellate court is permitted to review only the sufficiency of the evidence, a question of law. *Baltimore & Carolina Line, Inc. v. Redman*, 295 U.S. 654, 659, 55 S.Ct. 890, 892, 79 L.Ed. 1636 (1935).

* * *

In the instant case, the jury's finding of infringement was predicated on construction of claim 2. To obtain a reversal, Zink must demonstrate that no reasonable juror could have interpreted the claim in the fashion that supports the infringement finding, *e.g.*, in the fashion urged by McGill. * * *

CLAIM CONSTRUCTION—CLAIM AT ISSUE

The threshold requirement in claim construction is an examination of the claim at issue. In the instant case, McGill argues that the phrase "recovered liquid hydrocarbon absorbent" in the claim at issue means an undefined absorbent that is capable of recovering a substance called "recovered liquid hydrocarbon". Zink, on the other hand, argues that the phrase means that the recovered liquid hydrocarbon is being used as an absorbent. Thus, Zink's use of fresh gasoline in the absorption step would be an infringing use under McGill's interpretation and not an infringing use under Zink's.

* * *

Thus, the language of the claim at issue is in dispute, and Zink contends that other tools of claim construction must be used to interpret the claim.

CLAIM CONSTRUCTION—FILE HISTORY

In construing or interpreting claims, a whole host of factors may be considered. *Fromson v. Advance Offset Plate, Inc.*, 720 F.2d 1565, 219 USPQ 1137 (Fed.Cir.1983); *Autogiro*, 384 F.2d at 401, 155 USPQ at 705. One such factor is the prosecution history of the patent. The Court, in *Graham v. John Deere Co.*, 383 U.S. 1, 33, 86 S.Ct. 684, 702, 15 L.Ed.2d 545 (1966), stated that "an invention is construed not only in light of the claims, but also with reference to the file wrapper or prosecution history in the Patent Office."

In the instant case, McGill contends that prosecution history estoppel is inapplicable since the claim at issue and in particular, the phrase "recovered liquid hydrocarbon absorbent," was not amended or distinguished in response to a prior art rejection, citing *Hughes Aircraft Co. v. United States*, 717 F.2d 1351, 1362, 219 USPQ 473, 481 (Fed.Cir.1983).

* * *

Prosecution history may be used not only in an estoppel context but also as a claim construction tool. *Fromson, supra.* Where, as here, an unambiguous limitation such as the one that was present in original claim 8 was voluntarily added to a subsequent claim during prosecution, it may be used to construe the claim. In the instant case, the examiner twice remarked that original claim 9 would be allowed if it were rewritten in an independent form and included *all the limitations* present through dependency. The phrase "recovered liquid hydrocarbon absorbent" in original claim 8 was clearly a limitation, a limitation having the meaning: recovered liquid hydrocarbon being used as an absorbent. Since this condition for allowance was clear and the limitation of original claim 8 was clear on its face, the appearance of the phrase in new claim 14 was an indication, as interpreted by Zink, that the limitation of original claim 8 had been incorporated into the new claim.

CLAIM CONSTRUCTION—SPECIFICATION

Another factor in claim construction is the use of the patent specification. *McClain v. Ortmayer*, 141 U.S. 419, 12 S.Ct. 76, 35 L.Ed. 800 (1891); *Fromson*, 720 F.2d at 1569–70, 219 USPQ at 1140. Words which were defined in the specification must be given the same meaning when used in a claim. *General Electric Co. v. United States*, 572 F.2d 745, 753, 198 USPQ 65, 71 (Ct.Cl.1978). In *Autogiro*, 348 F.2d at 397–98, 155 USPQ at 702–3, the Court of Claims stated:

> In serving its statutory purpose, the specification aids in ascertaining the scope and meaning of the language employed in the claims inasmuch as words must be used in the same way in both the claims and the specification. U.S.Pat.Off. Rule 75(d). The use of the specification as a concordance for the claims is accepted by almost every court, and is a basic concept of patent law. [Footnotes omitted.]

In the specification of the patent at issue, the phrase "recovered liquid hydrocarbon absorbent" is not defined. However, the phrase "recovered liquid hydrocarbon" and the word "absorbent" are defined. For example, the specification states that the "[r]ecovered liquid hydrocarbon overflowing the weir 54 is withdrawn from separator 52 through line 62 connected between the lower portion of separator 52 and line 74 for use as a liquid absorbent [sic]." The specification then describes the direct countercurrent contact of the vapor hydrocarbon component and the recovered liquid hydrocarbon "introduced in the upper portion of the absorber via line 72." In addition, the specification discloses that a portion of the recovered liquid hydrocarbon discharged from absorber 70 is first cooled by cooler 82 and then pumped via line 72 to the top of absorber 70 "for use as absorbent." Thus, the specification discloses a process in which the absorbent is created internally within the system and not a process that utilizes an external liquid as its absorbent.

It is clear from the specification that the recovered liquid hydrocarbon functions as the absorbent in absorber 70. Contrary to McGill's construction, the phrase "recovered liquid hydrocarbon absorbent" does not mean an undefined absorbent that is capable of recovering a substance called "recovered liquid hydrocarbon." In addition, all of the drawings of the patent show only the use of internally-created recovered liquid hydrocarbon as the absorbent. *Dominion Magnesium Ltd. v. United States*, 320 F.2d 388, 394, 138 USPQ 306, 310 (Ct.Cl.1963). Thus, the phrase "recovered liquid hydrocarbon absorbent" in claim 2, as urged by Zink, has the meaning that was defined in the specification which is internally-created recovered liquid hydrocarbon being used as an absorbent.

CLAIM CONSTRUCTION—OTHER CLAIMS

A third factor in claim construction is the use of other claims in the patent to determine the scope of the claim at issue. *Fromson,* 720 F.2d at 1570, 219 USPQ at 1140–41; *General Electric,* 572 F.2d at 751, 198 USPQ at 70.

In dependent claim 3, the steps of cooling the recovered liquid hydrocarbon discharged by absorber 70 and the recycling of the cooled liquid to the absorber are claimed. The cooled recovered liquid hydrocarbon are recycled to absorber 70 "for use as absorbent in the absorption step." McGill contends that if independent claim 2 is interpreted to include an absorption step carried out with "recovered liquid hydrocarbon," then the second step of dependent claim 3 would be redundant. As such, it would be an improper reading of a limitation explicitly set forth in a dependent claim into an independent claim, citing *Environmental Designs, Ltd. v. Union Oil Co. of California,* 713 F.2d 693, 699, 218 USPQ 865, 871 (Fed.Cir.1983). We disagree.

McGill is misconstruing claims 2 and 3. It seems to be reading claim 2 to mean that something other than internally-created recovered liquid hydrocarbon was used as the absorbent in the initial or first absorption step. Then, in light of claim 3, only the *cooled* recovered liquid hydrocarbon is being recycled as the absorbent. Since the specification and drawings fail to show the use of anything but the internally-created recovered liquid hydrocarbon as the absorbent, Zink contends that this is a tortured reading. It interprets claim 3 to mean that the "recovered liquid hydrocarbon" of claim 2, already being used as the absorbent, is further cooled and recycled for the same use.

CLAIM CONSTRUCTION—EXPERT TESTIMONY

In addition to tools of claim construction such as file history, patent specification, and other claims in the patent, testimony by expert witnesses may be used to construe claims. *See Control Components, Inc. v. Valtek, Inc.,* 609 F.2d 763, 770, 204 USPQ 785, 791 (5th Cir.), *cert. denied,* 449 U.S. 1022, 101 S.Ct. 589, 66 L.Ed.2d 484 (1980). Such testimony is evidence of construction of the claims as they would be construed by those skilled in the art. *Fromson,* 720 F.2d at 1571, 219 USPQ at 1142. In this regard, experts for both sides testified as to their interpretation of the phrase "recovered liquid hydrocarbon absorbent."

McGill contends that the testimony of two of its experts, a co-inventor of the '423 patent and its patent law expert, supports its interpretation of claim 2. * * *

Zink, however, disputes the interpretation of McGill's experts. Its own patent law expert equated recovered liquid hydrocarbon with recovered liquid hydrocarbon absorbent. Zink also argues that even a Dr. Garwin, another one of McGill's experts, testified that the absorbent and the recovered liquid hydrocarbon were the same substance. In particular, Zink contends that its cross-examination of McGill's patent law expert raised questions regarding that expert's interpretation of claim 2.

CLAIM CONSTRUCTION—CONCLUSION

After considering the record taken as a whole, including the experts' testimony, *Hayes v. Department of the Navy,* 727 F.2d 1535, 1538 (Fed.Cir.1984); *see Control Components, supra; cf. Moraine Products v. ICI America, Inc.,* 538 F.2d 134, 146, 191 USPQ 65, 75 (7th Cir.), *cert. denied,* 429 U.S. 941, 97 S.Ct. 357, 50 L.Ed.2d 310 (1976), we are convinced that there is no set of facts, consistent with McGill's interpretation, that is supported by substantial evidence. Thus, McGill's interpretation of claim 2, a legal conclusion implied from the jury's finding of infringement, cannot be upheld, premised as it must be on facts which are not supported by substantial evidence.

* * *

McGill's claim 2 is limited, instead, to an absorbent which consisted of internally-created recovered liquid hydrocarbon. It is undisputed that fresh gasoline, as used by Zink to recover liquid hydrocarbon, is not "recovered liquid hydrocarbon" as that term is used in the '423 patent. As such, Zink's use of fresh gasoline as the absorbent is noninfringing. Accordingly, the district court should have granted Zink's motion for JNOV in relation to infringement and the district court's denial is reversed.

* * *

AMSTAR CORPORATION v. ENVIROTECH CORPORATION

United States Court of Appeals, Federal Circuit, 1984.
730 F.2d 1476, 221 USPQ 649.

MARKEY, CHIEF JUDGE.

Appeal from that part of a judgment of the United States District Court for the District of Utah finding non-infringement of U.S. Patent No. 3,523,889 ('889 patent). We *reverse* and *remand.*

* * *

The law of infringement requires that the asserted claims be compared with the products or processes accused of infringement. *Graver Tank & Mfg. Co. v. Linde Air Products Co.,* 339 U.S. 605, 70 S.Ct. 854, 94 L.Ed. 1097, 85 USPQ 328 (1950); *Rel-Reeves, Inc. v. United States,* 534 F.2d 274, 209 Ct.Cl. 595 (1976); *Astra-Sjuco, A.B. v. U.S. International Trade Commission,* 629 F.2d 682, 207 USPQ 1 (CCPA 1980). That was not done here. On the contrary, in the seven pages of the Memorandum Decision devoted to the infringement issue, it is made clear that the district court was led to take a wrong turn in determining the infringement issue.

Infringement is not determined by comparison between parts of the description in a patent and the accused process or product, or by comparison between commercial products sold by the parties. Accused products made, sold, or used, and accused processes performed, before suit must be compared with the claims. That products may have been modified after suit is brought, and may or may not be accused of infringement, does not remove the need for that comparison.

Modification by mere *addition* of elements of functions, whenever made, cannot negate infringement without disregard of the long-established, hornbook law expressed in *Cochrane v. Deener,* 94 U.S. 780, 786, 24 L.Ed. 139 (1876); *Eastern Rotorcraft Corp. v. United States,* 397 F.2d 978, 981, 104 Ct.Cl. 709, 154 USPQ 43, 45 (Ct.Cl.1968) (infringement not avoided by adding an additional element); *McCullough Tool Co. v. Well Surveys, Inc.,* 343 F.2d 381, 402, 145 USPQ 6, 22 (10th Cir.1965), *cert. denied* 383 U.S. 933, 86 S.Ct. 1061, 15 L.Ed.2d 851, 148 USPQ 772 (1966) ("But infringement cannot be avoided by the mere fact that the accused device is more or less efficient or performs additional functions."); *Acme Highway Products Corp. v. D.S. Brown Co.,* 473 F.2d 849, 855, 177 USPQ 130, 135 (6th Cir.), *cert. denied* 414 U.S. 824, 94 S.Ct. 125, 38 L.Ed.2d 57, 179 USPQ 321 (1973) ("An accused device cannot escape infringement by merely adding features, if it otherwise has adopted the basic features of the patent."). Further, the law recognizes the irrelevance of apparatus distinctions in determining infringement of process claims. *International Glass Co. v. United States,* 408 F.2d 395, 400, 187 Ct.Cl. 376, 161 USPQ 116 (Ct.Cl.1969).

Similarly, the presence of additional ("lamella") plates in some Envirotech drawings cannot negate infringement, lamella plates being irrelevant because they are not included in the accused products as sold, because they have no effect on the processes of claims 1 and 8, and because they are not an element of product claim 9.

Often, as here, consideration of the infringement issue may be benefitted by recognition of the findings made in considering the validity issue (Envirotech tried various schemes to "neutralize Enviro-clear's influence" and "counteract the Enviro-clear threat"; Envirotech's apparatus and process "[bear] a striking resemblance to the preferred embodiment of the Amstar apparatus and process described in the Eis patent".

* * *

The statute provides no support for the district court's statement that "the combinative nature of Amstar's patent rights effectively limits the scope of enforceable claims under the Eis patent". There is no separate classification of "combination patents" and no basis for considering claims to combinations of elements differently from any other. *Richdel, Inc. v. Sunspool Corp.,* 714 F.2d 1573, 1579, 219 USPQ 8, 12 (Fed.Cir.1983); *Medtronic, Inc. v. Cardiac Pacemakers,* 721 F.2d 1563, 220 USPQ 97, 100 (Fed.Cir.1983).

* * *

The record further illustrates that the modifications assertedly made by Envirotech, whenever they may have been made, are either irrelevant or fail to escape infringement. The accused products, including those modified, are the same, they perform the same function in the same way, and they achieve, as the district court found, the same result as the claimed inventions. *See Sanitary Refrigerator Co. v. Winters*, 280 U.S. 30, 41–42, 50 S.Ct. 9, 12–13, 74 L.Ed. 147, 3 USPQ 40, 44 (1929).

In this case, the merely colorable variations so vigorously pressed by Envirotech are of a kind with those described by the Supreme Court as fostering "the piracy" and consequent defeat of the disclosure purpose of the patent system. *Graver Tank, supra*, 339 U.S. at 607, 70 S.Ct. at 855, 85 USPQ at 330. Infringement is clear on this record.

* * *

GRAVER TANK & MFG. CO. v. LINDE AIR PRODUCTS CO.

Supreme Court of the United States, 1950.
339 U.S. 605, 70 S.Ct. 854, 94 L.Ed. 1097.

MR. JUSTICE JACKSON delivered the opinion of the Court.

* * *

At the outset it should be noted that the single issue before us is whether the trial court's holding that the four flux claims have been infringed will be sustained. Any issue as to the validity of these claims was unanimously determined by the previous decision in this Court and attack on their validity cannot be renewed now by reason of limitation on grant of rehearing. The disclosure, the claims, and the prior art have been adequately described in our former opinion and in the opinions of the courts below.

In determining whether an accused device or composition infringes a valid patent, resort must be had in the first instance to the words of the claim. If accused matter falls clearly within the claim, infringement is made out and that is the end of it.

But courts have also recognized that to permit imitation of a patented invention which does not copy every literal detail would be to convert the protection of the patent grant into a hollow and useless thing. Such a limitation would leave room for—indeed encourage—the unscrupulous copyist to make unimportant and insubstantial changes and substitutions in the patent which, though adding nothing, would be enough to take the copied matter outside the claim, and hence outside the reach of law. One who seeks to pirate an invention, like one who seeks to pirate a copyrighted book or play, may be expected to introduce minor variations to conceal and shelter the piracy. Outright and forthright duplication is a dull and very rare type of infringement. To prohibit no other would place the inventor at the mercy of verbalism and would be subordinating substance to form. It would deprive him of the benefit of his invention and would foster concealment rather than disclosure of inventions, which is one of the primary purposes of the patent system.

The doctrine of equivalents evolved in response to this experience. The essence of the doctrine is that one may not practice a fraud on a patent. Originating almost a century ago in the case of Winans v. Denmead (U.S.) 15 How. 330, 14 L.Ed. 717, it has been consistently applied by this Court and the lower federal courts, and continues today ready and available for utilization when the proper circumstances for its application arise. "To temper unsparing logic and prevent an infringer from stealing the benefit of the invention"[1] a patentee may invoke this doctrine to proceed against the producer of a device "if it performs substantially the same function in substantially the same way to obtain the same result." Sanitary Refrigerator Co. v. Winters, 280 U.S. 30, 42, 50 S.Ct. 9, 74 L.Ed. 147, 156. The theory on which it is founded is that "if two devices do the same work in substantially the same way, and accomplish substantially the same result, they are the same, even though they differ in name, form, or shape." Union Paper-Bag Machine Co. v. Murphy, 97 U.S. 120, 125, 24 L.Ed. 935, 936. The doctrine operates not only in favor of the patentee of a pioneer or primary invention, but also for the patentee of a secondary invention consisting of a combination of old ingredients which produce new and useful results. Imhaeuser v. Buerk, 101 U.S. 647, 655, 25 L.Ed. 945, although the area of equivalence may vary under the circumstances. See Continental Paper Bag Co. v. Eastern Paper Bag Co., 210 U.S. 405, 414, 415, 28 S.Ct. 748, 52 L.Ed. 1122, 1126, 1127, and cases cited; Seymour v. Osborne (U.S.) 11 Wall. 516, 556, 20 L.Ed. 33, 42; Gould v. Rees (U.S.) 15 Wall. 187, 192, 21 L.Ed. 39, 40. The wholesome realism of this doctrine is not always applied in favor of a patentee but is sometimes used against him. Thus, where a device is so far changed in principle from a patented article that it performs the same or a similar function in a substantially different way, but nevertheless falls within the literal words of the claim, the doctrine of equivalents may be used to restrict the claim and defeat the patentee's action for infringement. Westinghouse v. Boyden Power Brake Co., 170 U.S. 537, 568, 18 S.Ct. 707, 42 L.Ed. 1136, 1137. In its early development, the doctrine was usually applied in cases involving devices where there was equivalence in mechanical components. Subsequently, however, the same principles were also applied to compositions, where there was equivalence between chemical ingredients. Today the doctrine is applied to mechanical or chemical equivalents in compositions or devices. See discussions and cases collected in 3 Walker, Patents (Deller's ed. 1937) §§ 489–492; Ellis, Patent Claims (1949) §§ 59, 60.

What constitutes equivalency must be determined against the context of the patent, the prior art, and the particular circumstances of the case. Equivalence, in the patent law, is not the prisoner of a

1. L. Hand in Royal Typewriter Co. v. Remington Rand (C.A.2d Conn.) 168 F.2d 691, 692.

formula and is not an absolute to be considered in a vacuum. It does not require complete identity for every purpose and in every respect. In determining equivalents, things equal to the same thing may not be equal to each other and, by the same token, things for most purposes different may sometimes be equivalents. Consideration must be given to the purpose for which an ingredient is used in a patent, the qualities it has when combined with the other ingredients, and the function which it is intended to perform. An important factor is whether persons reasonably skilled in the art would have known of the interchangeability of an ingredient not contained in the patent with one that was.

A finding of equivalence is a determination of fact. Proof can be made in any form: through testimony of experts or others versed in the technology; by documents, including texts and treatises; and, of course, by the disclosures of the prior art. Like any other issue of fact, final determination requires a balancing of credibility, persuasiveness and weight of evidence. It is to be decided by the trial court and that court's decision, under general principles of appellate review, should not be disturbed unless clearly erroneous. Particularly is this so in a field where so much depends upon familiarity with specific scientific problems and principles not usually contained in the general storehouse of knowledge and experience.

In the case before us, we have two electric welding compositions or fluxes: the patented composition, Unionmelt Grade 20, and the accused composition, Lincolnweld 660. The patent under which Unionmelt is made claims essentially a combination of alkaline earth metal silicate and calcium fluoride; Unionmelt actually contains, however, silicates of calcium and magnesium, two alkaline earth metal silicates. Lincolnweld's composition is similar to Unionmelt's, except that it substitutes silicates of calcium and manganese—the latter not an alkaline earth metal—for silicates of calcium and magnesium. In all other respects, the two compositions are alike. The mechanical methods in which these compositions are employed are similar. They are identical in operation and produce the same kind and quality of weld.

The question which thus emerges is whether the substitution of the manganese which is not an alkaline earth metal for the magnesium which is, under the circumstances of this case, and in view of the technology and the prior art, is a change of such substance as to make the doctrine of equivalents inapplicable; or conversely, whether under the circumstances the change was so insubstantial that the trial court's invocation of the doctrine of equivalents was justified.

Without attempting to be all-inclusive, we note the following evidence in the record: Chemists familiar with the two fluxes testified that manganese and magnesium were similar in many of their reactions (R. 287, 669). There is testimony by a metallurgist that alkaline earth metals are often found in manganese ores in their natural state and that they serve the same purpose in the fluxes (R. 831–832); and a chemist testified that "in the sense of the patent" manganese could be included as an alkaline earth metal (R. 297). Much of this testimony was corroborated by reference to recognized texts on inorganic chemistry (R. 332). Particularly important, in addition, were the disclosures of the prior art, also contained in the record. The Miller patent, No. 1,754,566, which preceded the patent in suit, taught the use of manganese silicate in welding fluxes (R. 969,971). Manganese was similarly disclosed in the Armor patent, No. 1,467,825, which also described a welding composition (R. 1346). And the record contains no evidence of any kind to show that Lincolnweld was developed as the result of independent research or experiments.

It is not for this Court to even essay an independent evaluation of this evidence. This is the function of the trial court. And, as we have heretofore observed, "To no type of case is this * * * more appropriately applicable than to the one before us, where the evidence is largely the testimony of experts as to which a trial court may be enlightened by scientific demonstrations. This trial occupied some three weeks, during which, as the record shows, the trial judge visited laboratories with counsel and experts to observe actual demonstrations of welding as taught by the patent and of the welding accused of infringing it, and of various stages of the prior art. He viewed motion pictures of various welding operations and tests and heard many experts and other witnesses." 336 U.S. 271, 274, 275, 69 S.Ct. 535, 93 L.Ed. 672, 676, 677.

The trial judge found on the evidence before him that the Lincolnweld flux and the composition of the patent in suit are substantially identical in operation and in result. He found also that Lincolnweld is in all respects equivalent to Unionmelt for welding purposes. And he concluded that "for all practical purposes, manganese silicate can be efficiently and effectually substituted for calcium and magnesium silicates as the major constituent of the welding composition." These conclusions are adequately supported by the record; certainly they are not clearly erroneous.[2]

It is difficult to conceive of a case more appropriate for application of the doctrine of equivalents. The disclosures of the prior art made clear that manganese silicate was a useful ingredient in welding compositions. Specialists familiar with the problems of welding compositions understood that manganese was equivalent to and could be substituted for magnesium in the composition of the patented flux and their observations were confirmed by the literature of chemistry. Without some explanation or indication that Lincolnweld was developed by independent research, the trial court could properly infer that the accused flux is the result of imitation rather than experimentation or invention. Though infringement was not literal, the changes which avoid literal infringement are colorable only. We conclude that the

2. Rule 52(a), Federal Rules of Civil Procedure, provides in part: "Findings of fact shall not be set aside unless clearly erroneous, and due regard shall be given to the opportunity of the trial court to judge of the credibility of the witnesses."

trial court's judgment of infringement respecting the four flux claims was proper, and we adhere to our prior decision on this aspect of the case.

Affirmed.

CONTINENTAL PAPER BAG CO. v. EASTERN PAPER BAG CO.

Supreme Court of the United States, 1907.
210 U.S. 405, 28 S.Ct. 748, 52 L.Ed. 1122.

MR. JUSTICE MCKENNA delivered the opinion of the court:

* * *

* * * The lower courts did not designate the invention as either primary or secondary. They did, however, as we shall presently see, decide that it was one of high rank and entitled to a broad range of equivalents. It becomes necessary, therefore, to consider the point of law upon which petitioner contends the question of infringement depends. * * *

The right view is expressed in Miller v. Eagle Mfg. Co., 151 U.S. 186, 207, 14 S.Ct. 310, 38 L.Ed. 121, 130, as follows: "The range of equivalents depends upon the extent and nature of the invention. If the invention is broad or primary in its character, the range of equivalents will be correspondingly broad, under the liberal construction which the courts give to such inventions." And this was what was decided in Kokomo Fence Mach. Co. v. Kitselman, Cimiotti Unhairing Co. v. American Fur Ref. Co., and Computing Scale Co. v. Automatic Scale Co., 204 U.S. 609, 27 S.Ct. 307, 51 L.Ed. 645. It is from the second of those cases, as we have seen, that the citation is made which petitioner contends the point of law upon which infringement depends is formulated; but it was said in that case: "It is well settled that a greater degree of liberality and a wider range of equivalents are permitted where the patent is of a pioneer character than when the invention is simply an improvement, maybe the last and successful step, in the art theretofore partially developed by other inventors in the same field."

It is manifest, therefore, that it was not meant to decide that only pioneer patents are entitled to invoke the doctrine of equivalents, but that it was decided that the range of equivalents depends upon and varies with the degree of invention.

* * *

HUGHES AIRCRAFT COMPANY v. UNITED STATES

United States Court of Appeals, Federal Circuit, 1983.
717 F.2d 1351, 219 USPQ 473.

MARKEY, CHIEF JUDGE.

Hughes Aircraft Company (Hughes) appeals that part of a judgment of the United States Claims Court finding non-infringement of U.S. patent No. 3,758,051 (the Williams patent) by the government's "store and execute" (S/E) spacecraft. * * * We affirm-in-part, reverse-in-part, and remand for a determination of the quantum of recovery for infringement by the accused SKYNET II, NATO II, DSCS II, IMP (H and J), SOLRAD (9 and 10), and PIONEER (10 and 11) spacecraft.

*   *   *

Throughout the late 1950's and early 1960's, the Department of Defense and the National Aeronautics and Space Administration (NASA) engaged in an intense effort to build a synchronous communications satellite with an orbital period equalling the rotational period of the earth. The goal was a satellite moving in a west-to-east orbit with a radius of 22,750 nautical miles and having a linear velocity of 10,090 feet per second, so that it could "hover" above a fixed point on earth.

Despite huge expenditures, the government never solved the technical problem of attitude control. That problem is described as the need to orient the satellite in space, without exceeding weight limitations, while insuring that (1) its directional antennas were always pointed toward the earth, and (2) that it would obtain a reliable, adequate fuel supply from the sun.

Working for Hughes, Williams solved the problem. He created a practical system for attitude control of a spin-stabilized satellite. In the Williams system, signals sent by a ground crew control the satellite by causing a jet on the satellite to pulse at a selected satellite position in successive spin cycles, thereby "precessing" the satellite in a selected direction. Williams taught how a jet valve on the satellite's periphery could discharge gas in brief, successive pulses on command. He taught that an on-board V-beam sun sensor (vertical slit and canted slit) could collect raw data from the sun and transmit it to earth, enabling a ground crew to determine the satellite's existing and desired orientations.

When, using conventional radio signals, the ground crew pulses the attitude jet, torque is applied to the satellite and its spin axis is "precessed" parallel to the earth's axis, causing the beam of the satellite's antenna to point to the earth continuously during the 24-hour period of each orbit, and insuring that the satellite's solar cells receive maximum light from the sun.

*   *   *

II. INFRINGEMENT

(A) Literal Infringement

* * *

The trial judge correctly found, and it is here undisputed, that there are only two distinctions in the structure of the claimed Williams satellite from that of the S/E spacecraft: (1) the SKYNET II, NATO II, and DSCS II spacecraft do not include Williams' means for providing to the ground crew an indication of ISA position, having substituted computer-retention of that information; and (2) in all S/E systems, Williams' means for receiving synchronized control signals for immediate execution are substituted for by an on-board computer for receiving control signals and storing them for later execution. Because the claims speak of means for "providing an indication" of ISA position "to a location external" to the satellite, and to means for receiving from the external location firing signals "synchronized with said indication", there can be no literal infringement. At trial, Hughes conceded the absence of literal infringement and predicated its case for infringement on the doctrine of equivalents.

(B) Doctrine of Equivalents and Doctrine of File Wrapper Estoppel

The doctrine of equivalents comes into play only when actual literal infringement is not present. Under the doctrine of equivalents, an accused product that does not literally infringe a structural claim may yet be found an infringement "if it performs substantially the same function in substantially the same way to obtain the same result" as the claimed product or process. *Graver Tank & Mfg. Co. v. Linde Air Products Co.*, 339 U.S. 605, 608, 70 S.Ct. 854, 856, 94 L.Ed. 1097 (1950) (quoting from *Sanitary Refrigerator Co. v. Winters*, 280 U.S. 30, 42, 50 S.Ct. 9, 13, 74 L.Ed. 147). The doctrine is judicially devised to do equity. "Courts have also recognized that to permit imitation of a patented invention which does not copy every literal detail would be to convert the protection of the patent grant into a hollow and useless thing," *id.* 339 U.S. at 607, 70 S.Ct. at 856, and again, "The essence of the doctrine is that one may not practice a fraud on a patent," *id.* at 608, 70 S.Ct. at 856.

> As summarized by the Supreme Court: Equivalence, in the patent law, is not the prisoner of a formula and is not an absolute to be considered in a vacuum. It does not require complete identity for every purpose and in every respect. In determining equivalents, things equal to the same thing may not be equal to each other and, by the same token, things for most purposes different may sometimes be equivalents.

Id. at 609, 70 S.Ct. at 856–57.

Hughes, having the burden of proving infringement by a preponderance of the evidence, *Roberts Dairy Co. v. United States*, 530 F.2d 1342, 1357, 182 USPQ 218, 227 (Trial Div., Ct.Cl.1974), *aff'd* 198 USPQ 383 (Ct.Cl.1976), characterizes as "inconsequential" the differences in operation of the claimed invention and the accused S/E spacecraft. It asserts that the Williams satellite and S/E spacecraft are "obvious and exact equivalents". Hughes argues that: * * * (3) "[i]f there were doubt as to whether the S/E spacecraft are obvious and exact equivalents of Williams, the S/E spacecraft nevertheless fall within the broad range of equivalents to which the pioneer Williams patent is entitled."

Addressing the last argument first, we agree with the trial judge that Williams' invention is not of such "pioneer" status as to entitle the invention to the very broad range of equivalents to which pioneer inventions are normally entitled. McLean, not Williams, was the first to disclose the basic operational concept in which a pulsed jet is used to precess the spin axis of a spin-stabilized body. That does not mean, as discussed below, that the Williams invention is entitled to no range of equivalents. Nor is the Williams invention entitled only to that very narrow range of equivalents applicable to improvement patents in a crowded art.

Having chosen specific words of limitation to avoid the McLean disclosure, Hughes is estopped by the prosecution history of the application ("file wrapper estoppel"), from obtaining a claim interpretation so broad as to encompass the McLean structure, or to encompass all structures in which a pulsed jet is used to precess the spin axis of a spin-stabilized body. The doctrine of prosecution history estoppel precludes a patent owner from obtaining a claim construction that would resurrect subject matter surrendered during prosecution of his patent application. The estoppel applies to claim amendments to overcome rejections based on prior art, *Dwyer v. United States,* 357 F.2d 978, 984, 149 USPQ 133, 138 (Ct.Cl.1966), and to arguments submitted to obtain the patent, *Coleco Industries, Inc. v. ITC,* 573 F.2d 1247, 1257, 197 USPQ 472, 480 (Cust. & Pat.App.1978). Williams did not, of course, surrender subject matter related to employment of an on-board computer to accomplish in a differently timed manner what is accomplished by his disclosed structure.

An applicant for patent is required to disclose the best mode then known to him for practicing his invention. 35 U.S.C. § 112. He is not required to predict all future developments which enable the practice of his invention in substantially the same way.

The trial judge correctly stated that Hughes is estopped from asserting that the elements of its claims "are unnecessary to avoid the art". The relevant consideration, however, is not whether the claims avoid the art but whether the accused S/E spacecraft are equivalents of the inventions set forth in the claims interpreted in light of the prior art. The government is not claiming that its S/E spacecraft are built and operated in accord with the prior art, or that it is merely following the teachings of McLean. If it had followed those teachings in constructing its S/E spacecraft, there is no question that the range of equivalents to which Williams' claimed invention is entitled could not be broad enough to encompass such spacecraft.

Some courts have expressed the view that virtually any amendment of the claims creates a "file wrapper estoppel" effective to bar all resort to the doctrine of equivalents, and to confine patentee "strictly to the letter of the limited claims granted," *Nationwide Chemical Corp. v. Wright,* 584 F.2d 714, 718–19 (5th Cir.1978); *Ekco Products Co. v. Chicago Metallic Manufacturing Co.,* 347 F.2d 453, 455 (7th Cir.1965). We, as has the Supreme Court, reject that view as a wooden application of estoppel, negating entirely the doctrine of equivalents and limiting determination of the infringement issue to consideration of *literal* infringement alone. That view, as above indicated, fails to recognize that the doctrine of equivalents is unnecessary when literal infringement is present and is contrary to the guidance provided by the Supreme Court in *Graver,* supra.

Amendment of claims is a common practice in prosecution of patent applications. No reason or warrant exists for limiting application of the doctrine of equivalents to those comparatively few claims allowed exactly as originally filed and never amended. Amendments may be of different types and may serve different functions. Depending on the nature and purpose of an amendment, it may have a limiting effect within a spectrum ranging from great to small to zero. The effect may or may not be fatal to application of a range of equivalents broad enough to encompass a particular accused product. It is not fatal to application of the doctrine itself.

We adhere to the view expressed by our predecessor court in *Autogiro Co. of America v. United States,* 384 F.2d 391, 155 USPQ 697 (Ct.Cl.1967), and in *Garrett Corp. v. United States,* 422 F.2d 874, 164 USPQ 521 (Ct.Cl.), *cert. denied,* 400 U.S. 951, 91 S.Ct. 242, 27 L.Ed.2d 257 (1970). Discussing the relationship between the doctrines in *Autogiro,* the Court of Claims said:

> The doctrine of equivalence is subservient to file wrapper estoppel. It may not include within its range anything that would vitiate limitations expressed before the Patent Office. Thus a patent that has been severely limited to avoid the prior art will only have a small range between it and the point beyond which it violates file wrapper estoppel [Citations omitted].

384 F.2d at 400–01; 155 USPQ at 705.

Referring to the April 29, 1966 amendment described above, Hughes says: "All that Williams surrendered in order to avoid the prior art cited by the examiner were any claims that could be construed as applying to an automatic attitude control system not controllable from earth * * * [the] amendment did nothing but more accurately claim ground controllability as the point of novelty." We disagree. In that amendment, Williams did not submit claims broadly covering all ground controllable spacecraft, as he might have. Had he done so, and had such claims been allowed, literal infringement would have been present here. At the same time, Williams' amendment of the claims did not relate to any disclosure, in the prior art or elsewhere, in which the ISA position was stored in a computer along with command signals for later execution. Though we cannot agree that Williams' amendment left room for encompassing all ground-controlled spacecraft, it remains true that the operation of the Williams and S/E spacecraft involve control input from a ground crew, and McLean does not. That is an important consideration in applying the doctrine of equivalents. It does not *alone* establish infringement under that doctrine.

APPLICATION OF THE DOCTRINE OF EQUIVALENTS

* * *

In *Eastern Rotorcraft*, the Court of Claims afforded the patentee a limited application of the doctrine of equivalents, concluding that the range of equivalents of the claimed invention there encompassed the accused device. We hold that the trial judge erred as a matter of law in not so interpreting the scope of Williams' claims 1, 2, and 3 in their entirety, and in applying an appropriate range of equivalents to the entirety of the accused S/E spacecraft.

There are striking overall similarities between Williams' claimed satellite and the S/E spacecraft: * * * Clearly, the S/E spacecraft are much closer to Williams' satellite than they are to McLean's space vehicle. It is clear also that, in constructing its S/E spacecraft, the government followed the teachings of Williams much more than it did those of McLean. In following Williams' teachings, the government merely employed a modern day computer to do indirectly what Williams taught it to do directly.

The dispute as presented centers on what appears in paragraphs (e), (f), and (g), of representative claim 1: * * *

PARAGRAPH (E) "PROVIDING AN INDICATION"

Based on the testimony of its expert, Arthur E. Bryson, Jr., Hughes argues that the S/E spacecraft, with the ISA position indication retained on-board, are equivalents of Williams' claimed satellite, with the ISA position indication sent to ground, performance of the function involving the ISA position being substantially the same in each. We agree. Once an on-board computer became available, as Bryson said, "any intelligent engineer designing this [S/E] system would say 'Look, I don't need to send the value of that ISA position to the ground, it's right there in the spacecraft. I'll just key my firing signal to that on board the spacecraft'."

The S/E spacecraft are identical with the Williams satellite, except for the employment of sophisticated, post-Williams equipment (computers) to achieve attitude control in the basic manner taught by Williams. Advanced computers and digital communications techniques developed since Williams permit doing on-board a *part* of what Williams taught as done on the ground. As one of our predecessor courts, the Court of Claims, has thrice made clear, that partial variation in technique, an embellishment made possible by post-Williams technology, does not allow the accused spacecraft to escape the "web of infringement". *Bendix Corp. v. United States,* 600 F.2d 1364, 1382, 204 USPQ 617, 631 (Ct.Cl.1979); *see Decca Ltd. v. United States,* 544 F.2d 1070, 1080–81, 191 USPQ 439, 447–48 (Ct.Cl.1976); *Eastern Rotorcraft Corp. v. United States,* 397 F.2d at 981, 154 USPQ at 45. * * * Williams controls his satellite, and the government controls its S/E spacecraft, from the ground. That Williams does so in "real time" and the government does so in a delayed reaction made possible by the advent of computers does not establish that the S/E spacecraft do not perform the same function in substantially the same way to obtain the same result.

PARAGRAPHS (F) & (G) "DIRECT" VS. "INDIRECT" FIRING

The distinction emphasized by the government between "direct" firing and its own "indirect" firing, phrased also as a distinction between "external" and "internal" synchronization of command signals with ISA position, and as a distinction between firing in "fixed" time and in "computer-set" time, rests on the government's use of modern memory circuits on-board S/E spacecraft to store commands for later use. As above indicated, mere substitution of an embellishment made possible by post-Williams technology does not avoid infringement. *See Bendix Corp., Decca Ltd.,* and *Eastern Rotorcraft, supra.* Applying the guidance of those cases, along with that in *Graver, supra,* the range of equivalents of the present claims reaches the S/E spacecraft, wherein sun pulses, though retained on-board, are derived and used in the same way as in Williams to perform the same function, jet firing, which, though "indirect", is synchronized with ISA position precisely as taught by Williams.

The S/E spacecraft and the Williams claimed satellite each have on-board means for transmitting to ground the sun angle and spin rate. In each, the ground crew determines: (1) present orientation; (2) desired orientation; and (3) where in the spin cycle and how many times the jet must be pulsed to change (1) to (2). Each system, furthermore, provides for receipt of command signals to cause firing of the precession jet. The S/E spacecraft uses sun pulses retained on-board as reference points to fire the jet. Williams uses sun pulses sent to ground as reference points to fire the jet. The difference between operation by retention and operation by sending is achieved by relocating the function, making no change in the function performed, or in the basic manner of operation, or in the result obtained.

CONCLUSION ON EQUIVALENTS

The S/E spacecraft and the claimed Williams satellite reflect the precise circumstance envisaged in *Graver, supra,* for they perform the same function (receipt of and response to command signals from an external location to accomplish precession), in substantially the same way (jet firings synchronized, albeit later and internally, with ISA position) to obtain substantially the same result (controlled precession of spin axis in a predetermined direction to orient a hovering satellite).

At the same time, neither resembles as closely the self-guiding space vehicle of McLean or its purely automatic operation.

Accordingly, we hold that Hughes has proven that the government's S/E spacecraft infringe Williams' claims 1, 2, and 3 under the doctrine of equivalents.

* * *

SRI INTERNATIONAL v. MATSUSHITA ELECTRIC CORPORATION OF AMERICA

United States Court of Appeals, Federal Circuit, 1985.
775 F.2d 1107, 227 USPQ 577.

MARKEY, CHIEF JUDGE.

SRI International (SRI) appeals from a final judgment of the United States District Court for the Northern District of California granting summary judgment of non-infringement to Matshushita Electric Corporation (MEI). 591 F.Supp. 464, 224 USPQ 70 (1984). We reverse.

* * *

Availability of the reverse doctrine of equivalents was set forth by the Supreme Court in *Graver Tank & Mfg. Co., Inc. v. Linde Air Prods. Co., Inc.,* 339 U.S. 605, 608–09, 70 S.Ct. 854, 856–57, 94 L.Ed. 1097, 85 USPQ 328, 330 (1950):

> The wholesome realism of [the doctrine of equivalents] is not always applied in favor of a patentee but is sometimes used against him. Thus, where a device is so far changed in principle from a patented article that it performs the same or a similar function in a substantially different way, but nevertheless falls within the literal words of the claim, the doctrine of equivalents may be used [in reverse] to restrict the claim and defeat the patentee's action for infringement.

As made clear in *Graver Tank,* in which the Court upheld a finding of infringement under the doctrine of equivalents as "supported by the record" and "not clearly erroneous", the ultimate finding of infringement, or "actual infringement," may depend on facts and circumstances unique to the case.

* * *

There is no question, as the district court found and as SRI from the outset admitted, that MEI's filter and camera are so operated as to perform their functions in a way that differs from the way in which the structure of SRI's Figure 1 performs those functions. SRI and MEI had the right, however, to adduce documentary and testimonial evidence at trial in an effort to convince the fact finder that the MEI filter is or is not "so *far* changed in principle" that it performs "in a *substantially* different way."

The test mandated in *Graver Tank* leaves room for the fact finder's application to varying circumstances. Words like "so far", "principle" and "substantially" are not subject to rigid pre-definition; nor will the "principle" of a structural invention be always and immediately apparent. It is precisely the role of a trial to apply the test in light of all the live testimony and physical evidence adduced. * * * In sum, the key infringement question, i.e., whether a principle has been so *far* changed that the way is *substantially* different, depends on the evidence.

The Supreme Court supplied guidance useful here in *Graver Tank,* 339 U.S. at 609, 70 S.Ct. at 856–57, 85 USPQ at 330 (e.g., equivalence is not the prisoner of a formula, nor an absolute to be considered in a vacuum; it does not require identity in every purpose and respect; it is determined against the context of the patent, the prior art, and particular circumstances of the case; one factor is whether the accused product resulted from independent research; an important factor is whether persons reasonably skilled in the art would have known of the interchangeability of an ingredient not contained in the patent with one that was). A major factual dispute in this case, for example, is whether the parties employ substantially different ways of encoding color (MEI's position) or readily interchangeable ways long known to those skilled in the art for whom patents are written (SRI's position). *See Thomas & Betts Corp. v. Litton Systems, Inc.,* 720 F.2d 1572, 1580, 220 USPQ 1, 6 (Fed.Cir.1983) (known interchangeability of elements is evidence of equivalence).

* * *

The genuine and material fact question of whether MEI's filter and camera are "so far changed in principle" that they "perform the same or a similar function in a substantially different way" being present and disputed, the district court erred in granting summary judgment.

Reversed.

EXHIBIT SUPPLY CO. v. ACE PATENTS CORP.[p]

Supreme Court of the United States, 1941.
315 U.S. 126, 62 S.Ct. 513, 86 L.Ed. 736.

MR. CHIEF JUSTICE STONE delivered the opinion of the Court:

Respondent began the present litigation as three separate suits against the respective petitioners for infringement of the Nelson Patent No. 2,109,678 of March 1, 1938, for a "contact switch for ball rolling games." The defenses were noninvention in view of the prior art, anticipation by prior publication, use and sale, noninfringement and a file wrapper estoppel. The three suits were consolidated and tried together. Upon full consideration of the issues the District Court and the Circuit Court of Appeals for the Seventh Circuit held Claim 4 of the patent valid and infringed. 119 F.2d 349.

* * *

The patent relates to the structure of a resilient switch or circuit closer, so disposed on the board of a game table as to serve as a target

p. See exhibits at the end of this case.
The patent involved in this case is set out,
supra, page 609.

which, when struck by a freely rolling ball, will momentarily close an electrical circuit. Specifications and drawings disclose a target or switch comprising a conductor standard mounted in the table and carrying a coil spring having a leg pendantly disposed in a conductor ring located in the table and slightly offset from the standard. The standard and ring are wired in a circuit with a relay coil and a source of electrical energy. When a ball rolling on the table bumps the coil spring from any direction, the leg of the spring is deflected momentarily bringing it into contact with the ring, so as to close the circuit for operating the relay coil and any connected auxiliary game device. Any desired number of targets may be placed on the board in a suitably spaced relationship; in pin ball games a single ball may successively bump and close a number of the switch devices. In describing his invention the patentee declared it to be his intention "to cover all changes and modifications of the example of the invention herein chosen for purposes of the disclosure, which do not constitute departures from the spirit and scope of the invention."

The prior art as disclosed by the record shows no device in which the coil spring serves both as a target and a switch. The advantages of the device are said to be that the combination is peculiarly adapted to use in pin ball games; that the coil spring structure is so organized as to form both a switch for operating auxiliary recording or signalling devices and a target which is accessible from any direction.

Claim 4[1] claims as the elements of the invention the conductor standard anchored in the table, the coil spring surrounding the standard which carries the spring pendantly from its top, with the spring spaced from the standard to enable the spring to be resiliently flexed, "and conductor means in said circuit and embedded in the table at a point spaced from the standard and engageable by a portion of the spring when it is flexed to close the aforementioned circuit." The drawings of the patent show the "conductor means" last mentioned in the form of a ring or ferrule set in the table with its axis at right angles to the table and with its flange projecting slightly above the surface of the table. The leg pending from the coil spring is so disposed at the center of the annular ferrule that a ball striking the spring in any direction will bring the pendant leg into contact with the ring so as to close the circuit.

1. "4. In a ball rolling game having a substantially horizontal table over which balls are rollable, the combination with said table of a substantially vertical standard anchored in said table with its lower end carrying on the underside of the table a lead for an electric circuit and its upper end extending a substantial distance above the top surface of the table, a coil spring surrounding the standard, means carrying said spring pendantly from the upper portion of the standard above the table with the coils of the spring spaced from the standard to enable the spring to be resiliently flexed when bumped by a ball rolling on the table, said spring being in the aforementioned circuit and constituting a conductor, and conductor means in said circuit and embedded in the table at a point spaced from the standard and engageable by a portion of the spring when it is flexed to close the aforementioned circuit."

The six devices alleged to infringe the patent differ from the particular claim of the invention described in the specifications, only in the specific form and method of supporting the "conductor means" which is "engageable by a portion of the spring when it is flexed." In two of the accused devices, plaintiff's Exhibits 5 and 7, there is substituted for the ring conductor set in the table a nail or pin driven into the table and surrounded near its upper end by a ring attached to the end of the resilient coil spring, or formed there of the coil wire. When the spring is struck the circuit is closed by the contact of ring and nail at a point above the table. This arrangement contrasts with that of the conductors as shown in the patent drawings, in which a ring set in the table and the pendant leg of the coil form the contact at a point near or below the surface of the table. In the one case the ring conductor is supported by the table and the complementary conductor is attached to or is formed of the wire of the spring at its end. In the other the locations of the ring and of the complementary conductor are reversed.

Two others of the accused devices, plaintiff's Exhibits 6 and 10, show a further alteration. In Exhibit 6, the nail or pin, instead of being driven directly into the table, is affixed to and supported by a metal plate resting on the upper surface of the table with the coil spring standard passing through it and holding it firmly on the table. The conductor extends to the wire connection through a hole in the table underneath the plate. In Exhibit 10 the conductor is insulated from the plate, which is rigidly anchored to the coil spring standard, which in turn is anchored to the table.

In the remaining two accused devices, plaintiff's Exhibits 8 and 9, an insulating core or sleeve surrounds the coil standard and supports an annular or enveloping conductor wired in the circuit, spaced and insulated from the coil standard so that the circuit is closed by contact of the conductor and the coil when it is flexed. In Exhibit 8 the sleeve is electrically connected with a metal plate, held in position on the top of the table by the standard which passes through the plate. A wire leading from the plate passes through a hole in the table underneath the plate. In Exhibit 9 the annular conductor is located above the table top and a wire leading from it passes through a hole in the table.

Comparison of the several accused devices shows that in all but Exhibits 5 and 7 the conductor means complementary to the coil spring is not embedded in the table, but is supported by an insulated plate resting on the table or an insulating core held in position by the standard. In Exhibits 6 and 10 the conductor means passes to its wire connection through a hole in the table underneath the plate. In Exhibit 8 the connecting wire passes through a hole in the table to a metal plate resting on its surface, and in Exhibit 9 to the conductor means located above the surface of the table.

Petitioners insist that respondent is estopped to assert infringement by the file wrapper record in the Patent Office and in any event that estoppel can be avoided and infringement established only by resort to the doctrine of equivalents, which they assert is incompatible with the statutory requirements for the grant of a patent and with the doctrine that the patent claims measure the patented invention.

The file wrapper history, so far as now relevant, relates to Claim 7 which, after amendment, was allowed as Claim 4 now in issue. The original Claim 7 with its amendments is set forth as follows:

[Matter added by amendment in parentheses; matter stricken in italics and underscored.]

> (4) 7. In a ball rolling game having a substantially horizontal table over which balls are rollable, the combination with said table of a substantially vertical standard anchored in said table with its lower end carrying on the underside of the table a lead for an
>
> A¹ electric circuit and its upper end extending a substantial distance above the top surface of the table, a
>
> coil spring surrounding the standard, means carrying said spring pendantly from the upper portion of the standard
>
> per C (ABOVE THE TABLE) with coils of the spring spaced from the
>
> " " standard *and the lower end of the coil spring terminating*
>
> " " *at a distance above the top surface of the table* to enable the spring to be resiliently flexed when bumped
>
> by a ball rolling on the table, said spring being in the aforementioned circuit and constituting a conductor, and
>
> per B *other* conductor means (IN SAID CIRCUIT AND EMBEDDED IN) *carried by* the table at a point spaced from the standard and engageable by a portion of
>
> the spring when it is flexed to close the aforementioned circuit.

The original application contained six claims, all of which the examiner rejected because he thought no patentable significance had been shown. The inventor submitted certain amendments, and two new claims, 7 and 8, and induced the examiner to reconsider the patentability of the invention. Four of the claims were then allowed, but the examiner rejected Claim 7 as failing to claim the invention. He said: "It is old in the art to make an electrical contact by flexing a coil spring as shown by the art already cited in the case. In order to distinguish over the references therefor, the applicant's particular type of contact structure, comprising an extension on the coil spring adapted to engage an annular contact embedded in the table, must appear in the claims. * * *" Applicant rejected the examiner's suggestion that the "contact structure" be adapted to engage "an annular contact embedded in the table." Instead he cancelled "other" from the claim and substituted for "carried by" the phrase, "in said circuit and embedded in," saying Claim 7 has been "significantly amended" "to define the complementary conductor contact as being embedded in the table." He added that "it is too far to go to state that the specific leg 19 must be defined," and "the allowed claims can it seems, be very simply avoided by taking the leg 19, separating it from the spring 18 and embedding it as a pin in the table so that the spring when flexed would contact the pin.   *   *   * Claim 7 covers such alternative form and * * * in justice to applicant * * * should be allowed."

The examiner in reply recognized as "true" applicant's suggestion that if the leg pendant from the spring "were removed from the spring and embedded in the table an operative device would result," but pointed out that the device claimed by the amendment "would be inoperative as the coil spring could not both terminate at a distance above the table and extend into a ferrule embedded therein." Thereupon the applicant added to the claim the words "above the table" and cancelled the phrase, "and the lower end of the coil spring terminating at a distance above the top surface of the table." The claim as amended was then allowed as Claim 4.

The claim before amendment plainly read on plaintiff's Exhibits 5 and 7 in which the nail or pin conductor is driven into the table, since the nail or pin is a "conductor means carried by the table" "engageable by a portion of the spring when flexed." The claim thus read is for an operative device since the nail or pin projects above the table and may be engaged by the coil spring similarly located. The claim, as amended and allowed as Claim 4, likewise reads on Plaintiff's Exhibits 5 and 7 if the nail or pin conductor which is driven into the table is "embedded in the table."

*   *   *

We think that the word "embedded" as applied in Claim 4, must be taken to embrace any conductor means solidly set or firmly fixed in the table, whether or not it protrudes above or below the surface. Claim 7 before amendment read on the accused devices, plaintiff's Exhibits 5 and 7, which exhibit the nail or pin embedded in the table but protruding above its surface. Consequently the patentee by amending the claim so as to define the conductor means as embedded in the table did not exclude from the amended claim devices exemplified by these exhibits and they must be deemed to be infringements.

There remains the question whether respondent may rely upon the doctrine of equivalents to establish infringement by the four other accused devices. Respondent concedes that the conductor means in the four devices are not literally "embedded in the table," but insists that the changes in structure which they exhibit over that of plaintiff's Exhibits 5 and 7 are but the mechanical equivalents of the "conductor means embedded in the table" called for by the amended claim, and so are entitled to the protection afforded by the doctrine of equivalents. Petitioners do not seriously urge that the conductor means in the four accused devices are not mechanical equivalents of the conductor means embedded in the table which the patent claims. Instead they argue that the doctrine should be discarded because it does not satisfy the demands of the statute that the patent shall describe the invention. Rev.Stat. § 4888, 35 U.S.C.A. § 33.

We do not find it necessary to resolve these contentions here. Whatever may be the appropriate scope and application of the doctrine of equivalents, where a claim is allowed without a restrictive amendment, it has long been settled that recourse may not be had to that doctrine to recapture claims which the patentee has surrendered by amendment.

Assuming that the patentee would have been entitled to equivalents embracing the accused devices had he originally claimed a "conductor means embedded in the table," a very different issue is presented when the applicant in order to meet objections in the Patent Office, based on references to the prior art, adopted the phrase as a substitute for the broader one "carried by the table." Had Claim 7 been allowed in its original form it would have read upon all the accused devices since in all the conductor means complementary to the coil spring are "carried by the table." By striking that phrase from the claim and substituting for it "embedded in the table" the applicant restricted his claim to those combinations in which the conductor means, though carried on the table, is also embedded in it. By the amendment he recognized and emphasized the difference between the two phrases and proclaimed his abandonment of all that is embraced in that difference. Hubbell v. United States, 179 U.S. 77, 83, 21 S.Ct. 24, 45 L.Ed. 95, 99; Weber Electric Co. v. E.H. Freeman Electric Co., 256 U.S. 668, 677, 678, 41 S.Ct. 600, 65 L.Ed. 1162, 1167, 1168; I.T.S. Rubber Co. v. Essex Rubber Co., 272 U.S. 429, 440, 444, 47 S.Ct. 136, 71 L.Ed. 335, 341, 343; Smith v. Magic City Kennel Club, 282 U.S. 784, 789, 51 S.Ct. 291, 75 L.Ed. 707, 712; Schriber-Schroth Co. v. Cleveland Trust Co., 311 U.S. 211, 61 S.Ct. 235, 85 L.Ed. 132, cf. in case of disclaimer Altoona Publix Theatres v. American Tri-Ergon Corp., 294 U.S. 477, 492, 493, 55 S.Ct. 455, 79 L.Ed. 1005, 1015, 1016. The difference which he thus disclaimed must be regarded as material, and since the amendment operates as a disclaimer of that difference it must be strictly construed against him. Smith v. Magic City Kennel Club, supra (282 U.S. 790, 51 S.Ct. 291, 75 L.Ed. 712); Shepard v. Carrigan, 116 U.S. 593, 598, 6 S.Ct. 493, 29 L.Ed. 723, 724; Goodyear Dental Vulcanite Co. v. Davis, 102 U.S. 222, 228, 26 L.Ed. 149, 151. As the question is one of construction of the claim it is immaterial whether the examiner was right or wrong in rejecting the claim as filed. Hubbell v. United States, supra (179 U.S. 83, 21 S.Ct. 24, 45 L.Ed. 99); I.T.S. Rubber Co. v. Essex Rubber Co., supra (272 U.S. 443, 47 S.Ct. 136, 71 L.Ed. 342). It follows that what the patentee, by a strict construction of the claim, has disclaimed—conductors which are carried by the table but not embedded in it—cannot now be regained by recourse to the doctrine of equivalents, which at most operates, by liberal construction, to secure to the inventor the full benefits, not disclaimed, of the claims allowed.

Plaintiff's Exhibits 5 and 7 do, and its Exhibits 6, 8, 9 and 10 do not, infringe. The judgments will be modified accordingly.

Modified.

* * *

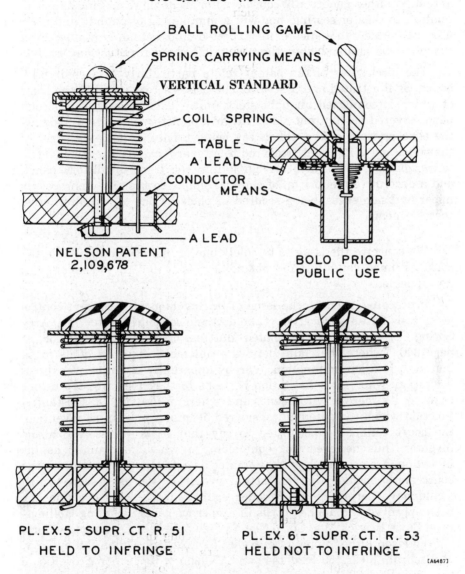

EXHIBIT SUPPLY CO. v. ACE PATENTS CORP.

315 U.S. 126 (1942)

BALL ROLLING GAME
SPRING CARRYING MEANS
VERTICAL STANDARD
COIL SPRING
TABLE
A LEAD
CONDUCTOR MEANS
A LEAD

NELSON PATENT 2,109,678

BOLO PRIOR PUBLIC USE

PL. EX. 5 - SUPR. CT. R. 51
HELD TO INFRINGE

PL. EX. 6 - SUPR. CT. R. 53
HELD NOT TO INFRINGE

[A6487]

AMERICAN SEATING CO. v. IDEAL SEATING CO.

United States Court of Appeals, Sixth Circuit, 1941.
124 F.2d 70, 52 USPQ 37.

SIMONS, CIRCUIT JUDGE. The patent, the validity of which and an asserted breadth of its claims are sought to be vindicated in the present suit, is one to Nordmark, No. 2,046,649, granted July 7, 1936, upon an application filed May 3, 1935. It is for a chair, particularly of the type used in theaters, and its object is to provide one having an improved back and improved means for mounting the back on its support.

* * *

It requires no historical review of the art to demonstrate its antiquity, either generically considered or in its more specific aspect in relation to theater seating, nor will a marshaling of patents and prior uses be needed to indicate its expected and actual crowding, even though it be assumed that there was left some room for invention.

The disclosures of the patent relate particularly to a chair back which, as illustrated and described, comprises a rear panel to the front of which is connected an upholstery unit. This consists of a second panel covered on its front side with an upholstery sheet and padding, the edge portions of the upholstery being turned around the edges of the panel and permanently secured to its rear face. The rear panel has screws passing forwardly through it into the front upholstery panel, and a decorative metal rim, of channel shape, covers and embraces its upper and side edges, being secured in place by one of two alternative specific means.

* * *

We conceive the issue to be solely one of infringement. While the court assumed validity it did not adjudicate it and the defendant has not appealed. * * *

Proceeding, then, to the issue of infringement, the present controversy calls for an application of the doctrine so clearly stated in D'Arcy Spring Co. v. Marshall Ventilated Mattress Co., 6 Cir., 259 F. 236, at page 240, "where the claim defines an element in terms of its form, material, location or function, thereby apparently creating an express limitation, where that limitation pertains to the inventive step rather than to its mere environment, and where it imports a substantial function which the patentee considered of importance to his invention, the court cannot be permitted to say that other forms, which the inventor thus declared not equivalent to what he claimed as his invention, are nevertheless to be treated as equivalent, even though the court may conclude that his actual invention was of a scope which would have permitted the broader equivalency." This doctrine has been approved and applied by us in numerous cases including Hollingshead Co. v. Bassick Mfg. Co., 6 Cir., 73 F.2d 543, 548; Directoplate Corp. v. Donaldson Lithographing Co., 6 Cir., 51 F.2d 199; Dillon Pulley Co. v. McEachran, 6 Cir., 69 F.2d 144; and Valjean v. Perfection Stove Co., 6 Cir., 103 F.2d 60.

It is clear to us, as it was to the District Judge, that in view of the prior art only a narrow range of equivalents is permitted to fall within the scope of the claims in suit. The essence of the invention lies in the precise retaining means and in their positioning. The defendant has not appropriated such retaining means and has not similarly positioned those it has employed so there is no room for the expansion of the claims by construction to bring the defendant's means within their ambit, by the application of the doctrine of equivalency.

* * *

Finally, Claim 4 recites, "means for fastening the retaining elements on the inner side of the forward member." The defendant fastens the retaining elements to the front face of the rear member. It is therefore contended that this is a mere reversal of parts. However, the language of the claim is specific as to location and it is clear that it was drafted to embrace an alternative construction and that the patentee considered this precise form important to his invention. There was not a mere reversal of parts, Sanitary Refrigerator Co. v. Winters, 280 U.S. 30, 42, 43, 50 S.Ct. 9, 74 L.Ed. 147. There was no infringement.

The decree below is affirmed.[s]

C. ACTS CONSTITUTING INFRINGEMENT

1. INTRODUCTION

The first Patent Act of 1790 provided that "if any person or persons shall devise, make, construct, use, employ, or vend within these United States * * * any invention or improvement * * * the sole and exclusive right of which shall be granted by patent * * *, without the consent of the patentee * * *, every person so offending shall forfeit and pay to the said patentee * * * such damages as shall be assessed by a jury * * *, which may be recovered in an action on the case founded on this act." Thus, violation of a patent right was a tort for which damages would lie.

This general definition of violation or infringement of a patent right by "making, using or selling" the patented invention was not more specifically defined by Congress until it passed the 1952 Patent Act. Indeed, even the aforesaid general definition of infringement was eliminated by the Patent Act of 1870. Accordingly, the courts have defined infringement and as would be expected there is some variation in judicial determinations of the outer limits of acts incurring liability for violating a patent right. Particular difficulty and uncertainty

---

s. Neither is it necessary that every embodiment be illustrated by the drawings unless the form of the device is the principle of the invention. Where the particular form is not an embodiment of the principle of the asserted invention, the patent is not restricted to the exact form of construction shown in the diagrammatical drawing. And a device infringes if it embodies the essential principles taught by the patent, even though there is a departure from the drawings to the extent of simple changes which would be readily conceived and made by a mechanic in the course of constructing a device on the patent. Johns-

Manville Corp. v. National Tank Seal Co., 10 Cir., 49 F.2d 142; Pangborn Corporation v. W.W. Sly Manufacturing Co., 4 Cir., 284 F. 217, certiorari denied 260 U.S. 749, 43 S.Ct. 249, 67 L.Ed. 495. Chicago Pneumatic Tool Co. v. Hughes Tool Co., 97 F.2d 945, 946, 38 USPQ 258, 259 (10th Cir., 1938).

See also: The Warner & Swasey Co. v. Universal Marion Corp., 237 F.Supp. 719, 742, 143 USPQ 371, 390, aff'd 354 F.2d 541, 148 USPQ 121 (D.C.Col.1964). Ackermans v. General Motors Corp., 202 F.2d 642, 646, 96 USPQ 281, 285 (4th Cir.1953).

occurred with the judicial concepts of inducing infringement and contributory infringement.

In the 1952 Patent Act, Congress addressed some of these problems in Section 271 which provides:

§ 271. Infringement of patent

(a) Except as otherwise provided in this title, whoever without authority makes, uses or sells any patented invention, within the United States during the term of the patent therefor, infringes the patent.

(b) Whoever actively induces infringement of a patent shall be liable as an infringer.

(c) Whoever sells a component of a patented machine, manufacture, combination or composition, or a material or apparatus for use in practicing a patented process, constituting a material part of the invention, knowing the same to be especially made or especially adapted for use in an infringement of such patent, and not a staple article or commodity of commerce suitable for substantial noninfringing use, shall be liable as a contributory infringer.

(d) No patent owner otherwise entitled to relief for infringement or contributory infringement of a patent shall be denied relief or deemed guilty of misuse or illegal extension of the patent right by reason of his having done one or more of the following: (1) derived revenue from acts which if performed by another without his consent would constitute contributory infringement of the patent; (2) licensed or authorized another to perform acts which if performed without his consent would constitute contributory infringement of the patent; (3) sought to enforce his patent rights against infringement or contributory infringement.

(e)(1) It shall not be an act of infringement to make, use, or sell a patented invention (other than a new animal drug or veterinary biological product (as those terms are used in the Federal Food, Drug, and Cosmetic Act and the Act of March 4, 1913)) solely for uses reasonably related to the development and submission of information under a Federal law which regulates the manufacture, use, or sale of drugs.

(2) It shall be an act of infringement to submit an application under section 505(j) of the Federal Food, Drug, and Cosmetic Act or described in section 505(b)(2) of such Act for a drug claimed in a patent or the use of which is claimed in a patent, if the purpose of such submission is to obtain approval under such Act to engage in the commercial manufacture, use, or sale of a drug claimed in a patent or the use of which is claimed in a patent before the expiration of such patent.

(3) In any action for patent infringement brought under this section, no injunctive or other relief may be granted which would prohibit the making, using, or selling of a patented invention under paragraph (1).

(4) For an act of infringement described in paragraph (2)—

(A) the court shall order the effective date of any approval of the drug involved in the infringement to be a date which is not earlier than the date of the expiration of the patent which has been infringed,

(B) injunctive relief may be granted against an infringer to prevent the commercial manufacture, use, or sale of an approved drug, and

(C) damages or other monetary relief may be awarded against an infringer only if there has been commercial manufacture, use, or sale of an approved drug.

The remedies prescribed by subparagraphs (A), (B), and (C) are the only remedies which may be granted by a court for an act of infringement described in paragraph (2), except that a court may award attorney fees under section 285. (Added September 24, 1984, Public Law 98–417, sec. 202, 98 Stat. 1603.)

(f)(1) Whoever without authority supplies or causes to be supplied in or from the United States all or a substantial portion of the components of a patented invention, where such components are uncombined in whole or in part, in such manner as to actively induce the combination of such components outside of the United States in a manner that would infringe the patent if such combination occurred within the United States, shall be liable as an infringer.

(2) Whoever without authority supplies or causes to be supplied in or from the United States any component of a patented invention that is especially made or especially adapted for use in the invention and not a staple article or commodity of commerce suitable for substantial noninfringing use, where such component is uncombined in whole or in part, knowing that such component is so made or adapted and intending that such component will be combined outside of the United States in a manner that would infringe the patent if such combination occurred within the United States, shall be liable as an infringer.

Paragraphs (a) through (d) were enacted in 1952 and remain unchanged. Paragraph (a) broadly defined infringement and was intended to be declaratory only of the general judicial definition. Paragraphs (b) through (d) were intended to change the then existing common law. Paragraphs (b) and (c) defined and limited inducing and contributory infringement and in conjunction with paragraph (d) defined their interface with the antithetical judicial doctrine of patent misuse.

Paragraph (e) was added in 1984 as part of the provisions relating to patented drugs and biological products subject to the regulations of the Federal Food, Drug, and Cosmetic Acts. Paragraph (f) was also added in 1984 in response to the decision of the United States Supreme Court in Deepsouth Packing Co. v. Laitram Corp., 406 U.S. 518, 92 S.Ct.

1700, 32 L.Ed.2d 273 (1972) which held that making and partial assembly in the United States, and completing assembly outside the United States, of the component parts of a patented combination of elements was not infringement.

2. DIRECT INFRINGEMENT

PAPER CONVERTING MACHINE COMPANY v. MAGNA–GRAPHICS CORPORATION

United States Court of Appeals, Federal Circuit, 1984.
745 F.2d 11, 223 USPQ 591.

NICHOLS, SENIOR CIRCUIT JUDGE.

* * *

With this case we are once again confronted with a situation which tests the temporal limits of the American patent grant. *See Roche Products, Inc. v. Bolar Pharmaceutical Co.*, 733 F.2d 858, 221 USPQ 937 (Fed.Cir.1984). We must decide here the extent to which a competitor of a patentee can *manufacture* and test during the life of a patent a machine intended solely for post-patent use. Magna-Graphics asserts that no law prohibits it from soliciting orders for, *substantially* manufacturing, testing, or even delivering machinery which, if *completely* assembled during the patent term, would infringe. We notice, but Magna-Graphics adds that it is totally irrelevant, that Paper Converting has lost, during the term of its patent, a contract for the patented machine which it would have received but for the competitor's acts.

* * *

The disjunctive language of the patent grant gives a patentee the "right to exclude others from making, using or selling" a patented invention during the 17 years of the patent's existence. 35 U.S.C. § 154. *See also* 35 U.S.C. § 271. Congress has never deemed it necessary to define any of this triad of excludable activities, however, leaving instead the meaning of "make," "use," and "sell" for judicial interpretation. *See Roche Products, Inc. v. Bolar Pharmaceutical Co., supra.* Nevertheless, by the terms of the patent grant, *no* activity other than the unauthorized making, using, or selling of the claimed invention can constitute direct infringement of a patent, *no matter* how great the adverse impact of that activity on the economic value of a patent. Judge Learned Hand stated, in *Van Kannell Revolving Door Co. v. Revolving Door & Fixture Co.*, 293 F. 261, 262 (S.D.N.Y.1920), that irrespective of where the equities may lie:

> [A] patent confers an exclusive right upon the patentee, limited in those terms. He may prevent any one from making, selling, or using a structure embodying the invention, but the monopoly goes no further than that. It restrains every one from the conduct so described, and it does not restrain him from anything else. If, therefore, any one says to a possible customer of a patentee, "I will make the article myself; don't buy of the patentee," while he may be doing the patentee a

wrong, and while equity will forbid his carrying out his promise, the promise itself is not part of the conduct which the patent forbids; it is not a "subtraction" from the monopoly. If it injures the plaintiff, though never performed, perhaps it is a wrong, like a slander upon his title, but certainly it is not an infringement of the patent.

Here, the dispositive issue is whether Magna-Graphics engaged in the making, use, or sale of something which the law recognizes as embodying an invention protected by a patent. Magna-Graphics relies on *Deepsouth Packing Co. v. Laitram Corp.*, 406 U.S. 518, 92 S.Ct. 1700, 32 L.Ed.2d 273, 173 USPQ 769 (1972). That case dealt with a "combination patent" covering machinery for shrimp deveining. The only active issue was whether certain export sales were properly prohibited in the district court's injunction and whether damages should include compensation for past infringement by these exports. The infringer had put in effect a practice of selling the machines disassembled for export, but with the subassemblies so far advanced, and with such instructions, that the foreign consignee could put them together on receipt in operable condition with an hour's work. The Supreme Court's five to four holding that these exports did not infringe was interwoven of three strands of thought: (1) that the patent laws must be construed strictly because they create a "monopoly" in the patentee; (2) that a "combination patent" is not infringed until its elements are brought together into an "operable assembly;" and (3) that an attempt to enforce the patent against a machine assembled abroad was an attempt to give it extraterritorial application and to invade improperly the sovereignty of the country where the final assembly and the intended use occurred.

Magna-Graphics' effort to apply *Deepsouth* as precedential runs into the obvious difficulty that the element of extraterritoriality is absent here, yet it obviously was of paramount importance to the *Deepsouth* Court. * * *

Although in *Deepsouth* the Court at times used broad language in reaching its decision, it is clear that *Deepsouth* was intended to be narrowly construed as applicable only to the issue of the extraterritorial effect of the American patent law. The Court so implied not only in *Deepsouth* ("[A]t stake here is the right of American companies to compete with an American patent holder *in foreign markets. Our patent system makes no claim to extraterritorial effect,* * * *" 406 U.S. at 531, 92 S.Ct. at 1708, 173 USPQ at 774 (emphasis added)), but in a subsequent decision as well ("The question under consideration [in *Deepsouth*] was whether a patent is infringed when unpatented elements are assembled into the combination *outside the United States.*" *Dawson Chemical Co. v. Rohm & Haas Co.*, 448 U.S. 176, 216, 100 S.Ct. 2601, 2623, 65 L.Ed.2d 696, 206 USPQ 385, 405 (1980) (emphasis added).). * * *

While there is thus a horror of giving extraterritorial effect to United States patent protection, there is no corresponding horror of a valid United States patent giving economic benefits not cut off entirely on patent expiration. Thus, we hold that the expansive language used in *Deepsouth* is not controlling in the present case. The facts in *Deepsouth* are *not* the facts here. Because no other precedent controls our decision here, however, we nevertheless look to *Deepsouth* and elsewhere for guidance on the issue of whether what Magna-Graphics did is an infringement of the '353 patent.

A further examination of the *Deepsouth* opinion reveals that the Court stated what was for it a most unusual reliance on a precedent established in an inferior court, the case being *Radio Corporation of America v. Andrea*, 79 F.2d 626 (2d Cir.1935). The reason for this was the eminently logical one that when in 1952 the Congress recodified the patent law, and specifically § 271, the most relevant precedent was *Andrea* as to the legal effect of exporting, unassembled, components that if exported assembled would infringe a "combination patent." Presumably the Congress accepted and enacted Judge Swan's interpretation in *Andrea*, absent any relevant pronouncement by our highest court.

Judge Swan's opinion on the appeal from a preliminary injunction is, indeed, a rather dramatic application of the view of the law he announced. The patents related to radio receiving sets. The alleged infringer, Andrea, exported them complete except for vacuum tubes exported *in the same package*, but not in their sockets. All the buyer had to do to have a patented set was, therefore, to put the tube in the socket designed to receive it. Swan's opinion does not mention any horror of extraterritoriality. Rather, the analysis is that the sale in this condition, even to domestic users, is not a direct infringement, but is only a contributory infringement. Thus, the practical impact of the Swan opinion, but not its reasoning, is limited to export sales, where contributory infringement is not logically applicable. Swan notes, however, as possible direct infringement evidence, that the alleged infringer put the tubes in their sockets to test them, and the sets generally, and then disassembled for export, and the reversal leaves it open to the trial court to look into this.

The trial court thereafter made further findings and entered its final judgment (then called its decree) and the case came up again, same name, 90 F.2d 612 (2d Cir.1937). Where previously the panel had consisted of only Swan and the subsequently ill-famed Manton, this time Circuit Judge Chase was added and Manton authored the opinion. The matter of testing was now clarified, and it was also now clear to the panel:

> The purchaser to connect the tube needs only insert it in the socket. No adjustment is required; no screw or nut need be tightened. Where the elements of an invention are thus sold in substantially unified and combined form, infringement may not be avoided by a separation or division of parts which leaves to the purchaser a simple task of integration. Otherwise a patentee would be denied adequate protection.

[*Id.* at 613.]

The court further noted that in part the sets were fully assembled for testing in the United States and that the sales of the completed though partly disassembled sets were made in the United States. The main problem dealt with in the second *Andrea* opinion was what "implied license" the infringer acquired when it bought the tubes separately.

Swan dissented, saying the holding that the sale of the disassembled parts in this country was an infringement overruled the decision in 79 F.2d 626. This history was, of course, not overlooked in the Supreme Court and is mentioned by Justice Blackmun in his dissent in *Deepsouth.*

What are we to make of all this? It does seem as if the concept of an "operable assembly" put forward by Justice White in his majority opinion is probably something short of a full and complete assembly; thus, if the infringer makes an "operable assembly" of the components of the patented invention, sufficient for testing, it need not be the same thing as the complete and entire invention. The other thing is, if the infringer has tested his embodiment of the invention sufficiently to satisfy him, this may be a "use," because as held in *Roche Products, Inc.,* "use" includes use for the purpose of testing. * * *

It is undisputed that Magna-Graphics intended to finesse Paper Converting out of the sale of a machine on which Paper Converting held a valid patent during the life of that patent. Given the amount of testing performed here, coupled with the sale and delivery during the patent-term of a "completed" machine (completed by being ready for assembly and with no useful noninfringing purpose), we are not persuaded that the district court committed clear error in finding that the Magna-Graphics' machine infringed the '353 patent.

To reach a contrary result would emasculate the congressional intent to prevent the making of a patented item during the patent's full term of 17 years. If without fear of liability a competitor can assemble a patented item past the point of testing, the last year of the patent becomes worthless whenever it deals with a long lead-time article. Nothing would prohibit the unscrupulous competitor from aggressively marketing its own product and constructing it to all but the final screws and bolts, as Magna-Graphics did here. We rejected any reduction to the patent-term in *Roche;* we cannot allow the inconsistency in the patent law which would exist if we permitted it here. Magna-Graphics built and tested a patented machine, albeit in a less than preferred fashion. Because an "operable assembly" of components was tested, this case is distinguishable from *Interdent Corp. v. United States,* 531 F.2d 547, 552 (Ct.Cl.1976) (omission of a claimed element from the patented combination avoids infringement) and *Decca Ltd. v. United States,* 640 F.2d 1156, 1168, 209 USPQ 52, 61 (Ct.Cl.1980) (infringement does not occur until the combination has been constructed and available for use). Where, as here, significant, unpatented assemblies of elements are tested during the patent term, enabling the infringer to deliver the patented combination in parts to the buyer, without testing the entire combination together as was the infringer's usual practice, testing the assemblies can be held to be in essence testing the patented combination and, hence, infringement.

That the machine was not operated in its optimum mode is inconsequential: imperfect practice of an invention does not avoid infringement. We affirm the district court's finding that "[d]uring the testing of the Fort Howard machine in July and August 1981, Magna-Graphics completed an operable assembly of the infringing rewinder."

* * *

3. INDUCING DIRECT INFRINGEMENT

FROMBERG, INC. v. THORNHILL

United States Court of Appeals, Fifth Circuit, 1963.
315 F.2d 407, 137 USPQ 84.

JOHN R. BROWN, CIRCUIT JUDGE.

This appeal by the Patentee of the Fromberg Patent of 1957 from an adverse judgment of the District Court presents questions of Defendant's liability for inducing others to infringe under 35 U.S.C.A. § 271(b) * * *

Fromberg discloses a simple device toward solving another one of the automotive age's problems—the repair of a puncture in the modern tubeless tire. The contribution—although hardly claimed to have been earth-shaking—is principally that the tire can be repaired without demounting the tire thus eliminating the risk of rim leaks. Recognizing the likelihood that Judges make poor patent draftsmen, we describe it loosely with like simplicity. In effect, the appliance is in two parts. One part is a hollow metal tube a couple of inches in length and, for varying repairs and tires, about one-quarter inch or so in diameter. The second part is a rubber cylindrical plug. This plug is inserted in the hollow tube for its whole length. This rubber insert is held firmly in place through compression. In its manufactured state, it is all in one piece—a solidly filled metal tube. In use it works this way. By a special tool, the assembly is inserted into the hole in the body of the tire. By manipulation of the special tool, the rubber plug insert is pushed out of the metal tube while the tube is being withdrawn from the tire. The result is two-fold. First, the hole in the tire is now filled with the rubber plug which, being released from compression of the metal tube, has expanded considerably to afford a seal. Second, the metal tube is now empty. In that condition, it has no further use as a tire repair.

It is at this stage that the Defendant's activities are alleged to (a) induce infringement by others and (b) additionally constitute contributory infringement on his part. The device manufactured and sold by the Defendant is called "Miracle-Plug."

The "Miracle-Plug" is a single piece of compressible rubber. Its main body is a cylinder approximately one-quarter inch in diameter and a couple of inches in length at which place it then tapers down to a one-eighth inch diameter tail about two to three inches in length. It is undisputed that by first inserting the tail into the empty Fromberg metal tube, the Miracle Plug can be forcibly drawn into the tube for its full length.　When the surplus body and tail parts protruding beyond the end of the metal tube are cut (by simple pocket knife), the result is a device identical with the original Fromberg appliance.

It is also uncontradicted that Defendant (1) knew of this capability and (2) sold Miracle Plugs with knowledge that at least a substantial number were being used with empty, spent, Fromberg metal tubes.

In a nutshell his justification for this was not a feigned innocence that such uses were actually being made of his Miracle Plug.　Rather, it was the bold and candid one that he had a legal right to do this. * * * As to inducing infringement, § 271(b), we conclude that the Patentee is entitled to a reversal.

Evaluation of the evidence as to that phase requires that we consider the conduct—and its legality—on the part of the Defendant's purchasers, the dealers.　To be sure, they are not now parties.　But their action bears on Defendant's culpability.　Moreover, we are freshly reminded that for contributory infringement, there must first be a *direct* infringement.　Aro Mfg. Co. v. Convertible Top Replacement Co., 1961, 365 U.S. 336, 341, 81 S.Ct. 599, 5 L.Ed.2d 592.

We think that this record shows irresistibly that the dealers are infringing the patent.　Infringement arises if one without permission (a) makes, (b) uses, or (c) sells a patented device.　35 U.S.C.A. § 271(a); and § 154.　The dealer (tire service station) does that here.　No one would question that if a dealer as an incipient Firestone and by his own ingenuity were to fill the empty Fromberg tube with compressible rubber, he is "making" a new appliance.　Likewise, he would "use" it were it employed in repairing a tire in his shop.　So far as the dealer is concerned, it does not matter what the source of the renewal rubber plug is.　When the renewal process is complete, the thing is exactly the same as when sold by Fromberg.

If, as would be the case here, the resulting product, that is the device, is the same as the patented one so that in appearance, form, fact and function, it is identical, it matters not how or in what manner that was brought about.　3 Walker, Patents § 453 (Deller ed. 1937).　The person who does that surely infringes, if the term has any meaning at all.　But civil culpability need not stop with the dealer who does the final act of making, using or selling.　The prohibition of the law, now codified in § 271(b), extends to those who induce that infringement.　Of course inducement has connotations of active steps knowingly taken— knowingly at least in the sense of purposeful, intentional, as distinguished from accidental or inadvertent.　But with that qualifying approach, the term is as broad as the range of actions by which one in fact causes, or urges, or encourages, or aids another to infringe a patent.[11]

11. See Walker, Patents (Deller ed. 1962 Suppl.) pp. 1764–1771: "Active inducement, which is considered to be part of the judge-made doctrine of contributory infringement, involves 'the actionable tort of knowingly aiding or abetting another to

On this phase the Defendant stands condemned by his own admissions and the overwhelming evidence from several witnesses, none of which so far reflects any helpful mitigation. Thus, in selling Miracle Plugs to several dealer-customers, the Defendant personally demonstrated how that Plug could be inserted in an empty Fromberg tube to recreate the original device which he knew to be patented. Without regard, then, to the separate question involved in the § 271(c) contributory infringement phase whether this was a staple product capable of other uses, the sales pitch for the Miracle Plug was obvious: here is a way to salvage empty Fromberg tubes to enable the dealer to obtain for his stock (and use) a Fromberg device at considerable savings in out-of-pocket cost [12] and the elimination of the economic waste in a useless, spent, tube. This brings it home to Defendant in a spectacular way. From his own motive to profit by sales of Miracle Plugs, he shows his customers how to poach upon another's patent so that the illicit user may likewise profit.[t]

* * *

4. CONTRIBUTORY INFRINGEMENT

DAWSON CHEMICAL COMPANY v. ROHM AND HAAS COMPANY

United States Supreme Court, 1980.
448 U.S. 176, 100 S.Ct. 2601, 65 L.Ed.2d 696.

MR. JUSTICE BLACKMUN delivered the opinion of the Court.

This case presents an important question of statutory interpretation arising under the patent laws. The issue before us is whether the owner of a patent on a chemical process is guilty of patent misuse, and therefore is barred from seeking relief against contributory infringe-

---

infringe a patent.' (Note 66 Yale Law Journal 132, 1956) * * * The enactment of Section 271(b), although ambiguous, was supposed to and has been considered to codify prior law. * * * Hence, active inducement or contributory infringement have been generally limited to those situations where the defendant has induced someone else to infringe the plaintiff's patent and when the defendant himself has not infringed the patent by making, using, or selling the invention. [Gould-National Batteries v. Sonotone Corp., 130 U.S.P.Q. 26; N.D.Ill.(1961).]"

"The following has been adjudged infringing conduct: licensing others to use infringing machines and processes * * *; fitting machinery for operation at the purchaser's plant; * * * converting machinery or adjusting operating parts * * *; passing on information intending to bring about infringement, (Jones v. Radio Corp. of America, 131 F.Supp. 82); furnishing

drawings and granting license (Weyerhauser Timber Co. v. Bostich, D.C., 178 F.Supp. 757, accused machines, Conmar Products Corp. v. Tibony, 63 F.Supp. 372); and granting immunity from suit to an infringer * * *." P. 1764, 1962 Supplement. The cited Jones v. RCA case gives a good summary of pre-1952 Code decisions as to acts inducing infringement even without sales.

12. The cost of a Miracle Plug was in the neighborhood of half that of a Fromberg device.

t. See General Electric Co. v. Sciaky Bros., Inc., 304 F.2d 724, 729, 134 USPQ 55, 59 (6th Cir.1962) where the court said: "In order to induce its customers to purchase these machines, which embodied the principle of Sciaky's inventions, General Electric executed save harmless agreements to indemnify them against loss by reason of patent infringement on account of their use of the machines."

ment of its patent rights, if it exploits the patent only in conjunction with the sale of an unpatented article that constitutes a material part of the invention and is not suited for commercial use outside the scope of the patent claims. The answer will determine whether respondent, the owner of a process patent on a chemical herbicide, may maintain an action for contributory infringement against other manufacturers of the chemical used in the process. To resolve this issue, we must construe the various provisions of 35 U.S.C. § 271, which Congress enacted in 1952 to codify certain aspects of the doctrines of contributory infringement and patent misuse that previously had been developed by the judiciary.

* * *

* * * To place § 271 in proper perspective, therefore, we believe that it is helpful first to review in detail the doctrines of contributory infringement and patent misuse as they had developed prior to Congress' attempt to codify the governing principles.

As we have noted, the doctrine of contributory infringement had its genesis in an era of simpler and less subtle technology. Its basic elements are perhaps best explained with a classic example drawn from that era. In *Wallace v. Holmes,* 29 F.Cas. 74 (No. 17,100) (CC Conn. 1871), the patentee had invented a new burner for an oil lamp. In compliance with the technical rules of patent claiming, this invention was patented in a combination that also included the standard fuel reservoir, wick tube, and chimney necessary for a properly functioning lamp. After the patent issued, a competitor began to market a rival product including the novel burner but not the chimney. *Id.,* at 79. Under the sometimes scholastic law of patents, this conduct did not amount to direct infringement, because the competitor had not replicated every single element of the patentee's claimed combination. Cf., *e.g., Prouty v. Ruggles,* 16 Pet. 336, 341, 10 L.Ed. 985 (1842). Yet the court held that there had been "palpable interference" with the patentee's legal rights, because purchasers would be certain to complete the combination, and hence the infringement, by adding the glass chimney. 29 F.Cas., at 80. The court permitted the patentee to enforce his rights against the competitor who brought about the infringement, rather than requiring the patentee to undertake the almost insuperable task of finding and suing all the innocent purchasers who technically were responsible for completing the infringement. *Ibid.* See also *Bowker v. Dows,* 3 F.Cas. 1070 (No. 1,734) (CC Mass.1878).

The *Wallace* case demonstrates, in a readily comprehensible setting, the reason for the contributory infringement doctrine. It exists to protect patent rights from subversion by those who, without directly infringing the patent themselves, engage in acts designed to facilitate infringement by others. This protection is of particular importance in situations, like the oil lamp case itself, where enforcement against direct infringers would be difficult, and where the technicalities of patent law make it relatively easy to profit from another's invention without risking a charge of direct infringement. See *Thomson-Houston Electric Co. v. Ohio Brass Co.*, 80 F. 712, 721 (CA6 1897) (Taft, Circuit Judge); Miller, Some Views on the Law of Patent Infringement by Inducement, 53 J.Pat.Off.Soc. 86, 87–94 (1971).

* * * In *Leeds & Catlin Co. v. Victor Talking Machine Co.*, 213 U.S. 325, 29 S.Ct. 503, 53 L.Ed. 816 (1909), the Court upheld an injunction against contributory infringement by a manufacturer of phonograph discs specially designed for use in a patented disc-and-stylus combination. Although the disc itself was not patented, the Court noted that it was essential to the functioning of the patented combination, and that its method of interaction with the stylus was what "mark[ed] the advance upon the prior art." *Id.*, at 330, 29 S.Ct., at 504. It also stressed that the disc was capable of use only in the patented combination, there being no other commercially available stylus with which it would operate. The Court distinguished the result in *Morgan Envelope* on the broad grounds that "[n]ot one of the determining factors there stated exists in the case at bar," and it held that the attempt to link the two cases "is not only to confound essential distinctions made by the patent laws, but essential differences between entirely different things." 213 U.S., at 335, 29 S.Ct., at 506.

The contributory infringement doctrine achieved its high-water mark with the decision in *Henry v. A.B. Dick Co.*, 224 U.S. 1, 32 S.Ct. 364, 56 L.Ed. 645 (1912). In that case a divided Court extended contributory infringement principles to permit a conditional licensing arrangement whereby a manufacturer of a patented printing machine could require purchasers to obtain all supplies used in connection with the invention, including such staple items as paper and ink, exclusively from the patentee. The Court reasoned that the market for these supplies was created by the invention, and that sale of a license to use the patented product, like sale of other species of property, could be limited by whatever conditions the property owner wished to impose. *Id.*, at 31–32, 32 S.Ct., at 373. The *A.B. Dick* decision and its progeny in the lower courts led to a vast expansion in conditional licensing of patented goods and processes used to control markets for staple and nonstaple goods alike.

This was followed by what may be characterized through the lens of hindsight as an inevitable judicial reaction. In *Motion Picture Patents Co. v. Universal Film Mfg. Co.*, 243 U.S. 502, 37 S.Ct. 416, 61 L.Ed. 871 (1917), the Court signalled a new trend that was to continue for years thereafter. The owner of a patent on projection equipment attempted to prevent competitors from selling film for use in the patented equipment by attaching to the projectors it sold a notice purporting to condition use of the machine on exclusive use of its film. The film previously had been patented but that patent had expired. The Court addressed the broad issue whether a patentee possessed the right to condition sale of a patented machine on the purchase of articles "which are no part of the patented machine, and which are not patented." *Id.,* at 508, 37 S.Ct., at 417. Relying upon the rule that the scope of a patent "must be limited to the invention described in the claims," *id.,* at 511, 37 S.Ct., at 419, the Court held that the attempted restriction on use of unpatented supplies was improper:

> "Such a restriction is invalid because such a film is obviously not any part of the invention of the patent in suit; because it is an attempt, without statutory warrant, to continue the patent monopoly in this particular character of film after it has expired, and because to enforce it would be to create a monopoly in the manufacture and use of moving picture films, wholly outside of the patent in suit and of the patent law as we have interpreted it." *Id.,* at 518, 37 S.Ct., at 421.

By this reasoning, the Court focused on the conduct of the patentee, not that of the alleged infringer. It noted that as a result of lower court decisions, conditional licensing arrangements had greatly increased, indeed, to the point where they threatened to become "perfect instrument[s] of favoritism and oppression." *Id.,* at 515, 37 S.Ct., at 420. The Court warned that approval of the licensing scheme under consideration would enable the patentee to "ruin anyone unfortunate enough to be dependent upon its confessedly important improvements for the doing of business." *Ibid.* This ruling was directly in conflict with *Henry v. A.B. Dick Co., supra,* and the Court expressly observed that that decision "must be regarded as overruled." 243 U.S., at 518, 37 S.Ct., at 421.

The broad ramifications of the *Motion Picture* case apparently were not immediately comprehended, and in a series of decisions over the next three decades litigants tested its limits. In *Carbice Corp. v. American Patents Corp.,* 283 U.S. 27, 51 S.Ct. 334, 75 L.Ed. 819 (1931), the Court denied relief to a patentee who, through its sole licensee, authorized use of a patented design for a refrigeration package only to purchasers from the licensee of solid carbon dioxide ("dry ice"), a refrigerant that the licensee manufactured. The refrigerant was a well-known and widely used staple article of commerce, and the patent in question claimed neither a machine for making it nor a process for using it. *Id.,* at 29, 51 S.Ct., at 334. The Court held that the patent holder and its licensee were attempting to exclude competitors in the refrigerant business from a portion of the market, and that this conduct constituted patent misuse. It reasoned:

> "Control over the supply of such unpatented material is beyond the scope of the patentee's monopoly; and this limitation, inherent in the patent grant, is not dependent upon the peculiar function or character of the unpatented material or on the way in which it is used. Relief is denied because the [licensee] is attempting, without sanction of law, to employ the patent to secure a limited monopoly of unpatented material used in applying the invention." *Id.,* at 33–34, 51 S.Ct., at 336.

The Court also rejected the patentee's reliance on the *Leeds & Catlin* decision. It found "no suggestion" in that case that the owner of the disc-stylus combination patent had attempted to derive profits from the sale of unpatented supplies as opposed to a patented invention. 283 U.S., at 34, 51 S.Ct., at 336.

Other decisions of a similar import followed. * * *

Although none of these decisions purported to cut back on the doctrine of contributory infringement itself, they were generally perceived as having that effect, and how far the developing doctrine of patent misuse might extend was a topic of some speculation among members of the patent bar. The Court's decisions had not yet addressed the status of contributory infringement or patent misuse with respect to nonstaple goods, and some courts and commentators apparently took the view that control of nonstaple items capable only of infringing use might not bar patent protection against contributory infringement. This view soon received a serious, if not fatal, blow from the Court's controversial decisions in *Mercoid Corp. v. Mid-Continent Investment Co.*, 320 U.S. 661, 64 S.Ct. 268, 88 L.Ed. 376 (1944) (*Mercoid I*), and *Mercoid Corp. v. Minneapolis-Honeywell Regulator Co.*, 320 U.S. 680, 64 S.Ct. 278, 88 L.Ed. 396 (1944) (*Mercoid II*). In these cases, the Court definitely held that any attempt to control the market for unpatented goods would constitute patent misuse, even if those goods had no use outside a patented invention. Because these cases served as the point of departure for congressional legislation, they merit more than passing citation.

Both cases involved a single patent that claimed a combination of elements for a furnace heating system. Mid-Continent was the owner of the patent, and Honeywell was its licensee. Although neither company made or installed the furnace system, Honeywell manufactured and sold stoker switches especially made for and essential to the system's operation. The right to build and use the system was granted to purchasers of the stoker switches, and royalties owed the patentee were calculated on the number of stoker switches sold. Mercoid manufactured and marketed a competing stoker switch that was designed to be used only in the patented combination. Mercoid had been offered a sublicense by the licensee but had refused to take one. It was sued for contributory infringement by both the patentee and the licensee, and it raised patent misuse as a defense.

In *Mercoid I* the Court barred the patentee from obtaining relief because it deemed the licensing arrangement with Honeywell to be an unlawful attempt to extend the patent monopoly. The opinion for the Court painted with a very broad brush. Prior patent misuse decisions had involved attempts "to secure a partial monopoly in supplies consumed * * * or unpatented materials employed" in connection with the practice of the invention. None, however, had involved an integral component necessary to the functioning of the patented system. 320 U.S., at 665, 64 S.Ct., at 271. The Court refused, however, to infer any "difference in principle" from this distinction in fact. *Ibid.* Instead, it stated an expansive rule that apparently admitted no exception:

"The necessities or convenience of the patentee do not justify any use of the monopoly of the patent to create another monopoly. The fact that the patentee has the power to refuse a license does not enable him to enlarge the monopoly of the patent by the expedient of attaching conditions to its use. * * * The method by which the monopoly is sought to be extended is immaterial. * * * When the patentee ties something else to his invention, he acts only by virtue of his right as the owner of property to make contracts concerning it and not otherwise. He then is subject to all the limitations upon that right which the general law imposes upon such contracts. The contract is not saved by anything in the patent laws because it relates to the invention. If it were, the mere act of the patentee could make the distinctive claim of the patent attach to something which does not possess the quality of invention. Then the patent would be diverted from its statutory purpose and become a ready instrument for economic control in domains where the anti-trust acts or other laws not the patent statutes define the public policy." *Id.,* at 666, 64 S.Ct., at 271.

The Court recognized that its reasoning directly conflicted with *Leeds & Catlin Co. v. Victor Talking Machine Co., supra,* and it registered disapproval, if not outright rejection, of that case. 320 U.S., at 668, 64 S.Ct., at 272. It also recognized that "[t]he result of this decision, together with those which have preceded it, is to limit substantially the doctrine of contributory infringement." *Id.,* at 669, 64 S.Ct., at 273. The Court commented, rather cryptically, that it would not "stop to consider" what "residuum" of the contributory infringement doctrine "may be left." *Ibid.*

* * *

What emerges from this review of judicial development is a fairly complicated picture, in which the rights and obligations of patentees as against contributory infringers have varied over time. We need not decide how respondent would have fared against a charge of patent misuse at any particular point prior to the enactment of 35 U.S.C. § 271. Nevertheless, certain inferences that are pertinent to the present inquiry may be drawn from these historical developments.

First, we agree with the Court of Appeals that the concepts of contributory infringement and patent misuse "rest on antithetical underpinnings." 599 F.2d, at 697. The traditional remedy against contributory infringement is the injunction. And an inevitable concomitant of the right to enjoin another from contributory infringement is the capacity to suppress competition in an unpatented article of commerce. See, *e.g., Thomson-Houston Electric Co. v. Kelsey Electric R. Specialty Co.,* 72 F. 1016, 1018–1019 (CC Conn.1896). Proponents of contributory infringement defend this result on the grounds that it is necessary for the protection of the patent right, and that the market for the unpatented article flows from the patentee's invention. They also observe that in many instances the article is "unpatented" only because of the technical rules of patent claiming, which require the placement of an invention in its context. Yet suppression of competition in unpatented goods is precisely what the opponents of patent misuse decry. If both the patent misuse and contributory infringement doctrines are to coexist, then, each must have some separate sphere of operation with which the other does not interfere.

Second, we find that the majority of cases in which the patent misuse doctrine was developed involved undoing the damage thought to have been done by *A.B. Dick.* The desire to extend patent protection to control of staple articles of commerce died slowly, and the ghost of the expansive contributory infringement era continued to haunt the courts. As a result, among the historical precedents in this Court, only the *Leeds & Catlin* and *Mercoid* cases bear significant factual similarity to the present controversy. Those cases involved questions of control over unpatented articles that were essential to the patented inventions, and that were unsuited for any commercial noninfringing use. In this case, we face similar questions in connection with a chemical, propanil, the herbicidal properties of which are essential to the advance on prior art disclosed by respondent's patented process. Like the record disc in *Leeds & Catlin* or the stoker switch in the *Mercoid* cases, and unlike the dry ice in *Carbice* or the bituminous emulsion in *Leitch,* propanil is a nonstaple commodity which has no use except through practice of the patented method. Accordingly, had the present case arisen prior to *Mercoid,* we believe it fair to say that it would have fallen close to the wavering line between legitimate protection against contributory infringement and illegitimate patent misuse.

* * *

A

The critical inquiry in this case is how the enactment of § 271 affected the doctrines of contributory infringement and patent misuse. Viewed against the backdrop of judicial precedent, we believe that the language and structure of the statute lend significant support to Rhom & Haas' contention that, because § 271(d) immunizes its conduct from the charge of patent misuse, it should not be barred from seeking relief. The approach that Congress took toward the codification of contributory infringement and patent misuse reveals a compromise between those two doctrines and their competing policies that permits patentees to exercise control over nonstaple articles used in their inventions.

Section 271(c) identifies the basic dividing line between contributory infringement and patent misuse. It adopts a restrictive definition of contributory infringement that distinguishes between staple and nonstaple articles of commerce. It also defines the class of nonstaple items narrowly. In essence, this provision places materials like the dry ice of the *Carbice* case outside the scope of the contributory infringement doctrine. As a result, it is no longer necessary to resort to the doctrine of patent misuse in order to deny patentees control over staple goods used in their inventions.

The limitations on contributory infringement written into § 271(c) are counterbalanced by limitations on patent misuse in § 271(d).

Three species of conduct by patentees are expressly excluded from characterization as misuse. First, the patentee may "deriv[e] revenue" from acts that "would constitute contributory infringement" if "performed by another without his consent." This provision clearly signifies that a patentee may make and sell nonstaple goods used in connection with his invention. Second, the patentee may "licens[e] or authoriz[e] another to perform acts" which without such authorization would constitute contributory infringement. This provision's use in the disjunctive of the term "authoriz[e]" suggests that more than explicit licensing agreements is contemplated. Finally, the patentee may "enforce his patent rights against * * * contributory infringement." This provision plainly means that the patentee may bring suit without fear that his doing so will be regarded as an unlawful attempt to suppress competition. The statute explicitly states that a patentee may do "one or more" of these permitted acts, and it does not state that he must do any of them.

In our view, the provisions of § 271(d) effectively confer upon the patentee, as a lawful adjunct of his patent rights, a limited power to exclude others from competition in nonstaple goods. A patentee may sell a nonstaple article himself while enjoining others from marketing that same good without his authorization. By doing so, he is able to eliminate competitors and thereby to control the market for that product. Moreover, his power to demand royalties from others for the privilege of selling the nonstaple item itself implies that the patentee may control the market for the nonstaple good; otherwise, his "right" to sell licenses for the marketing of the nonstaple good would be meaningless, since no one would be willing to pay him for a superfluous authorization. See Note, 70 Yale L.J. 649, 659 (1961).

Rohm & Haas' conduct is not dissimilar in either nature or effect from the conduct that is thus clearly embraced within § 271(d). It sells propanil; it authorizes others to use propanil; and it sues contributory infringers. These are all protected activities. Rohm & Haas does *not* license others to sell propanil, but nothing on the face of the statute requires it to do so. To be sure, the sum effect of Rohm & Haas' actions is to suppress competition in the market for an unpatented commodity. But as we have observed, in this its conduct is no different from that which the statute expressly protects.

The one aspect of Rohm & Haas' behavior that is not expressly covered by § 271(d) is its linkage of two protected activities—sale of propanil and authorization to practice the patented process—together in a single transaction. Petitioners vigorously argue that this linkage, which they characterize pejoratively as "tying," supplies the otherwise missing element of misuse. They fail, however, to identify any way in which this "tying" of two expressly protected activities results in any extension of control over unpatented materials beyond what § 271(d) already allows. Nevertheless, the language of § 271(d) does not explicitly resolve the question when linkage of this variety becomes patent misuse. In order to judge whether this method of exploiting the patent lies within or without the protection afforded by § 271(d), we must turn to the legislative history.

* * * It is the consistent theme of the legislative history that the statute was designed to accomplish a good deal more than mere clarification. It significantly changed existing law, and the change moved in the direction of expanding the statutory protection enjoyed by patentees. The responsible congressional Committees were told again and again that contributory infringement would wither away if the misuse rationale of the *Mercoid* decisions remained as a barrier to enforcement of the patentee's rights. They were told that this was an undesirable result that would deprive many patent holders of effective protection for their patent rights. They were told that Congress could strike a sensible compromise between the competing doctrines of contributory infringement and patent misuse if it eliminated the result of the *Mercoid* decisions yet preserved the result in *Carbice*. And they were told that the proposed legislation would achieve this effect by restricting contributory infringement to the sphere of nonstaple goods while exempting the control of such goods from the scope of patent misuse. These signals cannot be ignored. They fully support the conclusion that, by enacting §§ 271(c) and (d), Congress granted to patent holders a statutory right to control nonstaple goods that are capable only of infringing use in a patented invention, and that are essential to that invention's advance over prior art.

We find nothing in this legislative history to support the assertion that respondent's behavior falls outside the scope of § 271(d). To the contrary, respondent has done nothing that would extend its right of control over unpatented goods beyond the line that Congress drew. Respondent, to be sure, has licensed use of its patented process only in connection with purchases of propanil. But propanil is a *nonstaple* product, and its herbicidal property is the heart of respondent's invention. Respondent's method of doing business is thus essentially the same as the method condemned in the *Mercoid* decisions, and the legislative history reveals that § 271(d) was designed to retreat from *Mercoid* in this regard.

* * *

MR. JUSTICE WHITE, with whom MR. JUSTICE BRENNAN, MR. JUSTICE MARSHALL, and MR. JUSTICE STEVENS join, dissenting.

5. REPAIR AND RECONSTRUCTION

ARO MFG. CO. v. CONVERTIBLE TOP REPLACEMENT CO.

Supreme Court of the United States, 1961.
365 U.S. 336, 81 S.Ct. 599, 5 L.Ed.2d 592.

OPINION OF THE COURT

MR. JUSTICE WHITTAKER delivered the opinion of the Court.

On April 17, 1956, respondent, Convertible Top Replacement Co., Inc., acquired a "Territorial Grant" (coextensive with "the Commonwealth of Massachusetts") of all rights in Letters Patent No. 2,569,724, commonly known as the Mackie-Duluk patent, and 10 days later commenced this action against petitioners, Aro Manufacturing Co., Inc., and several of its officers, to enjoin the alleged infringement and contributory infringement of the patent and for an accounting of profits.

The patent—one for a "Convertible Folding Top with Automatic Seal at Rear Quarter"—covers the combination, in an automobile body, of a flexible top fabric, supporting structures, and a mechanism for sealing the fabric against the side of the automobile body in order to keep out the rain. Tops embodying the patent have been installed by several automobile manufacturers in various models of convertibles. The components of the patented combination, other than the fabric, normally are usable for the lifetime of the car, but the fabric has a much shorter life. It usually so suffers from wear and tear, or so deteriorates in appearance, as to become "spent," and normally is replaced, after about three years of use. The consequent demand for replacement fabrics has given rise to a substantial industry, in which petitioner, Aro Manufacturing Co., is a national leader. It manufactures and sells replacement fabrics designed to fit the models of convertibles equipped with tops embodying the combination covered by the patent in suit.

After trial without a jury, the court held that the patent was valid, infringed and contributorily infringed by petitioners. It accordingly enjoined them from further manufacture, sale or use of these replacement fabrics, and appointed a master to hear evidence concerning, and to report to the court on, the matter of damages. The Court of Appeals affirmed, 270 F.2d 200, and we granted certiorari, 362 U.S. 902, 80 S.Ct. 609, 4 L.Ed.2d 553.

The Court of Appeals, after holding that the patent was valid, stated that the "basic question" presented was whether petitioners' conduct constituted "making a permissible replacement of a part [the fabric] which expectedly became worn out or defective sooner than other parts of the patented combination" or whether such replacement constituted "a forbidden reconstruction of the combination." It then held that replacement of the fabric constituted reconstruction of the combination and thus infringed or contributorily infringed the patent.

It reached that conclusion principally upon the ground that "the life of the fabric is not so short, nor is the fabric so cheap, that we can safely assume that an owner would rationally believe that in replacing it he was making only a minor repair to his top structure." 270 F.2d at 202, 205.

Validity of the patent is not challenged in this Court. The principal, and we think the determinative, question presented here is whether the owner of a combination patent, comprised entirely of unpatented elements, has a patent monopoly on the manufacture, sale or use of the several unpatented components of the patented combination. More specifically, and limited to the particular case here, does the car owner infringe (and the supplier contributorily infringe) the combination patent when he replaces the spent fabric without the patentee's consent?

The fabric with which we deal here is an unpatented element of respondent's combination patent,[1] which covers only the combination of certain components, one of which is a "flexible top material."[2] The patent makes no claim to invention based on the fabric or on its shape, pattern or design. Whether the fabric or its shape might have been patentable is immaterial,[3] for the fact is that neither the fabric nor its shape has been patented. No claim that the fabric or its shape, pattern or design constituted the invention was made in the application or included in the patent.

Since the patentees never claimed the fabric or its shape as their invention, and the claims made in the patent are the sole measure of the grant,[4] the fabric is no more than an unpatented element of the combination which was claimed as the invention, and the patent did not confer a monopoly over the fabric or its shape. In Mercoid Corp. v. Mid-Continent Invest. Co., 320 U.S. 661, 667, 64 S.Ct. 268, 88 L.Ed. 376, 382, this Court ruled the point as follows:

> "The patent is for a combination only. Since none of the separate elements of the combination is claimed as the invention, none of them when dealt with separately is protected by the patent monopoly."

And in Mercoid Corp. v. Minneapolis-Honeywell Regulator Co., 320 U.S. 680, 684, 64 S.Ct. 278, 88 L.Ed. 396, 399, the Court said:

1. There are 10 claims in the patent. Claims 1 through 9 of the patent each specifically begin: "In a convertible automobile body, the combination of ∗ ∗ ∗." Claim 10 does not contain the word "combination" but nevertheless equally claims only a combination.

2. Among other elements in the claims are the automobile body structure or tonneau, a folding bow structure, a sealing strip, and a wiping arm.

3. Graver Tank & Mfg. Co. v. Linde Air Products Co., 336 U.S. 271, 277, 69 S.Ct. 535, 93 L.Ed. 672, 677; Universal Oil Prod-

ucts Co. v. Globe Oil & Ref. Co., 322 U.S. 471, 484, 64 S.Ct. 1110, 88 L.Ed. 1399, 1406; Milcor Steel Co. v. George A. Fuller Co., 316 U.S. 143, 145, 146, 62 S.Ct. 969, 86 L.Ed. 1332, 1334.

4. Mercoid Corp. v. Mid-Continent Invest. Co., 320 U.S. 661, 667, 64 S.Ct. 268, 88 L.Ed. 376, 381; Mercoid Corp. v. Minneapolis-Honeywell Regulator Co., 320 U.S. 680, 684, 64 S.Ct. 278, 88 L.Ed. 396, 399; McClain v. Ortmayer, 141 U.S. 419, 423, 424, 12 S.Ct. 76, 35 L.Ed. 800, 802; Pennock v. Dialogue (U.S.) 2 Pet. 1, 16, 7 L.Ed. 327, 332.

"The fact that an unpatented part of a combination patent may distinguish the invention does not draw to it the privileges of a patent. That may be done only in the manner provided by law. However worthy it may be, however essential to the patent, an unpatented part of a combination patent is no more entitled to monopolistic protection than any other unpatented device."

See also McClain v. Ortmayer, 141 U.S. 419, 423, 424, 12 S.Ct. 76, 35 L.Ed. 800, 802; Pennock v. Dialogue (U.S.) 2 Pet. 1, 16, 7 L.Ed. 327, 332.

It follows that petitioners' manufacture and sale of the fabric is not a *direct* infringement under 35 U.S.C.A. § 271(a). Cimiotti Unhairing Co. v. American Fur Ref. Co., 198 U.S. 399, 410, 25 S.Ct. 697, 49 L.Ed. 1100, 1105; Eames v. Godfrey (U.S.) 1 Wall. 78, 79, 17 L.Ed. 547, 548; Prouty v. Ruggles (U.S.) 16 Pet. 336, 341, 10 L.Ed. 985, 987; U.S. Industries, Inc. v. Otis Engineering Corp., 254 F.2d 198, 203 (C.A.5th Cir.). But the question remains whether petitioners' manufacture and sale of the fabric constitute a *contributory* infringement of the patent under 35 U.S.C.A. § 217(c). It is admitted that petitioners know that the purchasers intend to use the fabric for replacement purposes on automobile convertible tops which are covered by the claims of respondent's combination patent, and such manufacture and sale with that knowledge might well constitute contributory infringement under § 271(c), if, but only if, such a replacement by the purchaser himself would in itself constitute a *direct* infringement under § 271(a), for it is settled that if there is no *direct* infringement of a patent there can be no *contributory* infringement. In Mercoid v. Mid-Continent Invest. Co. supra, it was said: "In a word, if there is no infringement of a patent there can be no contributory infringer," 320 U.S. 661, 677, and that "if the purchaser and user could not be amerced as an infringer certainly one who sold to him * * * cannot be amerced for contributing to a non-existent infringement." Id. 320 U.S. at 674. It is plain that § 271(c)—a part of the Patent Code enacted in 1952—made no change in the fundamental precept that there can be no contributory infringement in the absence of a direct infringement. That section defines contributory infringement in terms of direct infringement—namely the sale of a component of a patented combination or machine for use "in an infringement of such patent." And § 271(a) of the new Patent Code, which defines "infringement," left intact the entire body of case law on direct infringements. The determinative question, therefore, comes down to whether the car owner would infringe the combination patent by replacing the worn-out fabric element of the patented convertible top on his car, or even more specifically, whether such a replacement by the car owner is infringing "reconstruction" or permissible "repair."

This Court's decisions specifically dealing with whether the replacement of an unpatented part, in a patented combination, that has worn out, been broken or otherwise spent, is permissible "repair" or infringing "reconstruction," have steadfastly refused to extend the patent monopoly beyond the terms of the grant. Wilson v. Simpson

(U.S.) 9 How. 109, 13 L.Ed. 66—doubtless the leading case in this Court that deals with the distinction—concerned a patented planning machine which included, as elements, certain cutting knives which normally wore out in a few months' use. The purchaser was held to have the right to replace those knives without the patentee's consent. The Court held that, although there is no right to "rebuild" a patented combination, the entity "exists" notwithstanding the fact that destruction or impairment of one of its elements renders it inoperable; and that, accordingly, replacement of that worn-out essential part is permissible restoration of the machine to the original use for which it was bought. 9 How., at 123. The Court explained that it is "the use of the whole" of the combination which a purchaser buys, and that repair or replacement of the worn-out, damaged or destroyed part is but an exercise of the right "to give duration to that which he owns, or has a right to use as a whole." Ibid.

The distilled essence of the Wilson Case was stated by Judge Learned Hand in United States v. Aluminum Co. of America, 148 F.2d 416, 425 (C.A.2d Cir.): "The [patent] monopolist cannot prevent those to whom he sells from * * * reconditioning articles worn by use, unless they in fact make a new article." Instead of applying this plain and practical test, the courts below focused attention on operative facts not properly determinative of the question of permissible repair *versus* forbidden reconstruction. The Court of Appeals found that the fabric "is not a minor or relatively inexpensive component" of the patented combination, or an element that would expectedly wear out after a very short period of use—although its "expectable life span" is shorter than that of the other components—and, for these reasons, concluded that "an owner would [not] rationally believe that * * * he was making only a minor repair" in replacing the worn-out fabric, but that, instead, the replacement "would be counted a major reconstruction." 270 F.2d, at 205. We think that test was erroneous.

Respondent has strenuously urged, as an additional relevant factor, the "essentialness" of the fabric element to the combination constituting the invention. It argues that the particular shape of the fabric was the advance in the art—the very "heart" of the invention—which brought the combination up to the inventive level, and, therefore, concludes that its patent should be held to grant it a monopoly on the fabric. The rule for which respondent contends is: That when an element of a patented machine or combination is relatively durable— even though not so durable as the entire patented device which the owner purchased—relatively expensive, relatively difficult to replace, and is an "essential" or "distinguishing" part of the patented combination, any replacement of that element, when it wears out or is otherwise spent, constitutes infringing "reconstruction," and, therefore, a new license must be obtained from, and another royalty paid to, the patentee for that privilege.

We cannot agree. For if anything is settled in the patent law, it is that the combination patent covers only the totality of the elements in the claim and that no element, separately viewed, is within the grant. See the Mercoid Cases, supra (320 U.S. at 667; 320 U.S. at 684). The basic fallacy in respondent's position is that it requires the ascribing to one element of the patented combination the status of patented invention in itself. Yet this Court has made it clear in the two Mercoid Cases that there is no legally recognizable or protected "essential" element, "gist" or "heart" of the invention in a combination patent. In Mercoid Corp. v. Mid-Continent Invest. Co., supra, the Court said:

> "That result may not be obviated in the present case by calling the combustion stoker switch the 'heart of the invention' or the 'advance in the art.' The patent is for a combination only. Since none of the separate elements of the combination is claimed as the invention, none of them when dealt with separately is protected by the patent monopoly." 320 U.S. at 667.

And in Mercoid Corp. v. Minneapolis-Honeywell Regulator Co. supra, the Court said:

> "The fact that an unpatented part of a combination patent may distinguish the invention does not draw to it the privileges of a patent. That may be done only in the manner provided by law. However worthy it may be, however essential to the patent, an unpatented part of a combination patent is no more entitled to monopolistic protection than any other unpatented device." 320 U.S. at 684.

No element, not itself separately patented, that constitutes one of the elements of a combination patent is entitled to patent monopoly, however essential it may be to the patented combination and no matter how costly or difficult replacement may be. While there is language in some lower court opinions indicating that "repair" or "reconstruction" depends on a number of factors, it is significant that each of the three cases of this Court, cited for that proposition, holds that a license to use a patented combination includes the right "to preserve its fitness for use so far as it may be affected by wear or breakage." Leeds & Catlin Co. v. Victor Talking Mach. Co., 213 U.S. 325, 336, 29 S.Ct. 503, 53 L.Ed. 816, 820; Heyer v. Duplicator Mfg. Co., supra (263 U.S. at 102); and Wilson v. Simpson, supra ((U.S.) 9 How. at 123). We hold that maintenance of the "use of the whole" of the patented combination through replacement of a spent, unpatented element does not constitute reconstruction.

The decisions of this Court require the conclusion that reconstruction of a patented entity, comprised of unpatented elements, is limited to such a true reconstruction of the entity as to "in fact make a new article," United States v. Aluminum Co. of America, supra (148 F.2d at 425), after the entity, viewed as a whole, has become spent. In order to call the monopoly, conferred by the patent grant, into play for a second time, it must, indeed, be a second creation of the patented entity, as, for example, in Cotton-Tie Co. v. Simmons, 106 U.S. 89, 1 S.Ct. 52, 27 L.Ed. 79, supra. Mere replacement of individual unpatented parts, one at a time, whether of the same part repeatedly or different parts successively, is no more than the lawful right of the owner to repair his property.

Measured by this test, the replacement of the fabric involved in this case must be characterized as permissible "repair," not "reconstruction."

Reversed.

[Concurring and dissenting opinions omitted.]

ARO MFG. CO. v. CONVERTIBLE TOP REPLACEMENT CO.

Supreme Court of the United States, 1964.
377 U.S. 476, 84 S.Ct. 1526, 12 L.Ed.2d 457.

MR. JUSTICE BRENNAN delivered the opinion of the Court.

Respondent Convertible Top Replacement Co., Inc., (CTR) acquired by assignment from the Automobile Body Research Corporation (AB) all rights for the territory of Massachusetts in United States Patent No. 2,569,724, known as the Mackie-Duluk patent. This is a combination patent covering a top-structure for automobile "convertibles." Structures embodying the patented combination were included as original equipment in 1952–1954 models of convertibles manufactured by the General Motors Corporation and the Ford Motor Company. They were included in the General Motors cars by authority of a license granted to General Motors by AB; Ford, however, had no license during the 1952–1954 period, and no authority whatever under the patent until July 21, 1955, when it entered into an agreement, discussed later, with AB; Ford's manufacture and sale of the automobiles in question therefore infringed the patent. Petitioner Aro Manufacturing Co., Inc. (Aro), which is not licensed under the patent, produces fabric components designed as replacements for worn-out fabric portions of convertible tops; unlike the other elements of the top-structure, which ordinarily are usable for the life of the car, the fabric portion normally wears out and requires replacement after about three years of use. Aro's fabrics are specially tailored for installation in particular models of convertibles, and these have included the 1952–1954 General Motors and Ford models equipped with the Mackie-Duluk top-structures.

* * *

CTR contends, and the Court of Appeals held, that since Ford infringed the patent by making and selling the top-structures without authority from the patentee, persons who purchased the automobiles from Ford likewise infringed by using and repairing the structures; and hence Aro, by supplying replacement fabrics specially designed to be utilized in such infringing repair, was guilty of contributory infringement under 35 U.S.C.A. § 271(c).

* * *

[T]o determine whether Aro committed contributory infringement, we must first determine whether the car owners, by replacing the worn-out fabric element of the patented top-structures, committed direct infringement. We think it clear under § 271(a) of the Patent Code and the "entire body of case law on direct infringement" which that section "left intact," that they did.

Section 271(a) provides that "whoever without authority makes, uses or sells any patented invention * * * infringes the patent." It is not controverted—nor could it be—that Ford infringed by making and selling cars embodying the patented top-structures without any authority from the patentee. If Ford had had such authority, its purchasers would not have infringed by using the automobiles, for it is fundamental that sale of a patented article by the patentee or under his authority carries with it an "implied license to use." Adams v. Burke, 17 Wall. 453, 456, 21 L.Ed. 700, 703; United States v. Univis Lens Co., 316 U.S. 241, 249, 250–251, 62 S.Ct. 1088, 86 L.Ed. 1408, 1417, 1418. But with Ford lacking authority to make and sell, it could by its sale of the cars confer on the purchasers no implied license to use, and their use of the patented structures was thus "without authority" and infringing under § 271(a). Not only does that provision explicitly regard an unauthorized user of a patented invention as an infringer, but it has often and clearly been held that unauthorized use, without more, constitutes infringement. Birdsell v. Shaliol, 112 U.S. 485, 5 S.Ct. 244, 28 L.Ed. 768; Union Tool Co. v. Wilson, 259 U.S. 107, 114, 42 S.Ct. 427, 66 L.Ed. 848, 852; see Sanitary Refrigerator Co. v. Winters, 280 U.S. 30, 32–33, 50 S.Ct. 9, 74 L.Ed. 147, 151; General Talking Pictures Corp. v. Western Electric Co., 305 U.S. 124, 127, 59 S.Ct. 116, 83 L.Ed. 81, 83.

If the owner's *use* infringed, so also did his *repair* of the top-structure, as by replacing the worn-out fabric component. Where use infringes, repair does also, for it perpetuates the infringing use.

"No doubt * * * a patented article may be repaired without making the repairer an infringer, * * * but not where it is done for one who is. It is only where the device in patented form has come lawfully into the hands of the person for or by whom it is repaired that this is the case. In other words, if one without right constructs or disposes of an infringing machine, it affords no protection to another to have merely repaired it; the repairer, by supplying an essential part of the patented combination, contributing by so much to the perpetuation of the infringement." Union Special Mach. Co. v. Maimin, 161 F. 748, 750 (C.C.E.D.Pa.1908), aff'd, 165 F. 440 (C.A.3d Cir.1908).

Accord, Remington Rand Business Serv., Inc. v. Acme Card System Co., 71 F.2d 628, 630 (C.A.4th Cir.1934), cert. denied, 293 U.S. 622, 55 S.Ct. 236, 79 L.Ed. 710; 2 Walker, Patents (Deller ed. 1937), at 1487. Consequently replacement of worn-out fabric components with fabrics sold by Aro, held in Aro I to constitute "repair" rather than "reconstruction" and thus to be permissible in the case of licensed General Motors cars, was not permissible here in the case of unlicensed Ford cars. Here, as was not the case in Aro I, the direct infringement by the car owners that is prerequisite to contributory infringement by Aro was unquestionably established.

We turn next to the question whether Aro, as supplier of replacement fabrics for use in the infringing repair by the Ford car owners, was a contributory infringer under § 271(c) of the Patent Code.

* * *

We think Aro was indeed liable under this provision.

Such a result would plainly have obtained under the contributory-infringement case law that § 271(c) was intended to codify.[6] Indeed, most of the law was established in cases where, as here, suit was brought to hold liable for contributory infringement a supplier of replacement parts specially designed for use in the repair of infringing articles. In Union Tool Co. v. Wilson, supra, 259 U.S. at 113–114, 66 L.Ed. at 852, the Court held that where use of the patented machines themselves was not authorized, "There was, consequently, no implied license to use the spare parts in these machines. As such use, unless licensed, clearly constituted an infringement, the sale of the spare parts to be so used violated the injunction [enjoining infringement]."

As early as 1897, Circuit Judge Taft, as he then was, thought it "well settled" that "where one makes and sells one element of a combination covered by a patent with the intention and for the purpose of bringing about its use in such a combination he is guilty of contributory infringement and is equally liable to the patentee with him who in fact organizes the complete combination." Thomson-Houston Elec. Co. v. Ohio Brass Co., 80 F. 712, 721 (C.A.6th Cir.1897).

While conceding that in the case of a machine purchased from the patentee, one "may knowingly assist in assembling, repairing, and renewing a patented combination by furnishing some of the needed parts," Judge Taft added: "but, when he does so, he must ascertain, if he would escape liability for infringement, that the one buying and using them for this purpose has a license, express or implied, to do so." Id., at 723. See also National Brake & Elec. Co. v. Christensen, 38 F.2d 721, 723 (C.A.7th Cir.1930), cert. denied, 282 U.S. 864, 51 S.Ct. 36, 75

---

6. The section was designed to "codify in statutory form principles of contributory infringement" which had been "part of our law for about 80 years." H.R.Rep. No. 1923 on H.R. 7794, 82d Cong., 2d Sess., at 9; see also Congressman Rogers' statement, Hearings before Subcommittee No. 3 of House Judiciary Committee on H.R. 3760, 82d Cong., 1st Sess., at 159:

"Then in effect this recodification, particularly as to section 231 [which became § 271 in the Patent Code of 1952], would point out to the court, at least that it was the sense of Congress that we remove this question of confusion as to whether contributory infringement existed at all, and state in positive law that there is such a thing as contributory infringement, or at least it be the sense of Congress by the enactment of this law that if you have in the Mercoid case [320 U.S. 661, 680] done away with contributory infringement, then we reinstate it as a matter of substantive law of the United States and that you shall hereafter in a proper case recognize or hold liable one who has contributed to the infringement of a patent.

"That is the substantive law that we would write if we adopted this section 231 as it now exists. Is that not about right?"

Mr. Giles S. Rich, now judge of the Court of Customs and Patent Appeals, then spokesman for proponents of § 271(c), answered that the statement of the bill's purpose was "very excellent." Ibid. See also 98 Cong.Rec. 9323, 82d Cong., 2d Sess., July 4, 1952 (colloquy of Senators Saltonstall and McCarran).

L.Ed. 764; Reed Roller Bit Co. v. Hughes Tool Co., 12 F.2d 207, 211 (C.A.5th Cir.1926); Shickle, Harrison & Howard Iron Co. v. St. Louis Car-Coupler Co., 77 F. 739, 743 (C.A.8th Cir.1896), cert. denied, 166 U.S. 720, 17 S.Ct. 998, 41 L.Ed. 1186. These cases are all authority for the proposition that "The right of one, other than the patentee, furnishing repair parts of a patented combination, can be no greater than that of the user, and he is bound to see that no other use of such parts is made than that authorized by the user's license." National Malleable Casting Co. v. American Steel Foundries, 182 F. 626, 641 (C.C.D.N.J.1910).

In enacting § 271(c), Congress clearly succeeded in its objective of codifying this case law. The language of the section fits perfectly Aro's activity of selling "a component of a patented * * * combination * * *, constituting a material part of the invention, * * * especially made or especially adapted for use in an infringment of such patent, and not a staple article or commodity of commerce suitable for substantial noninfringing use." Indeed, this is the almost unique case in which the component was hardly suitable for *any* noninfringing use.[7] On this basis both the District Court originally, 119 USPQ, at 124, and the Court of Appeals in the instant case, 312 F.2d at 57, held that Aro was a contributory infringer within the precise letter of § 271(c). See also Aro I, 365 U.S. at 341, 5 L.Ed.2d at 596.

However, the language of § 271(c) presents a question, apparently not noticed by the parties or the courts below, concerning the element of knowledge that must be brought home to Aro before liability can be imposed. It is only sale of a component of a patented combination "*knowing* the same to be especially made or especially adapted for use in an infringement of such patent" that is contributory infringement under the statute. Was Aro "knowing" within the statutory meaning because—as it admits, and as the lower courts found—it knew that its replacement fabrics were especially designed for use in the 1952–1954 Ford convertible tops and were not suitable for other use? Or does the statute require a further showing that Aro knew that the tops were patented, and knew also that Ford was not licensed under the patent so that any fabric replacement by a Ford car owner constituted infringement?

On this question a majority of the Court is of the view that § 271(c) does require a showing that the alleged contributory infringer knew that the combination for which his component was especially designed was both patented and infringing.[8] With respect to many of the replacement-fabric sales involved in this case, Aro clearly had such

7. Aro's factory manager admitted that the fabric replacements in question not only were specially designed for the Ford convertibles but would not, to his knowledge, fit the top-structures of any other cars.

8. This view is held by The Chief Justice and Justices Black, Douglas, Clark and White. See the opinion of Mr. Justice Black, post, pp. 490–492, and of Mr. Justice White, post, pp. 484, 485.

Justices Harlan, Brennan, Stewart and Goldberg dissent from this interpretation of the statute. They are of the view that the knowledge Congress meant to require was simply knowledge that the component was especially designed for use in a combination and was not a staple article suitable

knowledge. For by letter dated January 2, 1954, AB informed Aro that it held the Mackie-Duluk patent; that it had granted a license under the patent to General Motors but to no one else; and that "It is obvious, from the foregoing and from an inspection of the convertible automobile sold by the Ford Motor Company, that anyone selling ready-made replacement fabrics for these automobiles would be guilty of contributory infringement of said patents." Thus the Court's interpretation of the knowledge requirement affords Aro no defense with respect to replacement-fabric sales made after January 2, 1954. It would appear that the overwhelming majority of the sales were in fact made after that date, since the oldest of the cars were 1952 models and since the average life of a fabric top is said to be three years. With respect to any sales that were made before that date, however, Aro cannot be held liable in the absence of a showing that at that time it had already acquired the requisite knowledge that the Ford car tops were patented and infringing. When the case is remanded, a finding of fact must be made on this question by the District Court, and, unless Aro is found to have had such prior knowledge, the judgment imposing liability must be vacated as to any sales made before January 2, 1954. As to subsequent sales, however, we hold, in agreement with the lower courts, that Aro is liable for contributory infringement within the terms of § 271(c).

In seeking to avoid such liability, Aro relies on the Mercoid Cases. Mercoid Corp. v. Mid-Continent Investment Co., 320 U.S. 661, 64 S.Ct. 268, 88 L.Ed. 376; Mercoid Corp. v. Minneapolis-Honeywell Regulator Co., 320 U.S. 680, 64 S.Ct. 278, 88 L.Ed. 396. Since those cases involved essentially an application of the doctrine of patent misuse, which is not an issue in this case, they are not squarely applicable to the contributory infringement question here. On the other hand, they are hardly irrelevant. The Court in Mercoid said, among other things, that the principle that "he who sells an unpatented part of a combination patent for use in the assembled machine may be guilty of contributory infringement" could no longer prevail "against the defense that a combination patent is being used to protect an unpatented part from competition." 320 U.S. at 668, 88 L.Ed. at 382. As the Court recognized, its definition of misuse was such as "to limit substantially the doctrine of contributory infringement" and to raise a question as to "what residuum may be left." 320 U.S. at 669, 88 L.Ed. at 383. See Report of the Attorney General's National Committee to Study the Antitrust Laws (1955), at 252. The answer to Aro's argument is that Congress enacted § 271 for the express purpose of reinstating the doctrine of contributory infringement as it had been developed by decisions prior to Mercoid, and of overruling any blanket invalidation of the doctrine that could be found in the Mercoid opinions. See, e.g., 35 U.S.C.A. §§ 271(c), (d); Hearings, supra, n. 6, at 159, 161–162; and the Aro I opinions of Mr.

for substantial other use, and not knowledge that the combination was either patented or infringing.

[Their reasons are summarized in a lengthy footnote not reproduced here.]

Justice Black, 365 U.S. at 348–349 and nn. 3–4, 5 L.Ed.2d at 600, 601; Mr. Justice Harlan, id., at 378, n. 6; 5 L.Ed.2d at 618; and Mr. Justice Brennan, id., at 365–367, 5 L.Ed.2d at 610, 611. Hence, where Aro's sale of replacement fabrics for unlicensed Ford cars falls squarely within § 271(c), and where Aro has not properly invoked the misuse doctrine as to any other conduct by CTR or AB, Mercoid cannot successfully be employed to shield Aro from liability for contributory infringement.

Thus we hold that, subject to the reservation expressed at pp. 469–471, supra, with respect to sales made before January 2, 1954, and subject to the further reservations set forth in succeeding Parts of this opinion, Aro's sales of replacement fabrics for use in the Ford cars constituted contributory infringement under § 271(c).

* * *

FROMBERG, INC. v. THORNHILL

United States Court of Appeals, Fifth Circuit, 1963.
315 F.2d 407, 137 USPQ 84.

JOHN R. BROWN, C. JUDGE * * * Of course implicit in this discussion—Defendant's culpability based on direct infringement by the dealer—is the assumption that the dealer had no legal right to recreate the Fromberg device. In the light of contemporary developments, that may be a big assumption. What has been tentatively assumed must now be established. This turns on the problem so often epitomized in the verbal symbol "repair or reconstruction."

Where once the ultimate question seems to have been fractured into a series of subsidiary inquiries as to the length of life, cost, etc. of the replaced element of a combination patent in relation to other elements or the completed device as a whole, it has now been reduced to the simpler one: does this really *make* a new device? Aro Mfg. Co. v. Convertible Top Replacement Co., 1961, 365 U.S. 336, 81 S.Ct. 599, 5 L.Ed.2d 592. Of course it does not take long to recognize that such simplicity is beguiling, and in the process of a judicial determination a number of factors must be considered. Not the least of these will be those in the analogous area of misuse of patents. Akin to these are strong underlying policies against trusts and monopolies. Thus the patent monopoly does not extend to unpatented materials which are used in, or consumed by, the patented machine, process or device. And the effort to achieve that result, or the similar one of limiting the source of an unpatented element in a combination patent, through conditions for the grant of a license constitutes patent misuse.

This makes it essential therefore to examine the Fromberg device to determine its function and purpose. The principal point of this inquiry is whether, when sold by the Patentee, it is reasonably contemplated that the device will be repeatedly used. The patent is for a tire repair unit. The patent is not for a *means* by which a rubber plug can be inserted efficiently in a tire. If that were so, the patent would essentially cover only the hollow metal tube—an ancient and certainly non-novel thing. Designed, manufactured and sold as a unit, it is likewise used as a unit. Once the rubber plug is extruded into the tire, that part cannot ordinarily be used again. Nor is it expected that the metal tube will be. It has a single-shot function and purpose for a one-time use.

That brings the case precisely within American Cotton Tie Co. v. Simmons, 1882, 106 U.S. 89, 1 S.Ct. 52, 27 L.Ed. 79.[15] There the patent was on metal bands used to bind cotton bales. To open the cotton bale, the metal bands were cut. The Defendant followed the practice of buying the cut bands with buckles as scrap from various compresses. Thereafter the salvage bands were pieced and spliced together by rivets and with the original tie buckles were sold to the trade for their original purpose.

The situation presented was later summarized by the Court: "It is evident that the use of the tie was intended to be as complete a destruction of it as would be the explosion of a patented torpedo. In either case, the repair of the band or the refilling of the shell would be a practical reconstruction of the device." Morgan Envelope Co. v. Albany Perforated Wrapping Paper Co., 1894, 152 U.S. 425, 434, 14 S.Ct. 627, 631, 38 L.Ed. 500. In the tie case itself the Court stated: "What the defendants did in piecing together the pieces of the old band was not a repair of the band or the tie in any proper sense. The band was voluntarily severed by the consumer at the cottonmill because the tie had performed its function of confining the bale of cotton in its transit from the plantation or the press to the mill. Its capacity for use as a tie was voluntarily destroyed. As it left the bale it could not be used again as a tie. As a tie the defendants reconstructed it, although they used the old buckle without repairing that." 106 U.S. 89, 93–94, 1 S.Ct. 52, 56.

For these reasons we hold that on this record the Defendant was guilty of inducing infringement by others under § 271(b). The judgment is accordingly reversed and rendered as to that with directions to the District Court to grant appropriate relief on remand.

6. TEMPORARY PRESENCE IN UNITED STATES

35 U.S.C.A. § 272. Temporary Presence in the United States

The use of any invention in any vessel, aircraft or vehicle of any country which affords similar privileges to vessels, aircraft or vehicles of the United States, entering the United States temporarily or accidentally, shall not constitute infringement of any patent, if the invention is used exclusively for the needs of the vessel, aircraft or vehicle and is not sold in or used for the manufacture of anything to be sold in or exported from the United States.

---

15. The decision is very much alive as authoritative. It is cited and relied on in the majority, the concurring, and the dissenting opinions in Aro Mfg. Co. v. Convertible Top Replacement Co., 1961, 365 U.S. 336, see at 346, 355, 367, 369, and 373, 81 S.Ct. 599, at 604, 609, 615, 616, and 619, supra. Of course little reliance can be placed on the fact that the metal ties bore the legend "Licensed to use once only."

Chapter Seven

DESIGN PATENTS

A. INTRODUCTION

Design patents provide protection for the ornamental features of an article of manufacture. Ornamental designs are a component of the useful arts and complement the subject matter defined by 35 U.S.C.A. § 101 of so-called "utility" patents.

The first design patent statute was enacted in 1842 and provided protection for any new and original design for a manufacture; a printing of woolen, silk, cotton, or other fabric; a bust, statue, or bas relief; an impression or ornament formed in marble or other material; a useful pattern, print, or picture to be worked into or worked on, or printed, painted, or cast on, any article of manufacture; and any shape or configuration of any article of manufacture. Early versions of the statute contained the word "useful" in reference to designs, but this was replaced in 1902 by the word "ornamental." [a]

The requirements for a valid design patent are essentially the same as those for a utility patent except that the design must be "ornamental", rather than having some practical utility. The following are the statutory provisions of the 1952 Patent Act which specifically relate to design patents:

35 U.S.C.A. § 171. Patents for Designs

Whoever invents any new, original and ornamental design for an article of manufacture may obtain a patent therefor, subject to the conditions and requirements of this title.

The provisions of this title relating to patents for inventions shall apply to patents for designs, except as otherwise provided.

35 U.S.C.A. § 172. Right of Priority

The right of priority provided for by section 119 of this title and the time specified in section 102(d) shall be six months in the case of designs.

35 U.S.C.A. § 173. Term of Design Patent

Patents for designs shall be granted for the term of fourteen years.

---

a. The history of the design patent statutes is discussed in: 2 Deller's Walker on Patents 729–733 (2d Ed. 1964); Hudson, A Brief History of the Development of Design Patent Protection in the United States, 30 J.P.O.S. 380 (1948); and Sokolski, Is Our Design Patent Statute Adequate?, 42 J.P. O.S. 496 (1960).

B. STATUTORY SUBJECT MATTER

In general, design patents are for ornamental features of an article and are "intended to give encouragement to the decorative arts" contemplating "not so much utility as appearance." [b] The subject matter of an ornamental design should not be the result of purely functional requirements and the by-product thereof.[c] As stated by Judge Kaufman in Hygienic Specialties Co. v. H.G. Salzman, Inc., 302 F.2d 614, 133 USPQ 96 (2d Cir.1962):

> [T]he Hygienic soap dish patent is invalid for another reason; it is not ornamental. In order to qualify for a patent a design "must be the product of aesthetic skill and artistic conception." Blisscraft of Hollywood v. United Plastics Co., supra; Burgess Vibrocrafters, Inc. v. Atkins Industries, Inc., 204 F.2d 311, 313 (7th Cir.1953). The inventor of the soap dish design, Barnet D. Kaplan, admitted that the only design element not resulting from a mechanical function was a group of horizontal lines on the side of the dish. A design dictated solely by mechanical or functional requirements is not patentable, Hopkins v. Waco Products, Inc., 205 F.2d 221, 223 (7th Cir.1953); Blisscraft of Hollywood v. United Plastics Co., 189 F.Supp. 333, 337 (S.D.N.Y.1960), affirmed 294 F.2d 694 (2d Cir.1961), and Hygienic's soap dish, much like the Blisscraft pitcher,
>
> > "has no particular aesthetic appeal in line, form, color, or otherwise. It contained no dominant artistic motif either in detail or in its overall conception. * * * The reaction which [it] inspires is simply that of the usual, useful and not unattractive piece of kitchenware." 294 F.2d 696.

There may, however, be a mixture of functional and ornamental configurations. The Patent Office Board of Appeals dealt with this aspect in Ex parte Levinn, 136 USPQ 606, 607 (1962) stating:

> * * * A rejection of a design application as being functional, i.e., dictated by the function to be performed thereby, is only proper when every part or substantially every part of the shape is dictated by the utility to be performed * * * [d]

Note also the language of Judge Hough in Dietz Co. v. Burr & Starkweather Co., 243 Fed. 592, 594 (2d Cir.1917):

> While design patents are not intended to protect a mechanical function, or to secure to the patentee monopoly in any given mechanism or manufacture as such, it is immaterial that the subject of the design may embody a mechanical function, provided that the design per se is pleasing, attractive, novel, useful and the result of invention.

b. Gorham Mfg. Co. v. White, 81 U.S. 511, 20 L.Ed. 731 (1872).

c. Spaulding v. Guardian Light Co., 267 F.2d 111, 121 USPQ 288 (7th Cir.1959); Bliss v. Gotham Industries, Inc., 316 F.2d 848, 137 USPQ 189 (9th Cir.1963).

d. See: Megley, Design and Mechanical Patents Relating to the Same Subject Matter, 44 J.P.O.S. 309 (1962); Brown v. DeBell, 243 F.2d 200, 113 USPQ 172 (9th Cir.1957); Bentley v. Sunset House Distributing Corp., 359 F.2d 140, 149 USPQ 152 (9th Cir.1966).

Ashley v. Weeks, etc., Co., 220 Fed. at 901, 136 C.C.A. 465. But it is the design that is patented, not the mechanism dressed in the design.

Applying these rules to the matter in hand, we are of opinion that McArthur's lantern, or any lantern looking like that of the design, does not appeal to the aesthetic sense, and represents nothing more than a convenient shape for an article always purchased and used for what it will do—not for its looks.

The design to be ornamental does not have to "have curlicues on it or embossed roses" but it must be "pleasing to the eye." [e] "The law does not require that the device be attractive to us; judges are part of the laity insofar as artistic judgment is concerned." Bentley v. Sunset House Distributing Corp., 359 F.2d 140, 149 USPQ 152 (9th Cir.1966). It is generally true that a design on a natural form is not patentable [f] but a departure from the natural form may be, for example, a caricature of an animal.[g] A portion of a device may not be protected, such as the forward corner of an automobile, since such front corner is never manufactured and sold as a separate article of manufacture.[h]

Usually it is held that a device which is concealed in use may not be the subject of a design patent [i] but the Board of Appeals of the Patent Office permitted a design patent on a tire despite the fact that ornamental portions in the form of a bead would be concealed in use:

We believe the appearance of the subject matter involved here is of material concern to the general public. It is true that the bead portions of the tire may be concealed during its use but the tire does, in many cases, have an extended use as an attraction to the general public and during this use the bead forms an element affecting the overall appearance. It is our opinion that an impression, favorable or unfavorable, will be aroused by the appearance of the tire and in many cases be effective in a sale determination. The appearance of cars in general and tires in particular have become more important in the minds of the public in recent years, as witnessed by the advent of the sport cars and white side wall tires on many cars, and it therefore behooves the manufacturer to design a tire with aesthetic values in mind. It is these features which are of definite concern to both a manufacturer and the general public which have led to an ornamental design for an article of manufacture which seems to us to comply with the statute (35 U.S.C.A. 171) even though the tire may have a later or even prior use in which a portion is concealed during that use. We

e. Brunswick-Balke-Collender Co. v. Kuehne Mfg. Co., 110 USPQ 481 (N.D.Ill. 1956) (Not reported in Federal System).

f. In re Smith, 77 F.2d 514, 25 USPQ 360 (CCPA 1935).

g. R.M. Palmer Co. v. Luden's, Inc., 236 F.2d 496, 111 USPQ 1 (3d Cir.1956), supra, page 325.

h. Ex Parte Northrup, 1934 C.F.D. 29, 24 USPQ 63 (P.O. Bd. of Appeals, 1932);

also Philco Corp. v. Admiral Corp., 199 F.Supp. 797, 131 USPQ 413 (D.C.Del.1961).

i. In re Stevens, 173 F.2d 1015, 81 USPQ 362 (CCPA 1949); Ex parte Jaffe, 147 USPQ 45 (P.O.Bd.App.1964) (Printed circuit board for frequency shift tonekeyer); Ex parte Fesco, 147 USPQ 74, 75 (P.O.Bd.App.1965) (Disposable vacuum cleaner bag).

will not sustain the rejection as improper subject matter for a design patent. [Ex parte Wolfer, 121 USPQ 319, 321 (1958)][j]

Designs on tire treads have been rejected on the basis that allowance would be giving protection to mechanical excellences and that the primary object of the design was not to please the eye or decorate but to accomplish certain functions in use.[k] Some decisions of the Patent Office have said that a design patent cannot properly issue on a device having moving parts such as fire equipment[l] but this generalization was challenged in Chandler Adjustable Chair & Desk Co. v. Heywood Bros., 91 Fed. 163 (Mass.Cir.Ct.1898) validating a design patent for a furniture support. A full discussion of these cases is found in a decision of the Court of Customs and Patent Appeals, In re Koehring, 37 F.2d 421, 4 USPQ 169 (1930) in which a design patent was allowed for a Concrete Mixer.

APPLICATION OF HRUBY

United States Court of Customs and Patent Appeals, 1967.
54 CCPA 1196, 373 F.2d 997, 153 USPQ 61.

RICH, JUDGE. These appeals are from split decisions of the Patent Office Board of Appeals wherein the majority affirmed the rejection of appellant's claims in four design patent applications, serial Nos. 70,815, 70,816, 70,827, 70,828, all filed July 6, 1962, each entitled "Water Fountain."

The appeals of the four applications were argued as one, before both the board and this court, and the single issue in each is the same: is the subject matter sought to be patented within the statutory subject matter designated in 35 U.S.C. 171, namely, "an article of manufacture"?

The single claim in each application reads:

The ornamental design for a water fountain as shown and described.

As illustrative of the nature of the designs it will suffice to reproduce the drawings from one of the cases as typical, serial No. 70,816:

j. See also Ex parte Levinn, 136 USPQ 606 (P.O.Bd.Appeals, 1962).

k. North British Rubber Co., Ltd. v. Racine Rubber Tire Co., 271 Fed. 936 (2d Cir.1921); Pashek v. Dunlop Tyre & Rubber Co., 8 F.2d 640 (D.C.Ohio, 1925).

l. Ex parte Steck, 1902 C.D. 9; Ex parte Adams, 1898 C.D. 115.

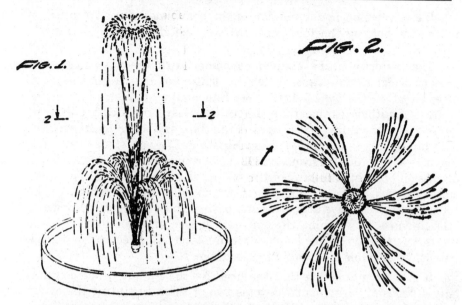

The full description, referred to in the claim, consisted, when filed, of the drawings and the following:

Fig. 1 is a perspective view of a water fountain showing my new design and showing in broken lines a catch basin and a fountain producing device; and

Fig. 2 is a cross section through the water fountain taken upon a plane indicated on Fig. 1 by line 2–2, and including a directional arrow which shows that the water fountain rotates.

* * *

No references are relied on.

The sole rejection was that the claim in each case does not define an article of manufacture. The precise question before us, therefore, is whether that portion of a water fountain which is composed entirely of water in motion is within the statutory term "article of manufacture." This appears to be a question of first impression without any closely analogous case.

* * *

Fountains are what appellant (or someone connected with him) sells. At oral argument, counsel presented us with a stereoscopic film-slide card, a sales device showing fountains like those here involved in three-dimensional pictures as offered for sale. There is no doubt in our minds that prospective buyers of these fountains would select them for the decoration of buildings or grounds according to specific, reproducible designs, intending to use them as permanent decoration. The fountains are certainly made by man (manufactured) for sale to and use by such buyers. They certainly carry into effect the plain intent of the design patent statute, which is to give encouragement to the decorative arts. Gorham Mfg. Co. v. White, 14 Wall. 511, 81 U.S. 511, 524, 20 L.Ed. 731 (1871).

We fail to find in the opinion of the board majority any sufficient reason for holding the fountains are not "articles of manufacture."

* * *

The majority board opinion concludes with the view that "the present design is not drawn to subject matter coming within the terms or spirit of 35 U.S.C.A. § 171." We find in the opinion, however, no citation of authority other than the statute itself, no indication that the *terms* mean anything other than what they say, no reason why the fountain is not "an article of manufacture" other than the board majority's inability to conceive that it could be, and certainly no discussion of what the *spirit* of the statute is. We think its spirit is as stated by the Supreme Court in Gorham Mfg. Co. v. White, to encourage the decorative arts, over and beyond those classically known as "the fine arts." We think the appellant has contributed to the decorative arts. Surely, if he is told he cannot have protection by design patent, he and his like will be discouraged.

It is most interesting that the brief for the Patent Office contains only 4 pages of "argument," devotes two of them to stating the evolution of the statute from 1842 to 1902, when it took its present form, cites no authority to support the rejection but does cite the *Hadden* case for the proposition we cited it for above, and makes but a single argument in support of the contention the fountains *should* not be considered to be "an article of manufacture." It is, as the examiner contended, that water sprays "cannot exist of themselves," being dependent on the existence of the nozzles and the water under pressure. Only because of this *dependence* are we asked to affirm the rejection.

We fail to see any force in this argument. It is not denied that *designs* exist. It is perfectly clear that these designs are of the three-dimensional or configuration-of-goods type. The "goods" in this instance are fountains, so they are made of the only substance fountains can be made of—water.[4] We see no necessary relation between the dependence of these designs made of water upon the means for producing them and their being articles of manufacture. A majority of this court recently held patentable a grille for a radio cabinet with a circularly brushed *appearance* which also had evenly-spaced small perforations. The peculiarity of this grille was that *"with variations in viewing angle and ambient lighting"* (emphasis added) a varying moiré effect was produced and the majority felt that this effect made the ornamental appearance unobvious and patentable. The design was thus *dependent,* insofar as the feature which made it patentable was concerned, on something outside itself, it did not exist alone, because without the proper angles of ambient lighting and viewing there was no moiré effect. In re Boldt, 344 F.2d 990, 52 CCPA 1283 (1965). For an older moiré effect case in a serrated rubber doormat, see New York Belting & Packing Co. v. New Jersey Car Spring & Rubber Co., 137 U.S.

---

4. We are aware that fountains of sorts have been made of other fluids such as Martinis and Manhattans, on a small scale; but speaking practically, decorative fountains of the type we are discussing must be made of water.

445, 11 S.Ct. 193, 34 L.Ed. 741 (1890). We do not see that the dependence of the existence of a design on something outside itself is a reason for holding it is not a design "for an article of manufacture." Many such designs depend upon outside factors for the production of the appearance which the beholder observes. The design of a lamp-shade may not be apparent unless the lamp is lighted. The design of a woman's hosiery is not apparent unless it is in place on her legs. The designs of inflated articles such as toy balloons, water toys, air mattresses, and now even buildings are not apparent in the absence of the compressed air which gives them form, as the water pressure here gives shape to the fountain. Even the design of wall paper is not always fully apparent in the commodity as it is sold and requires a wall and the services of a paperhanger to put it into condition for enjoyment by the beholder, which is the ultimate purpose of all ornamental design.

Finding, as we do, that the examiner, the majority of the board, and the Solicitor for the Patent Office have produced no argument of substance or any authority in support of their view, that the dissenting member of the board has made cogent arguments in opposition to it, and believing that the primary objectives of the design patent statute will be carried out by protecting these designs for water fountains, if they otherwise meet the requirements of the statutes, we hold they meet the "article of manufacture" requirement of 35 U.S.C.A. § 171.

The decisions of the board are reversed.

Reversed.

MARTIN, J., participated in the hearing of this case but died before a decision was reached.

WORLEY, CHIEF JUDGE (dissenting).

It is inconceivable that Congress could possibly have intended Sec. 171, in letter or spirit, to allow an individual to remove from the public domain and monopolize mere sprays of water. To do so, one must necessarily rely on strained semantics at the expense of common sense. The instant sprays, so evanescent and fugitive in nature, presumably subject to the whims of wind and weather, incapable of existing in and of themselves, are merely the *effect* flowing from articles of manufacture, but certainly are no more articles of manufacture per se than are the vapor trails of jets, wakes of ships or steam from engines.

It appears that appellant presently enjoys patent protection on the mechanical elements of the fountains, but apparently not satisfied with that, now seeks to monopolize certain configurations of moving water, whether produced by a garden hose or otherwise. It is not difficult to image the potential harassment that could result from such a monopoly.

I would affirm.

C. ACTUAL REDUCTION TO PRACTICE

FITZGERALD v. ARBIB

United States Court of Customs and Patent Appeals, 1959.
268 F.2d 763, 122 USPQ 530.

MARTIN, JUDGE. This is an appeal from the decision of the Board of Patent Interferences of the United States Patent Office awarding priority of invention of the involved subject matter to the senior party, Arbib et al., appellee here. The interference involves Design Patent No. 175,143, granted to Arbib et al. on July 19, 1955, on an application filed November 4, 1954, and an application of the junior party Fitzgerald, Design Serial No. 36,893, filed on July 11, 1955. The invention in issue is an ornamental escutcheon plate for a lock.

Since Fitzgerald's application was copending with that of Arbib et al., he has the burden of proving priority by a preponderance of the evidence. Gaiser v. Linder, 253 F.2d 433, 45 CCPA 846. Arbib et al., having taken no testimony, are confined to their filing date for conception and reduction to practice.

Fitzgerald submitted evidence showing a completion of a pencil drawing of the design in issue on May 21, 1954, a colored drawing thereof on June 3, 1954, an orthographic layout on December 2, 1954, a dimensioned detailed drawing for making an actual escutcheon dated January 13, 1955, and a wooden pattern on March 22, 1955.

The Board of Patent Interferences held, as a matter of law, that the May 21 and June 3 drawings were evidence only of conception and not of a reduction to practice of the invention here in issue. The Board found the decision of this court in Dieterich v. Leaf, 89 F.2d 226, 24 CCPA 1138, to be a controlling authority standing for the proposition that to have an actual reduction to practice " * * * in the case of a design for a three-dimensional article, it is 'required' that it 'should be embodied in some structure other than a mere drawing' * * *."

* * *

Appellant contends that the drawings in question constitute reductions to practice of the invention and that, accordingly, the rule in Dieterich v. Leaf, supra, should be narrowed to its particular facts, or in the alternative, overruled. It is urged that the rough line drawing in that case "did not disclose with the necessary fidelity 'the intended effect on the eye of the observer' * * *" of the design for the ice cream cones there involved, whereas the eye-pleasing multi-color perspective drawing of June 3, 1954, fully discloses the invention here in issue.

* * *

The color drawing of June 3, 1954, depicts the design very attractively and gives a better picture of the artist's conception than the original pencil drawing. However, this drawing does not constitute a completion of the invention any more than the original drawing because of the further activity necessary to produce a physical embodiment of the design.

The dimensioned detail drawing, showing both elevation and plan views, which was prepared by appellant in December, 1954, after the senior party filed, to be used by the pattern maker, and the pattern itself, demonstrate how much more activity was necessary.

Also, appellant's own statements concerning the design indicate that he found many problems in working with it and anticipated more before a physical embodiment of the design could be realized. For instance, he stated:

> "I had numerous conversations and visits to foundries and I was extremely interested in the shell molding process as having possibilities of [sic] high as cast finish on this; *because it was obvious that the intricacies of this design would pose serious finishing problems; and I felt that if the design were to succeed, it would have to reach the finishing process in a high—in a relatively high state of surface smoothness; otherwise it would be prohibitive to manufacture.*" [Emphasis added.]

Aside from the above mentioned case law, appellant's own testimony, as hereinabove set forth, indicates how much more was needed to perfect or complete the invention, not in terms of mental activity, but in the sense of actually making an article embodying the design, available for use by the public.

In similar circumstances, this court and its predecessor in patent jurisdiction have held that the reduction to practice of a three-dimensional design invention requires the production of an article embodying that design. Tyler v. St. Amend, 17 App.D.C. 464, 1901 C.D. 301, 94 O.G. 1969; Dieterich v. Leaf, supra. Under this law, the drawing of June 3, 1954, was not an actual reduction to practice of the invention in issue by Fitzgerald.

* * *

For the above reasons, the decision of the Board of Patent Interferences is affirmed.

Affirmed.

* * *

RICH, JUDGE (concurring).

* * *

D. SPECIFICATION

The specification of a design patent must comply with 35 U.S.C.A. § 112 and is generally very simple. It consists of a drawing of the ornamental design of the article, a description which essentially includes a title, a very brief identification of each figure of the drawing, and a single pro forma claim which defines the device in terms of the drawing. For example, in the following case, the claim is simply: "The ornamental design for a terminal box face plate assembly as shown."

EX PARTE REINER

United States Patent Office Board of Appeals, 1964.
142 USPQ 283.

FRIEDMAN, EXAMINER IN CHIEF. This is an appeal involving a design. Since appellant's proposed amendment submitted October 15, 1963 has not been entered by the examiner, the claim on appeal reads as follows:

The ornamental design for a terminal box face plate assembly as shown.

* * *

As stated by the examiner:

"The claim stands finally rejected because of lack of complete disclosure since the back of the claimed article has not been shown. Failure to disclose the back is believed to preclude one skilled in the art from making and using such an article."

The examiner bases this position on the decision of Philco Corp. v. Admiral Corp., 131 USPQ 413.[a]

Upon careful consideration of the issues involved, we are not inclined to agree with the instant rejection.

We do not find the case of Philco v. Admiral, supra, relied upon by the examiner, to be persuasive or controlling here. In that case, there was involved a design patent for a portable television receiver, having a front perspective view of the receiver as the sole figure of the patent, and a description stating that "the back is unornamented." The Court found that while from such presentation in the patent there would arise a reasonable inference that the back of the receiver was intended to be plain and relatively flat, this would be inconsistent with technical requirements for a television receiver such as picture tube length and the size of other components. Accordingly, it was reasoned that a back "of substantial configuration" would be required, and that this might have several different forms. It was held that under these circumstances the configuration of the receiver back would constitute a significant part of a design such as that involved, and that the failure to disclose some particular such configuration was a fatal defect of disclosure. Manifestly, an inherent factor forming part of the basis for such holding was the visibility in normal use of the back portion of the particular type of entity which was the subject of the design in suit.

We do not have a similar situation before us. We think that here the figures of the drawing, particularly Figures 3 and 4 and the absence of any dotted line denotation therein, when considered in relation to the other figures, would give rise to an inference as in the Philco v. Admiral case that the back of appellant's device was intended to be flat and unadorned. However, in the instant situation, in contradistinction from that in Philco v. Admiral, there is nothing to disturb this inference, there being no technical factors connected with the type of device

a. 199 F.Supp. 797 (D.C.Del.1961).

here involved presenting any particular configurational requirements. Moreover, as denoted by appellant, the rear portion of the instant design would be essentially irrelevant and of no significant import, since it would be hidden in the normal use of the device.

Under the circumstances outlined, we are impelled to the conclusion that the instant rejection is untenable, and accordingly, we will not sustain said rejection.

The decision of the examiner is reversed.

APPLICATION OF RUBINFIELD

United States Court of Customs and Patent Appeals, 1959.
47 CCPA 701, 270 F.2d 391, 123 USPQ 210.

WORLEY, CHIEF JUDGE. This is an appeal from the decision of the Board of Appeals of the United States Patent Office affirming the Primary Examiner's rejection of the three claims of appellant's application for a patent on a design for a floor waxer. The appealed claims are as follows:

1. The ornamental design for a Floor Waxer substantially as shown in Figures 1 to 4, inclusive.

2. The ornamental design for a Floor Waxer substantially as shown in Figures 5 to 8, inclusive.

3. The ornamental design for a Floor Waxer having the common appearance substantially as shown in Figures 1 to 8, inclusive.

Appellant's application discloses designs of two floor waxers of generally similar but specifically different appearance, one being shown in Figures 1 to 4 and the other in Figures 5 to 8.

No references have been cited and there is no issue as to whether appellant's designs involve patentable invention.

* * *

The board in its opinion stated the ground of rejection as being "that a multiplicity of designs are claimed" and limited its discussion to the *disclosure* of two embodiments of the design, no express statement being made that plural *claiming* was bad per se. However, since the examiner raised the issue of multiple claiming as well as multiple disclosure, and since the board entered a general affirmance of the examiner's decision, the former issue is before this court as well as the latter. * * * It is well settled that a design patent may be infringed by articles which are specifically different from that shown in the patent, Gorham Co. v. White, 81 U.S. 511; Borgfeldt & Co. v. Weiss, 265 F. 268, and it has been repeatedly held that a patent will be refused on an application claiming a design which is not patentably different from, or involves the same inventive concept as, a design claimed in a patent granted to the same inventor, even on a copending application. In re Bigelow, 39 CCPA 835, 194 F.2d 550, 93 USPQ 17; In re Russell, 44 CCPA 716, 239 F.2d 387, 112 USPQ 58, and cases there cited. It seems evident, therefore, that the inventive concept of a design is not limited to the exact article which happens to be selected for illustration in an application or patent.

While the exact issue under consideration here has not previously been before this court, In re William Schnell, 18 CCPA 812, 46 F.2d 203, 8 USPQ 19, 26, contains the following language clearly indicating the opinion that the disclosure of more than one specific embodiment of a design invention in a single application may be proper:

> * * * Furthermore, we know of no statutory or other reason why he [a design applicant] may not be permitted to submit drawings of more than one article if his design applies to more than one article and if it seems necessary and essential to use more than one drawing in order that he may teach the manner of applying the same to different articles. * * *

> * * * If he is entitled to certain protection under the enforcement provision, why is he not entitled by some appropriate words in the claim and drawing to disclose all that he is entitled to in order that others may be warned of the probable scope of applicant's invention?

> * * *

It seems anomalous to hold that two specifically different articles may represent a single inventive concept so far as double patenting or infringement is concerned, and yet may not be disclosed in a single application.

* * *

As above indicated, when similar designs or embodiments are presented by an inventor in separate applications, the Patent Office does not leave the determination as to whether they are distinct inventions to the courts, but, if it finds only one inventive concept to be involved, allows a patent on one application and rejects the others on the ground of double patenting. It is not apparent, therefore, why that office should refuse to undertake a similar determination when different embodiments are presented in a single application. No doubt, as was said by the Commissioner in Ex parte Lunken, 1896 C.D. 22, 76 O.G. 785, "it would be convenient for the office to dispose of the question summarily by requiring but one invariable form to be shown and patented" but, as was further, and we think correctly, pointed out by the Commissioner in that case, such convenience cannot take precedence over the rights of applicants.

For the reasons given, we are of the opinion that it cannot be stated as an invariable rule that a design application cannot disclose more than one embodiment of the design. Whether such disclosure is improper must depend upon the particular circumstances of the individual case involved, and a blanket rejection on the ground of "multiplicity," without considering such circumstances, is not proper. On this particular point we are unable to agree with the board.

* * *

It has been consistently held for many years that it is the appearance of a design as a whole which is controlling in determining questions of patentability and infringement. Gorham Company v. White, 81 U.S. 511; In re Schraubstadter, 26 App.D.C. 331, 1906 C.D. 541; In re Bonnell, 29 CCPA 1104, 129 F.2d 520, 54 USPQ 202; In re Campbell, 41 CCPA 896, 212 F.2d 606, 101 USPQ 406; and In re Russell, 44 CCPA 716, 239 F.2d 387, 112 USPQ 58. Under such circumstances, as was pointed out by the Commissioner in Ex parte Wiessner, 1898 C.D. 236, 85 O.G. 937, no useful purpose could be served by the inclusion of more than one claim in a design application or patent.

* * *

The fact that it may be permissible, in a proper case, to illustrate more than one embodiment of a design invention does not require or justify more than one claim

* * *

We find no sound reason for disturbing the long-standing practice of the Patent Office, embodied in Rule 153, which limits design applications to a single claim.

The decision of the Board of Appeals must, therefore, be affirmed insofar as it is predicated on the ground that plural claims cannot be allowed.

E. NOVELTY

Like utility inventions, to be patentable, an ornamental design must be new or novel and nonobvious. Nearly all of the design cases decided under the 1952 Patent Act interpret novelty as meaning simply different than any single prior art reference or device and evaluate, usually under Section 103, innovation or obviousness as a separate issue. Prior art is the type of materials defined by Section 102 and the statutory bar of 102(b) is applicable. Of course, the disclosure of a utility patent can be used to negate the novelty of an ornamental design and vice versa.[a]

APPLICATION OF BARTLETT ET AL.
United States Court of Customs and Patent Appeals, 1962.
49 CCPA 969, 300 F.2d 942, 133 USPQ 204.

RICH, JUDGE. This appeal is from the affirmance by the Patent Office Board of Appeals of the rejection of appellants' single claim, which is in prescribed form, for "The ornamental design for a Plastic Floor Tile as shown." Appellants' application is Ser. No. D–46,680, filed June 21, 1957.

The rejection is that the design is unpatentable over a single reference:

a. H.C. White Co. v. Morton E. Converse & Son, 20 F.2d 311 (2d Cir.1927); In re Hoffmann, 68 F.2d 978, 20 USPQ 304 (CCPA 1934); In re Jennings, 182 F.2d 207, 86 USPQ 68 (CCPA 1950).

"Sweet's Architectural File Catalog for 1954, Section 12i, Catalog Ke, page 5, Item ONYX (423)."

The reference is an illustration of a single square rubber floor tile which is predominantly black, with irregular, sometimes wavy, randomly distributed streaks, blobs and traces of white of varying degrees of intensity [1] appearing on its surface. The white and gray surface decoration is of the general type sometimes referred to as "marbled." It would not be too far afield to compare it to the inter-mixture of fat and lean in meat, which is one of the examples given in defining "marbling" by Webster's New Collegiate Dictionary. The inclusions of white in the reference tile appear to have a general orientation parallel to one edge of the tile, which orientation is barely definite enough to be recognizable as such. Furthermore, whatever parallelism with an edge exists, it does not appear to go in either direction and may be described as bidirectional.

The "drawing" of the application at bar, Fig. 1, is a plan view in the form of a photographic reproduction of a square floor tile showing a pattern of figures of mixed white and gray coloration on a black background. The pattern has a random, as distinguished from a regular, design and looks as though one had deposited drops of white and gray pigments on a black base and had then wiped them, in a partly dried condition, all in one direction parallel to one edge of the tile. The result is smeared blobs, the tails of which stream out behind them. Appellants have described them as "comet-like bodies." The effect is distinctly unidirectional, like burning embers falling through darkness if viewed with the comet tails up, not merely one of general parallelism with one edge of the tile.[2]

The Patent Office appears to have derived from this court's opinion in In re Johnson, 175 F.2d 791, 36 CCPA 1175 (1949), relied on by both the board and the solicitor, a point of law or legal test for determining the patentability of designs. Appellants accept the so-called test and both parties have argued the case on the basis of it, reaching diametrically opposite conclusions. The supposed test, quoting from the solicitor's brief which substantially quotes from the board's opinion, is, "that the degree of difference [from the prior art] required to establish a

1. A sample of such tile having been produced at the argument, it can be seen therefrom that the white material which is mixed into the black base material to form the surface pattern is sometimes visible on the surface while being slightly submerged below a thin surface layer of black base, somewhat obscuring the white material and giving it a gray cast. Thus the pattern is a mixture of white and gray on black.

2. While the application presents the design in black, white and gray, samples of tiles exhibited by appellants' counsel at the argument show that the design is executed, commercially, in a variety of color combinations as is usual in the tile business. For example, one tile has a light brown base color and the smeared blobs are of white, two darker shades of brown, and olive; another tile has a light gray base color and the smeared blobs are of black, brown, olive, yellow and a color resembling that of tomato juice. Thus the *design*, as a matter of surface ornamentation, which applicant seeks to protect, appears to be independent of specific color and inclusive of dark pattern on light background as well as light pattern on dark background. We so regard it.

patentable distinction occurs when the average observer takes the new design for a different, and not a modified, already-existing design." (Our emphasis.)

A *careful* reading of the Johnson opinion and an inspection of Shoemaker, Patents for Designs, page 76, which it cites, will show that the court was not stating a test for patentability at all, but a test only for *novelty* of the design. In fact what the court said, though not presented as a quotation, is a quotation from Shoemaker's section 46, the first section in his Chapter V, on novelty. He said:

> "If the general or ensemble appearance-effect of a design is different from that of others in the eyes of ordinary observers, *novelty* of design is deemed to be present. The degree of difference required to establish *novelty* occurs when the average observer takes the new design for a different, and not a modified already-existing, design." [Emphasis ours.]

This court accepted that as sound law in 1949 and we do now. But novelty, as the Johnson opinion was careful to point out, is only one of the prerequisites to patentability and finding compliance with the above test for novelty is not sufficient, in itself, to determine patentability, or the existence of a "patentable distinction."

It is not altogether clear in this case whether the rejection rests on lack of novelty. The examiner said in his answer:

> "It is the examiner's position that the instant design is substantially anticipated by the Sweet's item and that no patentable distinction is seen thereover. It is further the examiner's belief that while the exact shape and arrangements of the paint spatter-like bodies may be discernible upon a close and detailed analysis the same is not deemed to provide the present design with any new, distinctive or ornamental appearance such as would warrant the grant of a design patent, the general overall appearance still being that of Sweet's design." [He then cited the Johnson case *novelty* test.]

In affirming, the board, after citing the Johnson case as giving a test for a *patentable* distinction from the prior art and saying that mere novelty of detail is not sufficient to warrant a holding of "patentable unobviousness over the prior art," concluded that "the instant design is but a modification of the prior art." It then held:

> "We do not believe that new and patentably distinct effect has been achieved; * * * we are of the opinion that the over-all effect is not significantly or unobviously different so as to create a patentably different design."

We are left wondering whether, by the Johnson case test, the board held that the instant design is not novel. If it believed that it was not, there was no need for the board to speak of unobviousness or patentable difference. We shall assume, however, because of the uncertainty, that the Patent Office rejection is based on both lack of novelty (by the Johnson case test) and obviousness in view of the reference disclosure and shall deal with both issues.

By the Johnson case test, adopted from Shoemaker, the appellants' design appears to us to be clearly novel. The average observer, in our judgment, would inevitably take appellants' design to be a different design from that shown in Sweet's catalog, rather than a modification of the latter. The two appearances, created by the tile in Sweet's catalog and by applicants' tile respectively, are not only easily distinguished by the practiced eye but they make different overall impressions so that purchasers might very well have preferences for one over the other. In short, they do not look alike and the existence of statutory novelty is beyond question.

But there remains the issue of unobviousness of appellants' design in view of the reference. Its solution, as has always been recognized, is not easy and as the solicitor realistically concludes in his brief, "the determination of patentability in design cases must finally rest on the subjective conclusion of each judge." Whether the design is unobvious is a question not unrelated to novelty, however, and the differences in degree and in kind which one can observe are the only criteria of decision available to us. As stated above, we see no overall similarity, as did the board. Appellants have produced a distinctly new and different impression. They did not do so by modifying what is shown in the reference but by adopting a new approach. We cannot better describe it than to say that instead of using a marbleizing technique which produces a bidirectional pattern they adopted a blob-smearing technique which produces a distinctive and strongly unidirectional pattern. Judging, as we must, from the basis that the single reference depicts the most relevant prior art, what we see is that appellants' design was obviously the result of creative rather than imitative efforts, origination rather than close copying. The difference in kind between the designs is, in our opinion, such as to eliminate the possibility that the prior art contains a suggestion of the design sought to be patented. We are unable, therefore, to conclude that it was obvious.

The decision of the board is reversed.

Reversed.

F. NONOBVIOUSNESS

In the last portion of the preceding case, Judge Rich dealt with the issue of unobviousness in design inventions. In an earlier case,[a] he said of a design for ornamental iron work, "We see no aping here, or mere development. Something from the creativity of the artist impinges itself on our consciousness which we are unable to equate with the concept of obviousness."

Many of the problems in determining non-obviousness under Section 103 of utility inventions are also present in cases involving design inventions. In addition, with design inventions, the determination of

a. Application of Braun, 275 F.2d 738, 125 USPQ 192 (CCPA 1960).

non-obviousness must be based in large measure on visual observations of the ornamental design, the prior art, and the differences between them. In making this determination, the concepts useful in relation to utility patents, namely, improved usefulness, unexpected results, and mechanically unrelated or non-analogous art, are of little, if any, value, since appearance, not use, is controlling.[b] As the Court of Customs and Patent Appeals said in Application of Boldt, 52 CCPA 1283, 344 F.2d 990, 991, 145 USPQ 414, 415 (1965):

> [T]he question in design cases is not whether the references sought to be combined are in analogous arts in the mechanical sense, but whether they are so related that the appearance of certain ornamental features in the one would suggest application of those features in the other.

Moreover, many of the secondary considerations associated with utility inventions are seldom, if ever, associated with design inventions. As the court noted in Plantronics, Inc. v. Roanwell Corp., 403 F.Supp. 138, 187 USPQ 489 (D.C.S.D.N.Y.1975):

> "Unfortunately, in an action for infringement of a design patent there are rarely any of the 'signposts' of patentability which enable an objective evaluation of the obviousness vel non of utility inventions. Since the design patent covers only optional esthetic features, there is never a long-felt need or an unsuccessful search, and it is rarely possible to allocate the specific portions of the profits on a commercial product which are respectively attributable to its utilitarian advantages and to its visual appeal. Thus, in the final analysis, a court's evaluation of the patentability of a design is essentially subjective and personal artistic tastes are unpredictable and inexplicable—one viewer's mural is another's graffiti."

SIDEWINDER MARINE INC. v. STARBUCK KUSTOM BOATS AND PRODUCTS, INC.

United States Court of Appeals, Tenth Circuit, 1979.
597 F.2d 201, 202 USPQ 356.

[Excerpt Only]

The Standard for Obviousness

Plaintiff Sidewinder next contends that the trial court erred in assessing the obviousness issue according to how an "ordinary designer" would view it rather than from the perspective of the "ordinary intelligent man." The importance of this distinction to plaintiff is that under the "ordinary designer" standard, the trial court found that previously-existing automobile designs may properly be taken into account as developments in an analogous field which a boat designer could reasonably be expected to be aware of, and we accept that finding. Under the "ordinary intelligent man" standard, the trial court felt that only prior boat designs would be relevant. See 418 F.Supp. at 229–30.

---

b. Application of Glavas, 230 F.2d 447, 109 USPQ 50 (CCPA 1956); Blumcraft v. Brenner, 247 F.Supp. 978, 147 USPQ 385 (D.C.D.C.1965).

While the trial court applied both tests and found the Sidewinder design obvious even under the "ordinary intelligent man" standard preferred by plaintiff,[8] we have considerable doubt as to the result under that standard alone. Since the result might be different under the two standards, we feel that we should determine which standard applies and then proceed on that basis.

> Title 35 U.S.C. § 103, provides in part: A patent may not be obtained though the invention is not identically disclosed or described as set forth in section 102 [concerning "novelty"], if the differences between the subject matter sought to be patented and the prior art are such that the subject matter as a whole would have been *obvious* at the time the invention was made *to a person having ordinary skill in the art to which said subject matter pertains.* [emphasis added]

As written, and as interpreted in cases dealing with utility patents, the statutory non-obviousness requirement focuses not on some hypothetical "ordinary" person, or layman, but on one "reasonably skilled" in the applicable art. Dann v. Johnston, 425 U.S. 219, 229, 96 S.Ct. 1393, 47 L.Ed.2d 692. There is disagreement among the Circuits, however, when the non-obviousness requirement is carried over—as it must be according to 35 U.S.C.A. § 171—into the design patent area. As noted, the Ninth Circuit in Schwinn Bicycle Co. v. Goodyear Tire & Rubber Co., supra, 444 F.2d at 299, applied the level of knowledge of an "ordinary intelligent man" as the standard by which obviousness or non-obviousness of a design should be determined, following the lead of the Court of Customs and Patent Appeals, which had said concerning obviousness in In re Laverne, 356 F.2d 1003, 1006, 53 C.C.P.A. 1158:

> The test is inherently a visual test, for the design is nothing more than appearance, and the appearance is that of the article as a whole.
> * * * *No special skill is required* to determine what things look like, though individuals react differently. It is bound to be an individual reaction. (Emphasis added).

See also In re Johnson, 175 F.2d 791, 792, 36 C.C.P.A. 1175.

On the other hand, the Second, Third, Sixth, Eighth, and District of Columbia Circuits have phrased their standard for design obviousness in terms of the "worker of ordinary skill in the art" or the "ordinary designer," though those courts recognize that novelty and ornamentality—distinct requirements of design patentability contained in 35 U.S.C.A. § 171—are to be assessed from the viewpoint of the "ordinary observer." See Clark Equipment Co. v. Keller, 570 F.2d 778, 799 (8th Cir.), cert. denied, 439 U.S. 825, 99 S.Ct. 96, 58 L.Ed.2d 118; Schnadig Corp. v. Gaines Manufacturing Co., 494 F.2d 383, 389 (6th Cir.); Fields v. Schuyler, 153 U.S.App.D.C. 229, 472 F.2d 1304, 1306, cert. denied, 411 U.S. 987, 93 S.Ct. 2270, 36 L.Ed.2d 965; Hadco Products, Inc. v. Walter Kidde & Co., 462 F.2d 1265, 1272 (3d Cir.); G.B. Lewis Co. v. Gould

---

8. The trial judge stated that he believed that the "ordinary designer" test is the better approach, but that since neither the Supreme Court nor this court has ruled upon which test should be applied, he had analyzed the prior art references under both standards of non-obviousness. 418 F.Supp. at 229.

Products, Inc., 436 F.2d 1176, 1178 (2d Cir.). See also 2 Walker, Patents, § 161 at 757.

We are persuaded that the proper standard is that of the "ordinary designer" in the field in question. Not only does this standard hew more closely to the statutory wording in § 103, but, as pointed out in Fields v. Schuyler, supra at 1306, it serves as a "more objective reference point" concerning obviousness than the "ordinary observer" standard.[9] If the latter standard were adopted, as again pointed out in *Fields,* commercial success of the design among the mass of "ordinary" consumers would be a "virtually conclusive determinant" of non-obviousness, rather than the secondary consideration it is supposed to be under the rule of Graham v. John Deere Co., 383 U.S. 1, 17, 86 S.Ct. 684, 15 L.Ed.2d 545.[10]

In sum, we cannot agree with plaintiff Sidewinder that the proper standard is that of the ordinary intelligent man. We feel instead that the standard to apply is that of an ordinary designer in the sport and pleasure boat field.

Notes

1. In re Nalbandian, 661 F.2d 1214, 211 USPQ 782 (CCPA 1981): The court held that the tests for determining validity of a design patent pursuant to 35 U.S.C.A. § 171 are identical to those for determining validity of a utility patent. The standard determining "obviousness" under 35 U.S.C.A. § 103 is the "designer of ordinary skill who designs articles of the type in question." In re Laverne, 356 F.2d 1003, 148 USPQ 674 (CCPA 1966), which established the "ordinary observer" test, was reversed.

2. Federal Circuit cases applying the Nalbandian standard are Litton Systems, Inc. v. Whirlpool Corp., 728 F.2d 1423, 221 USPQ 97 (Fed.Cir.1984) and Peterson Mfg. Co. v. Central Purchasing, Inc., 740 F.2d 1541, 222 USPQ 562 (Fed.Cir.1984).

9. We acknowledge the necessarily subjective element in any determination of the obviousness or non-obviousness of designs. See In re Bartlett, 300 F.2d 942, 944, 49 C.C.P.A. 969. Nevertheless, the skill and knowledge of the "ordinary designer" are capable of some proof in court (as by the testimony of three workers in the field in the instant case), whereas the viewpoint of the "ordinary observer" resolves itself into an "eyeball test" to be carried out by the trial judge or the jury, whichever decides the facts.

10. We feel that the plaintiff's reliance on Smith v. Whitman Saddle Co., 148 U.S. 674, 680, 13 S.Ct. 768, 37 L.Ed. 606, and Gorham Co. v. White, 81 U.S. (14 Wall.) 511, 528, 20 L.Ed. 731 is misplaced. Gorham Co. v. White did apply the test of substantial similarity in the eye of an ordinary observer, but only in deciding the question of infringement of the patented design.

It is true that in Smith v. Whitman Saddel Co., 148 U.S. 674, 679–80, 13 S.Ct. 768, 37 L.Ed. 606 (1893), in discussing patentability generally the Court referred to the test of identity of design as being that of sameness of appearance to the eye of an ordinary observer, citing Gorham Manufacturing Co. v. White, *inter alia.* However, we do not feel that this statement is controlling here since it was made long before the enactment of § 103 on obviousness with its standard of "a person having ordinary skill in the art * * *" and long before the clear reference in Graham v. John Deere Co. to "the level of ordinary skill in the pertinent art * * *" in applying the 1952 statute. 383 U.S. at 17, 86 S.Ct. at 694.

G. INFRINGEMENT

In determining patent infringement, the basic question is whether the accused process, article, or composition embodies the patented invention. In a utility patent, the invention is claimed by a written statement pointing out and defining the patentable invention.

However, in a design patent, the invention is claimed by reference to a drawing illustrating the patented ornamental design. Thus, the determination of infringement of utility and design patents involves quite different concepts. To determine whether a design patent is infringed, a visual comparison and evaluation is made of the similarity in overall appearance between the patented ornamental design and the accused article.

GORHAM MFG. CO. v. WHITE

Supreme Court of the United States, 1872.
81 U.S. (14 Wall.) 511, 20 L.Ed. 731.

[Excerpts Only]

We are now prepared to inquire what is the true test of identity of design. Plainly, it must be sameness of appearance, and mere difference of lines in the drawing or sketch, a greater or smaller number of lines, or slight variances in configuration, if insufficient to change the effect upon the eye, will not destroy the substantial identity. * * * The court below was of opinion that the test of a patent for a design is not the eye of an ordinary observer. The learned judge thought there could be no infringement unless there was "substantial identity," "in view of the observation of a person versed in designs in the particular trade in question"—

* * *

There must, he thought, be a comparison of the features which make up the two designs. With this we cannot concur. Such a test would destroy all the protection which the act of Congress intended to give.

* * *

The purpose of the law must be effected if possible; but, plainly, it cannot be if, while the general appearance of the design is preserved, minor differences of detail in the manner in which the appearance is produced, observable by experts but not noticed by ordinary observers, by those who buy and use, are sufficient to relieve an imitating design from condemnation as an infringement.

We hold, therefore, that if, in the eye of an ordinary observer, giving such attention as a purchaser usually gives, two designs are substantially the same, if the resemblance is such as to deceive such an observer, inducing him to purchase one supposing it to be the other, the first one patented is infringed by the other.

* * *

In the White designs this inner line is wanting on the stem of the handle, though not on the broad part, but as the single line is wider it presents much the same appearance as it would present if divided into two. There are other small differences which it is needless to specify. What we have mentioned are the most prominent. No doubt to the eye of an expert they are all real. Still, though variances in the ornament are discoverable, the question remains: Is the effect of the whole design substantially the same? Is the adornment in the White design used instrumentally to produce an appearance, a distinct device, or does it work the same result in the same way, and is it, therefore, a colorable evasion of the prior patent, amounting at most to a mere equivalent? In regard to this we have little doubt, in view of the evidence. Both the White designs, we think, are proved to be infringements of the Gorham patent.

* * *

LITTON SYSTEMS, INC. v. WHIRLPOOL CORPORATION

United States Court of Appeals, Federal Circuit, 1984.
728 F.2d 1423, 221 USPQ 97.

NICHOLS, SENIOR CIRCUIT JUDGE.

This is an appeal from a judgment entered on April 28, 1983, in which the United States District Court for the District of Minnesota, after a bench trial, held valid a United States utility patent and a United States design patent, both owned by Litton Systems. The district court also found that certain microwave ovens manufactured and sold by Whirlpool Corporation infringe these two patents * * *

WHIRLPOOL Model 7600 Oven (PX–36)

* * *

THE '990 DESIGN PATENT

Whirlpool takes issue with the district court's holding that the '990 design patent is valid, arguing that the design would have been obvious. Whirlpool also disputes the trial court's finding that Whirlpool microwave ovens infringe the design patent.

This is the design claimed by the design patent in suit:

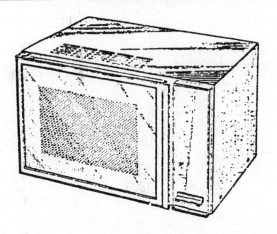

D-226,990
Wolfe, Tapper (5/23/73)
<u>Litton</u>

We affirm on validity, but reverse on the issue of infringement.

A. VALIDITY

* * *

We show these prior art ovens here (issuing date in parentheses).

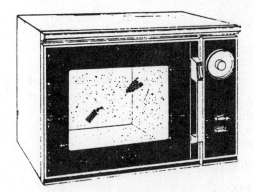

D-228,607
Binzer, Schmitt, Wooding,
Sugunoya and Miyake (10/16/73)
General Electric

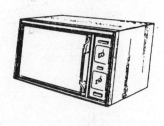

D-228,313
Sugunoya and Miyake
(9/4/73)
Sharp

D-225,579
Sugunoya and Miyake
(12/19/72)
Sharp

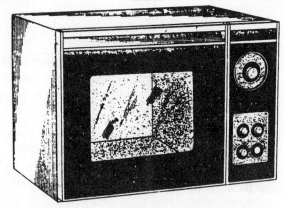

D-225,780
Binzer, Schmitt & Wooding
(1/2/73)
General Electric

728 F.2d—33

     * * * the trial court held that the ordinary designer would not have found Litton's microwave oven design, as a whole, obvious in light of the differences between the prior art and the claimed design. In reaching its decision, the court correctly gave the design patent, which had survived the scrutiny of the PTO, the same statutory presumption of validity it would give a utility patent pursuant to 35 U.S.C. § 282.

     When we compare the prior art with the '990 design, however, we find that the prior art references *all* show doors as "slim appearing" as the door claimed in the '990 patent. There is, in addition, no justification whatever for the trial court's finding that the '990 patent design shows a "light-weight" door, or even, a door more "light" than any of the prior art references. Finally, the prior art clearly discloses an uncluttered control layout. As to these "differences," therefore, we hold that the district court committed clear error. * * *

We also note that there are a large number of similarities between the Litton design and that of the prior art. The fact that similarities exist, however, does not, and cannot, control our decision. It is the difference between the subject matter sought to be patented and the prior art which matters. Since differences do exist, we hold that Whirlpool has failed to convince us that the trial court committed reversible error in holding that a person of ordinary designer skill would not have found the design, *as a whole,* obvious. The district court's holding that the '990 patent is valid is affirmed.

B. INFRINGEMENT

More than one hundred years ago, the Supreme Court established a test for determining infringement of a design patent which, to this day, remains valid. *Gorham Co. v. White,* 81 U.S. (14 Wall.) 511, 20 L.Ed. 731 (1871). This test requires that "if, in the eye of an ordinary observer, giving such attention as a purchaser usually gives, two designs are substantially the same, if the resemblance is such as to deceive such an observer, inducing him to purchase one supposing it to be the other, the first one patented is infringed by the other." *Id.* at 528, 20 L.Ed. 731.

For a design patent to be infringed, however, no matter how similar two items look, "the accused device must appropriate the novelty in the patented device which distinguishes it from the prior art." *Sears, Roebuck & Co. v. Talge,* 140 F.2d 395, 396 (8th Cir.1944); *Horwitt v. Longines Wittnauer Watch Co.,* 388 F.Supp. 1257, 1263, 185 USPQ 123, 128 (S.D.N.Y.1975). That is, even though the court compares two items through the eyes of the ordinary observer, it must nevertheless, to find infringement, attribute their similarity to the novelty which distinguishes the patented device from the prior art. (This "point of novelty" approach applies only to a determination of infringement. *See, e.g., Medtronic, Inc. v. Cardiac Pacemakers, Inc.,* 721 F.2d 1563, 1567, 220 USPQ 97, 101 (Fed.Cir.1983). This court has avoided the point of novelty approach in other contexts. *See, e.g., Carman Industries, Inc. v. Wahl,* 724 F.2d 932 at 940 (Fed.Cir.1983) (double patenting); *In re Gulack,* 703 F.2d 1381, 1385 n. 8, 217 USPQ 401, 403 n. 8 (Fed.Cir.1983) (unobviousness).)

The novelty of the '990 patent consists, in light of our analysis in the previous section on the '990 patent's validity, of the combination on a microwave oven's exterior of a three-stripe door frame, a door without a handle, and a latch release lever on the control panel. The district court expressly found, however, that the Whirlpool design had none of these features.

We recognize that minor differences between a patented design and an accused article's design cannot, and shall not, prevent a finding of infringement. In this case, however, "while there is some similarity between the patented and alleged infringing designs, which without consideration of the prior art might seem important, yet such similarity as is due to common external configuration is no greater, if as great, between the patented and challenged designs as between the former and the designs of the prior art." *Applied Arts Corp. v. Grand Rapids Metalcraft Corp.*, 67 F.2d 428, 430 (6th Cir.1933). Where, as here, a field is crowded with many references relating to the design of the same type of appliance, we must construe the range of equivalents very narrowly.

We hold, therefore, that the scope of protection which the '990 patent affords to a microwave oven is limited in application to a narrow range: the three-stripe effect around a door with no handle and the latch release mounted on the control panel. The Whirlpool ovens, therefore, do not infringe the '990 design patent. The contrary conclusion of the district court is clearly erroneous, being attributable to its failure to apply the correct legal standard of infringement in design patent cases.

Chapter Eight

PLANT PATENTS

Since May 23, 1930, the Patent Act has had a section directed to the protection of plants. During the consideration of the original act by Congress, the question arose as to whether a discoverer of a new plant variety was an inventor or a discoverer within the meaning of the constitutional provision. Why would such a discovery be protected any more than the discovery of a new mineral? A Congressional report treats the matter this way: [a]

> The mineral is created wholly by nature unassisted by man and is likely to be discovered in various parts of the country; and, being the property of all those on whose land it may be found, its free use by the respective owners should of course be permitted. On the other hand, a plant discovery resulting from cultivation is unique, isolated, and is not repeated by nature, nor can it be reproduced by nature unaided by man, and such discoveries can only be made available to the public by encouraging those who own the single specimen to reproduce it asexually and thus create an adequate supply.

The plant patent statute as presently amended reads as follows:

35 U.S.C.A. § 161. Patents for Plants

Whoever invents or discovers and asexually [b] reproduces any distinct and new variety of plant, including cultivated sports, mutants, hybrids, and newly found seedlings, other than a tuber propagated plant or a plant found in an uncultivated state, may obtain a patent therefor, subject to the conditions and requirements of this title.

The provisions of this title relating to patents for inventions shall apply to patents for plants, except as otherwise provided.

35 U.S.C.A. § 162. Description, Claim

No plant patent shall be declared invalid for noncompliance with section 112 of this title if the description is as complete as is reasonably possible.

The claim in the specification shall be in formal terms to the plant shown and described.

a. Deller's Walker on Patents (2nd Ed.) Vol. 3, Section 192.

b. Editor's Note: Asexual reproduction may be accomplished by grafting, budding, cuttings, layering, inarching, division and similar horticultural procedures.

667

35 U.S.C.A. § 163. Grant

In the case of a plant patent the grant shall be of the right to exclude others from asexually reproducing the plant or selling or using the plant so reproduced.

35 U.S.C.A. § 164. Assistance of Department of Agriculture

The President may by executive order direct the Secretary of Agriculture, in accordance with the requests of the Commissioner, for the purpose of carrying into effect the provisions of this title with respect to plants (1) to furnish available information of the Department of Agriculture, (2) to conduct through the appropriate bureau or division of the Department research upon special problems, or (3) to detail to the Commissioner officers and employees of the Department.

7 U.S.C.A. § 2402. Right to Plant Variety Protection; Plant Varieties Protectable

(a) The breeder of any novel variety of sexually reproduced plant (other than fungi, bacteria, or first generation hybrids) who has so reproduced the variety, or his successor in interest, shall be entitled to plant variety protection therefor, subject to the conditions and requirements of this title unless one of the following bars exists: * * *

7 U.S.C.A. § 2483. Contents and Term of Plant Variety Protection

(a) Every certificate of plant variety protection shall certify that the breeder (or his successor in interest) his heirs or assignees, has the right, during the term of the plant variety protection, to exclude others from selling the variety, or offering it for sale, or reproducing it, or importing it, or exporting it, or using it in producing (as distinguished from developing) a hybrid or different variety therefrom, to the extent provided by this chapter. If the owner so elects, the certificate shall also specify that in the United States, seed of the variety shall be sold by variety name only as a class of certified seed and, if specified, shall also conform to the number of generations designated by the owner. Any rights, or all rights except those elected under the preceding sentence, may be waived; and the certificate shall conform to such waiver. The Secretary may at his discretion permit such election or waiver to be made after certificating and amend the certificate accordingly, without retroactive effect.

(b) The term of plant variety protection shall expire eighteen years from the date of issue of the certificate in the United States. If the certificate is not issued within three years from the effective filing date, the Secretary may shorten the term by the amount of delay in the prosecution of the application attributed by the Secretary to the applicant.

(c) The term of plant variety protection shall also expire if the owner fails to comply with regulations, in force at the time of certificating, relating to replenishing seed in a public repository: *Provided, however,* That this expiration shall not occur unless notice is mailed to the last owner recorded as provided in section 2531(d) of this title and he fails, within the time allowed thereafter, not less than three months, to comply

with said regulations, paying an additional fee to be prescribed by the Secretary.

Plant patents have not issued in large numbers and the total number of patents issued in the first 50 years since the enactment of the statute is about 6,000 by June of 1987. The filing of plant patent applications is limited to a very few attorneys who have specialized in the field. Details relative to the nature of disclosure for flowers and plants, involving a description of blooming habits, buds, bloom, petals, sexual organs, fruit, foliage, wood, thorns, etc. may be found in Deller's Walker on Patents (2nd Ed.) and other references specific to the subject.

It is not within the scope of this casebook to explore in detail the field of plant patents. The following cases will illustrate some of the issues which arise in the obtaining and enforcement of plant patents. By way of introduction to these cases, it has been held that a plant patent cannot be issued for the discovery of a variety of plant which exists in nature but which has previously not been catalogued by botanists. An applicant who had found a variety of syngonium plant in South America was denied protection by the Patent Office Board of Appeals in Ex parte Foster, 90 USPQ 16 (1951), the decision stating:

> A different interpretation cannot be given to the words "invented or discovered" and "new" in connection with plants than is given to these words in connection with other classes of patentable subject matter since plants are recited in the same sentence of the statute as the other classes of patentable subject matter, and there is nothing in the language of the statute to indicate that the words occurring in the sentence mean one thing for one class and another thing for another.

> In this case applicant may have found a variety of plant hitherto unrecognized by botanists, but it is not seen that such a plant can be patented under the law.

The above interpretation of the statute as it relates to plants is borne out by the legislative history of the plant patent act, which shows that Congress specifically intended to exclude from the scope of the statute newly found plants existing in nature.

YODER BROS., INC. v. CALIFORNIA–FLORIDA PLANT CORP.

United States Court of Appeals, Fifth Circuit, 1976.
537 F.2d 1347.

* * *

Before reaching the issues on appeal, we make a final comment about the requirement of asexual reproduction. It has been described as the "very essence" of the patent. Langrock, Plant Patents—Biological Necessities in Infringement Suits, 41 J.Pat.Off.Soc. 787 (1959). Asexual reproduction is literally the only way that a breeder can be sure he has reproduced a plant identical in every respect to the parent. It is quite possible that infringement of a plant patent would occur only if stock obtained from one of the patented plants is used, given the

extreme unlikelihood that any other plant could actually infringe. See Cole Nursery Co. v. Youdath Perennial Gardens, Inc., N.D.Ohio 1936, 17 F.Supp. 159, 160; Ex parte Weiss, Bd.App.1967, 159 U.S.P.Q. (dictum); Langrock, supra, at 788–89.

If the alleged infringer could somehow prove that he had developed the plant in question independently, then he would not be liable in damages or subject to an injunction for infringement. This example illustrates the extreme extent to which asexual reproduction is the heart of the present plant patent system: the whole key to the "invention" of a new plant is the discovery of new traits *plus* the foresight and appreciation to take the step of asexual reproduction. See Nicholson v. Bailey, S.D.Fla.1960, 182 F.Supp. 509; Ex parte Moore, 115 U.S.P.Q. 145 (1957); Dunn v. Ragin v. Carlile, 50 U.S.P.Q. 472 (1941).

[The Court concluded with a finding of validity and infringement.]

EX PARTE MOORE

United States Patent Office Board of Appeals, 1957.
115 USPQ 145.

TAYLOR, EXAMINER IN CHIEF.

This is an appeal from the final rejection of the following claim:

The new and distinct variety of peach tree as shown and described, characterized by its hardiness and resistance to cold and the late time of ripening of the fruit.

No references are relied on by the examiner, the rejection being solely on the ground that appellant is not the "original, first and sole inventor or discoverer" of the new and distinct variety of peach tree defined in the claim as averred in the oath accompanying his application as filed. The facts of the case are as follows.

Mr. Francis Miller built a house in 1918 and the following year he noticed a small peach tree growing in his yard which he believed sprang from a peach seed planted by one of the men who worked on the house the preceding year. He protected the tree from injury and watered and fertilized it along with the grass and other vegetation in the yard. The tree lived some twelve years or more and bore annual crops of large, luscious peaches. During all of this time Miller had no idea that the peach tree in his yard was a new variety. In so far as he was concerned, it was just a peach tree.

In 1928, when the tree was about ten years old and after it had borne seven annual crops, Mr. William Moore, the applicant in the application here on appeal, who was a friend of Miller and an orchardist and developer of new varieties of orchard trees by profession, saw the peach tree in Miller's yard and recognized that it was a new variety. He requested permission to take grafts for the purpose of asexually reproducing the tree on his own farm and with Miller's consent he took ten scions and grafted them on native root stock and had produced several successive generations from the original tree at

the time the instant application was filed, thus demonstrating that the peach tree was in fact a new variety.

*   *   *

If the word "discovers," as used in the statute, is to be construed as meaning—finds—, and "finds" is construed as merely becoming aware of the existence of a plant without any appreciation that it is a new variety and no attempt is made to perpetuate the variety by asexual reproduction, it seems to us that the constitutional objective of advancing the progress of science and useful arts will to a large degree be nullified in so far as found seedlings are concerned. To illustrate; had the matter been left entirely in Miller's hands he would have done nothing to preserve the variety because, although he knew it was a peach tree, so far as he was aware, it had no unusual characteristics and was just an ordinary peach tree. When it had lived out its life span of twelve years and died, the new variety would have been lost for all time. Miller found a peach tree but he did not discover a new variety.

As pointed out above, the statute says that "Whoever invents or discovers and asexually reproduces any distinct and new variety of plant, * * * may obtain a patent therefor, * * *." It seems to us that although one may find a plant, he has not discovered a new variety if he has no appreciation that the plant is a distinct and new variety. We think that in the instant case appellant is the one who discovered a new variety of seedling because he appreciated that it was distinct and new and took steps to prove that fact by asexual reproduction through several generations and thus preserved for posterity a variety that otherwise would have been lost. It seems to us that what appellant did satisfies the terms of the statute and also carries out the constitutional objective of the patent law of promoting progress. The rejection on the ground that appellant is not the "original, first and sole inventor or discoverer" of the new and distinct variety of peach tree is not sustained.

*   *   *

The decision of the examiner is reversed.

———

Ownership of the plant may determine ownership of the plant patent in the absence of permission to take the plant. The Oregon Supreme Court in Mix v. Newland, 273 Or. 362, 541 P.2d 136, 196 USPQ 506, 507 (1975), had this to say:

"If the right to the sport rested solely upon who first discovered it, defendant's contention might have some merit. But plaintiff need not and does not rest his claim upon this ground. It is plaintiff's theory, and the theory of the trial court as we interpret it, that plaintiff's ownership of the initial plant found in his nursery determines the ownership of any product of that plant, including the commercial value attributable to its uniqueness as a separate specie of chrysanthemum. We agree with plaintiff's contention. Even assuming that defendant had first discovered the unique plant, his discovery would be of no value to him if he could not obtain the plant in order to test and determine its value as a true sport. Defendant's appropriation of the plant for this purpose would constitute a conversion in the absence of plaintiff's permission.[1]

"We cannot conceive of any rational system of law which would condone the conversion of an owner's goods to advance the interests of those claiming a monopoly through first discovery. Since this is primarily a question of the extent to which protection should be extended to existing property ownership and only secondarily a question of the rights acquired by first discovery, we are of the opinion that the matter is within the jurisdiction of the state courts and is not preempted by federal law for adjudication by the Patent Office.

"The decree of the trial court is affirmed."

NICHOLSON v. BAILEY

United States District Court of Florida, 1960.
182 F.Supp. 509, 125 USPQ 157.

FREEMAN, DISTRICT JUDGE.

This case is before the court on defendant's motion for summary judgment. * * * The complaint, in essence, alleges infringement of plaintiff's U.S. Plant Patent 625 relating to a certain navel orange tree producing oranges designated as "Dream Navels," as well as unfair competition in aggravation of the infringement, and seeks damages and a permanent injunction.

* * *

The plaintiff is a recently retired citrus grower and plant breeder in Orlando, Florida. On December 3, 1941, he applied for a plant patent covering a "seedless navel orange tree," which patent was duly issued to the plaintiff on April 25, 1944, and designated as "U.S. Plant Patent 625." In it, the plaintiff claims the following:

"A new and distinct variety of navel orange tree substantially as described, characterized particularly by its much heavier juice content; its larger amount of acidity; its absence of dry juice-cells and ability to hold its juices; its higher ratios of sugars to acids; its higher content of soluble solids; its different flavor; its shorter maturing period after flowering, which is 6 to 6½ months; and its higher rate of productivity on sour orange rootstock; all as compared with the Washington navel orange."

Disclosure in Plant Patents is treated in Section 162, supra, and extensively discussed in Application of LeGrice, a decision of the Court of Customs and Patent Appeals, 301 F.2d 929, 133 USPQ 365 (CCPA 1962).

1. If plaintiff had given defendant permission to take the plant, the result might well be different. Cf., Ex parte Moore, 115 U.S.P.Q. 145 (Patent Office Board of Appeals 1937).

This same court has placed an additional responsibility on the applicant in a case dealing with a variety of Bermuda Grass Plant. We quote from Application of Greer, 484 F.2d 488, 179 USPQ 301, 303 (CCPA 1973):

"Nevertheless, we do not agree that it was contemplated by Congress that its incorporation into R.S. 4888 of the matter which is the statutory predecessor to § 162 would operate to allow an applicant to allege characteristics which might be capable of distinguishing one variety of plant from another without sufficient disclosure to establish that these characteristics are indeed present in the claimed plant and absent in the varieties to which it is most closely related. In fact, the portion of the legislative history relied upon by the board makes it clear that the applicant bears the burden of clearly and precisely describing those characteristics which define the new variety.

"In the instant case we do not doubt that Bermuda grass having *different* reproductive properties, disease resistance, etc., when compared to the same properties of known varieties, would be a distinct variety of Bermuda grass. However, if, as is true in this case, the characteristics chosen to define the new plant are meaningless unless compared with predecessor plant varieties, it is incumbent upon the applicant to provide information of such a character that a meaningful comparison can be made. It is our view that the Patent Office in this case was justified in its conclusion that the criteria used to support the claim did not allow for such a meaningful comparison."

The Chrysanthemum industry, the legislative history of the Plant Patent Act, together with issues of antitrust violations, validity and infringement are fully discussed in Yoder Bros., Inc. v. California-Florida Plant Corp., 537 F.2d 1347, 193 USPQ 264 (5th Cir.1976). In adapting the case law of utility patents to the plant patents, the court said:

"Rephrasing the *John Deere* tests for the plant world, we might ask about (1) the characteristics of prior plants of the same general type, both patented and nonpatented, and (2) the differences between the prior plants and the claims at issue. We see no meaningful way to apply the third criterion to plants—i.e. the level of ordinary skill in the prior art. Criteria one and two are reminiscent of the 'distinctness' requirement already in the Plant Patent Act. Thus, if we are to give obviousness an independent meaning, it must refer to something other than observable characteristics.

"We think that the most promising approach toward the obviousness requirement for plant patents is reference to the underlying constitutional standard that it codifies—namely, invention.

"The general thrust of the 'invention' requirement is to ensure that minor improvements will not be granted the protection of a seventeen year monopoly by the state. In the case of plants, to develop or discover a new variety that retains the desirable qualities of the parent stock and adds significant improvements, and to preserve the new specimen by asexually reproducing it constitutes no small feat.

"[The court suggested an analogy to the drug industry where the therapeutic value of the drug is examined.]

"The same kind of shift in focus would lead us to a more productive inquiry for plant patents. If the plant is a source of food, the ultimate question might be its nutritive content or its prolificacy. A medicinal plant might be judged by its increased or changed therapeutic value. Similarly, an ornamental plant would be judged by its increased beauty and desirability in relation to the other plants of its type, its usefulness in the industry, and how much of an improvement it represents over prior ornamental plants, taking all of its characteristics together.[35] "

EX PARTE HIBBERD

Patent and Trademark Office Board of Appeals and Interferences, 1985.
227 USPQ 443.

SMITH, EXAMINER-IN-CHIEF.

This is an appeal from the examiner's decision finally rejecting claims 239 through 243, 249 through 255 and 260 through 265 as unpatentable under 35 USC 101. Claims 1 through 238 have been cancelled, and claims 244 through 248, 256 through 259, and 266 through 270 have been allowed.

The subject matter on appeal relates to maize plant technologies, including seeds (claims 239 through 243), plants (claims 249 through 255) and tissue cultures (claims 260 through 265) which have increased free tryptophan levels, or which are capable of producing plants or seeds having increased free tryptophan levels, or which are capable of producing plants or seeds having increased tryptophan content.

* * *

There are no rejections based on prior art; rather, claims 239 through 243, 249 through 255 and 260 through 265 are rejected solely under 35 USC 101. It is the examiner's position that the claims drawn to seeds and plants, 239 through 243 and 249 through 255, respectively, comprise subject matter which is inappropriate for protection under 35 USC 101 because the subject matter of plants and seeds is within the purview of the Plant Variety Protection Act of 1970 administered by the U.S. Department of Agriculture, 7 USC 2321 *et seq.* The examiner's position with respect to claims 260 through 265 drawn to tissue cultures is that such subject matter is inappropriate for protection under 35 USC 101 because it is within the purview of the Plant Patent Act of 1930, 35 USC 161. The examiner asserts that, to the extent that

---

35. We suspect that part of our problem in applying patent concepts to the facts before us lies in the fact that we are dealing with ornamental plants. Beauty for its own sake is not often a goal of inventors—indeed, even ornamental plant breeders might be more aptly described as seekers of beauty for profit. Nevertheless, the statute does not exempt ornamental plants, and so we are bound to treat them on a par with more "useful" botanical creations.

the claimed subject matter can be protected under the Plant Variety Protection Act (PVPA) or the Plant Patent Act (PPA), protection under 35 USC 101 is not available.

* * *

The examiner acknowledges in his answer that, in view of the decision in *Diamond v. Chakrabarty, supra,* it appears clear that Section 101 includes man-made life forms, including plant life. Moreover, the examiner's allowance of claims drawn to hybrid seeds and hybrid plants is a further indication that the examiner considers the scope of Section 101 to include man-made plant life. The examiner asserts in his answer, however, that by enacting the PPA in 1930 and the PVPA in 1970 "Congress has specifically set forth how and under what conditions plant life covered by these Acts should be protected." The examiner contends that the only reasonable statutory interpretation is that the PPA and the PVPA, which were later in time and more specific than Section 101, each carved out from Section 101, for specific treatment, the subject matter covered by each. Thus, it is the position of the examiner that the plant-specific Acts (PPA and PVPA) are the *exclusive* forms of protection for plant life covered by those acts.

We disagree with these contentions that the scope of patentable subject matter under Section 101 has been narrowed or restricted by the passage of the PPA and the PVPA and that these plant-specific Acts represent the exclusive forms of protection for plant life covered by those acts. The position taken by the examiner presents a question of statutory construction concerning the scope of patentable subject matter under 35 USC 101, i.e., has the scope of Section 101 been narrowed or restricted by reason of the enactment of the plant-specific Acts.

In cases of statutory construction we begin, as did the Court in *Diamond v. Chakrabarty, supra,* with the language of the statutes. The language of Section 101 has been set forth, *supra,* and has been interpreted by the Supreme Court to include everything under the sun that is made by man. The examiner does not point to any specific language in the plant-specific Acts to support his position that the plant-specific Acts restrict the scope of patentable subject matter under Section 101. We have examined the provisions of the PPA and the PVPA and we find, as did appellants, that neither the PPA nor the PVPA expressly excludes any plant subject matter from protection under Section 101. Accordingly, we look next to the legislative histories of the plant-specific Acts to determine whether there is any clear indication of congressional intent that protection under the plant-specific Acts be exclusive.

* * * However, as noted by appellants at page 17 of their brief, there is nothing in the legislative histories of the plant-specific Acts from which one could conclude that Congress intended to remove from protection under Section 101 any subject matter already within the scope of that section. Rather, the Senate Committee on the Judiciary concluded on September 29, 1970 in its Report on Senate bill S.3070 in which it recommended passage of the Plant Variety Protection Act that ". . . it does not alter protection currently available within the patent system."

The Supreme Court in *Diamond v. Chakrabarty, supra,* addressed the legislative history and purpose of the plant-specific Acts and noted that prior to 1930 there were two obstacles to obtaining patent protection on plants. The first was the belief that plants, even those artificially bred, were products of nature not subject to patent protection; the second was the fact that plants were thought not amenable to the "written description" requirement of the patent law. The Supreme Court noted that Congress addressed both of these obstacles in enacting the PPA. Congress explained at length its belief that the work of the plant breeder "in aid of nature" was patentable invention, and it relaxed the written description requirement in favor of a description "as complete as is reasonably possible." In our view, the Supreme Court's analysis of the legislative history of the plant-specific Acts makes it clear that the legislative intent of these acts was to extend patent protection to plant breeders who were stymied by the two noted obstacles.

* * *

In an attempt to show a conflict, the examiner points in his answer to provisions of the plant-specific Acts which differ from Section 101. He notes, for example, that (1) the PVPA contains both research (experimental use) and farmer's crop exemptions, while Section 101 does not explicitly contain such exemptions; (2) the PVPA spells out infringement in great detail and includes a compulsory licensing provision, while no such congressional guidance exists under Section 101 protection; (3) the PVPA limits protection to a single variety, whereas the opportunity for greater and broader exclusionary rights exists under Section 101 protection; (4) under 35 USC 162 (PPA), the applicant is limited to one claim in formal terms to the plant described, whereas there is no such limitation on coverage under Section 101; and (5) under 35 USC 163 (PPA), the plant patent conveys the right to exclude others from asexually reproducing the plant, or selling or using the plant so produced. However, this analysis by the Examiner merely serves to indicate that there are differences in the scope of protection offered by Section 101 and the plant-specific Acts. In our view, such differences fall far short of what could be required to find an irreconcilable conflict or positive repugnancy that would mandate a partial repeal of Section 101 by implication.

Nor does the fact that subject matter patentable under Section 101 overlaps with subject matter protectable under the plant-specific Acts provide a basis for concluding that there is irreconcilable conflict between the statutes. * * *

In his rejection of claims 260 through 265 drawn to tissue cultures, the examiner contends that the claims to tissue cultures are drawn to "asexual propagating material" and may, therefore, be protected under the PPA under Section 161. We disagree, and the rejection of claims 260 through 265 is, therefore, *reversed* for the additional reason that tissue cultures are not "plants" within the purview of 35 USC 161. The Court of Customs and Patent Appeals in its decision in *In re Bergy,* 596 F.2d 952, 201 USPQ 352 (CCPA 1979), *vacated as moot sub nom. Diamond v. Chakrabarty, supra,* interpreted the meaning and scope of the term "plant" in the PPA as having its common, ordinary meaning which is limited to those things having roots, stems, leaves and flowers or fruits. In our view, tissue cultures manifestly do not come within the noted "common, ordinary meaning" of the term "plants" and are, therefore, not within the scope of the PPA (35 USC 161).

* * *

Notes

1. *Additional Cases of Interest:*

In re Arzberger, 112 F.2d 834, 46 USPQ 32 (CCPA 1940). (Bacteria not patentable).

Application of LeGrice, 301 F.2d 929, 133 USPQ 365 (CCPA 1962).

Bourne v. Jones, 114 F.Supp. 413, 98 USPQ 206 (S.D.Fla.1951), affirmed 207 F.2d 173 (5th Cir.1953).

Kim Bros. v. Hagler, 167 F.Supp. 665, 120 USPQ 210 (S.D.Cal.1958).

Armstrong Nurseries, Inc. v. Smith, 170 F.Supp. 519, 120 USPQ 220 (E.D. Texas 1958) (Rose plants).

2. *Articles:*

Allyn, Plant Patent Queries, 15 J.P.O.S. 180 (1933).

Kneen, Plant Patents Enrich Our World, National Geographic Magazine, March 1948, p. 357.

Magnuson, A Short Discussion on Various Aspects of Plant Patents, 30 J.P. O.S. 493 (1948).

Langrock, Plant Patents—Biological Necessities in Infringement Suits, 41 J.P.O.S. 787 (1959).

Botanical Plant Patent Law, 11 Cleveland-Marshall Law Review 430 (1962).

Jeffrey, The Patentability and Infringement of Sport Varieties: Chaos or Clarity? 59 J.P.O.S. 645 (1977).

Chapter Nine

PROPERTY AND CONTRACT
INTERESTS IN PATENTS

A. STATUTORY PROVISIONS

35 U.S.C.A. § 261. Ownership; Assignment

Subject to the provisions of this title, patents shall have the attributes of personal property.

Applications for patent, patents, or any interest therein, shall be assignable in law by an instrument in writing. The applicant, patentee, or his assigns or legal representatives may in like manner grant and convey an exclusive right under his application for patent, or patents, to the whole or any specified part of the United States.

A certificate of acknowledgment under the hand and official seal of a person authorized to administer oaths within the United States, or, in a foreign country, of a diplomatic or consular officer of the United States or an officer authorized to administer oaths whose authority is proved by a certificate of a diplomatic or consular officer of the United States, shall be prima facie evidence of the execution of an assignment, grant or conveyance of a patent or application for patent.

An assignment, grant or conveyance shall be void as against any subsequent purchaser or mortgagee for a valuable consideration, without notice, unless it is recorded in the Patent and Trademark Office within three months from its date or prior to the date of such subsequent purchase or mortgage.

35 U.S.C.A. § 262. Joint Owners

In the absence of any agreement to the contrary, each of the joint owners of a patent may make, use or sell the patented invention without the consent of and without accounting to the other owners.

35 U.S.C.A. § 281. Remedy for Infringement of Patent

A patentee shall have remedy by civil action for infringement of his patent.

35 U.S.C.A. § 100. Definitions

When used in this title unless the context otherwise indicates—

(d) The word "patentee" includes not only the patentee to whom the patent was issued but also the successors in title to the patentee.

678

35 U.S.C.A. § 4.　Restrictions on Officers and Employees as to Interest in Patents

Officers and employees of the Patent and Trademark Office shall be incapable, during the period of their appointments and for one year thereafter, of applying for a patent and of acquiring, directly or indirectly, except by inheritance or bequest, any patent or any right or interest in any patent, issued or to be issued by the Office. In patents applied for thereafter they shall not be entitled to any priority date earlier than one year after the termination of their appointment.

B.　GENERALLY

Deller, in his Second Edition of Walker on Patents, introduces the nature of title to patents and methods of acquisition as follows:

> Titles to patent rights are capable of two independent classifications. One relates to the nature of title, and the other relates to the methods by which title may be acquired. In the first of these aspects, titles are divisible into those which are purely legal, those which are purely equitable, and those which are both legal and equitable. In the second aspect, they are divisible into those: [1] by occupancy, [2] by assignment, [3] by grant, [4] by creditor's bill, [5] by bankruptcy, and [6] by death. Titles which are both legal and equitable may be acquired by any of these methods. Titles which are purely equitable may be acquired by any, except the first; and those which are purely legal may be transferred by any, except the first, fourth and fifth.[a]

In addition to the above means of acquiring a complete or undivided part of title to a patent, a contract interest can be acquired by license. A license does not ordinarily create any rights normally associated with ownership. It merely creates rights between the parties, and allows the licensee to perform certain acts he otherwise might not be able to perform without infringing the licensor's patent.

A reading of Section 261 of Title 35 U.S.C.A. indicates the necessity of a written assignment, and the desirability of both an acknowledgment under the hand and seal of an authorized person and a recordation of the assignment within three months of execution. The former provides prima facie evidence of the execution. The latter guarantees enforceability against subsequent purchasers for a valuable consideration without notice.

The states may exercise their traditional controls where patent rights are involved. There are two aspects. First, the states may police patent transactions against fraud. They may not, however, prohibit sales of patents or interfere with assignments which are ruled by federal law. Second, the states have jurisdiction over matters arising under contracts of assignment or license, or under mortgages, wills, etc. State courts may even determine "patent questions" collateral to an issue of state law. But while there is a wide area in which

---

a. Deller's Second Edition of Walker on Patents, Vol. 4, Sec. 333, p. 337 (1965).

state law is applicable, the federal-state dividing line has been shifting in favor of federal law in recent years. The question of federal preemption is considered elsewhere in this book (Part V). See generally, Cooper, State Law of Patent Exploitation, 56 Minnesota Law Review 313 (1972).

As indicated by the opening sentence of Section 261, patents have the attributes of personal property, but the patent property is in many ways unique. The right of an inventor to make, use, or vend his invention is a common law right. The statute does not confer that right; it merely allows an inventor an exclusivity for which the common law did not provide. Chief Justice Taft in Crown Die & Tool Co. v. Nye Tool & Machine Works, 261 U.S. 24, 36, 43 S.Ct. 254, 257, 67 L.Ed. 516, 529 (1922) said:

> * * * the patent confers on such common-law right the incident of exclusive enjoyment, and it is the common-law right, with this incident, which a patentee or an assignee must have. This is the implication of the descriptive words of the grant "the exclusive right to make, use and vend the invention." The Government is not granting the common-law right to make, use and vend, but is granting the incident of exclusive ownership of that common-law right, which cannot be enjoyed save with the common-law right.

The unique nature of patent property is demonstrated by Judge Nott's statement in Solomons v. United States, 21 Ct.Cl. 479, 483 (1886):

> This new form of property, the mindwork of the inventor, though its constitutional existence is now well nigh a century old, is still a novelty in the law. The wisdom of the common law gives neither maxims nor precedents to guide, and the American cases which deal with it, though numerous enough, run in a narrow, statutory groove. Though the most intangible form of property, it still, in many characteristics, is closer in analogy to real than to personal estate. Unlike personal property, it cannot be lost or found; it is not liable to casualty or destruction; it cannot pass by manual delivery. Like real property, it may be disposed of, territorially, by metes or bounds; it has its system of conveyancing by deed and registration; estates may be created in it, such as for years and in remainder; and the statutory action for infringement bears a much closer relation to an action for trespass than to action in trover and replevin. It has, too, what the law of real property has, a system of user by license.

C. ASSIGNMENTS

1. GENERALLY

Assignments are transfers of title in a patent or an undivided part thereof. The assignee should receive substantially the powers, duties, and privileges possessed by the grantor. An assignment of an undivided part of the full interest creates the legal effect of a joint tenancy. But co-ownership of patents differs substantially from ordinary co-tenancy.

At present there is no requirement that assignments be recorded in the Patent and Trademark Office. It is merely permissive. There has been some agitation for compulsory recordation. This has been prompted by a belief by some that patents are used in a widespread number of cases in schemes to circumvent the anti-trust laws. These recommendations have often been made in conjunction with anti-patent biases. One such view was expressed by Hamilton, T.N.E.C. Monograph No. 31, at page 147:

> At present the use of patents is enmeshed in a network of legal instruments. Inventors assign patents to corporations; corporations lease them out to other corporations; all sorts of terms and conditions attend the lease. Such arrangements may do no more than put an invention to use; they determine the amount and distribute into shares the revenue which it yields; they provide mechanisms through which technology is indentured to money-making. The grant appoints lines to the private claim and, through usage which derives from the resulting contracts, its boundaries may be changed. The legal documents which the latter brings into being are thus of as much concern to the public as they are to the persons who sign them. It follows, almost as of course, that all assignments, leases, and documents correlative thereto, should be public records. Congress should, therefore, require all instruments giving effect to a patent to be filed with the Federal Trade Commission, where they can be consulted by all who are, or come to be, in interest. The very fact of publicity will cause concerns to use greater care to hew to the line and will constitute an effective instrument of police. In addition Congress should instruct the courts, in all legal controversies, to treat as null and void all contracts in respect to patents not so filed.

TALBOT v. QUAKER–STATE OIL REFINING CO.
United States Court of Appeals, Third Circuit, 1939.
104 F.2d 967, 41 USPQ 1.

KIRKPATRICK, DISTRICT JUDGE.

* * *

* * * It is true that between cotenants of land or other tangible property there is neither privity nor identity of interest, and a judgment rendered in a suit affecting the common property brought by or against only one of the cotenants is not binding upon his associate. Property in patents, however, is of a peculiar character and, while the theory of separate and distinct undivided interests is preserved, there is actually a much closer interrelationship between the rights of co-owners and a much nearer approach to substantial identity of interests than with tangibles or ordinary choses in action. In its essence all that the Government confers by the patent is the right to exclude others from making, using or vending the invention (Crown Co. v. Nye Tool Works, 261 U.S. 24, 35, 43 S.Ct. 254, 67 L.Ed. 516), and as to this essential attribute of the property each joint owner is in a very real sense at the mercy of any other. Each of them may use or license others to use the invention without the consent of his fellows, and without responsibility to such fellows for the profits arising from such use or license. McDuffee v. Hestonville M. & F.R. Co., 3 Cir., 162 F. 36, 39. This unlimited right to license others may, for all practical purposes, destroy the monopoly and so amount to an appropriation of the whole value of the patent. Vose v. Singer, 4 Allen, Mass., 226, 230, 81 Am.Dec. 696.

* * *

WHY CORP. v. SUPER IRONER CORP.

United States Court of Appeals, Sixth Circuit, 1942.
128 F.2d 539, 53 USPQ 609.

MARTIN, CIRCUIT JUDGE. Appellant, claiming ownership of Patent No. 1,624,698, brought an infringement suit against appellee. The validity of the patent and the manufacture and sale by appellee of machines embodying the invention were admitted; but, defensively, appellee asserted its own title to the patent. The district court sustained the defense and dismissed appellant's action on the merits.

* * *

The patentee, by instrument dated October 24, 1927, assigned to his father, T.J. Watts, title to the patent. This assignment was recorded in the United States Patent Office on July 6, 1937. By an unrecorded, but duly acknowledged, instrument dated November 1, 1928, the patentee's father, signing as Timothy J. Watts, assigned the patent to Watts Laundry Machinery Company, a corporation of which the father was president and controlling stockholder.

By instrument dated and acknowledged April 10, 1929, Watts Laundry Machinery Company reassigned the patent to T.J. Watts, who was still president and owner of the controlling stock interest in the assignor corporation. This reassignment was not authorized by the directors of the Watts Laundry Machinery Company and was not recorded in the Patent Office. * * *

During 1928, T.J. Watts, without authority, had withdrawn from the corporate funds $40,000 in excess of his salary and expenses. * * *

On March 30, 1929, minority stockholders received from an audit report their first information that T.J. Watts had assigned the patent to the company in liquidation of the amount improperly withdrawn by him. In the latter part of [1929, he] * * * was dropped from the board of directors and, on February 28, 1930, was superseded in the presidency.

On April 7, 1931, the Watts Laundry Machinery Company executed a duly acknowledged bill of sale, granting and conveying to appellee, Super Ironer Corporation, for a consideration of $200, the receipt whereof was acknowledged, Patent No. 1,624,698, and other patents. The instrument recited that "the Certificates representing said Patents have been lost or mislaid, and in the event that said Certificates are found, the same will be duly assigned and transferred to the second party." This assignment was executed under seal of the Watts Laundry Machinery Company, was authorized by the corporation's directors, and complied with formal requisites. It was not recorded in the United States Patent Office until June 30, 1938. The date of recordation of this assignment, however, preceded the assignment on September 16, 1938, by T.J. Watts of his right, title and interest in the patent in controversy to Harry Koplin, who, on September 24, 1938, recorded his assignment in the Patent Office.

On February 9, 1939, Harry Koplin assigned his title to the patent to David Koplin, who, in turn, recorded his assignment on February 13, 1939. On December 5, 1939, David Koplin assigned his right, title and interest in the patent to appellant, Why Corporation, which recorded its assignment in the United States Patent Office on December 9, 1939.

For its title to the patent in suit, appellant relies upon the assignment from the patentee to T.J. Watts and upon the assignment, dated September 16, 1938, from T.J. Watts to Harry Koplin; and upon the subsequent mesne assignments described above.

The district court found, as a matter of fact, that the appellee corporation, on April 7, 1931, purchased the patent in suit for a valuable consideration, without actual or constructive notice or knowledge by any of its officers or directors of the prior unrecorded assignment of April 10, 1929, by Watts Laundry Machinery Company to T.J. Watts.

*   *   *

The assignment of the patent from the Watts Laundry Machinery Company to appellee antedated the assignment by T.J. Watts to Harry Koplin by more than seven and a half years; and the assignment of the patent to appellee was recorded two and one-half months prior to the assignment by T.J. Watts to Harry Koplin. Harry Koplin was put on notice by the recorded assignment that appellee's assignor had acquired title to the patent by an unrecorded instrument. At his peril, he failed to make appropriate inquiry as to this representation. The minor discrepancy in the recorded instrument as to the date of the unrecorded instrument seems immaterial. Information that there was extant an unrecorded assignment to the assignor named in the recorded instrument was the material fact to be gleaned from inspection of the Patent Office records.

The assignment from Watts Laundry Machinery Company to appellee dated April 7, 1931, and recorded June 30, 1938, was executed for a valuable consideration, without notice of the prior unrecorded assignment of April 10, 1929, from Watts Laundry Machinery Company to T.J. Watts. Appellee, having recorded its assignment prior to the subsequent purchase of the patent by Harry Koplin from T.J. Watts on September 16, 1938, is vested with the title to the patent in suit.

This is a logical sequitur from the language of the recordation statute, hereinbefore quoted, when applied to the salient facts which have been stated without elaboration.

The judgment of the district court is affirmed.

PETERSON v. FEE INT'L LTD.

United States District Court of Oklahoma, 1974.
381 F.Supp. 1071, 182 USPQ 264.

DAUGHERTY, CHIEF JUDGE.

Plaintiffs claim Defendants are guilty of patent infringement, false marking and unfair competition, the latter under both Federal and State Statutes. Plaintiffs claim to own U.S. Patent No. 3,555,939 (939) which Defendants are alleged to have infringed and U.S. Patent No. 3,368,432 (432) which patent number Defendants are alleged to have used in the false marking claim. 939 covers an open-end or "crescent" type wrench which is helix operated by a knob running up and down the handle.

By way of defense, Defendants claim they (Resco) own 939 and if this is not so they are not guilty of infringement because 939 is invalid over published prior art and Halls (the inventor by patent office records) was not the true inventor and that Halls abandoned the invention. Defendants deny wilful mismarking of any consequence. Defendants have also filed a counterclaim in which they assert that Plaintiffs are violating the Schlote Patent No. 2,795,987 (987) which Defendants own. As the issues have been drawn, the Court will consider in order the matter of title, patent validity, infringement, patent mismarking, unfair competition and the counterclaim.

TITLE

The evidence overwhelmingly shows 939 Patent ownership in Plaintiffs. The Court finds the assignments relied on by Defendants to be false documents and to constitute a fraud. Halls assigned this patent to Western Tool Company of Denver, Colorado who assigned the same to Central Control Corporation who assigned the same to Helix Tool Company (Helix) who assigned the same to Plaintiff Eugene E. Petersen (Petersen) on April 14, 1970. This latter assignment was filed of record by Petersen in the United States Patent Office on May 18, 1970 and Petersen's name appeared as the assignee of record on the face of the patent when it was issued on January 19, 1971.

The Defendants' claimed assignment of Helix to Resco under date of February 27, 1970 is clearly false and fraudulent. Plaintiff Petersen who owned seventy (70%) per cent of Helix knew nothing of this Helix to Resco assignment which was signed by Leslie D. and Rex Elder, as President and Secretary of Helix until June 1, 1972 when he was deposed herein. It was not accomplished or authorized by the Corporation as required by Nebraska law and amounts to a breach of a fiduciary obligation by the Elders. Eleven days prior to the date of said assignment Helix, by a document signed by the Elders, granted an option to one George I. Rosenthal on the 939 patent which option did not expire until April 2, 1970, over a month after the alleged date of the Helix to Resco assignment. The February 27, 1970 assignment from Helix to Resco contained some identical language which was not composed and put on certain of the patent papers by counsel for Helix until April 14, 1970. The alleged consideration from Helix to Resco was not delivered for eleven months after February 27, 1970 and then was never delivered to Helix by the Elders. The Elders joined in the April 14, 1970 assignment from Helix to Petersen and told Petersen nothing of the alleged earlier assignment to Resco. This Resco assignment was not recorded in the United States Patent Office for over two years or until May 20, 1972 and not within three months of its date as provided by 35 U.S.C.A. § 261. The second Helix to Resco assignment of March 7, 1972 was but a further fraudulent move of Les Elder and the Defendants. At this time Helix was a dissolved company and Petersen was the known assignee of the patent and the record owner in the United States Patent Office. The Helix to Resco assignments of February 27, 1970 and March 7, 1972 are the most clearly established case of falsity and fraud as this Court has experienced in nearly twenty years of trial experience. Plaintiffs are found to be the owners of Patent Nos. 939 and 432. Defendants do not own the same and their claims of ownership of 939 are false and fraudulent. The Court further finds from the evidence that Plaintiffs did not reach an agreement or understanding with the Defendants or any of them whereby Defendants would undertake the manufacture of the Helix wrench in Japan or the Far East. Nor did Helix reach any such agreement. The most that occurred was a discussion on this point which never ripened into an agreement. Nor did Plaintiffs or Helix authorize Defendants to spend large sums of money as Defendants claim in investigating this possibility thereby causing Defendants to become a licensee of 939. Under the evidence the Court specifically rejects Defendants' contention that such an agreement was entered into which was binding on Plaintiffs and Helix.

VALIDITY

The Plaintiffs claim Defendants are infringing claims 1 through 5 of 939 by their wrench manufactured in and imported from Japan. Notice of infringement and false marking was given by Plaintiffs to Defendants on December 2, 1971. 35 U.S.C.A. § 287. It is clear and Defendants concede that all of claims 1 through 5 of 939 cover their wrench sold under the name "Quali-Kraft". Indeed, it was made from Halls' drawings given Defendants by the Elders.

First, the Court finds that the Defendants are estopped to challenge the validity of 939 by their false and fraudulent claims to own the same by the Helix to Resco assignments. Though, ordinarily, there is no estoppel to deny the validity of a patent, Lear, Incorporated v. Adkins, 395 U.S. 653, 89 S.Ct. 1902, 23 L.Ed.2d 610 (1969); Scott Paper Co. v.

Marcalus Co., 326 U.S. 249, 66 S.Ct. 101, 90 L.Ed. 47 (1945), this case presents those most extraordinary circumstances as heretofore set forth, which require the application of the doctrine of estoppel. Nordhaus, Patent, Trademark & Copyright Infringement, 1971. See Keystone Driller Co. v. General Excavator Co., 290 U.S. 240, 54 S.Ct. 146, 78 L.Ed. 293 (1933). The case of Lear, Incorporated v. Adkins, supra, is distinguished and does not prevent estoppel as the Court specifically finds that Defendants are not licensees of Plaintiffs as to the 939 Patent.

Moreover, the Court finds claims 1 through 5 of the Patent to be valid, not to have been obvious by the prior art, that Halls was the true inventor and such patent was not abandoned by Halls.

* * *

Plaintiffs are therefore entitled to Judgment finding them to be the owner of Patent 939, that said patent is a valid patent and Defendants' claims of invalidity, that Halls is not the true inventor thereof and that Halls abandoned the invention are all without merit, that Defendants are infringing on Patent 939 with their "Quali-Kraft" wrench, that Defendants are guilty of mismarking some of their wrenches with Patent 432 which patent is owned by Plaintiffs, that Defendants are guilty of unfair competition against Plaintiffs in violation of both Federal and State Statutes and that Defendants are not entitled to assert infringement of 987 by 939 by reason of patent misuse of 987 and additionally that 939 does not infringe on 987.

* * *

2. WARRANTIES

It is important to distinguish between two related concepts. On the one hand, there are warranties, express and implied, in contracts of assignment. While a warranty of title is implied in the grant, there is no implied warranty, as demonstrated in the following cases, that the assigned patent is valid, or that it does not infringe other patents. A warranty is a guarantee by the assignor that a certain legal relationship can be enforced by the assignee against the world.

On the other hand, we have estoppel concepts, which are based on considerations of fairness in business dealings. The court in Stubnitz-Greene Spring Corp. v. Fort Pitt Bedding Co., 110 F.2d 192, 196, 45 USPQ 52, 56 (6th Cir.1940) expressed the estoppel rationale this way:

> Its vitality is only present where but for its application an utterance by a party would convict him of previous falsehood, and authorize him to deny an affirmation upon which persons have dealt and pledged their credit or expended their money.

Estoppel operates only against parties who have equitably foreclosed a claim which all others are free to raise.

LEESE v. GLOEKLER CO.

Supreme Court of Pennsylvania, 1926.
287 Pa. 295, 135 A. 206.

PER CURIAM, November 22, 1926. Plaintiff claimed to be the inventor of a patented article, which invention and patent rights he sold to defendant, the transaction being evidenced by a written offer wherein, after reciting the patent in question, plaintiff stated, "I will sell, assign and transfer to you [defendant], or your assigns, my entire interest for the sum of $5,000," and by a receipt signed by plaintiff and delivered to defendant reading as follows: "Received from the Bernard Gloekler Company the sum of One Hundred ($100) Dollars, as part payment of Five Thousand ($5,000) Dollars, for U.S. Letter Patent No. 1,314,003, dated August 26th, 1919, for Fluid Regulating Valve. Balance to be paid upon delivery of assignment by me." Plaintiff claimed that the above-recited papers and payment on account closed the bargain between him and defendant. On the other hand, defendant claimed that the bargain never was closed between it and plaintiff; that the receipt accepted by its representative was not read by him, and that the $100 thereby acknowledged was not paid on account of the alleged sale but was advanced as a loan to plaintiff; that, "after necessary investigation, it was found that plaintiff's invention was an infringement on other patents and that the patent rights and invention of plaintiff were of no value," and for that reason defendant had declined to pay plaintiff for such patent rights. Plaintiff sued to recover the balance of the $5,000. All of the issues thus raised were submitted to the jury in a well-balanced charge, and found against defendant company, which prosecutes this appeal.

Appellant's principal contention is that the court below erred in refusing to charge that, because of an implied warranty in the sale, plaintiff could not recover; but it is not plain just what warranty defendant relies on. The court told the jury that, if there was a total failure of consideration, in the sense that the "thing that was to be sold" had no value whatever, the verdict should be for defendant; and, under the evidence, this, at the most, was all appellant was entitled to. At trial, counsel for defendant stated his position to be that "the valve was an infringement of another article and would involve us in lawsuits if we purchased it"; but the only testimony to sustain this contention was that the use of the valve might "possibly subject" defendant "to an injunction," since the patent "was practically of the same principle as the Hale and might infringe on the Hale patent rights." The jury having found in favor of plaintiff, we must assume the existence of the written contract claimed by him; it contains no express warranty, and implies no warranty, that the invention does not infringe prior patents. The law upon this subject is stated in 30 Cyc. at p. 949, thus: "The assignment of a patent creates an implied warranty of title in the assignor but no warranty that the patent is valid or that the invention does not infringe prior patents." See Gilmore v. Aiken, 118 Mass. 94,

97; Otto v. Singer, 62 L.T.Rep.,N.S. (Eng.) 220, 223, and other authorities mentioned in Cyc. as above cited.

The assignments of error are all overruled and the judgment is affirmed.

Note

Deller's Walker on Patents, 2nd Ed. (1965), § 406:

* * * In the absence of a covenant to protect the license against infringers there is no obligation on the part of the licensor to do so.

3. ASSIGNMENTS AND ESTOPPEL

Law dictionaries provide many definitions of estoppel. Black's Law Dictionary states that "estoppel" is a bar or impediment raised by law which precludes a man from alleging or denying a certain fact or state of facts, in consequence of his previous allegation or denial or conduct or admission. Estoppel by deed "occurs when a party has executed a deed, an assignment or writing of some sort reciting a certain fact and is thereby precluded from denying, in any action brought upon that instrument, the fact so recited." Equitable estoppel (estoppel *in pais*) is said to arise when a party makes a false representation or a concealment of material facts, with knowledge of the facts, to a party ignorant of the truth with the intention that the other party shall act upon it, and that other party does act in reliance on such representation and is injured thereby. (Black's Law Dictionary, Fourth Edition).

If the owner of a patent assigns his patent knowing of facts which would render it invalid, such as a prior public use or an invalidating reference, this clearly raises an estoppel against the assignor and may also provide a basis for rescission of the contract by the assignee. However, assume that a patent owner assigns a patent in good faith for valuable consideration not knowing of any invalidating facts. Does "estoppel by deed" prevent him later from asserting facts which would invalidate the patent? The question frequently arises when the former patent owner decides to infringe the patent he has assigned and is sued for infringement by his assignee. Should the assignor be permitted to make all available defenses despite his previous ownership and assignment?

Section D, immediately following in the casebook, deals with Licenses. Should a person who is operating under a license of a patent be permitted to challenge the validity of the patent? Should he be permitted to accept the benefits of the license and immunity from infringement suits while at the same time challenging the validating of the licensed patent?

Quasi-estoppel is defined as the principle which precludes a party from asserting, to another's disadvantage, a right inconsistent with a position previously taken by him. Is a licensee prevented by quasi-estoppel from attacking the patent under which he is licensed?

The following case reviews the history of estoppel in patent assignment and license cases.

LEAR, INC. v. ADKINS

Supreme Court of the United States, 1969.
395 U.S. 653, 89 S.Ct. 1902, 23 L.Ed.2d 610.

MR. JUSTICE HARLAN delivered the opinion of the court.

[Factual background set forth at page 961, infra.]

*   *   *

II.

Since the California Supreme Court's construction of the 1955 licensing agreement is solely a matter of state law, the only issue open to us is raised by the court's reliance upon the doctrine of estoppel to bar Lear from proving that Adkins' ideas were dedicated to the common welfare by federal law. In considering the propriety of the State Court's decision, we are well aware that we are not writing upon a clean slate. The doctrine of estoppel has been considered by this Court in a line of cases reaching back into the middle of the 19th century. Before deciding what the role of estoppel should be in the present case and in the future, it is, then, desirable to consider the role it has played in the past.

A.

While the roots of the doctrine have often been celebrated in tradition, we have found only one 19th century case in this Court that invoked estoppel in a considered manner. And that case was decided before the Sherman Act made it clear that the grant of monopoly power to a patent owner constituted a limited exception to the general federal policy favoring free competition. Kinsman v. Parkhurst, 18 How. 289, 15 L.Ed. 385 (1856). Curiously, a second decision often cited as supporting the estoppel doctrine points clearly in the opposite direction. St. Paul Plow Works v. Starling, 140 U.S. 184, 11 S.Ct. 803, 35 L.Ed. 404 (1891), did not even question the right of the lower courts to admit the licensee's evidence showing that the patented device was not novel. A unanimous Court merely held that, where there was conflicting evidence as to an invention's novelty, it would not reverse the decision of the lower court upholding the patent's validity.

In the very next year, this Court found the doctrine of patent estoppel so inequitable that it refused to grant an injunction to enforce a licensee's promise never to contest the validity of the underlying patent. "It is as important to the public that competition should not be repressed by worthless patents, as that the patentee of a really valuable invention should be protected in his monopoly *   *   *." Pope Manufacturing Co. v. Gormully, 144 U.S. 224, 234, 12 S.Ct. 632, 36 L.Ed. 414, 418 (1892).

Although this Court invoked an estoppel in 1905 without citing or considering Pope's powerful argument, United States v. Harvey Steel

Co., 196 U.S. 310, 25 S.Ct. 240, 49 L.Ed. 492, the doctrine was not to be applied again in this Court until it was revived in Automatic Radio Manufacturing Co. v. Hazeltine Research, Inc., supra, which declared, without prolonged analysis, that licensee estoppel was "the general rule." 339 U.S., at 836, 94 L.Ed. at 1320. In so holding, the majority ignored the teachings of a series of decisions this Court had rendered during the 45 years since Harvey had been decided. During this period, each time a patentee sought to rely upon his estoppel privilege before this Court, the majority created a new exception to permit judicial scrutiny into the validity of the Patent Office's grant. Long before Hazeltine was decided, the estoppel doctrine had been so eroded that it could no longer be considered the "general rule," but was only to be invoked in an ever-narrowing set of circumstances.

B.

The estoppel rule was first stringently limited in a situation in which the patentee's equities were far more compelling than those presented in the typical licensing arrangement. Westinghouse Electric & Manufacturing Co. v. Formica Insulation Co., 266 U.S. 342, 45 S.Ct. 117, 69 L.Ed. 316 (1924), framed a rule to govern the recurring problem which arises when the original patent owner, after assigning his patent to another for a substantial sum, claims that the patent is worthless because it contains no new ideas. The courts of appeals had traditionally refused to permit such a defense to an infringement action on the ground that it was improper both to "sell and keep the same thing," Faulks v. Kamp, 3 F. 898, 902 (1880). Nevertheless, Formica imposed a limitation upon estoppel which was radically inconsistent with the premises upon which the "general rule" is based. The Court held that while an assignor may not directly attack the validity of a patent by reference to the prior state of the art, he could introduce such evidence to *narrow* the claims made in the patent. "The distinction may be a nice one but seems to be workable." 266 U.S. at 351, 69 L.Ed. at 322. Workable or not, the result proved to be an anomaly: if a patent had *some* novelty Formica permitted the old owner to defend an infringement action by showing that the invention's novel aspects did not extend to the inclusion of the old owner's products; on the other hand, if a patent had *no* novelty at all, the old owner could not defend successfully since he would be obliged to launch the direct attack on the patent that Formica seemed to forbid. The incongruity of this position compelled at least one court of appeals to carry the reasoning of the Formica exception to its logical conclusion. In 1940 the Seventh Circuit held that a licensee could introduce evidence of the prior art to show that the licensor's claims were not novel at all and thus successfully defend an action for royalties. Casco Products Corp. v. Sinko Tool & Manufacturing Co., 116 F.2d 119.

In Scott Paper Co. v. Marcalus Manufacturing Co., 326 U.S. 249, 66 S.Ct. 101, 90 L.Ed. 47 (1945), this Court adopted a position similar to the Seventh Circuit's, undermining the basis of patent estoppel even more than Formica had done. In Scott, the original patent owner had attempted to defend an infringement suit brought by his assignee by proving that his product was a copy of an expired patent. The Court refused to permit the assignee to invoke an estoppel, finding that the policy of the patent laws would be frustrated if a manufacturer was required to pay for the use of information which, under the patent statutes, was the property of all. Chief Justice Stone, for the Court, did not go beyond the precise question presented by a manufacturer who asserted that he was simply copying an expired patent. Nevertheless it was impossible to limit the Scott doctrine to such a narrow compass. If patent policy forbids estoppel when the old owner attempts to show that he did no more than copy an expired patent, why should not the old owner also be permitted to show that the invention lacked novelty because it could be found in a technical journal or because it was obvious to one knowledgeable in the art? As Justice Frankfurter's dissent indicated, id., at 258–264, 90 L.Ed. at 53–56, there were no satisfactory answers to these questions. The Scott exception had undermined the very basis of the "general rule."

C.

At about the time Scott was decided, this Court developed yet another doctrine which was profoundly antithetic to the principles underlying estoppel. In Sola Electric Co. v. Jefferson Electric Co., 317 U.S. 173, 63 S.Ct. 172, 87 L.Ed. 165 (1942), the majority refused to permit a licensor to enforce the license's price-fixing provisions without permitting the licensee to contest the validity of the underlying patent. Since the price-fixing clause was per se illegal but for the existence of a valid patent, this narrow exception could be countenanced without compromising the general estoppel principle. But the Sola Court went further: it held that since the patentee had sought to enforce the price-fixing clause, the licensee could also avoid paying royalties if he could show that the patent was invalid. Five years later, the "anti-trust exception" was given an even more extensive scope in the Katzinger and MacGregor cases.[12] Here, licensors were not permitted to invoke an estoppel despite the fact that they sought only to collect their royalties. The mere existence of a price-fixing clause in the license was held to be enough to bring the validity of the patent into question. Thus in the large number of cases in which licensing agreements contained restrictions that were arguably illegal under the antitrust laws, the doctrine of estoppel was a dead letter. Justice Frankfurter, in dissent, went even further, concluding that Katzinger and MacGregor had done all but repudiate the estoppel rule: "If a doctrine that was vital law for more than ninety years will be found to have now been deprived of life, we ought at least to give it decent public burial." 329 U.S., at 416, 91 L.Ed. at 390.

---

12. Edward Katzinger Co. v. Chicago Metallic Manufacturing Co., 329 U.S. 394, 67 S.Ct. 416, 91 L.Ed. 374 (1947); MacGregor v. Westinghouse Electric & Manufacturing Co., 329 U.S. 402, 67 S.Ct. 421, 91 L.Ed. 380 (1947).

[The opinion continues in a lengthy discussion with a final conclusion that the licensee was not estopped to deny the validity of the licensor's patent rights despite the absence of any price fixing clause on the contract.] [19]

Notes

1. If the assignor knew at the time of making the assignment that the patent was invalid, he would be guilty of fraud, and the assignee would have a remedy on that ground. Hiatt v. Twoney, 1 N.C. (Dev. & B.Ed.) 243 (1836).

2. An assignee of an issued patent may disaffirm if it later is found to be invalid, and he may refuse to make further payments, on the ground of failure of consideration. Fitzgerald v. McFadden, 88 F.2d 639 (2d Cir.1937).

D. LICENSES

1. GENERALLY

Licenses are contractual arrangements between a patentee and one who is granted a right to make, use, or sell under the patent. The rules governing license formation, enforcement, and termination are not provided by the patent statutes. They are instead a product of general contract law. As with contracts, generally they may take any form and convey any right within the patent grant subject to public policy. Any grant of a right under a patent which falls short of an assignment is a license. Licenses can be either exclusive or non-exclusive. Whereas an assignment passes a property interest in the patent and thus a right in the assignee to exclude others from making, using or selling, a non-exclusive license provides the licensee merely an assurance that the patent right of exclusion will not be exercised against him. The non-exclusive license only allows the licensee to do what would constitute acts of infringement without a license. Non-exclusive licenses may be granted to more than one party.

An exclusive license essentially includes a promise by the licensor not to grant licenses to others. There may be, however, other prior non-exclusive licenses outstanding and in this case the exclusive license would be subject to these licenses. An exclusive license can be granted either with or without the right to grant sub-licenses thereunder. The licensor will not retain the right to make, use or sell under the patent if he grants an exclusive license without expressly reserving such right.

---

19. Adkins suggests that any decision repudiating licensee estoppel as the general rule should not be retroactively applied to contracts concluded before such a decision is announced. Given the extent to which the estoppel principle had been eroded by our prior decisions, we believe it clear that the patent owner—even before this decision—could not confidently rely upon the continuing vitality of the doctrine. Nor can we perceive that our decision today is likely to undermine any existing legitimate business relationships. Moreover, the public's interest in the elimination of specious patents would be significantly prejudiced if the retroactive effect of today's decision were limited in any way.

License contract drafting requires precision because courts in their attempts equitably to supply missing terms have, at times, construed the agreement contrary to the expectations of one or both parties. The term of the license will not be limited to less than the term of the patent unless expressly provided for in the contract. With respect to implied warranties, a license generally does not imply that the patent is valid or that the licensee will be free of infringement suits by third parties. A mere warranty of title in the licensor is implied. Any further warranties must be provided for in the license.

2. CREATION AND EFFECT

WATERMAN v. MACKENZIE

Supreme Court of the United States, 1891.
138 U.S. 252, 11 S.Ct. 334, 34 L.Ed. 923.

MR. JUSTICE GRAY delivered the opinion of the court.

Every patent issued under the laws of the United States for an invention or discovery contains "a grant to the patentee, his heirs and assigns, for the term of seventeen years, of the exclusive right to make, use and vend the invention or discovery throughout the United States and the Territories thereof." Rev.Stat. § 4884. The monopoly thus granted is one entire thing, and cannot be divided into parts, except as authorized by those laws. The patentee or his assigns may, by instrument in writing, assign, grant and convey, either, 1st, the whole patent, comprising the exclusive right to make, use and vend the invention throughout the United States; or 2d, an undivided part or share of that exclusive right; or, 3d, the exclusive right under the patent within and throughout a specified part of the United States. Rev.Stat. § 4898. A transfer of either of these three kinds of interests is an assignment, properly speaking, and vests in the assignee a title in so much of the patent itself, with a right to sue infringers; in the second case, jointly with the assignor; in the first and third cases, in the name of the assignee alone. Any assignment or transfer, short of one of these, is a mere license, giving the licensee no title in the patent, and no right to sue at law in his own name for an infringement. Rev.Stat. § 4919; Gayler v. Wilder, 10 How. 477, 494, 495; Moore v. Marsh, 7 Wall. 515. In equity, as at law, when the transfer amounts to a license only, the title remains in the owner of the patent; and suit must be brought in his name, and never in the name of the licensee alone, unless that is necessary to prevent an absolute failure of justice, as where the patentee is the infringer, and cannot sue himself. Any rights of the licensee must be enforced through or in the name of the owner of the patent, and perhaps, if necessary to protect the rights of all parties, joining the licensee with him as a plaintiff. Rev.Stat. § 4921. Littlefield v. Perry, 21 Wall. 205, 223; Paper Bag Cases, 105 U.S. 766, 771; Birdsell v. Shaliol, 112 U.S. 485–487. And see Renard v. Levinstein, 2 Hem. & Mil. 628.

Whether a transfer of a particular right or interest under a patent is an assignment or a license does not depend upon the name by which it calls itself, but upon the legal effect of its provisions. For instance, a grant of an exclusive right to make, use and vend two patented machines within a certain district, is an assignment, and gives the grantee the right to sue in his own name for an infringement within the district, because the right, although limited to making, using and vending two machines, excludes all other persons, even the patentee, from making, using or vending like machines within the district. Wilson v. Rousseau, 4 How. 646, 686. On the other hand, the grant of an exclusive right under the patent within a certain district, which does not include the right to make, and the right to use, and the right to sell, is not a grant of a title in the whole patent right within the district, and is therefore only a license. Such, for instance, is a grant of "the full and exclusive right to make and vend" within a certain district, reserving to the grantor the right to make within the district, to be sold outside of it. Gayler v. Wilder, above cited. So is a grant of "the exclusive right to make and use," but not to sell, patented machines within a certain district. Mitchell v. Hawley, 16 Wall. 544. So is an instrument granting "the sole right and privilege of manufacturing and selling" patented articles, and not expressly authorizing their use, because, though this might carry by implication the right to use articles made under the patent by the licensee, it certainly would not authorize him to use such articles made by others. Hayward v. Andrews, 106 U.S. 672. See also Oliver v. Rumford Chemical Works, 109 U.S. 75.

An assignment of the entire patent, or of an undivided part thereof, or of the exclusive right under the patent for a limited territory, may be either absolute, or by way of mortgage and liable to be defeated by non-performance of a condition subsequent, as clearly appears in the provision of the statute, that "an assignment, grant or conveyance shall be void as against any subsequent purchaser or mortgagee for a valuable consideration without notice, unless it is recorded in the Patent Office within three months from the date thereof." Rev.Stat. § 4898.

Notes

1. "[T]he patentee may assign his exclusive right within and throughout a specified part of the United States, and upon such an assignment the assignee may sue in his own name for an infringement of his rights. But in order to enable him to sue, the assignment must undoubtedly convey to him the entire and unqualified monopoly which the patentee held in the territory specified—excluding the patentee himself, as well as others. And any assignment short of this is a mere license. For it was obviously not the intention of the Legislature to permit several monopolies to be made out of one, and divided among different persons within the same limits. Such a division would inevitably lead to fraudulent impositions upon persons who desired to purchase the use of the improvement, and would subject a party who, under a mistake as to his rights, used the invention without authority,

to be harassed by a multiplicity of suits instead of one, and to successive recoveries of damages by different persons holding different portions of the patent right in the same place. Unquestionably, a contract for the purchase of any portion of the patent right may be good as between the parties as a license, and enforced as such in the courts of justice. But the legal right in the monopoly remains in the patentee, and he alone can maintain an action against a third party who commits an infringement upon it." Gayler v. Wilder, 51 U.S. (10 How.) 477, 494, 13 L.Ed. 504, 511 (1850).

2. "If the owner of a patent being within the jurisdiction refuses or is unable to join an exclusive licensee as coplaintiff, the licensee may make him a party defendant by process and he will be lined up by the court in the party character which he should assume.

* * *

"The owner beyond the reach of process may be made coplaintiff by the licensee, but not until after he has been requested to become such voluntarily. If he declines to take any part in the case, though he knows of its imminent pendency and of his obligation to join, he will be bound by the decree which follows. We think this result follows from the general principles of res judicata.

* * *

"By a request to the patent owner to join as coplaintiff, by notice of the suit after refusal and the making of the owner a coplaintiff, he is given a full opportunity by taking part in the cause to protect himself against any abuse of the use of his name as plaintiff, while on the other hand the defendant charged with infringement will secure a decree saving him from multiplicity of suits for infringement. Of course, a decree in such a case would constitute an estoppel of record against the patent owner if challenged only after evidence of the exclusive license, the request to join as coplaintiff and the notice of the suit." Independent Wireless Tel. Co. v. Radio Corp. of America, 269 U.S. 459, 468–74, 46 S.Ct. 166, 169–171, 70 L.Ed. 362–65 (1926).

3. An exclusive licensee may sue in his own name the owner of the licensed patent, for the owner's infringement thereof. Littlefield v. Perry, 88 U.S. (21 Wall.) 205, 223, 22 L.Ed. 577, 579 (1875).

4. A non-exclusive licensee cannot join with the patent owner in an action for infringement of the licensed patent. Blair v. Lippincott Glass Co., 52 Fed. 226 (D.Ind.1892).

5. An assignee of the right to sue certain individuals for past and future infringement of a patent who is not an owner of the patent cannot sue such individuals for patent infringement in his own name. Crown Die & Tool Co. v. Nye Tool & Machine Works, 261 U.S. 24, 43 S.Ct. 254, 67 L.Ed. 516 (1923).

DE FOREST RADIO TEL. & TEL. CO. v.
UNITED STATES

Supreme Court of the United States, 1927.
273 U.S. 236, 47 S.Ct. 366, 71 L.Ed. 625.

MR. CHIEF JUSTICE TAFT delivered the opinion of the Court.

This is an appeal from a judgment of the Court of Claims dismissing the petition of the appellant, on the 4th of May, 1925. This was before the effective date of the Act of February 13, 1925, c. 229, 43 Stat. 936, by which direct appeals from the Court of Claims under §§ 242 and 243 of the Judicial Code were repealed and the review by certiorari was substituted.

The De Forest Radio Telephone & Telegraph Company filed its petition in the Court of Claims against the United States, seeking to recover for an alleged unlawful use by the Government of certain patented vacuum tubes or audions, used in radio communication. The suit was brought under the Act of June 25, 1910, c. 423, 36 Stat. 851, as amended by the Act of July 1, 1918, c. 114, 40 Stat. 704, 705. The Act of 1910 provided that whenever an invention described in and covered by a patent of the United States should thereafter be used by the Government without license of the owner or lawful right to use it, the owner could recover reasonable compensation for the use in the Court of Claims, provided that the United States could avail itself of all defenses, general or special, which might be pleaded by any other defendant charged with infringement. * * *

The petition was demurred to, the demurrer was sustained and the petition dismissed. It is conceded by the parties that, on the face of the petition, with the contracts which were made exhibits, the De Forest Company and the American Telephone & Telegraph Company had each the right to license to the United States the making and use of these audions, and that, if either did so license them, it would be a complete defense to a claim by the other for damages for the tort of infringement.

The sole question, therefore, which the Court of Claims considered, and decided against the appellant, was whether on the facts recited in the petition the American Telephone & Telegraph Company had in fact given a license to the United States to have made and to use these audions, covered by the patents. In other words, was the claim which the American Telephone & Telegraph Company had against the United States for the manufacture and use of the audions, based on a contract, or was it based on a tort? If it was the former, it was a full defense to any claim by the De Forest Company. If it was the latter, the De Forest Company was entitled to recover under the Act of 1918.

The appellant says that the necessary effect of the allegations of its petition is, that the Telephone Company said to the United States, in answer to the United States' notice that it wished to make and use the audions, "You will be infringing my rights. I shall not stop you but I notify you that I shall hold you for such infringement," and therefore that the subsequent acts of the United States and its manufacturers were torts. We think a different construction should be given the allegations. The agreement by the Telephone Company that it would not do anything to interfere with the immediate making of the audions for the United States, interpreted in the light of its subsequent action in assisting the United States to a prompt making of the audions for its use, in furnishing the needed information and drawings and blueprints for such manufacture, and in giving to the experts of the United States and its manufacturers the opportunity to witness and study the manufacture of audions by the Telephone Company, to the end that the audions might be more promptly manufactured and delivered to the United States for use in the war, made such conduct clearly a consent to their manufacture and use, and a license, and this without any regard to the effect of the subsequent release by the Telephone & Telegraph Company of compensation for such manufacture and use. No formal granting of a license is necessary in order to give it effect. Any language used by the owner of the patent, or any conduct on his part exhibited to another from which that other may properly infer that the owner consents to his use of the patent in making or using it, or selling it, upon which the other acts, constitutes a license and a defense to an action for a tort. Whether this constitutes a gratuitous license, or one for a reasonable compensation, must of course depend upon the circumstances; but the relation between the parties thereafter, in respect of any suit brought, must be held to be contractual and not based on unlawful invasion of the rights of the owner. Concede that if the owner had said, "If you go on and infringe my patent, I shall not attempt to enjoin you, but I shall subsequently sue you for infringement," the tort would not be waived—that is not this case. Here the circumstances show clearly that what the Company was doing was not only fully consenting to the making and using by the United States of the patent, but was aiding such making and using and, in doing so, was licensing it, only postponing to subsequent settlement what reasonable compensation, if any, it might claim for its license. The case of Henry v. Dick, 224 U.S. 1, in its main point was overruled in the Motion Picture Patents Company v. Universal Film Company, 243 U.S. 502; but that does not shake the authority of the language of the Court in the following passage (p. 24):

> "If a licensee be sued, he can escape liability to the patentee for the use of his invention by showing that the use is within his license. But if his use be one prohibited by the license, the latter is of no avail as a defense. As a license passes no interest in the monopoly, it has been described as a mere waiver of the right to sue by the patentee," citing Robinson on Patents, §§ 806 and 808.

In this case the language used certainly indicated the purpose of the Telephone Company not to seek an injunction against infringement, and not to sue for damages therefor, but only to sue or seek for an amicable settlement by payment of just compensation. Such action by the Telephone Company was a license, and constituted a complete defense against a suit for infringement by the De Forest Company.

Judgment affirmed.

3. EMPLOYER–EMPLOYEE RELATIONSHIPS

UNITED STATES v. DUBILIER CONDENSER CORP.

Supreme Court of the United States, 1933.
289 U.S. 178, 53 S.Ct. 554, 77 L.Ed. 1114, 85 A.L.R. 1488.

MR. JUSTICE ROBERTS delivered the opinion of the Court.

Three suits were brought in the District Court for Delaware against the respondent as exclusive licensee under three separate patents issued to Francis W. Dunmore and Percival D. Lowell. The bills recite that the inventions were made while the patentees were employed in the radio laboratories of the Bureau of Standards, and are therefore, in equity, the property of the United States. The prayers are for a declaration that the respondent is a trustee for the Government, and, as such, required to assign to the United States all its right, title and interest in the patents; for an accounting of all moneys received as licensee, and for general relief. The District Court consolidated the cases for trial, and after a hearing dismissed the bills. The Court of Appeals for the Third Circuit affirmed the decree.

* * *

In the fall of 1921 both Dunmore and Lowell were considering the problem of applying alternating current to broadcast receiving sets. This project was not involved in or suggested by the problems with which the radio section was then dealing and was not assigned by any superior as a task to be solved by either of these employees. It was independent of their work and voluntarily assumed.

* * *

Dunmore and Lowell were permitted by their chief, after the discoveries had been brought to his attention, to pursue their work in the laboratory and to perfect the devices embodying their inventions. No one advised them prior to the filing of applications for patents that they would be expected to assign the patents to the United States or to grant the Government exclusive rights thereunder.

The respondent concedes that the United States may practice the inventions without payment of royalty, but asserts that all others are excluded, during the life of the patents, from using them without the respondent's consent. The petitioner insists that the circumstances require a declaration either that the Government has sole and exclusive property in the inventions or that they have been dedicated to the public so that anyone may use them.

* * *

A patent is property and title to it can pass only by assignment. If not yet issued an agreement to assign when issued, if valid as a contract, will be specifically enforced. The respective rights and obligations of employer and employee, touching an invention conceived by the latter, spring from the contract of employment.

One employed to make an invention, who succeeds, during his term of service, in accomplishing that task, is bound to assign to his employer any patent obtained. The reason is that he has only produced that which he was employed to invent. His invention is the precise subject of the contract of employment. A term of the agreement necessarily is that what he is paid to produce belongs to his paymaster. Standard Parts Co. v. Peck, 264 U.S. 52, 44 S.Ct. 239, 68 L.Ed. 560, 32 A.L.R. 1033. On the other hand, if the employment be general, albeit it cover a field of labor and effort in the performance of which the employee conceived the invention for which he obtained a patent, the contract is not so broadly construed as to require an assignment of the patent. Hapgood v. Hewitt, 119 U.S. 226, 7 S.Ct. 193, 30 L.Ed. 369; Dalzell v. Dueber Watch Case Mfg. Co., 149 U.S. 315, 13 S.Ct. 886, 888, 37 L.Ed. 749. In the latter case it was said [p. 320]:

> "But a manufacturing corporation, which has employed a skilled workman, for a stated compensation, to take charge of its works, and to devote his time and services to devising and making improvements in articles there manufactured, is not entitled to a conveyance of patents obtained for inventions made by him while so employed, in the absence of express agreement to that effect."

The reluctance of courts to imply or infer an agreement by the employee to assign his patent is due to a recognition of the peculiar nature of the act of invention, which consists neither in finding out the laws of nature, nor in fruitful research as to the operation of natural laws, but in discovering how those laws may be utilized or applied for some beneficial purpose, by a process, a device or a machine. It is the result of an inventive act, the birth of an idea and its reduction to practice; the product of original thought; a concept demonstrated to be true by practical application or embodiment in tangible form. Clark Thread Co. v. Willimantic Linen Co., 140 U.S. 481, 489, 11 S.Ct. 846, 35 L.Ed. 521; Symington Co. v. National Castings Co., 250 U.S. 383, 386, 39 S.Ct. 542, 63 L.Ed. 1045; Pyrene Mfg. Co. v. Boyce, (C.C.A.) 292 F. 480, 481.

Though the mental concept is embodied or realized in a mechanism or a physical or chemical aggregate, the embodiment is not the invention and is not the subject of a patent. This distinction between the idea and its application in practice is the basis of the rule that employment merely to design or to construct or to devise methods of manufacture is not the same as employment to invent. Recognition of the nature of the act of invention also defines the limits of the so-called shop-right, which shortly stated, is that where a servant, during his hours of employment, working with his master's materials and appliances, conceives and perfects an invention for which he obtains a patent, he must accord his master a non-exclusive right to practice the invention. McClurg v. Kingsland, 1 How. 202, 11 L.Ed. 102; Solomons

v. United States, 137 U.S. 342, 11 S.Ct. 88, 34 L.Ed. 667; Lane & Bodley Co. v. Locke, 150 U.S. 193, 14 S.Ct. 78, 37 L.Ed. 1049. This is an application of equitable principles. Since the servant uses his master's time, facilities and materials to attain a concrete result, the latter is in equity entitled to use that which embodies his own property and to duplicate it as often as he may find occasion to employ similar appliances in his business. But the employer in such a case has no equity to demand a conveyance of the invention, which is the original conception of the employee alone, in which the employer had no part. This remains the property of him who conceived it, together with the right conferred by the patent, to exclude all others than the employer from the accruing benefits. These principles are settled as respects private employment.

Second. Does the character of the service call for different rules as to the relative rights of the United States and its employees?

[The court proceeds to answer this question in the negative.]

USHAKOFF v. UNITED STATES
United States Court of Claims, 1964.
164 Ct.Cl. 455, 327 F.2d 669, 140 USPQ 341.

[Opinion of Commissioner Lane]

The need for a means of providing drinking water on the open seas became apparent early in World War II when reports of the agonies faced by men cast adrift at sea were made known. During 1942 plaintiff Alexis E. Ushakoff, hereafter referred to as Ushakoff, became aware of the problem and began experiments to investigate the possibility of using solar distillation of sea water to provide drinking water. A short time later Ushakoff entered the employ of Higgins Industries as Director of Research and was charged with the responsibilities of developing a research department and working on projects then being developed at Higgins Industries. In negotiating his employment, Ushakoff informed Andrew J. Higgins, the head of Higgins Industries and hereafter referred to as Higgins, that he was working on several projects of his own, including specifically the solar still, and that as one condition of his employment it must be agreed that he would receive some share of the profits on these inventions. The condition was apparently accepted. The employment agreement was never reduced to a written contract.

After his employment by Higgins Industries, Ushakoff continued the development of the solar still along with his regular duties and he utilized Higgins Industries personnel and equipment. As the development of the solar still progressed, numerous experimental models were constructed and tested. Frequently the models were submitted to the Air Corps, which was actively attempting to find an effective solar still. The Air Corps ran various tests and experiments on the solar stills in an attempt to determine if they were effective, and then reported the deficiencies to Ushakoff at Higgins Industries. As the development of

Ushakoff's solar still proved more promising, the Air Corps encouraged Higgins Industries to continue working on it and entered a *purchase order* in September, 1944, for 15 solar stills to enable Higgins Industries to obtain a priority for the purchase of plastic film which was in short supply and was slowing down the development. After the priority was received, development proceeded at a much faster rate. While the contract called for 15 solar stills, some 36 were actually sent. These solar stills were delivered a few at a time, and, as the Air Corps comments were received, the solar stills were modified so that actually very few of the solar stills sent to the Air Corps under the contract were identical to any of the others. Even the last of the solar stills which were delivered to the Air Corps on February 5, 1945, incorporated improvements over those delivered in the preceding shipment. All of the solar stills delivered to the Air Corps up to February 5, 1945 were for tests and experiments of various sorts.

Early in 1945 Ushakoff further pressed Higgins for a written contract covering their agreement with respect to the inventions. A draft agreement was prepared by Ushakoff which Higgins refused to accept. Later, Higgins presented Ushakoff with a memorandum agreement which Ushakoff refused. Both proposed agreements called for the payment of royalties to Ushakoff, and neither of them called for an assignment of Ushakoff's patent rights to Higgins Industries. The relationship between Ushakoff and Higgins deteriorated rapidly and finally Ushakoff's employment was terminated on April 3, 1945.

* * *

The defendant also alleges that it received a license from Higgins Industries to use the invention as part of the *production contract* of June 21, 1945, calling for 172,678 solar stills. A necessary presupposition to this allegation is that Higgins Industries had the right to grant such a license. There is no evidence of any assignment by Ushakoff to Higgins Industries of the patent rights to the invention, nor is there any evidence that Ushakoff agreed to make such an assignment of the invention. If Higgins Industries has any rights in the patent they must have arisen from the circumstances of Ushakoff's employment. The courts have, in certain circumstances, recognized the right of an employer to an assignment of his employee's invention even in the absence of an agreement to that effect in the employment contract. These circumstances require, however, that the employee be hired to secure certain defined results. Marshall v. Colgate-Palmolive-Peet Co., 175 F.2d 215 (3rd Cir.1949). As explained by Mr. Justice Roberts:

> "One employed to make an invention, who succeeds, during his term of service, in accomplishing that task, is bound to assign to his employer any patent obtained. The reason is that he has only produced that which he was employed to invent. His invention is the precise subject of the contract of employment." United States v. Dubilier Condenser Corp., 289 U.S. 178, 187, 53 S.Ct. 554, 557, 77 L.Ed. 1114 (1933).

Such circumstances have not been proved in the instant case. Ushakoff was employed as Director of Research by Higgins Industries, and at the time of his employment he made it known that he was working on several projects of his own and wanted to retain an interest in any profits obtained therefrom. Ushakoff's job involved the normal duties of a Director of Research as well as working on projects then being developed at Higgins Industries. The solar still project was initiated by Ushakoff on his own, and it was not until after Ushakoff's initial work that Higgins Industries became actively interested in it. Ushakoff was not employed for the purpose of inventing a solar still, and hence the circumstances of the instant case do not warrant a finding that Ushakoff was obliged to assign the invention to Higgins Industries. The circumstances of the instant case would appear to more correctly fall within the equitable "shop rights" doctrine which gives the employer the right to practice the invention because the employee developed the invention during the hours of employment and has used the employer's materials and equipment. However, it is unnecessary to decide here if Higgins Industries has acquired such a shop right, since this right does not carry with it the right to grant licenses. Therefore, defendant cannot rely for defense on any license or sublicense from Higgins Industries.

* * *

NORTH BRANCH PRODUCTS, INC. v. FISHER

United States District Court of Appeals, District of Columbia, 1961.
131 USPQ 135, affirmed per curiam 312 F.2d 880, 136 USPQ 28 (D.C.Cir.1962).

McGARRAGHY, DISTRICT JUDGE.

FINDINGS OF FACT

1. Plaintiff, North Branch Products, Inc. is a corporation organized and existing under the laws of the State of Michigan, and has its principal place of business at Millington, Michigan.

2. Defendant, W. Reuen Fisher, is a citizen of the United States, residing in Alberta, Canada.

3. Plaintiff is engaged almost exclusively in the manufacture for sale and in selling through a wholly owned subsidiary, Revere Fisher Manufacturing Company a line of drill guide bushings characterized by a usually replaceable helical coil type insert or liner, as described and claimed in one or more letters patents, No. 2,766,084, No. 2,744,424, No. 2,737,425, No. 2,852,322, and No. 2,766,083, all issued to the defendant. The circumstances under which the plaintiff became thus engaged are as related in the following paragraphs.

4. In the early part of 1949, the defendant approached Dr. E.C. Swanson, a medical doctor and suggested the acquisition of the facilities of the existing North Branch Products, Inc. and using them to manufacture and sell what defendant described as a revolutionary type of drill guide bushing which defendant represented to Swanson he had invent-

ed and had ready for the market and as represented by patent applications theretofore filed by him. Swanson in turn interested Dr. Edward L. Grimm, an educator, in the venture, and later, other persons. Thereupon and by the end of March, 1949, defendant secured the assignment of the outstanding stock of North Branch Products, Inc., to himself as trustee for the initial investors, and purchased machinery from funds supplied by himself, Dr. Swanson and others.

*   *   *

6. Following the acquisition of the stock of the plaintiff, the first shareholders meeting of the reorganized company was held on April 1, 1949 at which Swanson was elected President, Grimm as Vice President, and Fisher as Secretary-Treasurer.

*   *   *

8. Upon acquisition of the shares of stock in plaintiff corporation as recited in finding 4 hereof, defendant became and continues to be a principal stockholder of the corporation. He also served intermittently as a director and officer until April 17, 1957. He was in sole charge of all phases of manufacture and sales of drill guide bushings and also was in sole charge of experimentation, research and engineering with respect to development of said bushings. At various times until termination of his office as General Manager on April 17, 1957, he held the title of Secretary-Treasurer and General Manager. He was the only person connected with either plaintiff or its subsidiary with any experience and knowledge in the field of drill guide bushings. At all times defendant was paid a salary for his work.

9. All other officers and directors of plaintiff were non-technical men who relied entirely upon the knowledge, training, experience and representations of the defendant with respect to experimentation, development, research, manufacture and sales of its products.

10. The bushings which defendant had represented to Swanson were a revolutionary new type *   *   * were of no commercial value. For this reason, much time was spent by defendant and other employees of plaintiff in an effort to develop a bushing which would sell. The inventions claimed in the patents which are the subjects of this suit were developed by the defendant by the use of plaintiff's machinery, plant facilities, material, employees, on company time and with company funds. At least a portion of the expense of applying for and obtaining the patents was paid out of plaintiff's funds. This experimental work resulted in applications for and issuance of letters patent as follows:

> Patent No. 2,744,424, application filed January 10, 1952 and patent issued May 8, 1956.

> Patent No. 2,737,425, application filed March 27, 1953 and patent issued March 6, 1956.

> Patent No. 2,766,083, application filed March 27, 1953 and patent issued October 9, 1956.

Patent No. 2,766,084, application filed July 29, 1953 and patent issued October 9, 1956.

Patent No. 2,852,322, application filed July 29, 1953 and patent issued September 16, 1958.

11. Prior to issuance of the aforesaid patents, defendant refused and failed to give any information to plaintiff's other officers and directors with respect to the existence and/or status of patent applications. The defendant pursued a course designed to, and which did, in fact, conceal such information from the other officers and directors. Efforts by them to obtain such information were consistently frustrated by the defendant. It was not until March, 1957, when the defendant left Michigan for Canada, that the other officers and directors were able to determine the status and facts with respect to the patents.

* * *

13. There are approximately 170 stockholders in plaintiff corporation who paid approximately $500,000.00 for their stock. In at least one instance, defendant assured the prospective purchaser of stock, before he purchased, that the company owned the patents.

CONCLUSIONS OF LAW

* * *

2. By reason of defendant's status and position as principal shareholder, officer, director and general manager in sole charge of experimentation, research, development, manufacture and sales, defendant was in a fiduciary relationship with the plaintiff at the time the inventions claimed in the patents were developed and the applications for said patents were filed by, and the patents issued to, defendant.

3. The defendant violated his fiduciary relationship with the company.

* * *

5. The plaintiff has the equitable right to the patents and patent applications in suit and is entitled to a decree declaring it to be the owner of the legal title thereto.[a]

4. ASSIGNMENT OF LICENSES AND SUBLICENSING

Robinson on Patents—Sec. 823

* * * Clearly a licensee, unless receiving express authority to that effect, would have no right to multiply his privileges by sublicenses, and thus increase the number of the individuals who could lawfully practise the invention. His authority to divide his rights, and to apportion them to others must be measured by the circumstances of each case, and be so limited that the sum of all the rights distributed shall be no greater than his own. In view of the abuses likely to arise from the practical exercise of such powers of alienation, and the difficulties attending any attempt to vindicate the rights of the licensor,

a. See Dowse v. Federal Rubber Co., 254 F. 308 (D.C.N.D. Illinois, 1918).

the courts have held that a license is not assignable unless it affirmatively appears that such was the intention of the parties.   *   *   *

UNARCO INDUS., INC. v. KELLEY CO., INC.

United States Court of Appeals, Seventh Circuit, 1972.
465 F.2d 1303, 175 USPQ 199.

DUFFY, SENIOR CIRCUIT JUDGE.

This is a suit for declaratory relief seeking the proper construction of a written agreement. The critical question is whether or not the patent license herein considered was assignable without the consent of the licensor. The District Court held the agreement to be assignable. A motion to restrain production and sale of the patented product pending a decision by the District Court was held in abeyance and finally denied.

The principal product manufactured by Kelley Company, Inc., the defendant herein, is based upon a patent granted to Garrett P. Kelley. The Company produced material-handling equipment known as "dockboard." This product permits the movement of merchandise from the bed of a truck to a loading dock.

In 1964, Kelley became aware that Unarco, a large corporation, was marketing and selling a dockboard which Kelley believed infringed its patented invention.

Kelley Company sued Unarco in the Federal District Court in Tennessee for patent infringement. This litigation became protracted and thus very expensive. Settlement discussions were held, and it became apparent to all that it would be for the best interest of both parties to enter into a nonexclusive license agreement terminating the litigation.

It became apparent that Unarco was not a serious competitor in the dockboard industry. Unarco's principal interest was to use dockboard as a selling tool for its principal product which was shelving. The settlement permitted Unarco to manufacture annually a few hundred dockboards without paying a royalty. While operating under this agreement, Unarco never exceeded the minimum number of royalty-free dockboards anticipated by the parties to the agreement.

Thereafter, the President of a Texas conglomerate named Overhead Door attempted to buy or merge with Kelley Company because of its desire to operate in the dockboard field. No agreement was reached.

Overhead Door then contacted Unarco with respect to the possible purchase of Unarco's dockboard division [Sturdi-bilt]. On August 4, 1969, Overhead Door and Unarco entered into a contract whereby Overhead Door agreed to purchase and Unarco agreed to sell Unarco's dockboard business and all the assets used in connection therewith. In this contract, Unarco agreed not to compete for at least five years in the dockboard business with Overhead Door, and furthermore warranted that "Every contract, license agreement or other intangible included among Dock Board Assets is assignable by UNARCO without prior consent of any other person. * * *'"

Subsequently, in a letter dated August 13, 1969, the attorney for Kelley was notified by a newspaper article of the contemplated acquisition of the Sturdi-bilt (dockboard) division of Unarco by Overhead Door. Overhead Door was advised by Kelley's attorney that their license agreement for the patents "was and is limited to Unarco."

On October 20, 1969, Unarco and Overhead Door commenced this action in District Court for a declaratory judgment with respect to the assignability of the nonexclusive patent license.[3]

The District Court held that the compromise agreement was a simple contract to be construed under the common law of the State of Illinois. Further, that as Illinois common law views a liberal construction of the assignability of all contracts, the license of the patent was assignable.

Defendant Kelley points out that the nonexclusive license agreement or contract between Kelley and Unarco was not only the result of a compromise settlement but it was, in fact, a forbearance.

Kelley points out that if the judgment of the District Court is sustained, Kelley's refusal to sell out to Overhead Door will be circumvented, and Overhead Door would, indirectly, obtain Kelley's patent rights which Kelley had consistently refused to sell to Overhead Door.

The threshold question before our Court is whether the law of the State of Illinois, where the contested agreement was consummated, applies, or whether determination of this issue in federal court falls within one of the exceptions to the doctrine of Erie R. Co. v. Tompkins, 304 U.S. 64, 58 S.Ct. 817, 82 L.Ed. 1188 (1938) requiring the application of federal common law.[4]

The Supreme Court considered this exception to Erie in Sola Electric Co. v. Jefferson Co., 317 U.S. 173, 176, 63 S.Ct. 172, 87 L.Ed. 165 (1942). In that opinion regarding patent license litigation, the Supreme Court also considered the application of estoppel and whether estoppel in litigation concerning patent licenses and the Sherman Act was a state or federal question. The Court held that estoppel as applied was a federal question where, if invoked, it would thwart the purposes of statutes of the United States. The *Erie* doctrine was circumvented by the Court in *Sola Electric Co.,* supra, by the following passage:

> "It is familiar [doctrine] that the prohibition of a federal statute may not be set at naught, or its benefits denied, by state statutes or

---

3. On October 23, 1969, three days after commencing this action, Unarco entered into an assignment of licensing agreement with Overhead Door, assigning to Overhead all their rights to royalties from Kelley under that agreement for the use of Unarco's patents.

4. The exception to application of state law to outcome determinative questions appears on page 78 of 304 U.S., on page 822 of 58 S.Ct. of *Erie,* supra "Except in matters [governed] by the Federal Constitution or by Acts of Congress, the law to be applied in any case is the law of the state."

state common law rules. In such a case our decision is not controlled by Erie R. Co. v. Tompkins, 304 U.S. 64 [58 S.Ct. 817, 82 L.Ed. 1188, 114 A.L.R. 1487.] There we followed state law because it was the law to be applied in the federal courts. But the doctrine of that case is inapplicable to those areas of judicial decision within which the policy of the law is so dominated by the sweep of federal statutes that legal relations which they affect must be deemed governed by federal law having its source in those statutes, rather than by local law. Royal Indemnity Co. v. United States, 313 U.S. 289, 296 [61 S.Ct. 995, 997, 85 L.Ed. 1361;] Prudence [Realization] Corp. v. Geist, 316 U.S. 89, 95 [62 S.Ct. 978, 982, 86 L.Ed. 1293;] Board of Comm'rs. [of Jackson County] v. United States, 308 U.S. 343, 349 [350, 60 S.Ct. 285, 287, 288, 84 L.Ed. 313;] cf. O'Brien v. Western Union Telegraph Co. [1 Cir.,] 113 F.2d 539, 541. * * * To the federal statute and policy, conflicting state law and policy must yield."

Article I, Section 8, Clause 8 of the United States Constitution provides that Congress has been granted the power " * * * [T]o promote the Progress of Science and useful Arts, by securing for limited Times to Authors and Inventors the exclusive Right to their respective Writings and Discoveries." This exclusive and personal concept of patents was considered by Congress upon implementation of the Patent Act of 1952 and other legislation aimed at federal control of patent regulation. When an inventor or person holding patent rights desires to license or relinquish any part of the patent monopoly, such person is utilizing the monopoly of rights intended by the framers of the Constitution and the legislation of Congress to reward invention and originality. This monopoly conferred by federal statute as well as the policy perpetuating this monopoly, so affects the licensing of patents, and the policy behind such licensing is so intertwined with the sweep of federal statutes, that any question with respect thereto must be governed by federal law.

We are of the opinion that the question of assignability of a patent license is a specific policy of federal patent law dealing with federal patent law. Therefore, we hold federal law applies to the question of the assignability of the patent license in question.

We agree with Kelley that we are here considering a specific policy of the patent law dealing with federal patent rights, and in that respect our problem does not involve the general state of Illinois contract law.

The long standing federal rule of law with respect to the assignability of patent license agreements provides that these agreements are personal to the licensee and not assignable unless expressly made so in the agreement. Troy Iron & Nail Factory v. Corning, 55 (14 How.) U.S. 193, 14 L.Ed. 383 (1852); Hapgood v. Hewitt, 119 U.S. 226, 7 S.Ct. 193, 30 L.Ed. 380 (1886); Lane & Bodley Co. v. Locke, 150 U.S. 193, 14 S.Ct. 78, 37 L.Ed. 1049 (1893); Wood Harvester Co. v. Minneapolis Harvester Co., 61 F. 256 (8 Cir., 1894); Bowers v. Lake Superior Contracting, 149 F. 983 (8 Cir., 1906). See also Deller's Walker on Patents, Sec. 409 (2d Ed.1965).

In Wood Harvester Co. v. Minneapolis Harvester Co., supra, the license agreement said nothing pertaining to assignability. That Court said 61 F. on page 258: " * * * I think the absence of any words of assignability in this license shows an intent to make it run to [licensees] alone, as clearly as if words of nonassignability had been incorporated therein." In post-Erie federal decisions, this rule of non-assignability has been unquestioned. Rock-Ola Mfg. Corp. v. Filben Mfg. Co., 168 F.2d 919 (8 Cir., 1948), cert. den. 335 U.S. 892, 69 S.Ct. 249, 93 L.Ed. 430.

This rule on non-assignability absent consent has been adhered to by state and federal courts. We therefore hold the District Court was in error in departing from this well established rule.

We hold the nonexclusive license agreement which was, in fact, a forbearance of suit, here in question was personal, and that it was not assignable without Kelley's consent. Further, the attempted assignment by Unarco Industries, Inc. to Overhead Door was and is void.

The judgment of the District Court is

Reversed.

Note

E.I. du Pont de Nemours & Co., Inc. v. Shell Oil Co., 498 A.2d 1108, 227 USPQ 233 (Del.Sup.1985): Shell held a non-exclusive license under a duPont patent which included the rights to "have made" and "sell" the invention but not to grant sublicenses. Shell entered into a "toll conversion/sale-back agreement" with Union Carbide under which Carbide would make the invention for Shell, and Shell would sell back to Carbide, the product never leaving Carbide's plant. The court held that this effectively constituted a sublicense and violated the duPont/Shell agreement. But see Lisle Corp. v. Edwards, 777 F.2d 693, 227 USPQ 894 (Fed.Cir.1985).

5. SCOPE OF THE LICENSEE'S OBLIGATIONS

BRISTOL LOCKNUT COMPANY v. SPS TECHNOLOGIES, INC.

United States Court of Appeals, Ninth Circuit, 1982.
677 F.2d 1277, 216 USPQ 867.

FARRIS, CIRCUIT JUDGE.

* * *

III. THE PARTIES' CLAIMS FOR ROYALTIES

A. Background

Under the licensing agreement, Bristol Locknut agreed to pay SPS a royalty based on a percentage of the sales of Skidmore locknuts and locknuts manufactured by the Burt tool. In return, SPS agreed not to sue for patent infringement.

The original agreement was signed on December 11, 1970. Bristol Locknut started making royalty payments in 1971. It was purchased by Frank Klaus in late 1972 and sales were thereafter underreported and the royalties consequently underpaid. On January 28, 1977, Bristol Locknut wrote to SPS, explaining it was delaying payment of the fourth quarter 1976 royalties until it received copies of SPS's licensing agreements with other locknut manufacturers. Bristol Locknut never resumed payment of royalties, but soon thereafter filed this action, on March 22, 1977, for a declaratory judgment that both patents were invalid and not infringed. SPS's separate action for breach of contract and infringement of its patents and trademark was consolidated. Bristol Locknut sued for a return of all royalties it had paid, and SPS sued for the unpaid royalties that accrued during the two fiscal quarters before the action was filed. SPS also sued for the underpaid royalties Bristol Locknut was obligated to pay. The parties stipulated that the total amount of underreported and unpaid royalties that accrued to the date of filing totalled $69,396.43.

The district court left the parties as they were. It held that since both patents were invalid and the trademark not infringed, SPS was not entitled to any additional royalties. We assume the court concluded that the holding of invalidity terminated Bristol Locknut's obligation to pay any further royalties. The court also held that, under the rationale of *Lear, Inc. v. Adkins,* 395 U.S. 653, 89 S.Ct. 1902, 23 L.Ed.2d 610 (1969), and *St. Regis Paper Co. v. Royal Industries,* 552 F.2d 309 (9th Cir.), *cert. denied,* 434 U.S. 996, 98 S.Ct. 633, 54 L.Ed.2d 490 (1977), Bristol Locknut was not entitled to a reimbursement of royalties already paid.

We agree that Bristol Locknut was not entitled to a refund of royalties paid, but we reverse the holding that it owes no further royalties. Bristol Locknut is obligated to pay SPS the full amount of underreported royalties and the unpaid royalties which accrued before it challenged the patents' validity by bringing this action.

B. Return of Royalties Paid by the Licensee

Bristol Locknut argues that it is entitled to a refund of royalties paid under an invalid, and therefore void patent. We reject the argument.

In *St. Regis Paper Co. v. Royal Industries,* 552 F.2d 309, 314 (9th Cir.), *cert. denied,* 434 U.S. 996, 98 S.Ct. 633, 54 L.Ed.2d 490 (1977), we held that a licensee was not entitled to a refund of royalties paid before it challenged the patent's validity. *St. Regis* involved the typical situation in which a license agreement was entered into after the patent was issued. After four years, the licensee stopped paying royalties. Nine months later, it filed an action contesting the patent's validity and sought a return of royalties paid under the agreement. We found that the federal policy in favor of the prompt and early adjudication of the validity of patents, as articulated in *Lear, Inc. v. Adkins,* 395 U.S. 653, 89 S.Ct. 1902, 23 L.Ed.2d 610 (1969), overrode countervailing state laws:

> [T]he possibility of a royalty refund might delay such a determination [of a patent's validity]. The possibility of obtaining a refund of all royalties paid might induce a manufacturer to accept a license based on a patent of doubtful validity, derive the benefits of suppressed competition which the patent affords, and challenge validity only after the patent's expiration. The licensee would have a chance to regain all the royalties paid while having enjoyed the fruits of the license agreement. Therefore, if a refund were permitted, licensees who were only recently unmuzzled by *Lear* would again be silenced by economic self-interest rather than by state law.

St. Regis, 552 F.2d at 314.

Other circuits have also read *Lear* to deny a refund of royalties paid by a licensee. *E.g., American Sterilizer Co. v. Sybron Corp.,* 614 F.2d 890 (3d Cir.), *cert. denied,* 449 U.S. 825, 101 S.Ct. 88, 66 L.Ed.2d 29 (1980); *USM Corp. v. Standard Pressed Steel Co.,* 524 F.2d 1097 (7th Cir. 1975); *PPG Industries, Inc. v. Westwood Chemical, Inc.,* 530 F.2d 700 (6th Cir.), *cert. denied,* 429 U.S. 824, 97 S.Ct. 76, 50 L.Ed.2d 86 (1976).

Bristol Locknut argues that it is entitled to a reimbursement of all royalties because the district court found both patents not infringed, as well as invalid. Unlike patent validity questions, infringement is a question of fact, not law. Bristol Locknut contends that since both parties were operating under a mutual mistake of fact, the licensing agreement should therefore be rescinded and all royalties returned. We understand but reject the argument. We affirm the holding of invalidity and need not review the finding of noninfringement, *Schwinn Bicycle Co. v. Goodyear Tire & Rubber Co.,* 444 F.2d 295, 301 (9th Cir. 1970), since noninfringement here would not affect our holding that Bristol Locknut is not entitled to a reimbursement of royalties. Because an invalid patent cannot be infringed, *Wham-O-Mfg. Co. v. Paradise Manufacturing Co.,* 327 F.2d 748, 751 (9th Cir.1964), Bristol Locknut's logic would permit every licensee who successfully challenged the validity of a patent to demand a reimbursement of royalties because of the consequent noninfringement of that patent. Such a result would undermine the stated policies of *Lear* and *St. Regis,* and would also promote an injustice where, as here, both issues of invalidity and noninfringement rest on the same asserted technical defects in the patents.

Bristol Locknut's argument is novel and, under these facts, unpersuasive. Here, Bristol Locknut fully "enjoyed the fruits of the license agreement." *St. Regis,* 552 F.2d at 314. We do not decide whether in a different situation involving a valid but not infringed patent, the argument would also fail.

C. Payment of Royalties Until the Patents' Validity Was Challenged

A licensee remains obligated to pay all royalties under a licensing agreement which accrue until it takes an affirmative step that would prompt the early adjudication of the validity of the patent, such as filing an action contesting the patent's validity or notifying the licensor that the payments were being stopped because the patent was believed to be invalid.[7] *PPG Industries, Inc. v. Westwood Chemical, Inc.,* 530 F.2d 700, 701 (6th Cir.), *cert. denied,* 429 U.S. 824, 97 S.Ct. 76, 50 L.Ed. 2d 86 (1976); *accord, American Sterilizer Co. v. Sybron Corp.,* 614 F.2d 890, 895–98 (3d Cir.), *cert. denied,* 449 U.S. 825, 101 S.Ct. 88, 66 L.Ed.2d 29 (1980) (the crucial date for terminating the obligation to pay royalties occurs when the licensee makes a prompt challenge to the patent, not necessarily when the action is filed); *cf. St. Regis,* 552 F.2d at 314 (a licensee is "not entitled to the refund of royalties paid before it challenged the validity of the patent"); *Kraly v. National Distillers & Chemical Corp.,* 502 F.2d 1366, 1372 (7th Cir.1974) (the obligation to pay royalties stopped when the licensee repudiated the license agreement by ceasing to represent that its product was licensed under the patent); *see also USM Corp. v. Standard Pressed Steel Co.,* 524 F.2d 1097, 1099–100 (7th Cir.1975).

Here, Bristol Locknut stopped paying royalties seven weeks before it filed suit. Because its letter to SPS did not prompt the early adjudication of the patents' validity, it remained obligated to pay royalties until it filed this declaratory judgment action to contest the patents' validity.

D. *Payment of the Underreported Royalties*

Before it ceased paying royalties because of doubts about the patents' validity, Bristol Locknut engaged in a deliberate and systematic underreporting of sales, thereby reducing the royalties paid to SPS. Bristol Locknut contends it has no obligation to pay royalties on the underreported sales that would otherwise be due if the patents were valid and not infringed. We reject the argument. To permit Bristol Locknut to retain the royalties it owed SPS would be inequitable and would undermine federal patent law policy. Bristol Locknut's contractual obligation to pay royalties terminated only after it ceased paying royalties and clearly notified SPS it was contesting the patents' validity. Just as the subsequent determination of the patents' invalidity did not affect Bristol Locknut's duty to pay royalties before it challenged the patents' validity, it does not affect the duty to pay the full amount of royalties owed under the contract. *Cf. Ransburg Electro-Coating Corp. v. Spiller & Spiller, Inc.,* 489 F.2d 974, 978 (7th Cir.1973) (an infringement settlement agreement was enforced even though the patent was later declared not infringed, since a contrary result would be inconsistent with the *Lear* policy favoring early challenges to patent validity).

---

7. Either method of giving adequate notice would fulfill the strong federal policy of prompting an early adjudication of patent validity. To mechanically require that a lawsuit be filed in order to suspend the obligation to pay royalties would place an undue burden on the courts, hinder settlement, and is not the only means of effectuating federal patent law policy.

A contrary result would also be inequitable. Here, Bristol Locknut received the full benefit of the licensing agreement despite the later adjudication of the patents' invalidity. Bristol Locknut was licensed to sell the locknuts without being sued by SPS for infringement. For six years Bristol Locknut enjoyed the benefits of the patent and developed a substantial business, economies of scale, and customer goodwill. It cannot avoid its contractual obligation by deliberately underreporting its sales. *See Kraly v. National Distillers & Chemical Corp.*, 502 F.2d 1366, 1372 (7th Cir.1974).

* * *

MEEHAN v. PPG INDUSTRIES, INC.

United States Court of Appeals, Seventh Circuit, 1986.
802 F.2d 881, 231 USPQ 400.

CUMMINGS, CHIEF JUDGE.

* * *

The facts in this case are undisputed. The plaintiff, John Meehan, invented a method and apparatus for the packaging and dispensing of anti-icing products, which when added to fuels in internal combustion engines prevent ice formation. In a contract executed January 30, 1964, Meehan conveyed exclusive rights in the invention to Hoffman-Taff Corporation. Hoffman-Taff's rights and obligations under the agreement were subsequently assumed by defendant PPG Industries.

At the time that the agreement was entered into Meehan had not filed a patent application for the invention. But the contract did require PPG to determine immediately whether the invention was patentable and, if so, to pursue an application for a U.S. patent. Meehan was required to assist in a technical capacity, as well as to furnish the necessary information and complete the necessary documents in the patent application process. The contract also transferred the patent, once it issued, to PPG.

Ultimately patents were granted in the United States, Canada, and the United Kingdom. The three patents expired in the following sequence: British patent, November 11, 1981; U.S. patent, January 4, 1983; Canadian patent, December 19, 1984. Since the U.S. patent expired, PPG has made no royalty payments on sales of plaintiff's invention in the United States.

Meehan sued PPG for breach of contract in 1984. The contract was interpreted as requiring PPG to continue paying plaintiff royalties on all sales until the last patent expired, or in December of 1984. PPG defended, asserting that any obligation it had to continue paying plaintiff royalties beyond the life of the U.S. patent was unenforceable under federal patent law. The district court agreed with PPG and granted summary judgment in its favor. We affirm.

1. DISCUSSION

Article I § 8 of the Constitution empowers Congress to grant inventors limited monopoly rights in their discoveries. Congress exercised that power by giving inventors the right to exclude others from making, using, or selling the idea for 17 years. 35 U.S.C. § 154. The policy behind this federal patent law is to give a 17-year monopoly to inventors in exchange for release of the invention to the public upon expiration of the patent. *Scott Paper Co. v. Marcalus Mfg. Co.,* 326 U.S. 249, 255, 67 USPQ 193, 196; *Singer Mfg. Co. v. June Mfg. Co.,* 163 U.S. 169, 185. Thus for a limited time the inventor may profit exclusively from the invention on condition that the invention goes public after 17 years. Even this limited monopoly right has extensive social and economic consequences for the public and therefore the courts are ever watchful of the possibility that patent monopolies will overstep their bounds. *Precision Instrument Mfg. Co. v. Automotive Maintenance Machinery Co.,* 324 U.S. 806, 816, 65 USPQ 133, 138. Consequently the policy and purpose of the patent laws is undermined by any attempt to extend or preserve the patent monopoly beyond the 17 years. *Scott Paper,* 326 U.S. at 255–256, 67 USPQ at 196.

Accordingly, in *Brulotte v. Thys Co.,* 379 U.S. 29, 143 USPQ 264, the Supreme Court held that licensing agreements extending royalty payments beyond the life of an issued patent was unlawful. In *Brulotte,* an owner of patents on hop-picking techniques sold machines to farmers for a flat sum. With each sale the owner also executed a licensing agreement requiring payment of a royalty. All of the patents expired before the licenses; nonetheless, the terms of the licenses remained identical both before and after the last patent expired. When the hop farmers eventually refused to pay the royalties, the owner sued to enforce the licenses under state contract law. The farmers defended claiming misuse of the patents. The Supreme Court held that the owner has improperly used the leverage of his patent to extend the monopoly. *Id.* at 32, 143 USPQ at 265. The Court based its conclusion on the unchanging nature of the license agreement terms after the patent expired; continuation of patent protection limitations and identical amounts of royalties due. *Id.* Because the terms failed to distinguish between the pre-expiration and post-expiration periods, the Court was unable to determine whether or not the post-expiration royalties were subject to the leverage of the patent. *Id.* Without evidence that the post-expiration royalties were not tied to the payment, the Court assumed that they were. "In light of those considerations, we conclude that a patentee's use of a royalty agreement that projects beyond the expiration date of the patent is unlawful *per se.*" *Id.*

The Eleventh Circuit's decision in *Pitney Bowes, Inc. v. Mestre,* 701 F.2d 1365, 218 USPQ 987 (1983), certiorari denied, 464 U.S. 893, applied *Brulotte's* rule of *per se* invalidity to an agreement specifically encompassing both patent and trade secret rights and where the patents were only pending at the time the agreement was entered into. In *Pitney,* the inventor had applied and was awaiting patents for his inventions. The prospective patent owner executed four licenses granting exclusive right to make and sell different paper handling machines. Like *Brulotte,* the royalty and use provisions did not distinguish between rates of payment for the pre-expiration and post-expiration periods or between royalties attributable to patent rights and those for trade secret rights. These hybrid royalty payments extended beyond the life of the patent. The Eleventh Circuit ruled that once the patent issued the conflicting and indistinguishable trade secret provisions were unenforceable. Thus, the *Pitney* Court held that misuse of the leverage afforded by a pending patent was subject to the *Brulotte* rule of *per se* invalidity. See also *Aronson v. Quick Point Pencil Co.,* 440 U.S. 257, 264–265, 201 USPQ 1, 5. In *Pitney,* the court reasoned that the anticipation of the issuance of a patent provided sufficient bargaining power to warrant application of the *Brulotte per se* analysis.

The Sixth Circuit, relying on *Brulotte* and *Pitney,* took the analysis one step further in *Boggild v. Kenner Products,* 776 F.2d 1315, 228 USPQ 130 (6th Cir.1985), certiorari denied, 106 S.Ct. 3284. *Boggild* involved a set of facts remarkably similar to the case presented before this Court. In *Boggild,* the plaintiffs invented a toy extruder to be used with Play-Doh. These plaintiffs sold an exclusive license to make, use, and sell the extruder to Kuto Products, which subsequently assigned its rights to Kenner Products. No patents for the extruder had been applied for when the agreement was executed. However, the agreement required the plaintiffs to apply promptly for mechanical and design patents on the extruder. Patents were subsequently issued. The agreement required Kenner Products to make royalty payments for 25 years, regardless of whether the patents issued. The Sixth Circuit held that the *Brulotte* rule of *per se* invalidity precluded enforcement of license terms that were entered into in anticipation of patent protection and that required royalty payments beyond the life of the patent. *Id.* at 1319, 228 USPQ at 133. Because the agreement did not contain provisions for reduction of post-expiration royalties and because the use restrictions on the extruder were the same in the post-expiration and pre-expiration periods, it was held unlawful. *Id.* at 1321, 228 USPQ at 134.

Aronson v. Quick Point Pencil Co., 440 U.S. 257, 201 USPQ 1, is not to the contrary. In *Aronson,* the Supreme Court reversed an Eighth Circuit decision applying *Brulotte* to an agreement in which the patent applications, although anticipated, ultimately failed. The *Aronson* Court held that absent an issued patent, federal patent law will not preempt state contract law. *Id.* at 265, 201 USPQ at 5. The Court explicitly noted, however, that had the patent issued, enforcement of the royalty for exclusive rights beyond the life of the patent would have been precluded. *Id.* at 263–264, 201 USPQ at 5.

2. Application of Law to Facts

We agree with the Sixth Circuit's holding that the *Brulotte* rule should be extended to agreements entered into in anticipation of applying for patents. * * *

Meehan then argues that the right to apply for a patent is not a patent right. Therefore, the argument continues, this contract does not involve a transfer of patent rights and *Brulotte* does not apply. This is but semantics; Meehan transferred the only patent interest he had at the time. What plaintiff fails to recognize is that *Brulotte* is not concerned with restrictions on the sale of patent rights but rather the impact of such arrangements on the policies and purposes of the federal patent laws. Meehan could not have transferred a "patent right" because he did not have one yet. It is the issuance of the patent that triggers *Brulotte's* application, not the transfer of the rights. See *Boggild,* 776 F.2d at 1319, 228 USPQ at 133; see also *Aronson,* 440 U.S. at 261, 201 USPQ at 4.

* * * *Brulotte* stated that when the license provisions fail to distinguish between post- and pre-expiration royalty amounts, the royalties do not constitute deferred payment for use during the pre-expiration period or long-term payments on a sale of unpatented products. 379 U.S. at 31–32, 143 USPQ at 265. Identical payments in the post-expiration period are "a telltale sign that the licensor was using the licenses to project its monopoly beyond the patent period. They forcefully negate the suggestion that we have here a bare arrangement for a sale or a lease at an undetermined price, based on use." *Id.* at 32, 143 USPQ at 265.

* * *

Even when an inventor has not yet applied for a patent, the right to apply for and obtain those protections is valuable.[1] Such a right places the inventor in a strong bargaining position. It is that abuse of that leverage over which the Supreme Court expressed concern in *Brulotte.* We agree with the Sixth Circuit that:

> the same violations of patent law arising from abuse of the leverage attached to a pending or issued patent can arise from abuse of the leverage afforded by an expressly anticipated application for a patent.

776 F.2d at 1320, 228 USPQ at 134.

* * *

"In our view, the absence of a patent application is, under the circumstance, irrelevant to the analysis under *Brulotte.*" *Boggild,* 776 F.2d at 1321, 228 USPQ at 134.

The terms of the contract must be examined before deciding whether Mehan abused this leverage from the anticipated patent. As in *Brulotte, Pitney,* and *Boggild,* this contract fails to distinguish between pre-expiration and post-expiration royalties. The exclusive rights conferred by the contract do not change in the post-expiration period. Although it is true, as Meehan argues, that parties can contract for trade secret payments to extend beyond the life of a patent, there must be some provision that distinguishes between patent royalties and trade secret royalties. *Brulotte,* 379 U.S. at 31–33, 143 USPQ at 265–66. * * *

DWIGHT AND LLOYD SINTERING CO., INC. v. AMERICAN ORE RECLAMATION CO.

United States District Court of New York, 1937.
44 F.Supp. 391.

BONDY, DISTRICT JUDGE. This suit was brought for the cancellation and rescission of patent licensing agreements and for an accounting of royalties. The defendant counterclaimed for an injunction against the termination of the agreements by the plaintiff, against plaintiff's competing with the defendant in a field exclusively set over to the defendant by the licensing agreements and for an accounting of plaintiff's profits and defendant's damages arising out of plaintiff's alleged competition with the defendant and plaintiff's neglect in bringing suit against alleged infringers of the patent.

By an order of reference made on consent, the Special Master was authorized to hear and determine the issues of fact and of law with the same effect as if tried by the court. The order provided that on the filing of the report of the Special Master, judgment should be entered in conformity therewith. Upon the court's advising the parties of difficulties which would arise upon an appeal from a judgment entered pursuant to this order, it was amended to provide that the Special Master should hear the issues and report to the court.

By an agreement dated April 7, 1911, defendant's assignors acquired from plaintiff's assignor an exclusive license of patents covering a process and apparatus for the sintering of ores, including the right to grant sublicenses in the iron and steel field. The licensees agreed to keep accurate records of the tonnage produced under each sublicense and to pay stipulated royalties to the licensor at stated intervals. The licensor received $35,000 in full paid nonassessable common stock of the defendant and was granted the privilege of naming one of the defendant's directors. The licensees agreed to pay as royalty three cents for each ton produced under the licensed process and apparatus by them and their sublicensees, and a minimum royalty increasing from $3,000 in the first year to $15,000 after the fifth year.

The defendant entered upon the business of exploiting plaintiff's patents in the iron and steel industry and it succeeded in doing a large business with the principal producers of iron and steel.

In 1931, defendant induced the United States Steel Corporation to accept a license under patents which it owned instead of a sublicense under plaintiff's patents. It is plaintiff's contention that the licensing agreements impliedly obligated defendant to work plaintiff's patents with due diligence and to refrain from exploiting a competing patent. The execution of the Steel Corporation license, it is urged, constituted a violation of both implied obligations.

The Special Master, on this issue, ruled that the agreements did not impose any obligations on defendant other than those expressed therein. He held that since the agreements contained no provision concerning the acquisition and use by defendant of other patents, no obligation preventing such acquisition and use could be implied. He predicated his ruling upon the fact that the agreements were carefully drafted by competent attorneys who sought to cover every contingency by explicit language. Consequently he felt that any omission in the agreements should be deemed to have been intentional and that the parties should be bound only by promises expressly made. Accordingly, he did not dispose of the sharply controverted question of fact concerning the defendant's actions and motives in connection with its license to United States Steel Corporation.

In arriving at this conclusion, the Special Master relied on Dixie Cotton Picker Co. v. Bullock, C.C.Ill., 188 F. 921, 923; Thomson Spot Welder Co. v. National Electric Co., D.C.N.D.Ohio, 260 F. 223, 225, each decided by a single judge; Thorn Wire Hedge Co. v. Washburn & Moen Mfg. Co., 159 U.S. 423, 16 S.Ct. 94, 40 L.Ed. 205; Eclipse Bicycle Co. v. Farrow, 199 U.S. 581, 26 S.Ct. 150, 50 L.Ed. 317.

Though there is language to the contrary in these cases, the court considers itself bound by the language and reasoning used subsequently by the Circuit Court of Appeals in this Circuit in Re Waterson, Berlin & Snyder Co., 2 Cir., 48 F.2d 704, followed in Driver-Harris Co. v. Industrial Furnace Corporation, D.C., 12 F.Supp. 918 and reiterated in Tesra Co. v. Holland Furnace Co., 6 Cir., 73 F.2d 553, 555. In the Waterson, Berlin & Snyder case [48 F.2d 709] Judge Augustus N. Hand stated: "In both countries [United States and England], where there has been a conveyance upon an agreement to pay the grantor sums of money based upon the earnings of the property transferred, the courts have implied a covenant to render the subject-matter of the contract productive—if the property was a mine, a covenant to mine, quarry or drill; if it consisted of a patent or copyright, a covenant to work the patent or copyright."

There is no valid distinction in principle between an assignment or conveyance and the exclusive license before the court. In each the entire fate of the subject of the assignment or license is in the hands of the grantee.

Nor does the provision for a minimum royalty payable whether or not the licensees actually used the patents affect the conclusion. In Driver-Harris Co. v. Industrial Furnace Corporation, D.C., 12 F.Supp. 918, the court followed the Waterson case, although the agreement there in suit provided for a minimum royalty. The effect of the minimum royalty provision however was not discussed by the court. It was discussed with the same result in Telegraph Dispatch and Intelligence Co. v. McLean, 8 Ch.App. 658. Cf. In re Railway and Electric Appliances Co., 57 L.J.Ch. 1027.

The circumstances surrounding the making of the agreements herein all indicate that the licensor intended to secure the exploitation of important patents by a company equipped to work them on a large scale, and intended not merely to grant a license which would yield the licensor a return dependent upon whether the licensee saw fit to use or not to use the patent.

The obligation to exploit diligently does not necessarily exclude all competition by the licensee with the licensed patent. Thorn Wire Hedge Co. v. Washburn & Moen Mfg. Co., 159 U.S. 423, 16 S.Ct. 94, 40 L.Ed. 205; Eclipse Bicycle Company v. Farrow, 199 U.S. 581, 26 S.Ct. 150, 153, 50 L.Ed. 317. In the latter case the court stated: "Due business diligence would not require it [the assignee] to enter into a hopeless contest, and would not prevent it from avoiding such a contest by purchase" of a patent for a competing article.

These decisions make it clear that mere ownership and use of a competing patent do not necessarily in themselves constitute a violation of the implied obligation to use due diligence in working the patent. Whether due diligence has been exercised is a question of fact to be determined in each case. The validity of the plaintiff's patents, their possible infringement by the defendant's patents, their value in competition with defendant's patents, the extent to which they are used by the defendant and the extent to which they must be used in sintering ore, the defendant's alleged bad faith and misrepresentations and all other circumstances surrounding the making of the license under the defendant's patents to the United States Steel Corporation must be considered.

These issues accordingly are referred back to the Special Master who heard the testimony and who was designated by the parties to pass on all issues in the first instance to report whether the defendant's action in making its agreement with the United States Steel Corporation, or its action in securing control of the patents involved in the license to the United States Steel Corporation were in violation of its implied agreement to work the plaintiff's patents with reasonable diligence.

The question whether the contract should be rescinded or whether less drastic relief is appropriate is also referred to the Special Master whose determination obviously will depend upon his findings on the question of breach.

* * *

The suit is referred back to the Special Master for additional findings in accordance with this opinion. Specific exceptions will be ruled on after submission of the final report of the Master.

Notes

1. An implied obligation of the exclusive licensee to make "good faith" or reasonable use of the invention is not extended to a non-exclusive licensee. When an exclusive license is granted, without an implied obliga-

tion to exploit the invention, the licensee would have the power to suppress the invention. This inequitable result would not come about in the case of a non-exclusive license because the licensor could license another party if he thought the first licensee was not diligently exploiting the invention.

2. "There is one well recognized exception to the doctrine as it has previously been applied. That is where there is outside competition which the exclusive licensee cannot meet with reasonable chance of success with the licensed article * * * If such competition comes from something not better commercially than the licensed device, he must meet it by means of the latter. If he sees fit to overcome the competition by purchasing the right to make the competing article, he cannot substitute the latter for the licensed device without thereby violating his covenant to exploit so long as he retains an exclusive license. But if competition comes from a better article than the one licensed, he is under no obligation to try with no hope of success to meet it with the licensed device. Faced with such a business situation he may, if he can, obtain and exercise the right to make or use the competing article without violating any obligation to exploit under his exclusive license." Mechanical Ice Tray Corp. v. General Motors Corp., 144 F.2d 720, 725, 726, 62 USPQ 397, 402 (2d Cir.1944).

3. " * * * [S]ince the defendant company has failed to perform its part of the agreement and has ceased manufacturing and has apparently abandoned its rights thereunder, it would be inequitable to further deprive complainant of the use of the patent and there should be a decree that the agreement is null and void and is cancelled." American Mechanical Improvement Co. v. Des Lauriers Aircraft Corp., 119 A. 179, 94 N.J.Ed. 197, 219 (1922).

4. For a discussion of many of the cases on licensee obligations, see Comment, Licensee's Obligations, 49 Michigan Law Review 738, 745–748 (1951). See also, Ellis, Patent Assignments and Licenses, Baker, Voohries & Co., Inc. (1943), Deller's Walker on Patents, 2nd Edition, Vol. 4, Chapters XIV, XV, Title and Licenses.

6. OBSERVATIONS ON NEGOTIATING AND PREPARING LICENSE AGREEMENTS

The drafting of a licensing contract is like the drafting of any contract, in that it requires clear foresight of every possibility of dispute which may conceivably arise concerning the agreements, and specific provisions in the writing for solution of the dispute. Suppose, for example, a carelessly drawn license gives the licensee an exclusive privilege of manufacture at a fixed royalty per unit manufactured; for reasons of advantage to himself the licensee manufactures no units at all. Because the licensee's privilege is "exclusive" the licensor has precluded himself from licensing anyone else. Because the licensee chose not to exercise his privilege he owes the patentee-licensor nothing, in the absence of appropriate provision; the patent is in effect valueless so long as the exclusive licensee wishes to keep it so. A provision for minimum royalty regardless of nonmanufacture, or a requirement for manufacture of a minimum number of units, or a right retained by the patentee to license others in case of nonmanufacture, or any one of various other possible provisions would protect the licensor. A competent draftsman will foresee such needs and will express in the contract the most advisable protection.

So also, dispute may arise, if not foreseen and precluded, over the right of a licensee to transfer his license, or to sublicense others. And if he is privileged to sublicense, is the patentee-licensee; or must he rely on the financial responsibility of his own licensee? Many other matters, such as the time limit of the license, or its geographical limits, or its various other possibly desirable limitations, must be thought out and explicitly stated. The time and manner of payment of royalties will rarely be overlooked in drafting the license, but the consequences of nonpayment, the right of the licensor to revoke the license, or his limitation to suit for breach of contract, are not so invariably dealt with.

From the licensee's point of view, also, a variety of problems must be preventively anticipated. Controversy which should have been unnecessary has in fact reached the courts because inept draftsmanship has neglected to state whether or not the patentee is obligated to protect his licensee against infringement. No manufacturer wants to pay royalties for what competitors are manufacturing royalty free. If the licensor does agree to protect his licensee, what if he fails in that duty? May the licensee withdraw from his own obligations; or seek some other remedy? If the licensor does protect the licensee, can the costs be divided? Even if there be no problem of infringers, what of other licensees? Can the licensor hold his first licensee to an agreed royalty while permitting competitors of that licensee to manufacture at a lower royalty? A wisely drawn agreement will cover such possibilities. Some license agreements may obligate the licensee to push the product by advertising, others may leave it to the licensor. Some will set up standards to which the manufactured product must conform, by way of protecting the patentee's good will. There may be provision for inspection by the licensor of the licensee's books should the amount of royalties due come into question.

These, and an infinite variety of other provisions, must be conned over in the proper drafting of license agreements; but time does not permit their discussion here. Nor would the illustrative cases with which the reports abound serve a sufficiently valuable purpose herein.

There are, however, many conditions and limitations in license contracts which have been thought of by the draftsmen, and which have been brought into litigation on the allegation of legal invalidity. In respect of these, problems not merely of foresight and wisdom but of law are raised. Other restrictions have not yet come before the courts as to their legality, but are likely sooner or later to be brought into question. As to these, it is imperative for a draftsman to know what the courts have said, or are likely to say.[b]

b. Waite, Cases on Patent Law, pp. 290–91 (1949).

ROBERTS v. SEARS, ROEBUCK AND CO.

United States Court of Appeals, Seventh Circuit, 1978.
573 F.2d 976, 197 USPQ 516, cert. denied 199 USPQ 640, 439 U.S. 860, 99
S.Ct. 179, 58 L.Ed.2d 168 (1978).

SPRECHER, CIRCUIT JUDGE.

The major issues in this case are whether the district court proper-ly declined to decide the validity of plaintiff's patent in a suit for fraud, breach of a confidential relationship and negligent misrepresentation in defendant's procurement of an assignment of plaintiff's patent rights and whether the district court properly concluded that plaintiff had elected his legal remedies and, therefore, was barred from seeking his equitable remedies of rescission and restitution.

I

This case involves the efforts of one of this nation's largest retail companies, Sears, Roebuck & Co. (Sears), to acquire through deceit the monetary benefits of an invention of a new type of socket wrench created by one of its sales clerks during his off-duty hours. That sales clerk, Peter M. Roberts (Plaintiff), initiated the unfortunate events that led to this appeal in 1963, when at the age of 18 he began work on a ratchet or socket wrench that would permit the easy removal of the sockets from the wrench. He, in fact, designed and constructed a prototype tool with a quick-release feature in it that succeeded in permitting its user to change sockets with one hand. Based on that prototype, plaintiff filed an application for a United States patent. In addition, since he was in the employ of Sears, a company that sold over a million wrenches per year, and since he had only a high school education and no business experience, he decided to show his invention to the manager of the Sears store in Gardner, Massachusetts where he worked. Plaintiff was persuaded to submit formally his invention as a suggestion to Sears. In May 1964, the prototype, along with a complet-ed suggestion form, was sent to Sears' main office in Chicago, Illinois. Plaintiff, thereafter, left Sears' employ when his parents moved to Tennessee.

It was from this point on that Sears' conduct became the basis for the jury's determination that Sears appropriated the value of the plaintiff's invention by fraudulent means. Plaintiff's evidence proved that Sears took steps to ascertain the utility of the invention and that based on the information it acquired, Sears became convinced that the invention was in fact valuable. Sears had two sets of tests run on plaintiff's wrench by its custom manufacturer of wrenches, Moore Drop Forging Co. (Moore). The first test was conducted in July 1964, and it proved that the wrench operated normally and that the quick-release feature did not substantially weaken the structure of the wrench. The second test, conducted in May 1965, showed that actual mechanics liked the quick-release feature. Moore reported the results of these tests to Sears.

Based presumably on these tests, and the expert opinion of its senior tool buyer, Arthur Griesbaum, Sears in March 1965, had Moore design a fine-tooth wrench with the quick-release feature built into it. In addition, at about the same time, Sears put in motion plans to incorporate the quick-release feature into then-existing wrench models that constituted 74.27 percent of all the wrenches Sears sold. Thus, by early 1965, it was clear to Sears that this invention was very useful and probably would be quite profitable.

Sears also received reports from Moore regarding the manufacturing cost of plaintiff's quick-release feature. In the initial prototype built by Moore, the cost was 44 cents per unit. By June of 1965, Sears had received a report indicating that the cost could be reduced to 20 cents per unit. Thus, early in 1965, Sears learned that the feature was relatively inexpensive to manufacture.

Sears also took pains to ascertain the patentability of the quick-release feature. In April 1965, it received outside patent counsel's advice that there was "some basis for limited patentability" (defendant's Exhibit 9). It had previously learned in February 1965 from plaintiff's lawyer, Charles Fay, that he believed the invention was patentable based on a limited search. In addition, Sears was informed in early May 1965, by plaintiff's lawyer that a patent had been issued to plaintiff.[1]

With all of this information either available or soon to be available, Sears contacted plaintiff in January 1965, and began negotiations regarding the purchase of rights to use plaintiff's invention. During these negotiations, conducted with plaintiff's attorney, Sears' lawyer, Leonard Schram, made various representations to plaintiff that serve as the essential basis for plaintiff's complaint. In April 1965, in a letter seeking merely a license, Schram first told plaintiff that the invention was not new and that the claims in any patent that would be permitted would be "quite limited" (plaintiff's Exhibit 34). Second, Schram told plaintiff that the cost of the quick-release feature would be 40–50 cents. Third, he told plaintiff the feature would sell only to the extent it would be promoted and thus $10,000 was all that the feature was worth. Finally, and perhaps most ironically, Schram wrote to plaintiff that "[o]nce we have paid off the royalty expense, then we would probably take the amount previously allocated to said expense and use it for promotional expenses *if we desire to maintain sales on the item.*" (Emphasis added).

Based on this letter, plaintiff entered into the agreement on July 29, 1965, which provided for a two cent royalty per unit up to a maximum of $10,000 to be paid in return for a complete *assignment* of all of plaintiff's rights. In fact, for no extra charge, plaintiff's attorney

1. We might note here that Mr. Fay contacted Sears before informing plaintiff that a patent had issued. In addition, it was shown that Sears had contacted Mr. Fay during the period of these negotiations about doing some work for it and that he, in fact, did perform a couple of routine matters for Sears, thus raising some doubt about the independence of his advice to plaintiff.

gave Sears all of plaintiff's foreign patent rights. A provision was included in the contract regarding what would happen if Sears failed to sell 50,000 wrenches in a given year, thus reinforcing the impression that the wrenches might not sell very well. Also, a provision was inserted dealing with the contingency that a patent might not be issued, notwithstanding that Sears already knew, and plaintiff did not, that the patent had been granted.

By July, Sears knew that it planned to sell several hundred thousand wrenches with a cost per item increase of only 20 cents, that a patent had issued and that this product in all likelihood would have tremendous appeal with mechanics. Nonetheless, it entered into this agreement both having failed to disclose vital information about the product's appeal and structural utility and having made representations to plaintiff that were either false at the time they were made or became false without disclosure prior to the time of the signing of the contract.

Within days after the signing of the contract, Sears was manufacturing 44,000 of plaintiff's wrenches per week—all with plaintiff's patent number prominently stamped on them—and within three months, Sears was marketing them as a tremendous breakthrough. Within *nine months,* Sears had sold over 500,000 wrenches and paid plaintiff his maximum royalty thereby acquiring all of plaintiff's rights. Between 1965 and 1975, Sears sold in excess of 19 million wrenches, many at a premium of one to two dollars profit because no competition was able to market a comparable product for several years. To say the least, plaintiff's invention has been a commercial success.

Plaintiff, a Tennessee resident, filed suit against Sears, an Illinois Corporation, in federal district court in December 1969, based on diversity jurisdiction, seeking alternatively return of the patent and restitution or damages for fraud, breach of a confidential relationship and negligent misrepresentation. A jury trial was held from December 20, 1976, until January 18, 1977. During the trial plaintiff basically proved the facts as presented above. Sears argued that it did not misrepresent any facts to plaintiff, that he had a lawyer and thus there was no confidential relationship and that the success of the wrenches was a function of advertising and the unforeseeable boom in do-it-yourself repairs, and thus Sears did not misrepresent the salability of plaintiff's wrenches. The jury was instructed on each of the three counts in plaintiff's complaint and told that it could award plaintiff profits [2] for Counts I and II and could consider a reasonable royalty as a

2. The court instructed the jury on damages for Counts I and II, fraud and breach of a confidential relationship, as follows:

The award of money damages you make may equal the net profits which you find the defendant gained as a result of its merchandising of wrenches incorporating Plaintiff's quick release invention and idea, minus any expenditures which you find the defendant has proved it incurred which it would have incurred had it not merchandised such wrenches incorporating plaintiff's quick release invention and idea from the time of the contract in question to the present.

(Tr. at 3469).

remedy for Count III. The jury apparently believed the plaintiff's evidence because it found Sears guilty on all three counts and entered judgment for one million dollars on each count, but the award was not cumulative.

Both parties filed post-trial motions. Sears filed for judgment NOV and plaintiff sought rescission of the contract and restitution. The district court denied both motions holding as to Sears' motion that the jury verdict was in accordance with the evidence and that the damages award was reasonable and holding as to plaintiff's motion that when he permitted the case to go to the jury he had elected his legal remedy and could not later also seek his equitable relief. Plaintiff appealed seeking equitable relief and Sears cross-appealed the one million dollar judgment against it. Since Sears' cross-appeal raises basic issues of liability, we will deal with it first. We will subsequently consider plaintiff's appeal on the issues of the appropriate remedy.

II

Sears' primary argument in its cross-appeal is that the district court erred in not determining conclusively the validity of plaintiff's patent as a precondition to trying plaintiff's claims for fraud, breach of a confidential relationship and misrepresentation. Relying on Lear, Inc. v. Adkins, 395 U.S. 653, 89 S.Ct. 1902, 23 L.Ed.2d 610 (1969), Sears contends that if the district court had concluded that the patent was invalid, then plaintiff could not have been injured by any fraud Sears may have committed since it paid $10,000 for a "worthless" invention.

Sears' analysis, however, misconceives the Supreme Court's holding in *Lear*. There the Court held that a patent licensee was not estopped to contest the validity of the licensor's patent, and, in fact, was not required to pay the contractually-provided royalties for the license on the invalid patent during the pendency of the litigation. Contrary to Sears' implication, the *Lear* Court did not hold that the potentially invalid patent was worthless and thus the royalties offered in exchange for the right to use that patent would be unjustified. Instead, the Court explicitly recognized that there was significant economic value in the rights to an unchallenged patent. 395 U.S. at 669, 89 S.Ct. 1902. In this regard the Court stated that "the existence of an unchallenged patent may deter others from attempting to compete with the licensee," thereby creating a monopoly in fact if not in law. Id.[3]

Other courts have also acknowledged that significant economic value attaches to the rights to an uncontested patent. The Supreme Court recognized this recently in an opinion by Chief Justice Burger: "[E]ven though a discovery may not be patentable, that does not 'destroy the value of the discovery * * *.'" Kewanee Oil Co. v. Bicron Corp., 416 U.S. 470, 482, 94 S.Ct. 1879, 1886, 40 L.Ed.2d 315 (1974). Similarly, this court has held that "[w]hile there are paradoxi-

3. This valuable benefit was available even in the case of a non-exclusive license because the royalty charged to the licensee "serves as a barrier to entry." 395 U.S. 669 n. 16, 89 S.Ct. 1910.

cal aspects of allowing recovery to arise from illegal interference with the sale of something which ultimately was proven to have no sales value, it cannot be said that there was no such value during the period of the presumptive validity of the patent." Moraine Products v. ICI America, Inc., 538 F.2d 134, 149 (7th Cir.1976).[4]

The facts of this case, by themselves, make abundantly clear both that Sears believed that the uncontested patent had significant economic value as a deterrent to competitors and that the patent, in fact, did serve to deter competitors. Sears had the patent number stamped on all of its wrenches with plaintiff's quick-release feature, which presumably was done for the purpose of scaring off competitors. Also, Sears' competitors did not enter this lucrative market for several years after it became clear that this product had genuine sales appeal, which can only be explained by the existence of the patent.

It is at least somewhat disingenuous for Sears to argue before this court that plaintiff's patent was valueless when it made every effort in its marketing to exploit the economic value of the uncontested patent, received the benefits of a factual monopoly for several years because of that uncontested patent and to this day has refused to return the patent rights to plaintiff in return for the $10,000 originally paid to acquire these "valueless" rights. We, therefore, have little difficulty finding that Sears' deception caused plaintiff to be injured in fact.

The issue remains whether the public interest, recognized in *Lear,* in having patent validity challenged is of such significance that we should extend *Lear* to cover this case. The *Lear* Court held that a licensee should be permitted to contest the validity of a licensor's patent because "[l]icensees may often be the only individuals with enough economic incentive to challenge the patentability of an inventor's discovery." 395 U.S. at 670, 89 S.Ct. at 1911. Thus, the Court feared that if licensees "are muzzled, the public may continually be required to pay tribute to would-be monopolists, without need or justification." Id.[5]

---

4. The court subsequently defined more specifically the nature of the economic value created by the uncontested patent during the period of its presumptive validity:

> While Moraine was the holder of a presumptively valid patent, it could legally entertain the expectation, unless it had in some manner deprived itself thereof, of receiving royalties from licensing arrangements which in final analysis are agreements in which the licensee is purchasing the right to be free from infringement litigation, which Moraine did have to sell during the period of validity.

538 F.2d at 149.

5. The policy against deterring licensees from attacking the validity of the licensor's patent also justified not requiring the licensee to pay royalties under the license agreement during the litigation. The Court reasoned:

> Enforcing this contractual provision would give the licensor an additional economic incentive to devise every conceivable dilatory tactic in an effort to postpone the day of final judicial reckoning. * * * [T]he cost of prosecuting slow-moving trial proceedings and defending an inevitable appeal might well deter many licensees from attempting to prove patent invalidity in the courts.

395 U.S. at 673, 89 S.Ct. at 1912.

We believe that the reasoning in *Lear* does not extend to this case for two reasons. First, we deal here with a complete assignment of plaintiff's patent rights to Sears. See generally Heltra, Inc. v. Richen-Gemco, Inc., 395 F.Supp. 346, 352 (D.S.C.1975), rev'd on other grounds, 540 F.2d 1235 (4th Cir.1976); Arnold & Goldstein, Life Under Lear, 48 Texas L.Rev. 1235, 1244 (1970). Thus, the primary evil that the Court in *Lear* sought to end—that the public might have to pay tribute to a "would-be monopolist"—is completely irrelevant to this case. Plaintiff has no legal basis for exacting any "tribute" until the patent rights are returned to him. At that point in time, the patent's validity can be tested either in an infringement suit or after plaintiff enters into a licensing agreement. The public's interest would not be injured by our decision to bar Sears from contesting this patent at this time.

Second, and perhaps even more fundamentally, the Court's analysis in *Lear* initiated with an assessment of "the spirit of contract law, which seeks to balance the claims of promisor and promisee in accord with the requirements of *good faith.*" 395 U.S. at 670, 89 S.Ct. at 1911. (emphasis added). Only after the Court satisfied itself that the equities were balanced on each side did it proceed to a consideration of the needs of patent law and the public interest. Sears' actions in this matter have violated completely the basic assumption in *Lear* that there was good faith in the dealings between the parties. There is no balance of equities between Sears and plaintiff in their contractual relations. For this court to employ the public interest in patent law to sanction Sears' conduct is unjustifiable. Certainly nothing in patent law requires this court to permit fraud to go unremedied. Cf. Kewanee Oil Co. v. Bicron Corp., 416 U.S. 470, 487, 94 S.Ct. 1879, 40 L.Ed.2d 315 (1974) (nothing in patent law discourages states from preventing industrial espionage). We, therefore, hold that the district court properly concluded that Lear, Inc. v. Adkins, is no bar to plaintiff's recovery.

III

Having determined that the district court properly declined to decide the validity of the plaintiff's patent, we can readily dispose of Sears' second contention in its cross-appeal. Sears argues that the district court erred in not permitting the introduction of certain evidence dealing with the prior art surrounding plaintiff's invention. Sears, however, attempted to introduce all of the prior art evidence at issue (defendant's Exhibits 25, 26, 29, 33, 34, 39, 40, 41, 42 and 43) for the purpose of proving that the patent was invalid. Since that contention was irrelevant to the case, it seems, *a fortiori,* that the materials introduced to prove it must also be deemed irrelevant to this case.

Sears, however, argues that the district court recognized that patent validity was a relevant issue. By citing materials out of context, Sears has severely mischaracterized the district court's analysis. During the trial, the district court properly recognized that some evidence of prior art was relevant for the issue of Sears' intent. Prior art was relevant to the limited extent that if Sears could prove it knew about the prior art at the time it was negotiating with plaintiff then the jury might conclude that Sears had not intentionally deceived plaintiff about the novelty and value of his invention.

The best example of this reasoning by the district court was with regard to the Carpenter patent (defendant's Exhibit 29). In considering its relevance the court asked when Sears had become aware of the patent. Counsel for Sears stated that the Carpenter patent was not discovered until 1971, after the law suit was initiated (Tr. at 2409). Since it was clear that the Carpenter patent had not entered into Sears' assessment of the value of plaintiff's invention when it made its representations to plaintiff, the district court properly concluded the patent was irrelevant and refused to admit it into evidence (Tr. at 2425). We have examined the record concerning the other prior art evidence that was not admitted and about which Sears complains, and we conclude that the district court properly applied its rule of limited relevance and thereby correctly excluded all of it.

IV

Sears' final argument in its cross-appeal is that plaintiff failed to prove the existence of a confidential relationship between himself and Sears. In assessing that argument, we recognize at the outset that there are no hard and fast rules for determining whether a confidential relationship exists. See G. Bogert, The Law of Trusts and Trustees § 482 (2d ed. 1960). The trier of fact must examine all of the circumstances surrounding the relationship between the parties and determine whether "one person reposes trust and confidence in another who thereby gains a resulting influence and superiority over the first." Kester v. Crilly, 405 Ill. 425, 91 N.E.2d 419, 423 (1950).

Various factors have been recognized judicially as being of particular relevance to that inquiry. Among them are disparity of age, education and business experience between the parties. Melish v. Vogel, 35 Ill.App.3d 125, 343 N.E.2d 17, 26 (1975). Additional factors are the existence of an employment relationship and the exchange of confidential information from one party to the other. See Yamins v. Zeitz, 322 Mass. 268, 76 N.E.2d 769, 772 (1948). All five of those factors are present in this case. In addition, one of Sears' witnesses admitted that the company expected plaintiff to "believe" and to "rely" on various representations that Sears made to him (Tr. at 1981). Obviously, this question is best left to the trier of fact, and this court under any circumstances would hesitate to disturb the jury's findings. That hesitation is especially strong here where so many factors suggest that a confidential relationship in fact existed.

Sears argues, however, that there are two factors involved here that eliminate any possible confidential relationship. They are that plaintiff never proved that Sears had knowledge of the confidential relationship upon which plaintiff was relying and that plaintiff retained counsel to guide him, and therefore, did not rely on Sears. We find neither factor sufficient to justify overturning the jury's verdict on this issue.

Sears cites several cases that emphasize that a confidential relationship cannot be thrust upon an unknowing party. See Broomfield v. Kosow, 349 Mass. 749, 212 N.E.2d 556 (1965); Yamins v. Zeitz, supra; Comstock v. Livingston, 210 Mass. 581, 97 N.E. 106 (1912). That proposition, however, does not lead to the conclusion that a plaintiff must demonstrate by direct evidence that the defendant actually was aware of the confidential relationship. All that must be proved is that the parties engaged in activities under circumstances that created a confidential relationship and that defendant breached that relationship.

In the cases cited by Sears, all of the circumstances surrounding the transactions that were being attacked suggested an arms-length arrangement, and thus the plaintiffs in those cases attempted to thrust a confidential relationship on the unknowing defendants after the fact. Here, Sears' knowledge is circumstantially proved by all of the facts surrounding its dealings with plaintiff. In addition, as suggested above, there was direct testimony to the effect that Sears expected plaintiff to rely on its representations.[6]

With regard to the existence of counsel representing plaintiff, we conclude that that is merely one factor to be considered along with all of the others. In fact, once plaintiff established the existence of a confidential relationship through proof of the five factors previously discussed, the burden was on Sears to prove that plaintiff had competent and independent advice. See Jones v. Washington, 412 Ill. 436, 107 N.E.2d 672, 674 (1952). The judge instructed the jury on this issue (Tr. at 3467) and it obviously rejected Sears' argument. There is no basis for this court to disturb that determination. Thus, we conclude that a jury could reasonably find that a confidential relationship existed between the parties and that Sears breached its duties created by that relationship.

For all of the above-stated reasons, we find no merit to any of the issues raised in Sears' cross-appeal. We, therefore, affirm the district court's judgment of liability against Sears on all three counts of plaintiff's complaint.

V

Plaintiff, in his appeal, seeks review of the district court's decision that he elected his legal remedies by taking the case to the jury, and therefore, is barred from pursuing his equitable remedies of rescission and restitution. Plaintiff argues that the district court, as a court of equity, should have accepted the jury's liability determination, but

---

6. Sears also argues that the district court failed to instruct the jury on the issue of Sears' knowledge of the confidential relationship. In view of our holding that knowledge does not have to be proved as an element of the tort, we find no basis for requiring any specific mention of this factor. In our view, the district court's instructions on the confidential relationship issue were proper.

should have disregarded its damages verdict and instead should have granted rescission and restitution.[7]

Before considering the substance of the doctrine of election of remedies, we should determine what law, state or federal, should control our decision. Sears relies almost exclusively on Illinois decisions in arguing that after plaintiff takes his case to the jury in a court of law he cannot thereafter seek rescission of the contract from a court of equity. We, however, conclude that federal courts are not bound by the Illinois election of remedies doctrine.

* * *

[The court discusses the doctrines of election of remedies and the choice of law in diversity cases.]

> "With regard to an election between the profits awarded by the jury and return of the patent based on rescission, however, we see no basis for invoking the election of remedies doctrine. Based on the jury instruction, plaintiff will receive one million dollars as the measure of *past* profits earned by Sears up to the time of trial. That award, however, is not inconsistent with return of the patent so that plaintiff can receive the *future* benefits of the patent that Sears fraudulently acquired. There will be neither a double recovery nor a factual inconsistency between these remedies. See Prudential Oil Corp., supra at 257; G. Bogert, The Law of Trusts and Trustees § 946 (2d ed. 1962). Therefore, we conclude that going to the jury under a past profits instruction did not bar plaintiff from seeking rescission and thereby possibly recovering his patent. Whether rescission is appropriate, however, is an issue that should be decided in the first instance by the district court.

> "For the reasons stated above, we affirm the district court's judgment against Sears on all three counts in plaintiff's complaint and the court's decision not to alter plaintiff's monetary award, but reverse the court's determination that it lacked the power to award rescission and remand to the district court for a determination of whether rescission is appropriate under the facts of this case.

> "Affirmed in part; Reversed in part; and Remanded."

On remand to the District Court, the contract between Roberts and Sears was rescinded, reassignment of the patent was ordered, and Sears was ordered to account for "all of the profits it has earned from the use of the quick release device." Roberts v. Sears, Roebuck & Co., 471 F.Supp. 372, 202 USPQ 727 (D.C.Ill.1979). However, this decision was

-----

7. Plaintiff asks this court to leave undisturbed his one million dollar judgment in Count III, negligent misrepresentation, because that is an action at law and therefore was properly given to and decided by the jury.

As to Counts I and II, plaintiff claims that the evidence proves that Sears' profits on the sale of quick-release wrenches was in excess of 40 million dollars. Sears argues that that figure is based on a misinterpretation of Sears' sales techniques. Given our disposition of this case, we need not resolve this dispute, although we do agree with the district court that the jury's damage award was not unreasonable.

vacated on appeal, 617 F.2d 460, 205 USPQ 788 (7th Cir.1980). The Circuit Court "clarified" its earlier opinion noting that, by "rescission" of the fraudulent assignment, it had meant "cancellation" of the assignment or "reassignment" of the patent so that Roberts could obtain the benefits of patent ownership from the date of the court's decree. Roberts was held to have elected the damage remedy for past activity. In a subsequent suit against Sears for patent infringement, the patent was held invalid, 697 F.2d 796, 217 USPQ 675 (7th Cir.1983), on rehearing 723 F.2d 1324, 221 USPQ 504 (7th Cir.1983).

Chapter Ten

LITIGATION PROCEDURE, REMEDIES, DEFENSES AND JUDGMENTS

A. PATENT INFRINGEMENT ACTIONS AND DECLARATORY JUDGMENTS

1. INTRODUCTION

The United States Court of Claims has exclusive subject matter jurisdiction of all actions for patent infringement by or for the United States. The United States District Courts have exclusive subject matter jurisdiction of all other patent infringement and patent declaratory judgment actions.

The usual rules for *in personam* jurisdiction over the defendant are applicable. In addition, a nonresident patent holder may designate in writing a person residing in the United States on whom process may be served in a proceeding affecting his patent, and, if such person cannot be found or has not been designated, the District Court for the District of Columbia has the equivalent of *in personam* jurisdiction over the patent holder.

The following are the statutory provisions relating to jurisdiction and venue.

28 U.S.C.A. § 1338. Patents, Plant Variety Protection, Copyrights, Trade-marks, and Unfair Competition

(a) The district courts shall have original jurisdiction of any civil action arising under any Act of Congress relating to patents, plant variety protection, copyrights and trade-marks. Such jurisdiction shall be exclusive of the courts of the states in patent, plant variety protection and copyright cases.

(b) The district courts shall have original jurisdiction of any civil action asserting a claim of unfair competition when joined with a substantial and related claim under the copyright, patent, plant variety protection or trade-mark laws.

28 U.S.C.A. § 1400. Patents and Copyrights

(a) (Copyrights). (b) Any civil action for patent infringement may be brought in the judicial district where the defendant resides or where the defendant has committed acts of infringement and has a regular and established place of business.

731

28 U.S.C.A. § 2201.   Creation of Remedy

In a case of actual controversy within its jurisdiction, except with respect to Federal taxes, * * * any court of the United States, upon the filing of an appropriate pleading, may declare the rights and other legal relations of any interested party seeking such declaration, whether or not further relief is or could be sought. Any such declaration shall have the force and effect of a final judgment or decree and shall be reviewable as such.

28 U.S.C.A. § 1391.   Venue Generally

(a) A civil action wherein jurisdiction is founded only on diversity of citizenship may, except as otherwise provided by law, be brought only in the judicial district where all plaintiffs or all defendants reside, or in which the claim arose.

(b) A civil action wherein jurisdiction is not founded solely on diversity of citizenship may be brought only in the judicial district where all defendants reside, or in which the claim arose, except as otherwise provided by law.

(c) A corporation may be sued in any judicial district in which it is incorporated or licensed to do business or is doing business, and such judicial district shall be regarded as the residence of such corporation for venue purposes.

(d) An alien may be sued in any district.

35 U.S.C.A. § 293.   Nonresident Patentee; Service and Notice

Every patentee not residing in the United States may file in the Patent and Trademark Office a written designation stating the name and address of a person residing within the United States on whom may be served process or notice of proceedings affecting the patent or rights thereunder. If the person designated cannot be found at the address given in the last designation, or if no person has been designated, the United States District Court for the District of Columbia shall have jurisdiction and summons shall be served by publication or otherwise as the court directs. The court shall have the same jurisdiction to take any action respecting the patent or rights thereunder that it would have if the patentee were personally within the jurisdiction of the court.

28 U.S.C.A. § 1498.   Patent and Copyright Cases

(a) Whenever an invention described in and covered by a patent of the United States is used or manufactured by or for the United States without license of the owner thereof or lawful right to use or manufacture the same, the owner's remedy shall be by action against the United States in the United States Claims Court for the recovery of his reasonable and entire compensation for such use and manufacture.

2. JURISDICTION AND VENUE

TELECHRON, INC. v. PARISSI

United States Court of Appeals, Second Circuit, 1952.
197 F.2d 757, 93 USPQ 492.

SWAN, CHIEF JUDGE. This appeal from an order striking certain matter from the complaint in a declaratory judgment action raises questions as to the district court's jurisdiction to hear a non-federal claim with a federal claim, when there is no diversity of citizenship between the parties. The complaint sought (1) a declaration that three patents issued to the defendant are invalid and were not infringed, (2) a declaration that neither of the plaintiffs has violated any other rights of the defendant, including rights based upon any alleged disclosure of any of the subject matter of the patents, and (3) an injunction against the bringing of suit by the defendant charging infringement of the patents, or charging that other rights of the defendant have been violated by the plaintiffs. Federal jurisdiction with respect to the patents was founded on 28 U.S.C.A. §§ 2201 and 1338(a) and with respect to the other claim on § 1338(b). The order on appeal struck from the complaint all matter relating to the defendant's non-patent rights and dismissed the claim set forth in the matter so stricken.

The patents in suit relate to flashing light alarm clocks and clock controlled switches. Litigation between the parties was initiated by the patentee, Parissi. In November 1950 he sued General Electric Company in the Supreme Court of Albany County, New York. His complaint alleged that before applying for the patents later issued to him, he had disclosed his invention to General Electric Company in confidence, that it had thereafter wrongfully appropriated his invention and realized profits therefrom to which he was justly entitled and for which he sought an accounting. After removing this suit to the federal court, General Electric and Telechron brought the present declaratory judgment action against Parissi. He promptly moved to dismiss it and also moved to remand the removed action. Both motions were argued before Judge Brennan, who granted the motion to remand, 97 F.Supp. 333 and denied the motion to dismiss, 97 F.Supp. 355. Thereafter on the first day of the trial of the declaratory judgment action, which came on before Judge Foley, Parissi made the motion to strike on which was entered the order now before us on appeal. Ruling on the motion was deferred until the plaintiffs rested their case. It was then granted in an oral opinion in which Judge Foley concluded that Judge Brennan's prior opinions had decided that the court lacked jurisdiction of the non-patent claim and also that Judge Brennan had exercised his discretion not to take jurisdiction over that part of the complaint "involving the confidential disclosure and unjust enrichment." Judge Foley added that in the exercise of his own discretion, if he had discretion, he would exercise it in favor of the defendant Parissi. Hence the questions presented on appeal are (1) whether the district court has jurisdiction of the non-patent claim, and (2) if it has, whether discretion was abused in refusing to hear it.

* * *

Turning to the merits of the appeal, the first question for consideration is the jurisdiction of the district court. * * * Although the district court referred to the complaint as alleging a patent claim and a non-patent claim, close examination of the complaint discloses, we think, that in reality three claims are averred as to which the plaintiffs sought declarations of rights and injunctive relief: (1) a claim that the patents are invalid and have not been infringed;[5] (2) a claim that the alleged inventions were not disclosed to the plaintiffs in confidence; (3) a claim that the alleged inventions were not disclosed subject to any understanding, express or implied, that compensation would be paid therefor to defendant. The second and third claims involve common law rights and, since diversity of citizenship is lacking, jurisdiction must depend upon the applicability of 28 U.S.C.A. § 1338(b). This court has recently considered the problem of dependent jurisdiction in Kleinman v. Betty Dain Creations, 2 Cir., 189 F.2d 546 and Schreyer v. Casco Products Corp., 2 Cir., 190 F.2d 921, certiorari denied 342 U.S. 913, 72 S.Ct. 360. In the former two causes of action were asserted, one for patent infringement, the other for breach of contract to pay for use of the patented article. It was held, Judge Clark dissenting, that a failure to make payments under a licensing agreement does not constitute the tort of unfair competition and therefore the claim for breach of contract was not within the dependent jurisdiction of § 1338(b). In the Schreyer case the complaint charged both infringement of a patent and unfair competition consisting in the use of information which had been confidentially disclosed to the defendants during negotiations concerning the granting of a license to them. We held that the use of confidentially disclosed information to invade the plaintiff's market was unfair competition and that jurisdiction existed under § 1338(b). In the case at bar, the non-patent claim referred to above as claim (2) falls squarely within the Schreyer decision, and the claim referred to as claim (3) within the Betty Dain decision.

In differentiating Betty Dain in the later Schreyer case, the court said, 190 F.2d at page 924: "Unlike the situation in Kleinman v. Betty Dain Creations, Inc., 2 Cir., 189 F.2d 546, 548, this dependent cause of action does not 'sound primarily in contract.'" The difference between the two cases as we read them is that the duty in one rested on a contract based on a consensual undertaking, while the duty in the other depended on a contract implied in law because the relations between the parties were such that it would be unjust for the recipient of the information to use it to the detriment of the person who imparted it. Why this difference in the nature of the obligation should be important in determining whether the violator of the obligation has engaged in "unfair competition" within the meaning of section 1338(b) is not

5. This claim is plainly within the court's jurisdiction by virtue of 28 U.S.C.A. § 1338(a), as Judge Brennan held in 97 F.Supp. 355.

expounded in the Schreyer case, and is not apparent to the court as now constituted. Whether the obligation is a fictional contract implied in law or a consensual contract not to use confidential information to invade the plaintiff's market of a patented device to which the information related, the wrong done is the same, and the claim asserting it would seem as truly a "claim of unfair competition" in the one case as the other. In our opinion the Betty Dain case was in substance overruled by the Schreyer decision, since the attempted distinction between them cannot logically be supported. We follow the later case and hold that the district court had dependent jurisdiction of both non-patent claims.

The district court also rested dismissal of the non-patent claims on the exercise of his discretion, if he had power to exercise discretion. This brings us to the question whether discretion was abused in not retaining jurisdiction of these claims. The appellants concede that in actions for declaratory judgment the court has wide discretion in refusing to exercise jurisdiction where another adequate remedy is available. The reasons which moved the court to exercise discretion in favor of the state court action are stated in his opinion. The primary reason appears to be the priority in point of time of Parissi's state court action. As this court recognized in Hammett v. Warner Bros. Pictures, 2 Cir., 176 F.2d 145, 150, the determination of priorities between pending cases on the basis of dates of filing is not to be applied in a mechanical way regardless of other considerations. See also Kerotest Mfg. Co. v. C-O-Two Fire Equipment Co., 342 U.S. 180, 72 S.Ct. 219. The state court cannot deal with Parissi's patent claim; the federal court can dispose of that as well as the non-patent claims. In other words, it can terminate the litigation completely. The case had been on trial for 16 days before the court rendered its decision granting the motion to dismiss the non-patent claims. The evidence is not before us but the appellants' brief states that "Proofs covering every aspect of the confidential disclosure case had been presented by the appellants and to the extent that Parissi wished, by him." Under the circumstances it would seem to conserve judicial effort and save expense to the parties to dispose of the entire controversy in the federal court rather than to send the non-patent claims to the state court where the same evidence would have to be again presented.

Accordingly the order is reversed and the cause remanded for further proceedings.

KEROTEST MFG. CO. v. C-O-TWO FIRE EQUIPMENT CO.

Supreme Court of the United States, 1952.
342 U.S. 180, 72 S.Ct. 219, 96 L.Ed. 200.

MR. JUSTICE FRANKFURTER delivered the opinion of the Court.

The C-O-Two Fire Equipment Company, the respondent here, owns two patents, one issued on November 23, 1948, and the other reissued on August 23, 1949, for squeeze-grip valves and discharge heads for portable fire extinguishers. C–O–Two, incorporated in Delaware, has offices in Newark, New Jersey. On January 17, 1950, it commenced in the District Court for the Northern District of Illinois an action against the Acme Equipment Company for "making and causing to be made and selling and using" devices which were charged with infringing C–O–Two's patents.

On March 9, 1950, the petitioner Kerotest began in the District Court of Delaware this proceeding against C–O–Two for a declaration that the two patents sued on in the Illinois action are invalid and that the devices which Kerotest manufactures and supplies to Acme, the Illinois defendant, do not infringe the C–O–Two patents. Kerotest, a Pennsylvania corporation, has its offices in Pittsburgh, but was subject to service of process in Illinois. C–O–Two on March 22, 1950, filed an amendment to its complaint joining Kerotest as a defendant in the Illinois action.

In Delaware, C–O–Two moved for a stay of the declaratory judgment action and Kerotest sought to enjoin C–O–Two from prosecuting the Illinois suit "either as against Kerotest alone, or generally, as [the Delaware District Court might] deem just and proper." The District Court stayed the Delaware proceeding and refused to enjoin that in Illinois, subject to reexamination of the questions after 90 days. 85 USPQ 185. On appeal by Kerotest, the Court of Appeals for the Third Circuit affirmed, holding that the District Court had not abused its discretion in staying the Delaware action for 90 days to permit it to get "more information concerning the controverted status of Kerotest in the Illinois suit." 182 F.2d 773, 775.

During the 90–day period the Illinois District Court allowed the joinder of Kerotest as a defendant, denying a motion by Acme to stay the Illinois proceeding pending disposition of the Delaware suit, and Kerotest made a general appearance. After 90 days both parties renewed their motions in Delaware, with Kerotest this time asking that C–O–Two be enjoined from prosecuting the Illinois suit only as to Kerotest. The District Court, a different judge sitting, enjoined C–O–Two from proceeding in the Illinois suit against Kerotest, and denied the stay of the Delaware action, largely acting on the assumption that rulings by its own and other Courts of Appeals required such a result except in "exceptional cases," since the Delaware action between C–O–Two and Kerotest was commenced before Kerotest was made a defendant in the Illinois suit. 92 F.Supp. 943. On appeal, the Court of Appeals for the Third Circuit reversed, saying in part:

"* * * the whole of the war and all the parties to it are in the Chicago theatre and there only can it be fought to a finish as the litigations are now cast. On the other hand if the battle is waged in the Delaware arena there is a strong probability that the Chicago suit nonetheless would have to be proceeded with for Acme is not and cannot be made a party to the Delaware litigation. The Chicago suit when adjudicated will bind all the parties in both cases. Why should there be two litigations where one will suffice? We can find no adequate reason. We assume, of course, that there will be prompt action in the Chicago theatre." 88 USPQ 335, 337.

A petition for rehearing was granted and the Court of Appeals, the seven circuit judges sitting *en banc,* in an expanded opinion from which two judges dissented, adhered to the views of the court of three judges. 189 F.2d 31, 89 USPQ 411. Inasmuch as a question of importance to the conduct of multiple litigation in the federal judicial system was involved, we granted certiorari. 342 U.S. 810, 72 S.Ct. 48.

The Federal Declaratory Judgments Act,[1] facilitating as it does the initiation of litigation by different parties to many-sided transactions, has created complicated problems for coordinate courts. Wise judicial administration, giving regard to conservation of judicial resources and comprehensive disposition of litigation, does not counsel rigid mechanical solution of such problems. The factors relevant to wise administration here are equitable in nature. Necessarily, an ample degree of discretion, appropriate for disciplined and experienced judges, must be left to the lower courts. The conclusion which we are asked to upset derives from an extended and careful study of the circumstances of this litigation. Such an estimate has led the Court of Appeals twice to conclude that all interest will be best served by prosecution of the single suit in Illinois. Even if we had more doubts than we do about the analysis made by the Court of Appeals, we would not feel justified in displacing its judgment with ours.

It was strongly pressed upon us that the result below may encourage owners of weak patents to avoid real tests of their patents' validity by successive suits against customers in forums inconvenient for the manufacturers, or selected because of greater hospitality to patents. Such apprehension implies a lack of discipline and of disinterestedness on the part of the lower courts, hardly a worthy or wise basis for fashioning rules of procedure. It reflects an attitude against which we were warned by Mr. Justice Holmes, speaking for the whole Court, likewise in regard to a question of procedure: "Universal distrust creates universal incompetence." Graham v. United States, 231 U.S. 474, 480, 34 S.Ct. 148, 151, 58 L.Ed. 319. If in a rare instance a district judge abuses the discretionary authority the want of which precludes an effective, independent judiciary, there is always the opportunity for corrective review by a Court of Appeals and ultimately by this Court.

The manufacturer who is charged with infringing a patent cannot stretch the Federal Declaratory Judgments Act to give him a paramount right to choose the forum for trying out questions of infringement and validity. He is given an equal start in the race to the courthouse, not a headstart. If he is forehanded, subsequent suits against him by the patentee can within the trial court's discretion be

[1]. 48 Stat. 955, 28 U.S.C.A. §§ 2201–2202.

enjoined pending determination of the declaratory judgment suit, and a judgment in his favor bars suits against his customers.[5] If he is anticipated, the court's discretion is broad enough to protect him from harassment of his customers. If the patentee's suit against a customer is brought in a district where the manufacturer cannot be joined as a defendant, the manufacturer may be permitted simultaneously to prosecute a declaratory action against the patentee elsewhere. And if the manufacturer is joined as an unwilling defendant in a *forum non conveniens,* he has available upon an appropriate showing the relief provided by § 1404(a) of the Judicial Code. 62 Stat. 869, 937, 28 U.S. C.A. § 1404(a).

The judgment below must be

Affirmed.

The CHIEF JUSTICE and MR. JUSTICE BLACK dissent.

Note

Codex Corp. v. Milgro Electronic Corp., 553 F.2d 735, 737–8 (1st Cir. 1977). While the first-filed rule may ordinarily be a prudent one, it is so only because it is sometimes more important that there be a rule than that the rule be particularly sound. Accordingly, an exception to the first-filed rule has developed in patent litigation where the earlier action is an infringement suit against a mere customer and the later suit is a declaratory judgment action brought by the manufacturer of the accused devices * * *. At the root of the preference for a manufacturer's declaratory judgment action is the recognition that, in reality, the manufacturer is the true defendant in the customer suit. In spite of (patentee's) vigorous protests to the contrary, it is a simple fact of life that a manufacturer must protect its customers, either as a matter of contract, or good business, or in order to avoid the damaging impact of an adverse ruling against its products.

* * *

[I]t seems to us only too clear that the district court's decision effectively compels [the manufacturer] to renounce its right not to be sued in a forum where it could not have been sued for infringement [under] 28 USC 1400(b) * * *

Venue rights, contrary, perhaps, to the view of the district court, which did not mention them at all, are important, particularly in patent litigation * * * In these circumstances, while we do not say that there should be an inflexible rule, we would recognize a rebuttable presumption that a manufacturer's declaratory judgment action, in its home form, at least if brought no later than promptly after a customer action, should take precedence over a mere customer action in a jurisdiction in which the manufacturer could not have been sued.

  5. Kessler v. Eldred, 206 U.S. 285, 27 S.Ct. 611, 51 L.Ed. 1065.

KORATRON CO. v. DEERING MILLIKEN, INC.

United States Court of Appeals, Ninth Circuit, 1969.
418 F.2d 1314, 164 USPQ 6, cert. denied 398 U.S. 909, 90 S.Ct. 1692,
26 L.Ed.2d 68 (1970).

HUFSTEDLER, CIRCUIT JUDGE.   Pursuant to leave granted by this court (28 U.S.C.A. § 1292(b)), appellant Deering Milliken, Inc. ("Milliken"), appeals from an interlocutory order of the District Court for the Northern District of California denying Milliken's motions to dismiss, to transfer, or to stay the action filed against it by Koratron Company, Inc. ("Koratron").

Milliken contends that venue was improperly laid because the gravamen of Koratron's action is patent infringement for which an action may be brought only "in the judicial district where the defendant resides, or where the defendant has committed acts of infringement and has a regular and established place of business" 28 U.S.C.A. § 1400(b) and that the Northern District of California, in which the suit was brought, is not such a district. Koratron replies that its suit is not one for patent infringement, or even an action arising under the patent laws; rather, it is an action founded on a common law tort, and federal jurisdiction rests solely upon diversity of citizenship. Alternatively, Koratron argues that even if the suit is for patent infringement, the record supports the laying of venue in the Northern District of California.

Koratron holds two process patents dealing with the manufacture of permanent press garments. It has licensed some 200 garment makers to practice the patents upon payment of royalties. Milliken manufactures fabrics ("Visa," "Milstar," and "Milliset"), which are sold to garment makers who, in turn, may use the fabrics to make permanent press garments.

In its original complaint, Koratron alleged the following controversy between it and Milliken: Milliken claims that by using its Visa, Milstar, and Milliset fabrics a garment manufacturer can in all other respects follow one of the Koratron process patents without falling within the scope of that patent, which claim Koratron denies; Milliken threatens to tell Koratron's licensees that they can avoid paying royalties to Koratron by using Milliken's fabrics, unless Koratron acknowledges in writing that the use of Milliken's fabrics is outside the scope of the patent; Milliken had already advised one or more of Koratron's licensees to that effect; and Milliken's purpose in these actions was to induce the licensees not to pay royalties to Koratron. Koratron prayed for judgment declaring, *inter alia,* that the scope of its patent includes the making of garments from the described Milliken fabrics, that Milliken be enjoined from asserting to the contrary, and that it be awarded compensatory damages for its loss of royalties and $5,000,000 punitive damages.

Thereafter Koratron filed an amendment to its complaint to include an after-acquired improvement patent and to add averments that Milliken also claims "that *non*-licensees of Koratron will escape being guilty of infringement of the patent by using Visa, Milstar or Milliset." (Emphasis added.)

* * *

The central issue is the proper characterization of Koratron's complaint. If it is a "civil action for patent infringement" the narrow venue provisions of section 1400(b) apply; if, on the other hand, the action is either a common law tort claim, triable in the federal courts solely by reason of diversity, or a patent suit, other than an action for infringement, the parties agree that venue is proper in the Northern District of California under the more liberal provisions of section 1391(c). Koratron asserts that its complaint states a good cause of action under California law for interference with contract and for interference with prospective economic advantage. (E.g., Collins v. Vickter Manor, Inc. (1957) 47 Cal.2d 875, 306 P.2d 783; Uptown Enterprises v. Strand (1961) 195 Cal.App.2d 45, 15 Cal.Rptr. 486.) Milliken argues, however, that the substance of Koratron's complaint is contributory infringement under 35 U.S.C.A. § 271(b): "Whoever actively induces infringement of a patent shall be liable as an infringer." Since the substance and not the form of the complaint is controlling, Milliken argues, the suit should be construed as one for patent infringement.

The appeal presents a novel issue, for the parties have cited no case, and we have found none, in which a patent holder has attempted to avoid the venue provisions of section 1400(b) by waiving its action for contributory infringement and proceeding solely under an interference theory.

Judge Kaufman faced a similar problem in Bradford Novelty Co. v. Manheim (S.D.N.Y.1957) 156 F.Supp. 489, but there the plaintiff had pleaded both an infringement action and a common law action for unfair competition. Defendant moved to dismiss for lack of venue and established that the provisions of section 1400(b) were not met. Plaintiff contended, however, that "its action against Eppy for unfair competition is independently founded on diversity of citizenship and is, therefore, properly brought in this district, § 1400 being inapplicable to common law actions for unfair competition." Because venue was proper for one of the causes of action, plaintiff argued, the court can properly hear the related claim of infringement. Judge Kaufman was not convinced:

> "[T]he gravamen of the present complaint is patent infringement; unfair competition, if a separate cause of action at all, being a subsidiary issue dependent on the prior determination of the action for patent infringement. The Supreme Court has gone so far as to conclude that claims of infringement and unfair competition are not separate causes of action at all but are different grounds asserted in support of the

same action. Hurn v. Oursler, 1933, 289 U.S. 238, 247, 53 S.Ct. 586, 77 L.Ed. 1148. Since unfair competition can almost always be charged in a patent infringement action, if plaintiff were to prevail in its argument, it would be a simple matter of pleading for a party to evade the venue limitation imposed by § 1400." (156 F.Supp. at 492.)

* * * The only real difference between the instant case and *Bradford Novelty* is that Koratron has gone one step further than did the plaintiff in *Bradford* by omitting altogether the infringement action from its complaint. Although this is "a simple matter of pleading," we hold that it is sufficient to make section 1400 inapplicable.

Our conclusion is compelled by a line of Supreme Court cases beginning in 1850 with the decision of Wilson v. Sandford, 51 U.S. (10 How.) 99, 13 L.Ed. 344 and culminating in 1926 with Luckett v. Delpark, Inc., 270 U.S. 496, 46 S.Ct. 397, 70 L.Ed. 703. In each of the cases in the line, the central question was jurisdictional: Was the action one "arising under" the patent laws and thus triable exclusively in the federal courts under the statutory predecessor to 28 U.S.C.A. § 1338(a). The Court consistently said "No," despite the fact that in each instance the scope or the validity of a patent, or both, was directly in issue. According to these decisions, characterization of the action as a patent or nonpatent suit within the meaning of section 1338(a) turns on the form in which the plaintiff has chosen to cast his complaint: "[T]he plaintiff is absolute master of what jurisdiction he will appeal to; * * *. Jurisdiction generally depends upon the case made and relief demanded by the plaintiff; * * *." (Healy v. Sea Gull Specialty Co. (1915) 237 U.S. 479, 480, 35 S.Ct. 658, 659, 59 L.Ed. 1056; see also The Fair v. Kohler Die & Specialty Co. (1913) 228 U.S. 22, 25, 33 S.Ct. 410, 57 L.Ed. 716.)

The plaintiffs in *Luckett* and *Wilson,* although adding infringement counts, chose to frame their actions as ones in contract and to seek contract relief primarily. In American Well Works Co. v. Layne & Bowler Co. (1916) 241 U.S. 257, 36 S.Ct. 585, 60 L.Ed. 987, the action sounded in tort, although plaintiff could just as easily have sued for infringement. The plaintiff initiated the action in state court, charging that it had a valid patent on a certain pump, that defendants asserted that plaintiff's patent infringed defendants' pump patent, and that defendants were suing and threatening to sue plaintiff's licensees for infringement. Defendants removed the case to federal court as an action arising under the patent laws. The Supreme Court reversed, holding that the case did not arise under the patent laws. "Of course," said the Court, "the question depends upon plaintiff's declaration." (241 U.S. at 258, 36 S.Ct. 585.) The Court later observed:

"What makes the defendants' act a wrong is its manifest tendency to injure the plaintiff's business; and the wrong is the same whatever the means by which it is accomplished. But whether it is wrong or not depends upon the law of the state where the act is done, not upon the patent law, and therefore the suit arises under the law of the state. A suit arises under the law that creates the cause of action. The fact that the justification may involve the validity and infringement of a patent is no more material to the question under what law the suit is brought than it would be in an action of contract." (241 U.S. at 260, 36 S.Ct. at 586.)

Interference with contract and interference with prospective economic advantage are state causes of action. When the subject matter of the contract interfered with is a patent or the prospective economic advantage relates to a patent, questions of patent law will often arise in the controversy. But that fact does not make the action one arising under the patent laws. (See also Pratt v. Paris Gas Light & Coke Co. (1897) 168 U.S. 255, 259, 18 S.Ct. 62, 42 L.Ed. 458; Lear Siegler, Inc. v. Adkins (9th Cir.1964) 330 F.2d 595, 600.)

Koratron intended to plead its case as a common law action. It strained out all patent infringement language from its pleading. It did not seek treble damages and attorneys' fees available in a patent infringement suit; it sought compensatory and lump sum punitive damages appropriate to a common law claim. The complaint, as amended, stated a cause of action for common law relief. The facts stated also would have sustained a claim for patent infringement had Koratron elected that remedy, but it did not do so, and it cannot be compelled to do so. (See Henry v. A.B. Dick Co. (1912) 224 U.S. 1, 15, 32 S.Ct. 364, 56 L.Ed. 645.)

* * *

We hold that Koratron's action does not arise under the patent laws and *a fortiori* it is not a patent infringement suit subject to the narrow venue provisions of section 1400(b).

The Supreme Court's decisions in Schnell v. Peter Eckrich & Sons, Inc. (1961) 365 U.S. 260, 81 S.Ct. 557, 5 L.Ed.2d 546; Fourco Glass Co. v. Transmirra Prods. Corp. (1957) 353 U.S. 222, and Stonite Prods. Co. v. Melvin Lloyd Co. (1942) 315 U.S. 561, 62 S.Ct. 780, 86 L.Ed. 1026 do not support a contrary result. In each of those cases the claim for relief pleaded was patent infringement, and in each, the Court held that the narrow venue provisions of section 1400(b), or its predecessor statute, applied to the exclusion of the general venue statute. An integral part of the Court's rationale in those cases is that section 1400(b) expresses a federal policy limiting venue in patent infringement cases to prevent infringers from being subjected to suit in districts where the defense of the action would entail an unnecessarily oppressive burden. However strong that policy may be once the action has been characterized as an infringement action, the Court has never applied it to limit the manner in which a plaintiff can plead his cause. The Court's reading of section 1400(b) cannot be wholly reconciled with its reading of the "arising under" clause of section 1338(a) for the effect of the latter often, although not always, is to broaden the number of districts to which a plaintiff has initial access. But so long as the Supreme Court distinguishes the two situations, we are obliged to follow that bifocal vision.

The order denying Milliken's motion is affirmed, and the cause is remanded to the District Court for further proceedings.

Notes

1. "There is a clear distinction between a case and a question arising under the patent laws. The former arises when the plaintiff in his opening pleading—be it a bill, complaint or declaration—sets up a right under the patent laws as ground for a recovery. Of such the state courts have no jurisdiction. The latter may appear in the plea or answer or in the testimony. The determination of such question is not beyond the competency of the state tribunals." Pratt v. Paris Gaslight & Coke Co., 168 U.S. 255, 259, 18 S.Ct. 62, 42 L.Ed. 458 (1897).

2. The venue provision of 28 U.S.C.A. § 1400(b) is the sole determinent in a patent infringement action of proper venue for defendants residing in the United States. It is not to be read together with 28 U.S.C.A. § 1391(c) dealing with venue generally in civil actions against corporations. Fourco Glass Co. v. Transmirra Products Corp., 353 U.S. 222, 77 S.Ct. 787, 1 L.Ed.2d 786 (1957). However, in a patent infringement action against an alien, venue is proper in any district under 28 U.S.C.A. § 1391(d). Brunette Machine Works, Ltd. v. Kockum Indus., Inc., 406 U.S. 706, 92 S.Ct. 1936, 32 L.Ed.2d 428 (1972). Moreover, the general venue provisions of 28 U.S.C.A. § 1391 are applicable in an action for a declaratory judgment of patent invalidity and non-infringement.

3. The venue provision of 28 U.S.C.A. § 1400(b) is not to be read liberally. Grantham v. Challenge-Cook Bros., Inc., 420 F.2d 1182, 164 USPQ 259 (7th Cir.1969); Schroeder v. Owens-Corning Fiberglas Corp., 326 F.Supp. 594, 170 USPQ 62 (D.C.Cal.1971).

3. JURY TRIALS

BEACON THEATRES, INC. v. WESTOVER

Supreme Court of the United States, 1959.
359 U.S. 500, 79 S.Ct. 948, 3 L.Ed.2d 988.

[Excerpt]

This * * * is required by the provision in the Rules that "[t]he right to trial by jury as declared by the Seventh Amendment to the Constitution or as given by a statute of the United States shall be preserved * * * inviolate."

If there should be cases where the availability of declaratory judgment or joinder in one suit of legal and equitable causes would not in all respects protect the plaintiff seeking equitable relief from irreparable harm while affording a jury trial in the legal cause, the trial court will necessarily have to use its discretion in deciding whether the legal or equitable cause should be tried first. Since the right to jury trial is a constitutional one, however, while no similar requirement protects trials by the court, that discretion is very narrowly limited and must, wherever possible, be exercised to preserve jury trial. As this Court said in Scott v. Neely, 140 U.S. 106, 109, 110, 35 L.Ed. 358, 360,

11 S.Ct. 712: "In the Federal courts this [jury] right cannot be dispensed with, except by the assent of the parties entitled to it, nor can it be impaired by any blending with a claim, properly cognizable at law, of a demand for equitable relief in aid of the legal action or during its pendency." This long-standing principle of equity dictates that only under the most imperative circumstances, circumstances which in view of the flexible procedures of the Federal Rules we cannot now anticipate, can the right to a jury trial of legal issues be lost through prior determination of equitable claims. See Leimer v. Woods (C.A.8 Mo.) 196 F.2d 828, 833–836. As we have shown, this is far from being such a case.

KENNEDY v. LAKSO CO., INC.

United States Court of Appeals, Third Circuit, 1969.
414 F.2d 1249, 163 USPQ 136.

FREEDMAN, CIRCUIT JUDGE.

The issue presented is whether trial by jury is available in a suit for patent infringement which seeks both monetary and injunctive relief.

The complaint, filed on November 29, 1967, claims that defendant infringed plaintiffs' patents for article counting and loading machines. The pleadings show that plaintiffs had licensed their patents to defendant from March 27, 1962 until October 5, 1965, when, according to the plaintiffs, the agreement was terminated. The claim is that defendant thereafter made and sold machines similar to those which it had made under the license. Plaintiffs sought the following relief:

(1) An injunction against the infringement;

(2) An "accounting" for "profits" as well as "damages" resulting from the infringement;

(3) Judgment for $200,000 for the infringement "in case the total profits made by the sale of the infringing machines do not aggregate that sum;"

(4) Trebling of the damages for infringement;

(5) Surrender for destruction of the infringing machines; and

(6) Recovery of plaintiffs' costs and attorneys fees.

After the pleadings were in, defendant successfully moved to strike the plaintiffs' demand for jury trial, made in the complaint,[1] on the ground that the action was essentially one in equity and therefore was not triable by jury.

Prior to the Patent Act of 1952 (35 U.S.C.A. §§ 1–293), R.S. § 4919 provided a remedy at law for damages for patent infringement, and R.S.

1. Rule 38(b) of the Federal Rules of Civil Procedure: "Any party may demand a trial by jury of any issue triable of right by a jury by serving upon the other parties a demand therefor in writing at any time after the commencement of the action and not later than 10 days after the service of the last pleading directed to such issue. Such demand may be indorsed upon a pleading of the party."

§ 4921 provided the remedy of injunction. In patent cases under R.S. § 4919 jury trials were held available because of its provision that "Damages for the infringement of any patent may be recovered by action on the case ＊ ＊ ＊." The basis of the decisions was that the statutory authorization of an action on the case established a common law remedy which fell within the Seventh Amendment provision that "In Suits at common law, where the value in controversy shall exceed twenty dollars, the right of trial by jury shall be preserved ＊ ＊ ＊." It also came to be settled that where suit was brought for equitable relief under R.S. § 4921 there was no right to a jury trial even though damages were also sought for past infringement. The basis for this was the well-established doctrine that once equity assumed jurisdiction it would round out the entire controversy and grant full relief.

The merger of actions at law and in equity in a single "civil action" under Rule 2 of the Federal Rules of Civil Procedure did not obliterate the distinction between them in determining the right to jury trial. Rule 38(a) preserves inviolate the right to trial by jury "as declared by the Seventh Amendment to the Constitution or as given by a statute of the United States," and Rule 38(b) provides that any "party may demand a trial by jury of any issue triable of right by a jury. ＊ ＊ ＊"

The rules did not alter the principle that a civil action in the nature of an action at law was triable by jury and one in the nature of an action in equity was not triable by jury. This view of the draftsmen was recognized shortly after the rules went into effect in Bellavance v. Plastic-Craft Novelty Co., 30 F.Supp. 37 (D.D.Mass.1939). The court there held that the rules did not change the prior law and that the plaintiff, who sought injunctive relief under R.S. § 4921, was not entitled as of right to a jury trial.

It is in this state of the law that the Patent Act of 1952 was adopted. Various sections of the new Act incorporated the provisions of R.S. § 4919 and § 4921. Section 281 provides a remedy for infringement by civil action, § 283 authorizes injunctions and § 284 provides for recovery of damages. In providing for the recovery of damages for infringement, § 284 goes on to declare: "When the damages are not found by a jury, the court shall assess them. In that event the court may increase the damages up to three times the amount found or assessed." It is clear from this language alone that the draftsmen of the Patent Act of 1952 contemplated that damages would in some cases be determined by a jury. The use of the term "civil action" in § 281 was taken from the Federal Rules of Civil Procedure and used in place of the similar description in § 4919 of an action on the case with the studied understanding by the draftsmen that this would continue the right to jury trial where no equitable relief was sought.

We therefore must reject defendant's contention that § 281 of the Patent Act of 1952 expressed an intention to overthrow the well-settled principle that jury trials are available in actions for damages for infringement, simply because it does not reiterate the language of R.S. § 4919 which described such proceeding as an action on the case.

The recognition of the existence of the right to trial by jury in patent infringement actions for damages leaves the significant question whether a jury trial still must be denied if the plaintiff also seeks equitable relief. Since the Patent Act of 1952 was adopted the Supreme Court has given far-reaching recognition and encouragement to the right of jury trial in Beacon Theatres, Inc. v. Westover, 359 U.S. 500, 79 S.Ct. 948, 3 L.Ed.2d 988 (1959), Dairy Queen, Inc. v. Wood, 369 U.S. 469, 82 S.Ct. 894, 8 L.Ed.2d 44 (1962), and Fitzgerald v. United States Lines, 374 U.S. 16, 83 S.Ct. 1646, 10 L.Ed.2d 720 (1963). In *Beacon Theatres* and *Dairy Queen* the Supreme Court held that even in a case which in form is equitable the right to a trial by jury must be recognized as to those issues which traditionally are triable at law by a jury.

As a result of the decisions, the doctrine that an action which seeks both damages and equitable relief is predominately equitable and therefore may not be tried by a jury, has been reversed. In *Dairy Queen* Mr. Justice Black said: "The holding in *Beacon Theatres* was that where both legal and equitable issues are presented in a single case, 'only under the most imperative circumstances, circumstances which in view of the flexible procedures of the Federal Rules we cannot now anticipate, can the right to a jury trial of legal issues be lost through prior determination of equitable claims.' That holding, of course, applies whether the trial judge chooses to characterize the legal issues presented as 'incidental' to equitable issues or not." 369 U.S. at 472–473, 82 S.Ct. at 897. The Supreme Court carried forward this view in *Fitzgerald*, where it was held error to refuse plaintiff a jury trial of his claim for maintenance and cure coincident with a jury trial of his claims under the Jones Act for negligence and under maritime law for unseaworthiness. The Court based its decision on the fundamental factors of simplicity, utility to litigants and the interest of justice in having one tribunal decide the three claims which in general arise from a unitary set of circumstances. Since Congress has recognized the right to jury trial in the Jones Act negligence claim the Court declared that the jury must also be permitted to try the claims for maintenance and cure and for unseaworthiness.

The rule under these decisions has been applied to patent infringement cases and where there are issues which ordinarily would be triable at law before a jury the right to jury trial is not lost because equitable relief also is sought.

It follows that no distinction can be drawn which would justify recognition of the right to jury trial for "damages" and its denial in a claim for "profits" on the theory that "damages" are recoverable in an action at law whereas "profits" have their origin in equitable principles which hold the infringer a trust for the patent holder. For whether the patentee's recovery is based upon "damages"—the loss to him, or upon "profits"—the unjust enrichment of the infringer, the underlying issue remains essentially the same—infringement. It is similarly indecisive whether plaintiff affixes the label of "accounting" to the remedy he seeks. For the plaintiff must always establish the amount which he is entitled to recover. While it is true that equity traditionally has had jurisdiction in actions for an accounting, it has always been recognized that there may be a suit for accounting at law and indeed the essential ingredient of equity's jurisdiction has been the complicated nature of the accounting. The claim for an accounting, therefore, does not, on its face, destroy the right to a jury trial now that it is recognized to exist in cases where the court itself may also fashion equitable relief.

There is nothing on the present record to indicate that the accounting between the parties in the determination of profits or damages will be so complicated as to be beyond the power of a jury to determine. Indeed, the decision of the District Court was based not upon any complication in accounting, or even on any supposed difficulty in a jury's determination of validity or infringement. It was founded, rather, on the view that since plaintiffs demanded equitable relief the action could not be heard by a jury.

We hold that on the record before us plaintiff is entitled to have a jury decide the factual issue in the case.

The claims for treble damages and for counsel fees are outside the range of the right to jury trial. We made clear in Randolph Laboratories, Inc. v. Specialties Development Corp., 213 F.2d 873, 875 (3 Cir.), cert. denied 348 U.S. 861, 75 S.Ct. 91, 99 L.Ed. 678 (1954), that even though damages are found by a jury, their "increase * * * up to three times the amount found" (Patent Act of 1952, § 284) is for the court and not for the jury, as is also the question of counsel fees.

The order of the District Court striking off plaintiffs' demand for jury trial will be reversed and the case remanded for further proceedings in accordance with this opinion.

Notes

1. On the use of detailed special interrogatories when submitting mixed questions of law and fact to a jury, such as the issues of obviousness under 35 USC 103 and inequitable conduct during prosecution before the Patent Office, see Connell v. Sears, Roebuck & Co., 722 F.2d 1542, 220 USPQ 193 (Fed.Cir.1983) and American Hoist & Derrick Co. v. Sowa & Sons, Inc., 725 F.2d 1350, 220 USPQ 763 (Fed.Cir.1984). As stated in Connell at 1547, 220 USPQ at 197:

"So long as the Seventh Amendment stands, the right to a jury trial should not be rationed, nor should particular issues in particular types of cases be treated differently from similar issues in other types of cases. Scholarly disputes over use of jury trials in technically complex cases relate to the right to trial by jury itself, and center on whether lay juries are capable of making correct fact determinations, not over the propriety of submitting legal questions to juries. The obviousness issue may be in some cases complex and complicated, on both fact and law, but no more so than equally complicated, even technological, issues in product liability, medical injury, antitrust, and similar cases. Indeed, though the analogy like most is not perfect, the role of the jury in determining obviousness is not unlike its role in reaching a legal conclusion respecting negligence, putting itself in the shoes of one "skilled in the art" at the time the invention was made in the former and in the shoes of a "reasonable person" at the time of the events giving rise to the suit in the latter.

"When a jury merely reports a general verdict for one of the parties, as above indicated, the decision on a motion for JNOV or on direct appeal requires assumptions respecting its consideration of the evidence. Submission of the obviousness question to the jury should therefore be accompanied by detailed special interrogatories designed to elicit responses to at least all the factual inquiries enumerated in Graham, supra, and based on the presentations made in the particular trial."

2. "This case is an excellent illustration of the wisdom of this court's observation that "members of the Patent Bar have wisely avoided jury trials in patent litigation." A persuasive clue as to the jury's misunderstanding of what was involved in this case is provided by the fact that it found infringement by a chair which everyone agrees did not infringe. Perhaps the statement of this court quoted above should be modified to include an exception for those members of the Patent Bar who recognize a weakness in their position on the issue of obviousness and who might be aided by possible confusion on the part of a jury." Dual Mfg. & Engineering, Inc. v. Burris Indus., Inc., 202 USPQ 708, 712 (7th Cir.1979).

4. APPEALS

28 U.S.C.A. § 1295. Jurisdiction of the United States Court of Appeals for the Federal Circuit

(a) The United States Court of Appeals for the Federal Circuit shall have exclusive jurisdiction—

(1) of an appeal from a final decision of a district court of the United States, the United States District Court for the District of the Canal Zone, the District Court of Guam, the District Court of the Virgin Islands, or the District Court for the Northern Mariana Islands, if the jurisdiction of that court was based, in whole or in part, on section 1338 of this title, except that a case involving a claim arising under any Act of Congress relating to copyrights or trademarks and no other claims under section 1338(a) shall be governed by sections 1291, 1292, and 1294 of this title;

* * *

(3) of an appeal from a final decision of the United States Claims Court;

(4) of an appeal from a decision of—

(A) the Board of Patent Appeals and Interferences of the Patent and Trademark Office with respect to patent applications and interferences, at the instance of an applicant for a patent or any party to a patent interference, and any such appeal shall waive the right of such applicant or party to proceed under section 145 or 146 of title 35;

(B) the Commissioner of Patents and Trademarks or the Trademark Trial and Appeal Board with respect to applications for registration of marks and other proceedings as provided in section 21 of the Trademark Act of 1946 (15 U.S.C. 1071); or

(C) a district court to which a case was directed pursuant to section 145 or 146 of title 35;

(5) of an appeal from a final decision of the United States Court of International Trade;

(6) to review the final determinations of the United States International Trade Commission relating to unfair practices in import trade, made under section 337 of the Tariff Act of 1930 (19 U.S.C. 1337);

* * *

(8) of an appeal under section 71 of the Plant Variety Protection Act (7 U.S.C. 2461);

* * *

28 U.S.C.A. § 1292. Interlocutory Decisions

(c) The United States Court of Appeals for the Federal Circuit shall have exclusive jurisdiction—

(1) of an appeal from an interlocutory order or decree described in subsection (a) or (b) of this section in any case over which the court would have jurisdiction of an appeal under section 1295 of this title; and

(2) of an appeal from a judgment in a civil action for patent infringement which would otherwise be appealable to the United States Court of Appeals for the Federal Circuit and is final except for an accounting.

PANDUIT CORP. v. ALL STATES PLASTIC MANUFACTURING CO., INC.

United States Court of Appeals, Federal Circuit, 1984.
744 F.2d 1564, 223 USPQ 465.

PER CURIAM.

This is an appeal from an order of the United States District Court for the Northern District of Illinois (No. 76 C 4012), entered by Judge Grady on September 16, 1983. The district court disqualified Robert Conte and the firm of Laff, Whitesel, Conte & Saret (the "Laff Firm") from representing appellant, All States Plastic Manufacturing Co., Inc. ("All States"). We reverse-in-part, vacate-in-part, and remand.

* * *

ISSUES

1. Whether or not this court has jurisdiction to review the disqualification order?

2. Which law to apply in this case?

3. Whether or not the district court erred in disqualifying Robert Conte and the Laff Firm from further representation of All States?

OPINION

I

JURISDICTION

As a threshold matter, Panduit argues that the district court's order is not appealable under 28 U.S.C. § 1295(a)(1) (1982). It asserts, citing the recent case of *Flanagan v. United States,* 465 U.S. 259, 104 S.Ct. 1051, 79 L.Ed.2d 288 (1984), that a pre-trial grant of a motion to disqualify counsel is interlocutory and is, therefore, not an immediately appealable final decision. We disagree.

* * *

The Court of Customs and Patent Appeals, one of our predecessor courts, has ruled that a grant of a motion to disqualify counsel is an immediately appealable decision. *Ah Ju Steel Co. v. Armco, Inc.,* 680 F.2d 751, 753 (CCPA 1982). This result has also been reached in the Seventh Circuit. *See Freeman, supra.* Accordingly, the order disqualifying counsel before us in this case is immediately appealable.

II

CHOICE OF LAW

After considering the jurisdictional question, we must then decide the choice of law question. In our recent opinion of *Litton Systems, Inc. v. Whirlpool Corp.,* 728 F.2d 1423, 1445, 221 USPQ 97, 110–11 (Fed.Cir. 1984), we noted, *sua sponte,* the choice of law question in relation to pendent matters, but found it unnecessary to decide that question.[9] In the instant appeal, we again note, and decide, the choice of law question in relation to procedural matters that do not pertain to the patent issues.

As stated in 28 U.S.C. § 1295(a), this court has *exclusive* jurisdiction of, *inter alia,*

> an appeal from a final decision of a district court if the jurisdiction of that court was based, in whole or in part, on section 1338 of this title

* * *.

Since our jurisdiction to review a district court's decision is predicated on the presence of a bona fide patent claim in that action, we, naturally, have the exclusive jurisdiction to review any other matters which were tried below. One of such other matters is disqualification of counsel.

---

9. This court has jurisdiction over pendent matters when they are attached to a patent claim pursuant to 28 U.S.C. §§ 1295(a) and 1338. Pendent matter jurisdiction in the Federal Circuit encompasses both: (1) the traditional pendent state matters, *United Mine Workers v. Gibbs,* 383 U.S. 715, 86 S.Ct. 1130, 16 L.Ed. 2d 218 (1966), *see* n. 19, *infra;* and (2) pendent federal matters such as copyright or trademark claims under section 1338, or antitrust claims. *Walker Process Equip., Inc. v. Food Mach. & Chem. Corp.,* 382 U.S. 172, 86 S.Ct. 347, 15 L.Ed.2d 247 (1965) (Sherman Act); *Hughes v. Novi American, Inc.,* 724 F.2d 122, 220 USPQ 707 (Fed.Cir. 1984) (Copyright Act); *Litton, supra* (Trademark Act); and *American Hoist & Derrick Co. v. Sowa & Sons,* 725 F.2d 1350, 220 USPQ 763 (Fed.Cir.1984) (Sherman Act).

We recognize, as did Congress, the unique jurisdictional grant of this court—specific, nationwide subject matter jurisdiction. This jurisdictional grant, however, places practitioners and district courts in a unique posture: they are accountable to two different courts of appeals. Such a posture raises questions relating to *stare decisis* and certainty in the law. *See generally* 1B *Moore's Federal Practice* ¶ 0.402[1]. Since a district court is bound by the law of its circuit, *see Hasbrouck v. Texaco, Inc.*, 663 F.2d 930, 933 (9th Cir.), *cert. denied*, 459 U.S. 828, 103 S.Ct. 63, 74 L.Ed.2d 65 (1982), a district court exercising jurisdiction pursuant to 28 U.S.C. § 1338 is bound by the substantive patent law of this circuit. The requirement to obey the law of its circuit causes practitioners and district judges, in general, to follow the substantive patent law as set forth by this court in "patent" cases and to follow the "general" laws as set forth by their regional circuit court in non-patent cases. That requirement, however, is the result that Congress sought to achieve in creating the Federal Circuit.

Such obedience, however, creates a problem that was possibly unforeseen by Congress. That problem is which law must a district court apply in matters that are procedural in nature such as the attorney disqualification question in the instant case. In a case where this court does not have appellate jurisdiction, the district court would be deciding that question in light of the law of its regional circuit court. Since we have jurisdiction to review all matters in a case that is appealable to us, the district court would then be obligated to decide that question in light of our precedents. Such bifurcated decisionmaking is not only contrary to the spirit of our enabling legislation but also the goal of the federal judicial system to minimize confusion and conflicts.

Since our enabling statute fails to enunciate any guidance for this question, an analysis of the legislative history must be made. *United States v. John C. Grimberg Co.*, 702 F.2d 1362 (Fed.Cir.1983) (in banc).

The purpose of this court's enabling act, the Federal Courts Improvement Act of 1982 (the "FCIA"), Pub.L. 97–164, 96 Stat. 25, is to provide:

> [A] forum that will increase doctrinal stability in the field of patent law. Based on the evidence it had compiled, the Hruska Commission singled out patent law as an area in which the application of the law to the facts of a case often produces different outcomes in different courtrooms in substantially similar cases. Furthermore, in a Commission survey of practitioners, the patent bar indicated that uncertainty created by the lack of national law precedent was a significant problem * * *.
>
> *   *   *   *   *   *   *   *   *
>
> The testimony received by the committee also supported the basic objective of providing for uniformity of doctrinal development in the patent area. * * *
>
> *   *   *   *   *   *   *   *   *

The creation of the Court of Appeals for the Federal Circuit will produce desirable uniformity in this area of the law.

S.Rep. 97–275, 97th Cong., 1st Sess. 5, *reprinted in* 1982 U.S.Code Cong. & Ad.News 11, 15.

It is, therefore, clear that one of the primary objectives of our enabling legislation is to bring about uniformity in the area of patent law. "[T]he central purpose [of the FCIA] is to reduce the widespread lack of uniformity and uncertainty of legal doctrine that exist in the administration of patent law." H.R.Rep. 97–312, 97th Cong., 1st Sess. 23. This court was created, as contemplated by the Congress, to achieve uniformity and to reduce uncertainties in this area. This court, thus, has a mandate to achieve uniformity in patent matters.

The fundamental underpinning for uniformity was Congress' abhorrence of conflicts and confusion in the judicial system. That was the underlying motivation for the creation of this court, and it must remain the spirit and guiding principle of this court. We must, therefore, be cognizant of the guidance provided by the legislative history and the underlying Congressional motivation as we resolve the choice of law question.

In addition to the guidance provided by the legislative history, we must resolve this choice of law question by considering the general policy of minimizing confusion and conflicts in the federal judicial system. Where, as here, a procedural question [12] that is independent of the patent issues is in dispute, practitioners within the jurisdiction of a particular regional circuit court should not be required to practice law and to counsel clients in light of two different sets of law for an identical issue due to the different routes of appeal. An equal, if not more important, consideration is that district judges also should not be required to decide cases in this fashion. For instance, practitioners and district judges in the Seventh Circuit should not be saddled with two different sets of requirements regarding attorney disqualification, one for cases appealed to the Seventh Circuit and one for cases appealed to this court. The possibility of different requirements should be minimized especially where a dispute is totally unrelated to patent issues and the resolution of that dispute does not impinge on the goal of patent law uniformity. The standard for attorney disqualification, relating to a district court's power to supervise and to conduct local operating procedure, should not be different just because the reviewing path on such matter is different.

We, therefore, rule, as a matter of policy, that the Federal Circuit shall review procedural matters, that are not unique to patent issues,

---

12. Procedure is defined as "the judicial process for enforcing rights and duties recognized by substantive law and for justly administering remedy and redress for disregard or infraction of them." *Sibbach v. Wilson & Co.,* 312 U.S. 1, 14, 61 S.Ct. 422, 426, 85 L.Ed. 479 (1941). Whereas the "substantive law relates to rights and duties which give rise to a cause of action," procedure is defined as either "the machinery for carrying on the suit" or "the modes of conduct of litigation and judicial business." *Jones v. Erie R.R. Co.,* 106 Ohio St. 408, 412–13, 140 N.E. 366, 368 (1922).

under the law of the particular regional circuit court where appeals from the district court would normally lie.[14] This policy is within the intent and spirit of not only our enabling statute but also the general desire of the federal judicial system to minimize confusion and conflicts. Since our mandate is to eliminate conflicts and uncertainties in the area of patent law, we must not, in doing so, create unnecessary conflicts and confusion in procedural matters.

* * *

This policy, however, does not preclude this court from following existing or creating new law regarding any and all matters in cases where this court has *exclusive* jurisdiction over *all appeals* from a particular court. *See* 28 U.S.C. §§ 1295(a)(3) and 1295(a)(5) (1982). For example, the attorney disqualification standard enunciated in the *Ah Ju Steel* case is applicable for this court as well as the Court of International Trade and the Claims Court. We may, in future cases, alter or extend the *Ah Ju Steel* standard irrespective of our views in this case or other cases if they are from forums within our exclusive jurisdiction over all appeals from a particular court. The viewpoints regarding attorney disqualification that we take in the instant case do not preclude us from taking a contrary viewpoint when deciding the identical issue in a case where we have exclusive jurisdiction over all appeals from a particular court.

When we review procedural matters that do not pertain to patent issues, we sit as if we were the particular regional circuit court where appeals from the district court we are reviewing would normally lie. We would adjudicate the rights of the parties in accordance with the applicable regional circuit law. * * *

Notes

1. In its first decision, the CAFC adopted the decisions of its predecessor courts, the United States Court of Customs and Patent Appeals and United States Court of Claims, as binding precedent. South Corp. v. United States, 690 F.2d 1368, 215 USPQ 657 (Fed.Cir.1982).

2. The CAFC has exclusive appellate jurisdiction from a district court whose jurisdiction was based in part on 28 U.S.C.A. § 1338(b), even when the appeal itself involves no patent issue. Atari, Inc. v. JS & A Group, Inc., 747 F.2d 1422, 223 USPQ 1074 (Fed.Cir.1984) (preliminary injunction against copyright infringement).

3. In Wyden v. Commissioner of Patents and Trademarks, 807 F.2d 934, 231 USPQ 918 (Fed.Cir.1986), the CAFC affirmed its jurisdiction in an appeal from a district court review under 35 U.S.C.A. § 32 of refusal to

---

14. This policy is not inconsistent with our prior decisions in which procedural matters that do pertain to patent issues, such as whether proof of non-experimental use is necessary to establish a prima facie defense of an on-sale bar, must conform to Federal Circuit law. *See Barmag Barmer Maschinenfabrik v. Murata Machinery Ltd.*, 731 F.2d 831, 839, 221 USPQ 561, 567–68 (Fed.Cir.1984). Since those procedural matters are related to patent issues, they have a direct bearing on the outcome of those determinations.

register Wyden to practice before the Office. In dissent, Chief Judge Markey characterized the court's apparent assertion of jurisdiction in any case "relating to patents" as "an illegitimate exercise of raw judicial power."

B. INJUNCTIONS, DAMAGES AND COSTS

1. STATUTORY PROVISIONS

35 U.S.C.A. § 281. Remedy for Infringement of Patent

A patentee shall have remedy by civil action for infringement of his patent.

35 U.S.C.A. § 100. Definitions

When used in this title unless the context otherwise indicates—

(d) The word "patentee" includes not only the patentee to whom the patent was issued but also the successors in title to the patentee.

35 U.S.C.A. § 283. Injunction

The several courts having jurisdiction of cases under this title may grant injunctions in accordance with the principles of equity to prevent the violation of any right secured by patent, on such terms as the court deems reasonable.

35 U.S.C.A. § 284. Damages

Upon finding for the claimant the court shall award the claimant damages adequate to compensate for the infringement but in no event less than a reasonable royalty for the use made of the invention by the infringer, together with interest and costs as fixed by the court.

When the damages are not found by a jury, the court shall assess them. In either event the court may increase the damages up to three times the amount found or assessed.

The court may receive expert testimony as an aid to the determination of damages or of what royalty would be reasonable under the circumstances.

35 U.S.C.A. § 285. Attorney Fees

The court in exceptional cases may award reasonable attorney fees to the prevailing party.

35 U.S.C.A. § 286. Time Limitation on Damages

Except as otherwise provided by law, no recovery shall be had for any infringement committed more than six years prior to the filing of the complaint or counterclaim for infringement in the action.

In the case of claims against the United States Government for use of a patented invention, the period before bringing suit, up to six years, between the date of receipt of a written claim for compensation by the department or agency of the Government having authority to settle such claim, and the date of mailing by the Government of a notice to the claimant that his claim has been denied shall not be counted as part of the period referred to in the preceding paragraph.

35 U.S.C.A. § 287. Limitation on Damages; Marking and Notice

Patentees, and persons making or selling any patented article for or under them, may give notice to the public that the same is patented, either by fixing thereon the word "patent" or the abbreviation "pat.", together with the number of the patent, or when, from the character of the article, this can not be done, by fixing to it, or to the package wherein one or more of them is contained, a label containing a like notice. In the event of failure so to mark, no damages shall be recovered by the patentee in any action for infringement, except on proof that the infringer was notified of the infringement and continued to infringe thereafter, in which event damages may be recovered only for infringement occurring after such notice. Filing of an action for infringement shall constitute such notice.

35 U.S.C.A. § 288. Action for Infringement of a Patent Containing an Invalid Claim

Whenever, without deceptive intention, a claim of a patent is invalid, an action may be maintained for the infringement of a claim of the patent which may be valid. The patentee shall recover no costs unless a disclaimer of the invalid claim has been entered at the Patent and Trademark Office before commencement of the suit.

35 U.S.C.A. § 289. Additional Remedy for Infringement of Design Patent

Whoever during the term of a patent for a design, without license of the owner, (1) applies the patented design, or any colorable imitation thereof, to any article of manufacture for the purpose of sale, or (2) sells or exposes for sale any article of manufacture to which such design or colorable imitation has been applied shall be liable to the owner to the extent of his total profit, but not less than $250, recoverable in any United States district court having jurisdiction of the parties.

Nothing in this section shall prevent, lessen, or impeach any other remedy which an owner of an infringed patent has under the provisions of this title, but he shall not twice recover the profit made from the infringement.

2. INJUNCTIONS

SMITH INTERNATIONAL, INC. v. HUGHES TOOL COMPANY

United States Court of Appeals, Federal Circuit, 1983.
718 F.2d 1573, 219 USPQ 686, certiorari denied 104 S.Ct. 493 (1983).

SKELTON, SENIOR CIRCUIT JUDGE.

This is an appeal from an order of the United States District Court for the Central District of California, which denied a motion of defendant-appellant Hughes Tool Company (Hughes) for the entry of a preliminary injunction against plaintiff-appellee, Smith International,

Inc. (Smith) to prevent the further infringement by Smith of two patents owned by Hughes, which the Ninth Circuit Court of Appeals had previously declared valid, and which Smith had admitted it had infringed and was continuing to infringe. For reasons stated below, we reverse the decision of the district court and remand the case with instructions to issue the preliminary injunction.

* * *

The constitutional provision, which is the basis of patent law, grants Congress the power to award "inventors the exclusive right to their * * * discoveries." U.S. Const. art. 1, § 8, cl. 8. Congress has exercised this power by enacting the Patent Statute, which provides that patents shall have the attributes of personal property (35 U.S.C. § 261) and grants to the patentee the right to exclude others from making, using or selling the invention for a period of seventeen years (35 U.S.C. § 154). The grant of a patent is the grant of the right to invoke the state's power in order to exclude others from utilizing the patentee's discovery without his consent. *Zenith Radio Corp. v. Hazeltine Research*, 395 U.S. 100, 135, 89 S.Ct. 1562, 1582, 23 L.Ed.2d 129 (1969); *Sears, Roebuck & Co. v. Stiffel Co.*, 376 U.S. 225, 229, 84 S.Ct. 784, 787, 11 L.Ed.2d 661, *reh. denied*, 376 U.S. 973, 84 S.Ct. 1131, 12 L.Ed.2d 87 (1964); *Continental Paper Bag Co. v. Eastern Paper Bag Co.*, 210 U.S. 405, 430, 28 S.Ct. 748, 756, 52 L.Ed. 1122 (1908). Protection of this right to exclude has been provided by Congress through 35 U.S.C. § 283, *inter alia*, which provides that injunctions may be granted under the principles of equity to "prevent the violation of any rights secured by patent, on such terms as the court deems reasonable." Without this injunctive power of the courts, the right to exclude granted by the patent would be diminished, and the express purpose of the Constitution and Congress, to promote the progress of the useful arts, would be seriously undermined. The patent owner would lack much of the "leverage," afforded by the right to exclude, to enjoy the full value of his invention in the market place. Without the right to obtain an injunction, the right to exclude granted to the patentee would have only a fraction of the value it was intended to have, and would no longer be as great an incentive to engage in the toils of scientific and technological research. *See* I. KAYTON, KAYTON ON PATENTS, ch. 1, pp. 17–20 (1979).

However, courts have over the years developed a reluctance to resort to preliminary injunctions in patent infringement cases, and have constructed a rather strict standard for the granting of this form of equitable relief. It is generally recognized that the grant or denial of a preliminary injunction in a patent case is a matter committed to the sound discretion of the district court. *Pacific Cage and Screen Co. v. Continental Cage Corp.*, 259 F.2d 87, 88 (9th Cir.1958); *Superior Electric Company v. General Radio Corp.*, 194 F.Supp. 339 (D.N.J.) *aff'd*, 321 F.2d 857 (3rd Cir.), *cert. denied*, 376 U.S. 938, 84 S.Ct. 793, 11 L.Ed.2d 659, *reh. denied*, 376 U.S. 973, 84 S.Ct. 1134, 12 L.Ed.2d 88 (1964). The standard for granting such relief has been characterized as "unusually stringent." *Rohm & Haas Co. v. Mobil Oil Co.*, 525 F.Supp. 1298, 1302 (D.Del.1981). A preliminary injunction will normally issue only for the purpose of preserving the status quo and protecting the respective rights of the parties pending final disposition of the litigation. *Superior Electric Company v. General Radio Corp., supra.* The usual requirement of a showing of probability of success on the merits before a preliminary injunction will issue has historically been even stronger in a patent case. Besides having to prove title to the patent, it has been stated as a general proposition that the movant must show that the patent is beyond question valid and infringed. *Mayview Corp. v. Rodstein*, 480 F.2d 714, 717 (9th Cir.1973); *Bose Corporation v. Linear Design Labs, Inc.*, 467 F.2d 304, 307 (2d Cir.1972); *Eli Lilly and Company v. Generix Drug Sales, Inc.*, 460 F.2d 1096, 1099 (5th Cir.1972); *Carter-Wallace, Inc. v. Davis-Edwards Pharmacal Corp.*, 443 F.2d 867, 871 (2d Cir.), *cert. denied*, 412 U.S. 929, 93 S.Ct. 2753, 37 L.Ed.2d 156 (1973). In order to meet the burden of showing validity, the movant has sometimes been required to show either that his patent has previously been adjudicated valid, that there has been public acquiescence to its validity, or that there is conclusive direct technical evidence proving its validity. *Carter Wallace Inc. v. Davis Edwards Pharmacal Corp., supra*, at 871–874; *Jenn-Air Corporation v. Modern Maid Company*, 499 F.Supp. 320, 323 (D.Del.), *aff'd*, 659 F.2d 1068 (3rd Cir.1981). However, other courts have employed a less stringent standard of proof on the issue of validity. *See Eli Lilly and Co. v. Premo Pharmaceutical Labs.*, 630 F.2d 120, 136 (3rd Cir.), *cert. denied*, 449 U.S. 1014, 101 S.Ct. 573, 66 L.Ed.2d 473 (1980); *Tyrolean Handbag Co. v. Empress Hand Bag, Inc.*, 122 F.Supp. 299, 302 (S.D.N.Y.1954). The basis for the more severe rule appears to be both a distrust of and unfamiliarity with patent issues and a belief that the ex parte examination by the Patent and Trademark Office is inherently unreliable. Duft, *Patent Preliminary Injunctions and the United States Court of Appeals for the Federal Circuit*, 65 J.Pat.Off.Soc'y # 131 (1983).

As with preliminary injunctions in other types of cases, the movant is also required to demonstrate in a patent case that he will suffer immediate irreparable harm if the injunction is not granted. *Singer Co. v. P.R. Mallory & Co., Inc.*, 671 F.2d 232, 234 (7th Cir.1982). Some courts refuse to find irreparable injury where the alleged infringer is solvent and money will adequately compensate the injury. *Nuclear-Chicago Corp. v. Nuclear Data, Inc.*, 465 F.2d 428 (7th Cir.1972); *Rohm & Haas Co. v. Mobil Oil Corp., supra* at 1307; *Jenn-Air Corp. v. Modern Maid Co., supra* at 333. However, at least one court is of the opinion that where the showing on patent validity is very strong, invasion of the inventors right to exclude granted by the patent laws should be sufficient irreparable harm without a showing that the infringer is financially irresponsible. *Zenith Laboratories, Inc. v. Eli Lilly and Co.*, 460 F.Supp. 812 (D.N.J.1978).

Finally, where relevant, the court should take into account both the possibility of harm to other interested persons from the grant or denial of the injunction, and the public interest. *Eli Lilly and Co. v. Premo Pharmaceutical Labs., supra* at 136. In reaching its decision, the district court must consider the above factors and balance all of the elements. No one element will necessarily be dispositive of the case. *Id.* at 136.

* * *

The district court, while recognizing that infringement occurred, nonetheless declined to grant an injunction until the *extent* of the infringement was shown. We have found no case in our research that places such a burden on one seeking a preliminary injunction in a patent infringement case, and none has been cited to us. Such a requirement would make the standard practically impossible to meet. This inquiry is better left for the accounting proceeding, and the district court erred in making such a requirement of Hughes.

* * *

* * * The very nature of the patent right is the right to exclude others. Once the patentee's patents have been held to be valid and infringed, he should be entitled to the full enjoyment and protection of his patent rights. The infringer should not be allowed to continue his infringement in the face of such a holding. A court should not be reluctant to use its equity powers once a party has so clearly established his patent rights. We hold that where validity and continuing infringement have been clearly established, as in this case, immediate irreparable harm is presumed. To hold otherwise would be contrary to the public policy underlying the patent laws.

Upon balancing the requisite factors, we hold that the district court erred in denying Hughes' motion for a preliminary injunction. It committed a clear error of law in requiring proof of the extent of infringement prior to granting the preliminary injunction. The extent of infringement relates to damages and is a question to be determined at the trial on the merits. In addition, there do not appear to be any equitable considerations in this case that could in any way offset the strong showing of validity and infringement made by Hughes, coupled with the presumption of irreparable harm. Smith argues that public policy and the balance of hardship are in its favor, because it is a substantial competitor and has on hand a large inventory of the rock bits at issue here, and it would be unfair to disrupt its activities with an injunction. But it is clearly established that Smith knew of the Hughes patents when it designed the F series bits and took a calculated risk that it might infringe those patents. It instituted this action in an attempt to invalidate its competitor's patents, and, having failed, it will not now be heard to say that public policy is in its favor. To the contrary, public policy favors protection of the rights secured by the valid patents. Under these circumstances, we hold that the denial of a preliminary injunction was based on a clear error of law and constituted an abuse of discretion.[8]

* * *

8. Though the parties and the district court treated the matter as involving a "preliminary" injunction, and we have reviewed the case in those terms, we intend

CITY OF MILWAUKEE v. ACTIVATED SLUDGE

United States Court of Appeals, Seventh Circuit, 1934.
69 F.2d 577, 21 USPQ 69.

[The District Court for the Eastern District of Wisconsin held the process patents in suit valid and infringed by appellant's (City of Milwaukee) sewage treatment plant and the Court of Appeals affirmed this holding.]

SPARKS, CIRCUIT JUDGE. * * *

The decree in this case enjoins appellant from operating its plant. Ordinarily courts will protect patent rights by injunctive process. In determining whether that process shall be made permanent, the equities of all parties concerned should be considered. In the instant case both parties have strong equities, and there are many others who are indirectly concerned whose equities are even stronger than those of the parties. The damages of appellee may be compensated by a money judgment, and yet it has been subjected to great delay, and perhaps may yet suffer further delay, and greater than it otherwise would if the injunction were made permanent. It is only fair to say that these delays have been caused by the enormous amount of work necessarily occasioned by the issues involved. If, however, the injunction ordered by the trial court is made permanent in this case, it would close the sewage plant, leaving the entire community without any means for the disposal of raw sewage other than running it into Lake Michigan, thereby polluting its waters and endangering the health and lives of that and other adjoining communities. It is suggested that such harmful effect could be counteracted by chemical treatment of the sewage, but where, as here, the health and the lives of more than half a million people are involved, we think no risk should be taken, and we feel impelled to deny appellee's contention in this respect. This view is sustained by the group of cases to which appellant has called our attention in which injunctive relief was denied on the ground that it was not absolutely essential to preserve the rights of the patentee, and would cause the infringer irreparable damage. In none of those cases were the facts as serious or might the results have been as dangerous as in the case at bar. See Thacher v. Mayor & City Council of Baltimore (D.C.) 219 F. 909; Landis Tool Company v. Ingle (C.C.A.) 286 F. 5; McCreery Engineering Company v. Massachusetts Fan Company (C.C.) 180 F. 115; Ballard v. City of Pittsburgh (C.C.) 12 F. 783; Blake v. Greenwood Cemetery, 3 Fed.Cas. page 594, No. 1,497.

The decree is affirmed except as to the injunction, and as to the decree is reversed.

* * *

no implication that a patentee is not entitled to a permanent injunction against the infringer in the case upon final judicial determination that the involved patent is valid and has been infringed by that infringer. Such an injunction prohibits infringement by any product, not just those involved in the original suit. The burden of avoiding infringement at the risk of contempt falls upon the one enjoined.

3. DAMAGES, INTEREST AND ATTORNEY FEES

a. Generally

RADIO STEEL & MFG. CO. v. MTD PRODUCTS, INC.

United States Court of Appeals, Federal Circuit, 1986.
788 F.2d 1554, 229 USPQ 431.

FRIEDMAN, CIRCUIT JUDGE.

These are an appeal and a cross-appeal from a judgment of the United States District Court for the Northern District of Ohio, awarding damages in the accounting phase of a patent infringement suit. The infringer contends that the damages were excessive. The patentee contends that the damages were inadequate because the district court should have held that the infringement was willful and awarded enhanced damages and attorney fees. We affirm.

* * *

Following a trial in the accounting phase of the case, the district court awarded Radio Steel damages of $588,719.93 plus post-judgment interest and costs. The court found that "[t]he overwhelming majority of MTD's sales of the infringing wheelbarrows was to three retail store chains: White Stores, Montgomery Ward, and K-Mart." It determined that Radio Steel was entitled to recover lost profits on MTD's sales to K-Mart and the White Stores, which it calculated at $296,937.21. On MTD's sales to stores other than those two, the court ruled that Radio Steel was entitled to a reasonable royalty of ten percent, which amounted to $155,634.81.

The district court's combined damage award of $588,719.93 included prejudgment interest. The court rejected MTD's contention that Radio Steel was not entitled to prejudgment interest because it had allowed patent notices to remain on its wheelbarrows after the patent had expired.

The court held that MTD's infringement was not willful and therefore declined to enhance the damages or to award attorney fees.

II

In its appeal, MTD contends that (A) the award of lost profits was improper, (B) the ten percent royalty rate was excessive, and (C) Radio Steel's failure to remove patent markings from its wheelbarrows after the patent had expired barred the award to it of prejudgment interest.

A. *Lost Profits.* In awarding lost profits, the district court applied the standard announced in *Panduit Corp. v. Stahlin Bros. Fibre Works, Inc.,* 575 F.2d 1152, 197 USPQ 726 (6th Cir.1978), which we implicitly approved in *Central Soya Co., Inc. v. George Hormel & Co.,* 723 F.2d 1573, 220 USPQ 490 (Fed.Cir.1983). Under *Panduit,* to receive lost profits a patent owner must prove:

(1) demand for the patented product, (2) absence of acceptable noninfringing substitutes, (3) his manufacturing and marketing capability to

exploit the demand, and (4) the amount of the profit he would have made.

Panduit, supra at 1156, 197 USPQ at 730. The district court found that Radio Steel had proved the four elements of *Panduit with respect to sales MTD made to K-Mart and the White Stores.*

On appeal, MTD challenges only the district court's finding that there were no acceptable noninfringing substitutes. That was a finding of fact that we can reverse only if it is clearly erroneous. *Gyromat Corp. v. Champion Spark Plug Co.,* 735 F.2d 549, 222 USPQ 4 (Fed.Cir. 1984); *see also Anderson v. City of Bessemer,* 470 U.S. 564, 105 S.Ct. 1504, 84 L.Ed.2d 518 (1985). MTD has not shown that the finding has that fatal flaw.

The district court found that

the patented wheelbarrow has several attributes which demonstrate an absence of substitutes. The patented wheelbarrow could be shipped unassembled, thereby allowing more compact shipping with lower shipping costs. The wheelbarrows could be easily assembled at the stores. * * * The absence of the "shin scraper" brace along the rear of the legs, which was necessary in other wheelbarrows to achieve structural regidity [sic], also added to the popularity of the patented wheelbarrow. * * * Although other noninfringing contractor-type wheelbarrows exist in the market, such wheelbarrows are not acceptable substitutes for the patented product.

MTD contends, however, that

wheelbarrows for many years past * * * perform the *same function* of transporting a load contained in a bowl or tray on one wheel propelled by an operator holding the handles on which the bowl or tray is mounted and propelling the assembly on the single wheel. All wheelbarrows which have been on the market produce this result and are available acceptable substitutes.

Some of these wheelbarrows * * * have two-piece handles which facilitate packaging of the parts of the wheelbarrow, and these too are available acceptable non-infringing wheelbarrows.

This argument is another formulation of the contention, rejected twice by the district court and once by this court, that the patent simply was a combination of old elements. It ignores the district court's earlier ruling in the liability phase that "[i]t is the totality of all the elements and their interaction with each other which is the inventor's contribution to the art of wheelbarrow making." 566 F.Supp. at 619, 220 USPQ at 43. It also ignores the statement in our prior opinion that "as the district court held, the '600 patent 'descri[bed] * * * a new and improved complete wheelbarrow.'" 731 F.2d at 845, 221 USPQ at 661. The various wheelbarrows to which MTD refers incorporate only some, but not all, of the elements of the patent. They do not establish that the district court's finding that these were not acceptable noninfringing substitutes is clearly erroneous.

B. *Reasonable Royalty.* The district court's determination that ten percent was a reasonable royalty on MTD's sales to stores other than K-Mart or White Stores reflected the court's own independent judgment and was not based upon the court's acceptance of the evidence of either party. Indeed, the court rejected the reasonable royalty figures of both parties.

The district court rejected MTD's estimate of two percent, stating that it did not find that figure to be a reasonable royalty. It observed that Radio Steel lost sales not only of the patented wheelbarrows, but also of collateral items that are normally attendant to the sales of wheelbarrows, such as garden carts and lawn mowers. The court also noted that MTD made substantial sales to White Stores, Montgomery Ward, and K-Mart of noninfringing wheelbarrows with the sale of the infringing wheelbarrows.

The court rejected Radio Steel's figure of twenty-one percent, indicating its view that that amount, which is two-thirds of Radio Steel's incremental profit, was too high a royalty for a patent that would expire in three years. The court also expressed concern that Radio Steel's twenty-one percent figure would allow the company to collect unreasonably high royalties from MTD's sales to Montgomery Ward, with whom Radio Steel had been unable to establish a regular and consistent merchandising arrangement. The court concluded that

> [c]onsidering the age of the patent, the patent's novelty and contribution to the industry, Radio Steel's unwillingness to license, the profit margin on the wheelbarrows, the availability of wheelbarrows from other manufacturers, and the collateral sale benefits, the Court finds 10% to be a reasonable royalty on MTD's sale of wheelbarrows to other than K-Mart and the White Stores.

MTD challenges the ten percent royalty on two grounds.

1. MTD asserts that ten percent is unreasonably high because it far exceeds the profit MTD actually made on the infringing wheelbarrows. It relies on testimony by its treasurer that the profit MTD made on the sale of infringing wheelbarrows was low, and that in one year it had a loss on those sales.

The determination of a reasonable royalty, however, is based not on the infringer's profit, but on the royalty to which a willing licensor and a willing licensee would have agreed at the time the infringement began. *Panduit*, 575 F.2d at 1158, 197 USPQ at 731. Moreover, the district court could well have discounted MTD's profit figures because the treasurer also testified that the infringing wheelbarrows might have been utilized as loss-leaders at various times during the period of infringement.

2. MTD contends that ten percent is not commensurate with the "patent's novelty and contribution" to the industry. * * *

This is but another phrasing of the argument, which we have rejected in our discussion of lost profits, that the patent is only a combination of old elements and that their aggregation constituted a "minuscule" and "meager" contribution to the art.

The record fully supports the district court's selection of a ten percent reasonable royalty. MTD's treasurer testified that at the time of infringement, MTD expected to make a net profit of about six percent on its sale of infringing wheelbarrows. Radio Steel's vice president of finance testified that its net profit from its sales of patented wheelbarrows was ten plus-or-minus two percent. On this record we have no basis for rejecting the district court's selection of ten percent as a reasonable royalty rate. *Deere & Co. v. International Harvester Co.,* 710 F.2d 1551, 218 USPQ 481 (Fed.Cir.1983).

C. *Prejudgment Interest.* MTD contends that Radio Steel was equitably barred from receiving prejudgment interest because it failed to remove its patent notice from its wheelbarrows for one-and-one-half years after the patent expired. The district court rejected this contention because "MTD has not shown it suffered from such actions of Radio Steel, and the Court fails to see the relevance of such actions to the infringement in question."

We agree with that ruling.

MTD argues that *General Motors Corp. v. Devex Corp.,* 461 U.S. 648, 103 S.Ct. 2058, 76 L.Ed.2d 211 (1983), indicated that prejudgment interest may be denied to a prevailing patentee in an infringement suit under certain circumstances. The only example the Supreme Court gave was a case in which a patentee unduly delays the prosecution of an infringement suit. *Id.* at 657, 103 S.Ct. at 2063. The actual holding in *General Motors* was that "prejudgment interest should be awarded under § 284 absent some justification for withholding such an award." *Id.* The justification to which the Supreme Court referred must have some relationship to the award of prejudgment interest, which award the Court held "is necessary [in the typical case] to ensure that the patent owner is placed in as good a position as he would have been in had the infringer entered into a reasonable royalty agreement." *Id.* at 655, 103 S.Ct. at 2062 (footnote omitted).

* * *

III

In its cross-appeal, Radio Steel contends that the district court should have found that the infringement was willful and therefore should have awarded enhanced damages under 35 U.S.C. § 284 (1982) and attorney fees under 35 U.S.C. § 284 (1982) and attorney fees under 35 U.S.C. § 285 (1982).

* * *

The record shows that MTD's patent counsel gave his opinion on validity and infringement at a meeting held shortly after Radio Steel gave the notice of infringement to MTD. At that meeting, counsel examined the patent, an accused MTD wheelbarrow, and some MTD drawings. Counsel, however, did not review the prior art or the prosecution history of the patent. Counsel concluded that the accused wheelbarrow literally infringed the Radio Steel patent but that the patent was invalid. He suggested a design modification to avoid literal infringement. The opinion he gave at the meeting was not reduced to writing.

Radio Steel argues that under *Kori Corp. v. Wilco Marsh Buggies & Draglines, Inc.*, 761 F.2d 649, 225 USPQ 985 (Fed.Cir.1985), *cert. denied*, ___ U.S. ___, 106 S.Ct. 230, 88 L.Ed.2d 229 (1985), *Rosemount, Inc. v. Beckman Instruments, Inc.*, 727 F.2d 1540, 221 USPQ 1 (Fed.Cir.1984), *Central Soya Co., Inc. v. George A. Hormel & Co.*, 723 F.2d 1573, 220 USPQ 490 (Fed.Cir.1983), and *Underwater Devices, Inc. v. Morrison-Knudsen Co.*, 717 F.2d 1380, 219 USPQ 569 (Fed.Cir.1983), "an infringer may not in good faith, justifiably rely on the opinion of counsel and proceed in the face of a known patent unless counsel's advice is 'competent', 'authoritative', or 'contains sufficient internal indicia of credibility to remove any doubt that (the infringer) in fact received a competent opinion.'"

As we have indicated, however, the various factors we have discussed in those cases are just that: factors the district court is to consider in determining willfulness. In making that determination, it "is necessary to look at 'the totality of the circumstances presented in the case.'" *Central Soya*, 723 F.2d at 1577, 220 USPQ at 492.

In those cases we referred to the facts relating to opinions by patent counsel to explain why the factual finding in each case of willful infringement was not clearly erroneous. *Underwater Devices, supra* at 1390, 219 USPQ at 576. We have never suggested that unless the opinion of counsel met all of those requirements, the district court is required to find that the infringement was willful.

In this case, the district court found that MTD, after being notified of possible infringement on its part, obtained a validity and infringement opinion from an outside patent attorney. Based on that opinion, MTD made the design modifications its patent attorney suggested, to avoid possible infringement of the patent. The district court held that "MTD was acting under the good faith belief that its wheelbarrow did not infringe the patent."

*   *   *

UNDERWATER DEVICES INCORPORATED v. MORRISON–KNUDSEN COMPANY, INC.

United States Court of Appeals, Federal Circuit, 1983.
717 F.2d 1380, 219 USPQ 569.

KASHIWA, CIRCUIT JUDGE.

*   *   *

DISTRICT COURT PROCEEDING

In April, 1981, the district court found that the '417 and reissue patents were valid. In addition, the court found that M–K willfully infringed both claim 1 of the '417 patent and claims 1–4 of the reissue patent during the Sand Island project.

The district court then found $200,000 to be a reasonable royalty under 35 U.S.C. § 284 and awarded such an amount to UDI as damages. The court based its finding on the estimated royalty fee, $200,000, quoted in UDI's letter to prospective bidders. In addition, the court stated:

> [T]he application of the formulae in the earlier agreements entered into by UDI, and especially the agreement with Hood Corporation dated March 15, 1974, would have resulted in a royalty of about $200,000.

After trebling the $200,000 damage award to $600,000 for willful infringement, the district court assessed prejudgment interest of 10% uncompounded interest on the entire $600,000 amount.

*   *   *

III. PREJUDGMENT INTEREST

The appellant further argues that the district court erroneously awarded prejudgment interest on the punitive or enhanced portion of the damages. We agree.

Contrary to appellees' contention, citing *Brian Jackson Associates, Inc. v. San Manuel Copper Corp.*, 305 F.Supp. 66, 163 USPQ 198 (D.Ariz. 1969) and *Corometrics Medical Systems, Inc. v. Berkeley Bio-Engineering, Inc.*, 193 USPQ 467 (N.D.Cal.1977), that the award of prejudgment interest on the punitive or enhanced portion was proper, we hold that prejudgment interest can only be applied to the primary or actual damage portion and not to the punitive or enhanced portion.

Prejudgment interest is awarded to the patent owner for the purpose of making him whole, not only for the value of the actual damage suffered but also for the loss of any possible use of the money between the time of the infringement and the date of the judgment. *General Motors Corp. v. Devex Corp.*, 461 U.S. 648, 655, 103 S.Ct. 2058, 76 L.Ed.2d 211, 217 USPQ 1185, 1189 (1983). It is awarded to compensate for the delay in payment of the damages, and not to punish the infringer. In *Trio Process Corp. v. L. Goldstein's Sons, Inc.*, 638 F.2d 661 (3d Cir.1981), where the district court had doubled the damage award for willful infringement pursuant to section 284, the Third Circuit concluded that the enhanced portion was punitive in character. As such, it held that prejudgment interest could not be assessed on the enhanced portion of the damage award. The Third Circuit stated:

> [I]t is clear that the rationale for awarding prejudgment interest on a remedially enhanced damage award, to the extent such a rational exists, also implies that no prejudgment interest be awarded on a punitively enhanced portion of damages.

Id., at 663. *Accord H.K. Porter Co. v. Goodyear Tire & Rubber Co.*, 536 F.2d 1115, 1124, 191 USPQ 486, 493 (6th Cir.1976); *General Electric Co.*

v. Sciaky Brothers, Inc., 415 F.2d 1068, 1076, 163 USPQ 257, 263 (6th Cir.1969).

In the instant case, the enhanced portion of the damage award, $400,000, is punitive in character since it was assessed by the district court for M–K's willful infringement of UDI's patents. *See infra.* We therefore reverse the district court's award of prejudgment interest on the enhanced or punitive portion of the damage award.

IV. WILLFUL INFRINGEMENT

Last, the appellant argues that the district court's finding of willful infringement was erroneous. We disagree.

The district court's finding of willful infringement is a finding of fact, and as such, the standard of review is the clearly erroneous standard. F.R.Civ.P. 52(a). The appellant, however, has failed to show that the district court's finding was clearly erroneous. *United States v. United States Gypsum Co.,* 333 U.S. 364, 68 S.Ct. 525, 92 L.Ed. 746 (1948). *See also Kalman v. Kimberly-Clark Corp.,* 713 F.2d 760, 218 USPQ 781 (Fed.Cir.1983).

Where, as here, a potential infringer has actual notice of another's patent rights, he has an affirmative duty to exercise due care to determine whether or not he is infringing. *See Milgo Electronic Corp. v. United Business Communications, Inc.,* 623 F.2d 645, 666, 206 USPQ 481, 497 (10th Cir.1980), *cert. denied,* 449 U.S. 1066, 101 S.Ct. 794, 66 L.Ed.2d 611 (1980). Such an affirmative duty includes, *inter alia,* the duty to seek and obtain competent legal advice from counsel *before* the initiation of any possible infringing activity. *See General Electric, supra,* at 1073–74, 163 USPQ at 261; *Marvel Specialty Co. v. Bell Hosiery Mills, Inc.,* 386 F.2d 287, 155 USPQ 545 (4th Cir.1967), *cert. denied,* 390 U.S. 1030, 88 S.Ct. 1409, 20 L.Ed.2d 286 (1968). In this case, M–K obtained its counsel's advice *after* it commenced its infringing activities. Although Mr. Schlanger did order a patent search and received the results of that search in late 1973, he did not evaluate the validity or infringement of the Robley patents before M–K began the infringing activities. Such an evaluation would generally include an analysis of the file history of the patent. Mr. Schlanger, however, did not order the file histories of the Robley patents until September 5, 1974, well after the infringement had begun. Moreover, M–K did not receive the opinion of its patent counsel until November 30, 1974, long after infringement had commenced and even after the complaint for the instant case was filed.

Contrary to appellant's contention that it proceeded with the infringing activities in good faith based on the advice of its counsel, Mr. Schlanger, we disagree. Rather, M–K knew or should have known that it proceeded without the type of competent legal advice upon which it could justifiably have relied. M–K knew that the attorney from whom it sought advice was its own in-house counsel. While this fact alone does not demonstrate M–K's lack of good faith, it is a fact to be weighed. *See Western Electric Co. v. Stewart-Warner Corp.*, 631 F.2d 333, 337, 208 USPQ 183, 187 (4th Cir.1980), *cert. denied*, 450 U.S. 971, 101 S.Ct. 1492, 67 L.Ed.2d 622 (1981). In addition, M–K knew or should have known that Mr. Schlanger was not a patent attorney. Again, this fact alone is not controlling, but does bear on the question whether M–K, when it sought advice, did so in good faith.

Although M–K might have demonstrated to the district court that despite any inference arising from these circumstances, it was in fact justified in believing Mr. Schlanger was capable of rendering an independent and competent opinion because he did take the steps normally considered to be necessary and proper in preparing an opinion, it failed to do so. As stated previously, Mr. Schlanger did not order the file histories until September, 1974, such step being a normal and necessary preliminary to a validity or infringement opinion. In addition, M–K might have demonstrated to the district court that its counsel's opinion, without an analysis of the file histories, was in fact thorough and competent. Although the December, 1973 memorandum may be considered legal advice, it was not legal advice upon which the appellant was justified in relying, since it was not based on an evaluation of the validity or infringement of the Robley patents. The May, 1974 memorandum is similarly inadequate. It contains only bald, conclusory and unsupported remarks regarding validity and infringement of the Robley patents. Had it contained within its four corners a patent validity analysis, properly and explicitly predicated on a review of the file histories of the patents at issue, and an infringement analysis that, *inter alia,* compared and contrasted the potentially infringing method or apparatus with the patented inventions, the opinion may have contained sufficient internal indicia of creditability to remove any doubt that M–K in fact received a competent opinion. What these memoranda clearly demonstrated was M–K's willful disregard for the Robley patents. The appellant clearly failed to exercise its affirmative duty. Accordingly, the district court's finding that infringement was willful, in the totality of the circumstances presented in this case, is not clearly erroenous and the district court did not abuse its discretion in awarding treble damages. *Milgo, supra,* at 665, 206 USPQ at 497.

* * *

ROHM & HAAS COMPANY v. CRYSTAL CHEMICAL COMPANY

United States Court of Appeals, Federal Circuit, 1984.
736 F.2d 688, 222 USPQ 97, cert. denied 469 U.S. 851, 105 S.Ct. 172,
83 L.Ed.2d 107 (1984).

RICH, CIRCUIT JUDGE.

Crystal Chemical Company and Joe C. Eller (hereinafter Crystal), appellants, have filed:

(1) Appellants' Application for Attorney Fees and Expenses Incurred on Appeal Pursuant to 35 U.S.C. § 285.

(2) Appellants' Motion for Costs on Appeal Pursuant to FRAP Rule 39 and for Reconsideration of Assessment of Costs.

We consider these two matters seriatim.

I. ATTORNEY FEES

* * *

The awarding of attorney fees under § 285 for an "exceptional" *appeal* is a question of first impression in this court. It is also an issue that was rarely addressed by other circuits. Because of these circumstances, we first review the evolution of the statutory and case law on this subject and examine its public policy underpinnings, before considering the merits of Crystal's application for attorney fees.

The federal courts of the United States early adopted what has become known as the "American Rule" in the handling of attorney fee requests. Unlike countries which follow the "English Rule," our courts do not routinely assess attorney fees against the losing party. The American Rule was recognized by the Supreme Court as early as 1796 in *Arcambel v. Wiseman,* 3 U.S. (3 Dall.) 306, 1 L.Ed. 613, and, simply put, proscribes the award of fees absent statutory authorization or particularly compelling circumstances. The policy behind the Rule is fundamental—to avoid penalizing a party "for merely defending or prosecuting a lawsuit." *Fleischmann Distilling Corp. v. Maier Brewing Co.,* 386 U.S. 714, 718, 87 S.Ct. 1404, 1407, 18 L.Ed.2d 475 (1967).

* * *

Other statutory provisions have been enacted so as to further equitable considerations, in suits where encouragement of citizen suits is not applicable, as in the case of the present patent statute, § 285, and its predecessor for the purpose of enabling a court to prevent gross injustice.

Prior to 1946, the Supreme Court, following the American Rule, had held that the award of attorney fees based upon equitable considerations was not available in patent cases. However, in that year Congress amended § 4921 of the Revised Statutes to alter the type of damages recoverable for infringement, and added an attorney fee provision to that section:

> The court may in its discretion award reasonable attorney's fees to the prevailing party upon the entry of judgment on any patent case
> * * *.

The Senate Report concerning this provision noted its applicability to prevailing patentees as well as to prevailing alleged infringers, and emphasized that the award should not become "an ordinary thing":

> It is not contemplated that the recovery of attorney's fees will become an ordinary thing in patent suits, but the discretion given the court in this respect, in addition to the present discretion to award triple damages, will discourage infringement of a patent by anyone thinking that all he would be required to pay if he loses the suit would be a royalty. The *provision is also made general so as to enable the*

court to prevent a gross injustice to an alleged infringer. [Emphasis added.]

Subsequent to the 1946 amendments, attorney fee awards were granted by the courts, in their discretion, primarily upon findings of extraordinary circumstances. An early and leading decision ably summarized the policy behind this statutory waiver of the American Rule for attorney fees in the patent law context:

> Thus, the payment of attorney's fees for the victor is not to be regarded as a penalty for failure to win a patent infringement suit. *The exercise of discretion* in favor of such an allowance *should be bottomed upon* a finding of *unfairness or bad faith in the conduct of the losing party,* or some other equitable consideration of similar force, *which makes it grossly unjust that the winner of the particular law suit be left to bear the burden of his own counsel fees* which prevailing litigants normally bear. [Emphasis added.]

The next and most recent revision of the pertinent section of the patent statutes, the Patent Act of 1952, codified the attorney fee provision in 35 U.S.C. § 285, which omits explicit reference to the court's discretion but adds the qualifier that the court *may* award reasonable attorney fees in *"exceptional cases."* The Revision Note to this section, as restated later by its author, shows that:

> Section 285, providing for the recovery of attorney fees by the prevailing party, is substantially the same as the corresponding sentence of the old statute, with the addition of "in exceptional cases" to express the intention of the old statute as shown by its legislative history and as interpreted by the courts.[6]

Cases decided under § 285 have noted that "the substitution of the phrase "in exceptional cases' has not done away with the discretionary feature." *Hoge Warren Zimmerman Co. v. Nourse & Co.,* 293 F.2d 779, 783, 130 USPQ 382, 386 (6th Cir.1961).

Cases awarding attorney fees to prevailing patentees have typically found "exceptional" circumstances in willful and deliberate infringement by an infringer, or in the prolongation of litigation in bad faith. When prevailing alleged infringers are awarded attorney fees, "exceptional" cases have involved litigation in bad faith by the patentee, or fraud or other inequitable conduct during prosecution before the PTO. We are also cognizant of the frequently-cited policy considerations in support of the award of attorney fees to a party who succeeds in invalidating "fraudulent" patents, *cf. True Temper Corp. v. CF & I Steel Corp.,* 601 F.2d 495, 509, 202 USPQ 412, 423 (10th Cir.1979); and *Monolith Portland Midwest Co. v. Kaiser Aluminum & Chemical Co.,* 407 F.2d 288, 294, 160 USPQ 577, 581 (9th Cir.1969). We support this proposition only to the extent that a prevailing alleged infringer should

---

6. P.J. Federico, Commentary on the New Patent Act, Title 35, United States Code Annotated, page 1, at 56.

be awarded attorney fees only when it would be unjust not to make such an award.

Neither § 285 nor its legislative history distinguishes between awarding attorney fees in the district court and in the appellate court. We recognize that the district court is the forum in which requests for attorney fees are almost invariably made. We also recognize that the American rule against the award of attorney fees, in the absence of a statute or compelling circumstances, developed in order to avoid penalizing parties for asserting their legal rights. In section 285 we have an exception to the American rule, and it was enacted to further a different policy, that of preventing injustice to a party involved in a patent suit, as detailed above. We construe the language of § 285 as applicable to cases in which the appeal itself is exceptional, in furtherance of the latter policy.

* * *

To date, our experience in this court with the award of attorney fees under § 285, although limited, is representative of the developed case law for this section of the Patent Act. None of the cases so far has dealt with attorney fees on the appeal. We have upheld a district court's awarding of attorney fees under § 285 to patentees where willful infringement had been proved. *Rosemount, Inc. v. Beckman Instruments, Inc.*, 727 F.2d 1540, 221 USPQ 1 (Fed.Cir.1984); and *Lam, Inc. v. Johns-Manville Corp.*, 718 F.2d 1056, 219 USPQ 670 (Fed.Cir. 1983). Section 285 also permits the prevailing party to recover certain disbursements incurred during preparation for a case. *Central Soya Co. v. Geo. A. Hormel & Co.*, 723 F.2d 1573, 220 USPQ 490 (Fed.Cir. 1983).

Attorney fee awards have also been affirmed by this court when the basis for finding the case to be "exceptional" was "fraud" in procuring the patent sued upon as well as misconduct during suit and a bad faith assertion of infringement. *Hughes v. Novi American, Inc.*, 724 F.2d 122, 125, 220 USPQ 707, 710 (Fed.Cir.1984). Additionally, we have held that cases may be deemed exceptional for reasons other than inequitable conduct during prosecution, *Orthopedic Equipment Co. v. All Orthopedic Appliances*, 707 F.2d 1376, 1384, 217 USPQ 1281, 1287 (Fed.Cir.1983), such as persisting with a suit in the face of knowledge that the asserted patent is invalid, *Hughes*, supra, or "some finding of unfairness, bad faith, or inequitable conduct on the part of" a patentee unsuccessfully bringing an infringement suit, *Stevenson* (supra note 9).

We have affirmed the denial of attorney fees in several cases as well. For instance, the denial of fees has been affirmed on the basis that a motion, although meritless, was neither frivolous nor brought only for harassment or delay. *CTS Corp. v. Piher International Corp.*, 727 F.2d 1550, 221 USPQ 11 (Fed.Cir.1984). *See also, Stickle v. Heublein, Inc.*, 716 F.2d 1550, 1564, 219 USPQ 377, 388 (Fed.Cir.1983), in which an attorney fee award was vacated because the record did not show that numerous defenses had been used vexatiously or for dilatory purposes. Also in *Stickle,* part of the award related to work on non-patent issues, the fees for which are not allowable under § 285.

On the basis of the preceding review of the state of the law regarding the award of attorney fees under § 285, we now address the present case. We recognize that our previous holding on the merits, that, as a matter of law, R & H had not cured its earlier fraud in the prosecution of the application for the patent asserted on appeal, breaks new ground on the subject of fraud in the PTO and sets new standards in this area of the law. Under the circumstances of this case, we cannot hold that R & H's failure to follow this new standard makes it unjust for Crystal to bear its own counsel fees on this appeal from the lower court's decision in favor of R & H. We furthermore do not agree with Crystal that the record designations of R & H have "snowed" this court with a mountain of irrelevant information, nor do we feel that the conduct of R & H has frustrated presentation of this case.

We hold, therefore, that Crystal shall bear its own attorney fees on this appeal and its request is denied. We do not decide here whether or not attorney fees may be warranted for the trial below, because considerations other than the invalidity of the R & H patent may bear on the propriety of awarding attorney fees, and we cannot be as familiar with the proceedings below as is the district court. Thus, any question of attorney fees below must be decided, in the first instance, by that court, exercising its own discretion.

* * *

Notes

1. The statutory measure of damages does not provide for a recovery of an infringer's profits, although it did prior to August 1, 1946. An infringer's profits may, however, be an element in the determination of general damages in appropriate fact situations. Ric-Wil Co. v. E.B. Kaiser Co., 179 F.2d 401, 84 USPQ 121 (7th Cir.1950).

2. "Another word should be added concerning the position of McCulloch to the effect that the simple finding of wilfulness *compels* an award of *treble* damages. There is no such provision in the statute. The statute limits the damages up to three times the amount of actual damages. Additional damages may be awarded in any sum less than that amount." McCulloch Motors Corp. v. Oregon Saw Chain Corp., 245 F.Supp. 851, 857, 147 USPQ 175, 187 (S.D.Cal.1965).

3. "In this kind of action the successful patentee is entitled either to an established royalty rate, if there is one, or, if not, a reasonable royalty rate. * * * A reasonable royalty is one which a licensee would be willing to pay and still make a reasonable profit out of use of the patented article." Beatty Safway Scaffold Co. v. Up-Right, Inc., 306 F.2d 626, 134 USPQ 379, 384 (9th Cir.1962).

4. "Where the infringer was a former licensee of the patent, royalty may be a factor related to profits and hence an element of damages sustained by the holder of the patent. * * * Profits of the infringer are

evidence of the damages sustained by the holder of the patent and may be the measure of damages. * * * Where, as here, the infringer's profits are taken as the measure of the plaintiff's loss, a royalty should not be included to increase the award of damages." Henry Hanger & Display Fixture Corp. v. Sel-O-Rak Corp., 270 F.2d 635, 123 USPQ 3, 9 (5th Cir. 1959).

5. "The general rule, of course, is that the monopoly of a patent which entitles a patentee to damages for infringement commences only when the patent is granted; but where, in advance of the granting of a patent, an invention is disclosed to one who, in breach of the confidence thus reposed, manufactures and sells articles embodying the invention, such person should be held liable for the profits and damages resulting therefrom, not under the patent statutes, but upon the principle that equity will not permit one to unjustly enrich himself at the expense of another. * * * It would be a reproach to any system of jurisprudence to permit one who has received a disclosure in confidence to thus appropriate the ideas of another without liability for the wrong." Hoeltke v. C.M. Kemp Mfg. Co., 80 F.2d 912, 26 USPQ 114, 125–26 (4th Cir.1935). See also, e.g., Ackermans v. General Motors Corp., 202 F.2d 642, 96 USPQ 281 (4th Cir.1953).

6. "In sum, Dennison's presentation on appeal is disingenious, containing mischaracterizations, misleading statements, and improper submissions. It has unnecessarily burdened the court with extraordinary need to check the record in respect to each of its assertions, only to find in too many instances a lack of candor. Accordingly, Panduit is awarded double its costs on appeal." Panduit Corp. v. Dennison Mfg. Co., 774 F.2d 1082, 1102, 227 USPQ 337, 351 (Fed.Cir.1985). See also The D.L. Auld Co. v. Chroma Graphics Corp., 753 F.2d 1029, 224 USPQ 737 (Fed.Cir.1985) where attorney fees were awarded under 35 U.S.C.A. § 285 where appellant "had no reasonable basis for believing that its constitutional argument had any likelihood of prevailing before this court."

7. "It is undisputed that GTE did not obtain advice of counsel on whether the accused Cusack reed probe infringed. However, the district court heard Murray's testimony on cross-examination that '[GTE] was very conscious of the need not to infringe any patents with its probe head,' and that GTE believed 'with respect to Cusack's reed probe that there wouldn't be any patent problem because [the probe] was different.' * * *

"It is by now well settled that where a potential infringer has actual notice of another's patent rights he has an affirmative duty of due care. *Underwater Devices,* supra; *CPG,* supra. That affirmative duty will normally entail the obtaining of competent legal advice of counsel before infringing or continuing to infringe; that does not mean, however, that absence of an opinion of counsel alone *requires* in every case a finding of willful infringement. As this court stated in Kloster Speedsteel AB, 793 F.2d at 1579, 230 USPQ at 90–91: 'Though it is an important consideration, not every failure to seek an opinion of competent counsel will mandate an ultimate finding of wilfulness.' See King Instrument Corp. v. Otari Corp., 767 F.2d 853, 867, 226 USPQ 402, 412 (Fed.Cir.1985) (court 'should always look at the totality of the circumstances'), cert. denied, 106 S.Ct. 1197

(1986); see also Central Soya Co., Inc. v. George A. Hormel & Co., 723 F.2d 1573, 1577, 220 USPQ 490, 492 (Fed.Cir.1984).

"In respect of willfulness there cannot be hard and fast *per se* rules. The district court, considering the evidence before it and the testimony and demeanor of the witnesses, must in each case determine whether an infringer has discharged its affirmative duty of exercising due care. Here, the district court found, in light of the totality of the circumstances, that GTE had recognized and discharged that duty. See also Radio Steel & Manufacturing Co. v. MTD Products, Inc., 788 F.2d 1554, 1558–59, 229 USPQ 431, 434–35. Though the question is not totally free of doubt, that finding has not been shown to have been clearly erroneous." Rolls-Royce Ltd. v. GTE Valeron Corp., 800 F.2d 1101, 1109–1110, 231 USPQ 185, 191 (Fed.Cir.1986).

b. *Marking and Notice*

WINE RY. APPLIANCE CO. v. ENTERPRISE RY. EQUIPMENT CO.

Supreme Court of the United States, 1936.
297 U.S. 387, 56 S.Ct. 528, 80 L.Ed. 736.

MR. JUSTICE MCREYNOLDS delivered the opinion of the Court.

In 1922, respondent, Equipment Company, sued the petitioner for infringing certain patents. April 25, 1923, petitioner, Appliance Company, by counterclaim, charged that respondent had infringed its patents and asked for damages. The District Court dismissed both bill and counterclaim. The Circuit Court of Appeals held one of petitioner's patents valid and infringed and remanded the cause for an accounting.

The master reported (June 17, 1932) that profits amounting to $18,002.83 had been realized on the infringing device and recommended judgment for that sum. Of this total he attributed $5,490.77 to the period preceding the filing of the counterclaim and $12,512.06 to the subsequent one. The District Court approved; but the Circuit Court of Appeals, after citing many conflicting opinions by other Federal Courts, held no recovery could be had for anything done prior to the counterclaim. This ruling is challenged. To determine the issue, we must construe § 4900 R.S.; U.S.C.A., Title 35, § 49, which provides—

> "It shall be the duty of all patentees, and their assigns and legal representatives, and of all persons making or vending any patented article for or under them, to give sufficient notice to the public that the same is patented; either by fixing thereon the word 'patented,' together with the day and year the patent was granted; or when, from the character of the article, this can not be done, by fixing to it, or to the package wherein one or more of them is inclosed, a label containing the like notice; and in any suit for infringement, by the party failing so to mark, no damages shall be recovered by the plaintiff, except on proof that the defendant was duly notified of the infringement, and continued, after such notice, to make, use, or vend the article so patented."

* * *

Neither petitioner nor another with its consent has ever manufactured or vended an article under the infringed patent. No actual notice of infringement was given respondent prior to the counterclaim.

Counsel for petitioner affirm that under § 4900, whenever a patented article is made or vended by one of those therein specified it becomes his duty to give sufficient notice to the public "that the same is patented" either by placing thereon or upon the label the word "Patented." Also, that, as penalty for failure therein, the defaulter is deprived of the right to recover damages for infringement, except upon proof that after notice, the defendant continued to make, use or vend. This construction, it is said, correctly we think, gives effect to every word in the section and carries out the legislative purpose.

Counsel for respondent submit—

Section 4900 requires a patentee or patent owner, whether or not he makes or vends, to give notice in one of the two alternative methods, (marking the article, or giving actual notice to the defendant) as therein specified. By plain language, the duty to give notice of infringement is imposed without limitation upon "all patentees and their assigns and legal representatives." Then the statute proceeds and imposes this upon "all persons making or vending any patented article for or under them." The duty to give notice is required not only of patentees and their assigns and legal representatives, but also the duty is imposed upon all persons making or vending under them.

* * *

Obviously, but for § 4900, a patentee might recover for all damages suffered through infringement without giving prior actual notice to the infringer. That section subtracts something and creates an exception.

If respondent's position is correct, process patents and patents under which nothing has been manufactured may be secretly infringed with impunity, notwithstanding injury to owners guilty of no neglect. Only plain language could convince us of such an intent.

The idea of a tangible article proclaiming its own character runs through this and related provisions. Two kinds of notice are specified—one to the public by a visible mark, another by actual advice to the infringer. The second becomes necessary only when the first has not been given; and the first can only be given in connection with some fabricated article. Penalty for failure implies opportunity to perform.

If the word "patentees" is not qualified by "making or vending any patented article," the section would seem to impose on such persons a duty to the public impossible of performance when no article is made or vended by them. Also, if these words do not qualify patentees, then the words "same" and "thereon," are not easily understood.

[The court here reviews the statutory history.]

All these acts reveal the purpose to require that marks be put on patented articles for the information of the public. They undertook to specify those charged with the duty to attach such marks. In this regard, the meaning of the Act of 1861 is not open to question. The different language found in the Act of 1870 was intended, we think, to delimit the term "a person under the protection of letters patent," to describe the members of the class more definitely, and not to impose a new and different burden upon non-producing patentees. We find nothing adequate to support the notion that such patentees were deprived of the right theretofore existing to claim damages from an infringer unless and until he could be run down and served with actual notice.

* * *

Under the interpretation which we accept, § 4900, R.S., provides protection against deception by unmarked patented articles, and requires nothing unreasonable of patentees. By admission, the Act of 1861 did not require a patentee who did not produce to give actual notice to an infringer before damages could be recovered; and there is nothing in the language or history of the Act of 1870 sufficient to indicate an intent to alter his position in this regard. This conclusion is in harmony with the language of Dunlap v. Schofield, 152 U.S. 244, 247, 14 S.Ct. 576, 38 L.Ed. 426.

The challenged judgment must be reversed. The judgment of the District Court is affirmed.

Reversed.

OIL WELL IMPROVEMENTS CO. v. ACME FOUNDRY & MACHINE CO.

United States Court of Appeals, Eighth Circuit, 1929.
31 F.2d 898, 900.

[Excerpt Only]

STONE, CIRCUIT JUDGE. [W]hen should the period for estimating the damages begin? This depends upon the time of notice to the infringer. The appellee contends that no notice was given by marking the patented article as required by section 4900, R.S. (35 U.S.C.A. § 49), and, therefore, no recovery could be had for the period before this action was filed. Also, that the burden of proof is on appellant to show notice. It is certainly true that such burden of proof is on appellant. It is equally true, as impliedly conceded by appellee, that notice may be given otherwise than by the statutory method. The statutory method is merely supplemental—amounting to "legal" notice, analogous to that of recordation statutes. The essential matter, where the statutory method is not used to supply the deficiency, is actual notice to the infringer that the product of the patentee is patented.

KAPLAN v. HELENHART NOVELTY CORP.

United States Court of Appeals, Second Circuit, 1950.
182 F.2d 311, 85 USPQ 285.

[In an action for Declaratory Judgment to have a patent held invalid, the plaintiff complained that defendant had improperly notified customers of infringement and a temporary injunction was issued by the District Court. On appeal, the Circuit Court stated in part as follows:]

The plaintiffs brought this suit on October 7, 1949. It is asserted in an affidavit in opposition to the plaintiffs' motion for a temporary injunction that no suit was brought against the plaintiffs because of the expense involved, because of the pendency of another patent application by the individual defendant on which he would like to sue at the same time if suit were brought and because "during about the last five or six months of 1948 and until very recently, that is until about the 15th of September of this year, I was unaware of any sales by Mr. Kaplan and his partner of the football puzzle referred to in Mr. Price's letters and therefore believed that they had discontinued the manufacture and sale of these puzzles."

The judge did not consider such excuses an adequate explanation of the defendants' failure to sue in vindication of their rights as asserted in the notices, which he accordingly found to have been given in bad faith. He thus granted the temporary injunction.

As will be seen, this phase of the appeal turns on whether such a finding was justified on this record, since it is not an actionable wrong for one in good faith to make plain to whomsoever he will that it is his purpose to insist upon what he believes to be his legal rights, even though he may misconceive what those rights are.

* * *

While the privilege to try by notice to persuade acquiescence in one's assertions of his rights may not be exercised in bad faith, some confusion has at times crept into findings of bad faith because the distinction between the lack of an honest belief in the legal rights asserted and the lack of any intention to vindicate them by a timely suit has not been kept clear. Unreasonable lapse of time after notice given is evidence of lack of intention to sue and, to a lesser degree, of lack of an honest belief in the validity of the asserted right. Before the Declaratory Judgment Act, 28 U.S.C.A. § 2201, became effective and was construed to permit suit for declaration of invalidity or noninfringement, unreasonable delay in bringing suit after notice was alone sufficient to end the privilege. It really made no practical difference, as long as the giver of the notice could alone decide whether and when suit would be brought, whether he honestly believed in his rights but was unwilling to sue for some other reason or whether he was unwilling to sue because he was too doubtful of them to risk litigation. Consequently, unreasonable lapse of time without suit after notice would lay the basis for an injunction against further notices. Adriance, Platt & Co. v. National Harrow Co., 2 Cir., 121 F. 827.

We have no hesitation in reaching the conclusion that this record contains no substantial evidence to show that the defendants did not and do not reasonably believe that their patent is valid and has been infringed as they have asserted. The patent is presumptively valid; the Patent Office file wrapper and contents of the patent show, defendants' counsel avers, that all of the claims of the patent were allowed, as filed, without the citation of any prior art; and the allegations of infringement do not appear to be frivolous. Thus, the only evidence of bad faith is the defendants' failure to sue promptly. But the plaintiffs have continuously had a plain and complete remedy for any wrong done them, in that they could have brought this suit whenever they pleased after the first notice was given, instead of waiting as they did, since an actual controversy between the parties existed at least during all that time. Any delay in putting the defendants' asserted rights to the test of actual litigation was, therefore, only what the plaintiffs chose to permit, and, as the suit is as timely as they chose to make it, their motion for a temporary injunction stands no differently than it would have if the defendants had sued promptly after notice given.

* * *

Injunction dissolved and cause remanded.

Notes

1. Actual knowledge of the patent in suit by defendant at the time of infringement was held to relieve plaintiff of the burden of proving proper marking in T.C. Weygandt Co. v. Van Emden, 40 F.2d 938, 5 USPQ 521 (S.D.N.Y.1930); Nicholson v. Bailey, 182 F.Supp. 509, 125 USPQ 157 (S.D. Fla.1960). But, contrary is Carlisle v. Estes, 157 USPQ 6 (D.C.Colo.1967).

2. " * * * [T]he marking required by 35 U.S.C.A. § 287 has no application to an alleged infringement of a process patent only." Dairy Foods Inc. v. Farmers Co-operative Creamery, 298 F.Supp. 774, 161 USPQ 26, 27 (D.Minn.1969). See also Bandag, Inc. v. Gerrard Tire Co., 704 F.2d 1578, 217 USPQ 977 (Fed.Cir.1983) (no application to article made by patented process) and Coupe v. Royer, 155 U.S. 565, 15 S.Ct. 199, 39 L.Ed. 263 (1895) (no application to articles made by patented apparatus). The patent in Hanson v. Alpine Valley Ski Area, Inc., 718 F.2d 1075, 219 USPQ 679 (Fed.Cir.1983) included claims directed to a method of making artificial snow and to an article or device for making snow according to the claimed method. However, the patentee sued only for infringement of the method claims. The court held that failure of the exclusive licensee to mark the patented article did not bar recovery for infringement of the method claim.

3. "That a patentee may lawfully issue warnings to infringers of its patent is clear. Virtue et al. v. Creamery Package Manufacturing Co., et al., (8 Cir.1910) 179 F. 115, aff'd 227 U.S. 8, 33 S.Ct. 202. The only limitation on such right is the requirement of good faith, which carries with it the absence of express malice. Kemart Corp. v. Printing Arts Research Laboratories, (9 Cir.1959) 269 F.2d 375, 122 USPQ 56. That the

patentee is eventually found to be incorrect in his contentions of validity and infringement is of no importance so long as he honestly and reasonably believes that which he asserts. Eastern States Petroleum Co. v. Asiatic Petroleum Corp. (2 Cir.1939) 103 F.2d 315. The burden of establishing bad faith is upon the party asserting it. Heuser v. Federal Trade Comm'n, (7 Cir.1925) 4 F.2d 632." Jenkel-Davidson Optical Co. v. Roberts Instrument Co., 137 USPQ 644 (D.C.Missouri 1963).

4. MISCELLANEOUS ACTIONS AND REMEDIES

a. *False Marking*

35 U.S.C.A. § 292. False Marking

(a) Whoever, without the consent of the patentee, marks upon, or affixes to, or uses in advertising in connection with anything made, used, or sold by him, the name or any imitation of the name of the patentee, the patent number, or the words "patent," "patentee," or the like, with the intent of counterfeiting or imitating the mark of the patentee, or of deceiving the public and inducing them to believe that the thing was made or sold by or with the consent of the patentee; or

Whoever marks upon, or affixes to, or uses in advertising in connection with any unpatented article, the word "patent" or any word or number importing that the same is patented, for the purpose of deceiving the public; or

Whoever marks upon, or affixes to, or uses in advertising in connection with any article, the words "patent applied for," "patent pending," or any word importing that an application for patent has been made, when no application for patent has been made, or if made, is not pending, for the purpose of deceiving the public—

Shall be fined not more than $500 for every such offense.

(b) Any person may sue for the penalty, in which event one-half shall go to the person suing and the other to the use of the United States.

FILMON PROCESS CORP. v. SPELL–RIGHT CORP.

United States Court of Appeals, District of Columbia, 1968.
131 U.S.App.D.C. 374, 404 F.2d 1351, 158 USPQ 533.

Before BASTIAN, SENIOR CIRCUIT JUDGE, and LEVENTHAL and ROBINSON, CIRCUIT JUDGES.

LEVENTHAL, CIRCUIT JUDGE. * * *

1. We first consider, and reject, defendants' contention that the judgment is not appealable. It is urged that 35 U.S.C.A. § 292(b) is a criminal statute, that the double jeopardy clause prohibits appellate review of a finding of not guilty in a criminal case where the United States is the prosecutor, and that the same rule bars an appeal challenging the correctness of a judgment against a private party bringing a qui tam action to enforce 35 U.S.C.A. § 292. We put aside the question whether the double jeopardy question is the same when the appeal is by a private person rather than the Government. In our

view the double jeopardy clause does not apply where the nub of the action is civil qui tam enforcement of essentially remedial provisions. We are in agreement with the judicial pronouncements that 35 U.S. C.A. § 292(b), while penal, is not a criminal statute. In our view, that position is a sound basis for rejecting the double jeopardy claim in case of an action by an informer for misuse of his patent mark without his consent. That provision is designed to protect the exclusiveness of the use of the invention granted to the patentee. The patentee is given this remedy to protect his patent position, and as a practical matter, the patentee is the only likely enforcer of it, as recovery requires proof that the statements were made without his consent. We think the statute's remedial purposes outweigh the conceptual difficulties posed by the ostensibly non-compensatory character of the penalty relief awarded against a defendant who appropriates a patentee's mark. Further, although the point pressed herein was not discussed, appellate courts have frequently reviewed claims that a finding of no violation of 35 U.S. C.A. § 292 was clearly erroneous.

2. Defendant prevails, however, on the point that the record amply supports the trial judge's determination that requisite wrongful intention was lacking. Such a determination can be disturbed, as clearly erroneous, only in rare instances.

* * *

Notes

1. Placement of a method patent number on an unpatented article to be used in performing the patented method was not considered false marking in Ansul Co. v. Uniroyal, Inc., 306 F.Supp. 541 (S.D.N.Y.1969), affirmed 448 F.2d 872 (2d Cir.1971).

2. "As a general proposition, there can be no violation of § 292 absent an evidentiary showing that the false marking or mismarking was 'for the purpose of deceiving the public.' Furthermore, the *omission* of 'applicable patents' from a label listing patents purporting to cover the contents of a box of course cannot, in itself, be a violation of the *false* marking statute.

"The district court properly held any action based on the 1973 label, used only until 1978, to be time barred by the applicable statute of limitations, 28 USC 2462, which imposes a 5–year limit on any action for the enforcement of 'any civil fine.'"—Arcadia Machine & Tool, Inc. v. Sturm, Ruger & Co., Inc., 786 F.2d 1124, 1125, 229 USPQ 124, 125 (Fed.Cir. 1986).

b. Infringement by United States

28 U.S.C.A. § 1498. Patent and Copyright Cases

(a) Whenever an invention described in and covered by a patent of the United States is used or manufactured by or for the United States without license of the owner thereof or lawful right to use or manufacture the same, the owner's remedy shall be by action against the United States in the Court of Claims for the recovery of his reasonable and entire compensation for such use and manufacture.

For the purposes of this section, the use or manufacture of an invention described in and covered by a patent of the United States by a contractor, a subcontractor, or any person, firm, or corporation for the Government and with the authorization or consent of the Government, shall be construed as use or manufacture for the United States.

* * *

MOTOROLA, INC. v. UNITED STATES

United States Court of Appeals, Federal Circuit, 1984.
729 F.2d 765, 221 USPQ 297.

KASHIWA, CIRCUIT JUDGE.

* * *

This is a 28 U.S.C. § 1498 action, and as such, the patent owner is seeking to recover just compensation for the Government's unauthorized taking and use of his invention. The theoretical basis for his recovery is the doctrine of eminent domain. Crozier v. Fried. Krupp Aktiengesellschaft, 224 U.S. 290 (1912); Irving Air Chute Co. v. United States, 93 F.Supp. 633, 635, 87 USPQ 246, 248 (Ct.Cl.1950). In this context, the United States is not in the position of an ordinary infringer, United States v. Berdan Fire-Arms Manufacturing Co., 156 U.S. 552, 565–66 (1895); Carter-Wallace, Inc. v. United States, 449 F.2d 1374, 1390, 171 USPQ 359, 370 (Ct.Cl.1971) (Nichols, J., concurring), but rather a compulsory, nonexclusive licensee. Crozier, supra; Irving Air Chute, supra.

As occurs frequently in section 1498 patent actions, the parties in the instant appeal are presenting and arguing the case as if it were an action brought under Title 35. Although concepts, phrases and words commonly used in the patent field may connote or denote a panoply of rights and remedies under Title 35, the same concepts, phrases and words do not and cannot always connote or denote the same meaning under section 1498. Although a section 1498 action may be similar to a Title 35 action, it is nonetheless only parallel and not identical. Calhoun v. United States, 453 F.2d 1385, 1391, 172 USPQ 438, 443 (Ct.Cl. 1972).[3]

3. There are numerous examples of where the patent statutes are inapplicable in an eminent domain context. For instance, increased damages and attorneys fees available against private infringers under 35 U.S.C. §§ 284 and 285 are not permitted in an eminent domain proceeding. Leesona Corp. v. United States, 599 F.2d 958, 202 USPQ 424 (Ct.Cl.), cert. denied, 444 U.S. 991 (1979). In addition, injunctive relief under 35 U.S.C. § 283 is not available to a patent owner in a § 1498 action. Id. at 968, 202 USPQ at 434; see Belknap v. Schild, 161 U.S. 10 (1896). Moreover, the Government (treated as a licensee) has a right to replace (repair) an unpatented element in a patented combination without paying additional royalty.

Calhoun v. United States, 453 F.2d 1385, 1391, 172 USPQ 438, 443 (Ct.Cl.1972). As a compulsory, nonexclusive licensee, the Government is treated as an Aro I (Aro Mfg. Co. v. Convertible Top Replacement Co., 365 U.S. 336, 128 USPQ 354 (1961) voluntary licensee, and not as an Aro II (Aro Mfg. Co. v. Convertible Top Replacement Co., 377 U.S. 476, 483–85, 141 USPQ 681, 684–686 (1964)) private, unlicensed infringer. Further, the Government can only be sued for any direct infringement of a patent (35 U.S.C. § 271(a)), and not for inducing infringement by another (section 271(b)) or for contributory infringement (section 271(c)). Decca Ltd. v. United States, 640 F.2d 1156, 1167, 209 USPQ 52,

35 U.S.C. § 287 advises a patent owner to mark his patented article with a notice of his patent rights. Failure to do so limits his recovery of damages to the period after the infringer receives notice of the infringement. Wine Railway Appliance Co. v. Enterprise Railway Equipment Co., 297 U.S. 387, 395–97 (1936); Olsson v. United States, 72 Ct.Cl. 72, 103–5, 9 USPQ 111 and 11 USPQ 13, 13–14 (1931). The appellee argues and the lower court held that 28 U.S.C. § 1498 incorporates section 287 as a defense for the Government. The lower court stated:

> The Revisor's Notes appended to § 1498 stated that "[i]n absence of a statutory restriction, *any defense* available to a private party is equally available to the United States." * * * [S]ince section 287 is a limitation on the recovery of damages for patent infringement and thus, similar in effect to a defense, incorporating section 287 into 28 U.S.C. § 1498 appears to be within the spirit of the Revisor's Notes. [Emphasis in original.]

In addition, the appellee argues that at the time section 4900 of the Revised Statutes, the predecessor of section 287, was enacted in 1910, failure to mark was treated as a defense. It cites United States Printing Co. v. American Playing-Card Co., 70 Fed. 50, 53–54 (C.C.W.D. Mich.1895); Sessions v. Romadka, 21 Fed. 124, 133 (C.C.E.D.Wis.1884), rev'd in part on other grounds, 145 U.S. 29 (1892) for this proposition. We disagree.

* * *

Another indication that the marking and notice statute was never thought of as defense is the subsequent addition of the title "limitation on damages" to its successor, 35 U.S.C. § 287. Since the text of section 4900 was not changed when codified, the addition of the title supports this interpretation. Brotherhood of Railroad Trainmen v. Baltimore & Ohio Railroad Co., 331 U.S. 519, 529 (1947); Motor Coach Industries, Inc. v. United States, 536 F.2d 930, 936 (Ct.Cl.1976) ("[W]hile titles or headings 'cannot limit the plain meaning of the text,' they are to be considered in resolving ambiguity").

* * *

In light of this policy, a notice to the Government would be meaningless since the contracting agency must award the contract to the lowest bidder regardless of any patent infringement problems. This policy, therefore, does not take into consideration a fundamental rationale supporting section 287—supplying notice in order to prevent innocent infringement. Wine Railway, 297 U.S. at 394. Since the Government does not consider the question whether the device it takes by eminent domain is protected by patents or not, requiring a patent owner to mark his device or give notice pursuant to section 287 would be meaningless in this context. Accordingly, section 287 is not incorporated into section 1498 by government procurement policy.

60 (Ct.Cl.1980), cert. denied, 454 U.S. 819 (1981).

CONCLUSION

In light of our analysis, we interpret 28 U.S.C. § 1498 as not incorporating 35 U.S.C. § 287. The statutory construction of section 1498, the statutory history of section 1498, or the government procurement policy supports this interpretation. Since the Government is not a putative infringer but is deemed a licensee, section 287 has no application in an eminent domain taking. Accordingly, we reverse the Claims Court's judgment and remand for accounting of the just compensation owing to the appellant.

TVI ENERGY CORPORATION v. BLANE

United States Court of Appeals, Federal Circuit, 1986.
806 F.2d 1057, 1 USPQ2d 1071.

DAVIS, CIRCUIT JUDGE.

* * *

The sole issue before us is whether a private party which infringes another's patent during Government bidding activities such as those present here is immune under 28 U.S.C. § 1498 from a District Court infringement action for that test demonstration. In other words, was Blane acting "by or for" the United States and "with its authorization or consent" when it demonstrated the allegedly infringing targets at Fort Knox for the sole purpose of responding to the Government's demand for a "Product Demonstration," with the objective of acquiring a Government contract?

28 U.S.C. § 1498 was adopted originally in 1910 and later amended in 1918. The Congressional history of § 1498 makes it clear that the policy behind the 1918 amendment was to relieve private Government contractors from expensive litigation with patentees, possible injunctions, payment of royalties, and· punitive damages. The amendment provided that the patentees' sole remedy was a suit against the United States in the Court of Claims. The Act was amended in 1918 at the behest of the Secretary of the Navy who cited difficulties in procuring goods from private manufacturers necessary to meet military requirements of World War I. H.R. 10858, 65th Cong., 2d Sess., 36 Cong.Rec. 7961 (1918). *See Richmond Screw Anchor Co. v. United States,* 275 U.S. 331, 339 (1928); *Leesona Corp. v. United States,* 599 F.2d 958, 967, 220 Ct.Cl. 233, 248–49 [202 USPQ 424, 433–34] (1979); *Calhoun v. United States,* 453 F.2d 1385, 1391 [172 USPQ 438, 443] (Ct.Cl.1972).

Appellant's argument that Blane's activities were outside the scope of § 1498, because Blane was merely a *competitor* for a Government contract and not yet an approved Government *source,* is meritless. The significant point is that Blane was *required* to demonstrate the allegedly infringing targets as part of the Government's bidding procedure. Appellees' only purpose in demonstrating the targets was to comply with the Government's bidding requirements. In these circumstances, we can come to no other conclusion than that this demonstration fell within the scope of § 1498 as being "for the United States" and "with its approval." *Cf. Selma, Inc. v. Bridge Electronics Co.,* 300 F.2d 761, 132 USPQ 665 (3d Cir.1962).

* * *

c. *Interfering Patents*

35 U.S.C.A. § 291. Interfering Patents

The owner of an interfering patent may have relief against the owner of another by civil action, and the court may adjudge the question of the validity of any of the interfering patents, in whole or in part. The provisions of the second paragraph of section 146 of this title shall apply to actions brought under this section.

The second paragraph of Section 146 relates to jurisdiction, venue and service of process for civil actions in interferences.

Note

"Under any construction of § 291, it is impossible to conceive how it could be any clearer that interference between patents is a sine qua non of an action under § 291. Absent interference, a court has no power *under § 291* to adjudicate the validity of any patent. We hold that the court has no jurisdiction under § 291 unless interference is established. Mere citation of that statute or recitation in a pleading as a basis for suit is not enough. When challenged, the pleader must establish that interference does in fact exist.

"If the statute leaves a doubt that interference is a jurisdictional prerequisite under § 291, it should have long since been dispelled by P.J. Federico, the principal drafter of the 1952 Patent Act, in his 'Commentary on the New Patent Act,' published as a prologue to 35 USCA (West 1954), at p. 57:

Section 291 relates to interfering patents. When there are interfering patents, the owner of one may file a civil action against the owner of the other and the court may adjudge either or both the patents invalid. The new section has considerably condensed the language of the old statute. Under the old statute, interfering patents arose mostly if not always when a second patent for the same invention, with identical claims, was granted to another inventor who had won an interference with the first patentee in the Patent Office. The losing patentee could not file a civil action against the winning applicant, but could file an interfering patents suit against the winning applicant after the second patent had been granted. In view of the change in the civil action to review an interference decision which permits a losing patentee to file such action (section 146) and the change in the interference section relating to cancellation of the claims of a losing patentee when the interference decision becomes final (section 135), the mentioned occasion for interfering patents will no longer arise, and there will be little or no use for section 291.

The small number of cases decided under § 291 since 1952 bears out the accuracy of Mr. Federico's appraisal of its continued usefulness. More importantly for this case, his comments verify that the existence of interfering patents is intrinsically and inextricably a premise of a § 291 claim.

If that premise fails, then the § 291 claim dependent thereon fails as well." Albert v. Kevex Corp., 729 F.2d 757, 760–61, 221 USPQ 202, 205–06 (Fed. Cir.1984).

d. Unfair Importation

19 U.S.C.A. § 1337. Unfair Practices in Import Trade—Unfair Methods of Competition Declared Unlawful

(a) Unfair methods of competition and unfair acts in the importation of articles into the United States, or in their sale by the owner, importer, consignee, or agent of either, the effect or tendency of which is to destroy or substantially injure an industry, efficiently and economically operated, in the United States, or to prevent the establishment of such an industry, or to restrain or monopolize trade and commerce in the United States, are declared unlawful, and when found by the Commission to exist shall be dealt with, in addition to any other provisions of law, as provided in this section.

Exclusion of Articles From Entry

(d) If the Commission determines, as a result of an investigation under this section, that there is violation of this section, it shall direct that the articles concerned, imported by any person violating the provision of this section, be excluded from entry into the United States, unless, after considering the effect of such exclusion upon the public health and welfare, competitive conditions in the United States economy, the production of like or directly competitive articles in the United States, and United States consumers, it finds that such articles should not be excluded from entry. The Commission shall notify the Secretary of the Treasury of its action under this subsection directing such exclusion from entry, and upon receipt of such notice, the Secretary shall, through the proper officers, refuse such entry.

19 U.S.C.A. § 1337a. Same; Importation of Products Produced Under Process Covered by Claims of Unexpired Patent

The importation for use, sale, or exchange of a product made, produced, processed, or mined under or by means of a process covered by the claims of any unexpired valid United States letters patent, shall have the same status for the purposes of section 1337 of this title as the importation of any product or article covered by the claims of any unexpired valid United States letters patent.

* * *

Section 337 of the Tariff Act provides a vehicle for domestic industry to restrain "unfair competition" through importation of articles into the United States. Importation of articles which infringe a patent, trademark or copyright of a domestic industry are examples of possible "unfair competition". However, the latter term is broader than strict patent, trademark or copyright infringement. For example, importation of an article manufactured abroad by a patented process can be "unfair competition" even though not patent infringement. (Legislation is periodically introduced in Congress which would make such importation infringement of the process patent.)

In general, proceedings are begun by filing a complaint with the International Trade Commission alleging unfair competition by importation to the detriment of a domestic company. The ITC must rule on the complaint in one year, or one and one-half years in complex cases. Discovery is similar to that in Federal courts, and the usual defenses of noninfringement, invalidity, etc. may be asserted. The CAFC has exclusive jurisdiction on appeal from ITC decisions. If the ITC rules in favor of the complainant, the articles in question may be excluded from importation. However, the ITC's exclusive order is subject to disapproval by the President, whose decision is not appealable.

C. DEFENSES

1. STATUTORY PROVISIONS

35 U.S.C.A. § 282. Presumption of Validity; Defenses

A patent shall be presumed valid. Each claim of a patent (whether in independent or dependent form) shall be presumed valid independently of the validity of other claims; dependent claims shall be presumed valid even though dependent upon an invalid claim. The burden of establishing invalidity of a patent or any claim thereof shall rest on the party asserting it.

The following shall be defenses in any action involving the validity or infringement of a patent and shall be pleaded:

(1) Noninfringement, absence of liability for infringement, or unenforceability,

(2) Invalidity of the patent or any claim in suit on any ground specified in part II of this title as a condition for patentability,

(3) Invalidity of the patent or any claim in suit for failure to comply with any requirement of sections 112 or 251 of this title,

(4) Any other fact or act made a defense by this title * * *

2. IN GENERAL

The general statutory defenses are treated throughout this book and will not be considered separately here. There has been a noticeable increase in the use of equitable defenses in recent years which carefully check the conduct of a patentee who seeks judicial aid. An example is patent misuse which springs from the equitable doctrine of unclean hands and the public policies of promoting the useful arts and free and open competition in all unpatentable goods. In general, patent misuse involves an attempt to protect subject matter outside of the patent's scope, such as use of a combination patent in an attempt to monopolize manufacture of an unpatented element of the combination.

Some others are the unenforceability of fraudulently procured patents and the high degree of candor required of patent attorneys and agents in dealing with the Patent Office considered in Part II, Chapter

Four.   Another example not previously considered is the equitable defense of laches in bringing suit which is illustrated by the following cases.

3. LACHES AND EQUITABLE ESTOPPEL

STUDIENGESELLSCHAFT KOHLE mbH v. EASTMAN KODAK COMPANY

United States Court of Appeals, Fifth Circuit, 1980.
616 F.2d 1315.

COLEMAN, CHIEF JUDGE.

* * *

Studiengesellschaft Kohle mbH (SGK) charged Eastman Kodak Company (Eastman) with infringement of patents obtained by Professor Karl Ziegler covering certain chemical catalysts useful in the polymerization of hydrocarbons. * * * At the conclusion of these extensive proceedings, the Court found that Eastman had not infringed the remaining patents, held that certain claims of the '792 patent were invalid, and concluded, alternatively, that SGK's claims were barred by laches. *Studiengesellschaft Kohle v. Eastman Kodak,* 450 F.Supp. 1211 (E.D.Tex.1977).

* * *

Laches and estoppel are equitable defenses whose appropriateness must be determined in each case under its particular factual situation. *Advanced Hydraulics, Inc. v. Otis Elevator Co.,* 525 F.2d 477, 479 (7th Cir.) *cert. denied,* 423 U.S. 869, 96 S.Ct. 132, 46 L.Ed.2d 99 (1975); *Potash Co. of America v. International Minerals & Chemical Corp.,* 213 F.2d 153, 155 (10th Cir.1954); *Shaffer v. Rector Well Equipment Co.,* 155 F.2d at 345.   Whether the plaintiff should be barred by laches or estoppel is to be determined by the trial judge in the exercise of judicial discretion, and his findings will be reversed only if they are clearly erroneous. *Baker Manufacturing Co. v. Whitewater Manufacturing Co.,* 430 F.2d 1008, 1009 (7th Cir.1970) *cert. denied,* 401 U.S. 956, 91 S.Ct. 978, 28 L.Ed.2d 240 (1971); *General Electric Co. v. Sciaky Brothers, Inc.,* 304 F.2d 724, 727 (6th Cir.1962); *Potash Co. of America v. International Minerals & Chemical Corp.,* 213 F.2d at 155.

Although laches and estoppel are related concepts, there is a clear distinction between the two. *TWM Manufacturing Co., Inc. v. Dura Corp.,* 592 F.2d at 349–50; *Advanced Hydraulics, Inc. v. Otis Elevator Co.,* 525 F.2d at 479; *Continental Coatings Corp. v. Metco, Inc.,* 464 F.2d 1375, 1379 (7th Cir.1972).   The defense of laches may be invoked where the plaintiff has unreasonably and inexcusably delayed in prosecuting its rights and where that delay has resulted in material prejudice to the defendant.   The effect of laches is merely to withhold damages for infringement which occurred prior to the filing of the suit. *Advanced Hydraulics, Inc. v. Otis Elevator,* 525 F.2d at 479; *American Home Products Corp. v. Lockwood Manufacturing Co.,* 483 F.2d 1120, 1122 (6th

Cir.1973), *cert. denied,* 414 U.S. 1158, 94 S.Ct. 917, 39 L.Ed.2d 110 (1974); *Shaffer v. Rector Well Equipment Co.,* 155 F.2d at 345.

Estoppel, on the other hand, "arises only when one has so acted as to mislead another and the one thus misled has relied upon the action of the inducing party to his prejudice." *Lebold v. Inland Steel Co.,* 125 F.2d 369, 375 (7th Cir.1941); *see also Advanced Hydraulics, Inc. v. Otis Elevator Co.,* 525 F.2d at 479; *Armstrong v. Motorola, Inc.,* 374 F.2d 764 (7th Cir.1967). Estoppel forecloses the patentee from enforcing his patent prospectively through an injunction or through damages for continuing infringement. *Advanced Hydraulics, Inc. v. Otis Elevator Co.,* 525 F.2d at 479; *Continental Coatings Corp. v. Metco, Inc.,* 464 F.2d at 1379; *George J. Meyer Manufacturing Co. v. Miller Manufacturing Co.,* 24 F.2d 505, 507 (7th Cir.1928).

In considering whether plaintiff's delay in litigating his claim makes him guilty of laches, courts use the six-year statutory period for damages as a frame of reference, *TWM Manufacturing Co., Inc. v. Dura Corp.,* 592 F.2d at 348; *General Electric Co. v. Sciaky Brothers, Inc.,* 304 F.2d at 727; *Whitman v. Walt Disney Productions, Inc.,* 263 F.2d 229, 231 (9th Cir.1958); but laches may also bar a suit brought within the period specified by the corresponding statute of limitations. *Whitman v. Walt Disney Productions, Inc.,* 263 F.2d at 232.

Mere delay in bringing suit is not, of itself, sufficient to constitute laches in a patent infringement action. *Maloney-Crawford Tank Corp. v. Rocky Mountain Natural Gas Co., Inc.,* 494 F.2d 401, 403 (10th Cir. 1974); *Jenn-Air Corp. v. Penn Ventilator Co.,* 464 F.2d 48, 50 (3rd Cir. 1972). Instead, two elements must be established: (1) that the delay was unreasonable or inexcusable; (2) that the defendant has suffered injury or prejudice as a result of the delay. *Advanced Hydraulics, Inc. v. Otis Elevator Company,* 525 F.2d at 479; *Maloney-Crawford Tank Corp. v. Rocky Mountain Natural Gas Co., Inc.,* 494 F.2d at 403; *American Home Products Corp. v. Lockwood Manufacturing Co.,* 483 F.2d at 1122; *Jenn-Air Corp. v. Penn Ventilator Co.,* 464 F.2d at 50; *Potash Co. of America v. International Minerals & Chemical Corp.,* 213 F.2d at 154; *Shaffer v. Rector Well Equipment Co.,* 155 F.2d at 345; *Technitrol, Inc. v. Memorex Corp.,* 376 F.Supp. 828, 830–31 (N.D.Ill. 1974), *affirmed,* 513 F.2d 1130 (7th Cir.1975) (per curiam).

Although at one time the courts seemed divided over the relative burdens the parties must bear under a laches defense, recent cases reflect a growing unanimity among the circuits. Where the plaintiff's delay has exceeded the statutory six-year period, the delay is presumed unreasonable, and the plaintiff has the burden of justifying the delay. Similarly, when the delay exceeds six years, injury to the defendant is presumed, and the defendant need not necessarily produce additional evidence of prejudice. *TWM Manufacturing Co., Inc. v. Dura Corp.,* 592 F.2d at 349; *Continental Coatings Corp. v. Metco, Inc.,* 464 F.2d at 1378; *Baker Manufacturing Co. v. Whitewater Manufacturing Co.,* 430 F.2d at 1009; *Technitrol, Inc. v. Memorex Corp.,* 376 F.Supp. 828, 831 (N.D.Ill.

1974), *affirmed,* 513 F.2d 1130 (7th Cir.1975) (per curiam). Where the action is brought within the analogous limitation period, however, the defendant must show both that the delay is unreasonable and that he has suffered injury. *Maloney-Crawford Tank Corp. v. Rocky Mountain Natural Gas Co., Inc.,* 494 F.2d at 404. *Jenn-Air Corp. v. Penn Ventilator Co.,* 464 F.2d at 50.

To determine the length of plaintiff's delay, the court must look not to the date on which the patent issued but rather to the time at which the plaintiff knew or, in the exercise of reasonable diligence, should have known of the defendant's alleged infringing action. *See TWM Manufacturing Co., Inc. v. Dura Corp.,* 592 F.2d at 349 (period of delay begins to run from the notice of infringement given to defendant); *Maloney-Crawford Tank Corp. v. Rocky Mountain Natural Gas Co., Inc.,* 494 F.2d at 403 (where known infringement began before plaintiff obtained title to patent, delay is measured from time title was obtained); *Moore v. Schultz,* 491 F.2d 294, 300–01 (10th Cir.1974) (period begins when plaintiff became aware of the possible infringement); *Potash Co. of America v. International Minerals & Chemical Corp.,* 213 F.2d at 155 (laches will not be imputed to one who has been justifiably ignorant of facts which create his right of action, but he must be diligent and make such inquiry and investigation as the circumstances reasonably suggest).

The Courts have recognized a variety of factors which constitute prejudice to the defendant because of plaintiff's delay. Chief among these are the fact that important witnesses have died, that the memories of other witnesses have been dulled, that relevant records have been destroyed or are missing, and that the defendant has made heavy capital investments in its facilities in order to expand production connected with the alleged infringing article. *See, e.g., Advanced Hydraulics, Inc. v. Otis Elevator Co.,* 525 F.2d at 482; *Continental Coatings Corp. v. Metco, Inc.,* 464 F.2d at 1378; *Potash Co. of America v. International Minerals & Chemical Corp.,* 213 F.2d at 160; *Brennan v. Hawley Products Co.,* 182 F.2d 945, 948 (7th Cir.1950).

The factors which will excuse delay in bringing an infringement suit are less clear. The chief subject of dispute in this area is the plaintiff's activity in pursuing other infringement suits during the period of delay. * * * Where the plaintiff is engaged in other litigation involving the patent, to escape a defense of laches he must at least inform the potential infringer of his intent to pursue his rights under the patent.

* * *

Eastman argues that there is no evidence that the existence of litigation prevented Ziegler from instituting the present suit. We know of no appellate case which has established a rule requiring the plaintiff affirmatively to demonstrate that the other litigation prevented the prosecution of a patent claim. Quite the contrary, as we noted earlier, the cases have worked from the assumption that a patentee is not required to litigate against all his potential infringers simultaneously. *See e.g., Clair v. Kastar, Inc.,* 148 F.2d at 646; *Montgomery Ward v. Clair,* 123 F.2d at 883. The most the cases have required, in dicta, is that the defendant be informed of the pending litigation and of the plaintiff's intent to pursue his rights against a possible infringer. *See Advanced Hydraulics, Inc. v. Otis Elevator Co.,* 525 F.2d at 481; *American Home Products Corp. v. Lockwood Manufacturing Co.,* 483 F.2d at 1123. Those requirements have been met here.

As we pointed out earlier, estoppel—the preclusion of prospective or continuing relief—requires not only delay by the plaintiff and prejudice to the defendant but also misleading action by the plaintiff which causes the defendant to engage in conduct which would result in its injury if the suit were allowed to go forward. The plaintiff must have made representations or engaged in conduct which justifies an inference of abandonment of the patent claim or which has induced the infringer to believe that its business would be unmolested. As the Sixth Circuit observed in *TWM Manufacturing Co., Inc. v. Dura Corp.,* 592 F.2d at 350, for silence to work an estoppel, "some evidence must exist to justify an inference that the silence was sufficiently misleading to amount to 'bad faith.'" *See also Continental Coatings Corp. v. Metco, Inc.,* 464 F.2d at 1379–80.

* * *

4. STATUTE OF LIMITATIONS

35 U.S.C.A. § 286. Time Limitation on Damages

Except as otherwise provided by law, no recovery shall be had for any infringement committed more than six years prior to the filing of the complaint or counterclaim for infringement in the action.

In the case of claims against the United States Government for use of a patented invention, the period before bringing suit, up to six years, between the date of receipt of a written claim for compensation by the department or agency of the Government having authority to settle such claim, and the date of mailing by the Government of a notice to the claimant that his claim has been denied shall not be counted as part of the period referred to in the preceding paragraph.

THE STANDARD OIL CO. v. NIPPON SHOKUBAI KAGAKU KOGYO CO., LTD.

United States Court of Appeals, Federal Circuit, 1985.
754 F.2d 345, 224 USPQ 863.

RICH, CIRCUIT JUDGE.

* * *

The patent claims a process for making acrolein, in which process a bismuth molybdate catalyst is employed. Rohm and Haas Company and its subsidiary Rohm and Haas Texas, Incorporated (collectively R & H) have practiced the process, obtaining the catalyst from Nippon. The first use of the process by R & H was in 1973 in an experimental or pilot plant operation in Philadelphia in which a relatively small amount (about 200 pounds) of the catalyst was required. Subsequently R & H built a production plant in Texas and obtained from Nippon a large quantity of catalyst which has been described as "a full charge and one-half of catalyst" for the new Texas plant. This large quantity was shipped to R & H in Texas by Nippon in July, August, and November, 1975. Operation of that Texas plant began on November 18, 1976. The record shows no sale or delivery of catalyst by Nippon to R & H after 1975 and none is alleged. This suit was commenced against R & H and Nippon on November 18, 1982, six years "to a day," as Sohio's counsel said, after the alleged infringement by R & H in Texas by use of the Callahan process of the '007 patent.[3] Having delayed that long, Sohio counsel explained that suit was then brought because "the statute of limitations came upon us. And that is the reason we ultimately did file it." Another statement of counsel was, "We were forced by the statute of limitations to file this lawsuit against Rohm and Haas and N.S.K.K. else we would lose our right under the statute of limitations."

This so-called statute of limitations, referred to by counsel, in section 286 of the Patent Act of 1952, Title 35 USC, which reads in pertinent part:

§ 286. TIME LIMITATION ON DAMAGES

Except as otherwise provided by law, no recovery shall be had for any infringement committed more than six years prior to the filing of the complaint or counterclaim for infringement in the action.

* * *

The only act of Nippon alleged to constitute any kind of infringement of the '007 patent is the selling to R & H of catalyst for use in the Callahan process covered by the patent. The sale of catalyst does not, of course, constitute practice of the patented process and is not direct infringement. Nippon has not been charged with direct infringement but only with "inducing infringement" or "contributory infringement." See 35 USC 271(b) and (c). There is no discussion in the briefs of what, if anything, Nippon has done other than the sale of catalyst to constitute such forms of infringement and therefore we need not discuss these sometimes difficult questions.

The determinate fact here is that all of the acts of Nippon complained of took place and were over and done with before the end of 1975. This suit was filed November 18, 1982, at least six years, nine months, and eighteen days thereafter. At that time, the '007 patent had been long expired so no prospective relief, such as injunction or a holding of infringement by sale of catalyst subsequent to June 14, 1977, is a possibility. A possible award of damages by reason of the sales already affected is the only matter to be considered. Assuming in-

---

3. Sohio's counsel conceded that any recovery for infringement of the '007 patent in the 1973 Philadelphia operation is barred.

fringement, arguendo, and consequent damage, we turn now to a discussion of the effect of § 286, quoted above.

Black's law dictionary (4th Ed.1968) defined a statute of limitations thus:

A statute prescribing limitations to the right of action on certain described causes of action; that is, declaring that *no suit shall be maintained* on such cause of action unless brought within as specified period after the right accrued. Statutes of limitation are statutes of repose. [Emphasis ours.]

Reading § 286 in light of this definition shows that this statute is not a statute of limitations barring suit in the usual meaning of the term. It does not say that "no suit shall be maintained." Take, for example, the situation of R & H in this case as it was before the district court. R & H was allegedly continuing the use of the '007 patent process. Waiting for more than six years after that use commenced did not create a bar under § 286 to the *bringing of a suit* for infringement or *maintaining* the suit. Assuming a finding of liability, the only effect § 286 has is to prevent any "recovery * * * for any infringement committed more than six years prior to the filing of the complaint * * * *" Therefore, suit could be maintained and recovery of damages could be had for infringement taking place *within* the six years prior to the filing of the complaint. This assumes, of course, no other impediment to recovery or maintenance of the suit such an application of the doctrine of laches.

Since § 286 cannot properly be called a "statute of limitations" in the sense that it defeats the right to bring suit, it cannot be said that the statute "begins to run" on some date or other. In the application of § 286, one starts from the filing of a complaint or counterclaim and counts *backward* to determine the date before which infringing *acts* cannot give rise to a right to recover damages.

With respect to Nippon, the situation is different from that of R & H. No act of Nippon within the six years prior to suit is complained of. By reason of § 286, no recovery against Nippon can be had, as the district court properly held. The complaint against it was therefore properly dismissed by the district court. Since that suffices to sustain the judgment of dismissal, it is unnecessary for us to reach the other ground relied on, laches, and we do not do so or express any opinion thereon.

* * *

D. EFFECT OF JUDGMENTS

MISSISSIPPI CHEMICAL CORPORATION v. SWIFT AGRICULTURAL CHEMICALS CORPORATION

United States Court of Appeals, Federal Circuit, 1983.
717 F.2d 1374, 219 USPQ 577.

On Petition for a Writ of Mandamus

Friedman, Circuit Judge.

This is a petition for a writ of mandamus directing a United States District Judge to grant a motion for summary judgment of patent invalidity in a patent infringement suit. The motion, based on *Blonder-Tongue Laboratories, Inc. v. University of Illinois Foundation*, 402 U.S. 313, 91 S.Ct. 1434, 28 L.Ed.2d 788 (1971), urges that the patentee be estopped from relitigating the validity of the patent at issue in the present case because it has already been declared invalid in a prior case after a full and fair trial. We grant the petition, and direct the district judge to grant the motion.

* * *

A. In 1974, Swift filed in the United States District Court for the Eastern District of Louisiana an infringement suit against Usamex Fertilizers. After trial, the district court held the patent valid and infringed. *Swift Chemical Co. v. Usamex Fertilizers, Inc.*, 197 USPQ 10 (E.D.La.1977). Usamex noted an appeal, which was dismissed in March 1978 after the parties had settled the outstanding issues in the case, and the court had entered a consent judgment on damages.

* * *

B. In 1978, Swift filed in the United States District Court for the District of Kansas an infringement suit against Farmland Industries. After an eight-day trial, the district court held the Kearns patent invalid because the patented invention was anticipated by the prior art and would have been obvious, and not infringed. *Swift Agricultural Chemicals Corp. v. Farmland Industries, Inc.*, 499 F.Supp. 1295, 210 USPQ 137 (D.Kan.1980). The court noted the prior contrary decision in the *Usamex* case. It pointed out, however, that the unsuccessful argument for invalidity pressed in *Usamex* was based upon different contentions from the argument urged by Farmland, which the district court accepted. 499 F.Supp. at 1305–06, 210 USPQ at 146. The court also pointed out that since one of the grounds upon which it held the patent invalid for obviousness had not been raised in *Usamex*, "there was evidently no evidence introduced [in *Usamex*] on the question of whether representatives of the prior art might have" shown obviousness on that ground. *Id.* at 1305, 210 USPQ at 146.

* * *

A. In *Blonder-Tongue*, the Supreme Court held that where a patent has been declared invalid in a proceeding in which the "patentee has had a full and fair chance to litigate the validity of his patent" (402 U.S. at 333, 91 S.Ct. at 1445), the patentee is collaterally estopped from relitigating the validity of the patent. If an alleged infringer raises the defense of collateral estoppel, the burden is on the patentee "to demonstrate, if he can, that he did not have 'a fair opportunity procedurally, substantively and evidentially to pursue his claim the first time'" (*quoting Eisel v. Columbia Packing Co.*, 181 F.Supp. 298, 301 (D.Mass. 1960)). *Id.* See also *Carter-Wallace, Inc. v. United States,* 496 F.2d 535, 538–39, 204 Ct.Cl. 341 (1974). Among the factors to be considered in determining whether the patentee had a full and fair opportunity to litigate the validity of the patent in the prior case are

> whether the opinions filed by the District Court and the reviewing court, if any, indicate that the prior case was one of those relatively rare instances where the courts wholly failed to grasp the technical subject matter and issues in suit; and whether without fault of his own the patentee was deprived of crucial evidence or witnesses in the first litigation.

Blonder-Tongue, 402 U.S. at 333, 91 S.Ct. at 1445 (footnote omitted).

In denying Mississippi Chemical's motion for summary judgment of patent invalidity, which was based on collateral estoppel, the district judge did not find that Swift had not had a "full and fair chance" to litigate the validity of its patent in the *Farmland* case, or that the courts in that case "wholly failed to grasp the technical subject matter and issues in suit." To the contrary, the judge specifically deleted from Swift's proposed findings (which, as indicated, he otherwise adopted verbatim) statements that would have reflected that conclusion. The judge rejected the following language in Swift's proposed finding 9, which dealt with an affidavit of C. Marshall Dann, a former Commissioner of the Patent and Trademark Office:

> Mr. Dann testified clearly and unequivocally through his uncontradicted Affidavit that the courts in the Tenth Circuit wholly failed to grasp the technical subject matter and issues in the *Swift v. Farmland* suit. Defendant has not submitted any evidence to rebut this affidavit.

The judge also rejected proposed finding 10, which stated:

> Based on the record before this Court it appears that the Kansas courts wholly failed to grasp the technical subject matter of the Kearns invention, nor did they even consider why the Kearns process worked while all the prior attempts of others failed.

The district judge's refusal to adopt the foregoing findings presumably reflects the fact that Swift did not establish, by affidavit or otherwise, that it was denied a full and fair opportunity to litigate the validity of its patent in the *Farmland* case. There was an eight-day trial before the district court, and apparently there is no contention that in that trial Swift "was deprived of crucial evidence or witnesses. . . ." *Blonder-Tongue,* 402 U.S. at 333, 91 S.Ct. at 1445. The district court rendered a detailed and careful opinion, in which it discussed the evidence at length and explained why it concluded that the patented invention was anticipated and obvious. The court of appeals similarly explained in detail the reasons for its affirmance. Although there may be basis for disagreement with the *Farmland* decision of invalidity, such disagreement is not enough to establish that in the trial and appeal Swift did not have a full and fair opportunity to litigate the validity of its patent. *See Carter-Wallace*, 496 F.2d at 542; *Blumcraft of Pittsburgh v. Kawneer Co.*, 482 F.2d 542, 546–48, 178 USPQ 513, 516–18 (5th Cir.1973).

* * *

Indeed, *Blonder-Tongue* itself recognized the inappropriateness of extensive litigation on "the question whether the party to be estopped had a full and fair opportunity to litigate his claim in the first action." 402 U.S. at 347, 91 S.Ct. at 1452. The Court stated that "the accused infringer should have available an estoppel defense that can be pleaded affirmatively and determined on a pretrial motion for judgment on the pleadings or summary judgment." *Id.* at 348, 91 S.Ct. at 1452.

B. The reasons the district judge gave for rejecting the collateral estoppel defense are unconvincing, and do not justify the exception he created to the *Blonder-Tongue* principle.

1. The judge stated that the "entire basis and rationale" of *Blonder-Tongue* "are considerations of efficiency and economy," and that "[t]hese considerations of economy are obviously not present in this case * * *." The Supreme Court relied upon those considerations, however, as part of its reasoning for the principle it announced in *Blonder-Tongue*. The decision in that case does not contemplate or sanction the determination, on a case-to-case basis, whether considerations of efficiency and economy warrant application of collateral estoppel in the particular situation before the court. The approach of the district judge in this case would virtually nullify the *Blonder-Tongue* rule and its purpose to prevent relitigation of patent validity once the patent has been held invalid in a case in which the patentee had a full and fair opportunity to litigate the issue.

2. The district judge concluded that it would be "fundamentally offensive" to deny Swift "the opportunity" to relitigate the validity of its patent in view of the fact that the courts of the Fifth Circuit "in a full and fair fight" had held the patent valid. In *Stevenson v. Sears Roebuck & Co.*, 713 F.2d 705 at 710 (Fed.Cir.1983), we recently held that under *Blonder-Tongue*, where there have been inconsistent prior determinations of validity, the only permissible inquiry for the district court is "whether the patentee had a full and fair opportunity to litigate the validity of his patent in the prior unsuccessful suit." We followed and quoted with approval from *Blumcraft of Pittsburgh v. Kawneer Co.*, 482 F.2d 542, 548–49, 178 USPQ 513, 517–18 (5th Cir.1973), where the court stated:

> The fact that a prior inconsistent ruling of validity raises a question as to the correctness of the invalidity determination does not create an exception to *Blonder-Tongue* and in fact is fully supported by

the facts in *Blonder-Tongue*. . . . [T]he fact of a *prior* successful suit, as here, should not in itself be permitted to undermine the numerous policy reasons expounded in *Blonder-Tongue* in favor of applying estoppel. [Emphasis in original.]

Thus, as we concluded in *Stevenson,* the existence of a prior inconsistent decision on validity of the patent "should serve only as a 'red flag warning' to the court to apply the full and fair criteria more carefully." At 711.

* * *

C. The short of the matter is that under *Blonder-Tongue,* the only inquiry open to the district judge is whether the patentee had a full and fair opportunity to litigate the validity of the patent in the prior case in which it was held invalid. Unless the district judge finds that the patentee did not have that opportunity, the judge must treat the prior determination of invalidity as estopping the patentee from relitigating that question. The judge cannot permit relitigation because of equitable considerations. *See Blumcraft,* 482 F.2d at 547, 178 USPQ at 516; *Kaiser Industrial Corp. v. Jones & Laughlin Steel Corp.,* 515 F.2d 964, 978–79, 185 USPQ 343, 355–56 (3d Cir.1975), *cert. denied,* 423 U.S. 876, 96 S.Ct. 150, 46 L.Ed.2d 110 (1975); *Carter-Wallace,* 496 F.2d at 542. Although the Supreme Court in *Blonder-Tongue* referred to the "trial courts' sense of justice and equity" (402 U.S. at 334, 91 S.Ct. at 1445), "the only discretion left to the district court's 'sense of equity and justice' by *Blonder-Tongue* is in the determination of whether the plaintiff had a full and fair opportunity to litigate in the prior suit finding invalidity." *Blumcraft,* 482 F.2d at 547, 178 USPQ at 516. *Accord, Kaiser Industrial Corp.,* 515 F.2d at 978–79, 185 USPQ at 355–56.

* * *

BOUTELL v. VOLK

United States Court of Appeals, Tenth Circuit, 1971.
449 F.2d 673, 171 USPQ 668.

WILLIAM E. DOYLE, CIRCUIT JUDGE.

This appeal, by the plaintiff in the district court, involves a patent infringement action pertaining to Claim 6 of U.S. Patent No. 2,674,957, which was issued April 13, 1954. It pertains to the combination of front and rear wheel axle assemblies on a roller coaster type of amusement car which are designed so as to insure that the car will remain on the track at relatively high speeds while executing sharp substantially banked curves.

* * *

III

The remaining matter to consider is the contention of Boutell that Volk is now estopped to question the validity of the Miller patent in view of the Wisconsin litigation, Boutell v. Miler, 67–C–259 (D.C.E.D. Wis.), wherein the patent was ruled valid following a settlement in which Boutell was given a license and a consent judgment of validity was entered. Appellant would have us apply Blonder-Tongue Laboratories, Inc. v. University of Illinois Foundation, 402 U.S. 313, 91 S.Ct. 1434, 28 L.Ed.2d 788 (1971). Appellant does not argue that Volk was a participant in the Wisconsin case whereby he is on this account precluded from again litigating, for it is obvious that Volk was not a party directly or indirectly in the Wisconsin litigation. Instead, he contends that *Blonder-Tongue* has eliminated all need for privity in a patent case.[6] This is a grossly inaccurate appraisal.

* * *

Neither the actual decision of the Supreme Court nor the language of the opinion suggests that the mutuality requirement is relaxed as to a new infringer following an adjudication of validity. To so hold would deprive the alleged infringer of a trial. Thus, the obvious distinction is that it is not inequitable to relax mutuality in a situation in which the patentee has fired his best shot, so to speak, and has missed. On the other hand, it is grossly inequitable to bind a party to a judgment of *validity* rendered in an action against some other party.

The Supreme Court also made clear that the decision was not dictated by judicial administration considerations, but rather the justice and equity of permitting a patentee to shop interminably for a district in which he can secure a favorable adjudication. In any event, there is nothing in the very careful opinion of Mr. Justice White which in any way intimates that the patentee is free to obtain a judgment of validity and thrust it upon non-participating parties in other litigation. To do so would be contrary to the very matters which were weighed and considered in arriving at the final conclusion in *Blonder-Tongue*.

Moreover, there are no underlying policy considerations which would justify the interpretation which is advanced by the appellant here, for although the holder of a valid patent is entitled to all of the limited monopoly rights granted by law, there is no policy which favors the extending of his monopoly beyond the legal borders which have been established. In summary, then, we see no support in *Blonder-Tongue* for plaintiff's interpretation, and we therefore conclude that the district court was entirely correct in refusing in these conditions to give effect to the Wisconsin judgment.

The judgment is affirmed.

Notes

1. Where a previous suit had been dismissed because plaintiff lacked the capacity to sue, this will not work an estoppel against a plaintiff in privity. Grantham v. McGraw-Edison Co., 444 F.2d 210, 170 USPQ 201 (7th Cir.1971).

6. Appellants' brief explains *Blonder-Tongue* as:

The requirement of mutuality being overruled in patent cases to reduce crowded dockets.

2. Blonder-Tongue has been cited as a reason why summary judgments should be used only sparingly in patent suits. Black, Sivalls & Bryson, Inc. v. National Tank Co., 445 F.2d 922, 171 USPQ 17 (10th Cir. 1971).

3. Nothing in Blonder-Tongue indicates that a validity holding can't be good against a class of alleged infringers in a class action suit or that class actions aren't to be used after Blonder-Tongue. Dale Electronics, Inc. v. R.C.L. Electronics, Inc., 53 F.R.D. 531 (D.N.H.1971).

4. "As a general rule, while due process requires that a person shall have an opportunity to be heard by a court of competent jurisdiction upon a matter which affects his interest, parties are precluded by the doctrine of res judicata from relitigating controversies which have been settled by a valid final judgment of such a court. The principles underlying this doctrine have been so often stated and are so universally recognized that the citation of authorities is unnecessary. Under the doctrine of collateral estoppel, an aspect of res judicata, though the causes of action be different a decision by a court of competent jurisdiction in respect to any essential fact or question in one action is likewise conclusive between the same parties in all subsequent actions, and this applies to a state court judgment upon a contested issue which is sought to be applied in a suit between the same parties in a federal court. The doctrine has been applied to state court judgments involving patent rights and such judgments have been held to bar relitigation of the identical issues in the federal court. There is no logical reason why this rule should not apply to a state court judgment adjudicating an infringement question.

* * * It necessarily follows, we think, that a finding by a state court in a suit for royalties under a license agreement that the licensee's product was not within the claims of the patent must be given the effect of collateral estoppel in a subsequent infringement suit between the same parties in the federal court to the extent of precluding assertion by the patent owner that the same product infringes the claims of the same patent. The fact of noninfringement must be taken as conclusively established. Beyond this, however, the federal court is not bound by the judgment of the state court but may frame its own judgment consistently with all the facts of the case, the established fact of noninfringement as well as any others." Vanderveer v. Erie Mallable Iron Co., 238 F.2d 510, 111 USPQ 292 (3d Cir.1956).

5. "It has been settled doctrine in federal courts for at least seventy-five years that when a person not a party to the action takes over its defence, he may take advantage of the judgment if he wins, and he will be bound by it if he loses, exactly as though he were a party of record (Lovejoy v. Murray, 3 Wall. 1, 18, 19). To this has been added a gloss, certainly valid if he would take advantage of the judgment, that his defence must be open and avowed. Souffront v. Compagnie des Sucreries, 217 U.S. 473, 487." Minneapolis-Honeywell Regulator Co. v. Thermoco Inc., 116 F.2d 845, 846, 48 USPQ 221, 222 (2d Cir.1941).

6. "May a judgment be res judicata as to a person not a party who defended the suit on behalf of the record defendant where such participa-

tion was not open and avowed to the knowledge of the plaintiff during the pendency of the suit?

* * *

"If Caterpillar had lost in the Nevada litigation and International were now endeavoring to take advantage of the rule of res judicata against the unsuccessful plaintiff, then the open and avowed rule would be applicable. The reason is that to allow the secret defendant to have the advantage of the rule would be 'to force a plaintiff to prosecute to the utmost suits which, for personal or pecuniary reasons, he wishes to let slide.' 39 Columbia Law Review 1251, 1252.

* * *

"But it does not follow that because the defendant's participation must be known in order for him to have the benefit of the judgment, that his participation must be known in order that he be bound by it.

* * *

"We conclude that both fairness to the parties involved and the general public policy back of the rules of res judicata preclude the defendant in this case from relitigating the issues already contested and settled in the Nevada action." Caterpillar Tractor Co. v. International Harvester Co., 120 F.2d 82, 84–85, 49 USPQ 479, 481–82 (3d Cir.1941).

Part III

COPYRIGHTS

A. INTRODUCTION

The word "copyright" can be inverted to "the right to copy", which is the right traditionally protected by common law and statutes in this field. Bowker [a] states, with respect to the subject matter of copyrights, that "there is * * * no kind of property which is so dependent on the help of law for the protection of the real owner." Although historians attribute to the American Indians personal rights to songs composed by the individual warriors and used at ceremonial dances, the history of copyright protection can be said to originate only after literary works began to be reproduced by copying or printing.

One of the earliest statutes for the protection of authors is found in the records of Venice (1545): [b]

> It is decreed that henceforth no printer of this city shall dare to print * * * any words * * * unless * * * the author or his heirs * * * have declared their consent and requested the printing.

In Great Britain the book Licensing Act, which expired in 1679, was succeeded by the Statute of Anne effective in 1710 to provide protection to authors and booksellers by granting "the sole right and liberty of printing such book and books for the term of one and twenty years."

The concept of protection for authors was also carried to colonial America as evidenced by a statute of the Massachusetts Bay Colony passed in 1672 providing that no printer shall reproduce copies except as agreed upon by the owner or with his consent. By 1786 twelve of the original states, pursuant to a resolution of the Continental Congress, had enacted statutes providing protection for the writings of authors for a limited period of time. Thus, a foundation was laid for the United States Constitutional provision [c] upon which is based the present day

a. Bowker, Copyright—Its History and Its Law, Houghton and Mifflin Co. (1912).

b. Prager, History of Intellectual Property, 26 J.P.O.S. 711, 750 (1944).

c. Prager, History of Intellectual Property, 26 J.P.O.S. 711, 758 (1944).

federal copyright statute. Article I, Section 8, Clause 8 of the Constitution provides:

> The Congress shall have Power * * * to promote the Progress of Science and useful Arts, by securing for limited times to Authors and Inventors the exclusive Right to their respective Writings and Discoveries.

The question may arise as to whether copyrightable subject matter must "promote the progress of science" using the latter word in its original and archaic sense "of knowing or knowledge." However, to date the federal courts have merely required that the subject matter be originated or created by the author.

A common law exclusive right in unpublished writings and related creative works was recognized by the United States Supreme Court in the first copyright case it decided in 1834 [d] and was preserved by all federal copyright statutes prior to the 1976 Copyright Act. However, Section 301 of the 1976 Copyright Act preempted this common law right and exclusively governs by federal law all rights in federally copyrightable subject matter both before and after publication.

In general, under the common law this exclusive right in unpublished works vanished upon an unrestricted publication. What amounts to publication may vary with different works and situations. For example, printing and distribution to the public of a book without restriction is clearly a publication, but oral delivery of a lecture, or a public performance of a play, may not be considered a publication.[e]

The rationale for copyright protection is summed up rather well by Benjamin Kaplan [f] as follows:

> * * * I find one temptation easy to resist, and that is to sum up copyright with just the word "property" or "personality" or any one of the other essences to which scholars, foreign and domestic, have been trying to reduce the subject since before the time of Mansfield. To say that copyright is "property," although a fundamentally unhistorical statement, would not be badly misdescriptive if one were prepared to acknowledge that there is property and property, with few if any legal consequences extending uniformly to all species and that in practice the lively questions are likely to be whether certain consequences ought to attach to a given piece of so-called property in given circumstances. In the same way we might make do with "personality" or some other general characterization of copyright. But characterization in grand terms then seems of little value: we may as well go directly to the policies actuating or justifying the particular determinations.

> Copyright law wants to give any necessary support and encouragement to the creation and dissemination of fresh signals or messages to stir human intelligence and sensibilities: it recognizes the importance

d. Wheaton v. Peters, 33 U.S. (8 Pet.) 591, 8 L.Ed. 1055 (1834).

e. Kaplan, An Unhurried View of Copyright, Columbia University Press, 84, 85 (1967).

f. Kaplan, supra, pp. 74, 75 (1967).

of these excitations for the development of individuals and society. Especially is copyright directed to those kinds of signals which are in their nature "fragile"—so easy of replication that incentive to produce would be quashed by the prospect of rampant reproduction by free-loaders. To these signals copyright affords what I have called "head-start," that is, a group of rights amounting to a qualified monopoly running for a limited time. The legal device has been considered not too complex for administrative purposes and on the whole easier to handle than alternatives such as government subventions.[g]

A copyright claim may be registered for a work, whether published or unpublished, by depositing the required number of copies of the work with the Copyright Office along with an application and the requisite fee ($10.00 in 1987). The Copyright Office provides simple application forms for various categories of subject matter, and it is a relatively easy matter to learn how to fill out these forms and forward them with the proper number of copies and the nominal fee to the Copyright Office in Washington, D.C.

Thus, registration of a claim of copyright is inexpensive and simple, and this, taken with a term in excess of fifty years is a significant factor in considering the relative merits of collateral protection by patent or by trademark.

While there are attorneys who specialize in Copyright Law, even a general patent practice usually involves a fair number of copyright matters such as giving advice on how properly to mark materials for publication, assisting in the registration of copyright claims, and dealing with licensing, sale of rights, infringement questions and litigation. Thus, patent attorneys need at least a fair working understanding of copyright law.

Inventors and manufacturers can find a very practical use for copyright protection. The propensity of people to copy rather than create is unlimited. From the point of view of a manufacturer, copyright protection is available on catalogues, advertising leaflets, labels, jewelry, works of art, and other business devices. Since this protection is inexpensive and rather easy to obtain, by proper marking upon publication followed by a deposit in the Copyright Office, it is available as an effective tool to discourage those who might otherwise copy with impunity.

The Copyright Act of 1976 (Public Law 94–553, 90 Stat. 2541, 17 U.S.C.A. § 101ff) became effective January 1, 1978. This Act is too extensive to reprint here and, indeed, the comprehensive revision of the copyright laws contained in this Act can be the subject of an independent course of study. However, the following treatment is a brief

g. But see Collingwood, Principles of Art, Clarendon Press, Oxford (1938), wherein the author advocates getting rid of the conception of artistic ownership to permit freedom to borrow and plagarize: "Let every artist make a vow, and here among artists I include all such as write or speak on scientific or learned subjects, never to prosecute or lend himself to a prosecution under the law of copyright. * * * It would not be many years before the law was a dead letter * * *."

review intended to give the student some of the flavor of the 1976 Act, particularly in relation to the law of patents and trademarks. Even though some of the Sections of the Act are reprinted, if possible, the student should be furnished with a copy of the complete Act as a supplement to this text.

B. ORIGINALITY AND COPYRIGHTABLE SUBJECT MATTER

The Copyright Act of 1976 continues the longstanding criteria that copyrightable works be original and fixed in a tangible medium of expression (17 U.S.C.A. § 102). These criteria are derived from and undoubtedly required by the copyright clause of the Federal Constitution which is both a grant and limitation of Congressional power to promote the "Progress of Science * * * by securing for limited times to *Authors* * * * the exclusive Right to their * * * *Writings* (Emphasis added)."

In general, originality simply requires that a work be created by or "owes its origin" to the "author" [a] and the new Copyright Act incorporates without change the standard of originality previously established by the courts.[b] However, as would be expected, the federal courts have neither defined nor applied the requirement for originality uniformly. Under this new act, fixation of a work in a tangible form of expression, not publication, is the dividing line between common law and federal statutory protection of copyrightable subject matter (17 U.S.C.A. § 301).

The drafters of the new Copyright Act, in defining the subject matter in which federal copyright protection can be obtained, used the phrase "original works of authorship" rather than the phrase "all the writings of an author" of the prior act, to avoid using the full scope of Congressional power of the Constitutional copyright clause and to avoid the uncertainty of the courts as to whether the scope of the prior act and the Constitutional clause were coextensive.[c] In view of the broad language of Section 102 of the Copyright Act, and in view of the fact that its categories of works are "illustrive and not limitative" (§ 101), it remains to be seen whether the federal courts will find any significant differences between the subject matter scope of Section 102 and the Constitutional copyright clause. In any event the Constitutional scope of the words "authors" and "writings" has already been defined to include creators of many things other than the written word.

Under both the new act and its predecessor, musicians, compilers, lecturers, playwrights, composers, arrangers, artists, sculptors, jewelry designers, map makers, photographers, architects, label designers, movie directors, computer programmers, and numerous other creative per-

a. Burrow-Giles Lithographic Co. v. Sarony, 111 U.S. 53, 57–58, 4 S.Ct. 279, 281, 28 L.Ed. 349 (1884).

b. H.R.Rep. No. 94–1476, 94th Cong., 2d Sess. 51 (1976).

c. H.R.Rep. No. 94–1476, 94th Cong., 2d Sess. 51 (1976).

sons have obtained copyright protection for their various works. Moreover, in accordance with the decision of the United States Supreme Court in Mazer v. Stein, 347 U.S. 201, 74 S.Ct. 460, 98 L.Ed. 630 (1954) the new act explicitly provides copyright protection for works of applied art and denies protection to works of industrial design (§§ 101, 106 and 113).[d] The new act also provides limited copyright protection for fixed aggregations of sound or sound recordings which first received interim federal statutory protection under Public Law 92–140 effective February 15, 1972.

While minimal writing may be subject to copyright protection such as, for example, a two-line poem, nevertheless, protection of titles of books, plays, movies, and similar works is not available.[e] Accordingly, resort must be had to the law of unfair competition for the protection of titles.[f] The late Dr. W.J. Derenberg, an authority on trademarks, has taken the position in an article "Commercial Prints and Labels" (Yale Law Journal, May 1940, p. 1224) that copyright protection on trademarks and tradenames is not available, but an opposite view is expressed by Benjamin, "Copyright in Word Trademarks" (32 T.M.Rep. 136, 1942):

> There is no law permitting copyright protection only for writings over a certain minimal length. Literary property cannot and should not be measured with a yardstick. A short trade-mark or slogan may have more originality and intellectual quality than a fiction story of a hundred or more pages. Evidence of that are the high sums not seldom paid for the creation of trade-marks.[g]

For the first time the new Copyright Act in § 102(b) also expressly states and codifies the judicial doctrine that copyright protection is limited to the author's form of expression and does not prevent others from using the ideas, concepts, principles, processes or procedures described or disclosed in a copyrighted work.

17 U.S.C.A. § 102. Subject Matter of Copyright: In General

(a) Copyright protection subsists, in accordance with this title, in original works of authorship fixed in any tangible medium of expression, now known or later developed, from which they can be perceived, repro-

---

d. H.R.Rep. No. 94–1476, 94th Cong., 2d Sess. 54, 55, 105 (1976).

e. National Picture Theatres v. Foundation Film Corp., 266 F. 208 (2d Cir.1920); Warner Bros. Pictures, Inc. v. Majestic Pictures Corp., 70 F.2d 310, 21 USPQ 405 (2d Cir.1934); Jackson v. Universal Int'l Pictures, Inc., 36 Cal.2d 116, 222 P.2d 433, 87 USPQ 131 (1950). See also John, Peter C., Literary Titles, Copyrightable or Trademarkable, 11 Villanova Law Review 796 (1966).

f. Brandon v. Regents of the Univ. of California, 441 F.Supp. 1086, 196 USPQ

163, 168 (D.C.D.Mass.1977). I am persuaded that plaintiff has proved each of the essential elements of a cause of action under 15 U.S.C.A. § 1125(a) and that EMC's distribution of the Far West film under the title "Anything They Want To Be" constituted and constitutes unfair competition, entitling plaintiff to all relief available under Section 1125(a).

g. Reprinted with permission as it appeared in The Trademark Reporter, Volume 32 T.M.Rep. 136 of 1942.

duced, or otherwise communicated, either directly or with the aid of a machine or device. Works of authorship include the following categories:

(1) Literary works;

(2) musical works, including any accompanying words;

(3) dramatic works, including any accompanying music;

(4) pantomimes and choreographic works;

(5) pictorial, graphic, and sculptural works;

(6) motion pictures and other audiovisual works; and

(7) sound recordings.

(b) In no case does copyright protection for an original work of authorship extend to any idea, procedure, process, system, method of operation, concept, principle, or discovery, regardless of the form in which it is described, explained, illustrated, or embodied in such work.

17 U.S.C.A. § 103. Subject Matter of Copyright: Compilations and Derivative Works

(a) The subject matter of copyright as specified by section 102 includes compilations and derivative works, but protection for a work employing preexisting material in which copyright subsists does not extend to any part of the work in which such material has been used unlawfully.

(b) The copyright in a compilation or derivative work extends only to the material contributed by the author of such work, as distinguished from the preexisting material employed in the work, and does not imply any exclusive right in the preexisting material. The copyright in such work is independent of, and does not affect or enlarge the scope, duration, ownership, or subsistence of, any copyright protection in the preexisting material.

MITCHELL BROTHERS FILM GROUP v. CINEMA ADULT THEATER

United States Court of Appeals, Fifth Circuit, 1979.
604 F.2d 852, 203 USPQ 1041.

GODBOLD, CIRCUIT JUDGE:

This is a copyright infringement suit, arising under the now-superseded Copyright Act of 1909. But it is more than the usual commercial contest between copyright holder and alleged infringer. The infringers asserted as an affirmative defense that the copyrighted material—a movie—was obscene, and that, therefore, under the equitable rubric of "unclean hands" plaintiffs were barred from relief. After viewing the film the court found it obscene, adopted the unclean hands rationale, and denied relief to the copyright owners. Review of this holding requires us to consider the constitutional limits upon the power granted to Congress to issue copyrights, the manner in which Congress has chosen to exercise that power, and the applicability of the unclean hands doctrine.

Plaintiffs-appellants owned a properly registered copyright on a motion picture titled "Behind the Green Door," issued under the 1909 Act, 17 U.S.C. § 34 (1970) (repealed).

* * *

The statutory provision that controls in this case reads:

The works for which copyright may be secured under this title shall include all the writings of an author.

17 U.S.C. § 4 (1970) (repealed). Motion pictures are unquestionably "writings" under the Copyright Act.

The district court did not base its decision on standards found within the Act, which it described as "silent as to works which are subject to registration and copyright." The Act is not "silent." Rather, the statutory language "all the writings of an author" is facially all-inclusive, within itself admitting of no exceptions. There is not even a hint in the language of § 4 that the obscene nature of a work renders it any less a copyrightable "writing." There is no other statutory language from which it can be inferred that Congress intended that obscene materials could not be copyrighted.

Moreover, there is good reason not to read an implied exception for obscenity into the copyright statutes. The history of content-based restrictions on copyrights, trademarks, and patents suggests that the absence of such limitations in the Copyright Act of 1909 is the result of an intentional policy choice and not simply an omission. *See generally* 74 Colum.L.Rev. 1351, 1354 n. 27 (1974). From the first copyright act in 1790, Congress has seldom added restrictions on copyright based on the subject matter of the work, and in each instance has later removed the content restriction. These congressional additions and subsequent deletions, though certainly not conclusive, suggest that Congress has been hostile to content-based restrictions on copyrightability. In contrast Congress has placed explicit content-related restrictions in the current statutes governing the related areas of trademarks and patents. The Lanham Act prohibits registration of any trademark that "[c]onsists of or comprises immoral, deceptive, or scandalous matter," 15 U.S.C. § 1052(a), and inventions must be shown to be "useful" before a patent is issued. *See* 35 U.S.C. § 101.

The legislative history of the 1976 Act reveals that Congress intends to continue the policy of the 1909 Act of avoiding content restrictions on copyrightability. In recommending passage of the 1976 Act, the House Judiciary Committee stated:

The phrase "original works of authorship," [§ 102] which is purposely left undefined, is intended to incorporate without change the standard of originality established by the courts under the present copyright statute. This standard does not include requirements of novelty, ingenuity, or *esthetic merit,* and there is no intention to enlarge the standard of copyright protection to require them.

H.R.Rep. No. 1476, 94th Cong., 2d Sess. 51, *reprinted in* [1976] U.S.Code Cong. & Admin.News pp. 5659, 5664 (emphasis added).

It appears to us that Congress has concluded that the constitutional purpose of its copyright power, "[t]o promote the Progress of Science and useful Arts," U.S. Const. art. 1, § 8, cl. 8, is best served by allowing all creative works (in a copyrightable format) to be accorded copyright protection regardless of subject matter or content, trusting to the public taste to reward creators of useful works and to deny creators of useless works any reward. It is not surprising that Congress would choose to rely on public acceptability as a measure of a work's worth rather than on the judgment of such public officials as the Register of Copyrights and federal and state judges. As Justice Holmes said, in rejecting the argument that under an earlier version of the Copyright Act the courts had a duty to pass upon the artistic merits of engravings and prints,

> It would be a dangerous undertaking for persons trained only to the law to constitute themselves final judges of the worth of pictorial illustrations, outside of the narrowest and most obvious limits. At the one extreme, some works of genius would be sure to miss appreciation. Their very novelty would make them repulsive until the public had learned the new language in which their author spoke. It may be more than doubted, for instance, whether the etchings of Goya or the paintings of Manet would have been sure of protection when seen for the first time. At the other end, copyright would be denied to pictures which appealed to a public less educated than the judge. Yet if they command the interest of any public, they have a commercial value,—it would be bold to say that they have not an aesthetic and educational value,—and the taste of any public is not to be treated with contempt.

Bleistein v. Donaldson Lithograph Co., 188 U.S. 239, 251–52, 23 S.Ct. 298, 300, 47 L.Ed. 460, 462 (1903). The Ninth Circuit has recently voiced similar concerns in rejecting the defense of fraudulent content in copyright infringement actions:

> There is nothing in the Copyright Act to suggest that the courts are to pass upon the truth or falsity, the soundness or unsoundness, of the views embodied in a copyrighted work. The gravity and immensity of the problems, theological, philosophical, economic and scientific, that would confront a court if this view were adopted are staggering to contemplate. It is surely not a task lightly to be assumed, and we decline the invitation to assume it.

Belcher v. Tarbox, 486 F.2d 1087, 1088 (CA9, 1973).

In our view, the absence of content restrictions on copyrightability indicates that Congress has decided that the constitutional goal of encouraging creativity would not be best served if an author had to concern himself not only with the marketability of his work but also with the judgment of government officials regarding the worth of the work.

Further, if Congress were receptive to subject matter restrictions on copyright, there are many reasons why it would be unlikely to choose obscenity as one of those restrictions. Obscenity law is a concept not adapted for use as a means for ascertaining whether creative works may be copyrighted. Obscenity as a constitutional doctrine has developed as an effort to create a tolerable compromise between First Amendment considerations and police power. It is an awkward, barely acceptable concept that continues to dog our judicial system and society at large. The purpose underlying the constitutional grant of power to Congress to protect writings is the promotion of original writings, an invitation to creativity. This is an expansive purpose with no stated limitations of taste or governmental acceptability. Such restraints, if imposed, would be antithetical to promotion of creativity. The pursuit of creativity requires freedom to explore into the gray areas, to the cutting edge, and even beyond. Obscenity, on the other hand, is a limiting doctrine constricting the scope of acceptability of the written word.

* * *

Judging by this standard, it is obvious that although Congress could require that each copyrighted work be shown to promote the useful arts (as it has with patents), it need not do so. As discussed in the previous section, Congress could reasonably conclude that the best way to promote creativity is not to impose any governmental restrictions on the subject matter of copyrightable works. By making this choice Congress removes the chilling effect of governmental judgments on potential authors and avoids the strong possibility that governmental officials (including judges) will err in separating the useful from the nonuseful. Moreover, unlike patents, the grant of a copyright to a non-useful work impedes the progress of the sciences and the useful arts only very slightly, if at all, for the possessor of a copyright does not have any right to block further dissemination or use of the ideas contained in his works.[20] *See Baker v. Selden,* 101 U.S. 99, 25 L.Ed. 841 (1879).

The all-inclusive nature of the 1909 Act reflects the policy judgment that encouraging the production of wheat also requires the protection of a good deal of chaff. We cannot say this judgment was so unreasonable as to exceed congressional power. We conclude that the protection of all writings, without regard to their content, is a constitutionally permissible means of promoting science and the useful arts.

* * *

ALFRED BELL & CO. v. CATALDA FINE ARTS

United States Court of Appeals, Second Circuit, 1951.
191 F.2d 99, 90 USPQ 153.

FRANK, CIRCUIT JUDGE. 1. Congressional power to authorize both patents and copyrights is contained in Article 1, § 8 of the Constitution. In passing on the validity of patents, the Supreme Court recurrently

---

20. This is not true in the patent area, where an inventor has the right to prevent others from using his discovery. Thus Congress and the courts have been careful to require that each patented invention advance the useful arts in some way. *See generally Brenner v. Manson,* 383 U.S. 519, 86 S.Ct. 1033, 16 L.Ed.2d 69 (1966); *Alfred Bell & Co. v. Catalda Fine Arts, Inc.,* 191 F.2d 99 (CA2, 1951).

insists that this constitutional provision governs. On this basis, pointing to the Supreme Court's consequent requirement that, to be valid, a patent must disclose a high degree of uniqueness, ingenuity and inventiveness, the defendants assert that the same requirement constitutionally governs copyrights. As several sections of the Copyright Act—e.g., those authorizing copyrights of "reproductions of works of art," maps, and compilations—plainly dispense with any such high standard, defendants are, in effect, attacking the constitutionality of those sections. But the very language of the Constitution differentiates (a) "authors" and their "writings" from (b) "inventors" and their "discoveries." Those who penned the Constitution, of course, knew the difference. The pre-revolutionary English statutes had made the distinction.[3] In 1783, the Continental Congress had passed a resolution recommending that the several states enact legislation to "secure" to authors the "copyright" of their books. Twelve of the thirteen states (in 1783–1786) enacted such statutes. Those of Connecticut and North Carolina covered books, pamphlets, maps, and charts.

Moreover, in 1790, in the year after the adoption of the Constitution, the first Congress enacted two statutes, separately dealing with patents and copyrights.

Thus legislators peculiarly familiar with the purpose of the Constitutional grant, by statute, imposed far less exacting standards in the case of copyrights. They authorized the copyrighting of a mere map which, patently, calls for no considerable uniqueness. They exacted far more from an inventor. And, while they demanded that an official should be satisfied as to the character of an invention before a patent issued, they made no such demand in respect of a copyright. In 1884, in Burrow-Giles Lithographic Co. v. Sarony, 111 U.S. 53, 57, 4 S.Ct. 279, 28 L.Ed. 349, the Supreme Court, adverting to these facts said: "The construction placed upon the constitution by the first act of 1790 and the act of 1802, by the men who were contemporary with its formation,

---

3. The Act of Anne 8, c. 19, was entitled "An Act for the encouraging of learning, by vesting of the copies of printed books in the authors or purchasers of such copies, during the times therein mentioned."

The previous history shows the source of the word "copyright." See 1 Laddas, The International Protection of Literary and Artistic Property (1938) 15:

"In England, the royal grants of privilege to print certain books were not copyrights. They were not granted to encourage learning or for the benefit of authors; they were commercial monopolies, licenses to tradesmen to follow their calling. As gradually monopolies became unpopular, the printers sought to base their claims on other grounds, and called the 'right of copy' not a monopoly, but a property right. The Stationers Company had a register in which its members entered the titles of the works they were privileged to print. A custom developed by which members refrained from printing the books which stood on the register in the name of another. Thus members respected each other's 'copy,' as it was called, and there grew up a trade recognition of 'the right of copy' or copyright. This right was subsequently embodied in a by-law of the Stationers Company. The entry in the register was regarded as a record of the rights of the individual named, and it was assumed that possession of a manuscript carried with it the right to print copies." See also Sheavyn, The Literary Profession in the Elizabethan Age (1909) 52–53, 64–65, 70–71, 76–80.

many of whom were members of the convention which framed it, is of itself entitled to very great weight, and when it is remembered that the rights thus established have not been disputed during a period of nearly a century, it is almost conclusive." Accordingly, the Constitution, as so interpreted, recognizes that the standards for patents and copyrights are basically different.

The defendants' contention apparently results from the ambiguity of the word "original." It may mean startling, novel or unusual, a marked departure from the past. Obviously this is not what is meant when one speaks of "the original package," or the "original bill," or (in connection with the "best evidence" rule) an "original" document; none of those things is highly unusual in creativeness. "Original" in reference to a copyrighted work means that the particular work "owes its origin" to the "author." No large measure of novelty is necessary. Said the Supreme Court in Baker v. Selden, 101 U.S. 99, 102–103, 25 L.Ed. 841: "The copyright of the book, if not pirated from other works, would be valid without regard to the novelty, or want of novelty, of its subject-matter. The novelty of the art or thing described or explained has nothing to do with the validity of the copyright. To give to the author of the book an exclusive property in the art described therein, when no examination of its novelty has ever been officially made, would be a surprise and a fraud upon the public. That is the province of letters-patent, not of copyright. * * *"

In Bleistein v. Donaldson Lithographing Co., 188 U.S. 239, 250, 252, 23 S.Ct. 298, 47 L.Ed. 460, the Supreme Court cited with approval Henderson v. Tompkins, C.C., 60 F. 758, where it was said, 60 F. at page 764: "There is a *very broad distinction between what is implied in the word 'author,' found in the constitution, and the word 'inventor.' The latter carries an implication which excludes the results of only ordinary skill, while nothing of this is necessarily involved in the former.* Indeed, the statutes themselves made broad distinctions on this point." * * *

It is clear, then, that nothing in the Constitution commands that copyrighted matter be strikingly unique or novel. Accordingly, we were not ignoring the Constitution when we stated that a "copy of something in the public domain" will support a copyright if it is a "distinguishable variation"; or when we rejected the contention that "like a patent, a copyrighted work must be not only original, but new", adding, "That is not * * * the law as is obvious in the case of maps or compendia, where later works will necessarily be anticipated." [11] All that is needed to satisfy both the Constitution and the statute is that the "author" contributed something more than a "merely trivial" variation, something recognizably "his own." Originality in this context "means little more than a prohibition of actual copying." No matter how poor artistically the "author's" addition, it is enough if it be

11. Sheldon v. Metro-Goldwyn Pictures Corp., 2 Cir., 81 F.2d 49, 53. See also Ricker v. General Electric Co., 2 Cir., 162 F.2d 141, 142.

his own.   Bleistein v. Donaldson Lithographing Co., 188 U.S. 239, 250, 23 S.Ct. 298, 47 L.Ed. 460.

On that account, we have often distinguished between the limited protection accorded a copyright owner and the extensive protection granted a patent owner.[17]   So we have held that "independent reproduction of a copyrighted * * * work is not infringement", where as it is *vis a vis* a patent.   Correlative with the greater immunity of a patentee is the doctrine of anticipation which does not apply to copyrights: The alleged inventor is chargeable with full knowledge of all the prior art, although in fact he may be utterly ignorant of it.   The "author" is entitled to a copyright if he independently contrived a work completely identical with what went before;   similarly, although he obtains a valid copyright, he has no right to prevent another from publishing a work identical with his, if not copied from his.   * * *

* * *

2.   We consider untenable defendants' suggestion that plaintiff's mezzotints could not validly be copyrighted because they are reproductions of works in the public domain.   Not only does the Act include "Reproductions of a work of art", but—while prohibiting a copyright of "the original text of any work * * * in the public domain"—it explicitly provides for the copyrighting of "translations, or other versions of works in the public domain".   The mezzotints were such "versions."   They "originated" with those who made them, and—on the trial judge's findings well supported by the evidence—amply met the standards imposed by the Constitution and the statute.   There is evidence that they were not intended to, and did not, imitate the paintings they reproduced.   But even if their substantial departures from the paintings were inadvertent, the copyrights would be valid.[23] A copyist's bad eyesight or defective musculature, or a shock caused by a clap of thunder, may yield sufficiently distinguishable variations. Having hit upon such a variation unintentionally, the "author" may adopt it as his and copyright it.

Accordingly, defendants' arguments about the public domain become irrelevant.   They could be relevant only in their bearing on the issue of infringement, i.e., whether the defendants copied the mezzotints.   But on the findings, again well grounded in the evidence, we see no possible doubt that defendants, who did deliberately copy the mezzotints, are infringers.   For a copyright confers the exclusive right to copy the copyrighted work—a right not to have others copy it.   Nor were the

---

17.   35 U.S.C.A. § 73 requires that for a design patent the design shall be "not known or used by others in this country before" the "invention thereof, and not * * * described in any printed publication in this or any foreign country before" the "invention thereof."

23.   See Kallen, Art and Freedom (1942) 977 to the effect that "the beauty of the human singing voice, as the western convention of music hears it, depends upon a physiological dysfunction of the vocal cords. * * *"

Plutarch tells this story: A painter, enraged because he could not depict the foam that filled a horse's mouth from champing at the bit, threw a sponge at his painting; the sponge splashed against the wall—and achieved the desired result.

copyrights lost because of the reproduction of the mezzotints in catalogues.

*   *   *

BOOTH v. COLGATE–PALMOLIVE CO.

United States District Court of New York, 1973.
362 F.Supp. 343, 179 USPQ 819.

[Action by actress against advertiser and advertising agency to recover compensatory and exemplary damages on ground that she was damaged by reason of defendants' unfair competition and defamation in imitating the voice she had used in television comedy series on defendants' television commercial.]

BONSAL, DISTRICT JUDGE

[Excerpt Only]

The Court of Appeals for the Ninth Circuit had occasion, before *Goldstein,* to assess the effect of *Sears* and *Compco* on the common law of unfair competition in Sinatra v. Goodyear Tire and Rubber Co., 435 F.2d 711 (9th Cir.), cert. denied, 402 U.S. 906, 91 S.Ct. 1376, 28 L.Ed.2d 646 (1970). That case presented a factual situation similar to that presented here. The plaintiff in that case was a professional entertainer and had made a popular recording of a copyrighted song entitled "These Boots Are Made For Walking." Defendants were a tire manufacturer and an advertising company, which had conceived of an advertising campaign using as its theme the phrase "Wide Boots" as a descriptive term for defendant's tires. Radio and television commercials were made which featured a female singer, who was not identified in the commercials, singing "These Boots Are Made For Walking" under license from the copyright holder. Defendants admitted for purposes of the motion that the vocal rendition was an imitation of plaintiff's recorded performance of the song in question. The district court granted summary judgment for defendants, and the Court of Appeals, citing *Sears* and *Compco,* affirmed on the grounds that imitation alone does not give rise to a cause of action.

In Columbia Broadcasting System, Inc. v. DeCosta, 377 F.2d 315 (1st Cir.1967), the Court of Appeals for the First Circuit refused to grant protection, in the absence of federal copyright protection, to the character "Paladin" and his "Have Gun, Will Travel" motif, which had been created by the plaintiff. Citing *Sears* and *Compco,* the Court of Appeals held that the federal policy of allowing free access to copy whatever the federal patent and copyright laws leave in the public domain prevailed over the plaintiff's interest in his creations.

Moreover, there are persuasive reasons of public policy for refusing to recognize a performer's right of protection against imitators. The policing of a performance or the creation of a performer in playing a role would present very difficult, if not impossible, problems of supervision for a court of equity. In addition, the recognition of a performer's right in a copyrighted work would impose undue restraints on the potential market of the copyright proprietor since a prospective licensee would have to gain permission from each of possibly many performers who might have rights in the underlying work before he could safely use it. Such a right could also conflict with the Constitutional policy of permitting exclusive use of patented and copyrighted works for only a limited period of time. Finally, the vesting of a monopoly in the performer and the prevention of others from imitating his postures, gestures, voices, sounds, or mannerisms may impede, rather than "promote the Progress of * * * useful Arts." U.S. Const., art. I, § 8. See *Sinatra,* supra at 717–718 of 435 F.2d; *DeCosta,* supra at 320 of 377 F.2d; Comment, The Twilight Zone: Meanderings in the Area of Performers' Rights, 9 U.C.L.A.L.Rev. 819 (1962).

For the foregoing reasons, the court finds that the imitation by defendants of plaintiff's voice without more, does not constitute unfair competition under New York law.

MAZER v. STEIN

Supreme Court of the United States, 1954.
347 U.S. 201, 74 S.Ct. 460, 98 L.Ed. 630.

MR. JUSTICE REED delivered the opinion of the Court.

This case involves the validity of copyrights obtained by respondents for statuettes of male and female dancing figures made of semivitreous china. The controversy centers around the fact that although copyrighted as "works of art," the statuettes were intended for use and used as bases for table lamps, with electric wiring, sockets and lamp shades attached.

Respondents are partners in the manufacture and sale of electric lamps. One of the respondents created original works of sculpture in the form of human figures by traditional clay-model technique. From this model, a production mold for casting copies was made. The resulting statuettes, without any lamp components added, were submitted by the respondents to the Copyright Office for registration as "works of art" or reproductions thereof under §§ 5(g) or (h) of the copyright law, and certificates of registration issued. Sales (publication in accordance with the statute) as fully equipped lamps preceded the applications for copyright registration of the statuettes. 17 U.S.C.A. (Supp. V, 1952) §§ 10, 11, 13, 209; Rules and Regulations, 37 CFR, 1949, §§ 202.8 and 202.9. Thereafter, the statuettes were sold in quantity throughout the country both as lamp bases and as statuettes. The sales in lamp form accounted for all but an insignificant portion of respondents' sales.

* * *

Petitioners, charged by the present complaint with infringement of respondents' copyrights of reproductions of their works of art, seek here a reversal of the Court of Appeals decree upholding the copyrights. Petitioners in their petition for certiorari present a single question:

"Can statuettes be protected in the United States by copyright when the copyright applicant intended primarily to use the statuettes in the form of lamp bases to be made and sold in quantity and carried the intentions into effect?

"Stripped down to its essentials, the question presented is: Can a lamp manufacturer copyright his lamp bases?"

* * *

In answering that issue, a review of the development of copyright coverage will make clear the purpose of the Congress in its copyright legislation. * * *

The successive acts, the legislative history of the 1909 Act and the practice of the Copyright Office unite to show that "works of art" and "reproductions of works of art" are terms that were intended by Congress to include the authority to copyright these statuettes. Individual perception of the beautiful is too varied a power to permit a narrow or rigid concept of art. As a standard we can hardly do better than the words of the present Regulation, § 202.8, supra, naming the things that appertain to the arts. They must be original, that is, the author's tangible expression of his ideas. Compare Burrow-Giles Lithographic Co. v. Sarony, 111 U.S. 53, 59, 60, 4 S.Ct. 279, 281, 282, 28 L.Ed. 349, 351, 352. Such expression, whether meticulously delineating the model or mental image or conveying the meaning by modernistic form or color, is copyrightable. What cases there are confirm this coverage of the statute.

The conclusion that the statues here in issue may be copyrighted goes far to solve the question whether their intended reproduction as lamp stands bars or invalidates their registration. This depends solely on statutory interpretation. Congress may after publication protect by copyright any writing of an author. Its statute creates the copyright. It did not exist at common law even though he had a property right in his unpublished work.

But petitioners assert that congressional enactment of the design patent laws should be interpreted as denying protection to artistic articles embodied or reproduced in manufactured articles.

* * *

As we have held the statuettes here involved copyrightable, we need not decide the question of their patentability. Though other courts have passed upon the issue as to whether allowance by the election of the author or patentee of one bars a grant of the other, we do not. We do hold that the patentability of the statuettes, fitted as lamps or unfitted, does not bar copyright as works of art. Neither the Copyright Statute nor any other says that because a thing is patentable it may not be copyrighted. We should not so hold.

Unlike a patent, a copyright gives no exclusive right to the art disclosed; protection is given only to the expression of the idea—not the idea itself. Thus, in Baker v. Selden, 101 U.S. 99, 25 L.Ed. 841 (1879) the Court held that a copyrighted book on a peculiar system of book-keeping was not infringed by a similar plan which achieved similar results where the alleged infringer made a different arrangement of the columns and used different headings. * * * The dichotomy of protection for the aesthetic is not beauty and utility but art, for the copyright, and, the invention of original and ornamental design, for design patents. We find nothing in the copyright statute to support the argument that the intended use or use in industry of an article eligible for copyright bars or invalidates its registration. We do not read such a limitation into the copyright law.

Nor do we think the subsequent registration of a work of art published as an element in a manufactured article, is a misuse of the copyright. This is not different from the registration of a statuette and its later embodiment in an industrial article.

"The copyright law, like the patent statutes, makes reward to the owner a secondary consideration." United States v. Paramount Pictures, 334 U.S. 131, 158, 68 S.Ct. 915, 92 L.Ed. 1260, 1292. However, it is "intended definitely to grant valuable, enforceable rights to authors, publishers, etc., without burdensome requirements; 'to afford greater encouragement to the production of literary [or artistic] works of lasting benefit to the world.'" Washingtonian Pub. Co. v. Pearson, 306 U.S. 30, 36, 59 S.Ct. 397, 83 L.Ed. 470, 473.

The economic philosophy behind the clause empowering Congress to grant patents and copyrights is the conviction that encouragement of individual effort by personal gain is the best way to advance public welfare through the talents of authors and inventors in "Science and useful Arts." Sacrificial days devoted to such creative activities deserve rewards commensurate with the services rendered.

Affirmed.

[Opinion of Mr. Justice Douglas, in which Mr. Justice Black concurs relating to copyrightable material omitted.]

Notes

1. Copyright Office Regulation (37 CFR) 202.10(c): "If the sole intrinsic function of an article is its utility, the fact that the article is unique and attractively shaped will not qualify it as a work of art. However, if the shape of a utilitarian article incorporates features, such as artistic sculpture, carving or pictorial representation, which can be identified separately and are capable of existing independently as a work of art, such features will be eligible for registration." Upheld in Eltra Corp. v. Ringer, 579 F.2d 294, 198 USPQ 321 (4th Cir.1978) (registration of typeface design refused) and Esquire, Inc. v. Ringer, 591 F.2d 796 199 USPQ 1 (D.C.Cir.1978) (registration on outdoor lamp refused.)

Section 101 of the 1976 Act states that "the design of a useful article, as defined in this section, shall be considered a pictorial, graphic or sculptural work only if, and only to the extent that, such design incorporates pictorial, graphic or sculptural features that can be identified separately from, and are capable of existing independently of, the utilitarian aspects of the article." Such separability may occur either "physically or conceptually." 1976 US Code Cong. & Admin. News at 5668. A self-proclaimed case "on the razor's edge of copyright law" is Kieselstein-Cord v. Accessories by Pearl, Inc., 632 F.2d 989 (2d Cir.1980) in which a divided court upheld a copyright registration on an artistic belt buckle.

2. The relationship between copyrights and design patents is discussed in the "Spiro Agnew Watch Case"—Application of Yardley, 493 F.2d 1389, 181 USPQ 331 (CCPA 1974).

3. It is now well settled that computer programs, in all forms, are copyrightable subject matter. See Stern Electronics, Inc. v. Kaufman, 669 F.2d 852, 213 USPQ 443 (2d Cir.1982) (computer source code as literary works); Williams Electronics, Inc. v. Artic Int'l, Inc., 685 F.2d 870, 215 USPQ 405 (3d Cir.1982), Midway Mfg. Co. v. Strohon, 564 F.Supp. 741, 219 USPQ 42 (N.D.Ill.1983), and Tandy Corp. v. Personal Micro Computers, Inc., 524 F.Supp. 171, 214 USPQ 178 (N.D.Cal.1981), (routines stored as "firmware" on ROM), Apple Computer, Inc. v. Formula Int'l, Inc., 562 F.Supp. 775, 218 USPQ 47 (C.D.Cal.1983), affirmed 725 F.2d 521, 221 USPQ 762 (9th Cir.1984) and GCA Corp. v. Raymond Chance, 217 USPQ 718 (N.D.Cal.1982) (copyright on source code covers object code); Hubco Data Products Corp. v. Management Assistance, Inc., 219 USPQ 450 (D.Idaho 1980) (operating systems as well as application programs). See also Whelan Assoc., Inc. v. Jaslow Dental Laboratory, Inc., infra.

4. The telephone white pages directory "derived from information compiled and generated" by the author's efforts contains the requisite originality for copyright protection. Hutchinson Telephone Co. v. Fronteer Directory Co., 770 F.2d 128, 132, 228 USPQ 537, 539 (8th Cir.1985). However, an arbitrary part numbering system "falls short of even threshold originality." The Toro Co. v. R & R Products Co., 787 F.2d 1208, 1213, 229 USPQ 282, 286 (8th Cir.1986).

5. "The leading case on the issue of whether a map is copyrightable is Amsterdam v. Triangle Publications, Inc., 189 F.2d 104 (3rd Cir.1951). Under the rule of that case plaintiff's maps are not entitled to copyright protection unless the plaintiff performed sufficient original work. To be subject to copyright a map must be the result of some original work. Merely synthesizing a map from those previously published by various governmental agencies is insufficient. Amsterdam v. Triangle Publications, Inc., supra, 105–106. There must be originality resulting from the independent effort of the maker to acquire a reasonably substantial portion of the information. Marken & Bielfeld, Inc. v. Baughman Co., 162 F.Supp. 561 (E.D.Va.1957). Some actual original work of surveying, calculating or investigating must exist; merely obtaining the names of streets from real estate developers is insufficient. Amsterdam v. Triangle Publications, Inc., supra, 189 F.2d 106." Alaska Map Serv., Inc. v. Roberts, 368 F.Supp. 578, 579, 181 USPQ 296 (D.Alaska 1973).

C. FEDERAL PREEMPTION

17 U.S.C.A. § 307. Preemption With Respect to Other Laws

(a) On and after January 1, 1978, all legal or equitable rights that are equivalent to any of the exclusive rights within the general scope of copyright as specified by section 106 in works of authorship that are fixed in a tangible medium of expression and come within the subject matter of copyright as specified by sections 102 and 103, whether created before or after that date and whether published or unpublished, are governed exclusively by this title. Thereafter, no person is entitled to any such right or equivalent right in any such work under the common law or statutes of any State.

(b) Nothing in this title annuls or limits any rights or remedies under the common law or statutes of any State with respect to—

(1) subject matter that does not come within the subject matter of copyright as specified by sections 102 and 103, including works of authorship not fixed in any tangible medium of expression; or

(2) any cause of action arising from undertakings commenced before January 1, 1978; or

(3) activities violating legal or equitable rights that are not equivalent to any of the exclusive rights within the general scope of copyright as specified by section 106.

Since the first Copyright Act of 1790 in the United States there has been common law protection for all unpublished works and federal statutory protection for most published works. However, the Copyright Act of 1976, effective January 1, 1978, created a single system of federal protection for all published and unpublished "original works of authorship fixed in a tangible medium of expression" (17 U.S.C.A. § 102) and preempted common law protection for such unpublished works (17 U.S.C.A. § 301).

This federal preemption is of limited scope and in general is inapplicable to subject matter outside the scope of the Copyright Act such as causes of action arising prior to January 1, 1978, sound recordings fixed before February 15, 1972, and violations of rights which are not equivalent to the exclusive rights of federal copyright protection. Thus, the Copyright Act of 1976 does not preempt state common law or statutory protection for works not fixed in a tangible medium of expression such as extemporaneous speech, unrecorded pantomime and unrecorded choreography, and most trade secrets and varieties of unfair competition.

In International News Serv. v. Associated Press, 248 U.S. 215, 239, 39 S.Ct. 68, 72, 63 L.Ed. 211 (1818) the Supreme Court held that the prior federal copyright law and policy did not preclude common law protection of printed news dispatches of International News Service for a short period of time from appropriation and publication by its rival news agency, the Associated Press, saying:

> [D]efendant, by its very act, admits that it is taking material that has been acquired by complainant as the result of organization and the expenditure of labor, skill, and money and which is salable by complainant for money, and that defendant, in appropriating it and selling it as its own, is endeavoring to reap where it has not sown, and by

disposing of it to newspapers that are competitors of complainant's members is appropriating to itself the harvest of those who have sown. Stripped of all disguises, the process amounts to an unauthorized interference with the normal operation of complainant's legitimate business precisely at the point where the profit is to be reaped, in order to divert a material portion of the profit from those who have earned it to those who have not, with special advantage to defendant in the competition because of the fact that it is not burdened with any part of the expense of gathering the news. The transaction speaks for itself, and a court of equity ought not to hesitate long in characterizing it as unfair competition in business.

*   *   *

The contention that the news is abandoned to the public for all purposes when published in the first newspaper is untenable. Abandonment is a question of intent, and the entire organization of the Associated Press negatives such a purpose. *   *   *

It is to be observed that the view we adopt does not result in giving to complainant the right to monopolize either the gathering or the distribution of the news; or, without complying with the Copyright Act, to prevent the reproduction of its news articles; but only postpones participation by complainant's competitor in the processes of distribution and reproduction of news that it has not gathered, and only to the extent necessary to prevent that competitor from reaping the fruits of complainant's efforts and expenditure, *   *   *.[a]

The International News Service case was, however, found not to provide a basis in the Second Circuit for enjoining a manufacturer of silks from copying designs and patterns which had been sold by the plaintiff in Cheney Bros. v. Doris Silk Corp.[b] Judge Learned Hand stated:

True, it would seem as though the plaintiff had suffered a grievance for which there should be a remedy, perhaps by an amendment of the Copyright Law, assuming that this does not already cover the case which is not urged here. It seems a lame answer in such a case to turn the injured party out of court, but there are larger issues at stake than his redress. Judges have only a limited power to amend the law; when the subject has been confided to a Legislature, they must stand aside, even though there be an hiatus in completed justice.

The House Judiciary Committee Report[c] indicates that earlier Senate and House drafts of Section 301(b)(3) of the Copyright Act of 1976 also contained specific examples of rights and remedies excluded from federal preemption and committee commentary approving the continuing vitality of the common law of unfair competition of Interna-

---

a. See also Pottstown Daily News Pub. Co. v. Pottstown Broadcasting Co., 411 Pa. 383, 192 A.2d 657, 138 USPQ 406 (1963) where the state court ruled in favor of a local newspaper when its local news items were being appropriated by an unrelated radio station.

b. 35 F.2d 279, 3 USPQ 162 (2d Cir. 1929), cert. denied 281 U.S. 728, 50 S.Ct. 245, 74 L.Ed. 1145 (1930).

c. H.R.Rep. No. 94–1476, 94th Cong.2d Sess. 132 (1976).

tional News Service. However, these specific examples were deleted from the new act by the Conference Committee without any explanation for such deletion.[d] Thus, the legislative history with respect to federal preemption of the common law of International News Service may be subject to various interpretations.

ROTH v. PRITIKIN

United States Court of Appeals, Second Circuit, 1983.
710 F.2d 934.

KAUFMAN, CIRCUIT JUDGE.

* * *

Prior to the enactment of the 1978 Act, copyright interests in published works were controlled by the 1909 Copyright Act. Unpublished material enjoyed virtually perpetual protection under state common law. *See Goldstein v. California,* 412 U.S. 546, 93 S.Ct. 2303, 37 L.Ed.2d 163 (1973); *Meltzer v. Zoller,* 520 F.Supp. 847, 853 (D.N.J.1981). This dual system proved unwieldy, particularly in view of technological advances which diminished the importance of publication as the principal factor determining which body of law applied. Cognizant of these shortcomings in existing law, Congress passed the 1978 Act to implement a uniform system of copyright protection applicable to all creative works. The statutory language upon which Roth relies merely indicates that all copyrights, whether previously governed by the common law or by the 1909 Act, were thereafter to be controlled by the provisions of the 1978 statute.

The legislative history of § 301 makes clear a congressional intent to preempt previous law and replace the labyrinth of statutory and common law authority with a single, generally applicable federal statute.

> Instead of a dual system of "common law copyright" for unpublished works and statutory copyright for published works, * * * the bill adopts a single system of Federal statutory copyright from creation * * *. Common law copyright protection for works coming within the scope of the statute would be abrogated, and * * * a single Federal system [would be substituted for] the present anachronistic, uncertain, impractical, and highly complicated dual system.

H.R.Rep. No. 94–1476, 94th Cong., 2d Sess. 129 (1976), *reprinted in* [1976] U.S.Code Cong. & Ad.News 5659, 5745; *see also* H.R.Conf.Rep. No. 94–1733, 94th Cong.2d Sess. 78–79 (1976), *reprinted in* [1976] U.S. Code Cong. & Ad.News 5810, 5819–20.

* * *

d. Conf.Rep. No. 94–1733, 94th Cong.2d Sess. 79 (1976).

AVCO CORPORATION v. PRECISION AIR PARTS, INC.

United States District Court, M.D. Alabama, N. Division, 1980.
210 USPQ 894, affirmed 676 F.2d 494, 216 USPQ 1086 (11th Cir.1982).

VARNER, DISTRICT JUDGE,

Before the Court is Defendant's motion to dismiss or, in the alternative, motion for summary judgment filed herein January 21, 1980. In its complaint filed herein June 12, 1979, Plaintiff alleged State causes of action for misappropriation of trade secrets, unfair competition and common law copyright infringement. Defendant contends that Plaintiff's State causes of action are preempted by the Copyright Revision Act of 1976, 17 U.S.C. § 301. Upon consideration of the aforesaid motion, the affidavits, the answers to interrogatories and the briefs filed herein, this Court is of the opinion that, in this case of first impression, the Defendant's motion for summary judgment should be granted.

The claim of common law copyright infringement is premised upon Plaintiff's allegation that, "on information and belief", the Defendant has "copied or duplicated, or caused additional copies or duplications to be made from, such original Lycoming drawings and specifications", which Defendant has used to obtain PMAs from the FAA (Complaint, ¶ 20).

For a cause of action to be preempted by the federal statute, the facts must relate to rights that are equivalent to the exclusive rights belonging to a copyright holder as specified in 17 U.S.C. § 106, the works of authorship must be fixed in a tangible medium of expression and the facts must concern a work which is within the subject matter of copyright as specified by §§ 102 and 103.

The essence of Plaintiff's complaint is that Defendant has copied its drawings and specifications and prepared derivative works based upon those drawings and specifications. Thus, the complaint fits squarely into § 106(1) and (2). It is undisputed that the drawings and specifications are "fixed in a tangible medium of expression". Finally, the drawings and specifications in issue could certainly be characterized as pictorial or graphic works. Thus, this Court is of the opinion that the requirements of 17 U.S.C. § 301(a) are satisfied by the facts in this case.

The Congressional intent behind the Copyright Revision Act was to "preempt and abolish any rights or statutes of a state that are equivalent to copyright and that extend to works coming within the scope of the Federal copyright law" (Notes of Committee on the Judiciary, House Report No. 94–147). Thus, not only are common law copyright infringement actions preempted, but those actions "equivalent to copyright" are also preempted.

* * *

Even though Plaintiff's causes of actions alleged in Count I of its complaint are based on the same set of facts as the common law copyright infringement claim in Count II, Plaintiff contends that they are not equivalent to copyright and, thus, not preempted by 17 U.S.C. § 301. This Court disagrees.

In Count I of its complaint, the Plaintiff has alleged State causes of action for misappropriation of trade secrets and unfair competition. Plaintiff relies heavily on the contention that, while Alabama does not have any statutes concerning misappropriation of trade secrets, it has adopted the view as expressed by the RESTATEMENT OF TORTS, §§ 757 and 759. * * * However, if Alabama has adopted the RESTATEMENT view, jurisdiction is preempted—as in conflict with federal law—where it is based on a right within the scope of copyright or on a right equivalent thereto [8] or does not require the elements of an invasion of privacy, a trespass, a breach of trust or a breach of confidentiality.[9] This Court has already determined that Plaintiff's rights allegedly violated by Defendant—copying Plaintiff's drawings and specifications and preparing derivative works therefrom—are within the scope of copyright. 17 U.S.C. § 106(1) and (2). Plaintiff has not even alleged, much less shown that Defendant has committed any of the elements that allow the common law rights of "trade secrets" to avoid preemption. Thus, this Court is of the opinion that Plaintiff's cause of action for "misappropriation of trade secrets" is preempted by the Copyright Revision Act of 1976.

                              * * *

While a State may require that precautionary steps be taken to prevent customers from being misled as to the source of products, i.e., "palming off", it cannot prevent the copying of unpatented and uncopyrighted articles, since to do so would conflict with the federal patent and copyright laws.

> "To forbid copying would interfere with the federal policy, found in Art. I, § 8, I. 8, of the Constitution and in the implementing federal statutes, of allowing free access to copy whatever the federal patent and copyright laws leave in the public domain. * * * But if the design is not entitled to a design patent or other federal statutory protection, then it can be copied at will." Compco Corp. v. Day-Brite Lighting, 376 U.S. 234, 237, 140 USPQ 528 (1964).

Thus, this Court is of the opinion that Plaintiff's unfair competition is preempted and is due to be dismissed.

                              * * *

8. " 'Misappropriation' is not necessarily synonymous with copyright infringement, and thus a cause of action labelled 'misappropriation' is not preempted if it is fact based neither on a right within the general scope of copyright as specified by section 106 [section 106 of this title] nor on a right equivalent thereto." Notes of Committee on the Judiciary, House Report No. 94–1476.

9. The common law rights of "trade secrets" are not preempted by the Copyright Revision Act of 1976 so long as the cause of action contains elements, "such as an invasion of personal rights or a breach of trust or confidentiality, that are different in kind from copyright infringement." Notes of Committee on the Judiciary, supra.

Notes

1. The California Resale Royalties Act, Cal.Civil Code § 986, provides a royalty to authors on resale of "works of fine art" such as sculptures or paintings. This Act was upheld as constitutional and not preempted by the 1909 Copyright Act in Morseburg v. Balyon v. Mayer, 621 F.2d 972 (9th Cir. 1980) in which the court relied heavily upon Goldstein v. California, infra. Under the 1976 Copyright Act, however, Warren, "Droit de Suite: Only Congress Can Grant Royalty Protection for Artists," 9 Pepperdine Law Rev. 111, takes the position suggested by the article title.

2. "Nor do we believe that a possible exception to the general rule of preemption in the misappropriation area—for claims involving 'any form of commercial immorality,' 1 Nimmer on Copyright, § 1.01[B] 1, at 1–20 to 1–21 (1986), quoting Metropolitan Opera Ass'n v. Wagner-Nichols Recorder Corp., 199 Misc. 786, 101 N.Y.S.2d 483 [87 USPQ 173], aff'd, 279 App.Div. 632, 107 N.Y.S.2d 795 (1951)—should be applied here. We believe that no such exception exists and reject its use here. Whether or not reproduction of another's work is 'immoral' depends on whether such use of the work is wrongful. If, for example, the work is in the public domain, then its use would not be wrongful. Likewise, if, as here, the work is unprotected by federal law because of lack of originality, then its use is neither unfair nor unjustified." Financial Information, Inc. v. Moody's Investors Service, Inc. 808 F.2d 204, 208, 1 USPQ 2d 1279, 1282 (2d Cir.1986).

D. EXCLUSIVE RIGHTS AND DURATION

Pursuant to the copyright clause of the Federal Constitution, each copyright act has granted specified exclusive rights for a limited period of time. The trend of these acts has been to expand both the scope and duration of these exclusive rights.

The general approach of the Copyright Act of 1976 is, in Section 106, to define broadly the basic exclusive rights in copyrighted works, and, in Sections 107 through 118, to limit, qualify, and provide exclusions from these exclusive rights. Section 106 defines the five basic exclusive rights: namely, reproduction, adaptation, public distribution, public performance, and public display. These exclusive rights are independent, cumulative, and in some instances overlapping.

The first three of these exclusive rights are applicable to all kinds of copyrighted works while the rights of public performance and public display are limited to certain kinds of works. The Copyright Act of 1976, for the first time, expressly grants the exclusive right of public display. This act also expands the kinds of works for which the exclusive right of public performance is granted. It also eliminates the limitation of its predecessor that the public performance be "for profit," and, in lieu of such limitation, provides specific exemptions (§ 110) for certain educational, governmental, religious, and other specific nonprofit purposes.

The judicial doctrine of fair use is embodied in statutory form for the first time in Section 107 which, along with Section 108, is discussed subsequently in connection with infringement of copyrighted works. Detailed consideration of the limitations on exclusive rights for secondary transmissions (§ 111) including cable television systems, ephemeral recordings (§ 112), and noncommercial broadcasting (§ 118) is beyond the scope of this text. In these sections, Congress excluded some secondary transmissions, and ephemeral recordings from liability for copyright infringement under certain circumstances. Congress also imposed liability and compulsory royalty bearing licensing under certain circumstances for secondary transmissions by cable television systems, and established a procedure for determining reasonable royalty rates and terms for use of certain copyrighted works by noncommercial broadcasters when they cannot voluntarily negotiate satisfactory royalty bearing licenses. Congress created a legislative Copyright Royalty Tribunal (§§ 801–810) to determine these royalty rates and terms, and to adjust, periodically, both these and the secondary transmission compulsory license royalty rates.

Section 114 limits copyright protection for a sound recording to the particular "sounds fixed in the recording" and excludes "any right of performance." This copyright protection neither precludes a separate recording of another performance, imitating or simulating as closely as possible such fixed sounds, nor grants performers any rights.[a]

With several modifications from the prior act, Section 115 continues the royalty bearing compulsory license to third parties for making and distributing phonorecords of a nondramatic musical work, after the copyright owner, or anyone under his authority, distributes phonorecords of such work to the public in the United States. This license does not permit unauthorized copying of the fixed sounds of such phonorecord or require the owner of the original or master of such phonorecord to authorize or license copying of the fixed sounds thereof.

The Copyright Act of 1976 eliminated the jukebox exemption of its predecessor and makes the public performance of a copyrighted nondramatic musical work in a phonorecord by a jukebox an infringement unless, pursuant to Section 116, a compulsory license is obtained for the jukebox for a statutory fee of eight dollars per calendar year. Copyright owners claiming to be entitled to such license fees can file their claims with the Copyright Royalty Tribunal which will determine the distribution of the fees to the copyright owners. Consideration of the provisions of Section 116 is beyond the scope of this text.

Sections 101 and 117 were amended in 1980 (P.L. 96–517) to define and to limit exclusive rights in computer programs. Specifically, a lawful owner of a program copy may make an archival copy, and may

a. 17 U.S.C.A. § 114(b) and H.R.Rep.
No. 94–1476, 94th Cong., 2d Sess. 106
(1976).

make copies and adaptations as are required to permit use by the owner.

Under all prior acts federal copyright protection began either upon publication of works with notice, or upon registration of unpublished works, and continued for a fixed period of years, which period could be renewed once for a further period by re-registration. Under the prior act these periods were each 28 years making a total potential term of 56 years. The period of common law protection for unpublished works was unlimited.

The Copyright Act of 1976 eliminates the renewal provision, extends the term of federal copyright protection, changes the scheme on which the term is based, and limits the term of unpublished works fixed in a tangible medium of expression. Section 302 provides that copyright protection, for a work created after January 1, 1978, subsists from creation of the work for the life of the author plus fifty years, or, if the work is anonymous, pseudonymous, or made for hire, for the lesser of 100 years from creation or 75 years from publication of the work. A work is created when it is fixed in a copy or phonorecord for the first time. Euphemistically, the protection is said to start when the pen is lifted from the paper.

Sections 303 and 304 are transitional provisions for unpublished works created, and copyrights existing, before the effective date of the Copyright Act of 1976. The term of protection of unpublished works created before January 1, 1978, which have not been copyrighted, endures until the later of December 31, 2002 or the time provided by Section 302. As an inducement to publish before the end of 2002, the term of such works, if so published, is extended 25 years to the end of 2027.[b]

Copyrights already subsisting in their first term on January 1, 1978 may upon application be extended 47 years for a total term of 75 years, and copyrights already in, or registered for, their renewal term on January 1, 1978, are automatically extended for a total term of 75 years (§ 304). Section 304(c) grants a living author of a work not made for hire, and certain of his heirs, the right to terminate any transfer or license, executed before January 1, 1978, of the renewal copyright effective any time during the five year period after the latter of January 1, 1978, or the end of 56 years from the date the copyright was originally secured.

The purpose of this provision is to permit living authors or their specified heirs to terminate disadvantageous transfers after the 28 year renewal term under the prior act has expired, and to reclaim and benefit from the remaining portion of the extended term provided by the Copyright Act of 1976.[c] This provision is the companion to the termination provision of Section 203 discussed hereinafter.

b. H.R.Rep. No. 94–1476, 94th Cong., 2d Sess. 139 (1976).

c. H.R.Rep. No. 94–1476, 94th Cong., 2d Sess. 140, 141 (1976).

17 U.S.C.A. § 106.   Exclusive Rights in Copyrighted Works

Subject to sections 107 through 118, the owner of copyright under this title has the exclusive rights to do and to authorize any of the following:

(1) to reproduce the copyrighted work in copies or phonorecords;

(2) to prepare derivative works based upon the copyrighted work;

(3) to distribute copies or phonorecords of the copyrighted work to the public by sale or other transfer of ownership, or by rental, lease, or lending;

(4) in the case of literary, musical, dramatic, and choreographic works, pantomimes, and motion pictures and other audiovisual works, to perform the copyrighted work publicly; and

(5) in the case of literary, musical, dramatic, and choreographic works, pantomimes, and pictorial, graphic, or sculptural works, including the individual images of a motion picture or other audiovisual work, to display the copyrighted work publicly.

17 U.S.C.A. § 109.   Limitations on Exclusive Rights: Effect of Transfer of Particular Copy or Phonorecord

(a) Notwithstanding the provisions of section 106(3), the owner of a particular copy or phonorecord lawfully made under this title, or any person authorized by such owner, is entitled, without the authority of the copyright owner, to sell or otherwise dispose of the possession of that copy or phonorecord.

(b) Notwithstanding the provisions of section 106(5), the owner of a particular copy lawfully made under this title, or any person authorized by such owner, is entitled, without the authority of the copyright owner, to display that copy publicly, either directly or by the projection of no more than one image at a time, to viewers present at the place where the copy is located.

(c) The privileges prescribed by subsections (a) and (b) do not, unless authorized by the copyright owner, extend to any person who has acquired possession of the copy or phonorecord from the copyright owner, by rental, lease, loan, or otherwise, without acquiring ownership of it.

17 U.S.C.A. § 110.   Limitations on Exclusive Rights: Exemption of Certain Performances and Displays [Omitted]

17 U.S.C.A. § 114.   Scope of Exclusive Rights in Sound Recordings

(a) The exclusive rights of the owner of copyright in a sound recording are limited to the rights specified by clauses (1), (2), and (3) of section 106, and do not include any right of performance under section 106(4).

(b) The exclusive right of the owner of copyright in a sound recording under clause (1) of section 106 is limited to the right to duplicate the sound recording in the form of phonorecords, or of copies of motion pictures and other audiovisual works, that directly or indirectly recapture the actual sounds fixed in the recording. The exclusive right of the owner of copyright in a sound recording under clause (2) of section 106 is limited to the right to prepare a derivative work in which the actual sounds fixed in the sound recording are rearranged, remixed, or otherwise altered in sequence or quality. The exclusive rights of the owner of copyright in a sound recording under clauses (1) and (2) of section 106 do not extend to the making or duplication of another sound recording that consists entirely of an independent fixation of other sounds, even though such sounds imitate or simulate those in the copyrighted sound recording. The exclusive rights of the owner of copyright in a sound recording under clauses (1), (2), and (3) of section 106 do not apply to sound recordings included in educational television and radio programs (as defined in section 397 of title 47) distributed or transmitted by or through public broadcasting entities (as defined by section 118(g)): *Provided,* That copies or phonorecords of said programs are not commercially distributed by or through public broadcasting entities to the general public.

(c) This section does not limit or impair the exclusive right to perform publicly, by means of a phonorecord, any of the works specified by section 106(4).

[Subpart (d) omitted]

17 U.S.C.A. § 302. Duration of Copyright: Works Created on or After January 1, 1978

(a) **In General.** Copyright in a work created on or after January 1, 1978, subsists from its creation and, except as provided by the following subsections, endures for a term consisting of the life of the author and fifty years after the author's death.

(b) **Joint Works.** In the case of a joint work prepared by two or more authors who did not work for hire, the copyright endures for a term consisting of the life of the last surviving author and fifty years after such last surviving author's death.

(c) **Anonymous Works, Pseudonymous Works, and Works Made for Hire.** In the case of an anonymous work, a pseudonymous work, or a work made for hire, the copyright endures for a term of seventy-five years from the year of its first publication, or a term of one hundred years from the year of its creation, whichever expires first. If, before the end of such term, the identity of one or more of the authors of an anonymous or pseudonymous work is revealed in the records of a registration made for that work under subsections (a) or (d) of section 408, or in the records provided by this subsection, the copyright in the work endures for the term specified by subsection (a) or (b), based on the life of the author or authors whose identity has been revealed. Any person having an interest in the copyright in an anonymous or pseudonymous work may at any time record, in records to be maintained by the Copyright Office for that purpose, a statement identifying one or more authors of the work; the statement shall also identify the person filing it, the nature of that person's interest, the source of the information recorded, and the particular work affected, and shall comply in form and content with requirements that the Register of Copyrights shall prescribe by regulation.

(d) **Records Relating to Death of Authors.** Any person having an interest in a copyright may at any time record in the Copyright Office a statement of the date of death of the author of the copyrighted work, or a statement that the author is still living on a particular date. The statement shall identify the person filing it, the nature of that person's interest, and the source of the information recorded, and shall comply in form and content with requirements that the Register of Copyrights shall prescribe by regulation. The Register shall maintain current records of information relating to the death of authors of copyrighted works, based on such recorded statements and, to the extent the Register considers practicable, on data contained in any of the records of the Copyright Office or in other reference sources.

(e) **Presumption as to Author's Death.** After a period of seventy-five years from the year of first publication of a work, or a period of one hundred years from the year of its creation, whichever expires first, any person who obtains from the Copyright Office a certified report that the records provided by subsection (d) disclose nothing to indicate that the author of the work is living, or died less than fifty years before, is entitled to the benefit of a presumption that the author has been dead for at least fifty years. Reliance in good faith upon this presumption shall be a complete defense to any action for infringement under this title.

E. OWNERSHIP AND TERMINATION OF TRANSFERS AND LICENSES

17 U.S.C.A. § 101. Definitions

* * *

A "work made for hire" is—

(1) a work prepared by an employee within the scope of his or her employment; or

(2) a work specially ordered or commissioned for use as a contribution to a collective work, as a part of a motion picture or other audiovisual work, as a translation, as a supplementary work, as a compilation, as an instructional text, as a test, as answer material for a test, or as an atlas, if the parties expressly agree in a written instrument signed by them that the work shall be considered a work made for hire. * * *

17 U.S.C.A. § 201. Ownership of Copyright

(a) **Initial Ownership.** Copyright in a work protected under this title vests initially in the author or authors of the work. The authors of a joint work are coowners of copyright in the work.

(b) **Works Made for Hire.** In the case of a work made for hire, the employer or other person for whom the work was prepared is considered the author for purposes of this title, and, unless the parties have expressly agreed otherwise in a written instrument signed by them, owns all of the rights comprised in the copyright.

(c) **Contributions to Collective Works.** Copyright in each separate contribution to a collective work is distinct from copyright in the collective work as a whole, and vests initially in the author of the contribution. In the absence of an express transfer of the copyright or of any rights under it, the owner of copyright in the collective work is presumed to have acquired only the privilege of reproducing and distributing the contribution as part of that particular collective work, any revision of that collective work, and any later collective work in the same series.

(d) **Transfer of Ownership.**

(1) The ownership of a copyright may be transferred in whole or in part by any means of conveyance or by operation of law, and may be bequeathed by will or pass as personal property by the applicable laws of intestate succession.

(2) Any of the exclusive rights comprised in a copyright, including any subdivision of any of the rights specified by section 106, may be transferred as provided by clause (1) and owned separately. The owner of any particular exclusive right is entitled, to the extent of that right, to all of the protection and remedies accorded to the copyright owner by this title.

(e) **Involuntary Transfer.** When an individual author's ownership of a copyright, or of any of the exclusive rights under a copyright, has not previously been transferred voluntarily by that individual author, no action by any governmental body or other official or organization purporting to seize, expropriate, transfer, or exercise rights of ownership with respect to the copyright, or any of the exclusive rights under a copyright, shall be given effect under this title except as provided under Title 11.

17 U.S.C.A. § 202. Ownership of Copyright as Distinct From Ownership of Material Object

Ownership of a copyright, or of any of the exclusive rights under a copyright, is distinct from ownership of any material object in which the work is embodied. Transfer of ownership of any material object, including the copy or phonorecord in which the work is first fixed, does not of itself convey any rights in the copyrighted work embodied in the object; nor, in the absence of an agreement, does transfer of ownership of a copyright or of any exclusive rights under a copyright convey property rights in any material object.

———

The Copyright Act of 1976 restates the basic principles of the prior law that a copyright in a work is initially owned by its author [§ 201(a)], but the person for whom a work is made for hire is the owner of the copyright and is considered the author for purposes of the Copyright Act absent an agreement to the contrary [§ 201(b)]. This Act, unlike its predecessor, requires any agreement to the contrary to be expressed in a writing signed by the parties [§ 201(b)], and defines specific categories of specially ordered or commissioned works which, if the parties agree in writing, will be considered as works made for hire [§ 101].

In restating prior law that authors of a joint work are co-owners of its copyright [§ 201(a)], Congress intended to leave undisturbed the settled law treating co-owners as tenants in common, each having the right to use and license others to use the work, and the duty to account to all other co-owners for any profits absent an agreement to the contrary.[a] In Section 201(c) Congress intended to restate the prior law of rights in collective works, and clarify and more equitably define rights in contributions to collective works.[b]

Contrary to prior law, Section 201(d) expressly provides that the exclusive rights in a copyright are divisible, may be transferred and owned separately, and the owner of any separate exclusive right is entitled to bring suit for its enforcement. What effect, if any, this provision has on capital gains tax treatment for owners of separate exclusive rights remains to be seen. Section 201(e) reaffirms that a copyright of an individual author is his, and hence, except for mortgage foreclosures, bankruptcy and the like, cannot be involuntarily transferred such as by seizure, decree, or expropriation by a foreign government.[c]

Section 202 restates the federal law that copyright and material objects embodying the copyrighted work are separate and distinct and transfer of one does not of itself carry or transfer any rights in the other. However, by virtue of the federal preemption of Section 301, this section reverses the common law rule that authors are presumed to transfer their common law rights when they sell their original works unless such rights are specifically reserved.[d]

Sections 204 and 205 are broadened, modified and somewhat liberalized counterparts of the prior act relating to the transfer, recordation, and constructive notice of copyright ownership.[e] Section 205(d) for the first time requires recordation of transfers as a prerequisite to an infringement suit. Section 205(f) generally restates the prior judicial rule that unrecorded nonexclusive licenses prevail over subsequent transfers of ownership and prior unrecorded transfers if taken in good faith and without notice.

The Copyright Act of 1976 eliminated the contingent rights of authors and specified others in the renewal period for works not made for hire. These contingent renewal rights were intended to safeguard the authors of such works from unremunerative transfers of their copyrights. In practice, these provisions became complex and failed to achieve their intended purpose, at least partially, because the courts held these contingent renewal rights were assignable prior to renewal of the copyright. In lieu of such renewal rights Congress provided, in Section 203, the right to terminate transfers and licenses of a copyright in works not made for hire after a period of time and under specified conditions. Congress provided this right of termination because of the unequal bargaining position of authors due in part to the impossibility of determining the value of a work before it has been exploited.[f]

a. H.R.Rep. No. 94–1476, 94th Cong., 2d Sess. 121 (1976).

b. H.R.Rep. No. 94–1476, 94th Cong., 2d Sess. 122 (1976).

c. H.R.Rep. No. 94–1476, 94th Cong., 2d Sess. 123, 124 (1976).

d. H.R.Rep. No. 94–1476, 94th Cong., 2d Sess. 124 (1976).

e. H.R.Rep. No. 94–1476, 94th Cong., 2d Sess. 128, 129 (1976).

f. H.R.Rep. No. 94–1476, 94th Cong., 2d Sess. 124 (1976).

This right of termination applies only to copyrights in works not made for hire and is limited to grants of transfers and licenses executed only by the author while living. It cannot be waived, assigned, or contracted away. A grant may be terminated only during the five year period beginning, either 35 years after its execution, or, if the grant included the right of publication, the earlier of 35 years after publication or 40 years after its execution. This right of termination is inapplicable to grants expressly limited to a period of lesser duration but, unless a grant provides otherwise or this right of termination is exercised, it continues in effect for the full term of the copyright.

A written notice specifying the date of the intended termination must be served within two to ten years before such date and recorded in the Copyright Office before such date as a condition of effective termination. The persons who must sign this notice, who can exercise this right of termination, and to whom the terminated grant reverts, are specified in Sections 203(a)(1) and (2). A detailed consideration of the provisions of Section 203 is beyond the scope of this text.

Notes

1. "Defendants next argue that plaintiff Hammer was not a proprietor of copyright in 'Whatever Happens' until January 7, 1973, the date she was officially recorded in the Copyright Office as a joint owner. The district court found that Hammer, together with Pye and LeBlanc 'created and wrote the original words and music' to 'Whatever Happens' and that 'at all times herein applicable plaintiffs, Consuelo Pye and Iris Hammer, have each been and still each are sole proprietors' of 'Whatever Happens.' We uphold the trial court's conclusion that Hammer was a proprietor of an undivided one-third interest in 'Whatever Happens' even though she was not a proprietor of record.

"If a work is a product of joint authorship, each co-author automatically becomes a holder of an undivided interest in the whole. 1 Nimmer on Copyright § 69 (1976). There is abundant evidence in support of the finding that Hammer co-authored 'Whatever Happens.' When LeBlanc secured copyright for the composition on March 8, 1972 in his and Pye's names only, he did not divest Hammer of her interest in the music she had co-authored. In a similar situation where the defendant and plaintiff had jointly 'conceived, compiled, and created' a book and its parts for which defendant had obtained the related copyrights in her name only, this circuit found that the defendant held the copyright in trust for the co-author-plaintiff. Richmond v. Weiner, 353 F.2d 41 (9th Cir.1965), cert. denied, 384 U.S. 928, 86 S.Ct. 1447, 16 L.Ed.2d 531 (1966). Likewise, LeBlanc and Pye held the copyright in trust for Hammer." Pye v. Mitchell, 574 F.2d 476, 198 USPQ 264 (9th Cir.1978).

2. "The Copyright Act provides that 'in the case of a work made for hire the employer or other person for whom the work was prepared is considered the author.' 17 U.S.C. § 201(b). In Aldon Accessories, Ltd. v. Spiegel, Inc., 738 F.2d 548, 222 USPQ 951 (1984), cert. denied 469 U.S. 982, 105 S.Ct. 387, 83 L.Ed.2d 321 (1984), the Second Circuit, faced with an

argument analogous to defendants', had occasion to construe the scope of the 'work for hire' doctrine under the 1976 Copyright Act. The court concluded that subdivision (1) of the definition of 'work made for hire' in section 101 of the 1976 Act did not effect a change from the 1909 Act and the decisions construing it. Thus a contractor who works under the supervision and direction of the hiring party is considered to be an 'employee' acting 'within the scope of employment.' Id. at 552, 222 USPQ at 953; see also Picture Music, Inc. v. Bourne, Inc., 457 F.2d 1213, 1216–17, 173 USPQ 449, 450–51 (2d Cir.), cert. denied, 409 U.S. 997, 175 USPQ 577 (1972) (the fact that one acts in the capacity of an independent contractor does not preclude a finding that a work was done for hire)." Iris Arc v. S.S. Sarna, Inc., 621 F.Supp. 916, 919–20, 229 USPQ 25, 27 (E.D.N.Y.1985). See also Evans Newton, Inc. v. Chicago Systems Software, 793 F.2d 889, 230 USPQ 166 (7th Cir.1986). In Baltimore Orioles, Inc. v. Major League Baseball Players Assn., 805 F.2d 663, 231 USPQ 673 (7th Cir.1986), the players were held to be employees acting within the scope of their employment so that the baseball clubs owned all rights in the broadcast performances.

"A 'work made for hire' is defined, for purposes of this case, as 'a work prepared by an employee within the scope of his or her employment. . . . ,' id., § 101, but for statutory copyright purposes generally, the employment relationship giving rise to a copyright is somewhat more expansive than the master-servant relationship found in the common law of agency. Under the Act one may be an employee 'regardless of whether he is paid on the basis of a conventional periodic salary, on a piece work basis, on a fee or royalty basis, or even if [he works] as an accommodation with no compensation at all.' 1 Nimmer on Copyright, § 5:03[B][1][a] (1985). If the putative 'employer' was either the 'motivating factor' in the production of the work, or possessed the right to 'direct and supervise' the manner in which the work was done, the copyright is his no matter the degree of creative license actually exercised by the artist-employee. Id.; Murray v. Gelderman, 566 F.2d 1307, 1310–11 (5th Cir.1978); see Aldon Accessories Ltd. v. Spiegel, Inc., 738 F.2d 548, 552 [222 USPLQ 951, 953–954] (2d Cir.), cert. denied, 105 S.Ct. 387 (1984); Town of Clarkstown v. Reeder, 566 F.S.pp. 137, 141–42 (S.D.N.Y.1983).

"It is indisputable on this record that plaintiff CCNV was the motivating factor in the procreation of 'Third World America.' Snyder and his colleagues not only conceived the idea of a contemporary Nativity scene to contrast with the national celebration of the season, they did so in starkly specific detail. They then engaged Reid to utilize his representational skills, rather than his original artistic vision, to execute it. And while much was undoubtedly left to his discretion in doing so, CCNV nevertheless directed enough of his effort to assure that, in the end, he had produced what they, not he, wanted, notwithstanding his creative instincts may have been in harmony with theirs. Finally, they paid in full for the work, making their final payment only when satisfied, upon delivery, that the statute did, indeed, convey the message they had intended for it."

Community for Creative Nonviolence v. Reid, 652 F.Supp. 1453, 2 USPQ2d 1149, 1152 (D.C.D.C.1987).

3. Where basic character of Superman comic strip, including his miraculous powers, was completely developed by creators of the strip long before employment relationship between the creators and publisher was instituted, and where revisions directed by publisher were simply to accommodate the strip to magazine format, the strip was not a work made for hire. Siegel v. National Periodical Publications, Inc., 508 F.2d 909, 184 USPQ 257 (2d Cir.1974).

4. An assignment of all motion picture rights to the copyrighted play Maytime includes the right to license a broadcaster to televise the motion picture of the play.

"In the end, decision must turn, as Professor Nimmer has suggested, The Law of Copyright § 125.3 (1964), on a choice between two basic approaches more than on an attempt to distill decisive meaning out of language that very likely had none. As between an approach that 'a license of rights in a given medium (e.g., "motion picture rights") includes only such uses as fall within the unambiguous core meaning of the term (e.g., exhibition of motion picture film in motion picture theaters) and exclude any uses which lie within the ambiguous penumbra (e.g., exhibition of motion picture film on television)' and another whereby 'the licensee may properly pursue any uses which may reasonably be said to fall within the medium as described in the license,' he prefers the latter. So do we. But see Warner, Radio and Television Rights § 52 (1953). If the words are broad enough to cover the new use, it seems fairer that the burden of framing and negotiating an exception should fall on the grantor; if Bartsch or his assignors had desired to limit 'exhibition' of the motion picture to the conventional method where light is carried from a projector to a screen directly beheld by the viewer, they could have said so. A further reason favoring the broader view in a case like this is that it provides a single person who can make the copyrighted work available to the public over the penumbral medium, whereas the narrower one involves the risk that a deadlock between the grantor and the grantee might prevent the work's being shown over the new medium at all. * * * The risk that some May might find the nation's television screens bereft of the annual display of "Maytime," interlarded with the usual liberal diet of commercials, is not one a court can take lightly." Bartsch v. Metro-Goldwyn-Mayer, Inc., 391 F.2d 150, 157 USPQ 65 (2d Cir.1968), cert. denied 393 U.S. 826, 89 S.Ct. 86, 21 L.Ed.2d 96.

5. In an exclusive license to perform the copyrighted play Peg O' My Heart, a covenant is implied that the licensor cannot destroy the value of the right granted by producing or licensing others to produce the play in motion pictures. Manners v. Marosco, 252 U.S. 317, 40 S.Ct. 335, 64 L.Ed. 590 (1920).

6. "The parties have not cited, nor has the Court's research uncovered, a single case holding that a copyright *assignment* on file with the Copyright Office is prima facie evidence of the facts stated therein. In fact, a recent decision of the Second Circuit casts severe doubts over that proposition. See Epoch Producing Corp. v. Killiam Shows, Inc., 522 F.2d 737 (2d Cir.1975), cert. denied, 424 U.S. 955, 96 S.Ct. 1429, 47 L.Ed.2d 360 (1976), wherein the court rejected assertions that * * * a certificate of

copyright *renewal* is prima facie proof of the facts contained therein. Cf. Rose v. Bourne, Inc., 176 F.Supp. 605, 610 (S.D.N.Y.1959) (Dimock, J.) (execution and recording of a copyright assignment does not create a legal ownership in the publication that did not already exist). Assuming, *arguendo,* the correctness of defendants' position, this merely places upon the opposing party the burden of producing evidence to rebut the presumption of validity * * * which burden plaintiff has satisfied. See Epoch Producing Corp. v. Killiam Shows, Inc., 522 F.2d 737, 746 (2d Cir.1975), cert. denied, 424 U.S. 955, 96 S.Ct. 1429, 47 L.Ed.2d 360 (1976); Kingsrow Enterprises, Inc. v. Metromedia, Inc., 397 F.Supp. 879, 881 (S.D.N.Y.1975) (Frankel, J.); Baron v. Leo Feist, Inc., 78 F.Supp. 686, 692 (S.D.N.Y.1948), aff'd, 173 F.2d 288 (2d Cir.1949); Edward B. Marks Music Corp. v. Wonnell, 61 F.Supp. 722, 725 (S.D.N.Y.1945) (Conger, J.).

"Sweatman executed the assignment as 'executor of the estate of Scott Joplin.' There is no proof, however, that Sweatman was the executor of an estate of Scott Joplin, nor were records of the administration of such an estate ever located by the parties. Moreover, although the Trust instrument gave Sweatman the power to convey trust assets, he made this assignment to his own Music Publishing Company without consultation with the Trust's counsel, without any consideration to the Trust and without even making a record of the transfer in the Trust's files.

"The Court concludes that, under all of the facts and circumstances of this case, the assignment is invalid." Lottie Joplin Thomas Trust v. Crown Publishers, Inc., 456 F.Supp. 531, 195 USPQ 49 (D.C.S.D.N.Y.1977), aff'd 592 F.2d 651, 199 USPQ 449 (2d Cir.1978).

7. "Though defendant has priority in point of time, plaintiff would still prevail if it could claim the status of a bona fide purchaser for value under the recording statute (17 U.S.C.A. § 30 [now § 205]) since the 1936 assignment to defendant was never recorded. The 1942 assignment to plaintiff was duly recorded and plaintiff had no knowledge in 1942 of defendant's assignment of 1936. However, the court below held that plaintiff had not paid value within the meaning of the recording section. We agree with this holding.

"The court found as a fact that the one dollar consideration recited in the 1942 assignment had never been paid. Even if it had been paid, such nominal consideration would not constitute value under section 30. See Rossiter v. Vogel, 2 Cir., 1945, 148 F.2d 292, 293.

"Nor did plaintiff's promise to pay [the assignor] Lyman royalties constitute value. Rossiter v. Vogel, 2 Cir., 1943, 134 F.2d 908, 911. Recording statutes are designed to protect those who have actually made payment without notice of a prior conveyance. 4 American Law of Property § 17.10 (1952); Annotation, 1937, 109 A.L.R. 163; see also 3 Scott on Trusts § 302 (2d Ed. 1156).

'Under [the doctrine of innocent purchaser for value] relief is denied to a purchaser without notice who has not paid value, on the ground that his equity arises, not out of his mere lack of notice, but out of injury to him, through an innocent change of position to his prejudice. It is therefore denied where the matter of the payment remains executory between purchaser and seller, and there is no irrevocable change of position.' La Fon v. Grimes, 5 Cir., 1936, 86 F.2d 809, 812–813, 109 A.L.R. 156.

"So far as appears plaintiff's promise to pay royalties has remained executory. Plaintiff has not shown that it ever paid any royalties to Lyman.

"Affirmed." Venus Music Corp. v. Mills Music, Inc., 261 F.2d 577, 119 USPQ 360 (2d Cir.1958).

F. NOTICE, DEPOSIT AND REGISTRATION

17 U.S.C.A. § 401. Notice of Copyright: Visually Perceptible Copies

(a) **General Requirement.** Whenever a work protected under this title is published in the United States or elsewhere by authority of the copyright owner, a notice of copyright as provided by this section shall be placed on all publicly distributed copies from which the work can be visually perceived, either directly or with the aid of a machine or device.

(b) **Form of Notice.** The notice appearing on the copies shall consist of the following three elements:

(1) the symbol © (the letter C in a circle), or the word "Copyright", or the abbreviation "Copr."; and

(2) the year of first publication of the work; in the case of compilations or derivative works incorporating previously published material, the year date of first publication of the compilation or derivative work is sufficient. The year date may be omitted where a pictorial, graphic, or sculptural work, with accompanying text matter, if any, is reproduced in or on greeting cards, postcards, stationery, jewelry, dolls, toys, or any useful articles; and

(3) the name of the owner of copyright in the work, or an abbreviation by which the name can be recognized, or a generally known alternative designation of the owner.

(c) **Position of Notice.** The notice shall be affixed to the copies in such manner and location as to give reasonable notice of the claim of copyright. The Register of Copyrights shall prescribe by regulation, as examples, specific methods of affixation and positions of the notice on various types of works that will satisfy this requirement, but these specifications shall not be considered exhaustive.

17 U.S.C.A. § 402. Notice of Copyright: Phonorecords of Sound Recordings

(a) **General Requirement.** Whenever a sound recording protected under this title is published in the United States or elsewhere by authority of the copyright owner, a notice of copyright as provided by this section shall be placed on all publicly distributed phonorecords of the sound recording.

(b) **Form of Notice.** The notice appearing on the phonorecords shall consist of the following three elements:

(1) the symbol ℗ (the letter P in a circle); and

(2) the year of first publication of the sound recording; and

(3) the name of the owner of copyright in the sound recording, or an abbreviation by which the name can be recognized, or a generally known alternative designation of the owner; if the producer of the sound recording is named on the phonorecord labels or containers, and if no other name appears in conjunction with the notice, the producer's name shall be considered a part of the notice.

(c) **Position of Notice.** The notice shall be placed on the surface of the phonorecord, or on the phonorecord label or container, in such manner and location as to give reasonable notice of the claim of copyright.

17 U.S.C.A. § 405. Notice of Copyright: Omission of Notice

(a) **Effect of Omission on Copyright.** The omission of the copyright notice prescribed by sections 401 through 403 from copies or phonorecords publicly distributed by authority of the copyright owner does not invalidate the copyright in a work if—

(1) the notice has been omitted from no more than a relatively small number of copies or phonorecords distributed to the public; or

(2) registration for the work has been made before or is made within five years after the publication without notice, and a reasonable effort is made to add notice to all copies or phonorecords that are distributed to the public in the United States after the omission has been discovered; or

(3) the notice has been omitted in violation of an express requirement in writing that, as a condition of the copyright owner's authorization of the public distribution of copies or phonorecords, they bear the prescribed notice.

(b) **Effect of Omission on Innocent Infringers.** Any person who, innocently infringes a copyright, in reliance upon an authorized copy or phonorecord from which the copyright notice has been omitted, incurs no liability for actual or statutory damages under section 504 for any infringing acts committed before receiving actual notice that registration for the work has been made under section 408, if such person proves that he or she was misled by the omission of notice. In a suit for infringement in such a case the court may allow or disallow recovery of any of the infringer's profits attributable to the infringement, and may enjoin the continuation of the infringing undertaking or may require, as a condition or (sic) for permitting the continuation of the infringing undertaking, that the infringer pay the copyright owner a reasonable license fee in an amount and on terms fixed by the court.

(c) **Removal of Notice.** Protection under this title is not affected by the removal, destruction, or obliteration of the notice, without the authorization of the copyright owner, from any publicly distributed copies or phonorecords.

Every prior federal copyright act has required that the public be notified of every work in which a copyright is claimed, and, since 1802, the copyright laws have required published copies of a work to bear a specified notice as a condition of copyright protection. The statute required that this notice contain a claim of copyright, the copyright owner's name, and, for most types of works, the year of first publication. This requirement delineated which published works were in the public domain and hence freely usable by anyone, informed the public of works claimed to be copyrighted, identified the copyright owner or claimant, and, in most instances, informed the public of the date of first publication.

This notice requirement was strictly applied by the courts [a] and resulted in many copyrights being invalidated and placed in the public domain by unintentional omission of, or even minor errors in, the copyright notice. Copyrights were frequently invalidated when such omissions or errors occurred only in relatively few published copies of the work.[b] In the Copyright Act of 1976, Congress made a major change in the law of notice requirements to ameliorate the harsh effects of the prior law while trying to retain the principal advantages of a notice requirement. Sections 405 and 406 provide that omission of, or errors in, the copyright notice under certain circumstances do not invalidate the copyright, and limit the liability of innocent infringers who were misled by such omission or errors.

Section 405(a) enumerates only three specific circumstances under which omission of a required copyright notice does not invalidate a copyright. Thus, given the prior judicial history of strict application of notice requirements, it remains to be seen whether the courts will agree with the view of the House Judiciary Committee that "a work published without any copyright notice will still be subject to statutory protection for at least five years whether the omission was partial or total, unintentional or deliberate." [c]

Both the notice requirements of Sections 401 and 402, and the omission provision of Section 405(a), are applicable only to copies and phonorecords publicly distributed "by authority of the copyright owner". Section 405(a)(3) provides that omission of notice does not invalidate the copyright, if the omission is in violation of an express written requirement that notice be applied to copies or phonorecords as a condition of the copyright owner's authorization of their public distribution. The House Judiciary Committee stated:

> The intention behind this language is that, where the copyright owner authorized publication of the work, the notice requirements would not be met if copies or phonorecords are publicly distributed without a notice, even if he expected a notice to be used. However, if the copyright owner authorized publication only on the express condition that all copies or phonorecords bear a prescribed notice, the provision of section 401 or 402 and of section 405 would not apply since the

---

a. Dejonge & Co. v. Breuker & Kessler Co., 235 U.S. 33, 35 S.Ct. 6, 59 L.Ed. 113 (1914) and Wheaton v. Peters, 33 U.S. (8 Pet.) 591, 8 L.Ed. 1055 (1834).

b. H.R.Rep. No. 94–1476, 94th Cong., 2d Sess. 147 (1976).

c. H.R.Rep. No. 94–1476, 94th Cong., 2d Sess. 147 (1976).

publication itself would not be authorized. This principle is stated directly in section 405(a)(3).

Thus, if transfers and licenses of copyright interests are appropriately drafted, there may be a basis for courts holding that the grantor has no obligation to police or supervise the grantee's application of notice, and that the copyright is not invalidated by any omission of notice by the grantee from copies and phonorecords made and published by the grantee.

The provisions of Section 405(b), limiting the liability of innocent infringers who relied upon an authorized copy from which notice was omitted, are broader and liberalized modifications of similar provisions of the prior act. While this section speaks of being mislead by reliance on a copy from which notice was omitted as the controlling criteria, the House Judiciary Committee report [d] indicates that anyone who intends to engage in infringing activity extending over a period of time should check the Copyright Office registration records before he starts to copy, despite the fact that copies have been published without notice. Thus, there may be some doubt as to whether publishing houses and the like may rely on this provision without checking the Copyright Office registration records. This legislative history also indicates that the last sentence of Section 405(b) is intended to give the courts broad discretion in balancing the equities in determining whether to enjoin the innocent infringer or decree a reasonable royalty license.

Section 405(c) restates the majority judicial rule under prior acts that unauthorized obliteration of the notice does not invalidate the copyright.

Section 406 prescribes the effect of errors in the name or date of the copyright notice. Since the Copyright Act of 1976 eliminated the requirement that the elements of notice "accompany" each other, if the copies with a defective notice have the name and date on other portions thereof, Section 406(c) may be relied on in some circumstances to cure the defective notice.[e]

Sections 401 and 402 prescribe the general requirement of notice for visually perceptible copies and phonorecords, respectively, and the form and location of the notice. These sections retain the three elements of notice of the predecessor act and utilize a more liberal and flexible approach to location of the notice.[f] The notices for phonorecords and copies use different symbols (Ⓟ and ©) to avoid confusion and distinguish between copyright of fixed sounds and other copyrighted subject matter appearing on the phonorecord or its label, liner, jacket, cover or the like, and also to comply with the Phonograms Convention to which the United States is a party. Since a "phonorecord" is not a "copy" it is unnecessary to place a Section 401 notice

d. H.R.Rep. No. 94–1476, 94th Cong., 2d Sess. 147, 148 (1976).

e. H.R.Rep. No. 94–1476, 94th Cong., 2d Sess. 150 (1976).

f. H.R.Rep. No. 94–1476, 94th Cong., 2d Sess. 144, 145 (1976).

on a phonorecord to protect the literary or musical works embodied in its fixed sounds.[g] Similarly, since a public performance or display of a work is neither a publication nor a distribution of copies or phonorecords, a notice should not be required.

Section 404, in conjunction with Section 201(c), clarifies and defines a more equitable approach to the law on contributions to collective works which was a troublesome problem area under the prior law. The approach of Section 404 is (1) to permit but not require a separate contribution to bear its own notice, (2) to make a notice for the collective work satisfy the notice requirement for each separate contribution thereof, and (3) to protect an innocent infringer of a contribution without a separate notice by applying the provisions of Section 406(a).[h]

Since 1846, deposit of copies of published copyrighted works for use of the Library of Congress has been required. The 1909 Copyright Act treated this deposit and the furnishing of copies for the purpose of copyright registration as the same thing. However, the current copyright act separates these deposits, and, in Section 407, continues the mandatory deposit requirement for the Library of Congress, provides fines and a procedure for acquiring copies if the deposit is not made, and eliminates the penalty of the prior act of voiding the copyright for failure to deposit copies.[i]

Under Section 408, registration of a claim of copyright is permissive and is not a condition for protection except for § 405 works published without notice. This section somewhat liberalized prior law by providing for group registration and group renewal under certain conditions of works all first published in a periodical [§ 408(c)], and for supplemental registrations to correct errors and amplify information in prior registrations [§ 408(d)].[j] Section 408(e) eliminates the requirement of the predecessor act of re-registration of a published work previously registered as an unpublished work, but permits such re-registration.

Registration is applied for by delivering a specified number of copies or phonorecords of a work along with an application and fee to the Copyright Office (§ 408). If the Copyright Office finds the work contains copyrightable subject matter, and the other requirements of the act have been complied with, it issues a certificate of registration (§ 410). This application, unlike one under the prior act, must include a statement by any claimant who is not the author as to how ownership was obtained, and, if a compilation or derivative work, requires identification of any preexisting works and a brief statement of the additional material covered by the claim being registered (§ 409). This latter provision is intended to reveal any portions of the work already in the

g. H.R.Rep. No. 94–1476, 94th Cong., 2d Sess. 145 (1976).

h. H.R.Rep. No. 94–1476, 94th Cong., 2d Sess. 146 (1976).

i. H.R.Rep. No. 94–1476, 94th Cong., 2d Sess. 151 (1976).

j. H.R.Rep. No. 94–1476, 94th Cong., 2d Sess 154, 155 (1976).

public domain and the copyright status of all other previous publications;[k] and thus, the scope of the claim being registered.

Section 410 restates with modifications the prior law that a certificate of registration is prima facie evidence of the facts stated therein and the validity of the copyright. Most courts interpret this as shifting the burden of going forward with proofs to the party challenging validity of the copyright, with the ultimate burden of persuasion remaining with the copyright owner.

While registration is permissive, registration or refusal thereof, except for sound recordings being fixed simultaneously with broadcasting, is a prerequisite to an infringement suit (§ 411). Section 411(a) overturns some prior court decisions by permitting a copyright claimant who was refused registration, to file a suit for copyright infringement and serve a copy of the complaint on the Register of Copyrights, rather than be required to first sue the Register and obtain a registration, as a prerequisite to a suit for copyright infringement.[l]

Under Section 412, registration is also a prerequisite to recovery of statutory damages and attorney fees for infringement of unpublished works. This limitation also applies to infringement commenced after first publication and before application for the registration, unless the registration is applied for within three months after the first publication. This section is intended to encourage registration and limit the remedies for unregistered works to those available at common law prior to the present Copyright Act.[m]

Notes

1. Actual damages and profits may be recovered for copyright infringement occurring prior to deposit of copies and the effective date of registration. Washingtonian Pub. Co. v. Pearson, 306 U.S. 30, 59 S.Ct. 397, 83 L.Ed. 470 (1939).

2. Even a copyright owner may controvert the statements in a certificate of registration particularly where the statements are being relied on to invalidate the copyright. Baron v. Leo Feist, Inc., 78 F.Supp. 686, 78 USPQ 41 (S.D.N.Y.1948), affirmed 173 F.2d 288, 80 USPQ 535 (2d Cir.1949).

3. Action for infringement of the copyrighted poem Desiderata in which the court held its author Max Ehrman had abandoned the copyright.

"Abandonment of a copyright occurs if the owner intends to give up his copyright protection. Some overt act is necessary to evidence such an intent, National Comics v. Fawcett Pub., 191 F.2d 594 (2d Cir.1951), mere inaction is not enough, Hampton v. Paramount Pictures, 279 F.2d 100 (9th Cir.1960). The presence of a notice is strong evidence of an intent not to abandon, Stuff v. E.C. Pub., 342 F.2d 143 (2d Cir.1965). A limited distribu-

k. H.R.Rep. No. 94–1476, 94th Cong., 2d Sess. 156 (1976).

l. H.R.Rep. No. 94–1476, 94th Cong., 2d Sess. 157 (1976).

m. H.R.Rep. No. 94–1476, 94th Cong., 2d Sess. 158 (1976).

tion, even if not widespread enough to effect a forfeiture, can, coupled with the requisite intent, cause an abandonment.

"On the basis of the facts outlined above, the court finds that Max Ehrman abandoned his copyright protection. The acts of sending out Christmas cards and authorizing Moore's distribution certainly are strong evidence that the author did not endeavor to protect a commercial property. Even in his diary, the author opines that he has left a 'gift' to the world." Bell v. Combined Registry Co., 397 F.Supp. 1241, 188 USPQ 707 (E.D.Ill.1975), affirmed 536 F.2d 164, 191 USPQ 493 (7th Cir.1976).

4. "Considering first the Imperial fabric without the Dover copyright, it is well established that Imperial's publication without the Dover notice does not invalidate the copyright 'unless it is shown that such publication occurred by or under the authority of the copyright proprietor.' 1 Nimmer on Copyright § 82 (1973). The court is unwilling to find on this record that plaintiff had authorized Imperial's publication as a licensee without a proper notice. In the context of a licensing agreement where the affixing of a proper copyright notice is an express condition, this abandonment theory is of little utility since publication without notice is normally not authorized. In such circumstances, the courts have consistently refused to invalidate the copyright. National Comics Publications, Inc. v. Fawcett Publications, Inc., 191 F.2d 594, 600–601 (2 Cir.1951); American Press Ass'n v. Daily Story Pub. Co., 120 F. 766 (7 Cir.1902), appeal dismissed, 193 U.S. 675, 24 S.Ct. 852, 48 L.Ed. 842 (1904); National Council of Young Israel, Inc. v. Feit Company, Inc., 347 F.Supp. 1293, 1297 (S.D.N.Y.1972).

"An abandonment of a copyright requires some overt act by the copyright owner 'which manifests his purpose to surrender his rights in the "work," and to allow the public to copy it.' A licensing agreement containing an express provision of the type evidenced here can hardly be said to be such an act; 'to the contrary, it indicates a positive and continuing purpose to maintain one's rights.' " Judscott Handprints, Ltd. v. Washington Wall Paper Co., Inc., 377 F.Supp. 1372, 182 USPQ 601 (E.D. N.Y.1974).

5. "Obviously a deck of playing cards is a single commercial unit, the parts of which—the individual cards—cannot be separately used or exploited in the play of bridge or the other games in which playing cards are employed. Therefore it would seem that the notice on the ace of spades is sufficient. 1 Nimmer on Copyright, § 87.8, at p. 327 (1972); Uneeda Doll Co. v. Goldfarb Novelty Co., 373 F.2d 851, 153 USPQ 88 (2d Cir.1967), cert. dismissed, 389 U.S. 801, 155 USPQ 768.

"Moreover, as a general policy 'the courts have been liberal in overlooking defects in the copyright notice when it is obvious that the proprietor has substantially, and in good faith, complied with the statutory requirements, and the defendant has not relied to his prejudice on the notice as it appears on the copyrighted work.' Davis v. du Pont de Nemours & Company, 240 F.Supp. 612, 625, 145 USPQ 258, 268 (S.D.N.Y. 1965). This is so because,

" '[t]he purpose of a copyright notice is to prevent innocent persons who are unaware of the existence of the copyright from incurring the penalties of infringers by making use of the copyrighted work.' Shapiro,

Bernstein & Co. v. Jerry Vogel Music Co., 161 F.2d 406, 409, 71 USPQ 286, 288 (2d Cir.1946), cert. denied, 331 U.S. 820, 73 USPQ 550 (1947).

"In the instant case plaintiff made a good faith attempt to place a proper copyright notice on his cards. From the evidence it is apparent that Grolier and Goren knew of the Bridgepoint cards and of plaintiff's claim of copyright protection in the cards. Therefore, I find that Grolier and Goren have no valid claim of lack of notice." Freedman v. Grolier Enterprises, Inc., 179 USPQ 476 (S.D.N.Y.1973).

6. "In effect, § 405(a)(2) allows a person who publishes a copyrightable work without notice to hold a kind of incipient copyright on the work for five years thereafter; if the omission is cured in that time through registration and the exercise of "a reasonable effort * * * to add notice to all copies * * * that are distributed to the public in the United States after the omission has been discovered," the copyright is perfected and valid retroactively for the entire period after cure; if the omission is not cured in that time, the incipient copyright never achieves enforceability.

* * *

"On its face, § 405(a)(2) is not restricted to unintentional omissions * * * The difference between the broad language of § 405 and the more limited language of § 21 of the 1909 Act * * * shows that Congress no longer wanted to deal only with omissions of notice due to accident or mistake. Moreover, the legislative history of the 1976 Act affords ample demonstration that Congress intended to bring deliberate omissions within the ambit of § 405(a)(2)." Hasbro Bradley, Inc. v. Sparkle Toys, Inc., 780 F.2d 189 (2d Cir.1985). But see Beacon Looms, Inc. v. S. Lichtenberg & Co., 552 F.Supp. 1305 (S.D.N.Y.1982).

7. "The district court held as a matter of law that the section 405(a)(1) exception was not available to Lifshitz because of the number of copies distributed without copyright notice. Lifshitz concedes that, between 1979 and 1981, he distributed some 6,000 copies of his product, representing approximately 40% of his total sales, without any copyright notice whatsoever. Thereafter, he added a copyright notice bearing the year 1981. The date in a copyright notice, however, must be the 'year of first publication of the work.' 17 U.S.C. § 401(b)(2). Here, the first year of publication was 1979. Lifshitz argues on appeal that 1981 was the correct year because the instruction sheet represented a compilation or, alternatively, that no date was required in the notice because the work in question was pictorial. See 17 U.S.C. § 401(b)(2). We need not address these arguments, however, since they were raised for the first time on appeal. United States v. Moody, 778 F.2d 1380, 1383 (9th Cir.1985). As the date in the copyright notice Lifshitz added in 1981 is more than one year later than the year in which first publication occurred, copies of his work bearing such a notice are deemed by statute to have been published without any notice. 17 U.S.C. § 406(b). Lifshitz did not discover this date error until the year after the final sales of his hors d'oeuvre maker. It is clear, therefore, that all copies of Lifshitz's product, numbering approximately 15,000, were distributed, actually or constructively, without any copyright notice. The exception in section 405(a)(1) for cases in which only a 'relatively small' number of copies were distributed does not apply to this case. Donald

Frederick Evans & Associates, Inc. v. Continental Homes, Inc., 785 F.2d 897, 909 [229 USPQ 321, 329] (11th Cir.1986) (Evans); Canfield v. Ponchatoula Times, 759 F.2d 493, 499 [226 USPQ 112, 116–17] (5th Cir. 1985) (*Canfield*).

"Lifshitz also contends that the section 405(a)(2) exception saves his copyright. This exception contains two requirements. The first is that copyright registration be made within five years of the publication without notice. It is undisputed that Lifshitz fulfilled this requirement by registering his copyright in November of 1982, well within the permissible period. The second requirement is that a 'reasonable effort' be made to add notice to 'all copies * * * distributed to the public * * * after the omission has been discovered.' 17 U.S.C. § 405(a)(2). Etna argues that Lifshitz does not meet this requirement because he failed to add proper notice to some 3,000 copies of his product in the possession of one of his distributors, Starcrest of California (Starcrest), and because the notice he added to copies still in his possession was invalid.

* * *

"It is undisputed that Lifshitz made no attempt to add copyright notice to the roughly 3,000 copies of his product that were still in the hands of his distributor Starcrest at the time be discovered the omission of the copyright notice. The question is whether or not copies held by Starcrest had already been 'distributed to the public' in the sense contemplated in section 405(a)(2) and therefore whether or not Lifshitz should have made a reasonable effort to add notice to them.

"Lifshitz argues that the copies in question had been distributed to the public because they were owned by an independent entity, and were wholly under its control. We do not agree that these copies had been 'distributed to the public' in the sense envisioned by the statute's draftsmen. In enacting sections 401 *et seq.* of the 1976 Copyrights Act, Congress sought to balance the substantial benefits obtained from requiring copyright notice and its desire to encourage such notice against the problem posed by 'arbitrary and unjust forfeitures * * * resulting from the unintentional or relatively unimportant omissions or errors in the copyright notice.' H.R.Rep., supra at 143. For this reason, section 405 provided that, under certain circumstances, publication without notice would not result in a forfeiture of the copyright. One of these circumstances is where the copyright holder has registered the copyright and made a 'reasonable effort' to correct his omission on copies subsequently distributed to the public. Id. at 146–47. Congress apparently required only a 'reasonable effort' here because it wished to avoid forcing the copyright holder to undertake unduly burdensome and impracticable steps in order to preserve his copyright. It was for this reason that it chose to limit the scope of the required efforts to add proper notice to copies distributed within the United States. Id. at 147. The addition of proper notice to copies held by foreign licensees, or to ones already widely disseminated among the public, would, in a high proportion of cases, prove extremely difficult if it were possible at all. See Videotronics, Inc. v. Bend Electronics, 586 F.Supp. 478, 483–84 n. 11 [223 USPQ 936, 940 n. 11] (D.Nev.1984) (*Videotronics*). It seems reasonable to infer, therefore, that when Congress used the phrase 'distributed to the public' and then required only 'reasonable efforts' to effect a cure despite its strong interest in encouraging the use of proper copyright notice, it was contemplating a situation where offending copies were scattered among the public and difficult if not impossible to correct.

"In the situation before us, in contrast, the copies in question were not widely dispersed among the public, and locating them posed little, if any, burden. We hold, therefore, that they had not yet been 'distributed to the public' in the sense intended by section 405(a)(2). It is certainly possible that Starcrest, being an independent entity, would have declined to cooperate with Lifshitz in his efforts to add proper copyright notice to these copies. The statute, however, required only that Lifshitz make reasonable efforts, not that he succeed. Under the circumstances, Lifshitz should have made efforts to remedy his notice omission on the copies of the product still in the hands of his distributor. He made none." Lifshitz v. Walter Drake & Sons, Inc., 806 F.2d 1426, 1432–1434, 1 USPQ2d 1254, 1258–60 (9th Cir. 1986).

8. "Defendants' second contention is that Holland's alleged copyright is invalid and unenforceable because Holland intentionally published the design without copyright notice, and this omission was not cured pursuant to 17 U.S.C. § 405 (1982). It is well settled that if a copyright notice is required, and its omission is not excused or cured, the legal consequence is to inject the work into the public domain. *Shapiro & Son Bedspread Corp. v. Royal Mills Associates,* 568 F.Supp. 972 [223 USPQ 264] (S.D.N.Y.1983) citing 2 M. Nimmer, *Nimmer on Copyright* § 7.10[c] (1983). Holland concedes that the initial printings of Pattern No. 44252 did not contain any copyright notice. However, plaintiff asserts that in November 1984 it began to print copyright notices on the fabric, and thereby cured its omission. Defendant maintains that plaintiff's attempted cure was inadequate since the copyright notice was, as a matter of law, inadequate.

"According to plaintiff's own statements, after the company decided in November 1984 to register the pattern, 'it was then that the logo "Holland Fabrics c." was imprinted' on the fabric. Affidavit of Martin Levine at 3. This certainly is not proper copyright notice as is required under section 401(b) of the Copyright Act. The notation 'c.' is not the proper symbol for a copyright. Rather, the letter 'c' with a circle around it is acceptable, as is the word 'Copyright' or the abbreviation 'Copr.' 17 U.S.C. § 401(b)(1) (1982). As noted by the defendants, not only is the notation 'c.' by itself not recognizable as a copyright symbol, it is also ambiguous. The symbol 'c.' could be read as an abbreviation for the word company or color, or for a style or grade designation (e.g. Holland Fabrics grade a. b. or c., etc.). Further, Holland's notation, 'Holland Fabrics c.' does not satisfy the requirement of indicating the year of first publication. 17 U.S.C. § 401 (1982). Thus, Holland's printing of this 'logo' onto fabric with Pattern No. 44252 could not possibly have cured Holland's prior omission since the new notice did not itself comply with the requirements of the copyright laws. Nor did the notation which Holland printed on the third printing of Pattern No. 44252, which read 'kenrich inc. o', comply with any of the three notice requirements set out in § 401(b) of the Copyright Act.

"Holland has not indicated that it had any excuse for not complying with these requirements. Indeed, there is substantial evidence which indicates that Jack Levine, President of Holland, is well-versed in copyright law. Accordingly, since Holland's omission of the copyright notice was not excused pursuant to § 405(a)(1) or § 405(a)(3), or cured pursuant to § 405(a)(2), the 'legal consequence is the forfeiture of the copyright and the release of the work into the public domain.' *Beacon Looms, Inc. v. S. Lichtenberg & Co. Inc.*, 552 F.Supp. 1305, 1309 (S.D.N.Y.1982); 17 U.S.C. § 405(a) (1982)."

Holland Fabrics, Inc. v. Delta Fabrics, Inc., 2 USPQ2d 1157, 1157–8 (S.D. N.Y.1987).

9. "According to 17 U.S.C. § 404, a single notice of copyright for a collective work can in some instances fulfill the notice requirements as to the individual works collected therein, regardless of who owns the copyrights of the individual works. The statute, however, specifically excludes from such protection 'advertisements inserted on behalf of persons other than the owner of copyright in the collective work.' 17 U.S.C. § 404(a). Congress explained that this exclusion was justified by the special circumstances resulting from the common practice of publishing the same advertisement in several different collective works. House Report, supra, at 146, *reprinted in* 1976 U.S.Code Cong. & Ad.News at 5762. Congress intended that separate copyright notices be required for most advertisements included in collective works and stated that the requirement would not impose an undue burden on copyright owners. Id.; see also Southern Bell Telephone & Telegraph Co. v. Associated Telephone Directory Publishers, 756 F.2d 801, 811, 225 USPQ 899, 905–06 (11th Cir.1985). Whether the Sentinel's notice of copyright served as a notice for the drawings of Evans' designs contained in the accompanying supplement therefore depends on whether the drawings were advertisements." Donald Frederick Evans & Assoc. v. Continental Homes, Inc., 785 F.2d 897, 906–7, 229 USPQ 321, 327 (11th Cir. 1986).

G. INFRINGEMENT AND FAIR USE

17 U.S.C.A. § 501. Infringement of Copyright

(a) Anyone who violates any of the exclusive rights of the copyright owner as provided by sections 106 through 118, or who imports copies or phonorecords into the United States in violation of section 602, is an infringer of the copyright.

(b) The legal or beneficial owner of an exclusive right under a copyright is entitled, subject to the requirements of sections 205(d) and 411, to institute an action for any infringement of that particular right committed while he or she is the owner of it. The court may require such owner to serve written notice of the action with a copy of the complaint upon any person shown, by the records of the Copyright Office or otherwise, to have or claim an interest in the copyright, and shall require that such notice be served upon any person whose interest is likely to be affected by a decision in the case. The court may require the joinder, and shall permit the intervention, of any person having or claiming an interest in the copyright.

(c) For any secondary transmission by a cable system that embodies a performance or a display of a work which is actionable as an act of infringement under subsection (c) of section 111, a television broadcast station holding a copyright or other license to transmit or perform the same version of that work shall, for purposes of subsection (b) of this section, be treated as a legal or beneficial owner if such secondary transmission occurs within the local service area of that television station.

(d) For any secondary transmission by a cable system that is actionable as an act of infringement pursuant to section 111(c)(3), the following shall also have standing to sue: (i) the primary transmitter whose transmission has been altered by the cable system; and (ii) any broadcast station within whose local service area the secondary transmission occurs.

17 U.S.C.A. § 107. Limitations on Exclusive Rights: Fair Use

Notwithstanding the provisions of section 106, the fair use of a copyrighted work, including such use by reproduction in copies or phonorecords or by any other means specified by that section, for purposes such as criticism, comment, news reporting, teaching (including multiple copies for classroom use), scholarship, or research, is not an infringement of copyright. In determining whether the use made of a work in any particular case is a fair use the factors to be considered shall include—

(1) the purpose and character of the use, including whether such use is of a commercial nature or is for nonprofit educational purposes;

(2) the nature of the copyrighted work;

(3) the amount and substantiality of the portion used in relation to the copyrighted work as a whole; and

(4) the effect of the use upon the potential market for or value of the copyrighted work.

17 U.S.C.A. § 108. Limitations on Exclusive Rights: Reproduction by Libraries and Archives [Not Included]

COPYRIGHT INFRINGEMENT

Copyright infringement is a tort and all persons who unite in infringing acts are jointly and severally liable. The Copyright Act of 1976 provides for the first time in statutory form that an infringer is anyone who violates any of the exclusive rights defined by the statute (§ 501) or imports copies or phonorecords into the United States without authorization of the copyright owner (§ 602). This is merely a general restatement of prior judicial decisions which must still be considered in determining the test for infringement.

In a copyrighted work there is no definitive claim, as there is in a patent, which can be used in determining infringement, and, if two persons each independently create the same work, each is entitled to protection and neither one is an infringer of the other's work.[a] In general the judicially developed test for infringement is whether the accused work was copied from and has such substantial similarity to the copyrighted work that it invades an exclusive right of copyright protection. Where copying cannot be proved directly it may be inferred from access to the copyrighted work and similarities between the copyrighted and accused works. The test for substantial similarity is whether an ordinary lay observer would recognize the accused work as having been appropriated from the copyrighted work.[b] Thus, while expert testimony on similarities is seldom excluded, it is often frowned upon and considered to be of little value, particularly since Judge Learned Hand's criticism of its use in Nichols v. Universal Pictures Corp.[c]

As in the law of patents, one, who with knowledge of copyrighted material, causes or materially contributes to the infringing conduct of another is liable for inducing infringement or as a contributory infringer.[d] Moreover, persons such as owners of halls, nightclubs, theaters, stadiums, and the like, who actively operate or supervise operation of the place where an infringing public performance by an independent contractor occurs, and who expect commercial gain from the performance, are vicariously liable for the infringing performance even though they had no knowledge that the performance would be infringement.[e] In drafting the Copyright Act of 1976 the House Judiciary Committee expressly considered and rejected changing the rule of vicarious liability for an infringing public performance as an unwarranted "erosion of the public performance right."[f]

In some circumstances copying from copyrighted works has been permitted under the judicial doctrine of fair use. Thus, use of an excerpt of a copyrighted work for purposes such as review, comment, criticism, scholarship, teaching, parody, burlesque, and the like has been found under some circumstances to be a non-infringing fair use.

The equitable doctrine of fair use and the criteria usually considered in its application are restated in statutory form for the first time in Section 107. The purpose of this restatement was generally to approve of the fair use doctrine without either changing or freezing the doctrine in its present state of development.[g] This fair use doctrine also applies to libraries, and Congress, in Section 108 even specifically authorized, for libraries and archives, certain copying practices which

a. Axelbank v. Rony, 277 F.2d 314 (9th Cir.1960) and Russel v. Trimfit, Inc., 428 F.Supp. 91 (D.C.Pa.1977), aff'd 568 F.2d 770 (3d Cir.1978).

b. Ideal Toy Corp. v. Fab-Lu, Ltd., Inc., 360 F.2d 1021, 1022, 149 USPQ 800, 801 (2d Cir.1966).

c. 45 F.2d 119, 123, 7 USPQ 84 (2d Cir. 1930).

d. Gershwin Pub. Corp. v. Columbia Artists Management, Inc., 443 F.2d 1159

(2d Cir.1971) and Universal Pictures Co. v. Harold Lloyd Corp., 162 F.2d 354 (2d Cir. 1947).

e. Gershwin Pub. Corp. v. Columbia Artists Management, Inc., supra.

f. H.R.Rep. No. 94–1476, 94th Cong., 2d Sess. 159, 160 (1976).

g. H.R.Rep. No. 94–1476, 94th Cong., 2d Sess. 66 (1976).

may not have been fair uses.[h] In so doing, Congress struck what it believes is the proper balance between the "rights of creators and the needs of users." Detailed consideration of the provisions of § 108 is beyond the scope of this text.

WHELAN ASSOCIATES, INC. v. JASLOW DENTAL LABORATORY, INC.

United States Court of Appeals, Third Circuit, 1986.
797 F.2d 1222, 230 USPQ 481.

Cert. denied ___ U.S. ___, 107 S.Ct. 877, 93 L.Ed.2d 831 (1987).

BECKER, CIRCUIT JUDGE.

This appeal involves a computer program for the operation of a dental laboratory, and calls upon us to apply the principles underlying our venerable copyright laws to the relatively new field of computer technology to determine the scope of copyright protection of a computer program. More particularly, in this case of first impression in the courts of appeals, we must determine whether the structure (or sequence and organization) of a computer program is protectible by copyright, or whether the protection of the copyright law extends only as far as the literal computer code.

* * *

As this brief summary demonstrates, the coding process is a comparatively small part of programming. By far the larger portion of the expense and difficulty in creating computer programs is attributable to the development of the structure and logic of the program, and to debugging, documentation and maintenance, rather than to the coding. *See* Frank, *Critical Issues in Software* 22 (1983) (only 20% of the cost of program development goes into coding); Zelkowitz, *Perspective on Software Engineering,* 10 Computing Surveys 197–216 (June, 1978). *See also Info World,* Nov. 11, 1985 at 13 ("the 'look and feel' of a computer software product often involves much more creativity and often is of greater commercial value than the program code which implements the product * * *"). The evidence in this case is that Ms. Whelan spent a tremendous amount of time studying Jaslow Labs, organizing the modules and subroutines for the Dentalab program, and working out the data arrangements, and a comparatively small amount of time actually coding the Dentalab program.

IV. LEGAL BACKGROUND

A. *The elements of a copyright infringement action* —To prove that its copyright has been infringed, Whelan Associates must show two things: that it owned the copyright on Dentalab, and that Rand Jaslow copied Dentalab in making the Dentacom program. *Sid & Marty Krofft Television Prods., Inc. v. McDonald's Corp.,* 562 F.2d 1157, 1162 (9th Cir.1977); *Reyher v. Children's Television Workshop,* 533 F.2d 87,

h. H.R.Rep. No. 94–1476, 94th Cong., 2d Sess. 74 (1976).

90 (2d Cir.), *cert. denied,* 429 U.S. 980, 97 S.Ct. 492, 50 L.Ed.2d 588 (1976); 3 *Nimmer On Copyright* § 13.01 (1985) [referred to hereinafter as "Nimmer"]. Although it was disputed below, *see supra* 1226, the district court determined, and it is not challenged here, that Whelan Associates owned the copyright to the Dentalab program. We are thus concerned only with whether it has been shown that Rand Jaslow copied the Dentalab program.

As it is rarely possible to prove copying through direct evidence, *Roth Greeting Cards v. United Card Co.,* 429 F.2d 1106, 1110 (9th Cir. 1970), copying may be proved inferentially by showing that the defendant had access to the allegedly infringed copyrighted work and that the allegedly infringing work is substantially similar to the copyrighted work. *Ferguson v. National Broadcasting Co.,* 584 F.2d 111, 113 (5th Cir.1978); *Sid & Marty Krofft Television Prods. Inc., supra; Universal Athletic Sales Co. v. Salkeld,* 511 F.2d 904, 907 (3d Cir.), *cert. denied,* 423 U.S. 863, 96 S.Ct. 122, 46 L.Ed.2d 92 (1975); *Midway Mfg. Co. v. Strohon,* 564 F.Supp. 741, 753 (N.D.Ill.1983). The district court found, and there it is uncontested that Rand Jaslow had access to the Dentalab program, both because Dentalab was the program used in Jaslow Labs and because Rand Jaslow acted as a sales representative for Whelan Associates. *See Whelan Associates v. Jaslow Dental Laboratory,* 609 F.Supp. at 1314. Thus, the sole question is whether there was substantial similarity between the Dentcom and Dentalab programs.[23]

B. *The appropriate test for substantial similarity in computer program cases*—The leading case of *Arnstein v. Porter,* 154 F.2d 464, 468–69 (2d Cir.1946), suggested a bifurcated substantial similarity test whereby a finder of fact makes two findings of substantial similarity to support a copyright violation. First, the fact-finder must decide whether there is sufficient similarity between the two works in question to conclude that the alleged infringer used the copyrighted work in making his own. On this issue, expert testimony may be received to aid the trier of fact. (This is called the "extrinsic" test of substantial similarity. *Sid & Marty Krofft Television Prods., Inc. v. McDonald's Corp.,* 562 F.2d at 1164–65.) Second, if the answer to the first question is in the affirmative, the fact-finder must decide without the aid of expert testimony, but with the perspective of the "lay observer," whether the copying was "illicit," or "an unlawful appropriation" of the copyrighted work. (This is called an "intrinsic" test of substantial similarity. *Id.*) The *Arnstein* test has been adopted in this circuit. *See Universal Athletic Sales Co.,* 511 F.2d at 907.

---

23. Although not an issue in this case, *see infra* n. 47, it is important to note that even the showing of substantial similarity is not dispositive, for it is still open to the alleged infringer to prove that his work is an original creation, *see supra* n. 7, or that the similarities between the works was not on account of copying but because both parties drew from common sources that were part of the public domain. The cause of the substantial similarity—legitimate or not—is a question of fact.

The district court heard expert testimony. *See supra* 1227; *infra* at 1247–1249. It did not bifurcate its analysis, however, but made only a single finding of substantial similarity. *See Whelan Associates v. Jaslow Dental Laboratory,* 609 F.Supp. at 1321–22. It would thus appear to have contravened the law of this circuit. Nevertheless, for the reasons that follow, we believe that the district court applied an appropriate standard.

The ordinary observer test, which was developed in cases involving novels, plays, and paintings, and which does not permit expert testimony, is of doubtful value in cases involving computer programs on account of the programs' complexity and unfamiliarity to most members of the public. *See* Note, *Copyright Infringement of Computer Programs: A Modification of the Substantial Similarity Test,* 68 Minn. L.Rev. 1264, 1285–88 (1984). *Cf.* Note, *Copyright Infringement Actions: The Proper Role for Audience Reactions in Determining Substantial Similarity,* 54 S.Cal.L.Rev. 385 (1981) (criticizing lay observer standard when objects in question are intended for particular, identifiable audiences). Moreover, the distinction between the two parts of the *Arnstein* test may be of doubtful value when the finder of fact is the same person for each step: that person has been exposed to expert evidence in the first step, yet she or he is supposed to ignore or "forget" that evidence in analyzing the problem under the second step. Especially in complex cases, we doubt that the "forgetting" can be effective when the expert testimony is essential to even the most fundamental understanding of the objects in question.

On account of these problems with the standard, we believe that the ordinary observer test is not useful and is potentially misleading when the subjects of the copyright are particularly complex, such as computer programs. We therefore join the growing number of courts which do not apply the ordinary observer test in copyright cases involving exceptionally difficult materials, like computer programs, but instead adopt a single substantial similarity inquiry according to which both lay and expert testimony would be admissible. *See E.F. Johnson Co. v. Uniden Corp.,* 623 F.Supp. 1485, 1493 (D.Minn.1985); *Hubco Data Products Corp. v. Management Assistance Inc.,* 2 Copyright L.Rep. (CCH) ¶ 25,529 (D. Idaho Feb. 3, 1983) (enunciating bifurcated test, but relying entirely on expert testimony); *Midway Mfg. Co. v. Strohon,* 564 F.Supp. 741, 752–53 (N.D.Ill.1983) (relying entirely on expert testimony to find substantial similarity); *see also* Fed.R.Evid. 702 ("If [expert testimony] will assist the trier of fact to understand the evidence or to determine a fact in issue, a witness * * * may testify thereto in the form of an opinion or otherwise."). That was the test applied by the district court in this case.

C. *The arguments on appeal* —On appeal, the defendants attack on two grounds the district court's holding that there was sufficient evidence of substantial similarity. First, the defendants argue that because the district court did not find any similarity between the "literal" elements (source and object code) of the programs, but only similarity in their overall structures, its finding of substantial similarity was incorrect, for the copyright covers only the literal elements of computer programs, not their overall structures. Defendants' second argument is that even if the protection of copyright law extends to "non-literal" elements such as the structure of computer programs, there was not sufficient evidence of substantial similarity to sustain the district court's holding in this case. We consider these arguments in turn.

V. The Scope of Copyright Protection of Computer Programs

It is well, though recently, established that copyright protection extends to a program's source and object codes. *Stern Elecs., Inc. v. Kaufman*, 669 F.2d 852, 855 n. 3 (2d Cir.1982) (source code); *Apple Computer, Inc. v. Franklin Computer Corp.*, 714 F.2d 1240, 1246–47 (3d Cir.1983) (source and object code), *cert. dismissed*, 464 U.S. 1033, 104 S.Ct. 690, 79 L.Ed.2d 158 (1984); *Williams Elecs., Inc. v. Artic International, Inc.*, 685 F.2d 870 (3d Cir.1982) (object code). In this case, however, the district court did not find any copying of the source or object codes, nor did the plaintiff allege such copying. Rather, the district court held that the Dentalab copyright was infringed because the *overall structure* of Dentcom was substantially similar to the overall structure of Dentalab. *Whelan Associates v. Jaslow Dental Laboratory*, 609 F.Supp. at 1321–22. The question therefore arises whether mere similarity in the overall structure of programs can be the basis for a copyright infringement, or, put differently, whether a program's copyright protection covers the structure of the program or only the program's literal elements, *i.e.*, its source and object codes.

Title 17 U.S.C. § 102(a)(1) extends copyright protection to "literary works," and computer programs are classified as literary works for the purposes of copyright. *See* H.R.Rep. No. 1476, 94th Cong., 2d Sess. 54, *reprinted in* 1976 U.S.Code Cong. & Ad.News 5659, 5667. The copyrights of other literary works can be infringed even when there is no substantial similarity between the works' literal elements. One can violate the copyright of a play or book by copying its plot or plot devices. *See, e.g., Twentieth Century-Fox Film Corp. v. MCA, Inc.*, 715 F.2d 1327, 1329 (9th Cir.1983) (13 alleged distinctive plot similarities between *Battlestar Galactica* and *Star Wars* may be basis for a finding of copyright violation); *Sid & Marty Krofft Television Productions, Inc.*, 562 F.2d at 1167 (similarities between McDonaldland characters and H.R. Pufnstuf characters can be established by " 'total concept and feel' " of the two productions (quoting *Roth Greeting Cards v. United Card Co.*, 429 F.2d 1106, 1110 (9th Cir.1970)); *Sheldon v. Metro-Goldwyn Pictures Corp.*, 81 F.2d 49, 54–55 (2nd Cir.1936); *Nichols v. Universal Pictures Corp.*, 45 F.2d 119, 121 (2d Cir.1930) (copyright "cannot be limited literally to the text, else a plagiarist would escape by immaterial variations"). By analogy to other literary works, it would thus appear that the copyrights of computer programs can be infringed even absent copying of the literal elements of the program.[26] Defendants contend, however, that what is true of other literary works is not true of computer programs. They assert two principal reasons, which we consider in turn.

A. *Section 102(b) and the dichotomy between idea and expression*—It is axiomatic that copyright does not protect ideas, but only expressions of ideas. This rule, first enunciated in *Baker v. Selden,* 101 U.S. (11 Otto) 99, 25 L.Ed. 841 (1879), has been repeated in numerous cases. *See, e.g., Mazur v. Stein,* 347 U.S. 201, 217, 74 S.Ct. 460, 470, 98 L.Ed. 630 (1954) ("Unlike a patent, a copyright gives no exclusive right to the art disclosed; protection is given only to the expression of the idea—not the idea itself." (citation omitted)); *Universal Athletic Sales Co.,* 511 F.2d at 906; *Dymow v. Bolton,* 11 F.2d 690, 691 (2d Cir.1926); *see generally* A. Latman, *The Copyright Law* 31–35 (5th ed. 1979); 1 Nimmer § 2.03[D]. The rule has also been embodied in statute. Title 17 U.S.C. § 102(b) (1982) states:

> In no case does copyright protection for an original work of authorship extend to extend to any idea, procedure, process, system, method of operation, concept, principle, or discovery, regardless of the form in which it is described, explained, illustrated, or embodied in such work.

The legislative history of this section, adopted in 1976, makes clear that § 102(b) was intended to express the idea-expression dichotomy. *See* H.R.Rep. No. 1476 at 57 *reprinted in* 1976 U.S.Code Cong. & Ad.News at 5670 (§ 102(b) is intended to "restate * * * that the basic dichotomy between expression and idea remains unchanged.") *See also Apple Computer, supra,* 714 F.2d at 1252.

Defendants argue that the structure of a computer program is, by definition, the idea and not the expression of the idea, and therefore that the structure cannot be protected by the program copyright. Under the defendants' approach, any other decision would be contrary to § 102(b). We divide our consideration of this argument into two parts. First, we examine the caselaw concerning the distinction between idea and expression, and derive from it a rule for distinguishing idea from expression in the context of computer programs. We then apply that rule to the facts of this case.

* * *

The Court's test in *Baker v. Selden* suggests a way to distinguish idea from expression. Just as *Baker v. Selden* focused on the end

---

26. Professor Nimmer distinguishes two ways that one work might be substantially similar to another: comprehensive nonliteral similarity, and fragmented literal similarity. 3 Nimmer at § 13.03[A]. *See also Warner Bros. v. American Broadcasting Cos.,* 720 F.2d 231, 240 (2d Cir.1983) (noting distinction); *Smith v. Weinstein,* 578 F.Supp. 1297, 1303 (S.D.N.Y.) (same), *aff'd,* 738 F.2d 419 (2d Cir.1984). The titles are suggestive of their meanings: comprehen- sive nonliteral similarity means "a similarity not just as to a particular line or paragraph or other minor segment, but [that] the fundamental essence or structure of one work is duplicated in another," 3 Nimmer at 13–20.1, while fragmented literal similarity means occasional, but not complete, word-for-word similarity. *Id.* In Professor Nimmer's terminology, we are concerned here only with comprehensive nonliteral similarity.

sought to be achieved by Selden's book, the line between idea and expression may be drawn with reference to the end sought to be achieved by the work in question. In other words, *the purpose or function of a utilitarian work would be the work's idea, and everything that is not necessary to that purpose or function would be part of the expression of the idea. Cf. Apple Computer, Inc. v. Formula Int'l, Inc.,* 562 F.Supp. 775, 783 (C.D.Ca.1983) ("Apple seeks here not to protect *ideas* (i.e. making the machine perform particular functions) but rather to protect their particular *expressions* * * * "), *aff'd,* 725 F.2d 521 (9th Cir.1984). Where there are various means of achieving the desired purpose, then the particular means chosen is not necessary to the purpose; hence, there is expression, not idea.

Consideration of copyright doctrines related to *scenes a faire* and fact-intensive works supports our formulation, for they reflect the same underlying principle. *Scenes a faire* are "incidents, characters or settings which are as a practical matter indispensable * * * in the treatment of a given topic." *Atari, Inc. v. North American Philips Consumer Elecs. Corp.,* 672 F.2d 607, 616 (7th Cir.), *cert. denied,* 459 U.S. 880, 103 S.Ct. 176, 74 L.Ed.2d 145 (1982). *See also See v. Durang,* 711 F.2d 141, 143 (9th Cir.1983). It is well-settled doctrine that *scenes a faire* are afforded no copyright protection.

Scenes a faire are afforded no protection because the subject matter represented can be expressed in no other way than through the particular *scene a faire.* Therefore, granting a copyright "would give the first author a monopoly on the commonplace ideas behind the *scenes a faire." Landsberg v. Scrabble Crossword Game Players, Inc.,* 736 F.2d at 489.[30] This is merely a restatement of the hypothesis advanced above, that the purpose or function of a work or literary device is part of that device's "idea" (unprotectible portion). It follows that anything necessary to effecting that function is also, necessarily, part of the idea, too.

Fact intensive works are given similarly limited copyright coverage. *See, e.g., Landsberg,* 736 F.2d at 488; *Miller v. Universal City Studios, Inc.,* 650 F.2d 1365, 1372 (5th Cir.1981). Once again, the reason appears to be that there are only a limited number of ways to express factual material, and therefore the purpose of the literary work—telling a truthful story—can be accomplished only by employing one of a limited number of devices. *Landsberg,* 736 F.2d at 488. Those devices therefore belong to the idea, not the expression, of the historical or factual work. * * * The issue in a copyrighted case is simply whether the copyright holder's expression has been copied, not how difficult it was to do the copying. Whether an alleged infringer spent

---

30. *Hoehling,* 618 F.2d at 979 (explaining the *scenes a faire* doctrine as follows: "Because it is virtually impossible to write about a particular historical era or fictional theme without employing certain 'stock' or standard literary devices, we have held that *scenes a faire* are not copyrightable as a matter of law."); *cf. Dymow v. Bolton,* 11 F.2d at 691 ("[I]f the same idea can be expressed in a plurality of totally different manners, a plurality of copyrights may result * * * ").

significant time and effort to copy an original work is therefore irrelevant to whether he has pirated the expression of an original work.[32]

* * *

We are not convinced that progress in computer technology or technique is qualitatively different from progress in other areas of science or the arts. In balancing protection and dissemination, *see supra* at 1235 & n. 27, the copyright law has always recognized and tried to accommodate the fact that all intellectual pioneers build on the work of their predecessors. Thus, copyright principles derived from other areas are applicable in the field of computer programs.

2. *Application of the general rule to this case* —The rule proposed here is certainly not problem-free. The rule has its greatest force in the analysis of utilitarian or "functional" works, for the purpose of such works is easily stated and identified. By contrast, in cases involving works of literature or "non-functional" visual representations, defining the purpose of the work may be difficult. Since it may be impossible to discuss the purpose or function of a novel, poem, sculpture or painting, the rule may have little or no application to cases involving such works. The present case presents no such difficulties, for it is clear that the purpose of the utilitarian Dentalab program was to aid in the business operations of a dental laboratory. *See supra* 1224. It is equally clear that the structure of the program was not essential to that task: there are other programs on the market, competitors of Dentalab and Dentcom, that perform the same functions but have different structures and designs.

* * *

Our solution may put us at odds with Judge Patrick Higginbotham's scholarly opinion in *Synercom Technology, Inc. v. University Computing Co.,* 462 F.Supp. 1003 (N.D.Tex.1978), which dealt with the question whether the "input formats" of a computer program—the configurations and collations of the information entered into the program—were idea or expression. The court held that the input formats were ideas, not expressions, and thus not protectible.

* * *

The premise does not apply in other areas of copyright infringement. There is no general requirement that most of each of two works be compared before a court can conclude that they are substantially similar. In the cases of literary works—novels, movies, or plays, for example—it is often impossible to speak of "most" of the work. The substantial similarity inquiry cannot be simply quantified in such instances. Instead, the court must make a qualitative, not quantitative judgment about the character of the work as a whole and the impor-

---

32. Even if the product of the alleged infringer's efforts is a mixture of old and new elements, that would not protect it from the charge of infringement. Parodies, for example, mix copied elements with originality, yet they can violate the copyright of the work being parodied. *See generally* Note, *The Parody Defense to Copyright Infringement: Productive Fair Use After* Betamax, 97 Harv.L.Rev. 1395 (1984).

tance of the substantially similar portions of the work. *See, e.g., Harper & Row Publishers, Inc. v. Nation Enterprises,* 471 U.S. 539, 565–566 & 565 n. 8, 105 S.Ct. 2218, 2233–34 & 2233 n. 8, 85 L.Ed.2d 588 (1985); *Atari, Inc. v. North American Phillips Consumer Electronics Corp.,* 672 F.2d 607, 618 (7th Cir.) ("When analyzing two works to determine whether they are substantially similar, courts should be careful not to lose sight of the forest for the trees."), *cert. denied,* 459 U.S. 880, 103 S.Ct. 176, 74 L.Ed.2d 145 (1982); *Hoehling v. Universal City Studios, Inc.,* 618 F.2d 972, 979–80 (2d Cir.) (warning against same danger), *cert. denied,* 449 U.S. 841, 101 S.Ct. 121, 66 L.Ed.2d 49 (1980). *See also Universal Pictures v. Harold Lloyd Corp.,* 162 F.2d 354 (9th Cir.1947) (finding copyright violation for copying of 20% of plaintiff's film); *In re Personal Computers and Components Thereof,* 1983–84 Copyright L.Dec. (CCH) ¶ 25,651 at 18,931 (Int'l Trade Comm'n Mar. 9, 1984) (18%–25% identity is sufficient for substantial similarity). *Compare Elsmere Music, Inc. v. National Broadcasting Co.,* 482 F.Supp. 741, 744 (S.D.N.Y.), *aff'd,* 623 F.2d 252 (2d Cir.1980) (similarity uncontested by defendants where four notes out of 100 measures and two words out of 45 were identical) *with Jewel Music Publishing Co. v. Leo Feist, Inc.,* 62 F.Supp. 596, 597 (S.D.N.Y.1945) (finding no substantial similarity where three bars of an eight-bar line were identical and the line appeared 24 times in both songs).

Computer programs are no different. Because all steps of a computer program are not of equal importance, the relevant inquiry cannot therefore be the purely mechanical one of whether most of the programs' steps are similar. Rather, because we are concerned with the overall similarities between the programs, we must ask whether the most significant steps of the programs are similar. *See Midway Mfg. Co. v. Strohon, supra,* 564 F.Supp. at 753. * * *

FAIR USE

MAXTONE–GRAHAM v. BURTCHAELL

United States Court of Appeals, Second Circuit, 1986.
803 F.2d 1253, 231 USPQ 534.

Cert. denied, ___ U.S. ___, 107 S.Ct. 2201, 95 L.Ed.2d 856 (1987).

KAUFMAN, CIRCUIT JUDGE.

Nearly half a century ago, a distinguished panel of this Court including Learned Hand called the question of fair use "the most troublesome in the whole law of copyright," *Dellar v. Samuel Goldwyn, Inc.,* 104 F.2d 661, 662, 42 USPQ 164, 165 (2d Cir.1939) (per curiam). That description remains accurate today. Since Judge Hand's time, the common law doctrine has been inscribed into the Copyright Act, but the fair use inquiry continues to require a difficult case-by-case balancing of complex factors. The purpose of fair use is to create a limited exception to the individual's private property rights in his expression—rights conferred to encourage creativity—to promote certain productive uses of existing copyrighted material. Fair use has been defined as "a privilege in others than the owner of the copyright to use the copyrighted material in a reasonable manner without his consent, notwithstanding the monopoly granted to the owner [by the copyright]." [1]

In this case, we are asked to decide whether the district court properly granted summary judgment in favor of the defendants on the basis of the affirmative defense of fair use in an action for copyright infringement. Plaintiff had published a book of interviews with women discussing their experiences with abortion and unwanted pregnancy. Several years later, defendant Burtchaell was preparing a series of essays on abortion, and requested permission to quote extensively from plaintiff's interviews. Despite the denial of permission, he included numerous verbatim quotations in his book.

* * *

In the first few pages of his essay, Burtchaell explained that he regarded Maxtone-Graham's interviews as helpful source material, but that his own intention was to move beyond anecdotal reflection and offer a framework for analysis of the women's experiences. In a deposition, Burtchaell said he considered paraphrasing from the interviews, but felt "it [was] essential for the credibility of my essay that the words of abortion veterans themselves appear." He also decided that, as a Catholic priest, conducting his own interviews would pose credibility problems and that his book would be perceived as fairer if he relied on interviews conducted by those who sympathize with the "pro-choice" view of abortion.

The first essay in *Rachel Weeping* was approximately 37,000 words long, and about 7,000 of these were direct quotations from the interviews in Pregnant by Mistake. Burtchaell's book contains 325 pages of text, and the title essay filled 60 pages. The district court found that *Rachel Weeping* includes 4.3 percent of the words in *Pregnant by Mistake*.

* * *

C. THE FAIR USE DEFENSE

The roots of what we now know as "fair use" are firmly planted in the early English common law, where the defense was known as "abridgment." One of the earliest cases to raise the issue was *Gyles v. Wilcox*, 2 Atk. 141 (1740) (No. 130), a decision upon a bill for an injunction to stay the publication of a legal treatise. Lord Chancellor Hardwicke evaluated the defense of abridgment:

> Where books are colourably shortened only, they are undoubtedly within the meaning of the [copyright act], and are a mere evasion of the statute, and cannot be called an abridgment.

> But this must not be carried so far as to restrain persons from making a real and fair abridgment; for abridgments may, with great propriety, be called a new book, because not only the paper and print, but the invention, learning, and judgment of the author is shewn in

them, and in many cases are extremely useful, though in some instances prejudicial, by mistaking and curtailing the sense of an author.

Id. at 143. From the earliest days of the doctrine, courts have recognized that when a second author uses another's protected expression in a creative and inventive way, the result may be the advancement of learning rather than the exploitation of the first writer.

Fair use made its debut in American law with Justice Story's opinion in *Folsom v. Marsh,* 9 F.Cas. 342 (C.C.D.Mass.1841) (No. 4,901). *Folsom* involved a dispute over two biographical works about George Washington. The following passage is probably the most frequently cited one from Justice Story's discussion:

> In short, we must often, in deciding questions of this sort, look to the nature and objects of the selections made, the quantity and value of the materials used, and the degree in which the use may prejudice the sale, or diminish the profits, or supersede the objects, of the original work.

Id. at 348. He framed his analysis in terms of two extremes. At one extreme was the studied evasion, in which "the whole substance of one work has been copied from another, with slight omissions and formal differences only * * *." *Id.* at 344. At the other extreme was the use of verbatim portions of an earlier work to review or criticize. Justice Story wrote of this type of use:

> [N]o one can doubt that a reviewer may fairly cite largely from the original work, if his design be really and truly to use the passages for the purposes of fair and reasonable criticism. On the other hand, it is as clear, that if he thus cites the most important parts of the work, with a view, not to criticise, but to supersede the use of the original work, and substitute the review for it, such a use will be deemed in law a piracy.

Id. at 344–45.

As Justice Story observed, however, many uses would fall somewhere in between the two extremes. To evaluate cases falling in the gray area, he proposed an inquiry into the infringer's creative effort. In order to have a lawful abridgment, he said,

> [t]here must be real, substantial condensation of the materials, and intellectual labor and judgment bestowed thereon; and not merely the facile use of the scissors; or extracts of the essential parts constituting the chief value of the original work.

Id. at 345.

D. THE FOUR-PART INQUIRY OF SECTION 107

It is remarkable how much of the flavor of Justice Story's analysis remains intact in Section 107 of the Copyright Act of 1976. In enacting the legislation, Congress noted that its purpose was to "restate the present judicial doctrine of fair use, not to change, narrow, or enlarge it in any way." H.R.Rep. No. 1476, 94th Cong., 2d Sess. 66 (1976) *reprinted in* 1976 U.S.Code Cong. & Admin.News 5659, 5680 ("House Report"); S.Rep. No. 473, 94th Cong., 1st Sess. 62 (1975). At the same time, however, the legislature expressed its intention to give courts the freedom to adapt the doctrine to particular situations on a case-by-case basis, in light of changing technology. 17 U.S.C. Sec. 107 reads as follows:

* * * The factors listed in the statute are not intended to be exclusive: "[S]ince the doctrine is an equitable rule of reason, no generally applicable definition is possible, and each case raising the question must be decided on its own facts." House Report at 65, *quoted in Harper & Row, Publishers, Inc. v. Nation Enterprises,* 105 S.Ct. 2218, 2231, 225 USPQ 1073. They are, however, particularly relevant to the fair use question. We address each factor separately.

1. PURPOSE AND CHARACTER OF USE

The fair use provision of the Copyright Act expressly mentions "criticism" and "comment" as favored under the statute, and we think it indisputable that Burtchaell employed the material from *Pregnant by Mistake* for just such purposes. Certainly, *Rachel Weeping* is not merely the product of "the facile use of the scissors," to borrow Justice Story's phrase in *Folsom.* Rather, Burtchaell's work takes portions of the free form interviews and organizes them into a topical framework to make the case against abortion. One need not agree with the merit, methodology or conclusions of *Rachel Weeping* to recognize that Burtchaell applied substantial intellectual labor to the verbatim quotations, continually offering his own insights and opinions. As the district court found, Burtchaell drew upon published primary sources "to write persuasively and without arousing the suspicion of the reader . . . ." We also agree with Judge Brieant that "[a]n objective reader of *Rachel Weeping* would never confuse that work with the original *Pregnant by Mistake,* nor find that its author intended to supplant that work in the marketplace with his own.

a. COMMISSION OF ERROR

Maxtone-Graham argues, however, that Burtchaell's scholarly purpose is contradicted by inaccuracies that riddle his use of the quotations. She alleges that *Rachel Weeping* contains scores of minor mistakes involving capitalization, punctuation and so forth, and dozens more serious errors in which statements were taken out of context or distorted. The district court failed to consider the element of error, but after comparing the two books, we conclude that many of appellant's charges are well-founded—especially those relating to the muddling of adoption and abortion experiences. Burtchaell's scholarship clearly leaves something to be desired, and it is equally unfortunate that the numerous inaccuracies in *Rachel Weeping* escaped the editors' attention.

The commission of errors in borrowing copyrighted material is a proper ingredient to consider in making the fair use determination. 560 F.2d at 1071, 195 USPQ at 280. It is, however, but one of many factors. In view of our evaluation of the other fair use elements, we conclude that the errors in *Rachel Weeping* do not place the work beyond the pale of fair use. In *Gyles v. Wilcox,* the court noted that an otherwise "fair abridgment" might sometimes be "prejudicial, by mistaking and curtailing the sense of an author." 2 Atk. at 143. Furthermore, as a judicial body, we consider it highly undesirable to hinge a legal determination solely on the relative truth or accuracy of statements made in the context of debate on a highly volatile social issue. *See New York Times Co. v. Sullivan,* 376 U.S. 254, 278–83 (1964). Nor do we think it wise to give much legal relevance to whether the allegedly infringing work may be labeled "scholarly" or "dogmatic," for the dogma of one individual may be the original scholarship of another. Only where the distortions were so deliberate, and so misrepresentative of the original work that no reasonable person could find them to be the product of mere carelessness would we incline toward rejecting a fair use claim. The errors in *Rachel Weeping* do not cross that threshold.

b. Commercial Use

The Supreme Court recently addressed the question of fair use in *Sony Corp. v. Universal City Studios, Inc.,* 464 U.S. 417, 447–55, 220 USPQ 665, 680–684 (1984) (time-shifting by owners of home video tape recorders constitutes fair use) and in *Harper & Row, supra* (magazine's appropriation of right of first publication of former President Ford's unpublished manuscript not a fair use). These cases include discussion of how a commercial use affects the fair use inquiry. Maxtone-Graham maintains that *Sony Corp.* and *Harper & Row* require judgment against Burtchaell. We address the Supreme Court's recent pronouncements to show why appellant's suggestion that any income-producing use is unfair virtually by definition falls wide of the mark. In *Sony Corp.,* the Court stated:

> *Although not conclusive,* the first factor requires that "the commercial or nonprofit character of an activity" be weighed in any fair use decision. * * * [A]lthough every commercial use of copyrighted material is presumptively an unfair exploitation of the monopoly privilege that belongs to the owner of the copyright, noncommercial uses are a different matter.

464 U.S. at 448–49, 451, 220 USPQ at 680–682 (emphasis added). Appellant makes much of the last sentence, but we do not read it as altering the traditional multi-factor fair use inquiry. Indeed, the Court relied on a House report which states that the statutory language requiring consideration of "whether such use is of a commercial nature or is for nonprofit educational purposes" was

> not intended to be interpreted as any sort of not-for-profit limitation on educational uses of copyrighted works. It is an express recognition that, as under the present law, the commercial or non-profit character of an activity, while not conclusive with respect to fair use, can and should be weighed along with other factors in fair use decisions.

464 U.S. at 449 n. 32, 220 USPQ at 681 (quoting House Report at 66). This understanding was reflected in *Harper & Row,* in which the Court noted: "The fact that a publication was commercial as opposed to non-profit is a separate factor that *tends to* weigh against a finding of fair use." 105 S.Ct. at 2231 (emphasis added). Only an unduly narrow reading of the language in *Sony Corp.* and an inattention to the context could lead to the conclusion that the Court intended to attach heightened significance to the element of commerciality.

It is undisputed that Burtchaell was paid for his efforts and that his publishers were not motivated by purely charitable intentions. But the inquiry does not end there. We do not read Section 107(1) as requiring us to make a clear-cut choice between two polar characterizations, "commercial" and "non-profit." Were that the case, fair use would be virtually obliterated, for "[a]ll publications presumably are operated for profit * * *." *Koussevitzky v. Allen, Towne & Heath,* 188 Misc. 479, 483, 68 N.Y.S.2d 779, 783, *aff'd,* 272 App.Div. 759, 69 N.Y.S.2d 432 (1st Dept.1947), *quoted in Rosemont Enterprises,* 366 F.2d at 307, 150 USPQ at 719. The commercial nature of a use is a matter of degree, not an absolute, and we find that the educational elements of *Rachel Weeping* far outweigh the commercial aspects of the book. While *Rachel Weeping* involved some commercial aspects, it was first and foremost an essay expressing a certain point of view on the abortion issue. With sales of 6,000 copies, it was hardly a commercial blockbuster and, by all indications, was never intended as such. Of course, even a minimal level of commercial use weighs against a finding of fair use, but whether it affects the ultimate determination depends on the totality of factors.

2. THE NATURE OF THE COPYRIGHTED WORK

The second factor to be considered is the nature of *Pregnant by Mistake.* As we have noted, the book is a collection of verbatim interviews and, in the district court's words, "essentially reportorial in nature." We agree with Judge Brieant, however, that *Pregnant by Mistake* cannot be characterized as the product of mere "diligence," like the index in *New York Times Co. v. Roxbury Data Interface, Inc.,* 434 F.Supp. 217, 221, 194 USPQ 371, 374–375 (D.N.J.1977). *Pregnant by Mistake,* like all interviews, contains elements of creative journalistic effort. "Creation of a nonfiction work, even a compilation of pure fact, entails originality." *Harper & Row,* 105 S.Ct. at 2224, 225 USPQ at 1073. Nevertheless, Maxtone-Graham's book was essentially factual in nature, and, as the district court correctly noted, subsequent authors may rely more heavily on such works. As we have said in another context:

> Biographies, of course, are fundamentally personal histories and it is both reasonable and customary for biographers to refer to and utilize earlier works dealing with the subject of the work and occasionally to quote directly from such works * * *. This practice is permitted because of the public benefit in encouraging the development of histori-

cal and biographical works and their public distribution, e.g., so "that the world may not be deprived of improvements, or the progress of the arts be retarded."

Rosemont Enterprises, 366 F.2d at 307 (quoting *Sayre v. Moore,* 105 Eng. Rep. 138, 139 (K.B.1801)). Like the biography, the interview is an invaluable source of material for social scientists and later use of verbatim quotations within reason is both foreseeable and desirable.

3. THE VOLUME OF QUOTATION

We next turn to the quantitative assessment of the amount and substantiality of the excerpts in relation to the copyrighted work as a whole. There are no absolute rules as to how much of a copyrighted work may be copied and still be considered a fair use. In some instances, copying a work wholesale has been held to be fair use, *Sony Corp.; Williams & Wilkins Co. v. United States,* 487 F.2d 1345, 180 USPQ 49 (Ct.Cl.1973), *aff'd* (per curiam), 420 U.S. 376, 184 USPQ 705 (1975), while in other cases taking only a tiny portion of the original work has been held unfair. Questions of fair use may turn on qualitative assessments. "One writer might take all the vital part of another's book, though it might be but a small proportion of the book in quantity." *Bramwell v. Halcomb,* 3 My. & Cr. (Ch.) 736, 738 (1837). In *Harper & Row,* the Supreme Court found that although the words quoted were an insubstantial portion of former President Ford's manuscript, "the Nation took what was essentially the heart of the book." 105 S.Ct. at 2233, 225 USPQ 1073 (quoting 557 F.Supp., at 1072). *See Meeropol v. Nizer,* 560 F.2d 1071, 195 USPQ 280 (copyrighted letters comprised less than one percent of infringing work but were featured prominently in promotional materials); *Roy Export Co. Establishment of Vaduz, Liechtenstein, Black Inc. v. Columbia Broadcasting System, Inc.,* 503 F.Supp. 1137, 1145, 208 USPQ 580, 586–587 (S.D.N.Y.1980) (jury could have found that taking 55 seconds of one hour, 29 minute film was qualitatively substantial), *aff'd,* 672 F.2d 1095, 215 USPQ 289 (2d Cir.), *cert. denied,* 459 U.S. 826 (1982).

We agree with the district court that Burtchaell's inclusion of 4.3 percent of the words in *Pregnant by Mistake* in his own book is not incompatible with a finding of fair use. Burtchaell testified that he relied upon the verbatim quotations to make his own work more persuasive and because conducting his own interviews would have been impractical because he is a Catholic priest. Nor can it be said that Burtchaell took the heart of *Pregnant by Mistake,* since Maxtone-Graham's book consists of narratives by 17 women, and has no identifiable core that could be appropriated.

4. EFFECT ON THE MARKET

The final factor that we are required to consider is "the effect of the use upon the potential market for or value of the copyrighted work." The Supreme Court recently referred to the impact on the market as "undoubtedly the single most important element of fair use."

Harper & Row, 105 S.Ct. 2234, 225 USPQ at 1073. The Court also had occasion to comment upon the market effect in *Sony Corp.* It said:

> Actual present harm need not be shown; such a requirement would leave the copyright holder with no defense against predictable damage. Nor is it necessary to show with certainty that future harm will result. What is necessary is a showing by a preponderance of the evidence that *some* meaningful likelihood of future harm exists. If the intended use is for commercial gain, that likelihood may be presumed. But if it is for a noncommercial purpose, the likelihood must be demonstrated.

464 U.S. at 451, 220 USPQ at 682. Curiously, however, this bifurcated analysis was not employed by the Court when, only a year later, the issue of fair use resurfaced in *Harper & Row.* Despite the Court's finding that the Nation's stated purpose in publishing the excerpts was to scoop the forthcoming extracts in Time, the Court made no presumption of harm. Instead, it focused its inquiry on *actual* damages and assessed the likelihood of future harm.

The Court held that "to negate fair use one need only show that if the challenged use 'should become widespread, it would adversely affect the *potential* market for the copyrighted work.'" 105 S.Ct. at 2234–35, 225 USPQ at 1073 (quoting *Sony Corp.,* 464 U.S. at 451, 220 USPQ at 682). Harm to derivative works must be taken into account, *see Meeropol v. Nizer,* 560 F.2d at 1070, 195 USPQ at 279–280; *Roy Export v. Columbia Broadcasting System, Inc.,* 503 F.Supp. at 1145–46, 208 USPQ at 586–587, as must any effect on the value of adaptation and serialization rights. 3 Nimmer Sec. 13.05(B).

In view of our conclusion that the noncommercial elements of *Rachel Weeping* overwhelm its commercial aspects, it is not clear that the dicta from *Sony Corp.* regarding the presumption of market harm governs here. Fortunately, we need not settle that issue here, for whether we presume harm, or search for proof of it, it is abundantly clear that *Rachel Weeping* poses no more than an insignificant threat of economic damage to Maxtone-Graham.[8] Although she has uncrystallized plans to publish a small second edition to satisfy requests for the book, *Rachel Weeping* has not affected these plans. Indeed, it is unthinkable that potential customers for a series of sympathetic interviews on abortion and adoption would withdraw their requests because a small portion of the work was used in an essay sharply critical of abortion. This conclusion is supported by our finding that the two works served fundamentally different functions, by virtue both of their

---

8. We also note that *Pregnant by Mistake* was out of print when *Rachel Weeping* was published. While this factor is not essential to our affirmance of the district court's finding of fair use, it certainly supports our determination. The legislative reports have provided some guidance on this issue:

A key, though not necessarily determinative, factor in fair use is whether or not the work is available to the potential user. If the work is "out of print" and unavailable for purchase through normal channels, the user may have more justification for reproducing it than in the ordinary case. * * *

S.Rep. No. 94–473, 94th Cong., 1st Sess. 64 (1965); H.R.Rep. No. 94–1476, 94th Cong., 2d Sess. 67 (1976).

opposing viewpoints and disparate editorial formats. Moreover, it is not beyond the realm of possibility that Burtchaell's book might stimulate further interest in *Pregnant by Mistake*. Nor do we believe Maxtone-Graham can credibly argue that the use of the quotations has harmed potential markets for her work. She is unable to point to a single piece of evidence portending future harm, and the fact that *Pregnant by Mistake* was published a full decade before the appearance of *Rachel Weeping* makes any such claim far too speculative to sustain upon mere allegation.

5. OTHER FACTORS

The additional points raised by Maxtone-Graham do not affect our analysis of the fair use question. Although bad faith by the user of copyrighted material suggests unfairness, Burtchaell's decision to publish despite Maxtone-Graham's denial of permission does not deserve that characterization. Unlike the *Harper & Row* case, where materials were purloined and portions subsequently published, Burtchaell obtained *Pregnant by Mistake* through legitimate channels and made repeated attempts to obtain permission to quote from it. He was willing to pay the customary price, and in fact did so for the rights to quote from The *Ambivalence of Abortion*. Burtchaell should not be penalized for erring on the side of safety.

Finally, appellant argues that there is a material dispute concerning her purpose in withholding permission. She maintains that she was honoring her pledge to the interviewees, while the district court suggests that she was engaging in a form of content-based censorship. We accept her version of the facts, but also note that the issue is, at best, marginally relevant to our inquiry.

We find no genuine dispute on material issues of fact in this case, and conclude from our evaluation of the factors that the fair use defense was properly sustained as a matter of law. Burtchaell's use of *Pregnant by Mistake* was precisely the type of criticism of or comment on copyrighted materials anticipated by Section 107. * * *

HARPER & ROW PUBLISHERS, INC. v. NATION ENTERPRISES

United States Supreme Court, 1985.
471 U.S. 539, 105 S.Ct. 2218, 85 L.Ed.2d 588, 225 USPQ 1073.

JUSTICE O'CONNOR delivered the opinion of the Court.

This case requires us to consider to what extent the "fair use" provision of the Copyright Revision Act of 1976, 17 U.S.C. § 107 (hereinafter the Copyright Act), sanctions the unauthorized use of quotations from a public figure's unpublished manuscript. In March 1979, an undisclosed source provided The Nation magazine with the unpublished manuscript of "A Time to Heal: The Autobiography of Gerald R. Ford." Working directly from the purloined manuscript, an editor of The Nation produced a short piece entitled "The Ford

Memoirs—Behind the Nixon Pardon." The piece was timed to "scoop" an article scheduled shortly to appear in Time magazine. Time had agreed to purchase the exclusive right to print prepublication excerpts from the copyright holders, Harper & Row Publishers, Inc. (hereinafter Harper & Row) and Reader's Digest Association, Inc. (hereinafter Reader's Digest). As a result of The Nation article, Time canceled its agreement. Petitioners brought a successful copyright action against The Nation. On appeal, the Second Circuit reversed the lower court's finding of infringement, holding that The Nation's act was sanctioned as a "fair use" of the copyrighted material. We granted certiorari, 467 U.S. 1214, 104 S.Ct. 2655, 81 L.Ed.2d 362 (1984), and we now reverse.

* * *

Respondents, however, contend that First Amendment values require a different rule under the circumstances of this case. The thrust of the decision below is that "[t]he scope of [fair use] is undoubtedly wider when the information conveyed relates to matters of high public concern." *Consumers Union of the United States, Inc. v. General Signal Corp.*, 724 F.2d 1044, 1050 (CA2 1983) (construing *Harper & Row Publishers, Inc. v. Nation Enterprises*, 723 F.2d 195 (CA2 1983) (case below), as allowing advertiser to quote Consumer Reports), cert. denied, 467 U.S. 1214, 104 S.Ct. 2655, 81 L.Ed.2d 362 (1984). Respondents advance the substantial public import of the subject matter of the Ford memoirs as grounds for excusing a use that would ordinarily not pass muster as a fair use—the piracy of verbatim quotations for the purpose of "scooping" the authorized first serialization. Respondents explain their copying of Mr. Ford's expression as essential to reporting the news story it claims the book itself represents. In respondents' view, not only the facts contained in Mr. Ford's memoirs, but "the precise manner in which [he] expressed himself was as newsworthy as what he had to say." Brief for Respondents 38–39. Respondents argue that the public's interest in learning this news as fast as possible outweighs the right of the author to control its first publication.

The Second Circuit noted, correctly, that copyright's idea/expression dichotomy "strike[s] a definitional balance between the First Amendment and the Copyright Act by permitting free communication of facts while still protecting an author's expression." 723 F.2d, at 203. No author may copyright his ideas or the facts he narrates. 17 U.S.C. § 102(b). See, *e.g., New York Times Co. v. United States*, 403 U.S. 713, 726, n. *, 91 S.Ct. 2140, 2147, n. *, 29 L.Ed.2d 822 (1971) (BRENNAN, J., concurring) (Copyright laws are not restrictions on freedom of speech as copyright protects only form of expression and not the ideas expressed); 1 Nimmer § 1.10[B][2]. As this Court long ago observed: "[T]he news element—the information respecting current events contained in the literary production—is not the creation of the writer, but is a report of matters that ordinarily are *publici juris;* it is the history of the day." *International News Service v. Associated Press*, 248 U.S. 215, 234, 39 S.Ct. 68, 71, 63 L.Ed. 211 (1918). But copyright assures those who write and publish factual narratives such as "A Time to Heal" that they may at least enjoy the right to market the original expression contained therein as just compensation for their investment. Cf. *Zacchini v. Scripps-Howard Broadcasting Co.*, 433 U.S. 562, 575, 97 S.Ct. 2849, 2857, 53 L.Ed.2d 965 (1977).

Respondents' theory, however, would expand fair use to effectively destroy any expectation of copyright protection in the work of a public figure. Absent such protection, there would be little incentive to create or profit in financing such memoirs and the public would be denied an important source of significant historical information. The promise of copyright would be an empty one if it could be avoided merely by dubbing the infringement a fair use "news report" of the book. See *Wainwright Securities Inc. v. Wall Street Transcript Corp.*, 558 F.2d 91 (CA2 1977), cert. denied, 434 U.S. 1014, 98 S.Ct. 730, 54 L.Ed.2d 759 (1978).

Nor do respondents assert any actual necessity for circumventing the copyright scheme with respect to the types of works and users at issue here. Where an author and publisher have invested extensive resources in creating an original work and are poised to release it to the public, no legitimate aim is served by preempting the right of first publication. The fact that the words the author has chosen to clothe his narrative may of themselves be "newsworthy" is not an independent justification for unauthorized copying of the author's expression prior to publication. To paraphrase another recent Second Circuit decision:

> "[Respondent] possessed an unfettered right to use any factual information revealed in [the memoirs] for the purpose of enlightening its audience, but it can claim no need to 'bodily appropriate' [Mr. Ford's] 'expression' of that information by utilizing portions of the actual [manuscript]. The public interest in the free flow of information is assured by the law's refusal to recognize a valid copyright in facts. The fair use doctrine is not a license for corporate theft, empowering a court to ignore a copyright whenever it determines the underlying work contains material of possible public importance." *Iowa State University Research Foundation, Inc. v. American Broadcasting Cos., Inc.*, 621 F.2d 57, 61 (CA2 1980) (citations omitted).

Accord, *Roy Export Co. Establishment v. Columbia Broadcasting System, Inc.*, 503 F.Supp. 1137 (SDNY1980) ("newsworthiness" of material copied does not justify copying), aff'd 672 F.2d 1095 (CA2), cert. denied, 459 U.S. 826, 103 S.Ct. 60, 74 L.Ed.2d 63 (1982); *Quinto v. Legal Times of Washington, Inc.*, 506 F.Supp. 554 (DC 1981) (same).

In our haste to disseminate news, it should not be forgotten that the Framers intended copyright itself to be the engine of free expression. By establishing a marketable right to the use of one's expression, copyright supplies the economic incentive to create and disseminate ideas. This Court stated in *Mazer v. Stein:*

> "The economic philosophy behind the clause empowering Congress to grant patents and copyrights is the conviction that encouragement

of individual effort by personal gain is the best way to advance public welfare through the talents of authors and inventors in 'Science and useful Arts.' " 347 U.S. 201, 219, 74 S.Ct. 460, 471, 98 L.Ed. 630 (1954).

And again in *Twentieth Century Music Corp. v. Aiken:*

> "The immediate effect of our copyright law is to secure a fair return for an 'author's' creative labor. But the ultimate aim is, by this incentive, to stimulate [the creation of useful works] for the general public good." 422 U.S., at 156, 95 S.Ct., at 2043.

It is fundamentally at odds with the scheme of copyright to accord lesser rights in those works that are of greatest importance to the public. Such a notion ignores the major premise of copyright and injures author and public alike. "[T]o propose that fair use be imposed whenever the 'social value [of dissemination] * * * outweighs any detriment to the artist,' would be to propose depriving copyright owners of their right in the property precisely when they encounter those users who could afford to pay for it." Gordon, Fair Use as Market Failure: A Structural and Economic Analysis of the *Betamax* Case and its Predecessors, 82 Colum.L.Rev. 1600, 1615 (1982). And as one commentator has noted: "If every volume that was in the public interest could be pirated away by a competing publisher, . . . the public [soon] would have nothing worth reading." Sobel, Copyright and the First Amendment: A Gathering Storm?, 19 ASCAP Copyright Law Symposium 43, 78 (1971). See generally Comment, Copyright and the First Amendment; Where Lies the Public Interest?, 59 Tulane L.Rev. 133 (1984).

Moreover, freedom of thought and expression "includes both the right to speak freely and the right to refrain from speaking at all." *Wooley v. Maynard,* 430 U.S. 705, 714, 97 S.Ct. 1428, 1435, 51 L.Ed.2d 752 (1977) (BURGER, C.J.). We do not suggest this right not to speak would sanction abuse of the copyright owner's monopoly as an instrument to suppress facts. But in the words of New York's Chief Judge Fuld:

> "The essential thrust of the First Amendment is to prohibit improper restraints on the *voluntary* public expression of ideas; it shields the man who wants to speak or publish when others wish him to be quiet. There is necessarily, and within suitably defined areas, a concomitant freedom *not* to speak publicly, one which serves the same ultimate end as freedom of speech in its affirmative aspect." *Estate of Hemingway v. Random House,* 23 N.Y.2d 341, 348, 296 N.Y.S.2d 771, 776, 244 N.E.2d 250, 255 (1968).

Courts and commentators have recognized that copyright, and the right of first publication in particular, serve this countervailing First Amendment value. See *Schnapper v. Foley,* 215 U.S.App.D.C. 59, 667 F.2d 102 (1981), cert. denied, 455 U.S. 948, 102 S.Ct. 1448, 71 L.Ed.2d 661 (1982); 1 Nimmer § 1.10[B], at 1–70, n. 24; Patry 140–142.

In view of the First Amendment protections already embodied in the Copyright Act's distinction between copyrightable expression and uncopyrightable facts and ideas, and the latitude for scholarship and comment traditionally afforded by fair use, we see no warrant for expanding the doctrine of fair use to create what amounts to a public figure exception to copyright. Whether verbatim copying from a public figure's manuscript in a given case is or is not fair must be judged according to the traditional equities of fair use.

* * *

JUSTICE BRENNAN, with whom JUSTICE WHITE and JUSTICE MARSHALL join, dissenting.

The Court holds that The Nation's quotation of 300 words from the unpublished 200,000–word manuscript of President Gerald R. Ford infringed the copyright in that manuscript, even though the quotations related to a historical event of undoubted significance—the resignation and pardon of President Richard M. Nixon. Although the Court pursues the laudable goal of protecting "the economic incentive to create and disseminate ideas," *ante,* at 2230, this zealous defense of the copyright owner's prerogative will, I fear, stifle the board dissemination of ideas and information copyright is intended to nurture. Protection of the copyright owner's economic interest is achieved in this case through an exceedingly narrow definition of the scope of fair use. The progress of arts and sciences and the robust public debate essential to an enlightened citizenry are ill served by this constricted reading of the fair use doctrine. See 17 U.S.C. § 107. I therefore respectfully dissent.

* * *

III

The Court's exceedingly narrow approach to fair use permits Harper & Row to monopolize information. This holding "effect[s] an important extension of property rights and a corresponding curtailment in the free use of knowledge and of ideas." *International News Service v. Associated Press,* 248 U.S., at 263, 39 S.Ct., at 81 (Brandeis, J., dissenting). The Court has perhaps advanced the ability of the historian—or at least the public official who has recently left office—to capture the full economic value of information in his or her possession. But the Court does so only by risking the robust debate of public issues that is the "essence of self-government." *Garrison v. Louisiana,* 379 U.S., at 74–75, 85 S.Ct., at 215–216. The Nation was providing the grist for that robust debate. The Court imposes liability upon The Nation for no other reason than that The Nation succeeded in being the first to provide certain information to the public. I dissent.

FISHER v. DEES

United States Court of Appeals, Ninth Circuit, 1986.
794 F.2d 432, 230 USPQ 421.

SNEED, CIRCUIT JUDGE.

* * *

The plaintiffs-appellants, Marvin Fisher and Jack Segal (the composers), composed and own the copyright to the '50s standard "When Sunny Gets Blue" (the song). In late 1984, a law firm representing the defendants-appellees—disc jockey Rick Dees, Atlantic Recording Corp., and Warner Communications, Inc.—contacted Fisher and requested permission to use part or all of the music to "When Sunny Gets Blue" in order to create a comedic and inoffensive version of the song. Fisher refused the request.

A few months later, Dees released a comedy record album (also issued in cassette form) called *Put It Where the Moon Don't Shine.* One cut on the album, entitled "When Sonny Sniffs Glue" (the parody), is an obvious take-off on the composers' song. The parody copies the first six of the song's thirty-eight bars of music—its recognizable main theme. In addition, it changes the original's opening lyrics—"When Sunny gets blue, her eyes get gray and cloudy, then the rain begins to fall" to "When Sonny sniffs glue, her eyes get red and bulgy, then her hair begins to fall." The parody runs for 29 seconds of the approximately forty minutes of material on Dee's album.

* * *

A. *Copyright Infringement*

Dees urges affirmance of summary judgment on the claim for copyright infringement on the ground that the copying of the song for purposes of parody constituted a fair use.[2] We agree for the reasons discussed below.

* * *

1. *Overview of the fair-use doctrine*

* * *

Congress named parody as one of these activities. Nonetheless, parody was not classified as a *presumptively* fair use. *See Harper & Row,* 105 S.Ct. at 2231. Each assertion of the "parody defense" must be considered individually, in light of the statutory factors, reason, experience, and, of course, the general principles developed in past cases.

---

2. We reject out of hand the appellees' other two arguments for affirmance. The first one—that the first amendment gives parodists a blanket protection from copyright infringement actions—has previously been rejected by this circuit. *See Walt Disney Productions v. Air Pirates,* 581 F.2d 751, 758–59 (9th Cir. 1978) (holding that " 'the idea-expression line' " separating infringement from non-infringement " 'represents an acceptable definitional balance as between copyright and free speech interests' " (quoting *Sid & Marty Krofft Television Productions, Inc. v. McDonald's Corp.,* 562 F.2d 1157, 1170 (9th Cir. 1977))), *cert. denied,* 439 U.S. 1132, 99 S.Ct. 1054, 59 L.Ed.2d 94 (1979). The second one—that the taking from the song was *de minimis* and thus not violative of the composers' copyright—is not supported by the facts. As a rule, a taking is considered *de minimis* only if it is so meager and frag-

mentary that the average audience would not recognize the appropriation. *See, e.g., Elsmere Music, Inc. v. National Broadcasting Co.,* 482 F.Supp. 741, 744 (S.D.N.Y.) (holding that a parodist's copying of four notes in a 100-measure composition was not merely a *de minimis* taking where that musical phrase was the heart of the composition), *aff'd per curiam,* 623 F.2d 252 (2d Cir. 1980). Here, the appropriation would be recognized instantly by anyone familiar with the original. As an analytical matter, moreover, it would seem contradictory to assert that copying for parodic purposes could be *de minimis.* A parody is successful only if the audience makes the connection between the original and its comic version. To "conjure up" the original work in the audience's mind, the parodist must appropriate a substantial enough portion of it to evoke recognition.

There have been few cases in this circuit involving the parody branch of the fair-use doctrine. An early case, *Benny v. Loew's Inc.*, 239 F.2d 532 (9th Cir. 1956), *aff'd by an equally divided Court*, 356 U.S. 43, 78 S.Ct. 667, 2 L.Ed.2d 583 (1958), held that " 'a parodized or burlesqued taking [was] to be treated no differently from any other [copyright] appropriation,' " *id.* at 537 (quoting lower court opinion, 131 F.Supp. 165, 183 (S.D.Cal.1955)). This decision was criticized by contemporary commentators, *see Berlin v. E.C. Publications, Inc.*, 329 F.2d 541, 544–45 (2d Cir.) (listing critiques), *cert. denied*, 379 U.S. 822, 85 S.Ct. 46, 13 L.Ed.2d 33 (1964), and was essentially repudiated by Congress's recognition of parody in the notes to the Copyrights Act of 1976. *See* discussion, *supra*. Accordingly, in *Walt Disney Productions v. Air Pirates*, 581 F.2d 751 (9th Cir. 1978), *cert. denied*, 439 U.S. 1132, 99 S.Ct. 1054, 59 L.Ed.2d 94 (1979), we gave the *Benny* opinion a narrow interpretation and acknowledged that parody is a potential fair use subject to the multi-factor analysis codified in section 107. *See id.* at 756–58.

2. *Applying the fair-use test*

The composers advance five principal reasons why the parody before us is not a fair use: (1) the so-called parody is not actually a parody, or at least is not a parody of the composers' song; (2) Dees acted in bad faith; (3) Dees's use is commercial in nature; (4) the parody competes in the same market—record albums and tapes—as the song; and (5) the taking is more substantial than was reasonably necessary to "conjure up" the original in the mind of the audience.

In addition, the composers assert that the question of fair use is an issue for the jury. Even if the material facts pertaining to each factor in the fair-use test are undisputed, they maintain, the ultimate issue, fair use or no, is appropriate for determination on summary judgment only when no reasonable jury could have decided the question differently.

(a) *Judge or jury?*

We dispose of this last argument first, because it is completely undercut by the Supreme Court's recent decision in *Harper & Row, Publishers, Inc. v. Nation Enterprises*, ___ U.S. ___, 105 S.Ct. 2218, 85 L.Ed.2d 588 (1985). The Court held in that case that "[f]air use is a mixed question of law and fact", *id.* at 2231, and that "[w]here the District Court has found facts sufficient to evaluate each of the statutory factors," an appellate court may conclude as a matter of law— without remanding for further factfinding—" 'that [the challenged use] do[es] not qualify as a fair use of the copyrighted work,' " *id.* (quoting *Pacific & Southern Co. v. Duncan*, 744 F.2d 1490, 1495 n. 8 (11th Cir. 1984), *cert. denied*, ___ U.S. ___, 105 S.Ct. 1867, 85 L.Ed.2d 161 (1985)).

No material historical facts are at issue in this case. The parties dispute only the ultimate conclusions to be drawn from the admitted facts. Because, under *Harper & Row,* these judgments are legal in nature, we can make them without usurping the function of the jury.

(b) Substantive fair-use issues

We now turn to the composers' numerous substantive arguments as to why the fair-use defense is not available.

(1) The subject of the parody

The composers assert that the parody, although it borrows from the original work, was not "directed" at the original. That is, a humorous or satiric work deserves protection under the fair-use doctrine only if the copied work is at least partly the target of the work in question. *See Walt Disney Productions v. Air Pirates,* 581 F.2d 751, 758 n. 15 (9th Cir. 1978), *cert. denied,* 439 U.S. 1132, 99 S.Ct. 1054, 59 L.Ed.2d 94 (1979). Otherwise, there is no need to "conjure up" the original in the audience's mind and no justification for borrowing from it. *Id.; accord MCA, Inc. v. Wilson,* 677 F.2d 180, 185 (2d Cir. 1981).

We requested counsel to provide us with tapes of both Dees's parody and the original (as sung by Johnny Mathis). Although we have no illusions of musical expertise, it was clear to us that Dees's version was intended to poke fun at the composers' song, and at Mr. Mathis's rather singular vocal range. We reject the notion that the song was used merely as a vehicle to achieve a comedic objective unrelated to the song, its place and time. *Cf. id.* at 183–85 (purpose of saving the effort of composing original music); *infra* note 5.

(2) The propriety of Dees's conduct

One theme running through the composers' briefs is that Dees's alleged bad conduct should bar his use of the equitable defense of fair use. The principle invoked is sound. Because " '[f]air use presupposes "good faith" and "fair dealing," ' " *Harper & Row,* 105 S.Ct. at 2232 (quoting *Time Inc. v. Bernard Geis Associates,* 293 F.Supp. 130, 146 (S.D.N.Y.1968)), courts may weigh "the propriety of the defendant's conduct" in the equitable balance of a fair use determination, 3 M. Nimmer, *Nimmer on Copyright* § 13.05[A], at 13–72 to –73 (rev. ed. 1985).

Nonetheless, we conclude that the composers have failed to identify any conduct of Dees that is sufficiently blameworthy. For example, Fisher and Segal fault Dees for using the song after Fisher expressly refused him permission to do so. In their view, this shows bad faith on Dees's part. We cannot agree. Parodists will seldom get permission from those whose works are parodied. Self-esteem is seldom strong enough to permit the granting of permission even in exchange for a reasonable fee. *See* Note, *The Parody Defense to Copyright Infringement: Productive Fair Use After* Betamax, 97 Harv.L.Rev. 1395, 1397 n. 12 (1984) [hereinafter cited as *Parody Defense*]. The parody defense to copyright infringement exists precisely to make possible a use that generally cannot be bought. *See* 3 M. Nimmer, *supra,* § 13.05[C], at 13–89; Gordon, *Fair Use as Market Failure: A Structural and Economic*

Analyis of the Betamax *Case and its Predecessors,* 82 Colum.L.Rev. 1600, 1633 & n. 177. Moreover, to consider Dees blameworthy because he asked permision would penalize him for this modest show of consideration. Even though such gestures are predictably futile, we refuse to discourage them.

The composers also claim that the parody is immoral and thus unprotected by the fair-use doctrine. They cite the parody's irreverent references to drug addiction and its purported use of obscenities. Assuming without deciding that an obscene use is not a fair use, *but see Pillsbury Co. v. Milky Way Productions, Inc.,* 215 U.S.P.Q. 124, 131 & n. 10 (N.D.Ga.1981), we conclude, after listening to it, that the parody is innocous—silly perhaps, but surely not obscene or immoral.

(3) The purpose and character of the use

The first fair-use factor section 107 directs courts to consider is "the purpose and character of the use, including whether such use is of a commercial nature or is for' nonprofit educational purposes." 17 U.S.C. § 107(1) (1982). The parties agree that the parody is a commercial use of the song. This fact "tends to weigh against a finding of fair use," *Harper & Row,* 105 S.Ct. at 2231, because "every commercial use of copyrighted material is presumptively an unfair exploitation of the monopoly privilege that belongs to the owner of the copyright." *Sony Corp. v. Universal City Studios, Inc.,* 464 U.S. 417, 451, 104 S.Ct. 774, 793, 78 L.Ed.2d 574 (1984).

We recognize, however, that many parodies distributed commercially may be "more in the nature of an editorial or social commentary than . . . an attempt to capitalize financially on the plaintiff's original work." *Milky Way Productions,* 215 U.S.P.Q. at 131 (footnote omitted). In such cases, of which this is one, the initial presumption need not be fatal to the defendant's cause. The defendant can rebut the presumption by convincing the court that the parody does not unfairly diminish the economic value of the original. *See id.* & n. 9.

(4) The economic effect of the use

Thus, we must turn our attention to the fourth factor in the fair-use analysis—"the effect of the use upon the potential market for or value of the copyrighted work," 17 U.S.C. § 107(4). This factor, not surprisingly, "is undoubtedly the single most important element of fair use." *Harper & Row,* 105 S.Ct. at 2234 (footnote omitted).

In assessing the economic effect of the parody, the parody's critical impact must be excluded. Through its critical function, a "parody may quite legitimately aim at garroting the original, destroying it commercially as well as artistically." B. Kaplan, *An Unhurried View of Copyright* 69 (1967). Copyright law is not designed to stifle critics. " 'Destructive' parodies play an important role in social and literary criticism and thus merit protection even though they may discourage or discredit an original author." *Parody Defense,* 96 Harv.L.Rev. at 1411. Accordingly, the economic effect of a parody with which we are concerned is not its potential to destroy or diminish the market for the original—any bad review can have that effect—but rather whether it *fulfills the demand* for the original. Biting criticism suppresses demand; copyright infringement usurps it. Thus, infringement occurs when a parody supplants the original in markets the original is aimed at or in which the original is, or has reasonable potential to become, commercially valuable. *See, e.g., Air Pirates,* 581 F.2d at 756; *Berlin v. E.C. Publications, Inc.,* 329 F.2d 541, 545 (2d Cir.), *cert. denied,* 379 U.S. 822, 85 S.Ct. 46, 13 L.Ed.2d 33 (1964); *Parody Defense, supra,* at 1409–11.

This is not a case in which commercial substitution is likely. "When Sunny Gets Blue" is "a lyrical song concerning or relating to a woman's feelings about lost love and her chance for . . . happiness again." Appellants' Opening Brief at 3. By contrast, the parody is a 29-second recording concerning a woman who sniffs glue, which "ends with noise and laughter mixed into the song." *Id.* at 7. We do not believe that consumers desirous of hearing a romantic and nostalgic ballad such as the composers' song would be satisfied to purchase the parody instead. Nor are those fond of parody likely to consider "When Sunny Gets Blue" a source of satisfaction. The two works do not fulfill the same demand. Consequently, the parody has no cognizable economic effect on the original.

(5) The amount and substantiality of the taking

This court has also consistently focused on the third fair-use factor—the amount and substantiality of the taking, 17 U.S.C. § 107(3). *See Air Pirates,* 581 F.2d at 756. Thus far, however, we have provided few concrete guidelines; we have merely sketched the outer boundaries of the inquiry. On the one hand "substantial copying by a defendant, combined with the fact that the portion copied constituted a substantial part of the defendant's work," does not automatically preclude the fair use defense. *Id.* On the other hand, "copying that is virtually complete or almost verbatim" will not be protected. *Id.*

In *Air Pirates,* we ultimately based our analysis on the so-called "conjure up" test. *See Air Pirates,* 581 F.2d at 757 (citing *Berlin v. E.C. Publications, Inc.,* 329 F.2d 541 (2d Cir.), *cert. denied,* 379 U.S. 822, 85 S.Ct. 46, 13 L.Ed.2d 33 (1964), and *Columbia Pictures Corp. v. National Broadcasting Co.,* 137 F.Supp. 348 (S.D.Cal.1955)). As the *Air Pirates* opinion articulated it, the test asks "whether the parodist has appropriated a greater amount of the original work than is necessary to 'recall or conjure up' the object of his satire." *Id.* The composers interpret this test to limit the amount of permissible copying to that amount necessary to evoke only *initial* recognition in the listener.

We disagree with this rigid view. As the Second Circuit stated in *Elsmere Music, Inc. v. National Broadcasting Co.,* 623 F.2d 252 (2d Cir. 1980) (per curiam):

[T]he concept of "conjuring up" an original came into the copyright law not as a limitation on how much of an original may be used, but as a recognition that a parody frequently needs to be more than a fleeting evocation of an original in order to make its humorous point. A parody is entitled at least to "conjure up" the original.

Id. at 253 n. 1 (citation omitted). *Air Pirates* does not compel a different view. In that case—which concerned the near-verbatim copying of Disney characters in the defendants' underground comic book—we concluded that the defendants "took more than was necessary to place firmly in the reader's mind the parodied work and those specific attributes that [were] to be satirized," 581 F.2d at 758. We did not set a fixed limit on copying, but merely expressed our judgment that that particular parody could easily have been accomplished through more restricted means.

We singled out three considerations that we thought important in determining whether a taking is excessive under the circumstances—the degree of public recognition of the original work, the ease of conjuring up the original work in the chosen medium, and the focus of the parody. *See Air Pirates,* 581 F.2d at 757–58. Because the Disney characters were familiar and graphics was a relatively easy medium for parody, we concluded that close copying was impermissible. *See id.* But we expressly noted that media other than the graphic arts might justify greater leeway. We observed: "[W]hen the medium involved is a comic book, a recognizable caricature is not difficult to draw, so that an alternative that involves less copying is more likely to be available than if a speech, for instance, is parodied." *Id.* at 758.

The unavailability of viable alternatives is evident in the present case. Like a speech, a song is difficult to parody effectively without exact or near-exact copying. If the would-be parodist varies the music or meter of the original substantially, it simply will not be recognizable to the general audience. This "special need for accuracy," provides some license for "closer" parody. *See id.* To be sure, that license is not limitless: the parodist's desire to make the best parody must be "balanced against the rights of the copyright owner in his original expressions." [5] *Id.* We think the balance tips in the parodists' favor

---

5. Two music-related parody cases from the Second Circuit, *MCA, Inc. v. Wilson,* 677 F.2d 180 (2d Cir. 1981) and *Elsmere Music, Inc. v. National Broadcasting Co.,* 482 F.Supp. 741 (S.D.N.Y.), *aff'd per curiam,* 623 F.2d 252 (2d Cir. 1980), provide a useful contrast for purposes of assessing the amount and substantiality of various takings. In *MCA, Inc. v. Wilson,* the court held the doctrine of fair use inapplicable in the case of a song called "Cunnilingus Champion of Company C," which closely tracked the music an meter of the 40's standard, "Boogie Woogie Bugle Boy of Company B." The composers of "Champion," which was created for performance in the off-Broadway musical *Let My People Come,* admitted that the song was not orig-

inally conceived as a parody of "Bugle Boy." Rather, they had copied the original because it was " 'immediately identifiable as something happy and joyous and it brought back a certain period in our history when we felt that way.' " 677 F.2d at 184 (quoting uncited trial record). Central to the court's holding was the determination that "Champion" was *not* a parody of "Bugle Boy"; in copying "Bugle Boy" almost verbatim, the composers' purpose was simply to reap the advantages of a well-known tune and short-cut the rigors of composing original music. *See id.* at 183–85.

Elsmere Music, Inc. v. National Broadcasting Co., 482 F.Supp. 741 (S.D.N.Y.),

here. In view of the parody's medium, its purposes, and its brevity, it takes no more from the original than is necessary to accomplish reasonably its parodic purpose.

(6) Summation

We conclude that "When Sonny Sniffs Glue" is a parody deserving of fair-use protection as a matter of law. Thus, we affirm the district court's grant of summary judgment on the copyright claim.

* * *

Notes

1. "It will be seen that the problem of infringement is not simple in the present case. A very literal application of the *Peter Pan* test [Peter Pan Fabrics, Inc. v. Martin Weiner Corp., 274 F.2d 487 (2d Cir.1960)] would require a conclusion that there is no infringement here, because the aesthetic impression is not the same, and the difference in aesthetic impression is not accidental or the result of clumsy copying; it is, so far as one can judge from the comparison of the dolls, intentional and intended to improve the doll's sales appeal. Nor are the differences only such that an ordinary observer would be disposed to overlook them unless he set out to detect the disparities. The differences in the two dolls are plain enough and, as noted above, one would not be mistaken for the other. Yet observation of the two dolls together would convince an observer that one depends on the other, that one has drawn from the other, not merely unimportant features but the purposive combination of features that characterizes the body of the doll and comprises a considerable part of its character and appeal. It would be possible perhaps, in the language of the *Peter Pan* case, to say that the two dolls share no more than the idea of having a round bodied doll that nearly approaches spherical rotundity and has its arms and legs close molded to the body. But when that much has been said it remains that the particular expression, the specific treatment of that idea, has been copied. Here unless the 'idea' is defined with such refinement that it finally states the whole 'expression' or 'treatment' as well, the present case is one in which not only has the idea of a roly poly doll been taken but the mode of expression has been closely copied in its primary characteristics. The copier has not been slavish, but, if anything, a studious improver who has discarded one of the most conspicuously original features of plaintiff's doll, the head. Nevertheless, the Iwai doll maker is an infringer although he has not copied the whole, has not copied it slavishly and has not sought by his differences to disguise or hide the fact

aff'd per curiam, 623 F.2d 252 (2d Cir. 1980), concerned a Saturday Night Live parody of the song "I Love New York." The SNL version, entitled "I Love Sodom," was "sung *a cappella* by a chorus line of three SNL regulars to the tune of 'I Love New York,' with the words 'I Love Sodom' repeated three times." *Id.* at 743. Having first determined that the SNL song was indeed a parody of the original, the court went on to hold that the parodist's copying and repetition of a four-note phrase from the original—which it found to be the "heart of the composition," *id.* at 744—was not an excessive taking. In support of its decision, the court observed that (1) the repetition of the copied material served both to ensure viewer recognition and to satirize the frequent broadcasting of the original; and (2) the parodic use of the copied material lasted only 18 seconds, *see id.* at 747. The instant case is much closer to the facts of *Elsmere* than to those of *MCA*.

of copying. The fact of copying is plain." Uneeda Doll Co., Inc. v. Regent Baby Products Corp., 355 F.Supp. 438, 176 USPQ 73 (E.D.N.Y.1972).

2. "As a matter of the law in this circuit there can be little doubt that a three-dimensional object can infringe a copyright in a two-dimensional object. In 1914 the court of appeals held that a dramatic presentation involving characters introduced as 'Nutt' and 'Giff' infringed the copyright in the two-dimensional cartoon 'Mutt and Jeff.' Hill v. Whalen & Martell, Inc., 220 F. 359 (2d Cir.1914). Ten years later the court concluded that a three-dimensional reproduction of the horse 'Sparky' infringed the copyright in the cartoon 'Barney Google.' King Features Syndicate v. Fleischer, 299 F. 533 (2d Cir.1924). More recently, the court in Geisel v. Poynter Products, Inc., 295 F.Supp. 331 (S.D.N.Y.1968), found that three-dimensional dolls infringed the plaintiff's copyright in his 'Dr. Seuss' cartoons.

"Similarly, the law in this circuit is also clear that a copyright in a dramatic work such as a movie or a play can extend to cover the characters contained therein under certain circumstances. In the most famous statement on this subject, Judge Learned Hand drew upon Shakespeare for his example of the basic law:

'If Twelfth Night were copyrighted, it is quite possible that a second comer might so closely imitate Sir Toby Belch or Malvolio as to infringe, but it would not be enough that for one of his characters he cast a riotous knight who kept wassail to the discomfort of the household, or a vain and foppish steward who became amorous of his mistress. These would be no more than Shakespeare's "ideas" in the play, as little capable of monopoly as Einstein's Doctrine of Relativity, or Darwin's theory of the Origin of Species. It follows that the less developed the characters, the less they can be copyrighted; that is the penalty an author must bear for marking them too indistinctly.'

Nichols v. Universal Pictures Corp., 45 F.2d 119, 121 (2d Cir.1930), cert. denied, 282 U.S. 902, 51 S.Ct. 216, 75 L.Ed. 795 (1931). Thus, a court studying a claim of character infringement must first look to the degree to which the character is developed. M. Nimmer, Nimmer on Copyright § 30, at 134.2 (1976) ('Nimmer'). Professor Nimmer concludes that '[a] character is most readily protectible where both the original work and the copied work consist of cartoons or other graphic representations rather than "word portraits." ' Id. at 135. This analysis is appropriate here where the characters said to be protected are visually depicted in the movie." Ideal Toy Corp. v. Kenner Products Div. of Gen. Mills Fun Group, Inc., 443 F.Supp. 291, 197 USPQ 738 (S.D.N.Y.1977).

3. "In terms of an architectural drawing, the Baker v. Selden rationale would assert that no architect who copyrights his blueprints could thereby acquire a monopoly on the right to build a house with 2 × 4s or with a pitched roof or with a slab foundation or any other particular feature, no matter how unique. The court was concerned that copyright privileges might result in vesting exclusive use rights which only a patent could confer. We therefore interpret this decision as holding that a descriptive copyright may not extend an exclusive right to the use of the described art itself lest originality of description should preempt non-novel invention. Thus, no copyrighted architectural plans under § 5(i) may

clothe their author with the exclusive right to reproduce the dwelling pictured. However, nothing in Baker v. Selden prevents such a copyright from vesting the law's grant of an exclusive right to make copies of the copyrighted plans so as to instruct a would-be builder on how to proceed to construct the dwelling pictured.

" * * * we do not hold that the Lamonts were in anywise restricted by the existence of Imperial's copyright from reproducing a substantially identical residential dwelling. All we hold is that if copyrighted architectural drawings of the originator of such plans are imitated or transcribed in whole or in part, infringement occurs." Imperial Homes Corp. v. Lamont, 458 F.2d 895, 173 USPQ 519 (5th Cir.1972).

4. "Generally, the fact that a building, after construction, is open to public view does not constitute a general publication of the *plans* for the building, even though the interior or exterior is copyable by anyone with sufficient ability. Krahmer v. Luing, 127 N.J.Super. 270, 317 A.2d 96, 98–99; Nucor Corporation v. Tennessee Forging Steel Service, Inc., 8 Cir., 476 F.2d 386, 390–391, 177 USPQ 353, 355–356; Edgar H. Wood Associates, Inc. v. Skene, supra, at 895, 141 USPQ at 460; and Smith v. Paul, supra, at 553–554, 123 USPQ 463, cf. Masterson v. McCroskie, Colo.App., 556 P.2d 1231, 1233–1234. We agree with this view and hold it to represent the better-reasoned conclusion. The fact that a building exterior can be copied by anyone, is not to say that such copying *with the assistance of another's plans* is permissible. Use of the plans is what brings on an infringement, no matter how slight the infringement." Seay v. Vialpando, 567 P.2d 285, 196 USPQ 794 (Wyo.1977).

5. "It is clear that before one may be held liable as a vicarious infringer, absent a special relationship, such as agency or partnership, he must have had the right and ability to supervise the infringing activities, as well as a direct financial interest in those activities. Gershwin Publishing Corp. v. Columbia Artists Management, Inc., 443 F.2d 1159 (2d Cir.1971); Shapiro, Bernstein & Co. v. H.L. Green Co., 316 F.2d 304 (2d Cir.1963).

"However, in the present case, plaintiffs neither show benefit to the University, nor do they refute defendants Trustees' assertion that the University received no financial benefit from the two showings of the bootleg film. Plaintiffs, thus, fail to establish a vital element to their claim that the University is a vicarious infringer." Roy Export Co. Establishment v. Trustees of Columbia Univ., 344 F.Supp. 1350, 175 USPQ 349 (S.D. N.Y.1972).

6. "This lawsuit, brought by the National Football League (NFL) and the St. Louis Football Cardinals (Cardinals), alleges that defendants, the owners of several St. Louis restaurants, violated federal copyright and communications law by showing Cardinals' home games which had been 'blacked out' in the St. Louis area. According to plaintiffs, defendants picked up the signals for such games by means of satellite dish antennae. * * *

"The home-use exemption was included in the 1976 Copyright Act specifically in response to the Supreme Court's decision in Twentieth Century Music Corp. v. Aiken, 422 U.S. 151, 186 USPQ 65 (1975). *Aiken* held that the owner of a small fried-chicken restaurant was not 'performing' copyright works when he played a conventional radio through four in-the-ceiling speakers for the benefit of customers and employees. According to the legislative history of the 1976 Act, an act such as Aiken's would be considered a performance; to decide whether an infringement had occurred, the critical question instead would be the type of equipment used by the putative infringer. Calling 'the use of a home receiver with four ordinary loudspeakers * * * the outer limit of the exemption,' the drafters then said: the clause would exempt small commercial establishments whose proprietors merely bring onto their premises standard radio or television equipment and turn it on for their customers' enjoyment, but it would impose liability where the proprietor has a commercial 'sound system' installed or converts a standard home receiving apparatus * * * into the equivalent of a commercial sound system.

H.R.Rep. No. 94–1476 at 87, 94th Cong., 2d Sess., *reprinted in* 1976 U.S. Code Cong. & Ad.News 5659, 5701. Common sense alone says that it does not matter how well speakers amplify a performance if a receiver cannot pick up the signal in the first place. Moreover, both the legislative history and the plain language of the statute—which speaks of a "receiving set"—contemplate that how the signal is captured will be as much at issue under the exemption as how good the captured signal sounds or looks. There is no indication that the portion of a system which receives should be considered separately from that which displays.

"The factors listed in the legislative history do speak of the size of the area where the transmission will be played and 'the extent to which the receiving apparatus is altered * * * for the purpose of improving the aural or visual quality of the performance,' id * * *. The question in this instance, therefore, is how likely the average patron who watches a blacked-out Cardinals game at one of the defendant restaurants is to have the ability to watch the same game at home? If it is likely—that is, if such systems are the 'kind commonly used in private homes'—then the Section 110(5) exemption applies.

* * *

"Given these facts, the Court's finding that satellite dishes are not 'commonly found in private homes' is not clearly erroneous. There was testimony that the number of such receivers has been growing rapidly, Tr., Preliminary Hearing (November 29, 1984), Vol. II at 104–105, and while some day these antennae may be commonplace, they are not now." NFL v. McBee & Bruno's Inc., 792 F.2d 726, 727–730–1, 230 USPQ 30, 31, 33–34 (8th Cir.1986).

7. Columbia Pictures Ind., Inc. v. Aveco, Inc., 800 F.2d 59, 230 USPQ 869 (3d Cir.1986)—Defendant who rents private rooms to public for view of video cassettes has violated the public performance rights of video cassette copyright owner.

8. Pacific and Southern Co. v. Duncan, 744 F.2d 1490, 224 USPQ 131 (11th Cir.1986), cert. denied 471 U.S. 1004, 105 S.Ct. 1867, 85 L.Ed.2d 161 (1985)—video taping of newscasts and sale of "news clips" violated station's copyright rights.

9. State sovereign immunity under the 11th Amendment is discussed in BV Eng. v. UCLA, 34 P.T.C.J. 124 (C.D.Cal.1987).

H. REMEDIES AND EQUITABLE DEFENSES

17 U.S.C.A. § 502. Remedies for Infringement: Injunctions

(a) Any court having jurisdiction of a civil action arising under this title may, subject to the provisions of section 1498 of title 28, grant temporary and final injunctions on such terms as it may deem reasonable to prevent or restrain infringement of a copyright.

(b) Any such injunction may be served anywhere in the United States on the person enjoined; it shall be operative throughout the United States and shall be enforceable, by proceedings in contempt or otherwise, by any United States court having jurisdiction of that person. The clerk of the court granting the injunction shall, when requested by any other court in which enforcement of the injunction is sought, transmit promptly to the other court a certified copy of all the papers in the case on file in such clerk's office.

17 U.S.C.A. § 503. Remedies for Infringement: Impounding and Disposition of Infringing Articles

(a) At any time while an action under this title is pending, the court may order the impounding, on such terms as it may deem reasonable, of all copies or phonorecords claimed to have been made or used in violation of the copyright owner's exclusive rights, and of all plates, molds, matrices, masters, tapes, film negatives, or other articles by means of which such copies or phonorecords may be reproduced.

(b) As part of a final judgment or decree, the court may order the destruction or other reasonable disposition of all copies or phonorecords found to have been made or used in violation of the copyright owner's exclusive rights, and of all plates, molds, matrices, masters, tapes, film negatives, or other articles by means of which such copies or phonorecords may be reproduced.

17 U.S.C.A. § 504. Remedies for infringement: Damages and Profits

(a) *In General*—Except as otherwise provided by this title, an infringer of copyright is liable for either—

(1) the copyright owner's actual damages and any additional profits of the infringer, as provided by subsection (b); or

(2) statutory damages, as provided by subsection (c).

(b) *Actual Damages and Profits*—The copyright owner is entitled to recover the actual damages suffered by him or her as a result of the infringement, and any profits of the infringer that are attributable to the infringement and are not taken into account in computing the actual damages. In establishing the infringer's profits, the copyright owner is required to present proof only of the infringer's gross revenue, and the infringer is required to prove his or her deductible expenses and the elements of profit attributable to factors other than the copyrighted work.

(c) *Statutory Damages—*

(1) Except as provided by clause (2) of this subsection, the copyright owner may elect, at any time before final judgment is rendered, to recover, instead of actual damages and profits, an award of statutory damages for all infringements involved in the action, with respect to any one work, for which any one infringer is liable individually, or for which any two or more infringers are liable jointly and severally, in a sum of not less than $250 or more than $10,000 as the court considers just. For the purposes of this subsection, all the parts of a compilation or derivative work constitute one work.

(2) In a case where the copyright owner sustains the burden of proving, and the court finds, that infringement was committed willfully, the court in its discretion may increase the award of statutory damages to a sum of not more than $50,000. In a case where the infringer sustains the burden of proving, and the court finds, that such infringer was not aware and had no reason to believe that his or her acts constituted an infringement of copyright, the court at its discretion may reduce the award of statutory damages to a sum of not less than $100. The court shall remit statutory damages in any case where an infringer believed and had reasonable grounds for believing that his or her use of the copyrighted work was a fair use under section 107, if the infringer was: (i) an employee or agent of a nonprofit educational institution, library, or archives acting within the scope of his or her employment who, or such institution, library, or archives itself, which infringed by reproducing the work in copies or phonorecords; or (ii) a public broadcasting entity which or a person who, as a regular part of the nonprofit activities of a public broadcasting entity (as defined in subsection (g) of section 118) infringed by performing a published nondramatic literary work or by reproducing a transmission program embodying a performance of such a work.

17 U.S.C.A. § 505. Remedies for Infringement: Costs and Attorney's Fees

In any civil action under this title, the court in its discretion may allow the recovery of full costs by or against any party other than the United States or an officer thereof. Except as otherwise provided by this title, the court may also award a reasonable attorney's fee to the prevailing party as part of the costs.

17 U.S.C.A. § 506. Criminal offenses

(a) *Criminal infringement—*Any person who infringes a copyright willfully and for purposes of commercial advantage or private financial gain shall be punished as provided in section 2319 of title 18. (Amended May 24, 1982, Public Law 97–180, sec. 5, 96 Stat. 93.)

(b) *Forfeiture and Destruction—*When any person is convicted of any violation of subsection (a), the court in its judgment of conviction shall, in addition to the penalty therein prescribed, order the forfeiture and destruction or other disposition of all infringing copies or phonorecords and all implements, devices, or equipment used in the manufacture of such infringing copies or phonorecords.

(c) *Fraudulent Copyright Notice*—Any person who, with fraudulent intent, places on any article a notice of copyright or words of the same purport that such person knows to be false, or who, with fraudulent intent, publicly distributes or imports for public distribution any article bearing such notice or words that such person knows to be false, shall be fined not more than $2,500.

(d) *Fraudulent Removal of Copyright Notice*—Any person who, with fraudulent intent, removes or alters any notice of copyright appearing on a copy of a copyrighted work shall be fined not more than $2,500.

(e) *False Representation*—Any person who knowingly makes a false representation of a material fact in the application for copyright registration provided for by section 409, or in any written statement filed in connection with the application, shall be fined not more than $2,500.

17 U.S.C.A. § 507. Limitations on Actions

(a) **Criminal Proceedings.** No criminal proceeding shall be maintained under the provisions of this title unless it is commenced within three years after the cause of action arose.

(b) **Civil Actions.** No civil action shall be maintained under the provisions of this title unless it is commenced within three years after the claim accrued.

18 U.S.C.A. § 2318. Trafficking in Counterfeit Labels for Phonorecords, and Copies of Motion Pictures or Other Audiovisual Works

(a) Whoever, in any of the circumstances described in subsection (c) of this section, knowingly traffics in a counterfeit label affixed or designed to be affixed to a phonorecord, or a copy of a motion picture or other audiovisual work, shall be fined not more than $250,000 or imprisoned for not more than five years, or both.

(b) As used in this section—

(1) the term "counterfeit label" means an identifying label or container that appears to be genuine, but is not;

(2) the term "traffic" means to transport, transfer or otherwise dispose of, to another, as consideration for anything of value or to make or obtain control of with intent to so transport, transfer or dispose of; and

(3) the terms "copy", "phonorecord", "motion picture", and "audiovisual work" have, respectively, the meanings given those terms in section 101 (relating to definitions) of title 17.

(c) The circumstances referred to in subsection (a) of this section are—

(1) the offense is committed within the special maritime and territorial jurisdiction of the United States; or within the special aircraft jurisdiction of the United States (as defined in section 101 of the Federal Aviation Act of 1958);

(2) the mail or a facility of interstate or foreign commerce is used or intended to be used in the commission of the offense; or

(3) the counterfeit label is affixed to or encloses, or is designed to be affixed to or enclose, a copyrighted motion picture or other audiovisual work, or a phonorecord of a copyrighted sound recording.

(d) When any person is convicted of any violation of subsection (a), the court in its judgment of conviction shall in addition to the penalty therein prescribed, order the forfeiture and destruction or other disposition of all counterfeit labels and all articles to which counterfeit labels have been affixed or which were intended to have had such labels affixed.

(e) Except to the extent they are inconsistent with the provisions of this title, all provisions of section 509, title 17, United States Code, are applicable to violations of subsection (a).

18 U.S.C.A. § 2319. Criminal Infringement of a Copyright

(a) Whoever violates section 506(a) (relating to criminal offenses) of title 17 shall be punished as provided in subsection (b) of this section and such penalties shall be in addition to any other provisions of title 17 or any other law.

(b) Any person who commits an offense under subsection (a) of this section—

(1) shall be fined not more than $250,000 or imprisoned for not more than five years, or both, if the offense—

(A) involves the reproduction or distribution, during any one-hundred-and-eighty-day period, of at least one thousand phonorecords or copies infringing the copyright in one or more sound recordings;

(B) involves the reproduction or distribution, during any one-hundred-and-eighty-day period, of at least sixty-five copies infringing the copyright in one or more motion pictures or other audiovisual works; or

(C) is a second or subsequent offense under either of subsection (b)(1) or (b)(2) of this section, where a prior offense involved a sound recording, or a motion picture or other audiovisual work;

(2) shall be fined not more than $250,000 or imprisoned for not more than two years, or both, if the offense—

(A) involves the reproduction or distribution, during any one-hundred-and-eighty-day period, of more than one hundred but less than one thousand phonorecords or copies infringing the copyright in one or more sound recordings; or

(B) involves the reproduction or distribution, during any one-hundred-and-eighty-day period, of more than seven but less than sixty-five copies infringing the copyright in one or more motion pictures or other audiovisual works; and

(3) shall be fined not more than $25,000 or imprisoned for not more than one year, or both, in any other case.

(c) As used in this section—

(1) the terms "sound recording", "motion picture", "audiovisual work", "phonorecord", and "copies" have, respectively, the meanings set forth in section 101 (relating to definitions) of title 17; and

(2) the terms "reproduction" and "distribution" refer to the exclusive rights of a copyright owner under clauses (1) and (3) respectively of section 106 (relating to exclusive rights in copyrighted works), as limited by sections 107 through 118, of title 17.

The traditional discretionary powers of federal courts to grant temporary and permanent injunctions restraining copyright infringement and to impound and dispose of infringing articles and means of producing infringing articles are restated in Sections 502 and 503. Section 503(b) is intended to provide greater flexibility in making a final disposition of infringing articles and their means of production by expressly authorizing for the first time any "reasonable disposition", such as ordering "the infringing articles sold, delivered to plaintiff, or disposed of in some other way that would avoid needless waste and best serve the ends of justice." [a]

The monetary award provisions of § 504 were enacted to avoid the confusion and uncertainty of the prior law and give the courts express directions concerning determination of monetary awards while still preserving reasonable discretion to adjust the amount of the award to the circumstances of the case.[b] Thus, as a general rule the copyright owner's actual damages and any additional infringer's profits may be recovered or, in lieu thereof, and at the option of the copyright owner, statutory damages may be recovered. Actual damages are awarded to compensate the copyright owner for his losses due to the infringement, and profits are awarded to prevent the infringer from being enriched by or benefitting from his wrongful acts.

Where applicable the statutory damage provisions assure the copyright owner of a minimum recovery and limit the maximum amount a court in its discretion may award for willful and deliberate infringement. Statutory damages are precluded in certain circumstances by Sections 504(c)(2) and 412.

As under the prior act, in most suits the court has discretion to award costs and reasonable attorney fees (§ 505). Criminal offenses, three year limitations on actions, prohibitions on importation and various other remedies, are provided in Sections 506 through 510 and 601 through 603. Consideration of these sections is beyond the scope of this text.

Even valid copyrights which are being infringed are subject to the usual equitable defenses, such as laches and estoppel. In addition, a use in violation of the antitrust laws, or in inequitable and unjust ways, may constitute misuse and hence result in unenforceability. Moreover, failure to disclose all relevants facts when obtaining a copyright may result in unclean hands or even fraud on the Copyright Office, making the copyright unenforceable.

a. H.R.Rep. No. 94–1476, 94th Cong., 2d Sess. 160 (1976).

b. H.R.Rep. No. 94–1476, 94th Cong., 2d Sess. 161 (1976).

DOWLING v. UNITED STATES

United States Supreme Court, 1985.
473 U.S. 207, 105 S.Ct. 3127, 87 L.Ed.2d 152, 226 USPQ 529.

JUSTICE BLACKMUN delivered the opinion of the Court.

The National Stolen Property Act provides for the imposition of criminal penalties upon any person who "transports in interstate or foreign commerce any goods, wares, merchandise, securities or money, of the value of $5,000 or more, knowing the same to have been stolen, converted or taken by fraud." 18 U.S.C. § 2314. In this case, we must determine whether the statute reaches the interstate transportation of "bootleg" phonorecords, "stolen, converted or taken by fraud" only in the sense that they were manufactured and distributed without the consent of the copyright owners of the musical compositions performed on the records.

* * *

In contrast, the Government's theory here would make theft, conversion, or fraud equivalent to wrongful appropriation of statutorily protected rights in copyright. The copyright owner, however, holds no ordinary chattel. A copyright, like other intellectual property, comprises a series of carefully defined and carefully delimited interests to which the law affords correspondingly exact protections. "Section 106 of the Copyright Act confers a bundle of exclusive rights to the owner of the copyright," which include the rights "to publish, copy, and distribute the author's work." *Harper & Row, Publishers, Inc. v. Nation Enterprises*, 471 U.S. 539, 546–47, 105 S.Ct. 2218, 2224, 85 L.Ed.2d 588 (1985). See 17 U.S.C. § 106. However, "[t]his protection has never accorded the copyright owner complete control over all possible uses of his work." *Sony Corp. v. Universal City Studios, Inc.*, 464 U.S. 417, 432, 104 S.Ct. 774, 784, 78 L.Ed.2d 574 (1984); *id.*, at 462, 104 S.Ct., at 780 (dissenting opinion). For example, § 107 of the Copyright Act "codifies the traditional privilege of other authors to make 'fair use' of an earlier writer's work." *Harper & Row, supra*, 471 U.S., at 547, 105 S.Ct., at 2224. Likewise, § 115 grants compulsory licenses in nondramatic musical works. Thus, the property rights of a copyright holder have a character distinct from the possessory interest of the owner of simple "goods, wares, [or] merchandise," for the copyright holder's dominion is subjected to precisely defined limits.

It follows that interference with copyright does not easily equate with theft, conversion, or fraud. * * * The infringer invades a statutorily defined province guaranteed to the copyright holder alone. But he does not assume physical control over the copyright; nor does he wholly deprive its owner of its use. While one may colloquially like infringement with some general notion of wrongful appropriation, infringement plainly implicates a more complex set of property interests than does run-of-the-mill theft, conversion, or fraud. As a result, it fits but awkwardly with the language Congress chose—"stolen, converted or taken by fraud"—to describe the sorts of goods whose interstate shipment § 2314 makes criminal. "And, when interpreting a criminal statute that does not explicitly reach the conduct in question, we are reluctant to base an expansive reading on inferences drawn from subjective and variable 'understandings.'" *Williams v. United States,* 458 U.S., at 286, 102 S.Ct., at 3092.

* * *

Thus, the history of the criminal infringement provisions of the Copyright Act reveals a good deal of care on Congress' part before subjecting copyright infringement to serious criminal penalties. First, Congress hesitated long before imposing felony sanctions on copyright infringers. Second, when it did so, it carefully chose those areas of infringement that required severe response—specifically, sound recordings and motion pictures—and studiously graded penalties even in those areas of heightened concern. This step-by-step, carefully considered approach is consistent with Congress' traditional sensitivity to the special concerns implicated by the copyright laws.

* * *

D

The broad consequences of the Government's theory, both in the field of copyright and in kindred fields of intellectual property law, provide a final and dispositive factor against reading § 2314 in the manner suggested. For example, in *Harper & Row, supra,* this Court very recently held that The Nation, a weekly magazine of political commentary, had infringed former President Ford's copyright in the unpublished manuscript of his memoirs by verbatim excerpting of some 300 words from the work. It rejected The Nation's argument that the excerpting constituted fair use. Presented with the facts of that case as a hypothetical at oral argument in the present litigation, the Government conceded that its theory of § 2314 would permit prosecution of the magazine if it transported copies of sufficient value across state lines. Tr. of Oral Arg. 35. Whatever the wisdom or propriety of The Nation's decision to publish the excerpts, we would pause, in the absence of any explicit indication of congressional intention, to bring such conduct within the purview of a criminal statute making available serious penalties for the interstate transportation of goods "stolen, converted or taken by fraud."

Likewise, the field of copyright does not cabin the Government's theory, which would as easily encompass the law of patents and other forms of intellectual property. If "the intangible idea protected by the copyright is effectively made tangible by its embodiment upon the tapes," *United States v. Gottesman,* 724 F.2d 1517, 1520 (CA11 1984), phonorecords, or films shipped in interstate commerce as to render those items stolen goods for purposes of § 2314, so too would the intangible idea protected by a patent be made tangible by its embodiment in an article manufactured in accord with patented specifications. Thus, as the Government as much as acknowledged at argument, Tr. of

Oral Arg. 29, its view of the statute would readily permit its application to interstate shipments of patent-infringing goods. Despite its undoubted power to do so, however, Congress has not provided criminal penalties for distribution of goods infringing valid patents. Thus, the rationale supporting application of the statute under the circumstances of this case would equally justify its use in wide expanses of the law which Congress has evidenced no intention to enter by way of criminal sanction.[20] This factor militates strongly against the reading proffered by the Government. Cf. *Williams v. United States,* 458 U.S., at 287, 102 S.Ct., at 3093.

* * * In sum, Congress has not spoken with the requisite clarity. Invoking the "time-honored interpretive guideline" that "ambiguity concerning the ambit of criminal statutes should be resolved in favor of lenity,'" *Liparota v. United States,* 471 U.S. 419, 427, 105 S.Ct. 2084, 2089, 85 L.Ed.2d 434 (1985), quoting *Rewis v. United States,* 401 U.S. 808, 812, 91 S.Ct. 1056, 1059, 28 L.Ed.2d 493 (1971), we reverse the judgment of the Court of Appeals.

It is so ordered.

JUSTICE POWELL, with whom THE CHIEF JUSTICE and JUSTICE WHITE join, dissenting.

The Court holds today that § 2314 does not apply to this case because the rights of a copyright holder are "different" from the rights of owners of other kinds of property. The Court does not explain, however, how the differences it identifies are relevant either under the language of § 2314 or in terms of the purposes of the statute. Because I believe that the language of § 2314 fairly covers the interstate transportation of goods containing unauthorized use of copyrighted material, I dissent.

* * * The difficulty the Court finds with the application of § 2314 here is in finding a theft, conversion, or fraudulent taking, in light of the intangible nature of a copyright. But this difficulty, it seems to me, has more to do with its views on the relative evil of copyright infringement versus other kinds of thievery, than it does with interpretation of the statutory language.

* * *

Notes

1. Actual damages for defendant's use of plaintiff's copyrighted architectural plans was a reasonable architect's fee less the amount normally allocated to supervision during construction. Nucor Corp. v. Tennessee Forging Steel Serv., Inc., 513 F.2d 151, 185 USPQ 332 (8th Cir.1975).

20. The Government's rationale would also apply to goods infringing trademark rights. Yet, despite having long and extensively legislated in this area, see federal Trademark Act of 1946 (Lanham Act), 15 U.S.C. § 1051 *et seq.,* in the modern era Congress only recently has resorted to criminal sanctions to control trademark infringement. See Trademark Counterfeiting Act of 1984, Pub.L. 98–473, ch. XV, 98 Stat. 2178. See also S.Rep. No. 98–526, pp. 1–2, 5 (1984); 2 J. McCarthy, Trademarks and Unfair Competition § 30.39 (2d ed. 1984).

2. If neither the copyright holder's actual damages nor the infringer's profits are proven with reasonable certainty, the "in lieu" award of statutory damages is mandatory. Sid & Marty Krofft Television Productions, Inc. v. McDonald's Corp., 562 F.2d 1157, 196 USPQ 97 (9th Cir.1977).

3. In determining the amount of statutory damages, the court considers infringer's profits, degree of innocence of the infringer, copyright owner's higher profit margin and selling price, number of infringing articles sold and delay of the copyright owner in giving a notice of infringement. L. and L. White Metal Casting Corp. v. Cornell Metal Specialties Corp., 353 F.Supp. 1170, 175 USPQ 464 (E.D.N.Y.1972).

4. "To summarize, to find a willful infringement for profit, as made criminally punishable by 17 U.S.C. § 104, the following elements are required to be found:

'First, that the sound recording allegedly infringed was validly copyrighted. In order to so find, you must find that the sounds on that recording allegedly infringed had a fixation date of on or after February 15, 1972.

'Second, that the Defendant infringed the copyrighted recording as I have defined the arrangement.

'Third, that in infringing, the Defendant acted willfully.

'Fourth, that the act of infringement by Defendant was for profit.'

'Profit' includes the sale or exchange of the infringing work for something for value in the hope of some pecuniary gain. It is irrelevant whether the hope of gain was realized or not. The requirement of profit is intended to delineate commercial infringements from infringements for merely personal use and philanthropic infringements." United States v. Taxe, 380 F.Supp. 1010, 184 USPQ 5 (C.D.Cal.1974), affirmed except rev. of order imposing costs 540 F.2d 961, 192 USPQ 204 (9th Cir.1976).

5. "Normally, after a finding of price-fixing, the remedy is an injunction against the price-fixing—in this case, the blanket license. We think, however, that if on remand a remedy can be fashioned which will ensure that the blanket license will not affect the price or negotiations for direct licenses, the blanket license need not be prohibited in all circumstances. The blanket license is not simply a 'naked restraint' ineluctably doomed to extinction. There is not enough evidence in the present record to compel a finding that the blanket license does not serve a market need for those who wish full protection against infringement suits or who, for some other business reason, deem the blanket license desirable. The blanket license includes a practical covenant not to sue for infringement of any ASCAP copyright as well as an indemnification against suits by others.

"Our objection to the blanket license is that it reduces price competition among the members and provides a disinclination to compete. We think that these objections may be removed if ASCAP itself is required to provide some form of per use licensing which will ensure competition among the individual members with respect to those networks which wish to engage in per use licensing." Columbia Broadcasting System v. American Soc'y of Composers, Authors and Publishers, 562 F.2d 130, 195 USPQ 209 (2d Cir.1977).

6. A copyright may be unenforceable if the application for registration failed to comply with what is now § 409(9).

"The equitable maxim of unclean hands is applicable in determining the enforceability of copyright registrations; and it has been held, in a suit challenging the copyright of a brochure, to be inequitable conduct not to inform the Copyright Office of earlier publications.

'The Court finds that as to this defendant in connection with defendant's manufacture, sale and marketing of its device, the plaintiff's design patent and copyright registrations are unenforceable due to plaintiff's unclean hands and inequitable conduct in connection therewith.

'A substantial portion of Plaintiff's copyrighted material incorporates text and photographs that were previously published and copyrighted by Plaintiff in 1954 and 1955 in connection with its earlier Infra-Massage device * * * Plaintiff did not inform the Copyright Office of its earlier publications in its application to register the copyrights here in suit. That part of the copyright application, Item 7, which requires a listing of the "New Matter In This Version" of the material sought to be copyrighted was left blank by Plaintiff in each of the copyright certificates in suit.' International Biotical Corp. v. Associated Mills, Inc., 239 F.Supp. 511, 514 (N.D.Ill.1964).

"The plaintiff in this case left Item # 7 in the copyright application blank. This was not an insubstantial omission when one considers the identical nature of the two rings. If this item had been completed, the Copyright Office would have had the opportunity to evaluate whether or not the plaintiff had made any copyrightable changes." Vogue Ring Creations, Inc. v. Hardman, 410 F.Supp. 609, 190 USPQ 329 (D.R.I.1976).

7. "The statutory language provides that the allowance of fees to the prevailing party is not mandated in every case but is entrusted to the evaluation of the district court. The proper limits within which that discretion must be exercised remain unclear despite more than three-quarters of a century of experience with the statute.

"Cases in the Court of Appeals for the Ninth Circuit have established a finding of bad faith as a prerequisite for a grant of fees. Cooling Systems and Flexibles, Inc. v. Stuart Radiator, Inc., 777 F.2d 485, 493, 228 USPQ 275, 282 (9th Cir.1985); Jartech, Inc. v. Clancy, 666 F.2d 403, 407, 213 USPQ 1057, 1060 (9th Cir.1982). The Court of Appeals for the Eleventh Circuit has taken a less restrictive position. In Original Appalachian Artworks, Inc. v. Toy Loft, Inc., 684 F.2d 821, 832, 215 USPQ 745, 755 (11th Cir.1982), the court concluded that 'a showing of bad faith or frivolity' is not required for an award. The 'only preconditions * * * [are] that the party receiving the fee be the 'prevailing party' and that the fee be reasonable.' Id. at 832, 215 USPQ at 755.

* * *

"Given the lack of guidance from our earlier decisions, discussion of some of the relevant criteria may assist the district court on remand. We recognize at the outset that the statutory authorization is broad and evidences an intent to rely on the sound judgment of the district courts.

Had Congress intended to condition the award of fees on the presence of bad faith, the statutory provision would have been surplusage. '[E]ven under the American common-law rule attorney's fees may be awarded against a party who has proceeded in bad faith.' Christiansburg Garment Co. v. EEOC, 434 U.S. 412, 419 (1978). We think that limiting assessments to those cases where bad faith is shown unduly narrows the discretion granted to the district judges. Finding no indication either in statutory language or legislative history that bad faith should be a prerequisite to a fee award, we decline to so limit the conditions under which an assessment may be made.

* * *

"Thus we do not require bad faith, nor do we mandate an allowance of fees as a concomitant of prevailing in every case, but we do favor an evenhanded approach. The district courts' discretion may be exercised within these boundaries. Factors which should play a part include frivolousness, motivation, objective unreasonableness (both in the factual and in the legal components of the case) and the need in particular circumstances to advance considerations of compensation and deterrence. We expressly do not limit the factors to those we have mentioned, realizing that others may present themselves in specific situations. Moreover, we may not usurp that broad area which Congress has reserved for the district judge.

"Having decided that fees should be awarded, the district court must then determine what amount is reasonable under the circumstances." Lieb v. Topstone Ind., Inc., 788 F.2d 151, 154–6, 229 USPQ 426, 427–429 (3d Cir.1986).

8.   "This exclusive distribution right [under section 106] is limited by section 109(a) of the Act, which provides that: Notwithstanding the provisions of section 106(3), *the owner of a particular copy * * * lawfully made* under this title, or any person authorized by such owner, is entitled, without the authority of the copyright owner, to sell or otherwise dispose of the possession of that copy * * *. 17 U.S.C. section 109(a) (emphasis added).

* * *

"Our analysis would not be complete, however, without considering which party bears the burden of proof under section 109(a). Legislative history indicates that section 109(a) is a defense in civil copyright cases. After criticizing a district court opinion in a civil case which placed on the plaintiff the burden of proving that a copy had been unlawfully made or acquired, the House Committee on the Judiciary stated that 'in an action to determine whether a defendant is entitled to the privilege established by Sec. 109(a) * * * the burden of proving whether a particular copy was lawfully made or acquired should rest on the defendant.' H.R.Rep. No. 94–1476, 94th Cong., 2d Sess. 80–81, *reprinted in* 1976 U.S.CODE CONG. & AD.NEWS 5659, 5694–95.

"The first sale doctrine developed under section 27 of the former Copyright Act, which provided in pertinent part that 'nothing in this title shall be deemed to forbid, prevent, or restrict the transfer of any copy of a copyrighted work the possession of which has been lawfully obtained.' Interpreting former section 27, courts held that a copyright owner's exclusive vending right extended only to the first sale of a copy. If a legally made copy had been the subject of a first sale, then further distribution of that copy did not infringe the copyright owner's exclusive vending right. See generally 2 Nimmer on Copyright, Sec. 8.12 (1985)." United States v. Goss, 803 F.2d 638, 643, 231 USPQ 730, 733 (11th Cir.1986).

I. SEMICONDUCTOR CHIP PROTECTION

The Semiconductor Chip Protection Act of 1984 (Pub.L. 98–620, Nov. 8, 1984, 98 Stat. 3347) seeks to protect semiconductor chip products "in such a manner as to reward creativity, encourage innovation, research and investment in the semiconductor industry, prevent piracy, while at the same time protecting the public," (House Report No. 98–781, 1984 U.S.Code Cong. and Adm.News, p. 5750).

A semiconductor chip may include over 100,000 transistors photographically etched onto a silver substrate (Id. at 5751). Creation of a chip design involves a number of stages, including preparation of electrical drawings of the desired circuitry, layout of the circuitry in three-dimensional form with imposed size limitations, such as ¼–inch square, and creation of a stencil or mask for each layer of the three-dimensional design. The chip is then manufactured by depositing one or more layers of material onto a substrate, exposing the material to radiation through an appropriate mask, and removal of the unexposed material. The deposition, exposure and removal steps are repeated in conjunction with successive masks to form the desired three-dimensional circuit. Development of a single chip may require several years and cost up to $100 million (Id.). However, once a chip is introduced into the marketplace (or even earlier for the less scrupulous), the chip masks may be readily recreated by simply photographing and removing each layer in turn. This process, which may be completed in a few months at a cost of less than $50,000, allows a competitor to duplicate the chip exactly, but at only a fraction of the development cost. To allow the continuation of this practice may make it increasingly difficult for the semiconductor industry to continue to invest in development of new chips (Id. at 5752).

Patent law does protect the electronic circuity embodied in a chip, but typically does not protect the particular layout or design because of absence of "inventive level" (Id.). Copyright law does not cover strictly utilitarian objects such as chips (See Mazer v. Stein, 347 U.S. 201, 74 S.Ct. 460, 98 L.Ed. 630 (1954) and 17 U.S.C.A. § 101 discussed supra). Congress initially considered an extension of copyright law to encompass chips, but opted instead in favor of "a sui generis form of protection [which] represents * * * appropriate recognition of the industrial nature of mask work designs and avoids conceptual confusion in copyright law to accommodate a form of intellectual property which is better protected by reference to the background and practices of the semiconductor industry" (Id. at 5756). Thus, "[r]ather than risk confusion and uncertainty in, and distortion of, existing copyright law as a result of attempting to modify fundamental copyright principles to suit the unusual nature of chip design, the (Congressional) Committee concludes that a new body of statutory and decisional law should be developed" (Id. at 5759). The Semiconductor Chip Protection Act was therefore enacted, pursuant to the constitutional power of Congress "to promote the progress of science and the useful arts" (Id. at 5753–4), as Chapter 9, sections 901–912 of Title 17 U.S.C.A.

The Act does not protect the chip itself, but protects an original "mask work" that is used to make the chip. Section 901 defines a "mask work" as "a series of related images . . . having or representing the predetermined, three-dimensional pattern of metallic, insulating or semiconductor material present or removed from a semiconductor chip product." The "mask work" thus represents the three-dimensional topography of the chip "however encoded"—i.e., as an optical mask on glass or an "electronic mask" in a computer. A mask work must be "fixed" in a chip product from which it can be perceived or reproduced. An owner of a protected work may affix a notice of mask work protection. However, such notice is not a prerequisite to protection, even when the mask work is embodied in commercially exploited chips (§ 909). The notice, when used, "shall consist of—(1) the words "mask work", the symbol "M" or the symbol M; and the name of the owner or owners of the mask work or an abbreviation by which the name is recognized as or is generally known" (Id.).

To obtain protection, the mask work must be registered with the Copyright Office within two years of commercial exploitation (§ 908(a))—i.e., "distribution to the public for commercial purpose" including a written offer to sell or transfer a chip following "fixation" (§ 901(a)(5)). Registration is a prerequisite to a suit for infringement (§ 910(b)(1)). The mask work is protected for ten years from the date of registration or commercial exploitation, whichever is first (§ 904). The Copyright Office has issued regulations governing the registration process (§ 901; 37 C.F.R., Part 211). In general, registration is made by the owner on the appropriate Office form (Form MW, 37 C.F.R. § 211.4), accompanied by the prescribed fee ($20.00, 37 C.F.R. § 211.3), and a deposit of "identifying material." For works that have been commercially exploited, "identifying material" includes four actual chips plus a visually perceptible representation of each mask work layer. Where trade secret protection is claimed in specific layers, the owner may in some circumstances submit other identifying materials (37 C.F.R. § 211.5).

A mask work is eligible for protection under the Act only if: (1) first commercially exploited in the United States; or (2) on the date of commercial exploitation or registration, the owner is a national or domiciliary of the U.S. or a party to a treaty with the U.S. affording similar protection, a stateless person, or a national or domiciliary of a country covered by Presidential proclamation of effective reciprocal eligibility (§ 902(a)). However, the Secretary of Commerce may extend protection to nationals or domiciliaries of other nations under § 914 if such nation is making progress toward extending reciprocal protection to U.S. nationals and domiciliaries, if nationals or domiciliaries of the nation are not misappropriating mask works, and if such an order would promote international comity and protection of mask works. Under this authority, which has been delegated to the Commissioner of Patents and Trademarks, and which expires on Nov. 8, 1987, interim orders of protection have been granted on behalf of citizens of Japan, Sweden, Australia, the United Kingdom, Netherlands, Canada and the European Communities as of June 1, 1987.

Suit for infringement may be brought in Federal Court (§§ 911(a) and 912(d)), and maximum statutory damages is $250,000 (§ 911(c)). There is a three-year statute of limitations (§ 911(d)). The court may award an injunction and costs including attorneys' fees, and may order impoundment and destruction of chips, masks or other means of production. The test of "substantial similarity" as applied by the courts in cases regarding fact-based works, compilations and directories provides possible precedents (1984 U.S.Code Cong. and Adm.News, p. 5775). Section 906 of the Act limits exclusive rights in cases of "reverse engineering"—i.e., reproduction "solely for the purpose of teaching, analyzing or evaluating the concepts or techniques embodied in the mask work or the circuitry, logic plan or organization of components"— even where such conduct is for the purpose of incorporating the results in a new mask work.

It is the intent of the Committee to permit, under the reverse engineering limitation, the "unauthorized" creation of a second mask work whose layout, in substantial part, is similar to the layout of the protected mask work—if the second mask work was the product of substantial study and analysis, and not the mere result of plagarism accomplished without such study or analysis.

* * *

In examining whether a given reproduction qualifies for the reverse engineering privilege of section 906(a) it is the intent of the Committee that the doctrine be developed and adapted on a case by case basis, like the copyright doctrine of fair use. As with the fair use doctrine, reverse engineering is an affirmative defense. (Id. at 5771–2).

A number of witnesses testified [at Committee hearings] as to the practice in the semiconductor industry of reverse engineering a chip, and how to distinguish between chip piracy and legitimate reverse engineering. They emphasized the evidentiary importance of the "paper trail" of legitimate reverse engineering that helps to distinguish it from mere piracy. The Committee intends that the courts, in interpreting section 906(a), should place great weight on objective documentary evidence of this type. (Id. at 5770).

The Chip Protection Act in no way affects rights under Federal copyright or patent law (§ 912(a)). However, state law is preempted "to the extent those laws provide any rights or remedies * * * which are equivalent to those provided by this chapter" (§ 912(c)).

Part IV

TRADEMARKS

A. INTRODUCTION

The law of trademarks can be a speciality in itself and some lawyers practice trademark law exclusively. Usually, however, it is an adjunct to the practice of patent law, and a natural one, since the development of new products frequently requires the selection and protection of trademarks for use in the marketing activities.

Accordingly, a patent attorney may serve in an advisory capacity in helping the client select a proper mark and in searching the records to determine if the mark has been previously used by others. He can also assist in the protection of a newly selected mark by his advice on how the mark should be used in commerce and how it can be protected by available state and federal registration procedures.

It is not the purpose of this casebook to develop the entire law of trademarks. However, the following text material and cases will give the student some background on this area of the law as ancillary to the study of patent law.

The marking of commercial products goes back thousands of years when symbols were placed on certain goods to identify the source. Initially and for many years, the devices used as trademarks were pictures, designs, or trade symbols since most purchasers were illiterate. Even today in countries where illiteracy is prevalent, the pictures on labels are more significant than the words.[a]

Originally, the marking of goods was for identification as to ownership. In the case of ship-wrecked goods, ownership fell to the Crown unless the goods could be identified. In more recent history, during the logging days in America, various logging companies developed ownership brands to enable separation of their timber at the end of a river

a. For an excellent treatment of the history of Trademarks, see Schechter, The Historical Foundations of the Law Relating to Trade Marks, Columbia University Press, 1925. See also Nims, Unfair Competition and Trademarks, 4th Edition, 1947. See also: The Historical Development of Trademarks, Sidney A. Diamond, 65 T.M. Reporter 265 (1975).

transport. However, early use of marks to establish product reliability began with the guilds in Europe where an artisan, as a guild member, was held responsible for the quality of his output. His assigned mark would enable the guild to trace the article in the event proper standards were not met. It appears that bakers were particularly beset by quality and weight requirements and that marking was established for the purpose of accountability in the case of short weight or faulty quality.[aa]

As trade developed beyond local communities, the trademark began to assume the function it has today, namely, to serve, not only to reflect quality of the manufacturer, but also as a shortcut for the consumer who can rely on the mark as a substitute for testing of each particular product he buys in normal trade channels.

In the United States in 1791 the makers of sail-cloth petitioned Congress for assistance in the protection of their trademarks. The petition was referred to the then Secretary of State, Thomas Jefferson, who reported that the protection sought "would, in his opinion, contribute to fidelity in the execution of manufacturers to secure to every manufactory, an exclusive right to some mark on its wares to itself." The petition and report brought response from a Philadelphia manufacturer in a letter printed in a Boston newspaper on December 24, 1791, which read in part:

> It is with real pleasure and satisfaction that I behold the application of the proprietors of the sail cloth manufactory in the town of Boston to the Congress of the United States, for an act to secure them against the losses they are likely to sustain by persons counterfeiting their marks on sail cloth of an inferior quality. * * * For it is of the greatest importance to the rising prosperity, commerce, opulency, and of course greatness of this country, that the manufacturer should be secured in the benefit and profit of his ingenuity, labour and industry, being an incitement to that industrious, enterprising, and useful set of men, to carry on, persevere in and bring to the greatest possible perfection the various goods and articles by them undertaken and manufactured.

> There is no greater check to this laudable spirit of enterprise, industry and home manufacture, than that of imposters fraudulently counterfeiting of marks, and imposing and selling bad and spurious articles for good, real and genuine. It effectually cools the ambition of excelling and becoming serviceable to one's country, and is highly prejudicial to the good repute of our manufactures in foreign parts, consequently has a tendency to lessen instead of to increase our commerce. * * *

Despite the above-mentioned petition of the sailmakers for a federal statute on trademarks, the protection of trademark owners was and still is essentially a matter of commonlaw. The first federal statutes of 1870 and 1876 relating to registration of trademarks were held uncon-

---

aa. Schechter, op. cit., p. 51.

stitutional in 1879 in United States v. Steffens et al. (The Trademark
Cases).[b] In these cases the Supreme Court, in commenting on the
relationship to the constitutional provision directed to inventions, discoveries, and writings, said this:

> Any attempt, however, to identify the essential characteristics of a
> trade-mark with inventions and discoveries in the arts and sciences, or
> with the writings of authors, will show that the effort is surrounded
> with insurmountable difficulties.

> The ordinary trade-mark has no necessary relation to invention or
> discovery. The trade-mark recognized by the common law is generally
> the growth of a considerable period of use, rather than a sudden
> invention. It is often the result of accident rather than design, and
> when under the Act of Congress it is sought to establish it by registra-
> tion, neither originality, invention, discovery, science or art is in any
> way essential to the right conferred by that Act. If we should endeav-
> or to classify it, under the head of writings of authors, the objections
> are equally strong. In this, as in regard to inventions, there is
> required originality. And while the word writings may be liberally
> construed, as it has been, to include original designs for engravings,
> prints, etc., it is only such as are original, and are founded in the
> creative powers of the mind. The writings which are to be protected
> are the fruits of intellectual labor, embodied in the form of books,
> prints, engravings and the like. The trade-mark may be and, general-
> ly, is, the adoption of something already in existence as the distinctive
> symbol of the party using it. At common law the exclusive right to it
> grows out of the use of it, and not its mere adoption. By the Act of
> Congress this exclusive right attaches upon registration. But in
> neither case does it depend upon novelty, upon invention, upon discov-
> ery, or upon any work of the brain. It requires no fancy or imagina-
> tion, no genius, no laborious thought. It is simply founded on priority
> of appropriation. We look in vain in the statute for any other
> qualification or condition. If the symbol, however plain, simple, old or
> well known, has been first appropriated by the claimant as his distinc-
> tive trade-mark, he may, by registration, secure the right to its exclu-
> sive use. While such legislation may be a judicious aid to the common
> law on the subject of trade-marks, and may be within the competency
> of Legislatures whose general powers embrace that class of subjects, we
> are unable to see any such power in the constitutional provision
> concerning authors and inventors, and their writings and discoveries.

With respect to the commerce clause of the Constitution, the court
stated:

> The other clause of the Constitution supposed to supply the requi-
> site authority in Congress is the third of the same section, which, read
> in connection with the granting clause, is as follows: "The Congress
> shall have power to regulate commerce with foreign nations, and
> among the several States, and with the Indian Tribes."

b. 100 U.S. 82, 25 L.Ed. 550 (1879).

The argument is, that the use of a trade-mark—that which alone gives it any value—is to identify a particular class or quality of goods as the manufacture, produce or property of the person who puts them in the general market for sale; that the sale of the article so distinguished is commerce; that the trade-mark is, therefore, a useful and valuable aid or instrument of commerce, and its regulation by virtue of the above provision of the Constitution belongs to Congress, and that the Act in question is a lawful exercise of this power.

It is not every species of property which is the subject of commerce, or which is used or even essential in commerce, which is brought by this clause of the Constitution within the control of Congress.

* * *

When, therefore, Congress undertakes to enact a law, which can only be valid as a regulation of commerce, it is reasonable to expect to find on the face of the statute, or from its essential nature, that it is a regulation of commerce with foreign nations, among the several States, or with the Indian Tribes. If it is not so limited, it is in excess of the power of Congress. If its main purpose be to establish a regulation applicable to all trade; to commerce at all points, especially if it is apparent that it is designed to govern the commerce wholly between citizens of the same State, it is obviously the exercise of a power not confided to Congress.

* * *

The questions in each of these cases being an inquiry whether these statutes can be upheld in whole or in part as valid and constitutional, must be answered in the negative; and it will be so certified to the proper Circuit Courts.

Subsequent trademark statutes passed in 1881, 1905 and 1946 (Lanham Act) have been limited to the regulation of trademarks used in commerce which can be regulated by the United States Congress, and, accordingly, have been accepted as having a proper constitutional basis.

B. COMMON LAW PROTECTION

HANOVER STAR MILLING COMPANY v. METCALF

United States Supreme Court, 1916.
240 U.S. 403, 36 S.Ct. 357, 60 L.Ed. 713.

MR. JUSTICE PITNEY delivered the opinion of the court:

* * *

It will be convenient to dispose first of No. 30. Here the bill is rested upon alleged trademark infringement, pure and simple, and no question of unfair competition is involved. The decision of the court of appeals for the seventh circuit in favor of the Hanover Company and against the Allen & Wheeler Company was rested upon the ground that although the adoption of the Tea Rose mark by the latter antedated that of the Hanover Company, its only trade, so far as shown, was in territory north of the Ohio river, while the Hanover Company had adopted "Tea Rose" as its mark in perfect good faith, with no knowledge that anybody else was using or had used those words in such a connection, and during many years it had built up and extended its trade in the southeastern territory, comprising Georgia, Florida, Alabama, and Mississippi, so that in the flour trade in that territory the mark "Tea Rose" had come to mean the Hanover Company's flour, and nothing else. The court held in effect that the right to protection in the exclusive use of a trademark extends only to those markets where the trader's goods have become known and identified by his use of the mark; and because of the nonoccupancy by the Allen & Wheeler Company of the southeastern markets it had no ground for relief in equity. Let us test this by reference to general principles.

The redress that is accorded in trademark cases is based upon the party's right to be protected in the good will of a trade or business. The primary and proper function of a trademark is to identify the origin or ownership of the article to which it is affixed. Where a party has been in the habit of labeling his goods with a distinctive mark, so that purchasers recognize goods thus marked as being of his production, others are debarred from applying the same mark to goods of the same description, because to do so would in effect represent their goods to be of his production and would tend to deprive him of the profit he might make through the sale of the goods which the purchaser intended to buy. Courts afford redress or relief upon the ground that a party has a valuable interest in the good will of his trade or business, and in the trademarks adopted to maintain and extend it. The essence of the wrong consists in the sale of the goods of one manufacturer or vendor for those of another. [Citations Omitted]

This essential element is the same in trademark cases as in cases of unfair competition unaccompanied with trademark infringement. In fact, the common law of trademarks is but a part of the broader law of unfair competition. [Citations Omitted]

Common-law trademarks, and the right to their exclusive use, are, of course, to be classed among property rights (Trade-Mark Cases, 100 U.S. 82, 92, 93, 25 L.Ed. 550, 551); but only in the sense that a man's right to the continued enjoyment of his trade reputation and the good will that flows from it, free from unwarranted interference by others, is a property right, for the protection of which a trademark is an instrumentality. As was said in the same case (p. 94), the right grows out of use, not mere adoption. In the English courts it often has been said that there is no property whatever in a trademark, as such. [Citations Omitted] But since in the same cases the courts recognize the right of the party to the exclusive use of marks adopted to indicate goods of his manufacture, upon the ground that "a man is not to sell his own goods under the pretense that they are the goods of another man; he cannot be permitted to practice such a deception, nor to use the means which contribute to that end. He cannot therefore be allowed to use names, marks, letters, or other *indicia*, by which he may induce purchasers to believe that the goods which he is selling are the manufacture of another person" (6 Beav. 73); it is plain that in denying the right of property in a trademark it was intended only to deny such property right except as appurtenant to an established business or trade in connection with which the mark is used. This is evident from the expressions used in these and other English cases. Thus, in Ainsworth v. Walmsley, L.R. 1 Eq. 518, 524, Vice Chancellor Sir Wm. Page Wood said: "This court has taken upon itself to protect a man in the use of a certain trademark as applied to a particular description of article. He has no property in that mark *per se*, any more than in any other fanciful denomination he may assume for his own private use, otherwise than with reference to his trade. If he does not carry on a trade in iron, but carries on a trade in linen, and stamps a lion on his linen, another person may stamp a lion on iron; but when he has appropriated a mark to a particular species of goods, and caused his goods to circulate with this mark upon them, the court has said that no one shall be at liberty to defraud that man by using that mark, and passing off goods of his manufacture as being the goods of the owner of that mark."

In short, the trademark is treated as merely a protection for the good will, and not the subject of property except in connection with an existing business. The same rule prevails generally in this country, and is recognized in the decisions of this court already cited. [Citations Omitted]

Expressions are found in many of the cases to the effect that the exclusive right to the use of a trademark is founded on priority of appropriation. Thus, in Delaware & H. Canal Co. v. Clark, 13 Wall. 311, 323, 20 L.Ed. 581, 583, reference is made to "the first appropriator;" in McLean v. Fleming, 96 U.S. 245, 251, 24 L.Ed. 828, 830, to "the person who first adopted the stamp;" in Amoskeag Mfg. Co. v. Trainer, 101 U.S. 51, 53, 25 L.Ed 993, 994, the expression is "any symbol or devise, not previously appropriated, which will distinguish," etc. But these expressions are to be understood in their application to the facts of the cases decided. In the ordinary case of parties competing under the same mark in the same market, it is correct to say that prior appropriation settles the question. But where two parties independently are employing the same mark upon goods of the same class, but in separate markets wholly remote the one from the other, the question of prior appropriation is legally insignificant; unless, at least, it appear that the second adopter has selected the mark with some design inimical to the interests of the first user, such as to take the benefit of the reputation of his goods, to forestall the extension of his trade, or the like.

Of course, if the symbol or device is already in general use, employed in such a manner that its adoption as an index of source or origin would only produce confusion and mislead the public, it is not susceptible of adoption as a trademark. Such a case was Columbia Mill Co. v. Alcorn, 150 U.S. 460, 464, 37 L.Ed. 1144, 1146, 14 Sup.Ct.Rep. 151, affirming 40 Fed. 676, where it appeared that before complainant's adoption of the disputed word as a brand for its flour the same word was used for the like purpose by numerous mills in different parts of the country.

That property in a trademark is not limited in its enjoyment by territorial bounds, but may be asserted and protected wherever the law affords a remedy for wrongs, is true in a limited sense. Into whatever markets the use of a trademark has extended, or its meaning has become known, there will the manufacturer or trader whose trade is pirated by an infringing use be entitled to protection and redress. But this is not to say that the proprietor of a trademark, good in the markets where it has been employed, can monopolize markets that his trade has never reached, and where the mark signifies not his goods, but those of another. We agree with the court below (L.R.A.1916D, 136, 125 C.C.A. 515, 208 Fed. 519) that "since it is the trade, and not the mark, that is to be protected, a trademark acknowledges no territorial boundaries of municipalities or states or nations, but extends to every market where the trader's goods have become known and identified by his use of the mark. But the mark, of itself, cannot travel to markets where there is no article to wear the badge and no trader to offer the article."

* * *

It results from the general principles thus far discussed that trademark rights, like others that rest in user, may be lost by abandonment, nonuser, laches, or acquiescence. Abandonment, in the strict sense, rests upon an intent to abandon; * * *

INTERNATIONAL ORDER OF JOB'S DAUGHTERS v. LINDEBURG AND COMPANY

United States Court of Appeals, Ninth Circuit, 1980.
633 F.2d 912, 208 USPQ 718.

FLETCHER, CIRCUIT JUDGE:

Appellee, the International Order of the Daughters of Job (Job's Daughters), sued appellant Lindeburg and Co. (Lindeburg), for trademark infringement arising out of Lindeburg's manufacture and sale of jewelry bearing the Job's Daughters insignia. The district judge granted judgment for Job's Daughters. Lindeburg appeals, invoking appellate jurisdiction under 28 U.S.C. § 1291. We reverse and remand.

* * *

The parties have apparently assumed the existence of a general common law governing all trademark infringement cases brought in federal court. This assumption is incorrect. Save as an outgrowth of federal statutory or constitutional law, there is no federal common law. *Compare Erie R.R. Co. v. Tompkins*, 304 U.S. 64, 78, 58 S.Ct. 817, 822,

82 L.Ed. 1188 (1938) ("Except in matters governed by the Federal Constitution or by Acts of Congress, the law to be applied in any case is the law of the state * * *. There is no federal general common law."), *with Hinderlider v. La Plata River & Cherry Creek Ditch Co.,* 304 U.S. 92, 110, 58 S.Ct. 803, 810, 82 L.Ed. 1202 (1938) (applying "federal common law" to resolve a controversy regarding an interstate stream). *See generally,* P. Bator, P. Mishkin, D. Shapiro, & H. Wechsler, *The Federal Courts & The Federal System,* 756–832 (2d ed. 1973). Accordingly, to succeed, Job's Daughters must assert rights found either in state law or federal statutory law.

This seemingly simple proposition is rendered difficult by the complex relationship between state and federal trademark law. In general, the common law has been understood as protecting against the broad business tort of "unfair competition." Trademark infringement is a species of this generic concept. *See New West Corp. v. NYM Co. of California,* 595 F.2d 1194, 1201 (9th Cir.1979). The Lanham Act created a federal protection against two types of unfair competition, infringement of registered trademarks, 15 U.S.C. § 1114, and the related tort of false designation of the origin of goods, 15 U.S.C. § 1125(a). Federal courts have jurisdiction to hear suits invoking these protections. In addition, many states by statute or judge-made law protect against trademark infringement and other types of unfair competition, such as misappropriation of the fruits of another's labor, *see Zacchini v. Scripps-Howard Broadcasting Co.,* 433 U.S. 562, 97 S.Ct. 2849, 53 L.Ed. 2d 965 (1977); theft of trade secrets, *see Pachmayr Gunworks, Inc. v. Olin Mathieson Chemical Corp.,* 502 F.2d 802, 807–08 (9th Cir.1974); and trade disparagement, *see Kemart Corp. v. Printing Arts Research Laboratory, Inc.,* 269 F.2d 375, 388–94 (9th Cir.), *cert. denied,* 361 U.S. 893, 80 S.Ct. 197, 4 L.Ed.2d 151 (1959). These protections need not track those provided by the Lanham Act. *See Sears, Roebuck & Co. v. Stiffel Co.,* 376 U.S. 225, 232, 84 S.Ct. 784, 789, 11 L.Ed.2d 661 (1964); *John Wright, Inc. v. Casper Corp.,* 419 F.Supp. 292, 317 (E.D.Pa.1976), *modified sub nom. Donsco, Inc. v. Casper Corp.,* 587 F.2d 602 (3rd Cir. 1978); *Markel v. Scovill Mfg. Co.,* 471 F.Supp. 1244, 1249 (W.D.N.Y.), *aff'd,* 610 F.2d 807 (2d Cir.1979). If diversity factors exist, federal courts of course have jurisdiction to hear suits asserting these state law protections. Thus, a plaintiff complaining of trademark infringement in federal court may invoke either federal or state protections, or both.

Confusion as to the source of the substantive law is understandable because federal and state laws regarding trademarks and related claims of unfair competition are substantially congruent. *See K–S–H Plastics, Inc. v. Carolite, Inc.,* 408 F.2d 54, 59 n. 2 (9th Cir.), *cert. denied,* 396 U.S. 825, 90 S.Ct. 69, 24 L.Ed.2d 76 (1969); *Keebler Co. v. Rovira Biscuit Corp.,* 624 F.2d 366, 372 (1st Cir.1980); *Kentucky Fried Chicken Corp. v. Diversified Packaging Corp.,* 549 F.2d 368, 382 n. 14 (5th Cir.1977); *La Societe Anonyme des Parfums le Galion v. Jean Patou, Inc.,* 495 F.2d 1265, 1270 n. 5 (2d Cir.1974); *Maternally Yours, Inc. v. Your Maternity Shop, Inc.,* 234 F.2d 538, 540 n. 1 (2d Cir.1958). Therefore the choice of federal or state law frequently has no impact on the outcome, leading courts to avoid the issue. *See, e.g., K–S–H Plastics, Inc. v. Carolite, Inc.,* 408 F.2d 54, 59 n. 2 (9th Cir.1969); *Keebler Co. v. Rovira Biscuit Corp.,* 624 F.2d 366, 372 (1st Cir.1980). This does not, however, alter the fact that there are distinct federal and state rights.

* * *

This court held in *New West Corp. v. NYM Co. of California,* 595 F.2d 1194 (9th Cir.1979), that section 43 of the Lanham Act, 15 U.S.C. § 1125(a), created a federal remedy against the deceptive use of unregistered trademarks to designate falsely the origin of goods ("passing off"). 595 F.2d at 1198, 1201. *New West* also held that the test for false designation of origin was similar to that for infringement of a registered trademark under 15 U.S.C. § 1114. Both statutes preclude the use of another's trademark in a manner likely to confuse the public about the origin of goods. 595 F.2d at 1201. Thus, we must decide whether Lindeburg is likely to confuse the public about the origin of its jewelry by inscribing the Job's Daughters name and emblem on it.

Resolution of this issue turns on a close analysis of the way in which Lindeburg is using the Job's Daughters insignia. In general, trademark law is concerned only with identification of the maker, sponsor, or endorser of the product so as to avoid confusing consumers. Trademark law does not prevent a person from copying so-called "functional" features of a product which constitute the actual benefit that the consumer wishes to purchase, as distinguished from an assurance that a particular entity made, sponsored, or endorsed a product.

The distinction between trademarks and functional features is illustrated in *Pagliero v. Wallace China Co.,* 198 F.2d 339 (9th Cir.1952), where plaintiff, Wallace China, claimed trademark infringement on account of the use by others of the design it used on its china. The court found no trademark infringement because the design served primarily as a functional part of the product:

> Imitation of the physical details and designs of a competitor's product may be actionable, if the particular features imitated are "non-functional" and have acquired a secondary meaning. But, where the features are "functional" there is normally no right to relief. "Functional" in this sense might be said to connote other than a trade-mark purpose. If the particular feature is an important ingredient in the commercial success of the product, the interest in free competition permits its imitation in the absence of a patent or copyright. On the other hand, where the feature or, more aptly, design, is a mere arbitrary embellishment, a form of dress for the goods primarily adopted for purposes of identification and individuality and, hence, unrelated to basic consumer demands in connection with the product, imitation may be forbidden. * * * Under such circumstances, since effective competition may be undertaken without imitation, the law grants protection.

198 F.2d at 343 (citation omitted). *See also Famolare, Inc. v. Melville Corp.,* 472 F.Supp. 738, 742–45 (D.Hawaii 1979); *Boston Professional*

Hockey Ass'n, Inc. v. Dallas Cap & Emblem Mfg., Inc., 360 F.Supp. 459, 463–64 (N.D.Tex.1973), *rev'd, Boston Professional Hockey Ass'n, Inc. v. Dallas Cap & Emblem Mfg., Inc.*, 510 F.2d 1004 (5th Cir.), *cert. denied*, 423 U.S. 868, 96 S.Ct. 132, 46 L.Ed.2d 98 (1975); *Restatement of Torts* § 742, comment (a) (1938).

Application of the *Pagliero* distinction to this case has a special twist because the name "Job's Daughters" and the Job's Daughters insignia are indisputably used to identify the organization, and members of Job's Daughters wear the jewelry to identify themselves as members. In that context, the insignia are trademarks of Job's Daughters. But in the context of this case, the name and emblem are functional aesthetic components of the jewelry, in that they are being merchandised on the basis of their intrinsic value, not as a designation of origin or sponsorship.

It is not uncommon for a name or emblem that serves in one context as a collective mark or trademark also to be merchandised for its own intrinsic utility to consumers. We commonly identify ourselves by displaying emblems expressing allegiances. Our jewelry, clothing, and cars are emblazoned with inscriptions showing the organizations we belong to, the schools we attend, the landmarks we have visited, the sports teams we support, the beverages we imbibe. Although these inscriptions frequently include names and emblems that are also used as collective marks or trademarks, it would be naive to conclude that the name or emblem is desired because consumers believe that the product somehow originated with or was sponsored by the organization the name or emblem signifies.

Job's Daughters relies on *Boston Professional Hockey Ass'n, Inc. v. Dallas Cap & Emblem Mfg., Inc.*, 510 F.2d 1004 (5th Cir.), *cert. denied*, 423 U.S. 868, 96 S.Ct. 132, 46 L.Ed.2d 98 (1975), in which the Boston Bruins and other National Hockey League clubs brought a trademark infringement suit against a company that sold replicas of the NHL team emblems. The Fifth Circuit, applying the Lanham Act infringement test and focusing on the "likelihood of confusion," found infringement:

> The confusion or deceit requirement is met by the fact that the defendant duplicated the protected trademarks and sold them to the public knowing that the public would identify them as being the teams' trademarks. The certain knowledge of the buyer that the source and origin of the trademark symbols were the plaintiffs satisfies the requirement of the act. The argument that confusion must be as to the source of the manufacture of the emblem itself is unpersuasive, where the trademark, originated by the team, is the triggering mechanism for the sale of the emblem.

510 F.2d at 1012. Job's Daughters asserts that *Boston Hockey* supports its contention that even purely functional use of a trademark violates the Lanham Act. We reject the reasoning of *Boston Hockey*.

Interpreted expansively, *Boston Hockey* holds that a trademark's owner has a complete monopoly over its use, including its functional use, in commercial merchandising. But our reading of the Lanham Act and its legislative history reveals no congressional design to bestow such broad property rights on trademark owners. Its scope is much narrower: to protect consumers against deceptive designations of the origin of goods and, conversely, to enable producers to differentiate their products from those of others. *See Smith v. Chanel, Inc.,* 402 F.2d 562, 566–70 (9th Cir.1968). *See also HMH Publishing Co., Inc. v. Brincat,* 504 F.2d 713, 716 (9th Cir.1974); *Developments in the Law-Trademarks and Unfair Competition,* 68 Harv.L.Rev. 814, 816–17 (1955). The *Boston Hockey* decision transmogrifies this narrow protection into a broad monopoly. It does so by injecting its evaluation of the equities between the parties and of the desirability of bestowing broad property rights on trademark owners. A trademark is, of course, a form of business property. *See J. McCarthy, Trademarks and Unfair Competition* §§ 2:6–2:7 (1973). But the "property right" or protection accorded a trademark owner can only be understood in the context of trademark law and its purposes. A trademark owner has a property right only insofar as is necessary to prevent consumer confusion as to who produced the goods and to facilitate differentiation of the trademark owner's goods. *See id.* The *Boston Hockey* court decided that broader protection was desirable. In our view, this extends the protection beyond that intended by Congress and beyond that accorded by any other court. *Cf. Kentucky Fried Chicken Corp. v. Diversified Packaging Corp.,* 549 F.2d 368, 389 (5th Cir.1977) (rejecting the "notion that a trademark is an owner's 'property' to be protected irrespective of its role in the operation of our markets").

Indeed, the court in *Boston Hockey* admitted that its decision "may slightly tilt the trademark laws from the purpose of protecting the public to the protection of the business interests of plaintiffs." 510 F.2d at 1011. We think that this tilt was not slight but an extraordinary extension of the protection heretofore afforded trademark owners. It is an extension we cannot endorse. *See General Mills, Inc. v. Henry Regnery Co.,* 421 F.Supp. 359, 362 & n. 2, (N.D.Ill.1976). Instead, we agree with Judge Waterman of the Second Circuit, who recently said that under the Lanham Act "one can capitalize on a market or fad created by another provided that it is not accomplished by confusing the public into mistakenly purchasing the product in the belief that the product is the product of the competitor." *American Footwear Corp. v. General Footwear Co. Ltd.,* 609 F.2d 655, 662 (2d Cir.1979), *cert. denied,* 445 U.S. 951, 100 S.Ct. 1601, 63 L.Ed.2d 787 (1980) (finding that the manufacturer of a "Bionic Boot" did not infringe the trademark of the producers of the "Bionic Woman" television program).

Our holding does not mean that a name or emblem could not serve simultaneously as a functional component of a product and a trademark. *See Dallas Cowboys Cheerleaders, Inc. v. Pussycat Cinema, Ltd.,* 604 F.2d 200, 204 (2d Cir.1979). That is, even if the Job's Daughters' name and emblem, when inscribed on Lindeburg's jewelry, served primarily a functional purpose, it is possible that they could serve secondarily as trademarks if the typical customer not only purchased the jewelry for its intrinsic functional use and aesthetic appeal but also inferred from the insignia that the jewelry was produced, sponsored, or endorsed by Job's Daughters. *See generally*, Grimes & Battersby, *The Protection of Merchandising Properties,* 69 TMR 431, 441–45 (1980). We recognize that there is some danger that the consumer may be more likely to infer endorsement or sponsorship when the consumer is a member of the group whose collective mark or trademark is being marketed. Accordingly, a court must closely examine the articles themselves, the defendant's merchandising practices, and any evidence that consumers have actually inferred a connection between the defendant's product and the trademark owner.

The trial court made comprehensive findings of fact that provide an adequate record for this court to review the trial court's conclusion of law that the names and emblems were trademarks. *See Alpha Indus., Inc. v. Alpha Steel Tube & Shapes, Inc.,* 616 F.2d 440, 443–44 (9th Cir.1980); *AMF Inc. v. Sleekcraft Boats,* 599 F.2d 341, 346–47 (9th Cir.1979).

We conclude from our examination of the trial judge's findings and of the underlying evidence that Lindeburg was not using the Job's Daughters name and emblem as trademarks. The insignia were a prominent feature of each item so as to be visible to others when worn, allowing the wearer to publicly express her allegiance to the organization. Lindeburg never designated the merchandise as "official" Job's Daughters' merchandise or otherwise affirmatively indicated sponsorship. Job's Daughters did not show a single instance in which a customer was misled about the origin, sponsorship, or endorsement of Lindeburg's jewelry, nor that it received any complaints about Lindeburg's wares. Finally, there was evidence that many other jewelers sold unlicensed Job's Daughters jewelry, implying that consumers did not ordinarily purchase their fraternal jewelry from only "official" sources. We conclude that Job's Daughters did not meet its burden of proving that a typical buyer of Lindeburg's merchandise would think that the jewelry was produced, sponsored, or endorsed by the organization. The name and emblem were functional aesthetic components of the product, not trademarks. There could be, therefore, no infringement.

The judgment of the district court is reversed and the case is remanded for the entry of judgment in favor of appellant Lindeburg.

Notes

1. Holiday Inns, Inc. v. Trump, 617 F.Supp. 1443, 1469–1471, 229 USPQ 481, 500–501 (D.N.J.1985):

* * *

47.   Using a personal name as a service mark transforms the name by giving it a new identity as the symbol of commercial goodwill.   One who develops goodwill in a service mark acquires property rights in the mark. *See United States Drug Co. v. Theodore Rectanus Co.,* 248 U.S. 90, 97, 39 S.Ct. 48, 50, 63 L.Ed. 141 (1918) ("property in a trademark *   *   * [consists of] a right appurtenant to an established business or trade in connection with which the mark is employed.").   *Accord Family Circle, Inc. v. Family Circle Associates, Inc.,* 332 F.2d 534, 539 (3rd Cir.1964).   Plainly,

> a trademark [or service mark] is not property in the ordinary sense, but only a word or symbol indicating the origin of a commercial produce.   [However, t]he owner of the mark acquires the right to prevent the goods [or services] to which the mark is applied from being confused with those of others and to prevent his trade from being diverted to competitors through their use of misleading marks.

Industrial Rayon Corp. v. Dutchess Underwear Corp., 92 F.2d 33, 35 (2nd Cir.1937), *cert. denied,* 303 U.S. 640, 58 S.Ct. 610, 82 L.Ed. 1100 (1938) (per J. Learned Hand).   *Accord Dresser Industries, Inc. v. Heraeus Engelhard Vacuum, Inc.,* 395 F.2d 457, 464 (3rd Cir.), *cert. denied,* 393 U.S. 934, 89 S.Ct. 293, 21 L.Ed.2d 270 (1968).

* * *

50.   It is well established that there no longer exists any absolute right to use one's own name for commercial purposes.   *Taylor Wine Co. v. Bully Hill Vineyards, Inc.,* 569 F.2d 731, 734 (2nd Cir.1978); *John R. Thompson v. Holloway,* 366 F.2d 108, 113 (5th Cir.1966); *Caesars World, Inc. v. Caesar's Palace,* 490 F.Supp. 818, 826 (D.N.J.1980); 1 McCarthy, § 13.3.   "Once an individual's name has acquired a secondary meaning in the market place, a later competitor who seeks to use the same or similar name must take 'reasonable precautions to prevent [customer confusion].' "   *Taylor Wine Co. v. Bully Hill Vineyards, Inc., supra,* quoting *L.E. Waterman Co. v. Modern Pen Co.,* 235 U.S. 88, 94, 35 S.Ct. 91, 92, 59 L.Ed. 142 (1914). *Accord John R. Thompson v. Holloway, supra; David B. Findlay, Inc. v. Findlay,* 18 N.Y.2d 12, 271 N.Y.S.2d 652, 218 N.E.2d 531 (1966), *remittitur amd,* 18 N.Y.2d 676, 273 N.Y.S.2d 422, 219 N.E.2d 872, *cert denied,* 385 U.S. 930, 87 S.Ct. 289, 17 L.Ed.2d 212 (1966).

51.   The courts remain sympathetic to defendants' wishes to use their own names in the conduct of their businesses.   After all, to bar anyone from using his family name is to

> take away his identity: without it he cannot make known who he is to those who may wish to deal with him; and that is so grievous an injury that courts will avoid imposing it, if it possibly can.

Taylor Wine Co. v. Bully Hill Vineyards, Inc., supra, 569 F.2d at 735, *quoting Societe Vinicole de Champagne v. Mumm,* 143 F.2d 240, 241 (2nd Cir.1944).   *See also International Election Systems Corp. v. Shoup,* 452 F.Supp. 684, 713 (E.D.Pa.1978).   The court's task is to weigh this interest against the countervailing interests of the public, in avoiding confusion, and of the senior user of the mark (the Partnership), in preventing dilution of its goodwill in the mark.   *Taylor Wine Co. v. Bully Hill Vineyards, Inc., supra,* 569 F.2d at 736.   The relative strength of these interests determines what relief, if any, is appropriate.   *Id.*   *See International Election Systems Corp. v. Shoup, supra;* 1 McCarthy, § 13.3 at 588–95.   *But cf. A.W. Cox*

Dept. Store v. Cox's Inc., 159 W.Va. 306, 221 S.E.2d 539, 545 (1976) (favoring absolute injunctions in order to prevent confusion).

* * *

2. Carson v. Here's Johnny Portable Toilets, Inc., 698 F.2d 831, 834–5, 218 USPQ 1, 3–4 (6th Cir. 1983):

In an influential article, Dean Prosser delineated four distinct types of the right of privacy: (1) intrusion upon one's seclusion or solitude, (2) public disclosure of embarrassing private facts, (3) publicity which places one in a false light, and (4) appropriation of one's name or likeness for the defendant's advantage. Prosser, Privacy, 48 Calif.L.Rev. 383, 389 (1960). This fourth type has become known as the "right of publicity." Factors Etc., Inc. v. Pro Arts, Inc., 579 F.2d 215, 220, 205 USPQ 751, 755–56 (2d Cir. 1978), cert. denied, 440 U.S. 908 (1979); see Zacchini v. Scripps-Howard Broadcasting Co., 433 U.S. 562, 572, 205 USPQ 741, 746 (1977). Henceforth we will refer to Prosser's last, or fourth, category, as the "right of publicity."

* * *

The right of publicity has developed to protect the commercial interest of celebrities in their identities. The theory of the right is that a celebrity's identity can be valuable in the promotion of products, and the celebrity has an interest that may be protected from the unauthorized commercial exploitation of that identity. In Memphis Development Foundation v. Factors Etc., Inc., 616 F.2d 956, 205 USPQ 784 (6th Cir.), cert. denied, 449 U.S. 953 (1980), we stated: "The famous have an exclusive legal right during life to control and profit from the commercial use of their name and personality." Id. at 957.

The district court dismissed appellants' claim based on the right of publicity because appellee does not use Carson's name or likeness. 498 F.Supp. at 77, 209 USPQ at 270–71. It held that it "would not be prudent to allow recovery for a right of publicity claim which does not more specifically identify Johnny Carson." 498 F.Supp. at 78, 209 USPQ 271–72. We believe that, on the contrary, the district court's conception of the right of publicity is too narrow. The right of publicity, as we have stated, is that a celebrity has a protected pecuniary interest in the commercial exploitation of his identity. If the celebrity's identity is commercially exploited, there has been an invasion of his right whether or not his "name or likeness" is used. Carson's identity may be exploited even if his name, John W. Carson, or his picture is not used.

C. LIKELIHOOD OF CONFUSION

FRISCH'S RESTAURANTS, INC. v. ELBY'S BIG BOY

United States Court of Appeals, Sixth Circuit, 1982.
670 F.2d 642, 214 USPQ 15, cert. denied 459 U.S. 916, 103 S.Ct. 231, 74 L.Ed.
2d 182 (1982).

BAILEY BROWN, CIRCUIT JUDGE.

Marriott Corporation is the owner of the "Big Boy" trademark and service mark, which is used by a network of family restaurants around the country. The plaintiff, Frisch's Restaurants, Inc. (Frisch's), has the exclusive license from Marriott to use these marks in Ohio and currently operates eighty restaurants in Ohio under the Big Boy trademark. One of the defendants, The Boury Corporation, operates the network of "Elby's Family Restaurants" in western Pennsylvania (five restaurants), northern West Virginia, referred to in the record as "the panhandle," (seven restaurants), and eastern Ohio (eight restaurants in six different cities). The Boury Corporation holds the exclusive right to use the Big Boy trademark in the panhandle of West Virginia and in most of western Pennsylvania. Prior to 1971, the Elby's Restaurants in eastern Ohio were authorized under a franchise agreement with Frisch's to use the Big Boy trademark, but that agreement was terminated at Elby's request in late 1971.

* * *

Frisch's moved for a preliminary injunction on October 21, 1980, requesting that Elby's be enjoined from using the Big Boy trademark in "any advertising medium that reaches a not insubstantial number of Ohioans" without disclosing Ohio Elby's disaffiliation with the Big Boy restaurant organization. * * *

In *Toho Company, Ltd. v. Sears, Roebuck & Co.,* 645 F.2d 788 (9th Cir.1981), the Ninth Circuit delineated eight factors which are helpful in demonstrating that there is a likelihood of confusion among consumers:

In *AMF Inc. v. Sleekcraft Boats,* 599 F.2d 341, 348 (9th Cir.1979), we set forth eight factors that are relevant to the likelihood of confusion:

1. strength of the plaintiff's mark;

2. relatedness of the goods;

3. similarity of the marks;

4. evidence of actual confusion;

5. marketing channels used;

6. likely degree of purchaser care;

7. defendant's intent in selecting the mark;

8. likelihood of expansion of the product lines.

Id. at 790.

In considering these factors, the unique factual setting with which we are concerned militates strongly towards likelihood of confusion. Although the strength of the Big Boy mark was not addressed by the district court, we presume that it is a distinctive and desirable mark from Elby's attempts to implant in the public mind the idea that all of its restaurants are affiliated with the Big Boy mark. The parties are competing restaurant chains using the identical trademark to promote related if not identical goods; additionally, it is likely that the marketing methods used to promote the fast-food products served by both chains are substantially similar. All these factors contribute to the likelihood of confusion about the Ohio Elby's restaurants' association with the Big Boy trademark.

The district court determined that there was actual confusion among eastern Ohio consumers about the availability of Big Boy products at Ohio Elby's restaurants. 514 F.Supp. at 708–09. This finding was supported by evidence from Frisch's expert witness, who testified about a survey he conducted which indicated that Elby's television advertisements contributed to confusion over the connection of the Big Boy organization with the Ohio Elby's restaurants. The Fifth Circuit deduced that while "evidence of actual confusion is not necessary to a finding of likelihood of confusion, it is nevertheless the best evidence of likelihood of confusion." *Amstar Corp. v. Domino's Pizza, Inc.*, 615 F.2d 252, 263 (5th Cir.), *cert. denied*, 449 U.S. 899, 101 S.Ct. 268, 66 L.Ed.2d 129 (1980).[5]

The casual "degree of purchaser care" in selecting fast-food restaurants also supports a conclusion of likelihood of confusion. The "fast-food" products promoted by Elby's are not likely to be the object of intensive consumer research, but rather subject to "impulse buying;" therefore, it is highly unlikely that Ohio consumers will discover their mistake about the availability of Big Boy products in Ohio Elby's restaurants before patronizing Elby's.

The Fifth Circuit's comments on the intent factor are equally supportive of likelihood of confusion:

> *Intent:* we stated in *Amstar* that the "intent of defendants in adopting [their mark] is a critical factor, since if the mark was adopted with the intent of deriving benefit from the reputation of [the plaintiff,] *that fact alone may be sufficient to justify the inference that there is confusing similarity.*" *Amstar Corp., supra*, 615 F.2d at 263 (emphasis added).

Chevron Chemical Co., supra at 703–04. The district court found that "the defendants intentionally associate Ohio Elby's restaurants with the 'Big Boy' mark," since "the Ohio Elby's restaurants are in fact direct participants in the reciprocal advertising agreement with WTRF," they "actively encourage Ohio consumers to 'watch for Elby's specials on WTRF' * * * where the television advertisement frequently identifies the Elby's Family Restaurant with the 'Big Boy' mark" and "[a] variety of in-store promotional material including matchbooks and sacks also directs the Ohio consumer to WTRF." 514 F.Supp. at 710. The district court correctly inferred that Elby's improperly intended to "derive benefit" from the Big Boy trademark for their Ohio operations through coupling the entire chain to the trademark.

---

5. Indeed, it is difficult to conceive of a situation where a showing of substantial actual confusion would not result in a legal conclusion of likelihood of confusion. This is not a case involving "minimal" or "isolated" instances of actual confusion such as were involved in *Amstar Corp., supra* at 263.

Finally, the past association of the Ohio Elby's restaurants with the Big Boy trademark through their expired licensing agreement with Frisch's increases the likelihood that consumers would be confused about whether the Ohio Elby's restaurants continued to be linked with the Big Boy organization. It is evident from their actions that the Ohio Elby's restaurants hoped to reinforce the residual effects of Ohio consumer memories of their past affiliation with the Big Boy trademark by tying in with the legitimate West Virginia Big Boy advertisements, thereby obscuring their disaffiliation with the Big Boy trademark.

The preceding factors led the district court to conclude that a likelihood of confusion existed with regard to Elby's television advertisements. * * *

Elby's first argues that Frisch's does not have standing to bring this suit because Frisch's does not operate any restaurants in the eastern Ohio area where the confusion about Big Boy products is prevalent. However, it is evident that Frisch's suffers a cognizable injury in this instance because it would have to combat consumer misperceptions about the availability of Big Boy products if it were to expand into the area itself or license restaurants in that area to operate under the Big Boy trademark. The Ohio Supreme Court has recognized that a trademark is entitled to protection throughout the entire state even though its owner is currently operating only in one part of the state. *Younker v. Nationwide Mutual Ins. Co.*, 175 Ohio St. 1, 191 N.E.2d 145 (1963). More to the point, this court in *Socony-Vacuum Oil Co. v. Oil City Refiners, Inc.*, 136 F.2d 470 (6th Cir.), *cert. denied*, 320 U.S. 798, 64 S.Ct. 369, 88 L.Ed. 482 (1943), determined that the user of a trademark "was entitled to the exclusive use of the name within the entire state as territory which may reasonably be anticipated to be within normal business expansion * * *." *Id.* at 475. *Accord, Grocers Baking Co. v. Sigler*, 132 F.2d 498, 502 (6th Cir.1942).

* * *

This failure by the district court properly to apply the likelihood of confusion standard to the newspaper advertising was an error of law and therefore, to this extent, an abuse of discretion. *United States v. Colahan*, 635 F.2d 564 (6th Cir.1980), *cert. denied*, ___ U.S. ___, 102 S.Ct. 127, 70 L.Ed.2d 108 (1981). The question remains, however, whether a reversal and remand for a further factual determination is required or whether this court can determine on this record that Frisch's is entitled to injunctive relief as to the newspaper advertising.

The Ninth Circuit has developed a two-level test for reviewing lower court findings of likelihood of confusion.

In assessing whether there is likelihood of confusion, a court first considers numerous factors and then, based thereon, determines whether there exists a likelihood of confusion. With the analysis so structured, the *J.B. Williams [Co., Inc. v. Le Conté Cosmetics, Inc.*; 523 F.2d 187 (9th Cir.)], and *AMF, Inc.* courts held that the determination of what is the state of affairs regarding each factor (a "foundational fact") is a finding of fact reviewed on the clearly erroneous standard, but the further determination of likelihood of confusion based on those factors is a legal conclusion. *See J.B. Williams,* 523 F.2d at 191–92; *AMF, Inc.,* 599 F.2d at 348–54 (applying two-level test as described here).

Alpha Industries, Inc. v. Alpha Steel Tube & Shapes, Inc., 616 F.2d 440, 443–44 (9th Cir.1980).

Applying this test, with which we agree, to the facts that are not in dispute and as found by the district court, we conclude that Frisch's is entitled to injunctive relief as to the newspaper advertising.

*   *   *

Note

Elby's Big Boy of Steubenville v. Frisch's Restaurant, Inc., 459 U.S. 916, 103 S.Ct. 231, 74 L.Ed.2d 182 (1982):

"Justice White, dissenting from the denial of certiorari.

"One of the questions presented by this case is whether a district court's finding of a likelihood of confusion for purposes of § 43(a) of the Lanham Act, 15 U.S.C.A. § 1125(a) (1976) [15 USCS § 1125(a)], is reviewable under the 'clearly erroneous' standard, as a question of fact, or de novo, as a legal conclusion. Because there is a split in the lower courts on this question, compare Sun Banks of Florida, Inc. v. Sun Federal Savings & Loan Ass'n, 651 F.2d 311, 314–315 (CA5 1981) (applying 'clearly erroneous' standard); Squirtco v. Seven-Up Co. 628 F.2d 1086, 1091 (CA8 1980) (same); Keebler Co. v. Roviara Biscuit Corp. 624 F.2d 366, 377 (CA1 1980) (same), with Alpha Industries v Alpha Steel Tube & Shapes, Inc. 616 F.2d 440, 443–444 (CA9 1980) (reviewing court's conclusion that there was a likelihood of confusion de novo); Blue Bell, Inc. v Jaymar-Ruby, Inc. 497 F.2d 433, 435 n2 (CA2 1974) (same), I would grant certiorari to resolve the conflict."

SEARS, ROEBUCK AND CO. v. JOHNSON

United States Court of Appeals, Third Circuit, 1955.
219 F.2d 590, 104 USPQ 280.

STALEY, CIRCUIT JUDGE.   *   *   *

The following basic facts were found by the district court. Indeed, none of these facts were contradicted or disputed by defendants, who presented no evidence at the trial.

In 1926, plaintiff adopted "Allstate" as a trade name for automobile tires and tubes and has since extended this label to some 4,000 automobile accessories which it markets nationally. The articles sold by plaintiff under the registered trademark Allstate have attained throughout the United States a reputation for high quality and efficiency.

Millions of dollars have been spent in advertising these items through catalogues, sales books, newspapers, periodicals, store displays, circulars, and radio, and gross sales have been over a billion dollars. In the Philadelphia area alone, plaintiff marketed (exclusive of mail orders) over $17,000,000 worth of these items from 1946 through 1952, through its seven retail outlets. During that period about $48,000 a year was spent solely in local newspaper advertising.

In addition to the sale of automobile tires, accessories, parts and services in connection therewith, plaintiff, since 1931, through a wholly-owned subsidiary, Allstate Insurance Company, has continuously engaged in the business of selling automobile insurance of all types, under the name Allstate. The Allstate Insurance Company has maintained an office in Philadelphia since 1943. In 1952 the premium volume of the Philadelphia office was over $5,000,000, of which 40 per cent was in the Philadelphia metropolitan area. The company has organized the Allstate Foundation for Driving Education, which makes grants to universities for research in driving improvement and driver training, and grants scholarships to colleges for high school teachers to be trained in the giving of driving instruction. Discounts from regular insurance rates are granted to high school students who pass certain approved driving courses. The discount program has been widely publicized in every high school in the country. In the Philadelphia area, the program has been publicized by radio, displays at county fairs, and by direct contact with schools and civic organizations.

A survey conducted in the Philadelphia area indicated that of all persons orally interviewed, 74 per cent thought that the All-State Driving School was owned and operated by Sears, Roebuck and Company.

The court also found that, by virtue of the extensive use of the name Allstate by plaintiff and its wholly-owned subsidiary in connection with the sale of automobile products and services, and the extensive advertising of the name by plaintiff and its wholly-owned subsidiary, the name Allstate has become identified in the public mind with plaintiff and has acquired a secondary meaning as identifying the products and services of plaintiff.[3]

Whether state or federal law is applicable to the present situation we need not decide, for there would be no difference here. Campbell Soup Co. v. Armour & Co., 3 Cir., 1949, 175 F.2d 795. Pennsylvania, in fact, looks to federal decisions and precedents for its law of tradename infringement. Goebel Brewing Co. v. Esslingers, Inc., 1953, 373 Pa. 334, 95 A.2d 523. The Restatement of the Law of Torts, Sec. 729 (1938), sets forth the generally accepted factors to be considered in determining

3. Plaintiff made a request that the court find "In the course of the past three years between 150 and 200 telephone calls have been received by Allstate Insurance Company by persons inquiring as to All-State School of Driving." There was uncontradicted testimony to sustain this proposed finding. The court said that this request was answered in its opinion. The opinion does not explicitly affirm or deny this request, but does seem to indicate that the court accepted the testimony but did not think it warranted an inference of widespread public confusion. Even without this evidence, however, we think the other clearly found facts sufficient to sustain our decision.

whether a particular designation is confusingly similar to another's trade name:

"(a) the degree of similarity between the designation and the trademark or trade name in

"(i) appearance;

"(ii) pronunciation of the words used;

"(iii) verbal translation of the pictures or designs involved;

"(iv) suggestion;

"(b) the intent of the actor in adopting the designation;

"(c) the relation in use and manner of marketing between the goods or services marketed by the actor and those marketed by the other;

"(d) the degree of care likely to be exercised by purchasers."

In regard to the similarity of the names here involved, it need only be said that they are not just similar. They are practically identical. There is no difference in pronunciation, and the interpolation of a hyphen into the word Allstate will hardly distinguish the two names. Much less similarity between names has been found sufficient. Goebel Brewing Co. v. Esslingers, Inc., 1953, 373 Pa. 334, 95 A.2d 523 (Goebel and Goblet); Thomson-Porcelite Co. v. Harad, 1947, 356 Pa. 121, 51 A.2d 605 (Porcelite and Porcelene).

Defendants emphasize the point that plaintiff does not provide the same services they do, and therefore there could be no confusion. The fact that two parties market the same goods or services and are in direct competition with each other is important. But the absence of these factors is not conclusive. Restatement, Torts § 730 (1938); Bond Stores, Incorporated v. Bond Stores, Inc., 3 Cir., 1939, 104 F.2d 124; Duro Co. v. Duro Co., 3 Cir., 1928, 27 F.2d 339.

When we consider that all the services of plaintiff rendered under the Allstate label relate to automobiles, as to defendants' services, that plaintiff, through its financial grants and insurance discounts, is closely associated with the field of driving instruction, and that the services of plaintiff and defendants have the same prospective common purchasers, we think there is sufficient probability that confusion will result in the public's mind. Nor do we think the types of services involved are such that the public is likely through its own due care to ascertain the different sources of the driving instruction and other automotive services. Although there is no direct evidence as to defendants' intent, this is only one of the factors to be considered, and it is not an indispensable requirement. Defendants remained silent as to their reasons for using the name All-State. They say they did so because it was unnecessary for them to produce evidence when plaintiff had not proved its case. But their silence was nonetheless at their own peril, for they and not plaintiff had the burden of producing evidence on the question of intent; especially is this so where, as here, the name which they selected was practically identical to the one plaintiff had been using for over twenty years. Goebel Brewing Co. v. Esslingers, Inc., 373 Pa. 334, 95 A.2d 523; Lambert Pharmacal Co. v. Bolton Chemical Corp., D.C.S.D.N.Y.1915, 219 F. 325, 326; 2 Wigmore, Evidence § 285 (3d ed., 1940). We think that plaintiff has made out a very clear case of trade-name infringement.

The decree of the district court will be reversed and the cause remanded for further proceedings not inconsistent with this opinion.

THE GREAT SCOTT FOOD MARKET, INC. v. SUNDERLAND WONDER INC.

Supreme Judicial Court of Massachusetts, 1965.
144 USPQ 333.

The defendant has appealed from a final decree enjoining it "from using the name 'Big G' in any form or combination similar to the mark as registered by the plaintiff in connection with any food store within the County of Worcester, Commonwealth of Massachusetts." The evidence is reported.

1. The plaintiff bases its claim to relief on G.L. c. 110, § 7A, inserted by St.1947, c. 307, which provides: "Likelihood of injury to business reputation or of dilution of the distinctive quality of a trade name or trademark shall be a ground for injunctive relief in cases of trademark infringement or unfair competition notwithstanding the absence of competition between the parties or of confusion as to the source of goods or services." Under the principles stated in Jays Inc. v. Jay-Originals Inc., 321 Mass. 737, 740, 76 USPQ 238, and cases cited, we are of opinion that the plaintiff might in this instance be entitled to relief without reference to the statute. We note also, but express no view on, the possible applicability of the doctrine of reasonably expectable expansion of business. See Restatement 2d: Torts (Tent. draft No. 8, April 22, 1963), § 732. Since some question is present as to whether the defendant is or is likely to become a business rival of the plaintiff (see Skil Corp. v. Barnet, 337 Mass. 485, 488, 117 USPQ 461, 463), we conclude that the disposition of this case calls for application of the statute and that the plaintiff, falling within its express terms, is entitled to the relief granted by the trial court.

* * *

3. The defendant's contention that the name "Big G" is not sufficiently unique to warrant protection is without merit. "[A] trade name is not to be resolved into its component parts, and each part analyzed separately in cases of this sort." Food Fair Stores, Inc. v. Food Fair, Inc., 177 F.2d 177, 185, 83 USPQ 14, 20 (1st Cir.), affirming 83 F.Supp. 445, 79 USPQ 114 (D.Mass.). That relief under the statute is not dependent on uniqueness of name is supported by the statutory history of § 7A. See Skil Corp. v. Barnet, 337 Mass. 485, 489, n. 1, 117 USPQ 461, 463.

4. The defendant challenges the finding that its use of "Big G" has caused and will cause injury to the plaintiff's business reputation and dilution of its trade name. Although the plaintiff operated no stores within the Worcester trading area, the defendant's appropriation

of the name "Big G" endangered the plaintiff's reputation and good will.

* * *

The statute upon which the plaintiff relies has expressly withdrawn "competition between the parties" and "confusion as to the source of goods or services" as prerequisites to injunctive relief. Indeed "[t]he gravamen of a dilution complaint is that the continuous use of a mark similar to plaintiff's works an inexorably adverse effect upon the distinctiveness of the plaintiff's mark * * *. This injury differs materially from that arising out of the orthodox confusion." Callmann, The Law of Unfair Competition and Trademarks (2d ed.) § 84.2, p. 1643. Cf. Polaroid Corp. v. Polaraid, Inc., 319 F.2d 830, 138 USPQ 265 (7th Cir.), construing the Illinois antidilution statute.

5. Our view of the statute and the field to which it relates has been cogently expressed by Judge Learned Hand who, speaking in Yale Elec. Corp. v. Robertson, Commr. of Patents, 26 F.2d 972, 974 (2d Cir.), said: "[I]t has of recent years been recognized that a merchant may have a sufficient economic interest in the use of his mark outside the field of his own exploitation to justify interposition by a court. His mark is his authentic seal; by it he vouches for the goods which bear it; it carries his name for good or ill. If another uses it, he borrows the owner's reputation, whose quality no longer lies within his own control. This is an injury, even though the borrower does not tarnish it, or divert any sales by its use; for a reputation, like a face, is the symbol of its possessor and creator, and another can use it only as a mask. And so it has come to be recognized that, unless the borrower's use is so foreign to the owner's as to insure against any identification of the two, it is unlawful."

We conclude that the plaintiff is entitled to relief and that any use by the defendant within Worcester County of the name "Big G" will endanger the plaintiff's business reputation and cause the distinctive quality of its trade name to be diluted.

Decree affirmed with costs of appeal to the plaintiff.[a]

AMBASSADOR EAST, INC. v. ORSATTI, INC.[b]

United States Court of Appeals, Third Circuit, 1958.
257 F.2d 79, 118 USPQ 47.

GOODRICH, CIRCUIT JUDGE. * * *

The plaintiff complains of the defendant's use of the term "Pump Room." Plaintiff's "Pump Room" is a dining room in its hotel in Chicago and has been operated as such since 1938. The name is taken

a. Other states having Anti-Dilution Statutes are: Arkansas, California, Connecticut, Florida, Georgia, Idaho, Illinois, Iowa, New Hampshire, New Mexico, New York; see also: Callmann, Unjust Enrichment in the Law of Unfair Competition, 55 Harvard Law Review 595 (1942); Derenberg, The Problem of Dilution and the Anti-Dilution Statute, 44 California Law Review 439 (1956); Day, State Anti-Dilution Without a Statute, 54 Trademark Reporter 590 (1964); McAuliffe, The Dilution Concept in International Trade, 61 Trademark Reporter 76 (1971).

b. Beef & Brew, Inc. v. Beef & Brew, Inc., 389 F.Supp. 179, 185 USPQ 531 (D.C. Or.1974).

from the Pump Room in Bath, England, with the consent and approval of the proprietors of that establishment. Plaintiff's room is bizarre, garish and expensive; the cuisine specializes in dishes served on flaming swords and other exotic items. It is a room where quite evidently patrons go to see and be seen. It has been advertised nationally and publicized through other media.

The defendant is a restaurant proprietor in Philadelphia and has been since 1942. The name "Orsatti's Pump Room" and the insignia of a pump was adopted about 1951. * * *

The heart of the plaintiff's claim is that through the years and at great expense it has built up about the name "Pump Room" a distinctive reputation. It may not be the kind of reputation which would meet the approval of Cromwell's Puritans or their modern successors if any. But, nevertheless, because of it, the name has developed a business value which the plaintiff is entitled to have protected. See 3 Restatement, Torts 597–98 (1938).

Judge Learned Hand has described the controlling principle in words which are characteristically apt in a paragraph which has been quoted over and over again by courts in this type of case.[2] We can do no better than to quote it ourselves. He said:[3]

> "His mark is his authentic seal; by it he vouches for the goods which bear it; it carries his name for good or ill. If another uses it, he borrows the owner's reputation, whose quality no longer lies within his own control. This is an injury, even though the borrower does not tarnish it, or divert any sales by its use; for a reputation, like a face, is the symbol of its possessor and creator, and another can use it only as a mask. And so it has come to be recognized that, unless the borrower's use is so foreign to the owner's as to insure against any identification of the two, it is unlawful."

The learned district judge was willing to allow the plaintiff some measure of protection. He insisted that the name "Orsatti" be put ahead of the term "Pump Room." It is there now on the outside marquee of Orsatti's in Philadelphia but the photographs in evidence show pretty clearly that "Pump Room" is very prominent and the "Orsatti's" is not. The judge also thought that if the plaintiff wanted to establish a restaurant within ninety miles of Philadelphia and call it "Pump Room" that the defendant should then be restrained from using the term. Both these contentions too narrowly restrict the plaintiff's protection. It is entitled to have its name protected in full, not modified by other people's qualifying names and, at least on the facts before us, not limited by distance. The distance point in expressly

2. See Ambassador East, Inc. v. Shelton Corners, Inc., D.C.S.D.N.Y.1954, 120 F.Supp. 551, 554; Stork Restaurant v. Sahati, 9 Cir., 166 F.2d 348, 355; and cases cited in Annotation 1944, 148 A.L.R. 12, 55, note 212.

3. Yale Elec. Corp. v. Robertson, 2 Cir., 1928, 26 F.2d 972, 974.

covered by the cases cited below. See also Callmann, op.cit. supra § 76.3(b)(1), particularly at 1204.[4]

Interestingly enough, this problem of protection of names of eating places has come up in quite a number of cases involving restaurants whose proprietors have claimed to have built up far-reaching reputations for themselves. In every instance but one [5] to which our attention has been called the plaintiff has received full protection for the value of his name. Stork Restaurant, Inc. v. Sahati, 9 Cir.1948, 166 F.2d 348; Nagrom Corp. v. Cock 'N Bull, Inc., D.C.1957, 149 F.Supp. 217; Ambassador East, Inc. v. Shelton Corners, Inc., D.C.S.D.N.Y.1954, 120 F.Supp. 551; Stork Restaurant, Inc. v. Marcus, D.C.E.D.Pa.1941, 36 F.Supp. 90; Brass Rail, Inc. v. Ye Brass Rail of Massachusetts, Inc., D.C.Mass.1938, 43 F.Supp. 671; 51 West Fifty-First Corp. v. Roland, 1946, 139 N.J.Eq. 156, 50 A.2d 369; Maison Prunier v. Prunier's Restaurant & Cafe, Inc., Sup.Ct.1936, 159 Misc. 551, 288 N.Y.S. 529; see Bill's Gay Nineties, Inc. v. Fisher, Sup.Ct.1943, 180 Misc. 721, 41 N.Y.S.2d 234; cf. Pike v. Ruby Foo's Den, Inc., 1956, 98 U.S.App.D.C. 126, 232 F.2d 683.

The judgment of the district court will be reversed and the case remanded for further proceedings not inconsistent with this opinion.[e]

Tiffany & Co. v. Boston Club, Inc., 231 F.Supp. 836, 143 USPQ 2, 8 (D.C.Mass.1964). Plaintiff in the retail jewelry business in New York City since 1837 obtained injunction against Defendant operating a local restaurant in Boston under the name "Tiffany's". The court said: "This is not a case where a trader has plucked a word 'with favorable connotations for his goods or services out of the general vocabulary and apportionate it to his exclusive use.' Esquire, Inc. v. Esquire Slipper Mfg. Co., 243 F.2d 540, 543, 113 USPQ 237, 240.

Notes

1. Ameritech, Inc. v. American Information Technologies Corp., 811 F.2d 960, 964–65, 1 USPQ2d 1861, 1864–5 (6th Cir.1987):

Although trademark protection may have had its start in common law as an action in fraud, over the past one hundred fifty years it has come to

4. For a general discussion of the territorial scope of trademark and trade name protection, see Annotation, 1944, 148 A.L.R. 12, 92–125. See also 3 Restatement, Torts § 732 and Com. a (1938).

5. El Chico, Inc. v. El Chico Cafe, 5 Cir., 1954, 214 F.2d 721; cf. Faciane v. Starner, 5 Cir., 1956, 230 F.2d 732.

e. See also: Vaudable v. Montmartre, Inc., 20 MSC 2d 757, 193 N.Y.S.2d 332; 123 USPQ 357, 358 (1959). Plaintiff, owner of French restaurant in Paris known as Maxim's, sued Defendant operating a restaurant in New York City under same name. The court said: "It is obvious that defendants' purpose is to appropriate the good will plaintiffs have created in the name Maxim's as a restaurant establishment. The fact that they are not in present actual competition is immaterial. Maison Prunier v. Prunier's Restaurant & Cafe, Inc., 159 Misc. 551. A wrongful attempt to suggest an association or connection of some sort is sufficient to warrant relief to prevent confusion in the public mind as well as dilution of plaintiffs' trade name (Burrough, Ltd. v. Ferrara, 8 Misc.2d 819, 113 USPQ 233); and the more distinctive and unique the name, the greater the need for protection from dilution of its distinctive quality. Tiffany & Co. v. Tiffany Productions, Inc., 147 Misc. 679, aff'd 237 App. Div. 801, aff'd 262 N.Y. 482."

focus also on protecting property interests in trademarks themselves. This shift is the result of the recognition of the purposes trademarks serve in the modern, impersonal economy. They act as a means of identifying a product as coming from or being associated with a particular, although anonymous, source, and inducing subsequent purchases by customers. As a commentator pointed out sixty years ago:

The fact that through his trademark the manufacturer or importer may "reach over the shoulder of the retailer" and across the latter's counter straight to the consumer cannot be over-emphasized, for therein lies the key to any effective scheme of trademark protection . . . . [A trademark is] not merely the symbol of good will but often the most effective agent for the creation of good will, imprinting upon the public mind an anonymous and impersonal guaranty of satisfaction, creating a desire for further satisfactions. The mark actually *sells* the goods.

Schecter, *The Rational Basis of Trademark Protection*, 40 Harv.L.Rev. 812, 818–19 (1927) (emphasis original).

Thus, trademark law now pursues two related goals—the prevention of deception and consumer confusion, and, more fundamentally, the protection of property interests in trademarks. As a means of achieving these goals, the common law had developed a number of types of infringement actions. The first and most common is "palming off." This occurs between directly competing goods and the confusion is over their source of origin. Similar marks on these goods can cause the consumer to mistakenly buy the infringing defendant's product as the plaintiff's; the defendant tries to "palm off" his goods as the plaintiff's. *See, e.g., Seven-Up Co. v. Get Up Corp.*, 340 F.2d 954 [144 USPQ 171] (6th Cir.), *cert. denied*, 382 U.S. 901 [147 USPQ 541] (1965).

A second kind of infringement is confusion of sponsorship, which occurs where the goods do not directly compete. In this situation, the goods are unrelated enough that no inference arises that they originated from the same source, but the similarity of the trademarks erroneously suggests a connection between the sources; the defendant seeks to capitalize on the plaintiff's goodwill and established reputation. *See e.g., Conan Properties, Inc. v. Conans Pizza, Inc.*, 752 F.2d 145, 150 [225 USPQ 379, 382] (5th Cir.1985) (ordinary consumer might well believe defendant restaurant was affiliated with owners of fictional character "Conan The Barbarian" through licensing).

A third kind of infringement is reverse confusion of sponsorship. A reverse confusion claim differs from the stereotypical confusion of source or sponsorship claim. Rather than seeking to profit from the goodwill captured in the senior user's trademark, the junior user saturates the market with a similar trademark and overwhelms the senior user. The public comes to assume the senior user's products are really the junior user's or that the former has become somehow connected to the latter. The result is that the senior user loses the value of the trademark—its product identity, corporate identity, control over its goodwill and reputation, and ability to move into new markets. *See, e.g., Big O Tire Dealers, Inc. v. Goodyear Tire & Rubber Co.*, 561 F.2d 1365, 1371–72 [195 USPQ 417, 422] (10th Cir.1977), *cert. dismissed*, 434 U.S. 1052 (1978); *Plus Products v. Plus Discount Foods,*

Inc., 722 F.2d 999, 1003–04 [222 USPQ 373, 376–77] (2d Cir.1983). *See also International News Service v. Associated Press*, 248 U.S. 215, 247 (1948) (Holmes, J., concurring) ("The ordinary case, I say, is palming off the defendant's product as the plaintiff's; but the same evil may follow from the opposite falsehood,—from saying, whether in words or implication, that the plaintiff's product is the defendant's . . . [T]he principle that condemns one condemns the other.")

A fourth kind of infringement is dilution. Under this theory, an infringement can occur even where the products are non-competing and no confusion is possible. Rather than focusing on consumer confusion, the dilution theory seeks to protect the senior user's interests in the trademark. Dilution occurs when the senior user possesses a distinctive mark, the junior use of which might not, in the short run, result in loss of sales or loss of control over reputation, but might cause a gradual diminution in the mark's distinctiveness, effectiveness and, hence, value. This kind of infringement corrodes the senior user's interest in the trademark by blurring its product identification or by damaging positive associations that have attached to it. *See* 3A R. Callmann, *Unfair Competition, Trademarks & Monopolies* § 21.11, at 33–34 (4th ed. 1981); 2 J. McCarthy, *Trademarks and Unfair Competition* § 24.13, at 215 (2d ed. 1984). *See, e.g., Vogue Co. v. Thompson-Hudson Co.*, 300 F. 509 (6th Cir.1924), *cert. denied*, 273 U.S. 706 (1926); *Pro-Phy-Lac-Tic Brush Co. v. Jordan Marsh Co.*, 165 F.2d 549, 553 [76 USPQ 146, 149–50] (1st Cir.1948).

2. Dreyfus Fund, Inc. v. Royal Bank of Canada, 525 F.Supp. 1108, 1123, 213 USPQ 872, 883 (S.D.N.Y.1981):

The federal courts have refused to recognize a cause of action under the Lanham Act for dilution caused by an otherwise infringing use in connection with noncompeting goods so unrelated to those of the senior owner that there can be no likelihood or prospect of confusion of any kind. See, e.g., Avon Shoe Co. v. David Crystal, Inc., 279 F.2d 607, 125 USPQ 607 (2d Cir.1960); G.B. Kent & Sons, Ltd. v. P. Lorillard Co., 114 F.Supp. 621, 98 USPQ 404 (S.D.N.Y.1953), aff'd on opinion below, 210 F.2d 953, 101 USPQ 161 (2d Cir.1954). See generally 3 Callmann, supra, § 84.2, at 953–64; Note, Dilution: Trademark Infringement or Will-O'-the-Wisp? 77 Harv.L.Rev. 520 (1964).

3. Calvin Klein Cosmetics Corp. v. Lenox Laboratories, Inc., 815 F.2d 500, 2 USPQ2d 1285, 1287–8 (8th Cir.1987):

The parties do not dispute that Lenox may copy, if it can, the scent marketed as OBSESSION. *See, e.g., Smith v. Chanel, Inc.*, 402 F.2d 562, 563 & n.3 [159 USPQ 388, 389 n.3] (9th Cir.1968). Moreover, the parties agree that the issue here is not whether to completely bar Lenox from any use of the OBSESSION mark. A trademark is not a monopoly on the use of a name or a phrase. Rather, the legal relevance of a trademark is to show the source, identity, sponsorship, or origin of the product. *See Prestonettes, Inc. v. Coty*, 264 U.S. 359, 368 (1924) (Holmes, J.) (use of originator's registered trademark by firm that repackaged originator's cosmetics products upheld); *Chanel*, 402 F.2d at 566 [159 USPQ at 391] (use of originator's mark to market copy of Chanel No. 5 perfume upheld). An imitator may use in a truthful way an originator's trademark when advertising that the imitator's product is a copy so long as that use is not likely to create confusion in the consumer's mind as to the source of the product being sold. *Chanel*, 402 F.2d at 563 [159 USPQ 389]; *Societe Comptoir de L'Industrie Cotonniere Etablissements Boussac v. Alexander's Department Stores, Inc.*, 299 F.2d 33, 36 [132 USPQ 475, 477] (2d Cir.1962) (use of French couturier's name—Christian Dior—on copies of Dior designs upheld); 15 U.S.C. § 1114(1) (registered mark cannot be used without registrant's consent if such use is likely to cause confusion or mistake, or to deceive). The underlying rationale is that an imitator is entitled to truthfully inform the public that it believes that it has produced a product equivalent to the original and that the public may benefit through lower prices by buying the imitation. *Saxlehner v. Wagner*, 216 U.S. 375, 380–81 (1910) (Holmes, J.); *Chanel*, 402 F.2d at 567–68 [159 USPQ at 392].

* * *

D. FEDERAL REGISTRATION

A trademark or service mark employed in interstate or foreign commerce, and otherwise complying with prerequisites to registerability (see Section E infra), may be registered on the Principal or Supplemental Register of the U.S. Patent and Trademark Office by filing an application for registration and satisfying applicable regulations.

15 U.S.C.A. § 1072. Registration as Constructive Notice of Claim of Ownership

Registration of a mark on the principal register provided by this chapter or under the Act of March 3, 1881, or the Act of February 20, 1905, shall be constructive notice of the registrant's claim of ownership thereof.

15 U.S.C.A. § 1115. Registration on Principal Register as Evidence of Exclusive Right to Use Mark; Defenses

(a) Any registration issued under the Act of March 3, 1881, or the Act of February 20, 1905, or of a mark registered on the principal register provided by this chapter and owned by a party to an action shall be admissible in evidence and shall be prima facie evidence of registrant's exclusive right to use the registered mark in commerce on the goods or services specified in the registration subject to any conditions or limitations stated therein, but shall not preclude an opposing party from proving any legal or equitable defense or defect which might have been asserted if such mark had not been registered.

* * *

"Exclusive right to use" means the right to exclude others from using the registered mark, not a positive grant of a right to use. Holiday Inn v. Holiday Inns, Inc., 534 F.2d 312, 189 USPQ 630 (CCPA 1976).

15 U.S.C.A. § 1114. Remedies; Infringement; Innocent Infringement by Printers and Publishers

(a) Any person who shall, without the consent of the registrant—

(1) use in commerce any reproduction, counterfeit, copy, or colorable imitation of a registered mark in connection with the sale, offering for sale, distribution, or advertising of any goods or services on or in connection with which such use is likely to cause confusion, or to cause mistake, or to deceive; or

(2) reproduce, counterfeit, copy, or colorably imitate a registered mark and apply such reproduction, counterfeit, copy, or colorable imitation to labels, signs, prints, packages, wrappers, receptacles or advertisements intended to be used in commerce upon or in connection with the sale, offering for sale, distribution, or advertising of goods or services on or in connection with which such use is likely to cause confusion, or to cause mistake, or to deceive; shall be liable in a civil action by the registrant for the remedies hereinafter provided. Under subsection (b) of this section, the registrant shall not be entitled to recover profits or damages unless the acts have been committed with knowledge that such imitation is intended to be used to cause confusion, or to cause mistake, or to deceive.

* * *

GEORATOR CORP. v. UNITED STATES

United States Court of Appeals, Fourth Circuit, 1973.
485 F.2d 283, 179 USPQ 450, cert. denied 417 U.S. 945, 94 S.Ct. 3069, 41
L.Ed.2d 665, 182 USPQ 65.

[In a case presenting the question whether for federal income tax purposes a fee incurred while resisting a petition to cancel registration of a trademark would be deductible as an ordinary business expense or must be treated as a capital expenditure, the court had this to say about trademark registration.]

Registration of a trademark in the Patent Office, while not enlarging the common law rights of a trademark, does confer very real benefits upon the holder of such trademark. Those benefits include: (1) constructive notice of the registrant's claim of ownership of the trademark; (2) prima facie evidence of the validity of the registration, of the registrant's ownership of the mark, and of his exclusive right to use the mark in commerce as specified in the certificate; (3) the possibility that, after five years, registration will become incontestible and constitute conclusive evidence of the registrant's right to use the mark; (4) the right to request customs officials to bar the importation of goods bearing infringing trademarks; (5) the right to institute trademark actions in federal courts without regard to diversity of citizenship or the amount in controversy; and (6) treble damage actions against infringing trademarks and other remedies. 15 U.S.C.A. § 1051 et seq. Registration is effective initially for twenty years, but the possibility of renewal at the end of that time makes a determination of the effective life span impossible. Since the benefits of trademark registration are of indeterminate duration and likely to extend over several tax periods, the costs of registration have been held to be capital expenditures. Duesenberg, Inc. of Delaware, 31 B.T.A. 922 (1934), aff'd on other grounds, 84 F.2d 921 (7 Cir.1936); see also our discussion of Section 177 of the Internal Revenue Code, 26 U.S.C.A. § 177, infra.

In our view, legal costs incurred resisting cancellation of a trademark registration must be treated in the same manner as the costs of the original registration.

MISTER DONUT OF AMERICA, INC. v. MR. DONUT, INC.

United States Court of Appeals, Ninth Circuit, 1969.
418 F.2d 838, 164 USPQ 67.

McNichols, District Judge. * * *

The following chronology and factual situation is established by the record:

Plaintiff began to use the mark, Mister Donut in August, 1955; made sales in interstate commerce and applied to the United States Patent Office for registration of the mark pursuant to the provisions of the Trademark Act of 1946, codified as 15 U.S.C.A., Sec. 1051, et seq., and popularly known as the Lanham Act (hereinafter the "Act" or the "Lanham Act"). * * *

In October, 1957 * * *, defendant, without any actual knowledge of any prior use of the mark by anyone, first adopted the mark and, as indicated above, opened its first retail doughnut shop in California in December of that year.

On October 21, 1958, plaintiff secured a certificate of registration of the Mister Donut mark. (The trial court, rejecting the recording of the Ragsdale assignment, held that this date was the date of constructive notice of plaintiff's claim to the mark). By this time plaintiff had shops operating in Massachusetts, New York, Florida, Michigan and Virginia.

March 1, 1959, defendant franchised a second shop in Orange County and thereafter five more, in adjacent portions of the county, the opening being spaced over the following several years.

It appears that neither party was aware of the activities of the other until about 1963. In 1965, plaintiff opened a Western district office in Palo Alto, California and on April 23, 1966 the first California doughnut shop came into existence at Campbell, California. During 1966, three more shops were opened in California, not however, in Orange County. Plaintiff now proposes to establish retail doughnut shops in the Los Angeles and Orange County area. Undisputed evidence was presented at the trial to the effect that bona fide prospective franchisees, interested in operating in Orange County and the Los Angeles area, have, after discovering the competitive use of the mark by defendant, abandoned plans to open shops in the area.

* * *

We come now to the most troublesome aspect of this appeal. The district judge determined "that defendants' activities were and are outside the Lanham Act because they do not affect interstate commerce". He therefore concluded that defendants' intrastate use of plaintiff's federally registered mark was not an infringement for which relief should be granted under the Lanham Act. In arriving at this holding, the District Court relied exclusively on the authority of Fairway Foods v. Fairway Markets, 227 F.2d 193 (9th Cir.1955).

In *Fairway Foods,* the question facing the court was whether a large midwest grocery chain could enjoin the use of its federally registered trademark by a grocer doing business out of one store in California. The chain had no outlets in that state and no plans to locate any there in the foreseeable future. The District Court refused to issue an injunction because there was no present competition between the parties, and no likelihood of any in the future. This court in affirming that decision agreed that the conduct of the intrastate grocer would not warrant an injunction under the common law action for unfair competition, unless by operation of the Lanham Act. The panel of this Circuit then went on to hold that the activities of a purely intrastate grocer could not be made subject to the provisions of the Act unless these activities had a substantial effect on interstate commerce.

No such substantial effect was demonstrated as the parties were dealing in totally remote markets without any foreseeable likelihood of competition. Therefore it was held in *Fairway Foods* that the court should not enjoin the California grocer's activities.

We think *Fairway Foods* is good law, but is to be interpreted within the very narrow limits of its factual situation. This is borne out by the following excerpts from the opinion:

> "* * * It will be important to note that plaintiff has not and never has had any outlet for its merchandise in California, nor within 1500 miles of defendant's one seat of business. (at p. 195)"

> * * *

Fairway Foods thus stands for the rule that where the federal registrant and the intrastate user of conflictingly similar trade marks are using the respective marks in geographically separate and distinct market areas, with no real competition between them, and where there is no present likelihood that the federal registrant will expand his use into the area of use of the intrastate user, there is no cause shown for injunctive relief based on infringement. The instant case is readily distinguishable from *Fairway Foods* as the facts are nowise similar: Plaintiff has firmly established its nationwide doughnut shop business in California and is now competing with the defendant for shop locations in the same market area, i.e., Orange County. Each party has plans to expand throughout southern California and thus increase the competitive situation.

The trial court erred in determining that *Fairway Foods* was controlling in this case.

We hold that where a federal registrant has expanded its business to the point that the use of the conflictingly similar marks by the registrant and the unauthorized user are no longer confined to separate and distinct market areas and there is established the likelihood of public confusion, the federal registrant is entitled under the authority of the Lanham Act to injunctive relief. Dawn Donut Company v. Hart's Food Stores, Inc., 267 F.2d 358, 365 (C.A.2 1959); and Cf. John R. Thompson Co. v. Holloway, 366 F.2d 108 (C.A.5 1966); American Foods, Inc. v. Golden Flake, Inc., 312 F.2d 619 (C.A.5 1963); Drop Dead Co. v. S.C. Johnson & Son, Inc., 326 F.2d 87 (C.A.9 1963).

It is necessary that we remand the case to the District Court to determine the area of use by the defendant which was developed prior to October, 1958 when plaintiff's initial certificate of registration became effective. As to this area, defendant has perfected the defense provided in the Act by Sec. 1115(b)(5). Thereafter the District Court will grant such injunctive relief as is required consonant with the rules laid down in this opinion.

One additional issue merits brief discussion. Plaintiff seeks to obviate the effect of the defense provided in Sec. 1115(b)(5) of the Act by attempting to interject California state law. This issue was not presented to the trial court and we would be justified in refusing to consider it now. Keegan v. United States, 385 F.2d 260 (9 Cir.1967). However, since the matter is to go back to the District Court, we choose to comment.

Plaintiff claims that, since it first adopted the mark outside of California, it is the original owner and entitled under California law to exclusive right to the use of the mark regardless whether or not defendant was aware of the prior use. Reliance for this assertion is based on the California Business and Professions Code, Div. 6, Sec. 14270, which provided at the time of trial as follows:

> "Original owner. Any person who has first adopted and used a trademark, whether within or beyond the limits of this State, is its original owner."

What the effect of this California statutory provision might be if the Lanham Act had not been passed by Congress, we need not decide. The Lanham Act has pre-empted the field of trademark law and controls. It follows that the defense provided in Sec. 1115(b)(5) of the Act cannot be voided by state statute. Burger King of Florida, Inc. v. Hoots, 403 F.2d 904 (C.A.7 1968).

The judgment appealed from is affirmed in part and reversed in part. The cause is remanded to the District Court for further proceedings in accordance with our holdings.[a]

a. "Prior to the passage of the Lanham Act courts generally held that the owner of a registered trademark could not sustain an action for infringement against another who, without knowledge of the registration, used the mark in a different trading area from that exploited by the registrant so that public confusion was unlikely. By being the first to adopt a mark in an area without knowledge of its prior registration,

SPRINGFIELD FIRE & MARINE INS. CO. v. FOUNDERS' FIRE & MARINE INS. CO.

United States District Court of California, S.D., 1953.
115 F.Supp. 787, 99 USPQ 38.

GOODMAN, DISTRICT JUDGE. This case tenders the novel question, whether or not the plaintiff Insurance Company, which uses a picturization of a "covered wagon," drawn by oxen, on its insurance policies, stationery, and advertising media and which registered the picturization as a "service" mark pursuant to the provisions of the Lanham Act, 60 Stat. 427, 15 U.S.C.A. §§ 1051–1127, may enjoin the defendant Insurance Company from using a similar picturization on its policies, stationery, and advertising matter.

Prior to July 5, 1947, the effective date of the Lanham Act, there was no federal statutory provision for registering any mark used in connection with the sale or advertising of "services." Theretofore the federal registering of "trade-marks" had been confined to those affixed to tangible commodities.

Section 45 of the Lanham Act indicates the distinction between "trade-marks" and "service marks" as follows: It defines the term "trade-mark" as any word, name, symbol or device used by a manufacturer or merchant to identify his goods and distinguish them from those manufactured or sold by others. It defines the term "service mark" to mean a mark used in the sale or advertising of services to identify the services of one person and distinguish them from the services of others.

Plaintiff's complaint sets forth two causes of action. One alleges what might be termed technical "service mark" infringement, i.e. that the defendant's picturization of a "covered wagon" is a colorable imitation of the plaintiff's registered mark.

The second is for unfair competition. It is based upon the ground that the plaintiff's mark has acquired secondary meaning in the indus-

a junior user of a mark could gain the right to exploit the mark exclusively in that market.

"But the Lanham Act, 15 U.S.C.A. § 1072, provides that registration of a trademark on the principal register is constructive notice of the registrant's claim of ownership. Thus, by eliminating the defense of good faith and lack of knowledge, § 1072 affords nationwide protection to registered marks, regardless of the areas in which the registrant actually uses the mark." Dawn Donut Co., Inc. v. Hart's Food Stores, Inc., 267 F.2d 358, 362, 121 USPQ 430, 433 (2d Cir.1959).

"It is not disputed that plaintiff registered the mark "SAFEWAY" with the United States Patent Office effective September 19, 1961. Such registration puts even innocent users on constructive notice of plaintiff's claim of ownership of the mark after that date. However, defendants' innocent continuous use of the mark prior to that date can be and is a defense, " * * * *Provided, however,* That this defense * * * shall apply only for the area in which such continuous prior use is proved * * *." (15 U.S.C.A. § 1115(b)(5)).

"In the case at bar, we hold defendants should be protected in their prior innocent use of the mark "SAFEWAY" and that they may continue to use such mark in the areas where defendants operated and conducted their businesses prior to September 19, 1961." Safeway Stores, Inc. v. Safeway Quality Foods, Inc., 433 F.2d 99, 103, 166 USPQ 112, 115 (7th Cir. 1970).

try and that the defendant competes unfairly by using a similar mark. The second cause of action may be summarily disposed of. The ultimate test for unfair competition under the applicable California law [1] is: is the consuming public likely to be deceived. Silvers v. Russell, D.C., 113 F.Supp. 119, 125 and cases there cited. The evidence fails to show that plaintiff's mark has acquired any secondary meaning.

* * *

Plaintiff has adopted and used the covered-wagon picturization to symbolize that it was a pioneer company in the insurance business. Whether plaintiff's use of this symbolic mark entitles the mark to the trademark protection, sought in the first cause of action under the Lanham Act, is a novel question. The Lanham Act created, for the first time, federal substantive rights in registered trademarks and extended these rights to registered marks used in the sale or advertisement of services. Plaintiff's cause depends upon the scope of the protection Congress intended to afford by the Lanham Act. The Congressional intent must be considered against the background of the common law philosophy of trademark protection.

Trade-marks have always been regarded by the law as a means by which the seller seeks to distinguish his goods from those of another. A trade-mark has been treated as a right which is appurtenant to a business or trade in which the mark is employed or to the commodity with which it is identified. The right to the mark grows out of its use.

Today, a trade-mark performs a threefold function: (1) to indicate origin; (2) to guarantee; and (3) to advertise and sell. Historically, the function of indicating origin was the first to develop. The trade-mark came to mean that a certain manufacturer made the goods that bore the mark. Today, the trade-mark still serves to indicate origin, but the identity of the origin is often unknown to the consumer. The mark merely indicates to him that goods bearing the mark come from the same origin, whatever that origin may be.

Later in their historical development, trade-marks took on the function of guaranteeing to the consumer that the quality of goods bearing the mark was the same as previous goods which bore the same mark.

As modern advertising developed, trade-marks assumed their third function of creating and perpetuating a market for goods through use of the advertising. Consumers are now induced to try a product because

1. The cause of action for unfair competition has been argued by the parties upon the theory that it is governed by California law under the doctrine of Erie R. Co. v. Tompkins, 304 U.S. 64, 58 S.Ct. 817, 82 L.Ed. 1188. There are in the Lanham Act certain sweeping provisions, designed to implement various International Conventions to which the United States is a party, which might be construed to create a federal statutory law of unfair competition. See sections 44(h) and 44(i), and the discussion of these sections in Robert, The New Trade-Mark Manual (Washington, D.C. 1947) at xiii–xx and 165–180. But, however that may be, there is nothing in these statutory provisions nor in the International Conventions which would sustain plaintiff's claim of unfair competition under the circumstances of this case.

of the inherent appeal of the trade-mark used in advertising the product.[8]

The common law was originally shaped to protect trade-marks in their functions of indicating origin and guaranteeing quality to the consuming public. There was much discussion in the early cases as to whether protection was accorded a trade-mark merely to prevent the public from being deceived as to origin and quality, or also to prevent loss to the trade-mark owner of his market. The more recent cases have recognized that protection is afforded a trade-mark both for the benefit of the public and the trade-mark owner. The express purpose of the Lanham Act is to assure the trade-mark owner the advantages rightfully accruing to him from his use of the mark as well as to protect the public from deceit.

Because a trade-mark performs none of its functions apart from its use in connection with the sale of goods or services, the common law did not protect a mark as a trade-mark unless it was *in fact in use*. It is clear that the Lanham Act did not change the law in this respect. Registration under the Act does not in itself constitute a grant of the exclusive right to control a mark. The mark must be in use as a trade-mark or service-mark to entitle it to registration under the Act, and it must remain in use in order to receive the protection afforded by the Act. Sections 1, 3, 14, 45.

* * *

But, in cases where the sale of the marked goods were sporadic or few, or where it was not clear that the mark was affixed for the purpose of indicating origin, the mark was denied trade-mark protection in the absence of a showing that the mark had become associated with the goods in the mind of the consuming public. See for example, MacMahan Pharmacal Co. v. Denver Chemical Mfg. Co., 8 Cir., 1901, 113 F. 468, where in 10 years there had been but 362 sales of a drug marked "Antiphlogistine;" Kipling v. G.P. Putnam's Sons, 2 Cir., 1903, 120 F. 631, 65 L.R.A. 873, where a single edition of Kipling's works had been stamped with an ornamental device without any notice that it was intended as a trade-mark; Capewell Horse Nail Co. v. Putnam Nail Co., C.C.Mass.1905, 140 F. 670, where a check pattern was stamped upon nail heads but no public attention was called to it in the advertisements of the plaintiff nor upon its cartons; but compare the later case of Capewell Horse Nail Co. v. Mooney, C.C.N.D.N.Y.1909, 167 F. 575, where, upon other evidence, the court held the check pattern to be a valid trade-mark.

The Lanham Act has not significantly altered the common-law requirement that a trade-mark must be affixed to the goods which it identifies. The Act does permit the registration as trade-marks of marks used "or the displays associated" with goods. Section 45. But

---

8. For excellent discussions of the nature and history of trade-marks, see Robert, The New Trade-Mark Manual (Bureau of National Affairs, Washington, D.C.1947); Schechter, The Rational Basis of Trademark Protection, 40 Harvard Law Review 813 (1927).

even this use necessitates a close physical association between the mark and the goods. Thus the Lanham Act preserves the requirement of actual physical association between trade-mark and goods which tends to assure that a mark which is accorded trade-mark protection actually performs its function of identifying the goods to the consuming public.

The common law did not afford trade-mark protection to marks used in connection with the sale of services because the mark could not be affixed to the services. Such protection as these marks received was accorded under the general principles of unfair competition. See e.g., Atlas Assurance Company v. Atlas Insurance Company, 1907, 138 Iowa 228, 112 N.W. 232, 114 N.W. 609, 15 L.R.A.,N.S., 625. In extending trade-mark protection to service-marks, the Lanham Act does not specify any type of physical association that must exist between the service and the mark. The Act permits the registration, as a service-mark, of marks "used in the sale or advertising of services to identify the services of one person and distinguish them from the services of others * * *." Section 45. The Act goes on to specify that such service mark "includes without limitation the marks, names, symbols, titles, designations, slogans, character names, and distinctive features of radio or other advertising used in commerce." Section 45. This latter provision was intended primarily to protect the titles, theme songs, character names, and other distinctive features of radio programs. However, it is expressly not limited to radio advertising, although it was suggested at the Congressional committee hearings on the Lanham bill that it should be so limited. The Lanham Act thus emphasizes the advertising and selling function of a service-mark.

* * *

Thus for relief to be granted plaintiff, it must appear that defendant's use of the similar covered-wagon mark is likely to cause confusion as to the source of origin of the services. There is no evidence of any actual instance of such confusion, nor any evidence of any instance from which an inference as to such confusion could be drawn. As was said by Justice Hand in Miles Shoes, Inc., v. R.H. Macy & Co., Inc., 2 Cir., 1952, 199 F.2d 602, 603, in the absence of such actual instances of confusion, "in the final analysis the decision must rest on the court's conviction as to possible confusion." The Court's conviction in this case is that there could not possibly be any confusion. * * *

For any broker who would select an insurance carrier because its policies or advertising material carried an imprint of a covered wagon, or a pine tree, or an elephant, would obviously soon be seeking his living in other fields.

This case, despite the interesting legal problem it has presented, really is "Much Ado About Nothing." The pleasure and pride of the plaintiff in the use of the ornamental picture of the covered wagon is understandable. But that is, per se, a far cry to granting judicial aid to stop another insurance company from using similar adornments or ornaments. In the absence of any evidence showing any confusion or likelihood of confusion, there is no need or cause for the drastic sanction of injunctive relief.

Judgment for defendant upon findings of fact and conclusions of law to be presented pursuant to the rules.

PARK 'N FLY, INC. v. DOLLAR PARK AND FLY, INC.

United States Supreme Court, 1985.
469 U.S. 189, 105 S.Ct. 658, 83 L.Ed.2d 582, 224 USPQ 327.

JUSTICE O'CONNOR delivered the opinion of the Court.

In this case we consider whether an action to enjoin the infringement of an incontestable trade or service mark may be defended on the grounds that the mark is merely descriptive. We conclude that neither the language of the relevant statutes nor the legislative history supports such a defense.

* * *

The Court of Appeals for the Ninth Circuit reversed. 718 F.2d 327 (1983). The District Court did not err, the Court of Appeals held, in refusing to invalidate petitioner's mark. *Id.,* at 331. The Court of Appeals noted, however, that it previously had held that incontestability provides a defense against the cancellation of a mark, but it may not be used offensively to enjoin another's use. *Ibid.* Petitioner, under this analysis, could obtain an injunction only if its mark would be entitled to continued registration without regard to its incontestable status. Thus, respondent could defend the infringement action by showing that the mark was merely descriptive. Based on its own examination of the record, the Court of Appeals then determined that petitioner's mark is in fact merely descriptive, and therefore respondent should not be enjoined from using the name "Park and Fly." *Ibid.*

The decision below is in direct conflict with the decision of the Court of Appeals for the Seventh Circuit in *Union Carbide Corp. v. Ever-Ready Inc.,* 531 F.2d 366, cert. denied, 429 U.S. 830, 97 S.Ct. 91, 50 L.Ed.2d 94 (1976). We granted certiorari to resolve this conflict, 465 U.S. 1078, 104 S.Ct. 1438, 79 L.Ed.2d 760 (1984), and we now reverse.

II

Congress enacted the Lanham Act in 1946 in order to provide national protection for trademarks used in interstate and foreign commerce. S.Rep. No. 1333, 79th Cong., 2d Sess., 5 (1946). Previous federal legislation, such as the Federal Trademark Act of 1905, 33 Stat. 724, reflected the view that protection of trademarks was a matter of state concern and that the right to a mark depended solely on the common law. S.Rep. No. 1333, at 5. Consequently, rights to trademarks were uncertain and subject to variation in different parts of the country. Because trademarks desirably promote competition and the maintenance of product quality, Congress determined that "a sound public policy requires that trademarks should receive nationally the greatest protection that can be given them." *Id.*, at 6. Among the new protections created by the Lanham Act were the statutory provisions that allow a federally registered mark to become incontestable. §§ 15, 33(b), 15 U.S.C. §§ 1065, 1115(b).

The provisions of the Lanham Act concerning registration and incontestability distinguish a mark that is "the common descriptive name of an article or substance," from a mark that is "merely descriptive." §§ 2(e), 14(c), 15 U.S.C. §§ 1052(e), 1064(c). Marks that constitute a common descriptive name are referred to as generic. A generic term is one that refers to the genus of which the particular product is a species. *Abercrombie & Fitch Co. v. Hunting World, Inc.*, 537 F.2d 4, 9 (CA2 1976). Generic terms are not registrable, and a registered mark may be cancelled at any time on the grounds that it has become generic. See §§ 2, 14(c), 15 U.S.C. §§ 1052, 1064(c). A "merely descriptive" mark, in contrast, describes the qualities or characteristics of a good or service, and this type of mark may be registered only if the registrant shows that it has acquired secondary meaning, *i.e.*, it "has become distinctive of the applicant's goods in commerce." §§ 2(e), (f), 15 U.S.C. §§ 1052(e), (f).

This case requires us to consider the effect of the incontestability provisions of the Lanham Act in the context of an infringement action defended on the grounds that the mark is merely descriptive. Statutory construction must begin with the language employed by Congress and the assumption that the ordinary meaning of that language accurately expresses the legislative purpose. See *American Tobacco Co. v. Patterson*, 456 U.S. 63, 68, 102 S.Ct. 1534, 1537, 71 L.Ed.2d 748 (1982). With respect to incontestable trade or service marks, § 33(b) of the Lanham Act states that "registration shall be conclusive evidence of the registrant's exclusive right to use the registered mark" subject to the conditions of § 15 and certain enumerated defenses. Section 15 incorporates by reference subsections (c) and (e) of § 14, 15 U.S.C. § 1064. An incontestable mark that becomes generic may be cancelled at any time pursuant to § 14(c). That section also allows cancellation of an incontestable mark at any time if it has been abandoned, if it is being used to misrepresent the source of the goods or services in connection with which it is used, or if it was obtained fraudulently or contrary to the provisions of § 4, 15 U.S.C. § 1054, or §§ 2(a)–(c), 15 U.S.C. §§ 1052(a)–(c).

One searches the language of the Lanham Act in vain to find any support for the offensive/defensive distinction applied by the Court of Appeals. The statute nowhere distinguishes between a registrant's offensive and defensive use of an incontestable mark. On the contrary, § 33(b)'s declaration that the registrant has an "exclusive right" to use the mark indicates that incontestable status may be used to enjoin infringement by others. A conclusion that such infringement cannot be enjoined renders meaningless the "exclusive right" recognized by the statute. Moreover, the language in three of the defenses enumerated in § 33(b) clearly contemplates the use of incontestability in infringement actions by plaintiffs. See §§ 33(b)(4)–(6), 15 U.S.C. §§ 1115(b)(4)–(6).

The language of the Lanham Act also refutes any conclusion that an incontestable mark may be challenged as merely descriptive. A mark that is merely descriptive of an applicant's goods or services is not registrable unless the mark has secondary meaning. Before a mark achieves incontestable status, registration provides prima facie evidence of the registrant's exclusive right to use the mark in commerce. § 33(a), 15 U.S.C. § 1115(a). The Lanham Act expressly provides that before a mark becomes incontestable an opposing party may prove any legal or equitable defense which might have been asserted if the mark had not been registered. *Ibid.* Thus, § 33(a) would have allowed respondent to challenge petitioner's mark as merely descriptive if the mark had not become incontestable. With respect to incontestable marks, however, § 33(b) provides that registration is *conclusive* evidence of the registrant's exclusive right to use the mark, subject to the conditions of § 15 and the seven defenses enumerated in § 33(b) itself. Mere descriptiveness is not recognized by either § 15 or § 33(b) as a basis for challenging an incontestable mark.

The Court of Appeals in discussing the offensive/defensive distinction observed that incontestability protects a registrant against cancellation of his mark. 718 F.2d, at 331. This observation is incorrect with respect to marks that become generic or which otherwise may be cancelled at any time pursuant to §§ 14(c) and (e). Moreover, as applied to marks that are merely descriptive, the approach of the Court of Appeals makes incontestable status superfluous. Without regard to its incontestable status, a mark that has been registered five years is protected from cancellation except on the grounds stated in §§ 14(c) and (e). Pursuant to § 14, a mark may be cancelled on the grounds that it is merely descriptive only if the petition to cancel is filed within five years of the date of registration. § 14(a), 15 U.S.C. § 1064(a). The approach adopted by the Court of Appeals implies that incontestability adds nothing to the protections against cancellation already provided in § 14. The decision below not only lacks support in the words of the statute, but it effectively emasculates § 33(b) under the circumstances of this case.

III

*   *   *

These arguments are unpersuasive. Representative Lanham's remarks, if read in context, clearly refer to the effect of the *defenses* enumerated in § 33(b). There is no question that the Lanham Act altered existing law concerning trademark rights in several respects. For example, § 22, 15 U.S.C. § 1072, provides for constructive notice of registration and modifies the common-law rule that allowed acquisition of concurrent rights by users in distinct geographic areas if the subsequent user adopted the mark without knowledge of prior use. See

Hanover Star Milling Co. v. Metcalf, 240 U.S. 403, 415–416, 36 S.Ct. 357, 361, 60 L.Ed.2d 713 (1916) (describing pre-Lanham Act law). Similarly, § 14 cuts off certain grounds for cancellation five years after registration and thereby modifies the previous rule that the validity of a trademark could be attacked at any time. See *White House Milk Products Co. v. Dwinell-Wright Co.,* 111 F.2d 490 (CCPA 1940). Most significantly, Representative Lanham himself observed that incontestability was one of "the valuable new rights created by the act." 92 Cong.Rec. 7524 (1946).

* * *

The dissent echoes arguments made by opponents of the Lanham Act that the incontestable status of a descriptive mark might take from the public domain language that is merely descriptive. *Post,* at 672–673. As we have explained, Congress has already addressed concerns to prevent the "commercial monopolization," *post,* at 672, of descriptive language. The Lanham Act allows a mark to be challenged at any time if it becomes generic, and, under certain circumstances, permits the non-trademark use of descriptive terms contained in an incontestable mark. Finally, if "monopolization" of an incontestable mark threatens economic competition, § 33(b)(7), 15 U.S.C. § 1115(b)(7), provides a defense on the grounds that the mark is being used to violate federal antitrust laws. At bottom, the dissent simply disagrees with the balance struck by Congress in determining the protection to be given to incontestable marks.

IV

Respondent argues that the decision by the Court of Appeals should be upheld because trademark registrations are issued by the Patent Office after an *ex parte* proceeding and generally without inquiry into the merits of an application. This argument also unravels upon close examination. The facts of this case belie the suggestion that registration is virtually automatic. The Patent Office initially denied petitioner's application because the examiner considered the mark to be merely descriptive. Petitioner sought reconsideration and successfully persuaded the Patent Office that its mark was registrable.

More generally, respondent is simply wrong to suggest that third parties do not have an opportunity to challenge applications for trademark registration. If the Patent Office examiner determines that an applicant appears to be entitled to registration, the mark is published in the Official Gazette. § 12(a), 15 U.S.C. § 1062(a). Within 30 days of publication, any person who believes that he would be damaged by registration of the mark may file an opposition. § 13, 15 U.S.C. § 1063. Registration of a mark provides constructive notice throughout the United States of the registrant's claim to ownership. § 22, 15 U.S.C. § 1072. Within five years of registration, any person who believes that he is or will be damaged by registration may seek to cancel a mark. § 14(a), 15 U.S.C. § 1064(a). A mark may be cancelled at any time for certain specified grounds, including that it was obtained fraudulently or has become generic.   § 14(c), 15 U.S.C. § 1064(c).

* * *

JUSTICE STEVENS, dissenting.

* * *

Note

The trademark statute (Sec. 29) permits designation of a registered mark with the symbol ® or the words "Registered in U.S. Patent Office" as notice to the public.   Failure to so mark may cause a loss of profits and damages which may have accrued prior to actual notice.   On the other hand, false marking can result in penalties to a plaintiff as evidenced by the following:

"At the hearing plaintiff placed in evidence a number of exhibits. Exhibits 2, 3, 7, 9, 10 and 11 all contain only a purported trade or service mark, consisting of a running red fox with the words 'Fox Photo' imprinted thereon.   Additionally, the trademark displayed in each of these instances contained the letter 'R' surrounded by a circle, which normally and routinely is used to signify the existence of a valid trademark by the party using the trademark.   I find that plaintiff does not own a trademark for a running red fox with the words 'Fox Photo' imprinted thereon, and that plaintiff has no legal right whatsoever to represent to the public at large, by use of the letter 'R' within a circle, that it does own a valid trademark. It is a familiar principle of equity that a party seeking injunctive relief must come into court with clean hands, and I rule that the illegal use of this trademark by plaintiff by and of itself is a violation of the clean hands doctrine of such a serious magnitude as to disqualify plaintiff from obtaining injunctive relief in this court.   New York, New Haven & Hartford R R Co., et al. v. Pierce Coach Lines, Inc., et al., 281 Mass. 479."   Fox-Stanley Photo Products, Inc. v. Otaguro, 339 F.Supp. 1293, 174 USPQ 257 (D.Mass.1972).

E.   MARKS SUBJECT TO PROTECTION

Very frequently an attorney is in a position to assist in the selection of a trademark.   This requires imagination and a use of the basic doctrine that a "strong" mark consists of a word which is fanciful, invented, or arbitrary such as Kodak, Oxydol, Dreft while a "weak" mark is characterized as a mark which is essentially descriptive or in common use by others.   There are several organizations in the United States and in some foreign countries which specialize in searching trademarks and tradenames.   For a reasonably nominal sum in comparison with investments in labels, cartons, and advertising, there can be a determination with respect to previous federal or state registrations of possible conflicting marks and also a check of pertinent listings in trade and telephone books.

Once a trademark has been used in connection with the goods, it can be registered in the Patent and Trademark Office and also in the various States. Federal registration provides prima facie evidence of the validity of the registration (15 U.S.C.A. § 1057b), constructive notice of the registrant's claim of ownership (15 U.S.C.A. § 1072), and the right to bring suit for damages and injunction in the federal courts (15 U.S.C.A. §§ 1116, 1117, 1121).

The basic registration section of Title 15 relating to trademarks (15 U.S.C.A. § 1052) reads:

No trademark by which the goods of the applicant may be distinguished from the goods of others shall be refused registration on the principal register on account of its nature unless it—

(a) consists of or comprises immoral, deceptive, or scandalous matter; or matter which may disparage or falsely suggest a connection with persons, living or dead, institutions, beliefs, or national symbols, or bring them into contempt, or disrepute;

(b) consists of or comprises the flag or coat of arms or other insignia of the United States, or of any State or municipality, or of any foreign nation, or any simulation thereof;

(c) consists of or comprises a name, portrait, or signature identifying a particular living individual except by his written consent, or the name, signature, or portrait of a deceased President of the United States during the life of his widow, if any, except by the written consent of the widow;

(d) consists of or comprises a mark which so resembles a mark registered in the Patent and Trademark Office or a mark or trade name previously used in the United States by another and not abandoned, as to be likely, when applied to the goods of the applicant, to cause confusion, or to cause mistake, or to deceive: * * *

(e) consists of a mark which, (1) when applied to the goods of the applicant is merely descriptive or deceptively misdescriptive of them, or (2) when applied to the goods of the applicant is primarily geographically descriptive or deceptively misdescriptive of them, except as indications of regional origin may be registrable under section 4 hereof, or (3) is primarily merely a surname;

(f) except as expressly excluded in paragraphs (a), (b), (c), and (d) of this section, nothing herein shall prevent the registration of a mark used by the applicant which has become distinctive of the applicant's goods in commerce. The Commissioner may accept as prima facie evidence that the mark has become distinctive, as applied to the applicant's goods in commerce, proof of substantially exclusive and continuous use thereof as a mark by the applicant in commerce for the 5 years next preceding the date of the filing of the application for its registration (Amended Oct. 9, 1962, 76 Stat. 769). (Jan. 2, 1975, 88 Stat. 1949).

ABERCROMBIE & FITCH COMPANY v. HUNTING WORLD, INCORPORATED

United States Court of Appeals, Second Circuit, 1976.
537 F.2d 4, 189 USPQ 759.

FRIENDLY, CIRCUIT JUDGE:

This action in the District Court for the Southern District of New York by Abercrombie & Fitch Company (A & F), owner of well-known stores at Madison Avenue and 45th Street in New York City and seven places in other states, against Hunting World, Incorporated (HW), operator of a competing store on East 53rd Street, is for infringement of some of A & F's registered trademarks using the word 'Safari'. It has had a long and, for A & F, an unhappy history. On this appeal from a judgment which not only dismissed the complaint but canceled all of A & F's 'Safari' registrations, including several that were not in suit, we relieve A & F of some of its unhappiness but not of all.

*   *   *

II.

It will be useful at the outset to restate some basic principles of trademark law, which, although they should be familiar, tend to become lost in a welter of adjectives.

The cases, and in some instances the Lanham Act, identify four different categories of terms with respect to trademark protection. Arrayed in an ascending order which roughly reflects their eligibility to trademark status and the degree of protection accorded, these classes are (1) generic, (2) descriptive, (3) suggestive, and (4) arbitrary or fanciful. The lines of demarcation, however, are not always bright. Moreover, the difficulties are compounded because a term that is in one category for a particular product may be in quite a different one for another,[6] because a term may shift from one category to another in light of differences in usage through time,[7] because a term may have one meaning to one group of users and a different one to others,[8] and because the same term may be put to different uses with respect to a single product.[9] In various ways, all of these complications are involved in the instant case.

A generic term is one that refers, or has come to be understood as referring, to the genus of which the particular product is a species. At common law neither those terms which were generic nor those which were merely descriptive could become valid trademarks, see *Delaware & Hudson Canal Co. v. Clark,* 80 U.S. (13 Wall.) 311, 323, 20 L.Ed. 581

---

6. To take a familiar example "Ivory" would be generic when used to describe a product made from the tusks of elephants but arbitrary as applied to soap.

7. See, e.g., *Haughton Elevator Co. v. Seeberger,* 85 U.S.P.Q. 80 (1950), in which the coined word 'Escalator', originally fan-

ciful, or at the very least suggestive, was held to have become generic.

8. See, e.g., *Bayer Co. v. United Drug Co.,* 272 F. 505 (S.D.N.Y.1921).

9. See 15 U.S.C. § 1115(b)(4).

(1872) ("Nor can a generic name, or a name merely descriptive of an article or its qualities, ingredients, or characteristics, be employed as a trademark and the exclusive use of it be entitled to legal protection"). The same was true under the Trademark Act of 1905, *Standard Paint Co. v. Trinidad Asphalt Mfg. Co.*, 220 U.S. 446, 31 S.Ct. 456, 55 L.Ed. 536 (1911), except for marks which had been the subject of exclusive use for ten years prior to its enactment. 33 Stat. 726. While, as we shall see, p. 10 infra, the Lanham Act makes an important exception with respect to those merely descriptive terms which have acquired secondary meaning, see § 2(f), 15 U.S.C. § 1052(f), it offers no such exception for generic marks. The Act provides for the cancellation of a registered mark if at any time it "becomes the common descriptive name of an article or substance," § 14(c). This means that even proof of secondary meaning, by virtue of which some "merely descriptive" marks may be registered, cannot transform a generic term into a subject for trademark. As explained in *J. Kohnstam, Ltd. v. Louis Marx and Company,* 280 F.2d 437, 440, 47 CCPA 1080 (1960), no matter how much money and effort the user of a generic term has poured into promoting the sale of its merchandise and what success it has achieved in securing public identification, it cannot deprive competing manufacturers of the product of the right to call an article by its name. See, accord, *Application of Preformed Line Products Co.*, 323 F.2d 1007, 51 CCPA 775 (1963); *Weiss Noodle Co. v. Golden Cracknel and Specialty Co.*, 290 F.2d 845, 48 CCPA 1004 (1961); *Application of Searle & Co.*, 360 F.2d 650, 53 CCPA 1192 (1966). We have recently had occasion to apply this doctrine of the impossibility of achieving trademark protection for a generic term, *CES Publishing Corp. v. St. Regis Publications, Inc.*, 531 F.2d 11 (1975). The pervasiveness of the principle is illustrated by a series of well known cases holding that when a suggestive or fanciful term has become generic as a result of a manufacturer's own advertising efforts, trademark protection will be denied save for those markets where the term still has not become generic and a secondary meaning has been shown to continue. *Bayer Co. v. United Drug Co.*, 272 F. 505 (2 Cir. 1921) (L. Hand, D.J.); *DuPont Cellophane Co. v. Waxed Products Co.*, 85 F.2d 75 (2 Cir.) (A.N. Hand, C.J.), *cert. denied,* 299 U.S. 601, 57 S.Ct. 194, 81 L.Ed. 443 (1936); *King-Seeley Thermos Co. v. Aladdin Industries, Inc.*, 321 F.2d 577 (2 Cir.1963). A term may thus be generic in one market and descriptive or suggestive or fanciful in another.

The term which is descriptive but not generic [11] stands on a better basis. Although § 2(e) of the Lanham Act, 15 U.S.C. § 1052, forbids the

---

11. See, e.g., *W.E. Bassett Co. v. Revlon, Inc.*, 435 F.2d 656 (2 Cir.1970). A commentator has illuminated the distinction with an example of the "Deep Bowl Spoon":

"Deep Bowl" identifies a significant characteristic of the article. It is "merely descriptive" of the goods, because it informs one that they are deep in the bowl portion * * *. It is not, however, "the common descriptive name" of the article [since] the implement is not a deep bowl, it is a spoon * * *. "Spoon" is not merely descriptive of the article—it identifies the article—[and therefore] the term is generic.

Fletcher, Actual Confusion as to Incontestability of Descriptive Marks, 64 Trademark Rep. 252, 260 (1974). On the other hand, registration of a mark which, when applied to the goods of the applicant, is "merely descriptive," § 2(f) removes a considerable part of the sting by providing that "except as expressly excluded in paragraphs (a)–(d) of this section, nothing in this chapter shall prevent the registration of a mark used by the applicant which has become distinctive of the applicant's goods in commerce" and that the Commissioner may accept, as prima facie evidence that the mark has become distinctive, proof of substantially exclusive and continuous use of the mark applied to the applicant's goods for five years preceding the application. As indicated in the cases cited in the discussion of the unregistrability of generic terms, "common descriptive name," as used in §§ 14(c) and 15(4), refers to generic terms applied to products and not to terms that are "merely descriptive." In the former case any claim to an exclusive right must be denied since this in effect would confer a monopoly not only of the mark but of the product by rendering a competitor unable effectively to name what it was endeavoring to sell. In the latter case the law strikes the balance, with respect to registration, between the hardships to a competitor in hampering the use of an appropriate word and those to the owner who, having invested money and energy to endow a word with the good will adhering to his enterprise, would be deprived of the fruits of his efforts.

The category of "suggestive" marks was spawned by the felt need to accord protection to marks that were neither exactly descriptive on the one hand nor truly fanciful on the other—a need that was particularly acute because of the bar in the Trademark Act of 1905, 33 Stat. 724, 726, (with an exceedingly limited exception noted above) on the registration of merely descriptive marks regardless of proof of secondary meaning. See *Orange Crush Co. v. California Crushed Fruit Co.*, 54 U.S.App.D.C. 313, 297 F. 892 (1924). Having created the category the courts have had great difficulty in defining it. Judge Learned Hand made the not very helpful statement:

> It is quite impossible to get any rule out of the cases beyond this: That the validity of the mark ends where suggestion ends and description begins.

Franklin Knitting Mills, Inc. v. Fashionit Sweater Mills, Inc., 297 F. 247, 248 (2 Cir.1923), aff'd *per curiam*, 4 F.2d 1018 (2 Cir.1925)—a statement amply confirmed by comparing the list of terms held suggestive with those held merely descriptive in 3 Callmann, Unfair Competition, Trademarks and Monopolies § 71.2 (3d ed.). Another court has observed, somewhat more usefully, that:

> A term is suggestive if it requires imagination, thought and perception to reach a conclusion as to the nature of goods. A term is descriptive if it forthwith conveys an immediate idea of the ingredients, qualities or characteristics of the goods.

"Deep Bowl" would be generic as to a deep bowl.

Stix Products, Inc. v. United Merchants & Manufacturers Inc., 295 F.Supp. 479, 488 (S.D.N.Y.1968)—a formulation deriving from *General Shoe Corp. v. Rosen,* 111 F.2d 95, 98 (4 Cir.1940). Also useful is the approach taken by this court in *Aluminum Fabricating Co. of Pittsburgh v. Season-All Window Corp.,* 259 F.2d 314 (2 Cir.1958), that the reason for restricting the protection accorded descriptive terms, namely the undesirability of preventing an entrant from using a descriptive term for his product, is much less forceful when the trademark is a suggestive word since, as Judge Lumbard wrote, 259 F.2d at 317:

> The English language has a wealth of synonyms and related words with which to describe the qualities which manufacturers may wish to claim for their products and the ingenuity of the public relations profession supplies new words and slogans as they are needed.

If a term is suggestive, it is entitled to registration without proof of secondary meaning. Moreover, as held in the *Season-All* case, the decision of the Patent Office to register a mark without requiring proof of secondary meaning affords a rebuttable presumption that the mark is suggestive or arbitrary or fanciful rather than merely descriptive.

It need hardly be added that fanciful or arbitrary terms [12] enjoy all the rights accorded to suggestive terms as marks—without the need of debating whether the term is "merely descriptive" and with ease of establishing infringement.

In the light of these principles we must proceed to a decision of this case.

III.

We turn first to an analysis of A & F's trademarks to determine the scope of protection to which they are entitled. We have reached the following conclusions: (1) applied to specific types of clothing 'safari' has become a generic term and 'mini-safari' may be used for a smaller brim hat; (2) 'safari' has not, however, become a generic term for boots or shoes; it is either "suggestive" or "merely descriptive" and is a valid trademark even if "merely descriptive" since it has become incontestable under the Lanham Act; but (3) in light of the justified finding below that 'Camel Safari,' 'Hippo Safari' and 'Safari Chukka' were devoted by HW to a purely descriptive use on its boots, HW has a defense against a charge of infringement with respect to these on the basis of "fair use." We now discuss how we have reached these conclusions.

* * *

12. As terms of art, the distinctions between suggestive terms and fanciful or arbitrary terms may seem needlessly artificial. Of course, a common word may be used in a fanciful sense; indeed one might say that only a common word can be so used, since a coined word cannot first be put to a bizarre use. Nevertheless, the term "fanciful", as a classifying concept, is usually applied to words invented solely for their use as trademarks. When the same legal consequences attach to a common word, i.e., when it is applied in an unfamiliar way, the use is called "arbitrary."

IV.

We find much greater difficulty in the court's broad invalidation of A & F's trademark registrations. Section 37 of the Lanham Act, 15 U.S.C. § 1119, provides authority for the court to cancel those registrations of any party to an action involving a registered mark. The cases cited above, p. 13, establish that when a term becomes the generic name of the product to which it is applied, grounds for cancellation exist. The relevant registrations of that sort are Nos. 358,781 and 703,279. Although No. 358,751 dates back to July 20, 1938, and No. 703,279 was registered on August 23, 1960, and an affidavit under § 15(3), 15 U.S.C. § 1065(3), was filed on October 13, 1965, cancellation may be decreed at any time if the registered mark has become "the common descriptive name of an article or substance," § 14(c), see also § 15(4), 15 U.S.C. §§ 1064(c) and 1065(4). The whole of Registration No. 358,781 thus was properly canceled. With respect to Registration No. 703,279 only a part has become generic and cancellation on that ground should be correspondingly limited. Such partial cancellation, specifically recognized by § 37, accords with the rationale by which a court is authorized to cancel a registration, viz, to "rectify" the register by conforming it to court judgments which often must be framed in something less than an all-or-nothing way.

* * *

COCA–COLA CO. v. SEVEN–UP CO.

United States Court of Customs and Patent Appeals, 1974.
497 F.2d 1351, 182 USPQ 207.

MARKEY, CHIEF JUDGE.

This is an appeal from the decision of the Trademark Trial and Appeal Board, 178 USPQ 309 (1973), adhered to on reconsideration, dismissing the opposition of appellant to the registration by appellee of THE UNCOLA for soft drinks. Appellant relied, inter alia, on registrations of its well-known mark COCA–COLA. We affirm.

The opinion of the board sets out the massive volume of use and advertising of COCA–COLA and THE UNCOLA. No question of priority of use is involved, appellant having begun use of its mark more than three-quarters of a century prior to appellee's first use of the mark sought to be registered.

* * *

Appellant's second attack on the board's finding of secondary meaning is based on appellant's survey indication that the *public* uses THE UNCOLA infrequently in ordering appellee's product. The board correctly pointed out, however, that use by purchasers is not essential in establishing secondary meaning, particularly where a well-known mark, such as 7–UP, is available. We would add that many marks, including slogans and designs, are perfectly valid trademarks though their nature virtually precludes their use in ordering the goods with which they are associated. * * *

We see no need to determine the presence of secondary meaning herein. The word "secondary" in the phrase "secondary meaning" does not mean lesser in importance. Because a secondary meaning in this context is an acquired meaning, it is necessarily created later in time. It is created in a new environment, namely the marketplace, where its "secondary" meaning is of "primary" importance. The judicially developed concept of "secondary meaning," expressed in Section 2(f) as "has become distinctive," relates to a term which had earlier served only to describe or to locate geographically or as a surname. At that time such a term would not be registrable, in view of the prohibitions of Section 2(e). At some later time, the term may *become* distinctive of a seller's goods in commerce and, as such, become registrable under the provisions of Section 2(f). It is said that such a term has acquired a "secondary meaning," i.e., a "marketplace meaning," which is an indication of origin of the goods with which the term is associated in the market place. In the present case, THE UNCOLA has never served only to describe. From its origin, the mark was used only in connection with appellee's product to distinguish it (as to source) from the products of others. No question of "secondary meaning" arises in such a situation.

In summary, the record clearly establishes that THE UNCOLA was coined by appellee, has never been used by anyone else for any purpose and is not merely descriptive of soft drinks. The decision of the board must therefore be affirmed.

A.J. CANFIELD CO. v. VESS BEVERAGES, INC.

United States Court of Appeals, Seventh Circuit, 1986.
796 F.2d 903, 230 USPQ 441, 443.

[Excerpt Only].

A term is merely descriptive if it specifically describes a characteristic or an ingredient of a product. *Miller,* 561 F.2d at 79. By acquiring secondary meaning such a term can become a valid trademark. 15 U.S.C. § 1052(f); *Miller,* 561 F.2d at 79. *Abercrombie,* 537 F.2d at 10. A term acquires secondary meaning when the consumer associates it with the producer rather than the product. *Wesley-Jessen Div. of Shearing Corp. v. Bausch & Lomb, Inc.,* 698 F.2d 862 (7th Cir. 1983); *Harlequin Enterprises, Ltd. v. Gulf & Western Corp.,* 644 F.2d 946, 949 (2d Cir.1981). The focus is the attitude of the consuming public toward the designation. *Walt-West Enterprises, Inc. v. Gannett Co.,* 695 F.2d 1050, 1057 (7th Cir.1982) (primary significance of the term in the minds of the public is not the product but the producer).

APPLICATION OF SWIFT & CO.
United States Court of Customs and Patent Appeals, 1955.
42 CCPA 1048, 223 F.2d 950, 106 USPQ 286.

* * *

The Examiner-in-Chief was of the opinion that appellant's polka dot banding was merely the background ornamentation of its label and, as such, could not function as a technical trade-mark, citing In re Burgess Battery Co., 112 F.2d 820, 27 CCPA, Patents, 1297.

A specimen label (no colors shown) with the alleged mark thereon as actually used by appellant and the drawing accompanying the application for registration are reproduced herewith.

* * *

We think that in a trade-mark sense appellant's polka dot banding is an artistic and unique design or pattern which may be constituted a trade-mark "device" within the meaning of Section 45, supra, if it is used primarily to perform the office of a trade-mark and is, in fact, by virtue of any distinctiveness it may possess, capable of so doing.

[A6490]

[A6490]

In the case of In re Burgess Battery Co., supra [112 F.2d 822], the mark sought to be registered was for use on dry batteries and flash light cases and consisted of alternating black and white stripes, unrestricted as to number or length or as to the shape or size of area covered by the striping. The specimens accompanying the application showed the stripes applied entirely about the goods and packages by placing thereon labels upon which the striped design was printed. In holding such mark to be unregistrable, we said:

"We think it is apparent from the record that appellant's alleged trademark is a mere 'dress' which gives a distinctive external appearance to appellant's goods; that it is such distinctive appearance which is recognized by 'some' of the purchasing public as indicating appellant's goods; and that appellant's design is merely a colored label or dress of black and white alternating stripes, the office of which (design) is not to point out distinctly the origin or ownership of the articles to which the label is affixed. ∗ ∗ ∗" See also In re Burgess Battery Company, 142 F.2d 466, 31 CCPA, Patents, 1039.

∗ ∗ ∗

The Examiner-in-Chief also cited Campbell Soup Co. v. Armour & Co., 3 Cir., 175 F.2d 795, 798, as authority for denying registration to appellant's trademark. In that case, the Circuit Court of Appeals for the Third Circuit was called upon to consider whether the plaintiff had exclusive trade-mark rights to a red and white label used on food products. One portion of the label (substantially half) was white and the remainder red, the colors appearing on the label in the form of an endless band running around the entire container. After stating the well settled rule that trade-mark rights cannot be acquired in color alone, the court said:

"Plaintiffs cite to us a number of cases, however, in which various color combinations as trade-marks have been upheld. Here, too, the law is well settled. Color is a perfectly satisfactory element of a trademark if it is used in combination with a design in the form, for example, of a picture or a geometrical figure. The Barbasol case is typical [Barbasol Co. v. Jacobs, 7 Cir., 1947, 160 F.2d 336]. Here was a package using several colors but in a distinct and arbitrary design. The mere division of a label into two background colors, as in this case, is not, however, distinct or arbitrary, and the District Court so found.

"When we say that plaintiffs cannot have exclusive right to a trademark of a red and white label, we are by no means denying their right to acquire a trade-mark when the color is combined with other things in a distinctive design. ∗ ∗ ∗"

We think it is apparent that the legal principles in the above case have no application to the factual situation here. While as actually used the banding of appellant's design appears in red and the polka dots thereon imposed are in white. These colors act only in association or combination with a design which is in itself distinctive and arbitrary as applied to household cleanser. As indicated, we think appellant's polka dot banding design is a trade-mark "device" distinguishing its product from articles of like kind sold by others, and that it is so recognized by the public as a primary means of identification. That it is entitled to registration on the Principal Register is clear from Section 2 of the Trade-Mark Act of 1946, 15 U.S.C.A. § 1052, which provides:

"No trade-mark by which the goods of the applicant may be distinguished from the goods of others shall be refused registration on the principal register on account of its nature unless it—* * *."

* * *

APPLICATION OF SIMMONS CO.

United States Court of Customs and Patent Appeals, 1960.
47 CCPA 963, 278 F.2d 517, 126 USPQ 52.

WORLEY, CHIEF JUDGE. This appeal is from the decision of the Trademark Trial and Appeal Board of the United States Patent Office affirming the examiner's refusal to register appellant's alleged trademark for mattresses on the supplemental register.

As shown by the drawing of appellant's application, the mark comprises a series of horizontally spaced pairs of vertical rows of stitches which are applied on an outer vertical face of the mattress. The spacing between the pairs of rows of stitches is approximately six times the spacing between the rows of each pair.

As shown by the record, appellant has attempted, by advertising on a national scale, to cause the public to associate the stitches with its product. Typical advertisements contain the statement, "Look for the border with the vertical double stitch lines—it identifies the Beautyrest Mattress." Also of record are two affidavits, one by a mattress salesman and one by a purchaser, in which they state that they recognize the double stitch lines as identifying Beautyrest mattresses. There are two affidavits by an attorney associated with appellant's counsel, to the effect that five employees interviewed in a Chicago store recognized the double stitched border as identifying one of appellant's mattresses.

Appellant originally sought registration on the principal register, but was advised by the examiner that the proposed mark "at this time does not appear to distinguish the goods of applicant from similar goods of others." The examiner suggested that the application might be transferred to the supplemental register and that "the evidence submitted may support a holding that the mark is 'capable of distinguishing.'" However, when applicant transferred to the supplemental register, the same examiner refused registration on the ground that the mark was not capable of distinguishing appellant's goods in a trademark sense.

The board agreed with the examiner stating that

"The record fails to show that average purchasers recognize such stitching as a trademark or that they are in any way moved, by the stitching, to buy applicant's mattresses. It seems clear from the record that purchasers are moved by the trademark 'Beautyrest' to buy applicant's mattresses, and having decided on that brand, the stitching presented here for registration enables the salesmen to locate applicant's mattresses on the floor."

That statement appears to involve two misconceptions. In the first place, it is not the function of a trademark to "move" prospective purchasers to buy goods, but to identify and distinguish them from the goods of others. A trademark may or may not "move" purchasers to buy the goods.

Second, and of more importance here, the quoted statement suggests that a mark cannot be placed on the supplemental register unless it can be shown that the "average purchaser" recognizes it as a trademark. However, that is not the test set forth in the applicable statute (15 U.S.C. § 1091, 15 U.S.C.A. § 1091), which provides, with certain exceptions not pertinent here, that "All marks *capable of distinguishing* applicant's goods or services and not registrable on the principal register" may be registered on the supplemental register. The test is not whether the mark, when registration is sought, is actually recognized by the average purchaser, or is distinctive of the applicant's goods in commerce, but whether it is *capable of becoming* so. In fact a mark which has become distinctive of an applicant's goods, if not otherwise barred, is registrable on the principal register, hence is expressly barred from the supplemental register.

The board has not held that the mark is inherently functional or advanced any other specific reason why appellant's mark is *not* capable of distinguishing its goods from those of others, and we see none. So far as appears from the record, the double rows of stitching are quite distinct in appearance from the stitching on the mattresses of others, the attention of the public has been directed to this feature as distinctive of appellant's goods, and affidavits have been presented to the effect that they identify appellant's goods by such stitching. On the basis of such facts we cannot hold that the mark is *incapable* of distinguishing.

On the facts here we conclude that appellant is entitled to registration of its mark on the supplemental register. The decision appealed from is reversed.[a][b]

Reversed.

a. Stitching design in jockey shorts can serve as a trademark, In re Jockey Int'l, Inc., 192 USPQ 579, (TM Trial & Appeal Bd. 1976); "Levi's" pocket tab is a good trademark, Levi Strauss & Co. v. Blue Bell, Inc., 200 USPQ 434 (D.C.Cal.1978); Shape of guitar bowl registrable as non-functional feature, 201 USPQ 116 (P.O. Trial & Appeal Bd. 1978).

b. In connection with the trademark "Beer Nuts", the Circuit Court of Appeals of the Sixth Circuit has held that a picture of an overflowing stein of beer can be an infringement of the word mark, Beer Nuts, Inc. v. King Nut Co., 477 F.2d 326, 177 USPQ 609 (6th Cir.1973). The court concluded: It is well settled that words and their pictorial representation are treated the same in determining the likelihood of confusion between two marks. Shunk Mfg. Co. v. Tarrant Mfg. Co., 318 F.2d 328, 137 USPQ 881 (CCPA 1963); Pink Lady Corp. v. L.N. Renault & Sons, Inc., 265 F.2d 951, 121 USPQ 465 (CCPA 1959). As the picture in the present case is to be given the same effect as the word "beer", we conclude that the District Court's determination was correct.

Even as a trademark right is gained by use, it may also be lost by lack of use. If the use of a trademark is discontinued with an intention not to resume, the trademark rights immediately wither and die. The Lanham Trademark Act permits cancellation of a registration on an abandoned mark, Sec. 14 (15 U.S.C.A. § 1064c) and defines abandonment in Sec. 45 (15 U.S.C.A. § 1127) "when its use has been discontinued with intent not to resume." Trademark rights may also be lost when a mark becomes the common descriptive name of an article or substance. Such well-known marks as "Cellophane" and "Aspirin" have been so lost.[m] Owners of well-known trademarks maintain careful vigilance over uses of their marks by others to assure that the mark is not being used in a descriptive or generic sense.

The courts have also held that a "naked" license of a trademark, that is, a license with no provision for control of quality may have an adverse effect on a trademark.[n]

However, the Lanham Act of 1946 codifies a more general attitude that a license wherein provision is made to control quality will be valid and enforceable and will not detract from the value of the trademark to the original owner. See Section 45 (15 U.S.C.A. § 1127). Reliance upon the integrity of a licensee has been held to be sufficient in some cases.[o]

Can a trademark right be obtained in a product which has been or is the subject of a design patent? The Court of Customs and Patent Appeals in the case of In re Mogen David Wine Corporation, 328 F.2d 925, 140 USPQ 575 (CCPA 1964), indicated that protection could be obtained on a container by registration, but the Patent Office Trademark Trial and Appeal Board has refused registration on products which have been the subject of design protection.[p]

APPLICATION OF E.I. DUPONT DE NEMOURS & CO.

United States Court of Appeals Federal Circuit, 1973.
476 F.2d 1357, 1364, 177 USPQ 563, 569.

Decisional maxims like "the right to register follows the right to use," sometimes defended as "reflecting the realities of the market-

m. DuPont Cellophane Co. v. Waxed Products Co., 85 F.2d 75, 30 USPQ 332 (C.A.2, 1936); Bayer v. United Drug Co., 272 F. 505 (D.C.N.Y.1921); Nims, Unfair Competition and Trademarks, 4th Ed., Vol. 2, Pg. 1308; Callman, Unfair Competition, Trademarks, and Monopolies, Third Ed., Vol. 3, Sec. 79.1.

n. E.I. DuPont DeNemours & Co. v. Celanese Corp., 167 F.2d 484, 489, 77 USPQ 364 (CCPA 1948). See also: Nims, Unfair Competition and Trademarks, 4th Ed., Vol. 1, page 122; Callman Unfair Competition, Trademarks and Monopolies, Third Ed., Vol. 3, Sec. 98.3(c); Dawn Donut Co. v.

Hart's Food Stores, Inc., 267 F.2d 358, 366, 121 USPQ 430, 436 (2d Cir.1959).

o. Land O'Lakes Creameries, Inc. v. Oconomowoc Canning Co., 330 F.2d 667, 670; 141 USPQ 281, 283 (7th Cir.1964); Syntex Laboratories, Inc. v. Norwich Pharmacal Co., 315 F.Supp. 45, 166 USPQ 312, 320 (D.C.S.D.N.Y.1970) (aff'd 437 F.2d 566, 169 USPQ 1 (2d Cir.1971).

p. In re World's Finest Chocolate, Inc., 166 USPQ 63 (1970); In re Honeywell, 169 USPQ 619 (1971); See also Kellogg Co. v. National Biscuit Co., 305 U.S. 111, 59 S.Ct. 109, 83 L.Ed. 73 (1938).

place," founder on their non-universality of application and the existence of Sec. 2(d). As attractive as that approach appears in In re National Distillers Products Co., 297 F.2d 941, 49 CCPA 854 (1962) and in the dissents in Ultra-White Company, Inc. v. Johnson Chemical Industries, Inc., 465 F.2d 891, 59 CCPA __ (1972), In re Avedis Zildjian Co., 394 F.2d 860, 55 CCPA 1126 (1968) and In re Continental Baking Co., 390 F.2d 747, 55 CCPA 967 (1968), it is recognized as a goal and that the phrase "as nearly as possible" must be read into it. Clearly, a right to use is not a right to confuse. The rights to use and register are not identical. Alfred Dunhill of London, Inc. v. Dunhill Tailored Clothes, Inc., 293 F.2d 685, 49 CCPA 730 (1961), cert. den., 369 U.S. 864, 82 S.Ct. 1030, 8 L.Ed.2d 84 (1962). Many marks, including those described in Sec. 2(a), (b), and (c), merely descriptive terms and those on labels defective under other laws (Rule 2.69), might all be used but not registered.

Although a naked right to use cannot always result in registration, the Act does intend, as we said above, that registration and use be coincident so far as possible. Post-Lanham Act opinions relating to Sec. 2(d) which maintain an iron curtain between the rights to use and register do not contribute to stability in the law. Treating those rights as totally divorced entities only perpetuates the "arbitrary provisions" respecting confusion that the Congress thought it was eliminating more than twenty-five years ago.

Whether offered in response to a right-to-use argument or against any of the evidentiary considerations listed above, citation of "the public interest" as a basis for refusal of registration is a bootless cry. We need add little to the shattering of that shibboleth in the concurring opinion in *National Distillers, supra,* and in the dissents in *Ultra-White, Zildjian* and *Continental Baking, supra.* Writers and scholars listed in those reported opinions have also shown the fallacy in the notion that the Patent Office is somehow guarding the public against confusion when it refuses a registration. After a likelihood of confusion is found (and the case thus decided) citation of the public interest is unnecessary.

The Patent Office does have a guardianship role under Sec. 2(d). It lies not in a negative, nay-saying of refusal alone, but in the protection of a mark by registering it and then rejecting later improper attempts, of which the registrant is unaware, to register it or a similar mark. Refusal to register cannot prevent confusion. At most, it *might* discourage further use. Refusal can, under certain circumstances, encourage potential confusion. Absence of a registration of RALLY for auto cleansers in the present case may, for example, lead others to adopt and use that or a similar mark for auto cleansers. Granting a registration will not produce confusion. Use alone can do that and neither we nor the Patent Office can grant or deny a right to use.

Presumably, everything the Patent Office and this court does is in the public interest. We find no place for "the guardianship of the public interest" as support for refusals to register under Sec. 2(d).

F. REMEDIES FOR TRADEMARK INFRINGEMENT

The federal Trademark Act of 1946 expressly provides that injunctions restraining trademark infringement may be granted according to the usual principles of equity (15 U.S.C.A. § 1116), and all infringing labels, signs, prints, packages, wrappers, receptacles, and the like and all plates, molds, or other means of producing them shall be delivered up and destroyed (15 U.S.C.A. § 1118). Furthermore, with respect to damages, 15 U.S.C.A. § 1117 provides:

> When a violation of any right of the registrant of a mark registered in the Patent Office shall have been established in any civil action arising under this Act, the plaintiff shall be entitled, subject to the provisions of sections 29 and 32 and subject to the principles of equity, to recover (1) defendant's profits, (2) any damages sustained by the plaintiff, and (3) the costs of the action. The court shall assess such profits and damages or cause the same to be assessed under its direction. In assessing profits the plaintiff shall be required to prove defendant's sales only; defendant must prove all elements of cost or deduction claimed. In assessing damages the court may enter judgment, according to the circumstances of the case, for any sum above the amount found as actual damages, not exceeding three times such amount. If the court shall find that the amount of the recovery based on profits is either inadequate or excessive the court may in its discretion enter judgment for such sum as the court shall find to be just, according to the circumstances of the case. Such sum in either of the above circumstances shall constitute compensation and not a penalty (Amended Oct. 9, 1962, 76 Stat. 769).

Two interesting trademark cases awarding millions of dollars in damages are Borg-Warner Corp. v. York-Shipley, Inc., 293 F.2d 88, 130 USPQ 294 (7th Cir.1961), on remand 136 USPQ 255 (1963), cert. denied 368 U.S. 939, 82 S.Ct. 381, 7 L.Ed.2d 338, 131 USPQ 498 (1961); and Big O Tire Dealers, Inc. v. Goodyear Tire & Rubber Co., 408 F.Supp. 1219, 189 USPQ 17 (D.C.Colo.1976), modified 561 F.2d 1365, 195 USPQ 417 (10th Cir.1977).

IN THE MATTER OF VUITTON ET FILS S.A.

United States Court of Appeals, Second Circuit, 1979.
606 F.2d 1.

PER CURIAM

*   *   *

On January 16, 1979, Vuitton filed a complaint in the disrict court seeking preliminary and permanent injunctions against the defendants, Dame Belt & Bag Co., Inc. and an individual named Morty Edelstein, and requesting damages. The gist of the complaint was that the defendants had infringed Vuitton's trademark and engaged in unfair competition by offering for sale luggage and handbags identical in appearance to those merchandised by Vuitton. Accompanying the complaint was an affidavit by Vuitton's attorney explaining why service of process had not been effected and requesting that an *ex parte* temporary restraining order be issued against the defendants under Fed.R.Civ.P. 65(b). Vuitton explains its need for an *ex parte* order in the following terms:

Vuitton's experience, based upon the 84 actions it has brought and the hundreds of other investigations it has made * * * has led to the conclusion that there exist various closely-knit distribution networks for counterfeit Vuitton products. In other words, there does not exist but one or two manufacturers of counterfeit merchandise, but rather many more, but a few of which have been identified to date.

Vuitton's experience in several of the earliest filed cases also taught it that once one member of this community of counterfeiters learned that he had been identified by Vuitton and was about to be enjoined from continuing his illegal enterprise, he would immediately transfer his inventory to another counterfeit seller, whose identity would be unknown to Vuitton.

* * * [I]n most Vuitton cases defendants maintain few, if any, records. The now too familiar refrain from a "caught counterfeiter" is "I bought only a few pieces from a man I never saw before and whom I have never seen again. All my business was in cash. I do not know how to locate the man from whom I bought and I cannot remember the identity of the persons to whom I sold."

* * * If after Vuitton has identified a counterfeiter with an inventory of fake merchandise, that counterfeiter is permitted to dispose of that merchandise with relative impunity *after* he learns of the imminence of litigation but *before* he is enjoined from doing so, Vuitton's trademark enforcement program will be stymied and the community of counterfeiters will be permitted to continue to play its "shell game" at great expense and damage to Vuitton.

A hearing on this application was held the next day, January 17, 1979, before Judge Brieant. Counsel for Vuitton explained: "All we seek this Court to do but for a few hours is to maintain the status quo, namely the defendants' inventory of counterfeit Vuitton merchandise." Vuitton also explained that, if notice of the pending litigation was required, "by the time this Court entered an order, most if not all of the merchandise would have been removed from the premises." Because Vuitton was capable of giving the defendants in this action notice, however, a matter readily conceded by Vuitton, the district court declined to grant the request. That decision is, of course, not appealable, *Austin v. Altman,* 332 F.2d 273, 275 (2d Cir.1964). The district court denied certification of the question presented by this case under 28 U.S.C. § 1292(b), and this petition followed. For the reasons that follow, we instruct the district court to grant an appropriate *ex parte* temporary restraining order pursuant to Fed.R.Civ.P. 65(b), narrow enough and of brief enough duration to protect the interests of the defendants, the precise terms of which shall be determined by the district court.

Rule 65(b) provides in relevant part as follows:

A temporary restraining order may be granted without written or oral notice to the adverse party or his attorney only if (1) it clearly appears from specific facts shown by affidavit or by the verified complaint that immediate and irreparable injury, loss, or damage will result to the applicant before the adverse party or his attorney can be heard in opposition, and (2) the applicant's attorney certifies to the court in writing the efforts, if any, which have been made to give the notice and the reasons supporting his claim that notice should not be required.

As explained by the Supreme Court in *Granny Goose Foods, Inc. v. Teamsters,* 415 U.S. 423, 438–39, 94 S.Ct. 1113, 39 L.Ed.2d 435 (1974), "[t]he stringent restrictions imposed * * * on the availability of *ex parte* temporary restraining orders reflect the fact that our entire jurisprudence runs counter to the notion of court action taken before reasonable notice and an opportunity to be heard has been granted both sides of a dispute. *Ex parte* temporary restraining orders are no doubt necessary in certain circumstances, * * * but under federal law they should be restricted to serving their underlying purpose of preserving the status quo and preventing irreparable harm just so long as is necessary to hold a hearing, and no longer."

* * *

Assuming that all of the other requirements of Rule 65 are met, the rule by its very terms allows for the issuance of an *ex parte* temporary restraining order when (1) the failure to issue it would result in "immediate and irreparable injury, loss, or damage" and (2) the applicant sufficiently demonstrates the reason that notice "should not be required." In a trademark infringement case such as this, a substantial likelihood of confusion constitutes, in and of itself, irreparable injury sufficient to satisfy the requirements of Rule 65(b)(1). *See P. Daussa Corp. v. Sutton Cosmetics (P.R.) Inc.,* 462 F.2d 134, 136 (2d Cir. 1972); *Robert Stigwood Group Ltd. v. Sperber,* 457 F.2d 50, 55 (2d Cir. 1972); *Omega Importing Corp. v. Petri-Kine Camera Co.,* 451 F.2d 1190, 1195 (2d Cir.1971); *Miller Brewing Co. v. Carling O'Keefe Breweries,* 452 F.Supp. 429, 437–38 (W.D.N.Y.1978). Here, we believe that such a likelihood of product confusion exists. The allegedly counterfeit Vuitton merchandise is virtually identical to the genuine items. Indeed, the very purpose of the individuals marketing the cheaper items is to confuse the buying public into believing it is buying the true article.

We also believe that Vuitton has demonstrated sufficiently why notice should not be required in a case such as this one. If notice is required, that notice all too often appears to serve only to render fruitless further prosecution of the action. This is precisely contrary to the normal and intended role of "notice," and it is surely not what the authors of the rule either anticipated or intended.

Accordingly, we hold that, when a proper showing is made, such as was made in this case, and when the rule is otherwise complied with, a plaintiff is entitled to have issued an *ex parte* temporary restraining order. Such an order should be narrow in scope and brief in its duration. The petition is granted.

UNITED STATES v. BAKER

United States Court of Appeals, Fifth Circuit, 1986.
807 F.2d 427, 1 USPQ2d 1485.

REAVLEY, CIRCUIT JUDGE.

Paul Baker appeals his conviction for trafficking in counterfeit goods, claiming that an element of the offense is knowledge of the criminality of the conduct and that the jury should have been so charged. We reject his contention and affirm his conviction.

I

Prior to 1984 trademark counterfeiting was addressed by the civil penalties found in the Lanham Act, 15 U.S.C. §§ 1051–1127. In 1984, however, Congress determined that "penalties under [the Lanham] Act have been too small, and too infrequently imposed, to deter counterfeiting significantly." S.Rep. No. 526, 98 Cong., 2d Sess. 5 (1984), *reprinted in* 1984 U.S.Code Cong. & Ad.News 3182, 3627, 3631. Accordingly, Congress enacted the Trademark Counterfeiting Act of 1984, Pub.L. No. 98–473, tit. 11, chap. XV, 98 Stat. 2178, criminalizing much of the conduct that formerly had been subject only to civil penalties. The statute subjects to criminal penalties anyone who

> intentionally traffics or attempts to traffic in goods or services and knowingly uses a counterfeit mark on or in connection with such goods or services.

Id. § 1502(a) (codified at 18 U.S.C. § 2320).

Paul Baker was convicted under this new statute for dealing in counterfeit watches. He does not dispute that he intentionally dealt in the watches. He also admits that he knew the "Rolex" watches he sold were counterfeit. His contention is that the statute requires that he act with knowledge that his conduct is criminal. He asserts that he did not know trafficking in counterfeit goods is criminal and that he would not have done so had he known he was committing a crime.

* * *

Although this is a case of first impression as to this statute, the underlying legal principles are well established. "The definition of the elements of a criminal offense is entrusted to the legislature, particularly in the case of federal crimes, which are solely creatures of statute." *Liparota v. United States,* 471 U.S. 419, 105 S.Ct. 2084, 2087, 85 L.Ed.2d 434 (1985). Thus our job on this appeal is to determine what Congress intended when it enacted the statute under which Baker was convicted. Both the language of the statute and the legislative history lead to the inescapable conclusion that Baker need not have known his conduct was a crime.

The statute clearly sets out the elements of the crime and the mental state required for each element. The defendant must intentionally deal in goods and he must knowingly use a counterfeit mark in connection with those goods. There is no ambiguity in this language and nothing in the statute suggests that any other mental state is required for conviction. The plain language of the statute—"the most reliable evidence of its intent," *United States v. Turkette,* 452 U.S. 576, 593, 101 S.Ct. 2524, 2534, 69 L.Ed.2d 246 (1981)—thus counsels us to reject Baker's position. As we have earlier stated, "we will not presume from congressional silence that Congress intended to make knowledge a prerequisite to violating the statutory provision." *United States v. Schmitt,* 748 F.2d 249, 252 (5th Cir.1984), *cert. denied,* 471 U.S. 1104, 105 S.Ct. 2333, 85 L.Ed.2d 850 (1985).

*   *   *

It is not surprising that Congress would allow conviction of one who knows that he is selling bogus "Rolex" watches even though he does not know his conduct is punishable as a crime. While it is true that "the general principle that ignorance or mistake of law is no excuse is usually greatly overstated" (American Law Institute, Model Penal Code § 2.02 comment 131 (Tent. Draft no. 4 1955)), the principle continues to be valid to the extent that ordinarily "the criminal law does not require knowledge that an act is illegal, wrong, or blameworthy." *United States v. Freed,* 401 U.S. 601, 612, 91 S.Ct. 1112, 1119, 28 L.Ed.2d 356 (1971) (Brennan, J., concurring). Baker's claim is merely that, even though he had the mental states required by the face of the statute, he should not be convicted because he did not know that Congress had passed a statute criminalizing his conduct. This clearly is not the law. A defendant cannot "avoid prosecution by simply claiming that he had not brushed up on the law." *Hamling v. United States,* 418 U.S. 87, 123, 94 S.Ct. 2887, 2911, 41 L.Ed.2d 590 (1974).

*   *   *

Notes

1. "Proposed subsection 18 U.S.C. § 2320(d)(1)(A)(iii) states that a 'counterfeit mark' must be one the use of which is likely 'to cause confusion, to cause mistake, or to deceive.' This is the key phrase in the remedial section of the Lanham Act, 15 U.S.C. § 1114, and its inclusion here is intended to ensure that no conduct will be criminalized by this act that does not constitute trademark infringement under the Lanham Act. As a practical matter, however, this element should be easily satisfied if the other elements of a 'counterfeit mark' have been proven—since a counterfeit mark is the most egregious example of a mark that is likely to cause confusion." *Cong.Rec.* H12878 (daily ed. Oct. 10, 1984).

2. Coalition to Preserve the Integrity of American Trademarks v. United States, 790 F.2d 903, 904, 907–908, 229 USPQ 641, 644 (D.C.Cir. 1986), cert. granted 33 P.T.C.J. (No. 86–675 Dec. 8, 1986):

This case concerns the validity of regulations issued by the U.S. Customs Service permitting the importation of so-called "grey-market goods" in certain instances. These are goods manufactured abroad bearing legitimate foreign trademarks that are identical to American trademarks.

* * *

We turn, then, to the appellants' challenge to the Customs Service's failure to exclude all grey-market goods. The appellants claim that the Customs regulations permitting the importation of such goods where the American and foreign trademarks are owned by the same or related entities, or where the American trademark owner has authorized the use of the trademark, see 19 C.F.R. § 133.21(c)(1)–(3) (1985), are contrary to the statutes they purport to implement, Section 526 of the Tariff Act of 1930 and Section 42 of the Lanham Trade-Mark Act of 1946. We conclude that the regulations simply cannot be squared with Section 526 and are thus invalid.

* * *

Section 526(a) provides:

Except as provided in subsection (d) of this section, it shall be unlawful to import into the United States any merchandise of foreign manufacture if such merchandise, or the label, sign, print, package, wrapper, or receptacle, bears a trademark owned by a citizen of, or by a corporation or association created or organized within, the United States, and registered in the Patent and Trademark Office by a person domiciled in the United States, * * * and if a copy of the certificate of registration of such trademark is filed with the Secretary of the Treasury, * * * unless written consent of the owner of such trademark is produced at the time of making entry.

19 U.S.C. § 1526(a) (1982).

Section 526 does not, on its face, admit of any exceptions based upon the relationship of the American and foreign trademark owners or upon whether the American owner has authorized the use of the trademark abroad.

In accord: Premier Dental Products Co. v. Darby Dental Supply Co., Inc., 794 F.2d 850, 230 USPQ 233 (3d Cir.1986). Contra: Olympus Corp. v. United States, 792 F.2d 315, 230 USPQ 123 (2d Cir.1986); United States v. Eighty-Nine Bottles of "Eau de Joy," 797 F.2d 767, 230 USPQ 775 (9th Cir. 1986). See Also, Original Appalachian Artworks, Inc. v. Granada Electronics, Inc., 816 F.2d 68, 2 USPQ2d 1343 (2d Cir.1987); Coggio et al., "The History and Present Status of Gray Goods," 75 T.M.R. 433 (1985).

3. On application of the private civil-damage provisions of the Racketeer Influenced and Corrupt Organizations (RICO) Act, 18 U.S.C.A. § 1946, to trademark actions, see Ford Motor Co. v. B. & H. Supply, Inc., 646 F.Supp. 975 (D.Minn.1986); Cooley, "RICO: Treble Damages and Attorney Fees in Trademark Counterfeiting Actions," 73 T.M.R. 476 (1983).

4. San Francisco Arts & Athletics, Inc. v. United States Olympic Committee, 55 U.S.L.W. 5061 (1987) discusses the Committee's rights under the 1978 Amateur Sports Act (36 U.S.C.A. § 380) in the word "Olympic".

G. SECTION 43(a) OF THE LANHAM ACT OF 1946

The Lanham Act of 1946 constituted a complete revision of the Federal Trademark Statutes and supplanted all previous federal legislation relating to trademarks. Section 43(a) of this Act deals with false descriptions or representations as to goods in interstate commerce. The section was not immediately appreciated by the Patent and Trademark Bar but, in 1954, Judge Hastie of the Third Circuit Court of Appeals pointed out (L'Aiglon Apparel, Inc. v. Lana Lobell, Inc., 214 F.2d 649, 102 USPQ 94 (3rd Cir.1954)) that this section of the statute was not merely a codification of existing case law but was a definition of a statutory civil wrong. He stated:

> But however similar to or different from pre-existing law, here is a provision of a federal statute which, with clarity and precision adequate for judicial administration, creates and defines rights and duties and provides for their vindication in the federal courts. For illuminating discussions of Section 43(a) and its relation to precedent law, see Callman, False Advertising as a Competitive Tort, 1948, 48 Col.L.Rev. 876, 877–886; Bunn, The National Law of Unfair Competition, 1949, 62 Harv.L.Rev. 987, 998–1000.

The following cases are illustrative of the developing law relative to Section 43(a).

FRISCH'S RESTAURANTS, INC. v. ELBY'S BIG BOY

United States Court of Appeals, Sixth Circuit, 1982.
670 F.2d 642, 214 USPQ 15, cert. denied 459 U.S. 916, 74 L.Ed.2d 182, 103 S.Ct. 231 (1982).

BAILEY BROWN, CIRCUIT JUDGE.

* * *

Section 43(a) of the Lanham Act, 15 U.S.C. § 1125(a) (1976), provides:

> Any person who shall * * * use in connection with any goods or services * * * a false designation of origin, or any false description or representation, including words or other symbols tending falsely to describe or represent the same, and shall cause such goods or services to enter into commerce * * * shall be liable to a civil action by any person doing business in the locality falsely indicated as that of origin or in the region in which said locality is situated, or by any person who believes that he is or is likely to be damaged by the use of any such false description or representation.

The intent of the Lanham Act is set forth in § 45 thereof, 15 U.S.C. § 1127 (1976):

> The intent of this chapter is to regulate commerce within the control of Congress by making actionable the deceptive and misleading use of marks in such commerce * * * [and] to protect persons engaged in such commerce against unfair competition * * *.

It has been suggested that § 43(a) of the Lanham Act "created a *sui generis* federal statutory cause of action for 'false representation,'" *Chevron Chemical Co. v. Voluntary Purchasing Groups, Inc.*, 659 F.2d 695, 702 (5th Cir.1981). The Fifth Circuit also concluded that "§ 43(a) proscribes not only what had been considered 'false advertising' but also what had been differentiated as 'unfair competition.'" *Id.* In addition, the *Chevron Chemical* court described the distinctions between these two concepts:

> In sum, the essential misrepresentation in "false advertising," which we have noted forms the basis of the "false representation" leg of § 43(a), is fundamentally different from the essential misrepresentation in "unfair competition": in the former case, the defendant makes no secret of the origin of the goods in himself, but merely misrepresents certain qualities or characteristics that his goods may or may not have; in the latter case, the defendant misrepresents his goods to be those of another.

Id. at 701 (footnote omitted).

It is undisputed that Elby's has a right to use the Big Boy trademark in connection with its West Virginia operations; indeed, it has an obligation to promote the Big Boy trademark in the panhandle of West Virginia under its licensing agreement with Marriott. It is also undisputed that the Ohio Elby's restaurants have no right to use the Big Boy trademark. Frisch's contends that the Ohio Elby's restaurants, through their participation in Elby's West Virginia advertisements which have substantial exposure in eastern Ohio, are improperly using the Big Boy trademark to promote their products, thereby creating a "false designation of origin" or a "false description or representation" of their goods as being sponsored by the Big Boy organization in the minds of Ohio consumers in violation of § 43(a).

We conclude that Frisch's contentions are properly within the scope of § 43(a) of the Lanham Act. Frisch's primary concern is that Ohio consumers will assume that all Elby's restaurants, including the Ohio Elby's, sell food which is sponsored by or originates from the "Big Boy" chain of restaurants. This court previously concluded that false representations about the "origin of source or manufacture" of goods are prohibited by the "false designation of origin" clause of § 43(a). *Federal-Mogul-Bower Bearings, Inc. v. Azoff*, 313 F.2d 405, 408 (6th Cir. 1963). "[F]alse representations of the source of a product constitute the common-law tort of 'unfair competition,' or, as it is otherwise known, 'passing off.'" *Chevron Chemical Co., supra,* at 701.[3] Passing off

---

3. The Fifth Circuit has tied passing off to the "false description or representation" strand of § 43(a), contending that a "false designation of origin" refers only to misrepresentations of geographic origin and not manufacture or source origin. *Chevron Chemical, supra* at 700. However, this court held that passing off can be considered a "false designation of origin." *Feder-* *al-Mogul-Bower Bearings, supra* at 408. Nevertheless, whether characterized as a "false description or representation" or a "false designation of origin," there is no disagreement that § 43(a) would apply to prohibit an attempt by Elby's to pass off the food products of its Ohio restaurants as Big Boy sponsored goods. *See, e.g., Chevron Chemical, supra; Warner Bros., Inc. v.*

involves "defendant's use of plaintiff's well-known product name, symbol, or familiar packaging to attract the public to the product under the assumption that it is the plaintiff's product which is bought." Comment, *The Present Scope of Recovery for Unfair Competition Violations Under Section 43(a) of the Lanham Act,* 58 Neb.L.Rev. 159, 163 (1978). As we have previously determined, attempts at passing off are prohibited by § 43(a); indeed, the Lanham Act provides:

> a right of action to persons engaged in interstate and foreign commerce, against * * * deceptive and misleading use of words, names, symbols, or devices, or any combination thereof, which have been adopted by a manufacturer or merchant to identify his goods and distinguish them from those manufactured by others, where such misleading use is carried on, in the channels of interstate and foreign commerce, which is subject to regulation by Congress.

Federal-Mogul-Bower Bearings, supra at 409.

The district court properly held that the standard of proof needed to prevail in a § 43(a) action for injunctive relief was a showing of "likelihood of confusion."

> Although it is necessary to prove that the buying public was actually deceived in order to recover damages under § 43(a) of the Lanham Act, *Skil Corp. v. Rockwell International Corp.,* 375 F.Supp. 777 (N.D.Ill.1974), only a likelihood of confusion or deception need be shown in order to obtain equitable relief. *Dallas Cowboys Cheerleaders, Inc. v. Pussycat Cinema, Ltd.,* [604 F.2d 200 (2d Cir.1979)]. Here, since equitable relief is sought, only the likelihood of confusion need be shown, and not proof of actual confusion as was required by the District Court.

Warner Bros., Inc., supra at 79. This likelihood of confusion need not arise from intentional conduct; furthermore, a mere showing that advertisements tend to create a false impression is sufficient to warrant injunctive relief.

> Under § 43(a) of the Lanham Act it is not necessary to show that any false description or representation is wilful or intentional. *Parkway Baking Co. v. Freihofer Baking Co.,* 255 F.2d 641, 648 (3d Cir.1958). All that is required is that the representation or descriptions either be "false" or such as is "tending falsely to describe or represent the goods or services in question." *Ames Publishing Co. v. Walker-Davis Publications, Inc.,* 372 F.Supp. 1, 11 (E.D.Pa.1974). Thus, liability is not restricted solely to descriptions which are literally false, but extends to instances where the defendant creates a false impression. *Id.*

Walker-Davis Publications, Inc. v. Penton/IPC, Inc., 509 F.Supp. 430, 435 (E.D.Pa.1981).[4]

* * *

Gay Toys, Inc., 658 F.2d 76 (2d Cir.1981) (toy manufacturer's attempt to pass off its toy automobiles as sponsored by popular television series prohibited by § 43(a)); *Federal-Mogul-Bower Bearings, supra.*

4. *Accord, CBS, Inc. v. Springboard International Records,* 429 F.Supp. 563 (S.D. N.Y.1976); *CBS, Inc. v. Gusto Records, Inc.,* 403 F.Supp. 447 (M.D.Tenn.1974); *Rich v. RCA Corp.,* 390 F.Supp. 530 (S.D.N.Y.1975)

SKIL CORP. v. ROCKWELL INT'L CORP.

United States District Court of Illinois, 1974.
375 F.Supp. 777, 183 USPQ 157.

III.

A. CAUSE OF ACTION UNDER THE LANHAM ACT

Enacted in 1946, Section 43(a) of the Lanham Act created a new federal statutory remedy for various types of unfair competition in interstate commerce. It grew out of a recognition by Congress of the necessity to break with the restrictive guidelines laid down in such relics as American Washboard Co. v. Saginaw Manufacturing Co.[7] because of foreign trademark and patent treaty commitments. Furthermore, Congress undoubtedly recognized and intended to remedy the destructive effect that Erie v. Tompkins, 304 U.S. 64, 58 S.Ct. 817, 82 L.Ed. 1188 (1938) had upon the development of a uniform federal common law of unfair competition which was essential in a nation where interstate commerce was dominant. Nevertheless, presumably because of the case law which preceded enactment of Section 43(a), the response to the provision was sluggish—so much so that at least one Judge surmised that the practicing bar had yet to realize the potential impact of the statute. Maternally Yours v. Your Maternity Shop, 234 F.2d 538, 546 (2d Cir.1956) (Clark, C.J., concurring).

Section 43(a) (15 U.S.C.A. § 1125(a)) provides in pertinent part:
* * * The governing case law in this Circuit points directly to the conclusion that Section 43(a) creates a cause of action for conduct such as that alleged here.

In Bernard Food Industries v. Dietene Company, 415 F.2d 1279 (7th Cir.1969), cert. denied, 397 U.S. 912, 90 S.Ct. 911, 25 L.Ed.2d 92 (1970), the Court held that where the defendant, in comparing its food product to plaintiff's, made false representations of fact as to *plaintiff's* product,

(release of collection of old Charlie Rich recordings done in his old style with a current photograph of Charlie Rich on the cover created false impression that record was done in Rich's contemporary style; violation of § 43(a) found by three separate district courts); J. McCarthy, Trademarks & Unfair Competition, § 27:7 at 255 (1973).

7. 103 F. 281 (6th Cir.1900). There, the plaintiff was a manufacturer of an aluminum washboard which had gained a measure of popularity with the public. Suit was brought to enjoin defendant from labeling and selling its galvanized iron washboard as an aluminum one. Relief was sought not on the ground that defendant was "palming off" its product as that of the plaintiff, but because defendant was deceiving the public. The Court reflected the then prevailing law, saying:

"It is doubtless morally wrong and improper to impose upon the public by the sale of spurious goods, but this does not give rise to a private right of action unless the property rights of the plaintiff are thereby invaded. There may be many wrongs which can only be righted through public prosecution, and for which the legislature, and not the courts, must provide a remedy. Courts of equity, in granting relief by injunction, are concerned with the property rights of complainant." 103 F. at 285.

Because plaintiff did not have a "property right" in the form of a trademark and because, in the Court's opinion, lost future sales were not "property", the Court affirmed the dismissal of the lawsuit.

a cause of action did *not* arise under Section 43(a). However, the Court clearly indicated that a cause of action would have arisen if defendant, in its comparison advertising, had also made false statements about its *own* product, saying:

> "Further support for the view that the Act does not embrace misrepresentations about a competitor's product but only false or deceitful representations which the manufacturer or merchant makes about his own goods or services is contained in L'Aiglon Apparel v. Lana Lobell, Inc., 214 F.2d 649 (3d Cir.1954), and General Pool Corp. v. Hallmark Pool Corp., 259 F.Supp. 383 (N.D.Ill.1966)." 415 F.2d at 1284.

Thus, we hold that Bernard Food Industries v. Dietene Company, supra, requires plaintiff to allege the following elements in order to state a claim upon which relief may be granted under Section 43(a) of the Lanham Act: (1) in its comparison advertisements, defendant made false statements of fact about its own product; (2) those advertisements actually deceived or have the tendency to deceive a substantial segment of their audience; (3) such deception is material, in that it is likely to influence the purchasing decision; (4) defendant caused its falsely advertised goods to enter interstate commerce; and (5) plaintiff has been or is likely to be injured as the result of the foregoing either by direct diversion of sales from itself to defendant, or by lessening of the goodwill which its products enjoy with the buying public. See Weil, Protectability of Trademark Values Against False Competitive Advertising, 44 Cal.L.Rev. 527, 537 (1956). In order to recover *damages* under Section 43(a), plaintiff must establish that the buying public was actually deceived; in order to obtain *equitable relief,* only a likelihood of deception need be shown. Hesmer Foods, Inc. v. Campbell Soup Company, 346 F.2d 356, 359 (7th Cir.1965), cert. denied, 382 U.S. 839, 86 S.Ct. 89, 15 L.Ed.2d 81. We hold that Count I of the Complaint sets forth the above five elements. We further find that it states a claim upon which both damages and equitable relief may be recovered.

The extent to which Section 43(a) of the Lanham Act can be used is yet to be determined. It becomes critical when no Federal Trademark registration is available to provide Federal jurisdiction. In Beech-Nut, Inc. v. Warner Lambert Co., 480 F.2d 801, 178 USPQ 385 (2d Cir.1973), the breath mints, "Clorets" and "Certs", were pitted against "Breath Savers" the cousin to "Life Savers" of Beech-Nut, Inc. Judge Moore stated:

> Despite considerable doubt created by the language of the statute as to whether Section 43(a) of the Lanham Act (15 U.S.C. § 1125(a)) covers mere trademark infringement and unfair competition, the many cases decided since its enactment leave no doubt that, as construed by the courts, the claims advanced here may properly be brought under this section. Therefore, the claims set forth in the complaint could have been brought under Section 43(a)—hence, "removal was not improper."

Part V

FEDERAL PRE-EMPTION

A. IN GENERAL

When the United States Constitution was adopted, there were many states which had patent and copyright laws but these soon fell into disuse. Nevertheless, there remained many areas of protection of intellectual property which depended on the common law of the states. Trade secrets, common law copyright matters, trademark infringement questions, unfair competition and palming-off cases, all were matters dealt with in state courts where the common law of the state controlled. When a Federal Court obtained jurisdiction of a case of this kind, it may have, under the doctrine of Swift v. Tyson,ᵃ developed and applied rules of federal common law independent of the common law of the particular state in which the matter arose even though the Judiciary Act of 1789 provided that "The laws of the several States, * * * shall be regarded as rules of decision in trials at common law, in the courts of the United States, in cases where they apply." This was permissible because in 1842 the Supreme Court, in Swift v. Tyson, interpreted the Judiciary Act of 1789 as encompassing only the statutory law of the states saying:

> "The laws of a State are more usually understood to mean the rules and enactments promulgated by the legislative authority thereof, or long established customs having the force of laws."

In 1938, however, the Supreme Court reviewed this matter and, in Erie Railroad Co. v. Tompkins,ᵇ overruled Swift v. Tyson stating:

> Except in matters governed by the Federal Constitution or by Acts of Congress, the law to be applied in any case is the law of the State. And whether the law of the State shall be declared by its Legislature in a statute or by its highest court in a decision is not a matter of federal concern. There is no federal general common law.

> Congress has no power to declare substantive rules of common law applicable in a State whether they be local in their nature or "gener-

---

a. 41 U.S. (16 Pet.) 1, 10 L.Ed. 865 (1842).

b. 304 U.S. 64, 58 S.Ct. 817, 82 L.Ed. 1188, 1194 (1938).

al," be they commercial law or a part of the law of torts. And no clause in the Constitution purports to confer such a power upon the federal courts.[c]

A corollary to the Erie doctrine [d] was established in Clearfield Trust Co. v. United States [e] to the effect that when a matter is within the scope of the powers of the federal government, the federal courts can, in the absence of a controlling federal statute, "fashion the governing rule of law according to their own standards" and should do so where a uniform federal rule is desirable. More recently in Wallis v. Pan American Petroleum Corp.[f] the Supreme Court articulated an interest analysis test for determining whether federal law should be applied saying:

> In deciding whether rules of federal common law should be fashioned, normally the guiding principle is that a significant conflict between some federal policy or interest and the use of state law in the premises must first be specifically shown. It is by no means enough that, as we may assume, Congress could under the Constitution readily enact a complete code of law governing transactions in federal mineral leases among private parties. Whether latent federal power should be exercised to displace state law is primarily a decision for Congress. Even where there is related federal legislation in an area, as is true in this instance it must be remembered that "Congress acts * * * against the background of the total corpus juris of the states * * *." Hart & Wechsler, The Federal Courts and the Federal System 435 (1953).

Where there is a substantial conflict between federal and state laws, policies or interests, within the scope of the constitutional powers of the federal government, the supremacy clause of Article VI of the Federal Constitution permits subordination of the state interest to the federal interest. Thus, in the absence of controlling federal legislation, the Federal Courts can determine whether the desirability of a uniform rule, the comparative strength of the state and federal interests, the feasibility of creating a workable judicial rule and other similar factors require a federal common law rule. Federal common law rules can relate either to substantive law or conflicts of law.

The judicial displacement or subordination of a state law, policy or interest to a federal one is often referred to as federal pre-emption. The following materials have been selected to illustrate some of the federal pre-emption decisions relating to intellectual property.

c. Cooper, State Law of Patent Exploitation, 56 Minnesota L.R. 313 (1972).

d. Hanna v. Plummer: Erie Reshaped, 51 Virg.L.R. 884 (1965).

e. 318 U.S. 363, 63 S.Ct. 573, 87 L.Ed. 838 (1943).

f. 384 U.S. 63, 86 S.Ct. 1301, 16 L.Ed.2d 369 (1966).

KELLOGG CO. v. NATIONAL BISCUIT CO.

Supreme Court of the United States, 1938.
305 U.S. 111, 59 S.Ct. 109, 83 L.Ed. 73 (1939).

MR. JUSTICE BRANDEIS delivered the opinion of the Court:

This suit was brought in the federal court for Delaware [1] by National Biscuit Company against Kellogg Company to enjoin alleged unfair competition by the manufacture and sale of the breakfast food commonly known as shredded wheat. The competition was alleged to be unfair mainly because Kellogg Company uses, like the plaintiff, the name shredded wheat and, like the plaintiff, produces its biscuit in pillow-shaped form.

* * *

The plaintiff concedes that it does not possess the exclusive right to make shredded wheat. But it claims the exclusive right to the trade name "Shredded Wheat" and the exclusive right to make shredded wheat biscuits pillow-shaped. It charges that the defendant, by using the name and shape, and otherwise, is passing off, or enabling others to pass off, Kellogg goods for those of the plaintiff. Kellogg Company denies that the plaintiff is entitled to the exclusive use of the name or of the pillow-shape; denies any passing off; asserts that it has used every reasonable effort to distinguish its product from that of the plaintiff; and contends that in honestly competing for a part of the market for shredded wheat it is exercising the common right freely to manufacture and sell an article of commerce unprotected by patent.

First. The plaintiff has no exclusive right to the use of the term "Shredded Wheat" as a trade name. For that is the generic term of the article, which describes it with a fair degree of accuracy; and is the term by which the biscuit in pillow-shaped form is generally known by the public. Since the term is generic, the original maker of the product acquired no exclusive right to use it. As Kellogg Company had the right to make the article, it had, also, the right to use the term by which the public knows it. Compare Saxlehner v. Wagner, 216 U.S. 375, 30 S.Ct. 298, 54 L.Ed. 525; Holzapfel's Compositions Co. v. Rahtjen's American Composition Co., 183 U.S. 1, 22 S.Ct. 6, 46 L.Ed. 49. Ever since 1894 the article has been known to the public as shredded wheat. For many years, there was no attempt to use the term "Shredded Wheat" as a trade-mark.

* * *

Moreover, the name "Shredded Wheat," as well as the product, the process and the machinery employed in making it, has been dedicated

1. The federal jurisdiction rests on diversity of citizenship—National Biscuit Company being a New Jersey corporation and Kellogg Company a Delaware corporation. Most of the issues in the case involve questions of common law and hence are within the scope of Erie R. Co. v. Tompkins, 304 U.S. 64, 58 S.Ct. 817, 82 L.Ed. 1188, 114 A.L.R. 1487 (1938). But no claim has been made that the local law is any different from the general law on the subject, and both parties have relied almost entirely on federal precedents.

to the public. The basic patent for the product and for the process of making it, and many other patents for special machinery to be used in making the article, issued to Perky. In those patents the term "shredded" is repeatedly used as descriptive of the product. The basic patent expired October 15, 1912; the others soon after. Since during the life of the patents "Shredded Wheat" was the general designation of the patented product, there passed to the public upon the expiration of the patent, not only the right to make the article as it was made during the patent period, but also the right to apply thereto the name by which it had become known. As was said in Singer Mfg. Co. v. June Mfg. Co., 163 U.S. 169, 185, 16 S.Ct. 1002, 41 L.Ed. 118, 124:

> "It equally follows from the cessation of the monopoly and the falling of the device into the domain of things public, that along with the public ownership of the device there must also necessarily pass to the public the generic designation of the thing which has arisen during the monopoly. * * *

> "To say otherwise would be to hold that, although the public had acquired the device covered by the patent, yet the owner of the patent or the manufacturer of the patented thing had retained the designated name which was essentially necessary to vest the public with the full enjoyment of that which had become theirs by the disappearance of the monopoly."

* * *

Second. The plaintiff has not the exclusive right to sell shredded wheat in the form of a pillow-shaped biscuit—the form in which the article became known to the public. That is the form in which shredded wheat was made under the basic patent. The patented machines used were designed to produce only the pillow-shaped biscuits. And a design patent was taken out to cover the pillow-shaped form. Hence, upon expiration of the patents the form, as well as the name, was dedicated to the public. As was said in Singer Mfg. Co. v. June Mfg. Co., supra (163 U.S. 185, 16 S.Ct. 1002, 41 L.Ed. 124):

> "It is self-evident that on the expiration of a patent the monopoly created by it ceases to exist, and the right to make the thing formerly covered by the patent becomes public property. It is upon this condition that the patent is granted. It follows as a matter of course that on the termination of the patent there passes to the public the right to make the machine in the form in which it was constructed during the patent. We may, therefore, dismiss without further comment the complaint, as to the form in which the defendant made his machines."

Where an article may be manufactured by all, a particular manufacturer can no more assert exclusive rights in a form in which the public has become accustomed to see the article and which, in the minds of the public, is primarily associated with the article rather than a particular producer, than it can in the case of a name with similar connections in the public mind. Kellogg Company was free to use the pillow-shaped form, subject only to the obligation to identify its product lest it be mistaken for that of the plaintiff.

Third. The question remains whether Kellogg Company in exercising its right to use the name "Shredded Wheat" and the pillow-shaped biscuit, is doing so fairly. Fairness requires that it be done in a manner which reasonably distinguishes its product from that of plaintiff.

Each company sells its biscuits only in cartons. The standard Kellogg carton contains fifteen biscuits; the plaintiff's twelve. The Kellogg cartons are distinctive. They do not resemble those used by the plaintiff either in size, form, or color. And the difference in the labels is striking. The Kellogg cartons bear in bold script the names "Kellogg's Whole Wheat Biscuit" or "Kellogg's Shredded Whole Wheat Biscuit" so sized and spaced as to strike the eye as being a Kellogg product. It is true that on some of its cartons it had a picture of two shredded wheat biscuits in a bowl of milk which was quite similar to one of the plaintiff's registered trade-marks. But the name Kellogg was so prominent on all of the defendant's cartons as to minimize the possibility of confusion.

* * *

It is urged that all possibility of deception or confusion would be removed if Kellogg Company should refrain from using the name "Shredded Wheat" and adopt some form other than the pillow-shape. But the name and form are integral parts of the goodwill of the article. To share fully in the goodwill, it must use the name and the pillow-shape. And in the goodwill Kellogg Company is as free to share as the plaintiff. Compare William R. Warner & Co. v. Eli Lilly & Co., 265 U.S. 526, 528, 530, 44 S.Ct. 615, 68 L.Ed. 1161, 1163, 1164. Moreover, the pillow-shape must be used for another reason. The evidence is persuasive that this form is functional—that the cost of the biscuit would be increased and its high quality lessened if some other form were substituted for the pillow-shape.

Kellogg Company is undoubtedly sharing in the goodwill of the article known as "Shredded Wheat"; and thus is sharing in a market which was created by the skill and judgment of plaintiff's predecessor and has been widely extended by vast expenditures in advertising persistently made. But that is not unfair. Sharing in the goodwill of an article unprotected by patent or trade-mark is the exercise of a right possessed by all—and in the free exercise of which the consuming public is deeply interested. There is no evidence of passing off or deception on the part of the Kellogg Company; and it has taken every reasonable precaution to prevent confusion or the practice of deception in the sale of its product.

* * *

MR. JUSTICE MCREYNOLDS and MR. JUSTICE BUTLER are of opinion that the decree of the Circuit Court of Appeals is correct and should be affirmed. To them it seems sufficiently clear that the Kellogg Company is fraudulently seeking to appropriate to itself the benefits of a goodwill built up at great cost by the respondent and its predecessors.

SEARS, ROEBUCK & CO. v. STIFFEL CO.

Supreme Court of the United States, 1964.
376 U.S. 225, 84 S.Ct. 784, 11 L.Ed.2d 661.

MR. JUSTICE BLACK delivered the opinion of the Court.

The question in this case is whether a State's unfair competition law can, consistently with the federal patent laws, impose liability for or prohibit the copying of an article which is protected by neither a federal patent nor a copyright. The respondent, Stiffel Company, secured design and mechanical patents on a "pole lamp"—a vertical tube having lamp fixtures along the outside, the tube being made so that it will stand upright between the floor and ceiling of a room. Pole lamps proved a decided commercial success, and soon after Stiffel brought them on the market Sears, Roebuck & Company put on the market a substantially identical lamp, which it sold more cheaply, Sears' retail price being about the same as Stiffel's wholesale price. Stiffel then brought this action against Sears in the United States District Court for the Northern District of Illinois, claiming in its first count that by copying its design Sears had infringed Stiffel's patents and in its second count that by selling copies of Stiffel's lamp Sears had caused confusion in the trade as to the source of the lamps and had thereby engaged in unfair competition under Illinois law. There was evidence that identifying tags were not attached to the Sears lamps although labels appeared on the cartons in which they were delivered to customers, that customers had asked Stiffel whether its lamps differed from Sears', and that in two cases customers who had bought Stiffel lamps had complained to Stiffel on learning that Sears was selling substantially identical lamps at a much lower price.

The District Court, after holding the patents invalid for want of invention, went on to find as a fact that Sears' lamp was "a substantially exact copy" of Stiffel's and that the two lamps were so much alike, both in appearance and in functional details, "that confusion between them is likely, and some confusion has already occurred." On these findings the court held Sears guilty of unfair competition, enjoined Sears "from unfairly competing with [Stiffel] by selling or attempting to sell pole lamps identical to or confusingly similar to" Stiffel's lamp, and ordered an accounting to fix profits and damages resulting from Sears' "unfair competition."

The Court of Appeals affirmed. 313 F.2d 115. That court held that, to make out a case of unfair competition under Illinois law, there was no need to show that Sears had been "palming off" its lamps as Stiffel lamps; Stiffel had only to prove that there was a "likelihood of confusion as to the source of the products"—that the two articles were sufficiently identical that customers could not tell who had made a particular one. Impressed by the "remarkable sameness of appearance" of the lamps, the Court of Appeals upheld the trial court's findings of likelihood of confusion and some actual confusion, findings which the appellate court construed to mean confusion "as to the source of the lamps." The Court of Appeals thought this enough under Illinois law to sustain the trial court's holding of unfair competition, and thus held Sears liable under Illinois law for doing no more than copying and marketing an unpatented article. We granted certiorari to consider whether this use of a State's law of unfair competition is compatible with the federal patent law. 374 U.S. 826, 83 S.Ct. 1868, 10 L.Ed.2d 1050.

Before the Constitution was adopted, some States had granted patents either by special act or by general statute, but when the Constitution was adopted provision for a federal patent law was made one of the enumerated powers of Congress because, as Madison put it in The Federalist No. 43, the States "cannot separately make effectual provision" for either patents or copyrights.

* * *

Thus the patent system is one in which uniform federal standards are carefully used to promote invention while at the same time preserving free competition. Obviously a State could not, consistently with the Supremacy Clause of the Constitution, extend the life of a patent beyond its expiration date or give a patent on an article which lacked the level of invention required for federal patents. To do either would run counter to the policy of Congress of granting patents only to true inventions, and then only for a limited time. Just as a State cannot encroach upon the federal patent laws directly, it cannot, under some other law, such as that forbidding unfair competition, give protection of a kind that clashes with the objectives of the federal patent laws.

In the present case the "pole lamp" sold by Stiffel has been held not to be entitled to the protection of either a mechanical or a design patent. An unpatentable article, like an article on which the patent has expired, is in the public domain and may be made and sold by whoever chooses to do so. What Sears did was to copy Stiffel's design and to sell lamps almost identical to those sold by Stiffel. This it had every right to do under the federal patent laws. That Stiffel originated the pole lamp and made it popular is immaterial. "Sharing in the goodwill of an article unprotected by patent or trade-mark is the exercise of a right possessed by all—and in the free exercise of which the consuming public is deeply interested." Kellogg Co. v. National Biscuit Co., supra, 305 U.S. at 122, 83 L.Ed. at 80. To allow a State by use of its law of unfair competition to prevent the copying of an article which represents too slight an advance to be patented would be to permit the State to block off from the public something which federal law has said belongs to the public. The result would be that while federal law grants only 14 or 17 years' protection to genuine inventions, see 35 U.S.C.A. §§ 154, 173, States could allow perpetual protection to articles too lacking in novelty to merit any patent at all under federal constitutional standards. This would be too great an encroachment on the federal patent system to be tolerated.

Sears has been held liable here for unfair competition because of a finding of likelihood of confusion based only on the fact that Sears' lamp was copied from Stiffel's unpatented lamp and that consequently the two looked exactly alike. Of course there could be "confusion" as to who had manufactured these nearly identical articles. But mere inability of the public to tell two identical articles apart is not enough to support an injunction against copying or an award of damages for copying that which the federal patent laws permit to be copied. Doubtless a State may, in appropriate circumstances, require that goods, whether patented or unpatented, be labeled or that other precautionary steps be taken to prevent customers from being misled as to the source, just as it may protect businesses in the use of their trademarks, labels, or distinctive dress in the packaging of goods so as to prevent others, by imitating such markings, from misleading purchasers as to the source of the goods. But because of the federal patent laws a State may not, when the article is unpatented and uncopyrighted, prohibit the copying of the article itself or award damages for such copying. Cf. G. Ricordi & Co. v. Haendler, 194 F.2d 914, 916 (C.A.2d Cir.1952). The judgment below did both and in so doing gave Stiffel the equivalent of a patent monopoly on its unpatented lamp. That was error, and Sears is entitled to a judgment in its favor.

Reversed.

Separate Opinion

Mr. Justice Harlan, concurring in the result.

In one respect I would give the States more leeway in unfair competition "copying" cases than the Court's opinions would allow. If copying is found, other than by an inference arising from the mere act of copying, to have been undertaken with the dominant purpose and effect of palming off one's goods as those of another or of confusing customers as to the source of such goods, I see no reason why the State may not impose reasonable restrictions on the future "copying" itself. Vindication of the paramount federal interest at stake does not require a State to tolerate such specifically oriented predatory business practices. Apart from this, I am in accord with the opinions of the Court, and concur in both judgments since neither case presents the point on which I find myself in disagreement.

In a companion case to Sears, Justice Black, speaking for the Supreme Court, said:

> As we have said in Sears, while the federal patent laws prevent a State from prohibiting the copying and selling of unpatented articles, they do not stand in the way of state law, statutory or decisional, which requires those who make and sell copies to take precautions to identify their products as their own. A State of course has power to impose liability upon those who, knowing that the public is relying upon an original manufacturer's reputation for quality and integrity, deceive

the public by palming off their copies as the original. That an article copied from an unpatented article could be made in some other way, that the design is "nonfunctional" and not essential to the use of either article, that the configuration of the article copied may have a "secondary meaning" which identifies the maker to the trade, or that there may be "confusion" among purchasers as to which article is which or as to who is the maker, may be relevant evidence in applying a State's law requiring such precautions as labeling; however, and regardless of the copier's motives, neither these facts nor any others can furnish a basis for imposing liability for or prohibiting the actual acts of copying and selling. Cf. Kellogg Co. v. National Biscuit Co., 305 U.S. 111, 120, 59 S.Ct. 109, 83 L.Ed. 73, 79 (1938). And of course a State cannot hold a copier accountable in damages for failure to label or otherwise to identify his goods unless his failure is in violation of valid state statutory or decisional law requiring the copier to label or take other precautions to prevent confusion of customers as to the source of the goods. Compco Corp. v. Day-Brite Lighting, Inc., 376 U.S. 234, 238–39, 84 S.Ct. 779, 11 L.Ed.2d 669, 672–73 (1964).

Lower courts did not hesitate in concluding that the law of unfair competition had survived the Sears and Compco decisions as indicated in the following:

The doctrine of the recent cases of Sears, Roebuck & Company v. Stiffel Company, 376 U.S. 225, 140 USPQ 524, and Compco Corporation v. Day-Brite Lighting, Inc., 376 U.S. 234, 140 USPQ 528, relied upon by defendant, prevents plaintiff from complaining of the copying of the contents of its books, but it does not preclude state courts from protecting "businesses in the use of their trademarks, labels, or distinctive dress in the packaging of goods so as to prevent others, by imitating such markings, from misleading purchasers as to the source of the goods." 376 U.S. 225, 232, 140 USPQ 524, 528.

What appears on the covers of the books of the respective parties is not functional. It constitutes their "dress" within the meaning of the word as used in the above quotation and in the cases on unfair competition. Defendant is not free to copy what appears as plaintiff's covers, including the title, format, & c., to such a substantial extent as to mislead the purchasing public. The copying has even included the size of the covers. Pet Needs, Inc. v. T.F.H. Publications, Inc., 156 USPQ 479, 480 (N.Y.Sup.Ct., N.Y. County 1967).

Another approach is to pursue a federal cause of action under Section 43(a) of the Lanham Act. As stated by District Judge Herlands:

The thrust of plaintiff's complaint is that defendant has purposefully and intentionally copied plaintiff's brochure sheets, which function as labels for its product, with the intent to achieve so close a simulation in appearance as to cause confusion in the minds of prospective purchasers of garment bags and cause them to purchase defendant's garment bags when their intent is to purchase plaintiff's garment bags.

* * *

Defendant contends that by virtue of the decisions in Compco Corp. v. Day-Brite Lighting, Inc., 376 U.S. 234, 84 S.Ct. 779, 11 L.Ed. 669 (1964) and Sears, Roebuck & Co. v. Stiffel Co., 376 U.S. 225, 84 S.Ct. 784, 11 L.Ed.2d 661 (1964), the unfair competition law of a state "cannot prevent the copying of works unprotected by design patents and copyright which nevertheless are subject to such federal protection" (Plaintiff's Memorandum, pp. 4–5). See generally Symposium, Product Simulation: A Right Or A Wrong?, 64 Colum.L.Rev. 1178 (1964). However, plaintiff's claim is predicated not on state unfair competition law but upon a Congressionally-created right of action for a particular kind of unfair competition. [Lanham Act § 43(a)] We do not reach the question of whether a valid claim for relief could be predicated on the unfair competition law of New York State.

Citing the *Sears* and *Compco* cases, supra, defendant also contends that Section 43(a) of the Lanham Act would be unconstitutional if it is interpreted to prevent a competitor from copying a copyrightable but uncopyrighted label. (Defendant's Memorandum, pp. 5–7). Whatever the merits of that contention may be, the substance of the wrong the complaint alleges, and which Section 43(a) seeks to prevent, is the use of any words or symbols which constitute a false designation of the origin of goods, not the mere act of copying another's label. Bogene Inc. v. Whit-Mor Manufacturing Co., 253 F.Supp. 126, 127–128, 149 USPQ 672, 673–674 (D.C.S.D.N.Y.1966).

In Illinois, where the Sears and Compco cases originated, Justice McNamara of the Illinois Appellate Court indicated that the vitality of the International News Service Case, [248 U.S. 215, 39 S.Ct. 68, 63 L.Ed. 211 (1918)] was not impaired by the Sears doctrine saying:

Plaintiff Capitol Records Inc. filed a complaint in the Circuit Court against defendant Gary A. Spies, doing business as Tape-A-Tape, alleging that Spies was pirating certain performances from recordings made by Capitol and praying that he be temporarily and permanently enjoined from such further action. After a hearing, the chancellor denied Capitol's motion for a temporary injunction, and it brings this interlocutory appeal.

* * *

We believe that the facts of the instant case are clearly distinguishable from the Sears and Compco decisions, and we find that the chancellor erred in denying Capitol's motion for a temporary injunction. Whereas in those cases the court was concerned with the copying of products which were not patented, in the instant case Spies was actually appropriating another's property. Rather than the Sears and Compco decisions, we find that the case of International News Service v. Associated Press, 248 U.S. 215 (1918), is controlling. In that case, plaintiff gathered news at substantial cost to itself and distributed it to its members. Defendant would take the distributed news and sell it to its subscribers. The Supreme Court held that defendant was engaged in unfair competition and should be enjoined from pursuing such activity.

* * *

Consequently we hold that the Sears and Compco decisions do not apply to the case at bar. The evidence reveals that Spies was not merely copying unpatented or uncopyrighted articles, but that he was actually taking and appropriating Capitol's product itself—the actual sounds recorded on the albums. Spies was thus relieved of the necessity of contracting with various performers so that he might produce a recording; he needed only to wait until a particular rendition produced by Capitol became popular and then was able to take advantage of the existing market. It seems evident that the Supreme Court in Sears and Compco did not intend to condone this form of unfair competition. Capitol Records, Inc. v. Spies, 264 N.E.2d 874, 167 USPQ 489, 490, 491 (App.Ct. 1st Div.1970)

A different view of the survival of the International News Service case is found in a decision of the Fifth Circuit Court of Appeals [g] where Circuit Judge Coffin said:

This is an appeal by defendants from jury verdicts in the total amount of $150,000 awarded plaintiff on his claim that he created, and the defendants misappropriated, the character of Paladin, the protagonist of the CBS television series entitled "Have Gun Will Travel".

* * *

From the beginning plaintiff indulged a penchant for costume. He was already equipped with a moustache. He soon settled on a black shirt, black pants, and a flat-crowned black hat. * * * He adopted the name Paladin after an onlooker of Italian descent had hurled an epithet at him containing the word "Paladino".

* * *

The finishing touches were a chess knight, bought for fifteen cents at an auction, which plaintiff thought was a good symbol, and which he used on a business card along with the words "Have", "Gun", "Will", "Travel", and "Wire Paladin, N. Court St., Cranston, R.I.", hand-printed with separate rubber stamps; a silver copy of the chess piece on his holster; and an antique derringer strapped under his arm. So accoutered, he would appear in parades, the openings and finales of rodeos, auctions, horse shows, and a pony ring he once operated. From time to time at rodeos he would stage a western gunfight, featuring his quick draw and the timely use of his hidden derringer. He would pass out photographs of himself and cards—printed versions soon replacing the rubber-stamped ones. * * *

* * * witnesses for the defendants all testified that they had never seen DeCosta [Plaintiff] or any of his cards. The jury obviously disbelieved at least this much of their testimony, and we think it clear that they were amply justified. Thus, the plaintiff has had the satisfaction of proving the defendants pirates. But we are drawn to conclude that that proof alone is not enough to entitle him to a share of the plunder. Our Paladin is not the first creator to see the fruits of his creation harvested by another, without effective remedy; and

g. Columbia Broadcasting System v. DeCosta, 377 F.2d 315, 153 USPQ 649 (1st Cir.1967), cert. denied 389 U.S. 1007, 88 S.Ct. 565, 19 L.Ed.2d 603 (1967).

although his case is undeniably hard, to affirm the judgments below would, we think, allow a hard case to make some intolerably bad law.

* * *

[T]he leading case affording a remedy for mere copying, International News Serv. v. Associated Press, 1918, 248 U.S. 215, 39 S.Ct. 68, 63 L.Ed. 211, is no longer authoritative for at least two reasons: it was decided as a matter of general federal law before the decision in Erie R. R. v. Tompkins, 1938, 304 U.S. 64, 58 S.Ct. 817, 82 L.Ed. 1188; and, as it prohibited the copying of published written matter that had not been copyrighted (indeed, as news it could not be copyrighted, 248 U.S. at 234, 39 S.Ct. 68, 63 L.Ed. 211), it has clearly been overruled by the Supreme Court's recent decisions in Sears * * * and Compco * * * Congress has established a procedural scheme of protection by notice and registration. The necessary implication of this approach, we conclude, is that, absent compliance with the scheme, the federal policy favoring free dissemination of intellectual creations prevails. Thus, if a "writing" is within the scope of the constitutional clause, and Congress has not protected it, whether deliberately or by unexplained omission, it can be freely copied * * * [I]n view of the federal policy of encouraging intellectual creation by granting a limited monopoly at best, we think it sensible to say that the constitutional clause extends to any concrete, describable manifestation of intellectual creation; and to the extent that a creation may be ineffable, we think it ineligible for protection against copying *simpliciter* under either state or federal law.

Second and third causes of action for trademark infringement and unfair competition were dealt with in DeCosta v. Columbia Broadcasting System, Inc., 520 F.2d 499 (1st Cir.1975) where the First Circuit Court of Appeals denied relief saying:

"We recognize that plaintiff has lost something of value to him. The very success of defendants' series saturated the public consciousness and in time diluted the attractiveness of plaintiff's creation, although he continued his appearances longer than defendants' first run. While he was not injured financially, there can be no doubt that he has felt deprived. As a commentator has observed, '[I]t could be argued that the most appropriate measure of damages would be the emotional harm that he suffered when CBS exploited his character and lured his audience away.' 66 Mich.L.Rev. at 1034. But to give any relief, however tailored, we need a predicate of liability. Absent the ultimate fact of confusion, we cannot find a basis for liability for common law service mark infringement or unfair competition.* "

* Further unraveling of Sears—Compco: of Patches, Paladin and Laurel and Hardy, Laff and Saret, 66 T.M.Rep. 427 (1976).

LEAR, INC. v. ADKINS

Supreme Court of the United States, 1969.
395 U.S. 653, 89 S.Ct. 1902, 23 L.Ed.2d 610.

MR. JUSTICE HARLAN delivered the opinion of the Court.

In January of 1952, John Adkins, an inventor and mechanical engineer, was hired by Lear, Incorporated, for the purpose of solving a vexing problem the company had encountered in its efforts to develop a gyroscope which would meet the increasingly demanding requirements of the aviation industry. * * * Shortly after Adkins was hired, he developed a method of construction at the company's California facilities which improved gyroscope accuracy at a low cost. Lear almost immediately incorporated Adkins' improvements into its production process to its substantial advantage.

The question that remains unsettled in this case, after eight years of litigation in the California courts, is whether Adkins will receive compensation for Lear's use of those improvements which the inventor has subsequently patented. At every stage of this lawsuit, Lear has sought to prove that, despite the grant of a patent by the Patent Office, none of Adkins' improvements were sufficiently novel to warrant the award of a monopoly under the standards delineated in the governing federal statutes. Moreover, the company has sought to prove that Adkins obtained his patent by means of a fraud on the Patent Office. In response, the inventor has argued that since Lear had entered into a licensing agreement with Adkins, it was obliged to pay the agreed royalties regardless of the validity of the underlying patent.

The Supreme Court of California unanimously vindicated the inventor's position. While the court recognized that generally a manufacturer is free to challenge the validity of an inventor's patent, it held that "one of the oldest doctrines in the field of patent law establishes that so long as a licensee is operating under a license agreement he is estopped to deny the validity of his licensor's patent in a suit for royalties under the agreement. The theory underlying this doctrine is that a licensee should not be permitted to enjoy the benefit afforded by the agreement while simultaneously urging that the patent which forms the basis of the agreement is void." 67 Cal.2d 882, 891, 435 P.2d 321, 325–326 (1967).

Almost 20 years ago, in its last consideration of the doctrine, this Court also invoked an estoppel to deny a licensee the right to prove that his licensor was demanding royalties for the use of an idea which was in reality a part of the public domain. Automatic Radio Manufacturing Co. v. Hazeltine Research, Inc., 339 U.S. 827, 836, 70 S.Ct. 894, 94 L.Ed. 1312, 1320 (1950). We granted certiorari in the present case, 391 U.S. 912, 88 S.Ct. 1810, 20 L.Ed.2d 651, to reconsider the validity of the Hazeltine rule in the light of our recent decisions emphasizing the strong federal policy favoring free competition in ideas which do not merit patent protection. Sears, Roebuck v. Stiffel Co., 376 U.S. 225, 84

S.Ct. 784, 11 L.Ed.2d 661 (1964); Compco Corp. v. Day-Brite Lighting Inc., 376 U.S. 234, 84 S.Ct. 779, 11 L.Ed.2d 669 (1964).

* * *

On February 4, 1954, Adkins filed an application with the Patent Office in an effort to gain federal protection for his improvements. At about the same time, he entered into a lengthy period of negotiations with Lear in an effort to conclude a licensing agreement which would clearly establish the amount of royalties that would be paid.

These negotiations finally bore fruit on September 15, 1955, when the parties approved a complex 17–page contract which carefully delineated the conditions upon which Lear promised to pay royalties for Adkins' improvements. The parties agreed that if "the U.S. Patent Office refuses to issue a patent on the substantial claims [contained in Adkins' original patent application] or if such a patent so issued is subsequently held invalid, then in any of such events Lear at its option shall have the right forthwith to terminate the specific license so affected or to terminate this entire Agreement * * *." § 6. (2 App. 138.)

As the contractual language indicates, Adkins had not obtained a final Patent Office decision as to the patentability of his invention at the time the licensing agreement was concluded. Indeed, he was not to receive a patent until January 5, 1960. This long delay has its source in the special character of Patent Office procedures.

* * *

During the long period in which Adkins was attempting to convince the Patent Office of the novelty of his ideas, however, Lear had become convinced that Adkins would never receive a patent on his invention and that it should not continue to pay substantial royalties on ideas which had not contributed substantially to the development of the art of gyroscopy. In 1957, after Adkins' patent application had been rejected twice, Lear announced that it had searched the Patent Office's files and had found a patent which it believed had fully anticipated Adkins' discovery. As a result, the company stated that it would no longer pay royalties on the large number of gyroscopes it was producing at its plant in Grand Rapids, Michigan (the Michigan gyros). Payments were continued on the smaller number of gyros produced at the company's California plant (the California gyros) for two more years until they too were terminated on April 8, 1959.

* * *

II.

Since the California Supreme Court's construction of the 1955 licensing agreement is solely a matter of state law, the only issue open to us is raised by the court's reliance upon the doctrine of estoppel to bar Lear from proving that Adkins' ideas were dedicated to the common welfare by federal law. In considering the propriety of the State Court's decision, we are well aware that we are not writing upon a clean slate. The doctrine of estoppel has been considered by this Court in a line of cases reaching back into the middle of the 19th century. Before deciding what the role of estoppel should be in the present case and in the future, it is, then, desirable to consider the role it has played in the past.

* * *

III.

The uncertain status of licensee estoppel in the case law is a product of judicial efforts to accommodate the competing demands of the common law of contracts and the federal law of patents. On the one hand, the law of contracts forbids a purchaser to repudiate his promises simply because he later becomes dissatisfied with the bargain he has made. On the other hand, federal law requires that all ideas in general circulation be dedicated to the common good unless they are protected by a valid patent. Sears, Roebuck v. Stiffel Co., supra; Compco Corp. v. Day-Brite Lighting, Inc., supra. When faced with this basic conflict in policy, both this Court and courts throughout the land have naturally sought to develop an intermediate position which somehow would remain responsive to the radically different concerns of the two different worlds of contract and patent. The result has been a failure. Rather than creative compromise, there has been a chaos of conflicting case law, proceeding on inconsistent premises. Before renewing the search for an acceptable middle ground, we must reconsider on their own merits the arguments which may properly be advanced on both sides of the estoppel question.

A.

It will simplify matters greatly if we first consider the most typical situation in which patent licenses are negotiated. In contrast to the present case, most manufacturers obtain a license after a patent has issued. Since the Patent Office makes an inventor's ideas public when it issues its grant of a limited monopoly, a potential licensee has access to the inventor's ideas even if he does not enter into an agreement with the patent owner. Consequently, a manufacturer gains only two benefits if he chooses to enter a licensing agreement after the patent has issued. First, by accepting a license and paying royalties for a time, the licensee may have avoided the necessity of defending an expensive infringement action during the period when he may be least able to afford one. Second, the existence of an unchallenged patent may deter others from attempting to compete with the licensee.

Under ordinary contract principles the mere fact that some benefit is received is enough to require the enforcement of the contract, regardless of the validity of the underlying patent. Nevertheless, if one tests this result by the standard of good-faith commercial dealing, it seems far from satisfactory. For the simple contract approach entirely ignores the position of the licensor who is seeking to invoke the court's assistance on his behalf. Consider, for example, the equities of the licensor who has obtained his patent through a fraud on the Patent

Office. It is difficult to perceive why good faith requires that courts should permit him to recover royalties despite his licensee's attempts to show that the patent is invalid. Compare Walker Process Equipment, Inc. v. Food Machinery & Chemical Corp., 382 U.S. 172, 86 S.Ct. 347, 15 L.Ed.2d 247 (1965).

Even in the more typical cases, not involving conscious wrongdoing, the licensor's equities are far from compelling. A patent, in the last analysis, simply represents a legal conclusion reached by the Patent Office. Moreover, the legal conclusion is predicated on factors as to which reasonable men can differ widely. Yet the Patent Office is often obliged to reach its decision in an ex parte proceeding, without the aid of the arguments which could be advanced by parties interested in proving patent invalidity. Consequently, it does not seem to us to be unfair to require a patentee to defend the Patent Office's judgment when his licensee places the question in issue, especially since the licensor's case is buttressed by the presumption of validity which attaches to his patent. Thus, although licensee estoppel may be consistent with the letter of contractual doctrine, we cannot say that it is compelled by the spirit of contract law, which seeks to balance the claims of promisor and promisee in accord with the requirements of good faith.

Surely the equities of the licensor do not weigh very heavily when they are balanced against the important public interest in permitting full and free competition in the use of ideas which are in reality a part of the public domain. Licensees may often be the only individuals with enough economic incentive to challenge the patentability of an inventor's discovery. If they are muzzled, the public may continually be required to pay tribute to would-be monopolists without need or justification. We think it plain that the technical requirements of contract doctrine must give way before the demands of the public interest in the typical situation involving the negotiation of a license after a patent has issued.

We are satisfied that Automatic Radio Manufacturing Co. v. Hazeltine Research, Inc., supra, itself the product of a clouded history, should no longer be regarded as sound law with respect to its "estoppel" holding, and that holding is now overruled.

B.

The case before us, however, presents a far more complicated estoppel problem than the one which arises in the most common licensing context. The problem arises out of the fact that Lear obtained its license in 1955, more than four years before Adkins received his 1960 patent. Indeed, from the very outset of the relationship, Lear obtained special access to Adkins' ideas in return for its promise to pay satisfactory compensation.

Thus, during the lengthy period in which Adkins was attempting to obtain a patent, Lear gained an important benefit not generally obtained by the typical licensee. For until a patent issues, a potential licensee may not learn his licensor's ideas simply by requesting the information from the Patent Office. During the time the inventor is seeking patent protection, the governing federal statute requires the Patent Office to hold an inventor's patent application in confidence. If a potential licensee hopes to use the ideas contained in a secret patent application, he must deal with the inventor himself, unless the inventor chooses to publicize his ideas to the world at large. By promising to pay Adkins royalties from the very outset of their relationship, Lear gained immediate access to ideas which it may well not have learned until the Patent Office published the details of Adkins' invention in 1960. At the core of this case, then, is the difficult question whether federal patent policy bars a State from enforcing a contract regulating access to an unpatented secret idea.

Adkins takes an extreme position on this question. The inventor does not merely argue that since Lear obtained privileged access to his ideas *before 1960,* the company should be required to pay royalties accruing *before 1960* regardless of the validity of the patent which ultimately issued. He also argues that since Lear obtained special benefits before 1960, it should also pay royalties during the entire patent period (1960–1977), without regard to the validity of the Patent Office's grant. We cannot accept so broad an argument.

Adkins' position would permit inventors to negotiate all important licenses during the lengthy period while their applications were still pending at the Patent Office, thereby disabling entirely all those who have the strongest incentive to show that a patent is worthless. While the equities supporting Adkins' position are somewhat more appealing than those supporting the typical licensor, we cannot say that there is enough of a difference to justify such a substantial impairment of overriding federal policy.

Nor can we accept a second argument which may be advanced to support Adkins' claim to at least a portion of his post-patent royalties, regardless of the validity of the Patent Office grant. The terms of the 1955 agreement provide that royalties are to be paid until such time as the "patent * * * is held invalid," § 6, and the fact remains that the question of patent validity has not been finally determined in this case. Thus, it may be suggested that although Lear must be allowed to raise the question of patent validity in the present lawsuit, it must also be required to comply with its contract and continue to pay royalties until its claim is finally vindicated in the courts.

The parties' contract, however, is no more controlling on this issue than is the State's doctrine of estoppel, which is also rooted in contract principles. The decisive question is whether overriding federal policies would be significantly frustrated if licensees could be required to continue to pay royalties during the time they are challenging patent validity in the courts.

It seems to us that such a requirement would be inconsistent with the aims of federal patent policy. Enforcing this contractual provision would give the licensor an additional economic incentive to devise every conceivable dilatory tactic in an effort to postpone the day of final judicial reckoning. We can perceive no reason to encourage dilatory court tactics in this way. Moreover, the cost of prosecuting slow-moving trial proceedings and defending an inevitable appeal might well deter many licensees from attempting to prove patent invalidity in the courts. The deterrent effect would be particularly severe in the many scientific fields in which invention is proceeding at a rapid rate. In these areas, a patent may well become obsolete long before its 17–year term has expired. If a licensee has reason to believe that he will replace a patented idea with a new one in the near future, he will have little incentive to initiate lengthy court proceedings, unless he is freed from liability at least from the time he refuses to pay the contractual royalties. Lastly, enforcing this contractual provision would undermine the strong federal policy favoring the full and free use of ideas in the public domain. For all these reasons, we hold that Lear must be permitted to avoid the payment of all royalties accruing after Adkins' 1960 patent issued if Lear can prove patent invalidity.

C.

Adkins' claim to contractual royalties accruing before the 1960 patent issued is, however, a much more difficult one, since it squarely raises the question whether, and to what extent, the States may protect the owners of *unpatented* inventions who are willing to disclose their ideas to manufacturers only upon payment of royalties. The California Supreme Court did not address itself to this issue with precision, for it believed that the venerable doctrine of estoppel provided a sufficient answer to all of Lear's claims based upon federal patent law. Thus, we do not know whether the Supreme Court would have awarded Adkins recovery even on his pre-patent royalties if it had recognized that previously established estoppel doctrine could no longer be properly invoked with regard to royalties accruing during the 17–year patent period. Our decision today will, of course, require the state courts to reconsider the theoretical basis of their decisions enforcing the contractual rights of inventors and it is impossible to predict the extent to which this re-evaluation may revolutionize the law of any particular State in this regard. Consequently, we have concluded, after much consideration, that even though an important question of federal law underlies this phase of the controversy, we should not now attempt to define in even a limited way the extent, if any, to which the States may properly act to enforce the contractual rights of inventors of unpatented secret ideas. Given the difficulty and importance of this task, it should be undertaken only after the state courts have, after fully focused inquiry, determined the extent to which they will respect the contractual rights of such inventors in the future. Indeed, on remand, the California courts may well reconcile the competing demands of patent and contract law in a way which would not warrant further review in this Court.

IV.

We also find it inappropriate to pass at this time upon Lear's contention that Adkins' patent is invalid.

Not only did Lear fail to raise this issue in its petition for certiorari, but the California Supreme Court has yet to pass on the question of patent validity in that clear and unequivocal manner which is so necessary for proper adjudication in this Court. * * * In this context, we believe that Lear must be required to address its arguments attacking the validity of the underlying patent to the California courts in the first instance.

The judgment of the Supreme Court of California is vacated and the case is remanded to that court for further proceedings not inconsistent with this opinion.

It is so ordered.

SEPARATE OPINIONS

MR. JUSTICE BLACK, with whom THE CHIEF JUSTICE and MR. JUSTICE DOUGLAS join, concurring in part and dissenting in part.

I concur in the judgment and opinion of the Court, except for what is said in Part III, C, of the Court's opinion. What the Court does in this part of its opinion is to reserve for future decision the question whether the States have power to enforce contracts under which someone claiming to have a new discovery can obtain payment for disclosing it while his patent application is pending, even though the discovery is later held to be unpatentable. This reservation is, as I see it, directly in conflict with what this Court held to be the law in Sears, Roebuck v. Stiffel Co., 376 U.S. 225, 84 S.Ct. 784, 11 L.Ed.2d 661 (1964), and Compco Corp. v. Day-Brite Lighting, Inc., 376 U.S. 234, 84 S.Ct. 779, 11 L.Ed.2d 669 (1964). Brother Harlan concurred in the result in those cases, saying—contrary to what the Court held—"I see no reason why the State may not impose reasonable restrictions on the future 'copying' itself." Compco, supra, at 239, 11 L.Ed.2d at 668. Consequently, the Court is today joining in the kind of qualification that only Mr. Justice Harlan was willing to make at the time of our Stiffel and Compco decisions.

I still entertain the belief I expressed for the Court in Stiffel and Compco that no State has a right to authorize any kind of monopoly on what is claimed to be a new invention, except when a patent has been obtained from the Patent Office under the exacting standards of the patent laws. One who makes a discovery may, of course, keep it secret if he wishes, but private arrangements under which self-styled "inventors" do not keep their discoveries secret, but rather disclose them, in return for contractual payments, run counter to the plan of our patent laws, which tightly regulate the kind of inventions that may be protected and the manner in which they may be protected. The national policy expressed in the patent laws, favoring free competition and narrowly limiting monopoly, cannot be frustrated by private agreements among individuals, with or without the approval of the state.[h]

GOLDSTEIN v. STATE OF CALIFORNIA

Supreme Court of the United States, 1973.
412 U.S. 546, 93 S.Ct. 2303, 37 L.Ed.2d 163.

MR. CHIEF JUSTICE BURGER delivered the opinion of the Court.

We granted certiorari to review petitioners' conviction under a California statute making it a criminal offense to "pirate" recordings produced by others.

In 1971, an information was filed by the State of California, charging petitioners in 140 counts with violating § 653h of the California Penal Code. The information charged that, between April 1970 and March 1971, petitioners had copied several musical performances from commercially sold recordings without the permission of the owner of the master record or tape. Petitioners moved to dismiss the complaint on the grounds that § 653h was in conflict with Art. I, § 8, cl. 8, of the Constitution, the "Copyright Clause," and the federal statutes enacted thereunder. Upon denial of their motion, petitioners entered pleas of

h. "We think the rationale of Lear requires us to hold that the covenant of Golden State and Gold, in the settlement agreement of July 23, 1962, not to contest the validity of MCA's patent, is void on its face and unenforceable. It is in just as direct conflict with the 'strong federal policy' referred to repeatedly in Lear, as was the estoppel doctrine and the specific contractual provision struck down in that decision.

* * *

"We think it unimportant that in our case the covenant is part of a settlement agreement rather than of a typical patent licensing agreement. Were we to recognize such a distinction it would, in practice, be less than workable. * * * [I]t would be just as easy to couch licensing arrangements in the form of settlement agreements. If the recognized policy favoring settlement of disputes might be hindered by our holding on this question, that policy, in our opinion, must give way to the policy favoring free competition in ideas not meriting patent protection." Masillon-Cleveland-Akron Sign Co. v. Golden State Advertising Co., Inc., 444 F.2d 425, 427, 170 USPQ 440, 442 (9th Cir.1971).

"We believe that the policy considerations which underlie Blonder-Tongue, Lear, Sears and Compco lead inescapably to the conclusion that the defendants'

agreement to accept the validity of plaintiff's patent is unenforceable. We so hold.

"Plaintiff's estoppel argument rests on more than a private agreement between the parties. In addition, plaintiff claims the benefit of an adjudication because the determination of validity was included in a judicial decree entered after three days of trial in which a genuine issue of validity had been raised.

"Although the first case was partially tried, it does not appear that Judge Marovitz actually decided the issue of validity. Moreover, since the decree recited that the accused products did not infringe, there was no necessity for a determination of validity. In these circumstances, as the Second Circuit has held, a consent decree does not create an estoppel on the issue of validity. Addressograph Multigraph Corp. v. Cooper, 156 F.2d 483, 70 USPQ 272 (2nd Cir. 1946). A contrary result could not be reconciled with 'the public interest in a judicial determination of the invalidity of a worthless patent.' Id. at 485, 70 USPQ at 273–274." Business Forms Finishing Service Inc. v. Carson, 452 F.2d 70, 75, 171 USPQ 519, 522–23 (7th Cir. 1971).

nolo contendere to 10 of the 140 counts; the remaining counts were dismissed. On appeal, the Appellate Department of the California Superior Court sustained the validity of the statute. After exhausting other state appellate remedies, petitioners sought review in this Court.

I

* * *

The challenged California statute forbids petitioners to transfer any performance fixed on a tape or record onto other records or tapes with the intention of selling the duplicates, unless they have first received permission from those who, under state law, are the owners of the master recording.

* * *

Article I, § 8, cl. 8, of the Constitution gives to Congress the power—

> "To promote the Progress of Science and useful Arts, by securing for limited Times to Authors and Inventors the exclusive Right to their respective Writings and Discoveries * * *."

The clause thus describes both the objective which Congress may seek and the means to achieve it. The objective is to promote the progress of science and the arts. As employed, the terms "to promote" are synonymous with the words "to stimulate," "to encourage," or "to induce." To accomplish its purpose, Congress may grant to authors the exclusive right to the fruits of their respective works. An author who possesses an unlimited copyright may preclude others from copying his creation for commercial purposes without permission. In other words, to encourage people to devote themselves to intellectual and artistic creation, Congress may guarantee to authors and inventors a reward in the form of control over the sale or commercial use of copies of their works.

The objective of the Copyright Clause was clearly to facilitate the granting of rights national in scope. While the debates on the clause at the Constitutional Convention were extremely limited, its purpose was described by James Madison in the Federalist:

> "The utility of this power will scarcely be questioned. The copyright of authors has been solemnly adjudged, in Great Britain, to be a right of common law. The right to useful inventions seems with equal reason to belong to the inventors. The public good fully coincides in both cases with the claims of individuals. The States cannot separately make effectual provision for either of the cases, and most of them have anticipated the decision of this point, by laws passed at the instance of Congress."

The difficulty noted by Madison relates to the burden placed on an author or inventor who wishes to achieve protection in all States when no federal system of protection is available. To do so, a separate application is required to each state government; the right which in turn may be granted has effect only within the granting State's borders. The national system which Madison supported eliminates the need for multiple applications and the expense and difficulty involved. In effect, it allows Congress to provide a reward greater in scope than any particular State may grant to promote progress in those fields which Congress determines are worthy of national action.

Although the Copyright Clause thus recognizes the potential benefits of a national system, it does not indicate that all writings are of national interest or that state legislation is, in all cases, unnecessary or precluded. The patents granted by the States in the 18th century show, to the contrary, a willingness on the part of the States to promote those portions of science and the arts which were of local importance. Whatever the diversity of people's backgrounds, origins, and interests, and whatever the variety of business and industry in the 13 Colonies, the range of diversity is obviously far greater today in a country of 210 million people in 50 States. In view of that enormous diversity, it is unlikely that all citizens in all parts of the country place the same importance on works relating to all subjects. Since the subject matter to which the Copyright Clause is addressed may thus be of purely local importance and not worthy of national attention or protection, we cannot discern such an unyielding national interest as to require an inference that state power to grant copyrights has been relinquished to *exclusive* federal control.

The question to which we next turn is whether, in actual operation, the exercise of the power to grant copyrights by some States will prejudice the interests of other States. As we have noted, a copyright granted by a particular State has effect only within its boundaries. If one State grants such protection, the interests of States which do not are not prejudiced since their citizens remain free to copy within their borders those works which may be protected elsewhere.

* * * in the case of state copyrights, except as to individuals willing to travel across state lines in order to purchase records or other writings protected in their own State, each State's copyrights will still serve to induce new artistic creations within that State—the very objective of the grant of protection. We do not see here the type of prejudicial conflicts which would arise, for example, if each State exercised a sovereign power to impose imposts and tariffs; nor can we discern a need for uniformity such as that which may apply to the regulation of interstate shipments.

Similarly, it is difficult to see how the concurrent exercise of the power to grant copyrights by Congress and the States will necessarily and inevitably lead to difficulty. At any time Congress determines that a particular category of "writing" is worthy of national protection and the incidental expenses of federal administration, federal copyright protection may be authorized. Where the need for free and unrestricted distribution of a writing is thought to be required by the national interest, the Copyright Clause and the Commerce Clause would allow Congress to eschew all protection. In such cases, a conflict would develop if a State attempted to protect that which Congress intended to be free from restraint or to free that which Congress had protected. However, where Congress determines that neither federal protection nor freedom from restraint is required by the national interest, it is at liberty to stay its hand entirely. Since state protection would not then conflict with federal action, total relinquishment of the States' power to grant copyright protection cannot be inferred.

* * *

* * * We therefor conclude that, under the Constitution, the States have not relinquished all power to grant to authors "the exclusive Right to their respective Writings."

* * *

III

Our conclusion that California did not surrender its power to issue copyrights does not end the inquiry. We must proceed to determine whether the challenged state statute is void under the Supremacy Clause. No simple formula can capture the complexities of this determination; the conflicts which may develop between state and federal action are as varied as the fields to which congressional action may apply. "Our primary function is to determine whether, under the circumstances of this particular case, [the state] law stands as an obstacle to the accomplishment and execution of the full purposes and objectives of Congress." Hines v. Davidowitz, 312 U.S. 52, 67, 61 S.Ct. 399, 404, 85 L.Ed. 581 (1941). We turn, then, to federal copyright law to determine what objectives Congress intended to fulfill.

By Art. I, § 8, cl. 8, of the Constitution, the States granted to Congress the power to protect the "Writings" of "Authors." These terms have not been construed in their narrow literal sense but, rather, with the reach necessary to reflect the broad scope of constitutional principles. While an "author" may be viewed as an individual who writes an original composition, the term, in its constitutional sense, has been construed to mean an "originator," "he to whom anything owes its origin." Burrow-Giles Lithographic Co. v. Sarony, 111 U.S. 53, 58, 4 S.Ct. 279, 281, 28 L.Ed. 349 (1884). Similarly, although the word "writings" might be limited to script or printed material, it may be interpreted to include any physical rendering of the fruits of creative intellectual or aesthetic labor. Ibid.; Trade-Mark Cases, 100 U.S. 82, 94, 25 L.Ed. 550 (1879). Thus, recordings of artistic performances may be within the reach of Clause 8.

While the area in which Congress *may* act is broad, the enabling provision of Clause 8 does not require that Congress act in regard to all categories of materials which meet the constitutional definitions. Rather, whether any specific category of "Writings" is to be brought within the purview of the federal statutory scheme is left to the discretion of the Congress. The history of federal copyright statutes indicates that the congressional determination to consider specific classes of writings is dependent, not only on the character of the writing, but also on the commercial importance of the product to the national economy. As our technology has expanded the means available for creative activity and has provided economical means for reproducing manifestations of such activity, new areas of federal protection have been initiated.

Petitioners contend that the actions taken by Congress in establishing federal copyright protection preclude the States from granting similar protection to recordings of musical performances. According to petitioners, Congress addressed the question of whether recordings of performances should be granted protection in 1909; Congress determined that any individual who was entitled to a copyright on an original musical composition should have the right to control to a limited extent the use of that composition on recordings, but that the record itself, and the performance which it was capable of reproducing were not worthy of such protection. In support of their claim, petitioners cite the House Report on the 1909 Act, which states:

> "It is not the intention of the committee to extend the right of copyright to the mechanical reproductions themselves, but only to give the composer or copyright proprietor the control, in accordance with the provisions of the bill, of the manufacture and use of such devices."
> HR Rep No. 2222, 60th Cong, 2d Sess, 9 (1909).

To interpret accurately Congress' intended purpose in passing the 1909 Act and the meaning of the House Report petitioners cite, we must remember that our modern technology differs greatly from that which existed in 1909. The Act and the report should not be read as if they were written today, for to do so would inevitably distort their intended meanings; rather, we must read them against the background of 1909, in which they were written.

In 1831, Congress first extended federal copyright protection to original musical compositions. An individual who possessed such a copyright had the exclusive authority to sell copies of the musical score; individuals who purchased such a copy did so for the most part to play the composition at home on a piano or other instrument. Between 1831 and 1909, numerous machines were invented which allowed the composition to be reproduced mechanically. For example, one had only to insert a piano roll or disc with perforations in appropriate places into a player piano to achieve almost the same results which previously required someone capable of playing the instrument. The mounting sales of such devices detracted from the value of the copyright granted for the musical composition. Individuals who had use of a piano roll and an appropriate instrument had little, if any, need for a copy of the sheet music. The problems which arose eventually reached this Court in 1908 in the case of White-Smith Music Publishing Co. v. Apollo Co., 209 U.S. 1, 28 S.Ct. 319, 52 L.Ed. 655. There, the Apollo Company had manufactured piano rolls capable of reproducing mechanically compositions covered by a copyright owned by appellant. Appellant contended that the piano rolls constituted "copies" of the copyrighted composition and that their sale, without permission, constituted an infringement of the copyright. The Court held that piano rolls, as well as records, were not "copies" of the copyrighted composition, in terms of the federal copyright statutes, but were merely component parts of a machine which executed the composition. Despite the fact that the piano rolls employed the creative work of the composer, all protection was denied.

It is against this background that Congress passed the 1909 statute. After pointedly waiting for the Court's decision in *White-Smith Music Publishing Co.* Congress determined that the copyright statutes should be amended to insure that *composers of original musical works* received adequate protection to encourage further artistic and creative effort. Henceforth, under § 1(e), records and piano rolls were to be considered as "copies" of the original composition they were capable of reproducing, and could not be manufactured unless payment was made to the *proprietor of the composition copyright.* The section of the House Report cited by petitioners was intended only to establish the limits of *the composer's* right; composers were to have no control over the recordings themselves. Nowhere does the report indicate that Congress considered records as anything but a component part of a machine, capable of reproducing an original composition or that Congress intended records, as *renderings of original artistic performance,* to be free from state control.

Petitioners' argument does not rest entirely on the belief that Congress intended specifically to exempt recordings of performances from state control. Assuming that no such intention may be found, they argue that Congress so occupied the field of copyright protection as to pre-empt all comparable state action. Rice v. Santa Fe Elevator Corp., 331 U.S. 218, 67 S.Ct. 1146, 91 L.Ed. 1447 (1947). This assertion is based on the language of 17 U.S.C.A. §§ 4 and 5, and on this Court's opinions in Sears, Roebuck & Co. v. Stiffel Co., 376 U.S. 225, 84 S.Ct. 784, 11 L.Ed.2d 661 (1964), and Compco Corp. v. Day-Brite Lighting, 376 U.S. 234, 84 S.Ct. 779, 11 L.Ed.2d 669 (1964).

Section 4 of the federal copyright laws provides:

"The works for which copyright may be secured under this title shall include all the writings of an author." 17 U.S.C.A. § 4.

Section 5, which lists specific categories of protected works, adds:

"The above specifications shall not be held to limit the subject-matter of copyright as defined in section 4 of this title * * *." 17 U.S.C.A. § 5.

Since § 4 employs the constitutional term "writings," it may be argued that Congress intended to exercise its authority over all works to which the constitutional provision might apply. However, in the more than 60 years which have elapsed since enactment of this provision, neither the Copyright Office, the courts, nor the Congress has so interpreted it. The Register of Copyrights, who is charged with administration of the statute, has consistently ruled that "claims to exclusive rights in mechanical recordings * * * or in the performances they reproduce" are not entitled to protection under § 4. 37 CFR § 202.8(b) (1972). With one early exception, American courts have agreed with this interpretation; and in 1971, prior to passage of the statute which extended federal protection to recordings fixed on or after February 15, 1972, Congress acknowledged the validity of that interpretation. Both the House and Senate Reports on the proposed legislation recognized that recordings qualified as "writings" within the meaning of the Constitution, but had not previously been protected under the federal copyright statute. H.R.Rep. No. 92–487, pp. 2, 5 (1971); S.Rep. No. 92–72, p. 4 (1971); U.S.Code Cong. & Admin.News p. 1566. In light of this consistent interpretation by the courts, the agency empowered to administer the copyright statutes, and Congress itself, we cannot agree that §§ 4 and 5 have the broad scope petitioners claim.

Sears and *Compco,* on which petitioners rely, do not support their position. In those cases, the question was whether a State could, under principles of a state unfair competition law, preclude the copying of mechanical configurations which did not possess the qualities required for the granting of a federal design or mechanical patent. The Court stated:

> "[T]he patent system is one in which uniform federal standards are carefully used to promote invention while at the same time preserving free competition. Obviously a State could not, consistently with the Supremacy Clause of the Constitution, extended the life of a patent beyond its expiration date or give a patent on an article which lacked the level of invention required for federal patents. To do either would run counter to the policy of Congress of granting patents only to true inventions, and then only for a limited time. Just as a State cannot encroach upon the federal patent laws directly, it cannot, under some other law, such as that forbidding unfair competition, give protection of a kind that clashes with the objectives of the federal patent laws." Sears, Roebuck & Co. v. Stiffel Co., 376 U.S., at 230–231, 84 S.Ct., at 788 (footnotes omitted).

In regard to mechanical configurations, Congress had balanced the need to encourage innovation and originality of invention against the need to insure competition in the sale of identical or substantially identical products. The standards established for granting federal patent protection to machines thus indicated not only which articles in this particular category Congress wished to protect, but which configurations it wished to remain free. The application of state law in these cases to prevent the copying of articles which did not meet the requirements for federal protection disturbed the careful balance which Congress had drawn and thereby necessarily gave way under the Supremacy Clause of the Constitution. No comparable conflict between state law and federal law arises in the case of recordings of musical performances. In regard to this category of "Writings," Congress has drawn no balance; rather, it has left the area unattended, and no reason exists why the State should not be free to act.

IV

* * *

* * * The California statutory scheme evidences a legislative policy to prohibit "tape piracy" and "record piracy," conduct that may adversely affect the continued production of new recordings, a large industry in California. Accordingly, the State has, by statute, given to recordings the attributes of property. No restraint has been placed on the use of an idea or concept; rather, petitioners and other individuals remain free to record the same compositions in precisely the same manner and with the same personnel as appeared on the original recording.

* * *

We conclude that the State of California has exercised a power which it retained under the Constitution, and that the challenged statute, as applied in this case, does not intrude into an area which Congress has, up to now, preempted. Until and unless Congress takes further action with respect to recordings fixed prior to February 15, 1972, the California statute may be enforced against acts of piracy such as those which occurred in the present case.

Affirmed.

Note

As noted in Part III, supra, the current Copyright Act specifically provides protection to "sound recordings" (17 U.S.C.A. § 102(a)(7)), and precludes "reproduction or distribution" of "phonorecords" without authorization of the copyright owners. The 1976 Copyright Act also expressly "preempts" all "equivalent rights" under common or state law (17 U.S.C.A. § 301(a)).

KEWANEE OIL CO. v. BICRON CORP.

Supreme Court of the United States, 1974.
416 U.S. 470, 94 S.Ct. 1879, 40 L.Ed.2d 315, 181 USPQ 673.

MR. CHIEF JUSTICE BURGER delivered the opinion of the Court.

We granted certiorari to resolve a question on which there is a conflict in the courts of appeals: whether state trade secret protection is pre-empted by operation of the federal patent law.[1] In the instant case the Court of Appeals for the Sixth Circuit held that there was preemption.[2] The Courts of Appeals for the Second, Fourth, Fifth, and Ninth Circuits have reached the opposite conclusion.[3]

1. 414 U.S. 818, 94 S.Ct. 70, 38 L.Ed.2d 50 (1973).

2. 478 F.2d 1074 (1973).

3. Painton & Co. v. Bourns, Inc., 442 F.2d 216 (CA2 1971); Servo Corp. of America v. General Electric Co., 337 F.2d 716 (CA4 1964), cert. denied, 383 U.S. 934, 86 S.Ct. 1061, 15 L.Ed.2d 851 (1966); Water Services, Inc. v. Tesco Chemicals, Inc., 410 F.2d 163 (CA5 1969); Winston Research Corp. v. Minnesota Mining & Mfg. Co., 350 F.2d 134 (CA9 1965); Dekar Industries, Inc. v. Bissett-Berman Corp., 434 F.2d 1304 (CA9 1970), cert. denied, 402 U.S. 945, 91 S.Ct. 1621, 29 L.Ed.2d 113 (1971).

Harshaw Chemical Co., an unincorporated division of petitioner, is a leading manufacturer of a type of synthetic crystal which is useful in the detection of ionizing radiation. In 1949 Harshaw commenced research into the growth of this type crystal and was able to produce one less than two inches in diameter. By 1966, as the result of expenditures in excess of $1 million, Harshaw was able to grow a 17–inch crystal, something no one else had done previously. Harshaw had developed many processes, procedures, and manufacturing techniques in the purification of raw materials and the growth and encapsulation of the crystals which enabled it to accomplish this feat. Some of these processes Harshaw considers to be trade secrets.

The individual respondents are former employees of Harshaw who formed or later joined respondent Bicron. While at Harshaw the individual respondents executed, as a condition of employment, at least one agreement each, requiring them not to disclose confidential information or trade secrets obtained as employees of Harshaw. Bicron was formed in August 1969 to compete with Harshaw in the production of the crystals, and by April 1970, had grown a 17–inch crystal.

Petitioner brought this diversity action in United States District Court for the Northern District of Ohio seeking injunctive relief and damages for the misappropriation of trade secrets. The District Court, applying Ohio trade secret law, granted a permanent injunction against the disclosure or use by respondents of 20 of the 40 claimed trade secrets until such time as the trade secrets had been released to the public, had otherwise generally become available to the public, or had been obtained by respondents from sources having the legal right to convey the information.

The Court of Appeals for the Sixth Circuit held that the findings of fact by the District Court were not clearly erroneous, and that it was evident from the record that the individual respondents appropriated to the benefit of Bicron secret information on processes obtained while they were employees at Harshaw. Further, the Court of Appeals held that the District Court properly applied Ohio law relating to trade secrets. Nevertheless, the Court of Appeals reversed the District Court, finding Ohio's trade secret law to be in conflict with the patent laws of the United States. The Court of Appeals reasoned that Ohio could not grant monopoly protection to processes and manufacturing techniques that were appropriate subjects for consideration under 35 U.S.C.A. § 101 for a federal patent but which had been in commercial use for over one year and so were no longer eligible for patent protection under 35 U.S.C.A. § 102(b).

We hold that Ohio's law of trade secrets is not pre-empted by the patent laws of the United States, and, accordingly, we reverse.

* * *

The first issue we deal with is whether the States are forbidden to act at all in the area of protection of the kinds of intellectual property which may make up the subject matter of trade secrets.

Article I, § 8, cl. 8, of the Constitution grants to the Congress the power

"to promote the Progress of Science and useful Arts, by securing for limited Times to Authors and Inventors the exclusive Right to their respective Writings and Discoveries * * *."

In the 1972 Term, in Goldstein v. California, 412 U.S. 546, 93 S.Ct. 2303, 37 L.Ed.2d 163 (1973), we held that the cl. 8 grant of power to Congress was not exclusive and that, at least in the case of writings, the States were not prohibited from encouraging and protecting the efforts of those within their borders by appropriate legislation. The States could, therefore, protect against the unauthorized rerecording for sale of performances fixed on records or tapes, even though those performances qualified as "writings" in the constitutional sense and Congress was empowered to legislate regarding such performances and could preempt the area if it chose to do so. * * *

The question of whether the trade secret law of Ohio is void under the Supremacy Clause involves a consideration of whether that law "stands as an obstacle to the accomplishment and execution of the full purposes and objectives of Congress." Hines v. Davidowitz, 312 U.S. 52, 67, 61 S.Ct. 399, 85 L.Ed. 581 (1941). See Florida Lime & Avocado Growers, Inc. v. Paul, 373 U.S. 132, 141, 83 S.Ct. 1210, 1216, 10 L.Ed.2d 248 (1963). We stated in Sears, Roebuck & Co. v. Stiffel Co., 376 U.S. 225, 229, 84 S.Ct. 784, 11 L.Ed.2d 661 (1964), that when state law touches upon the area of federal statutes enacted pursuant to constitutional authority, "it is 'familiar doctrine' that the federal policy 'may not be set at naught, or its benefits denied' by the state law. Sola Elec. Co. v. Jefferson Elec. Co., 317 U.S. 172, 173, 176, 63 S.Ct. 172, 173, 87 L.Ed. 165 (1942). * * *"

Certainly the patent policy of encouraging invention is not disturbed by the existence of another form of incentive to invention. In this respect the two systems are not and never would be in conflict. Similarly, the policy that matter once in the public domain must remain in the public domain is not incompatible with the existence of trade secret protection. By definition a trade secret has not been placed in the public domain.[13]

The more difficult objective of the patent law to reconcile with trade secret law is that of disclosure, the *quid pro quo* of the right to exclude. Universal Oil Co. v. Globe Co., 322 U.S., at 484, 64 S.Ct. at 1116, 88 L.Ed. 1339. We are helped in this stage of the analysis by Judge Henry Friendly's opinion in Painton & Co. v. Bourns, Inc., 442 F.2d 216 (CA2 1971). There the Court of Appeals thought it useful, in determining whether inventors will refrain because of the existence of

---

13. An invention may be placed "in public use or on sale" within the meaning of 35 U.S.C.A. § 102(b) without losing its secret character. Painton & Co. v. Bourns, Inc., 442 F.2d, at 224 n. 6; Metallizing Engineering Co. v. Kenyon Bearing & Auto Parts Co., 153 F.2d 516, 520 (CA2), cert. denied, 328 U.S. 840, 66 S.Ct. 1016, 90 L.Ed. 1615 (1946).

trade secret law from applying for patents, thereby depriving the public from learning of the invention, to distinguish between three categories of trade secrets:

"(1) the trade secret believed by its owner to constitute a validly patentable invention; (2) the trade secret known to its owner not to be so patentable; and (3) the trade secret whose valid patentability is considered dubious." Id., at 224.

Trade secret protection in each of these categories would run against breaches of confidence—the employee and licensee situations—and theft and other forms of industrial espionage.

As to the trade secret known not to meet the standards of patentability, very little in the way of disclosure would be accomplished by abolishing trade secret protection. As with trade secrets of nonpatentable subject matter, the patent alternative would not reasonably be available to the inventor. * * *

Even as the extension of trade secret protection to patentable subject matter that the owner knows will not meet the standards of patentability will not conflict with the patent policy of disclosure, it will have a decidedly beneficial effect on society. Trade secret law will encourage invention in areas where patent law does not reach, and will prompt the independent innovator to proceed with the discovery and exploitation of his invention. Competition is fostered and the public is not deprived of the use of valuable, if not quite patentable, invention.

Even if trade secret protection against the faithless employee were abolished, inventive and exploitive effort in the area of patentable subject matter that did not meet the standards of patentability would continue, although at a reduced level. Alternatively with the effort that remained, however, would come an increase in the amount of self-help that innovative companies would employ. Knowledge would be widely dispersed among the employees of those still active in research. Security precautions necessarily would be increased, and salaries and fringe benefits of those few officers or employees who had to know the whole of the secret invention would be fixed in an amount thought sufficient to assure their loyalty. Smaller companies would be placed at a distinct economic disadvantage, since the costs of this kind of self-help could be great, and the cost to the public of the use of this invention would be increased. The innovative entrepreneur with limited resources would tend to confine his research efforts to himself and those few he felt he could trust without the ultimate assurance of legal protection against breaches of confidence. As a result, organized scientific and technological research could become fragmented, and society, as a whole, would suffer.

* * *

Nothing in the patent law requires that States refrain from action to prevent industrial espionage. In addition to the increased costs for protection from burglary, wiretapping, bribery, and the other means used to misappropriate trade secrets, there is the inevitable cost to the basic decency of society when one firm steals from another. A most fundamental human right, that of privacy, is threatened when industrial espionage is condoned or is made profitable; the state interest in denying profit to such illegal ventures is unchallengeable.

The next category of patentable subject matter to deal with is the invention whose holder has a legitimate doubt as to its patentability. The risk of eventual patent invalidity by the courts and the costs associated with that risk may well impel some with a good-faith doubt as to patentability not to take the trouble to seek to obtain and defend patent protection for their discoveries, regardless of the existence of trade secret protection. Trade secret protection would assist those inventors in the more efficient exploitation of their discoveries and not conflict with the patent law.

* * *

Eliminating trade secret law for the doubtfully patentable invention is thus likely to have deleterious effects on society and patent policy which we cannot say are balanced out by the speculative gain which might result from the encouragement of some inventors with doubtfully patentable inventions which deserve patent protection to come forward and apply for patents. There is no conflict, then, between trade secret law and the patent law policy of disclosure, at least insofar as the first two categories of patentable subject matter are concerned.

The final category of patentable subject matter to deal with is the clearly patentable invention, i.e., that invention which the owner believes to meet the standards of patentability. It is here that the federal interest in disclosure is at its peak; these inventions, novel, useful and nonobvious, are " 'the things which are worth to the public the embarrassment of an exclusive patent.' " Graham v. John Deere Co., supra, at 9, 86 S.Ct., at 689, 15 L.Ed.2d 545 (quoting Thomas Jefferson). The interest of the public is that the bargain of 17 years of exclusive use in return for disclosure be accepted. If a State, through a system of protection, were to cause a substantial risk that holders of patentable inventions would not seek patents, but rather would rely on the state protection, we would be compelled to hold that such a system could not constitutionally continue to exist. In the case of trade secret law no reasonable risk of deterrence from patent application by those who can reasonably expect to be granted patents exists.

Trade secret law provides far weaker protection in many respects than the patent law.[18] While trade secret law does not forbid the discovery of the trade secret by fair and honest means, e.g., independent creation or reverse engineering, patent law operates "against the world," forbidding any use of the invention for whatever purpose for a significant length of time. The holder of a trade secret also takes a substantial risk that the secret will be passed on to his competitors, by

18. Water Services, Inc. v. Tesco Chemicals, Inc., 410 F.2d, at 172.

theft or by breach of a confidential relationship, in a manner not easily susceptible of discovery or proof. Painton & Co. v. Bourns, Inc., 442 F.2d, at 224. Where patent law acts as a barrier, trade secret law functions relatively as a sieve. The possibility that an inventor who believes his invention meets the standards of patentability will sit back, rely on trade secret law, and after one year of use forfeit any right to patent protection, 35 U.S.C.A. § 102(b) is remote indeed.

Nor does society face much risk that scientific or technological progress will be impeded from the rare inventor with a patentable invention who chooses trade secret protection over patent protection. The ripeness of time concept of invention, developed from the study of the many independent multiple discoveries in history, predicts that if a particular individual had not made a particular discovery others would have, and in probably a relatively short period of time. If something is to be discovered at all very likely it will be discovered by more than one person. Singletons and Multiples in Science (1961), in R. Merton, The Sociology of Science 343 (1973); J. Cole & S. Cole, Social Stratification in Science 12–13, 229–230 (1973); Ogburn & Thomas, Are Inventions Inevitable?, 37 Pol.Sci.Q. 83 (1922). Even were an inventor to keep his discovery completely to himself, something that neither the patent nor trade secret laws forbid, there is a high probability that it will be soon independently developed. If the invention, though still a trade secret, is put into public use, the competition is alerted to the existence of the inventor's solution to the problem and may be encouraged to make an extra effort to independently find the solution thus known to be possible. The inventor faces pressures not only from private industry, but from the skilled scientists who work in our universities and our other great publicly supported centers of learning and research.

We conclude that the extension of trade secret protection to clearly patentable inventions does not conflict with the patent policy of disclosure. Perhaps because trade secret law does not produce any positive effects in the area of clearly patentable inventions, as opposed to the beneficial effects resulting from trade secret protection in the areas of the doubtfully patentable and the clearly unpatentable inventions, it has been suggested that partial pre-emption may be appropriate, and that courts should refuse to apply trade secret protection to inventions which the holder should have patented, and which would have been, thereby, disclosed. However, since there is no real possibility that trade secret law will conflict with the federal policy favoring disclosure of clearly patentable inventions partial pre-emption is inappropriate. Partial pre-emption, furthermore, could well create serious problems for state courts in the administration of trade secret law. As a preliminary matter in trade secret actions, state courts would be obliged to distinguish between what a reasonable inventor would and would not correctly consider to be clearly patentable, with the holder of the trade secret arguing that the invention was not patentable and the misappropriator of the trade secret arguing its undoubted novelty, utility, and nonobviousness. Federal courts have a difficult enough time trying to determine whether an invention, narrowed by the patent application procedure and fixed in the specifications which describe the invention for which the patent has been granted, is patentable. Although state courts in some circumstances must join federal courts in judging whether an issued patent is valid, Lear, Inc. v. Adkins, supra, it would be undesirable to impose the almost impossible burden on state courts to determine the patentability—in fact and in the mind of a reasonable inventor—of a discovery which has not been patented and remains entirely uncircumscribed by expert analysis in the administrative process. Neither complete nor partial pre-emption of state trade secret law is justified.

Our conclusion that patent law does not pre-empt trade secret law is in accord with prior cases of this Court. Universal Oil Co. v. Globe Co., 322 U.S., at 484, 64 S.Ct., at 1116; United States v. Dubilier Condenser Corp., 289 U.S., at 186–187, 53 S.Ct., at 557; Becher v. Contoure Laboratories, 279 U.S. 388, 391, 49 S.Ct. 356, 357, 73 L.Ed. 752 (1929); E.I. DuPont de Nemours Powder Co. v. Masland, 244 U.S. 100, 102, 37 S.Ct. 575, 61 L.Ed. 1016 (1917); Dr. Miles Medical Co. v. John D. Park & Sons Co., 220 U.S. 373, 402–403, 31 S.Ct. 376, 382–383, 55 L.Ed. 502 (1911); Board of Trade v. Christie Grain & Stock Co., 198 U.S. 236, 250–251, 25 S.Ct. 637, 639–640, 49 L.Ed. 1031 (1905). Trade secret law and patent law have co-existed in this country for over one hundred years. Each has its particular role to play, and the operation of one does not take away from the need for the other. Trade secret law encourages the development and exploitation of those items of lesser or different invention than might be accorded protection under the patent laws, but which items still have an important part to play in the technological and scientific advancement of the Nation. Trade secret law promotes the sharing of knowledge, and the efficient operation of industry; it permits the individual inventor to reap the rewards of his labor by contracting with a company large enough to develop and exploit it. Congress, by its silence over these many years, has seen the wisdom of allowing the States to enforce trade secret protection. Until Congress takes affirmative action to the contrary, States should be free to grant protection to trade secrets.

Since we hold that Ohio trade secret law is not preempted by the federal patent law, the judgment of the Court of Appeals for the Sixth Circuit is reversed, and the case is remanded to the Court of Appeals with directions to reinstate the judgment of the District Court.

It is so ordered.

* * *

ARONSON v. QUICK POINT PENCIL CO.

Supreme Court of the United States, 1979.
440 U.S. 257, 99 S.Ct. 1096, 59 L.Ed.2d 296, 201 USPQ 1.

OPINION OF THE COURT

MR. CHIEF JUSTICE BURGER delivered the opinion of the Court.

We granted certiorari to consider whether federal patent law preempts state contract law so as to preclude enforcement of a contract to pay royalties to a patent applicant, on sales of articles embodying the putative invention, for so long as the contracting party sells them, if a patent is not granted.

In October 1955 the petitioner Mrs. Jane Aronson filed an application, Serial No. 542677, for a patent on a new form of keyholder. Although ingenious, the design was so simple that it readily could be copied unless it was protected by patent. In June 1956, while the patent application was pending, Mrs. Aronson negotiated a contract with the respondent, Quick Point Pencil Company, for the manufacture and sale of the keyholder.

The contract was embodied in two documents. In the first, a letter from Quick Point to Mrs. Aronson, Quick Point agreed to pay Mrs. Aronson a royalty of 5% of the selling price in return for "the exclusive right to make and sell keyholders of the type shown in your application. Serial No. 542677." The letter further provided that the parties would consult one another concerning the steps to be taken "[i]n the event of any infringement."

The contract did not require Quick Point to manufacture the keyholder. Mrs. Aronson received a $750 advance on royalties and was entitled to rescind the exclusive license if Quick Point did not sell a million keyholders by the end of 1957. Quick Point retained the right to cancel the agreement whenever "the volume of sales does not meet our expectation." The duration of the agreement was not otherwise prescribed.

A contemporaneous document provided that if Mrs. Aronson's patent application was "not allowed within five (5) years, Quick Point Pencil Co. [would] pay two and one half percent (2½%) of sales * * * so long as you [Quick Point] continue to sell same." *

In June 1961, when Mrs. Aronson had failed to obtain a patent on the keyholder within the five years specified in the agreement, Quick

---

* In April 1961, while Mrs. Aronson's patent application was pending, her husband sought a patent on a different keyholder and made plans to license another company to manufacture it. Quick Point's attorney wrote to the couple that the proposed new license would violate the 1956 agreement. He observed that: "your license agreement is in respect of the dis-closure of said Jane [Aronson's] application (not merely in respect of its claims) and that even if no patent is ever granted on the Jane [Aronson] application, *Quick Point Pencil Company is obligated to pay royalties in respect of any keyholder manufactured by it in accordance with any disclosure of said application.*" (Emphasis added.)

Point asserted its contractual right to reduce royalty payments to 2½% of sales. In September of that year the Board of Patent Appeals issued a final rejection of the application on the ground that the keyholder was not patentable, and Mrs. Aronson did not appeal. Quick Point continued to pay reduced royalties to her for 14 years thereafter.

The market was more receptive to the keyholder's novelty and utility than the Patent Office. By September 1975 Quick Point had made sales in excess of seven million dollars and paid Mrs. Aronson royalties totalling $203,963.84; sales were continuing to rise. However, while Quick Point was able to pre-empt the market in the earlier years and was long the only manufacturer of the Aronson keyholder, copies began to appear in the late 1960's. Quick Point's competitors, of course, were not required to pay royalties for their use of the design. Quick Point's share of the Aronson keyholder market has declined during the past decade.

In November 1975 Quick Point commenced an action in the United States District Court for a declaratory judgment, pursuant to 28 U.S. C.A. § 2201, that the royalty agreement was unenforceable. Quick Point asserted that state law which might otherwise make the contract enforceable was pre-empted by federal patent law. This is the only issue presented to us for decision.

* * *

No decision of this Court relating to patents justifies relieving Quick Point of its contract obligations. We have held that a state may not forbid the copying of an idea in the public domain which does not meet the requirements for federal patent protection. Compco Corp. v. Day-Brite Lighting, Inc., 376 U.S. 234, 84 S.Ct. 779, 11 L.Ed.2d 669 (1964); Sears Roebuck & Co. v. Stiffel Co., 376 U.S. 225, 84 S.Ct. 784, 11 L.Ed.2d 661 (1964). Enforcement of Quick Point's agreement, however, does not prevent anyone from copying the keyholder. It merely requires Quick Point to pay the consideration which it promised in return for the use of a novel device which enabled it to pre-empt the market.

In Lear, Inc. v. Adkins, 395 U.S. 653, 89 S.Ct. 1902, 23 L.Ed.2d 610 (1969), we held that a person licensed to use a patent may challenge the validity of the patent, and that a licensee who establishes that the patent is invalid need not pay the royalties accrued under the licensing agreement subsequent to the issuance of the patent. Both holdings relied on the desirability of encouraging licensees to challenge the validity of patents, to further the strong federal policy that only inventions which meet the rigorous requirements of patentability shall be withdrawn from the public domain. Id., at 670–671, 673–674, 89 S.Ct. 1902, at 1911, 1912–1913, 23 L.Ed.2d 610. Accordingly, neither the holding nor the rationale of Lear controls when no patent has issued, and no ideas have been withdrawn from public use.

Enforcement of the royalty agreement here is also consistent with the principles treated in Brulotte v. Thys Co., 379 U.S. 29, 85 S.Ct. 176, 13 L.Ed.2d 99, 3 A.L.R.3d 761 (1964). There, we held that the obligation to pay royalties in return for the use of a patented device may not extend beyond the life of the patent. The principle underlying that holding was simply that the monopoly granted *under a patent* cannot lawfully be used to "negotiate with the leverage of that monopoly." The Court emphasized that to "use that leverage to project those royalty payments beyond the life of the patent is analogous to an effort to enlarge the monopoly of a patent. * * *" Id., at 33, 85 S.Ct. 176 at 179, 13 L.Ed.2d 99, 3 A.L.R.3d 761. Here the reduced royalty which is challenged, far from being negotiated "with the leverage" of a patent, rested on the contingency that no patent would issue within five years.

No doubt a pending patent application gives the applicant some additional bargaining power for purposes of negotiating a royalty agreement.

* * *

This case does not require us to draw the line between what constitutes abuse of a pending application and what does not. It is clear that whatever role the pending application played in the negotiation of the 5% royalty, it played no part in the contract to pay the 2½% royalty indefinitely.

Our holding in Kewanee Oil Co., supra, puts to rest the contention that federal law pre-empts and renders unenforceable the contract made by these parties. There we held that state law forbidding the misappropriation of trade secrets was not pre-empted by federal patent law. We observed:

> "Certainly the patent policy of encouraging invention is not disturbed by the existence of another form of incentive to invention. In this respect the two systems [patent and trade secret law] are not and never would be in conflict." Id., 416 U.S., at 484, 94 S.Ct. 1879, 1887, 40 L.Ed.2d 315, 69 Ohio Ops.2d 235.

Enforcement of this royalty agreement is even less offensive to federal patent policies than state law protecting trade secrets. The most commonly accepted definition of trade secrets is restricted to confidential information which is not disclosed in the normal process of exploitation. See Restatement of Torts § 757, comment b (1939). Accordingly, the exploitation of trade secrets under state law may not satisfy the federal policy in favor of disclosure, whereas disclosure is inescapable in exploiting a device like the Aronson keyholder.

Enforcement of these contractual obligations, freely undertaken in arm's length negotiation and with no fixed reliance on a patent or a probable patent grant, will:

> "encourage invention in areas where patent law does not reach, and will prompt the independent innovator to proceed with the discovery and exploitation of his invention. Competition is fostered and the public is not deprived of the use of valuable, if not quite patentable, invention." [Footnote omitted.] Id., at 485, 94 S.Ct. 1879, at 1888, 40 L.Ed.2d 315, 69 Ohio Ops.2d 235.

The device which is the subject of this contract ceased to have any secrecy as soon as it was first marketed, yet when the contract was negotiated the inventiveness and novelty were sufficiently apparent to induce an experienced novelty manufacturer to agree to pay for the opportunity to be first in the market. Federal patent law is not a barrier to such a contract.

Reversed.

BOGGILD v. KENNER PRODUCTS

United States Court of Appeals, Sixth Circuit, 1985.
776 F.2d 1315, 228 USPQ 130.

KEITH, CIRCUIT JUDGE.

* * *

Over twenty years ago, the plaintiffs-appellees, Robert Boggild and William Dale, invented a toy extruder to be used with the modeling substance called Play-Doh. In January 1963, the plaintiffs granted Kutol Products, Inc. an exclusive license to make, use and sell the extruder in conjunction with its line of Play-Doh products. Kutol subsequently assigned its rights and obligations under the 1963 license agreement to the defendant-appellant, Kenner Products. At the time the plaintiffs executed the agreement, no patents on the extruder had been issued or applied for. However, under Article II of the agreement, upon execution of the license the plaintiffs were required to promptly apply for mechanical and design patents on the extruder. The plaintiffs' patent applications were subsequently issued with expiration dates of March 2, 1979 for the design patent and August 9, 1983 for the mechanical patent.

Under the agreement, Kenner, the licensee, was required to pay royalty payments for a minimum of twenty-five years from the date of the license, or January 18, 1988, regardless of whether the anticipated patents issued or not. Thus, the agreement required the royalty payments to continue four and a half years beyond the latest patent expiration date.

* * *

The underlying policy of patent law grants a seventeen year monopoly to an inventor in exchange for release of the invention to the public upon expiration of the patent. *Scott Paper Co. v. Marcalus Manufacturing Co.,* 326 U.S. 249, 255, 66 S.Ct. 101, 104, 90 L.Ed. 47 (1945); *see Kewanee Oil Co. v. Bicron Corp.,* 416 U.S. 470, 480–81, 94 S.Ct. 1879, 1885–86, 40 L.Ed.2d 315 (1974); *Lear, Inc. v. Adkins,* 395 U.S. 653, 673–74, 89 S.Ct. 1902, 1912–13, 23 L.Ed.2d 610 (1969); *Brulotte v. Thys Co.,* 379 U.S. 29, 30–31, 85 S.Ct. 176, 178, 13 L.Ed.2d 99 (1964); *Prestole Corp. v. Tinnerman Products, Inc.,* 271 F.2d 146, 155 (6th Cir. 1959), *cert. denied,* 361 U.S. 964, 80 S.Ct. 593, 4 L.Ed.2d 545 (1960). Thus, for a limited time, the inventor exclusively reaps any material rewards from the invention on condition that she disclose it to the public upon expiration of the patent. *Scott Paper Co. v. Marcalus*

Manufacturing Co., 326 U.S. at 255, 66 S.Ct. at 104. The extensive social and economic consequences of the patent "give the public a paramount interest in seeing that patent monopolies are kept within their legitimate scope." *Precision Instrument Mfg. Co. v. Automotive Maintenance Machinery Co.,* 324 U.S. 806, 816, 65 S.Ct. 993, 998, 89 L.Ed. 1381 (1945). Hence, efforts to extend or reserve the patent monopoly beyond the seventeen years contravene the policy and purpose of the patent laws. *Scott Paper Co.,* 326 U.S. at 255–56, 66 S.Ct. at 104; *Prestole Corp. v. Tinnerman Products, Inc.,* 271 F.2d at 155.

Accordingly, in *Brulotte v. Thys Co.,* 379 U.S. 29, 85 S.Ct. 176, 13 L.Ed.2d 99 (1964), the Supreme Court found that an owner of patents on hop-picking techniques who executed licensing agreements requiring royalty payments beyond the life of the patent had improperly used the leverage of his patents to extend the monopoly. * * * The Supreme Court concluded that under these circumstances the patent owner had abused the leverage of the monopoly to project royalties into the post-expiration period; the agreement, therefore, was unlawful *per se. Id.*

In the case at bar, the district court reasoned that the *Brulotte* rule of *per se* invalidity was inapplicable because, unlike the hop-picking patents in *Brulotte,* the toy extruder patents had not been issued at the time the parties entered into the licensing agreement. *Boggild v. Kenner Products,* 576 F.Supp. at 536–37. Thus, the district court distinguished the present case as one involving patents which issued after the agreement and which conferred "hybrid" rights entailing trade secrets as well as "potential patent rights in part." *Id.* The district court then rejected the Eleventh Circuit's holding in *Pitney Bowes, Inc. v. Mestre,* 701 F.2d 1365 (11th Cir.), *cert. denied,* 464 U.S. 893, 104 S.Ct. 239, 78 L.Ed.2d 230 (1983), which concluded that the *Brulotte* rule of *per se* invalidity could be applied to hybrid agreements executed while applications for patents were pending:

> In our view the Eleventh Circuit over extended the *Brulotte* rule. It is clear from that early case that the Supreme Court found that the agreement, on its face, revealed an improper leveraging of the patent monopoly. In *Brulotte,* the patents had issued; thus the patentee had something that he could leverage. Here, no application had been made. We recognize that, regardless of whether an application has been made, one might improperly leverage the possibility that a patent might issue if the parties believe there is a substantial likelihood that a patent might issue. Under those circumstances, however, application of a per se rule is inappropriate. We hold, therefore, that the per se rule of *Brulotte* does not extend to the case where no patent application has been made at the time the agreement is negotiated even if an application is contemplated.

576 F.Supp. at 536–37. We reverse this judgment and hold that the *Brulotte* rule of *per se* invalidity precludes enforcement of license provisions which were developed in anticipation of patent protection and which require royalty payments for use, sale or manufacture of a patented item beyond the life of the patent.

The Eleventh Circuit's decision in *Pitney Bowes, Inc. v. Mestre,* is significant for several reasons.   *   *   * The Eleventh Circuit affirmed, ruling moreover that *Brulotte* was applicable to hybrid agreements and that issuance of the pending patent precluded enforcement of conflicting trade secret provisions. The circuit court found that under *Brulotte,* the agreement was invalid *per se* because the agreement's terms for royalty payments and exclusive use applied equally before and after expiration of the patent. 701 F.2d at 1373. Thus, the Eleventh Circuit found improper leveraging of the patent monopoly by applying *Brulotte's* rationale of *per se* invalidity to an agreement where the patents had not issued at the time of licensing but were pending and where trade secret rights were expressly included with patent rights.

We agree with the Eleventh Circuit that once the pending patent issues, enforcement of royalty provisions for other rights which conflict with and are indistinguishable from royalties for patent rights, is precluded. As noted in *Mestre,* the Supreme Court has upheld enforcement of potentially conflicting state trade secret provisions in hybrid agreements *only where no patents ever issued. See Aronson v. Quick Point Pencil Co.,* 440 U.S. 257, 99 S.Ct. 1096, 59 L.Ed.2d 296 (1979);[5] *Kewanee Oil Co. v. Bicron Corp.,* 416 U.S. 470, 94 S.Ct. 1879, 40 L.Ed.2d 315 (1974). Upon issuance of the patent, however, federal supremacy requires directly conflicting provisions to be resolved under federal patent law. *Pitney Bowes, Inc. v. Mestre,* 701 F.2d at 1372.

* * *

Thus, the tenor of the licensing agreement compels us to find that the possibility of forthcoming patents on the toy extruder substantially contributed to the formation of the licensing agreement and that the parties assumed a high likelihood that valid patents would issue. The terms of the licensing agreement compel the conclusion that, at the time the parties executed the license, the plaintiffs exerted considerable leverage from the anticipated patents. In our view, the absence of a filed patent application is, under these circumstances, irrelevant to the analysis under *Brulotte.*

Having established the leverage from anticipated patents, our inquiry next focuses on whether such leverage was misused to project

---

5. In our view, *Aronson,* lends further support to the contention that the *Brulotte* rule of *per se* invalidity is applicable to hybrid agreements in which royalties for patent rights are indistinguishable from those for other rights. * * * The Supreme Court reversed and held that absent issuance of a patent, federal patent law does not preempt state contract law. The Court concluded the terms of the agreement contravened no purpose under the federal patent system and that the reduced royalty was not negotiated with the leverage of a patent. 440 U.S. at 265, 99 S.Ct. at 1100. In so holding, however, the Court specifically noted that had the patent is-sued, enforcement of the higher 5% royalty rate for exclusive rights beyond the life of the patent would have been precluded:

"Mrs. Aronson attempted to obtain a patent for over five years. It is quite true that had she succeeded, she would have received a 5% royalty only on keyholders sold during the 17–year life of the patent."

440 U.S. at 263–64, 99 S.Ct. at 1099–1100. Thus, the Court would presumably have applied *Brulotte* to a "hybrid" agreement embodying rights conferred under both state law and the federal patent law.

the monopoly beyond the life of the patent. In *Brulotte* the Supreme Court found a *per se* projection of the monopoly where the provisions protecting the exclusive rights conferred by the patent applied without change to the post expiration period and where royalties for use during the patent were indistinguishable from royalties due after expiration. *Brulotte v. Thys Co.,* 379 U.S. at 32, 85 S.Ct. at 179. In the case at bar, the agreement calls for royalties on the sales of the patented extruder for a minimum of twenty-five years. As in *Brulotte,* the agreement contains neither provisions for reduction of royalties in the event valid patents never issued nor terms for reduction of post-expiration royalties. The provisions for use of the extruder and payment of royalties are applicable to both the pre-expiration and post-expiration periods. Therefore, under *Brulotte,* the agreement is unlawful *per se.*

Accordingly, the district court's grant of partial summary judgment to the plaintiffs is hereby reversed.

MORSEBURG v. BALYON v. MAYER

United States Court of Appeals, Ninth Circuit, 1980.
621 F.2d 972.

SNEED, CIRCUIT JUDGE.

Appellant is an art dealer. On March 24, 1977, he sold two paintings under such circumstances as to require him to pay royalties under the California Resale Royalties Act (California Act), which is set forth in full in the margin. He thereupon brought suit challenging the Act's constitutionality, claiming that it is preempted by the 1909 Copyright Act and that it violates due process and the Contracts Clause of the Constitution. The lower court rejected these contentions. We affirm.

* * *

With respect to preemption the Supreme Court's emphasis varies from time to time. At times the preemption doctrine has been applied with nationalistic fervor while during other periods with generous tolerance of state involvement in areas already to some extent the subject of national concern. *See* Note, *The Preemption Doctrine: Shifting Perspectives on Federalism and the Burger Court,* 75 Colum.L.Rev. 623 *passim* (1975). Without regard to the emphasis of the period certain basic doctrinal notions repeatedly are used in applying preemption. Thus, the extent to which the federal law has "occupied the field" and the presence of "conflict" between the federal and state law have always been focuses of analytic attention. The nature of the Court's emphasis at a particular time is revealed by whether "occupation of the field" and "conflict" are easily found to exist or not. "Occupation" can require no more than the existence of a federal law generally applicable to a significant portion of the area in question to no less than an express statement demonstrating an intention to occupy the area duly enacted by Congress. "Conflict," likewise, can require no more than a mechanical demonstration of potential conflict between federal and state law to no less than a showing of substantial frustration of an important purpose of the federal law by the challenged state law. When the emphasis is to protect and strengthen national power "occupation" and "conflict" are easily found while not so easily found when the emphasis is to promote federalism.

Although there is a discernable cyclical character in the Supreme Court's choice of emphasis, it is also true that, without regard to the particular point in the cycle at which a preemption issue arises, the choice of emphasis is heavily influenced by the area of the law in which the issue arises. Thus, when the area concerns foreign affairs, as in *Hines v. Davidowitz*, 312 U.S. 52, 61 S.Ct. 399, 85 L.Ed. 581 (1941), or labor relations, as in *San Diego Building Trades Council v. Garmon*, 359 U.S. 236, 79 S.Ct. 773, 3 L.Ed.2d 775 (1959), the emphasis, not surprisingly, is on the national interest, while when the area is protection of consumers of commodities, as in *Florida Lime & Avocado Growers, Inc. v. Paul*, 373 U.S. 132, 83 S.Ct. 1210, 10 L.Ed.2d 248 (1963), the emphasis understandably is upon the state's interest particularly and the imperatives of federalism generally. *See* Note, *The Preemption Doctrine: Shifting Perspectives on Federalism and the Burger Court*, *supra* at 638–39.

Fortunately, the Supreme Court provided clear guidance with respect to the emphasis proper for this case. This was done in *Goldstein v. California*, 412 U.S. 546, 93 S.Ct. 2303, 37 L.Ed.2d 163 (1973), in which the Court held valid a California statute making it a criminal offense to "pirate" recordings produced by others, an activity against which the copyright holder at that time had no protection. The interests of California in particular and of federalism in general were given emphasis. The Court refused to read the Copyright Clause of the Constitution to foreclose the existence of all state power "to grant to authors the exclusive Right to their respective Writings." *Id.* at 560, 93 S.Ct. at 2311. Also it held that the 1909 Copyright Act did not preempt the California statute. In support of this conclusion the Court observed that Congress had not exercised its full power under the Copyright Clause and that it was not required to do so. In addition, Congress had evidenced no intent, either expressly or impliedly, to bar the states from exercising their power. As a consequence, the area was not fully occupied by the federal government. This was supported additionally by the Court's explicit conclusion that no conflict between the national and state law existed because state law regulated a matter not covered by the federal Copyright Act of 1909 in a manner that did not disturb a careful balance struck by Congress between those matters deserving of protection and those things that should remain free. *Id.* at 567–70, 93 S.Ct. at 2315–2316. Both *Sears, Roebuck & Co. v. Stiffel Co.*, 376 U.S. 225, 84 S.Ct. 784, 11 L.Ed.2d 661 (1964), and *Compco Corp. v. Day-Brite Lighting, Inc.*, 376 U.S. 234, 84 S.Ct. 779, 11 L.Ed.2d 669 (1964), cases in which state unfair competition laws were held to be preempted by the federal patent law, were distinguished on the ground that in each case the state law upset the federally struck balance between protection and freedom. Finally, the Court in *Goldstein* held that California's statute did not restrain the use or expression of knowledge, truths ascertained, conceptions, or ideas.

We hold that *Goldstein* governs this case. The Copyright Clause does not prevent the enactment by California of the Resale Royalties Act. Nor has the Copyright Act of 1909 explicitly forbidden the enactment of such an act by a state. A bar by implication cannot be found in the word "vend" in section 1 of the 1909 Act. Doubt concerning the correctness of this conclusion disappears when the rights of the artist who creates a work of fine art are analyzed. Prior to the initial sale he holds title to the work and, assuming proper steps have been taken, all rights given to him by reason of his copyright. None of these provide the right afforded to him by the California Resale Royalties Act. This is an additional right similar to the additional protection afforded by California's anti-pirating statute upheld in *Goldstein*. It is true that under the California Act the right it bestows cannot be waived or transferred. This limits the right created by state law but not any right created by the copyright law.

* * *

Nor can we conclude that section 27 of the 1909 Act by implication precludes the enactment of resale royalty acts by the states. Technically speaking such acts in no way restrict the transfer of art works. No lien to secure the royalty is attached to the work itself, nor is the buyer made secondarily liable for the royalty. The work can be transferred without restriction. The fact that a resale may create a liability to the creator artist or a state instrumentality and, at the same time, constitute an exercise of a right guaranteed by the Copyright Act does not make the former a legal restraint on the latter. It is true, of course, that the imposition of the royalty may well influence the duration of a purchaser's holding period of a work of fine art. To cover the royalty the holder may defer selling until the work's value has appreciated to a greater extent than otherwise might have been the case. The aggregate volume of business done by the relevant art markets may be diminished somewhat. Moreover, the possibility of the imposition by the state of very high royalty rates and more than one state "taxing" a single sale suggests that resale royalty acts under certain circumstances could make transfer of the work of fine art a practical impossibility. Without regard to how the preemption argument should fare under those circumstances, we are not confronted with them here. We explicitly restrict our holding to the facts before us.

These observations permit us to conclude that the 1909 Copyright Act has not occupied the area with which we are concerned and that the California Act is not in conflict with it. A resale royalty is not provided by the 1909 Act; no hostility toward such a royalty is expressed by the Act; and, on the facts before us, the obligation to pay a resale royalty does not impermissibly restrict resales by the owners of works of fine art. The teaching of *Goldstein* is not limited to situations in which the matter regulated by state law is not covered by the 1909 Act. *Kewanee Oil Co. v. Bicron Corp.*, 416 U.S. 470, 94 S.Ct. 1879, 40 L.Ed.2d 315 (1974), makes this clear. The crucial inquiry is not whether state law reaches matters also subject to federal regulation, but whether the two laws function harmoniously rather than discordantly. We find no discord in this instance. For these reasons we distinguish *Sears* and *Compco* in the same manner as was done in *Goldstein*.

* * *

In Hampton v. Blair Mfg. Co., 374 F.2d 969, 153 USPQ 323 (8th Cir. 1967), the Court of Appeals reversed the District Court's order permanently enjoining Kelly Ryan's ex-employee Hampton from manufacturing farm implements covered by Kelly Ryan's blueprints, drawings and tracings, saying at page 973:

> The reasoning of *Sears* and *Day-Brite* and the holdings therein compels the holding here that Hampton cannot be permanently enjoined from duplicating or copying Kelly Ryan unpatented implements. Hampton's conduct in his surreptitiously obtaining possession and copying the blue prints and drawings of Kelly Ryan and its failure to obey the orders of the court to turn over such documents and not use them is indefensible and warrants the fashioning of appropriate equitable relief. While a fact dispute exists, substantial evidentiary support exists for the court's finding that Hampton retained some copies of the blue prints and drawings and made use thereof in manufacturing feeder wagons substantially the same as those manufactured by Kelly Ryan. Such use of the plans accelerated the time in which Hampton was able to produce the wagons. Hampton had possession of a Kelly Ryan feeder wagon and it seems clear from the evidence that it would be possible in the course of time for mechanics skilled in the field to draw necessary plans for the parts needed to construct the feeder wagons and to build such a wagon from the available model. It is difficult to say just how much time the use of the plans accelerated the production.

We believe that under the facts here the court would have been justified in restraining the production of substantially similar implements for the period that would have been required to reproduce such items without the aid of the plans.[i]

---

i. "In Shellmar Products Co. v. Allen-Qualley Co., 87 F.2d 104, 32 USPQ 24 (7th Cir.1936), this Court permitted an injunction to continue against the wrongful user of a trade secret after a patent later made the information public. Shellmar was not a suit for damages and did not involve Wisconsin law. It did not bar this district judge from holding, as a matter of first impression, that under Wisconsin law an improper use of a trade secret is an actionable wrong only prior to the issuance of the patent. [Citations omitted] This holding may even be required by the Supreme Court's decisions in Sears, * * * and Compco * * * delineating the preemptory relationship between federal patent law and state unfair competition law." Forest Laboratories, Inc. v. Pillsbury Co., 452 F.2d 621, 624, Footnote 4, 171 USPQ 731 (7th Cir.1971).

B. RECONCILIATION OF CONCURRENT PROTECTION RELATIVE TO DESIGNS, COPYRIGHTS AND TRADEMARKS

APPLICATION OF MOGEN DAVID WINE CORP.

United States Court of Customs and Patent Appeals, 1964.
51 CCPA 1260, 328 F.2d 925, 140 USPQ 575.

ALMOND, JUDGE. Mogen David Wine Corporation appeals from the decision of the Trademark Trial and Appeal Board, 134 USPQ 576, refusing registration of the configuration of a decanter bottle, as a trade-mark for wines, on the Principal Register established by the Trademark Act of 1946.

The application,[1] alleging use since November 1956, seeks registration of the following:

Appellant is the owner by assignment of an existing design patent[2] described by the board as "covering the decanter bottle for which it seeks registration."

Specimens filed in the Patent Office with the application comprise photographs of the bottle as actually used. While some differences may be noted among the bottles depicted in the drawings of the design patent, the application drawing, and the photographic specimens, no issue was raised below as to whether all three relate to substantially the same configuration.

* * *

The examiner took the position that the "container per se did not in fact function as a trademark to indicate origin of the goods in the applicant," stating that:

"* * * Since it does not appear from the record * * * that applicant has at any time, * * * by any * * * means, referred to the container per se as an indication of origin in applicant, the identical or substantially-identical form affidavits from consumers and dealers are not convincing that the container presented for registration does in fact function as a trademark to identify and distinguish applicant's wines from like goods of others."

The board in sustaining the examiner's refusal of registration rejected the reasoning applied by the examiner in denominating the issue as solely one of fact, attributing it to the examiner's misconstruction of or apparent confusion relative to the "law pertaining to the registration of the subject matter of an existing design patent on the Principal Register as distinguished from the registration of said matter on the Supplemental Register."

1. Serial No. 73,406 filed May 11, 1959.

2. Des.Pat. No. 158,213 issued Apr. 18, 1950 for a term of 14 years.

The board, citing In re The Pepsi-Cola Company, 120 USPQ 468 (TT & A Bd., 1959), and noting that the design patent here is due to expire in 1964, reasoned that inasmuch as registration on the Supplemental Register affords the owner no presumptive right to exclusive use, it could not extend the monopoly which the registrant enjoys under the grant of the design patent, while registration on the Principal Register avails to the owner thereof prima facie evidence of ownership of the mark and exclusive right to use it in commerce in connection with the recited goods with the consequent right to exclude others from the use and registration of the same or similar design for like or similar goods, for the duration of the registration, which is renewable every twenty years. The board concluded that issuance of the registration sought by appellant would be inimical to the rights of others conditioned under the patent grant to make fair use of the subject matter after expiration of the patent and would thereby, in effect, extend the monopoly of the patent contrary to the intent and purpose of the patent law.

* * *

It is clear that the board refrained from passing judgment on the factual issue as to whether the evidence submitted served to establish that appellant's mark functions as a trademark to identify and distinguish appellant's wines.

The ultimate issue posed here, therefore, is whether or not, as a matter of law, appellant is precluded from obtaining registration for its recited goods on the Principal Register for its bottle configuration trademark during the life of its design patent. This precise question is one of first impression in this court.

We believe that a proper resolution of the issue here requires recognition of the distinction in purpose underlying the protection accorded designs under the patent laws and that protection accorded trademarks under the common law of unfair competition, including the law of trademarks which is a part of it, and the statutory trademark law, on the basis of secondary meaning.

This distinction is recognized by a number of leading text writers in the field of patent and trademark law. In support of its contention in this respect appellant cites Nims, in Vol. 1, Unfair Competition and Trade-Marks (4th Edition, 1947), at page 390, where it is stated:

> "The good will of the patentee survives the patent. His popularity as manufacturer or merchant may create a demand for the product as made by him which may be represented by a trade-mark, by non-functional decorative features which have acquired a secondary meaning, or by dress such as a label or wrapper of peculiar design by which the article and its maker have become associated in the public mind. These features have nothing to do with the patent rights. They are property of the patentee which survives the patent. As to them, the general rules with regard to trade-marks and the dress of the goods apply as though no patent were involved. As a manufacturer, one may

make any unpatented article, but as a vendor, he may be restricted in the interest of fair competition."

A further citation of similar purport is Callmann in Vol. 1, "Unfair Competition and Trademarks" (2d Edition, 1950), at pages 252–253:

"A design patent is a hybrid which combines in itself features of both a patent and a copyright. From the patent it borrows the peculiarity that it is industrial and that its exclusive right is one to 'make, use and vent' as distinguished from the copyright which reserves the right to copy and represent the work to the public. Similar to the copyright its purpose is not to protect a technical idea but to protect an artistic or ornamental form. The design must be ornamental and is, of course, non-functional in nature; during and after the life of the patent protection may be granted against unfair competition on the ground of secondary meaning."

In further advancement of its thesis that "patent protection does not, in principle, exclude trademark protection or what is tantamount thereto, namely, protection under the law relating to unfair competition where secondary meaning has been established," appellant cites the following cases: Lucien Lelong, Inc. v. George W. Button Corporation, 50 F.Supp. 708 (D.C.S.D.N.Y.1943); Oneida, Ltd. v. National Silver Co., 25 N.Y.S.2d 271 (N.Y.Sup.Ct., 1940); Prince Matchabelli Inc. v. Anhalt & Co., Inc., 40 F.Supp. 848 (D.C.S.D.N.Y., 1941), and Falcon Industries, Inc. et al. v. R.S. Herbert Co., Inc., et al., 128 F.Supp. 204 (D.C.E.D.N.Y., 1955).

In Lucien Lelong imitation by defendant of the design of a bottle covered by an unexpired design patent was enjoined under the law of unfair competition.

[A6486]

In Oneida, Ltd. plaintiff secured injunctive relief in a state court, on the ground of unfair competition, against defendant's copying a silverware pattern covered by a design patent.

In Prince Matchabelli the patent involved covered a purse kit. Injunctive relief was granted pendente lite on the ground of unfair competition by reason of defendant's imitation of plaintiff's purse kit. The court stated:

" * * * the purse kit of the patent has 'become so associated with the plaintiff in the mind of the public as to acquire a secondary meaning and cause any bag of the same appearance to be ascribed to the plaintiff as the source of production'."

In the English case of In re United States Playing Card Company's Application, 1 Ch. 197 (1908), the application was for registration of a trademark consisting of a pattern on the backs of playing cards. Registration was refused on the ground that the mark, if protectable at all, would have to be registered under the Designs section. Reversal was had on appeal. Appellant quotes the court as stating:

"There is nothing in the Trade Marks Act of 1905 to prevent it being registered as a trademark merely because it is capable of being registered as a design.

"In my opinion registration as a design and registration as a trademark are not mutually exclusive, and it is not a fatal objection to an application to register something that is claimed as a trademark that the subject matter of the application is capable of being registered as a design."

While it is to be observed that the issue before us was not treated by these authorities, yet they bear a substantial relationship and relevancy in that they support the thesis advanced by appellant that "the law recognizes that the protection accorded to a design under the patent laws and that accorded to what amounts to a trademark under the common law doctrine of secondary meaning are separate and distinct, and that the rights conferred by law in the one in no way exclude the rights conferred by law in the other."

The underlying purpose and the essence of patent rights are separate and distinct from those appertaining to trademarks. No right accruing from the one is dependent upon or conditioned by any right concomitant to the other. The longevity of the exclusivity of one is limited by law while the other may be extended in perpetuity.

* * *

We recognize the distinction between registrations on the Principal and Supplemental Registers and their legal effects. However, we can find no supportable reasons in the purposes or philosophies of patent and trademark law to support the conclusion the board bases on that distinction. In our opinion, trademark rights, or rights under the law of unfair competition, which happen to continue beyond the expiration of a design patent, do not "extend" the patent monopoly. They exist independently of it, under different law and for different reasons. The termination of either has no legal effect on the continuance of the other. When the patent monopoly ends, it ends. The trademark rights do not extend it. We know of no provision of patent law, statutory or otherwise, that guarantees to anyone an absolute right to copy the subject matter of any expired patent. Patent expiration is nothing more than the cessation of the patentee's right to exclude held under the patent law. Conversely, trademarks conceivably could end through nonuse during the life of a patent. We doubt it would be argued that the patent rights should also expire so as not to "extend" them.

* * *

It was within the province of Congress to write an exception in the provisions of the statute to preclude use of the subject matter of a design patent during the life of the patent as trademark use. It did not see fit to do so.

* * * To hold, as did the board, that an existing design patent precludes even distinctive marks from registration would be tantamount to writing an exception into the statute excluding consideration of use during the life of a design patent. This we cannot do.

Furthermore, the decision of the board would in effect nullify or suspend the provisions of Section 1, supra, relating to date of first use and first use in commerce, which makes no exception as to use during the life of a design patent.

The board, as did the solicitor, cited In re The Deister Concentrator Company, Inc., 289 F.2d 496, 48 CCPA 952. The facts and the issue presented in In re Deister readily distinguish that case from the facts and issues here under consideration. The applicant in Deister sought Principal Register registration for a specific rhomboidal outline shape for ore concentrating and coal cleaning tables on which it had obtained apparatus patents showing the deck having the shape described in the trademark application. This court sustained the board's denial of registration "because the shape is *in essence* utilitarian" (289 F.2d 501, 48 CCPA 968).

* * *

We have not overlooked the case of In re McIlhenny Co., 278 F.2d 953, 47 CCPA 985. Here, as distinguished from the McIlhenny case, the decanter bottle design may be inherently distinctive.

* * *

Here, the design of the decantor bottle, when associated in the purchasing public's mind with appellant's wines, may have acquired the attributes of a registrable trademark. This essential factor was lacking in the McIlhenny case.

For the foregoing reasons, we are of the opinion that the decision of the board refusing registration of appellant's bottle configuration as a trademark for wines is in error.

We are further of the opinion that the board committed error in its holding that "use of the subject matter of a design patent during the life of the patent cannot properly be considered as trademark use."

The decision of the Trademark Trial and Appeal Board is *reversed* and the case *remanded* to the board for decision on the factual issue as to whether the evidence submitted is sufficient to establish that appellant's bottle design functions as a trademark to indicate origin.

Reversed and remanded.

WORLEY, CHIEF JUDGE, concurs in the result.

[Concurring Opinion of Judge Rich discussing Deister Case is omitted.]

EPILOGUE

We have been reading statutes, and decision after decision of lower courts and appellate courts, but through it all we have been beneficiaries to the real and unmentioned heroes who built the records upon which the decisions were based. In each contested case, there were trial lawyers on the losing and winning side. The records they created, by discovering and selecting exhibits, by finding and handling witnesses, by examination and cross-examination, by timely objection and lucid argument, are the true basis for the entire structure of the law. As the web of the law continues to be torn, repaired, rewoven and expanded, lawyers contribute by two important functions: First, by attempting to synthesize the decisions to give advice in advance of contest in an effort to avoid litigation. Second, when litigation comes, to use the knowledge of the past as a basis for constructing a record which will at once be logical, factual, consistent, and well founded in legal theory and precedent while yet being directed to judges as persons who must assimilate and adjudicate. In the field of patents, which involves, at times, complicated and complex technical subjects, the task is often a difficult one. Many and varied visual aids can be used to demonstrate and clarify in a trial where time is at a premium. While all lawyers cannot be trial attorneys, there are many opportunities to participate in the building of a record. To this end we study, to this end we continue to practice.

*

Index

†